PUBLIC PAPERS OF THE PRESIDENTS
OF THE UNITED STATES

PUBLIC PAPERS OF THE PRESIDENTS

OF THE UNITED STATES

Jimmy Carter

1980-81

(IN THREE BOOKS)

BOOK II—MAY 24 TO SEPTEMBER 26, 1980

UNITED STATES GOVERNMENT PRINTING OFFICE

WASHINGTON : 1982

Published by the
Office of the Federal Register
National Archives and Records Service
General Services Administration

For sale by the Superintendent of Documents, U.S. Government Printing Office
Washington, D.C. 20402

Foreword

The four months of 1980 covered by the papers in this volume were particularly challenging. Our Nation was confronted by serious violations of human rights and of national sovereignty by Iran and the Soviet Union. Our determination to meet these challenges is revealed in the following pages.

I am proud that this volume also reveals that our Nation remained firmly committed to peace and to international cooperation. Notable events included the completion of normalization of relations with the People's Republic of China and the convening of the Venice Economic Summit Conference.

The publication of the Global 2000 Report to the President indicated our concern for the future of the world's population, natural resources, and environment. At home, the passage of the Energy Security Act was the highlight of our efforts to develop and implement the Nation's first comprehensive energy policy.

These public papers of my Presidency contain some items of a routine nature that could have emanated from any form of government. Yet as a whole they are unique to our free government. They include numerous unedited transcripts of my open exchanges with the press and the people of America. The give-and-take of the 1980 campaign for the Presidency is recorded for history. It is a pleasure for me to have a part in ensuring that the American people continue to have access to the records of their government.

Jimmy Carter

Preface

This book contains the papers and speeches of the 39th President of the United States which were issued by the White House Press Office during the period May 24–September 26, 1980. A third Public Papers book completing President Carter's fourth year in office will be available later in 1982. The material has been compiled and published by the Office of the Federal Register, National Archives and Records Service, General Services Administration.

The material is presented in chronological order within each week, and the dates shown in the headings are the dates of the documents or events. In instances when the release date differs from the date of the document itself, that fact is shown in the textnote. Every effort has been made to ensure accuracy. Tape recordings are used to protect against errors in transcription of Presidential remarks, and signed documents are checked against the original to verify the correct printing. Textnotes, footnotes, and cross references have been provided by the editors for purposes of identification or clarity. Speeches were delivered in Washington, D.C., and other documents released there, unless indicated. All times noted are local times.

The index covers both Books I and II of the 1980–81 volume. In addition to the usual subject-matter entries in the index, the material has been classified in categories reflecting the type of Presidential activity or document. For example, a reader interested in the President's speeches will find them listed in the index under "Addresses and Remarks." An index accounting for all the materials for 1980–81 will be included in Book III.

The Public Papers series was begun in 1957 in response to a recommendation of the National Historical Publications Commission. An extensive compilation of messages and papers of the Presidents covering the period 1789 to 1897 was assembled by James D. Richardson and published under congressional authority between 1896 and 1899. Since then, various private compilations have been issued, but there was no uniform publication comparable to the Congressional Record or the United States Supreme Court Reports. Many Presidential papers could be found only in the form of mimeographed White House releases or as reported in the press. The Commission therefore recommended the establishment of an official series in which Presidential writings, addresses, and remarks of a public nature could be made available.

The Commission's recommendation was incorporated in regulations of the Administrative Committee of the Federal Register, issued under section 6 of the Federal Register Act (44 U.S.C. 1506), which may be found in Title 1, Part 10, of the Code of Federal Regulations.

Preface

A companion publication to the Public Papers series, the Weekly Compilation of Presidential Documents, was begun in 1965 to provide a broader range of Presidential materials on a more timely basis to meet the needs of the contemporary reader. Beginning with the administration of Jimmy Carter, the Public Papers series expanded its coverage to include all material as printed in the Weekly Compilation. That coverage provides a listing of the President's daily schedule and meetings, when announced, and other items of general interest issued by the White House Press Office. Also included are lists of the President's nominations submitted to the Senate, materials released by the Press Office which are not printed full-text in the book, and acts approved by the President. This information is compiled on a weekly basis and appears at the end of each week's coverage.

Volumes covering the administrations of Presidents Hoover, Truman, Eisenhower, Kennedy, Johnson, Nixon, and Ford are also available.

This series is under the direction of John E. Byrne, Director, Office of the Federal Register, and is produced by the Presidential Documents and Legislative Division, Robert E. Lewis, Director. Editors of this book were Katherine A. Mellody, Brenda A. Robeson, Kenneth R. Payne, Wilma P. Greene, and D. Michael Smith. The index was prepared by Walter W. Rice.

The frontispiece and photographs used in the portfolio were supplied by the White House Photo Office.

The typography and design of the volume were developed by the United States Government Printing Office under the direction of Danford L. Sawyer, Public Printer.

ROBERT M. WARNER
Archivist of the United States

GERALD P. CARMEN
Administrator of General Services
January 1982

Contents

Administration of Jimmy Carter

1980-81

Benefits for Members of the Armed Forces

**Letter to the Secretary of Defense.
May 23, 1980**

To Secretary Harold Brown

As you know from our previous discussions, I am committed to the principle that a career in the military should be at least as rewarding as a career elsewhere in our society. The Warner/Nunn amendment, which incorporates a number of the initiatives first proposed in our January budget, should be supported with the modifications you have indicated. We should also continue to seek enactment of the other legislative proposals we have submitted to the Congress.

In order to offset the many challenges and hardships of military duty, I would also like to make further improvements in the present health care program. For example, your suggestion of providing dental care for dependents seems to me a desirable step.

Finally, we should continue to press for Civil Service pay reform to allow us to reflect the differences between military and civilian government service in future pay decisions.

Sincerely,

JIMMY CARTER

NOTE: The text of the letter was released at Norfolk, Va., on May 26.

Nimitz Battle Group in the Indian Ocean

**Remarks on Board the U.S.S. Nimitz on the Battle Group's Return to the United States.
May 26, 1980**

Secretary Brown; Admiral Train; Captain Batzler, with this great ship, the Nimitz, and all the crew and officers; Captain Owens and the officers and crew of the Texas; Captain Smith and the officers and crew of the California:

It's good to have you back here at home away from the Gonzo Station.

We just flew over Pier 12 in Norfolk. There are hundreds of your family and friends already assembled there. In just a few hours, when you arrive, there will be literally tens of thousands of people there to welcome you home, including, I understand, 200 new Americans who've been born since you left.

Our Nation is grateful to you for what you have meant to our country, to freedom, and to the peace that has been maintained for the entire world by your courage and your dedication and your service to the U.S. Navy, to the Marines, and to our country.

It was my judgment that it would be better to have this welcoming ceremony to express the gratitude of our country at sea, while the *Nimitz* is still underway, so that we would not have any delay when you arrive at Pier 12 in letting you go down the gangplank and put your arms around the people who love you.

As you know, this ceremony is being broadcast to the other two ships in the *Nimitz* task force and also to those assembled at Pier 12 in Norfolk.

This is also Memorial Day, a day when our Nation pays tribute to those who've lost their lives in the service of our country in the military forces and also those who've worn the uniform in times of peace and in times of war.

History most often records the courage and dedication and sacrifice of those who have been in battle, when wars were won and lost and when heroism was apparent and well-publicized. But all of us know that the sacrifice and the courage and the dedication and the service in times of peace to prevent war are equally gratifying to those whom you have served so well.

I know what it means to be at sea for weeks and for months, both when our Nation was at war and also when our Nation was at peace. Quite often, it's even more lonesome for a service man or woman to serve in a sacrificial way in times of peace. The publicity is not there; quite often, the recognition is not there. But your sense of service and dedication in this particular time in the history of our country is particularly appreciated and known, not only by the people of our country but of the entire world.

Two weeks ago in the National Cemetery in Arlington, I offered my tribute on behalf of a nation to eight brave men who gave their lives in a lonely desert in Iran in the highest possible service that one human being can offer to another. They laid down their lives in a courageous way to save the lives of 50 hostages who have been held in an inhumane and unconscionable way by the Iranians, supported by their government, now for more than 6 months.

This was a time of soul searching for me and for our country as we look back on that tremendous act of heroism. All of you shared in that humanitarian commitment and that humanitarian mission. Since the rescue team returned to our country, I have met personally and shaken hands with almost all of them. Their uniform message to me was, first of all, "Mr. President, we regret that our mission was not completely successful." Second, they said, "We thank you from the bottom of our hearts for giving us this opportunity to serve and to offer our lives for the lives of the American hostages." And third, "Mr. President, we are ready to serve again whenever the time comes to bring those hostages home."

The three ships in this *Nimitz* Battle Group has literally made United States naval history: 270 days of deployment and, as you may have noticed, 144 days— [*laughter*]—at sea without any visit to any port. That is indeed service beyond the call of duty. But your presence in the Indian Ocean and in the Arabian Sea, a ship and an air wing constantly ready, constantly in training, serve to project the presence of the United States Government and its military forces at a time when your presence was crucial to the maintenance of peace and in the provision of a stability in that troubled region of the world vital to all nations on Earth.

You not only served to provide stability in the Persian Gulf, but I am absolutely convinced that your presence there— along with other United States ships and the fighting men on them—has been the major factor in protecting the lives of the 53 American hostages who are still held, because the clear knowledge of American military strength is the surest guarantee that when your presence was felt, stability prevailed, and the hostages were indeed protected in their lives.

There has been with your presence there no doubt about American strength, and I thank you from the bottom of my heart for exhibiting that strength so clearly and so well. I say on behalf of a grateful nation, again, "Well done," in this tremendous mission.

There can be no preservation of peace, there can be no maintenance of American strength, without patriotism and without sacrifice. You have not been the only ones to sacrifice because I know, as part of a Navy family myself, how sacrificial is the performance of duty of the members of your family who've had to wait so long for you to return. When our Nation is in debt to American military men, the highest possible officials of the Navy and the Government find it incumbent on us, and a grateful duty, to express the feelings of 220 million Americans who have seen you perform so well.

In the last 9 months we have seen tremendous, almost earthshaking events take place, which could have brought suffering and worldwide conflict had it not been for the service of men like yourselves. The Soviet invasion of Afghanistan was indeed a threat to the stability of Southwest Asia and the Persian Gulf region. This is a vital region, and the United States presence there help to mean that your mission of peace has been indeed successful.

Let those who wonder about the difference between freedom in our country and a life under the Soviet Communists compare the difference: in Afghanistan, Soviet troops at war with Moslem schoolgirls while you yourselves trained peacefully in a nearby ocean; in Afghanistan, tanks destroying helpless villages while Americans in the Caribbean provided a haven for those escaping from communism.

We see at this time:

—in Afghanistan, more than 800,000 refugees from communism and from tyranny;

—around the Ethiopian area, hundreds of thousands of others trying to escape from communism and from tyranny;

—around Kampuchea in Southeast Asia, hundreds of thousands of human beings trying to escape at the risk of their own lives from communism and from tyranny;

—in the Caribbean in our own hemisphere, literally hundreds of thousands of people, more than one tenth the population of Cuba, eager to escape the oppression of communism and tyranny.

Our Nation stands for freedom. Our Nation stands for human rights. Our Nation stands for democracy. Our Nation stands for peace. But there is no way for us to stand for these vital elements of the lives of human beings who love liberty without a strong military force.

As Commander in Chief, as the President of our country, I'm determined to maintain our military forces at the highest level of readiness, at the highest level of strength. In doing so, I realize quite clearly that the well-being of our military families is crucial. I understand and I'm committed to the principle that a career in the military should be as rewarding personally for those who serve as a career in any pursuit in the society that I represent.

We will therefore ask that the Congress move without delay to appropriate compensation, in addition to what's already provided, to give you more help when you move from one location to another, for reassignments; to provide more appropriate compensation for sea duty; to provide more compensation for flight duty; to provide more compensation for housing in high-cost areas in the United

States and other places where you have to serve; and to provide more compensation for the reenlistment bonuses of senior career enlisted personnel. Many of these improvements are already incorporated in legislation sponsored by Senator Nunn and Senator Warner, and I'll also ask the Secretary of Defense to provide legislation at the earliest possible moment, to provide under an expanded CHAMPUS program for dental care for your dependents in the future.

There is no way through pay or privileges adequately to reward you for offering your very lives in the service of our country. But I think you all realize, and will for the balance of the days you live, that the service that you've provided in the last 9 months is crucial not only to our country, as I mentioned several times, but to a particular group of Americans.

I would like now in closing my own remarks to introduce to you the wife of one of the hostages being held in Iran, Mrs. Louisa Kennedy, who will express to you the sentiments of the hostages' families for what you have meant to them personally as well as to our Nation.

Thank you. Welcome home. God bless everyone of you.

Mrs. Louisa Kennedy.

NOTE: The President spoke at 3:09 p.m. on the flight deck of the *Nimitz*. In his opening remarks, the President referred to Adm. Harry D. Train II, Commander-in-Chief, U.S. Atlantic Fleet.

Following his remarks, the President was given a private tour of the *Nimitz*.

Norfolk, Virginia

Remarks to Families Awaiting the Return of the Nimitz Battle Group. **May 26, 1980**

I can tell you first of all that I have just been out to greet the officers and men of the U.S.S. *Nimitz,* the U.S.S. *Texas,* and the U.S.S. *California.* They are not very far away. They are on their way home. And although they made me feel very welcome on the *Nimitz,* I know that you're the ones they are looking forward to putting their arms around and giving you their love and their appreciation.

It's hard for me this afternoon to express adequately my appreciation to the men on those three ships, but it's also difficult for me to let you know, the families of those who've served so well in the Indian Ocean and the Persian Gulf during the last number of months, during this time of crisis, for our country. I know that you realize that loved ones of service men and women are also on the frontlines of service to our country and on the frontlines of protecting liberty and preserving the peace. Like your hearts, my heart was with them when they were on duty protecting the interests of our Nation with courage and commitment and in a sense of dedication and sacrifice. And like their hearts, my heart was with you during this long time of waiting for your men to come home.

On Memorial Day there is a time both of gratitude and of sober reflection. It's a day of commemorating and expressing our appreciation in a special way for those during all the wars since the history of our country who gave their lives for the preservation of freedom. It's also a time to honor those who served in uniform in times of peace and in time of war. It takes as much dedication and sacrifice to serve in peacetime as it does in time of war, and quite often the service is even more lonely and sacrificial in nature, because your concern and your constant awareness of their commitment and courage and sacrifice is not always shared by the other millions of people who live in our Nation.

But in this particular instance when the *Nimitz,* the *Texas,* and the *California* were on station, the hearts of a grateful nation were with them. They were not only protecting the stability and the peace of a troubled region of the world, and therefore protecting our own stability and peace here in the continental United States, but their presence and the strength of our military forces represented by them was the best guarantee that the lives of the 53 American hostages in Iran would indeed be protected.

Let me say again that I'm grateful to them and welcome them home; I'm grateful to you and know that you will welcome them with open arms in just a few hours. They're approaching now; their hearts go out to you and vice versa. But on behalf of the other 220 million people in our country, let me say that all of us are glad to see you reunited with these heroic and courageous men, who served you and all Americans in our Nation so well.

God bless you all. Thank you for letting me be with you.

NOTE: The President spoke at 4:17 p.m. on Pier 12 at the Norfolk Naval Base.

Following his remarks, the President returned to Washington, D.C.

Delegation of Panama Canal Functions

Executive Order 12215.   May 27, 1980

By the authority vested in me as President of the United States of America by the Panama Canal Code (76A Stat. 1), as amended, by the Panama Canal Act of 1979 (93 Stat. 452; 22 U.S.C. 3601 *et seq.*), and by Section 301 of Title 3 of the United States Code, it is hereby ordered as follows:

1-1. The Secretary of Defense.

1-101. The Secretary of Defense shall develop for the President's consideration an appropriate legislative proposal as required by Section 3(d) of the Panama Canal Act of 1979 (93 Stat. 456; 22 U.S.C. 3602(d)). The Secretary of Defense shall coordinate development of this proposal with the Secretary of State and the heads of other interested Executive agencies.

1-102. The function vested in the President by Section 1212(d)(1) of the Panama Canal Act of 1979 (93 Stat. 464; 22 U.S.C. 3652(d)(1)) to exclude employees of, or positions within, the Department of Defense from coverage under any provision of subchapter II, Chapter 2 of Title I of the Panama Canal Act of 1979, is delegated to the Secretary of Defense.

1-103. The function vested in the President by Section 1281(b) of Title 6 of the Panama Canal Code (76A Stat. 455; 6 P.C.C. 1281(b)), as amended, with respect to areas and installations made available to the United States pursuant to the Agreement in Implementation of Article IV of the Panama Canal Treaty of 1977 is delegated to the Secretary of Defense.

1-104. The function vested in the President by Section 1701 of the Panama Canal Act of 1979 (93 Stat. 492; 22 U.S.C. 3801), with respect to regulations applicable within the areas and installations made available to the United States pursuant to the Agreement in Implementation of Article IV of the Panama Canal Treaty of 1977, is delegated to the Secretary of Defense.

1-105. The functions vested in the President by Sections 1243(c)(1) and 2401 of the Panama Canal Act of 1979 (93 Stat. 474 and 495; 22 U.S.C. 3681(c)(1) and 3851) are delegated to the Secretary of Defense.

1–106. The functions vested in the President by Section 1502(a) of the Panama Canal Act of 1979 (93 Stat. 488; 22 U.S.C. 3782(a)) are delegated to the Secretary of Defense.

1–2. Coordination of Pay and Employment Practices.

1–201. In order to coordinate the policies and activities of agencies under subchapter II of Chapter 2 of Title I of the Panama Canal Act of 1979 (93 Stat. 463; 22 U.S.C. 3651 *et seq.*), each agency shall periodically consult with the Secretary of Defense with respect to the establishment of rates of pay, in order to develop compatible or unified systems for basic pay. In addition, each agency shall consult with the Secretary of Defense on such other matters as the Secretary may deem appropriate in order to develop compatible or unified employment practices.

1–202. The head of each agency shall, upon approval by the Secretary of Defense, adopt a schedule of basic pay pursuant to Section 1215 of the Panama Canal Act of 1979 (93 Stat. 465; 22 U.S.C. 3655) and adopt regulations governing other matters relating to pay and employment practices.

1–203. The authority vested in the President by Section 1223(a) of the Panama Canal Act of 1979 to coordinate the policies and activities of agencies (93 Stat. 467; 22 U.S.C. 3663(a)) is delegated to the Secretary of Defense. The Secretary shall exercise such functions in a manner which is in accord with the provisions of Sections 1–201 and 1–202 of this Order.

1–3. Panama Canal Commission.

1–301. The functions vested in the President and delegated to the Secretary of Defense in this Section 1–3 of this Order shall be carried out by the Secretary of Defense, who shall, in carrying out the

said functions, provide, by redelegation or otherwise, for their performance, in a manner consistent with paragraph 3 of Article III of the Panama Canal Treaty of 1977, by the Panama Canal Commission.

1–302. The authority of the President under Section 1104 of the Panama Canal Act of 1979 (93 Stat. 457; 22 U.S.C. 3614) to fix the compensation of and to define the authorities and duties of the Deputy Administrator and the Chief Engineer is delegated to the Secretary of Defense.

1–303. The functions vested in the President by Sections 1418, 1801, and 2206 of the Panama Canal Act of 1979 (93 Stat. 487, 492, and 494; 22 U.S.C. 3778, 3811, and 3844) are delegated to the Secretary of Defense.

1–304. The authority of the President under Section 1701 of the Panama Canal Act of 1979 (93 Stat. 492; 22 U.S.C. 3801) with respect to regulations applicable within the areas and installations made available to the United States pursuant to the Agreement in Implementation of Article III of the Panama Canal Treaty of 1977 is delegated to the Secretary of Defense.

1–305. The function vested in the President by Section 1281(b) of Title 6 of the Panama Canal Code (76A Stat. 455; 6 P.C.C. 1281(b)), as amended, with respect to areas and installations in the Republic of Panama made available to the United States pursuant to the Agreement in Implementation of Article III of the Panama Canal Treaty of 1977 is delegated to the Secretary of Defense.

1–306. The functions vested in the President by Sections 82 and 86 of Title 3 of the Panama Canal Code (76A Stat. 54 and 55; 3 P.C.C. 82 and 86), as amended, are delegated to the Secretary of Defense.

1–307. The functions vested in the President by subsections (a), (b) and (c) of Section 8146 of Title 5 of the United States Code, as they apply to the employees of the Panama Canal Commission, are delegated to the Secretary of Defense.

1–308. Except to the extent heretofore delegated, the functions vested in the President pursuant to subchapter II of Chapter 2 of Title I of the Panama Canal Act of 1979 (93 Stat. 463) are hereby delegated to the Secretary of Defense.

1–4. Other Agencies.

1–401. The functions vested in the President by Sections 1111 and 3301 of the Panama Canal Act of 1979 (93 Stat. 459 and 497; 22 U.S.C. 3621 and 3871), are delegated to the Secretary of State. The Secretary shall perform these functions in coordination with the Secretary of Defense.

1–402. The functions vested in the President by Sections 1112(d), 1344(b), and 1504(b) of the Panama Canal Act of 1979 (93 Stat. 460, 484, and 488; 22 U.S.C. 3622(d), 3754(b), and 3784(b)) are delegated to the Secretary of State.

1–403. The functions vested in the President by Section 1243(a)(1) of the Panama Canal Act of 1979 (93 Stat. 473; 22 U.S.C. 3681(a)(1)) are delegated to the Director of the Office of Personnel Management.

1–404. Paragraphs (22) and (23) of Section 1 of Executive Order No. 11609, as amended, and Executive Order No. 11713 are revoked.

JIMMY CARTER

The White House,
May 27, 1980.

[Filed with the Office of the Federal Register, 3:44 p.m., May 27, 1980]

Food Stamp Act Amendments of 1980

Statement on Signing S. 1309 Into Law.
May 27, 1980

I am pleased to sign S. 1309, the Food Stamp Act Amendments of 1980.

Food stamps are vital to millions of Americans—the elderly and disabled, poor children, the unemployed, and working families who earn low wages. The food stamp program has been remarkably successful over the past 10 years in easing hunger and malnutrition in the Nation. I am proud of my administration's record of strong support for this program.

S. 1309 raises the food stamp authorization ceilings for fiscal years 1980 and 1981, helping ensure that the needy among us will not go hungry. I am pleased that Congress acted in time to avert a suspension of food stamps next month.

This legislation represents the kind of cooperation between the Congress and the administration we need to balance the budget and improve the operation of Federal programs.

The bill contains my proposals for reducing fraud and abuse in the food stamp program and for reducing the cost of the program. Revisions offered in the Congress will help focus the program's benefits on those most in need and will improve administration at the State level.

I am especially grateful to Chairmen Foley and Talmadge for their leadership in guiding S. 1309 through the Congress. They and their colleagues on the House and Senate Agriculture Committees are to be commended for their work on this legislation.

NOTE: As enacted, S. 1309 is Public Law 96–249, approved May 26.

White House Briefing for Community Leaders

Remarks at the Briefing.   May 27, 1980

Yesterday I joined Secretary of Defense Harold Brown and a few other dignitaries in going out to meet the U.S.S. *Nimitz* and the U.S.S. *Texas* and the U.S.S. *California*, a task force returning from the Indian Ocean and the Persian Gulf region after 270 days of deployment. They spent almost 150 days at sea without a port call, in our nuclear-powered strike force, designed to maintain stability in the Persian Gulf region of the world, and also to provide a show of force which is legitimate and peaceful in nature, to protect the lives of our hostages.

I spent most of the morning before leaving to go to the *Nimitz* working on this year's budget considerations, and how the Congress is dealing with them, and being concerned about legislation still not yet passed concerning energy. As I discussed matters of importance to all of us in this room, with Harold Brown and with others, it became vivid in my mind, as I looked into the faces of those young fighting men, willing to give their lives for our country if necessary, that they were dealing not just with stability and with peace in the Indian Ocean region but also were deeply involved in the questions of energy and the economy and economic strength of our Nation.

There is no way in this modern time and age in which we live to separate one consideration from another, because they are so intimately entwined; they're all so complex, complicated, rapidly changing, worldwide in nature. In every nation on Earth there has been felt in the last year and a half the impact of a 150-percent increase in the cost of oil in a period of 16 months. This means that on an annual average the price of oil has increased 10 percent per month. We've felt the impact of it, and we've seen how vulnerable we are to the instability brought about now as a threat by the Soviet invasion of Afghanistan and the instability of the Government of Iran.

As a President working closely with people like you throughout the country, I'm responsible for the accurate assessment of these challenges, and also the assessment of how well we can meet them. There is no doubt in my mind that our Nation is strong enough and resolved enough and unified enough and confident enough and determined enough to meet these challenges.

We are a world leader. Other nations look to us to set an example. We're on the cutting edge of change, and every time in our history we've ever been faced with rapid change that shook the foundations, economically or politically, of the world, we have been able to prevail. God has blessed us in a remarkable way.

We look on the OPEC nations, for instance, with some degree of trepidation and concern. How can they control the energy resources of the world and put us at their mercy? The fact is that all of them put together control about 6 percent of the world's energy reserves, almost entirely oil and natural gas. The United States, our country, controls 20 percent of the world's energy reserves; not just oil and natural gas but almost unlimited supplies of coal, geothermal supplies, deposits of shale, flowing water, richly productive land that can produce energy on a continuing basis for many centuries in the future, from growing crops and from the products derived from them.

Ours is a country that's the strongest on Earth—militarily, economically. We have a superb education system; a free enterprise system that values itself on human initiative, on competition, not only among ourselves but with others. We have never failed. The resiliency that is indicated in the lives of our country, both individuals and as a government, has been demonstrated over and over. And when we faced complicated questions or difficult pressures or serious problems, in the solution of them we've not only provided a guideline or path for the rest of the world, we've come out stronger every time.

There's no doubt in my mind that we'll do the same this time, but we must realize the situation accurately. It's not been easy for the American people to become convinced that for the first time we do have some limits on what we can use or waste.

More than 3 years ago, in April of 1977, I spoke to the American people in the so-called fireside chat and made an address to the Joint Session of the Congress, and referred to the energy crisis as the moral equivalent of war. It was discounted in much of the press, ridiculed by some. I was accused of exaggerating the problem. But as a matter of fact, instead of having world demand and world supply of energy meet in 1985 or so, it actually occurred in 1979, 5 or 6 years earlier than even I had anticipated.

And our country has responded well. Although the Congress delayed for many months in passing the legislation necessary for an energy policy, over a carefully phased period, to deregulate the price of oil and natural gas, to make them competitive, and to force Americans to save and also to force the government and the private enterprise system to search out for new alternative supplies of energy, we have made a lot of progress.

There was inordinate delay, but now we've got on the verge of success a massive, difficult effort to carve out a national energy policy, based on two simple facts.

The need is to cut down on oil imports.

The solution is, first, to save energy, to stop wasting energy, to conserve energy. And the second is to produce more energy in the United States. It's just that simple: to save energy and to produce more.

The drain on our economy is tremendous. This year, we'll send American money overseas to foreign countries to buy their oil—about $90 billion. That's hard to put in perspective. It's more than the net income of all the Fortune 500 corporations put together, and it amounts to more than $400 for every man, woman, and child in this country.

We're not only importing oil, we're importing inflation and also importing unemployment. We're in a transition phase, but the American people have responded well. The first 5 months of this year, as probably has already been pointed out to you, we have imported a million barrels of oil less every day. That's a tremendous saving in oil imports—12 percent less than last year at the same time, same months, same climate conditions. And last year, we used 5 percent less gasoline than the year before that. And this has been in spite of the fact that in previous years, we've been going up, up, up every year in how much oil we used and how much oil we imported.

So, again, we're setting an example for other major oil-consuming countries. We had a long way to go. We were more inefficient than some of them, because their oil prices have been very high for a number of years. Americans are able to accommodate change, however. We have never feared change in a morbid sense or a sense of paranoia. We've been able to say, "I'd rather things not change" if we're sitting on top of the world, "but if they change, I'll be ready." Americans have been remarkably united.

The other problem that I'd like to mention very briefly to you is this. Inflation has been a burden on the shoulders of Americans for a number of years; 10 or 12 years, we have been burdened with excessive inflation. There was one brief period of time right after the '73–'74 OPEC oil embargo when energy prices did not change for a number of months—I think more than a year. With that temporary dip, inflation has been going up by leaps and bounds ever since, and with a 150-percent increase in oil prices, we've had much more inflation earlier this year.

The second week in March, I put forward to the American people and to the Congress and to the Federal Reserve Board a proposal to control inflation, to bring down the enormously increasing interest rates and following that, of course, the inflation rate. Interest rates have dropped precipitously lately. At this time, some interest rates—Government securities and so forth—are lower than they were a year ago. The prime rate is coming down a little bit more slowly, but steadily. And home mortgage interest rates are also dropping now fairly rapidly. I hope they'll drop much more in the future.

And following that, we believe and I predict to you that during these next few months—during the summer months— we'll have a sharp drop in the inflation rate, which will be gratifying to all Americans, particularly those who are poor or who are old or who are living on fixed incomes and who are least able to pay that 15- or 20-percent tax on them caused by inflation.

In this process, we have prepared ourselves much better than in previous decades to deal with a family that is afflicted with the problem of unemployment, either temporary or extended unemployment. Government programs are much more effective, much more carefully designed to alleviate that problem for a family. And,

of course, we also have programs that are designed, on a targeted basis—very carefully focused basis—to provide jobs that are either in the public sector or supplemented in some way by the Government and held by an employee in the private sector.

As we go through this phase of controlling inflation with a balanced budget commitment and other measures on restraining consumer spending and building up savings, we must not permit the ravages of recession to damage the progress that we've made in providing jobs for our people and a restoration of the older and more deteriorating urban centers of our country.

This is what I fear about the Congress action recently on the first budget resolution. It hasn't gotten much publicity throughout the country, but it severely restrains some programs carefully designed for those purposes—for jobs, for cities, for training, for education—those very things that will prevent recession getting out of hand. And we cannot afford to slash those too deeply and add money to a budget for defense, for instance, which is more than we actually need. So, there must be a careful balancing of those forces as we go into the months ahead.

The last point I'd like to make to you is this: A government can obviously have a great effect on the course of a nation. We cannot expect to control inflation, for instance, unless the Government is willing to exercise, in a demonstrable way, self-discipline. We've been borrowing too much and our deficits have been too great.

In 1976, when I was running for President, we had a deficit of $66 billion. That was about 4½ percent of our gross national product. In January, when I proposed to the Congress a budget for '81, although it was not quite balanced, we had cut that 4½ percent down to six-tenths of 1 percent. And now the Congress is working on a balanced budget. So, to get the Government out of the deficit spending habit is not easy, but it does indicate that we ourselves, if we're determined here in Washington, can set an example for State and local governments and also for private citizens.

But the strength of our country is derived not from the Government, but from the people who comprise the basic resource of our Nation. And that's why it's so important for you to come here to listen to a discussion by my key advisers and Cabinet officers responsible for economics and for energy and to see how they tie in together with the other decisions that have to be made on national defense, on foreign policy, on training, on education, on jobs, on cities, on transportation, on agriculture, on exports and imports, monetary policy—they're all closely and intimately related.

I'm deeply grateful that you would come here. Each one of you is a leader in your own community. People listen to your voice; they know what you can do for them; you've proven yourselves in a highly competitive system. And I hope that when you leave here this afternoon, you will take with you part of the responsibility that I share with you to recognize the innate and undeviating, unchangeable strength of our country, our ability to accommodate change successfully, the responsibility we have to lead other countries, and the special problems that we do face during a transition time in world life where we can prevail, and make the greatest nation on Earth even greater in the future. That's what I hope you'll do when you leave here.

NOTE: The President spoke at 3:17 p.m. in the East Room at the White House.

Postal Rate Commission

Nomination of Janet Dempsey Steiger To Be a Commissioner.   May 27, 1980

The President today announced that he will nominate Janet Dempsey Steiger, of Oshkosh, Wis., to be a Commissioner of the Postal Rate Commission. She would replace Kieran O'Doherty, whose term is expiring.

Steiger has been vice president of The WorkPlace, Inc., a consulting firm servicing freelance professionals in Washington, since 1975. She has been a research associate of the National Academy for Public Administration since 1978.

Steiger was born June 10, 1939, in Oshkosh. She received a B.A. from Lawrence University in 1961. In 1965 she served as assistant to the legislative aide to the Governor of Wisconsin.

Community Services Administration

Nomination of Michael T. Blouin To Be an Assistant Director.   May 27, 1980

The President today announced that he will nominate Michael T. Blouin, of Dubuque, Iowa, to be Assistant Director of the Community Services Administration. He would replace Robert Smith, resigned.

Blouin is a former U.S. Representative from Iowa and was a consultant on Indian education to the Assistant Secretary of the Interior until earlier this year.

He was born November 7, 1945, in Jacksonville, Fla. He received a B.A. from Loras College, Dubuque, Iowa, in 1966.

From 1967 to 1969, Blouin taught fifth grade in Dubuque. From 1970 to 1974, he was an advertising consultant. He served in the Iowa House of Representatives from 1968 to 1972 and in the Iowa Senate from 1972 to 1974.

Blouin was elected to the U.S. House of Representatives in 1974 and reelected in 1976. He was a member of the House Education and Labor Committee and chairman of its Advisory Panel on Indian Education.

In 1979 Blouin was Director of the Information Security Oversight Office at the General Services Administration.

Claims of the Cow Creek Band of the Umpqua Indian Tribe

Statement on Signing S. 668 Into Law.
May 27, 1980

I have reluctantly approved S. 668, which permits the Cow Creek Band of the Umpqua Tribe of Indians to file with the United States Court of Claims any claim the band could have filed under the Indian Claims Commission Act of August 13, 1946.

This legislation permits the Cow Creek Band to file claims against the United States in the U.S. Court of Claims notwithstanding the statute of limitations. As a matter of general policy and equity, I do not favor and I will not sign further piecemeal waivers of the statute of limitations unless unique and special circumstances exist. In this instance, the circumstances were unique, and I have therefore signed S. 668.

NOTE: As enacted, S. 668 is Public Law 96–251, enacted May 26.

Trade With Romania, Hungary, and the People's Republic of China

Message to the Congress.   May 28, 1980

To the Congress of the United States:

In accordance with subsection 402(d) (5) of the Trade Act of 1974, I transmit herewith my recommendation for a further 12-month extension of the authority to waive subsections (a) and (b) of section 402 of the Act.

I include as part of my recommendation my determination that further extension of the waiver authority, and continuation of the waivers applicable to the Socialist Republic of Romania, the Hungarian People's Republic and the People's Republic of China will substantially promote the objectives of section 402.

This recommendation also includes my reasons for recommending the extension of waiver authority and for my determination that continuation of the three waivers currently in effect will substantially promote the objectives of section 402.

JIMMY CARTER

The White House,
   May 28, 1980.

RECOMMENDATION FOR EXTENSION OF
WAIVER AUTHORITY

I recommend to the Congress that the waiver authority granted by subsection 402(c) of the Trade Act of 1974 (hereinafter referred to as "the Act") be further extended for twelve months. Pursuant to subsection 402(d) (5) of the Act, I have today determined that further extension of the waiver authority granted by section 402(c) of the Act, and continuation of the waivers currently applicable to the Socialist Republic of Romania, the

Hungarian People's Republic and the People's Republic of China will substantially promote the objectives of section 402 of the Act. My determination is attached to this recommendation and is incorporated herein.

The general waiver authority conferred by section 402(c) of the Act has been of major importance in permitting and re-enforcing the expansion of relations between the United States and certain countries of Eastern Europe and the People's Republic of China. In the past year this authority has permitted the negotiation and entry into force of the U.S.-China Agreement on Trade Relations. This is a major step in the evolution of U.S.-Chinese relations. Moreover, the waiver authority has permitted us to conclude and maintain in force bilateral trade agreements with Romania and Hungary. These have been cornerstones in the strengthening of our political and economic relations with those countries, including our important and productive exchanges on human rights and emigration matters. Continuation of this authority may provide a basis for future steps to expand and improve our bilateral relations with other countries now subject to subsections 402(a) and (b) of the Act, should circumstances permit. I believe that all of these considerations fully justify this recommendation for extension of the general waiver authority.

I also believe that continuing the current waivers applicable to Romania, Hungary and the People's Republic of China will substantially promote the objectives of section 402.

Romania—Emigration from Romania to the United States has grown substantially since the waiver has been in effect and is now nearly four times as large as it was in 1974. This progress continued in 1979 and throughout the first four months of 1980. During this period, we have maintained an active dialogue with the Romanian Government concerning emigration matters, including our interest in sustained performance with respect to emigration to the United States and Israel. This interest was expressed, most recently, during high-level bilateral consultations in Washington in April within the framework of the Final Act of the Conference on Security and Cooperation in Europe and in the context of meetings of the U.S.-Romanian Joint Economic Commission.

During these meetings there was also a detailed examination of overall emigration trends for Romania and the question of binational marriages. We believe that discussions such as these, which take place within the context of the waiver under section 402 of the Act, will ensure continued favorable resolution of emigration and humanitarian problems.

Hungary—At the time of the initial waiver in 1978, the Hungarian Government indicated that it would continue to deal with emigration matters in a responsive and humanitarian manner. Since then, Hungarian actions have been consistent with this policy. Most Hungarians who apply to emigrate receive permission to do so without undue difficulty. The number of problem cases outstanding at any one time remains small, usually considerably fewer than a dozen at any time among persons seeking to come to the United States. We have found that we can discuss problem cases productively with the Hungarian Government, and that most eventually are resolved favorably.

People's Republic of China—During the past year, China has demonstrated its commitment to open emigration by simplifying its exit procedures and permitting over 1,500 students to study in the United States. The numerical limits imposed on entry to the U.S. by our immigration law are now a more significant impediment to immigration from China than are the Chinese Government's exit controls. China's commitment to open emigration is exemplified by the consular agreement concluded with the United States in January, 1979, in which China agreed to facilitate the reunion of families and to process all applications as quickly as possible. The Chinese Government is aware of the benefits of most favored nation status and of our interest in open emigration, and extension of the waiver will encourage the Chinese to maintain their current travel and emigration policy.

In light of all of these considerations, I have determined that continuation of the waivers applicable to Romania, Hungary and the People's Republic of China will substantially promote the objectives of section 402 of the Act.

Trade With Romania, Hungary, and the People's Republic of China

Memorandum From the President.
May 28, 1980

Presidential Determination No. 80–19

Memorandum for the Secretary of State
Subject: Determination under Subsection 402(d)(5) and (d)(5)(C) of the Trade Act of 1974—Continuation of Waiver Authority

Pursuant to the authority vested in me under the Trade Act of 1974, (Public Law 93–618, January 3, 1975; 88 Stat. 1978) (hereinafter "the Act"), I determine, pursuant to Subsections 402 (d)(5) and (d)(5)(C) of the Act, that the further

extension of the waiver authority granted by Subsection 402(c) of the Act will substantially promote the objectives of Section 402 of the Act. I further determine the continuation of the waivers applicable to the Socialist Republic of Romania, the Hungarian People's Republic and the People's Republic of China will substantially promote the objectives of Section 402 of the Act.

This determination shall be published in the FEDERAL REGISTER.

JIMMY CARTER

[Filed with the Office of the Federal Register, 4:02 p.m., June 2, 1980]

Federal Trade Commission Improvements Act of 1980

Statement on Signing H.R. 2313 Into Law.
May 28, 1980

I am today signing the Federal Trade Commission Improvements Act of 1980 into law. For the first time in 3 years there will be a specific authorization statute in effect for the Federal Trade Commission. The FTC can resume fulfilling its mandate to safeguard the integrity of our national marketplace.

This bill contains some valuable features patterned after my program to eliminate excessive regulation. It requires that FTC rules be based on sound economic analysis. Another provision directs the agency to find the least burdensome way of achieving its goals.

Other aspects of the legislation are less satisfactory. Section 21 provides for a two-house congressional veto of FTC final rules. This provision is both unwise and unconstitutional. I am signing this bill despite the congressional veto provision, because the very existence of this agency is at stake. Under the bill, a suit to test the legislative veto provision can be expedited, and I look forward to such a court challenge.

We need vigorous congressional oversight of regulatory agencies. But the reauthorization bills passed by the Senate and the House went beyond such oversight and actually required termination of specific, major, ongoing proceedings before the Commission. I am pleased that the conferees have modified these provisions. If powerful interests can turn to the political arena as an alternative to the legal process, our system of justice will not function in a fair and orderly fashion.

Enactment of this bill has been a complicated, often frustrating process for the House and Senate conferees and for the members and employees of the Federal Trade Commission. I appreciate the cooperation of Congressmen Scheuer and Broyhill, of Senators Ford and Danforth, and of Chairman Michael Pertschuk in molding a compromise bill that permits the FTC to continue to protect the consumers of our Nation.

NOTE: As enacted, H.R. 2313 is Public Law 96–252, approved May 28.

United States Ambassador to The Gambia

Nomination of Larry Gordon Piper.
May 28, 1980

The President today announced that he will nominate Larry Gordon Piper, of Burnet, Tex., to be Ambassador Extraordinary and Plenipotentiary of the United States to the Republic of Gambia. He would replace Herman J. Cohen, resigned. Piper has been Executive Director of the Executive Secretariat at the State Department since 1977.

He was born June 26, 1928, in Dallas,

Tex. He received a B.B.A. from Southwest Texas State College in 1949.

From 1949 to 1954, Piper was assistant manager of a food processing and distribution company, and from 1954 to 1963, he was senior accountant, then comptroller-manager, of a petroleum production and exploration company. From 1961 to 1963, he was U.S. consular agent in Las Palmas, Canary Islands. From 1963 to 1964, he was a cost analyst with an aerospace company.

Piper served as budget and fiscal officer at the U.S. Embassies in Salisbury (1964–66), Mogadishu (1966–67), and La Paz (1967–70). He was a budget officer (1970–72) and budget and management officer (1972–74) at the State Department.

From 1974 to 1977, Piper was administrative officer in Lagos. In 1977 he also served as Counselor for Administration at the U.S. Mission to the United Nations.

United States Ambassador to Guinea

Nomination of Allen Clayton Davis.
May 28, 1980

The President today announced that he will nominate Allen Clayton Davis, of Murfreesboro, Tenn., to be Ambassador Extraordinary and Plenipotentiary of the United States to the People's Revolutionary Republic of Guinea. He would replace Oliver S. Crosby, who is resigning. Davis has been minister-counselor and Deputy Chief of Mission in Kinshasa since 1977 and has been a Foreign Service officer since 1956.

He was born August 23, 1927, in Glencliff, Tenn. He received a B.S.F.S. from Georgetown University in 1956. He served in the U.S. Navy from 1947 to 1953.

Davis joined the Foreign Service in 1956 and was posted in Monrovia, at the U.S. Mission to the United Nations, and at the State Department. From 1966 to 1968, he was a political officer in Moscow, and from 1968 to 1970, he was counselor for political affairs and Deputy Chief of Mission in Ouagadougou.

From 1970 to 1973, Davis was counselor for political affairs in Algiers. He attended the Army War College in 1973–74 and was counselor and Deputy Chief of Mission in Dakar from 1974 to 1977.

Investigation of Hamilton Jordan

Statement by the President. May 28, 1980

My confidence in Hamilton Jordan's integrity has never wavered. I am gratified that after an exhaustive investigation the Special Prosecutor and the grand jury have now agreed with the Attorney General's conclusion last fall that the charges against Hamilton have not been substantiated.

NOTE: Special Prosecutor Arthur H. Christy concluded in a report that there was insufficient evidence to support allegations that Mr. Jordan, Assistant to the President, had used cocaine in a New York disco in June 1978 or in Los Angeles in October 1977.

Interview With the President

*Remarks and a Question-and-Answer Session With Newhouse Newspaper Editors.
May 28, 1980*

THE PRESIDENT. Well, first of all, let me welcome all of you to the White House. Some of you have been here before; a few of you have not. But you represent news media that are very important throughout our Nation, and I wanted to take a few minutes to outline one or two basic problems on which we are working at this time, and then spend what remaining minutes we have with my answering your questions.

ADMINISTRATION POLICIES

Domestically, we are going through a very severe transition phase from overdependence on foreign oil to the evolution of a very good, sound, adequate energy policy for our country based on two elements. One is to reduce consumption through conservation, and secondly, to produce more energy in our own Nation.

The unbelievable 150-percent increase in the price of oil in the last 18 months has had a severe adverse impact on inflation throughout the world, and obviously it's affected our country with both high inflation rates and high interest rates. These high interest rates in particular have adversely affected the production of things like automobiles and the building of homes.

The first part of March we put forward a good anti-inflation program, working with the Federal Reserve and the Congress, to go toward a balanced budget, to restrict consumer spending, and to take other action that's been very effective so far. Interest rates are dropping precipitously, and we believe that the inflation rates will drop substantially during the summer months and toward the second part of this year.

Now we're dealing with budget questions which are very difficult to handle. We are committed to a balanced budget; within that budget there must be a proper allotment of resources between defense and domestic programs. On our defense program, which I put to the Congress back in November and have committed to continue now for 5 years, we have built into it a 4-percent real growth in appropriations each year for 5 years. That's above and beyond the inflation rate. It's adequate; it's approved by the Joint Chiefs of Staff, the Secretary of Defense, and others.

The Congress, however, has added on top of that additional spending at the expense of domestic programs. And as we go through this time of recession which is now on us, we really need to have programs designed to keep Americans at work and to meet the needs of education, training, and the prevention of deterioration in our most severely impacted cities and communities around the Nation. We cannot afford to cheat the American people on domestic programs with an unnecessary allocation of funds from domestic programs to defense expenditures.

This is why I will oppose and have announced my opposition to the first budget resolution by the Congress. This is not a resolution that has to come to me, but with the so-called reconciliation language, it is severely binding in the coming weeks on the authorization committees and the appropriations committees. A final judgment is being made to an unprecedented degree by this first budget resolution as to what the Congress can do in the remainder of this year in preparing the 1981 fiscal year budget.

So, I'm committed to a budget that's balanced; a budget that is adequate for our defens needs, not only this next year but for the next 5 years; and which adequately meets domestic programs, particularly in view of the fact that we have a recession on us now and the prospects of excessive unemployment and deteriora-

tion in our communities if we don't meet those needs in the coming months.

Those are a few of the considerations that we are facing now on a domestic level. I'd be glad to answer your questions on this or any other item.

Anybody have a question?

QUESTIONS

PRESIDENT'S PRIMARY CAMPAIGNS

Q. Mr. President, Dave Rogers from Bay City Times. Senator Kennedy is in Ohio right now saying that you're not a real Democrat because of your policies against inflation are putting people out of work. How do you respond to that?

THE PRESIDENT. Well, I've run my campaign, as you know, in every State that's had either a primary or a caucus this year. We've not skipped from one part of the country to another, all the way from Hawaii and Alaska to the Virgin Islands and Puerto Rico and all the States in between. We've put our record on the line against any candidate who wanted to run against me.

The results have been gratifying. We've gotten more than 60 percent of all the delegates in the primary States and more than 60 percent of all the delegates in the caucus States—I think it's really about 65 percent.

I think that our administration has accurately represented the basic concepts and principles of the Democratic Party. We've had extraordinary improvements in those facets of American life that are particularly valuable to those who suffer most from deprivation historically. We've added 9 million new jobs to the American economy; a million of those are among blacks, a substantial number, of course, are among Hispanics and other minority groups. We've had an unprecedented increase in education, and I think we've got a good urban program. So, I think as far as our record in the past is concerned and the judgment of Democratic voters throughout the country this year, that claim that we don't accurately represent the party is inaccurate.

And last night we had four more difficult States in which we ran, difficult in that they face the same problems as the others in the country do; now, we ran a campaign, won in all four of them. We've won and lost some; I wish we could have won them all. But I don't think there's any doubt about the judgment of the Democratic electorate, and I also don't think there will be any doubt in November when we face the Republicans in the general election.

ADMINISTRATION ACCOMPLISHMENTS AND
FAILURES

Q. In the last year of your first term, in retrospect, what two or three major accomplishments are you most proud of, and what two or three major things might you have handled differently if you had it to do over again?

THE PRESIDENT. In the historic evolution of a nation, 4 years is a brief time. Not since Eisenhower has a President served two full terms, and I hope and expect that having turned the tide in many difficult areas, I'll be able to take advantage of that as the President next time.

We've never had an energy policy for our country. I proposed such a policy to the Congress and to the American people in April of 1977, more than 3 years ago. The effort that I made at that time, calling it the moral equivalent of war, was severely discounted and even ridiculed— maybe by some of you around this table, I don't know—but by some in the press

and the Congress. But we're now approaching the final decisions by the Congress on giving us an energy policy that will meet our needs. This is a notable achievement.

In 1979 our country was the only one of the major consuming nations that met an agreed goal of cutting down oil consumption by 5 percent below what was expected. In the first 5 months of this year, the American people have conserved by reducing imports more than a million barrels of oil per day. That's a 12-percent reduction. That policy is beginning to bite successfully on cutting down consumption, and with the new so-called fast-track method and a new synfuels bill, combined with the windfall profits tax, we will greatly escalate the production of American energy of all kinds, including oil and natural gas. So, the evolution of that program is a major achievement, by this administration and the Congress, of which I'm very proud.

We've kept our Nation at peace. We have faced successfully, sometimes as a lonely country, a superpower or leader, the question of strengthening our alliances, and I would guess that NATO now, with its new commitment to a 3-percent growth in real defense expenditures and with a new commitment to theater nuclear forces, is in as strong and united a position as it has been since the Second World War, since its foundation.

We've also extended our sphere of peaceful influence to the Middle East. We've made notable progress under the most severe difficulties between Israel and Egypt. We're now trying to make that into a comprehensive peace, without any definite assurance, of course, of success.

We've opened up vast areas of the world to new friendship with our own country which will pay rich dividends in the future. A fourth of the total population of the Earth, the People's Republic of China, now have normal relationships with this country. We've not severed our relationships or our trade with the people of Taiwan. As a matter of fact, the first quarter of this year, we increased trade 65 percent with Taiwan compared to what it was a year ago.

At the same time, I've opened up areas of American life to people who were previously deprived because of discrimination. I've appointed more Federal judges, for instance, who are black than all the previous Presidents in the 200-year history of our Nation. I've done the same thing with women, the same thing with Hispanics and others, not only in judgeships but in administrative positions in the regulatory agencies.

We've had a vast improvement in the allocation of our Nation's resources, not only for defense, having turned around a long slide downward in real defense expenditures, but also in domestic programs. And I think there's a new sense of viability now about the system of federalism—the relationship between the Federal, State, and local governments—that's most gratifying to me and will pay rich dividends in the future.

Some things move very slowly. We've not been successful in getting tax reform, which I think is necessary. We'll move on tax reduction, I believe, next year after we get assurance of a balanced budget. But the reform aspect, I have not been able to get that accomplished.

We have not yet been successful in getting the final stages of a Mideast peace agreement, and we have been disappointed in some respects because of the lack of adequate support for our position in opposing Soviet invasion of Afghanistan and the Iran question from some of our allies.

We face difficulties and challenges—there's no doubt about that—and we haven't solved all those problems. But our Nation is united. I think our Nation is proud. I think we are a nation that's been successful. We're still a leader. We're not timid, we're not afraid; we're confident. And I think that we have, to some degree, restored confidence of the American people back in the Government after Vietnam and Watergate.

So, it's a mixed bag. In general, I'm very pleased with the strength of our country and our successes, but I see a lot of items on the agenda for the future.

GOVERNOR RONALD REAGAN

Q. Mr. President, Martin Duggan from St. Louis. You visited us at the Globe-Democrat in the summer of 1975, and we were terribly impressed by your accurate forecast of what you were going to achieve in the Iowa caucuses, in New Hampshire, and more importantly, in the Florida primary, because Governor Wallace was still a factor at that time.

THE PRESIDENT. Yes.

Q. But in our private conversation that day, I brought up the name of Governor Reagan, and I sensed that you disliked Governor Reagan. Was that a fair impression on my part? I would be happy to remind you of what you said to me if— [*laughter*]——

THE PRESIDENT. I think I remember what I said. We were both Governors together——

Q. That's what you said.

THE PRESIDENT.——and during the times of Governors' meetings, many of us would work very hard for programs concerning education and programs concerning agriculture and environmental quality and trade. Governor Reagan was one who would come into a meeting without doing the long, tedious work in which most of us were involved, would call a press conference and, because of his fame, would attract a great deal of press attention and then he would be gone. That's, I believe, the only thing that I ever criticized about Governor Reagan.

I never have known him well. I've only seen him during those transient times when we were both Governors—he was a Republican, I was a Democrat—we didn't have much to do together in planning.

Q. Well, perhaps "dislike" was not proper——

THE PRESIDENT. No, I don't dislike him at all.

Q. Since I'll be seeing him Saturday, would you have any message for him at this point?

THE PRESIDENT. Tell him I look forward to meeting him in the debate and in the contest in the fall if we are both successful in getting the nominations. And I think we'll have a good solid presentation of the difference of our party platforms for the American people, and also a good referendum on what we've done in this administration and also a good judgment between what we've proposed for the next 4 years.

Q. Thank you.

THE PRESIDENT. But I approach that with a spirit of friendship, not dislike.

Q. Can I ask one more?

THE PRESIDENT. I think we'd probably——

Q. At what point will Governor Reagan be given briefings by national security people?

THE PRESIDENT. After he gets the nomination, I think would be a good time.

Q. You would?

THE PRESIDENT. Yes, that's when I was given them. And if he prefers some briefings prior to that time, I would make that available to him.

REPRESENTATIVE JOHN ANDERSON

Q. Mr. President, you mentioned debates. Jody Powell says it's not in your interest to face John Anderson in a debate. Why isn't it in your interest and what about your responsibility to the interests of the American voting public?

THE PRESIDENT. I guess there are probably dozens of Independent candidates, and I just have no desire to start deciding which of the Independent candidates I meet and which ones I don't. The debates in the past between Kennedy and Nixon and between myself and President Ford have set a good precedent; that is, the nominees of the two major parties, chosen through the primary and caucus system, are confirmed by conventions as recognized in U.S. law and custom, I think, is an adequate forum. This is my judgment, I'm going to stick to it, and I think it's a proper one.

Q. Isn't Mr. Anderson a greater threat to your base of support than he is to Reagan?

THE PRESIDENT. I think whatever strength Anderson has in November—and that's unpredictable at this time—will be more at my expense than at Reagan's expense.

RETURN OF ROYAL STANDARD TO CANADA

Q. Mr. President, a recent visit of the Toronto editors—Springfield, Massachusetts, where I'm from—focused our attention, however briefly, on the fact that we have never returned the Royal Standard which our troops seized in Toronto, seat of government, in the War of 1812. As a result of that, Congressman Boland has asked Secretary Muskie to make a recommendation to you to return the Royal Standard as evidence of our particular gratitude to Canada for the rescue of our six Embassy employees in Tehran.

I wanted to ask you, do you have a set policy against returning prizes of war, particularly from your alma mater—[*laughter*]—or would you consider that individually on its merits when it comes from Secretary Muskie?

THE PRESIDENT. I will consider it on its merits, but it has not yet been brought to my attention. I'll make a note of it here, and I'll check on it, but I'm not trying to prejudge my decision. But I will consider it on its merits.

CUBAN REFUGEES

Q. Mr. President, what would you like to say personally—my name is Lockwood, from the Jersey Journal—what would you like to say personally to the leaders of those municipalities which have large Cuban American populations and are anticipating additional flow of people?

THE PRESIDENT. The policy that I've established for the handling of Cubans wanting to leave Castro's regime, under the present prospects, will not result in any substantial new emigres to our country. I will only permit them to come into this country in accordance with legal screening processes to be worked out with the Cuban Government. The boats that were already in Cuban ports are very likely to continue to come to our country. They almost have all come here. We have prevented those captains of the ships from going back to Cuba for additional refugees or emigres.

So, the ones who are already here will be assimilated into the American popula-

tion. Their legal status has not yet been determined. The flow of additional emigres from Cuba will be severely curtailed, because they will have to come here in the future in accordance with American law and after a careful screening process.

OLYMPICS BOYCOTT

Q. Mr. President, I am Peter Harrigan from New York. Some 85 countries have ignored your request for a boycott of the summer Olympics. Do you think that this is a sign that the prestige and influence of the United States is declining?

THE PRESIDENT. No. We decided not to send athletes to the Soviet Union on our own. And the U.S. Olympic Committee and the Congress and the American people strongly support that position. Our preference was that the Olympics in Moscow not be held at all this summer, because it sends a signal, whether it's intended or not, of approbation for or acceptance of the Soviet invasion of their neighbors in Afghanistan.

Most of the governments in the Western Alliance did not prefer to have their athletes go to Moscow. They confirmed our position. The independent nature, however, of the national Olympic committees will permit some athletes to go from those countries.

There has been a substantial worldwide realization and dramatization of the condemnation of the Soviet Union's invasion, through the Olympic question; and also, of course, 104 members of the U.N. condemned the Soviet Union and called for their withdrawal. And of course, the Moslem countries, 35 or so of them, have also done the same thing unanimously. Our economic actions against the Soviet Union are another vivid demonstration of

989

our displeasure and our condemnation of that unwarranted invasion.

So, we never expected a unanimous compliance with our position. The vote of the U.S. Olympic Committee was in doubt; I have no control over the Olympic committees. But I think in countries like Italy and Great Britain and Australia and others, the governments did support our position that the athletes should not go; their national Olympic committees decided otherwise.

CUBAN REFUGEES

Q. Mr. President, Saul Kohler, Harrisburg, Pennsylvania. Mr. President, on the Cubans: We have 16,000 of them at Indiantown Gap near Harrisburg. And I speak not maliciously—my father was parolee under President Coolidge. We are now paying people $5.25 an hour to wash their dishes, make their beds, and sweep their barracks. Is there any reason we can't at least call for volunteers to do that and help balance your budget in that respect?

THE PRESIDENT. Saul, I think that's a good suggestion. I don't know the answer to it, but I will find out the answer.

As you know, we've got American law to follow. The official designation of those who've come here from Cuba and from Haiti and other countries has still not yet been determined. They are not classified as refugees; they are asylees so far. We're giving them a haven from Cuban persecution.

But the question you raise is one that would involve legality. It also is one that might involve American workers' rights in that area, and I'm not prepared to give you an answer to it. But I will find out the answer.

SOVIET RESPONSE TO U.S. HOSTAGES IN IRAN

Q. Mr. President, I'm Arnold Friedman from Springfield, Massachusetts. Is there any indication that the Soviet Union might respond differently to an American initiative in the United Nations, based on the fact that the Soviet judge at the World Court was one of those who voted unanimously in our case?

THE PRESIDENT. No. As a matter of fact, the Soviet judge in the International Court of Justice, I believe, and the Syrian judge, were the 2 among the 15 who voted against the recent decision. The vote was 13 to 2. There were three votes——

Q. [*Inaudible*]—as I read the wires, sir.

THE PRESIDENT. No, there were three votes; two of them were unanimous. The third vote was a 13-to-2 decision, and the Soviet and the Syrian judge voted no. I think Ray [1] can get you a summary of that if you want to go into it more thoroughly. But I believe that's accurate.

As you know, when the U.N. Security Council was voting on economic sanctions against Iran, the Soviet judge at that time had voted to condemn Iran's holding of the hostages and demanded they release them. The Soviet representative at the U.N. Security Council voted no, which vetoed the economic sanctions. I don't think there's any real, strong tie between a Soviet judge who's now independent of his own government's influence, ostensibly at least, on the International Court of Justice, and the Soviet Government's position.

Q. So you think that the Soviets would veto any initiative——

_____
[1] Ray Jenkins, Special Assistant to the President.

THE PRESIDENT. That would be my prediction. I would hope they would change, but I think they would veto.

Ms. BARIO. Thank you, Mr. President.

THE PRESIDENT. Maybe one more question.

DISASTER ASSISTANCE

Q. Mr. President, there have been a lot of disasters lately—I'm Roger Kullenberg from the Kalamazoo Michigan Gazette. One of the minor disasters is our own $50 million tornado. You declared us a disaster area. We've been reading lately that Congress may be out of money——

THE PRESIDENT. Yes.

Q. It's a small amount compared to Mount St. Helens and some of the other problems. Is there any assurance you can give me that aid that we need pretty badly will be available?

THE PRESIDENT. I have submitted a request to Congress for a supplemental appropriation for disaster relief, and the Congress has not yet acted. But to use the same word again, historically speaking, the Congress has always made those funds available as a very high priority. We don't yet know the extent of loss or damage relief funds that will be necessary for the major disaster in the Washington-Oregon-Montana-Idaho area from Mount St. Helens eruption, but at this time we are doing the best we can to alleviate the suffering of people.

Although the funds are not available, I am absolutely sure that the Congress will make them available with minimum delay.

NOTE: The interview began at 11:30 a.m. in the Cabinet Room at the White House. Patricia Y. Bario is a Deputy Press Secretary.

The transcript of the interview was released on May 29.

Vernon E. Jordan, Jr.

Statement by the President. May 29, 1980

I was shocked and saddened to learn of the shooting of Vernon Jordan, president of the National Urban League. Vernon is a valued leader and a personal friend. All of us are praying for his speedy and full recovery.

NOTE: Mr. Jordan was shot early on the morning of May 29 after stepping from a car outside the motel where he was staying in Fort Wayne, Ind.

Department of State

Nomination of Richard Lee McCall, Jr., To Be an Assistant Secretary. May 29, 1980

The President today announced that he will nominate Richard Lee McCall, Jr., of Virginia, to be Assistant Secretary of State for International Organization Affairs. He would replace Charles W. Maynes, Jr., resigned.

Mr. McCall is currently deputy staff director for the U.S. Senate Committee on Foreign Relations.

McCall was born May 6, 1942, in Detroit. He received a B.A. from Hastings College in 1964 and attended the University of Nebraska from 1964 to 1966.

In 1967 he was Wyoming field representative for the Teton National Life Insurance Co. He was a chemist for the Wyoming State Highway Department in 1968. From 1968 to 1971, McCall was a staff writer for United Press International.

From 1971 to 1977, he was legislative aide to Senator Gale McGee. He was legislative aide to Senators Hubert and

Muriel Humphrey from 1977 to 1978. In 1978 he became a professional staff member for the U.S. Senate Committee on Foreign Relations and was promoted to deputy staff director in 1979.

Columbus, Ohio

Remarks at a Carter/Mondale Campaign Rally.   May 29, 1980

Senator John Glenn, Commissioner Mike Dorrian, Dean Jeffers, ladies and gentlemen, my fellow Americans:

It is overwhelming to see this crowd here today. I've been waiting a long time for this moment. And there is no place in the world I would rather be right now than Columbus, Ohio, because there's no place that's any better to speak to the heart of America than right here in the heart of America. And I have to admit there are some other reasons that I'm glad to be here. [*Laughter*]

My final victory in the primary season in 1976 in Ohio convinced the Nation that I would win the nomination of the Democratic Party, and I want to thank Ohioans for that. Secondly, at the 1976 convention in New York, the delegate votes of Ohio put me over the top as the Democratic nominee. I want to thank you for that. And on election day in the fall of 1976, the votes in Ohio made the difference between another 4 years of Republicanism and the return of a Democrat to the White House, and I and the rest of the American people want to thank you for that.

And next Tuesday, Ohio will make a decision that will give me a nationwide majority of the Democratic delegates again, and I want to thank you for that in advance.

It is good to be back, and I could not ask for a better man to introduce me and to welcome me back—a bolder pioneer, a finer statesman, a great son of Ohio—than Senator John Glenn.

In the fall of 1944, when President Roosevelt was running for reelection, he said that he would not campaign, but he would take the occasion to correct any errors that his opponents made about him and his administration and his record. Although I will, of course, campaign this fall, now is a good time to set the record straight, not only about my own record but also about the strengths and the achievements of the United States of America.

Let me ask you a few questions. The answers might surprise you. Of all of the industrial powers, which nation has the highest productivity per worker? The United States is the answer. Another one: Of the major developed nations on Earth, which one was the only nation to meet our goal of reducing oil consumption by 5 percent in 1979, compared to 1978? Which nation did that? The answer is the United States. And during the 5 years since OPEC declared its oil embargo in 1973, among the major oil-consuming nations—our country, West Germany, France, Great Britain, Japan—listen closely to the question—which is the only nation to have a net increase in manufacturing employment? The answer is the United States, right.

Another question: During this exact same period, the same countries, which of these nations had the greatest increase in industrial production? Anybody know? You're right: the United States of America. Here's one you could probably answer just as well: Which nation has added in the last 3½ years more than 9 million new jobs? The United States, again. And I might say that 350,000 of those jobs was right here in Ohio. Which nation is the strongest and at peace? The United States. And which nation is going to stay the strongest and stay at peace? The United States.

I'm here today to talk sense to the people of Ohio and to the people of the United States of America. It is time to set the record straight about our Nation and about our future. We do live in a time of challenge; we do live in a time of change; we do live in a time of danger. But in every area of change, in every area of challenge, in every area of danger, because of our courage and strength, America is turning the tide.

We're turning the tide in energy from a nation which has been overly dependent on foreign oil to a nation which is determined to be energy secure. We're turning the tide on the economy from a nation suffering along with other nations of worldwide inflation and from escalating interest rates to a nation determined to bring inflation under control. And we're turning the tide in foreign policy as well from a nation which was paralyzed by a tragic Asian war and by a scandal at home to a nation which is determined to meet the challenge of the future no matter what it brings to keep the peace and a nation that's proud of protecting the principles on which our very lives are based.

First, let me tell you how we are turning the tide on foreign policy. For years, Americans were divided. We were unsure of our purpose in the world. But today we are united not only in defending our Nation but in defending the principles on which we stand. We're united in the determination that America must be strong; strong militarily, strong economically, and strong morally. And today, the people of the United States are not ashamed to say that we are proud and that we love our country.

We've got some challenges ahead of us,

there's no doubt about that. And I want to describe very briefly to you some of those challenges and what we have done and are doing to meet them.

For more than 15 years, as John Glenn well knows, the Soviet Union maintained a steady upward growth in its military strength, while our own Nation failed to meet this challenge adequately. Now the United States is leading its allies in a steady, sustained growth in defense expenditures, not just for the last 3 years but with a commitment to the next 5 years and beyond. We have turned the tide in military strength. As long as I'm President, our Nation will be ready and determined to use our great strength for peace, *for peace,* to stand up for security, to stand up for our people, and to stand up for our unchanging principles.

As a world leader—and that's what we are—as a superpower—and that's what we are—we are meeting aggression and terrorism with peaceful means. When possible, we meet these challenges with other nations at our side. But I can tell you that on occasion, if necessary, to meet those challenges of aggression and terrorism, we will stand alone if necessary.

Over the most difficult possible obstacles and with great predictions that we would fail, we are now turning the tide on energy. For years our Nation was more and more a captive of the oil-producing nations. Each year we imported more and more oil. Each year more of our wealth flowed out of our country to buy that oil. We paid a great price for this, and we are still paying that price. As we send billions of dollars overseas to pay for foreign oil, we import inflation, and we also import unemployment. We allow our Nation to become dependent on the undependable and addicted to the unaffordable.

To cut oil imports, we must do two things: We must produce more energy in

America, and we must conserve energy. Last year in this country, we cut gasoline consumption by more than 5 percent. So far this year, we have cut oil imports by 12 percent. That comes to a reduction of 1 million barrels of oil per day. Under new legislation—and I want to thank you for what you've done for that—under new legislation passed by the Congress with John Glenn's help, we are at long last moving in the right direction.

Now, for the first time in our Nation's history, we will have a national energy program to put us on the road to energy security. It's more ambitious than the space program, the Marshall plan, and the Interstate Highway System combined. It will replace foreign oil with American ingenuity and with Ohio coal. And it will take billions of dollars that now go to foreign countries to pay for their oil to create new energy sources and new American jobs here at home. This will be an exciting and a challenging time for all of us.

We're also turning the tide on the economy. The biggest single cause of our economic problems is energy. As long as we send those billions of dollars overseas to pay for foreign oil, we hurt ourselves, as I've said, in two ways: first, through inflation, because inflated oil prices go all the way through our economy and all the way through our land; and second, through unemployment, because the more money we send abroad, the less we have to invest and to spend at home to increase further the productivity of American workers.

High interest rates, as you well know, have hit the automobile and the homebuilding industries a severe blow. We are facing up to these economic problems. We have moved strongly on a broad-based front since the second week in March with an anti-inflation program, which is very

successful, to cut interest rates and inflation. The results speak for themselves. Interest rates are now moving down rapidly; the inflation rate is also beginning to come down. And I tell you flatly, with the perfect knowledge that if I make a mistake it's going to hurt me, I make this prediction: that the second half of this year, beginning in the summer, the inflation rate is going to go down too, and you can count on it.

For the first time in 12 years we are working to balance the Federal budget. But we must do it right, with fairness and with compassion. Within the context of a strong defense and a balanced budget, we are fighting right now, today, in Congress, to meet the recession that's impending with expanded Federal assisted housing, with new job programs for young people, and aid to distressed urban areas. Because we have taken the right steps, we are building a brighter economic future for our country, a future of stable economic growth and of self-reliance and a better life for all those who live in our great land.

In each area—in foreign policy, in energy, and in the economy—there are no easy answers. We face major challenges, but we are turning the tide. We are demonstrating what we can accomplish by what we have accomplished already, with your help. In every area of challenge, I'm convinced that America can finish the job. I'm convinced of that because I know what we have already done together.

Our Nation has acted with firmness and with determination against aggression in Afghanistan; against terrorism in Iran; against dangerous reliance on foreign oil; against inflationary government spending. And we've acted together as a nation also for peace here at home and in the Middle East; for human rights at home and abroad; for a strong defense; and for the

994

dignity of our senior citizens, our minority groups, our young people, and for all working men and women.

I'm not here to say that all my decisions have been right or popular. I know that they have certainly not all been easy ones. But I will say this: In the last 3½ years we have been tested under fire. We have never ducked nor hidden. We've tackled long-term problems that have been with us and overlooked or deliberately ignored for years. We've made tough decisions, and we've taken the heat when we made those decisions. But we've done what was right, and we've always told the truth.

As long as I'm President, and as long as Fritz Mondale is Vice President, that's something you can count on, the truth. We will always talk sense; we will always give it to you straight. And also as long as I'm President, the Government of the United States will be committed to those fundamental principles that hold our ever-stronger Nation together; freedom, democracy, compassion, and human rights. We'll remain committed to the full promise of America—the land of equal justice, the land of full opportunity, and the land of liberty for all Americans.

Thank you very much. God bless you all.

NOTE: The President spoke at 12:36 p.m. at the Nationwide Insurance Company Plaza. In his opening remarks, he referred to Dean Jeffers, chairman of the board and chief executive officer of the Nationwide Insurance Company.

Columbus, Ohio

Remarks at a Carter/Mondale Fundraising Luncheon. May 29, 1980

Both to Dean Jeffers and to John Galbreath, let me say I am deeply grateful to you personally and to all of you who are here.

I've been thinking, the last few minutes riding along in the car with Dean and with Bob Strauss and others, Bob tells me we just lack a few delegates from having a majority to go into the convention and be the nominee. If I had just had Dean Jeffers a few months ago instead of—[laughter]—would have been over the top already, but—[laughter]—

In 1976, as I said a few minutes ago at a wonderful rally, Ohio gave me your expression of confidence. It was a coincidence perhaps, or maybe fate, but at the Democratic convention in New York, it was the Ohio votes that finally gave me a majority. And as you well know, in November of 1976, it was the Ohio votes that were crucial in determining who would be the President. And I believe that Tuesday and again in November, you're going to continue that long, ancient, good tradition of Ohio politics and do it again.

Let me say that I'm very grateful that Bob would come out here with me. Bob's done a superb job in managing our campaign and being our campaign chairman. And I'm going to count on him all the way through November, and if any problems arise in the campaign or anything like that, don't call me, call Bob Strauss. [*Laughter*]

I'm not going to make another speech to you, because I've already made one. And I, however, do want to say just a couple of things.

This last decade was probably the most severe economic test of our Nation since the decade of the 1930's. We have survived. We've survived strong, united, determined, and with confidence. Our country has had to face very difficult problems; we've not flinched. We've not avoided them. Certainly the last 3½ years, we have never turned our head away when a difficult problem had to be solved or a difficult question had to be answered or an obstacle had to be overcome.

It's not always been an easy or a popular thing to do, but we've made tremendous progress, and the decade of the 1980's is going to test our Nation even further. We can meet that test. Our country has never failed when we were united and when we had a clear vision of the challenge to meet that challenge.

We hear a lot these days about temporary inconveniences or difference of opinion among government and other leaders, and perhaps transient disappointments. But if you go back down in history and look at the challenges that have faced our country in years and generations gone by, now we are blessed not with severe discouraged people who are suffering, but we're blessed with great gifts from God of a wonderful life. The testing of our country, not being anything new to us, is something that can result, as it always has in the past not only with a triumph but a better life.

This country is on the cutting edge of change, the cutting edge of progress. As I said in my speech a few minutes ago, just one segment of our future economic life, the production of more kinds of energy in our Nation—solar energy, all kinds of energy from Ohio and other coal, the new development of energy derived from growing crops, that one industry alone is greater in scope and concept and excitement and challenge than the space program, the Marshall plan, and the Interstate Highway System all put together. And you know which State is going to be particularly blessed in the future with this enormous opportunity to make a better life for Americans.

And what we do here in our country will shape the lives of people all over the world. In World War II we were challenged with a dormant approach to production of weapons and other goods, and Ohio perhaps more than any other State in the Nation, responded and turned the tide of that challenge from Hitler. And we also have become a breadbasket of the world. Well, the 1980's can hold for us and will hold for us not only an opportunity to meet a severe test but to triumph and give our Nation an even better life in the future.

Let me say in closing this: As we go through a time of rebuilding and revitalizing and necessarily changing our economic structure, our industrial base, we must not forget the human needs that exist among us. The Constitution of the United States spells this out very clearly for us; that we must have stability, public peace, as well as equal opportunity. And what has happened in Miami and what might happen in the future in different places where deprivation has existed is a challenge to all of us. And as we have a better life for those like the ones in this room have been blessed so greatly, we cannot forget those who haven't yet been blessed as well as we.

That's part of the challenge; it's part of the opportunity; it's part of a democratic life; it's part of the life of the greatest nation on Earth, which together you and, I believe, I as President will make even greater in the years to come.

Thank you again for helping me out. God bless you all.

NOTE: The President spoke at 1:12 p.m. in the Isabella Ballroom at the Sheraton-Columbus Hotel. In his opening remarks, he referred to Dean Jeffers, chairman of the board and chief executive officer of the Nationwide Insurance Company, and luncheon chairman, and John Galbreath, luncheon cochairman.

Parma, Ohio

Remarks and a Question-and-Answer Session With Community Leaders and Senior Citizens. May 29, 1980

What I'd like to do this afternoon, Mayor Petruska and other mayors and ladies and gentlemen, my friends, is to speak just for a few minutes to you and save some time at the end to answer a few questions that you might have on your mind and on your heart. It's really a delightful experience for me to be back here and to be with you and to see your friends outside, who can't get in, and to have a chance personally to visit with you.

I thought, as I prepared for this particular visit, about the best brief message I could bring to you. And I thought, just in a short period of time, I would try to put the challenges that we face in perspective, because quite often in our great country, there is too much of an overemphasis on the negative side of life. People complain about temporary inconveniences; they're concerned about being disturbed just temporarily. We have hot debates about issues that are important to all of us, but we must remember that in a democratic society, those kind of things are inevitable.

You represent many things in your own life: first a full life—a life of experience, a life of commitment, a life of sacrifice, a life of love—and in this particular community, you represent a life that has believed in the closeness of families and the closeness of communities and intense patriotism.

Our Nation is a nation of immigrants. People have come here from all over the world. We've come here for different reasons—my own family looking for a better chance in life, for religious freedom from Europe; perhaps yours for the same basic reasons. And after we got here, we were still proud of what our families had been.

We were proud of our religion; we were proud of our habits and our customs; we were proud of our blood relatives who still live in our old mother countries. But we wanted to give up those things at least where we formerly lived to bring the best parts of it to this great new country.

The United States is the strongest nation on Earth. We are strong because our people are strong; we are strong because we believe in the value of every single human life; we're strong because we believe in freedom, that each person should have a right to take whatever talent or ability God might have given that person and develop and to use it for one's own family, for one's own friend, for one's own self, but not ever forgetting the kind of large and small community in which we live, in Parma, in Ohio, in the United States, in the entire world.

We do have problems. Our country has problems that we can handle. The challenges that face us today are not nearly so severe as the ones that have been faced in the past. We don't know what's going to happen next. My ancestors had no idea what was going to happen next when they landed from Europe on the Atlantic Coast. The future was uncertain. But they had courage, and they had conviction, and they had confidence, and they had hope. And as they melded themselves together to form a new nation, they realized the dreams of their lives.

That's still going on. After 200 years or 300 years or 20 years or 2 years of living in this country, that concept does not change. We strive for a better life for ourselves, but we're also looking down the road in the future when our children and my grandchildren and your grandchildren will have an even better life—more opportunity, more time to be with each other, more time to love, a stronger country, more time to serve.

997

These kinds of things are still with us. Energy: difficult. The price of oil has been going for the last number of months, more than a year, an average of 10 percent a month. Oil's gone up in price in the last 18 months much more than it ever had in all the years since oil was first discovered. But our country has been strong enough to accommodate that and to make the change.

One thing that we're very proud of in our Nation is our ability to take care of those who need help. Most of that help has been provided ourselves, particularly the senior citizens who retire after a long year, a long lifetime of service, and an investment is made in our Nation in social security and other programs to give us security during our senior years. But those years must be productive, because our Nation cannot afford to waste the tremendous human resources represented by you in this room and by others like you all over the Nation.

Our country's budget is very large. More than one-third of it goes for programs for senior citizens. As we developed the budget for next year, we were very careful not to cut those programs one penny. In fact, they've all been increased—social security, SSI, Meals on Wheels, the Government programs to give better housing. Those kinds of things have been expanded and they ought to be expanded from year to year to accommodate the increased needs and also the increased investments that you have made.

So, to summarize, our Nation is strong; it's getting stronger. We face challenges now; we've faced more difficult challenges in the past. Our Nation is united, and you have a tremendous offering still to make to your own families and friends and to your small community here, to the Cleveland area, to Ohio, and to the Nation, and we cannot afford to waste what you have to offer.

As President, I'm very proud to be here. I don't know how many other Presidents have been in this hall—maybe not very many—but I hope some will be able to come back in the future. But I'm sorry I waited so long to come here as President. I was in this community when I was running for President.

Well, I'm not going to talk today about politics, although you might know that Tuesday there will be a very important election in Ohio—[*laughter*]—I just don't want you to forget. And I would like to point out that I'm a student of Ohio history as it relates to the Presidency. I'm not going to name how many Presidents have come from Ohio, but I'll start in 1976, because in 1976, one State put me over the top on the last primary day of the season, and that was Ohio.

When we got to the convention and they were calling the roll of the States, you remember, there was one State whose delegate votes gave me a majority and the Democratic nomination, and that State was Ohio. And then, in the general election in 1976, in November—it was a very close election, but there was one powerful State that gave me its votes again and put a Democrat in the White House, and that was Ohio again.

So, without making a political speech, but just making a historical speech, I want to make sure that Ohio does not break its record. And Tuesday, and also the first Tuesday in November, just remember what you did in '76—do the same thing in 1980, and I'll be perfectly satisfied, okay?

I've learned a lot since I've been in the White House. One thing is to make brief speeches. I've got a timer on my speaking platform, and I've spoken now for 8 minutes and 56 seconds, and I wanted to speak about 9 minutes. So, I'll stop and see if any of you have any questions that you'd like to ask me about domestic matters or foreign affairs. And I'll do the best I can to answer your questions. Does anybody have a question?

Mary Rose Oakar, isn't she great?

Q. I don't know whether everybody can hear me.

THE PRESIDENT. I'll repeat your question if I can hear it.

Q. All right. Mr. President, I'm concerned about our social security program. It seems inflation is steadily—[*inaudible*]—increases that come along in July. Many senior citizens are falling behind all the time. Now there is talk of taxing social security. Many seniors can't make it on what they get now. With more dollars—[*inaudible*]—in social security income, it means less dollars——

THE PRESIDENT. I'll repeat the question in a minute.

Q. ——for much needed survival needs. On behalf of all senior citizens, is this tax really needed? This is not a popular tax for the senior citizens.

Taxing interest income is another sorespot. Interest income is used to supplement social security payments.

THE PRESIDENT. The question was about the stability of the social security system, what might happen in the future as far as meeting the increased cost of living by those depending on social security and whether or not social security income would be taxed.

When I was campaigning around this Nation in 1975 and 1976, I never met with a senior citizens group that the most important single concern was a bankruptcy that then seemed to be inevitable for the social security system. I promised then as a candidate, and Democratic Congress and I together, and with Republican help, I'll admit, have put the social security system back on a sound financial basis. It has resulted in increased payments into the social security system.

But you can rest assured that as long as I am President and as long as Vice President Mondale is in office with me, the social security system will stay sound. And we will also have in the social security system built-in, indexed increases to take care of the increased cost of living for you as the inflation rate goes up. And there will be no taxation of your social security income.

Q. What are your future plans for the Cuban refugees?

THE PRESIDENT. The question: What are my future plans for the Cuban refugees?

For the last 2 weeks, we have not permitted any boats to go from the Miami, Key West area down to Cuba for the purpose of picking up additional Cuban refugees. I do not intend to let additional boats go down there as long as Fidel Castro keeps his same inhumane and unacceptable and widely condemned practices which he has initiated.

So, I believe that this is the best way to handle it in accordance with American law, in a stable, sound basis with anyone who wants to come to our country from Cuba or any other nation being carefully screened before they leave Cuba. So, we have stopped that series of boats going to Cuba. I do not intend to permit that series to start again.

Q. [*Inaudible*]

THE PRESIDENT. I understand the question.

I don't think so. It is hard for me to answer that question, but there are no immediate plans now to lower the social security age. As you know, we have removed, since I've been in office, with the strong work of many deeply committed Members of Congress—like former Senator Claude Pepper, who's in the House—the mandatory retirement age, which was making people stop working before they wanted to. But I don't know of any plans now to change the social security age beyond what's built into the present law.

Q. Mr. President, what can we do about the medical and hospital bills that are—[inaudible]?

THE PRESIDENT. This is a place where you can help me a great deal. As you know, we have had before the Congress for a number of months a hospital cost containment legislation that would limit the charges that hospitals can levy against those who go there for medical treatment. In some cases, in some States, hospital charges have gone up sometimes as much as twice as much as the inflation rate. We are now bringing the inflation rate down. My prediction to you—and you watch what I say and see if I'm accurate—is that during the summer months and toward the end of this year, we'll have a sharp reduction in the inflation rate. It'll help us all.

But we need a nationwide, comprehensive national health insurance program with built-in hospital cost containment. And I need you to help me get that through the Congress, so that we can put it into effect for all of our people.

Q. Mr. President, after the city of Parma is instrumental in electing you June 3 and after, once again in November, when we're able to get you elected President again, will you please come back and visit us?

THE PRESIDENT. It's hard for me to make out my exact schedule that far in advance, but I will put Parma right at the top of my list of those to be considered.

Maybe one more question, because there's an overflow crowd in another room, and I want to go in and speak to them too for a few minutes. So, maybe one more question.

Q. What are your plans for the CETA program?

THE PRESIDENT. For what program?

Q. The CETA program.

THE PRESIDENT. Oh, I see. What we've done since I've been in office is to take the CETA program and magnify it tremendously. It's more than twice as great as it was when I was elected President. We are now facing a decision in the Congress about whether or not the CETA program, like title VI, will be eliminated or kept as a viable program. The Senate-and the House-passed first budget resolution does away with title VI CETA program jobs. I'm fighting to get that decision in the Congress reversed, because we would like to protect not only the CETA program but other aspects of public service employment.

In addition, for young people, we are particularly interested in seeing the programs not only protected but expanded. We'll have the money available this summer for at least a million summer youth jobs, for kids, I believe, who—15 years old or above. I believe it'll be adequate to take care of all their needs. And I've also asked the Congress for an additional program to be implemented over the next 2 years, that costs 2 billion more dollars, to provide jobs for youth, and also training for jobs for young people who are inclined to drop out of high school.

So, we're trying to protect those job programs. We're going to have a difficult time in the Congress, particularly with title VI on CETA, and if you all have influence with other Members of the Congress, help me. Mary Rose Oakar, I'm sure, stands with us——

REPRESENTATIVE OAKAR. I'm for it all the way.

THE PRESIDENT. All the way, she says.

Let me say this in closing to you: Nothing would please me more than to stay in here with you, because it's an enjoyable experience. And as I look in your faces, it's an inspirational thing for me to know what you mean to our Nation and what our Nation means to you. We've faced difficult problems. We've faced them before. United, and not forgetting the principles on which our Nation was founded and on which it still rests, we need have no fear of the future. In my judgment, the greatest nation on Earth, with your help, will be even greater in the years to come. And I hope you have many of them.

God bless you, everyone. Thank you very much.

NOTE: The President spoke at 5 p.m. in the Parma Memorial Auditorium.

Following the meeting, the President attended a private reception at the home of Representative Mary Rose and James Oakar.

Cleveland, Ohio

Remarks at the Olivet Institutional Baptist Church. May 29, 1980

President George Forbes, my good friend Dr. Reverend Otis Moss, ladies and gentlemen, brothers and sisters:

I'm glad to be back here in this church. I came here as a candidate; I was received with open arms. I'm back here as President now, received again with open arms. Reverend Moss is a very discerning person. He knows protocol; he understands the status of human beings. The last time I was here, he took me into the community center, and this time, as President, he's let me come in the sanctuary. [*Laughter*]

He made a beautiful speech a few minutes ago, and I'm going to take it as my text. The first time I heard Reverend Moss preach was in a sad congregation at the time of the death of Martin Luther King, Sr.'s wife, Mrs. Martin Luther King, Sr. He only spoke 5 minutes. I believe it was the best sermon I have ever heard. I doubt that he's preached a 5-minute sermon since then. [*Laughter*] But it was beautiful.

And tonight, before I begin my own remarks, I would like to report to you that I have, just a few minutes ago, talked to Shirley Jordan, the wife of Vernon Jordan. His father, his mother are there with her in the Fort Wayne Hospital. I had a long conversation with Dr. Jeffrey Towles, who's the surgeon who has ministered to our brother, Vernon Jordan. He reports that he was the victim of a critical wound. He's in the intensive care center. He is in satisfactory condition. He needs intense medical care, and he needs our prayers. And I would like to ask all of you for just one minute to stand, and let's pray for the quick recovery of our brother, Vernon Jordan.

[*Pause for silent prayer.*]

I thank you very much. Amen.

My first thought when I heard about this attack, which I believe was an assassination effort—I was filled with a sense of outrage and a sense of sadness. I've known Vernon Jordan for a long time in Atlanta; we worked together. I was the Governor; he occupied a major position in shaping the lives of poor people and black people throughout the Southeast by giving them a right to vote. He was planning then to run for Congress. He later decided, as you know, to go to the Urban League. He's been a severe critic of mine on occasion, and I've listened to him very closely. I've been to his home; he's spent the night at my home, and we're close personal friends.

It's ironic that his life should be attacked, because he has spent it and will spend it in the future fighting against the causes of violence. He realizes that we must have an end to bloodshed and the hatred in this country, whether it's based on religion or race or ethnic divisions. That kind of hatred resulting in violence can destroy us all.

We live under a Constitution that promises us life, liberty, the pursuit of happiness, equal opportunity, but we also know that our Founding Fathers wrote in that we should ensure domestic tranquillity. Martin Luther King, Jr.—I know his wife was in this church recently—said, and I'd like to quote something I wrote in the hotel room a few minutes ago: "Every crisis has both its danger and its opportunities. The ultimate measure of a man is not where he stands in moments of comfort and convenience, but where he stands in moments of challenge and controversy."

We know where Vernon Jordan has always stood, and we know where, if our prayers are answered—and I believe they will be—he will stand in the years to come.

As President I have a great responsibility. I'm the chief law enforcement officer of our Nation. I'm the Commander in Chief of the Armed Forces. But I'm also the person charged with the responsibility to alleviate the causes of dissension and despair and hopelessness and hatred.

Reverend Otis Moss has helped me a lot. He's been to the White House twice in the last 2 weeks. The last time he came there I couldn't be with him, because a volcano erupted in the southern part of the State of Washington. I went out and saw the terrible destruction that resulted from that act of nature. It had the force of a hydrogen bomb, with 10 million tons of TNT, 500 times more powerful than the atomic bomb that was dropped on Hiroshima in Japan to end the Second World War; 150 square miles of beautiful forestland leveled, devastated. And I flew over

it. And I was impressed then with the power of God.

And I was also reminded of something else that Martin Luther King, Jr., said. He said man is not flotsam and jetsam on the river of life; man is the child of God. And the trust that we have in our institutions, in our families, in our communities, in our Nation and our religious faith, can tide us over difficult times. We are not the first ones who've faced difficult times; we're not the first ones that sought for full freedom; we're not the first ones who've sought to find the promised land.

Moses led the Israeli people out of Egypt to seek freedom, and they were happy and delighted when they crossed the Red Sea and wound up in what they thought was safety. But they wandered for a long time. They didn't reach their destination immediately. They turned against Moses. They began to complain about the manna and the quail and said, "We haven't got the things that we used to have: fruit and fish and wonderful foods." But they forgot about the freedom that they had found, and they forgot about the slavery that they had escaped. But they continued on a long, hard road.

As Otis Moss pointed out a few minutes ago, after 244 years the American people, and particularly the American black people, have not yet reached the promised land. But we're on the road toward the promised land.

To reach our goals is not going to be easy; it's not going to be simple—it never has. Sometimes it's required suffering, sometimes it's required patience. It's always required courage and determination and a sense of unity and a maintenance of our degree of faith.

We want our people to have good health. We don't yet have adequate health care in this country. But the programs for women and infants and children, if the present budget proposals are carried out, will be six times greater than they were the last time I stood in this church.

We're making progress down the road together, but I don't claim that we've yet reached the promised land. We want our children to have a good education and take the ability and the talent that God gives them and nourish it and develop it and then be able to use it.

God knows and you know and I know that one of the greatest deprivations ever perpetrated against black people in this country was the segregated schools and the absence of a quality education. Special programs for disadvantaged children are quite often not provided by local and State governments. Those have had to come from the Federal Government. In the last 3½ years, since the last time I stood in this church, we have increased those programs three times over. We've not yet done enough. We've not yet reached the promised land, but we're making progress together in a constant, steady, determined fashion.

We want our people—young people, in particular—to have jobs, because there's nothing more devastating to a human being than to have one life to live on this Earth and not be able to expend that life or use that life in a productive way to serve oneself, to serve one's family, to serve one's community, and, indeed, to serve one's nation. And to arrive at the age of 16 or 17 or 18 or 21 and not have a chance for gainful employment is a devastating blow to a young person—man or woman.

We've not solved all those problems. In the last 3½ years, we have added a net increase of 1 million jobs in our country for black people alone. The unemployment rate among young black people has gone down 14 percent. We have doubled the

programs in the Job Corps, the CETA programs. And now we're asking the Congress for the only major new domestic program of the year, an additional $2 billion to be spent to take those young people that might be ready to drop out of high school and give them extra training, either on the job or in the high school with a job, and let that be a permanent part of American life. We've not yet got it through the Congress. We're fighting for it, and with your help we will get it. This is important that we do it.

The Federal Government jobs have gone down since I've been in office, the total. But jobs for black people employed in the Federal Government have increased 20,000, and we now have 15 percent of the total employment in the Federal Government; black employees. We haven't yet reached the promised land. We need to do more, but we're making progress down the right road.

And we want our people to have food. I want to be sure that no one in this country goes hungry. We have had an adequate food stamp program evolved, but as you know, a few years ago, the last time I was in this church, you had to have money to buy the food stamps to go back and get food. We've eliminated that requirement. Now you get the food stamps. And this is a major step forward, but the Congress is still treading on dangerous ground in not fully funding the food stamp program. We almost lost it the 15th day of May. But with your help and many like you, including Otis Moss, George Forbes, Vernon Jordan, others, we're making progress to make sure that people don't suffer from a lack of food.

Housing also is needed for our families. We've increased allocation of funds for housing by 75 percent. Government-assisted housing in next year's budget will jump from 240,000 to 300,000; we're going back now to get a hundred more thousand homes. Making progress; we haven't yet reached the promised land—God knows we have not—but we're making progress down the road toward the goals that we all share.

We already have programs that will let any young person of college age in this country get a college education without regard to their family financial condition if they're qualified to do the academic work. A major step forward; a long way yet to go but we're making progress.

I could go on and on; I don't want to make my talk too long but I would like to say this. Those programs are good. They are needed. They're long overdue. But we've got to be sure that we have justice in other ways. The decisions are made not by a President, not by a Congress, not even by a member of the city council; but over a long period of time the decisions are made by the regulatory agencies and by the Federal courts.

I wanted to bring people that knew what deprivation was into the Government with me, and Otis has mentioned some of those people: Pat Harris and Drew Days. You've also got Eleanor Holmes Norton, and you know we've had Andy Young. And we've got the Secretary of the Army, who understands what it means to be deprived of an equal opportunity to serve in the Armed Forces of our country. But we also need more and more people to serve permanently for life.

We've had some good Presidents in the past—Franklin Roosevelt, Lyndon Johnson, John Kennedy, and others. I've only been in office now 3½ years, but I have been able to appoint more black Federal judges than all the previous Presidents put together since our Nation was founded. Next week we're going to have another one, George White. George, stand up a minute.

I'd like to say one other thing. This is a time of controversy; this is a time of challenge; this is a time of impatience; this is a time of inconvenience. But it's also a time of opportunity. It's a time to build on what we've already done. It's a time to look to the future with hope and with conviction that if we all pull together we'll continue to make progress.

I was in the Navy for 11 years, and if you put people that want to go in the same direction in a boat, and half of them are rowing forward and half of them are rowing backwards, the boat's not going very far. As a matter of fact, it could do worse than stand still. A President has got to face a lot of things: rampaging rivers, exploding volcanoes, Republicanism that might come back next November. And we don't want our boat to sink the first week in November, right? So, let's pull together.

Ours is a great country. We're all in it together. We never thought it would take this long to reach the promised land. When the civil rights bills were passed more than 15 years ago we thought the time would be short when full equality would be with us and when full equality of opportunity would be the lot of our families. We've not yet quite reached that goal. But we are moving in the right direction. It's going to take persistence, harmony, trust, conviction, and prayer.

James said "the effectual, fervent prayer of a righteous man availeth much," right? And that's what we're going to need in the future: effective, *fervent* prayer. And we've got to make sure we're righteous and we're doing what's right in the eyes of God. And in this great land of opportunity we're going to make sure that we don't fail as we try to availeth much together.

Thank you very much. God bless you all.

NOTE: The President spoke at 7:27 p.m. In his opening remarks, he referred to George Forbes, president of the Cleveland city council.

Cleveland, Ohio

Remarks at a Carter/Mondale Fundraising Dinner. May 29, 1980

As some of you may know, this is the fifth event I've had today in Ohio, and it's very nice to end an exciting day with a quiet little event, a few friends—[*laughter*]—particularly when they're Carter/Mondale Democrats, and particularly when you're led, as I am tonight, by that great poet and wonderful political organizer, Vince Marotta. [*Laughter*]

Bob Strauss and I were talking this afternoon on the way down here, and he was telling me what a tremendous job Vince has done for us ever since this campaign began. And he even admitted—and those of you who know Bob Strauss know that this was very difficult for him—that although we lack about 15 or 20 delegates now, and I know Ohio's going to put us over the top, he said, Bob Strauss said that if he had not been the campaign chairman and Vince Marotta had been the campaign chairman, we'd be over the top already. [*Laughter*]

I really enjoyed coming down the aisle and shaking hands with you. I saw a beautiful group of young ladies outside singing a beautiful song that I know you heard. The other night someone asked Rosalynn what was her favorite song. She said she agreed with John Kennedy—"Hail to the Chief" was right at the top. [*Laughter*] And I believe with your help, Rosalynn and I will be hearing it for the next 4 years, after 1980 has ended.

I'd like to talk to you very briefly tonight. I know you've had a long day and a long evening like I have, but I want to say a few things that are important to me in kind of a sober way from the viewpoint of the Oval Office, the highest elected office in the land, perhaps even in the world.

I just came from Olivet Baptist Church, a church that I had visited in 1976. I pointed out the history of this country going back 244 years, and Reverend Otis Moss pointed out that for 117 years, since the Emancipation Proclamation, the blacks and others have been waiting for full opportunities in this promised land. We pointed out that we hadn't yet reached the full promise of this great land of opportunity. But we're traveling the road together united, courageous, forceful, confident, filled with hope, because we've seen what we've accomplished in the past.

We do face now difficult challenges. A time of troubling change, not just in this country but particularly in other nations around the world. It's even a time of danger for Americans, citizens of a superpower, leaders of others who look to us for guidance, because we are on the cutting edge of the evolution of society in the finest possible way. We have never been afraid in a time of testing and trial and trouble much more severe than anything we face today.

In generations past, in years past, when Americans were united and when we saw a clear vision or a clear challenge, we have never failed to answer a difficult question; we have never failed to solve a troubling problem; we have never failed to overcome an apparently insurmountable obstacle.

Our Nation is the strongest on Earth, and our Nation is at peace, and we're trying to keep our Nation at peace through strength. And we're trying to extend the beneficial effects of our commitment to peace to other people. This was illustrated vividly at Camp David by Prime Minister Begin and President Sadat, two men leading nations hungry to end 30 years of war, when their young men and women have fallen in combat;

1005

nations that I have visited with tens of thousands of people on the street expressing their thanks, not to me personally, but to the United States of America. A nation not selfish; not divided; not trying to take advantage of other people; not trying to dominate other people, but trying to fulfill the full elements of world leadership.

Energy is a problem for us. I've talked about it several times today, and many times in the last 3½ years. In April of 1977 I said the energy problems were the moral equivalent of war. I was not exaggerating. Some of the press made a lot of fun of that statement and said I exaggerated. We were anticipating then that by 1984 or 1985 world demand for oil would match the world supply of oil, and we had to prepare for it. That did not happen in 1983 or 1984, 1985. It happened in 1979. And for the first time Americans had to shape up to the fact that our natural resources blessed for us by God were not unlimited.

It's not been an easy thing for us, but we have responded well, as we've always responded in the past. In 1979 the only nation on Earth that met a goal of cutting back energy consumption by 5 percent was the United States of America. And this year, the first 5 months, we have reduced oil imports 12 percent, 1 million barrels of oil less per day than we were importing a year ago. And we've done it without sacrificing the quality of our lives, because we know that we have to conserve energy, and—this is the exciting thing about it, particularly for Ohio—we're going to produce more energy in our own country in the future. We've committed to do this.

The Congress is finally putting the finishing touches on a comprehensive energy policy. We've never had one before.

And now we'll be developing energy in our own land; not just oil and natural gas but geothermal heat will be used; shale; solar power; and particularly coal, from Ohio. We've got the legislation on the books, signed into law, to finance this program: $227 billion during the next 10 years. And we're going to make synthetic fuels and solar power work. To give you the size of this program: If you take the total space program to put a man on the Moon and do everything else, the Marshall plan, which rebuilt Europe, plus the Interstate Highway System combined, the new energy program is bigger than all that put together.

And this will give us an excitement and a challenge and jobs and growth and a new life and new leadership for the entire world: a way to tap the tremendous natural and human resources of the greatest nation on Earth. And as we move into the future, we need not do it with doubt and trepidation and fear and concern and timidity, but with conviction and unity and courage and confidence.

It's typical of us. Your area of the country in particular is made up of different kinds of people who came here from almost every nation on Earth, priding ourselves that we are different one from another, but we come here, our ancestors came here, looking for a better life. And that search for a better life did not end the day we or our ancestors stepped off a boat on the east coast from Europe or wherever we came from—that search for a better opportunity, for more freedom, for better education, better housing, better health care, a better free enterprise system, better competition, better leadership, better democracy. Those challenges are still with us every day, and when we hear the evening news or on the radio or read the newspapers and we see about the debates or the differences of opinion or the temporary setbacks or the transient disappointments—they're nothing compared to the tremendous blessings that we Americans have in this Nation and also the tremendous ability that we have to overcome those differences and those debates and those disappointments and those temporary setbacks.

Look back in history over the generations. We ourselves and our mothers and fathers and our grandfathers have faced much more difficult questions or challenges than have we: the First World War, the Second World War, a divisive Vietnam war, Watergate, the greatest depression that the world has ever seen. When I grew up and many of you grew up, transforming social accommodation to eliminate racial discrimination and to minimize hatred among people who are of a different race—those things have not been easy. But we have triumphed, we've met the challenges; not in a dormant way, not just breaking even. But every time we've met one of those challenges and ended it, we have been stronger and we have benefited. And I'm thankful that in spite of a political season when every candidate is condemning our country for having failed and condemning our Government for having failed and condemning the President for having failed, the people have not lost the sound judgment and common sense and conviction and courage that's been the foundation for American success.

I'd like to say one other thing. There's a lot of comment in the news media about the fragmentation of our alliances—with Japan, with Australia, with New Zealand, with France and Germany, with Italy and Great Britain. That's a gross exaggeration. Our alliances in NATO have never been stronger than now; never been stronger than now since NATO was founded.

They are free people too; they're independent countries too; they have strong leadership too. And they have a right to their own opinion, and we don't have the ability nor the desire to dominate them. But when push comes to shove, when the difficult decisions are made, our allies are there, and they know we'll be there. And our potential adversaries know that we stand together.

If you have a globe at home, even a small grammar school or high school type globe, look at it. Put yourself in the position of the leader of the Soviet Union, and see how hard it is to get out to the open ocean. Look at your neighbors, and see if they're friendly like Canada and Mexico. See if you can trust your own allies to fight alongside you if they have a chance to escape. Assess how you would be if you had to keep massive troops and tanks in those allied countries just to assure yourself of the loyalties.

Look around the world at almost 3 million refugees; 900,000 people trying to escape from Afghanistan, not to Afghanistan. They didn't build the Berlin Wall to keep people out of East Germany. They built the Berlin Wall to keep people from escaping from East Germany. The Soviets have gone into Ethiopia. There are hundreds of thousands of people who love freedom and want a better chance in life who've escaped out of Ethiopia. Look at Kampuchea, a country dominated by the Vietnamese, financed by the Soviet Union. You don't see people trying to sneak into Kampuchea. Look at Cuba, completely dependent upon and dominated by the Soviet Union. You don't have boatloads of Americans trying to sneak into Cuba.

The fact is that those who came here when this country was being founded, and even 2 years or 20 years ago, knew what we were doing. We came to the greatest nation on Earth, because we saw an opportunity here not only for freedom but for the accommodation of change, and because we wanted our Government to match our spirit and to match our vision and to realize our dreams. And down through the years, Americans have never been disappointed. We've got the greatest nation on Earth, and it's going to be even greater in the future.

Thank you very much.

NOTE: The President spoke at 8:31 p.m. in the Grand Ballroom at the Cleveland Plaza Hotel. In his opening remarks, he referred to Vincent G. Marotta, chairman of the board of Mr. Coffee, and dinner chairman.

Scripps-Howard National Spelling Bee

Remarks on Greeting the Participants in the Contest. May 30, 1980

THE PRESIDENT. First of all, let me say how delighted I am to have you here. I have a lot of groups come to the White House where I, as President, feel inferior in their presence, but I think this is the most overwhelming superior group I ever had to face. I don't have any doubt that everyone here can spell better than I can. [*Laughter*] And also my staff is not invulnerable. I noticed this morning in recognizing Jacques Bailly, they misspelled his name. [*Laughter*] I bet it's not the first time it's happened, is it?

MR. BAILLY. No.

THE PRESIDENT. I am glad to have you here. I've thought a lot this morning, after I saw the news reports and have followed the contest throughout our Nation this year—you're fortunate in being sponsored by, I believe, 108 newspapers. Is that correct? And this contest in pretty

much its present form began in 1925, a year after I was born—55 years ago. And I know that you are the final superb product of one of the most intense competitions in the world.

As far as the number of contestants is concerned, I think beginning with roughly 8 million, a few thousand are chosen to compete in the final stages and ultimately a very tiny group come to the finals. So, you've been the product of a massive effort which culminates in a great achievement for all of you and a very gratifying moment for just one, and then everybody else suffers both the trauma of getting ready, the excitement of intermediate victories, and also experience a final defeat except one.

And that's kind of the way with life. We have in this country an opportunity to strive for excellence on our own, but with a lot of necessary help from teachers, from close family members, from those who work tedious hours, to make champions out of all of you. And when anybody succeeds in our competitive society, where each human being is so important, it requires those two things: one's own ability and initiative and hard work, and the support and encouragement of many others.

I'm very grateful that you would come and honor me today. We have observed with a great deal of interest the fact that Dr. Baker,[1] I believe—is Dr. Baker here? Dr. Baker began the contest this year, I think by reading the 12,555th word that he has read in these top competitions. And when a President speaks, people do listen at times, but when Dr. Baker says a word, people really listen to what he says. [*Laughter*]

Thank you, Dr. Baker.

How many of you knew what "elucu-

---

[1] Dr. Richard Baker, pronouncer for the national competition.

brate" meant before yesterday? [*Laughter*] Did you, Dr. Baker?

Dr. Baker. Not until I looked it up.

The President. Did you, Jacques?

Mr. Bailly. No.

The President. I didn't either. I looked it up this morning. How many of you know what it means now? I know what it means now. [*Laughter*]

Well, those kinds of words, to be able to spell them requires a great deal of knowledge—not about that particular word, but about the derivations of words. I think it came from a French word meaning to study by candlelight or something of that kind, didn't it? And it means, of course, to express something and to work on something—do you want to finish, Jacques?—[*laughter*]—by studious effort. And that's a good summary, I think, for the wonderful achievement that you've experienced.

Well, again, my thoughts are these: Congratulations to you. You represent the finest aspects of a wonderful country: competition, initiative, achievement, and a temporary disappointment in not being standing here with me where Jacques is, because not everybody can win the top prize. But in the process, you've learned a lot, and you've learned a lot about our country, you've learned a lot about one another. And I'm very grateful to be part of it. Jacques, would you like to say a word?

Mr. Bailly. No. [*Laughter*]

The President. No? Jim, would you like to say just a word?

Mr. Wagner. I would just like to say, if I can say it, that the hardest word I had to pronounce was "politicization." That means to politicize, which means those who want to make something political out of everything, and that's a good thing. [*Laughter*]

The President. That's a word I try to avoid. [*Laughter*]

Somebody asked a student once what does "synonym" mean. He said that it means trying to find the word that says what you want to say that you can spell, and I think that's true with politicization. It's got too many syllables in it. [*Laughter*]

But I want to thank you all for coming. Congratulations to you, and I'd like to go around the edge and shake hands with as many as I can. Thank you again. Congratulations to you all.

NOTE: The President spoke at 9:56 a.m. in the Rose Garden at the White House. James Wagner is director of the National Spelling Bee.

Northeast Corridor Appropriations Bill

Remarks on Signing S. 2253 Into Law.
May 30, 1980

The President. This is a good day for our entire country, and especially for the Northeast corridor and for those in the Middle West who have a real need for consistently good service in rail transportation.

Before I begin, let me express my thanks to Senators Cannon and Pell and Kassebaum, Pete Williams, to Representatives Florio, Madigan, and others, who have been so instrumental in passing this historic legislation through the Congress.

I waited a few minutes hoping that my friend, Governor Brendan Byrne, would get here. In the future, with a better Northeast corridor rail transportation, he'll be here on time. [*Laughter*] But he's been instrumental, as you know, in initiating this project, representing the Governors, because when he was chairman of the Conference of Northeast Governors, they made this Northeast corridor project their number one priority.

And also, I want to thank Governor Joe Garrahy, who's here, as well as Governor Ella Grasso who could not be with us today, but who currently holds the chairmanship of the Governor's conference on this particular item.

Americans sometimes forget that trains are the transportation system of the future, not the past. In a fast-changing world with energy costs, air pollution, deteriorating cities and communities that need to be revived, a need for efficiency, and the changing personal habits of our people, the prospect for rail transportation for people is extremely bright in the years to come.

This bill, Senate bill 2253, implements many of my administration's rail priorities. It provides, as many of you know, $750 million over the next 5 years for the Northeast corridor improvement projects to make possible a high-speed transportation corridor between Washington, D.C., and Boston, Massachusetts. It also provides $75 million in well-protected loan guarantees to the trustee of—to the Rock Island Railroad, which will provide an orderly transition for them in making sure that the workers there are protected. And there's $1½ million in here for worker training for new jobs. I've supported these provisions in the legislation, and I congratulate the Congress for having passed this bill and presented it to me for signing today.

My administration has been very concerned about the bankruptcy of the Rock Island Railroad and its adverse effect on crucial rail transportation for the Midwest. The aid for the Rock Island trustee is very important to protect workers who are affected by the bankruptcy of this line, and it will also help in providing an orderly transition for maintaining the essential services in the Midwest.

This investment in the Northeast corridor will provide in direct jobs 30,000 person-years of employment. This will be skilled labor. It will also have a heavy emphasis on minority and small business contractors and will provide, in addition, between forty and fifty thousand additional, indirect jobs associated with the improvements in the Northeast corridor.

It will also improve riding conditions for more than 50 percent of all the Amtrak passengers and then, by 1990, we anticipate an increase in rail passengers of 5¾ million riders because of this legislation.

And I think most importantly of all, it will provide the basis for a revitalization of our Nation's industrial base. It will provide land use and improve the analysis of how land can be used in crucial areas, because it will focus on businesses and workers who will be inclined to locate in the area of these vast improvements.

It will also help to revive the central cities of the Northeast which have declined partly because of deteriorating rail service which will now be repaired.

In short, the total $2½ billion authorized for the life of this corridor project is the largest public investment ever made in the Northeast part of the United States, and its impact is already profound and beneficial.

I'm especially pleased at the $140 million allocated for station improvements. This money will be tremendously magnified because of associated developments from the private industry sector near these new and improved railroad stations. For example, improvements in the Newark, New Jersey, station have already coincided with $125 million in nearby development. Newark has long needed an assist to commercial activity in that part of the city, and this appears to be accomplishing that goal. Also, South Station in Boston is becoming a major multimodal transportation center, and it will stimulate over $500 million in expected private development in that area.

Other benefits of this project, as I've mentioned very briefly in passing, will be lower operating costs, higher patronage by railroad riders, and less congestion of airports, less congestion on our highways, less use of oil, efficiency in the entire Nation's transportation system, and, of course, reduced air pollution—a lot of benefits from one bill.

In short, the $750 million in this authorization is vital not simply to the Northeast rail system but also to our Nation's businesses, our Nation's workers, all the cities of our country, and ultimately, of course, to all the American people.

So, again, I'm grateful to the Congress for having passed this legislation and for those private citizens like yourselves, men who've worked and women who've worked in the Governors' conferences and others, to make this day possible. It's with a great deal of gratitude and confidence that the future will be even brighter for our Nation that I now sign this important bill.

SENATOR CANNON. Thank you very much, Mr. President. This is a great day. It's a great day not only for the Northeast corridor but for those people affected by the Rock Island in the Midwest part of the United States. And I'm delighted that we were able to work the matter out between the Senate and the House conferees in a solution that I think is very compatible and will add to the rail service that we desperately need throughout all of the country. Thank you very much, sir.

CONGRESSMAN FLORIO. Mr. President, thank you very much. We're very pleased at the cooperation that's been received by the two Houses, with the executive branch. Your support of the Northeast corridor has been unquestioned straight

on through, and your administration deserves great credit, and we thank you for your help.

GOVERNOR GARRAHY. Mr. President, as perhaps representing the Northeast Governors here, I should like to thank you. We've worked very closely with you, as Governors, to see this project come to this particular day. And in a very personal sense, I'd like to thank you for the State of Rhode Island, because this is going to permit us to revitalize our downtown area. It's going to open up acreage of new space in downtown Providence. It'll provide for the relocation of our station in Providence and, of course, help us get back and forth to Washington much faster. Thank you, Mr. President.

THE PRESIDENT. I'm sorry, if people arrive late we do not give them a place on the program. [*Laughter*] But since part of his tardiness is because we have not yet completed the Northeast corridor, I will let Brendan say a word.

GOVERNOR BYRNE. Thank you very much, Mr. President. It's nice to be here. I'm sorry to be late; I had to wait for my wife to get dressed. She has a lot of influence on me, too. I just signed a bill allowing sex education in schools in New Jersey. That's the only thing I've done that she disagreed with. She said we mandate reading, and they can't read; and we mandate writing, and they can't write. Now we—[*laughter*]——

I assume you signed the bill that my note said you signed, Mr. President, and that's going to be very helpful to us. People want to get from Boston to Washington fast; some of them want to get there too fast, but—[*laughter*]——

This bill, Governor Garrahy, will help your State, will help all of the States along that corridor. It will also help the people of those States.

I've had several meetings in the past few months which stressed the fact that the cities in the Northeast will benefit, because those station improvements and the roadbed improvements are going to revitalize a number of our cities in the Northeast. That will help tremendously. Newark, for instance, is being revitalized, and the revitalization is spreading from that station.

Also, the more people you get on mass transportation, the better off we all are. The people in our section of the country use less gasoline per capita than the people from any other section, and so there's more gasoline to go around throughout the whole of the United States. So we're not celebrating—although the leadership came from men like Jim Florio and Senator Williams—we're not celebrating with you on a regional basis at all; we're celebrating a bill which you signed for the benefit of all of the citizens of these United States. And we congratulate you for doing it.

We congratulate you for the courageous stands you've taken on a number of things very recently, Mr. President, including the courageous stand you just took on a budget resolution.

Thank you very much.

THE PRESIDENT. Thank you all very much.

NOTE: The President spoke at 1:08 p.m. at the signing ceremony in the Rose Garden at the White House.

As enacted, S. 2253 is Public Law 96–254, approved May 30.

Gasoline Conservation Fee

Letter to the Speaker of the House and the Senate Majority Leader.   May 30, 1980

Dear Mr. Speaker (Dear Mr. Leader)

This is to reemphasize my long standing position that I cannot sign any bill

disapproving the gasoline conservation fee which I imposed April 2, 1980.

Thus I shall immediately veto any debt limit extension or other legislation that disallows the fee or that restricts my authority to impose such a fee.

Sincerely,

JIMMY CARTER

NOTE: This is the text of identical letters addressed to Thomas P. O'Neill, Jr., Speaker of the House of Representatives, and Robert C. Byrd, Majority Leader of the Senate.

Protection of Lake Tahoe
White House Statement.   May 30, 1980

Lake Tahoe is a national treasure and an area of national concern. The President believes it is critical that the environmental quality of the lake be protected.

Today, the President is taking action in three areas.

First, it is important for the Federal Government to ensure that its activities in the Lake Tahoe basin will not cause further environmental deterioration—to make sure that the Federal house is in order before making legislative demands on the State and local governments concerning Tahoe. Therefore, the President will issue an Executive order to establish a Lake Tahoe Federal Coordinating Council composed of Federal agencies with responsibilities and actions affecting the basin.

The Coordinating Council will review Federal proposals and programs which may affect the basin. Should the Council determine that a proposed action will have a significant adverse impact on the basin's environment, it will recommend to the responsible Federal agency not to approve the application or proposal. If there is disagreement, the matter will be referred to the Council on Environmental Quality for resolution.

Pending the adoption of basin environmental threshold standards, the Executive order will direct all Federal agencies to review their proposed programs and other actions which may affect the Lake Tahoe basin, and to defer action if such programs would significantly stimulate additional development in environmentally critical areas or would promote polluting auto traffic in the basin. In addition, Federal actions having potential effects on the basin's overall waste treatment plan, as required under section 208 of the Clean Water Act, should be reviewed to determine if they should be deferred until such plan is adopted by Nevada and California and has been approved by the Environmental Protection Agency.

Second, the President strongly supports and urges prompt enactment of legislation introduced by Congressmen Santini and Burton and Senators Cranston and Laxalt. This legislation provides for the sale of Federal lands near urban areas in Nevada with the bulk of the proceeds to be used as repayments of appropriations for acquisition of environmentally sensitive lands by the Secretary of Agriculture in the Lake Tahoe basin. These bills are important first-step measures and must be passed this session.

Third, the Federal Government will continue to work closely with the States and regional governments and others concerned to protect the unique qualities and environment of the Lake Tahoe basin. The President urges the States to try once again to work together to make the bi-State compact agreement effective. However, while the administration will immediately implement the announced executive actions and will support the legislation, the administration is also prepared to develop stronger legislative proposals if the current legislation and announced steps prove insufficient.

Digest of Other White House Announcements

The following listing includes the President's public schedule and other items of general interest announced by the White House Press Office and not included elsewhere in this issue.

May 26

The President left Camp David, Md., and went by helicopter to the U.S.S. *Nimitz,* which was en route to Norfolk, Va.

May 27

The President met at the White House with:

—Zbigniew Brzezinski, Assistant to the President for National Security Affairs;

—Frank B. Moore, Assistant to the President for Congressional Liaison;

—Charles L. Schultze, Chairman of the Council of Economic Advisers;

—Vice President Walter F. Mondale;

—Hedley W. Donovan, Senior Adviser to the President.

May 28

The President met at the White House with:

—David L. Aaron, Deputy Assistant for National Security Affairs;

—Mr. Moore;

—Geng Biao, Vice Premier of the State Council of the People's Republic of China, Leonard Woodcock, U.S. Ambassador to the People's Republic of China, Secretary of State Edmund S. Muskie, Secretary of Defense Harold Brown, Vice President Mondale, and Dr. Brzezinski.

The President announced that he has nominated Gen. David C. Jones for reappointment as Chairman of the Joint Chiefs of Staff for an additional 2-year term. General Jones, 58, was appointed Chairman of the Joint Chiefs of Staff in 1978. He was previously Chief of Staff of the United States Air Force.

The White House announced that at the invitation of the President of the Republic, Alessandro Pertini, the President and Mrs. Carter will pay a state visit to Italy from June 19–21. In the course of the visit, the President will also meet with the President of the Council of Ministers Francesco Cossiga.

The White House announced that the President will participate in the Venice Summit on June 22–23. The summit, the sixth such meeting, will be attended by heads of state or government of Canada, the Federal Republic of Germany, France, Great Britain, Italy, Japan, and the United States, and the President of the Commission of the European Community. At the conclusion of his stay in Rome on the morning of June 21, President Carter will visit the Vatican and call on His Holiness, Pope John Paul II. On the invitation of the Presidency of the Socialist Federal Republic of Yugoslavia, the President will visit Yugoslavia on June 24–25. The President will then travel to Spain on June 25–26 at the invitation of His Majesty Juan Carlos I. At the invitation of President António dos Santos Ramalho Eanes, the President will conclude his trip with a visit to Portugal on June 26. The President looks forward to the opportunity to exchange views with the many distinguished leaders he will meet during this trip.

May 29

The President met at the White House with:

—Dr. Brzezinski;

—the Democratic congressional leadership;

—Mr. Moore.

The White House announced that at the invitation of the President, His Majesty King Hussein of the Hashemite Kingdom of Jordan will pay an official visit to Washington on June 17–18. He will be joined by Her Majesty Queen Noor. A visit was proposed by the President and accepted in principle by King Hussein some time ago and dates have now been set. The two leaders last met in January 1978. Both leaders felt that this was a good time to exchange views on issues of interest to our two countries.

May 30

The President met at the White House with:

—Dr. Brzezinski;

—Hamilton Jordan, Assistant to the President, Lloyd N. Cutler, Counsel to the President, Secretary Muskie, Secretary Brown, Mr. Donovan, and Dr. Brzezinski;

—Mr. Moore;

—leaders of consumer organizations.

The President transmitted to the Congress the 1979 annual report on the administration of the Radiation Control for Health and Safety Act.

NOMINATIONS SUBMITTED TO THE SENATE

The following list does not include promotions of members of the Uniformed Services, nominations to the Service Academies, or nominations of Foreign Service officers.

Submitted May 28, 1980

LARRY GORDON PIPER, of Texas, a Foreign Service officer of Class two, to be Ambassador Extraordinary and Plenipotentiary of the United States of America to the Republic of The Gambia.

NOMINATIONS—Continued

Submitted May 28—Continued

ALLEN CLAYTON DAVIS, of Tennessee, a Foreign Service officer of Class two, to be Ambassador Extraordinary and Plenipotentiary of the United States of America to the People's Revolutionary Republic of Guinea.

GENERAL DAVID C. JONES, United States Air Force, for reappointment as Chairman of the Joint Chiefs of Staff for an additional term of 2 years.

DANIEL B. TAYLOR, of Massachusetts, to be Assistant Secretary for Vocational and Adult Education, Department of Education (new position).

RICHARD JOHN RIOS, of California, to be Director of the Community Services Administration, vice Graciela (Grace) Olivarez, resigned.

MICHAEL T. BLOUIN, of Iowa, to be an Assistant Director of the Community Services Administration, vice Robert Nathaniel Smith, resigned.

JANET DEMPSEY STEIGER, of Wisconsin, to be a Commissioner of the Postal Rate Commission for the term expiring October 14, 1986, vice Kieran O'Doherty, term expiring.

Submitted May 30, 1980

RICHARD LEE MCCALL, JR., of Virginia, to be an Assistant Secretary of State.

CHECKLIST OF WHITE HOUSE PRESS RELEASES

The following listing contains releases of the White House Press Office which are not included in this issue.

Released May 28, 1980

Statement: on the conclusion of the Special Prosecutor's investigation of allegations against Hamilton Jordan, Assistant to the President—by Mr. Jordan

Released May 30, 1980

Fact sheet: administration's actions to protect Lake Tahoe

Statements: support of the President's position on the House-Senate conference report on the first budget resolution for fiscal year 1981

Announcement: nomination of George Howard, Jr., to be a United States District Judge for the Eastern and Western Districts of Arkansas

CHECKLIST—Continued

Released May 30—Continued

Announcement: nomination of John E. Sprizzo to be a United States District Judge for the Southern District of New York

Announcement: nomination of Earl H. Carroll to be a United States District Judge for the District of Arizona

Announcement: nomination of Charles P. Kocoras to be a United States District Judge for the Northern District of Illinois

Announcement: nomination of Alfred C. Marquez to be a United States District Judge for the District of Arizona

ACTS APPROVED BY THE PRESIDENT

Approved May 26, 1980

S. 1309_____ Public Law 96–249
Food Stamp Act Amendments of 1980.

S.J. Res. 175_____ Public Law 96–250
A joint resolution to extend the expiration date of the Defense Production Act of 1950.

S. 668_____ Public Law 96–251
An act to permit the Cow Creek Band of the Umpqua Tribe of Indians to file with the United States Court of Claims any claim such band could have filed with the Indian Claims Commission under the Act of August 13, 1946 (60 Stat. 1049).

Approved May 28, 1980

H.R. 2313_____ Public Law 96–252
Federal Trade Commission Improvements Act of 1980.

Approved May 29, 1980

S. 2648_____ Public Law 96–253
An act to authorize appropriations for the Federal Election Commission for fiscal year 1981.

Approved May 30, 1980

S. 2253_____ Public Law 96–254
An act to amend the Railroad Revitalization and Regulatory Reform Act of 1976 to authorize additional appropriations for the Northeast Corridor improvement project and to require the Secretary of Transportation to begin development of energy efficient rail passenger corridors, to provide for the protection of the employees of the Rock Island Railroad, and for other purposes.

ACTS APPROVED—Continued

Approved May 30—Continued

H.R. 6615_____ Public Law 96–255 An act to amend the National Ocean Pollution Research and Development and Monitoring Planning Act of 1978 to authorize appropriations to carry out the provisions of

ACTS APPROVED—Continued

Approved May 30—Continued

such Act for fiscal years 1981 and 1982, and for other purposes.

H.R. 7471_____ Public Law 96–256 An act to extend the present public debt limit through June 5, 1980.

Special Central American Assistance Act of 1979

Statement on Signing H.R. 6081 Into Law.
May 31, 1980

I am pleased to sign into law the authorizing legislation for the Special Central American Assistance Act. The countries of Central America need U.S. assistance to improve the well-being of their people and to strengthen their ability to withstand interference from abroad. Nowhere is this need more urgent than in Nicaragua. This legislation reaffirms our commitment to assist in democratic development in Nicaragua and our determination to meet the Cuban challenge throughout the Central American region.

The United States provided substantial emergency assistance to the Nicaraguan Government and people immediately after the revolution. Through the Special Central American Assistance Act, we can now offer significant help in reconstructing the Nicaraguan economy and in rebuilding Nicaragua's active private sector. Through it, we demonstrate our sympathy with the aspirations of the Nicaraguan people for a better life and our desire to cooperate with those governments that share our interest in pluralism and democracy. This legislation will signal to the Cubans and others who might wish to interfere in Central America that the United States intends to resist their efforts throughout the region in order to support the forces of democracy.

The passage of the Central American Assistance Act will help to accelerate the pace of reconstruction in Nicaragua, promote mutual understanding between our two countries, and improve the prospects for progressive, peaceful solutions to problems in Central America.

NOTE: As enacted, H.R. 6081 is Public Law 96–257, approved May 31.

Interview With the President

Excerpt From a Question-and-Answer Session With Daniel Schorr and George Watson of the Cable News Network.
May 31, 1980

MR. SCHORR. Mr. President, on the tangled skein of international problems you could start almost anywhere——

THE PRESIDENT. Yes.

MR. SCHORR.——but let us start, because it's current, on the problem of Palestinian autonomy talks. They have reached a snag, if not broken down altogether. The Europeans now appear to be getting ready with some kind of initiative in which they're going to move ahead in a pro-Palestinian direction. Are you worried about it? If so, what can you do about it?

THE PRESIDENT. Yes, I'm worried about it and have been for the last 3 years or so. It's important to put this thing in perspective. Two years ago nobody thought that there would be any direct talks between an Arab country and the Israelis under any circumstances or that there could be peace between the major Arab nation of Egypt and Israel; or nobody dreamed that there would be diplomatic relations established and tourists flying back and forth between Tel Aviv and Jerusalem on the one hand, and Alexandria and Cairo on the other.

We've had enormous progress already made, because of the courage and the conviction of the Israeli and the Egyptian leaders. Before the Mideast peace treaty was signed in front of the White House here, a little more than a year ago, and before the Camp David agreement was reached, we had equally difficult and intransigent problems to address, and there was an equally discouraged attitude among some who didn't have faith in the peace process.

We've got to maintain the basis for the peace negotiations—twofold: One is United Nations Resolution 242, and secondly, the Camp David accords, which have become almost like a bible between Israel and Egypt as we get into these detailed negotiations.

As you know, there is a sharp difference of opinion now between Israel and Egypt about how rapidly to move forward on full autonomy, a common commitment; how rapidly to move forward on the withdrawal of the Israeli forces, military forces, and the administrative government there; how to set up the security locations on the West Bank to protect Israel from external aggression; and how to deal with water rights, how to deal with land rights. These kinds of things are extremely hard to resolve, but we are down to what you might call the nitty gritty now. The issues have been clearly defined.

Lately there's been a sharp difference of opinion evolved within the Government of Israel, and we are waiting now for Israel and Egypt to get back together. We're very eager to see this done. My prediction to you is that without very much more delay we will be back at the negotiating table, making progress again toward a Mideast peace treaty on that basis, and full autonomy for the West Bank, Gaza.

As far as the European nations are concerned, they have the same hope that we do: that the issue of autonomy on the West Bank, the resolution of the Palestinian problem, the provision of security for Israel, a permanent peace in the Middle East, comprehensively negotiated with Israel's neighbors—we have the same goals. I don't believe that the Europeans will make any move within the next couple of weeks.

MR. SCHORR. You don't?

THE PRESIDENT. No.

MR. SCHORR. They're meeting in Venice.

THE PRESIDENT. We will all meet in Venice, seven of us, the last part of June, June 22. The European Community members will meet, I think, the 12th or 13th of June. There will certainly, almost certainly, be no action by them before that date. We are encouraging the European allies not to intervene in the negotiations as long as we are meeting and are making progress toward a Mideast peace settlement.

I can't control them. They obviously have opinions of their own. That's been proven many times. Neither can I control Israel and Egypt. We have a conciliatory role to play and an intermediary role to play. We keep the talks going. Both nations depend on us. And to the extent that they trust me and trust our Nation's inclinations and commitments toward peace and toward fairness, to that extent we'll have the prospect of success.

So, to summarize: We have a good basis; the issues are clearly defined; Israel and Egypt both want a peace settlement.

We are asking the European allies not to get involved in it for the time being.

MR. SCHORR. Have they agreed not to?

THE PRESIDENT. I don't believe they'll do it for the next couple of weeks, which I believe will be enough time to get us back at the bargaining table. And even if they do come in, we will not permit in the United Nations any action that would destroy the sanctity of and the present form of U.N. 242.

MR. SCHORR. You've got a firm grip now on what happens in the United Nations?

THE PRESIDENT. Well, we've got a veto power that we can exercise, if necessary, to prevent this Camp David process from being destroyed or subverted, and I would not hesitate to use it if necessary.

NOTE: The interview began at approximately 9:30 a.m. in the Oval Office at the White House. It was videotaped for use on the Cable News Network on June 1, the first day of broadcasting for the new network.

Fort Wayne, Indiana

Remarks and a Question-and-Answer Session With Reporters Following a Visit With Vernon E. Jordan, Jr. June 1, 1980

THE PRESIDENT. I'm very pleased, on behalf of myself, my family, and all the people of this Nation, to come here to Indiana to find Vernon Jordan doing so well.

I've talked several times on the telephone with Dr. Towles and with Shirley Jordan, the wife of Vernon, to get progress reports. But today, again, I've been given a very accurate report from his own physicians that he's recovering well. His strength and his good health, his athletic attitude and ability have stood him in good stead, along with the prayers of

tens of thousands of people who believe in Vernon and who admire him very much and who've been concerned about him, and also, of course, the excellent care that he's gotten here in this superb hospital facility.

I've also had a chance to meet with the mayor, with the police officials from the local government, and with the director of the FBI regional headquarters here in Fort Bend [Wayne], and I think it's very good to point out that we have excellent cooperation and that they are getting along well with each other. The local officials are very grateful that the FBI is involved in the investigation of the case, and I'm not going to comment on the progress of the investigation except to point to you that there is nothing in their relationship except one of mutual appreciation and the very closest possible cooperation.

The mayor of Fort Wayne and others have done a superb job in making all the local officials available in this heavy burden on the community. And the attitude of the people along the highway as I came in from the airport was one of friendship and encouragement, which shows the deep concern of the people about this unfortunate incident and the hope that Vernon Jordan will do well and recover completely, which is a high prospect now, and that the perpetrators of this crime will be brought to justice.

It's obvious that what Vernon Jordan stands for is courage. His commitment to the plight of the poor and deprived people of all races has been appreciated by this Nation, and as President, I want to add my personal appreciation for what he has meant for our country and what he will continue to mean in the years ahead. Mr. Mayor, would you like to add any words?

MAYOR MOSES. That's fine.

REPORTER. Mr. President, what did you and Mr. Jordan talk about, even though you talked only very briefly?

THE PRESIDENT. We talked about the necessity for him to carry out the doctor's orders and directions. He gave me a report that he's getting along well, that he has received indirectly an outpouring of expressions of support and friendship and prayers from throughout the country. He has now been permitted to watch television. He can't have visitors outside of just myself and a few others in his family. He's not yet begun to read newspapers and so forth, but he will, I understand, tomorrow. And he, of course, doesn't have a telephone in his room. But he's interested in the continued progress of the Urban League while he is incapacitated, has complete confidence it will be done.

He primarily expressed his thanks to me for the outpouring of support and help for him and his family that has been exhibited here in Fort Wayne and throughout the State of Indiana and, indeed, the country.

Q. Mr. President, do you think this was a conspiracy?

THE PRESIDENT. I don't have any information that I want to divulge concerning the criminal investigation. I think that's best described by the legal officials.

Q. Well, Mr. President, you called this, the other day, an attempted assassination.

THE PRESIDENT. Yes.

Q. What does that word mean to you? Does it mean political? Does it rule out personal motives? What did you mean by that?

THE PRESIDENT. Well, after I got home, I looked it up in the dictionary—[laughter]—because some question had been raised by the press. It said, "the attempted murder of a prominent person," and this is all I meant. I was not trying to define the nature of the crime except that a prominent person was the subject of an attack.

Q. You weren't referring to motives at all?

THE PRESIDENT. I have no way to know what the motive is.

Q. Mr. President, you just said that you hoped that the perpetrators are brought to justice. You used the word plural. Does that reflect a belief by the Justice Department that there's still a feeling that there may be more than one person involved?

THE PRESIDENT. No, I was not trying to determine how many there might be— one or more.

Q. Mr. President, Vernon Jordan always travels alone, without security, because that's the American way. He wanted to be able to do that. Did you give him any advice to the contrary, or does he feel he's wrong? And also, is there any national, coordinated efforts to protect civil rights leaders right now?

THE PRESIDENT. No, there is no national, coordinated effort to protect prominent people who are active in the civil rights movement. This, I don't believe, is necessary now. Those people who are prominent and also courageous in dealing with controversial issues are always a possible subject of attack, but this is something I've not discussed with Vernon, as far as providing help or protection for other civil rights leaders. I don't think it's necessary at this time.

Q. Mr. President, is there anything you view about the circumstances of the shooting, what happened? Did he discuss the shooting—[inaudible]?

THE PRESIDENT. Just very briefly. Well, he just—I think the only comment that he made was that with people who are involved in public life, like he has been, that the possibility of an attack is something that one has to understand and accept, that the alternative is a withdrawal of one's service, that it was a danger that he was willing to accommodate in his own life, and that he was very thankful that the attack was not successful.

Q. Mr. President, do you think that this was in any way related to the events in Miami?

THE PRESIDENT. I don't have any reason to think that there is a relationship.

Q. Mr. President, 8 hours before the shooting Mr. Jordan gave local reporters here the impression that he was for challenging leaders in this country for trying to address problems, mainly domestic problems. Was there any mention of any assurances that you might try to give him if there would be another 4 years of your administration?

THE PRESIDENT. No, we didn't discuss that, but I observe very carefully Vernon's statements. I've known him for a long time. When he was in charge of voter registration in the southeastern region of our country, he was living in Atlanta. I was a State senator then. Vernon was planning to run for Congress from the Fifth District in Georgia; I was planning to run for Governor. We both wound up with different positions later on. And Vernon has sometimes been a very severe critic of policies of the Federal Government, actions of the Congress, actions by me, or failure to move rapidly enough to alleviate the concerns of the poor people about whom he's concerned. But, at the same time, we've always maintained our friendship. And I'm familiar with Vernon's speeches, the major thrust of them. I listen to them very carefully.

When I've made decisions in my own

administration, as President, concerning urban areas or housing or education or the provision of jobs for the poor or welfare programs, care for the aged, I've almost invariably called Vernon in to give me his advice and his counsel and, hopefully, his support if the program that we evolved met with his approval. And I've done this with just a few other leaders in the country. I've done this because of the position he holds, because of my confidence in his judgment, and also because of a personal friendship.

Q. Do you agree with other leaders, particularly black leaders, who have said that this—they hope this incident will be a little more of an impetus to do more for—[*inaudible*]?

THE PRESIDENT. This is obviously a time for us to recommit ourselves to the protection of the poor and minority groups, those who suffer in time of recession or in time of extremely high interest rates and inflation rates. The riots in Miami, this attack on Vernon Jordan— although I don't have any reason to think they are directly related—are certainly a reminder that we need to redouble our efforts to alleviate the problems of people of all races, in all locations in our country, who are suffering from economic deprivation or some kind of social or legal justice deprivation.

So, obviously it's a reminder, but I don't see that it's directly related to what we are doing. I'm trying to protect the domestic allocation of funds for jobs and for housing and for health and education in the budget dispute with the Congress right now, and I know that in this particular dispute, Vernon Jordan and what he stands for would be a major ally. But we did not discuss the particular programs in my brief visit with him.

Thank you very much.

NOTE: The President spoke at 5:22 p.m. at the Fort Wayne Hospital after visiting Mr. Jordan in his hospital room.

National Science Foundation
Nomination of Donald N. Langenberg To Be Deputy Director. June 2, 1980

The President today announced that he will nominate Donald N. Langenberg, of Bala-Cynwyd, Pa., to be Deputy Director of the National Science Foundation. He would replace George Claude Pimentel, who has resigned.

Langenberg has been a professor of physics at the University of Pennsylvania since 1967 and a professor of electrical engineering and science since 1976.

He was born March 17, 1932, in Devils Lake, N. Dak. He received a B.S. from Iowa State College in 1953, an M.S. from the University of California at Los Angeles in 1955, and a Ph. D. from the University of California at Berkeley in 1959.

Langenberg has been on the faculty of the University of Pennsylvania since 1960. He has served as director of the Laboratory for Research on the Structure of Matter and as vice provost for graduate studies and research. He has been a visiting professor or researcher at Oxford University, the École Normale Superieure, the California Institute of Technology, and the Technische Universität München.

Langenberg is currently chairman of the National Science Foundation Advisory Council and a member of the board of trustees of Associated Universities, Inc., of the Council on Governmental Relations, and of the National Commission on Research. His field is experimental condensed matter physics and materials science. He is the author of numerous articles.

United States-United Kingdom Reciprocal Fisheries Agreement
Message to the Senate Transmitting the Agreement. June 2, 1980

To the Senate of the United States:

I transmit herewith, for the advice and consent of the Senate to ratification, the Reciprocal Fisheries Agreement between the Government of the United States of America and the Government of the United Kingdom of Great Britain and Northern Ireland, 1979, with its Agreed Minute, done at London, March 27, 1979. The report of the Department of State is enclosed for the information of the Senate in connection with its consideration of the Agreement.

The Reciprocal Fisheries Agreement, which pertains to reciprocal fishing activities in the waters off the United States Virgin Islands and the British Virgin Islands, was concluded in order to replace the Reciprocal Fisheries Agreement between the Government of the United States of America and the Government of the United Kingdom of Great Britain and Northern Ireland, 1977, which expired on December 31, 1978. The purpose of the Agreement, like that of its predecessor, is to permit traditional, small-scale fishing operations in the Virgin Islands area to continue undisturbed. The United States will retain exclusive authority to enforce the provisions of the Agreement and applicable national fisheries regulations within the Fishery Conservation Zone, and the United Kingdom will retain similar authority within the exclusive fisheries zone of the British Virgin Islands. Without this Agreement, and as a consequence of the entry into force of the Fishery Conservation and Management Act of 1976 and of similar British legislation, such traditional fishing activity would have to cease. I therefore recommend that the Senate give early consideration to the Reciprocal Fisheries Agreement and its advice and consent to ratification.

JIMMY CARTER

The White House,
    June 2, 1980.

National Advisory Committee on Oceans and Atmosphere

Appointment of Paul Bock as a Member.
June 2, 1980

The President today announced the appointment of Paul Bock, of West Hartford, Conn., to be a member of the National Advisory Committee on Oceans and Atmosphere.

Bock is a professor of civil engineering at the University of Connecticut and a member of the Institute of Water Resources. He is chairman of the Committee on Space Hydrology of the American Geophysical Union.

National Advisory Council on Women's Educational Programs

Nomination of Six Members.   June 2, 1980

The President today announced that he will nominate six persons to be members of the National Advisory Council on Women's Educational Programs. They are:

MARIA CONCEPCION BECHILY, of Chicago, president of Ms. Executive Search, which specializes in finding women and Hispanic executives for major firms. She has worked as a counselor and placement specialist with the Chicago Alliance of Business and Manpower Services.

BARBARA M. CAREY, of Miami, Fla., assistant principal of Miami Edison Senior High School, a former teacher of speech and English at the junior high school and college levels.

VIRGINIA FOXX, of Banner Elk, N.C., assistant dean of the General College, instructor in sociology, and coordinator for developmental studies at Appalachian State University. She served previously as director of Upward Bound/Special Services at Appalachian State University.

K. JESSIE KOBAYASHI, of San Carlos, Calif., superintendent of the Murray School District in Dublin, Calif. She has also served as director of curriculum and as a classroom teacher.

RHINE LANA McLIN, of Dayton, Ohio, manager and funeral director of McLin Funeral Home and a substitute teacher in the Dayton Public Schools. She has also served as a divorce counselor and a vocational counselor.

JEWEL LIMAR PRESTAGE, of Baton Rouge, La., a professor and chair of the political science department at Southern University.

Bombing of Yugoslav Diplomat's Home

White House Statement.   June 3, 1980

President Carter strongly condemns the bombing last night of the home of Vladimir Sindjelic, the Minister-Counselor at the Yugoslav Embassy in Washington, and reaffirms the statement he made on May 4, on the occasion of President Tito's death: "I pledge again that this Government will not tolerate terrorist acts directed against Yugoslavia or its representatives here."

Carter/Mondale Committee Party

Remarks to Campaign Workers.
June 3, 1980

As I stand here before you, I have one deep feeling in my heart, and that is thanksgiving to all of you who turned what 8 months ago was a prediction of absolute defeat into a wondrous victory tonight. Thank you very much.

It has been a long campaign. We have not avoided presenting our issues and our platform and our record and our future to every single State and territory in this country. Many of you have had to campaign for me while I stayed at the White House to conduct the President's duties.

I've had two secret weapons: One is all of you out there who worked so hard, and the other one is my wife, who worked in the open and who is not a secret weapon anymore.

A few minutes ago, after the first returns came in from Ohio and from West Virginia and other States, I called Fritz Mondale on the phone to ask him if he would be my running mate in 1980. He said if I would debate him that he would join me in the campaign. [*Laughter*] Obviously, having a partner like Fritz Mondale is a tremendous advantage for a President who is an incumbent, taking care of the duties of this great Nation as President, and it's also a tremendous advantage for a candidate like myself, running for reelection.

This team spirit has been permeating throughout our whole campaign. And I'm now dedicated to bringing our Democratic Party back together, after we have faced two formidable candidates who ran tremendous campaigns on their own, to reach out a hand of friendship and cooperation for them and their supporters, to share the values and the commitments, to share the principles, and to share the future of the Democratic Party and what it stands for.

This is the end of a long primary season, and it's the early beginning of a general election campaign. I intend to be very active as a campaigner in the fall. And I look forward to meeting the Republican nominee—I presume it will be Governor Reagan—both on the campaign trail and in intense, head-on-head debates to let the American people choose whom they want.

It's time to set the record straight. It's time to present clearly to the American people what our Nation is, what it has been; the formidable challenges and problems which we face; the fact that there are no easy answers and there are no easy solutions; that we must be bound together in a spirit of partnership and mutual commitment to realize the tremendous potential of our country in the future.

We need not fear those questions or those problems or those obstacles. In times of trial and testing, our Nation has never failed. It's good in a democratic system to have the American people participate, and 15 million Democrats have participated so far in this primary season. Now it's time for the American people to clearly define the issues and to make a choice for the future.

As for myself, I have no doubt that our Nation will triumph and win a tremendous victory over the problems that face us now, because of our innate strength. And I have no doubt that together, you and I, and all other Democrats, will triumph in November and return a Democrat next year to the White House again, and I hope that Fritz Mondale will be my running mate there.

Again, in the general election campaign I need your support, your friendship, and your dedicated work, as you've already demonstrated you're eager to give. And I close my remarks the same way I began them: Thank you from the bottom of my heart. God bless every one of you. Thank you.

NOTE: The President spoke at 9:07 p.m. at Liberty Plaza, outside a restaurant named The Buck Stops Here. The party was sponsored by the Carter/Mondale Presidential Committee.

United States Ambassador to Burundi

Nomination of Frances D. Cook.   June 4, 1980

The President today announced that he will nominate Frances D. Cook, of Homestead, Fla., to be Ambassador Extraordinary and Plenipotentiary of the United States to the Republic of Burundi. She would replace Thomas J. Corcoran, who is resigning.

Cook has been Director of the Office of Public Affairs for the State Department's Bureau of African Affairs since 1978.

She was born September 7, 1924, in Charleston, W. Va. She received a B.A. from Mary Washington College in 1967 and an M.P.A. from John F. Kennedy School of Government, Harvard University, in 1978.

Cook joined the Foreign Service in 1967 as a public affairs trainee in Paris and served as special assistant to Ambassador Shriver and a member of the U.S. delegation to the Paris meetings on Vietnam from 1969 to 1971. She was cultural affairs officer in Sydney from 1971 to 1973 and in Dakar from 1973 to 1975.

From 1975 to 1977, Cook was a Foreign Service personnel officer in Washington. She took public administration training at Harvard University from 1977 to 1978.

United States Ambassador to Djibouti

*Nomination of Jerrold Martin North.
June 4, 1980*

The President today announced that he will nominate Jerrold Martin North, of Skokie, Ill., to be Ambassador Extraordinary and Plenipotentiary of the United States to the Republic of Djibouti. He would be the first American Ambassador since the independence of Djibouti in June 1977.

North has been Deputy Chief of Mission in Mogadishu since 1979.

He was born December 8, 1931, in Chicago, Ill. He received a B.S. from the United States Military Academy in 1954 and an M.S. from the University of Alabama in 1960. He served in the U.S. Army from 1954 to 1963.

North joined the Foreign Service in 1963 and was posted in Leopoldville, Bukavu, Brussels, and at the State Department. From 1971 to 1973, he was detailed to the Agency for International Development as an area development adviser in Saigon.

From 1973 to 1974, North was a program analyst officer at the State Department, and from 1974 to 1976, he was administrative officer in Lilongwe. From 1976 to 1979, he was Deputy Chief of Mission in Freetown.

United States Ambassador to the German Democratic Republic

*Nomination of Herbert Stuart Okun.
June 4, 1980*

The President today announced that he will nominate Herbert Stuart Okun, of Chevy Chase, Md., to be Ambassador Extraordinary and Plenipotentiary of the United States to the German Democratic Republic. He would replace David B. Bolen, who is resigning.

Okun has been the State Department representative to the Strategic Arms Limitation Talks since 1978 and has served as Deputy Head of the U.S. Delegation to the Comprehensive Test Ban talks since 1979.

He was born November 27, 1930, in New York City. He received an A.B. from Stanford University in 1951 and an M.P.A. from Harvard University in 1959. He served in the U.S. Army from 1952 to 1954.

Okun joined the Foreign Service in 1955 and was posted in Munich, Moscow, Belo Horizonte, Brasília, and at the State Department. He attended the Naval War College in 1968–69 and served as special assistant to the Secretary of State from 1969 to 1970.

From 1970 to 1973, Okun was Alternate Director of the Office of Soviet Affairs at the State Department. From 1971 to 1972, he was Deputy Chairman of the U.S. Delegation to the U.S.-U.S.S.R. Talks on Prevention of Incidents at Sea. From 1973 to 1974, he was political adviser to the Commander in Chief, Allied Forces Southern Europe, in Naples. From 1975 to 1978, he was Deputy Chief of Mission in Lisbon.

National Labor Relations Board

Nomination of Don Alan Zimmerman To Be a Member.   June 4, 1980

The President today announced that he will nominate Don Alan Zimmerman, of Bethesda, Md., to be a member of the National Labor Relations Board. He would replace Betty S. Murphy, who has resigned.

Zimmerman has been minority labor counsel to the U.S. Senate Committee on Labor and Human Resources since 1974.

He was born March 30, 1940, in Los Angeles, Calif. He received a B.A. from Pomona College in 1962 and a J.D. from George Washington University Law School in 1968. He served in the U.S. Army from 1962 to 1964.

From 1967 to 1971, Zimmerman was a legislative analyst with the Office of Management and Budget. From 1971 to 1972, he was special counsel to the trustees of the Penn Central Transportation Co., where his responsibilities included labor relations matters, including emergency labor disputes.

From 1972 to 1974, Zimmerman was a senior associate with the National Manpower Institute, a private nonprofit organization, where he directed the staff engaged in various studies and projects involving employment, training, and educational policies and programs.

United States-Morocco Agreement on Nuclear Energy

Message to the Congress Transmitting the Agreement.   June 4, 1980

To the Congress of the United States:

I am pleased to transmit to the Congress, pursuant to Section 123d of the Atomic Energy Act of 1954, as amended (42 U.S.C. 2153(d)), the text of the proposed Agreement Between the United States and the Kingdom of Morocco Concerning Peaceful Uses of Nuclear Energy, together with an accompanying agreed minute, my written approval, authorization and determination concerning the agreement, and the memorandum of the Director of the United States Arms Control and Disarmament Agency with the Nuclear Proliferation Assessment Statement concerning the agreement. The joint memorandum submitted to me by the Secretaries of State and Energy, which includes a summary analysis of the provisions of the agreement, and the views of the Director of the United States Arms Control and Disarmament Agency and of the Members of the Nuclear Regulatory Commission are also enclosed.

The Nuclear Non-Proliferation Act of 1978, which I signed into law on March 10, 1978, establishes certain requirements for new agreements for cooperation. In my judgment, the proposed agreement for cooperation between the United States and the Kingdom of Morocco, together with its agreed minute, meets all statutory requirements.

The Kingdom of Morocco is a strong supporter of the Non-Proliferation Treaty, having ratified it on November 27, 1970, and of international non-proliferation efforts generally. The proposed agreement reflects the desire of the Government of the United States and the Government of the Kingdom of Morocco to begin peaceful nuclear cooperation in a manner that recognizes both the shared non-proliferation objectives and the generally close relationship between our two countries. The proposed agreement will, in my view, further the non-proliferation and other foreign policy interests of the United States.

I have considered the views and recommendations of the interested agencies in reviewing the proposed agreement and have determined that its performance will promote, and will not constitute an unreasonable risk to, the common defense and security. Accordingly, I have ap-

proved the agreement and authorized its execution, and urge that the Congress give it favorable consideration.

JIMMY CARTER

The White House,
June 4, 1980.

Conservation Fee on Oil Imports

Remarks and a Question-and-Answer Session With Reporters. June 4, 1980

THE PRESIDENT. Back in March, after very close consultations with the leadership in both the House and Senate, I decided and announced to the public that I would impose an oil conservation fee on imported oil to this country. Both the congressional leaders and I decided then, and I still maintain and am convinced, that this is important for the energy security of our Nation, for the economic security of our Nation, and also for the national security of our country.

This is important, because we import too much oil. Now more than 40 percent of all of the oil we use is imported. As a matter of fact, we import and use more oil than all the other Western industrialized nations put together. That's our total consumption. When and if this import fee is imposed, it will save us about 100,000 barrels per day the first year, and after 3 years a quarter of a million barrels per day reduction in imported oil.

This is an important, tangible contribution to saving oil and also preventing the expenditure, this year for instance, of $90 billion of American money to buy foreign oil. Along with that oil, as I've said many times, we import both inflation and we import unemployment.

To the extent that we can convince the foreign nations, both the oil producers and consumers, that we mean business in conserving energy and reducing our imported oil, to that extent they will join with us in reducing world demand and also maintaining world production. A small investment now by us in reducing imported oil by the imposition of this fee will have great benefits in the future in holding down the price of imported oil and, therefore, gasoline to American people.

Most European countries and Japan and other Western democratic societies have a gasoline tax imposed by their federal government of between $1 and $2 per gallon. If this import fee is imposed, the total Federal tax will only be 14 cents. If the Congress should reverse this decision—which they are now attempting to do—it will send a clear signal to oil-producing nations and oil-consuming nations that we do not mean business, that we will not take a firm stand to conserve oil; and we will pay much higher prices for oil in the future because of that.

Soon a bill will get to my desk, I believe, that will reverse this decision to impose the conservation fee. If and when that happens, I intend to veto the bill immediately and send it back to the Congress. My hope is that the American people and the Congress will understand the importance of this. This is not a popular decision. It does involve an increase in the price of gasoline to American consumers now. But in my judgment it is right for our country, and it will also be right in holding down the price of gasoline in future years.

Thank you very much.

REPORTER. Mr. President, what's your alternative if they override the veto? Do you have other things that you could do?

THE PRESIDENT. There are some other alternatives. I hope that they will not override. But if I don't get but one vote on the Hill, I'm still going to veto this bill, because it's right and it's important to us to send to the American people and to the foreign countries a clear signal that we mean business in conserving oil.

Q. Sir, what will you say to Senator Kennedy when you see him tomorrow here?

THE PRESIDENT. I don't know. I intend to meet with Senator Kennedy. And I'll congratulate him on having run a good campaign and see what we can do together to work together in the future to meet the Republican challenge successfully.

Q. Are you going to ask him to join you as the nominee of the party?

THE PRESIDENT. I'll wait until I meet with him——

Q. What did he say to you on the phone today?

THE PRESIDENT. That he thought it would be important for us to get together at an early time to discuss the political situation.

Q. Did it sound like he's being conciliatory?

THE PRESIDENT. I wouldn't say that, no. [*Laughter*]

Q. Did he say he would persist in the campaign?

THE PRESIDENT. We didn't go into that.

Q. Did he say why it took him so long to answer the phone? [*Laughter*]

THE PRESIDENT. Well, he's been very busy, as have I, and he returned the call in adequate timely fashion.

Q. What's he been doing?

THE PRESIDENT. You'll have to ask Senator Kennedy. I think we'll have a good meeting.

Q. Do you think you'll have no problem of winning his support before the convention?

THE PRESIDENT. Well, that'll be a decision for him to make, Sam [Sam Donaldson, ABC News].

Q. Are you going to be able to offer him some help on the platform, so that some of his views could be expressed there?

THE PRESIDENT. Yes. Obviously, the views of Senator Kennedy and his supporters, Governor Brown and his supporters, and even individual Democrats who've not run for President, will be presented to the platform drafting committee first, and then to the full committee. And if there are still differences of opinion about what the platform should say, then the delegates on the floor of the convention will make the ultimate decision. That's a democratic process. It'll be open, and I think it'll be a healthy process.

Q. Governor Carey said again today that you hadn't won New York, you hadn't won New Jersey, you hadn't won major States that a Democratic nominee had to win. How do you answer that?

THE PRESIDENT. Can't win them all. I've won about three-fourths of the contests. But I wish I could have won a hundred percent, but I didn't, and that was because I had some formidable opponents and because we have some very difficult decisions to make. And I think we did much better than we thought we would 7 or 8 months ago.

Q. Did he say he's going to stay in the race until the convention?

THE PRESIDENT. We did not discuss that at all.

Q. At all? What did you actually say to the Senator?

THE PRESIDENT. We primarily just made arrangements to have a meeting tomorrow afternoon.

Q. Will it be cordial? Will it be strained?

THE PRESIDENT. Very cordial, not strained.

Q. Did he call you back, or did you place the call?

THE PRESIDENT. No, he called back. [*Laughter*]

Q. Do you feel relieved that the primaries are over now?

THE PRESIDENT. I am very relieved that the primaries are over. It's been a long, tough, tedious, difficult 7 or 8 months, and it's a great relief to be——

Q. Mr. President, Governor Reagan—how serious of a challenge can he mount against you?

THE PRESIDENT. I think a formidable challenge. He's shown what he can do in the Republican primary, caucus contest.

Q. But isn't he too old?

THE PRESIDENT. That's a judgment that the voters will have to make.

Q. Was there any discussion of whipping anything? [*Laughter*]

THE PRESIDENT. No discussion, except that maybe we'll whip the Republicans in the fall.

Q. Do you think that was a little over-ambitious statement back there in the winter?

THE PRESIDENT. I'll let you judge by yourselves.

Q. Are you going to plan your strategy now for the Reagan—for the campaign?

THE PRESIDENT. We've been working on that for a few weeks.

Q. How are you going to portray him?

THE PRESIDENT. I'll let you know later.

NOTE: The President spoke at 4:41 p.m. in the Oval Office at the White House.

Reception for Congressional Supporters of the Carter/Mondale Campaign

Remarks at the Reception.   June 4, 1980

THE PRESIDENT. This is the best day I've had in a long time. [*Laughter*] When Bob [1] came in tonight from California 2 or 3 hours earlier than I thought he was going to come, we were discussing his mission. His mission was to go out and carry the California primary for me yesterday. [*Laughter*] I asked him how it went, and he was a little slow in responding. He said, "I'd like to ask you, Mr. President, how you did with the oil conservation fee in the House?" [*Laughter*]

I hope we're going to correct both actions later on—California in November, and I'm counting on all of you to support me on the veto override in a day or two when it comes through on the gasoline tax.

Sometimes you get applause, sometimes you don't. [*Laughter*]

This has been a long 7 or 8 months. I think most of you—probably almost everyone under this tent—remembers how it looked for us back in October, November, early in December. The polls were abysmal in their content and prediction, and the prospects for my victory in the primary season were very low. And you were the ones who came forward and said, "Win or lose, Mr. President, we're with you." It's the kind of pledge and the kind of support, the kind of friendship, the kind of partnership I will never forget.

Some of you helped me in 1976. And that was a time when I was a lonely candidate and, again, didn't have a very bright prospect of winning. But this year

---

[1] Robert S. Strauss, chairman of the Carter/Mondale Presidential Committee.

has been a very difficult campaign. I think the issues have been fairly clearly drawn. The press has been very fair. I noticed every evening on the news, there was at least 1 minute for Bob Dole to talk about me and 1 minute for Howard Baker to talk about me and 1 minute for Crane to talk about me; Bush, 1 minute to talk about me; Reagan, 1 minute to talk about me; and 1 minute for Governor Brown to talk about me; a minute, at least, for Kennedy to talk about me. And then I got my minute—[*laughter*]—to discuss my inflation rate—[*laughter*]—or my interest rate or my progress in getting legislation through the Congress. But anyway, we've done very well, I think, with the American people under extremely difficult circumstances.

My commitment is to start planning now for a victory not only for myself in November but a victory for all of you. Our Nation will be well served to elect men of integrity and courage and women of integrity and courage like all of you.

This is not going to be an easy campaign. Ronald Reagan will be a formidable candidate. We still don't yet know how the people of the Nation will judge others who might run on an independent ticket or on organized, fairly minor parties. But I'm willing to face them all with conviction and with anticipation and with absolute confidence that together we will win again, not because of me or my qualities in particular, but because what we have espoused together and what our party stands for is what the American people need and, I believe, want.

It's my duty, as well as yours, to explain the issues clearly to them—to the people of this country. Their judgment, I feel very clearly today, is sound, and we have an opportunity to marshal all the forces of the Democratic Party and to pull our party back together before the convention.

Tomorrow afternoon I'll be meeting with Senator Kennedy. We'll have a discussion, probably just the two of us. My anticipation is that he will carry his forces and his popularity and his strength and his delegates and his deep belief in issues to the convention; that's part of the democratic process. It need not cause us fear or concern or trepidation. To the extent that we can agree on common ground, then the harmony will be quite early. To the extent that we don't agree through the platform committee, we'll let the delegates make a choice. And I look forward, again, to that contest, if necessary.

The Democrats have always been able to stand the public scrutiny of our party's principles and our party's ideals, our party's successes, even our party's failures. We have never been a group, as Democrats, fearful to address difficult issues. Many of the problems that have been solved or are still being solved now in 1980 were inherited in 1977 when the White House and the Oval Office changed hands.

Our record is a good one, and as the Majority Leader of the Senate pointed out this morning, what the Congress has done with me and for me is a formidable achievement. When those issues are clearly discussed and when our record is put on the line, I don't have any doubt about the outcome of the campaign.

I am really looking forward to the campaign season. I'll be there campaigning hard, remembering what I learned in 1976 and learning from Fritz Mondale and from my wife and from my mother and from Chip and from many of you what you've learned in 1980. I think we've done well so far. We'll have an even greater victory in November.

But from the bottom of my heart, I want to thank all of you for your trust and your friendship, your partnership. We're in it together; we will not fail. In November we'll win again.

Thank you very much.

Bob said if I would confine myself to one subject he would give me an encore. [*Laughter*]

This may not be the appropriate forum—because this is primarily to thank those in the Congress who've helped me—but I would particularly like to thank Bob Strauss. There is not a person here in this lovely setting who has not benefited from his sensitivity, his knowledge, his commitment to the same principles that bind us together. And in an unselfish, dedicated, and effective way, he's not only made me come through in a successful campaign, but he's helped many of you, and we're all in it together. And his help and assistance as the chairman of my own campaign will be of benefit to you all.

And I was going to come back up here after Bob, but I think I'll say now that we really want to thank the Tobins for being so good to us.

NOTE: The President spoke at 7:39 p.m. at the home of Mr. and Mrs. Maurice Tobin.

Transporting of Cuban Refugees to the United States

Statement by the President.   June 5, 1980

On Tuesday, June 3, a freighter of recent Panamanian registry landed at Key West, Florida, with 731 Cuban refugees on board. This boat was chartered by Cuban Americans apparently in direct violation of my order that the private boat flotilla from Cuba cease.

Any person who attempts to circumvent this order will be prosecuted to the full extent of the law.

Any shipowner, captain, or crewmember agreeing to travel from U.S. or foreign ports to Cuba to take refugees to the United States in violation of American immigration law will face the most severe penalties under the law. Ships engaged in such efforts will be seized regardless of the nation of registry. Ship captains will face criminal prosecutions and maximum civil fines. Those who charter boats for these purposes will also face criminal prosecution.

The penalties for aiding and abetting a conspiracy to smuggle aliens into the United States include prison sentences of up to 5 years and fines up to $2,000 per alien brought to the United States.

The captain of the freighter, the *Red Diamond,* and those responsible for chartering her services have been charged under these statutes. I have instructed the Justice Department to prosecute these cases vigorously.

There should be no misunderstanding of my intention. Illegal boat traffic in refugees is unacceptable to the United States. It will be stopped. Those who attempt to evade this order will pay very severe penalties under our laws.

Baltimore, Maryland

Remarks at the Opening Session of the White House Conference on Families. June 5, 1980

Thank you, Jim Guy Tucker, Bishop Stafford, Mayor Schaeffer, Coretta King, Mario Cuomo, Guadalupe Gibson, Maryann Mahaffey, and Senator Mathias and Senator Sarbanes, who came over here with me, members of the National Advisory Committee, and delegates to this first White House Conference on the Families:

I'm very pleased to see that there's no violence in the audience or on the outside of the assembly area.

As you probably know, I feel a deep sense of gratitude to all of you, particularly those who have helped to make successful the preparations for this first of three very important meetings. Jim Guy Tucker and John Carr [1] and thousands of others, including some of you, have helped to make this day possible. You have literally reached out to the heart of America, and not just to the professional experts but to hundreds of thousands of people, literally, who believe that the strong family is the basis for a strong America.

We've had meetings now in all the territories and in 48 of the 50 States. People have participated in laying the groundwork for this conference and the ones that will follow in Minneapolis and in Los Angeles. We are brought together by one thing: by our love and our concern for the families of our country. I don't know of a finer motivation, and I don't know of a more important motivation. Every family is different, unique. If I ever doubt that, I have to look at my own family. [*Laughter*]

Early in 1976 when the news reporters first recognized where Plains, Georgia, was and what it was, they were interviewing my brother, Billy, at his service station. And there had been some stories around town—all false, of course— [*laughter*]—that Billy was something of a character, and they were trying to probe what Billy was. And he said, "Listen." He said, "I've got one sister almost 50 years old, who spends every weekend on a mo-

[1] Executive Director, White House Conference on Families.

torcycle." He said, "I've got another sister, not quite so old, who's a holy roller preacher. I've got a mother that joined the Peace Corps when she was 68 years old." He said, "I've got a brother who thinks he's going to be President of the United States." [*Laughter*] He said, "I'm the only sane one in the whole family." [*Laughter*]

I would guess that each one of you can tell a story about the members of your family that would show the uniqueness of the interrelationship among those who are different, but who love one another. In fact, I was very fortunate in my family.

I grew up in a strong and a loving family. And I had the extra benefit of an extended family in Plains. About 7 miles south of Plains is a cemetery where my wife's grandparents are buried; the first one buried there was born in 1787. And about 7 miles north of Plains is the Carter family cemetery, and my ancestor, Wiley Carter, who is buried there, was born in 1798. We've not moved far.

And I had a community of friends who wished me well as a child and who gave me strength and who gave me support, who gave me confidence, who gave me encouragement. And when Rosalynn and I were married almost 34 years ago, we tried to pattern our own family on the family style of our parents and our grandparents.

Our deepest joys together now are when the other members of our family can join us. We've always shared the same hard work, the same pleasures, the same pains, the same successes, the same failures, the same excitement, the same boredom with each other. We've had our problems, we've had our struggles, we've had our sadnesses. I have to admit that we've even had some arguments. It hasn't hurt our family. In fact, those exciting experiences, some good and some bad, have strengthened our family ties.

A very beautiful picture in microcosm of a nation: with troubles, trials, tribulations, tests, boredom, excitement, achievement, disappointment—unified through trial into a stronger nation. Every family has similar experiences with ours. I know that we were very lucky, and we still are.

When we think of families, ordinarily we think of brothers and sisters and a father and a mother, with grandparents and uncles and aunts and nephews and nieces and cousins, perhaps. That's a standard that's been held up by many traditions, including of course the Judeo-Christian tradition, and also by thousands of years of human experience. But that same tradition and that same experience teaches us that there is really no such thing as a perfect family or one that should be used as a standard for all other families.

We find the essence of family life in the universal need for mutual support, for nurturing, a safe haven for children and for old people, and for love; a love that doesn't always ask questions or impose qualifications on others before it's given, a kind of unselfish love. People need that love, just as surely as people need food and shelter, and air to breathe.

That love can be found, obviously, in many different circumstances. For instance, Rosalynn's was a family of sorrow: When she was 13 years old, her father died. Her mother had four little children. She worked in the school cafeteria, and she was a seamstress for the other, more prosperous ladies of the community. Later on she got a job in the post office, and she kept her family together.

There were a lot of other single-parent families in Plains, probably 35 or 40, out of a population of just a few dozen. I saw the struggle they had emotionally and financially to keep their family together and to keep their family strong. They didn't always succeed. And I promised myself, when I entered politics as a State senator and later when I was Governor and when I was running for President, to help struggling families like that have a better chance.

I also saw families, black and white, that worked hard, but never quite had enough. I saw the strength that the family ties gave them as they struggled. And I saw men and women who reached the time in years when they deserved and had earned a secure retirement, but they had all too little to sustain them in those later years. And I vowed to do something about those kind of families too, if I ever had a chance.

You, friends and delegates, through this White House Conference on Families, we have a chance to help those kinds of families and also, at the same time, to help every single family in America. To do that we must face up to the real changes in our society, changes that present both new problems and, at the same time, new opportunities.

Some of us come from a history and an ethnic background where the family is still the center of existence, where the ownership of a home and to care for one another is paramount. Others come from a less rigidly structured family environment, where there's more freedom and more movement, more mobility, where children are not wedded so deeply to their parents in their later years.

More of our people are living longer. More women, particularly more mothers, are working now outside the home. There are more single-parent households because of divorce or death. Our people are more mobile. The average person lives in a particular place now less than 5 years. People are uprooted. Television—that electronic version of the man who came

to dinner and never went home—affects families in ways that we are only now beginning to understand. Inflation and recession both put additional burdens on family life. Problems like drugs, alcohol, unwanted pregnancies, even suicide have reached down to members of a family who are younger and younger. Tragic instances of family violence remind us that the bonds of kinship don't automatically make families a place of nurturing one another. Most violent crimes against a person are committed among those who know each other and often love each other.

Some laws, some government policies, tend to disrupt family structures. It's easy to list the problems associated with a modern, fast-changing, technological world, but we must not overlook the improvements that have been made in family life since I was a child and many of you were children.

Much of the death and disease that once stalked childhood—such as polio and diphtheria, typhus and typhoid—is now either conquered or greatly reduced.

More of our people are better educated than ever before. My father didn't finish high school. Neither did his father, nor any other in our family for five or six generations back.

More families have a chance to share cultural and leisure activities now than before. This was once a privilege of the few. Even 40 years ago, when I was still living on the farm, the workday was 16 or 17 or 18 hours. And with the sweatshops and the long working hours in urban areas, there was very little time for a family to be together, because the breadwinner had to be on the job.

We have made great progress in this country against racial discrimination, sexual discrimination, age discrimination, and we are fighting to make more progress. Both men and women are more free today to fulfill their own and their family's needs in new and exciting and challenging ways. Many fathers have discovered, for instance, the joys and responsibilities of being with his children more.

Family ties are based on more than blood kinship. There are also kinships of shared experiences and shared dreams and shared joys and sorrows. Most of all, they are based on love, love that can span vast distances and also span the barrier between generations. Families are or should be the first place that we ever learn. As Jim Guy quoted me, it's the first school. We can learn how to live in harmony and helpfulness with one another, and nourish the individuality of those who live in the same home; respect one another, even though we're different.

It's the first place that we learn to care and to nurture the child, and to recognize its centrality in any society. That has always been the special responsibility of the family. It's here that the motivation and the morals and goals of a life are first shaped. Habits that one carries through adulthood are quite often formed at a very early age in the family. In family life we also find the roots of crime and failure, and quite often a lifetime of health problems are started at an early age within the family. They are also the roots of good habits and achievements and happiness and a pattern of whether or not we are concerned about others or just ourselves.

I hope that we'll come out of this conference with a reaffirmation of families as the fundamental building blocks of our society. I hope we will unite around a commitment to strengthen and not weaken families, to help and not hinder families, to lift families up and not drag them down.

Four years ago, I called for this conference, because I was deeply concerned that official America had lost touch with family America—and I don't mean just government, but the private sector, the news media and all its ramifications need to be reminded of the importance of and the problems of and the opportunities of and the challenge of American families.

How many of our modern-day problems could be resolved if just a little could be done in each family to make it stronger? I want the conference to be a catalyst for a new awareness in the Government, which I head, and also in State and local governments throughout this Nation, of the importance of families and the needs of families and for a period of intense reassessment of programs and policies. Where government is helpful to families, let it be strengthened. Where government is harmful to families, let it be changed. And what you recommend will be studied very carefully.

No one wants government interference in our personal affairs. We don't want government in our kitchens, in our bedrooms, in our living rooms, monitoring—certainly not controlling—family life. But we know that regardless of that commitment that government does touch our families through the tax system, public education, social security, health, housing, human services, transportation—government touches our families.

As a Nation, we are faced with serious problems both at home and abroad, and almost every one of those problems that we address has a direct effect on an individual family. The solutions we've worked out will either strengthen or weaken those families—as I deal with inflation, as we bring down interest rates—touches every family in this country.

When we create jobs, it helps the families of this country. When we improve education, helps every family. Better health care helps every family. When we insist on equal justice under the law or equal rights under the Constitution for all people, we help the American family. And when we work for a secure nation and a peaceful world, we help the American family.

This country is looking to you in this conference for constructive suggestions on how our society can help, not just government but the entire society in all its public and private aspects, how we jointly can help American families of all kinds. I hope that you will recommend specifically things that the government can do or stop doing in order to strengthen families, but I hope you'll go much deeper. Look for creative and compassionate solutions to the problems of families that have already been presented by those hundreds of thousands of Americans, and those that will be presented to you, directly or indirectly, through these three conferences, and then consider who can best carry out your recommendations or how those recommendations can be carried out.

I hope that you will search your own hearts and minds to see what nongovernmental institutions might help with family life. Colleges, universities, other eleemosynary institutions, churches, synagogues—already done very much. And as you know, certain denominations or certain religious faiths concentrate specifically on families as a major, permanent project. It'll be good to remind all the churches that if they deal with family lives, their ultimate goals are much more likely to be realized.

I hope that we will consider not just the troubled families but the families that are okay now and might be troubled in the future. And I think the most important thing, perhaps, for us to remember is that the members of the families themselves are the most likely ones to make the best and the right decisions about their own lives.

I have no doubt that we can make our country a better place to rear a family. Starting today we can help imbue our Nation and its institutions with a new appreciation and a new sensitivity about families. We can build an America of stronger families, an America where home is a place of love and stability, where children are nurtured to a responsible citizenship; where husbands and wives can share love and growth; an America where in the home basic religious and ethical values are taught to children at an early age, and where they are lived by example for the children to observe among their elders; an America where each family is a wellspring of racial and ethnic and religious understanding, where people who look differently within the community from the members of the family are embraced, not only as neighbors but as brothers and sisters.

We can build an America where parents are partners with the schools in education. We can build an America where the tasks of the family life are valued and recognized as very important work. We can build an America where employees don't have to make the horrible choice between responsibilities as workers on the one hand, and responsibilities as parents on the other.

We can build an America where the powerful forces of inevitable change in a modern life don't endanger the basic structure of family life, but strengthen the foundation of family life. And we can build an America where the policies of our national life as a family grow out of the needs of millions of individual families that make up our great Nation.

I'll do all I can to ensure that your

work does not end just as a report on the shelves in Washington. I'd like to remind you that in the past, there have been very few White House Conferences. When there have been White House Conferences, they have almost invariably spurred this country to major and constructive change. Your deliberations and those that will follow in Minneapolis and Los Angeles are, therefore, extremely important.

Certainly American families face difficulties, and they look to us for strength and support in the 1980's. Your recommendations will be very important, but in the enthusiasm that has already gone into this event and the care with which it has been prepared, we can already see something else: We can see the strength of American families.

American families have been tested. They've survived. They are strong. They are there to be strengthened further, and we can see the commitment of Americans to their own families and to their national family. And we can see the love that will provide a better future for every family in our land.

Those are the things that we see together; those are the goals that we'll establish together. And I have no doubt that this White House Conference on Families will transform our Nation into a place where the hopes and ideals and the spirit and the commitment and the love of America will all be made stronger in the years to come.

Thank you very much.

NOTE: The President spoke at 3:04 p.m. in Hall D at the Baltimore Convention Center. In his opening remarks, he referred to Jim Guy Tucker, Chairperson, and Coretta King, Mario Cuomo, Guadalupe Gibson, and Maryann Mahaffey, Deputy Chairs, White House Conference on Families, and Bishop J. Francis Stafford, member of the Conference's National Advisory Committee.

Veto of Public Debt Limit Extension Bill

Remarks to Reporters on Signing the Message of Disapproval.   June 5, 1980

THE PRESIDENT. I have received from the Congress this afternoon a bill which cancels the imposition of the oil conservation fee that I imposed earlier last month. This was a decision made by me, as recommended by the leaders of the Congress, to save on imported oil, and to help on the control of inflation and unemployment in this Nation. I believe it was the right decision when I made it, and I believe it is the right decision now.

I cannot accept this action by the Congress without expressing my strong disapproval of it and my absolute conviction that it doesn't help for public officials to stand up and make speeches about conserving energy and controlling inflation and controlling unemployment, unless they are willing to face the political heat when the time comes to make a tough decision for the benefit of this country. So, because of the congressional action and because of my conviction that we must conserve energy, I am vetoing the legislation sent to me today by the Congress.

[*At this point, the President signed the message.*]

This veto message will be sent to the Congress immediately, and I hope that the Congress will uphold my veto and keep in effect the oil conservation fee which is so important for our country.

Q. Mr. President, can you tell us whether you intend to debate Senator Kennedy as he asked today? And could you tell us about your meeting with him?

THE PRESIDENT. No questions about the oil conservation? [*Laughter*]

Q. Sir, what do you think you will do

if they override your veto. What will you do then?

THE PRESIDENT. Well, I'll face that decision if and when that occasion arises. I don't know what the Congress will do. But I'll just have to make a judgment then.

I had a good——

Q. Mr. President, can we go back to the other subject, sir?

THE PRESIDENT. Yes. What was the subject? [*Laughter*]

Q. Senator Kennedy—he told us that he asked you again if you wouldn't debate him. And what did you tell him? And just generally, what about the meeting?

THE PRESIDENT. Well, the first exchange was a very friendly one. I congratulated him on a very forceful campaign, on the effectiveness of his campaign; pointed out to him, and we agreed, that the primary season was now over, that we still had some differences of opinion remaining on the number of delegates that he and I would have on the final vote. I'm convinced that I will be nominated, and he's not convinced of that fact yet.

We agreed that we had some differences of opinion on issues. The most important difference of opinion was that he thinks the best way to address these differences is through some sort of public debate, I presume on television for an hour or so. I pointed out to Senator Kennedy that since the primary season was over that my opinion was that the best way to address these differences which do still exist between him and me is through the platform process, with Senator Kennedy presenting his own views about what the Democratic Party platform should be on which the nominee will run; let me present my views to the platform committee, and others have the same opportunity if they choose; and then a drafting committee will come out, hopefully, with the resolution of some of these differences, because of the language used.

That recommendation from the drafting committee will then be made by the platform committee, and if there are still remaining differences and 25 percent of the platform committee believe them to be important, they can be taken to the floor of the convention itself.

There, the strongest possible spokesman that we can get to present my views and Senator Kennedy's views will be used to present those issues in a sharply defined form to all the delegates chosen at the convention, both representing him and me and let the delegates make an ultimate judgment on how the Democratic Party stands on this issue as decided by the representatives of the people in all the States and territories of this country.

So, that's the difference that remains, primarily, is whether or not the platform process, including a final vote on the convention, should decide the position of the party or whether there should be some public, televised debate between me and him.

Q. Mr. President, how are you going to persuade the Senator to drop out of the race?

THE PRESIDENT. I did not ask him to drop out of the race.

Q. How are you going to? Do you have any plans?

THE PRESIDENT. I have no—that's a judgment for him to make.

The final decision about who will be the nominee will be made by the delegates when they cast their official vote at the convention itself. I'm absolutely convinced that a substantial majority of the delegates will vote for me as the nominee. But the decision about dropping out or continuing or how to proceed between now and then is one for the Senator to make himself, and I respect his right to retain his delegates and to retain his campaign intact if that's his decision to do so.

I also pointed out and we had a very harmonious understanding that in allocating representatives on the rules committee, the credentials committee, the platform committee, and so forth, that we would bend over backwards to treat the Senator fairly, to make sure that his representatives had an adequate right to speak for him if there were disputes on the platform, credentials, or rules.

Q. How bad will this continued contest, however, in the Democratic Party hurt the chances of the nominee—you think it'll be you—in the fall against Ronald Reagan?

THE PRESIDENT. Well, obviously, the longer it takes for all of the Democrats to come together and harness our combined efforts toward a victory in November, the more difficult it will be. But in spite of any foreseeable difficulties, I'm convinced that Fritz Mondale and I will win in November against Ronald Reagan and whoever he chooses to be Vice President.

Q. If you're reelected, would you abide by the Democratic platform?

THE PRESIDENT. I'm sorry?

Q. If you're reelected, would you abide by the Democratic platform?

THE PRESIDENT. I'll have to reserve the judgment on that. There were a couple of items—I don't remember them now—from 1976 on which I did not agree, but I made my disagreement very clear to the delegates and to the public. But in general, my intention is to abide by the platform to the ultimate extent possible and, hopefully, to work out differences between me and Senator Kennedy and perhaps Governor Brown and others in that long and carefully contrived process according to what democracy is.

Q. Mr. President, was there anybody in the room besides you and he at this meeting?

THE PRESIDENT. No.

Q. Was there any progress, Mr. President, toward unity of the Democratic Party during this hour you spent with the Senator?

THE PRESIDENT. Yes, I think so. There was a sharing of respect, mutually I think, because of the effectiveness of the two campaigns run. There was a commitment on my part to the Senator that he and his supporters would be treated fairly in allocating delegates and in the procedures of the convention itself.

There was an acknowledgment that we share many commitments in common to minimize the adverse effect of economic circumstances on the families of this Nation who look to us for leadership, and there was also a common realization that the most important thing for us to do is to defeat the Republican nominee in the fall.

Q. Did he say, sir, that he would support you if you became the nominee of the party?

THE PRESIDENT. No, I didn't pin him down on that, but the final result of our meeting was that there were many things on which we agree. There was one basic thing on which we disagree: his desire to have a televised, I presume, public debate for an hour or so, and my belief that the differences between us on the issues, to the extent that they have not already been clearly defined in the campaign for the last 7 months, could best be judged by the delegates, ultimately, on the convention floor.

Q. When will he see you again?

THE PRESIDENT. I don't know. We agreed to stay in touch directly, if necessary, and through our appointed representatives, as the next days and weeks go by.

Q. Mr. President, do you think the differences on economic policy between you and the Senator can be reconciled by whatever process?

THE PRESIDENT. Yes, I think so. You have to remember, however, that anything I might espouse or propose would have to be tempered by the willingness of the Congress to adopt it. I've made many proposals to the Congress, as you know, since I've been in office, and so have all other predecessors in the Oval Office, that the Congress has not been willing to accept.

I'm adamantly opposed to mandatory wage and price controls. The Senator has endorsed mandatory wage and price controls. There is no authority for a President to impose mandatory wage and price controls. It is absolutely inconceivable that the Congress would pass any such legislation. So, in effect, that's a moot point. But I don't think there's any way that he and I could finally agree that we should or should not have wage and price controls of a mandatory nature.

So, if we word the platform or the mutual commitment on having as many jobs as possible for our people, protecting title VI CETA jobs, protecting a million summer youth jobs, having impact aid assistance for automobile workers and others laid off, adding $2 billion on for youth employment for a new program, those kind of things that I have proposed, I'm sure the Senator would espouse and would support. Whether he has additional proposals to make I don't know.

Q. Mr. President, can you win reelection without Senator Kennedy's support?

THE PRESIDENT. I think regardless of any foreseeable circumstance, yes, that I will win reelection.

Q. Do you have any reason to expect that he will tone down his personal criticism of you over the coming weeks and months?

THE PRESIDENT. Well, I certainly would think that now that the heat of the primary campaign is over that the personal debates and so forth would be minimized, yes. That's my expectation.

Q. Did he say that or did you——

THE PRESIDENT. That's a judgment for him to make.

Q. Mr. President, did he renew his offer to withdraw in exchange for a debate?

THE PRESIDENT. No, he didn't.

Q. Mr. President, what do you think of the primaries on Tuesday and the fact that there was a very high rating by many people that they didn't like you or Mr. Reagan?

THE PRESIDENT. Well, it's obvious that when voters are asked, "Do you want Reagan or Carter or none of the above?" a lot of people are going to say at this point, "None of the above." And also, there's a profound difference in the attitude of voters in a primary campaign than in the general election.

In a primary campaign there's an excitement about it and an inclination to keep the contest going, to express displeasure about the inflation rate or about the unemployment rate or about Iran or about Afghanistan or about the transportation problems. Those things are ordinarily expressed, quite often expressed, by voters who cast their ballot against an incumbent.

But when the voter goes into the polling booth in November to choose a President for the next 4 years, to determine whether or not our Nation will be at peace or whether we might be at war, whether a President is going to have a better effect on the quality of life of that voter or an adverse effect over a long 4-year period, those kind of things become a very serious matter. And I think the frivolity that often is associated with a primary campaign season will not exist in November.

The choice is going to be between the Democratic nominee and the Republican nominee, and I am convinced that the choice will be myself and that the voters will prove that I'm right.

Q. But, Mr. President, every indication that we polled indicates that if you are the nominee, the Democratic Party is going to be devastated——

THE PRESIDENT. That's not the case at all.

Q. Could I also ask you, did the Senator make the proposal that he and you would both withdraw in favor of another candidate?

THE PRESIDENT. No, he didn't make that proposal. And the presumption of your first question is erroneous.

Thank you.

NOTE: The President spoke at 6:03 p.m. in the Oval Office at the White House.

Veto of Public Debt Limit Extension Bill

Message to the House of Representatives Returning H.R. 7428 Without Approval. June 5, 1980

To the House of Representatives:

I am returning H.R. 7428, the Public Debt Limit Extension Bill, without my signature. I regret the need to take this action, because enactment of the debt limit bill is critically important to the financial operations of the Federal government. I urge the Congress in the strongest possible terms to return an acceptable bill to my desk promptly, so that unjust hardship to millions of Americans can be avoided.

My action in returning this critical bill is required by an unrelated and wholly unacceptable amendment which would prohibit the imposition of the oil import conservation fee that I announced as part of our comprehensive anti-inflation program on March 14.

As you will recall, that carefully conceived program was worked out in unusually close and detailed cooperation with the Congress. Both the Congressional leaders and I decided then, and I still maintain and am convinced, that a conservation fee on imported oil is important for the energy security, for the economic security, and for the national security of the United States.

We were also well aware that this step, however important to the interest of the Nation as a whole, might not be in the individual political interests of many Members, especially in this election year. I acted under my executive authority, thereby shielding the Congress from most of the immediate political repercussions. Thus there can be no doubt among those now attempting to override the oil import conservation fee that this reversal will only encourage more domestic energy consumption, add to our intolerable oil import bill, hinder our efforts for energy security, obstruct our fight against inflation, and be inconsistent with our responsibility for leadership among the oil consuming nations.

That is why I have stated clearly on several occasions, and repeated yesterday, that if legislation blocking my decision on the oil import conservation fee should be sent to me, I would be compelled to veto it—and it is for those very same reasons that I now do so.

The fee on imported oil is an integral part of energy, economic and foreign policy goals that hold important benefits both for the welfare of our citizens and for the security of our Nation.

• The fee reduces our imports of foreign oil by 100,000 barrels a day within the first year and much more in future years. Over 40 percent of all the oil consumed in this country is imported. Unless we take this kind of courageous action, we will remain dangerously vulnerable to severe economic disruptions from terrorism, accident, embargo, war or political strategy.

• The United States is a leader in trying to forge a joint program, with our allies, to secure greater energy independence. But we use about half of all the oil consumed in the Western industrial nations, and a larger proportion of gasoline than anywhere else in the world. The oil import fee is a symbol of our own willingness to take the painful steps needed to conserve oil. If we are to lead, we must act like a leader.

• With the full imposition of the oil import conservation fee the United States would have a 14 cent per gallon tax, one of the lowest in the Western world. The tax has been only 4 cents a gallon since 1959. In contrast, France has a $1.67 per gallon tax. Since the 1973 oil embargo, France has increased its gasoline tax by more than 160 percent. Italy has a $1.92 per gallon tax. Since the 1973 embargo, the Italian tax has been increased by more than 200 percent. Even with the fee, Americans will in fact be paying lower taxes this year relative to the price of gasoline than they did two decades ago.

• To the extent that we can convince foreign nations, both the oil producers and consumers, that we mean business in conserving energy and reducing our oil imports, to that extent they will join us in reducing world demand, and in maintaining oil production. A small investment in reducing imported oil now will return great benefits in the future by holding down the price of imported oil, and therefore gasoline, to the American people.

• Unless and until we can control our appetite for imported oil, we will not be able to solve our inflation problem. In 1979 alone, the price of each barrel of imported oil rose 120 percent—an average of 10 percent each month. More than 2 points of our Consumer Price Index (CPI) increase in 1979 can be attributed directly to the OPEC increases. As long as nearly one out of every two gallons of gasoline we consume comes from abroad, that inflationary "tax" levied by OPEC will continue. This year we will pay $90 billion for foreign oil—$400 for each person in the United States. Along with that $90 billion, we export jobs and import inflation.

• While the fee will cause a short-term, one-time increase in the CPI, the long-term effect of the fee is not inflationary— it is deflationary. First, the fee will save money that would otherwise be sent to OPEC. Second, the fee is a vital part of an anti-inflation package which is beginning to take hold. To the extent that part of this package is removed, the financial impact could be serious. The consequence could be an increase in overall inflationary pressures.

• The fee has been imposed for energy conservation reasons, but its revenue-raising effect cannot be ignored. The fee serves to allocate a small share of a realistic increase in gasoline prices, not to the energy companies or the exporting nations, but for public use. Without the oil import fee, our long struggle to achieve a balanced budget is in jeopardy, and it will be more difficult to find the resources for tax reduction and to provide needed incentives for investment and productivity when economic conditions warrant.

• Above all, my Administration and the Congress are together putting in place the energy policy America needs for energy security, for economic security, and for national security. Only by encouraging greater conservation, stimulating new production, and making alternative energy sources competitive, will we eventually stop the price of gasoline from rising. Only if we are prepared to take strong actions and make tough stands now—like this import conservation fee—can we assure adequate supplies of gasoline and limit the crippling escalation of gasoline prices later.

I recognize the political pressures. I know that this is a difficult issue for many Members of Congress. Nevertheless, the oil import conservation fee is good public policy, and it is good common sense. That was true when we agreed upon it. It is if anything even more true today, as we see the early tangible, measurable signs of successes in both our energy and inflation policies.

Therefore, I urge the Congress to join me in carrying on the work of enhancing America's energy security, economic security, and national security by sustaining my veto and upholding the oil import conservation fee.

JIMMY CARTER

The White House,
    June 5, 1980.

NOTE: On June 5, the House of Representatives voted to override the President's veto, and on June 6, the Senate also voted to override the veto. As enacted, H.R. 7428 is Public Law 96–264.

Veto of Ute Mountain Ute Tribe Benefits Bill

Message to the House of Representatives Returning H.R. 5036 Without Approval. June 6, 1980

To the House of Representatives:

I am returning, without my approval, H.R. 5036, a bill that would accord certain land and monetary benefits upon the Ute Mountain Ute Tribe, Colorado and New Mexico.

Specifically, the enrolled bill would require the Secretary of the Interior (1) to convey approximately 3,000 acres (esti-

mated value of $1,800,000) of public domain land in Colorado to the Ute Mountain Ute Tribe, and (2) to pay $5,840,000 to the tribe for economic development purposes. These benefits would be considered compensation to the tribe for the loss of oil and gas revenues allegedly resulting from an incorrect land survey by the United States Government.

The central issue raised by H.R. 5036 involves a land dispute in New Mexico between the Ute Mountain Ute Tribe and the Navajo Tribe. Both tribes claimed ownership of the same lands which formed a common boundary between their respective reservations. However, pursuant to the Navajo-Ute Boundary Dispute Act of 1968, the Supreme Court reviewed the case and ruled in favor of the Navajo Tribe in 1972. In addition, there is no legal claim against the United States and in light of the Supreme Court decision, I do not believe this legislation should be approved.

This legislative relief is unwarranted because of the preferential treatment and special advantage it would accord the Ute Mountain Ute Tribe vis-a-vis other tribes whose circumstances may be similar.

JIMMY CARTER

The White House,
    June 6, 1980.

White House Reception for Democratic Party State Chairmen

Remarks at the Reception.   June 6, 1980

You could tell that John White was practicing for the Democratic convention.[1] [*Laughter*] And I think he did very well, by the way.

---

[1] The President was introduced by the chairman of the Democratic National Committee.

There are a lot of smiles in this room. Quite often when I meet with groups in the Oval Office or in the Cabinet Room or here, I look around, at the beginning of those meetings, and there are very few smiles. But today the Democrats, the leaders in the different States appear to be approaching the convention and the fall campaign with a great deal of anticipation and determination and confidence. And I share those feelings with you.

But I would like to talk about a few things concerning the leadership, not just of a President but of our party itself. It's not easy, in a time of rapid change, to provide leadership without unity in our party. I have a quote from Adlai Stevenson. He said, "Even more important than winning an election is governing the Nation. When the tumult and the shouting die, there is a stark reality of responsibility in an hour history." These are hours of history, and the challenges that we have faced in the last 3½ years and the ones that we will face in the next 4½ years are formidable indeed.

The responsibility for governing this Nation, in the White House and on the Hill, lies with us Democrats. Some of that responsibility is pleasant and enjoyable; some of it is often unpleasant; all of it is difficult. The issues that arrive on my desk in the Oval Office are the ones that cannot be solved or resolved in the county courthouse, the city hall, the State capitols; often can't be resolved on the Hill.

In times like these it is important that we make decisions not based on what's popular and easy, but what is right for our Nation. The Founders of our country wondered if it was possible in a democracy to have those directly responsible to the American people on a daily basis make judgments concerning what was right in the long run that might be unpopular at that particular time. And they feared very

greatly, as you well know, a party system. That came later on.

A lot of Americans today are concerned with the spectacle of political leaders grappling with difficult issues with excessive timidity, with a concern about the adverse consequences from the electorate, when the fact is that the voters of this Nation, the electorate of a democratic nation like ours, expect and demand political courage.

We are a superpower. We're the leader, as John White says, of the free world. Other nations look to us for guidance. We're on the cutting edge of change. And when we are fearful or if we flinch, we are not the only ones who suffer. Demagoguery is not to be abided in this Nation. I anticipate hearing from the other side a great deal of demagoguery in the fall: simplistic answers to complicated questions, temporarily appealing solutions to issues which are extremely difficult. But I have been impressed in my own time in politics with the sound judgment and the maturity of the American people.

If they understand the issues clearly, they make the right decisions. That's the main reason the Democrats have been so successful in keeping our position of leadership. But even with a Democratic administration, the people often see a government which is not capable of moving as rapidly as we should. Powerful special interest groups mount formidable forces on Capitol Hill and delay or sometimes subvert decisions that are important to the American people.

The Congress is pushed in every direction by highly organized and well-financed groups, with attractive spokesmen who put forward a special, narrowly defined request. And there are those in this country, unless they get a hundred percent of what they want, they don't want anything. It is much easier to raise money and to mount a crusade for an extreme position that appeals to a narrow, fervent, hysterical group—and sometimes that decision, under pressure, is made to the disadvantage of the sound, moderate, carefully considered, broadly based solution, again, so important to our people.

Those kinds of solutions often appear almost like orphans, without friends, and the American people who don't have a highly paid lobbyist to represent them in Washington don't like it. And neither do I. Our country was not founded by people who say, "Me first, me last, me always. I'm grasping for some selfish advantage to the detriment of my neighbor."

And the Democrats have been strong, and we've been viable. When we have remembered that fact, honored those who trust us, been courageous in the face of difficult decisions, and not turned our heads away from sometimes politically unpopular action, we've been the ones who've enhanced individual liberty. We've been the ones who have enhanced the free enterprise system of our country. We have been the ones who enhanced human rights, equality of opportunity, forward progress. We've been the ones who met the uncertainty and the fear of change with confidence and with strength. And every time we've done it, we've prevailed, and our Nation has not become weaker, it's become stronger.

We have an opportunity in the next few weeks to pull our party together, to unite in a common effort, to face a formidable challenge. And, as you know from your studies this morning, we have a new opportunity to bind together in a true system of political federalism the proper interrelationship between the local, State, and the national Democratic Party effort. It'll strengthen us all. It will give you another, additional opportunity to help shape national policy and to make sure that the programs that we espouse or debates that we participate in, the positions that we assume, the commitments that we make during this general election campaign are compatible with what the people in your own communities want and expect from us.

We are free people. We do pride ourselves on our individuality. We are strongly in favor of a democratic convention process which settles disputes on credentials or rules or platform or the identity of the candidates, the nominees of our party, openly, honoring the commitments that have been made over a long, tedious, sometimes divisive, not always pleasant primary campaign season.

As the incumbent President, as a prior leader of the Democratic Party, I've not avoided a single State. We have been into each State to present our views and to be judged by the people. Sometimes we have won overwhelmingly, sometimes we have lost. But the decisions have been made by individual Democrats, more than 15 million of them, who went to vote in the primaries or who met in the caucuses. And now those decisions will be rendered officially when the Democratic convention meets.

This is a time for plain talk; it's a time for political courage. And I think we will see a Republican Party putting forward a leadership that claims they have quick fixes for our country, a kind of a laundry list of simplistic solutions which the American people will not trust. If we are able to present our case clearly to the American people, I have no doubt about the judgment that they will make.

I look forward to the contest, as do you, with anticipation and with confidence. When and if the convention makes a judgment that I'm the nominee, I intend to have Fritz Mondale as my running mate. I'll be covering this Nation, presenting our case as Democrats as best I can, working very closely with other national candidates for the U.S. Senate, for the U.S. Congress, supporting Democratic congressional candidates plus the State legislatures and the Governors, and tying ourselves together in an unprecedented way to provide a common effort and a common front.

I'm not asking you to support verbatim every recommendation I make. I'm eager to hear from you and to make sure that when I do make a judgment or make a statement or make a commitment, that to the optimum degree possible, it's compatible with what you want and what you expect our party to do and to be.

We've made a lot of progress in the last 3½ years. I'm not here to enumerate the challenges which we have met successfully. We have enough challenges still left to meet. But we've turned the corner on inflation. The figures that we got this morning on the Producer Price Index are the lowest ones since September of 1977. It was just a few weeks ago that we had an extremely high inflation rate and extremely high interest rates. The interest rates have been dropping now about 1 percent per week, and we hope that during the summer we'll have good statistics to present to the American people as a demonstration of our good stewardship on inflation and interest rates.

We do have a serious problem with a recession that's on us, but we're taking the proper action to minimize the damage to our people. And I think in a comparison between ourselves and the Republican Party, the working families of this Nation will know that the Democrats are much more likely to meet their needs and to maximize their quality of life much better than Ronald Reagan and the Republican Party, looking backward to the 1950's, rather than forward to the 1980's.

Every public official these days lives in Harry Truman's kitchen, and those who can't stand the heat ought not to be there. Most of them who couldn't stand the heat left our party and went to the other party. But they'll be facing the heat in November, when the people make a judgment about who they prefer to be President the next 4 years; who will be responsible for peace or war; who will be responsible for keeping the Americans at work or unemployed; who will be responsible for the quality of our environment; for the development of our great resources; for forming closer and closer alliances with our allies; for solving the long-range problems of energy, tapping the resources of the Sun; to enhance opportunities of individuals who've too long been deprived. Those kinds of basic decisions that affect the lives of a father and a mother and children and grandparents will be the prevailing factor in November. We have an inherent advantage because the Democratic Party is the party of the people.

Finally, I'd like to say that I am not asking for reelection as President simply because I want to live 4 more years in the White House. It's been an interesting experience living here. I've enjoyed it, and I look forward to it the next 5 years. But the important thing is what we are able to accomplish while the Democrats have the responsibility for governing this Nation. You are the leaders of our Democratic Party. You're the ones with the close connections to those who look to us for the results of that leadership. And you're willing to sacrifice, and I'm asking you to sacrifice, for a common effort. I'll make my part of the sacrifices as well, in time and commitment and study and in the use of whatever ability and talent God has given me.

We have a wonderful, dynamic, strong, confident united nation, and when an analysis is made of what we have done in the recent past, the judgment will be in our favor. There is no easy way, and we are not searching for the easy way. The democratic officials have never been elected because we've promised to avoid problems or to circumvent responsibility. Many of the problems that I inherited when I moved into this house were there because they had been avoided for 4 years or 8 years by the Republican leadership who lived here. We've not avoided those problems. We've worked very closely with the Democratic Congress. And when we inventory what we have done we'll all be very proud.

We are the majority party; that's one of our names. We are the party of the people; that's one of our names. And we have been successful in elections, because we believe in America, should be united by a common commitment to unchanging principles and to changing times. We've never been afraid to honor both. And although we do have the greatest nation on Earth, our determination is, through hope and confidence and unity and commitment and sacrifice and determination and strength and courage, to make a greater party and a greater nation in the years to come. And if we keep that commitment—and I'm sure we will—the Democrats will enjoy another tremendous victory in November of 1980.

I'm in it with you. I'm proud to have you as partners.

Thank you very much. God bless you.

NOTE: The President spoke at 3:34 p.m. in the East Room at the White House.

Committee for the Preservation of the White House

Appointment of Two Members.   June 6, 1980

The President today announced the appointment of two persons as members of the Committee for the Preservation of the White House. They are:

PAULINE L. HARRISON, of New York City, who is active in civic affairs and the arts;

ROBERT I. MILLONZI, an attorney in Buffalo, N.Y., who is an active member of the Board of the Kennedy Center and Cochairman of the Advisory Committee on the Arts for the Kennedy Center.

Library of Congress

Reappointment of Jane R. Engelhard as a Member of the Trust Fund Board.
June 6, 1980

The President today announced the reappointment of Jane R. Engelhard, of Far Hills, N.J., as a member of the Library of Congress Trust Fund Board.

Engelhard is chairman of the board of Engelhard Hanovia, Inc., director of Engelhard Minerals and Chemicals Corp., and was executive vice president of Holbrook Microfilming Co., which microfilmed records of the Library of Congress during World War II.

Smithsonian Institution

Appointment of Two Members of the National Armed Forces Museum Advisory Board.
June 6, 1980

The President today announced the appointment of two persons as members of the National Armed Forces Museum Advisory Board of the Smithsonian Institution. They are:

ANDREW J. GOODPASTER, Superintendent of the United States Military Academy;

THEODORE ROPP, a professor of history at Duke University who is currently a visiting professor at Singapore University and Australia National University. He has been a member of this Board since 1975 and is president and a trustee of the American Military Institute.

National Corporation for Housing Partnerships

Nomination of Kennon V. Rothchild To Be a Member of the Board of Directors.   June 6, 1980

The President today announced that he will nominate Kennon V. Rothchild, of Mahtomedi, Minn., for reappointment as a member of the Board of Directors of the National Corporation for Housing Partnerships.

Rothchild has been a member of this Board since 1978. He is chairman of the board and chief executive officer of H. & Val J. Rothschild, Inc., a mortgage banking firm, and of Rothschild Financial Corp.

Advisory Committee for Trade Negotiations

Appointment of Jiro Murase as a Member and Reappointment of 20 Members. June 6, 1980

The President today announced the reappointment of 20 members of the Advisory Committee for Trade Negotiations and the appointment of one new member.

The new member is Jiro Murase, senior partner in the New York firm of Wender, Murase & White, and legal counsel to approximately 200 leading U.S., European, and Japanese multinational corporations.

Those being reappointed are:

W. J. AMOSS, JR., of New Orleans, president of Lykes Brothers Steamship Co.;

NORBORNE BERKELEY, JR., president and director of Chemical New York Corp. and Chemical Bank;

JAMES H. BINGER, of Minneapolis, chairman of the executive committee of Honeywell, Inc.;

DAVID W. BROOKS, of Atlanta, Ga., chairman of the policy committee of Gold Kist, Inc.;

ALEX CHISHOLM, president of L & M Radiator, Inc., Hibbing, Minn.;

MURRAY H. FINLEY, president of the Amalgamated Clothing and Textile Workers Union;

MAURICE R. GREENBERG, president and chief executive officer of American International Group, Inc., and C. V. Starr & Co.;

KARL D. GREGORY, professor of economics and management at Oakland University in Michigan, and a management and economic consultant;

LOYD HACKLER, president of the American Retail Foundation;

RICHARD E. HECKERT, a director, senior vice president, and member of the executive committee of the du Pont Co.;

RUTH J. HINERFELD, of Larchmont, N.Y., vice president of the League of Women Voters;

ROBERT M. IVIE, president of Guild Wineries and Distilleries in San Francisco;

FRANKLIN A. JACOBS, of St. Louis, Mo., president, chairman of the board, and chief executive officer of Falcon Products, Inc.;

WILLIAM D. KNOX, president of W. D. Hoard & Sons Co., Fort Atkinson, Wis., which publishes "Hoard's Dairyman";

KENNETH D. NADEN, of Bethesda, Md., president of the National Council of Farmer Cooperatives;

CHARLES H. PILLARD, international president of the International Brotherhood of Electrical Workers;

MYER RASHISH, a Washington, D.C., consulting economist, who was an assistant to President John F. Kennedy from 1961 to 1963;

WILLIAM J. ROCHE, vice president of Texas Instruments Inc.;

JEAN HEAD SISCO, coordinator for business and community affairs at American University in Washington, D.C.;

C. WILLIAM VERITY, JR., chairman of the board of directors, Armco Steel Corp., in Middletown, Ohio.

Petroleum Import Licensing Requirements

Proclamation 4762. June 6, 1980

By the President of the United States of America

A Proclamation

By the authority vested in me as President by the Constitution and the laws of the United States, including Section 232 of the Trade Expansion Act of 1962, as amended (19 U.S.C. 1862), I hereby proclaim, effective immediately, that:

Any license for the importation of crude oil or gasoline as defined in Proclamation 4744 and issued thereunder shall remain valid, for purposes of Proclamation 3279, as amended, until 12:01 a.m. September 1, 1980, provided that the time period for which it was issued has not expired and that the volumes authorized to be imported under that license have not been entered into the United States.

IN WITNESS WHEREOF, I have hereunto set my hand this sixth day of June, in the year of our Lord nineteen hundred and eighty, and of the Independence of the United States of America the two hundred and fourth.

JIMMY CARTER

[Filed with the Office of the Federal Register, 9:48 a.m., June 9, 1980]

Digest of Other White House Announcements

The following listing includes the President's public schedule and other items of general interest announced by the White House Press Office and not included elsewhere in this issue.

May 31

The President met at the White House with Zbigniew Brzezinski, Assistant to the President for National Security Affairs.

The President went to the CBS News Washington Bureau, where he was interviewed for the program "Face the Nation" by CBS News correspondents George Herman and Lesley Stahl, and Walter Mears of the Associated Press. The interview was taped for broadcast on the CBS television and radio networks on June 1.

The President left the White House for a visit to Camp David, Md.

June 1

Following his visit with Vernon E. Jordan, Jr., in Fort Wayne, Ind., the President returned to the White House.

June 2

The President met at the White House with:

—Dr. Brzezinski;

—Frank B. Moore, Assistant to the President for Congressional Liaison.

The President transmitted to the Congress, the 1979 annual report on health activities under the Federal Mine Safety and Health Act of 1977 and the fourth annual report on the administration of the Genetic Diseases Program.

The White House announced that the President has designated Representative Lucien N. Nedzi of Michigan as his representative at the Poznan International Technical Fair to be held in Poland June 8–17.

June 3

The President met at the White House with:
—Dr. Brzezinski;
—Mr. Moore;
—representatives of the food processing industry to discuss pricing policies;
—a group of his advisers for an overview session on the fiscal year 1982 budget;
—Senators Dale Bumpers and David Pryor of Arkansas.

June 4

The President met at the White House with:
—Dr. Brzezinski;
—the Democratic congressional leadership;
—Representative Bill Tauzin of Louisiana, who was elected to fill the seat in the House of Representatives formerly held by Governor Treen;
—Mr. Moore;
—Vice President Walter F. Mondale;
—Thomas J. Watson, U.S. Ambassador to the Soviet Union, upon his return to Moscow after consultations in this country;
—George W. Stone, newly elected president of the National Farmers Union, to discuss farm issues;
—James T. McIntyre, Jr., Director of the Office of Management and Budget.

The President announced the appointment of Susan B. King, Chairman of the Consumer Product Safety Commission, as Vice Chairman of the Regulatory Council.

June 5

The President met at the White House with:
—Dr. Brzezinski;

—Secretary of the Treasury G. William Miller, Under Secretary of Labor John N. Gentry, Alonzo L. McDonald, Jr., Assistant to the President, Charles L. Schultze, Chairman of the Council of Economic Advisers, Alfred E. Kahn, Advisor to the President on Inflation and Chairman of the Council on Wage and Price Stability, R. Robert Russell, Director of the Council on Wage and Price Stability, Stuart E. Eizenstat, Assistant to the President for Domestic Affairs and Policy, and John P. White, Deputy Director of the Office of Management and Budget;
—Mr. Moore;
—representatives of the machinery industry to discuss pricing policies;
—Senator Edward M. Kennedy of Massachusetts.

The President participated in two separate briefings held in the East Room. One was given for members of the board of directors of the National Association of Broadcasters, and the other for Members of the 95th Congress.

The White House announced that the President has declared a major disaster for the State of Nebraska as a result of severe storms and tornadoes, beginning on or about June 3, which caused extensive property damage.

June 6

The President met at the White House with:
—Dr. Brzezinski;
—Vice President Mondale, Secretary of State Edmund S. Muskie, Secretary of Defense Harold Brown, Hedley W. Donovan, Senior Adviser to the President, Hamilton Jordan, Assistant to the President, and Dr. Brzezinski;
—Mr. Moore;

—Edward Stoll, 94, of Elwood, Nebr., who has been a volunteer cooperative weather observer for the National Weather Service for the past 74 years;

—Jacqueline Colvill, international president, and other representatives of the Juvenile Diabetes Foundation, accompanied by three juvenile diabetes poster children;

—Mrs. Carter, for lunch.

In a ceremony in the Oval Office, the President received diplomatic credentials from Ambassadors Sherif Fawaz Sharaf of Jordan, Jorge Pacheco Areco of Uruguay, Tamaiti Willie Star of Nauru, and Jacques Topande-Makombo of the Central African Republic.

The President left the White House for a weekend stay at Camp David.

The President transmitted to the Congress the 1979 annual report of the Department of Health, Education, and Welfare on occupational safety and health.

NOMINATIONS SUBMITTED TO THE SENATE

The following list does not include promotions of members of the Uniformed Services, nominations to the Service Academies, or nominations of Foreign Service officers.

Withdrawn June 2, 1980

CHARLES J. FAHEY, of New York, to be a member of the Federal Council on the Aging for a term expiring December 19, 1982, vice Nelson H. Cruikshank, term expired, which was sent to the Senate on May 2, 1980.

Submitted June 2, 1980

EARL H. CARROLL, of Arizona, to be United States District Judge for the District of Arizona, vice a new position created by P.L. 95–486, approved October 20, 1978.

ALFRED C. MARQUEZ, of Arizona, to be United States District Judge for the District of Arizona, vice a new position created by P.L. 95–486, approved October 20, 1978.

GEORGE HOWARD, JR., of Arkansas, to be United States District Judge for the Eastern

NOMINATIONS—Continued
Submitted June 2—Continued

and Western Districts of Arkansas, vice Richard S. Arnold, elevated.

CHARLES P. KOCORAS, of Illinois, to be United States District Judge for the Northern District of Illinois, vice Alfred Y. Kirkland, retired.

JOHN E. SPRIZZO, of New York, to be United States District Judge for the Southern District of New York, vice Charles H. Tenney, retired.

JAMES E. JONES, JR., of Wisconsin, to be Chairman of the Special Panel on Appeals for a term of 6 years (new position, P.L. 95–454).

CHARLES J. FAHEY, of New York, to be a member of the Federal Council on the Aging for a term expiring June 5, 1982 (reappointment).

Submitted June 3, 1980

The following-named persons to be members of the National Advisory Council on Women's Educational Programs for the terms indicated:

For terms expiring May 8, 1982

MARIA CONCEPCION BECHILY, of Illinois, vice Elizabeth Z. Fryer, term expired.

BARBARA M. CAREY, of Florida, vice Marjorie Bell Chambers, term expired.

VIRGINIA FOXX, of North Carolina, vice Marguerite C. Selden, term expired.

K. JESSIE KOBAYASHI, of California, vice Agnes I. Chan, term expired.

JEWEL LIMAR PRESTAGE, of Louisiana, vice Thera C. Johnson, term expired.

For a term expiring May 8, 1983

RHINE LANA McLIN, of Ohio, vice Gladys Gunn, resigned.

DONALD NEWTON LANGENBERG, of Pennsylvania, to be Deputy Director of the National Science Foundation, vice George Claude Pimentel, resigned.

Submitted June 4, 1980

FRANCES D. COOK, of Florida, a Foreign Service officer of Class three, to be Ambassador Extraordinary and Plenipotentiary of the United States of America to the Republic of Burundi.

JERROLD MARTIN NORTH, of Illinois, a Foreign Service officer of Class three, to be Ambassador Extraordinary and Plenipotentiary of the United States of America to the Republic of Djibouti.

NOMINATIONS—Continued

Submitted June 4—Continued

HERBERT STUART OKUN, of Maryland, a Foreign Service officer of Class one, to be Ambassador Extraordinary and Plenipotentiary of the United States of America to the German Democratic Republic.

SUSAN C. GETZENDANNER, of Illinois, to be United States District Judge for the Northern District of Illinois, vice a new position created by P.L. 95–486, approved October 20, 1978.

DON ALAN ZIMMERMAN, of Maryland, to be a member of the National Labor Relations Board for the term of 5 years expiring December 16, 1984, vice Betty Southard Murphy, resigned.

Submitted June 6, 1980

CYNTHIA G. BROWN, of the District of Columbia, to be Assistant Secretary for Civil Rights, Department of Education (new position).

EDWIN W. MARTIN, JR., of Virginia, to be Assistant Secretary for Special Education and Rehabilitative Services, Department of Education (new position).

CHECKLIST OF WHITE HOUSE PRESS RELEASES

The following listing contains releases of the White House Press Office which are not included in this issue.

Released May 30, 1980

Statement by the President: on signing S. 2253, the Northeast corridor appropriations bill, into law

Released June 3, 1980

Fact sheet: the President's meeting with representatives of food processing firms to discuss pricing policies

Released June 4, 1980

Announcement: nomination of Susan C. Getzendanner to be United States District Judge for the Northern District of Illinois

Released June 5, 1980

Advance text: remarks at the opening session of the White House Conference on Families in Baltimore, Md.

ACTS APPROVED BY THE PRESIDENT

Approved May 31, 1980

H.R. 6081_____ Public Law 96–257
Special Central American Assistance Act of 1979.

Approved June 3, 1980

H.R. 3807_____ Public Law 96–258
An act to amend subtitle IV of title 49, United States Code, to codify recent law and improve the Code without substantive change.

S. 662_____ Public Law 96–259
An act to provide for increased participation by the United States in the Inter-American Development Bank, the Asian Development Bank, and the African Development Fund.

H.R. 4088 _____ Public Law 96–260
An act to authorize the Secretary of Commerce to sell two obsolete vessels to Coast Line Company and for other purposes.

Approved June 4, 1980

H.J. Res. 554_____ Public Law 96–261
A joint resolution making an appropriation for the Federal Trade Commission for the fiscal year ending September 30, 1980.

Approved June 5, 1980

H.R. 4890_____ Public Law 96–262
An act to authorize appropriations for the Commercial Fisheries Research and Development Act of 1964 for fiscal years 1981, 1982, and 1983.

Approved June 6, 1980

H.R. 3789_____ Public Law 96–263
An act to amend section 16(b) of the Soil Conservation and Domestic Allotment Act, as amended, providing for a Great Plains conservation program.

EDITOR'S NOTE: The following bill became law over the President's veto of June 5 (see page 1041):

H.R. 7428_____ Public Law 96–264
An act to extend the present public debt limit through June 30, 1980.

Cuban Refugees

Statement by the White House Press
Secretary. June 7, 1980

Among the tens of thousands of people fleeing oppression in Cuba and seeking to reunite with their families and to seek freedom in the United States, Fidel Castro has very cynically thrown in several hundred hardened criminals from Cuban jails. These criminals will not be resettled or relocated in American communities under any circumstances. The administration will take the legal and necessary steps to make sure that this will not happen.

There is evidence that the Cuban Government exported these undesirable elements to the United States in a calculated effort to disguise the fact that the vast majority of those Cubans who have come to this country were and are law-abiding citizens whose only purpose was to seek freedom and to seek reunification with their families.

This action by the Cuban Government, in addition to its cynical and inhumane characteristics, is a direct and serious violation of international law. It would be an equally serious violation if the Government of Cuba should refuse to perform its obligations under international law to accept the return of these criminals. The President has directed the Secretary of State to press this issue urgently through diplomatic channels and in the appropriate international forum.

Unfortunately, a few of those who came to the United States seeking the right to live here in this country, to join a democratic and law-abiding society, have created disturbances and have violated the laws of the country in which they seek to live. These individuals will be dealt with in strict accordance with those laws.

The President has directed the Attorney General to take the following actions:

First, Cubans identified as having committed serious crimes in Cuba are to be securely confined. Exclusion proceedings will be expedited to the maximum extent consistent with constitutional requirements for due process of law.

Second, exclusion proceedings will also be started against those who have violated American law while waiting to be reprocessed or relocated. The Justice Department will investigate all serious violations of the law, and the Justice Department will bring prosecutions where justified. Those responsible for the disturbances at Fort Chaffee are confined and will be confined until fair decisions can be made on criminal prosecution or exclusion from this country or both. Similar measures will be taken in the event of any future disturbances.

NOTE: Press Secretary Jody Powell read the statement at approximately 12:30 p.m. to reporters assembled in the Briefing Room at the White House. A question-and-answer session followed the statement and is included in the press release.

Federal Agency Consumer Programs

Remarks Announcing the Release of 35 Agency Programs. June 9, 1980

Congressman Rosenthal, Congressman Scheuer, distinguished members of my Cabinet who will be appearing later on this program, Esther Peterson, and Americans who are interested in fairness and equity and the protection of consumers in our country:

This is a time of economic challenge for America, a time when decisions are difficult both to make and to implement. It's a time when many people are concerned about the future. It's a time when it's important, even imperative, that Government demonstrate its commitment to preserving the utmost degree of care and concern about troubled American families.

I'm delighted that so many of the top agency heads are here this morning to demonstrate their commitment to the consumer programs that we will outline for you today.

In my State of the Union speech a year ago last January, I pointed out that we must have a stronger voice for consumers in our Government and throughout the country. And last September, I signed an Executive order which is designed to put that commitment into motion.

Today, I'm pleased to share with you some of the fruits of a lot of hard work, both by those on the platform and those seated before me. This final publication by 35 different Federal agencies of their new programs and procedures for consumers will indeed be an historic development in our Government.

One of the things that I set out to do when I was first inaugurated, in fact when I was first a candidate for President, was to bring the Government closer to the people. This is one viable and forceful way to accomplish that goal.

For that closeness to be realized, the Government in all its aspects must listen to what people have to say. This is not always easy in the frantic daily life of even the most enlightened bureaucrat or the most enlightened President. The doors have got to be opened to Government, and the doors have got to be kept open, because of a lot of very highly paid and very competent lobbyists are determined to make sure that those doors are closed and kept closed.

In our working lives here in Washington and throughout the country, we all have different roles to play, but one thing we have in common—all of us are consumers. And when we protect consumers, we protect ourselves, and we protect those who look to us for leadership. That's what the consumers want, and that's what these consumer programs today will accomplish.

As you know, I fought side-by-side with almost everyone in this room to set up a separate consumer protection agency for the Government. This was not possible to accomplish because the special interest lobbyists pulled out all the stops, and they prevailed temporarily. But we've not yet lost that war.

Together, we've had to come up with some additional ways to accomplish as much as possible of the same goals that were envisioned with the consumer protection agency itself—the goal of making the ordinary citizen just get a fair deal, a fair shake from government.

Two years ago, I issued an Executive order designed to improve Government regulations. That order gave, among other things, consumers more time to comment and to express their own concerns before the order became final.

I created a Regulatory Council to bring together all the major regulatory agencies in the Federal Government under one organization, which is informal in nature but very effective, to set out a calendar for the issuing of regulations to let the people who would be affected by them comment and criticize and maybe even delay or cancel the regulations that were in prospect. The bringing together of all the regulatory agencies into one place for discussions of their future actions has indeed been a very successful event and helpful to us all.

I proposed a bill to the Congress to extend public participation funding throughout the Government. Quite often, those who suffer most by government action or by action from an unenlightened private sector representative are least able to pay for a trip to Washington or a voice that needs to be clearly heard. And in the meantime, before this bill passes, I've urged agencies to use their existing authority to aid all those who otherwise could not participate effectively in expressing their views to Government agencies and to others.

We've begun to install toll free telephone lines so that consumers throughout the Nation or representatives of consumer groups who are highly knowledgeable and who are constantly studying how best to present their views can have access to Government agencies and to consumer advisers in the Government without any cost to themselves and without the necessity of a trip to Washington. It also prevents them from getting the runaround because along with the toll free numbers is a clear description of how they can best approach the Government and to whom they will be speaking. And we've put into distribution now a Consumers Resource Handbook that lets people know how they can call in to the Government to get help and information and to express their displeasure or their suggestions.

So, the education program is now moving beyond the leadership positions themselves and is being distributed on a local basis throughout the Nation to those who have a crucial interest in dealing with the Government more effectively. The Executive order on Federal Consumer Programs, the one that has led to today's announcements, is a keystone of my commitment to consumers, pending the passage of consumer protection agency legislation in the future.

This order sets up a single, tough standard for the protection of consumer interests. And after months of hard work, 35 agencies are issuing their final consumer programs today. Each agency has named a senior person, as I requested, to look after consumer matters. That consumer representative will report directly to the head of the agency itself to make sure that there is a regular, routine, incisive, effective consumer representative at the top level within each agency. This will permit the agency head and, indirectly, myself to pay attention to the ways that the policy of that agency might affect adversely or beneficially the consumers of our country.

This arrangement, by the way, just coincidentally happens to be patterned after the arrangement between Esther Peterson and myself. She had some influence in devising the procedure and the organizational structure, and I can tell you without any doubt of being contradicted by anyone who knows us, that if the agencies themselves and their consumer representatives function as well as Esther makes me function as President, then the consumers will achieve great benefit from this entire arrangement, and this will be a bright new day for consumers.

She advises me, by the way, not just on narrowly focused consumer issues but on any other aspect of Government that has an adverse effect on American families or which can be beneficial to the quality of life of Americans. She works closely with other members of the White House staff. She's involved in the drafting of legislation. She's involved in the implementation of programs once they are authorized by law and financed through the appropriations committee, and she also makes sure that consumers have an identifiable person within the White House to whom they can relay suggestions or express their concerns. If and when this is done in each one of these 35 agencies, as a result of today's announcements, then there's no doubt in my mind that there will be a tremendous expansion of the beneficial influence of consumers throughout the Government itself.

We have, in effect, created a Government-wide system of Esther Petersons, and nothing could be better for the consumers.

Well, I'm going to leave it up to Esther to outline the program to you in detail. I know you are intensely interested in it, and I have asked Bill Miller, the Secretary of Treasury, to give you his analysis of the program from the perspective of a major Cabinet officer. Some of the other agency heads here may also want to participate in the program this morning.

Let me close by saying that I want to emphasize that these programs are important not just to you, but also they are very important to me.

I've informed the agencies directly of my personal concern about the effectiveness with which they will carry out the

Executive order and their present plans. There is no doubt in my mind that despite a stringent budget commitment which I share with the Congress, that these consumer programs will be implemented effectively. They have been very carefully developed; they are based on extensive consultation not only within the agencies and with me and Esther Peterson, but also extensive consultation with the public. They are designed in a very deliberate way to make the Government better able to address the needs of consumers.

We are trying to lock the consumer perspective into the basic structure of the Federal Government and not make this an ad hoc relationship that comes and goes only with a major or a minor crisis. I want the entire Federal Government to think like a consumer would think so that the relationship is continuous, it's natural, it's routine, and it's effective. That's our goal and, with your help, we've made major progress toward that goal.

Let me just add my thanks for all the work that has gone into the consumer programs that will be unveiled to you today—hard work by scores of top representatives in the agencies themselves, by consumer groups, and by individuals who took the time to comment on the draft proposals which were published last December, and especially by Esther Peterson and her staff. All of you are not only to be thanked but to be congratulated.

Our next task is to monitor very closely the progress that we make after today. If there are defects in the proposals made, if there are inadequacies in the care for the rights of consumers, I want you to let us know. Direct it to me or to the head of the agency involved, or the ultimate appeal would be to Esther Peterson herself.

From now on, the voice of consumers will be clear, and I hope the voice of consumers will be loud and it will be heard in the halls of Government.

This is a good day, in my opinion, for our country and for the consumers of our Nation, and I'm deeply grateful to Esther Peterson, whom I now present to you to speak for me, on her own, and for you.

Thank you very much.

NOTE: The President spoke at 9:45 a.m. in Room 450 of the Old Executive Office Building.

The consumer programs were published in the FEDERAL REGISTER of June 9, 1980, as Books 2 and 3.

Presidential Medal of Freedom

Remarks at the Presentation Ceremony.
June 9, 1980

THE PRESIDENT. It's a great privilege for us to have had Charles Brown Fisk play this morning. He's one of the winners of the Bach International Competition, the first American winner, I believe. He was playing the Introductory Movement of Bach's Italian Concerto for us. This is the world's first major competition devoted exclusively to Bach. And since it was begun in 1959, it has encouraged a whole generation of musicians to include some of the most challenging and exciting music in their own repertoires. We're very deeply grateful to you for beginning this program with such an excellent performance. Thank you very much.

As I'm sure you know, the Presidential Medal of Freedom is the highest civilian award given in this Nation. The medal was first presented by President Truman during the time of World War II to honor especially meritorious nonmilitary con-

tributions to national security and to world peace. Since I've been in office, I've given the Medal of Freedom to three people: Justice Arthur Goldberg, to Jonas Salk, and to Martin Luther King, Jr.

Over the years the qualifications were broadened to include cultural and other significant public and private endeavors. Past recipients have included our greatest composers, writers, scientists, performing and visual artists, religious and moral leaders of our time, appropriately covering the wide range of activities that a free people rightly consider to be invaluable contributions to the quality of our lives and to the peace and the cultural improvement of the lives of people everywhere.

The men and women to be honored here today reflect that broad range to an extraordinary degree: an admiral and an actor, who both came to symbolize the spirit of American individualism; a biologist and a birdwatcher; a dramatist and a dancer; a photographer, a poet, and a President; a coloratura and a civil rights leader; and a Senator from Minnesota whose enthusiasm and whose compassion inspired a generation of Americans. Their widely differing styles and careers are united by just one thing—their passionate commitment to their own convictions and the compatibility of their convictions with the enhancement of the quality of American life.

They have enriched our lives by broadening the scope of our vision and by deepening our understanding. They have, in their varying ways, aroused our rightful indignation at injustice and intolerance, at indifference and ignorance. They've made us look up to the birds in flight, down into the depths of ocean, and inward to probe the cruelty and the comedy, the courage and the compassion of the human heart. The rest of us have not always come up to the high standards that they've set for us. But because of them, our Nation is a little more secure, a little less careless, a little more literate, a little more loving than we might otherwise have been.

Now I'd like to read the names and the citations in alphabetical order, and as I read each citation, I would like to ask the honoree to come forward.

The first is Ansel Adams.

[At this point, the President read the citation, the text of which follows:

THE PRESIDENT OF THE UNITED STATES OF AMERICA AWARDS THIS PRESIDENTIAL MEDAL OF FREEDOM TO ANSEL ADAMS

At one with the power of the American landscape, and renowned for the patient skill and timeless beauty of his work, photographer Ansel Adams has been visionary in his efforts to preserve this country's wild and scenic areas, both in film and on Earth. Drawn to the beauty of nature's monuments, he is regarded by environmentalists as a monument himself, and by photographers as a national institution. It is through his foresight and fortitude that so much of America has been saved for future Americans.]

I'm very thankful that Ansel Adams is my personal friend. I have one of his beautiful photographs in my office. I enjoy it every day, and it reminds me and others who visit me there not only of the beauty of our country in the past and at the present time but the necessity for preserving that beauty for the future.

Although Ansel Adams and many others are presently responsible for the awareness of American people about the quality of our lives and our environment, perhaps the most significant single contribution was made by the next honoree, Rachel Carson. I'd like to ask her nephew and adopted son to come forward as I present this award to her.

[At this point, the President read the citation, the text of which follows:

THE PRESIDENT OF THE UNITED STATES OF AMERICA AWARDS THIS PRESIDENTIAL MEDAL OF FREEDOM TO RACHEL CARSON

Never silent herself in the face of destructive trends, Rachel Carson fed a spring of awareness across America and beyond. A biologist with a gentle, clear voice, she welcomed her audiences to her love of the sea, while with an equally clear determined voice she warned Americans of the dangers human beings themselves pose for their own environment. Always concerned, always eloquent, she created a tide of environmental consciousness that has not ebbed.]

The next honoree is Lucia Chase.

[At this point, the President read the citation, the text of which follows:

THE PRESIDENT OF THE UNITED STATES OF AMERICA AWARDS THIS PRESIDENTIAL MEDAL OF FREEDOM TO LUCIA CHASE

Ballerina Lucia Chase has been a one-woman show, devoting her lifework to sustaining the vitality of American dance. A dancer and ballet director both, she has interpreted roles and created them, and in every instance she has served to inspire the young, entertain the old and win for American talent its rightful place on the international stage of dance.]

On occasion in our lives, a certain person touches the heartstrings of our existence and inspires us all in a special, deeply human way. I'd now like to ask the wife of Hubert Humphrey to come forward. *[Applause]* If you'll permit me an aside, I think the applause is not only for the honoree but for Muriel Humphrey as well, who shared so much.

[At this point, the President read the citation, the text of which follows:

THE PRESIDENT OF THE UNITED STATES OF AMERICA AWARDS THIS PRESIDENTIAL MEDAL OF FREEDOM TO HUBERT H. HUMPHREY

Hubert H. Humphrey awed us with the scope of his knowledge; he inspired us with the depth of his sympathy; he moved us with his passion for social justice; he delighted us

with his joyous love of his fellow human beings. He brought honor and enthusiasm to
everything he did. He ennobled the political
process.]

One of the most exciting days of my
Presidency was a year or so ago when we
had this entire lawn almost filled with delighted Greek Americans who share with
me and others the admiration that we all
feel for the next honoree. I'd like to ask
Archbishop Iakovos to come forward.

*[At this point, the President read the citation,
the text of which follows:*

THE PRESIDENT OF THE UNITED STATES OF
AMERICA AWARDS THIS PRESIDENTIAL
MEDAL OF FREEDOM TO ARCHBISHOP
IAKOVOS

Greek Orthodox Archbishop Iakovos has
long put into practice what he has preached.
As a progressive religious leader concerned
with human rights and the ecumenical movement, he has marched with Dr. Martin Luther
King, Jr. and has met with the Pope. As the
Primate of the Greek Orthodox Church of
North and South America concerned with his
congregation, he has given guidance to
millions.]

It's hard to think of words adequate to
describe the profound impact made on
our Nation and the world by this next
honoree, a man who was big in every way,
a great influence, great heart, who literally transformed the attitudes of our country. I would like to ask Lady Bird Johnson
to come forward to accept the award for
Lyndon Baines Johnson.

*[At this point, the President read the citation,
the text of which follows:*

THE PRESIDENT OF THE UNITED STATES OF
AMERICA AWARDS THIS PRESIDENTIAL
MEDAL OF FREEDOM TO LYNDON BAINES
JOHNSON

Lyndon B. Johnson cared deeply about our
country, its citizens, and the condition of their
lives. He knew well how to translate concern
into action, and action into a national agenda.
He did more than any American of his time to
break the chains of injustice, illiteracy, poverty

and sickness. We are a greater society because
President Johnson lived among us and worked
for us.]

It may well be that Hubert Humphrey
and Lyndon Baines Johnson would not
have been so notably acclaimed had it not
been for the next gentleman who will be
honored. I'd like to ask Clarence Mitchell,
Jr., to come forward.

*[At this point, the President read the citation,
the text of which follows:*

THE PRESIDENT OF THE UNITED STATES OF
AMERICA AWARDS THIS PRESIDENTIAL
MEDAL OF FREEDOM TO CLARENCE M.
MITCHELL, JR.

Clarence M. Mitchell, Jr., for decades waged
in the halls of Congress a stubborn, resourceful
and historic campaign for social justice. The
integrity of this "101st Senator" earned him
the respect of friends and adversaries alike. His
brilliant advocacy helped translate into law the
protests and aspirations of millions consigned
too long to second-class citizenship. The hard-
won fruits of his labors have made America a
better and stronger nation.]

The combination of the love of our
natural heritage and the excitement and
pleasure that can be given to other Americans who can't share on a full-time basis
the delights of his own existence make this
next award especially significant. I'd like
to ask Roger Tory Peterson to come
forward.

*[At this point, the President read the citation,
the text of which follows:*

THE PRESIDENT OF THE UNITED STATES OF
AMERICA AWARDS THIS PRESIDENTIAL
MEDAL OF FREEDOM TO ROGER TORY
PETERSON

Roger Tory Peterson has achieved distinction as a consummate painter, writer, teacher
and scientist. As an unabashed lover of birds
and a distinguished ornithologist, he has fur-
thered the study, appreciation and protection
of birds the world over. And he has done more.
He has impassioned thousands of Americans,

and has awakened in millions across this land, a fondness for nature's other two-legged creatures.]

I've said many times to a close circle of friends that probably with the exception of my own father, no other person has had such a profound impact on my life than has the next honoree. A person who is personally responsible for the first full utilization of atomic power not for destruction but for peace, I would like to ask Admiral Hyman G. Rickover, U.S. Navy, to come forward.

This is one of the few times when Admiral Rickover has walked toward me that I didn't tremble in my shoes. [*Laughter*]

[*At this point, the President read the citation, the text of which follows:*

THE PRESIDENT OF THE UNITED STATES OF AMERICA AWARDS THIS PRESIDENTIAL MEDAL OF FREEDOM TO ADMIRAL HYMAN RICKOVER

Admiral Rickover exemplifies the American belief that freedom and responsibility are inseparable; the duty of the citizen is to contribute his best to the Nation's welfare and defense. His successful development and application of nuclear propulsion revolutionized naval warfare. The performance of our nuclear fleet over more than a quarter of a century is proof of his well-known commitment to excellence. This Nation's first civilian electric utility reactor, which he designed and developed in the 1950's is the technological forerunner of nearly all utility reactors subsequently built in this country. A keen observer of mankind, he has not hesitated to measure publicly the actions of government, industry, the professions, and our schools against the standard of responsibility.]

Not all of us have the benefit of world renown and excellence in our chosen profession, the ability to inspire others, and personal beauty as well, but the next honoree who means so much to America personifies all those characteristics. I'd like to ask Beverly Sills Greenough to come forward.

[*At this point, the President read the citation, the text of which follows:*

THE PRESIDENT OF THE UNITED STATES OF AMERICA AWARDS THIS PRESIDENTIAL MEDAL OF FREEDOM TO BEVERLY SILLS GREENOUGH

Beverly Sills has captured with her voice every note of human feeling, and with her superb dramatic talent projected them out to us with ringing clarity. Through her many and diverse roles, she tells and retells opera's intensely heightened stories of human folly, goodness, pain and triumph. She has touched and delighted audiences throughout the world as a performer, as a recording artist, and now as a producer—and of all her arts she is a master.]

On rare occasions, a person who has extraordinary talent finds that talent to be repeated in various aspects of human endeavor. Our next honoree certainly is a person of that kind who has inspired a Nation to assess very closely a standard of excellence which few others can equal. I would like to ask Robert Penn Warren to come forward for his citation.

[*At this point, the President read the citation, the text of which follows:*

THE PRESIDENT OF THE UNITED STATES OF AMERICA AWARDS THIS PRESIDENTIAL MEDAL OF FREEDOM TO ROBERT PENN WARREN

Robert Penn Warren excels as a poet, novelist, literary critic, and teacher. His textbooks, written with Cleanth Brooks, transformed the teaching of literature and writing in the United States. As a literary craftsman and a committed humanist Robert Penn Warren has undertaken a lifelong quest for self-knowledge and moral vision which has established him as one of America's greatest men of letters of the 20th Century.]

All of these are famous people, they're well-known throughout the world. But even including Vice Presidents and Presidents, noted singers and dancers and writers and ornithologists, I think the next would be the most famous of us all, including the one who reads this citation.

I would like to ask Mrs. John Wayne to come forward.

[At this point, the President read the citation, the text of which follows:

THE PRESIDENT OF THE UNITED STATES OF AMERICA AWARDS THIS PRESIDENTIAL MEDAL OF FREEDOM TO JOHN WAYNE

John Wayne was both an example and a symbol of true American grit and determination. Through his countless film roles, "The Duke" still leads millions on heroic adventures on behalf of fairness and justice. He embodies the enduring American values of individualism, relentless bravery and perseverance in pursuit of what is right. He was the quintessential patriot, and will especially be remembered whenever our Nation faces a challenge calling for steadfast courage.]

Sometimes a writer has such a special sensitivity about the human heart and the human spirit that their works literally burst forward not only with entertainment but with human comedy and the ability to epitomize what a character means, not only to those considered in the novel or short story but to us as well. I would now like to ask one of my favorite authors to come forward, Eudora Welty.

[At this point, the President read the citation, the text of which follows:

THE PRESIDENT OF THE UNITED STATES OF AMERICA AWARDS THIS PRESIDENTIAL MEDAL OF FREEDOM TO EUDORA WELTY

Eudora Welty's fiction, with its strong sense of place and triumphant comic spirit, illuminates the human condition. Her photographs of the South during the Depression reveal a rare artistic sensibility. Her critical essays explore mind and heart, literary and oral tradition, language and life with unsurpassed beauty. Through photography, essays and fiction, Eudora Welty has enriched our lives and shown us the wonder of human experience.]

A few days ago someone accused me of being prejudiced toward the South in the selection of these honorees. That is not the case, although Robert Penn Warren and Eudora Welty and the next honoree happen to be from the South. I'm very delighted to read the citation for this last of our group of honorees. His work is truly remarkable. The breadth of it is astonishing, and the enjoyment that people have derived during his own lifetime—and I'm sure for many decades or centuries in the future—will indeed be a reminder of what America is in its challenge, in its failures, in its dreams and hopes for the future. I'd like to ask Tennessee Williams to come forward.

[At this point, the President read the citation, the text of which follows:

THE PRESIDENT OF THE UNITED STATES OF AMERICA AWARDS THIS PRESIDENTIAL MEDAL OF FREEDOM TO TENNESSEE WILLIAMS

Tennessee Williams has shaped the history of modern American theater through plays which range from passionate tragedies to lyrical comedies. His masterpieces dramatize the eternal conflicts between body and soul, youth and death, love and despair through the unity of reality and poetry. Tennessee Williams shows us that the truly heroic in life or art is human compassion.]

I'd like to ask all of the honorees to come forward maybe for a photograph together with me. And, Rosalynn, would you join us? And then Rosalynn will have a special invitation to give you all.

MRS. CARTER. I want to congratulate all of these honorees and thank them for their great contributions to our country and to the world. I'm very pleased that you could all join us this morning for the ceremony, and now I want to invite everyone to come inside and have lunch. Thank you.

NOTE: The President spoke at 11:46 a.m. on the South Lawn of the White House. Following the ceremony, a luncheon was held in the State Dining Room for honorees and their guests.

Roger Christy accepted the medal and citation on behalf of Rachel Carson.

Social Security Disability Amendments of 1980

Statement on Signing H.R. 3236 Into Law.
June 9, 1980

Today I have signed H.R. 3236, the Social Security Disability Amendments of 1980. This bill is the product of several years of intensive study and review conducted by this administration and the Congress. It forms a balanced package, with amendments to strengthen the integrity of the disability programs, increase equity among beneficiaries, offer greater assistance to those who are trying to work, and improve program administration.

Since the mid-1950's the social security disability insurance (DI) program has offered protection to insured workers who have lost wages because of unexpected and often catastrophic disabilities. More recently, since 1974, the Supplemental Security Income (SSI) program has provided Federal financial assistance to needy disabled persons whether or not they are covered under the disability insurance program.

Despite their medical impairments, most disabled DI and SSI beneficiaries would like to work. Often they are able to find employment either in their previous occupations or in new jobs. But returning to work can now cause a recipient to lose all his cash and medical benefits, and this formidable financial risk deters many beneficiaries from seeking or accepting serious job offers.

H.R. 3236 is designed to help disabled beneficiaries return to work by minimizing the risks involved in accepting paid employment. It does this in several ways:

—by providing automatic reentitlement to benefits if an attempt to return to work fails within 1 year;

—by continuing medical protection for up to 3 years after a person returns to work, and by providing immediate reentitlement to medical benefits if the individual subsequently returns to the disability rolls;

—by taking account of an individual's disability-related work expenses in determining eligibility for benefits; and

—by continuing, on an experimental basis for 3 years, cash and medical benefits to SSI recipients with low earnings.

H.R. 3236 establishes a special pilot program that will provide $18 million over a 3-year period to allow States to offer medical and social services to employed handicapped people to help them continue working. It also gives the Social Security Administration new authority to test the effect of further changes in the law. Changes which show promise for helping DI and SSI beneficiaries can then be made a permanent part of the law.

H.R. 3236 adjusts the maximum limitation on disability insurance dependents' benefits. The adjustment addresses problems that exist because some disabled workers can receive cash disability benefits that are greater than their previous employment income. The adjusted benefit limitation will not apply to people currently receiving benefits. In fact, no person now receiving benefits will have his or her benefits reduced as a result of any provision in this bill. The final version of the limitation is more restrictive than the administration proposed and will impact adversely on some beneficiaries. Therefore, I will expect the Department of Health and Human Services to evaluate carefully its effect on new beneficiaries and be prepared to recommend any changes that may be needed.

A major provision of H.R. 3236 establishes a voluntary certification program for health insurance supplemental to Medicare—commonly referred to as "Medigap" policies—in States that do not have adequate programs of their own to control abuses in the sale of these policies. The new voluntary certification program, which I strongly and actively supported, will do the senior citizens of our country a great service. It will ensure that approved policies meet prescribed minimum standards, and it will set penalties for furnishing fraudulent or misleading information and for other abuses.

Finally, I would like to recognize the contributions made by Congressman Jake Pickle, Congressman Al Ullman, Congressman Jim Corman, Congressman Claude Pepper, Senator Gaylord Nelson, Senator Russell Long, and Senator Max Baucus. Their able leadership and cooperation were essential to the passage of this bill.

NOTE: As enacted, H.R. 3236 is Public Law 96–265, approved June 9, 1980.

American Committee on Italian Migration

Remarks to Participants in the Washington Symposium.   June 9, 1980

THE PRESIDENT. *Bishop Swanstrom and Father Cogo, Congressman Peyser, distinguished representatives of the Italian American Community:*

I'm very delighted to have you here. This is a wonderful day for me. We've had an opportunity within the last couple of hours to recognize a few outstanding Americans who have been given the American President's Medal of Freedom. This is done very rarely in our country, and it recognizes those people among us who have contributed with a special talent to the greatness of our country.

Today, I want to recognize an entire group of people, some of whom were never singled out individually for fame or for recognition, but who mean just as much to our country. We have great strength in our Nation—our agricultural productivity, our energy supplies, enormous educational system, technological advances—but our greatest strength, as you know, lies in the dynamism of America's people.

We've time and again encountered extraordinary questions, difficult obstacles to overcome and to face, challenges that have been too much for other people to meet successfully. And time and again Americans all together, united, courageous, determined, have prevailed. There's an important basis for this national strength derived from the people's dynamic approach to life.

First of all, we are a nation of immigrants. Our ancestors came here from many countries, many of us even as refugees coming here seeking a greater degree of freedom to worship as we chose, to raise our families as we prefer, and a better opportunity in life. We brought with us our own values, our customs, our strengths, our religious faith, our commitment to our family, a new commitment to new communities. And we brought something else, all of us, the hope for a better life, for those who first came here and our family and for their decendents now until this moment and also a better, hopeful life for children and our grandchildren who will come behind us.

For more than two centuries America has breathed life into these hopes and aspirations that were clutched within the hearts of individual immigrants to our

Nation. We began in 1976 [1776] as the one nation on Earth—the only one so far as I know—that made the pursuit of happiness a fundamental goal. We've invigorated that ambition for happiness with every succeeding generation. America is unique in this way. Unlike all the other nations on Earth, we're not united by either a single culture or a single place of national origin or by a single ethnic identity nor by a single language.

What unites a nation is an idea. It's the idea of what a free and equal people can accomplish together and what a free society can mean as an example to the rest of the world. It was Philip Mazzei, a contemporary of Thomas Jefferson, who gave shape to this idea. He was the one, an early Virginian, who having come to our country from Italy, as you may have guessed, drafted our most fundamental principle, that all men are created equal. He's the one who originated that thought.

It was his words that found their way into Thomas Jefferson's mind, into our Declaration of Independence, and into our history. "All men are created equal." It's symbolic that this ringing phrase that every American knows should have been drafted by an American of Italian heritage. Throughout our history, as you well know—and I'm sure no one here would disagree—Italian Americans have continued to contribute their efforts and their values, their talent, their commitment to every endeavor of American human life.

I'm happy to say that the United States will honor Philip Mazzei and his contribution in a stamp that will be issued in October of this year. It's a recognition that's long overdue.

We live in time of challenge; we live in a time of difficulty, a time of change, even a time of danger. It's important for us to understand the roots of our national strength and the roots of our ideals and the roots of our principles and the roots of our hopes. We need to know who we are and what we stand for as a people.

Since 1776 our Nation has been a great hope of people who suffered from religious persecution, from political repression, from economic deprivation. It still is. For 200 years our Nation has been a refuge for people committed to life and to liberty and to the pursuit of happiness, and it still is. The American Committee on Italian American Migration has helped to keep this American ideal a reality.

This committee on Italian migration has helped families to become reunited. It's helped immigrants to adjust to the American way of life. It's helped thousands and thousands of Italian immigrants to learn to speak English, to find jobs, to find a home, to learn how to vote, even to learn how to pay taxes. [*Laughter*] And for those who are new in our country, your work makes all the difference in the world—the difference between loneliness and a sense of being loved, the difference between despair and hope, the difference between misery and happiness, the difference between disappointment and success.

You fought long and hard to end the unfair system by which people were excluded from our country on the basis of specific national quotas. Your efforts helped to bring about this tremendously important legislation of 1965 abolishing these national quotas. Italian Americans, not coincidentally, have been the prime beneficiaries of this historic legislation. And as the benefits have gone to Italians who wanted to come here, those benefits obviously have been accrued by the United States of America.

During the past decade, the last 10 years, Italians were among the three nationalities, top nationalities, who immigrated to this country. But all Americans have benefited from this landmark legislation in social progress for our country. We have long believed that our country is the greatest on Earth. And with your help I am convinced that our Nation will be even greater in the future. Thank God for you and for the Italian Americans who provide the strength for our country.

Thank you.

BISHOP SWANSTROM. Mr. President, I just want to take a moment to thank you very sincerely on behalf of this representation of our membership drawn from all over the country. As you know, we're primarily interested in the migration of Italians, but we're equally interested in the migration of all people who feel that they can find a new life in the United States, refugees and migrants, and we're here to examine what's being put into the new law that Congress and yourself are proposing. And we just want you to know that, like yourself, we're interested. We feel that the family is the basic unit of our society, and we're particularly interested in that part of the legislation that provides for the reunion of families.

So, we pledge our cooperation. We're sure, under your leadership, the necessary reforms that are needed in our immigration law will take place. And so we thank you very kindly for your words of encouragement.

THE PRESIDENT. I want to come by and shake hands with those that I missed earlier. But in just a moment I'm going to have to leave here. And you might want to walk out just beyond the hedge and watch the helicopter take off. I go to Andrews Air Force Base and then take Air Force One. I'll be going to Florida and to the State of Washington and, probably, to Nebraska before I come back home.

I'm sure I'll see Italian Americans everywhere I go.

NOTE: The President spoke at 1:30 p.m. in the Rose Garden at the White House. In his opening remarks, he referred to Bishop Edward E. Swanstrom D.D., chairman of the board, and Father Joseph A. Cogo C.S., executive secretary, American Committee on Italian Migration.

Bureau of Mines

Nomination of Lindsay D. Norman, Jr., To Be Director.   June 9, 1980

The President today announced that he will nominate Lindsay D. Norman, Jr., of Harwood, Md., to be Director of the Bureau of Mines. He would replace Roger Markle, resigned.

Norman has been Acting Director of the Bureau of Mines since 1979 and was previously the Bureau's Assistant Director for Program Development and Evaluation.

He was born October 14, 1937, in Drexel Hill, Pa. He received a B.S. (1960), M.S. (1964), and Ph. D. (1969) from the University of Maryland.

Norman joined the Bureau of Mines in 1960, while in graduate school. He served as a metallurgical engineer and a research supervisor. In 1970 he worked on development of the Bureau's metallurgy program and from 1971 to 1975, he was the Bureau's Special Assistant for Environmental Activities and chief adviser on all mineral-related matters concerning development, research, legislation, and regulations.

Norman has received the Bureau's Superior Performance Award and has served as a consultant to the United Nations on developing mining guidelines for Third World countries. He is the author of numerous publications.

Federal Trade Commission

Nomination of Patricia P. Bailey To Be a Commissioner.   June 9, 1980

The President today announced that he will nominate Patricia P. Bailey, of Washington, D.C., for reappointment as a Federal Trade Commissioner.

Bailey, 42, has been a Commissioner of the Federal Trade Commission since 1979. She was previously executive legal assistant to the General Counsel of the Merit Systems Protection Board.

Miami Beach, Florida

Remarks at the Annual Convention of the Opportunities Industrialization Centers of America.   June 9, 1980

Thank you very much, Leon Sullivan. It's an honor to be introduced by a man who, along with you, has done so much for hundreds of thousands of Americans and given us all a better life. Thank you very much. I can't think of another fellow Baptist—[*laughter*]—who's done so much to take literally the song "We'll Work 'Til Jesus Comes." Right? [*Laughter*]

Not too long ago Leon Sullivan came into the White House, into the Oval Office, and he never walks in the Oval Office unless he walks out with something—[*laughter*]—never for himself, but always for others. One thing he wanted was for me to come down to be with you, and that's a favor he did for me. And another proposition he had to make was that he and I join forces as partners, the Federal Government and OIC, to try to put additional tens of thousands of Americans to work, and I'll tell you about it in just a few minutes.

But I'm delighted to be here at the 16th annual convention of the Opportunities Industrialization Centers. I congratulate you and I thank all of you in OEC——

AUDIENCE MEMBERS. OIC!

THE PRESIDENT. OIC. OIC. And I thank all of you in OIC for 16 years of great achievement.

All of us are meeting in a time of great importance in our Nation's history. They are still hard times, as you well know, for millions of Americans. These times challenge our minds and our courage, our commitment, our unity, and these times demand our concern and our compassion.

The inflation and the unemployment figures show that the almost inevitable recession has finally arrived, later than most economists had predicted, but with sharper increases in our unemployment rate than had been expected. The damaging effect of explosive OPEC oil prices and the sustained high interest rates and high inflation must be met by all of us together as we struggle to provide jobs for America, which is your commitment, and it's my commitment, too.

I'm well aware of the anxieties that exist, the uncertainty for hard-working, struggling families, and the discouragement of young people who are looking for their first job. There is nothing so damaging to a young person as to arrive at the adult working age, having talent and ability having been given by God, and not feeling a part of society; not being able to support oneself with one's own work; not being able to form a family of stability and achievement. We must not let them down, and we will not let them down.

Just as we've taken effective steps recently to reduce inflation, I want you to know, I want the country to know, that we have the existing proposals and the new programs to cushion the effects of this recession and that we are also fighting to care for the poor and the elderly and the afflicted. We cannot lose sight of our fundamental obligation to share what God has given us with those less fortunate than we are, even if it means sacrifice on the part of all. This is the reason I'm determined to maintain and to strengthen existing programs in the Federal Government and in the private sector that are in danger. And even during a period of stringent budget limitations, designed to hold down inflation, interest rates, we have new programs that we are pushing which are making good progress, and with your help we will not fail.

We've had to face many severe problems in the last few months. We've had to make difficult decisions. Not one of those decisions has been easy, but I've kept foremost my own determination, and I'm sure you agree, that we will not solve the problems of energy, inflation, and economic stagnation by imposing sacrifices on the poor.

Just last week, I notified the Congress that we must exercise constraint in controlling inflation and that I wanted a budget that is balanced, but one which is fair to the poor, to the cities, to the jobless, and to those who look for government, of necessity, to alleviate the deprivation and the discrimination that's in their lives, particularly in hard times.

I sent to the Congress a budget that is restrained, but is filled with compassion. We did not advocate and we do not advocate any spending cuts for the elderly, we've had substantial increases; for the disabled, substantial increases; and for our dependent children, again substantial increases. The 1981 budget, for instance, includes spending for women, infants, and children six times greater than it was 3½

years ago when I took the oath of office as President. I've set up a full food stamp program, and you need to help me protect it, after working with the Congress to eliminate the purchase requirement.

Housing: This year, 1980, which ends October 1, we've got 240,000 Federal-assisted housing being built, homes primarily for the poor and the middle-income persons—240,000. We expect to have another 160,000—almost double—in the 1981 budget.

These compassionate programs are being tested in Congress, but they are working, they're doing the job, and we will keep on doing this kind of job as long as I am President. And we must expand these programs, and the Congress is cooperating on many of them.

Our fight to bring down inflation must not be abandoned, because it will help everyone. It particularly eliminates a cruel burden on the poor, on the elderly who live on fixed incomes, on those who can least protect themselves, even the poor who sometimes must choose between a warm meal and a warm home, for the young people who need jobs and a career with a future. Inflation has steadily robbed these people for the last 12 years, and we must put an end to that.

I call on you today to keep the faith. We will not waver in our struggle to build an economy that sustains the hopes and the dreams of the forgotten people of this country.

As Leon Sullivan points out at every chance he gets, as is stated with facts and action in every OIC office, we must continue to create jobs, permanent jobs; some in government, yes, but most in the private sector. And as we control the wage and price spiral, we can build a permanent energy base that will make it impossible for unfriendly oil-producing countries to manipulate our economy and to decide our destiny.

I'm with you today to call for redoubled efforts to attack the root causes of economic misery. It's good for us not to forget the causes of our problems. We must improve an aging industrial base. At the present time the productivity of American workers is the highest in the world, but other countries are increasing how much their workers can produce faster than we are. We must maintain a proper balance between controlling inflation on the one hand, and providing full employment. And we must realize that when we cut down on inflation and cut down interest rates we let people buy refrigerators and stoves and sewing machines and automobiles and homes, which have to be produced, and therefore provide jobs.

We must call up the compassion on the one hand and the realism on the other which groups like OIC have always shown. There is no better place to continue this struggle than within the OIC's of America, for your concern has meant a hand up and not a handout. And Leon, if anybody asks you what my administration thinks about the OIC's, tell them about the $120 million in national and local CETA funds going to your centers this year. We're putting our money where it counts: in the OIC offices around this country.

On the way down here on the plane I was talking with Ernie Green, who heads up a $10 billion program in CETA, and he said, "Mr. President, there is no way that we can better spend limited job funds than with the OIC, because they do such a good job."

I told you a few minutes ago that when Leon Sullivan came in the Oval Office, he took something out with him. We've agreed with the OIC to mount a common

effort to place 100,000 more young people in jobs in the coming year. It'll be a close partnership arrangement with 10,000 of these jobs being placed in Federal agencies, and the other 90,000, with Federal help, along with your help, in the private sector. And I'm directing the Department of Labor and the Office of Personnel Management to work with OIC, and I'm asking also the business community—and I will be meeting in a few minutes with some of the top business leaders of the Miami area—to cooperate fully in this joint effort.

This is an unprecedented commitment. This is the largest single job placement effort ever undertaken in the history of this Nation by a community organization.

Let me quickly point out that I look upon this not as the Federal Government doing OIC a favor, but I look on it as OIC continuing to do this Nation a favor and the Federal Government providing help for you. That illustrates the kind of confidence I have in you, and it also illustrates the reason that I wanted to come to Miami to be at this convocation of this assembly to speak to you.

When Leon Sullivan spoke last fall before the youth employment task force, he said some powerful things, which I'm sure does not surprise any of you. And I'd like to quote him: He said, "We need an all-out effort. We need to declare war on joblessness, hopelessness, racial prejudice, and despair that are all part of the mounting unemployment youth tragedy, and we need, as Americans, to do it together."

I listened very carefully. He sounded like a good partner to me. And not long after that, with the help of my staff and Leon and many others on this podium with me, I announced a new jobs and training program that will add $2 billion to the $4 billion we're already spending for young people.

This will ultimately mean 500,000 youth jobs in our country, with a close working relationship between the new Department of Education, young people in the junior and senior years of high school, and private employers who will provide the jobs and part of the training while the schools do the rest. Now, I want to make sure that you understand that this is above and beyond the million summer jobs that we'll have this year and next year, and the 424,000 youth employment jobs that are already in place this year. It's nearly three times the amount being spent on youth employment and training when I took office 3½ years ago. You see, it pays to listen to Leon, because the country benefits from it.

This is a record that I'm very proud to relate. I might say that this new youth employment bill is making good progress in the House, and also the amount of money for it has already been approved in the House and Senate budget committee. So, it's got an excellent prospect of passing.

The number one domestic priority in my budget to Congress was to put young people to work. This commitment was emphasized before the recession came, and I'm fighting to keep it in place at every step in its progress through the Congress. Three years ago, with the help of Ernie Green, Leon, and others, we took over a CETA program that scattered its resources everywhere, and we made it into a concentrated effort against hardcore unemployment. Now CETA not only is twice the size that it was 3 years ago, but it reaches four times the number of disadvantaged Americans. We have concentrated on Americans who are out of work,

who needs it most, and now 95 percent of all the CETA jobs go to the disadvantaged. And I've made sure that CETA is placing people in the private job sector in career jobs, in permanent jobs, and that's the way CETA's going to continue to be run, with your help.

We've made some progress, but I don't want to overemphasize it, because we all know that too many people are still out of work. We never like that. But we also have to look beyond the percentages to the number of real jobs that have been added. We've had the largest growth in jobs in this country of any President's administration in history, and a million of those new jobs, a net increase of a million of those new jobs, have gone to black workers. About a million have gone to workers who speak Spanish. We have more minorities, more women, more young workers on the job than ever before in the history of this country.

Minority teenage employment has gone up 17 percent. As these young people and women and minority citizens got jobs, when they had previously given up hope, their neighbors and their friends saw them with new employment. And now we have hundreds of thousands of more Americans coming forward whose names have never been on the unemployment rolls, saying, "I want a job, too." That's good, because what we want is to put Americans to work. Everybody who's able to work ought to have a job.

We have made good progress, and we'll make more. But let me refer one more time in closing to the root causes of our economic problems, because you need to understand it in its entirety. The recession that we face is the inevitable result of inflation that has been fueled by a huge surge upward in OPEC oil prices. For more than a year, the world price of oil has gone up an average of 10 percent a month, and it's driven up the cost of everything else.

This year, we will spend in foreign countries $90 billion to buy their oil. That's a lot of money. It amounts to $1,500 for every family in this country— more than $400 for every man, woman, and child in this country sent out of our Nation to buy foreign oil. That's about nine times more than the total CETA program.

Just think, if we could cut down that oil import and quit sending our money overseas, how many new jobs we could create with investments, and a dynamic life and a better quality of life for all Americans. That's why it is so important that we save energy to start with, and produce more energy here at home. Twice in the last 6 years, we've seen OPEC price increases first bring on sky-high inflation, like it did this year and in 1974, and then an inevitable recession, and it may happen again unless we are able to free ourselves from our excessive dependence on foreign oil.

Finally, after a long period of time, there is some hope for energy security for our country. After 3 years of working with Congress, we are putting together now a national energy program. Oil imports are already on the way down. In previous years they'd been going up, up, up, every year. Last year we reduced our oil consumption by 5 percent, and so far this year, the first 5 months of 1980, we have cut down our oil imports 12 percent, which amounts to a million barrels of oil every day. That's a good savings.

In addition to that, the other side of it is to produce more. The only way you can cut down on what you import from overseas is to save energy, don't waste it, and produce more at home. There's no other way.

We have a new program, financed by a tax on the oil companies, that is going to be bigger than the space program, the Marshall plan that rebuilt Europe, and all the cost of the Interstate Highway System put together. And that's going to create a new industry in our Nation— very large, very complex, broad based, almost every community—to derive energy from not only oil and gas but from coal and shale and growing crops and directly from the Sun.

So, ahead of us is a time of hope and challenge and excitement and a better life, and we have no reason in this country to be afraid. We can now get off that economic rollercoaster that the OPEC oil nations have put us on. We've turned the tide on our energy problem, and we are beginning to turn the tide on inflation. It has been a very difficult question. Interest rates, as you well know, are down sharply. The prime interest rate charged by the banks has been dropping about 1 percent per week for the last month and a half or two. Price increases are also coming down. We will have good inflation news this summer. These favorable trends can build up consumer purchasing power and leave us more money in our pockets to buy things that have to be produced by Americans on the job.

The seeds of a lasting recovery in the falling interest rates and falling rates of inflation are encouraging, but we face some difficult weeks immediately ahead.

The programs that we've improved together are now in place to ease the harmful effects on families that are damaged by temporary or permanent disappointment, unemployment. We've got to protect those programs. And next we must turn our American production machine loose for the future, to increase productivity, to have new plants, new factories, new construction, new opportunities for us all. This is a great economic challenge for the 1980's. It can be exciting; it can be gratifying; it can be stimulating, as we face the future together.

A determined America, a united America can turn the economic tide and rebuild an economy in which people need not fight with one another to divide a shrinking pie. Our workers need more new and efficient tools. We need a better transportation system. We need new technology to tap our resources; better schools, better training. We need permanent and productive jobs for the millions of Americans who are in need of work. I have high ambitions for this country in the coming years, and I want to complete the job we've started together.

Three years ago I set out to extend the benefits of equal justice and equal opportunity. We've not yet in this country been fully successful in guaranteeing people equal justice, but we have come further than we've ever come before, because I've asked people like Pat Harris, Andy Young, Eleanor Holmes Norton, Drew Days, Clifford Alexander, Ernie Green, and many others to help me; people who are familiar with what OIC does and familiar with the challenge that we face together.

We're enforcing civil rights laws to the letter. We're making affirmative action work. We're enhancing human rights at home and abroad. In just a short $3\frac{1}{2}$ years I've been able to triple the number of black Federal judges. As a matter of fact, I've been lucky enough to appoint more black Federal judges than all the other Presidents who ever lived and served

in this country. This will help to ensure justice in our courts.

And together we brought close to enactment the Fair Housing Act amendments. This vital legislation, which can be the most significant civil rights legislation of this decade, will be coming to the House floor for a vote in Washington, probably on Wednesday. If every person who's up here with me on this stage would contact key Members of Congress, we'll have a good chance to pass this legislation, to make sure that we wipe out once and for all discrimination in housing, which was guaranteed in 1968, but which has never been enforced.

Despite the progress we've made, the recent tragedy in Miami is a reminder that we still have a long way to go. I'm determined that our system of justice be simply that—the same justice for all with no regard for race or color or creed or ethnic background or how rich a person might be. I'm also very saddened that those most hurt by the rioting here in Miami are those who already had the least. Burning down a business cannot create any jobs. Violence cannot breed justice. Hate can only poison and ultimately destroy our hopes for the future.

Our Constitution calls on the National Government to establish justice, including economic justice and social justice, but it also calls on us to ensure domestic tranquillity, and I'm committed along with you to doing both.

Martin Luther King, Jr., who knew how to accomplish great things without violence, said, "Man is not mere flotsam and jetsam in the river of life, but he's a child of God." All of us know that truth, and we know our responsibility to one another, and particularly to those less fortunate than we who would never think of sitting in a big ballroom like this in the Fontainebleau Hotel.

The staff of the OIC's, the board members, the business leaders who've taken part, all of you have made a great difference in the lives of others. Before you and me lies the rest of the job, and I ask you to join me in getting it done with renewed hope and renewed commitment and renewed courage and renewed determination. If we work together—and I'm determined that we shall—then we will not fail.

Thank you very much.

NOTE: The President spoke at 4:58 p.m. in the Grand Ballroom at the Fontainebleau Hotel. In his opening remarks, he referred to Leon Sullivan, chairman of the board of Opportunities Industrialization Centers of America.

Miami Beach, Florida

Remarks to Reporters Serving the Local Hispanic American Community.   June 9, 1980

THE PRESIDENT. Would you all rather that I read it in English or struggle in Spanish?

REPORTERS. Spanish.

THE PRESIDENT. Really? Okay. You might have to interpret what I say, but I'll try.

[*In Spanish*] It is a pleasure for me to be in Miami to speak to the Cuban-American community through the local Spanish language press.

These past weeks have been both rewarding and difficult for all of us. Over 100,000 Cubans have come to our shores in a spontaneous and dramatic expression of their faith in freedom, of their desire to escape the oppressive Castro regime, and a desire to reunite long-separated families.

We thank God that so few lives were lost during the dangerous sea voyages. The United States Coast Guard and the Navy have saved thousands of lives during the past 7 weeks. I join every American in congratulating both organizations for their good work. We could not permit this unsafe and uncontrollable flotilla to continue. That is why on May 14, I announced that we must replace it with a safe and orderly process of bringing close family members and political prisoners from Cuba to the United States.

We will continue to insist that the 362 Cubans in the U.S. Interest Section in Havana be allowed to depart for the United States immediately and that families be reunited and political prisoners be permitted to enter our country in complete accordance with our Nation's laws. We will not stand idly by while Castro willfully seeks to violate those laws or our immigration process.

Among the many people fleeing oppression in Cuba, Fidel Castro has cynically included several hundred hardened criminals from Cuban jails. We will take all legal steps to ensure that under no circumstances will these criminals be resettled or relocated in American communities. There is evidence that the Cuban Government exported these undesirable elements to the United States in a calculated effort to support a propaganda contention that all of those Cubans who have come to this country are undesirable. The truth is that the vast majority are law-abiding citizens whose only purpose is to seek freedom and to be reunited with their families.

This despicable action of Castro is a violation of international law and practice, and the government of Cuba is obligated to accept the return of those criminals. I have directed the Secretary of State to press these issues through diplomatic channels and in appropriate international forums.

With the help of the Cuban-American community and others throughout the country, we have already resettled more than half of the Cubans with their families. Others await resettlement at temporary staging centers. We are working diligently to locate sponsors for eligible people and to reunite families as quickly as possible. The continuing cooperation and support of the Cuban-American community are essential if these efforts are to be successful.

I will soon be making recommendations to the Congress concerning the legal status and benefits to be made available to those Cubans and Haitians who have come to our country over the last few months. I am mindful that the Federal Government must bear its fair share of the resettlement, and other costs, so that the particular State and local governments involved will not be unduly burdened by such costs. If we are to reunite more Cuban-American families and allow Cuban political prisoners to live free of persecution, we need your help.

The dangerous and disorderly flow of boats from Cuba is just about at an end. Only if it remains stopped will the Castro government have any reason to agree to orderly procedures that would allow other Cubans to find freedom.

We and other nations have already proposed to the Cuban Government the negotiation of such arrangements. We need the continued support and cooperation of Cuban Americans for these efforts to succeed.

During the last 20 years, the Cuban-American community has distinguished itself by its hard work, by its enterprise and patriotism, and has contributed greatly to our Nation. Our Nation now needs your help both in keeping the illegal flow from Cuba stopped and in resettling and assimilating the Cubans who have recently arrived. As your President, I call upon you for that help.

I am pleased to announce that Mr. Sergio Perrera, a Cuban American who is currently working in Dade County, will join my administration as an adviser to the State Department on the resettlement program.

Thank you very much.

[*The President answered questions in English.*]

Q. Mr. President, what's your position regarding Castro's demands of lifting the blockade on the Guantanamo Naval Base?

THE PRESIDENT. I don't know about any demand that we lift a blockade on the Guantanamo Base. There is no blockade on the Guantanamo Base.

Q. Castro is demanding the surrendering of the Guantanamo Base, the lifting of the economic blockade, and the stop of the recognition plans.

THE PRESIDENT. Well, we have a long-term agreement with Cuba, signed before Castro took power and confirmed by him after he became the leader of Cuba, that confirms our use of the Guantanamo Base. And this is an international agreement, confirmed under international law; and it is being carried out meticulously in accordance with its terms; and we have no intention of abandoning this agreement even though Castro demands it now, since he confirmed it himself after he became the leader of Cuba.

Thank you very much.

NOTE: The President spoke at 5:40 p.m. outside the Fontainebleau Hotel.

As printed above, the translation of the President's remarks in Spanish follows the press release.

Miami, Florida

Remarks to Reporters Following a Meeting With Community Leaders. June 9, 1980

THE PRESIDENT. I appreciate that comment. I've come here as President, representing our Federal Government, to tell the local and State officials and also those who are leaders in Liberty City and throughout this region, professional and business community leaders, that we all must share the responsibility for the guaranteeing of equal justice and equal opportunity, of the repair of damage, of the treatment of people in a fair manner, but that violence creates hatred which hurts us all, and destruction of property and business places doesn't create jobs; it destroys jobs.

We have a representative of the Federal Government here, Frank Jones, who will listen to all the voices that speak for this community that describe what will be done locally and the best way for the Federal programs to be used. He will make a report to me, and within the framework of the law and within the framework of appropriated funds, we will treat Liberty City and this region in a generous but fair fashion.

We have long-term problems here to address. The prime initiative must come from this community. It cannot come from Washington. And the community must realize that violence and dissension and destruction hurts most those who are least able to afford it.

The cooperative attitude that I have experienced this afternoon is very gratifying. There is a deep commitment here to assess the problem and also to solve the problem. And I will meet the proposals on the local basis for jobs, for construc-

tion, for loans, and for opportunity more than halfway from the Federal Government level. This will have to be a continuing process; it can't be a transient or a temporary process. And I have very great hopes that this visit has not only resulted in a deeper commitment by us all to make this a better community, but I have no doubt that I will be a better President and the Federal Government will be much more efficient and effective and sensitive in providing services for communities like this in the future because of my visit here.

Yes?

Q. Mr. Carter, why did you wait so long to come to Miami?

THE PRESIDENT. It's very important that before I come here we have a chance for the community to express itself. We've had Frank Jones down representing the Federal Government, working for me. And I've had either Gene Eidenberg or Jack Watson here representing me as well. They have been briefing me, and now Mr. Jones is putting together his full report. But I wanted to come before I sign-off on the final report, to get a personal assessment from the mayors involved and from the Governor's staff and others. I think this was a proper time to come.

Q. Mr. President, do you think 4 hours is enough time to assess the situation here?

THE PRESIDENT. No, it's obviously not enough time for me to assess the situation alone, but I have not only Frank Jones, who represents me on a broad scale contacting many agencies, but also we have labor representatives here, those who will be responsible for summer youth jobs, for CETA programs, for the Job Corps. We have education officials here who will be responsible for those programs. HHS that'll be responsible for Head Start. The

Small Business Administration people are here in the Miami area, responsible for loans and the rebuilding of this community where it has been destroyed. The transportation representatives will be allocating contracts that will help minority entrepreneurs and others in the construction of a rapid transit system. So, I've got permanent representatives here from many agencies in the Federal Government who are designed to solve the economic problems.

In addition, I have sent the Attorney General down here, and also Drew Days, to make sure that within the system of justice and confining our responsibility to what the Federal Government ought to do, that equality of opportunity in the courts is guaranteed. So, I have many people to speak for me and to listen for me. They make the recommendations, and I'll make the final judgments.

Q. Mr. President, have you as yet decided what action you will take or what you will recommend with regard to the legal status of the Haitians and the Cubans and, also, what kind of funding levels you will recommend, through special legislation or other means, to offset the costs?

THE PRESIDENT. One of those commitments has already been made, and that is to treat exactly the same the Haitians who come here and the Cubans who come here. This has been done for a number of weeks, and it will continue to be done. There will be no discriminatory difference drawn between Haitians and Cubans who've come to our shores. As far as the allocation of funds is concerned, an assessment is now being made through the Immigration and Naturalization Service and through the Office of Management and Budget, working with the local congres-

sional delegation, and that will be made as a recommendation to the appropriate appropriations committees in Washington. But you have to remember that the enormous expense involved in this influx of emigres from Cuba is not confined to this area. We have a staging area in northern Florida; we have another staging area in Wisconsin, another in Pennsylvania, and another one in Arkansas; and we're trying to place the Cuban Americans and the Haitians around the Nation, not to concentrate them here.

Q. I meant whether you have decided to grant them, or asked that they be granted, refugee status versus applicants for asylum.

THE PRESIDENT. That decision has not been made. The legislation that presently exists does not encompass arrival of emigres from another country. We have planned our actions, and the law was written with the idea that each person who comes to this country would be screened, either in their country of origin or in a third country, before they arrive on our shores. This has not been the case in this last instance.

I might point out, too, that the reception of the large number of Cuban Americans and the processing of them has been an extraordinary achievement. Many people lose sight of the fact that in the first 2 months of the large influx of Cubans here in 1965, we received a total of 3,000. And during the first 6 weeks of this incident, we were receiving 3,000 per day. It was an unbelievable challenge to many of us in the Federal Government and the local and State governments, and it was handled superbly.

I might say that we are now screening for placement in this Nation about a thousand of the Cuban emigres per day. So, we are working under very difficult circumstances, without a clear delineation of authority under the law, because the law was not designed for this circumstance. And we are committed to treating the Cubans and the Haitians equally.

Q. What is your response to the Black Caucus' ultimatum to you, saying that if you did not come up with a program for more jobs in 2 weeks—I think they said—that they would not support you politically?

THE PRESIDENT. I don't have any response to that, except we have a large number of job programs already on the books, that are being effectively administered, and additional requests to the Congress, like the youth employment bill and the protection of title VI, the CETA jobs, and others, that will add to job opportunities in the country.

Q. Many people on the streets of Miami have said that they did not want just a Presidential board, that they in fact wanted a specific dollar figure given to them, and that if you left here without giving that that there could be more unrest. Do you leave Miami tonight feeling secure that the black people have been answered?

THE PRESIDENT. It's not possible to give a final answer in a brief visit like this, but we have set into motion a procedure or a mechanism that will let us find the proper sharing of responsibility. The local and the State governments have a major responsibility, and so does the private sector. So do the people who live here who are looking for jobs and who must maintain peace. The Federal Government will more than meet its responsibility. But there has to be a coordinated effort, so that it's not just a transient commitment

that will die away after a few weeks. It will be a permanent commitment where jobs and careers are established and where justice is guaranteed and equality of treatment is given to all people, and they believe they'll have it.

So, you can't do this on a 1-day visit. It must be a continuing commitment, and I don't have any doubt that the mayors involved, of Dade County and Miami, the Governor and all his State agencies, the business and professional community, the Chamber of Commerce, the NAACP, and many others are now working jointly toward a common goal, and that is to guarantee the people who have been deprived and who have suffered from discrimination and who have been suffering from economic deprivation will have a better life.

So, we have a common goal, although we look at the same problem from a different perspective. But we are sharing now in a very constructive way, and the answers will not be delayed in forthcoming. They'll be made as quickly as they can possibly be assessed properly.

Maybe one more question.

Q. Mr. President, do you believe that what happened here in Miami is an indication of problems that exist all over America?—racism, discrimination, opportunities that are not equal for all.

THE PRESIDENT. Well, obviously there is racism in many places in America, in the minds of many Americans. There is discrimination. There is unemployment. There is dissatisfaction. There's also an inequitable allocation of the system of justice. That's inherent in any country, and I think it's minimal in our Nation compared to almost all other nations on Earth.

There was a remarkable confluence of circumstances here that precipitated this crisis. I don't know the details of the background, but there was a sense of extremely high unemployment, a sense that the black community did not have its adequate share of economic and political opportunity, a sense that there was not a fair treatment under the system of justice. Whether all of those beliefs were accurate I cannot say. But obviously, I think, all have learned that the violence was not constructive and the destruction hurt those least able to afford it, and the best way to resolve either actual or deeply felt beliefs that there is discrimination is to work together toward a common future.

So, I don't condone the violence that occurred here, but I do say that now that it has occurred, whether it had a sound basis or not in fact, we must redress any grievances that exist and have a very highly improved belief among all those who live in this community that the Government and the private sector is committed to a fair and equitable opportunity of life for all those who live here.

Q. Thank you, Mr. President.

THE PRESIDENT. Thank you.

Q. Why not meet with Cuban leaders today?

THE PRESIDENT. I met with the Cuban press earlier.

NOTE: The President spoke at 7:44 p.m. at the James E. Scott Community Association in Liberty City, a section of Miami.

Following his remarks, the President went to Miami International Airport, where he met with officials of the U.S. Coast Guard, the U.S. Immigration and Naturalization Service, the U.S. Customs Service, and the Federal Emergency Management Agency. He then left for Seattle, Wash.

Military Education for Yugoslav Officers in the United States

Memorandum From the President.
June 10, 1980

Presidential Determination No. 80–20

Memorandum for the Secretary of State

Subject: International Military Education and Training for Yugoslavia

By virtue of the authority vested in me by the Foreign Assistance Act of 1961, as amended (the Act):

I hereby find pursuant to section 620 (f) of the Act that the furnishing of assistance to Yugoslavia under chapter 5 of part II of the Act effective immediately is vital to the security of the United States, that Yugoslavia is not controlled by the international Communist conspiracy, and that such assistance will further promote the independence of Yugoslavia from international communism.

Pursuant to section 614(a) of the Act—

(a) I hereby determine that the furnishing of such assistance to Yugoslavia is important to the security of the United States; and

(b) I hereby authorize the furnishing of such assistance without regard to section 620(f) of the Act in the amount of $36,000 in fiscal year 1980 and $29,000 in fiscal year 1981, subject to the authorization and appropriation of funds. This determination shall be reported to the Congress and none of the funds provided for herein shall be furnished to Yugoslavia until ten days have elapsed after such report has been made, and fifteen days have elapsed after the notifications of reprogramming have been furnished to the

Congress in accordance with section 634A of the Act and the Joint Resolution on Continuing Appropriations (Public Law 96–123).

This determination shall be published in the FEDERAL REGISTER.

JIMMY CARTER

[Filed with the Office of the Federal Register, 9:56 a.m., July 3, 1980]

Seattle, Washington

Remarks at the Annual Conference of the U.S. Conference of Mayors. June 10, 1980

President and Mayor Richard Carver, Mayor Charles Royer, other distinguished leaders of the cities of our great Nation:

It's a pleasure to be with you. This has been an exciting and a gratifying trip. I've been looking forward to meeting with you for a long time. This is not an easy time in the history of our Nation, and you occupy, perhaps along with the President, some of the most difficult positions in public life.

I tried to think of a story that would illustrate what you and I got into when we took office. I have a favorite story that I've told before about the old man who was arrested for being drunk and setting a bed on fire in a hotel. He came before the judge. The judge accused him, and the man said, "I'm not guilty, Your Honor." He said, "I was drunk, but the bed was on fire when I got in it." [*Laughter*] I think about that story every now and then when I walk over to the Oval Office early in the morning. And I know you feel the same way, being mayors of our troubled cities, but our dynamic and competent and improving cities.

This morning I want to make a straightforward talk to you and a frank, unvarnished talk, about two things: what we have done together, the fundamental changes that have taken place in our cities the last few years, and the problems which we confront here and now. As we meet, as all of you so well know, there are hard times still for millions of Americans. Although we've been able to add millions of new jobs in the last 3½ years, the recent unemployment figures and the recent inflation figures cause us deep concern.

We know that the impending recession, which has been approaching for several years, almost inevitably has now arrived. Because of the damaging effect of inflation and unemployment, driven by skyrocketing oil prices, our unemployment rate has recently moved up quite rapidly.

I'm deeply and personally concerned about the hardship and the anxiety felt by families who are directly affected by these recessionary trends and the uncertainty for the hard-working and struggling families and about the new trials that this brings to the communities which you represent. But I want to remind you, and I want the Nation to know, that together we have put in place programs which are working to reduce the adverse impact of the recession, to sustain and improve these programs so important to you that care for the poor and the elderly and the afflicted and the unemployed and the troubled cities. You and I will—and I pledge to you—we will fight together to win, and we will not lose this battle.

We know that there are no quick solutions, there are no easy answers, and we must not mislead ourselves or those who listen to our voices. We have to deal with the root causes of inflation and unemployment.

I hope and I pray that the recession will be short and the worst of the unemployment soon behind us. If recession should deepen and unemployment continues to rise unabated, I will work closely with you and we will take other steps which may be necessary.

We will maintain fiscal discipline in Washington, and we will not take action which will refuel inflation. Now, however, we must protect and improve the programs that are being considered by Congress, which you and I have forged together.

Just last week, I reminded Congress that we must exercise constraint to control inflation and I wanted a budget which was balanced, but one which is fair to those who look to the government—to your local governments and to our Federal Government—for the lifelines that only government can provide in these hard times for troubled families.

I sent to the Congress the first balanced budget in 12 years. It's a budget that provides for a strong national defense, but it's also one of compassion and rebuilding. You reviewed the budget with me. You helped me make some of the tough decisions. I'm not blaming you for all the decisions that I made in the budget, but I would like to explain very briefly that it does provide for a 4-percent real increase in military spending sustained for the next 5 years. This is essential to strengthen NATO and to strengthen our own country for collective defenses in order to stop and to deter Soviet aggression, which has been exemplified so vividly for all those on Earth in the Soviet invasion of Afghanistan.

Some of you expressed your personal concern to me about defense expenditures and increases, but in spite of your expressions of concern I decided to stand firm because of the overriding need for national security. Above everything else, the number one responsibility on the shoulders of a President is to provide for and to guarantee our Nation's security, and through it to preserve peace for ourselves and peace for people around the world.

We are strong. We are growing stronger. We have nothing to fear. Our Nation is at peace. We are working daily to bring peace to others. These considerations are paramount. But I also stood firm with the Congress for what might be called the domestic security of our Nation. Within the balanced budget, we provided for a strong America on housing; a nation that's strong on jobs, strong on economic development, strong on public transportation, strong on fiscal aid, strong on social security, strong on the caring for the afflicted and the old and the poor. We must have a military budget, with steady, predictable and sustained growth, for ourselves and to set an example for others, both in expenditures this year and next year, and also an authority to make commitments which will result in expenditures later, when our defense equipment is delivered.

There must be a proper commitment along with this for government efficiency; for the prompt and equitable collection of taxes; for foreign aid; and for adequate domestic programs. As mayors, you have equivalent, difficult budget decisions to make. We share a lot in this common responsibility—a little difference in perspective, but there is no way to separate your responsibilities from mine, nor to separate my responsibilities from you.

I'm also fighting to bring down inflation. Early in March I announced to the

Nation, after consulting with you, an anti-inflation program to remove the cruel and the heavy burden on those who can least afford it. And this should not be forgotten by those who are concerned about the least among us. My program will bring down price increases and interest rates, and this will help everyone. But it's a program designed especially to help old people on fixed incomes, for the poor who must sometimes choose between a warm home and a warm meal, and for communities and neighborhoods that are struggling to restore their own vitality and to provide a better quality of life for those who live within them.

High inflation has robbed America for the last 12 years, and we simply must do everything we can to stop it. As partners we must not waver in our struggle. We must continue to provide jobs, permanent jobs. We must keep wages and prices reasonable. We must build a permanent energy base which will prevent unfriendly foreign oil producers from creating crises in our own economy and in our own lives and, indeed, threatening our Nation's security and helping to shape, against our will, our Nation's destiny.

I'm working with you today, not simply because of our immediate problems which challenge both our compassion and our realism but also because of the fundamental changes which will be made and which we can help to make for the 1980's. The decisions that I've described to you on defense, energy, self-discipline in Washington, will be carried out. You need to understand them. But this need not provide any obstacle between us in working for the alleviation of suffering, the caring for the poor, the rebuilding of our cities, or providing a better life for the same people that you represent, because

all of your constituents are my constituents, and they look to us jointly for responsibility and for leadership in facing the future not with cowardice or fear or trepidation or division or selfishness or concern, but with a common commitment, based on the strength of our country, the idealism and the foresight, the natural resources, the human resources, the unity, and the courage of the American people.

Four years ago I came before you. I studied your agenda beforehand. I came as a candidate, and I later proposed an ambitious urban policy based on your agenda, and pledged to build a partnership with the mayors, with the private sector, and with the Federal Government. In order to reverse the decline that was so evident 4 years ago and the quality of American cities, you've helped me; and I have kept that pledge to you.

Since I took office we've had a net increase of more than 8 million jobs in this country, the greatest expansion of jobs in the history of any administration, of any President who's ever served. A million of those jobs went to black Americans. Another million of those jobs, net increase, went to Americans who speak Spanish. More minorities, more women, more young people are at work today than ever before.

I'm not here to brag because this is obviously not enough. But we can be proud of the solid job growth in the last 3 years.

Within a year of taking office, again working very closely with you, I proposed the Nation's first urban policy to make sense out of the confusion that had been existing among Federal agencies in their inadequate interrelationship with you and your predecessors in the cities for which you are so deeply concerned and directly responsible.

I proposed that we reinsert the life-blood and the hope and confidence in cities, many of which were despairing and rapidly deteriorating. And I proposed, in addition to government, that we bring the private sector back into the cities.

When I took office, the Federal Government was spending $60 million a year to bring private investment to cities. This year, we will spend more than $1.8 billion—a 30-fold increase in just 3 years, to encourage private investment in the cities of our country. This is encouraging the investment by the private sector of $6 billion—not government money—and it creates over 400,000 new jobs and it also brings in to you more than $100 million in increased property taxes, because the property is worth more, and the people are making the profits to pay the taxes with.

We put in place the largest public jobs effort in our history, and we made sure that it concentrated on the hardcore unemployed. This has not previously been done.

CETA, this year and next year, is not only twice its total size of 3 years ago, it serves four times the number of disadvantaged people. At this moment, CETA jobs—95 percent of them—go to the disadvantaged.

We are launching a new, expanded nationwide effort against youth unemployment. I proposed $2 billion to the Congress above and beyond the $4 billion we presently spend to train, to hire, and to place young workers in permanent jobs, almost all of which will be in the private sector.

The Department of Labor and the Department of Education are working harmoniously, getting ready to implement this program. The money for it has been approved by the House and Senate in their budget deliberations. And the legislation is now making good progress through the House. Nearly three times the total amount spent on youth unemployment and training when I took office, will be spent when this program is effectuated this coming year.

Right now, there will be a million summer youth jobs, 425,000 year-round jobs for young people. And I want to tell you that these jobs will be allotted to meet the needs of the most needy in your communities. And I need for you as mayors to continue to make these programs effective and efficient in dealing with the hardships which we face together.

When cities faced massive budget crises, you came to me, and we doubled counter-cyclical aid, and we strongly supported local revenue sharing. For New York, as a special example, we replaced a punitive Federal policy with one that has helped to put the city back on its feet.

All of our problems have not been solved. All of New York City's problems have not been solved. All of your problems have not been solved. But we've placed in effect a good, intimate, permanent working relationship, adequately financed, accepted now by the American people, which I believe will be not only permanent but a base on which we can make much more exciting progress in the years to come.

Housing is a problem for you and for all of us. In the 2 years before I took office 15,000 subsidized housing units were started, 15,000. In the 2 years after that 265,000 were started, and hundreds of thousands more are on the way. This coming year, we have in our budget proposals 400,000 federally assisted housing units, a 25-fold increase within a 4-year period.

This has all been done with adequate consideration given to fiscal discipline in Washington and to reducing Federal deficits and in laying the groundwork for dealing with the threat of inflation and to accommodate the special challenge of energy which permeates my consciousness when I deal with any aspect of the American economy.

You asked for new programs on city parks and recreation and Community Development Block Grants. We put them into effect. We've expanded Federal aid to education by 75 percent, and we've targeted the neediest school districts, and there's hardly a college-age child now in this Nation who's qualified to do college work that cannot have a college education financed by some means. We've committed $50 billion in this current decade for urban mass transit, more than three times the amount that was spent in the 1970's.

Well, to summarize what I've said so far: In the last 3 years where there was a Federal hodge-podge, there's now a good, calm, solid, routine working relationship between the Federal Government and the local officials of our Nation. We have a coordinated, comprehensive policy. Where government formerly ignored private development, we now involve businesses closely. Where a city's problem in the past was the mayor's alone, it's now a problem that we share together. In short, we have stopped Federal neglect of our cities, and we can see the hard, tangible evidence of urban progress all around us. That's the achievement of a good partnership that we've formed, and we can all afford to be very proud of it. We have a lot left to do.

For the past 16 months we've seen the world price of oil go up an average of 10 percent a month. This has had a devastating impact on the economy of our own Nation and on the economy of many other nations. Some of them spend more on imported oil than their total national exports, and, of course, this drives up the price of everything. It's very difficult to accommodate it. This year we'll spend $90 billion in foreign countries to buy their oil. Because of the rapidly increasing price—it's much more than doubled—this is $30 billion more than we spent in 1979. It's nine times more than we spent on the total CETA program, which is about $10 billion. Just think of all the jobs that could be provided, all the investments that could be created, the improvement of American productivity, a stronger nation, a more confident country—if we can be successful in holding down oil imports.

Twice in the last 6 years we've seen the OPEC oil producers, with their price increases skyrocketing, drive inflation up at a precipitous rate, and then plunged us into recession. Unless we act as a nation, this same process could be repeated in the future, because of excessive dependence on foreign oil.

You all remember in April of 1977, my first few weeks in office, that I went to the country and to the Congress, talking about the moral equivalent of war. We expected then that the world demand would equal the world supply of oil in 1983 or '84 or '85. It happened in 1979, and that's one of the reasons that oil prices have skyrocketed, and the world has been afflicted because of it. Fortunately, now, after 3 years, too long a delay, we have nearly completed our Nation's first energy policy: to build a solid energy base for the years and the decades to come. There are only two ways to cut down on oil imports: one is to conserve what we have, to eliminate waste; and the other is to produce more energy in our own country. There are no other ways.

We have made good progress. After years of constantly increased oil imports every year, last year gasoline use went down 5 percent. So far this year, oil imports are down 12 percent below 1979. That's a saving every day in oil imports of 1 million barrels.

We are beginning to succeed in energy conservation and we now have approved by the Congress a windfall profits tax on the oil companies that can provide new and exciting opportunities for us in producing more energy, larger in scope, larger in size than the space program, the Marshall plan that rebuilt Europe, and the entire interstate highway system combined. Oil, natural gas, yes. Coal, yes. Shale, yes. Growing crops, energy from the Sun.

The complexity of this opportunity and the excitement of this opportunity is almost overwhelming and has not yet sunk into the consciousness of America, what it will mean to your city, to your colleges and schools, research, development, technology, jobs, better life, better homes, more security. It's been a difficult challenge the last 3½ years, dealing with the Congress, overcoming an established oil lobbying effect that was rooted so deeply on Capitol Hill, and having the consumers and you and others come forward and say, "Let's be fair for a change." But this accomplishment is notable, and we are now waiting to derive the benefits from it.

We've had to make some unpopular decisions in dealing with these tremendous challenges, both you and I. But that's something that every responsible public executive must do, as you know so well.

So, we are turning the tide on energy, and we're beginning to turn the tide on inflation. The two are intimately related. Interest rates are down sharply. The last time I met with a large group of mayors, you could not sell municipal bonds for any price. Lately, we've seen interest rates dropping, prime rate dropping an average of 1 percent per week. And I predict to you that during this summer you will see an equivalent sharp reduction in the inflation rate. This will let those consumers and others who wanted to buy a home or buy an automobile or buy a refrigerator or stove or television set now do so as the benefits of these lower interest rates and lower inflation rates permeate the consciousness of our Nation, and as they buy a new refrigerator this will mean that workers who produce those goods will be back on the job. It's going to take a while, but the self-correcting effect of energy discipline and lower interest rates and a lower inflation rate are there to be tapped, to ease the impact of recession, and to forestall a lot of suffering that would have been felt otherwise.

That, combined with the programs that you and I have shaped together to care for the families that are adversely affected by temporary or extended unemployment, will help to reduce the suffering in our country. But that's not enough. We face an additional challenge in the 1980's of building greater productivity into our economy. This is one of the greatest challenges of this decade.

We have the largest economy of any nation in the world. We have the most productive work force, which may be a surprise to you. The American worker produces more than any other worker on Earth, both private and public workers; but we also have the lowest rate of savings on Earth; one of the oldest industrial bases among major economies.

Of the 20 most modern and productive steel plants in the world, not a single one is in the United States. And our productivity advantage over other industrialized nations is narrowing fast. Their rate of increase in productivity is greater than our own.

So, our economic lead, which is a matter of great pride to us, is being reduced. Our workers do need more and more efficient tools. We need a better transportaton system. We need new technology to tap our tremendous human and natural resources. We need permanent and productive jobs for the millions of Americans who are still out of work. We need a healthy private sector to provide these jobs. I'm determined to restore economic leadership without turning our backs on the poor or the elderly or the afflicted or the deprived, or those who've suffered too long from the effects of racial or other discrimination.

I reject the easy promise that massive tax cuts and arbitrary roll-backs of government programs are the answer. Such facile, quick fixes should be recognized as political doubletalk and ideological nonsense.

There is no way for us to build prosperity in this country without justice and compassion. We cannot build a strong nation without demonstrably caring for those less fortunate than are we. But, at the same time, we cannot ignore the reality of rebuilding our economy, because as we control inflation, as we control interest rates, as we rebuild our economy, we directly help the poor and those who suffer most from recession.

We're all in it together. None of us can claim that it's someone else's problem. You cannot say that a strong national defense is the President's problem—not mine. And I cannot say that a deteriorating block in the central part of your city is your problem, not mine.

Together we have made good, solid progress the last 3½ years, and now we face an equally difficult and exciting and challenging continuing job of improving and strengthening the entire economy, sustain the partnership that we've forged, to continue to face our problems without flinching, to keep our commitments to the less fortunate, to deal with the energy question, to maintain a strong defense, and to revive the spirit of great enterprise which has always been a characteristic of bold and exciting Americans.

When future generations look back, I want them to see a people who built for the future, you and I; who turned the tides of adversity, you and I; and who left something good and lasting behind us. I want to make that future come true, and I ask you to join with me in this great undertaking that will transform the lives for the better, of those who live in the greatest nation on Earth.

Thank you very much.

NOTE: The President spoke at 10 a.m. in the Grand Ballroom at the Olympic Hotel. In his opening remarks, he referred to Mayor Richard E. Carver of Peoria, Ill., president of the U.S. Conference of Mayors, and Mayor Charles Royer of Seattle.

Earlier in the day, the President attended a buffet breakfast for members of the executive committee of the U.S. Conference of Mayors. He then met with Federal officials responsible for disaster relief efforts in connection with the Mount St. Helens eruption.

Interview With the President

Excerpt From a Question-and-Answer Session With Reporters on Board Air Force One. June 10, 1980

THE PRESIDENT. . . . The disturbance there, which I didn't know about—any rock throwing or anything—until after I got back to the plane, was something that could happen in any demonstration. I mean, I don't consider it to be significant, because—probably young people; I don't know whether it was.

Q. Did you realize when you went there that you might be going into a dangerous situation?

THE PRESIDENT. Well, not danger to the extent it caused me to be concerned, but it was obviously a volatile situation. We had the option of not going to Miami at all, or to the Liberty City region, but I thought it was important that I go there as President to show my concern, and that we're determined to work to help them, and also to let the rest of the country realize that—[*inaudible*]—try to help themselves.

So, I didn't feel any concern about it.

Q. We wondered why the mayors didn't applaud more. Do you feel that they lacked enthusiasm about the speech? You know, it was a very serious speech.

THE PRESIDENT. No, we didn't. You can easily design an applause line here and there, or you can plant people around the audience who just start applause or do that sort of thing. I thought it was——

Q. Did you ever do that?

THE PRESIDENT. I haven't; sometimes people do it for me.

But I don't think that this was that kind of speech. I wanted them to realize that we're in it together, that they're responsible for defense strength and for fiscal discipline as much as I am, and that I'm responsible for the employment and rebuilding of cities as much as they are. I think you'll see from the Democratic mayors and so forth, the fact that they'll vote for me and my programs very strongly—and there has been all during this year. Very few of the Democratic mayors around the Nation have not supported me.

I've got very strong expressions of support even from some Republican mayors. Richard Carver, for instance, sharply disagreed with the statement that John Anderson made about the politicization of Government programs yesterday. So, I feel that that's a solid group in support for me, both politically among the Democrats and also—[*inaudible*].

Q. You know, Senator Kennedy found another forum today, and he's proposing a $12 billion, massive Federal program to create jobs and to combat this particular recession.

THE PRESIDENT. Yes, I had heard about that.

Q. Will you, as you suggested in the speech today, if things got worse, you'd take another look? Are you going to have to reexamine this now?

THE PRESIDENT. No, I was very careful what I said in the speech about reexamination. If the recession deepens and if the increase in unemployment continues unabated—I believe that's the language I used—then I would work with the mayors, within the framework of fiscal discipline and noninflationary contributions, to resolve those unanticipated problems. But that's a very cautious statement.

Q. It means no more money within the framework of fiscal discipline.

THE PRESIDENT. No, because Congress has got to show that it can cut back on expenditures as the budget committees have done and as the Congress leaders have pledged; that any stimulative action that is taken, if it's required, would have to be noninflationary in nature.

Q. Would a $12 billion crash program be inflationary?

THE PRESIDENT. I don't know the details of it, but I would presume that the Congress is highly unlikely to support such a massive program. And I wouldn't feel that I could support it, either.

Q. Why do you think that Kennedy wanted to speak on the same day, and what was that all about, or what's your impression?

THE PRESIDENT. I don't know. I was told a week or so ago, or several days ago, that Reagan was going to speak on one day, and one day Anderson was going to speak, one day I was going to speak, and one day Kennedy was going to speak. And so, we would have come anyway, no matter what they did. But that was the understanding that we had. I don't know what went on with the Governors [Mayors] Conference. No one consulted me about it.

Q. But weren't you instrumental, though, in Kennedy's decision to bail out altogether?

THE PRESIDENT. No, I didn't have anything to do with it, didn't know anything about it.

Q. But the objections that Wexler[1] raised with the Mayors Conference staff, it was my understanding, played a role in his decision.

THE PRESIDENT. It may or may not have, I don't know. My understanding after it was all over was that he was invited to speak tomorrow instead of today,

---

[1] Anne Wexler, Assistant to the President.

and that was the standing for the past several days, and that he canceled his speech tomorrow. Why he wanted to speak today, if he did, I don't have any idea. But I would have come anyway. Nobody ever insinuated that we not come.

Q. You would have come and spoken on the same day?

THE PRESIDENT. Sure.

Q. Then there must have been a sort of a mix-up in, a snafu in the orders there.

THE PRESIDENT. [*Inaudible*]

PRESS SECRETARY POWELL. I don't think Anne or anybody else ever told the Mayors Conference that.

THE PRESIDENT. I would've come no matter what—[*inaudible*]—no question about my coming.

Q. Is this meeting in Washington set for the 28th among the Mideast negotiators?

THE PRESIDENT. I know that the Egyptians have offered to come and that Prime Minister Begin has announced that Mr. Burg would come. Whether the exact date's been set, I don't know.

Q. My office told me the 28th.

THE PRESIDENT. That sounds like the highest authority. [*Laughter*]

Q. We have to take it from the—[*inaudible*].

Q. But the reality is that they will resume in Washington soon?

THE PRESIDENT. Yes, that's our hope and also that is our expectation.

Q. Is it just to discuss how to discuss the—[*inaudible*]?

THE PRESIDENT. No, there's no way to separate the two. You're talking about Jerusalem and whether the ultimate status of Jerusalem will be determined through negotiations. I understand from Ed Muskie, early this morning, that Prime Minister Begin said that was the case.

His speech, which was very carefully drafted over the last week or 10 days by him and me and others—I think it's been well received both in the Arab world, particularly in Egypt, and also in Israel. It's a speech that delineates not only what we've accomplished and the present need for the continuation of the talks but also the issues still to be resolved—the definition of autonomy, land, water, security, and who will participate in the elections. I think those are the five issues.

So, the reason for our new initiative, that was done through diplomatic means, not publicly, and the reason for the Muskie speech, delivered yesterday, both reasons were to get the Egyptians and the Israelis at the negotiating table again. And I presume that that has been successful.

Q. And this was the Muskie speech that was well received in the Arab world and in—did he——

THE PRESIDENT. That was Ed's assessment this morning—[*laughter*]—on the phone, that it was well received, particularly—I haven't seen a report—I'm particularly talking about Egypt.

Q. Did he bring up the question of Jerusalem in the speech?

THE PRESIDENT. Yes, he did.

Q. What did he say? Was it on his own, or did——

THE PRESIDENT. He said it was an issue to be resolved ultimately through the negotiating process, and that we favored an undivided Jerusalem with free access to the holy places by persons of all faiths.

Q. Did you hear Muskie on "Meet the Press?"

THE PRESIDENT. Yes.

Q. He seemed very conciliatory toward the Clark mission. He said that the policy you set down was to try to protect Americans who were going to Iran and getting

hurt, not to punish them. That sort of flew in the face of what——

Q. That sort of suggested that you weren't going to go ahead full bore on prosecuting Clark.

THE PRESIDENT. My inclination is, within the bounds of the law, to go ahead and prosecute both Clark and the others who went against my directive, which was legal. My presumption is that the Attorney General will make a decision on whether that should be to seek civil penalties or criminal penalties. I would guess civil penalties would be more appropriate.

But there's no doubt that the restraint on travel will be assessed for legality and for the constitutionality of it. My information from my own legal advisers, including the Attorney General, is that the order was legal and that Clark and the others violated that order and, therefore, violated U.S. law.

Q. But you would guess it would be a civil case?

THE PRESIDENT. I'm not trying to make that decision. I just surmise that that would be the best of the two options. But the Attorney General and his people are now assessing the options. My inclination is to see that the directive is carried out, and when people do violate it, to seek punishment that's appropriate.

Q. He, of course, makes a first amendment defense, saying that he has the freedom under the first amendment to travel, to speak, et cetera.

THE PRESIDENT. There is a long history of restraint of travel. Only after I came into office as President were people permitted to go to places like North Korea or Vietnam or to Cuba and so forth. So, we have done what we could to liberalize travel when we thought that the travelers would be safe and that there was an adequate sense that there was nothing that they would be likely to do that would be contrary to the security interests of our country.

Q. Mr. President, beyond the law, do you think the Clark mission made things any more difficult over there for us now?

THE PRESIDENT. I don't have any way to know. I didn't see him on——

Q. "Issues and Answers."

THE PRESIDENT.——television—"Issues and Answers." But I understand that he reported a lot of doubt about whether his mission accomplished anything tangible. But who can say?

For the last month we've had a simultaneous, concerted diplomatic and other effort being mounted through the United Nations and other countries to get the hostages released. We did not approve and did not expect any beneficial results from this visit by Clark to a forum designed to prove the criminality of the United States.

Q. [*Inaudible*]

THE PRESIDENT. I don't think it helped anything.

Q. You don't think it helped the Iranian case with the Shah, to make a stand?

THE PRESIDENT. Well, the ones who organized the forum were Bani-Sadr and Ghotzbadeh and their basic supporters. They have been in favor of resolving the hostage issue for a long time. The more militant groups and the mullahs who are involved in politics over there have been, in general, more reluctant to solve the hostage issue, and I don't think they endorsed or supported the convention called to condemn the United States.

Q. You once said you thought July would be an excessive time for the hos-

tages to be held. You obviously were thinking of the raid, which we didn't know anything about, when you said that. So, I would now think that you've got to let that slip.

THE PRESIDENT. It always has been hard to set a time limit. We've tried, and it hasn't worked. So, I think to set another arbitrary time limit would be counterproductive.

Q. So, if I ask you how long can this go on, what would your answer be?

THE PRESIDENT. I would say the briefest time possible would suit me best.

Q. You know, your response on Clark is much more punitive than what Muskie—Muskie acted like you were trying to protect Americans and really telling Americans that go into these areas that the U.S. cannot protect them. But you sound like you want some revenge.

THE PRESIDENT. Well, there's a—I'm not a lawyer, and there's a legal basis for restraining American travel. I've tried to outline to you those bases. One is the safety of the Americans involved, particularly when we do not have a consulate or an embassy near a region where they'll be visiting, and where there's an animosity apparent among large segments of the foreign population that may cause problems for the visiting Americans. That's one aspect of it.

The other aspect of it is to enforce the economic sanctions that we've imposed against Iran, and the commerce and trade of travelers is a factor. We've worked hard to get other nations to join with us in that economic sanctions effort to induce the Iranians to release the hostages. And for American citizens to open up travel precedents that might grow in the future is in direct contravention to the order.

And the third thing is when our own national security is at stake, which it is in the Iranian crisis, whether the visit by misguided Americans like Clark might exacerbate an already serious situation and cause further damages either to the hostages or to the Iranian relationships with the outside world is an additional factor. So, those are the bases on which the order was issued.

I don't think Ed Muskie has any legal responsibility for determining to prosecute or not to prosecute. I do have some legal responsibility, working primarily through the Attorney General. And my own inclination is to enforce my directive, which I presume to be legal, and when people violate it, to see that an appropriate punishment is levied.

Q. So they would just be fined, presumably? There would just be a fine involved?

THE PRESIDENT. I'm not trying to discount the possibility of criminal prosecution. I just gave you my opinion, that as the Attorney General makes his recommendation, I would think the most likely move would be civil in nature, because we need to make the American people know and the rest of the world know that the order will be enforced, to discourage further violation of it in the future.

Q. What about the irony here, a former Attorney General—[*inaudible*]?

THE PRESIDENT. Well, the irony is apparent in a former Attorney General attending a conference designed to prove the criminality of his own nation. So, I think that's much more ironic than the fact that an Attorney General is being accused of violating the law.

Q. Other Attorney Generals have been accused of violating the law, you know.

THE PRESIDENT. That's right. But so far as I know, none other have ever attended an international conference designed to prove the criminality of their own country.

Q. Some have gone to jail.

THE PRESIDENT. That's right.

Q. Tell us about the summit. What do you expect from it? Will there be one? There isn't going to be any pulling away because of Ohira?

THE PRESIDENT. No. Ohira may or may not go. I think his doctors have advised him not to go. If he is able, I hope he will come. He's a very fine leader, and he will be missed. But if he doesn't go then he'll have a substitute there, probably the Finance Minister and the Foreign Minister.

NOTE: The question-and-answer session began at approximately 11:45 a.m. during the flight from Seattle to Grand Island.

As printed above, the item contains only the portion of the question-and-answer session made available by the White House Press Office.

Grand Island, Nebraska
Exchange with Reporters on Arrival.
June 10, 1980

Q. What is your view of what ought to happen now to Ramsey Clark?

THE PRESIDENT. It is both legal and constitutional to restrict travel to Iran for several reasons. The order was issued publicly and clearly, and my inclination is that it be carried out. We will make the ultimate decision on how to confront the people who violate the order—whether it should be a civil or criminal prosecution—but I think it is damaging to our Nation's foreign policy. It is damaging to carrying out the economic sanctions to

Iran. It is clear that a prohibition legally should be followed.

Q. Your guess is that it will be a civil or criminal?

THE PRESIDENT. I think whether it is civil or criminal should be the concern and judged by the Attorney General. I would guess that a civil penalty would be more appropriate, but I don't want to make that final decision now.

Q. Mr. President, on the issues of debate, are you now more willing than before to debate Mr. Anderson during the campaign?

THE PRESIDENT. Well, the primary concern I have is to be able to debate Governor Reagan, as the Republican nominee, one-on-one. I can represent my party, the Democratic Party, and he can represent his, the Republican Party, and we can have an uninterrupted debate on our own policies and also the past and present and future commitments of our parties.

This is an important thing. I don't want to sit there and debate against two Republicans. However, if we can have that assured and some forum is indicated where I could debate both Governor Reagan and other candidates, it might be defined in some fashion. My own thought is that if any candidate is theoretically able to get a majority of delegates by qualifying in enough States that that might be one way to establish whether he qualifies for a debate or he should not.

To summarize, I am willing to debate a candidate who might have enough delegates and the possibility to win the nomination, but I don't like to interfere with the direct, head-on-head, one-to-one debate against Governor Reagan.

Q. Mr. President, you go to Venice in a little over a week to talk about energy and the world economy. Will you go there

seen as a less effective leader because of not having won the oil import fee?

THE PRESIDENT. It would have been better for me and for our country, for my reputation as a leader and for our Nation's reputation as a leader, had the Congress supported the oil import fee that they themselves asked me to impose. That was my energy policy, and it was a mistake on the Congress' part to vote that way.

NOTE: The exchange began at approximately 3:30 p.m. at the Hall County Regional Airport.

Following his arrival at the airport, the President went to the Grand Island YMCA building to meet with Federal, State, and local officials and discuss relief efforts in connection with the tornado damage in the area.

As printed above, the item follows the text of the White House press release.

Grand Island, Nebraska

Remarks Following an Inspection Tour of Tornado Damage in the City.   June 10, 1980

As I come to the end of this brief visit in Grand Island and Hall County in your wonderful Cornhusker State, I want to say that I've been impressed not only with the courage that the people here have shown in face of a natural disaster that could have been much more serious as far as human life is concerned, but I also have been impressed with the unselfish nature of the people that has been exhibited in their eagerness to help one another.

There's been a close working coordination between all the people who live here and who had property damaged—the mayor and the city coordinating council that's been appointed by him, Governor Thorne, and the National Guard and all the State agencies. And I believe we've also had an excellent exhibition of leadership by Mr. Tobin, who represents the Federal Emergency Management Administration.

The loss of property and the loss of life is a sobering reminder to us that there is a need for us to work together in a time of challenge. This has been exhibited brilliantly by the attitude of the people in this community.

We have approved immediately when the Governor requested it, an emergency declaration to permit people to survive economically the damage to their property. And more recently, the Governor has asked me to let the Federal Government share on a 75-percent Federal, 25-percent State and local basis the cost of the cleaning up of the debris from the tornado and also the repair of public buildings.

We have a long way to go before the complete repair job is finished. I've talked to several groups informally. I've expressed my admiration to them for the extreme show of mutual support and help during this first week after the tornadoes hit, and I know that this will be a long, extended, disappointing, and frustrating period for many people. And I trust that this spirit of cooperation and mutual help and unselfishness will continue in the difficult days ahead.

The Federal Government will remain eager to help in any way possible. It's a continuing process for us, and I've assured the mayor and the Governor that I'm available at any time when there is a need for additional attention being given by the Federal Government to the needs here in Grand Island and Hall County. I don't believe that need will arise, but we will not abandon the people here. And my hope and my belief is that in a few months or perhaps years after hard work and con-

tinued dedication to one another, that Grand Island and Hall County will be even more beautiful and even more prosperous and even more a delightful place to live than it was before the tornadoes struck.

I'm overwhelmed. To close, I would like to repeat myself: I'm overwhelmed with the sense of courage and dedication that has been shown. It's an inspiration to me as President, and I wish all the people here well, and Godspeed in the days ahead.

Thank you very much.

NOTE: The President spoke at 6:34 p.m. at the Hall County Regional Airport.

National Mental Health Association

Remarks at the Association's Salute to Rosalynn Carter.   June 10, 1980

About 32 minutes ago I landed at Andrews Air Force Base, having hurriedly changed into a tuxedo on the plane before I disembarked and flew over to the reflecting pool and took a car here to be with you on this exciting and wonderful occasion.

Yesterday, at noon, I left to go to Miami to meet with groups responsible for the influx of Cubans and Haitians who've come to our shores seeking freedom and seeking a better way of life. Back in 1965 when we had the enormous influx of Cubans from the Castro regime, who were seeking to escape the persecution and the totalitarian government, we received and processed in the first 2 months, 3,000 Cubans.

During the recent 6 weeks period, we processed an average of 3,000 every day.

There is no way to do this with Government agencies. It can only be done with volunteers. We have also witnessed in recent hours the impact of riots in Liberty City, north of Miami, caused by the real or imagined deprivation of the people there of an equal opportunity, for justice and for economic progress, and for a voice in the shaping of their own future.

I met in a closed room for about an hour and a half with [about] [1] 50 people or more, almost all of whom spoke to me. With the exception of three or four elected officials, including two Congressmen, all of them were volunteers. Distinguished members of the business community, Chamber of Commerce, head of the NAACP, the SCLC, Voters' League—volunteers trying to shape for the people who were alienated from their own community the realization and conviction of a better life.

And then I flew out to the State of Washington, to Seattle, and had a report this morning from the people responsible for repairing the damage to human lives and to our natural resources from the explosion at Mount St. Helens. The Federal Government contribution to the cleanup that I've sent up to the Congress Appropriations Committee today is $917 million.

But compared to the enormous outpouring of human volunteer work this pales into insignificance. And then this afternoon after speaking to the mayors of our Nation, I came back by Grand Island, Nebraska, to see the devastation caused there by four simultaneous tornadoes that hovered over this one tiny community for 3 hours. I stood on a street corner where as far as you could see, there was no house

_____
[1] White House correction.

standing, just piles of rubble and literally dozens of people there working.

I walked up to two men who seemed to be the most burdened down with fatigue and sweat because I wanted the news cameras to get a good picture of me— [*laughter*]—and I said to them, "Do you live here on this block?" And they said, "No." And, I said, "Where do you live?" And one of them said, "I live in Kansas." And the other one said, "I live in South Dakota." They were in the heart of Nebraska. And I said, "Why did you come this far?" They said, "We heard about the tornadoes and we figured they might need some help." They were both Mennonites; they were both farmers.

I walked across the street to what was formerly a house. It was just a foundation about as high as this table, 30 inches high. The people are now finding shelter in the basement. It was covered over with plyboard. And I asked one of the men standing there if that was his home. He said, "No, I live about three blocks away." I said, "What are you doing down here?" He said, "Well, I came here because my house wasn't hit."

I know what you do in the Mental Health Association. You come because people need you and you come often because your home hasn't been hit. To stand with others, to shape better lives, of those who are deprived and alienated, who are forsaken, and who feel themselves that they are not part of our society, and that they have no way to use the talent or ability that God gave them in a fruitful fashion.

Our Government, since the first days of this Nation, has been responsible to some degree for those who have mental problems, but recently because of the help of those in this room and others like you, that tiny seed of assistance has been tremendously magnified. And now, there's a consciousness of volunteer effort that is successful and proven, and an improvement in human lives that's an inspiration to us all. There can be no higher honor, in my judgment, than to call someone an exemplary volunteer in mental health. And, in my judgment—not completely unprejudiced—you have chosen someone who could not be a better person to exemplify the love and the dedication. You've chosen the person that I love more than anyone else in the world, and I love her not only because of her personal relationship with me but because of what I know she means to other people.

I thank you on behalf of our family.

NOTE: The President spoke at 9:27 p.m. in the Regency Ballroom at the Shoreham Hotel.

The dinner was cosponsored by the National Mental Health Association and the Mental Health Association of the District of Columbia.

Department of Defense

Nomination of Jack R. Borsting To Be an Assistant Secretary.   June 11, 1980

The President today announced that he will nominate Jack R. Borsting, of Carmel, Calif., to be Assistant Secretary of Defense (Comptroller). He would replace Fred P. Wacker, resigned.

Borsting has been Provost and Academic Dean of the Naval Postgraduate School in Monterey, Calif., since 1974.

He was born January 31, 1929, in Portland, Oreg. He received a B.A. from Oregon State University in 1951 and an M.A. (1952) and Ph. D. (1959) from the University of Oregon. He served in the U.S. Air Force from 1954 to 1956 as a nuclear weapons project officer.

Borsting was an instructor in mathematics at Western Washington College in 1953–54 and a teaching fellow at the University of Oregon from 1956 to 1959. He joined the faculty of the Naval Postgraduate School in 1959 and served as a professor of mathematics, then professor and chairman of the Department of Operations Research and Administrative Sciences.

Borsting is past president of the Operations Research Society of America and honorary treasurer of the International Federation of Operations Research Societies. He is past president of the Military Operations Research Society.

Egyptian-Israeli Peace Negotiations

Announcement by the White House Press Secretary.   June 11, 1980

As you know, the United States has been holding discussions with both Egypt and Israel concerning the issues which have impeded a resumption of the autonomy talks. All parties recognize that it is essential to pursue the negotiations to a successful conclusion as expeditiously as possible.

Accordingly, the President is pleased to announce that Egypt and Israel have accepted the invitation of the United States to send their heads of delegation, Dr. Burg and Foreign Minister Ali, to Washington to meet with Ambassador Linowitz to prepare for the resumption of formal negotiations. A mutually agreeable date will be set for this meeting in the near future.

NOTE: Press Secretary Jody Powell read the announcement at 11:58 a.m. to reporters assembled in the Briefing Room at the White House.

Neighborhood Development

Remarks on Greeting Representatives of
Neighborhood Groups.   June 11, 1980

THE PRESIDENT. To the members of our National Neighborhood Commission, and to the distinguished Members of the Congress assembled behind me, both Senators and Congressmen, and to all of you, I want to say welcome to the White House. This is a good day for us, and a new and innovative program has been launched now in the country that I think will stand us all in good stead in making better lives for Americans.

I grew up in a very small town, in fact it's still a very small town, with a total population of about 500. As a matter of fact, I didn't live there. I lived about 3 miles west of Plains. But I could see in my early life, and later on as a State senator, and then as a Governor, and now as President, how in a very small town the people naturally pull together to meet common problems and to meet common concerns and common opportunities. And exactly the same thing prevails in the urban neighborhoods, around a block or a few blocks, around a central park, around a stop on a rapid transit system, around a school or around a church, quite often, or around some center for congregation of people.

In the past, too many times the government has not recognized the inherent strength of a neighborhood, built on strong families who share common problems and common opportunities. We've concentrated on bricks and mortars; we quite often have not concentrated on the soul of a community. Under the great leadership and advice of the National Neighborhood Commission, headed by some of the people behind me, Joe Timilty and others, this concept in government has been changed substantially. I think the key to the revitalization of our cities lies in volunteer work within the neighborhoods, aided by and encouraged by the government, the Federal, State, and local governments.

I'm very proud that the Federal Government has taken the initiative here. In 1978 Congress passed the Neighborhood Self-Help Development Act. And today we are honoring the first 70 grantees under that program. This has been the result of an intense competition, and many neighborhoods, as you know, many leaders, fought for this first allocation of funds. You are the ones who have been successful, because of the superb work you've done and the good programs that you've presented.

I won't go down the list of all 70, you'll be glad to know. [*Laughter*] But they are very diverse in nature. A Portland, Oregon, group has created a low-income housing unit that'll help people who live in that region. A Harlem group is creating a mental health clinic. An Hispanic group in Hartford, Connecticut, is building a new market complex. And farmers in Waynesboro, Georgia, are building a cannery to utilize the products that they grow on the farms in their community. So, I could go down the lists with the other 66 projects that have been approved; I won't do it. But you can see how broad and how valuable these projects are.

There's nothing better than a new place to live, or a mental health clinic, or a new market to sell and to buy products that are produced or consumed in that neighborhood, and also a cannery, for instance, to utilize farm products. Overall you will be receiving a little more than $8½ million in these neighborhood grant funds. That may not seem like an enormous amount on a nationwide basis, and it isn't, but each one of those dollars has attracted $17; a total of $145 million will be spent on these projects. That shows what can be done with cooperation from the private sector of our free enterprise system, working with interested citizens.

We have included Federal funds to provide that base. We've given technical aid or advice to people who want to take the initiative in their own communities. We've tried to prescribe policies for our country so that it will provide guidance for those in the future who seek these grants. And, of course, we'll be observing very closely to see how well you do. The ones that we trust in these first 70 grants—who quite often are experimental in nature, we can't guarantee success—but those that do work well, we'll find out why. And those that don't work so well, we'll also find out why, so that the future applicants can do an even better job and expend the money even better.

Another thing that we want is kind of a network of cooperating groups. I would hope that the ones in Hartford, Connecticut, and the ones in Oregon, the ones in Georgia, and the ones in Harlem, would share, maybe through Geno Baroni and others, your experiences, and kind of form an organization of helping not only your own neighborhood but other neighborhoods around you, in the same large city or perhaps even in adjacent cities.

The efforts that we've made have been initiated and invigorated by the neighborhood commission, the National Commission on Neighborhoods. This act, the Self-Help Development Act that provides these funds, is one of the results of their labor. We've extended the Home Mortgage Disclosure Act. And we are now voting, today as a matter of fact, in the House, on amendments to the Fair Housing Act, to remove the discrimination that still exists in the finding of homes by American families. And the emphasis on this technical assistance that goes to help you prepare and to carry out your proposals, and the public and private partnerships that have been formed with industry and with investors in your community, all have been initiated by this very fine National Commission on Neighborhoods. I'm going to urge all the Federal agencies to continue to assess and to carry out the recommendations that this fine Commission has made.

Our country does face many challenges, many problems, many obstacles. We have to answer many questions. This is not unique in American history. We've always been kind of on the cutting edge of change. We've never been afraid of change. We've been eager to work together. We are different, one from another. Those differences don't make us weak; they make us stronger, when we can put them together, and that's what we're trying to do with this particular program. And I want you to join in with me in reaffirming our faith in the greatest nation on Earth, and also reaffirming our commitment in the future to make it even greater.

God bless you, everyone. Congratulations on your success. Best wishes for the future.

ASSISTANT SECRETARY BARONI. Mr. President, we'd like to thank you for inviting all of us, and especially these neighborhood groups, to your neighborhood. And we hope that you're going to go and visit their neighborhoods and see the work they've done. And because of the special request, mostly of your wife and yourself, and because of your support for the neighborhood program, we've prepared a neighborhood self-help sampler, as you discussed, telling neighborhood groups what they can do, with government help, without government help. And these groups have autographed this first copy, which is being presented around the country today, to you and to Mrs. Carter.

Thank you very much.

THE PRESIDENT. Well, thank you very much.

Well, I appreciate this much. I won't comment to you on how much I like this neighborhood. I'd like to stay here a little bit longer. [*Laughter*]

NOTE: The President spoke at 2:05 p.m. in the Rose Garden at the White House. Monsignor Geno Baroni is Assistant Secretary of Housing and Urban Development for Neighborhoods, Voluntary Associations, and Consumer Protection.

The document presented to the President is entitled "Neighborhoods: A Self-Help Sampler" (Government Printing Office, 161 pages).

White House "Salute to Congress"

Remarks at the Buffet Dinner for Members of Congress and Their Families.   June 11, 1980

Well, first of all, let me say that we're very delighted to have all of you here tonight. We've got a 1-day winning streak in the House—[*laughter*]—so we decided not to cancel the party tonight. We made everybody check their political speeches at the gate, so there's not going to be anything tonight except good times, good music, good dancing, good food, good friendship. We're very delighted that you would bring your families with you. This is a very fine annual occasion for us. We hope to see you many more years here

on the same South Grounds. Thank you very much, have a good time.

Rosalynn said she'll dance with me, so we'll lead it off, and the rest of you join in with us.

NOTE: The President spoke at 8:06 on the South Lawn of the White House.

Death of Prime Minister Masayoshi Ohira of Japan

Statement by the President.   June 11, 1980

I am shocked and deeply saddened to learn of the death of Prime Minister Ohira. He was a great leader of his people, a good friend of the United States, and a friend I valued. I consider his death a great loss for Japan and for the world.

During the last year, Prime Minister Ohira and I met at bilateral summits here in Washington and in Tokyo, as well as at the Tokyo economic summit. He was one of the warmest people I have known, and I came to trust fully in his judgment and counsel.

The close friendship and alliance between the United States and Japan to which he contributed so much will, of course, continue as before. But we will all miss a cherished friend and partner.

On behalf of the American people, and for ourselves, Rosalynn and I extend our deepest condolences to Mrs. Ohira and her family, and to the people of Japan.

Department of State

Nomination of William J. Dyess To Be Assistant Secretary for Public Affairs. June 12, 1980

The President today announced his intention to nominate William J. Dyess, of Troy, Ala., to be Assistant Secretary of State for Public Affairs. He would replace Hodding Carter III, who is resigning. Dyess has been Deputy Assistant Secretary of State for Public Affairs since 1977 and has been a Foreign Service officer since 1958.

He was born August 1, 1929, in Troy, Ala. He received a B.A. (1950) and M.A. (1951) from the University of Alabama. He served in the U.S. Army from 1953 to 1956.

Dyess joined the Foreign Service in 1958 and served as an exchange program officer, then an intelligence research specialist, at the State Department. In 1960–61 he took Serbo-Croatian language training. He was political officer in Belgrade from 1961 to 1963 and in Copenhagen from 1963 to 1965.

In 1965–66 Dyess took Russian language training. He was posted in Moscow from 1966 to 1968 as administrative officer, then political officer, and in Berlin from 1968 to 1970 as political officer. From 1970 to 1975, he was an international relations officer at the State Department. From 1975 to 1977, he was Executive Director of the Bureau of Public Affairs at the State Department.

Department of Education

Nomination of James Bert Thomas, Jr., To Be Inspector General.   June 12, 1980

The President today announced that he will nominate James Bert Thomas, Jr., of McLean, Va., to be Inspector General of the Department of Education, a new position. Thomas has been Director of the Bureau of Accounts at the Interstate Commerce Commission (ICC) since 1977.

He was born March 16, 1935, in Tallahassee, Fla. He received a B.S. in business administration from Florida State University in 1957.

From 1957 to 1958, Thomas was an auditor analyst with the Florida State Department of Education. He was a special auditor with the Florida State Comptroller's USE Tax Division from 1958 to 1959. In 1959 he was a junior auditor with an accounting firm, and from 1959 to 1960, he was senior State auditor for the State of Florida.

Thomas was Assistant Director of Audit Operations with the Department of Housing and Urban Development from 1960 to 1971. He joined the ICC in 1971 as an accounting officer and then served as Assistant Director of the ICC's Bureau of Accounts from 1972 to 1975. From 1975 to 1977, he was Inspector General of the Department of Housing and Urban Development.

National Advisory Committee for Juvenile Justice and Delinquency Prevention

Appointment of Seven Members. June 12, 1980

The President today announced the appointment of seven persons as members of the National Advisory Committee for Juvenile Justice and Delinquency Prevention. They are:

MARY ELLEN CHAMBERLIN, of Davenport, Iowa, chairperson of the Scott County (Iowa) Juvenile Detention Planning Advisory Committee, who is very active in civic affairs, particularly activities dealing with youth and criminal justice;

AURISTELA FRIAS, of San Francisco, a drug abuse counselor and administrative assistant to the president of Delancey Street Foundation;

ROBERT D. GLASER, of New Orleans, a junior at Tulane University and counselor at the Greenhouse Crisis Center, Youth Alternatives, Inc.;

SONIA E. MELARA, of Sunnyvale, Calif., a foster home recruitment and educational coordinator with the Santa Clara County Department of Social Services;

DAVID HERRON MOSELEY, of Seattle, director of the City of Seattle Division of Youth Services and chairman of the National Youth Work Alliance;

DAVID GRAY ROSS, of Bowie, Md., an associate judge of the Seventh Judicial Circuit of Maryland and a former member of the Maryland General Assembly;

T. GEORGE SILCOTT, of Mount Kisco, N.Y., president of the Urban Research Planning and Conference Center and former executive director of the Wiltwyck School, a residential treatment center for emotionally disturbed or neglected children from poor homes.

Fair Housing Amendment of 1980

Statement on House Passage of the Legislation.   *June 12, 1980*

I congratulate the House of Representatives for passing the fair housing amendment of 1980 by a vote of 310–96. This is the most important civil rights bill to be considered by the Congress in more than a decade.

I would like to thank Representatives Donald Edwards, Robert Drinan, Peter Rodino, Thomas Railsback, and Hamilton Fish for their work on behalf of this measure. I particularly appreciate the efforts of Congressman Mike Synar, whose compromise amendment led to today's victory.

This bill provides the enforcement powers that the Nation's Fair Housing Act needs, and I hope the Senate will quickly approve it.

Combined Federal Campaign

Memorandum From the President.
June 12, 1980

Memorandum for the Heads of Executive Departments and Agencies

The Honorable Bob Bergland, Secretary of Agriculture, has agreed to serve again this year as Chairman of the Combined Federal Campaign for the National Capital Area. Secretary Bergland did an outstanding job as campaign chairman last year and I am pleased that he is willing to serve again.

Citizens working together through voluntary agencies can become partners in the effort to build better communities, a healthier nation, and a more peaceful world. This year, our help is needed more than ever. Voluntary organizations need the support of all Federal personnel in the National Capital Area to accomplish their important objectives.

I request that you serve personally as Chairman of the combined campaign in your organization and that you appoint a top assistant as your Vice Chairman. Please advise Secretary Bergland of the person you designate as your Vice Chairman.

JIMMY CARTER

Combined Federal Campaign

Memorandum From the President.
June 12, 1980

Memorandum for All Federal Employees and Military Personnel

America's character and tradition are deeply rooted in a spirit of neighborliness, of people banding together to do the things they see must be done.

Through the Combined Federal Campaign, Federal employees can show their individual concern for those who need help. This is an opportunity that comes only in a free society.

The Combined Federal Campaign covers in one single drive the campaigns of the United Way, the National Health Agencies, the International Service Agencies, the National Service Agencies and local non-federated voluntary agencies. These agencies help make our world a better place in which to live. They reflect the complex and dynamic vitality of American life, the traditional concern of the American people for the unfortunate, and the genius for voluntary service that has long been our pride and our strength.

The Combined Federal Campaign is a fine vehicle for expressing the American tradition of neighborliness and service. Let me urge you to continue this tradition through your contributions to the Combined Federal Campaign.

JIMMY CARTER

Standby Gasoline Rationing Plan

Message to the Congress Transmitting the Plan. June 12, 1980

To the Congress of the United States:

I am hereby transmitting to the Congress the Standby Gasoline Rationing Plan as required by Section 203 of the Energy Policy and Conservation Act (42 U.S.C. 6263) as amended by Section 103 of the Emergency Energy Conservation Act of 1979, P.L. 96–102. I have also directed the Secretary of Energy to publish the Plan in the FEDERAL REGISTER, as the final step in prescribing a gasoline rationing contingency plan by rule, as required by statute.

I am also transmitting today to the appropriate committees of Congress the "Progress Report to Congress on the Standby Motor Fuel Rationing Plans" required by Section 102 of the Emergency Energy Conservation Act. This report will provide further information on the development of the Standby Gasoline Rationing Plan.

The Standby Gasoline Rationing Plan responds to the concerns of the Congress expressed in the debates on last year's plan and in the Emergency Energy Conservation Act, as well as to the concerns expressed by the public during the comment period. In accordance with statutory requirements, the Plan is designed to deal with a serious shortage which will necessarily inconvenience large numbers of gasoline users. If circumstances arise that necessitate its implementation, the Plan will serve to allocate gasoline supplies equitably, stabilize the gasoline market and minimize economic dislocations.

The undependability of foreign sources of petroleum has been demonstrated by a long series of events, including the curtailment of oil supplies from Iran and the shortages of gasoline, diesel fuel and other products which we incurred during 1979. The current situation in the Middle East, particularly the continued retention of hostages by Iran and the Soviet occupation of Afghanistan, underscores the need for the United States to be well prepared to deal with periods of serious shortage. The Plan, in addition to the Standby Federal Emergency Energy Conservation Plan recently promulgated under the Emergency Energy Conservation Act of 1979, will provide important tools for the management of a severe gasoline shortfall.

I urge favorable review by the Congress.

JIMMY CARTER

The White House,
June 12, 1980.

NOTE: On the same day, the President transmitted copies of the progress report to Henry M. Jackson, chairman of the Senate Committee on Energy and Natural Resources, and Harley O. Staggers, chairman of the House Committee on Interstate and Foreign Commerce.

The plan is printed in the FEDERAL REGISTER of June 18, 1980.

Democratic National Committee

Remarks at a Reception for the Platform Committee. June 12, 1980

First of all, I thought I would recapitulate our own proposals on the platform since maybe you didn't—[laughter]—completely assimilate them today.

I've gotten very good results from the reports that have come concerning your work today. I understand that you've had a long, hard day, but very fruitful; that the sessions have been remarkably harmonious, almost as much as the campaigns during the primaries—[laughter]—and that there were some genuine and very fruitful and constructive exchanges between the presentations made by Senator Kennedy and his supporters and me and my supporters, and I know that you've had a long series of discussions around the nation.

Since you have had so many presentations and talks today, I'm going to be very brief, because I would like to shake hands and thank every one of you for the good work you've done.

We've got a major responsibility shared among those in this room. I'm extremely eager to see the rifts that are in our party, which are inevitable in a democratic society—particularly in a democratic party—healed but, at the same time, honoring the diversity that must exist among us that gives us a major part of our party's strength.

To me, there's a parallelism between our own party and its pride in individuality and the right of each person to speak forcefully for diverging views on the one hand, and our Nation, which is so strong because of its diversity on the other.

As I've said many times, ours is a nation of immigrants, a nation of refugees. We've come here—our families have—from almost every nation on Earth. We've preserved our heritage, our pride, our customs, our religion, quite often even our language, as a source of strength for us. But we've been able in this society, with a free enterprise system, with the nature of our government, with open and free discussions, to meld into a very strong, pliable, forceful, flexible nation, able to deal with constant change without fear and without failure.

Our country has faced the most difficult possible challenges. Because of the initiative of our people, we've always been on the cutting edge of change. When worldwide customs and circumstances had to be modified, we have not broken. Quite often we have found a way to accommodate those kinds of changes in our own lives that cause us so much consternation and sometimes trepidation and fear, and we've capitalized on them to move forward to an ever better quality of life.

In my judgment, this time of testing, this time of even international danger gives us another opportunity for that. The Nation is looking to the Democratic Party to find a way for our country, and other nations are looking to us as a country to find a way for them.

I'll be leaving next week, going to meet with the leaders of Japan and Italy, of Canada, England, and of France, Germany. I'll go then to Yugoslavia, then back to Portugal and Spain, and then return to our country. And I'm sure that in all those sessions, they will be extremely eager to learn what our Nation has done in the past, what we are doing now, what we will do in the future.

You're the ones who have listened to Americans all over this Nation. You've observed with particular sensitivity the debates that have taken place in the primaries and caucuses in all the States and territories. And now you have a major job of finding the common ground on which we agree, to narrow the differences as much as possible, and to sharpen those differences so that they can be clearly understood to point out to the Nation in a forceful, succinct, and accurate fashion what the Democratic Congress and the Democratic administration has done and, perhaps more importantly of all, to prescribe for us an agenda for the future.

I don't have any idea that all your discussions will be harmonious or that you will even get a clear, acceptable majority opinion that can be adopted by the minority members of the committee. If not, then of course, the debate will be shifted to the Democratic Convention floor. That need not cause us any fear or consternation, and the judgment of the delegates assembled in New York will be final as far as the platform of our party is concerned.

Members of Congress, Governors, other State officials, as well as the Democratic ticket running for President and Vice President will, of course, be guided by what you do. And I hope that all your deliberations will be open and that you will also let everyone express themselves thoroughly and that your decisions will be courageous. Courage requires not only an adherence to past statements but courage perhaps even to a higher degree requires some modification of past commitments and past statements when you are convinced that there is a better way. And when a group of people like you come together, there is obviously a need for compromise without the compromise of principle.

I'm eager to help you. Stu Eizenstat has presented our basic platform proposals. We will listen with great care to other proposals made both by Senator Kennedy and by the Members of Congress, Governors, and others, and we'll be eager to improve upon our own if we see an opportunity for it. David Rubenstein will represent me, with you, on a constant basis. And of course, if you have a question about foreign policy, Senator Muskie, now Secretary Muskie, is here with us, and Dr. Brzezinski and my entire staff will be available. We have Pat Harris and we have Secretary Bergland here; Secretary Duncan is here. I don't know what other Cabinet officers are present, but my entire Cabinet will be available to answer specific questions not only by the chairman of the committee but also by any of you who don't quite understand a proposal, or would like to have some facts about what our administration has done, or about the factors that must go into a decision. We are eager to have a very constructive and exciting result of your deliberations, and I have no doubt that that will provide a basis for a tremendous Democratic victory in November.

I am determined that the Democrats will win, and we have harnessed our efforts, along with those of candidates for Congress in 1978, in a remarkable and also successful fashion. During the '78 convention when I was not running for reelection, we made more than 1,100 trips to States and to congressional districts—that was my own personal staff, the members of my Cabinet, and the members of the families of myself and Fritz Mondale. And I think it paid rich dividends for us because we learned our Nation well, and it also, of course, helped many Democrats be elected.

We're in it together. We're a team. We belong to the same party, and together we'll make a great nation even greater in the future. I'm deeply grateful to all of you and now, if you would permit me, I'd like to meet you just outside the door to shake hands with each person and thank you from the bottom of my heart for the constructive effort that you've made already and for the even greater contribution that I feel sure you're going to make in the next few days.

Thank you very much.

NOTE: The President spoke at 6:35 p.m. in the East Room at the White House.

Interview With the President

Question-and-Answer Session With Arrigo Levi of La Stampa and Sergio Telmon of RAI-TV. June 12, 1980

Q. Mr. President, you are going to Italy very soon. What are your aims, your expectations, visiting our country?

THE PRESIDENT. Well, first of all, I'm very excited about going to Italy because of the great reception and hospitality that has been extended to the members of my family who have been there, both on offi-

cial visits and just visits to meet with friends.

Secondly, we will be having extensive discussions with the Italian leaders and with some of the representatives of the Italian private sector, to strengthen the bilateral relationships between our two countries and also to prepare for the conference in Venice involving seven international leaders.

Third is that we consider the relationship between our Nation and Italy to be extremely important to us and to world peace and to economic stability and to future progress. This will give me a chance to follow up on the meetings that I've had already this year with your Prime Minister Cossiga and also, of course, with your Foreign Minister, who was here just this week. And I look forward to paying my respects to President Pertini, who's a close friend of my mother's and whom I admire very much. And I'll be visiting again with the Pope at the Vatican to discuss international matters and also matters of morality and the spirit.

Q. Mr. President, then it will be on to Venice, and Venice will be a summit meeting of the Western Alliance. I wonder if I can ask a question about the state of the Western Alliance as seen by you, by the White House?

THE PRESIDENT. Yes.

Q. There have been in recent months quite a few misunderstandings—at least that's what the papers have written—we sometimes get it wrong; sometimes we get it right. There have been complaints. We Europeans complain of not being consulted enough by America, not being listened to enough. Americans—sometimes we read they complain about being betrayed by their allies. Is that correct?

THE PRESIDENT. No.

Q. Do you feel that is the state of affairs, the state of the Alliance? Is that as bad as all that?

THE PRESIDENT. No. In my judgment, the Alliance is much stronger now than it has been in many years, perhaps even since the Alliance was first formed.

We've initiated in the last 3 years, a long-range defense program to revitalize the NATO Alliance. This will extend over 15 years. It's a common commitment that all of us have made over very difficult obstacles. We've also pledged ourselves to strengthen the defense commitments in our nations. We've agreed among ourselves, again in a difficult way, to meet the growing Soviet threat, with their SS–20 missiles, with the theater nuclear force commitment. And in my judgment, we've got a very fine interrelationship among us in close consultation, not only on matters that relate to defense but also economic progress.

The attendance and the achievements in London in 1977, in Bonn in 1978, in Tokyo last year, and now this year in Venice, in my opinion help to bind us together in a very strong, structured fashion. We recognize that in a conference of democracies that there must be a recognition and an honoring of individuality, of national commitments and priorities. This is not a Warsaw Pact where there are dominant forces there from the Soviet Union; this is a matter of free exchange. Obviously, in a democracy an open discussion of issues quite often creates the impression of disharmony.

Q. It is just an impression, Mr. President?

THE PRESIDENT. I think just an impression as far as seriousness is concerned. We are extremely forceful in our own Nation in condemning and working to oppose the present and the future possibilities of Soviet aggression, exemplified in the invasion of Afghanistan. Some of the allies in Europe have not been quite so forceful as we in imposing sanctions against the Soviet Union and in moving to boycott the Olympics and so forth, but we recognize that there are reasons for them not to pattern their actions specifically after ours.

Q. What you mean is that you do not share the feeling which sometimes is voiced in America, that the allies are betraying America? You think that's wrong?

THE PRESIDENT. No. I think the word betrayal is completely an erroneous word.

Q. Or not supporting enough?

THE PRESIDENT. Sometimes they don't support us strongly enough, as judged from our perspective, but we recognize the difference that must exist between us. I'm sure sometimes some of our actions are not completely pleasing to our allies. But that's inevitable in an alliance of free and independent nations who are democratic in nature and who don't conceal differences with suppression of the press and suppression of free speech.

Obviously, we have nations that are attractive—there are no walls built around West Germany to keep people from escaping that nation. And if you look at the 4 million, roughly, refugees around the world, three-fourths of them are trying to escape from Soviet-inspired Communist domination. So the attractiveness of a free world is patently obvious, and the disharmonies that exist within a free world are because we believe in free speech and the importance of individuals.

Q. So that will not be one subject for discussions in Venice? You will not be discussing improvements in methods of consultation——

THE PRESIDENT. Yes, I think we will.

Q. You will?

THE PRESIDENT. Yes. We don't claim that the Alliance is perfect, and we also probe for ways to strengthen the Alliance and to create more harmony and better consultation. But one of the reasons for that commitment is my visit to Rome and also the subsequent meeting of the Alliance leaders, some of them in Venice.

Q. The Middle East, Mr. President——

THE PRESIDENT. Yes.

Q. The European Community is considering an initiative and, on the other hand, the United States is trying to get together again the Israelis and the Egyptians. What do you think at this point the situation will be?

THE PRESIDENT. It's important, very quickly, to look at this Mideast effort in perspective. Two years ago, it was inconceivable that Israel and Egypt would be sitting down together working on ways to alleviate tensions between them, with open borders and diplomatic recognition, exchange of ambassadors, tourism, trade being established.

The Camp David accords have brought that progress into being. Both Israel and Egypt will be meeting with us shortly, here in Washington, to resume the talks. The Camp David accords outline a way to resolve the Palestinian issue, to give the Palestinians a voice in the determination of their own future, to resolve the Palestinian question in all of its aspects.

These phrases that I've just quoted to you have been approved specifically not only by myself and President Sadat but also by Prime Minister Begin and, subsequently, ratified by the Israeli Knesset.

So, we have a basis here for progress. It is obvious to everyone that the relationship between Israel and her neighbors is crucial to the stability and the maintenance of peace in the Mideast. And this Camp David process is the only one in the last 30 years that has made any progress in guaranteeing to the Palestinians the realization of their own rights.

So, I'm committed to the Camp David process. If the European nations—the Community wants to take actions that are constructive, we will welcome this. But to subvert or to cancel or to bypass the Camp David process, we believe, would be a very serious mistake.

Q. Do you really hope in a breakthrough at this time?

THE PRESIDENT. Yes. We've had them before. When we went to Camp David there was no prospect then of an assured success, but almost miraculously, the Egyptians and the Israelis reached an agreement on basic principles, under which we are presently working. And later, when I went to the Mideast, it was to salvage what seemed to be a hopeless breakdown in their relationships, and from that came the peace treaty between Israel and Egypt with the return of the Sinai to Egypt and the establishment of these good relationships.

Now we do face difficulties and I can't guarantee success, but I guarantee that we will continue to work for success with the best possible avenue being the use of and the building upon the Camp David accords.

Q. Will you personally be involved again in it?

THE PRESIDENT. Yes. I am personally involved almost on a daily basis in directing the Secretary of State and our negotiators and in dealing directly with the

Prime Minister of Israel and the President of Egypt. And I'll be meeting with other leaders from time to time. We have a good correspondence with the Saudis, for instance, who have a beneficial influence on occasion. The King of Jordan will be here to meet with me for 2 days prior to the time that I come to Italy.

So, we are exploring every possible avenue of success in the Mideast and trying to provide stability there while the nations involved search for peace.

Q. Do you expect a meeting with Sadat and Begin?

THE PRESIDENT. Not any time soon, but they are always willing and eager to join me in discussions when it's necessary to meet at that highest level.

Q. Relations with the Soviet Union— 1 year ago, 12 months ago, in Vienna, you met Chairman Brezhnev and restated the principles of détente. There is a general feeling that détente in the meantime is more or less over—rightly or wrongly, I do not know. That's what most people say. They feel there is a new cold war fear and an unlimited arms race, and some people fear war. Do you still believe in détente? Do you still believe there will be peace in the nuclear age? And what are you planning to do—I mean, to improve the sort of relation with the Soviet Union—these two superpowers having such a heavy responsibility for maintaining peace in the world? Are you planning some initiative?

THE PRESIDENT. Yes, there is still détente. We are still at peace. We have a continuing, deep commitment to the control of nuclear weapons. The SALT process is still a viable process which we will continue to pursue. The problem is that the Soviets have interrupted the arms control process and also have damaged the progress in détente by their unwarranted and vicious invasion of a peace-loving nation, of Afghanistan.

The Soviets have made a serious mistake. One hundred and four members of the United Nations have condemned the Soviet Union's aggression and have demanded that the Soviets withdraw. The Afghan people, heroically, are still fighting for their own freedom against the Soviet invading forces. And we believe that when and if the Soviets do make any contribution toward the restoration of international stability by withdrawing their forces, that we can continue to make good progress on arms control and on the enhancement of détente.

There will always be a relationship of competition between the Western World and the Soviet-dominated or influenced nations, but there'll also be a commitment on our part for maximum cooperation in building on détente, on controlling nuclear weapons, and in cooperation with the Soviet Union every time they are willing to join with us in the maintenance of peace.

Q. We will see a new embrace between President Carter and Chairman Brezhnev as we saw in Vienna?

THE PRESIDENT. That's up to the Soviet Union. I would welcome nothing more than peace and harmony between us, as leaders, and between our nations. I am convinced that the Soviet people do not support the war-like activities which the Soviets have demonstrated in their invasion of Afghanistan, and I'm convinced the Soviet people do not support the war by surrogates which the Soviets are encouraging through the use of Vietnam forces in Kampuchea, and also the Cuban forces in several places in Africa.

Q. Mr. President, I know that your most important preoccupation is the release of the hostages from Iran.

THE PRESIDENT. Yes.

Q. Is there any new strategy you're working on?

THE PRESIDENT. No, we have tried, in every way since the hostages were taken, to protect the lives and the safety of the hostages and also to protect the principles of our Nation and to secure the hostages' release. We've explored in every way, direct relationships with the Iranian Government officials and others.

Now, I think the best avenue is through a multitude of diplomatic and economic efforts, being made through the United Nations and through other countries, to convince the Iranians that it is counterproductive for them to continue to hold these innocent people. This is an act of international terrorism, and it is condoned and supported by the official Government of Iran. And for other nations like Italy and the Europeans allies, Japan, and others, to join in with us to convince the Iranians that they are making a mistake and that the bringing of Iran back in to an acceptable position with other nations of the Earth, with an end to this act of terrorism, is very important.

That's why we consider a peaceful approach to Iran, but with some economic sanctions being imposed to encourage them to act is important. In the meantime, we are pursuing every avenue—through religious leaders, through private citizens, through the United Nations, and through other governments—to induce Iran to release the hostages so that normal relationships can be restored.

Q. Are military measures being excluded for the time being, or just being excluded full stop?

THE PRESIDENT. Military measures are not being considered.

Q. Are not being considered?

THE PRESIDENT. No.

Q. Mr. President, this is none of my business, but do you plan to attend the economic summit of '81?

THE PRESIDENT. [*Laughing*] Yes, I do intend to be there.

Q. You don't expect there's some Brutus waiting for you at the Ides of August? [*Laughter*]

THE PRESIDENT. Well, I've faced formidable political challenges in the past and have prevailed. My belief is that the Democratic Party is by far the most popular organization in our Nation, that the principles of our party are acceptable to the American people. I expect to be the nominee of our party, and in November I expect to win the election, and in 1981 I expect to be at the economic summit.

Q. Thank you very much, Mr. President.

THE PRESIDENT. Thank you very much. I enjoyed it. It's a pleasure.

NOTE: The interview, taped for later broadcast in Italy, began at 11:30 a.m. in the Map Room at the White House.

The transcript of the interview was released on June 13.

United States Ambassador to Bahrain

Nomination of Peter Adams Sutherland. June 13, 1980

The President today announced that he will nominate Peter Adams Sutherland, of Ashland, N.H., to be Ambassador Extraordinary and Plenipotentiary of the United States to the State of Bahrain. He would replace Robert H. Pelletreau, Jr., who has resigned. Sutherland was Deputy Chief of Mission in Kuwait from 1976 until earlier this year.

He was born May 10, 1933, in Rochester, N.Y. He received an A.B. from Harvard College in 1953, and an LL.B. from Harvard Law School and M.A. from Harvard Graduate School in 1960. He served in the U.S. Army from 1953 to 1956.

Sutherland joined the Foreign Service in 1961 and was posted in Amman, Port Said, Jidda, and at the State Department. He took language and area training in Beirut from 1966 to 1967 and was political officer in Jerusalem from 1967 to 1970.

From 1970 to 1972, Sutherland was political-economic officer in the Bureau of Near Eastern and South Asian Affairs at the State Department. From 1972 to 1973, he was on detail as a congressional intern. He was a personnel officer at the State Department from 1973 to 1974 and counselor for political affairs in Tunis from 1974 to 1976.

United States Ambassador to Cameroon and Equatorial Guinea

Nomination of Hume Alexander Horan.
June 13, 1980

The President today announced that he will nominate Hume Alexander Horan, of Cranford, N.J., to be Ambassador Extraordinary and Plenipotentiary of the United States to the United Republic of Cameroon and to the Republic of Equatorial Guinea. He would replace Mabel M. Smythe, who has resigned. Horan has been Deputy Assistant Secre-

tary of State for Consular Affairs since 1978.

He was born August 13, 1934, in Washington, D.C. He received an A.B. (1958) and A.M. (1963) from Harvard University. He served in the U.S. Army from 1954 to 1956.

Horan joined the Foreign Service in 1960 and was posted in Baghdad, Beirut, Baida, and at the State Department. He had a congressional fellowship in 1969–70. From 1970 to 1972, he was political officer in Amman.

From 1972 to 1977, Horan was Deputy Chief of Mission in Jidda. He was a member of the Foreign Service Institute's Executive Seminar in National and International Affairs in 1977–78.

United States Ambassador to Fiji, Tonga, and Tuvalu and United States Minister to Kiribati

Nomination of William Bodde, Jr.
June 13, 1980

The President today announced that he will nominate William Bodde, Jr., of Bethesda, Md., to be Ambassador Extraordinary and Plenipotentiary of the United States to Fiji, to the Kingdom of Tonga, and to Tuvalu, and Envoy Extraordinary and Minister Plenipotentiary of the United States to the Republic of Kiribati. He would replace John P. Condon, who has resigned, as Ambassador to Fiji, Tonga, and Tuvalu. He would be our first accredited Minister to Kiribati. Bodde has been Director of Pacific Island Affairs at the State Department since 1978.

He was born November 27, 1931, in Brooklyn, N.Y. He received a B.A. from

Hofstra College in 1961. He served in the U.S. Army from 1951 to 1954.

From 1954 to 1961, Bodde was with Newsday in Garden City, Long Island. He was a program analyst with the Housing and Home Finance Agency in 1961 and 1962. He joined the Foreign Service in 1962 and was posted in Vienna, Stockholm, and at the State Department.

From 1970 to 1973, Bodde was an international relations officer, then personnel officer, at the State Department. He was political officer in Berlin from 1973 to 1974 and in Bonn from 1974 to 1977. From 1977 to 1978, he was an international relations officer at the State Department.

United States Ambassador to Suriname

Nomination of John J. Crowley, Jr. June 13, 1980

The President today announced that he will nominate John J. Crowley, Jr., of Sutton, W. Va., to be Ambassador Extraordinary and Plenipotentiary of the United States to the Republic of Suriname. He would replace Nancy Ostrander, who has resigned. Crowley has been Deputy Chief of Mission in Caracas since 1977 and a Foreign Service officer since 1955.

He was born February 10, 1928, in Albuquerque, N. Mex. He received an A.B. from West Virginia University in 1949 and an M.A. from Columbia University in 1950. He served in the U.S. Army from 1946 to 1948.

From 1950 to 1952, Crowley was an instructor at the University of Puerto Rico. He was a public affairs assistant with the

International Communication Agency in Maracaibo from 1952 to 1955. He joined the Foreign Service in 1955 and was posted in Lima, Brussels, Quito, and at the State Department.

In 1969–70 Crowley attended the National War College. He was Deputy Chief of Mission in Santo Domingo from 1970 to 1974 and Director of the Office of Northern European Affairs at the State Department from 1974 to 1977.

Agency for International Development

Nomination of Jack Hood Vaughn To Be Assistant Administrator for Latin America and the Caribbean. June 13, 1980

The President today announced that he will nominate Jack Hood Vaughn, of Washington, D.C., to be Assistant Administrator of the Agency for International Development (AID) for Latin America and the Caribbean. He would replace Abelardo Lopez Valdez, who has been appointed Chief of Protocol.

Vaughn has been senior vice president of Pierce International since 1979. He is a former Assistant Secretary of State for Latin America and Peace Corps Director.

He was born August 18, 1920, in Columbus, Mont. He received an A.B. (1943) and M.A. (1947) from the University of Michigan. He served in the U.S. Marine Corps.

Vaughn was director of USIA's Binational Centers in Bolivia and Costa Rica from 1949 to 1952 and was an economist with the AID missions to Panama and Bolivia from 1949 to 1952. He taught economics at Johns Hopkins University from 1958 to 1959 and served as AID's program officer for Europe and Africa in 1959.

In 1959 and 1960, Vaughn was Acting AID Mission Director in Guinea and in 1960 and 1961, he was Mission Director in Senegal and Mauritania. He was Regional Director of the Peace Corps for Latin America from 1961 to 1964 and U.S. Ambassador to Panama from 1964 to 1965. From 1965 to 1966, he was Assistant Secretary of State for Latin America and U.S. Coordinator of the Alliance for Progress.

From 1966 to 1969, Vaughn was Director of the Peace Corps. From 1969 to 1970, he was Ambassador to Colombia. He was president of the National Urban Coalition from 1970 to 1971 and campaign manager of the Harris for President campaign in 1971.

Vaughn was dean of international affairs at Florida International University in 1972. He was director for international development of the Children's Television Workshop from 1972 to 1975, and was responsible for creation of the foreign language versions of "Sesame Street."

From 1975 to 1977, Vaughn was president of Planned Parenthood Foundation—World Population. From 1977 to 1979, he was vice president of Development and Resources Corp.

Vaughn served as chairman of the Inter-American Literacy Foundation from 1971 to 1977.

Alternative Approaches to Regulation

Memorandum From the President.
June 13, 1980

Memorandum for the Heads of Executive Departments and Agencies

Two years ago, I issued Executive Order 12044, "Improving Government Regulations". This Order directed regulatory agencies to find ways to achieve their goals with reduced burden on the private sector. The agencies have developed several new regulatory alternatives that provide flexibility and decentralized decisionmaking. Last year, I asked the Regulatory Council to study these ideas and develop a blueprint for applying them more widely.

The Council's survey of agency experience found eight techniques that show real promise:

- marketable rights;
- economic incentives;
- performance-based standards;
- market-oriented compliance measures;
- reduction of barriers to competition;
- information disclosure;
- voluntary standard setting; and
- adjustment of standards to distinguish among categories of regulated entities ("tiering").

These techniques are not always appropriate. In some cases, only the traditional approach of rigid, detailed "command-and-control" regulation adequately protects public health and safety. Often, however, alternatives that allow flexibility or use market forces can make regulation more cost-effective. Such approaches can cut cost and red tape without sacrificing legitimate regulatory goals. They can also promote innovation, putting private ingenuity to work finding better long-term solutions to regulatory problems.

Each of these alternatives is being used by several agencies and is producing substantial benefits. They are described in greater detail, with specific examples, in the attached summary report by the Council.

I am directing all agencies with regulatory responsibility to review their programs and find areas where these alternatives can be applied. In addition, each agency should expedite the development and implementation of flexible alternatives now under consideration.

The Regulatory Council will report to me on your progress on October 1, 1980. Council Chairman Douglas Costle and his staff will work with you to apply successful alternatives to new regulatory areas. Please designate a contact person for this program and tell the Council who it is.

I know I can count on your personal involvement and support to expand the use of these alternative approaches to regulation.

JIMMY CARTER

NOTE: On the same day, the President issued a similar memorandum to the heads of other Government agencies with regulatory responsibilities. The summary report of the U.S. Regulatory Council was sent with each memorandum.

Digest of Other White House Announcements

The following listing includes the President's public schedule and other items of general interest announced by the White House Press Office and not included elsewhere in this issue.

June 8

The President returned to the White House from Camp David, Md.

June 9

The President met at the White House with:

—Zbigniew Brzezinski, Assistant to the President for National Security Affairs;
—the Congressional Black Caucus;
—Frank B. Moore, Assistant to the President for Congressional Liaison.

June 11

The President met at the White House with:

—Dr. Brzezinski;
—the Democratic congressional leadership;
—Mr. Moore;
—Vice President Walter F. Mondale, Secretary of State Edmund S. Muskie, Stansfield Turner, Director of Central Intelligence, Hamilton Jordan, Assistant to the President, and Dr. Brzezinski;
—Minister of Foreign Affairs Emilio Colombo of Italy;
—Mrs. Richard M. Daley, Illinois State Senator Richard M. Daley, Jr., and members of the Daley family;
—Vice President Mondale.

The President greeted members of the National Rural Electric Cooperative Association's Youth Tour on the South Lawn of the White House.

The White House announced the following personnel changes in the White House staff:

—Hamilton Jordan, Assistant to the President and White House Chief of Staff will become Deputy Chairman of the Carter/Mondale Presidential Committee;
—Jack H. Watson, Jr., Assistant to the President for Intergovernmental Affairs and Secretary to the Cabinet, will become Assistant to the President and White House Chief of Staff;

—Eugene Eidenberg, Deputy Assistant to the President for Intergovernmental Affairs and Deputy Secretary to the Cabinet, will become Assistant to the President for Intergovernmental Affairs and Secretary to the Cabinet.

June 12

The President met at the White House with:

—Dr. Brzezinski;
—members of the Senate Labor and Human Resources Committee;
—Mr. Moore;
—Hedley W. Donovan, Senior Adviser to the President.

June 13

The President met at the White House with:

—Dr. Brzezinski;
—Secretary of Defense Harold Brown, Secretary Muskie, Deputy Secretary of State Warren M. Christopher, Lloyd N. Cutler, Counsel to the President, Mr. Jordan, Mr. Donovan, and Dr. Brzezinski;
—representatives of the American Jewish Press Association (transcript will be printed next week);
—the Regulatory Council.

The President left the White House for a weekend stay at Camp David.

The President declared an emergency for the Commonwealth of Pennsylvania as a result of severe storms and tornadoes, beginning on or about June 3, which caused extensive property damage.

NOMINATIONS SUBMITTED TO THE SENATE

The following list does not include promotions of members of the Uniformed Services, nominations to the Service Academies, or nominations of Foreign Service officers.

NOMINATIONS—Continued

Submitted June 9, 1980

KENNON V. ROTHCHILD, of Minnesota, to be a member of the Board of Directors of the National Corporation for Housing Partnerships for the term expiring October 27, 1982 (reappointment).

Submitted June 10, 1980

PATRICIA PRICE BAILEY, of the District of Columbia, to be a Federal Trade Commissioner for the term of 7 years from September 26, 1980 (reappointment).

LINDSAY D. NORMAN, JR., of Maryland, to be Director of the Bureau of Mines, vice Roger A. Markle, resigned.

Submitted June 11, 1980

JACK R. BORSTING, of California, to be an Assistant Secretary of Defense, vice Fred P. Wacker, resigned.

RICHARD C. ERWIN, of North Carolina, to be United States District Judge for the Middle District of North Carolina, vice a new position created by P.L. 95–486, approved October 20, 1978.

Submitted June 13, 1980

WILLIAM BODDE, JR., of Maryland, a Foreign Service officer of Class three, to be Ambassador Extraordinary and Plenipotentiary of the United States of America to Fiji and to serve concurrently and without additional compensation as Ambassador Extraordinary and Plenipotentiary of the United States of America to the Kingdom of Tonga and to Tuvalu, and as Envoy Extraordinary and Minister Plenipotentiary of the United States of America to the Republic of Kiribati.

JOHN J. CROWLEY, JR., of West Virginia, a Foreign Service officer of Class one, to be Ambassador Extraordinary and Plenipotentiary of the United States of America to the Republic of Suriname.

HUME ALEXANDER HORAN, of New Jersey, a Foreign Service officer of Class one, to be Ambassador Extraordinary and Plenipotentiary of the United States of America to the United Republic of Cameroon, and to serve concurrently and without additional compensation as Ambassador Extraordinary and Plenipotentiary of the United States of America to the Republic of Equatorial Guinea.

NOMINATIONS—Continued

Submitted June 13—Continued

PETER ADAMS SUTHERLAND, of New Hampshire, a Foreign Service officer of Class three, to be Ambassador Extraordinary and Plenipotentiary of the United States of America to the State of Bahrain.

JAMES BERT THOMAS, JR., of Virginia, to be Inspector General, Department of Education (new position).

CHECKLIST OF WHITE HOUSE PRESS RELEASES

The following listing contains releases of the White House Press Office which are not included in this issue.

Released June 9, 1980

Fact sheet: Federal agency consumer programs

Advance text: remarks at the annual convention of the Opportunities Industrialization Centers of America in Miami Beach, Fla.

Released June 10, 1980

Advance text: remarks at the annual conference of the U.S. Conference of Mayors in Seattle, Wash.

Released June 11, 1980

Fact sheet: President's meeting with neighborhood group representatives

CHECKLIST—Continued

Released June 11—Continued

Announcement: nomination of Richard C. Erwin to be United States District Judge for the Middle District of North Carolina

---

ACTS APPROVED BY THE PRESIDENT

Approved June 9, 1980

H.R. 3236_____ Public Law 96–265
Social Security Disability Amendments of 1980.

H.J. Res. 445_____ Public Law 96–266
A joint resolution to provide for designation of the week of September 21–27, 1980, as "National Cystic Fibrosis Week".

H.R. 6727_____ Public Law 96–267
An act to establish the Bon Secour National Wildlife Refuge.

Approved June 13, 1980

S. 1786_____ Public Law 96–268
An act to amend the Act of October 15, 1966 (80 Stat. 953; 20 U.S.C. 65a), relating to the National Museum of the Smithsonian Institution, so as to authorize additional appropriations to the Smithsonian Institution for carrying out the purposes of said Act.

S. 2517_____ Public Law 96–269
An act to rename certain buildings of the Library of Congress.

Interview With the President

*Remarks and a Question-and-Answer Session
With Representatives of the American Jewish
Press Association.   June 13, 1980*

THE PRESIDENT. First of all, let me say
that it's a pleasure to have all of you here
at the White House, both yesterday, to
some degree, and today.

What I'd like to do is what I ordinarily
do with members of editors groups or with
the media, electronic media, and that is
to outline very quickly a few items that
are important to me at this particular
time, and then to receive questions from
you on any subject that you might deem
suitable.

ADMINISTRATION POLICIES AND
ACTIVITIES

I'm preparing and will work this weekend on my briefing papers for the summit
meeting in Venice. I'll make prior to that
an official state visit to Italy, being in
Rome primarily, following which I'll go
to Yugoslavia, then to Spain and Portugal,
and back here.

Yesterday I had press interviews with
the media from both Italy and Yugoslavia
to lay down the basic elements of our bilateral relationship with them. We are
working hard to strengthen the support
for our opposition of the Soviet invasion
of Afghanistan and to strengthen our position on continuing economic sanctions
against Iran until they release the
hostages.

We'll also be dealing primarily at the
summit with economic matters relating to
energy—conservation and the production
of alternate forms of energy—and, in
general, how to deal with inflation and
unemployment and rate of growth of the
economies of the nations involved.

We have, in addition to this, a massive
schedule of legislation in Congress. We
had good results this week in the House
on the fair housing legislation. We won
the first test vote by one vote and had another narrow vote afterwards, but this is
a very important civil rights legislation,
perhaps the most important in the last 10
to 12 years. It'll now go to the Senate for
a decision.

We've also got a budget resolution, the
first budget resolution, agreed to, and we
are approaching the final stages of a comprehensive energy policy which will be a
major step forward in letting our Nation
prevent the rise and fall of our economic
status in an uncontrollable way imposed
on us by OPEC. As you know, I attempted
to impose a conservation fee on gasoline.
It should've been done. We need to set an
example for the American people, for our
allies who are oil consuming nations, and
also for the oil producing nations, that we
will indeed conserve fuel in this country.

We will complete shortly a mechanism
by which we can have a massive effort
made that will stimulate the American
economy and be an exciting thing for the
1980's in producing alternative forms of
energy in this Nation.

I'll be coordinating with Ed Muskie
the preparations for the resumption of the

Mideast peace talks. We will have Foreign Minister Ali and Mr. Burg coming to our country, I believe the first week in July— I think the 2d or 3d; this was still to be confirmed. And we'll be discussing with them in the meantime and with the heads of state involved, how to keep the Camp David process going in an effective fashion. There's no doubt in my mind that both the Israeli and Egyptian people are deeply committed to the peace process.

We are monitoring very closely what is being done by others, notably the European Community, to make sure that they don't do anything that would interfere with or subvert the progress of the Camp David procedure. We will protect the U.N. Security [Council] Resolution 242 with a veto if necessary. We will continue our own deep commitment to the Camp David process, and we've made good progress, I think, lately with the European allies in stopping their previously announced effort, at least by some, to go to the Security Council to change U.N. 242.

The last point I'd like to make is that we face the economic circumstances in this country with concern about the recession and growing unemployment, but with gratitude that we've had such notable success in recent weeks in getting interest rates down. And the inflation rate will come down very rapidly now. This will stimulate consumer spending and, I think, help to rejuvenate the construction industry, particularly home building, automobile purchases, and other items that will use up consumer goods and put our people back to work. It's a long-term possibility for this to be correcting; I don't think there's any doubt about the fact that it will help.

But we will observe very closely the development on this economic scene and,

within the bounds of a strict self-discipline being imposed by the Federal Government, and within the bounds that any action would be noninflationary in nature, we will take action, if necessary, in the future to help with the economy. And we are now protecting and enhancing the job opportunity bills that already are on the books or being considered by the Congress.

I think at this time it might be good to answer questions that you might have, and I'll be looking forward to it.

QUESTIONS

MIDDLE EAST: ISRAELI SETTLEMENTS

Q. I'm Leo Goldberger of The Hebrew Watchman of Memphis, Tennessee. Mr. President, Jordan occupied the West Bank when the armistice was signed following the war of 1948. No nation at that time or for 19 years later called for the autonomy for the Palestinians during that time. In 1967, Israel liberated Judea and Samaria, and the Israel Government started its settlements in that area. My question is, why do you call these settlements illegal, and what court or international body made this ruling on which you base your statement?

THE PRESIDENT. We consider these settlements to be contrary to the Geneva Convention, that occupied territories should not be changed by the establishment of permanent settlements by the occupying power. The ultimate status of the West Bank and Gaza area will be determined in accordance with the agreement reached at Camp David, through negotiations, after the self government is installed in the West Bank and Gaza.

We have long maintained this position under the administration of previous Presidents, back at least 15 years, that the establishment of settlements in that area was contrary to progress toward a comprehensive peace. I discussed this at length, as you can well imagine, with Prime Minister Begin and others in the Israeli Government. They obviously have a difference of opinion. And there's a strong difference of opinion, I might say, within Israel itself, about whether there should be a cessation of the construction of additional settlements until a peace agreement is reached. This is a very disturbing matter for the Egyptians and for others that would have to join in with Israel on a comprehensive peace agreement.

We have not changed the American policy since the time when Arthur Goldberg was our delegate to the United Nations and when U.N. 242 was hammered out. We've repeated this policy on our part. We have encouraged the Israelis to restrain themselves on the establishment of settlements.

I might point out that within the Camp David accords—and I wish all of you would reread the text, because this is the text that we follow meticulously—that was approved by Prime Minister Begin himself, that does call for the establishment of Israeli security posts at agreed locations [1] to make sure that Israel does have adequate protection against any sort of outside invasion, and there can be forward-based troops as determined by Israel and others which would protect Israel in case of an invasion. That's our basic policy. It has not changed for many, many years.

---

[1] The correct quotation is "specified locations." [White House correction.]

MIDDLE EAST: EUROPEAN PROPOSALS FOR PEACE PROCESS

Q. Mr. President, our European allies in a meeting already have taken the position which indicates that the PLO should be made a part of the negotiating process. How would you characterize this action in keeping with your earlier remarks that you would attempt to restrain our allies from taking steps that would be injurious to the Camp David process?

THE PRESIDENT. I haven't seen the text of what the allies have decided. My understanding is that the foreign minister level has recommended to the heads of state a draft proposal. This is a sharp division among the heads of state themselves. It wouldn't be proper for me to reveal what I know about their attitudes. Some of them do not want to refer to the PLO specifically, but just refer to Palestinians or Palestinian Arabs. We have avoided any reference to the PLO as a negotiating partner, but we have referred—in agreement with Prime Minister Begin and President Sadat—we've referred to Palestinians and to Palestinian Arabs.

We will not negotiate with the PLO, and we will not recognize the PLO status until after the PLO recognizes Israel's right to exist and until the PLO also recognizes that U.N. 242—resolution—is a basis for further progress for a comprehensive settlement.

So, whatever the European allies might do about this, our position is clear and as I've just stated to you.

MIDDLE EAST: KING HUSSEIN'S ROLE IN PEACE PROCESS

Q. Mr. President, Doris Sky from the Intermountain Jewish News in Denver. Mr. President, King Hussein will be in

Washington in a few days. Do you feel that at this time he may be ready to assume any active and public role in the Mideast peace process, and can you tell us if and how you plan to encourage him to take a more active role?

THE PRESIDENT. As you know, under the Camp David accords, as signed by all three heads of state, including myself, we call for Jordan to join the Camp David negotiations in two phases: The first phase is the one that's going on now, which would establish the self-governing authority, in effect, and with its very difficult but very important elements. And then following the establishment of that self-governing authority, there would be a period of 5 years under the self-governing authority, during which Israel and Jordan and the Palestinian Arabs who live in the West Bank/Gaza area would join in the negotiations to determine the permanent status of the West Bank and Gaza area.

I will certainly encourage King Hussein to join in these talks as soon as it's possible for him to agree to do so. This has been our position since the Camp David agreement was reached. I can't speak for him. His position has not been one of cooperation on the Camp David accords so far. One of the reasons that he states is that he was not adequately consulted before the terms of the Camp David accords were reached by me and Begin and Sadat and, therefore, this is an imposed agreement demanding that he join the talks when he was not involved in the decision itself.

But this will be the first time I've met personally with King Hussein since Camp David, and I'll use all of the persuasive power that I have to encourage him, within the bounds of his own decisions—of course, he represents an independent nation—to be constructive in bringing about a comprehensive peace. And I'll try to convince him that the best procedure for doing this is in accordance with the Camp David accord itself.

JEWISH EMIGRATION FROM THE SOVIET UNION

Q. Mr. President, the emigration of Jews from the Soviet Union is decreasing rapidly. There are some pessimists that believe that after the Olympics, it will dribble down to practically nothing. Now, in the light of the current status of relations between the United States and the Soviet Union, what leverage does the administration or Congress or anybody in the United States still have on the Soviet Union?

THE PRESIDENT. You know last year, I think, we reached the peak of Jewish emigration from the Soviet Union—about 50,000. So far this year, the early months, that rate has dropped off about 30 percent. It's still quite high compared to previous years, but not high enough. We have made some progress in the reuniting of divided families. This is a more generic concept involving other nationalities and those of other faiths. That's a glimmer of hope.

We have also a possibility and a duty at the Madrid Conference on the Helsinki Agreement, the CSCE conference, to point out any violations of human rights by the Soviet Union, including the restraint of emigration. The divided families being reunited is the triggering language under the Helsinki Agreement to encourage the Soviet Union, and to force them by worldwide public opinion, to permit out-migration of Jews from the Soviet Union.

We provide to the Soviets monthly—annually—and we just did it last month; that's why it's fresh on my mind—a list of all the families that are known to be divided, and this is done and has been done for the last 20 years. We'll continue that. And every time I have ever met with a Soviet leader—the Ambassador here or the Foreign Minister or Brezhnev himself—that has been near the top of our agenda, to encourage the Soviets to permit increased emigration from their country.

We will continue this process through every means of diplomatic persuasion ourselves and to encourage worldwide opinion to focus itself on the Soviet's deprivation of human rights by the restraint of out-migration.

MIDDLE EAST: EUROPEAN INVOLVEMENT IN PEACE PROCESS

Q. Mr. President, at the United Nations, our Representative vetoed once, abstained two times in the past few weeks, on matters relating to Israel and the Middle East. Now, we had in that process complete opposition from the international community, including Scandinavian countries, England, and France. What hope is there of regaining some sort of cooperation from the international community in behalf of a peaceful resolution of the serious issues in the Middle East?

THE PRESIDENT. You've described the situation accurately. The best hope that I can see is demonstrable progress under the Camp David process. One of the reasons why there's such an absence of support for Israel's position is that many of the former friends and allies of Israel don't think that the Camp David talks are going to succeed.

To the extent that we make progress, those European nations—the Scandinavian countries and others—I think will come back to a more balanced approach

to the question. And if we can ever get the Palestinian Arabs and the refugees represented in the talks through the West Bank mayors, the Gaza mayors, and others, I think this will alleviate tension considerably and not only will stop the rash of U.N. resolutions but also will strengthen support for a balanced decision on those matters.

So, I would say that—to answer your question—demonstrated progress on the Camp David accords, which we have reached at Camp David itself and with the Mideast peace talks, is the best solution to the problem.

ALLOCATION OF FUNDS FROM WINDFALL PROFITS TAX

Q. Mr. President?

THE PRESIDENT. Yes, sir?

Q. I'd like to ask you a question. Jimmy Wisch, Texas Jewish Post, Dallas and Fort Worth. The scourge of the Nation, of course, is inflation. We congratulate you on coming in with a balanced budget as of this morning's newspapers. We have a carrying charge of $82 billion on the national debt—the core of inflation. What would be wrong with the philosophy of using our windfall profits gasoline tax, say 50 percent of that, and telling the people at the gasoline pump that we're going to use 50 percent of that tax to go directly to reduce the national debt?

THE PRESIDENT. Well, the Congress, in passing the windfall profits tax, prescribed some guidelines. One of the major elements, the biggest single item to be used by the windfall profits tax, is to reduce taxes on the American people to stimulate growth and to create new jobs and to give a better quality of life in the future.

Another element of that commitment, the second largest, I believe, was to encourage the production of American energy—solar energy, increased exploration for natural gas through so-called unconventional means, the creation of synthetic oil and gas from coal and shale— these kind of things. And, in addition, there was a commitment expressed by Congress, which I share, to give the poorer families in our Nation some relief in heating their homes, in particular from the extremely high cost of energy which, as you know, on an international basis, has more than doubled in the last 12 months.

So, these are the basic thrusts. We have benefited so far and will benefit much more the rest of this year and next year by reduced interest rates. The prime rate, as you know, has been dropping about 1 percent a week for the last 6 weeks or so, and we hope this trend will continue downward to be followed very rapidly by inflation rate.

I don't think it would be possible to take the windfall profits tax specifically to pay off the existing Federal debt at this time. I can't say that that wouldn't be a good goal in the future, but the Congress has already expressed itself in the law on those——

Q. Would you be against that philosophy if it could be passed?

THE PRESIDENT. At this time, I would not put that above the priorities that the Congress has already prescribed—the production of more energy in this country, the helping of the poorer families, and the reduction of taxes. I think the priorities, so far, are proper.

FOREIGN INVESTMENTS IN THE UNITED
STATES

Q. Mr. President, I would like to know why you have not taken a more forceful stand with regard to Arab and other foreign investments in the United States, namely to demand full disclosure so the possible effects and influence on United States business and industry can be assessed?

THE PRESIDENT. Well, there are a couple of reasons. One is you can't single out a particular nationality or religious faith of a business or professional or financial person and say, "You have to disclose your holdings, but no one else does."

Q. How about across the board?

THE PRESIDENT. Well, you know—I think the way you phrased the question, though, you were just talking about Arabs, and I think if the same thing was done against Jews or against blacks or against the Baptists or against other specific groups, it would violate the equality of treatment under the law that's so precious to us.

Secondly, we export from the United States this year about $90 billion in cash money to OPEC nations to buy their oil— a grossly excessive figure. This amounts to about $400 for every person—man, woman, and child—in this Nation, and it would be a devastating blow to us if none of that money came back. As a matter of fact, the Arab countries—well, not just Arab countries but all the OPEC countries; some of them are not Arab as you know, like Venezuela and Nigeria—but the OPEC countries have to have a place to invest that money, and if they invested all of that money in countries other than ourselves, it would be a net drain from our economy of a greatly magnified and very damaging nature.

They do buy U.S. Government bonds, they do invest in American corporate stock, and on occasion, they buy property itself—a very small amount, by the way. The total foreign holdings in agricultural land, for instance, I believe is less than 1 percent. And quite often, an investment in a community by an Arab leader is a highly publicized fact, when a much larger investment by, say, a German corporation or a British or a Japanese corporation is publicized not at all or, if it is publicized, in a favorable light.

So, for those two reasons, that you cannot single out a particular religious faith and have a special law that puts restraints on them to the exclusion of others, and secondly, because we need the exported money to buy foreign oil to be reinvested in our country—those are the two major reasons.

And the third one is what I mention quite often—there is a very high publicized factor in Arab investments. I know that an Arab group here was going to buy, or might buy a bank—they bought one in Atlanta—and it was top headlines in all the newspapers. So, there is an inclination in the American press to publicize those Arab investments much more, I think, than any other nationality or group that I know.

MIDDLE EAST: ISRAELI MILITARY OUT-
POSTS AND CIVILIAN SETTLEMENTS

Q. Mr. President, may I take you back to an earlier statement you made, that military outposts will be, and I quote you correctly, I believe, "to be determined by Israel and others."

THE PRESIDENT. Yes.

Q. Who else, besides Israel, is to determine Israel's security on the West Bank, and the second part of the question is——

THE PRESIDENT. The phrase that's used in the Camp David accord is agreed locations,[2] and the presumption there is that Israel would make proposals about where those outposts were to be made, and if there is a comprehensive settle-

———
[2] The correct quotation is "specified locations." [White House correction.]

ment, the others would be involved. But I would say the primary choice of those outposts would be with Israel.

We discussed at Camp David, along with Mr. Weizman and Dayan and Prime Minister Begin, the possible location of those outposts and the possible level of military forces to be stationed there, but no decision was made. The tentative places and figures put forward by the military leaders seem to be generally acceptable. If Israel proposed a location or a series of locations that was not acceptable, then Israel would not have to agree to the overall settlement.

So, I would say that the basic presumption would be that Israel would make their choices, and the basic presumption is that within the framework of a comprehensive settlement—to be decided by Jordan and the Palestinian Arabs and others—that those choices would be approved, but nobody can take that away from Israel as the prime one.

Q. May I follow up on that, Mr. President, please? It could be possible, of course, and it has been the practice of Israeli governments, present and past, to establish settlements on the West Bank for security purposes.

THE PRESIDENT. I know that.

Q. And a civilian settlement could be for security, as well as a military-manned outpost.

THE PRESIDENT. Yes.

Q. Therefore, isn't it possible and legal, even under the Geneva Convention—and Israelis, many of them, think that the opposition to settlements is a political issue and not a legal issue—but apart from that, since a civilian settlement also could be considered military, would you then agree that it is worthwhile for Israel to establish settlements on the West Bank for defensive purposes?

THE PRESIDENT. In my opinion, the establishment of additional Israeli settlements on the West Bank is not necessary. It is an obstacle to peace, because it creates very serious problems in reaching a comprehensive agreement. In my opinion, the Camp David accords, signed by Prime Minister Begin and President Sadat and myself, prescribe an adequate commitment to Israel's security; that is, that the military government will be withdrawn and that security posts at agreed locations will be established.

We have not demanded from Israel that any settlements be dismantled. We have requested from Prime Minister Begin and others that the establishment of new settlements be ceased until after an agreement could be reached, in order to expedite the process. Israel disagrees. Their Government makes the decision, and they have so far carried those decisions out. What Prime Minister Begin has described to me is an extension of existing settlements, and he did agree to a temporary moratorium or delay in the establishment of new settlements after Camp David.

So, I would not be willing to endorse the concept of establishing civilian settlements on the West Bank, but I do endorse the concept that Jews should have a right to live where they choose and Jews should have a right to leave a place of their choosing.

The thing that is troubling about the establishment of settlements under the aegis and with the sponsorship and sometimes the financing of the Israeli Government is that it indicates to the Palestinian Arabs, to the Egyptians, and to others, that Israel will not carry out the principles of the Camp David accord in withdrawing their government, military government, and establishing the security

outposts. This is a long-time position of the United States. It's one that has been discussed clearly with Prime Minister Begin, and it does not mean at all that we oppose Jews living where they choose, including on the West Bank.

Ms. BARIO.[3] Thank you, Mr. President.

THE PRESIDENT. Just one more. I'll take one more.

Q. Mr. President, let me make one comment. I think the Camp David agreement talks about specified locations, not agreed locations. That was a clear difference that the Israelis had requested to make—at least from the Israeli point of view—clear that they were the ones that would specify the locations—there wouldn't be an agreement necessary.

THE PRESIDENT. You may be right. I'll let somebody bring the text back to you in just a few minutes and read it to you.

I need to go, but I would like to meet every one of you personally and thank you for coming and maybe get a quick photograph if you have no objections.

NOTE: The interview began at 11:30 a.m. in the Cabinet Room at the White House. The transcript of the interview was released on June 14.

50th Anniversary of the Veterans Administration
Proclamation 4763.   June 16, 1980

By the President of the United States of America

A Proclamation

Fifty years ago, on July 21, 1930, President Herbert Hoover established the Veterans Administration, fulfilling the

_____
[3] Patricia Y. Bario, Deputy Press Secretary.

words of Abraham Lincoln that our great Nation would "care for him who had borne the battle, and for his widow and orphan."

The world has seen much turbulence and suffering since that day, and American families have all touched in some sense the tragedy of war. Throughout this period, the Veterans Administration has set a standard of care and compassion.

On this 50th anniversary of the Veterans Administration, Americans take pride in having led the world in healing the physical and social wounds of war. Our system of assistance and care for veterans is the most comprehensive in the world. In medicine, the Veterans Administration has been a leader in innovation, research, and the quality of care. Its staff includes Nobel Prize winners and other men and women of international renown. Millions of Americans have been helped by Veterans Administration benefits and services, and protected by Veterans Administration life insurance. Veterans loan guarantees have made home ownership possible for tens of thousands of families, and GI Bill education has transformed the social fabric of America. These efforts express our appreciation and commitment to those who have sacrificed for our country and to the families of those who gave their lives in its service.

Now, THEREFORE, I, JIMMY CARTER, President of the United States of America, do hereby proclaim July 21, 1980, as Veterans Administration 50th Anniversary Day, and call upon State and local officials and all Americans to observe this day with appropriate activities.

IN WITNESS WHEREOF, I have hereunto set my hand this sixteenth day of June, in the year of our Lord nineteen hundred eighty, and of the Independence of the United States of America the two hundred and fourth.

JIMMY CARTER

[Filed with the Office of the Federal Register, 3:05 p.m., June 16, 1980]

Visit of King Hussein of Jordan

Remarks at the Welcoming Ceremony.
June 17, 1980

THE PRESIDENT. This morning it's my very pleasant duty, on behalf of the people of the United States, to welcome Their Majesties King Hussein of the Hashemite Kingdom of Jordan and Her Majesty Queen Noor.

There is a great deal in common between our two people, the Kingdom of Jordan and the United States of America: ties of friendship; the deep roots of shared experience; long years of consultation and cooperation, a cooperation based on mutual interest, which we both recognize, and on beliefs in the same basic principles and a foundation of mutual respect, one for another. This friendship, this relationship, has been tested in crisis, and it has stood all tests without damage.

We know that our people want the same things: peace, peace through strength; dignity of individual human beings; proper attention to human rights and the nurturing of the talent and ability of each person; economic progress; taking advantage of technological improvements in the world around us; and at the same time the preservation of the principles which never change. As is the case between independent nations, there are sometimes some differences of approach about how to deal with current crises, but we have always let these differences be properly aired. And as I've said earlier, they have never damaged the basic mutual commitment and the basic relationship which binds our two countries together.

We recognize that the Middle East, the cradle of recorded human history, has been torn and is torn now by tension, by an absence of understanding and trust, inadequate communications, turmoil, sometimes suffering from war too often, and also the threat of terrorism. We know that we must end these threats to peace and alleviate this tension and end the threat of terrorism and bloodshed. The conflict which has torn this region can be settled and must be settled with dignity and with justice. We share this commitment, and we share this belief, and we share these mutual goals, because we recognize the tremendous benefits, not only to the people of that region but to the people of almost every nation on Earth, to bring about peace and stability in this troubled land.

It is not an easy thing to accomplish. There are doubts about the prospects for peace, and there are differences about the route to take to achieve peace. His Majesty has shown in his enlightened rule over courageous people his commitment to progress, to economic development, to a better life for those who look to him for leadership. And at the same time he's been able to preserve, in the finest possible way, the traditional values of his people, of their religion, of their history, which never change.

We have the same basic challenge: to approach the future with confidence; to accommodate inevitable change; to provide better economic and other opportunities for our people, but to preserve basic values.

This year we join in the observation of the 14th centennial of the world of Islam, for the spiritual and intellectual and moral contributions of these worldwide worshipers mean so much to us all. It's an honor for us to participate in a proper way in this notable observance.

We are also mutually committed to the stability of the Persian Gulf region and to Southwest Asia, the preservation of peace, the honoring of international boundaries, the cohesion of nations, independence of people, and the preservation of their security. The search for peace is filled with difficulty and complexity, but there is no doubt that it's worthy of the most persistent and notable effort. It's vital for the future of all.

With these observations of our common commitments, it's an additional pleasure for me to welcome again Their Majesties representing the Hashemite Kingdom of Jordan. This is an honor for us and a pleasure on this beautiful day in the lives of two peoples bound together by so many common commitments, principles, ideals, and hope for the future.

Your Majesty, you're welcome.

THE KING. Mr. President, both Queen Noor and I feel happiness and pleasure at having this opportunity to visit the United States and to be with you here today, sir. We thank you and Mrs. Carter for making it possible for us to accept your kind invitation, to be amongst friends, to be once again in the United States.

Indeed it has been a march throughout the years by our peoples in many fields and in many areas with their dedication to the same aims and objectives, their following of the same principles and values and their sharing of a common vision of a better future—a future with dignity for mankind; a future of peace with justice; a future that will give the generations that follow us better opportunities, better times than those we have had to endure.

There is much indeed, sir, that we share. And regardless of the differences in terms of outlook regarding the route, as you say, to achieve an objective or to reach a goal, we do believe very much in the firm commitment of both our governments and peoples and ourselves to the same goals and the same objectives. Our world is facing enormous difficulties at this point in time. It's a privilege and a very, very great pleasure for me to have this opportunity to benefit from your wisdom, to convey to you our impressions, to share with you thoughts and ideas regarding the times ahead and the responsibilities that we bear towards the future.

I look forward to my meetings with you, sir, and with our friends here. And, once again, I, my government and people are proud that we have always adhered to the same principles, we've always upheld the same ideals on which this Nation, the greatest in our times, was created and stands for.

Thank you very, very much indeed, sir, for your courtesy and your kindness.

NOTE: The President spoke at 10:12 a.m. on the South Lawn of the White House.

Visit of King Hussein of Jordan

Statement by the White House Press Secretary. June 17, 1980

Let me begin with a few brief comments on the meeting between President Carter and King Hussein this morning.

They met this morning for about 2 hours, with advisers on both sides. A list of the participants will be posted at the conclusion of this briefing. They began their talks with a strategic overview of the entire area: the consequences for regional security of the Soviet invasion of Afghanistan; the situation in Iran, the Arabian Peninsula and the gulf, and Lebanon, as well as the West Bank.

Each leader discussed the measures that his government is taking to achieve the common objective of helping to preserve the stability and independence of states in the area. They also shared their analyses of current efforts to achieve a negotiated settlement of the Arab-Israeli conflict. They agreed—as was apparent from their statements at the arrival ceremonies this morning—that the objective of both countries is a comprehensive peace.

Their discussions, as you know, will continue tomorrow morning, and the King will be meeting with Secretary Muskie tomorrow as well.

Let me say in characterization that it is the view of the President that these discussions were both very frank and extremely cordial and constructive.

NOTE: Press Secretary Jody Powell read the statement at 1:35 p.m. at his regular briefing for reporters in the Briefing Room at the White House.

Participants in the bilateral meeting included:

American side

PRESIDENT JIMMY CARTER
SECRETARY OF STATE EDMUND S. MUSKIE
ZBIGNIEW BRZEZINSKI, Assistant to the President for National Security Affairs
AMBASSADOR NICHOLAS VELIOTIS, U.S. Ambassador to Jordan
AMBASSADOR SOL LINOWITZ, Personal Representative of the President for Middle East Peace Negotiations
HAROLD SAUNDERS, Assistant Secretary of State for Near Eastern and South Asian Affairs
ROBERT HUNTER, National Security Council staff member

Jordanian side

HIS MAJESTY HUSSEIN I, King of the Hashemite Kingdom of Jordan

HIS EXCELLENCY 'ABD AL-HAMID SHARAF, Prime Minister and Minister of Foreign Affairs of the Hashemite Kingdom of Jordan

HIS EXCELLENCY AHMAD LAWZI, Chief of Royal Court

LT. GEN. AMER KHAMMASH (Ret.), Minister of Court

LT. GEN. SHARIF ZAID BIN SHAKER, Commander in Chief of the Jordan Armed Forces

HIS EXCELLENCY FAWAZ SHARAF, Ambassador of the Hashemite Kingdom of Jordan to the United States

Adoption Assistance and Child Welfare Act of 1980

Statement on Signing H.R. 3434 Into Law. June 17, 1980

It is with great pleasure that I sign into law today H.R. 3434, the Adoption Assistance and Child Welfare Act of 1980. This legislation is the product of more than 3 years of cooperative effort by the administration and Congress. It makes great improvements in Title XX, the basic Federal social services program. It reforms our current crisis-ridden foster care program, creates a Federal adoption assistance program for children with special needs, and reinforces the child welfare services program.

The sad statistics underlying the need for this legislation are all too compelling— more than 500,000 children across the country are in foster care. Although foster care placements are supposed to be temporary, almost half of these children have been away from their families for longer than 2 years, and about 100,000 have spent more than 6 years of their young lives in foster care. Almost one-fourth of these children are awaiting adoption, yet no adoptive homes have been found for them, and the services and assistance these young people need have not been available.

This legislation holds the promise of dramatically improving the lives of these children and their families. By authorizing funding for services designed to prevent family breakup, we are placing a firm emphasis on helping families keep their children at home. By encouraging States to provide services designed to return children to their families where possible or to place them in permanent family-like settings, we are responding to the need for permanence and stability in children's lives.

H.R. 3434 provides important protections for children and their families, designed to ensure that children are not "lost" in foster care. It creates a new Federal adoption assistance program to build on the leadership and hard work of the States, and it authorizes additional incentive funds to assist States in providing services badly needed by children and their families.

I believe this legislation represents an important initiative in Federal policy. This legislation would not have succeeded on its long and often rocky road to enactment if not for the persistent and dedicated efforts of several Members of Congress: Representative George Miller, who began looking into the foster care system 5 years ago; Representatives Jim Corman and Bill Brodhead, who shepherded the bill through the Ways and Means Committee; and Senators Russell Long, Daniel Moynihan, and Alan Cranston, whose cooperation and legislative acumen made passage possible.

NOTE: As enacted, H.R. 3434 is Public Law 96–272, approved June 17.

Independence Day, 1980
Message of the President. June 17, 1980

Across the United States on Independence Day our citizens join in celebration of the freedoms we cherish, in thanksgiving for the blessings bestowed on us and in prayerful remembrance of those who do not share in our good fortune.

Rosalynn and I will be there in spirit with all our patriotic and proud fellow Americans who take part in the many commemorative events this historic day inspires.

We join you in a rededication to this nation's unbending commitment to human rights for all and in a reaffirmation of our nation's founding principles. We hope that each of the special programs and activities that mark this occasion will be inspiring, memorable and enjoyable.

JIMMY CARTER

Equal Employment Opportunity Commission
Nomination of Ethel Bent Walsh To Be a Member. June 17, 1980

The President today announced that he will nominate Ethel Bent Walsh, of Washington, D.C., for reappointment as a member of the Equal Employment Opportunity Commission. Walsh has been a member of the EEOC since 1971.

She was previously Director of Advisory Councils for the Small Business Administration and has over 20 years of business experience.

National Mediation Board
Nomination of Robert O. Harris To Be a Member. June 17, 1980

The President today announced that he will nominate Robert O. Harris, of Washington, D.C., for reappointment as a member of the National Mediation Board. Harris has been a member of the Board since 1977 and Chairman since 1979.

Visit of King Hussein of Jordan
Toasts at the State Dinner. June 17, 1980

THE PRESIDENT. A lot of people have accused me of inviting Their Majesties to Washington just so we could have Queen Noor visit the White House. [*Laughter*] That's not entirely accurate, because there are many reasons why we should want His Majesty, King Hussein, to come back to visit with us, as well as his beautiful bride and the new mother of his new child, to come with her parents and her brothers and sisters and to be with us this evening. It's a delightful experience for us, and her presence vividly demonstrates the close relationship and the unbreakable ties between our two countries.

The first time that King Hussein came to visit a President of the United States was in 1960, when President Eisenhower lived in this home. And he's been here many times since, a great leader, one who represents accurately the courage and the dynamism and the commitment and the progress of the people of Jordan.

He has led his nation over more than a quarter of a century, in good times and in dangerous times, in successful times and in disappointing times, but always with a deep commitment to what's best for his own people and the preservation of stability and peace and the honoring of human rights not only in Jordan but throughout the Middle East.

He's indeed been an inspiration to many people who have served as the leaders of other nations. This is a troubled time in the history of the world, and to have a leader like him, still young, but with deep experience, reaching out his hand of friendship and peace to those neighbors of Jordan who look to him with confidence and with admiration, is reassuring to us all.

We share a great deal in common—a commitment to the integrity of international boundaries; a commitment to the unity of nations in the Middle East, to the preservation of peace, to the security of all, and to the enhancement of those principles which guide human beings and which never change. But, at the same time, he has exhibited to a remarkable degree an ability to ensure economic progress and utilization of modern science and technology to give his people a better life.

King Hussein is a good counselor and adviser for other leaders of nations who meet with him. And although sometimes our two nations do disagree on the technique for achieving a goal, we share completely a common commitment to the same goals—to the realization of the full rights of the Palestinian people, to the security of Israel and all the nations in the Middle East, to the honoring of deep religious feelings, and to the knowledge that

people of good will ultimately, with courage and with perseverance, sometimes with patience, can triumph.

We have had good discussions so far today—much better than would have been expected—because of his frankness and because of his generosity, his eagerness to understand different points of view without yielding at all on the deep principles which have guided his life and which he holds so dear. We have expressed our concern about aggression demonstrated by the Soviets' invasion of Afghanistan. We've expressed our concern about international terrorism, exhibited in Iran with the unwarranted holding of innocent Americans hostage for many months, and we've expressed our commitment to stability in the Persian Gulf region and to peace in the Middle East.

I would like to say in closing that because of his own leadership and because of geographical circumstances of his own nation, Jordan will indeed play a central role in the realization of the hopes and dreams of all who want peace and stability and freedom and security in the Middle East.

At this time, I would like to propose a toast, if you will stand and join me. To Their Majesties, King Hussein and Queen Noor, to the friendship which binds our two nations and our two people together, and to the commitment to peace and the enhancement of human rights and a better life for all those of faith and good will everywhere throughout the world.

THE KING. *Mr. President, Mrs. Carter, ladies and gentlemen, my good friends:*

I'd like to thank you, sir, for your kind and warm words of friendship towards both Noor and I, towards a friendship that I value, towards the ties and relations that have grown between our two nations over many years, and through good and difficult times, the ties that we treasure, for the fact that there are links of people who uphold the same ideals and principles and are dedicated towards fulfilling the same objectives for a better tomorrow which, hopefully, will bring a preservation of dignity to human beings, peace, justice, and a better life.

It's true, sir, I have had the privilege of visiting the United States over many years. I'm a firm believer and have always been dedicated to the cause of friendship between our people, a better understanding, and I'm proud to have been able to serve this objective and will continue to do so to the end of my days.

Throughout these many years and many occasions, I've had the privilege of meeting with leaders of this great Nation. I said it today, and I've said it often: throughout all these meetings, none gave me more of his time to discuss the problems of our part of the world and indicated as much of an interest in the problems that we face in the area from which I came and the determination to contribute towards solutions to those problems as have your good selves.

It is true that we may have differences in approach, but we respect your dedication to the cause of peace in our part of the world. It's a dedication that we share. We look into the future with hope, with determination, to contribute our full share for the establishment of a just and durable peace in the Middle East which will affect not only those who live there but future generations there and elsewhere in the world.

We thank you for the opportunity to be with you, to have this opportunity to discuss our problems, to discuss all matters as friends, as brethren, and I'm convinced that this opportunity will enable us to address ourselves more adequately to the challenge in the times to come. We have been overwhelmed by the kindness and warmth with which we have been received once again, almost at home and amongst friends.

Thank you very much, sir, from both Noor, myself, and all who accompanied me from Jordan on this visit to the United States. May God bless you; may your efforts always meet with success in the times to come. Thank you, Mr. Carter.

Ladies and gentlemen, please, I call upon you to rise and join me in drinking a toast to the President and Mrs. Carter, to the United States, to friendship and fruitful cooperation in serving our mutual and common objectives. To peace and a better future.

THE PRESIDENT. Thank you very much.

NOTE: The President spoke at 8:08 p.m. in the State Dining Room at the White House.

President's Committee on the International Labor Organization

Executive Order 12216.   June 18, 1980

By the authority vested in me as President by the Constitution and statutes of the United States of America, and in order to create in accordance with the Federal Advisory Committee Act (5 U.S.C. App. I) an advisory committee on United States participation in the International Labor Organization, it is hereby ordered as follows:

1–1. *Establishment of Committee.*

1–101. There is established the President's Committee on the International Labor Organization (ILO). The members will be the Secretaries of Labor, State, and Commerce, the Assistant to the

President for National Security Affairs, and the Presidents of the AFL–CIO and the United States Council of the International Chamber of Commerce, or their designated representatives.

1–102. The Chairman of the Committee shall be the Secretary of Labor. The Committee shall meet at the request of the Chairman.

1–2. *Functions of the Committee.*

1–201. The Committee shall monitor and assess the work of the ILO.

1–202. The Committee shall make recommendations to the President or other officers of the Federal government, including the Secretary of Labor. With due recognition that in the ILO tripartite system, government, employer, and employee representatives retain the right to take positions independent of one another, the Committee shall exert its best efforts to develop a coordinated position as to United States policy on ILO issues.

1–203. The Committee shall also perform other functions relevant to relations with the ILO as requested by the President or the Committee Chairman.

1–3. *Funding and Expenses.*

1–301. Each member of the Committee who is not otherwise employed full-time by the Federal government may receive, to the extent permitted by law, compensation for each day he is engaged in the work of the Committee at a rate not to exceed the maximum daily rate now or hereafter prescribed by law, and may also receive transportation and travel expenses, including per diem in lieu of subsistence, as authorized by law (5 U.S.C. 5702 and 5703).

1–302. The Chairman of the Committee is authorized to establish such addi-tional advisory committees as may be deemed appropriate to carry out the purposes of this Order.

1–303. All necessary administrative staff services, support, facilities and expenses of the Committee shall be furnished by the Department of Labor to the extent permitted by law.

1–4. *General Provisions.*

1–401. Notwithstanding the provisions of any other Executive order, the functions of the President applicable to the Committee under the Federal Advisory Committee Act, as amended (5 U.S.C. App. I), except that of reporting annually to the Congress, are hereby delegated to the Secretary of Labor, who shall perform them in accordance with guidelines and procedures established by the Administrator of General Services.

1–402. The Committee shall terminate on December 31, 1980, unless this date is extended by further Executive order.

JIMMY CARTER

The White House,
June 18, 1980.

[Filed with the Office of the Federal Register, 3:15 p.m., June 18, 1980]

Budget Deferrals

Message to the Congress. June 18, 1980

To the Congress of the United States:

In accordance with the Impoundment Control Act of 1974, I herewith report two new deferrals of budget authority totalling $166.4 million and one revision to a previously transmitted deferral increasing the amount deferred by $20.6 million. These items affect programs in the Departments of Agriculture, Defense, and Transportation.

The details of the deferrals are contained in the attached reports.

JIMMY CARTER

The White House,
June 18, 1980.

NOTE: The attachments detailing the deferrals are printed in the FEDERAL REGISTER of June 20, 1980.

Department of the Interior

Nomination of Thomas W. Fredericks To Be an Assistant Secretary.   *June 18, 1980*

The President today announced that he will nominate Thomas W. Fredericks, of Boulder, Colo., to be Assistant Secretary of the Interior for Indian Affairs. He would replace Forrest J. Gerard, who has resigned.

Fredericks has been chief executive officer and a practicing attorney with the Boulder firm of Thomas W. Fredericks & Associates since 1979.

He was born March 9, 1943, in Elbowoods, N. Dak. He received a B.S. from Minot State College in 1965 and a J.D. from the University of Colorado School of Law in 1972.

From 1965 to 1966, Fredericks was a high school mathematics and physical education teacher. In 1970 he was organizer and part owner of the Native American Technical Assistance Corp., a management consulting firm. From 1972 to 1977, he was director of the Native American Rights Fund and from 1977 to 1979, he was Associate Solicitor for Indian Affairs at the Interior Department.

Fredericks is former president of the American Indian Lawyers Association.

Visit of King Hussein of Jordan

*Remarks Following a Meeting.
June 18, 1980*

THE PRESIDENT. I'd like to say this morning, after the discussion with His Majesty King Hussein and his advisers, that the talks have indeed been very fruitful. We've explored the common basis on which we will cooperate in the future, as we have in the past. We've had thorough discussions of what might be done to alleviate tensions in the Middle East and to deal with the threats to stability and security in the Persian Gulf and Southwest Asia regions. We've talked about the possibility of economic progress in the region, both before and after a full and comprehensive and just peace is realized.

His Majesty knows that the United States and Israel and Egypt are all determined to proceed with the Camp David process. We believe it has the best chance for success. His Majesty has expressed on many occasions his concern about the limitations of the Camp David process, and we've not tried to change each other's minds about the approach or the technique or the procedure to be used. But we do agree completely with the ultimate goals, that is, the solution of the Palestinian question in all its aspects, the right of the Palestinians to have a voice in the determination of their own future, the security of Israel, and a comprehensive and just peace for the region. So, in almost every instance our ultimate goals are parallel or the same, and we have explored ways to resolve the differences in our approach to the technique or the procedure to be used in reaching those goals.

I'm very deeply grateful for the visit by King Hussein to our country again. And the outpouring of affection that has been evidenced among the Americans who have welcomed him is indicative again of the high esteem in which he's held personally and of the strength of the friendships that bind our two nations and our two people together.

King Hussein, welcome again. And I'm very grateful to you for the progress that we've made and for your advice and counsel, which will be very beneficial to me in the future.

THE KING. Mr. President, I'd like to thank you once again, sir, for giving me this opportunity to visit with you; to have extremely fruitful and comprehensive talks on all matters of mutual interest regarding the problems within our area and within the world as a whole, and ways and means of closer cooperation, with some better understanding of our respective positions; to make our contributions, to overcome difficulties, and to make progress towards dear objectives. I've had the opportunity once again to express my feelings and the feelings of my countrymen of determination to see the friendship that has existed between our two countries hopefully grow stronger in all fields and areas, the feelings that these contacts between us are important and necessary and are of great benefit during these times and in the face of the challenge before us.

We understand better the United States position. We've had the chance and opportunity to bring to you and our friends in the United States our feelings that a just and comprehensive peace must come in the area. We will do all we can towards that end, but it can only come as a result of a solution to the Palestinian problem, which would give the people of Palestine their legitimate rights on their soil, rights of self-determination, rights to express themselves and forge their future, with all confidence that their desire and yearning is for peace, a life of dignity and peace and security. And in the area of security, what we seek once peace is established, a just peace, a lasting peace, a security for all, all there now, in the near future, and in the future in the broadest sense.

The challenge is there, the objectives are clear, we will do all we can, and hopefully we will respond to what is within us in the way of genuine and sincere feelings and the drive that is there and which is shared by the rest of the world and the world community as well.

I thank you very much indeed, sir, for all your kindness, for the warm reception—it's made us feel at home and amongst friends once again—for the privilege of being with you. And I look forward to the great pleasure of continuing our contacts and, hopefully, fruitful cooperation to serve our common objectives.

Thank you, sir, very, very much.

THE PRESIDENT. Thank you, Your Majesty.

NOTE: The President spoke at 12:13 p.m. on the South Grounds of the White House.

Visit of King Hussein of Jordan

Statement by the White House Press Secretary. June 18, 1980

The President and His Majesty met with their advisers this morning in the Cabinet Room for about 1 hour and 45 minutes to continue the discussions which they began yesterday. The participants in the second meeting were the same as we posted for the first meeting.

They had a useful and constructive exchange which showed similar perspectives on overall regional security questions.

On the Middle East peace process, they made progress in understanding each other's approaches to the problems of the region. The talks provided a good basis for working together in the future toward their common goal of a comprehensive peace in the Middle East.

NOTE: Press Secretary Jody Powell read the statement at 3:32 p.m. at his regular briefing for reporters in the Briefing Room at the White House.

National Athletic Boosters Week
Proclamation 4764. June 18, 1980

By the President of the United States of America

A Proclamation

The young people of America are one of our greatest natural resources, and their health and well-being are vital to the health and well-being of the Nation. The thousands of youth athletic programs run by communities, schools, and private groups all across this country promote physical fitness among our youth—and more. They also give the young people of this country invaluable training in sportsmanship, fair play, and team effort. They are the training ground for those who will eventually replace us—and surpass us.

Youth athletic programs are heavily dependent on voluntary contributions of funds and services from individuals. Thanks to the generosity of Americans throughout the United States, these programs continue to succeed in their crucial task. Such volunteers are a credit to their communities and to the Nation.

The Congress, by House Joint Resolution 442, has requested the President to proclaim the week beginning June 22, 1980, as National Athletic Boosters Week.

Now, THEREFORE, I, JIMMY CARTER, President of the United States of Amer-

ica, do hereby proclaim the week beginning June 22, 1980, as National Athletic Boosters Week, and I call upon the people of the United States to observe it with appropriate ceremonies and activities.

IN WITNESS WHEREOF, I have hereunto set my hand this eighteenth day of June, in the year of our Lord nineteen hundred and eighty, and of the Independence of the United States of America the two hundred and fourth.

JIMMY CARTER

[Filed with the Office of the Federal Register, 11:06 a.m., June 19, 1980]

Federal Compliance With Fuel Use Prohibitions
Executive Order 12217. June 18, 1980

By the authority vested in me as President by the Constitution and statutes of the United States of America, including Section 403(a) of the Powerplant and Industrial Fuel Use Act of 1978 (92 Stat. 3317; Public Law 95–620) and Section 301 of Title 3 of the United States Code, and to ensure Federal compliance with applicable requirements governing the construction or conversion of powerplants and major fuel-burning installations, it is hereby ordered as follows:

1-1. *Applicability of Fuel Use Requirements.*

1-101. The head of each Executive agency is responsible for compliance with applicable fuel use prohibitions established pursuant to, but not limited to, the following:

(a) Title II of the Powerplant and Industrial Fuel Use Act of 1978, with respect to new facilities.

(b) Title III of the Powerplant and Industrial Fuel Use Act of 1978, with respect to existing facilities.

1–102. The head of each Executive agency is also responsible for compliance with applicable pollution control standards, in accord with:

(a) Subtitle G of Title VII of the Powerplant and Industrial Fuel Use Act of 1978.

(b) Executive Order No. 12088 of October 13, 1978.

1–2. *Agency Coordination.*

1–201. Each Executive agency shall cooperate with the Secretary of Energy, hereinafter referred to as the Secretary, in the achievement of the requirements of the Powerplant and Industrial Fuel Use Act of 1978.

1–202. Each Executive agency shall consult with the Secretary concerning plans for the construction or conversion of electric powerplants and major fuel-burning installations.

1–203. The Secretary shall provide advice and assistance to Executive agencies in order to ensure their cost effective and timely compliance with applicable fuel use prohibitions.

1–3. *Fuel Use Conversion.*

1–301. Each Executive agency shall survey its electric powerplants and major fuel-burning installations in order to identify those subject to the Act and shall transmit the results of the survey to the Secretary. The Secretary shall establish guidelines for accomplishing the survey.

1–302. (a) Each Executive agency shall submit to the Director of the Office of Management and Budget, through the Secretary, an annual plan, including cost estimates, for the fuel use conversion of electric powerplants and major fuel-burning installations.

(b) The plan shall identify all powerplants and major fuel-burning installations which are subject to the fuel use prohibitions of the Powerplant and Industrial Fuel Use Act of 1978.

(c) The Secretary shall establish guidelines for developing such plans.

1–303. In preparing its plan, each Executive agency shall ensure that the plan provides for compliance with all applicable fuel use prohibitions.

1–304. The plan shall be submitted in accordance with any other instructions that the Director of the Office of Management and Budget may issue.

1–4. *Funding.*

1–401. The head of each Executive agency shall ensure that funds for compliance with applicable fuel use prohibitions are requested in the agency budget.

1–402. The head of each Executive agency shall ensure that funds appropriated and apportioned for the fuel use conversion of electric powerplants and major fuel-burning installations are not used for any other purpose unless permitted by law and specifically approved by the Office of Management and Budget.

1–5. *General Provisions.*

1–501. Exemptions from applicable fuel use prohibitions may only be granted under the provisions of the Powerplant and Industrial Fuel Use Act of 1978.

1–502. The Secretary of Energy shall prepare for the President's consideration and transmittal to the Congress the report required by Section 403(c) of the Act.

JIMMY CARTER

The White House,
June 18, 1980.

[Filed with the Office of the Federal Register,
11:07 a.m., June 19, 1980]

Equal Rights Amendment

Remarks at a Fundraising Dinner.
June 18, 1980

It's always a disappointment to an audience when anyone replaces Liz Carpenter at the microphone.[1] [*Laughter*]

I thought a lot about what I would say tonight. You know the statistics. You know the issue. But I thought that it would be good to put this challenge that we face in perspective maybe from a human point of view, a personal point of view.

In 1966 I gave up a seat in the Georgia Senate and ran for Governor. No one knew who I was when I began. I spent all the money I had. I borrowed more than I could afford. I lost 22 pounds. I missed making the runoff for Governor by 21,000 votes. It was a disappointment, I admit, but the morning after the 1966 election I met with a very small group of folks, and they asked me what I was going to do for the next 4 years. I said "I'm going to run for Governor." And in 1970 I was elected. I did not intend to lose.

In 1947 we had our first child, a son, who was born in Virginia. We wanted very much for the next child to be a daughter. But in 1950, in Hawaii, Chip was born, and we wanted very much for the next child to be a daughter. [*Laughter*] In 1952 Jeffery was born. It was a disappointment, I admit. That was in 1952. And 1955 went by and 1960 went by and 1965 went by. And finally came 1967, and the entire family burst into tears when Rosalynn announced—the doctor let her do it—that we finally had a daughter: Amy. We had some disappointments on the way, but we did not intend to lose.

---

[1] The President was introduced by ERA supporter and Assistant Secretary of Education for Public Affairs Elizabeth S. Carpenter.

In 1974 I announced that I was going to run for President. I invited some major political reporters down to Plains and to Atlanta to talk to me, and I made what I considered to be a major address to the Nation at the National Press Club. A few days later they had the miniconvention in Kansas City, December 3, 1974. I waited eagerly for the Gallup poll to come out. They had 36 names in the Gallup poll: more than a dozen Senators, several Members of the House, several Governors, Julian Bond, Ralph Nader, Benjamin Spock. [*Laughter*] They didn't have Jimmy Carter on the list. But less than 2 years later I was elected President. It was a difficult struggle, but I did not intend to lose.

Not too many months after that, we faced the prospect of continued war in the Middle East—in 30 years, four wars, thousands of young people killed on both sides, atmosphere filled with hatred. International borders were an insurmountable obstacle to communication and to peace. We went to Camp David—myself, President Sadat, Prime Minister Begin. After the first 3 days they did not speak to each other. For 10 solid days neither Begin nor Sadat talked to one another at all about the peace agreement.

Sunday morning we thought we had failed. It was a major disappointment. But Sunday afternoon we signed the Camp David accords, and not many months after, the peace treaty between Israel and the major Arab country. It was a disappointment along the way, but we did not intend to lose.

This afternoon in Illinois there was a vote, 102 to 71, a major majority: ERA was not ratified by the Illinois legislature, a major disappointment. But we do not intend to lose.

The history of our Nation is filled with personal reminiscences. Every one of you here could list things in your own life where you had a major goal or a major aspiration or a major hope or a yearning deep in your heart for something you thought was important—with obstacles and disappointments all along the way, plenty of chance to be discouraged, plenty of chance to blame others for a failure, plenty of chance to separate yourself from others who were involved in the same noble endeavor. But you persisted, and you triumphed.

Ours is the greatest nation on Earth, the greatest democratic experiment in the history of humankind. But for decades, generations, our Constitution permitted slavery of human beings. Americans were not given the right to vote directly for their own United States Senator; women were not permitted to vote. Had there been timidity on the part of Americans, had there been discouragement that brought an end to struggle, our Nation would never have improved.

We've almost wiped clean the legal, permissive discrimination against a group of human beings in our Nation. Not quite. There is only one group, as you well know, against whom laws can still be passed patently depriving Americans citizens of their civil or human rights, and that is against women. It's a noble struggle. It's difficult. Massive forces are mounted against us. The most abominable distortions are promulgated as the truth. Political pressures are exerted on often well-meaning members of State legislatures. It's not an easy task, but there is no reason for us to fail.

Six Presidents who lived before me in the White House have endorsed and supported the equal rights amendment. Thirty-five States, as you know, have already ratified the equal rights amendment. The Democratic and Republican platforms have endorsed the equal rights amendment. The overwhelming majority of Americans in almost every poll, or every one, so far as I know, favor the equal rights amendment. But discrimination still exists of a legal kind.

Women have not been deprived of responsibility. More than a fourth of all the households in this Nation are headed by women. Women have not been deprived of the burden of labor. Forty-three percent of our workforce is comprised of women. What women have been cheated of is equal wages, equal opportunities in education, equal opportunities under the law, equal opportunities to hold property, equal opportunities for human dignity, equal opportunities to realize the hopes of a human life and to utilize the talent that God has given.

This is a smirch on America, not yet to have succeeded in ratifying the equal rights amendment. I'm concerned about every one of you here, because I know what you go through. I meet every month with the presidents of most women's organizations, to share ideas and to share plans and to assign responsibilities, for telephone calls, for luncheons at the White House with the Governors and the speakers of the house and the majority leader and the minority leader of the State legislatures which still have not yet ratified the equal rights amendment. We make numerous calls. My whole family, my whole administration is committed to this struggle: to say that equality of rights under the law shall not be denied or abridged by the United States or any State on account of sex. A simple statement, but one with profound significance.

My message is, don't be discouraged. We have had a setback this afternoon. It means we'll have to struggle harder, we'll have to unify ourselves more closely. We'll have to realize that this is not a time to cast stones at one another or to try to assign blame for a disappointing day. It's a time for the marshaling of forces and to realize that together we will not fail.

We did not get in this fight to lose, and we do not intend to lose. We will ratify the equal rights amendment for the United States of America.

Thank you very much.

NOTE: The President spoke at 9:58 p.m. at the Mazza Gallerie.

The President's Trip to Europe

Remarks on Departure From the White House. June 19, 1980

THE VICE PRESIDENT. Mr. President and Rosalynn, today you begin a crucial trip at a crucial time. In Venice you will meet with the leaders of the Western world for the first time since the Soviet Union invaded Afghanistan.

That invasion is a challenge to the whole world: a challenge to peace, to the principles of international law, and to national sovereignty. To meet this challenge, the leading democratic nations of the world must speak with a common voice.

You also meet at a time when the problems of inflation and recession threaten the economies of every nation. These too require international cooperation and require all of us to speak with a common voice and to act with a common purpose.

Mr. President, you will also visit three major nations of southern Europe, each one of which stands on the threshold of a new beginning. Two of Europe's oldest, proudest and most illustrious countries, Spain and Portugal, are also two of the world's youngest democracies; and new leadership begins the new decade for the strong, united, and independent people of Yugoslavia. At this important point of their history you bring to each of these three nations the message of our respect, our good will, and friendship.

And when you visit Italy, your first stop, you'll be among people for whom America has a special affection. From the seeds that Italy planted, so much culture has blossomed in the Western world. From the shores of that country, so many people set off across the ocean to help build our own Nation. To Italy you return the warmth and esteem and love of the American people.

I know that I speak for all Americans, Mr. President, when I say that we wish— such historic talks before you, you leave with our wish for a safe and successful journey.

THE PRESIDENT. Thank you very much, Fritz.

I know that I do leave this Nation with a great deal of confidence that while I'm gone that you will administer the affairs of the Government well and that we will be in constant communication at all times; secondly, that the American people have their hearts and their minds attuned to the challenges of this extremely difficult visit: meeting with, in a short time, key leaders of the Western world and Japan, in more than 12 different consultations with them of great importance.

This is a trip that's fairly brief, but it's long in importance and long in difficulty and challenge. Our mission has many facets. We will examine such issues as energy dependence, the economics of emerging nations and of our own countries, a lasting peace for the Middle East. We'll discuss the clear-cut challenge of the Soviet invasion of Afghanistan, the question of terrorism and how to deal with Iran, the control of nuclear arms. And we will also discuss, in individual meetings with the leaders of all of those nations, the differences and common purposes and commitments of our nations. But throughout all these interrelated issues and delicate shades of difference, we will be guided by this knowledge: the power of free, democratic nations, who welcome diversity and who do not erect walls to imprison our own people; who exist to nurture human rights and human beings, not to enslave them. The power of democracy and freedom will shape the future of the world.

In Rome I'll meet with Italian leaders, President Pertini and Prime Minister Cossiga, to discuss diplomatic, energy, and security matters. And then Pope John Paul II and I will continue our work on human rights, on human needs, on refugees, and on arms control, which we began during his visit to Washington last October. And then I'll go to 2 days of meetings in Venice at the summit conference, the sixth such meeting among the major non-Communist and industrial nations.

The industrial democracies are meeting now very severe tests successfully. Let there be no misunderstanding about this anywhere in the world. We are not motivated by hostility against anyone, nor by any desire for reckless confrontation, nor for any return to the cold war. But we must sustain world opposition to Soviet aggression and not allow the Soviets to derive any permanent benefits from their invasion of the neutral nation of Afghanistan.

In working toward that response and for many other difficult solutions, America will be clear in voicing our own commitments, our needs, and we will also be eager to understand and to listen to the views of other countries. We are not the Warsaw Pact, held together by one nation's tanks. We are bound by shared ideals, shared goals, and shared respect for one another. Our alliance is based on understanding and not demands; on

listening to each other's voices, not dictating to each other. That's what makes these summit meetings so vital. That's also what makes these summit meetings so difficult at times.

We will work together on tough issues each nation faces at home: inflation, unemployment, rising oil prices, energy conservation, production of energy in our own countries—a host of problems that are interrelated and very intricate. It's important for Americans to remember that international understanding and cooperation on these issues is every bit as important to our security, to our jobs, to our quality of life, as anything that we can do by ourselves here at home.

Immediately following the Venice summit I'll travel to Yugoslavia, to Spain, and then to Portugal. I will assure the leaders and the people of Yugoslavia of America's unwavering support for the independence, the unity, and the territorial integrity of that great country, as well as our respect for Yugoslavia's constructive, nonaligned position.

America has watched with wonder and with deep appreciation and admiration, in both Spain and Portugal, as they've made a remarkable transition from autocracy to democracy in the last several years. I will express personally to them, to the leaders and to the people, the great pleasure that Americans feel at the success of these historic achievements.

I'll join with all these nations, with their leaders and, in some cases, with their people, in fulfilling the difficult and demanding agenda of peace, of working towards a solid economic foundation for the entire world, and adhering to the high ideals and the deep commitments of free people.

Finally, I might say that the difficult task of marshaling the democratic alliance to meet the challenges and dangers and opportunities of a new decade will call for courage, patience, knowledge, and persistence among the people of all our nations. There is no more important work for an American President, and I'm grateful for your support as we seek peace, security, and better life for ourselves and for all the world.

Thank you very much.

NOTE: The exchange of remarks began at 7:02 a.m. on the South Lawn of the White House.

Export of Special Nuclear Material and Components to India

Executive Order 12218. June 19, 1980

By the authority vested in me as President by the Constitution and statutes of the United States of America, including Section 126b. (2) of the Atomic Energy Act of 1954, as amended (42 U.S.C. 2155 (b) (2)), and having determined that withholding the exports proposed pursuant to Nuclear Regulatory Commission export license applications XSNM–1379, XSNM–1569, XCOM–0240, XCOM–0250, XCOM–0376, XCOM–0381 and XCOM–0395, would be seriously prejudicial to the achievement of United States non-proliferation objectives and would otherwise jeopardize the common defense and security, those exports to India are authorized; however, such exports shall not occur for a period of 60 days as defined by Section 130 g. of the Atomic Energy Act of 1954, as amended (42 U.S.C. 2159 (g)).

JIMMY CARTER

The White House,
June 19, 1980.

[Filed with the Office of the Federal Register, 11:08 a.m., June 19, 1980]

Export of Special Nuclear Material and Components to India

Message to the Congress. June 19, 1980

To the Congress of the United States:

I am transmitting with this message, pursuant to Section 126b. (2) of the Atomic Energy Act of 1954, as amended, an Executive Order authorizing the export of 39,718 kgs. of low-enriched uranium to India for use in fueling its Tarapur Atomic Power Station and authorizing the export of replacement parts for this station.

Two applications for licenses to export the fuel were submitted to the Nuclear Regulatory Commission in September 1978 and August 1979 respectively. After a careful review of these applications, and the applications for replacement parts for the Tarapur reactors, the Executive Branch concluded that the proposed exports would not be inimical to the common defense and security, that they met all applicable statutory criteria under the Atomic Energy Act, and that the licenses should be issued. The Commission was notified of these Executive Branch findings and recommendations on March 28, 1979, and on May 7, 1980.

On May 16, 1980, the Nuclear Regulatory Commission decided that it could not find that the criteria for issuing the licenses had been met. Pursuant to the law, the Commission then referred these applications to me.

In reaching its decision, the Commission argued that the full-scope safeguards export criterion of Section 128a of the Atomic Energy Act applies to these applications because they do not fall within the grace period provided in the law. The Department of State, on the other hand, concludes that this statutory criterion does not apply to these two applications

1137

because they were submitted before September 10, 1979, the cutoff date specified in the law, because the first shipment under each was reasonably planned to occur before March 10, 1980, and because there is no reason to believe that the applications were filed early as a way of circumventing the September 10, 1979, deadline.

In any event, the license criteria specified by statute, of which Section 128a is one, are not the same as the export criteria on the basis of which I must determine whether to issue an Executive Order. As the Commission noted, its inability to issue the licenses "should not be read as a recommendation one way or the other on the proposed exports." As the Commission noted further, in such cases the law provides that the President may authorize such exports by Executive Order if he determines that withholding them would be seriously prejudicial to the achievement of United States non-proliferation objectives or would otherwise jeopardize the common defense and security.

I have determined that to withhold these exports would be seriously prejudical to the achievement of United States non-proliferation objectives and would otherwise jeopardize the common defense and security. I have made this determination for the policy reasons discussed below. However, I want to make it clear that I do in fact regard these export applications as having fallen within the statutory grace period before the full-scope safeguards requirement of action 128a takes effect. Thus, my authorization of these exports does not constitute a precedent for an exception to the full-scope safeguards criterion. Further, this action in no way indicates a change in the high priority I attach to preventing the spread of nuclear explosives. On the contrary, this action reflects my judgment that non-proliferation would be set back, not advanced, by

withholding these exports, and that our failure to supply this fuel could seriously jeopardize other important U.S. interests.

India's failure to accept international safeguards on all its peaceful nuclear activities and its failure to commit itself not to conduct further nuclear explosions are of serious concern to me. These exports will help us to maintain a dialogue with India in which we try to narrow our differences on these issues.

The exports will avoid the risk of a claim by India that the United States has broken an existing agreement between the two governments and has thereby relieved India of its obligation to refrain from reprocessing the fuel previously supplied by the United States.

Supply of this fuel will also ensure the continuation of safeguards and other U.S. controls on disposition of U.S.-origin fuel that has been supplied to India.

Approval of these exports will help strengthen ties with a key South Asian democracy at a time when it is particularly important for us to do so. Insecurity in South and Southwest Asia has been greatly heightened by the crisis in Iran and the Soviet invasion of Afghanistan. We must do all we reasonably can to promote stability in the area and to bolster our relations with states there, particularly those that can play a role in checking Soviet expansionism.

When I signed the Nuclear Non-Proliferation Act of 1978, I expressed reservations about the constitutionality of provisions of law which purport to allow the Congress to overturn my decisions by actions not subject to my veto power. In transmitting this Executive Order, I also want to make it clear that I am not departing from those reservations.

JIMMY CARTER

The White House,
June 19, 1980.

Afghanistan Relief Week
Proclamation 4765. June 19, 1980

By the President of the United States of America

A Proclamation

From the beginning, the United States has been a shining symbol of hope to the oppressed and the destitute of the world. The lamp held high by the Statue of Liberty still sheds its light into the darkness of tyranny, poverty and war.

In the years since World War II, America has given substance to that symbol time after time. Our country has provided food, clothing, shelter and medicine to millions of people from Greece, Hungary, Czechoslovakia, Kampuchea, Bangladesh, Chile, Guatemala and many other places.

Last December, the non-aligned, Moslem nation of Afghanistan was suddenly and brutally invaded by almost a hundred thousand Soviet troops. Because of this act of aggression, which has earned the condemnation of the world, hundreds of thousands of Afghans have been forced to flee their country.

They have fled because their homes have been bombed, their crops and flocks have been destroyed, and their villages have been attacked with rockets, napalm, and other modern weaponry. Facing starvation, shelterless against the bitter cold of the mountain winter, some one million men, women and children have crossed the high passes to seek shelter in Pakistan, or have fled to Iran. Children and the old often die on the way. But despite the hardships, thousands more arrive each week.

The Afghans now constitute one of the largest concentrations of refugees in the world today. Most of them are destitute. They have been able to bring with them only their proud, resilient spirit of independence.

They desperately need shelter. And they need clothing, blankets, fuel and urgent medical care, especially for the women and children.

Americans can help—and Americans must help. I call upon all Americans to help the Afghan refugees through contributions to agencies involved in the relief efforts, both the UN High Commission for Refugees and the dedicated private voluntary agencies.

Now, THEREFORE, I, JIMMY CARTER, President of the United States of America, do hereby proclaim the week of July 21 through July 27, 1980, as Afghanistan Relief Week and urge my fellow citizens to join with international relief agencies in assisting and helping the Afghan refugees in their struggle for survival.

IN WITNESS WHEREOF, I have hereunto set my hand this nineteenth day of June, in the year of our Lord nineteen hundred and eighty, and of the Independence of the United States of America the two hundred and fourth.

JIMMY CARTER

[Filed with the Office of the Federal Register, 3:34 p.m., June 19, 1980]

Presidential Commission on World Hunger
Executive Order 12219. June 19, 1980

By the authority vested in me as President by the Constitution of the United States of America, and in order to extend the life of the Presidential Commission on World Hunger for two months, Section 1–402 of Executive Order No. 12078 of September 5, 1978, is hereby amended to read: "The Commission shall terminate on August 31, 1980.".

JIMMY CARTER

The White House,
June 19, 1980.

[Filed with the Office of the Federal Register, 3:35 p.m., June 19, 1980]

Imports of Petroleum and Petroleum Products

Proclamation 4766.   June 19, 1980

By the President of the United States of America

A Proclamation

Congress has terminated the Petroleum Import Adjustment Program (PIAP), which was designed to reduce the threat to our nation's security caused by our dependence on imported oil. Consistent with this Congressional action, I am rescinding Proclamation 4744 which established the PIAP.

The threat to national security, however, has not dissipated, and an effective means of reducing oil imports remains an imperative. I will work with Congress to reach this objective. In the meantime, the Mandatory Oil Import Program, which the PIAP had modified, will once again govern all importation of oil into this country. The small import fees associated with that Program were first imposed in 1973 and have been suspended since April 6, 1979. Under present circumstances, these fees would not fulfill the long term purposes for which they were originally adopted. I have therefore determined that a further six month suspension of these fees is consistent with the development of a more comprehensive program for reducing oil imports.

NOW, THEREFORE, I, JIMMY CARTER, President of the United States of America, by the authority vested in me by the Constitution and the laws of the United States, including Section 232 of the Trade Expansion Act of 1962, as amended (19 U.S.C. 1862), do hereby proclaim that:

SECTION 1–101. Proclamation 4744, as amended, is rescinded in its entirety, effective March 15, 1980.

SEC. 1–102. Proclamation 3279, as amended, is further amended in section 3(a)(1)(i) by deleting both the term "through June 30, 1979." and the clause following that term, and by substituting therefor: "through December 31, 1980;".

SEC. 1–103. Proclamation 3279, as amended, is further amended in section 3(a)(1)(ii) by deleting both the term "through June 30, 1979." and the clause following that term, and by substituting therefor: "through December 31, 1980;".

SEC. 1–104. Proclamation 3279, as amended, is further amended by deleting section 3(a)(1)(viii).

SEC. 1–105. (a) Proclamation 4762 is revoked.

(b) Section 1 of Proclamation 3279, as amended, is amended by adding a new subsection (f), to read as follows: "Except with respect to licenses issued pursuant to the next to last sentence of Section 4(b)(1) of this Proclamation, all licenses issued pursuant to this Proclamation which could be utilized to enter crude oil or gasoline pursuant to another Proclamation shall expire effective 12:01 a.m., April 24, 1980. Licenses issued for the entry of crude oil and gasoline pursuant to Proclamation 4744, as amended, shall be considered to have been and to be issued pursuant to the authority contained in this Proclamation and shall be subject to all of its terms and conditions (except for those in the preceding sentence), including those arising by virtue of the implementing regulations and interpretations.".

SEC. 1–106. Section 8 of Proclamation 3279, as amended, is amended by deleting the period at the end of the next to last paragraph and by adding at the end of that paragraph the following words: "; provided, that the system of issuing allocation and licenses with respect to exchanges under Section 4(b)(1) of this Proclamation shall remain in effect during any period in which a fee of $0.00, as provided in Section 3 of this Proclamation, is in effect.".

IN WITNESS WHEREOF, I have hereunto set my hand this nineteenth day of June, in the year of our Lord nineteen hundred and eighty, and of the Independence of the United States of America, the two hundred and fourth.

JIMMY CARTER

[Filed with the Office of the Federal Register, 10:29 a.m., June 20, 1980]

Renewable Resources of the United States

Letter to the Speaker of the House and the President of the Senate Transmitting a Statement of Policy and Related Documents. June 19, 1980

Dear Mr. Speaker: (Dear Mr. President:)

I am pleased to transmit a Statement of Policy, an Assessment of the Nation's Renewable Resources, and the Secretary of Agriculture's Recommended Program for Forest Service activities as required by the Forest and Rangeland Renewable

Resources Planning Act of 1974 as amended.

The Secretary of Agriculture's recommended program provides important guidance for the near and long-term management of the nation's natural resources. The wise use of these valuable natural resources is essential for providing continuing social and economic benefits to Americans. My Statement of Policy provides further guidelines for implementation of the Recommended Program.

I am proud of the progress we have made since the first RPA documents were transmitted to Congress in 1976. But there is much more to be done to assure our forest and range resources will continue to be properly managed in the 1980's and the decades beyond. The documents, which are being transmitted to the Congress today, will be useful in your consideration of natural resources policies, programs, and budgets.

I look forward to working with the Congress as you review these documents and my Statement of Policy in the coming months.

Sincerely,

JIMMY CARTER

STATEMENT OF POLICY

INTRODUCTION

Today, I am transmitting to the Congress my Statement of Policy regarding the management and use of the nation's renewable resources. This statement enunciates my policies for planning, budgeting, and implementing Forest Service programs between now and 1985. Accompanying this policy statement is the Renewable Resources Assessment and Renewable Resources Program prepared by the Secretary of Agriculture pursuant to the Forest and Rangeland Renewable Resources Planning Act. The RPA documents review in detail the current and prospective condition and uses of 1.6 billion acres of public and private forests and rangelands and recommend near and long-term programs that will improve the contribution of these resources to the welfare of the American people. These documents, the most comprehensive ever developed for this purpose, will provide an improved basis for managing our nation's natural resources, and balancing economic efficiency, environmental quality, and important social values. They reflect the contributions of a great many people in Federal and State agencies and in the private sector.

The Assessment provides estimates of present and prospective demand and supply for all renewable resources on public and private forest and rangeland. These resources are extremely important to the welfare of our nation. They include vast outdoor recreation resources, varied fish and wildlife habitats, livestock forage, surface and ground water, energy and mineral resources, extensive areas of pristine and scenic wilderness, and wood for housing, paper and energy.

These lands are part of our natural and national heritage. Our responsibilities for their management not only include the immediate needs of our nation, but also our long-term needs. Since I took office, we have worked together in many ways to protect and improve the productivity and environmental quality of forests and ranges. The Congress enacted and I signed into law the Soil and Water Resources Conservation Act, the Renewable Resources Research Act, the Public Rangelands Improvement Act, the Endangered American Wilderness Act, the Cooperative Forestry Assistance Act and many other important laws. I am proud

of this record of protecting and improving the environment and in fostering economic growth and productivity. In addition, my Administration has taken a number of actions to advance these objectives. I have delivered two comprehensive Environmental Messages. We have made considerable progress in building the National Wilderness Preservation System. Last year, we completed the comprehensive Roadless Area Review and Evaluation (RARE II) of the National Forest System. This review examined 62 million acres of undeveloped lands. From this review, I recommended to the Congress that over 15 million acres be designated as wilderness. My recommendations bring the total wilderness designated and proposed for the National Forest System to over 34 million acres. I directed the management of 36 million acres for other multiple use purposes and 10.6 million acres will be studied further for possible wilderness or other uses.

While we have made progress, there is much more to be done. Our forest and range resources have not yet been developed to their full potential. We have a basic need to continue to improve the overall productivity of our renewable resource base. It is the source of much of our nation's strength and prosperity.

Theodore Roosevelt once said that, "the nation behaves well if it treats the natural resources as assets which it must turn over to the next generation increased, and not impaired in value." The rich potential of our forest and rangeland resources have been confirmed in the RPA documents.

The "Assessment of the Forest and Range Land Situation in the United States" indicates that our nation's demands for renewable resources—outdoor recreation, wilderness, wildlife, and fish, range, timber, and water, will continue to increase. Demand for timber is expected to be particularly strong during the next decade. We have an opportunity to manage our nation's resources, both public and private, for increased productivity. Such increases would moderate upward price pressures on wood products and other forest-related commodities, decrease our dependency on foreign suppliers, and provide additional opportunities for our people to enjoy the outdoors, enhance wildlife habitat and improve water quality.

I believe it is important to make use of the potential of the National Forest System to contribute to the nation's supply of renewable resources in an economically efficient and environmentally sound manner. For this reason, last June I directed the Secretaries of Agriculture and Interior to "use maximum speed in updating land management plans . . . with the objective of increasing the harvest of mature timber through departure from the current non-declining evenflow policy." I further directed that ". . . all relevant economic and environmental implications must be taken into account." The updating of land management plans for national forests is underway and thus, accurate estimates of the potential for increased supply from this policy are not presently available. Consistent with multiple use requirements, such increases are to be reflected in the annual program proposals.

BASIC PRINCIPLES

The basic policy that I intend to pursue will seek a balance among three important principles:

—*Economic Efficiency.* Public investment in resource management should be directed toward maximizing net national benefits.

—*Environmental Quality.* Environmental values will be maintained and where possible enhanced. Legal requirements will be met, including those for air and water quality standards, and for protecting long-term soil productivity. Threatened and endangered species, and fish and wildlife habitat will continue to be protected.

—*Social Values.* The relationship of individual communities to the National Forest System with respect to employment, income and social amenities is important, and will be considered in management decisions. The concerns of those using the forests for recreation and aesthetic purposes will also be considered in management decisions.

To reach these goals, the Resources Planning Act and the Multiple Use-Sustained Yield Act provide important and appropriate guidance. The Multiple Use-Sustained Yield Act specifies ". . . management of all the various renewable surface resources of the national forests so that they are utilized in the combination that will best meet the needs of the American people . . . with consideration being given to the relative values of the various resources and not necessarily the combination of uses that will give the greatest dollar return . . .". The Resources Planning Act specifies a process for determining the best combination of uses of national forests lands and other Forest Service activities. It emphasizes determination of demand, supply, and price relationships and the comparison of benefits and costs of Federal activities. The Secretary's recommended program is based on this general guidance.

THE RECOMMENDED PROGRAM

The comprehensive planning process embodied in the 1980 RPA Program has important benefits. It provides a systematic look into the future to determine what actions may be required now or in the near term. It helps in managing complex programs. It facilitates achievement of uniform standards, policies, and procedures while also permitting management to be responsive to specific local and regional situations.

The 1980 Program recommended by the Secretary of Agriculture is presented as a range and will be used to guide budget proposals, land management planning and other government action. It reflects certain limitations in the data and analysis, and uncertainty about the economic conditions that we face in the future. Thus, it allows a reasonable degree of flexibility for considering differing views on resource management priorities.

The program being recommended by the Secretary of Agriculture is briefly described below:

National Forest Management. National Forests will continue to be managed under multiple-use sustained yield principles to assure a continuous flow of all goods and services, and to achieve the regional and national goals displayed in the Program. Specifically, it will include:

• *Recreation and Wilderness.* Dispersed recreation will continue to be emphasized in the National Forests. Recreation facilities will be maintained, improved and developed in a way that compliments dispersed recreation and encourages energy conservation by providing greater recreational opportunities to areas closest to urban areas. Additional areas will be considered for the wilderness system.

• *Wildlife and Fish.* Planning and support activities will be maintained as necessary to protect and enhance wildlife and fish habitats and to meet the needs of threatened and endangered species. Population targets will be established to guide the enhancement of wildlife and fish habitats. Forest and range landowners will be encouraged to practice

wildlife management within the context of multiple use. States will be encouraged to consider wildlife needs in the development of their forest resource plans.

• *Range.* The range program will be directed toward improving range conditions with emphasis on efficient forage production opportunities and protecting soil and water values.

• *Water.* On National Forest land, water quality goals specified in the Clean Water Act will be met.

• *Minerals.* There are extensive undeveloped energy and non-energy mineral resources in the National Forests. The development of mineral and geothermal resources will be emphasized within appropriate environmental constraints.

• *Timber.* Timber supplies from National Forest lands will be maintained through more complete utilization standards and intensive management on more productive sites. Timber sale contracts will be modified where feasible to increase utilization. A complete review of appraisal procedures and timber sale receipts will be conducted.

Research. An aggressive research program would be continued. Research to meet increasing demands for timber, energy, protection of riparian habitat and streams, air and water quality and recreation will be emphasized.

Cooperative Forestry. The assessment underscores the importance of commercial forestland held by non-industrial landowners for meeting future resource needs. Cooperative Forestry programs will promote improved management of State and private lands for timber production and other forest values.

SPECIFIC KEY CONCERNS

While greatly improved over the 1975 RPA, the present program is necessarily based on available data and analysis. This program will be strengthened further through the next generation of land management plans scheduled for completion in 1985. A broad array of options will be considered in each forest plan including options that may fall outside the boundaries of the recommended program.

In addition, I would like to stress the following special concerns:

• *Timber Production.* This nation's housing requirements during the next five years are expected to place major demands on the forest products industry to increase production of lumber and wood products. In the long run, private forestlands are expected to become a chief source of increased timber supply, but during this decade, careful consideration must be given to increased supplies from Federally-owned lands, particularly the National Forest System. The recommended program for the National Forests provides for timber harvest goals ranging between 11.0 and 12.5 billion board feet by 1985, based on the traditional planning guidelines. However, at my direction, the Secretary of Agriculture is accelerating national forest land management plans with the objective of increasing the harvest of mature timber through departure from the current nondeclining evenflow policy.

Increases in the state and private cooperative forestry program will be based on additional analyses of the effectiveness of existing and potential approaches that could efficiently improve productivity on these lands. This includes a joint review by the Agriculture and Treasury Departments of tax implications for forest land management.

• *Environmental Values.* My Administration has demonstrated a deep and abiding commitment to maintaining and enhancing the quality of our nation's environment. The importance of the values provided by water, recreation, fish and wildlife, wilderness and many others, is well recognized. Proper management of both timber and other resources, as outlined above, requires ongoing recognition and protection of environmental values. This will be done through my recommendations on expanding the wilderness system, and also by considering environmental values as an integral part of multiple-use management. This policy will be reflected in all actions to increase the economic efficiency and productivity of our nation's forests and rangelands. The recommended program is directed toward assuring long-term maintenance of these resources.

BUDGET POLICY

It is my intention that the Department of Agriculture manage the National Forest System and carry out research and cooperative forestry programs with a keen sensitivity to the anticipated difficult economic and budgetary choices confronting this nation over the next several years. Federal investment decisions must be made in accordance with the most urgent and pressing needs.

I anticipate that my budget proposals for fiscal years 1982 through 1985 and beyond will fall within the bounds of the recommended program totals. Funding for Forest Service programs will necessarily be considered in each year's economic and fiscal context, along with emerging resource needs, and the demands placed on our financial resources by our other national goals and interests. Consistent with my zero-based budget process, additional planning and analysis will be necessary to provide specific program justification.

CONCLUSION

I believe the RPA process is important and desirable. The 1980 assessment and program comprise major progress in developing a sound planning process. They provide a very useful picture of the status of our forestry resources, the projected demands on them and a realistic set of options for managing those resources to meet national needs. In this respect, the results represent a significant improvement over the 1975 RPA.

I commend the Secretary of Agriculture for his Department's efforts in preparing the Renewable Resources assessment and program, and for his responsiveness to the Forest and Rangeland Renewable Resources Planning Act.

JIMMY CARTER

NOTE: This is the text of identical letters and statements of policy addressed to Thomas P. O'Neill, Jr., Speaker of the House of Representatives, and Walter F. Mondale, President of the Senate.

The reports transmitted with the letter are entitled: "An Assessment of the Forest and Range Land Situation in the United States—January 1980" (Government Printing Office, 631 pages), and "The 1980 Report to Congress on the Nation's Renewable Resources" (Government Printing Office, 155 pages).

Administrative Conference of the United States

Appointment of Three Members of the Council and Designation of Joan Z. Bernstein as Vice-Chair of the Conference.
June 19, 1980

The President today announced his intention to appoint three persons as members of the Council of the Administrative Conference of the United States. They are:

Reuben B. Robertson III, of Washington, D.C., who is currently Director of the Bureau of Consumer Protection at the Civil Aeronautics Board. He will replace Margaret McKenna, resigned. The President has also announced he will nominate Robertson to be Chairman of the Administrative Conference.

Ronald B. Lewis, of Washington, D.C., Deputy Adviser for Regulatory Policies, Council on Wage and Price Stability.

Franklin M. Schultz, of Alexandria, Va., a partner in the Washington, D.C., law firm of Purcell & Nelson.

Lewis and Schultz will replace Betty Southard Murphy and Michael Eagan, resigned.

The President also announced he has designated Joan Z. Bernstein, of Chevy Chase, Md., as Vice-Chair of the Administrative Conference. She would replace Margaret McKenna, resigned.

Bernstein has been a member of the Council of the Administrative Conference since 1978. She is also General Counsel for the Department of Health and Human Services.

The Administrative Conference was created in 1964 to develop improvements in the legal procedures by which Federal agencies administer regulatory, benefit, and other Government programs. Its members include agency heads, other Federal officials, private lawyers, university professors, and other experts in administrative law and government.

The Council is the executive board of the Administrative Conference. It consists of 10 members in addition to the Chairman, all of whom are appointed by the President for 3-year terms.

Administrative Conference of the United States

Nomination of Reuben B. Robertson III To Be Chairman. June 19, 1980

The President today announced that he will nominate Reuben B. Robertson III, of Washington, D.C., to be Chairman of the Administrative Conference of the United States. He would replace Robert A. Anthony, resigned.

Robertson is currently Director of the Bureau of Consumer Protection at the Civil Aeronautics Board.

He was born September 24, 1939, in Cincinnati, Ohio. He received a B.A. from Yale College in 1961 and an LL.B. from Yale Law School in 1964. He took postgraduate studies at the London School of Economics in 1964–65.

Robertson is a member of the District of Columbia Bar and the American Bar Association's Section of Administrative Law, and he is vice-chairman of the ABA Aviation and Space Law Committee. He served as a member of the Civil Aeronautics Board Advisory Committee on Procedural Reform in 1975 and as a member of U.S. delegations in bilateral civil aviation negotiations in 1977–78.

From 1966 to 1968, he was associated with the law firm of Covington & Burling. He was a special assistant to the Chief Counsel of the Federal Highway Administration from 1968 to 1969. From 1969 to 1973, he was with the Center for the Study of Responsive Law, and from 1971 to 1978, he was legal director of the Aviation Consumer Action Project. From 1973 to 1978, he was senior attorney in the Public Citizen Litigation Group. In 1978 he was a consultant to the Office of Rail Public Counsel of the Interstate Commerce Commission. He became Director of the Bureau of Consumer Protection in 1978.

Trucking Industry Deregulation Legislation

Statement on House of Representatives Approval of the Legislation. June 19, 1980

The House of Representatives took a major step today in the fight against inflation by passing comprehensive legislation to reform economic regulation of the trucking industry. By increasing competition and ending irrational regulatory restrictions, the bill will save shippers and consumers billions of dollars each year and conserve hundreds of millions of gallons of fuel.

I commend the bipartisan efforts of Chairmen Harold Johnson and James Howard, and ranking minority members William Harsha and Bud Shuster in achieving the rapid passage of this important measure. I urge the House and Senate to resolve any differences promptly so that the benefits of this legislation can take effect as soon as possible.

Helen Keller Day

Proclamation 4767. June 19, 1980

By the President of the United States of America

A Proclamation

Stories of brave individuals battling seemingly insurmountable odds fire our imagination and pride as human beings. So it is with the remarkable life of Helen Keller. Her incredible fight against, and eventual triumph over, the multiple handicaps of deafness and blindness made her a world-famous symbol of hope for all handicapped people.

Today we honor the 100th anniversary of Helen Keller's birth. In so doing, we honor also the patience and understanding of her devoted teacher Anne Sullivan. Helen Keller refused to let her handicaps cut her off from a life of usefulness and service to others. Through her own determination and faith, she was able to develop and use her talents and demonstrate how much even the most severely handicapped individual can accomplish when proper training and rehabilitation opportunities are provided.

As a mark of respect for her achievements, the Congress, by joint resolution, has authorized the President to proclaim June 27, 1980, as "HELEN KELLER DAY".

Now, THEREFORE, I, JIMMY CARTER, President of the United States of America, do hereby designate June 27, 1980, as "HELEN KELLER DAY". I urge all appropriate Federal departments and agencies to foster the recognition of Helen Keller's achievements on that day with ceremonies, programs, and activities.

IN WITNESS WHEREOF, I have hereunto set my hand this nineteenth day of June, in the year of our Lord nineteen hundred and eighty, and of the Independence of the United States of America the two hundred and fourth.

JIMMY CARTER

[Filed with the Office of the Federal Register, 9:34 a.m., June 23, 1980]

NOTE: The text of the proclamation was released on June 20.

Council of Economic Advisers

Nomination of Stephen M. Goldfeld To Be a Member. June 20, 1980

The President today announced that he will nominate Stephen M. Goldfeld, of Princeton, N.J., to be a member of the Council of Economic Advisers. He would replace Lyle Gramley. Goldfeld has been on the faculty of Princeton University since 1963 and has been the Class of 1920 professor of economics and banking since 1971.

He was born August 9, 1940, in the Bronx, N.Y. He received an A.B. from Harvard College in 1960 and a Ph. D. in economics from Massachusetts Institute of Technology in 1963.

Goldfeld was a visiting research professor at C.O.R.E. Université Catholique de Louvain in 1970–71 and Ford visiting professor at the University of California at Berkeley in 1975–76. He has served as a consultant on economics to numerous government and private agencies and is the author of several books.

United States Ambassador to Senegal

Nomination of Walter C. Carrington. June 20, 1980

The President today announced that he will nominate Walter C. Carrington, of Roosevelt Island, N.Y., to be Ambassador Extraordinary and Plenipotentiary of the United States to the Republic of Senegal. He would replace Herman J. Cohen, who is being assigned to the State Department. Carrington has been executive vice president of the African American Institute since 1971.

He was born July 24, 1930, in New York City. He received an A.B. from Harvard College in 1952 and an LL.B. from Harvard Law School in 1955. He served in the U.S. Army from 1955 to 1957.

From 1957 to 1961, Carrington was a

partner in the law firm of Maples, Carrington and Rhuland. He was a commissioner of the Massachusetts Commission Against Discrimination from 1957 to 1961. He was with the Peace Corps from 1961 to 1971, serving as country director in Sierra Leone and Senegal and deputy director in Tunisia; deputy director of the Office of Planning and Program Review; deputy regional director for Africa and special assistant to the director of the Peace Corps for equal employment opportunity; and regional director for Africa.

Carrington is a member of the Advisory Committee on Voluntary Foreign Aid of the Agency for International Development. He was chairman of the 1974 United Nations Conference on the African Regional Plan for the Application of Science and Technology to Development.

Legal Services Corporation
Nomination of Five Members of the Board of Directors. June 20, 1980

The President today announced five persons whom he will nominate for reappointment as members of the Board of Directors of the Legal Services Corporation. They are:

STEVEN L. ENGELBERG, of Chevy Chase, Md., a partner in the Washington, D.C., firm of Grove, Engelberg & Gross, P.C.;

CECILIA D. ESQUER, of Tempe, Ariz., a partner in the firm of Esquer & Silvas;

HILLARY RODHAM, of Little Rock, Ark., an associate in the litigation division of Rose, Nash, Williamson, Carroll, Clay & Giroir;

RICHARD ALLAN TRUDELL, of Oakland, Calif., executive director of the American Indian Lawyer Training Program, Inc.;

JOSEPHINE WORTHY, of Holyoke, Mass., who is active in local legal services organizations and other community activities.

National Science Board
Nomination of Seven Members. June 20, 1980

The President today announced seven persons whom he will nominate to be members of the National Science Board. They are:

PETER T. FLAWN, of Austin, Tex., president of the University of Texas at Austin and a professor of geological sciences and public affairs;

MARY LOWE GOOD, of Sorrento, La., the Boyd professor of chemistry at the University of New Orleans;

PETER D. LAX, of New York City, an assistant professor at New York University and director of the Courant Institute of Mathematic Sciences;

HOMER A. NEAL, of Bloomington, Ind., dean of research and graduate development and professor of physics at Indiana University;

MARY JANE OSBORN, of Farmington, Conn., professor of microbiology at the University of Connecticut Health Center;

DONALD B. RICE, of Santa Monica, Calif., president of the Rand Corp. and a former assistant director of the Office of Management and Budget;

STUART A. RICE, of Chicago, Ill., chairman of the department and professor of chemistry at the University of Chicago.

Immigration and Naturalization Service
Nomination of Matt Garcia To Be Commissioner. June 20, 1980

The President today announced his intention to nominate Matt Garcia, of San Antonio, Tex., to be Commissioner of Immigration and Naturalization. He would replace Leonel J. Castillo, resigned.

Garcia has been a State Representative for District 57K, Bexar County, since 1973. He was born November 7, 1927, in

1149

San Antonio. He received an LL.B. from St. Mary's University in 1951.

Garcia also has been in private practice since 1951.

Digest of Other
White House Announcements

The following listing includes the President's public schedule and other items of general interest announced by the White House Press Office and not included elsewhere in this issue.

June 15

The President returned to the White House from Camp David, Md.

June 16

The President met at the White House with:

—Zbigniew Brzezinski, Assistant to the President for National Security Affairs;

—Frank B. Moore, Assistant to the President for Congressional Liaison.

The President greeted the graduating class of the Capitol Hill Page School in the Rose Garden at the White House.

The President went to the Japanese Embassy, where he signed a book expressing condolences at the death of Prime Minister Masayoshi Ohira.

June 17

The President met at the White House with:

—Dr. Brzezinski;

—Mr. Moore;

—James T. McIntyre, Jr., Director of the Office of Management and Budget.

The President announced that he has designated Michael J. Calhoun as Vice Chairman of the United States International Trade Commission. Calhoun has been a member of the Commission since 1979.

June 18

The President met at the White House with:

—Dr. Brzezinski;

—Mr. Moore;

—Vice President Walter F. Mondale, Secretary of State Edmund S. Muskie, Secretary of Defense Harold Brown, Deputy Secretary of State Warren M. Christopher, and Dr. Brzezinski;

—Vice President Mondale.

June 19–20

The President was in Rome, Italy, on a state visit. Releases issued during his trip to Europe begin on page 1153, and a chronology of his activities begins on page 1240.

NOMINATIONS SUBMITTED TO THE SENATE

The following list does not include promotions of members of the Uniformed Services, nominations to the Service Academies, or nominations of Foreign Service officers.

Submitted June 16, 1980

JACK HOOD VAUGHN, of the District of Columbia, to be an Assistant Administrator of the Agency for International Development, vice Abelardo Lopez Valdez.

Submitted June 17, 1980

ETHEL BENT WALSH, of the District of Columbia, to be a member of the Equal Employment Opportunity Commission for the term of 5 years expiring July 1, 1985 (reappointment).

ROBERT OBERNDOERFER HARRIS, of the District of Columbia, to be a member of the National Mediation Board for the term expiring July 1, 1983 (reappointment).

Submitted June 18, 1980

THOMAS W. FREDERICKS, of Colorado, to be an Assistant Secretary of the Interior, vice Forrest J. Gerard, resigned.

Submitted June 20, 1980

REUBEN B. ROBERTSON, of the District of Columbia, to be Chairman of the Administrative Conference of the United States for a term of 5 years, vice Robert Armstrong Anthony, resigned.

NOMINATIONS—Continued

Submitted June 20—Continued

DAVID VREELAND KENYON, of California, to be United States District Judge for the Central District of California, vice Albert Lee Stephens, Jr., retired.

CONSUELO B. MARSHALL, of California, to be United States District Judge for the Central District of California, vice Robert Firth, retired.

STEPHEN M. GOLDFELD, of New Jersey, to be a member of the Council of Economic Advisers, vice Lyle E. Gramley.

CHECKLIST OF WHITE HOUSE PRESS RELEASES

The following listing contains releases of the White House Press Office which are not included in this issue.

Released June 18, 1980

Fact sheet: Executive Order 12217, Federal compliance with fuel use prohibitions

Released June 19, 1980

Advance text: remarks on departing the White House for Europe

Fact sheet: Proclamation 4766, imports of petroleum and petroleum products

Released June 20, 1980

Announcement: nomination of David Vreeland Kenyon to be a United States District Judge for the Central District of California

Announcement: nomination of Consuelo B. Marshall to be a United States District Judge for the Central District of California

ACTS APPROVED BY THE PRESIDENT

Approved June 14, 1980

S. 1658_____ Public Law 96–270
Asbestos School Hazard Detection and Control Act of 1980.

Approved June 16, 1980

S. 2666_____ Public Law 96–271
An act to authorize appropriations for the International Natural Rubber Agreement for fiscal year 1981.

ACTS APPROVED—Continued

Approved June 17, 1980

H.R. 3434_____ Public Law 96–272
Adoption Assistance and Child Welfare Act of 1980.

H.R. 4453_____ Public Law 96–273
An act to amend the Saccharin Study and Labeling Act to extend to June 30, 1981, the ban on actions by the Secretary of Health, Education, and Welfare respecting saccharin.

H.R. 2102_____ Public Law 96–274
An act pertaining to the inheritance of trust or restricted land on the Standing Rock Sioux Reservation, North Dakota and South Dakota.

H.R. 6842_____ Public Law 96–275
An act to protect the confidentiality of Shippers' Export Declarations, and to standardize export data submission and disclosure requirements.

H.R. 6285_____ Public Law 96–276
Egg Research and Consumer Information Act Amendments of 1980.

H.R. 3979_____ Public Law 96–277
An act to repeal and amend certain laws regulating trade between Indians and certain Federal employees.

S.J. Res. 127_____ Public Law 96–278
A joint resolution to authorize and request the President to proclaim June 27, 1980, as "Helen Keller Day".

Approved June 18, 1980

H.J. Res. 442_____ Public Law 96–279
A joint resolution designating the week beginning June 22, 1980, as "National Athletic Boosters Week".

S.J. Res. 89_____ Public Law 96–280
A joint resolution permitting the supply of additional low enriched uranium fuel under international agreements for cooperation in the civil uses of nuclear energy, and for other purposes.

Approved June 19, 1980

S.J. Res. 183_____ Public Law 96–281
A joint resolution congratulating the Order of the Sons of Italy in America for their seventy-fifth anniversary and wishing the Order of the Sons of Italy in America success in future years and proclaiming June 22, 1980, as "National Italian-American Day".

EDITOR'S NOTE: For a chronology of the President's activities while in Europe, see the Digest of Other White House Announcements on page 1240.

Italy: State Dinner in Rome

Toasts of the President and President Alessandro Pertini of Italy. June 20, 1980

PRESIDENT PERTINI. Mr. President, I am particularly happy to welcome you, Mrs. Carter, and your entourage on your first visit to Italy, which falls at a particularly delicate and difficult moment in international affairs and on the eve of the Venice summit. Public opinion in our countries look to this opportunity for obtaining an unambiguous and reassuring answer to the problems and uncertainties which lie before us.

Although at many similar occasions and meetings in the past, we have sought to emphasize how numerous and how close are the traditional ties which unite our two peoples and nations, permit me, Mr. President, to once again recall our substantial convergence of views.

The ties of friendship between Italy and the United States are deep-rooted and immutable and extend back through history to one of my fellow countrymen who opened up the frontier with the New World. This long history tells of the irresistible passage of men and ideas across the vastness of the ocean.

I am thinking now of the influence that the American Revolution had on movements for Italian unification and independence, the political and cultural interaction between Italy and the United States in the first half of the nineteenth century, which witnessed the first mass emigration of Italian labor to the United States, particularly from the most depressed areas of the Italian South. From that emigration a whole group of your countrymen originated, those of Italian extraction who made their mark through their hard work, tenacity, patience, and affection, both for their country of adoption and their distant motherland in the Old World.

Nor can we Italians forget that at the darkest hour in our national history—and not ours alone—there came from the United States the decisive intervention against fascism and nazism, the moral support and the economic aid which permitted our ravaged and exhausted country to rebuild and regain its place within the international community.

Casting my mind back to our struggle, I am bound to recall that noble message which Franklin Delano Roosevelt delivered to the U.S. Congress in the wartime winter of 1944. His conception of liberty was the same for which we were fighting, we Italian patriots in the mountains, towns, and cities, and it was for this same liberty that the European resistance and the Allies fought. It was a total political and social conception of liberty which remains today the fundamental value for which, Mr. President, we and our two countries are still fighting today.

I want now to take two quotations from that Roosevelt speech on which we all should meditate:

1153

"This Republic had its beginning, and grew to its present strength, under the protection of certain inalienable political rights—among them the right of free speech, free press, free worship, trial by jury, freedom from unreasonable searches and seizures. They were our rights to life and liberty."

This great President then finalized this idea with these words:

"We have come to a clear realization of the fact that true individual freedom cannot exist without economic security and independence. Necessitous men are not free men. People who are hungry and out of a job are the stuff of which dictatorships are made. In our day these economic truths have become accepted as self-evident. We have accepted, so to speak, a second Bill of Rights under which a new basis of security and prosperity can be established for all—regardless of station, race or creed."

This conception of liberty, Mr. President, should be championed and consistently safeguarded in the international order also, in relations between all peoples, with the developing countries and with the Third World, which has so great a need for help from the industrialized nations to resolve the frequently life-and-death alternatives which encroach on all sides.

While I speak, millions of human beings are fighting against hunger. In 1979, 18 million children in the world died of malnutrition. This slaughter of the innocents is a condemnation which weighs heavily on the consciences of every statesman—and I am no exception. To resolve these agonizing problems means to strengthen that liberty proclaimed in the noble words of President Roosevelt.

To defend this liberty intact and indivisible, the United States have twice set foot on the old continent; these two memorable landings I myself lived through during the First and Second World Wars. And the gravestones recalling those American soldiers who laid down their lives that Europe might be free remain an everlasting monument to the defense of liberty.

These men indeed died for Europe's freedom, since the United States were not drawn to Europe by desire for conquest, but only by the firm resolution to stem the rising tide of authoritarian regimes. These men—I repeat—came to defend our liberty.

Mr. President, Italy is committed to a policy of dialog and détente in its awareness of the need for contacts which foster an understanding of the stances adopted by others and make its own position understood; this in the conviction that détente is the only possible way forward if a dangerous and complex spiral is to be avoided in international relations. Only an overall climate able to contribute to the maintenance of relations of friendship and confidence can effectively place relations between states in a framework within which elements of opposition and controversy can be settled and their causes progressively reduced.

This is the spirit which inspires our participation in the Atlantic Alliance, just as this is also the spirit which guides our staunch commitment to the creation of a politically unified Europe. Both these undertakings seem the surest means of removing the threats to peace, reducing tension, and achieving all those essential conditions for the peaceful and harmonious development of our peoples.

It is nevertheless necessary, particularly at a time when the future is so overshadowed with uncertainties, to succeed in expressing that Western solidarity to which we refer. This solidarity must therefore be translated into concerted and united positions on the major problems which confront us. If indeed a lesson can be learned from the analysis of the present political situation and outlook, it is surely the need—or urgency, rather—to strengthen ties, to create new forms of consultation and cooperation, in common recognition of the commitment which makes all of us equally indispensable to collective security.

It is for these reasons that we feel profound solidarity and sympathy with the feelings of the people of the United States and for the stand taken by the U.S. Government over the distressing issue of the Tehran hostages. I personally understand, Mr. President, the agony of your thoughts: to be forced to adopt embittered caution to avoid a global conflict. I have often asked myself what would have happened if the hostages had been of some other nationality. I am proud to have been the first to express full solidarity with you and to dispatch a firm protest to the Tehran authorities.

Our support of a friendly nation and ally is at this time inspired above all by concern for what is needed to restore as quickly as possible a situation of legality which has been so brutally overthrown. These events risk involving that overall climate of international relations in the overthrowal of rules which traditionally govern relations between states, when it is that climate which is the cornerstone of the very existence of states founded on the rule of law.

For these same reasons, Italy is opposed to any departure from the principle of constantly striving to safeguard détente. In particular, Italy deplores that most serious departure currently perpetrated in Afghanistan. This indeed jeopardizes not only local equilibria but also the general principles governing coexistence between peoples.

Yet again, therefore, we voice our firm protest against the brutal invasion of that country. With our own memories of the struggle against foreign powers who occupied and oppressed our country, we send out from this place, which is today honored by your presence, Mr. President, a message of brotherly solidarity to the Afghan patriots who are heroically pursuing their struggle against the invader. It would be cowardice to resign ourselves to the criminal act which has been committed, and cowardice is the main enemy not only of peace but also of democracy.

The task of defending peace and democracy in the world must be a common task. Europe must take its own responsibility for this onerous task if it is to survive; this responsibility can validly be undertaken by Europe to the degree to which the continent can succeed in achieving its unity. But this unity will never be obtained unless we learn to put aside our egotism and individual interests and permit the admission of nations such as Spain and Portugal to the European Community.

I still vividly recall my recent visit to Spain. This nation, which has without bloodshed made the transition from a long dictatorship to democracy, is today totally committed to its social and economic rebirth under the guidance of a young and wise sovereign.

A truly united Europe will never come into being while we continue to create restricted "executive boards," or worse, even more limited bodies. The nations of democratic Europe—all nations, without discriminations of any sort—must take their place with equal rights and equal obligations. Italy has shown that she can fulfill her obligation, but she intends to see her rights and, above all, her national dignity, properly safeguarded.

You are familiar, Mr. President, with discriminations which have been practiced or attempted towards Italy. The United States has supported us, and for this, Mr. President, we are grateful. Yet permit me, nevertheless, as a representative of Italy—this country to which I have dedicated my whole life—to lodge my protest.

These discriminations are senseless, because they do not take into consideration the strategic importance derived from the nation's geographical position. Italy is a democratic bridge uniting Europe with Africa and the Middle East, and in the alarming event that this bridge should be destroyed, not only would the Mediterranean area be destabilized but world peace itself placed in jeopardy. Moreover, the terrorism in our country is probably aimed at just this objective.

With equal rights and equal obligations for each member and without these absurd discriminations, European unity can be truly created. Then, and only then, Europe, which has been a battlefield for centuries, can become through its human, cultural, technological, and industrial potential, a land of solidarity. A Europe on these lines could truly contribute to the strengthening and defense of world peace.

With these intentions and these remarks, I propose this toast to ever closer ties between Italy and the United States, to your own personal well-being and that of Mrs. Carter and all those present.

PRESIDENT CARTER. *Mr. President, ladies and gentlemen:*

It's a great honor for me to be here on a trip of great economic importance to our Nation and also one of political and diplomatic significance to our two nations and also to the world.

My entire family has been here before me, and I have to admit that the best diplomat is not the one speaking to you. I remember when my mother arrived in Italy without any instructions from the diplomatic corps, she made three statements: First of all, she said she had always through her entire life wanted to meet the Pope; secondly, she congratulated Italy on choosing such a young President; and third she says, "I have never met an ugly Italian man." [*Laughter*]

I learn a lot from these visits. One piece of advice that I've gotten from the President is that when I go to Spain, I not go to bed too early, but be sure to see the flamenco dancers, and I intend to take your advice, Mr. President.

You have a text before you, but I would like to say these words to you, because they are so important to us. We have a lot in common. In each of our lands, a democracy has been born. Each has struggled to achieve the balance of unity and liberty that lead free societies to the highest form of human government—self-government.

Freedom and human rights have no firmer friend in thought and action than President Pertini. For personal liberty and democracy in this country, his country, he paid the price through years of cruel imprisonment. In fact, I understand that in 1940 he was not released from prison as he legally had a right to be, because he was considered especially dangerous. And so he remains today: dangerous to anyone who would threaten to destroy or to diminish the liberty of an individual, the rights of a group, or the life or livelihood of free people.

As chief of state, he was foremost in his appeal to Iranian authorities—the first of all—to release our diplomatic personnel from terrorists, and it gives me great pleasure on this personal occasion to express the gratitude which the American people and I feel for his unswerving support.

This morning, President Pertini and I discussed some of the central issues that are troubling world peace. Later I was able to discuss these questions with Prime Minister Cossiga, whose visit to Washington in January and whose presidency of the European Community have so deeply impressed us all.

Three basic ideas ran through our discussions today. The first is that the best possible policy for our countries, as we face a time of danger, change, and testing in the 1980's, is a policy that seeks both strong defense of national security and lasting world peace, for the plain truth is that the one is necessary to the other.

In decades past the West successfully resisted Soviet expansionism, both eastward and westward. Today we see the Soviet Union thrusting southward directly into Afghanistan and indirectly through Vietnam and Cambodia. This represents a strategic challenge to the vital interests of the West and to the industrial democracies. We must face it together. If we are firm in our resolve, we will define a position from which we can encourage détente. If we fail, we will have allowed the strategic, political, and economic balance to be gravely altered in favor of totalitarianism.

A second belief we share is that we cannot defend our common heritage of freedom by arms alone. Our future—the future of our way of life—is equally dependent upon our ability to provide economic opportunity and social justice for all our citizens and to create a decent world environment in which freedom can survive and prosper. We must be careful thinkers and practical politicians in our approach to energy independence, inflation, developing nations, arms control,

and peace in troubled regions, such as the Middle East.

The third basic idea that ran through our discussions today is that national security and world peace can only be achieved by maintaining a strong and united Atlantic Alliance. Just as the best form of government is self-government, so the strongest cement of any alliance is free will. Ours is an alliance of independent democracies. We draw strength both from our common traditions and our individual differences.

Mr. President, let us not be afraid to confront directly and in full public view the most fundamental challenges of our alliance today. We've heard a great deal recently about the differences and the disagreements among the Western democracies. Some voices in my country and in Europe talk about disarray. Some pessimists view debate among democratic nations as a signal of fatal weakness. They predict the decline of Western civilization, spreading pessimism, materialism, softness of will, and diminishing confidence in ourselves and in our institutions.

Our experience and reality itself shows clearly that these self-styled realists are wrong. Our open and public grappling with economic and social problems cannot obscure the extraordinary achievements of our society as a whole. The democratic nations are magnets for young students from all over the world. The democratic world is a center of intellectual and technological invention. It's a great focus of cultural creativity. It's undergoing a major resurgence of religious belief, and our political institutions establish and exhibit a resilience unmatched by any society in the totalitarian world.

It is not from democracy that millions of refugees have fled since 1945. It is not to escape democracy that people have risked their lives in small boats in the high seas during recent weeks. It is not from democracy that nearly 10 percent of the people of an entire Asian nation have left their ancient homeland. And it is certainly not from democracy, but from foreign oppression, that hundreds of thousands—almost a million—of men, women, and children have now fled Afghanistan. These votes of fleeting millions are being cast—as the voices of millions more are being raised—for the deeply rooted faith that gives democracy its unique dynamism: Our underlying belief in the inalienable rights and dignity of human beings.

Material accomplishments and cultural vitality alone cannot express the power of our spiritual heritage. Nor is the spirit of our society found simply in the enterprise, the skills, or success of our people. The fundamental desire for democracy rises from the very center of the human heart and the human soul. That's why the echo of the unsilenceable call for liberty is heard throughout the world. That call finds its voice in the nations assembling in Venice tomorrow.

Our faith in human rights—the freedom, the dignity, and the value of every individual—is the most compelling revolutionary concept of our times. It has produced a level of economic progress and intellectual creativity unmatched by any other political philosophy or idea. We have no reason to fear change, new ideas, or new problems. We do not rely on military invasions by so-called friendly neighbors, much less on terrorism, to sustain the idea of liberty. It stands on its own merit.

The search for freedom and democracy has spread throughout recent years—in Spain, in Portugal, in Greece, in Africa, in Latin America. Today the genuine human voice of democracy rings far more clearly than the rasping loudspeakers of authoritarian regimes.

But while liberty need not be imposed by force, we know all too well that once won, it must be defended. To quote from your statement, Mr. President, "Cowardice is the main enemy not only of peace but also of democracy." The search for peace demands strength, not weakness; firmness, not vacillation; pride, not arrogance. We do not seek to remake the world on the model of America or the West. We want the peoples of the world to decide their own destiny and to make their own choices. We are confident, because history is on the side of freedom.

Let there be no mistake about this: The West is not motivated by relentless hostility nor by a desire for indiscriminate confrontation nor a return to the cold war.

But for the Western alliance simply to accept foreign occupation and domination of Afghanistan as an accomplished fact would be a cynical signal to the world that could only encourage further aggression, further tension, and further danger to world peace. It is our responsibility to register in concrete terms our condemnation of the Soviet invasion for as long as that invasion continues.

We cannot know with certainty the motivations of the latest Soviet move, whether Afghanistan is the purpose or the prelude, but there can be no doubt that this invasion poses an increased threat to the independence of nations in the region and to the world's access to vital resources and to vital sealanes. The fact is that our democracies are dependent on oil supplies from a volatile region whose own security from internal divisions and from external threat is now in question. Unresolved, that security problem could change the way we live. Already it does touch directly or drastically the lives of all.

But our interest in peace and stability in the region goes far beyond economics. In this ever more interdependent world, to assume that aggression need be met only when it occurs at one's own doorstep is to tempt new and very serious adventures.

Détente with the Soviets remains our goal, but détente must be built on a firm foundation of deterring aggression. The Soviets must understand that they cannot recklessly threaten world peace or still enjoy the benefits of cooperation while pursuing a policy of armed intervention. Above all, everyone must know that efforts cannot succeed to divide our alliance nor to lull us into a false belief that somehow America or Europe can be an island of détente while aggression is carried out elsewhere.

We recognize, Mr. President, that our policy towards those who might threaten peace must be clear, it must be consistent, it must be comprehensible. There must be no room for any miscalculation. But let me be equally clear that the way to improved relations is open, and that is the path we prefer.

I'm confident that just as the American people want to sustain strong policies against Soviet aggression, they also want our strong efforts to continue at arms control. We know that the SALT II agreement can contribute directly to the security not only of the United States but of Europe and indeed of the entire world. It can help to restrain future arms competition, continue the historically important direction of nuclear arms limitation, and keep our faith that even the most dangerous differences can be resolved in a framework of cooperation. Especially now in this time of tension, observing the mutual constraints imposed by the treaty is in the best interest of every nation on Earth.

Therefore, I intend to honor the object and purpose of the treaty as long as the Soviet Union, as observed by us, does the same. I will remain in close consultation with our Congress with the goal of seeking the ratification of SALT II at the earliest opportune time.

Further, if the decade of the 1980's is not to become the decade of violence, we must work with our friends on renewed efforts to stabilize all aspects of arms competition and to widen the scope of arms control agreements.

In sum, I do not accept forecasts of weakness or failure for democracy in the world. Our societies, our values, our freedoms will decline only if we allow them to do so; only if we surrender to uncertainty about where we stand and in what we believe; only if we forget that each nation and each individual share a responsibility to pull together and defend those common beliefs which unite us—and I am convinced that none of us will ever surrender nor forget.

Mr. President, Mr. Prime Minister, ladies and gentlemen, just as within each democracy we must work to nourish the spirit of community which alone can make the whole of a nation larger than the sum of its parts, so within the alliance of free nations it is equally true that unless we work together we shall surely be vulnerable separately.

I pledge America's own unswerving commitment to our common interest of security and peace, and we depend on our European friends and allies to join us in that effort. Together we can and will defend the values and interests of our society. Historical experience counsels such a course. Present circumstances compels it.

It is in this spirit of alliance and partnership that I ask you to join me in a toast. If you would please rise. To President Pertini, to the traditions of two great nations that are at once parallel and intertwined, and to the unbreakable spirit of freedom, friendship, and the love of human life that will forever join our countries and our people.

NOTE: The exchange of toasts began at 9:35 p.m. in the Salon delle Feste at the Quirinale Palace. President Pertini spoke in Italian, and as printed above, the translation of his remarks follows the White House press release.

Italy: Conclusion of State Visit

Joint Press Statement. June 20, 1980

At the invitation of the President of the Italian Republic Sandro Pertini, the President of the United States of America, Jimmy Carter, paid a state visit to Rome June 19–21. The visit provided an opportunity for the two Presidents to have a productive exchange of views. Constructive meetings were also held between President Carter and the President of the Council of Ministers, Francesco Cossiga. The meetings were also attended by Minister of Foreign Affairs Emilio Colombo and Secretary of State Edmund Muskie.

The two sides noted with satisfaction the extremely close relations between the United States and Italy which are based on longstanding ties of friendship and kinship, a common commitment to democratic values and on ties which derive from the membership of the two countries in the Atlantic Alliance. In the course of the discussions, an exchange of views was held on key international issues of particular concern to both governments; these included the crisis in Afghanistan, the Middle East situation, the grave problem of the illegal detention of the hostages in Iran, and U.S.-Italian cooperation for the promotion of security and peace. President Carter expressed appreciation for the constructive role played by Prime

Minister Cossiga, in his capacity as President of the European Community for the current term.

The international situation created by the Soviet Union's armed intervention and continuing occupation of Afghanistan was examined in depth. It was agreed that this Soviet action, taken in flagrant violation of the United Nations Charter, constitutes a threat to peace, poses a grave challenge to the West and to its interests in Southwest Asia and the Persian Gulf, and that it has created a serious obstacle to the continuation of the process of detente.

As a result of this assessment, both sides view as indispensable a comprehensive Western political strategy designed to make clear to the Soviet Union by the application of tangible measures the necessity of a prompt and complete withdrawal of its troops from Afghanistan.

In line with that view, the two sides welcomed the concerted steps which NATO is now pursuing in order to strengthen the common defense in response to the strategic challenge faced by all the Western allies. The two governments confirmed their commitment to the earliest possible fulfillment of the goals embodied in NATO's long-term defense program. Both sides recognized that increased European attention to security requirements within the NATO treaty area assumes even greater urgency because of U.S. commitment of resources toward building a security framework in the region of Southwest Asia and the Persian Gulf.

President Carter and Prime Minister Cossiga expressed their satisfaction with the NATO decision to pursue the complementary objectives of arms control, and the deployment of theater nuclear forces. President Carter reiterated his admiration for Prime Minister Cossiga's leadership in this effort. Prime Minister Cossiga reaffirmed Italy's active support to implement the NATO offer of December 12, 1979, inviting the Soviet Union to begin negotiations on the limitation of long range theater nuclear weapons systems.

President Carter expressed his own appreciation and that of the entire American people for Italy's support of the international effort to secure the release of the American hostages held by Iran in violation of international law and universally accepted standards of decency. It was stressed that the principle of the rule of law, vital to the health and stability of the world community, is at stake in this crisis. The conviction was also expressed that the release of the hostages constitutes a precondition for reestablishing the international prestige of Iran and for the resumption of mutually beneficial relations with its government, including the revocation of economic sanctions.

Turning to other questions of common interest, President Carter reiterated the U.S. commitment for a comprehensive peace in the Middle East, including the resolution of the Palestinian problem in all its aspects. He reaffirmed his belief that the Camp David accords continue to provide the soundest framework for building on the significant progress which has already been achieved toward ending the decades of bitterness and conflict in the Middle East.

President Cossiga expressed Italy's full agreement with the objective of a comprehensive and durable peace with justice for all, for Israel as well as for the Arab countries and for the Palestinian people. This objective is shared by the United States. It is also endorsed by the countries of the European Community and was reconfirmed in the June 13 declaration of the European Council in Venice.

In the context of the efforts designed to achieve this objective he expressed the hope that significant progress could be made in the implementation of all aspects of the agreement reached at Camp David, thanks to the personal and courageous commitment of President Carter.

Both sides reaffirmed their commitment to work toward détente, based on principles of reciprocity and mutual restraint. They agreed that détente can be achieved only on condition that its comprehensive and indivisible character is acknowledged as indispensable.

An exchange of views on the agenda of the Venice Summit to be held June 22–23 followed. President Carter expressed his appreciation for the extensive preparations which Italy, as host, has made on behalf of the seven industrialized democracies which will participate in the Summit.

The two sides agreed on the need for closer consultations among the industrialized democracies to formulate a comprehensive strategy based on mutual security to meet the challenges of the eighties the crises, the instability and conflicts in the world frequently caused by poverty, underdevelopment and injustice.

To further the close bilateral relations between Italy and the United States it was agreed to intensify mutually advantageous cooperation in a variety of fields. The two governments announced their decision to cooperate in the design of the world's largest installation for the direct conversion of sunlight into electricity; a one megawatt photovoltaic plant to be located in Puglia. They agreed to carry forward other projects for research and information exchange in the solar field and in coal technologies, geothermal energy, nuclear safety and energy conservation.

In the social sector, it was agreed to continue cooperation to combat unemployment, particularly among the young. Satisfaction was also expressed for the positive impact of the Social Security Agreement. The two governments will continue to cooperate on both a bilateral and multilateral basis for the suppression of international narcotics traffic, together with the prevention and treatment of drug abuse.

Expanding knowledge of the languages of the two countries was considered. Having noted with satisfaction the results of the Memorandum of Agreement signed in Rome on May 4, 1978, both sides agreed to work together to produce television programs for the teaching of their respective languages. The Italian government announced its intention to increase its financial contribution to the Fulbright Program to match the U.S. contribution in the next years.

The decision recently announced by the Cini Foundation in Venice and by the Guggenheim Foundation in New York, to collaborate on the establishment of a major cultural center in Venice, was cited with satisfaction as a concrete and valid example of the contribution which the private sector offers to the development of bilateral relations between the United States and Italy.

Italian participants at the meeting at the Quirinale today:

PRESIDENT SANDRO PERTINI

EMILIO COLOMBO, Foreign Minister

ANTONIO MACCANICO, Secretary General of the Presidency of the Republic

PAOLO PANSA CEDRONIO, Italian Ambassador to the United States

Italian participants at the meeting at Villa Madama today:

FRANCESCO COSSIGA, President of the Council of Ministers

EMILIO COLOMBO, Foreign Minister

PAOLO PANSA CEDRONIO, Italian Ambassador to the United States

MINISTER SERGIO BERLINGUER, Diplomatic Adviser to the Prime Minister

AMBASSADOR FRANCESCO MARIA MALFATTI, Secretary General to the Foreign Ministry

American participants at both the meeting at the Quirinale and the Villa Madama:

THE PRESIDENT

EDMUND MUSKIE, Secretary of State

ZBIGNIEW BRZEZINSKI, Assistant to the President for National Security Affairs

GEORGE VEST, Assistant Secretary of State for European Affairs

RICHARD GARDNER, United States Ambassador to Italy

Italy: Visit to American Embassy

Remarks to Embassy Employees and Members of the American Community in Rome.
June 21, 1980

As I stand on this United States land in the midst of a friendly nation, I bring you greetings from the motherland and the deep thanks of all Americans for the wonderful work that you're doing here. Thank you from the bottom of our heart.

I would be remiss if I did not particularly thank Ambassador Richard Gardner and his wife, Danielle, who is from Venice and who will be helping us to see the beautiful city there beginning this afternoon.

As you know, there are about 20 million American citizens who have ties of blood and kinship with the people of Italy. They've come to our Nation over the last 200-year period, looking not only for a different life, a new life, an exciting life, but at the same time, retaining their hopes and their dreams, their deep commitment to their heritage and their religion. And those bonds of friendship and of kinship are very dear and very precious to all the citizens of our Nation.

During this last 2 days, I've had a chance to meet with the Prime Minister of Italy, Mr. Cossiga. I've had a chance to meet with all the leaders of the political parties that comprise the coalition which has formed such a close alliance with the United States of America—their predecessors, as well, in the coalition who were equally strong in their commitment to our Nation and to the strength of friendship and mutual purpose.

We've spent a lot of time with President Pertini, who has captured all the Carter women—my mother, my wife, my daughter, all of whom preceded me here, as you know. As we've had a chance to speak with him in quiet moments and in moments of ceremony, it's been an inspiration to know that for the cause of freedom and for the cause of democracy, he spent 15 of his years in prison, never yielding in his commitment to the principles and to the ideals which are the foundation for our own Nation's commitments for now and in the future.

Ours is a strong nation, the strongest nation on Earth. We're strong militarily, and we will remain so, because we know that peace can only be maintained through strength. But we are also strong economically, and we are strong politically. Our commitment to human rights, our commitments to morality and to the principles that guide the yearnings of the most insignificant and the most powerful

human beings is a basic element of the strength that does not change.

This is a troubled time. We are sometimes facing challenge. We are sometimes facing difficulty. We are sometimes facing change, which is unpredictable. We are sometimes even facing danger. I particularly want to express my thanks to all of you for being willing in a time of change and trouble and challenge—for being willing to serve our Nation in a foreign land.

The military here are a constant reminder to me of what has happened in Iran and in other places around the world when diplomatic personnel, knowing that they were in danger, served their nation without flinching and without complaint and effectively. We are thankful that the good relationships that exist with Italy remove that kind of danger from your lives. But I know that every day of my own life I think constantly about the 53 innocent Americans who are the victims of international terrorism, supported by the Government of Iran, and we never forget them in our prayers and in our considerations for the future.

As soon as I leave here I will go to meet with the Pope, who is a man revered and admired by Americans of all faiths.

His visit to our country was one of unbelievable triumph. In Chicago a million and a half people assembled to hear him speak and to perform the ceremony of the Mass. Many of those in Chicago, as you know, were Italian Americans. And this is a time of deep appreciation for what he means to the entire world—his commitment to peace, his commitment to the control of weapons, his commitment to the alleviation of suffering and hunger, his commitment to the plight of refugees who are seeking to escape from persecution and from totalitarian governments. These commitments of his are shared by us. The official position of our own Government mirrors exactly those kinds of commitments exemplified by the life of this wonderful religious leader.

And then this afternoon I'll go down to Venice to meet with our allies and friends in the industrialized nations of the West, not only the European allies but also our friends from Canada and from Japan. We'll be talking about how to give within the concept of peace a better life for all our people and, therefore, a better life for the people of the entire world.

Sometimes you hear or read in the press about the differences among our governments. Some differences do exist. They're the differences founded on independence, on free will, on the autonomy of nations. We're not a subservient group. Each one of us has our own ideas, our own perspective, our own ultimate goals. But the facet of this relationship that is overwhelmingly important is the common ground on which we stand together.

Those differences among us, highly publicized with a free press and freedom of speech, is a relatively insignificant part of the relationship that binds these Western allies together. We stand staunchly for freedom, for democracy, for progress, for peace through strength, with unchanging principles and unchanging moral commitments.

Those are the aspects of American life which you represent. And as you deal on a commercial basis, to control the spread of drugs, to search out common ground with the people of Italy, you carry out those principles in a fine, dedicated, sometimes even sacrificial way.

Again, to repeat my first phrases, from the bottom of my heart as President, and on behalf of Secretary Muskie, who's here with me, and the 220 million people who are very proud of you, thank you and may God bless you all.

NOTE: The President spoke at 9 a.m. in the courtyard of the Embassy.

Italy: Meeting With Pope John Paul II

Exchange of Remarks.   June 21, 1980

THE PRESIDENT. Your Holiness, as happy as I was to welcome you as the first Pope to visit in the White House, I'm equally happy today to be welcomed by you to your ancient and holy city.

Like millions before me, I'm moved by the beautiful works of Michelangelo, of Raphael, or Bernini, and many other great artists. They've left us proof that when our energies are expended away from destruction and toward creation, that we are able to do the work of the divine in the service of mankind. Today, as perhaps never before, heads of nations and leaders of religious faith as well stand in need of a shared commitment to serve humanity.

In the midst of a trip which I'm presently taking, whose objective is to promote peace and cooperation and common purpose with the close partners of my country, it has been a privilege today to meet with a man passionately dedicated to these same ideals.

I'm gratified that we share a belief that the struggle to enhance the dignity and decency of individual human lives gives meaning to history; that through our actions our beliefs are given life; that the role of a state is not to crush, but to free the spirit of its people; and that it is the duty of leaders to join together with all who would walk in the ways of peace.

Our common pilgrimage is more urgent than ever before. The world's resources, meant by God for the use of all, are diverted on a grand scale to finance means of destructon. Homeless people by the millions, often driven from their lands by violence and subjected to hunger and disease, wander the world in search of elemental dignity which has been denied to them.

We all share the responsibility for bringing these tragedies to an end. In the current world situation, we know it is fraught with conflictng interests that threaten bloodshed. It is also alive with possibilities for reconciliation, and we must seize these initiatives and use them.

Nations can begin by heeding a universal moral and political imperative that the protection of the human rights of each person is the premise and the purpose of governments. They can also respect as sacrosanct the sovereignty of other nations.

America's settlers were drawn to our own shores by the promise of freedom and of a better life. Over our long history, now more than 200 years, America has been guided by the traditions of that continuing quest, not only for ourselves but for all peoples. That's why the pursuit of individual freedom, the security of nations and the peace of the world are basic principles of American foreign policy. And that is why Americans feel such deep admiration and so much love for Pope John Paul II.

Americans of all faiths rejoiced in his visit to our country last year. It was one of the most remarkable events in the history of our Nation. And we have watched with respect and with gratitude as he's touched millions of lives in his further travels. His moral and spiritual leadership has focused the attention of the world upon those suffering from hunger, from poverty and disease; upon refugees in every corner of the Earth; and upon those laboring under political repression.

The United States shares these concerns of His Holiness. They are our unfinished tasks as well. America has responded generously to the men, women, and children of Kampuchea, and we are acting with justice and with charity toward those people escaping from intolerable conditions in the Caribbean. And we work with the international relief agencies, such as the Catholic Relief Services, in providing food and shelter for those who are displaced by warfare in Indochina, the Horn of Africa, and Afghanistan.

In addition, the United States is trying to provide new leadership toward a just and lasting peace in the Middle East. We are pleased to champion the cause of democracy and human development in Latin America, and we will continue to make the United States more worthy as a nation committed to social justice, to economic opportunity, and to religious freedom.

One thing more, and this is deeply important to me. On behalf of the American people, Your Holiness, I would like personally to thank you for your efforts toward the release of the 53 American hostages being held in Iran, victims of terrorism who are being held in continued defiance of international law and universally accepted standards of decency.

We do have many unfinished tasks, but we have many resources—of courage, patience, faith, strength, and love. We've renewed these sources in our meeting today. Together we are working toward a day when human beings shall not make others go homeless and hungry, when all people will have a voice in deciding their own destiny, when we will at last lift the terrible fear of nuclear destruction from our children and from their children, when the values and ideals of freedom are respected by all governments, and when humility and the service of the human spirit and the human condition is the high honor of ever human state.

Your Holiness, it's been an honor and a pleasure for me to be with you, and I go with the hope that your prayers will be with me.

THE POPE. Mr. President, it is a great pleasure for me to welcome you today. I am very happy to be able to reciprocate the warm welcome I received from you in Washington. The memories of my visit to the White House and of all my other contacts with the people of the United States are stored in my heart. They are recalled with joy and are frequently expressed in my prayers for America.

Your visit today to the Vatican as President of the United States is greatly appreciated. I am pleased to see in it an indication of your country's profound respect and esteem for ethical and religious values, a respect and esteem which are so characteristic of millions and millions of Americans of different faiths.

During my visit last October, I was a personal witness to the way these spiritual values find expression in the lives of your people, how they form the moral fabric of your nation, how they constitute the strength of the civil state which does not forget that it was founded on sound moral principles and which wishes to preserve its heritage as one nation under God.

All fields of human endeavor are enriched by true ethical values. During my pastoral journey I had occasion to speak of these values and to profess my own profound esteem for all who embrace them in national life. There is no sphere of activity that does not benefit when religious values are actively pursued. The political, social, and economic domains are authenticated and reinforced by the application of those moral standards that must be irrevocably incorporated into the tradition of every state.

The same principles that guide the internal destinies of a people should direct their relationships with other nations. I desire to express my esteem for all those who, at the national and international level, have exemplified the values of compassion and justice, of personal concern for others, and fraternal sharing in an effort to promote ever greater freedom, ever more authentic equality, and an ever more stable peace for a world craving for truth, unity, and love.

At the center of all sublime spiritual values is the worth of every human person worthy of respect, from the first moment of existence, endowed with dignity and rights, and called to share responsibility for every brother and sister in need. In the cause of dignity and human rights the Church is intent on offering to the world the contribution of the Gospel of Christ, proclaiming that man is created in the image and likeness of God and destined for life everlasting.

Although, as the Second Vatican Council emphasizes, the Church is not a political entity, she still serves together with the political community, but by a separate title, the personal and social evocation of the same human beings. And, while distinct from the socio-economic realm, the Church is called to serve it by proclaiming that man is the source and center and purpose of all socio-economic life.

In this area, as in so many others, the Church is happy to speak out in favor of the human person and for everything that is advantageous to humanity. Moreover, she gives the assurance of her support for all that is done for the good of mankind according to the distinctive contribution of each one. In this sense, church and state are called to collaborate in the cause of man and in the promotion of sacred human dignity.

This collaboration is eminently useful, and it corresponds to the truth about man. Through the ethical formation of true citizens who work side by side with their fellow citizens, the Church fulfills another aspect of her collaboration with the political community.

And today, in this context, Mr. President, I wish to assure you of my deep interest in every effort aimed at the betterment of humanity and devoted to world peace, and particularly the Middle East and neighboring regions occupy our common attention because of the immense importance they hold for international well-being. I offer my prayers that all worthy endeavors at reconciliation and cooperation may be crowned with success.

The question of Jerusalem, which during these very days attracts the attention of the world in a special way, is pivotal to a just peace in those parts of the world, since this holy city embodies interests and aspirations that are shared by different peoples in different ways. It is my hope that a common monotheistic tradition of faith will help to promote harmony among all those who call upon God. I would renew my earnest plea that just attention be given to the issues affecting Lebanon and the whole Palestinian problem.

The Holy See is aware of the worldwide aspect of the responsibility that falls to the United States. It is likewise conscious of the risks involved in facing this responsibility. But despite all inconveniences and problems, despite human limitations, governments of good will must continue to work for peace and for international understanding in the control and reduction of armaments, in the promotion of

the North-South dialog, and in furthering advancement of developing nations.

Just recently, on my visit to Africa, I was able to perceive personally the importance of that continent and the contribution it is called to make to the good of the world. But all this, in turn, requires the interests, support, and fraternal assistance of other peoples so that African stability, independence, and rightful autonomy will be safeguarded and reinforced.

The question of human dignity is particularly linked with efforts on behalf of justice. Any violation of justice anywhere is an affront to human dignity, and all effective contributions to justice are truly worthy of the greatest praise.

The purification of structures in the political, social, and economic fields cannot help but yield salutary results. I know of the interest of the United States in the situation in Central America, especially at this time. Persevering efforts are required and must be sustained until every brother and sister in that part of the world and elsewhere is secure in his or her dignity and free from manipulation by any power, overt or subtle, anywhere on Earth.

I hope that the United States will lend its powerful support to efforts which effectively uplift the human level of peoples in need.

As I mentioned, my contacts with the people of the United States are vivid in my memory. Enthusiasm and generosity, the will not to fall into enslaving materialism, in the pursuit of the common good at home and in the international field, and for Christians, the need to communicate justice and the peace of Christ—these are the forces that the Holy See encourages for the benefit of humanity.

Mr. President, my words today are meant to be an expression of appreciation for what has been done, and echo of the persistent needs of the world, a challenge of hope and confidence to the American people, whom I have known and loved so much. May God sustain you and bless the nation which you represent.

NOTE: The President spoke at 11:34 a.m. in the Papal Study at the Vatican.

Italy: Beatification of Kateri Takakwitha

Remarks of the President and the Pope to Americans Attending the Ceremony.
June 21, 1980

THE PRESIDENT. *Your Holiness, Your Eminences, Your Excellencies, and fellow Americans:*

Last October, John Paul II became the first Pope to visit in the White House. It was an historic occasion, a happy occasion, a day of solemn joy as we marked a milestone in the long and intertwined history of faiths and of nations.

Today marks a milestone of a different sort, but of similar significance. Once again we share a moment of reflection on the intertwinings of history and, I hope, a time of inspiration for the future.

Many of you have traveled here to mark a very special event: the recognition which the Roman Catholic Church is giving to five of her faithful. One of those five was a truly native American: Kateri Takakwitha. His Holiness and I have been practicing how to pronounce her name. [*Laughter*]

She was born a Mohawk, a member of the tribe that is the keeper of the eastern door of the great Iroquois confederacy. She spent her life in what is now New York State, but we willingly share her memory and her honor with our Canadian neighbors.

Although she lived three centuries ago—this year is the 300th anniversary of her death at only 24 years of age—she is still remembered for her selfless, steadfast faith that has transcended time and place and mere human mortality. Beatification has a public meaning for members of the Catholic Church, but people of many religious traditions and origins can feel the joy and the satisfaction of tomorrow's events.

I'm glad to be able to join you and to join Their Eminences John Cardinal Krol, Terence Cardinal Cooke, and William Cardinal Baum, and His Excellence Howard Hubbard, Bishop of Albany.

In sharing this joy and satisfaction with you, I want to say a word of greetings also to the others gathered here, to the students, the teachers, the officials of church and also of civil affairs who live and work here. Your activities contribute to the task of building peace and justice in the world. By making that contribution, you are witnesses to an essential element of the American spirit: concern for the world and its people, concern for human and humane values, concern for the religious impulse which seeks to put itself at the service of the highest human aspirations.

In this beautiful place we are surrounded by treasures. There are the tangible treasures: the statues and the priceless works of art. And there are the invisible treasures: the inspirational works of faith. These invisible treasures are what make this such a timeless place, so full of history, and such a boundless place, when its physical expanse is small. All of you here today bear witness to that. The dedication and commitment that you've come to honor is the kind that we must strive to rekindle.

Finally, let me say that in this trying time, when so many fall victim to violence, to hunger, and to tyranny, we need the integrity of words and actions. We need those who inspire, those whom we can emulate. Those whom you've come in pilgrimage to honor are such as that. So is the great world leader who honors us by his presence in this room.

Ladies and gentlemen, as President of our country, and as a Christian, it is a great honor for me to present to you His Holiness Pope John Paul II.

THE POPE. *Mr. President, Your Eminences, dear friends from the United States:*

Your visit today takes me back in spirit to America. I have already met this morning with the President of your country, and now your presence evokes the different categories of people that I met last October. A number of these groups are represented in the American community in Rome. My particular greetings go to Cardinal Krol, Cardinal Cooke, and to the bishops who have come especially for this occasion, and also for the occasion of beatification of the first Indian American blessed, to Cardinal Baum and to Bishop Machinkos, who assist me day after day in Rome, and to the large number of American seminarians.

Every gathering of Americans elicits some reference to your homeland and to the bountiful gifts that God has bestowed on your people, gifts of nature as well as spiritual and religious blessings. A few years ago, on the occasion of your Bicentennial celebration at which I was present in Philadelphia, you made a special effort to emphasize your heritage and to preserve the gifts you had received.

Every gift that comes from God creates a responsibility in the recipient. This is very true of America, where God's gifts have been abundant. One of the eminent gifts that constitute the special heritage of all your people, people of different backgrounds, ethnic origins, and creeds, is the gift of freedom, a gift to be guarded and perfected and a gift to be used, not as an absolute and in itself, but as a means of ensuring the pursuit of all the truly human values. And so, as people, you have a shared responsibility for preserving freedom and for purifying it.

Like so many other things of great value, freedom is fragile. Saint Peter recognized this when he told the Christians never to use their freedom as a pretext for evil. Any distortion of truth or dissemination of no truth is an offense against freedom. Any manipulation of public opinion, any abuse of authority or power or, on the other hand, just the omission of vigilance endangers the heritage of a free people.

But even more important, every contribution to promoting truth and charity consolidates freedom and builds up peace. When shared responsibility for freedom is truly accepted by all, a great new force is set at work for the service of humanity. The same need for shared responsibility exists for Christians in regard to the Gospel of Christ.

The Gospel is a sacred deposit to be guarded and told ever more effectively, a dynamic message to be lived and to be proclaimed by word and example. It is a gift that is given for the benefit of all. It requires effort from all.

In varying degrees everyone shares responsibility for the word of God, the word of divine truth, lifegiving truth, liberating truth. It is my hope and prayer today that the concerted contribution to freedom of the American community in Rome and the worthy fulfillment of Christian responsibility for the Gospel will become ever more effective for the good of humanity and the glory of God.

And may God bless you in your daily activities and give you joy and peace in His holy name. God bless America.

NOTE: The President spoke at 12:09 p.m. in the Clementine Room at the Vatican. The ceremony marking the beatification of Kateri Takakwitha was held on the following day.

Italy: Meeting With Chancellor Helmut Schmidt of the Federal Republic of Germany

Exchange With Reporters.   June 21, 1980

Q. How about telling us about your talk?

THE PRESIDENT. Very good.

Q. What did you discuss?

THE PRESIDENT. Well, we had a thorough discussion about many issues of interest to both countries. We discussed Afghanistan. We discussed the theater nuclear force question. We discussed the agenda for Chancellor Schmidt's upcoming trip to Moscow in just an outline form. We discussed some of the issues that will be coming up here at the Venice summit conference.

I might say that we have no differences between us about how to deal with Afghanistan. We both agree completely that the Soviets must withdraw all their troops from Afghanistan. As Chancellor Schmidt said, the presence of any of their troops there is unacceptable.

We also understand completely the situation on the theater nuclear force, and I assured Chancellor Schmidt that we have absolutely no doubt that he and the Federal Republic of Germany are completely committed to carry out the agreement that was reached back in December concerning the deployment of theater nuclear force for Western Europe.

Q. Why did you write him the letter then, sir, if you had no doubt about that?

THE PRESIDENT. We're not going to have a press conference, but I would say that I stated in my letter that there had been erroneous press reports, and I outlined the position of the United States concerning the theater nuclear force question.

CHANCELLOR SCHMIDT. I would like to underline any single sentence which the President just spoke, and there isn't really much to add from my side.

Q. Why were you responding to the President's letter, Mr. Chancellor?

THE CHANCELLOR. I am not going to answer press conference-type questions as much as the President did. There will be press conferences at the end of the summit.

Q. But you two agree, then—you do agree on things.

THE PRESIDENT. Yes.

Q. Well, then——

THE CHANCELLOR. I never thought that we did not agree in substance. Thank you very much.

Q. Did you discuss taking up the question of a deployment in Moscow?

Q. Should we write that you like each each other now or what?

THE PRESIDENT. Always have. Thank you very much.

Q. Are you going out tonight, Mr. President?

THE PRESIDENT. I don't know. I don't think so.

NOTE: The exchange began at approximately 8:45 p.m. on the steps of the Cipriani Hotel in Venice.

Venice Economic Summit Conference

Statement on Afghanistan.
June 22, 1980

In seeking here in Venice to define a global economic strategy and to show our united determination to make it a reality, we are consciously accepting the responsibility that falls to the three great industrialized areas of the world—North America, Western Europe and Japan—to help create the conditions for harmonious and sustained economic growth. But we cannot do this alone; others too have a part to play.

However, present circumstances oblige us to emphasize that our efforts will only bear fruit if we can at the same time preserve a world in which the rule of law is universally obeyed, national independence is respected and world peace is kept. We call on all countries to join us in working for such a world and we welcome the readiness of non-aligned countries and regional groups to accept the responsibilities which this involves.

We therefore reaffirm hereby that the Soviet military occupation of Afghanistan is unacceptable now and that we are determined not to accept it in the future. It is incompatible with the will of the Afghan people for national independence, as demonstrated by their courageous resistance, and with the security of the states of the region. It is also incompatible with the principles of the United Nations Charter and with efforts to maintain genuine détente. It undermines the very foundations of peace, both in the region and in the world at large.

We fully endorse in this respect the views already expressed by the overwhelming majority of the international community, as set out by the United Nations General Assembly in Resolution No. ES–6/2 of 14th January 1980 and by the Islamic Conference at both its recent sessions.

Afghanistan should be enabled to regain the sovereignty, territorial integrity, political independence and non-aligned character it once enjoyed. We therefore call for the complete withdrawal of Soviet troops and for the Afghan people to be left free again to determine their own future.

We have taken note of today's announcement of the withdrawal of some Soviet troops from Afghanistan. In order to make a useful contribution to the solution of the Afghan crisis, this withdrawal, if confirmed, will have to be permanent and continue until the complete withdrawal of the Soviet troops. Only thus will it be possible to reestablish a situation compatible with peace and the rule of law and thereby with the interests of all nations.

We are resolved to do everything in our power to achieve this objective. We are also ready to support any initiative to this end, such as that of the Islamic Conference. And we shall support every effort designed to contribute to the political independence and to the security of the states of the region.

Those Governments represented at this meeting which have taken a position against attendance at the Olympic Games vigorously reaffirm their positions.

NOTE: Prime Minister Francesco Cossiga of Italy, Chairman of the Conference, issued the statement to the press on behalf of the Conference participants.

As printed above, this item follows the text of the English translation made available by the White House. It was not issued as a White House press release.

Venice Economic Summit Conference

Statement on the Taking of Diplomatic Hostages.   June 22, 1980

Gravely concerned by recent incidents of terrorism involving the taking of hostages and attacks on diplomatic and consular premises and personnel, the Heads of State and Government reaffirm their determination to deter and combat such acts. They note the completion of work on the International Convention Against the Taking of Hostages and call on all States to consider becoming parties to it as well as to the Convention on the Prevention and Punishment of Crimes Against Internationally Protected Persons of 1973.

The Heads of State and Government vigorously condemn the taking of hostages and the seizure of diplomatic and consular premises and personnel in contravention of the basic norms of international law and practice. The Heads of State and Government consider necessary that all Governments should adopt policies which will contribute to the attainment of this goal and to take appropriate measures to deny terrorists any benefits from such criminal acts. They also resolve to provide to one another's diplomatic and consular missions support and assistance in situations involving the seizure of diplomatic and consular establishments or personnel.

The Heads of State and Government recall that every State has the duty under international law to refrain from organizing, instigating, assisting or participating in terrorist acts in another State or acquiescing in organised activities within its territory directed towards the commission of such acts, and deplore in the strongest terms any breach of this duty.

NOTE: Prime Minister Francesco Cossiga of Italy, Chairman of the Conference, issued the statement to the press on behalf of the Conference participants.

As printed above, this item follows the text of the English translation made available by the White House. It was not issued as a White House press release.

Venice Economic Summit Conference

Statement on Refugees.
June 22, 1980

The Heads of State and Government are deeply concerned at the plight of the ever-increasing number of refugees throughout the world. Hundreds of thousands have already left the Indochinese peninsula and Cuba, many of them taking the risk of fleeing across the open seas. Pakistan and Iran have received almost one million refugees from Afghanistan. In Africa refugees number several millions.

The Heads of State and Government note with great regret that the refugee population continues to grow and that, despite major international relief efforts, their suffering continues. They pay tribute to the generosity and forebearance with which countries in the regions affected have received refugees. For their part, the countries represented at this Summit have already responded substantially to appeals for assistance to and resettlement of refugees. They will continue to do so, but their resources are not unlimited. They appeal to others to join with them in helping to relieve this suffering.

But, however great the effort of the international community, it will be difficult to sustain it indefinitely. The problem of refugees has to be attacked at its root.

The Heads of State and Government therefore make a vigorous appeal to the Governments responsible for it to remove the causes of this widespread human tragedy and not to pursue policies which drive large numbers of their people from their own countries.

NOTE: Prime Minister Francesco Cossiga of Italy, Chairman of the Conference, issued the statement to the press on behalf of the Conference participants.

As printed above, this item follows the text of the English translation made available by the White House. It was not issued as a White House press release.

Venice Economic Summit Conference

Statement on Hijacking.
June 22, 1980

The Heads of State and Government expressed their satisfaction at the broad support of the international community for the principles set out in the Bonn

Declaration of July 1978 as well as in the international Conventions dealing with unlawful interference with civil aviation. The increasing adherence to these Conventions and the responsible attitude taken by States with respect to air-hijacking reflect the fact that these principles are being accepted by the international community as a whole.

The Heads of State and Government emphasize that hijacking remains a threat to international civil aviation and that there can be no relaxation of efforts to combat this threat. To this end they look forward to continuing cooperation with all other Governments.

NOTE: Prime Minister Francesco Cossiga of Italy, Chairman of the Conference, issued the statement to the press on behalf of the Conference participants.

As printed above, this item follows the text of the English translation made avaliable by the White House. It was not issued as a White House press release.

Venice Economic Summit Conference

Exchange With Reporters Following the First Two Sessions. June 22, 1980

THE PRESIDENT. We've completed our first full day of work here at the Venice summit conference. We've spent a great deal of time today talking about both the political and diplomatic interrelationships that bind us together, and also talking about the problem that we face in the 1980's with an almost inevitable reduction in the amount of oil that will be available to us by the end of this decade and the need to take strong, united, concerted conservation commitments among ourselves, and also increase the production of alternate forms of energy other than oil.

I was very pleased at the statement issued by the chairman and our host, Prime Minister Cossiga, this afternoon concern-

ing Afghanistan. This was a carefully worded statement that shows the unity among the seven nations assembled here, the condemnation of the Soviets' invasion of and occupation of Afghanistan, the commitment that we've jointly made to maintain our opposition to this invading force and our admiration for those freedom-fighters in Afghanistan who are seeking to liberate their country from the occupying forces.

We observe with interest the announcement by the Soviet Union that some of their military forces were being withdrawn from Afghanistan. If these reports are confirmed and if these withdrawals are permanent and if these withdrawals are just a first step in moving the Soviets toward a permanent and total withdrawal of their forces from Afghanistan, then of course, this will be a significant thing.

All of the nations who have expressed themselves against participation in the Olympics vigorously reaffirmed their positions today, and all of us were very pleased at the outcome of this first day's work.

Q. Mr. President, could you speak about the timing of the Soviet announcement on the pullout, coming as it did at the start of the summit?

THE PRESIDENT. I'll speak personally, not for the entire group.

My belief is that it's much more associated with a desire to get Olympic participation than it is to modify the wording of the communique to be issued here in Venice. The Soviets want very much to have athletes come to Moscow. The Olympic boycott has hurt them very badly in world opinion and also within their own country. They are now offering to pay the expenses of individual athletes who might be authorized to come to the Soviet Union. And my belief is that that is more of a factor than this summit conference, but we don't know yet, as I said earlier. The significance of any troop withdrawal would have to be decided

1173

only after the withdrawal itself is confirmed and after we are assured that this is just a step in the total withdrawal of troops from the Soviet Union.

Q. Mr. President, did President Giscard amplify in any way on this TASS announcement? He had a personal message from Brezhnev, and did he tell you more?

THE PRESIDENT. Yes.

Q. What did he tell you?

THE PRESIDENT. I would rather let him make those statements.

Q. [*Inaudible*]—say anything at all about your long conversation with Giscard d'Estaing? [*Inaudible*]

THE PRESIDENT. It could not have gone any better. President Giscard d'Estaing and I communicate frequently and regularly, either by telephone or by cable, and we meet together whenever we can. But we discussed a wide range of issues, bilateral issues between ourselves and France, matters concerning the European Community and also matters concerning the East Africa, Persian Gulf, and Southwest Asian region. This is an alliance and a relationship between our country and France that's very valuable to us and to them, and there are no differences, so far as I know, that are any cause for concern between our two countries.

Q. Mr. President, why don't you consider our withdrawal from the boycott of the Olympics if the Soviets withdraw from Afghanistan?

THE PRESIDENT. No. Our decision not to attend the Olympics was made back in February, and it is irrevocable as far as I'm concerned.

This question will be the last one.

Q. After speaking with President Giscard, do you have the feeling that the Soviet report or the Soviet talk about, of a pullback from Afghanistan is sincere or just a ploy to get Olympic participation?

THE PRESIDENT. I don't have any way

to know. All of us believe that this Soviet announcement can only be judged as significant if it's accurate, if it's permanent, and if it's a first step toward total withdrawal. A partial withdrawal of Soviet forces, of carefully selected units, would have very little significance.

But we don't know the answer to any of those questions yet. We'll have to learn that as time evolves.

Thank you very much.

REPORTER. Thank you, Mr. President.

NOTE: The exchange began at approximately 7:30 p.m. outside the Cipriani Hotel.

Venice Economic Summit Conference

Concluding Statements of the Participants.
June 23, 1980

PRIME MINISTER COSSIGA. May I thank, on behalf of all the heads of government— I thank all of you not only for being here but also for your collaboration in this summit through the information that you, the press, have provided. This is the final press conference, the traditional press conference we have after a summit, and it is up to me as chairman, president of this summit of the seven industrialized countries of the West.

The message, I think, emerging from this Venice summit, at the beginning of the 1980's, the beginning of a difficult decade, is a message of unity, solidarity, and cooperation.

You have before you the text of the final communique, or if not, it will be distributed to you. And yesterday you received the text on consultation that was taking place on the political themes. The problems that we've had to deal with in these 2 days, as you already understand, were numerous and by no means easy, and nobody, I think, would have maintained that we could give an immediate response or reply or final reply, because, of course, this is never reality, either in history or in politics.

The truth emerging from this summit is that the seven major industrialized countries are agreed on the strategy which should guide us in facing the challenges that we have before us. We also agree that our unity and solidarity is not enough in a world which is increasingly interdependent. We are all responsible for the fate of this world—industrialized countries and developing countries, oil-producing countries and oil-consuming countries. In the communique, I think you will find an appeal to this general sense of a joint responsibility.

As you already know, the central problem that we discussed was that of energy, and we have set out a strategy which involves specific actions to save oil, but also an accelerated or speedy effort to produce alternative sources of energy, alternative to oil, including nuclear energy, whose contribution is essential for a better balance between supply and demand in the energy field. We've decided on the general lines for the decade and how we are to monitor the execution of this program.

We have decided on the need to fight inflation, but we've also agreed that we will help investment to create more jobs, improving the economic structures in our countries. In particular, in the energy field, there will be new investments which can create new jobs, which is very important to solve what is a human, social, political problem; one of the most important, that of youth.

We also discussed in depth the problems of the less rich countries. And it is our intention to confirm our commitment, but at the same time, we wish to make aware of this commitment—what should be a general opinion, a general commitment, a general responsibility—the other industrialized countries, all of them, including the Communist industrialized countries and the oil-producer countries.

The increasing cost of oil doesn't only harm the industrialized countries but creates situations which sometimes are unbearable, especially in developing countries. And the problem cannot be solved merely through the recycling undertaken by private banks. In the final communique, you will find what other measures we intend to adopt in this field.

Venice has been the host in the past 10 days of two summit meetings, two important meetings at the highest political level. In the first, that of the nine heads of state, heads of government of the European Community, we found, in spite of the fears of many, the confirmation of the real vital unity of the Community. In this second meeting at the highest political level, which is drawing to an end today, we've taken economic and political decisions and indicated lines of action to reinforce international cooperation in the decade which is only now opened.

From Venice, then, we leave with a new spirit. We thank this marvelous city for its hospitality, with a spirit and a sense of openness to the world which has characterized the history of this beautiful city.

Thank you for your attention.

PRESIDENT GISCARD D'ESTAING. Thank you, Mr. President to the Council.

This meeting of the seven major industrialized nations here in Venice, of the summit—there are three things that I shall particularly bear in mind.

First of all, this summit has enabled us to issue joint statements on subjects as important as Afghanistan, the attitude to be adopted with regard to refugees throughout the world, and the problem of the holding of hostages. Also, this summit has clearly shown that there is agreement, converging views, with regard to not just the analysis, which is important, but particularly the measures that should be taken in order to resolve the economic difficulties with which we are currently faced.

And the third point is that this summit has been chaired so excellently by Italy, and we have enjoyed the finest Italian hospitality. And, Mr. President, Mr. Chairman, we thank you for both.

In the very short time available to us, there are two things to which I would like to refer: energy and development aid.

Last year in Tokyo our decisions aimed at establishing a ceiling and at reducing our oil imports. These were decisions that it was necessary for us to take, but which were of a defensive, negative nature.

In Venice we have taken a different decision, and I invite you to understand the importance of this. It's expressed by a sentence in our communique, and it is our decision to break the link between oil imports and economic growth. We have set ourselves a limit of 10 years in which to break this link, and in particular, in order to efface in public opinion the feeling of anxiety, the feeling of uncertainty about the economic growth of our countries, given a high level of oil imports.

We could have confined ourselves to expressing this in very general terms. And our communique, which I think will be distributed to you shortly, contains, in fact, quite specific indications with regard to energy savings. We have decided that we shall build no new generating stations which are oil fired. We have taken measures with regard to savings to be made in the heating of dwellings and public buildings, with regard to the consumption of petrol by automobiles and other motor vehicles.

We have also taken decisions with regard to the development of alternative energy sources. As you know, there are three main sources: coal, nuclear electricity, and new energy sources. And here

the target that we have set ourselves is to effect a saving by 1990 of between 15 and 20 million barrels a day of oil by using these new energy sources.

The Latin countries, that are more familiar with units expressed in millions of tons of petrol—this means that by 1990 our seven countries will, together, be producing the equivalent of 1 billion tons of oil in all equivalents— 1 billion tons.

This means that between 1980 and 1990 we shall be doubling our coal production. It means that we shall be carrying forward our efforts to develop nuclear powerplants. As you know, France is making a major effort in this respect, and we shall maintain these efforts. And lastly, it means that we shall develop alternative energy sources: biomass, geothermal energy, and solar energy. And lastly, we shall be lending assistance to new producer countries, developing countries that could develop new oil resources.

If we manage to achieve all of this, we shall in fact reduce the link that exists between oil imports and economic growth to the following extent. Up until the 1974 crisis, when we underwent the economic growth of 100, oil imports went up by 100. At the present time, subsequent to our initial efforts, when economic growth goes up by 100, our oil imports go up by 90 or even 80. And in 1990, when our economic growth goes up by 100, our oil imports will be going up by only 60. Thus, we shall have broken the link that exists between economic growth and oil imports.

We shall be reducing our oil share, that's currently at 53 percent of our imports down to 40 percent by 1990. And as far as France is concerned, this figure will be substantially less. The goal we set ourselves is to bring the oil share in our energy consumption down to a figure of between 28 and 33 percent by 1990; in other words, far beyond the common goals that we have set ourselves.

A second point—and I shall be very brief, Mr. Chairman; you've given us 5 minutes each—this is aid to development.

We've said, first of all, that aid to development in the world is a responsibility that we all must share, a responsibility that is shared by all countries. And we have decided to devote thought to the mechanisms which are appropriate to the development of states in the decade 1980 to 1990. And the conclusions of the thinking that we have devoted to this indeed will be at the forefront of our next summit, that is to say, in 1981.

And then lastly, we have emphasized that fact that we shall be making an active contribution to the very necessary dialog that must be established between North and South.

Here, Mr. Chairman, you have the main features of what I have noted from our work. And now, as I'm here with Helmut Schmidt and we are two of the founding fathers of these summit meetings, because we participated at the first in Rambouillet and each summit since, I would just like to say, by way of conclusion, that the Venice summit represents a very marked progress in this institution in the way in which it functions and in its usefulness.

And then, last of all, if you would allow me, I would like to say that I shall leave Venice in a short time with great regret, and it is with great joy and pleasure that one day I shall return.

Thank you.

PRESIDENT CARTER. Thank you, Mr. Chairman.

Our meeting is ending in a spirit of gratifying concord and mutual confidence. We have joined in unity to prepare an agenda for both individual and common action.

From the history of this beautiful city, we have drawn an important lesson, that even the most secure political powers must act in time in order to shape great changes. The republic of Venice left us with incomparable beauty, which we have observed to our great pleasure. Yet in the end, its leaders failed to meet the threats of change pressing in from the East and failed to seize the opportunities for change which were opening then in the West. We are determined not to repeat these same errors.

All of us who serve in positions of leadership recognize that the decade of the 1970's was a period of great difficulty and great challenge, of struggle against unpredictable and uncontrollable change. Yet we all recognize that the 1980's might very well be much more difficult, much more challenging, and much more unpredictable.

Free peoples face hard choices. The freedoms that make our nations strong are at risk in the decade of the 1980's. And we have pledged ourselves here, during this Venice conference, to secure those freedoms for the 1990's and even to the end of this century. The challenges are both political and economic in nature.

We've committed our combined strength and our influence and our voices against a ruthless power's invasion of its nearby defenseless neighbor, which threatens the stability of a crucial area of the world for us all. The Soviet aggression in Afghanistan is a profound assault against the laws of nations and a grave threat to the stability of that vital region.

We've pledged to oppose this Soviet invasion with the means at our disposal, and we do this because it is a moral imperative and also a strategic imperative. We also know that by resisting Soviet militarism and aggression in the present that we can reopen the paths of peace, détente, accommodation in the future.

We've demonstrated our almost unique unity in our opposition to terrorism, hijacking, to the attacks on innocent diplomatic personnel, and toward the alleviation of the suffering of many millions of refugees around the world.

We are also committed to the same unity of purpose in overcoming our common economic challenges. We continue to battle the inflationary forces that poison the confidence on which our economic systems are built. That battle, as we all know too well, is far from won. It compels us to a greater common effort.

Our own Nation has been effective, since the convention of this summit in Tokyo, in reducing oil imports, reversing a longstanding upward trend. I just received the figures today that the first months of this year our Nation's oil imports are down 13.4 percent below the same months last year, an indication not particularly of our own achievement, but of the results of these summits, which have been felt so tangibly on the lives of our people in the past.

We are resolved, as the President of France has said, to break the link between our economic growth and our oil consumption. We have set ambitious goals for alternative energy sources to replace oil, with coal, shale, energy deduced from the Sun, energy deduced from growing crops and trees, equivalent to between 15 and 20 million barrels of oil per day by the end of this decade. And we've agreed on concrete, definite actions with which to achieve this goal. It is a figure not idly given to the public. We feel this commitment binding on all of us.

Here, both in oil consumption and in the exploration and development of alternative energy sources, including our enormous coal reserves—six or seven times greater than all the known oil reserves in the world—is an adventure, an exciting opportunity for us, of our imagination and of our skill.

And finally, another challenge confronts us in the poor nations of the world, those nations who have been especially crippled by the unwarranted and excessive increases in the price of oil set by the OPEC nations. Here, again, we must match our concern with concrete action, for without such action, we will face an accelerating cycle of alienation and despair and disorder. We will study this question of aid, assistance, trade in great depth between now and next year when this summit conference is convened again.

We share responsibility with each other and with those developing nations to achieve a better life for all. We know that the hunger that afflicts many of these people is not only for food, which our Nation, thank God, has in abundance, but it's a hunger also for mutual respect, for mutual understanding, and for mutual support, which we are dedicated freely to give to one another. We recognize that hunger for equality of treatment and concern, and we've resolved to do everything we can do to alleviate it with dignity and with equal treatment.

What we do in facing these dangers and opportunities is a measure of our will to survive as free societies. There's no longer much real distinction that can be drawn between domestic affairs and foreign affairs, between military strength and energy or economic strength, between economic health and political vitality. These factors and the characteristics of a life in a nation are intimately entwined and inseparable. All these elements must be fused together to provide the basis for genuine security, security for the future as well as for the present.

Here in Venice, we have confronted

this broad range of challenges together, and together we have fashioned our responses. Our hosts, by their gift of hospitality, have opened this path and opportunity of harmony and tangible cooperation to us.

We owe our thanks to the authorities of the Italian Republic for preparing and coordinating our work, and particularly for our Chairman, Prime Minister Cossiga, for the people of Venice, who have made our stay here so pleasant. We leave this meeting thankful for their help, inspired by their example in solving problems for themselves, and committed to show in our common work how much we honor the sacrifices they have made for our own convenience.

We will now return to our own countries to ask more sacrifices of ourselves. There will undoubtedly be some who will oppose the pledges of action we've taken and given each other here. Some will seek to delay the implementation of our action. But I'm confident that our democratic societies will assume these burdens of freedom in freedom, rather than subsequently, if we fail, to have more crushing burdens imposed on us from outside.

We've reached our conclusions freely as befits an association of free peoples. We've agreed on the ways to ensure the security of our free world, now and urgently. We shall show that we can employ the tools of democracy in order to build a future of freedom.

This has been a very gratifying experience for me and one of great profit to our Nation. The association with these other leaders, representing their great countries, is indeed an important element in the future development of the lives of the people of the United States of America. I'm indebted to them and, particularly, Mr. Chairman, to you and the people of

Italy and the people of this beautiful community.

Thank you.

CHANCELLOR SCHMIDT. Mr. President of the Council, Mr. Chairman, first of all, I would like to support the excellent appreciation of President Giscard d'Estaing on this year's summit meeting. I think it is in the very nature of a meeting such as this with the press that we can't go over all the ground that the previous speakers have covered. But I would expressly like to support everything that has been said about the three previous speakers about the nature of our discussions.

And for me, there is another point, which is particularly relevant, in what President Carter said—the very great value we place upon our exchange of views.

Obviously, with regard to a series—given the current range of problems—the international links, the international political links played a perhaps greater role than in the past, took up a very great deal of our time, rather more than has been the case in earlier meetings. And in this respect, I have had an opportunity, after lengthy consultation with our Minister of Foreign Affairs, our diplomats, I have been able to report on the forthcoming visit of the Foreign Minister and myself to Moscow, the points that we shall be discussing.

We didn't ask for any mandate. We shall be speaking for our own country, but we have proceeded to a far-reaching consultation on all the areas that we wish to discuss, and we shall certainly inform ourselves in our discussions. These discussions will be informed by the points that we have covered with our colleagues. And we would like to thank our colleagues for their support.

There is one point in the comments made by President Giscard d'Estaing that

I would like to highlight—indeed, this was also raised by President Carter—this is our determination, our joint determination to break the link between economic growth on the one hand and growth in oil imports on the other hand. It's a very ambitious goal that we have set ourselves, but I am quite convinced it's a very realistic goal. And my country, like France, like the United States of America, like Italy, will be making the utmost efforts to achieve this goal, and we think that we have very good chances of achieving the goals we have set ourselves for 1990.

Energy problems, oil problems, oil price problems perhaps are of particular importance in the world at the present time. The balance of payments of oil-exporting countries and non-oil-producing countries, the industrialized countries, price rises, inflation. We have emphasized the necessity of carrying forward an anti-inflationary policy. This is very much in keeping with the policies that we pursue in my own country.

We have never before, at such a meeting, gone in such detail into the possibilities of economic relations with the developing countries, and we have set ourselves a target of doing this even more exhaustively next year. And I would very much like to emphasize the fact that we are convinced, as we have said in the communique, that the oil-exporting countries that currently have very high surpluses must directly participate in aid programs, in transfers to the non-oil-producing, developing countries.

Here, too, I would like to say that we looked at the possibility of a North-South summit with limited participation. And I'd like to say here what I said in our discussions. I certainly would intend to participate at such a meeting and would expect the oil-producing, exporting countries to do likewise.

Now, if I'm going to confine myself to the 5 minutes allowed to me, I must bring my remarks to a close. But I would very much like to thank our colleague, Francesco Cossiga. He has chaired brilliantly and most successfully two very important international meetings here in Venice within 10 days. And at this meeting, the meeting of the seven most important democratic, industrialized states in the world, we have had an extremely positive atmosphere, one of collaboration and cooperation. I am most grateful and appreciative of this.

And I would like to say to the ladies and gentlemen of the press, of the mass media that, of course, only part of the things that we have discussed have been able to go into the communique, but I certainly feel greatly enriched by the far-ranging discussions we have been able to have among ourselves.

I'd also like to express my thanks for the warm hospitality of Venice. Those of us who aren't Italians are very, very much impressed by the few days we've had the opportunity of spending here in Venice, in this remarkable city which is of importance to the culture of the whole world.

Thank you.

PRIME MINISTER THATCHER. [*Inaudible*]—I'd like to undertake four points. The first one is this: If you look back to Tokyo last year and think what has happened there, you'll see that the events since that time illustrate very vividly the kind of problems that we have to tackle. Those of you—[*inaudible*]—Tokyo will remember that we were then discussing the oil problem, which—[*inaudible*]. Then the price of a barrel of oil was $20; now it's $30 a barrel. We were worried then; we're much, much more worried now. That illustrates one of the continuing problems which we've had to tackle.

Another one of these is the taking of

hostages in Iran, a new one which came upon us suddenly and which we're doing all we can to assist President Carter to secure their release.[1]

The one continuing problem, one new one, and the third one, which was also discussed—for the invasion of Afghanistan, which many of us would call a continuing manifestation of an old problem and the fundamental divisions between East, West, and their political philosophies.

I mention these things as my first point to illustrate that in politics we're constantly having to deal both with short-term and long-term problems, but we try to deal with the short-term ones in a way that will contribute to the solution of the longer term problems. And we've discussed them all at this conference.

The second point will take up one of the first ones. How are we going to continue to deal with the oil problem? You've heard my colleagues give details of some of the things which we have agreed. Really, they all have this in common: From whatever countries we come, we're trying to reduce our dependence on oil and therefore make ourselves less vulnerable to the oil-producing countries being able to suddenly reduce their production and leave both our economies and our politics highly vulnerable.

So, everything we're doing is trying to reduce the dependence of our countries on oil and leave us less vulnerable to the acts of others. You will find them all detailed, but by and large, they boil down to that simple proposition. That means, of course, that we have to find other sources of energy. It means that in order to find the resources for developing other sources of energy, we shall have to let the price

---
[1] Due to a failure in transmission, the White House transcript does not include the first portion of Prime Minister Thatcher's statement.

rise of the energy we're using now and we shall have to have massive investment into alternative supplies, such as nuclear, among other things, and such as opening up new coal fields.

Now the third point I want to make is this: If we in the Western industrialized countries have found it difficult to rise to the problems of the increasing price of oil and if it's reduced our ability to help others, then the poorer countries have had the worst problem of the lot. We talk about recycling; we talk about aid. The fact is that some of the poorer countries just plain can't afford the oil they're having to import now. And if you look at the relationship of aid to the increasing prices of oil that they've had put upon them, you'll find the astonishing thing is that the aid that we all give them together from the whole of the Western world is not sufficient to match the increasing price of oil since 1978.

So, everything we can do in aid isn't enough to meet their very real problems. And that is why I think, instead of just talking about North-South dialog, I think most of us are very conscious that as well as involving the countries of the North in solving the problems of the countries of the South, we also have to involve the oil-rich countries, the oil-producing countries, because we really feel that it's not only a question of recycling money, it's also a question of giving new sources of aid to those poor countries.

And the fourth point, Mr. Chairman, is this: We have great ambitions; we have great wishes to help others, though we're only able to do so if each of us puts our own economies really in order.

For many of us, we have a very considerable inflation problem. Indeed, I think over the past 2 years, inflation has been a very much larger part of the problems, economical problems of Western societies. Indeed, some 2 years ago, the average of OECD inflation was 8 percent; now it's some 14 percent. And we're not going to be able to help other countries, let alone ourselves, as much as we would wish unless we tackle that problem.

So, you will find quite a considerable portion of the communique taken up with the old recipes for tackling inflation. They are the old ones; there aren't any new ones. It's just sometimes that the old ones haven't been tried for long enough to produce sound money and a basis for stable growth, except perhaps in the economy of Germany, which we all admire for its tenacity in holding to sound financial principles. So, we recognize that we will have to do that if we really intend to be in a position to help others.

Mr. Chairman, I think that our success in tackling the problems of the coming year will depend upon whether in our own countries we can raise our economic efficiency sufficiently to match the level of our international ideals. That will be the test that we have to undergo during the coming year, and doubtless you'll be keeping us up to it as to how well we're doing.

I would like to join my colleagues in saying thank you. We've had a wonderful Chairman, who's presided over our proceedings with very, very great ability. We've been visitors in a most beautiful city, and we've had a valuable and very rewarding conference.

We, all of us, talked about difficulties. I wouldn't like the message to go out of this conference just to be one of difficulties and problems. I think the result is that we believe the Western free societies can cope with those difficulties and that we'll all be back next year—perhaps with a new set of problems, perhaps with the same— but we believe we'll have made some progress in meeting them. And I'm sure

we'll all meet together, I believe, next year in Canada. We look forward to it.

PRIME MINISTER TRUDEAU. In facts and figures and conclusions, there is very little I can add, if anything, to the forceful and lucid statements which my colleagues have just made, indeed add to the very detailed communique which you will have before you. So, I thought, for those few of you who might be interested in mood pieces, that I would say a word about the mood of cautious optimism which, in my judgment, seems to have been present among us.

I notice that Prime Minister Thatcher just used words to that effect by saying that there is a belief that we can cope with our problems. And that seemed to me to be the mood which prevails here today— not a mood of wild enthusiasm or of great self-congratulation, but feeling that the industrialized democracies, challenged as they have been over the years with what seemed at each summit an intractable problem, has begun to find a way towards a solution.

One year it was the problem of recycling petro-dollars, and that seems to have been solved, at least until now, and we see the great danger for the future. There was also, another year, the discussion of the impending trade wars and protectionism to defend ourselves from each other, and that, too, seems to have been satisfactorily overcome, or at least held in abeyance. And I remember also we talked on one occasion of our slow growth and the danger that that might create cynicism and perhaps a measure of revolt amongst, particularly, of the young in our populations, and that, too, seems to have been averted for the time being.

And I think we must say that to the worries that might have existed as to the possibility for industrialized democracies to come to grips with these very intractable problems, that worry is somewhat in abeyance in the sense that we have managed, not to overcome all the crises, but we have managed to manage them in a certain sense. We have remained in a reasonable measure of control of our domestic economic environment.

Now, there is one problem which was intractable and which for the time being remains so; that is the problem of North-South relations. And we did discuss that again at this summit. I suppose it's fair to say that that is one problem that is not, of course, wholly within our control, since we must seek a measure of agreement with those countries of the Third World. I believe there were new steps taken at this summit towards a solution of those problems. Some of us, certainly myself, indicated an interest, if invited, in participating in the Brandt mini-summit.

We, as my colleagues have indicated, have called upon the oil-rich countries to help solve this problem with us, and we've called upon, also, the Soviet bloc to do something to bear a part of this burden, which it certainly is not doing now. But perhaps more important, we discussed among ourselves the fact that we hadn't really broken the back of this problem, and we were determined—you will see some words in the communique to that effect—we were determined to make sure that at next year's summit we would expend every effort to come to grips with that problem, hopefully with a beginning of success.

I would not wish to finish without making some reference to the political dimension of our discussions, to which reference has indeed already been made. We mentioned the four communiques of a political nature, or semi-political nature, of the refugees, hijacking, the taking of hostages, and above all, on Afghanistan.

I think it is important to underline that our summits are, first of all and above all, of an economic nature and should remain such. But we have had to become aware of this reality that the industrialized democracies, those represented at the summit, could not avoid realizing that in the political field, where there's been rather more disarray, rather less unity than in the economic field, and the political crises still seem to be somewhat more intractable, rather more insoluble than the economic crises or the economic challenges we've had to face. But there, too, a climate of moderate optimism is justified.

On Afghanistan, we made a declaration saying that as to the essentials we share the same view on the basis, the foundation of the problem, the main positions to be taken for the future. I think we shall also have to face these responsibilities. But as far as I'm concerned, I realize that we must do it marginally to the economic discussions, which are essential to the summit. We merely envisage the possibility of translating in the political domain this sort of political unity or this democratic approach which we've achieved in the economic field.

We could hope that this may pass over into the political field. This remains to be seen, and this no doubt remains to be seen at the Canadian summit next year, since we have agreed at this summit in Venice to meet next year in 1981 at the Canadian summit.

I must say, indeed I must warn my colleagues and those of you who will be there that we shall not be able to compete with the splendor of Venice and the hospitality of the Italian people, nor even the excellence of the masterly way in which our chairman has conducted the proceedings during the past 2 years. But I can tell you that you will all be welcome. And we think, all together, we shall be able to contribute further to the solutions of some of our serious problems.

FOREIGN MINISTER OKITA. So, I hope everybody's ready for earphones, except a few who understand Japanese.

Mr. Chairman, thank you. On behalf of government and people of Japan, I wish to take this opportunity to express our deep sense of gratitude and appreciation to the condolence expressed to the sudden demise of our late Prime Minister, Mr. Ohira, by the heads of government and state.

Prime Minister Ohira had particularly high valuation of the role of the summit in these difficult times of the world, and he had great expectations upon his participation. I truly regret that and miss his presence, but Prime Minister Cossiga and heads of state and government have given very kind and courteous attention to us so that the Japanese delegation has been able to participate in this meeting very productively.

Yesterday, by the way, we had general election in Japan. The results have come to be known to us by now. The party of which Prime Minister Ohira was representative enjoyed a landslide victory, increasing the number of seats of the Liberal Democratic Party from 258 to 284. I might take this opportunity to report that to you.

This summit in Venice I believe has accomplished a result that truly befits the first such summit in this decade of the eighties.

First, on the political question: Initially the summits were for economic discussions, but as other heads of government and state have commented, in these new, changing environments we have discussed political points, matters, particularly with regard to our position as regards Afghanistan. You all heard Prime Minister Cossiga yesterday in his press briefing.

The Government of Japan, since the outset of the Soviet military intervention in Afghanistan—the Government of Japan has persistently taken the view that Japan cannot tolerate such military intervention in that nation, and Japan shall continue to maintain this same attitude. I am gratified and find it very significant that among the heads of state and government in Venice, a common perception has ben confirmed about this question.

As regards economic questions, Japan came to Venice looking forward to fruitful and substantive discussions on inflation and energy and the so-called North-South situation, including the question of recycling of oil money. We are satisfied that we have seen long-term strategic discussion. First, in next year's Canada summit, further discussions we look forward to take place on North-South relations. We strongly support this forthcoming agenda item.

On energy, our view is that among the seven nations here, on the supply side—in other words, not only on demand side, on the supply side—our efforts must be further redoubled. This is the question that affects the oil market economies. We must demonstrate our resiliency and strength of market economies to the rest of the world. To that end, through investment, productivity must be increased, and through savings, inflation must be curtailed.

In other matters, that may involve political difficulties domestically, but for us industrialized nations to overcome the difficulty of paying such prices would be an essential condition for strengthening our democracies. This summit meeting has dealt with such a long-term question fully and squarely, and we find it very significant that we have done so.

Next, on the matter of relations with the developing nations, our present summit has paid greater attention than before to that matter; in this, it has been very meaningful. At the present, because of the sharp rise of the prices of oil, many non-oil-producing developing nations have met difficulties, and we must, of course, step up our cooperation with these nations.

In our relationship with the developing nations, we need long-term basic strategy; that is, we in the West need it. For Japan, we have, for some time, been emphasizing increased food production and building of better human resources for improving human skills and also development of energy resources in developing nations. On these matters, too, I'm glad we have had good discussions in the present summit.

For some time to come, in all of our respective nations, we will, I expect, continue to have difficult domestic economic situations, particularly on unemployment and recession respects. Nevertheless, we must resist any protectionistic pressure resolutely and squarely. And on that, too, we have seen convergence of opinion and consensus. Not only for this present generation but for our future generations, we must prove that our free democratic economies are indeed viable and strong. We must make every effort to demonstrate that, I believe.

Finally, may I say, Mr. Chairman, that we are very favorably impressed by this city of Venice. We regret our stay has been too short—only for 2 days—and too full of meetings, leaving us very little time to enjoy the beautiful sights of Venice. We think we have to come back in a more leisurely way if possible. I personally hope to bring my wife to Venice.

To the government of Italy and the municipal authorities of Venice and to all the citizens of Venice and to the entire population, friendly people of Italy, and to the host government who has been most courteous, warm, and considerate for successful management of the meeting, and to the most smooth chairmanship of Prime Minister Cossiga, I would like to express our deep appreciation.

Finally, for the end of my statement, I would like to say that at the beginning of yesterday's session, I mentioned that our seven nations are fellow passengers in the same gondola, we are riding in the same gondola. And this is the feeling that I have, once again, most strongly as I leave here.

Thank you.

PRESIDENT JENKINS. I'll be very brief. The central message of this summit meeting, in my view, has been that the stability of the world economy depends on all countries recognizing their mutual needs and accepting their mutual responsibilities.

The problem faced by the seven major industrial countries and the European Community, as such, cannot be separated from those of the world as a whole. For this reason, I greatly welcome the way in which at this summit we looked beyond the frontiers of the industrial countries and our own difficulties to the problems which concern the greater part of mankind.

No outside industrial country is so closely linked to the developing world as is the European Community. Our interest is closely joined to theirs. The disequilibrium between rich and poor is tolerable to neither; both are deeply vulnerable. The devastating impact of oil price rises on developing countries without oil of their own causes deficits which could not only deepen and prolong the existing recession but could touch the very vitals of our economic and monetary system.

On trade, the Tokyo round has been a battle won, but not the war. We still face a protectionist threat which could cause major and lasting damage to the trading system on which our jobs and our standard of living depend.

Here at Venice we have looked realistically at these problems. We tried to see our way forward into the somber decade of the eighties. We isolated some of the policies which should guide us and looked, as has been rightly said by Prime Minister Trudeau, with cautious optimism at the major changes which will be necessary. Above all, we recognized the common dangers and the common interests which should bind the world together.

Mr. President of the Council, I thank you for your outstanding chairmanship, and I thank the Italian Government and the people of Venice for their unforgettable hospitality.

NOTE: Prime Minister Francesco Cossiga of Italy, Chairman of the Conference, spoke at 3:40 p.m. in the Sala Degli Arazzi at the Cini Foundation. He spoke in Italian. President Valéry Giscard d'Estaing of France, Chancellor Helmut Schmidt of the Federal Republic of Germany, and Foreign Minister Saburo Okita of Japan also spoke in their native languages, and their remarks were translated by interpreters.

President Carter, Prime Minister Margaret Thatcher of the United Kingdom, Prime Minister Pierre Elliott Trudeau of Canada, and Roy Jenkins, President of the Commission of the European Communities, spoke in English.

Venice Economic Summit Conference

Declaration Issued at the Conclusion of the Conference. June 23, 1980

I. INTRODUCTION

1. In this, our first meeting of the 1980's the economic issues that have dominated our thoughts are the price and supply of energy and the implications for inflation and the level of economic activity in our own countries and for the world as a whole. Unless we can deal with the problems of energy, we cannot cope with other problems.

2. Successive large increases in the price of oil, bearing no relation to market conditions and culminating in the recent decisions by some members of the Organization of Petroleum Exporting Countries (OPEC) at Algiers, have produced the reality of even higher inflation and the imminent threat of severe recession and unemployment in the industrialised countries. At the same time they have undermined and in some cases virtually destroyed the prospects for growth in the developing countries. We believe that these consequences are increasingly coming to be appreciated by some of the oil exporting countries. The fact is that the industrialised countries of the free world, the oil producing countries, and the non-oil developing countries depend upon each other for the realisation of their potential for economic development and prosperity. Each can overcome the obstacles to that development, but only if all work together, and with the interests of all in mind.

3. In this spirit we have discussed the main problems that confront us in the coming decade. We are confident in the ability of our democratic societies, based on individual freedom and social solidarity, to meet these challenges. There are no quick or easy solutions; sustained efforts are needed to achieve a better future.

II. INFLATION

4. The reduction of inflation is our immediate top priority and will benefit all nations. Inflation retards growth and harms all sectors of our societies. Deter-

mined fiscal and monetary restraint is required to break inflationary expectations. Continuing dialogue among the social partners is also needed for this purpose. We must retain effective international coordination to carry out this policy of restraint, and also to guard against the threat of growing unemployment and worldwide recession.

5. We are also committed to encouraging investment and innovation, so as to increase productivity, to fostering the movement of resources from declining into expanding sectors so as to provide new job opportunities, and to promoting the most effective use of resources within and among countries. This will require shifting resources from government spending to the private sector and from consumption to investment, and avoiding or carefully limiting actions that shelter particular industries or sectors from the rigors of adjustment. Measures of this kind may be economically and politically difficult in the short term, but they are essential to sustained non-inflationary growth and to increasing employment which is our major goal.

6. In shaping economic policy, we need a better understanding of the long-term effects of global population growth, industrial expansion and economic development generally. A study of trends in these areas is in hand, and our representatives will keep these matters under review.

III. ENERGY

7. We must break the existing link between economic growth and consumption of oil, and we mean to do so in this decade. This strategy requires conserving oil and substantially increasing production and use of alternative energy sources. To this end, maximum reliance should be placed on the price mechanism, and domestic prices for oil should take into account representative world prices. Market forces should be supplemented, where appropriate, by effective fiscal incentives and administrative measures. Energy investment will contribute substantially to economic growth and employment.

8. We welcome the recent decisions of the European Community (EC), the International Energy Agency (IEA) and the Organization for Economic Cooperation and Development (OECD) regarding the need for long term structural changes to reduce oil consumption, continuing procedures to monitor progress, the possible use of oil ceilings to deal with tight market conditions, and coordination of stock policies to mitigate the effect of market disruption. We note that the member countries of the IEA have agreed that their energy policies should result in their collective 1985 net oil imports being substantially less than their existing 1985 group objective, and that they will quantify the reduction as part of their continuing monitoring efforts. The potential for reduction has been estimated by the IEA Secretariat, given existing uncertainties, at around 4 million barrels a day (MBD).

9. To conserve oil in our countries:

—We are agreed that no new base-load, oil-fired generating capacity should be constructed, save in exceptional circumstances, and that the conversion of oil-fired capacity to other fuels should be accelerated.

—We will increase efforts, including fiscal incentives where necessary, to accelerate the substitution of oil in industry.

—We will encourage oil saving investments in residential and commercial buildings, where necessary by financial incentives and by establishing insulation standards. We look to the public sector to set an example.

—In transportation, our objective is the introduction of increasingly fuel efficient vehicles. The demand of consumers and competition among manufacturers are already leading in this direction. We will accelerate this progress, where appropriate, by arrangements or standards for improved automobile fuel efficiency, by gasoline pricing and taxation decisions, by research and development, and by making public transport more attractive.

10. We must rely on fuels other than oil to meet the energy needs of future economic growth. This will require early, resolute, and wide-ranging actions. Our potential to increase the supply and use of energy sources other than oil over the next ten years is estimated at the equivalent of 15–20 MBD of oil. We intend to make a coordinated and vigorous effort to realise this potential. To this end, we will seek a large increase in the use of coal and enhanced use of nuclear power in the medium-term, and a substantial increase in production of synthetic fuels, in solar energy and other sources of renewable energy over the longer term.

11. We shall encourage the exploration and development of our indigenous hydrocarbon resources in order to secure maximum production on a long term basis.

12. Together we intend to double coal production and use by early 1990. We will encourage long term commitments by coal producers and consumers. It will be necessary to improve infrastructures in both exporting and importing countries, as far as is economically justified, to ensure the required supply and use of coal. We look forward to the recommendations of the International Coal Industry Advisory Board. They will be considered promptly. We are conscious of the environmental risks associated with increased coal production and combustion. We will do everything in our power to ensure that increased use of fossil fuels, especially coal, does not damage the environment.

13. We underline the vital contribution of nuclear power to a more secure energy supply. The role of nuclear energy has to be increased if world energy needs are to be met. We shall therefore have to expand our nuclear generating capacity. We will continue to give the highest priority to ensuring the health and safety of the public and to perfecting methods for dealing with spent fuels and disposal of nuclear waste. We reaffirm the importance of ensuring the reliable supply of nuclear fuel and minimizing the risk of nuclear proliferation.

14. The studies made by the International Nuclear Fuel Cycle Evaluation Group, launched at the London Summit in 1977, are a significant contribution to the use of nuclear energy. We welcome their findings with respect to: increasing predictable supplies; the most effective utilization of uranium sources, including the development of advanced technologies; and the minimization of proliferation risks, including support of International Atomic Energy Agency (IAEA) safeguards. We urge all countries to take these findings into account when developing policies and programmes for the peaceful use of nuclear energy.

15. We will actively support the recommendations of the International Energy Technology Group, proposed at the Tokyo Summit last year, for bringing new energy technologies into commercial use at the earliest feasible time. As far as national programmes are concerned, we will by mid-1981 adopt a two-phased approach; first, listing the numbers and types of commercial scale plants to be constructed in each of our countries by the mid-1980s, and, second, indicating quantitative projections for expanding production by 1990, 1995 and 2000, as a basis

for future actions. As far as international programmes are concerned, we will join others in creating an international team to promote collaboration among interested nations on specific projects.

16. A high level group of representatives of our countries and of the EEC Commission will review periodically the results achieved in these fields.

17. Our comprehensive energy strategy is designed to meet the requirements of the coming decade. We are convinced that it can reduce the demand for energy, particularly oil, without hampering economic growth. By carrying out this strategy we expect that, over the coming decade, the ratio between increases in collective energy consumption and economic growth of our countries will be reduced to about 0.6, that the share of oil in our total energy demand will be reduced from 53 percent now to about 40 percent by 1990, and that our collective consumption of oil in 1990 will be significantly below present levels so as to permit a balance between supply and demand at tolerable prices.

18. We continue to believe that international cooperation in energy is essential. All countries have a vital interest in a stable equilibrium between energy supply and demand. We would welcome a constructive dialogue on energy and related issues between energy producers and consumers in order to improve the coherence of their policies.

IV. Relations With Developing Countries

19. We are deeply concerned about the impact of the oil price increases on the developing countries that have to import oil. The increase in oil prices in the last two years has more than doubled the oil bill of these countries, which now amounts

to over $50 billion. This will drive them into ever increasing indebtedness, and put at risk the whole basis of their economic growth and social progress, unless something can be done to help them.

20. We approach in a positive spirit the prospect of global negotiations in the framework of the United Nations and the formulation of a new International Development Strategy. In particular, our object is to cooperate with the developing countries in energy conservation and development, expansion of exports, enhancement of human skills, and the tackling of underlying food and population problems.

21. A major international effort to help these countries increase their energy production is required. We believe that this view is gaining ground among oil-exporting countries. We ask the World Bank to examine the adequacy of the resources and the mechanisms now in place for the exploration, development and production of conventional and renewable energy sources in oil importing developing countries, to consider means, including the possibility of establishing a new affiliate or facility by which it might improve and increase its lending programmes for energy assistance, and to explore its findings with both oil-exporting and industrial countries.

22. We are deeply conscious that extreme poverty and chronic malnutrition afflict hundreds of millions of people of developing countries. The first requirement in these countries is to improve their ability to feed themselves and reduce their dependence on food imports. We are ready to join with them and the International Agencies concerned in their comprehensive long term strategies to increase food production, and to help improve national as well as international research

services. We will support and, where appropriate, supplement initiatives of the World Bank and of the Food and Agricultural Organization (FAO) and to improve grain storage and food handling facilities. We underline the importance of wider membership of the new Food Aid Convention so as to secure at least 10 million tons of food aid annually and of an equitable replenishment of the International Fund for Agricultural Development.

23. High priority should be given to efforts to cope with population growth and to existing United Nations and other programmes for supporting these efforts.

24. We strongly support the general capital increase of the World Bank, increases in the funding of the regional development banks, and the sixth replenishment of the International Development Association. We would welcome an increase in the rate of lending of these institutions, within the limits of their present replenishments, as needed to fulfill the programmes described above. It is essential that all members, especially the major donors, provide their full contributions on the agreed schedule.

25. We welcome the report of the Brandt Commission. We shall carefully consider its recommendations.

26. The democratic industrialised countries cannot alone carry the responsibility of aid and other different contributions to developing countries: it must be equitably shared by the oil exporting countries and the industrialised Communist countries. The Personal Representatives are instructed to review aid policies and procedures and other contributions to developing countries and to report back their conclusions to the next Summit.

V. MONETARY PROBLEMS

27. The situation created by large oil-generated payments imbalances, in particular those of oil-importing developing countries, requires a combination of determined actions by all countries to promote external adjustment and effective mechanisms for balance of payments financing. We look to the international capital market to continue to play the primary role in rechanneling the substantial oil surplus funds on the basis of sound lending standards. We support the work in progress by our monetary authorities and the Bank for International Settlements designed to improve the supervision and security of the international banking system. The private banks could usefully supplement these efforts.

28. Private lending will need to be supplemented by an expanded role for international institutions, especially the International Monetary Fund (IMF). We are committed to implementing the agreed increase in the IMF quotas, and to supporting appropriate borrowing by the Fund, if needed to meet financing requirements of its members. We encourage the IMF to seek ways in which it could, within its guidelines on conditionality, make it more attractive for countries with financing problems to use its resources. In particular, we support the IMF's examination of possible ways to reduce charges on credits to low-income developing countries. The IMF and the World Bank should work closely together in responding to these problems. We welcome the Bank's innovative lending scheme for structural adjustment. We urge oil-exporting countries to increase their direct lending to countries with financial problems thus reducing the strain on other recycling mechanisms.

29. We reaffirm our commitment to stability in the foreign exchange markets.

We note that the European Monetary System (EMS) has contributed to this end. We will continue close cooperation in exchange market policies so as to avoid disorderly exchange rate fluctuations. We will also cooperate with the IMF to achieve more effective surveillance. We support continuing examination by the IMF of arrangements to provide for a more balanced evolution of the world reserve system.

VI. Trade

30. We are resolved further to strengthen the open world trading system. We will resist pressures for protectionist actions, which can only be self-defeating and aggravate inflation.

31. We endorse the positive conclusion of the multilateral trade negotiations, and commit ourselves to early and effective implementation. We welcome the participation of some of our developing partners in the new non-tariff codes and call upon others to participate. We also call for the full participation of as many countries as possible in strengthening the system of the General Agreement on Tariffs and Trade. We urge the more advanced of our developing partners gradually to open their markets over the coming decade.

32. We reaffirm our determination to avoid a harmful export credit race. To this end we shall work with the other participants to strengthen the International Arrangement on Export Credits, with a view to reaching a mutually acceptable solution covering all aspects of the Arrangement by 1 December 1980. In particular, we shall seek to bring its terms closer to current market conditions and reduce distortions in export competition, recognising the differentiated treatment of developing countries in the Arrangement.

33. As a further step in strengthening the international trading system, we commit our governments to work in the United Nations toward an agreement to prohibit illicit payments to foreign government officials in international business transactions. If that effort falters, we will seek to conclude an agreement among our countries, but open to all, with the same objective.

VII. Conclusions

34. The economic message from this Venice Summit is clear. The key to success in resolving the major economic challenges which the world faces is to achieve and maintain a balance between energy supply and demand at reasonable levels and at tolerable prices. The stability of the world economy, on which the prosperity of every individual country relies, depends upon all of the countries concerned, recognising their mutual needs and accepting their mutual responsibilities. Those among us whose countries are members of the European Community intend to make their efforts within this framework. We, who represent seven large industrialised countries of the free world, are ready to tackle our own problems with determination and to work with others to meet the challenges of the coming decade, to our own advantage and to the benefit of the whole world.

NOTE: As printed above, this item follows the text of the declaration made available by the White House. It was not issued as a White House press release.

Venice Economic Summit Conference

Interview With Reporters Following the Conclusion of the Conference. June 23, 1980

THE PRESIDENT. Well, I think what I'll do is just make a couple of remarks to start with and then spend the time we have answering any questions that you might have.

I've had a chance to meet individually with the leaders of the nations and also with the President of the European Community, as well as to meet collectively with them on several occasions, as you know, to deal with the political and economic problems that our countries face collectively in the 1980's.

Basically, we continued the themes that I expressed in the State of the Union message, that I repeated in my Philadelphia speech on foreign affairs, and that I outlined in the toast in Rome this week, emphasizing the threat to the Western democracies, urging them to stand resolved against the Soviet invasion of Afghanistan, not to accept it in any way as a move that would be condoned by any nation, demanding absolute and total withdrawal of all Soviet troops, not to treat it as was treated their taking over of Czechoslovakia; calling on the nations to be as harmonious as possible in dealing with the energy question, to emulate what we have already done in passing through our Congress a new energy package based on both conservation and on the development of alternative forms of energy.

I've been very pleased at the strength of the resolutions and the harmony that does exist among us. This has been an opportunity for me to discuss many items of mutual interest, and I think this has probably been the best summit conference that I've attended so far.

I'll be glad to answer your questions.

Q. Mr. Carter, you have now been to three of these, and there have been discussion from Giscard and others about the format and whether it's a good thing and how they work and how it should be changed, if at all—more frequent, different format, political separate from eco-

nomic. I wonder what your thoughts are and how you rate this one.

THE PRESIDENT. This is my fourth one. It's obvious that as experience has been gained, with Henry Owen as my personal representative, the 6 solid months of preparation for these summit conferences have paid rich dividends. It's let us explore possible differences among us and resolve as best we could prior to the entry of the heads of state the answers to some of the questions.

We all believe that the maximum benefit comes from the frank discussion among the heads of state ourselves, possibly joined by the Foreign Ministers. And my guess is that in the conference to be held in Canada in 1981, there's likely to be a smaller entourage, and we probably will limit the questions to those that relate fairly exclusively to the head-of-state level that can't be resolved by the Finance Ministers or by the Ministers responsible for energy.

We have expanded this session more than ever before to a discussion of political and diplomatic measures, including all seven heads of state. In the past, we have had one breakfast meeting or one luncheon meeting with the four so-called Berlin powers. This time we decided to have the political aspects of Europe and the world discussed among all seven. And I think it worked well.

Q. Mr. President, what has happened here beyond the strong communique that we got yesterday that makes it any more likely that the Russians will be willing to either get out or negotiate an exit from Afghanistan? And do you expect them to negotiate an exit from Afghanistan?

THE PRESIDENT. It's hard to predict what the Soviets are doing. My experience has been not to be optimistic in expectations.

Well, we have, since the very beginning, taken unilateral steps and urged as many of our allies and friends in other countries to join us with the prohibition against Soviet fishing in American waters, the grain embargo, and the joint call by 104 nations for the Soviets to withdraw and demands of a similar nature made by the 34 to 36 nations in the Moslem world on two occasions.

We've asked our allies and friends not to replace goods or services that we did not sell to the Soviet Union, and we've asked them not to give special credit terms to the Soviets, as had been the case in the past, for instance, with the British and the Japanese. We've asked them to stand resolute in not recognizing as legitimate the Babrak Karmal, Babrak regime, and demanding total withdrawal of troops from Afghanistan by the Soviets—not a partial withdrawal—as an acceptable fact.

The more the Soviets realize that they do stand isolated in the world, that they are condemned by the world as an aggressive power and as long as we support the national liberation forces in Afghanistan with our words and our encouragement on a collective basis as we have done here, the more likely the Soviets are to decide they've made a serious mistake. I think the Soviets did underestimate the fervor and the courage of the freedom-fighters who are struggling for national liberation. I think they did underestimate the condemnation of the United Nations members and also the constant condemnation of the Moslem countries with whom the Soviets do want good relationships.

I think we have reconfirmed the position of all the nations on the Olympic boycott that had been stated before by them, even after we had the flurry of reports about the Soviet withdrawal.

So, for the Soviets to face a united commitment of all of us plus the other nations in the world of opposition to their ex-tended stay in Afghanistan will be an encouraging factor in the Soviets' decision to withdraw.

Q. Why did your joint statement not go into economic sanctions, Mr. President?

THE PRESIDENT. Pardon?

Q. Why did your joint statement on that not go into economic sanctions on Afghanistan?

THE PRESIDENT. We didn't go into specifics about what the nations would or would not do in withholding credit or the grain embargo or the fishing in waters or other matters relating to economics. Each nation over the last 6 months has decided on its own, working with parliaments and, in my case, working with the Congress, to make a stand on Afghanistan and to initiate sanctions of a varying degree of severity.

I think it's accurate to say that those exerted by the United States were the most severe, and they vary among the nations here. There has been no backing off, no change in the severity of the sanctions already imposed, but to enumerate the degree of the sanctions which do vary among the nations, I think, would have been a fruitless effort.

Q. Mr. President, could I ask about the hostages in Iran?

THE PRESIDENT. Yes.

Q. You've said that you wouldn't forget them, but there was no mention of the 53 Americans in the statement which came out of yesterday's meeting. And you did not refer to those hostages specifically in your closing remarks today. Could you tell us why they weren't mentioned, or were they discussed privately?

THE PRESIDENT. Yes, they were discussed privately, and I think some of the leaders did mention them. I think that Mrs. Thatcher, for instance, did.

We all see the international terrorism associated with the capture of the diplomats, of the Americans in Iran, as a pattern to be feared and condemned by the entire world. The essence of the hijacking and the terrorism, the capturing of diplomats, is that it's a phenomenon that's abhorrent to all of us and on which the nations represented here have stood resolutely.

All of them have joined in with us in sanctions against Iran. Those sanctions are being maintained, and there's no doubt about that fact. In my private discussions with the leaders, we covered, in each case, what the countries are doing to help us, either through the United Nations or through diplomatic or other means. Some still have personnel in Iran who are giving assistance to us.

So, that's a matter of great concern to all of us. There's no——

Q. But was there a conscious decision not to mention the 53 and Iran in the context of the statement and/or your statement?

THE PRESIDENT. No, there was no conscious decision——

Q. What have you determined, Mr. President, about what the Russians actually have done with their troops in— or out of Iran—not so much what the letters say.

THE PRESIDENT. Out of Afghanistan.

Q. Excuse me, out of Afghanistan— but what you know, have determined to be a fact about that?

THE PRESIDENT. We know what forces the Soviets claim are going to be moved out of Afghanistan, and we know that some of those forces are being moved, at least just across the border. The best information I have is that the Soviets have had about 85,000 armed troops in Afghanistan and 30 to 35 thousand on the borders of Afghanistan in Soviet territory.

They have probably ordered the withdrawal of less than 10 percent of those forces. And my own information is that the forces they have withdrawn have not been those that have seen action within the last several weeks or months and they can easily be put into Afghanistan without delay if the Soviets should suffer reverses there.

Q. But then you don't consider this any kind of a real withdrawal, to any extent, that would be a first step?

THE PRESIDENT. Well, I helped to word that part of the communique yesterday, and we put some very careful "ifs" in there. It will be significant if it is confirmed, if the withdrawal is permanent, and if this is a first step leading to total and complete withdrawal of Soviet forces. Under those circumstances, it will be significant.

Q. Then you're not able to judge yet?

THE PRESIDENT. Not yet.

Q. Mr. President, with regard to Chancellor Schmidt's coming visit to Moscow, how do you feel personally about the timing of that visit? Is it helpful, or does it run counter to current interests of keeping the Russians at arm's length until they show better faith about Afghanistan?

THE PRESIDENT. I think it's coming at a good time. After talking with President Giscard d'Estaing, I also believe that his visit with Brezhnev was a fruitful exchange. There was a very firm and forceful presentation by the French President of the position of their nation, as expressed in this communique, and I have no doubt that Chancellor Schmidt will make the same forceful presentation to the President of the Soviet Union.

And for the Soviet leaders to hear in an unvarnished fashion directly from European leaders the same kind of message they've been hearing by various means from us, I think, strengthens our own position and also sends a very clear signal to the Soviets that there is no variation among us in our condemnation of the Soviet invasion, and also that it's fruitless for them to try to drive a wedge between us and our European friends and allies.

Q. Mr. President, what merit do you think there is, if any, in Chancellor Schmidt's idea that by pointing out to the Soviets that we have 3 years before we'll be deploying theater nuclear forces in Western Europe—that that may give them an opportunity to pull back on their future weapons? Do you think there's any merit at all in that idea?

THE PRESIDENT. No, I don't. There is merit to the thought that the Soviets would unilaterally cease deploying the SS–20's. So far, the Soviets have built facilities and have deployed several dozen SS–20's, and they are continuing with that building and that deployment. If the Soviets would unilaterally stop that, it would be beneficial, and that's what Chancellor Schmidt expressed to me as his hope. However, for us to offer a quid pro quo, a quid for that quo, we would not be gaining anything at all.

We will start this summer locating sites, and we'll be going through the construction phase in 1981, 1982, and '83 of the deployment of theater nuclear forces just to meet an overwhelming threat that the Soviets have built up already. And for us to accept the proposition that there is any sort of equity or equality in the present arrangement is a mistake, and for us to agree not to deploy if they will just maintain their heavy existing deployment is not a fair exchange.

So, I do not agree with any freeze nor any prohibition against American and European continuation of our uninterrupted plans.

Q. On the Middle East——

Q. You seem to be holding out hope for something that I gather you don't agree is——

THE PRESIDENT. If the Chancellor's hopes are realized and if the Soviets unilaterally stop their present heavy construction and deployment plans, I would be pleased and I would also be surprised.

Q. On the Middle East, Mr. President——

Q. Mr. President, one of the subjects on which there was no statement in the summit was on the Middle East with regard to peace efforts.

THE PRESIDENT. Yes.

Q. Today there seems to be a new complicating circumstance in reports that Prime Minister Begin is supposed to be moving some office to East Jerusalem. Were there discussions here on the Middle East, and how did they come out?

THE PRESIDENT. Yes. We did not discuss that report, and I'm not prepared to discuss it, because I've not been briefed on it. But I explained to the European leaders very clearly what our position is. We are committed to the Camp David process, as long as the Egyptians and the Israelis agree with us that there is an ongoing chance of progress toward a comprehensive peace.

Obviously we have had some times of rapid movement and some times of dormancy in progress, and I cannot predict firmly what the future might hold. But at this time there is no alternative procedure that I can envision that could adequately replace the Camp David document, the basis provided for it in U.N. 242, nor the process of negotiating between Israel and Egypt and us with the invitation open to the Jordanians and Palestinians that might be acceptable to all sides. For us to terminate this process simply because we're not making rapid progress would be a mistake.

I have pointed out to the European leaders—and I don't think any have privately disagreed with me—that there is absolutely nothing in the Camp David accords that contradicts what the Palestinians and/or the Jordanians and other Arab leaders desire to see accomplished. Those difficult issues that presently divide the Israeli position from the Arab position are yet to be resolved through negotiation, and I pointed out to them the unpredicted progress that was made between Israel and Egypt, when Egypt was willing to sit down with the Israelis and negotiate in good faith under the most difficult of circumstances.

I had a long discussion earlier this week with King Hussein of Jordan about this.

It would please me—but I don't expect this to happen—if Jordan would join the peace talks. It has become difficult now for the Jordanians and other Arab leaders to acknowledge that the Camp David accords are the best approach. I don't have any doubt that they are.

If, in the future, the Egyptians become convinced or the Israelis become convinced or we become convinced that there is a better way to move toward a comprehensive peace in the Mideast, resolving the Palestinian question in all its aspects, giving the Palestinians a voice in the determination of their own future, guaranteeing mutual security, then of course we would explore that alternative route. But so far I do not see any alternative to what we are doing.

Q. Has the European resolution helped or hindered?

Q. What was that question?

THE PRESIDENT. "Has the European resolution helped or hindered."

It's hard to say. I did not encourage the passing of that resolution. It could have been worse in its wording. It was worded very cautiously, and I don't believe that it did any harm. But we will continue in an uninterrupted fashion along the course laid out by the Camp David agreement and the Camp David process.

Q. Do you think you've convinced anybody, Mr. President, on the Camp David argument here in Venice?

THE PRESIDENT. Yes, I think so. I would rather let them speak for themselves.

What they want to do is to express their belief that the Palestinian people should be represented as a final decision is made about the Middle East. We agree with that. This is included within the Camp David accord signed by Prime Minister Begin. So far, we've not been able to get the Jordanians, for instance, to join with Palestinian members of its delegation, and we've not yet been able to get a representative group of, say, the West Bank and Gaza mayors to say, "This is what we want to do in going toward full autonomy." I don't know if we'll be successful in that effort.

But I think the European leaders understand very well that there is no present alternative to the Camp David effort and we don't disagree with the fact that the Palestinian question must be resolved and that the Palestinian rights must be honored and that the Palestinians must have a voice in this decision.

Q. Prime Minister Trudeau said that while there was great unity on economic issues that you hadn't quite come to that sense of unity on the political front. Could you explain to us what some of the political differences were and where you see the major problems are?

THE PRESIDENT. Well, obviously the other leaders have different views about how rapidly to move on the resolution of the Mideast differences.

I think the French, for instance, would demand immediate and total withdrawal of all Israeli forces from the occupied territories of the West Bank. President Giscard d'Estaing has made this clear, that that is his option. That's easy to say, but how to go about inducing the Israelis to withdraw from the West Bank, which they've agreed to do, in U.N. 242, how far to withdraw, how to negotiate a final determination of the status of the West Bank, how to guarantee Israeli security in the meantime, those are the difficult aspects of it—how to accommodate the questions of water and land and the authority given to the interim self-governing body. So, I think there are differences about how and how rapidly to move, and there are differences about how to assess the ultimate status of the West Bank.

But those things are inevitable. They've been very clearly expressed to the public. There are no private disagreements among us that haven't been clearly discerned through the press and through the public.

Q. Mr. President, do you anticipate any repercussions at home about the conference's very unequivocal statement about the importance of expanding nuclear power?

THE PRESIDENT. No, I don't—well, I say I don't. Do I anticipate any differences? There are going to be some differences.

Our position on nuclear power is clear. We believe that nuclear power is going to have to play a viable part in the energy production in the United States. We consider nuclear power to be a source of last resort, in that to the extent that we can conserve energy in our country and provide alternative forms of energy, the dependence on nuclear power can be minimized. But there are many States and

communities that have a heavy dependence on nuclear power, and we believe that there's a viable demand for nuclear powerplants that will be honored in the future in our country.

We are working toward safer plants, better operation, better maintenance, better design, more standardization of construction.

Other countries that don't have the benefit of massive coal deposits and oil and gas and shale, like, for instance, France or Germany or Japan, have to depend much more heavily on nuclear power. So, the communique was worded very carefully to accommodate the special needs of seven nations who differ radically one from another in the natural resources with which they've been blessed.

We don't have any apology to make for the language. Our position has not changed on how nuclear power should be handled.

Q. Mr. President, following upon that, nuclear power is one aspect, but you all stressed the breaking of the link between oil consumption and economic growth. And one of you—or the communique spoke of this as a binding commitment. Now, some of the means to that end—doubling the use of coal and the use of synthetics from shale and so forth—also pose potential problems for the environment. My question is, do you foresee that our current environmental laws will have to be relaxed in some degree in order to meet that commitment?

THE PRESIDENT. No, I do not. There are two aspects of the energy thing. One is the ratio between the additional energy used in its totality, on the one hand, and the growth in our economy on the other hand. I think Valéry Giscard d'Estaing explained this better than anyone else, because he went into it in more depth.

At the present time, assuming 1980 as a base, if economic growth goes up 100 percent, then the amount of energy used will go up 100 percent, total energy. We set as a goal for ourselves that by the end of this decade, if economic growth goes up 100 percent in a certain year, as a base, then the amount of energy required to gain that growth would only go up 60 percent. That's the total amount of energy, regardless of where it comes from.

We can meet that goal. We've done a fairly good analysis of it, and we've made great progress already in our country reducing that energy level by about 30 or 40 percent since 1973, primarily in the commercial area where the profit and loss figures are so important in designing plants and in utilizing wasted energy.

The other aspect of it is how much oil to replace by other forms of energy, and we set as a goal for ourselves between 15 and 20 million barrels of oil per day by these seven nations in totality, that we will replace with coal, nuclear power, synthetic fuels, solar energy, and so forth. I believe that we can meet those goals.

I might say that we set some targets or goals a year ago in Tokyo that many people thought were too radically severe and that no one could meet. We have more than met our goals, and all the nations reported today that they will meet those goals in 1980.

Q. Sir, the progress that you cite that's been made in the United States, as I would understand it, has been largely through more efficiency.

THE PRESIDENT. Yes.

Q. And now, as you reach the end of the road on that and have to substitute other fuel than oil, do you still believe that this can be done without, one, damaging the environment or, two, having to relax environmental laws.

THE PRESIDENT. Yes, my answer to that question is still the same.

Obviously, you help the environment when you have a certain amount of economic growth or transport people so far with less energy, because you have less exhaust. And as you burn fuels cleaner, you have less air pollution, for instance, and less waste put into the water. And in addition to that, even though we have a very ambitious coal program, we will not lower our air pollution standards at all. In my approach to the coal people from the very first meeting I ever had with them was that they would be committing a very serious mistake if, in promoting the use of coal, they advocated the lowering of air pollution standards. And they have not done so at this point and do not anticipate doing so.

All of the changes, for instance, that would be made in the so-called Rockefeller report to convert existing utility companies from oil or gas to coal were approved ahead of time by the Environmental Protection Agency to make sure that they could make this change without lowering the air pollution standards.

Q. Mr. President, you say you haven't been briefed on the Begin report, but in general, do you not have a position on anything that Israel might do absent negotiations to make more permanent her presence in East Jerusalem?

THE PRESIDENT. I don't want to refer to East Jerusalem specifically, but we have issued a statement about a month ago through a speech that Ed Muskie made calling on both nations not to take any action of a permanent nature that would be incompatible with the Camp David process.

Q. Would it not be incompatible to do something that would make more permanent a presence in East Jerusalem, say?

THE PRESIDENT. I'll let you make the

judgment of that. Let me not go into East Jerusalem.

Q. Mr. President, you're going to Yugoslavia, I guess it's tomorrow. Did you have any regrets——

THE PRESIDENT. Let me get the question in the back.

Q.——about not going to the funeral?

Q. On the timing of Brezhnev's announcement of troop withdrawals, what do you think he expected, if anything, from this meeting here, announcing as you all gathered here in Venice?

THE PRESIDENT. It's hard to judge a reason for Brezhnev's announcement that, as you know, was made to the President of France through TASS News Agency, and then, I think, in general throughout the world.

The Soviets authorized President Giscard d'Estaing to notify us. We had already had this information before we were informed by President Giscard d'Estaing.

Q. You already had the information before Giscard told you?

THE PRESIDENT. Yes.

Q. How?

Q. CIA. [*Laughter*]

THE PRESIDENT. Well——

Q. Wiretaps.

THE PRESIDENT. It's hard—I think one thing is obviously a propaganda effort on the part of the Soviets to repair some of the damage that has been done to their reputation, because they claim to be a peace-loving nation, and they are occupying, by military force, a freedom-loving people and perpetrating very severe punishment on those people who are fighting to liberate their own country. And to give the impression in the world that they are withdrawing those forces—whether it's an accurate impression or not remains to be seen—would be a propaganda effort for them.

I believe another reason—and this was discussed among the leaders—is to induce some independent athletes to attend the Olympics. The Soviets have put out the word among their embassies throughout the world that they will pay all the expenses, for instance, of athletes who are willing to go to the Olympics. So, they are having a major recruitment effort to induce additional people to go to the Olympics.

What other reasons they might have I don't know. There may be some special consequences of their invasion in the Soviet Union with casualty figures. That could be a factor, but I have no way to know. It's just all this is surmise on my part.

Q. Mr. President?

THE PRESIDENT. Maybe a couple more questions.

Q. Why did they tell President Giscard before they told you?

THE PRESIDENT. I don't know.

Q. Or anybody?

THE PRESIDENT. Why? I have my own guess.

Q. Which is what?

THE PRESIDENT. But I don't know why.

Q. Mr. President, on Afghanistan again, there was some mention, too, about the courage of the Afghan rebels and the support for their movement. Is there going to be any efforts on the parts of the countries here to support those rebels with arms or any financial aid?

THE PRESIDENT. That's a question I would rather not answer.

Q. Could I ask you about the Tito funeral? You're going to Yugoslavia tomorrow. In hindsight, do you have any regrets about not going to the Tito funeral, and why did you choose not to go at the time when everybody else but Giscard went?

THE PRESIDENT. No, I don't have any regrets in hindsight. I might point out that the President of Mexico didn't go. The Prime Minister of Canada didn't go. The President of France didn't go. I didn't go.

I think there are 150 some nations on Earth. Forty-two of them went; some, heads of state, and some not. But there was certainly no absence of respect or reverence that I wanted to express to the people of Yugoslavia, and I believe that this trip to Yugoslavia will be much more beneficial a result than would have a visit by me to the country in the aftermath of President Tito's death.

I had an opportunity for television interviews and news interviews with Yugoslav press this past week and again expressed to the Yugoslavian people my admiration for President Tito, his reputation as a fighter for freedom, his leadership in the nonaligned movement, and my regrets to them over his death.

So, I don't have any apology to make, but I think I made the right decision.

Q. Mr. President, you said in your toast in Rome that there had to be a concrete demonstration of Western opposition to the Afghanistan invasion. Do you consider the statement that the leaders issued yesterday sufficient to meet that test, or would you hope and expect that some of the allies will take steps beyond what they've already done to let the Soviets know they do not approve of their behavior?

THE PRESIDENT. I think a communique alone would not be enough, and we certainly don't consider it to be enough in our own case, just to issue a communique. There are restraints presently and to be continued in the future on the transfer of technology to the Soviet Union, for instance. There has been an interruption of

former trade credits, beneficial terms and lower interest rates than ordinarily that have been granted to the Soviets that are no longer granted. These kinds of things will be maintained. And there'll also be the pressure of world opinion on the Soviet Union—an acknowledgment by us and other nations of the occupation.

So, this is just part of a broad gamut of actions that we and others are taking in a peaceful way to induce the Soviets to withdraw their forces.

Q. [*Inaudible*]—additional concrete steps in the nature of our own grain embargo by other nations?

THE PRESIDENT. I can't answer that question.

Q. When you say this wouldn't be enough in our own case, do you mean that we are going to take some other specific steps?

THE PRESIDENT. I meant we are already taking other steps in addition to the communique.

Q. Is it true that you and Schmidt crossed swords? According to a German official, he really—that said he lectured you for a half hour. Or was it all sweetness and light?

THE PRESIDENT. Well, it was sweeter and lighter at the end of the conversation than it was at the beginning. [*Laughter*]

Q. Are you going to the Ohira memorial service?

THE PRESIDENT. I don't know.

I think I made an appropriate statement after Helmut and I had our conversation. One was that the letter that I sent—which I consider to be a private letter and which he considers to be private—was sent with the best of intentions and consists of two basic parts. One was an acknowledgment that erroneous press reports concerning Schmidt's statement on the theater nuclear force agreement were causing problems. I personally put in the phrase "erroneous press reports," because they were erroneous.

Secondly, I wanted to explain to Chancellor Schmidt very clearly what the United States position is on any sort of moratorium or freeze concerning theater nuclear forces.

So, he understands me, and I understand him very well. And I think the meeting was fruitful, and we just never have to refrain from speaking frankly.

Q. What was astonishing about the letter?

THE PRESIDENT. I don't think the letter should have been astonishing, but I'd rather let Chancellor Schmidt tell you about that.

Q. What did you say about an Ohira memorial service? Are you going? I didn't hear you.

THE PRESIDENT. I don't—want to say anything on that—[laughter]——

Q. Did you have any fun in Venice, or was it all work?

THE PRESIDENT. I had a good time, yes. It's just an unbelievably beautiful city. And Rosalynn and Amy have been having a good time.

Q. Did you really have bread and cheese and water for breakfast——

THE PRESIDENT. Milk.

Q. Oh, milk. [Laughter]

Q. Did you have any trouble getting a word in?

THE PRESIDENT. This morning? [Laughter]

Well, I really enjoyed it. They have eight monks over there. This is an order that was founded in the year 982, and they formerly had 215 monks there, and now they only have 12. But they take care of St. Marks, as you know, which is

filled with treasures, and they minister to the congregation who comes there, primarily tourists and others who come. And then they also have duties out among the little islands, among the poor people.

They do scholarly work. One of them is a very noted scholar on Gregorian chants and has issued several publications that are used in recording the ancient Gregorian chants. It was a very delightful occasion for me.

The priest who's the head of the order formerly lived in Arkansas and Missouri and Wisconsin. He taught school there in the colleges. He's a musician, a pianist and an organist. And another one of the monks is from Brooklyn——

Q. A Jewish monk. [Laughter]

THE PRESIDENT. I asked him—he said he'd be there the rest of his life. When the monks join the order, they come prepared to stay forever.

Q. Are you going to retire there, Mr. President?

THE PRESIDENT. It sounds like a great idea.

They've also got some people who just come and live with the monks and who go out every day and do their work at the university, keeping books.

Q. Could the press learn something from those monks? [Laughter]

THE PRESIDENT. I have to admit that I looked on them with great envy.

Q. Did they try to convert you? They're Catholic.

THE PRESIDENT. I've already converted. [Laughter]

Q. Mr. President, do you really think that—I don't mean to get serious again——

THE PRESIDENT. That's all right.

Q.—— but do you really think it's a healthy trend that the Russians are now dealing with the French and the Germans and so forth?

THE PRESIDENT. Yes.

Q. And not just primarily with the United States?

THE PRESIDENT. I don't think they've ever dealt primarily with us. There's always been, I think, a legitimate effort on the part of the Soviet Union to work with and to discuss issues with and also to negotiate with the Europeans directly. But we've always had a custom since the Second World War to share the results of those exchanges.

As soon as Chancellor Schmidt completes his visit to Moscow, then Mr. Genscher, who's the Foreign Minister, will come to Washington to give Secretary Vance and myself a complete report——

Q. Who, who?

Q. Who, sir?

THE PRESIDENT. Genscher.

Q. Secretary who?

Q. Vance? You said Vance.

THE PRESIDENT. I'm sorry. My fault. Secretary Muskie. Secretary Muskie. [*Laughter*]

PRESS SECRETARY POWELL. Donaldson's [Sam Donaldson, ABC News] been drunk for 3 days. [*Laughter*]

Q. He's a better man for it.

Q. You don't think this looks like business as usual to the American public?

THE PRESIDENT. Well, it may.

Q. When we are blessing Schmidt going and you saying that there were fruitful results from Giscard going and that to the public it looks like——

THE PRESIDENT. But the fruitful part, I think I pointed out, was that Giscard told Brezhnev, in effect, the same things that were in this communique that was issued yesterday, and I don't have any way to know what reports President Brezhnev might get from his ambassadors in other countries, whether he knows that

the allies are this firm in condemning the occupation. So, in my judgment, it's both beneficial and also inevitable. We could not prevent it even if we wanted to, which I don't.

And when I have met with Brezhnev or when Secretary Muskie met with Gromyko recently, he immediately gave a report, a private report, to the Foreign Ministers of the other nations who were assembled there. This is a customary thing, and I think it's very good for us to keep having these communications open with the Soviet Union.

Q. But the only thing the Soviets see or hear that would increase their likelihood to want to withdraw is simply unity, right? I mean there aren't any new concrete steps that you're anticipating or any of them is anticipating—if I understood you correctly.

THE PRESIDENT. None that I could surmise.

Q. It's simply the impression that we are——

THE PRESIDENT. But that's important.

Q.——all together, and it won't be, as you said, another Czechoslovakia——

THE PRESIDENT. I think that all of us——

Q.——that it's supposed to make them take the idea of negotiating more seriously.

THE PRESIDENT. Yes. I think that all of us refuse to accept the Soviet invasion of Afghanistan as a permanent, accomplished fact, that we demand the Soviets' total withdrawal from Afghanistan, and that we are so closely united that the Soviet effort, if mounted, to divide us one from another and to deal individually with us on a separate basis would be fruitless. I think that's a very good and beneficial signal to send to the Soviets.

Q. Is there a problem, Mr. President, that the French, the German President have somewhat different home constituencies than you have——

The PRESIDENT. I'm sure they do.

Q.——that they have to sometimes speak to. You're going to be running against, probably, Governor Reagan. Schmidt has a problem on the left wing of his party and so on, so that you may agree in purpose, but when you express it sometimes, you've got to think of whom you are talking to at home.

THE PRESIDENT. Yes, I think everything you said is true. And I try to make a point, within limited bounds, of studying the German and the French and the British and the Japanese and other political party coalitions and the makeup of the individual party factions. This is important for me, when I have a bilateral meeting, to understand what they face.

We observed very closely this morning, for instance, the results of the Japanese election—the drastic reduction in the Communists' strength, a very unexpected victory for the conservative party, which has been the ruling party for a long time. So, I try to understand these things and also ask them questions in our private, more informal talks about politics in their country. They are quite interested in our Nation, knowing the general results of the primary season, what the issues were, how those might carry over into the general election. We're all politicians, and we all exchange experiences.

Q. Can you see any prospect that the Soviets could be seriously interested in negotiating withdrawal before November—I mean, that you could be engaged in serious discussions about it by the fall?

THE PRESIDENT. I really don't envision the Soviets negotiating a withdrawal. We don't know what the Soviets might do, but I can't imagine our being involved in a negotiation.

We have sent to the Soviets a very clear message that was known by our friends and allies here, telling them in effect that with the withdrawal of the Soviet forces in their entirety, that we would support an independent, nonaligned, neutral government of Afghanistan if it was acceptable in form to the Afghan people. And how that goal might be accomplished is something that the Soviets can assess, and whether they will attempt it, I can't predict.

Q. [*Inaudible*]—do you think more informal, where there's some real prospect that they would be talking about withdrawing by fall?

THE PRESIDENT. I think it's a possibility. As you know——

Q. But that's not your expectation, is that correct?

THE PRESIDENT. I don't predict it, but I would be pleased to see it happen.

The Moslem nations, as you know, have formed a three-person committee to explore those possibilities. And it may be, if the Soviets are very discouraged about their lack of success in subjugating the Afghan people, that they might be looking for some way to resolve this issue, and they might attach themselves to this Moslem country effort. But I don't have any way to know.

Q. Who are the Moslem countries?

THE PRESIDENT. Iran, Syria, and—anybody know?

MR. FRIENDLY.[1] Iran, Pakistan, and the secretary general of the Islamic Conference.

THE PRESIDENT. I know Ghotzbadeh is one of them.

Q. But you don't see our participating short of a total wihdrawal—I mean, if they were to begin—participating in neutralization.

---

[1] Alfred Friendly, National Security Council Press Officer.

THE PRESIDENT. Well, that's too con-
jectural——

Q. Well, a senior American official said
yesterday——

THE PRESIDENT.——because a commitment to a total withdrawal at a certain specified early time—you know, if it
can be monitored—would be a major
factor. I wouldn't say that we'll sit back
and——

Q. Have you noticed, Mr. President, as
some of us have, that as Reagan emerges
more clearly as the Republican candidate
that your stock in Europe goes up?

THE PRESIDENT. I hope it's not just in
Europe. [*Laughter*]

REPORTER. Thank you.

NOTE: The President spoke at approximately
6 p.m. at the Cipriani Hotel.

Interview With the President

*Question-and-Answer Session With Goran
Milic of Yugoslavian TV and Juri Gustinicic
of Politika. June 12, 1980*

U.S.-YUGOSLAV RELATIONS

Q. Mr. President, although American-
Yugoslav relations have been developing
favorably over a good many years——

THE PRESIDENT. Yes.

Q. ——it is widely believed that they
made particularly strong advances during
your Presidency. So, in this regard, how do
you view your first visit to Yugoslavia?
What do you expect from this visit?

THE PRESIDENT. First of all, I'm very
excited about going to Yugoslavia. We
were honored, as you know, with a visit
here by President Tito. And we benefited
so greatly from his visit and his advice
that that's obviously one of the bases for
the—I think, perhaps, the best relation-

ships we have had with Yugoslavia in
many years.

Secondly, we have had an undeviating
policy toward Yugoslavia, a commitment
to the independence, the territorial integrity, and the unity of Yugoslavia for more
than 30 years, since President Truman
was in this office.

And third, we have a broad range of
bilateral concerns: about peace and stability, the prevention of terrorism and
aggression, the role to be played by the
nonaligned movement nations, and also,
of course, to enhance trade and economic
relationships.

I'm particularly eager to meet with the
new leaders in Yugoslavia. And perhaps,
since it will follow the economic summit
conference in Venice, I can give them a
report on what the major Western developed countries believe about the future of
inflation and unemployment and energy
and trade. So, I think it's going to be an
exciting visit and also very profitable for
us.

PRESIDENT'S CORRESPONDENCE WITH PRESIDENT TITO

Q. The Yugoslav—and also the international public—has noticed a more than
usual intensity of personal correspondence
between you and President Tito.

THE PRESIDENT. Yes.

Q. Could you tell us how such an exchange of personal messages came about,
and what was the significance of it?

THE PRESIDENT. They were extremely
significant to me and to our country. I
have had a long admiration for President
Tito and his contribution to the development of independent nations and the preservation of peace and liberty of not only
the people of your country but, indeed, for
many others around the world. When I

became President I initiated this communication on a tentative basis, and he responded enthusiastically. And we exchanged many long letters that were private and confidential in nature, but extremely frank in our discussion of our two countries and our relationships and also matters that were of concern to us that happened in other nations.

His advice and counsel to me was profound, very thoughtful, and based upon his long years of experience in dealing with leaders of the world and with nations of the world that he knew much better than did I. When he came here on his official visit, we instantly got along very well, and again, we benefited greatly from it. So, this long series of communications back and forth, of private correspondence, I hope was of help to him in understanding our Nation and its current policies better. But it was extremely beneficial to me.

Q. I would be free to ask you, Mr. President, of course, if it is not a secret of state, is there any detail that you particularly remember from that personal correspondence with President Tito?

THE PRESIDENT. Well, as the relationship changed in the nonaligned movement, and as the relationship changed between ourselves and the Soviet Union, as we sought a basis for stronger détente and peace, and as we hammered out the principles of the SALT agreement to control nuclear weapons, and then later, of course, as the hostage question evolved, and the Soviets invaded Afghanistan—those kinds of current issues were discussed between us. I received his advice, and of course I gave him a response about what our own Nation's policies might be.

He was pleased with his visit here, and I don't have any doubt that he was very gratified at the outpouring of admiration for him that was so obvious among the people of my country.

THE NONALIGNED MOVEMENT

Q. You have already stressed, yourself, the importance of the nonaligned movement, of which Yugoslavia is a very active member. But one has the impression that lately, nonalignment is less frequently mentioned in American policy. Do you share this impression? And what is your position and your attitude to date to the nonalignment in world politics?

THE PRESIDENT. This was one of the subjects that President Tito and I discussed at length: the subversion of the nonaligned movement—which he initiated in its early days—by the later entry of influence, for instance, by the Cubans, who are obviously dominated by and aligned with the Soviet Union; and how the true nonaligned countries—India and Yugoslavia being leaders—could restore the integrity of the movement in the face of Cuban leadership there.

As he was preparing to go to the Havana conference, he outlined to me some of the principles that would be discussed and debated. And I think he won a notable success in the Havana nonaligned movement conference in trying to move the entire movement back to a true independence and true nonalignment.

We are deeply concerned about the integrity and the thrust of the nonaligned movement. I know that in his latter days President Tito [was], and now his successors are, very eager to see true nonalignment restored there. The Soviet invasion of Afghanistan is a serious departure from the respect for nonaligned countries. Although Afghanistan was not a signatory of the nonaligned movement charter, they were indeed a nonaligned country until the Soviets invaded them. And this encroachment on the integrity of the smaller and weaker nations was of great concern to him and is to me.

Q. But you do consider the nonaligned movement an important factor in today's politics?

THE PRESIDENT. Extremely valuable, yes, for the maintenance of peace and the stability of the world, and also for the meeting of economic challenges, such as the explosion in energy prices. What the nonaligned countries do and say is very important to our country, to the Soviet Union, I'm sure, and to the rest of the world.

THE INTERNATIONAL ECONOMY

Q. Your administration has recognized, Mr. President, the need for serious change in the structure of economic relations in the world. However, almost nothing has been done so far in this field. And how do you see the effective way out of this stagnation towards the new economical order?

THE PRESIDENT. Well, I believe it's accurate to say that we were making good progress on this economic development through the regional banks, the World Bank, the International Monetary Fund, through bilateral aid of an economic nature, through the enhancement of trade, through the elimination of protectionist barriers, through cultural exchanges. This applied to our relationship with Yugoslavia and to other countries, and among other nations that did not involve us directly.

The OPEC price increases, however, have added to the cost of energy so much that many nations now spend almost their entire export earnings just to buy oil from the OPEC countries at the exploded prices. For instance, in the 12-month pe-

riod, during 1979, OPEC oil prices more than doubled. They went up more than they had, the entire history, since oil was first discovered. And we have large energy supplies of our own, but we still are a large importing nation as well. But this has shocked the world economy, and now we're working on ways to conserve energy and also to produce alternative forms of energy that don't rely on oil.

But I think we are making progress over a long period of time, but we had a setback with the unanticipated explosion in oil prices.

Q. Some say that petrol is expensive, but some say that computers are expensive, too, so what shall we do with the countries who don't have computers and which don't have petrol as well?

THE PRESIDENT. Well, different nations have natural and human resources that they can tap with adequate financial investments and with adequate means to sell their products. My own belief is that our country's greatest asset, on a historical basis over many decades of time, is the extremely productive land that we have to produce food and fiber for the rest of the world. Obviously, we've been blessed by technological advances with our highly competitive free enterprise system, which was built upon almost unlimited natural resources of minerals and growing forests and the production of our agricultural lands.

But each country is different, and what we are trying to do now is to have a marketing arrangement in the world that eliminates trade barriers and protects those poorer countries which are quite vulnerable—some of them only have one or two export items that are available to bring in much needed purchasing power for them.

We also have mounted, under my leadership, a commission on world hunger, to try to deal with the more equitable distribution of food supplies and, also, to let those who have very ill-developed production techniques do a better job with better seeds, some irrigation principles, better fertilizers that we ourselves have developed in this country. And as we go with our technicians into those small and developing countries to help them, we learn a lot in the process and, therefore, are better off ourselves.

DÉTENTE

Q. There's a lot of talk today about a very difficult time in détente. You spoke about it, too. Now, assuming that certain critical issues cannot be resolved in the very near future, what is then, in your opinion, going to happen to détente in the meantime?

THE PRESIDENT. We are trying to preserve the essence of détente—that is, to oppose aggression and also to eliminate the threats to world peace. These must be done simultaneously.

There was a major setback to détente and to the prospects for world peace with the unwarranted Soviet invasion of Afghanistan. Even with this very serious development, however, we still are attempting in every possible way to preserve the peaceful nature of the world and to control the spread of nuclear weapons and, at the same time, to reestablish much better communications among nations who might see their relationships deteriorate, absent a sharing of hopes and dreams for a better and a more peaceful future.

In Africa, in Asia in particular, we've opened up new avenues of communication with nations like Nigeria, and before that, with Egypt which was formerly not a very close friend of ours, and more re-

cently with normalized relationships with China.

But we intend to continue to oppose aggression, the persecution of human beings as is taking place now in Kampuchea, in Ethiopia where many refugees have escaped—the same thing, of course, in Afghanistan, and now in Cuba—and, at the same, enhance human rights and human freedom.

So, the maintenance of peace, the provision of stability, the searching for a way to control nuclear weapons, the enhancement of communications among nations, and the protection of human rights—those are the bases that I see for the perpetuation and improvement of détente.

CONFERENCE ON SECURITY AND COOPERATION IN EUROPE

Q. We've heard your position on this, but can the European conference help to maintain certain positive achievements in international cooperation in détente, at least in Europe? How do you see the Madrid Conference?

THE PRESIDENT. Yes, I thought the conference in Belgrade was an historic development in letting nations search among themselves—different nations with different perspectives—for common ground on which they could predicate plans for the future.

We will go to Madrid with a commitment to enhance what was decided at Helsinki: to provide for better security among nations, for a more open relief of tension that might develop because of misunderstood intentions among the countries, for the enhancement of human rights, and for better economic relationships.

So, there will be differences at Madrid. I think that's an accurate prediction. But we believe that together we can carry out the principles and the spirit and the commitments made at Helsinki.

ADMINISTRATION'S ACCOMPLISHMENTS

Q. Mr. President, at the end I would like to ask a more personal question. You have now been in office for almost 4 years, and I remember when you started. You said on one occasion that it's a heavy burden and also that there are limitations to what a President can do. Now, looking ahead to a new term, would you feel more strongly the burden or the high hopes you had at the beginning?

THE PRESIDENT. I think I failed to anticipate the burdens, and I failed to anticipate the limitations on resolving the problems in the world. We are a superpower, but our dealings are with free and independent other nations who have a different perspective from us. And in a free world, where people can act on their own, when nations make their own decisions, there are bound to be these differences.

We have made progress, though. The world has basically been at peace. Our country has stayed at peace. We've made progress in hammering out the principles of the SALT II agreement, which we intend to see ratified, and then go on to SALT III and the control of theater nuclear forces. We've opened up new relationships with a fourth of the people on Earth, with the People's Republic of China. We've made notable progress under the most difficult circumstances in the Mideast, with peace treaties now between Israel and the major Arab nation, and now working under difficult circumstances, as I say, toward further progress. I think we've strengthened our NATO Alliance and, as you pointed out earlier, the relationship between ourselves and Yugoslavia has never been better.

So, we're making progress. We face issues frankly and without trepidation. We don't flinch when a difficult decision has to be made. And the damage that was done in our own country, because of the Vietnam war and because of the Watergate embarrassment, has substantially been repaired. We have a much stronger country in its spirit and in its unity and, although we have some economic problems, they are not nearly so severe as they are in many other nations.

So, in general, I'm pleased with the progress so far, and I hope that I'm reelected and will have a chance to serve 4 more years and, if so, we'll continue to make further progress.

Q. Thank you very much for this interview, Mr. President.

THE PRESIDENT. It's a pleasure, and I'm really looking forward to being in Yugoslavia.

NOTE: The interview, taped for later use in Yugoslavia, began at 1 p.m. in the Diplomatic Reception Room at the White House.

The transcript of the interview was released on June 23.

Yugoslavia: Arrival in Belgrade

Remarks at the Welcoming Ceremony at Surcin Airport.   June 24, 1980

Mr. President, Yugoslav and American friends:

I've looked forward to this day since March of 1978, when President Tito invited me to come to Yugoslavia. I'm very grateful to the Presidency of the Socialist Federal Republic of Yugoslavia for renewing that invitation.

My pleasure in visiting this proud and beautiful land is tempered by the sorrow we all feel at the passing of President

Tito. He was a great man, one of the greatest of the 20th century. He was one of a small handful of statesmen who can truly be said to have shaped the modern world and one of an even smaller handful who have shaped it for the better.

He was a man of extraordinary courage—physical, moral, and political courage. He was also a man of imagination and of a rare kind of practical vision, the kind of vision that sees not only what a better world might be like but also how the imperfect tools that we have can be used to help build a better world. President Tito's contribution to the development of a strong, independent, and nonaligned Yugoslavia was, of course, unparalleled, but his contribution to international peace and stability was no less important.

It was my privilege to have worked with President Tito. I've greatly valued his counsel, which was the product of so much wisdom and experience. He shared this wisdom with me very generously, both face to face and through the many letters that we exchanged.

I share your grief at his passing and your admiration for what he accomplished. President Tito left a precious legacy—a strong, independent, and nonaligned Yugoslavia. I have come to Belgrade to assure you of the friendship and support of the United States as you build on that legacy.

President Tito devoted a great deal of effort to forging good relations between our two countries. Today the foundation of those relations is firm and durable. In the past 3 years, moreover, the bonds between our two countries have grown visibly stronger, and I am eager to work with you to make them stronger still.

In this connection, Mr. President, I want to reaffirm to you today the basic continuity of American policy toward Yugoslavia. The United States supports and will continue to support the independence, territorial integrity and the unity of Yugoslavia. The United States wishes to see an economically prosperous and politically strong Yugoslavia. The United States respects Yugoslavia's nonalignment and admires Yugoslavia's constructive international role.

We stand ready to work closely with you to ensure the continued development of an independent Yugoslavia. But we know that your independence is a creation not of any outside force, but of the courage and sacrifice of the people of Yugoslavia. And we also know that the greatest bulwark of your independence is your own fierce determination to defend it. That determination is perhaps the key to the special role Yugoslavia plays in the world.

Yugoslavia was a pioneer of nonalignment and a founder of the nonaligned movement. Yugoslavia remains an important leader of that movement today, militarily, economically, and politically. Yugoslavia has pursued a policy of authentic nonalignment that has won the respect of the entire world. Especially now, at a time when the principles of equality, noninterference, and territorial inviolability are threatened, Yugoslavia's steadfast defense of the principles of the United Nations and of the nonaligned movement takes on new importance.

We know that Yugoslavia can make a significant contribution to the solution of international problems and to the further development of détente between East and West. The United States also wants to strengthen détente, and we will work hard toward that end. But détente must be based on reciprocity. It must be based on mutual restraint. It must be based on respect for the principles of sovereignty, territorial integrity, and noninterference in the affairs of other nations. These are the principles of international life for which Yugoslavia has always struggled.

At the same time, the United States strongly believes that efforts to reduce the chances of nuclear war must continue; so must the efforts to build an international system that helps to reduce tensions and to foster peace, security, freedom, and economic well-being.

Despite the crises that beset the world today, the United States remains committed to preserving the framework of détente and to maintaining a dialog between the nations of the world. Specifically, we support arms control and disarmament talks and negotiations wherever they can contribute to mutual security and to international stability. We also support the Madrid Review Conference of the Helsinki Final Act, which we feel can contribute to the full and frank review of progress to date and to balanced steps forward in all areas of the Final Act.

Mr. President, I'm looking forward to our discussions on these and other matters. We are eager to hear your ideas for ways in which Yugoslavia and the nonaligned movement can contribute to solving the many difficult problems the world faces. Mr. President, our time here is short and we have much to discuss, but we will be building on a foundation of mutual purpose. I'm very pleased to be here. I bring to you and to all the people of Yugoslavia the warmest good wishes of the people of the United States.

Thank you very much for this fine welcome.

NOTE: The President spoke at 8:50 a.m.

Yugoslavia: Meeting With President Cvijetin Mijatovic and Government Officials

White House Statement.   June 24, 1980

The two sides held a cordial and constructive meeting in a spirit of understanding and mutual respect. International issues including East-West relations, Afghanistan, Iran, the Middle East, and international economic problems were discussed. The strength of the bilateral relations between the two countries was confirmed. The two sides agreed to issue a joint statement at the conclusion of the visit.

Yugoslavia: Tour of Kalemegdan Park

Exchange With Reporters.   June 24, 1980

REPORTER. Ah, yes, nice.

THE PRESIDENT. You like that, eh?

Q. You could match this with the Coliseum.

Q. Yes. You could make a—[inaudible].

THE PRESIDENT. How'd the Coliseum turn out?

Q. Very good.

Q. It was beautiful.

Q. What'd you talk about in your private meetings, Mr. President?

THE PRESIDENT. Well it's beautiful—[inaudible]—very good. We talked about the results of the Venice conference, and we talked about the bilateral relationship between our countries, the strength of the Government as it continues following President Tito's tragic death, the importance of the nonaligned movement to be truly nonaligned in its character, and how President Tito, who organized the nonaligned movement, had been very influential in this. We talked about economic problems and—[*inaudible*]—problems—[*inaudible*]—of the Middle East. We had a general discussion of matters of importance to Yugoslavia. It was very harmonious, very good.

Q. Thank you.

THE PRESIDENT. What one has in Belgrade is the tragedy of war, because the city itself has been damaged and destroyed so much and so many of the population have been killed in the Second World War, the First World War, and down through the centuries. This site first became a fortress 2,000 years ago, right? And since then it's had to have fortifications. But we now see a good opportunity for maintaining world peace through good international relationships and frank discussions of difficult issues. But Belgrade has been given worldwide significance even beyond previous times, because of the great leadership of President Tito, and I think no one could come to Belgrade and see its historical significance without knowing what it means now to the entire world.

Q. Mr. President, does the Yugoslav leadership share your feelings of great concern about the Soviet invasion of Afghanistan?

THE PRESIDENT. I think the comments about that would best come from the Yugoslav leadership.

Q. All right, sir. Thank you, Mr. President.

NOTE: The exchange began at approximately 5:15 p.m.

Yugoslavia: State Dinner in Belgrade

Toast of the President.   June 24, 1980

Mr. President, American colleagues, and Yugoslav friends:

Although this is my first visit to your great country, Yugoslavia, the special relationship between our two countries has involved seven American Presidents, beginning with President Harry Truman. I'm here to confirm the continuity of that relationship. I'm here to reiterate our firm support of Yugoslavia's independence, territorial integrity, and unity and our respect for Yugoslavia's nonaligned position.

These are the principles which President Tito and I emphasized during his visit to the United States a little more than 2 years ago. I want you to know that they are just as central to American policy now as they were then, when our country was honored by the presence of this great leader.

It is with great sadness that I pay here tonight a personal tribute to President Tito. I regarded him as a friend, as well as a statesman of uncommon vision. I valued his counsel, his wisdom, and his perspective. I gained many insights from our personal correspondence, which continued even during the final months of his illness.

Great men of history sometimes leave the nations they have led ill equipped to face the world without them. What has impressed me in my brief visit here is how smoothly you have met the challenge of transition. That is a great tribute not only to the foresight of President Tito but also to the dedication and the patriotism of his political heirs.

A man like President Tito cannot be replaced. It is the nature of such men to be irreplaceable, but the courage and the creativity of the Yugoslav people guarantee that President Tito's life's work of building a strong, independent Yugoslavia will go forward in the years ahead.

Yugoslavia's unswerving defense of the principles of true nonalignment and nonintervention in the internal affairs of foreign states is particularly important in today's unstable and troubled world. The United States respects such a policy.

It has always been my hope as President that we could move on in many areas of the world from conflict to peace. I did look forward to significant contributions in arms control when the SALT II treaty was signed. Ratification of this treaty has been temporarily frustrated, but not abandoned.

We are deeply concerned that an unjustifiable act of armed aggression continues in Afghanistan, a founding member with you of the nonaligned movement, a small country, which, as you well know, constituted no threat to anyone. The vast majority of the countries of the world, in an extraordinary vote by the General Assembly of the United Nations, have called for the immediate and unconditional withdrawal of all foreign troops from Afghanistan. We want to see the restoration of an independent and nonaligned Afghanistan, which can live in peace with all its neighbors and contribute to the stability of the region.

With the withdrawal of all Soviet forces from Afghanistan, we would be prepared to join in assurances and arrangements to establish a truly independent, a truly nonaligned Afghanistan with a government acceptable to the Afghan people. We would be prepared to explore a transitional arrangement, to be implemented along with the prompt withdrawal of all Soviet troops from Afghanistan, for the purpose of restoring peace and tranquillity in that suffering country.

Mr. President, our talks today have also touched on the grave consequences of politically motivated terrorism. I speak for every American citizen when I say how much we appreciate Yugoslavia's forthright support for the release of the American diplomatic personnel who at this moment are held hostage in Iran, in violation of every tenet not only of international law but of simple decency.

For my part, I want to reiterate that my Government will not tolerate terrorist acts against Yugoslav officials and establishments in the United States and that we strongly oppose political efforts aimed at undermining Yugoslavia's unity and territorial integrity.

Mr. President, our talks today have confirmed my view that Yugoslavia's concept of nonalignment is not a passive or quiescent thing, but a bold, creative, imaginative approach to the problems of the world, particularly the problems of the developing nations. And our talks have confirmed something else, that both Yugoslavia and the United States want to strengthen the bilateral relationships that exist between us and that we want to do so on the basis of independence, equality, and mutual respect.

I would like to thank you, on behalf of my family and my colleagues, for your generous hospitality and friendship. I look forward to a continuing exchange with you on international issues, on which we share so many compatible views, and also on bilateral issues, on which we've made such great progress in recent years.

I would like to ask everyone to join me as I raise my glass in a toast: To the Presidency of the Socialist Federal Republic of Yugoslavia and to its President, his Excellency President Mijatovic; to a strong and prosperous Socialist Federal

Republic of Yugoslavia; to the peoples of Yugoslavia, whose love of independence we admire and support; and to the furthering, strengthening of American-Yugoslav friendship in the cause of peace and stability throughout the world.

NOTE: The President spoke at 9:31 p.m. in the Federal Hall of the Palace of the Federation in response to a toast by President Mijatovic.

Interview With the President

Responses to Written Questions Submitted by the EFE Spanish News Agency. June 24, 1980

SPAIN: DEMOCRATIC DEVELOPMENT

Q. Spanish democracy goes on, and the people there strongly desire its consolidation. How does your administration evaluate His Majesty's role in Spain's democratic development, and that of the political forces?

A. We in America share the desire of the Spanish people to see democracy flourish. True democracy frees its citizens to realize the best in themselves and to require the highest standard of their government.

Certainly, as you suggest, the role of His Majesty the King has been central in the development of democracy in Spain. At the same time, coming from a nation with a vigorous democratic tradition, I well appreciate the vital role played by responsible political parties, both in positions of leadership and of opposition, in developing and maintaining a viable and vigorous democracy.

Most important, of course, is the determination of a nation's people to maintain its free institutions. It is a continuing process and, in Spain, one which our Government and our people have watched with admiration and support.

THE PRESIDENT'S TRIP TO EUROPE

Q. Mr. President, could we have some general remarks on your forthcoming trip to the Mediterranean countries of Europe? What is going to be your agenda?

A. The initial purpose, of course, was to participate in the annual economic summit taking place in Italy this year. As I looked at the planning for the trip, it seemed to me a good opportunity to accept the generous invitations from the Governments of Spain, Portugal, and Yugoslavia to pay visits to these Mediterranean nations as well.

These visits, while not as lengthy as I would have liked, will provide an opportunity for me to exchange views on a range of subjects and at a time when consultation and cooperation among good friends are not only desirable but imperative.

There have been critical developments in recent months which affect our nations and our citizens. The Soviet invasion of Afghanistan carries strategic implications for the well-being of all nations which value peace and independence. Iran's holding of hostages threatens internationally accepted rules of civilized conduct among nations. We have questions on European defense and security, as well as other regional and bilateral issues to discuss. In brief, the agenda is full.

Moreover, I am delighted that an opportunity has arisen for me, personally, to express the admiration and support of the American people, so many of whom are of Hispanic origin, for Spain's historic transition to democratic government. This evolution is being carried out with maturity and sensitivity. It is one of the most inspiring political developments of our generation.

I anticipate with pleasure meeting again with His Majesty the King and with President Suárez, both of whom I have had the honor of receiving at the White House, and with other Spanish officials and citizens.

On a personal note, my wife and I have had a lifelong respect and admiration for Spanish life and culture, and we are delighted to have the opportunity, finally, to pay a visit to Spain.

SPAIN: RELATIONS WITH U.S. AND ROLE
IN WESTERN WORLD

Q. Mr. President, how do you assess, as of this moment, the relations between the United States and Spain? And how do you view Spain's role in Europe and the Western World?

A. Relations between Spain and the United States are better than at any time in recent memory. As democracies with shared interests and perceptions, our two countries consult frequently on the challenges facing the world today. We work together in many areas—political, military, and economic—and our cooperation has intensified with the advent of Spanish democracy. This warm spirit of friendship sets the tone for my visit to Spain.

In addition, we are bound by ties of family and culture. Hispanic peoples from various areas who have made their lives in the United States have enriched our society in ways beyond measure.

Moreover, Spain is an integral and important part of Europe and the Western World. With its rich history and culture, Spain has already given much to our civilization. As a young and vibrant democracy, it has much more to give. This is a role that we in the United States welcome and applaud. We look forward to increased cooperation with Spain in many areas where we can work together to meet the challenges to our common interests.

SPAIN: RELATIONS WITH ARAB AND
MEDITERRANEAN COUNTRIES

Q. Because of its historic ties, Spain feels linked by a special relationship to the Arab and Mediterranean countries. Could you comment on this attachment and similar close Spanish ties to Latin America?

A. While physically and politically part of Europe, Spain nonetheless has a unique perspective on the Arab and Mediterranean world. The complex reasons for this are rooted in history and geography. The resultant heritage has endowed Spain with a special insight into the Arab world. We understand this fact and appreciate the way in which it complements Spain's growing institutional relationship with the West.

For different, deep historical reasons Spain has a special relationship with the nations of Latin America, a role which the United States welcomes. Spain's interest in Latin American affairs, as exemplified by participation in the Andean Pact, is a salutary development. Spain has an important role to play in modern Latin America as an historic source of cultural energy and a contemporary example of democratic vigor.

CONFERENCE ON SECURITY AND
COOPERATION IN EUROPE

Q. The next round of talks of the Conference on Security and Cooperation in Europe will take place in Madrid next fall. Is the United States in favor of these talks to take place as planned? How do you view prospects for the meeting in general?

A. Although the Soviet invasion of Afghanistan has gravely damaged the climate of East-West relations, I consider the Madrid CSCE meeting to be in the interests of the signatories of the Helsinki

Final Act, including the United States. We do favor going ahead as planned.

The United States and other countries will use the important opportunity the CSCE meeting provides to call attention to how well or poorly the signatory countries have lived up to their obligation since the 1975 Helsinki summit. This review is particularly important with respect to the human rights and humanitarian provisions of the Final Act, where there have been serious failures by some countries to carry out their commitments.

Additionally, the Madrid meeting offers us the chance to work out further measures to improve the implementation of the Final Act by achieving balanced advances in all significant areas it touches. Finally, the meeting should ensure that the Helsinki process continues through a regular series of future review meetings such as that planned for Madrid.

LATIN AMERICA

Q. What are the present policies of your administration towards the Latin American countries?

A. From its inception, my administration has acted on the conviction that the Latin American countries play an important global role. The national aspirations of individual Latin American and Caribbean countries for independence, self-expression, and economic development are important both to the Third World and to the West, particularly to countries like Spain and the United States, which share with them a multitude of personal and historic ties.

U.S. policies seek relationships that support these traditions, these aspirations, and this potential. We maintain continuing dialogs that give balanced treatment to their interests and ours. I have personally emphasized the need to forge better

direct people-to-people ties that stress the basic values of our common civilization and take advantage of opportunities to create closer and more balanced relationships. I am encouraged by the improvement in respect for human rights in most Latin American countries and the trend towards democracy. We Americans strongly support this pattern.

CENTRAL AMERICAN AND CARIBBEAN REGION

Q. The present situation in Central America and the Caribbean area—does it deserve any special consideration for your administration?

A. Yes, of course. The nature of the Caribbean Basin is changing rapidly, and so is the structure of relationships between the nations of the region and the West. We believe the challenge before us is not to resist these changes—many of which are natural and inevitable—but to support them in new and constructive ways.

With other concerned nations, we are seeking to:

—encourage moderate and democratic forces throughout the area;

—facilitate economic development and the equitable distribution of wealth;

—promote observance of internationally accepted standards regarding human rights;

—rejuvenate processes of regional cooperation; and

—assure security against external aggression.

In *Nicaragua,* we are providing assistance to help the country recover from its devastating civil war and encourage the evolution of a pluralistic, truly independent Nicaragua.

In *El Salvador,* the Christian Democratic military government is carrying out unprecedented reforms in land-holding and banking. For that reason, we believe it offers the best hope for a moderate democratic outcome. We are supporting it, and believe it deserves the economic and political support of West Europeans.

The peaceful and democratic evolution of these countries and others in the Caribbean Basin is the only path to the establishment of self-sustaining democracies in this important area. It is also the path which we support, but the path which Cuba, in many ways and often with violence, seeks to obstruct. As in Spain, so in the Caribbean, the United States supports and applauds the strengthening of democracy.

Yugoslavia: Conclusion of State Visit

Joint Statement. June 25, 1980

At the invitation of the Presidency of the Socialist Federal Republic of Yugoslavia, President of the United States Jimmy Carter and Mrs. Carter paid an official visit to Yugoslavia June 24–25, 1980. During the visit, President Carter and President of the Presidency of the SFRY Cvijetin Mijatovic held cordial and constructive talks in an atmosphere of mutual respect, understanding, candor and friendship.

Participating in the talks were, on the American side:

Jimmy Carter, President of the United States

Lawrence S. Eagleburger, Ambassador to Yugoslavia

Zbigniew Brzezinski, Advisor to the President for National Security Affairs

Jody Powell, Press Secretary to the President

David Newsom, Under Secretary of State for Political Affairs

Richard Cooper, Under Secretary of State for Economic Affairs

Steve Larrabee, National Security Council Staff

On the Yugoslav side:

Cvijetin Mijatovic, President of the Presidency of the SFRY

Lazar Kolisevski, Member of the Presidency of the SFRY

Veselin Djuranovic, President of the Federal Executive Council

Josip Vrhovec, Federal Secretary for Foreign Affairs

Sinan Hasani, Vice President of the Federal Assembly

Budimir Loncar, Ambassador to the United States

Milivoje Maksic, Counselor to the President of the Presidency for International Affairs

Mirko Zaric, Office Director for North American Affairs, Federal Secretariat for Foreign Affairs

President Carter also met with other prominent Yugoslav officials.

President Carter expressed the profound sorrow of the American people at the death of President Tito, who was greatly admired and respected in the United States. President and Mrs. Carter on this occasion again expressed regret at the loss of a great statesman who, as one of the most prominent leaders of the Non-Aligned Movement, devoted his entire life's work to building a strong and independent Yugoslavia and to securing peace and progress in the world.

President Carter and the Presidency of Yugoslavia noted with satisfaction the very successful development of relations and cooperation between Yugoslavia and the United States. They agreed that the meeting held in Washington in March 1978 between President Carter and Tito and the document signed on that occasion represents a durable and stable basis for further strengthening of the cooperation between the two countries. Based firmly on the positions and principles set forth in that document, as well as the documents signed by the Presidents of the two countries in 1971 and 1975, the United States and Yugoslavia have made great progress in recent years in broadening and deepening their relations in all areas.

Both sides affirmed that in recent years significant expansion of the dialogue and consultations between the two countries has occured, in which a special role was played by the regular exchange of letters between Presidents Tito and Carter. There have also been frequent exchanges of visits at all levels, including productive contacts between members of the U.S. Congress and of the Federal Assembly of the SFRY as well as other mutually useful visits and exchanges. The United States and Yugoslavia affirmed their readiness to continue this useful practice, which has proven to be in the interests of both countries and of greater international understanding generally.

The two sides noted the importance of historical and cultural ties between the two peoples and the special role in strengthening the bonds of friendship and understanding played by Americans of Yugoslav descent. They also confirmed their mutual interest in facilitating the free flow of information and people between the two countries, endorsed governmental and non-governmental exchanges in the fields of science and technology, culture, and information, and agreed that even more can be done in these areas.

Turning to the increasingly important economic relations between the United States and Yugoslavia, President Carter and the Presidency of the SFRY noted with satisfaction the growth in trade and economic cooperation between Yugoslav and American enterprises and financial institutions. They stressed their mutual interest in further expansion of economic relations and agreed to intensify efforts to increase trade, while recognizing that the growth of Yugoslavia's exports will be an important factor in the satisfactory development of two-way trade. They also agreed that more should be done to promote other forms of economic cooperation including joint ventures and long-term cooperation. The American side expressed understanding for and a readiness to support the efforts of Yugoslavia toward stabilization and further development of its economy. Appreciation was expressed for the contribution already being made to strengthening U.S.-Yugoslav economic relations by the U.S.-Yugoslav Economic Council, the Yugoslav Chamber for Promotion of Economic Cooperation with the U.S., and the U.S.-Yugoslav economic working groups.

The two sides favorably noted the measures taken to prevent acts of violence against Yugoslavia and its diplomatic, consular and other representatives in the United States and in prosecuting the perpetrators. President Carter reiterated the commitment of the United States Government not to tolerate such terrorist activities, which are against the interests of the United States and are also against the good relations between the two countries.

President Carter and the President of the SFRY Presidency expressed great concern over the serious deterioration in the international situation which represents a threat to world peace. With the objective of halting the current dangerous trend in international relations, and of renewing the disrupted process of detente, they affirmed the need for strict respect for the spirit and principles of the U.N. Charter, especially those which refer to the inadmissibility of the application of force, of intervention and interference in the affairs of other countries, of the imposition of alien will on sovereign states, whatever the form or justification, and of the blocking of their independent internal development.

On these bases the two sides emphasized the importance of broadening the process of negotiations and cooperation in the world, as well as the need for a comprehensive process of detente which should include the largest possible number of countries, and be based on strict respect for the independence, sovereignty, and territorial integrity of all states. This was judged to be all the more significant as the world is undergoing great change requiring reciprocal restraint on the part of all countries from actions which disrupt world peace and stability. They reaffirmed the role of the U.N. as an essential instrument for preserving peace, for the peaceful settlement of disputes, and for strengthening cooperation in the world.

The discussion also encompassed general questions of security and cooperation in Europe. Both sides affirmed the obligation to implement all provisions of the Helsinki Final Act and stressed their determination to strengthen the CSCE process and to work for balanced progress in all areas at the Madrid meeting, in the conviction that doing so would improve security and cooperation among all signatories of the Final Act, and would have broader significance.

The two sides exchanged views on the consequences of further arms competition from the standpoint of preserving peace and security, the current worsening international situation, and the need for general economic development. They agreed on the need resolutely to pursue effective, equitable and verifiable arms limitation, arms reduction, and disarmament agree-

ments based on the principles of undiminished security of all states. The objective should be gradual reduction of armaments to the lowest possible level consistent with the security and stability of all nations, with the ultimate objective of general and complete disarmament under effective international control. The two sides took note of the significance of the U.S.-Soviet Strategic Arms Limitation Treaty. They also agreed upon the urgent need for further progress through negotiations, both bilateral and multilateral, toward the limitation and reduction of nuclear and conventional armaments.

Special attention was devoted in the discussions to the worsening situation of developing countries and of the international economic situation as a whole. Proceeding from the growing interdependence of all nations, it was mutually affirmed that there is an urgent need to seek solutions to unresolved questions and to seek the equitable harmonization of the economic interests of all countries. The two sides agreed on the far-reaching political importance of the continuation of a constructive dialogue between industrial and developing countries and on the furthering of international economic cooperation on a more stable and just basis. They especially emphasized the importance of greater support of the industrially developed countries for the more rapid development of developing countries and of the importance of the global negotiations on these questions. They expressed the hope that these negotiations will achieve productive results for the benefit of all, and particularly for developing countries, which would be in the interest of the more efficient functioning of the entire world economy.

Considering the various aspects of human rights, the two sides also agreed that efforts to enhance respect for human rights in all countries should proceed in accord with the provisions of the Charter of the U.N., the Universal Declaration of Human Rights, and the Helsinki Final Act.

Agreeing upon the need to invest decisive effort toward the equitable solution of both previously existing and new crises in the world, the U.S. and the Yugoslav sides assessed current developments in the Near East, South Africa, Southwest and Southeast Asia, and other areas.

The two sides expressed their special concern about the situation in the Middle East, which remains a source of great tension in international affairs. They agreed on the urgent need to find a comprehensive, just and lasting solution to the problems of the Middle East and explained in detail their respective views on the current situation.

Turning to Southern Africa, the American and Yugoslav sides condemned racism in all forms and the South African system of apartheid. They expressed their support for efforts directed at the achievement of majority rule and national independence in Namibia. They welcomed recent developments in Zimbabwe.

Both sides emphasized the need to respect the right of Iran to independence and to non-alignment, as well as its right to determine its own internal development and orientation in international affairs without outside interference and pressure. They agreed that the release of the U.S. diplomats held hostage in Iran and the peaceful resolution by the U.S. and Iran of the issues between them, on the basis of the principles of the U.N. Charter, would greatly contribute to peace and stability in this region.

The two sides called for an end to military intervention and all other forms of interference in the internal affairs of independent countries. Both sides emphasized the need for the foreign troops involved to be withdrawn and an end put to all causes of suffering and sacrifice in such countries. They also called for further humanitarian efforts by the international community to resolve the problems of refugees.

In this connection, each side elaborated its viewpoint on ways to resolve the situations which have arisen in Afghanistan and Kampuchea, emphasizing the need to respect the rights of all peoples to determine their own destiny.

President Carter and the President of the Presidency of the SFRY emphasized the significance of non-alignment as an independent factor in international affairs. President Carter affirmed that the United States respects the desire of the non-aligned states to determine their own internal development and orientation in international affairs.

President Carter reiterated the continuing respect and support of the United States for the independence, territorial integrity, and unity of Yugoslavia. The United States considers an independent and non-aligned Yugoslavia an important factor for balance, peace and stability in Europe and the world.

The two sides emphasized their determination further to expand and to enrich qualitatively the current successful development of friendly relations between the SFRY and the USA, on the basis of equality and with full mutual respect for the differences in each other's social system and international position.

President Carter extended an invitation to the President of the Presidency of the SFRY to visit the United States and the invitation was accepted with pleasure.

Yugoslavia: Departure From Belgrade

Text of the President's Departure Statement. June 25, 1980

I leave Yugoslavia with strong impressions of a brave and dedicated country.

I have been moved by the dignity and courage of the Yugoslav peoples at this time of national sorrow over the passing of President Tito. Just as strongly, I have been impressed by the determination of Yugoslavia's leaders as they face the challenges of the present and plan for the future.

My talks with President Mijatovic and other Yugoslav leaders have reminded me once again of Yugoslavia's steadfast commitment to the policies which have become its hallmark: independence and nonalignment abroad; brotherhood, unity, and self-management at home.

We have reviewed our bilateral relations—which I am happy to affirm are excellent.

We have also had an opportunity to discuss a number of aspects of the current international scene. There, as we had to agree, the picture remains deeply troubled.

We have seen in Afghanistan a gross violation of the sovereignty of a non-aligned nation. In response, the United States and Yugoslavia clearly have different roles to play, but both our countries are committed to upholding the principles of respect for independence and sovereignty, non-intervention and peaceful resolution of disputes—principles that are enshrined in the United Nations Charter and confirmed in the Helsinki Final Act.

As a leader and founder of the Non-aligned Movement, Yugoslavia plays a unique role in promoting the universal realization of these principles.

As I depart Yugoslavia, I want to express to you, Mr. President, and to your colleagues in the Presidency and Yugoslavia's other ruling bodies, and to the people of your great country, my sincere thanks for the hospitality you have shown us. Our visit has not only been useful, it has also been very enjoyable. We carry home to the United States many pleasant memories and reminders of the close friendship of our peoples.

Thank you and farewell.

NOTE: The President did not deliver departure remarks. As printed above, the statement follows the text released by the White House.

Communications Satellite Corporation

Nomination of Thomas R. Donahue To Be a Member of the Board of Directors. June 25, 1980

The President today announced that he will nominate Thomas R. Donahue, of Washington, D.C., to be a member of the Board of Directors of the Communications Satellite Corporation. He would replace the late George Meany.

Donahue is secretary-treasurer of the AFL–CIO and was executive assistant to Meany from 1973 to 1979. He was Assistant Secretary of Labor for Labor-Management Relations from 1967 to 1969.

Spain: State Luncheon in Madrid

Text of the President's Toast.   June 25, 1980

Your Majesties, Mr. President, friends of Spain and the United States:

This is a great moment for me to be here and to bring you and your people the warm good wishes of the Government and people of the United States of America. It is a special pleasure, because of my great personal interest in your language and culture.

Four hundred years ago, Spain was the superpower of the Western World, and the Spanish of that day left a legend of vision and courage that has never been forgotten. During that golden age, painters like El Greco and Velasquez and writers like Cervantes and Lope De Vega taught the world new ways to see and to feel. The Spanish explorers were the astronauts of their day, bravely probing new worlds with unforeseen dangers and difficulties. All of us have benefited from this greatness of Spain.

My own State of Georgia began as a very small outpost of the Spanish Empire. The first European to set foot there was Hernando de Soto, in 1540. Georgia was a Spanish colony for a much longer time than it was an English colony.

I speak of the historic influence of Spain because it is so obvious that Spain's courage and greatness prevail today. In little more than 4 years, you have created a vigorous, thriving democracy, with respect for human rights, individual liberties, and freedom of expression. The task has not been easy. You have had to contend with worldwide recession, with enormous increases in energy costs, and with ancient and sometimes divisive internal challenges. Yet you have succeeded brilliantly in rebuilding old institutions and creating new ones.

The growth of Spanish democracy has been a tonic for the entire Western World. Spain refutes the false contention that the sweep of history is invariably toward authoritarianism. So, Spain is a source of hope and inspiration to democrats everywhere. Spain's experience holds lessons about resolution, moderation, and self-control, lessons for other democracies and for new countries in the Third World which have found freedom and now are searching for models to follow in shaping their own societies.

In the past 4 years, Spain has also moved toward a new place of leadership in the world. Your Ministers have repeatedly made it clear that Spain stands side by side with the other Western democracies, as a full member-to-be of the European and Atlantic Communities. We are pleased that you have begun negotiations for entry into the European Communities, because we believe that Spain's accession will strengthen the Community, just as the Community strengthens Europe.

Similarly, we hope that Spain will see its own interests served by participating in the collective defense of the West. However, we fully recognize that this is a decision to be taken solely and exclusively by Spain, in its own time and in its own way. Our Nation will give full support to your decision once it has been made.

In addition, our two countries share a bilateral security partnership based on important common interests. We will begin a review this year of the security relationship that has well served the interests of both our countries and that will continue to serve our joint interests for many years to come.

Our significant economic relationship also links our peoples. American business leaders have demonstrated their faith in Spain's future by their high level of investments here in recent years. Exporters in each country have looked to the other as an important market for their products. What is absolutely clear is that the growing economic relationship is of very great benefit to both countries.

Spain's concern about energy supplies is fully shared in the United States. As you know, I took office as President at a time when the American people still largely believed that oil was an infinite resource. The central drama of American public life during the last 4 years has been the struggle to change that attitude and then to build a viable energy policy. The struggle goes on, but the foundations for such an energy policy are now nearly complete. This is crucial not only to the future of my own country but to the broader web of relationships of which both our countries are a part.

Our two countries also share a strong interest in democratic evolution and respect for human rights in other parts of the world. In Latin America we both have special ties. I appreciate the support and wise counsel we have often received from Spain with respect to difficult, frequently critical situations in Latin America and the Caribbean. We also appreciate the close consultations we have had and the assistance you have given us on the hostage crisis in Iran and other aspects of that delicate situation. In the Middle East and parts of Africa, we can look forward to further cooperation, especially valuable because of your historical knowledge of the Moslem world.

The United States has special reason to applaud Spain's emergence as a major partner in the unfinished tasks of peace. Her cultural and historical ties in so many areas of the world enable her to be a bridge between the Third World and the West. This is especially relevant as we take up the problems of the new decade, which in many ways will be more difficult and dangerous than any we have surmounted before.

Today the West confronts a strategic challenge of historic magnitude. From 1945 through the mid-1950's, we successfully resisted Soviet expansionary power westward and eastward. Today the Soviet Union is thrusting southward directly in Afghanistan, indirectly through Vietnam and Cambodia, and elsewhere by means of foreign proxies. The challenge is clear, and so is the question it poses for our democratic institutions: Do we permit aggression to proceed with impunity, or do we resist encroachment which affects our common vital interests? There is no doubt in my mind where both our countries stand on this issue.

The gratifying resurgence of Spanish influence throughout the world is an important source of confidence with which the West can approach the difficult decade of the 1980's. That confidence is fully justified. The vitality I have witnessed here attests to Spain's own sure sense of its future and the direction it has freely taken toward democracy, diversity, and the unfettered exercise of the human spirit.

Your Majesty, I would like to raise my glass: To you, to your lovely queen, to your President and all the leaders of the government and of the democratic opposition who have helped build Spanish democracy, and above all to the Spanish people, to whose spirit goes the bulk of the credit for the successes of the past several years. *Viva España!*

NOTE: The exchange of toasts began at approximately 3:15 p.m. in the State Dining Room of the Royal Palace.

Following the toast of King Juan Carlos I, the President delivered his response in Spanish. As printed above, the President's toast follows the advance text released by the White House.

Spain: Meeting With Prime Minister Adolfo Suárez and Government Officials

White House Statement.
June 25, 1980

President Carter and Prime Minister Suárez met this evening at the Moncloa Palace for a working dinner, preceded by an hour's private conversation. Their discussions in all lasted 2 hours and covered a broad range of international issues including Afghanistan, Iran, the Middle East, the Western Sahara, and the Madrid CSCE review conference, as well as issues of bilateral interest.

In addition to the two leaders, those present at the dinner included, on the U.S. side, Dr. Brzezinski, Under Secretaries of State Newsom and Cooper and Ambassador Todman; as well as on the Spanish side, Foreign Minister Oreja, Commerce Minister Gamir, Information Secretary Milia and Ambassador Llado.

Interview With the President

Responses to Written Questions Submitted by Wilton Fonseca of the Portuguese News Agency, ANOP.   June 25, 1980

PRESIDENT'S TRIP TO EUROPE

Q. Mr. President, you haven't traveled internationally for quite some time. Apart from your attendance at the Venice summit, what conditions have prompted your visits to Yugoslavia, Spain, and Portugal, and what do you hope to gain through these visits?

THE PRESIDENT. The visits I am making in Europe in addition to the economic summit meeting in Venice bring me to-gether with friends and allies for frank talk at a time of serious challenge to our common interests. The challenges are as familiar as they are grave: the crises in Iran and Afghanistan, the search for peace in the Middle East, the issue of energy dependence for the industrialized world, and the aspirations for economic justice of the developing nations. Thorough discussion of these and other matters is not only necessary, it is also helpful in making strong relationships stronger and in shaping consensus from diverse ideas and outlooks.

Within this overall context, I attach special importance to my visit to Portugal. On the personal side, I am very pleased to have the occasion to come to Lisbon, to visit a capital which no American President has been fortunate enough to visit since 1960. Moreover, I am anxious to use my time in Portugal to express the profound admiration which I and Americans generally feel for your nation's remarkable transition to democracy. Your experience and that of Spain confound those pessimists who profess to see democracy in retreat around the world. You give heart, instead, to those who espouse freedom and individual dignity as the surest avenue to social and political progress.

Beyond paying tribute to your example, I am also looking forward to consulting with the leaders of Portugal, who have managed the transition with such skill and wisdom.

The Portuguese Government's forthright support of the standards of international law and civilized conduct against those who are violating those standards in Iran and Afghanistan has established the foundation on which we can continue to cooperate in addressing those crises. Portugal's continuing ties with lusophone

Africa, moreover, assure me of valuable insights into ways we can work together on the pressing economic development needs of that continent.

Though the time is short, there is much to discuss, much to do, much to gain from talking and working together.

NORTH ATLANTIC TREATY ORGANIZATION

Q. Mr. President, as you know, Portugal has continued to maintain a strong interest in African developments (particularly its former colonies) simultaneously with its commitment to the Atlantic Alliance. Recognizing that many areas of international crisis today lie outside the traditional NATO regional concerns, could you comment on the advantages of NATO's adopting a more global strategy?

THE PRESIDENT. NATO was formed in 1949 in response to what was then viewed as the most visible threat—the Soviet Union's military buildup in Eastern Europe and designs on Western Europe. For over 30 years our Alliance has successfully resisted this expansionist threat to the NATO treaty area.

But throughout the years, our nations have also had to look beyond the NATO perimeter to Soviet actions elsewhere in the world and to their potential effect on European security. Such concerns have recurred throughout the history of the Alliance. For example, in June 1974 the North Atlantic Council Declaration in Ottawa—endorsed by all the heads of state later that month in Brussels—stated clearly that the interests of the Alliance could be affected by events in other regions of the world.

The Soviet invasion of Afghanistan has dramatized this reality more clearly than any other recent event. The invasion, although outside the NATO treaty area, has affected the fabric of East-West relations by posing a threat to Southwest Asia and the Persian Gulf, a region vital to the security of the entire Western Alliance.

This new challenge to peace is one which NATO, as an Atlantic alliance, meets best by pursuing its original, primary mission: the defense of Europe. At the same time, NATO's members and our other friends and allies must also be prepared, as partners in peace and security, to contribute according to their capabilities to cooperative security efforts in other parts of the world. The best way to preserve peace is firmly to oppose aggression.

DEMOCRACY IN PORTUGAL AND SPAIN

Q. How does the U.S. assess democratic development in the Iberian Peninsula, and, particularly in the case of Portugal? To what degree have these developments strengthened the country's security-defense role within the NATO structure?

THE PRESIDENT. The development of democracy in Iberia has strengthened the chances for lasting stability and economic progress in both Spain and Portugal. We have seen new constitutions with significant safeguards for human rights adopted in both countries enabling public opinion to play its vital political role.

In Spain, the transition to democracy passed a milestone when in December 1978 the Spanish people approved a new constitution establishing a constitutional monarchy with a sovereign parliament to which the President is responsible. Scarcely 4 years after Franco's death, the national parliament has been elected twice, and freely chosen municipal governments have taken office for the first time in many years.

Portugal's political development since the revolution of April 25, 1974, has been equally admirable. I am impressed by the rapidity with which the Portuguese people are recovering from the economic and political difficulties of the past several years. To have fashioned a constitution with as much concern for human rights as they have augurs well for the future of democracy in Portugal. The steady and consistent progress toward political stability sets the stage for major economic and social gains in the years to come.

The establishment of democratic institutions has, of course, accelerated the development of Portugal as a respected member of NATO. The actions of the Portuguese people in recent years have strengthened their standing and voice in the community of Atlantic nations. In recognition of Portugal's important role in the Alliance, the U.S. has assisted significantly toward equipping the Portuguese army and air force. Also, we are working with other allies in NATO to ensure their continuing effective contribution toward Portuguese force modernization in the interests of NATO's common defense.

IRAN; AFGHANISTAN

Q. In light of the current situation, what do you project as future U.S. steps to secure the release of the hostages in Tehran? To what extent do the situations in Southwest Asia (Iran and Afghanistan) threaten overall world peace?

THE PRESIDENT. Iran's holding of diplomats as hostages violates every standard of international law and civilized behavior. While we are continuing to pursue a variety of diplomatic avenues to secure our citizen's safe release, we are also, through economic measures taken with our allies and other nations, bringing home to Iran the tangible costs of such irresponsible behavior. If Iran's leadership truly has the interest of the Iranian nation and the well-being of its people as its primary goals, I am confident it will free the hostages.

Even apart from the hostage question, the instability in Iran creates another uncertain situation in a turbulent and vital region. The brutal Soviet invasion of Afghanistan threatens the strategic balance in this critical region. The actions taken by our allies, as well as by scores of other nations, serve to let the Soviet Union know that its aggression—and that is the only word for it—will not go unpunished. Certainly, our concerns for the security of Southwest Asia and the Persian Gulf will be high on the agenda in my talks with President Eanes and Prime Minister Sá Carneiro.

Portugal's principled response to the crises in Iran and in Afghanistan has been as welcome as it was courageous. But the crises continue, and we have much to discuss.

SOVIET INFLUENCE IN AFRICA

Q. What aspects of U.S. diplomacy in Africa do you feel represent the best chance of countering long-term Soviet influence or the influence of their surrogates on the continent?

THE PRESIDENT. Soviet activity in Africa is based on a mixture of geopolitical, strategic, and ideological motivations. The objective is to expand Soviet influence in any way possible, seizing opportunities as they arise and relying heavily on military rather than economic assistance. But the consequence in those areas where the Soviets have increased their influence the most—as in Ethiopia and Angola—is that conflict and suffering have only intensified. Refugees—like those we see fleeing from communism in Kampuchea, Afghanistan, and Cuba—are the innocent victims of this Soviet interference.

We believe Africans should be free to build their own futures. Accordingly, we pursue a policy which recognizes fundamental African aspirations and priorities; self-determination, an end to racism and white minority rule, the maintenance of territorial integrity, and economic development. We Americans can and do identify with these priorities, and we continue to give diplomatic and financial support to advance them.

This long-range approach is the most effective answer to attempts by the Soviets and their Cuban surrogates to win influence in Africa at the expense of Africa's interests and real needs.

NUCLEAR WEAPONS

Q. We Europeans are obviously concerned about the question of international nuclear weapons safeguards, whether in the context of SALT and other disarmament negotiations or the recent computer failure in the U.S. defense alert system. Could you comment upon the question of the safeguards and the possibilities of accidental war?

THE PRESIDENT. The pursuit of arms control is itself a measure to prevent accidental conflict. Negotiations, for example, make possible a dialog between adversaries which can provide greater understanding of military thinking and systems generally. Arms control agreements, moreover, work to increase confidence between the sides in specific areas, as, for example, in the SALT II provision for advance notification of certain ICBM flight-tests.

Although our own alert systems are fully adequate to discern an attack clearly, it is nevertheless useful to exchange information of this type as part of a process to build confidence. The notification procedures on large-scale troop movements

and exercises under the Helsinki accords of 1975 contribute in a somewhat similar fashion to security in Europe.

While we are concerned about the computer error, there was no possibility of aggressive response from the United States based on this isolated component indicator. During those two brief alarms our personnel followed standard procedures and immediately determined no attack was underway. We were not remotely close to launching any of our nuclear forces. All our warning sensors worked properly, as did our procedures for discriminating false from real alarms.

THE NATION'S ECONOMY

Q. The state of the economy has always played an important role in the outcome of U.S. Presidential elections. In the context of the current economic situation (e.g., recession, rising unemployment, etc.) will these domestic concerns outweigh U.S. foreign efforts both in terms of your own reelection and the possible direction of future U.S. priorities?

THE PRESIDENT. If you are suggesting that the United States will turn inward because of domestic economic concerns the answer is a clear no. We have a vital and responsible international role to play, as a member of the Atlantic Alliance, as a member of NATO, as a full partner in the Middle East peace process, as a responsible and constant force for conciliation and economic progress.

Our domestic economic situation, of course, would concern me whether or not this were an election year. In essence, our economic difficulties are no different from those affecting the other advanced nations of the world. Our agenda at the Venice summit addressed these economic issues, in particular the long-term issue of energy conservation, production, and resources, as well as the continuing struggle against inflation.

In our era domestic and international economic priorities cannot be separated. They must be addressed with as much responsibility and creativity at home as abroad. They call for frank assessments and sometimes difficult decisions that look beyond an election day.

NOTE: Mr. Fonseca met with the President at 1:10 p.m. on June 16 in the Oval Office at the White House and submitted the questions for the President's response.

Spain: Visit to American Embassy
Remarks to Embassy Employees and Members of the American Community in Madrid.
June 26, 1980

Buenos días a todos. Es una gran placer para nosotros estar aquí con ustedes. [Good morning, everyone, it's a pleasure for us to be here with you.]

In a few minutes we will have to leave Madrid after too short a visit and continue our journey to Portugal, and then later on this evening we'll be back in Washington.

It's impossible for a President to come to Madrid without remembering our first emissary to the great nation of Spain. While our country was still fighting for its own independence in 1777, the father of the Foreign Service came here to represent our great country. He was a diplomat of great ability, an author, a scientist, a thinker who was one of the great Americans of all times. I refer, of course, to Benjamin Franklin, who came here to marshal support for our Nation in a time of war, so that we might later enjoy blessings of peace.

He exemplified in his own life what you exemplify in yours—the ability and the dedication and the courage required in times of peace, through sound diplomacy accurately representing what our Nation is, to prevent or to reduce the prospects of war.

We have a lot of wonderful people in our Foreign Service around the world. We have great Ambassadors who serve us. There is none that I know of in any post in the world more accomplished and more competent and more effective than Terence Todman, and I'm very deeply grateful to him and to Doris for what they do.

I first knew him, during the few months when I began to be President, as an Assistant Secretary in charge of the entire region of Latin America. As you well know, this is a very important post, to be responsible for a whole region of the world. But because of the significance which we attached to Spain and the rapid evolution that Spain has demonstrated to the entire world in shifting toward a completely democratic government, we believed that this fine man should be stationed here. He agreed with the significance of this task, and his transfer to Spain was done with his full agreement and approval.

It's impossible for us to recognize how much diplomacy has changed. You're here, involved in testing military and peaceful relationships, preparing for every eventuality, studying the problem of narcotics, problems of space exploration, the problems of trade, communications, tourism—quite different from what they were as problems for diplomats in the time of Benjamin Franklin, but still exactly the same purpose: accurately and fruitfully to represent the greatest nation on Earth, the United States of America, in a great nation, an ally and a friend, the nation of Spain.

We have a lot of interests here, a lot of common commitments, a lot of common goals and ideals and principles. I've had a very fruitful period of discussions, both with King Juan Carlos and his beautiful wife and also, of course, with the Prime Minister, the President, and with the members of the Cabinet and the opposition parties, to try to assess personally, as best I could here in Spain, what we might do even to improve already excellent relationships.

Your duties are not easy. I understand that very well. In a way, I'm part of the diplomatic corps of our country. Secretary Muskie accompanied me on the first part of our trip to Rome and to Venice, and then he went to Ankara in Turkey to meet with the Foreign Ministers of the European nations, and then went to Kuala Lumpur to meet with the Foreign Ministers and leaders of the ASEAN nations in Southeast Asia.

This constant effort to project the good side of our country and to learn how best to deal with our friends and to minimize the impact of potential adversaries is an important part of your life and mine.

Your life is not only a difficult and dedicated one but also, at times, dangerous. In the last 6 years, for instance, four American Ambassadors have been killed in the line of duty. And I can never look into the faces of anyone who serves in the Foreign Service without thinking about the 53 American hostages, who are innocent, who are held as a horrible act of international terrorism, condoned and supported by the official Government of Iran.

This problem is constantly on my mind, and I never meet with a foreign leader or in a group of foreign leaders without very early raising this problem with them, urging them to do everything they possibly can, through diplomatic or private channels, to hasten the day when these 53 brave Americans will be free and will be back home where they belong.

Don't ever forget how deeply grateful the American people are to you for the fine service that you render here. I know that in addition to the difficulties and the challenge and sometimes the danger in some countries, there's also a great sense of gratitude that you can not only serve a great country but live in a foreign country which is also great and pleasant and exciting and a friend.

I want to add my personal thanks also to the citizens of Spain who work with you here in all the multitudinous duties of the American Embassy. On behalf of 220 million Americans who don't have the opportunity to come and stay in Spain, let me say that all of us are deeply grateful to you and wish for you God's greatest blessings.

NOTE: The President spoke at 8:45 a.m. at the Chancery at the Embassy.

Spain: Conclusion of State Visit

Press Statement Issued on the President's Departure.   June 26, 1980

At the invitation of His Majesty King Juan Carlos, the President of the United States Jimmy Carter paid an official visit to Spain on June 25–26.

During the visit the President of the United States held conversations with His Majesty the King. President Carter also had meetings with the President of the Government, Mr. Suarez, and with members of the Spanish Government.

President Carter's visit is the first by a President of the United States to democratic Spain. Accepting the Spanish

King's invitation, the President is returning visits to his country by His Majesty and by the President of the Spanish Government.

During the conversations between President Carter and His Majesty the excellent level of the close and friendly relations between the two countries was noted with satisfaction as were the harmonious points of view on various foreign policy subjects.

The two Chiefs of State expressed their concern with regard to the tensions existing in various parts of the world and set forth their desire and their intention to contribute in all appropriate ways to the reestablishment of peace and stability in those regions.

President Carter congratulated His Majesty on the favorable evolution of the Spanish democratic process which has earned the sincere support of the entire free world and for Spain's return to its proper place in the concert of nations. For its part the Spanish side expressed its appreciation for the work carried out by the United States in support of human rights and the cause of peace.

The international scene, with particular reference to the crises in Iran and Afghanistan and the situation in the Middle East, and bilateral relations were examined in President Carter's meeting with the President of the Spanish Government, Mr. Suarez. During these conversations, which were held within the framework of the consultations and contacts taking place among Western leaders, it became evident once again that Western solidarity constitutes one of the main principles of democratic Spain's foreign policy and that Spain will join its efforts with those of the other Western countries in the pursuit of peace and stability for all peoples.

In these contacts President Carter said he was pleased at progress toward Spain's entry into the European Community, which will reinforce Western solidarity and will complete the construction of a stronger and more united Europe.

Both leaders expressed the hope that the balanced development of the Madrid conference would permit the creation of a climate favorable to dialogue and cooperation, that it would favor the reestablishment of mutual confidence and make it possible to advance on the road toward detente and peace.

President Carter expressed his satisfaction for the important work that Spain is carrying out as host to the CSCE meeting in Madrid.

Both statesmen examined ways to strengthen Western solidarity in the face of the serious threat represented by Soviet aggression in Afghanistan. They examined the significance of the Soviet announcement of the withdrawal of some forces from Afghanistan and reaffirmed that only the total withdrawal of Soviet troops and guarantees for non-alignment and respect for the freedom of the Afghan people to express their political desires constitute the necessary elements for a definitive solution to the conflict.

President Carter expressed his understanding of Spain's role in its relations with the Arab world and of President Suarez' efforts in his international contacts and his trips to the Middle East. The two leaders expressed their common desire to contribute to a just and peaceful solution to the problems of the region.

President Carter expressed his appreciation and that of all the American people for Spain's support and activities on behalf of the prompt liberation of the American hostages being illegally held in Iran.

The President of the Spanish Government stated that Spain will continue its actions to support the international effort for the favorable solution of the problem.

The two Presidents agreed that respect for international law is indispensable for the proper conduct of international relations and for the solution of the present crisis.

President Carter described the results achieved in the recent Venice Summit. In view of the concern shared by both governments regarding the world energy crisis and its negative economic and social effects, President Carter showed his willingness that Spain cooperate in and benefit from research and development into alternate energy sources in which the United States is making an important effort.

The two statesmen agreed in the opinion on the threat which terrorism constitutes for the peace, stability and progress of today's world.

In the field of bilateral matters the two Presidents expressed pleasure at the state of our relations and set forth their satisfaction at the favorable attitude of both parties toward the search for a contractual framework for future relations between both countries, which will take account of Spain's new political circumstances.

The two sides examined the state of economic relations between the two countries and expressed their intention to maintain this trend, while, at the same time, striving to end the present imbalance in their commercial exchanges.

NOTE: As printed above, this item follows the text of the Spanish press statement as translated by the United States International Communication Agency. The statement was agreed to by the United States Government. It was not issued as a White House press release.

Portugal: Arrival in Lisbon

Remarks of the President and President António dos Santos Ramalho Eanes at the Welcoming Ceremony at Portela Airport. June 26, 1980

PRESIDENT EANES. Mr. President, on behalf of my wife, myself, and the Portuguese people, I would like to welcome you and express our warmest and most sincere greetings.

Your Excellency is the first President of the United States of America to pay a state visit to Portugal since the restoration of our democracy. As you have pointed out, the Portuguese people have demonstrated to the world its attachment to freedom and to democratic principles overthrowing a dictatorial regime and overthrowing—[*inaudible*]. And this, Mr. President, was achieved in the atmosphere of liberty and pluralism, of which we are justly proud.

This is a strong evidence that we will continue to be able to defend the democratic regime which shows the very will of our people and is also the greatest tradition of the American people.

[*Inaudible*]—meet today, as representatives of two countries sharing the highest ideals of freedom, justice, and human dignity. Based on these principles, the old friendship between Portugal and the United States became stronger than ever before. Considering this friendship and these future perspectives, I would like to express the appreciation of the Portuguese people and to greet on their behalf the great American mission that your Excellency symbolizes and represents here today.

PRESIDENT CARTER. I was extremely pleased to accept the invitation of President Eanes to visit Portugal on the occasion of my trip through Europe.

Portugal and the United States have an old and valued friendship. Our countries established diplomatic relations more than 200 years ago. We appointed a Vice Consul to Punta del Gada even before we had written our Declaration of Independence.

Beyond our official relations, the links between our two countries have been nurtured by Portugal's greatest gift to the United States, some of her people who came to our country with a pioneer spirit. Today there are many thousands of Americans who proudly preserve their family heritage brought to our country from Portugal.

Portugal and the United States are both members of a great alliance. That alliance helps to guarantee our mutual security. But it has become more than just a military defense pact. It reflects the basic commitment of all its members to freedom and to democracy.

Over the past 6 years Americans have watched and supported Portugal's successful struggle to build a democracy. That struggle has given hope to believers in democratic liberty throughout the entire world.

For all these reasons, I am grateful for the opportunity to visit Portugal and of being able to meet with your country's leaders.

As you know, I have just come from a meeting of heads of state in Venice. The need for consultation among allies has taken on a new urgency as this new decade begins. We've watched government-sponsored terrorism against American diplomats in Tehran. We've witnessed the Soviet invasion of Afghanistan, and we have seen hundreds of thousands of refugees driven by oppression from their homelands in Southwest Asia, Indochina, and Latin America.

In contrast, the peoples of both Portugal and the United States live in peace and freedom with respect for our neighbors and for our fellow citizens. Both our nations are engaged in helping the great numbers of human beings around the world who are oppressed or desperately poor. Both our nations are trying to build a better and a more humane world.

It is in that spirit that I look forward to these consultations with our Portuguese friends. In the name of my fellow countrymen, let me express the special friendship Americans feel for the people of Portugal. To all Portuguese I bring a warm American *abraço*.

Thank you very much.

NOTE: President Eanes delivered his welcoming remarks in Portuguese at 9:47 a.m., and his remarks were translated by an interpreter.

Portugal: State Luncheon in Lisbon

Toast of the President. June 26, 1980

Mr. President, let me thank you and Mrs. Eanes for this lovely luncheon in this most magnificent setting. Rosalynn and I have long looked forward to a chance to visit Portugal. The excitement of the visit started even before our plane landed as we came in over Lisbon and the Tagus River. As I looked down on this beautiful city and its monuments, I was vividly reminded of Portugal's rich history.

Just a few hours ago, I had a chance to visit the monastery which honors two of Portugal's greatest heroes, the poet Camoes and the explorer Vasco Da Gama. These men and others, like Ferdinand Magellan, are properly honored in our country as well as yours. Their courage and their vision paved a way for the extension of a great cultural heritage across the seas to other continents.

Portugal has reason for pride in these men. Now, 500 years later, we may have run out of seas never before navigated, as Camoes said, but I have seen that Portugal continues to be served by dedicated men. While their task is different from that of the discoverers, it is no less difficult. It's to build a strong and a new permanent democracy.

Portugal's democratic leaders had the courage of the explorers in the years after the 1974 revolution. Your nation's perseverance and your capacity have been severely tested by the stresses of the last 6 years—economic crises, the resettlement of hundreds of thousands of refugees, forging new ties with your former colonies, and challenges to democracy itself. But you have prevailed. You've built healthy and vigorous democratic parties. You've defended freedom to debate and to differ one from another, and you've conducted fair and free elections.

Many of you in this room have helped lay the foundations of a lasting democracy in Portugal. You, the democratic leaders, have personally borne the burdens of office. You've played the role of responsible opposition. You've organized, inspired, and led your people. Because of your personal involvement in creating democracy, you know better than most how precious it is. It's no wonder that Portugal was among the first of the world's nations to recognize and to respond to the threat which was posed to democratic societies everywhere by aggression in Afghanistan and official terrorism in Iran.

Your actions and your words demonstrated that people who value freedom cannot stand idly by while others' rights are ruthlessly suppressed and while a system of international order so dearly won and so delicately maintained is so callously attacked. It is at times such as these that friends and allies must stand together.

The Alliance has served us well, but it's now being tested by new challenges—a challenge to its most vital economic interests and a challenge to the principle that free people in independent nations should have the right to decide their future without outside interference. Will we be able to meet such threats? Do we have the will, the capacity, the resolve to make a common stand? I am confident that we can, and my confidence has been bolstered by the talks that I have had here today.

Consultations such as these and others that I've had with other nations on this trip are essential for us to maintain the strength and unity of our associations, for we are members of a voluntary association—the association of democratic nations. It's a source of great satisfaction to me and to my fellow American, Mr. President, to know that democracy is succeeding in Portugal and that Portugal is a steadfast member of the Atlantic Alliance.

Mr. President, I ask everyone to join me as I raise my glass to you and to Portugal's democratic leaders of all parties. You've set an example in your achievements at home and in your leadership abroad. I thank you for your hospitality. I wish you every success, and I look forward to our continued and close collaboration.

Mr. President, to you, to your lovely wife, and to the brave and courageous people of Portugal.

NOTE: The President spoke at 2:40 p.m. in the State Dining Room of the Ajuda Palace in response to a toast by President Eanes.

Portugal: Meetings With President Eanes and Government Officials

White House Statement. June 26, 1980

President Carter met today with President Eanes at Belem Palace on matters of mutual interest, including an overview of Portugal's experiences since the revolution and it successful progress to democracy. The two leaders also discussed ways and means of strengthening the North Atlantic Treaty Organization.

President Carter also met with Prime Minister Sá Carneiro at Ajuda Palace for discussions of a number of international issues, including Portugal's role in the Western Alliance. They gave special attention to the strategic challenge posed to Western security interests by the crisis in Afghanistan and to the long-term challenge to global stability posed by conditions in the Third World.

Portugal: Conclusion of State Visit

Joint Statement. June 26, 1980

President Jimmy Carter of the United States visited Lisbon on June 26 at the invitation of the President of Portugal, Antonio Ramalho Eanes. The visit provided an opportunity for meetings between the two Presidents and between President Carter and Prime Minister Francisco Sá Carneiro.

President Carter and his hosts noted with satisfaction the close relations between the U.S. and Portugal, based on long-standing ties of friendship, common commitment to democratic values, and partnership in the NATO Alliance. They discussed international issues, including the situation in Afghanistan, in Iran, and in the Middle East; new forms of coordination and consultation among the Western countries; and US-Portuguese cooperation in enhancing western security, including development and conservation of energy resources.

In emphasizing Portugal's very positive contributions to the Western Alliance, President Carter congratulated both the President and the Prime Minister for their vigorous leadership in the evolution of Portuguese democracy. He expressed particular appreciation for the prompt response of the Portuguese Government to the Soviet armed invasion and occupation of Afghanistan. The leaders agreed that this Soviet action, in flagrant violation of the United Nations charter, seriously threatens international peace and poses a major strategic challenge affecting vital western interests in Southwest Asia and the Persian Gulf region.

In accord with that shared strategic assessment, the leaders view as indispensable the application of concrete political, economic, and commercial measures to impress upon the Soviet Union the necessity of a prompt and complete withdrawal of its troops from Afghanistan.

In line with that view, the leaders welcomed the concerted steps which NATO is now pursuing in order to strengthen the common defense in response to the strategic challenge faced by all the Western Allies and they pledged their commitment to the earliest possible fulfillment of the goals embodied in NATO's long-term defense program. Bearing in mind the U.S. commitment of resources toward building a security framework in the region of Southwest Asia and the Persian Gulf, they further recognized the usefulness of adequate consultation among the Western Allies regarding security requirements within the NATO area.

President Carter also reiterated his appreciation and that of the entire American people for the forthright support given by Portugal to the international effort to secure release of American hostages held by Iran in defiance of international law and universally accepted standards of decency. The leaders stressed that the principle of the rule of law, vital to the health and stability of the world community, is at stake in this crisis. They agreed that continued detention of the hostages will further undermine Iran's international standing and they concurred in the necessity of maintaining economic sanctions on Iran as well as the efforts being pursued by international bodies as a way of convincing the Iranian authorities to release all the hostages unharmed.

Turning to other aspects of mutual interest, both sides recognized the importance of achieving a comprehensive and lasting peace in the Middle East which takes into consideration the interests of all the parties involved.

President Carter welcomed the constructive insights and suggestions which President Eanes and Prime Minister Sá Carneiro offered regarding critical issues affecting East-West and North-South relationships. In particular, President Carter praised Portugal's efforts to strengthen ties with Africa, and especially with the Lusophone African states. They agreed that it would be useful to intensify U.S.-Portuguese consultations on ways in which both countries can work for greater peace, freedom, and prosperity.

The President's Trip to Europe

Remarks on Arrival at Andrews Air Force Base, Md.   June 26, 1980

First of all, let me say that Rosalynn and I and Amy and all of us are very glad to be back here in the United States.

We've had a very long and, I think, productive and successful trip. Since I left this country a few days ago, I've had a chance to have extensive conversations with the leaders of nine different nations, not only the present heads of state but also, in some instances, the leaders of the opposition parties and those who will comprise the government in the present time and the future. We also met with the President of the European Community and had extensive discussions with the Pope at the Vatican.

In Yugoslavia we expressed our deep commitment to the integrity and the unity and the security of that country, which is now making good progress since the unfortunate death of President Tito. The new Government seems to be strong and firm, in control, dedicated. And of course, we gave our support to them and to the future stability and integrity of that great country.

In Italy we shared with Prime Minister Cossiga and President Pertini the common basis on which we predicate our own hopes for the future. The Italians did a superb job in preparing for the Venice conference, where I met with the leaders not only of Italy and the European Community but of Germany and France, Great Britain, Canada, and Japan.

I also was able to stop in the two new democracies, Spain and Portugal, both ancient countries, but new to the democratic process. I expressed to them the gratitude of our own Nation and our admiration for their rapid change into true democratic government, and was able to have fruitful discussions with them.

All of us were in a remarkable degree of harmony, understanding that we had had painful experiences in the 1970's, with rapidly changing economic and other circumstances, but that we face even greater challenges in the 1980's. All the leaders recognize that there must be some painful decisions made and that our people are strong enough and courageous enough and dedicated enough and united enough to make these decisions, even though they might involve some sacrifice on our part and some accommodation for the desires and needs of one another.

We recognize that we must break the relationship between economic growth in the future and our dependence on energy; in other words, to have more growth for less energy, through conservation and through the reduction, particularly, in the importation of oil. The one word that permeated all the discussions was oil. The smell of foreign oil has a profound impact on all our nations. Obviously our overdependence on foreign oil takes away our own basic security, the right that we have to make our own decisions.

The price of oil is crippling, not only to us, in bringing additional inflation but also unemployment; and for the less developed or poor countries, the new, rapidly increasing, excessive price of oil is particularly damaging to them and to their prospects. And oil politics is literally changing the interrelationship among nations, where we must stand united, cooperate whenever we can, and meet a common challenge to the security and the certainty of the future brought about by rapidly increasing, uncontrollable prices

of oil, and excessive dependence by all of us on imports of oil.

Finally, we had extensive political discussions. We were united in our commitment, in our statements to the public, that a major threat to peace had been perpetrated by the Soviet Union in their unwarranted invasion and present occupation of Afghanistan. We expressed our admiration for the freedom-fighters in Afghanistan, who are struggling for national liberation from the occupying Soviet forces. This major threat, we all agree, must be resolved by the withdrawal of Soviet forces, total withdrawal. The recent token withdrawal has relatively little strategic significance unless it is permanent and is rapidly followed by step-by-step withdrawal of all Soviet forces.

And finally, all the nations expressed their commitment to us as rapidly as possible to encourage the Iranian Government to end the act of international terrorism which they have perpetrated against 53 innocent Americans, against our Nation, and against the rest of the world, indeed. This holding of innocent hostages is unacceptable. It violates every principle of international law and human decency. All the nations have committed themselves again to us that they would do everything in the world they could, through private, diplomatic channels and through their public statements and actions, to secure the rapid release of the American hostages.

Finally, we recognize that among democratic nations, free people, there are bound to be some differences. But the common understanding which we have and the agreements which we have reached show a remarkable degree of unity as we face present problems and prepare for the future.

The best thing about the trip is coming back home. We are glad to be back in the United States of America, the greatest nation, by far, on Earth.

Thank you very much.

NOTE: The President spoke at 6:17 p.m.

Riots in Miami, Florida

Announcement of Federal Assistance in Rebuilding Areas Damaged During the Riots. June 27, 1980

The White House today announced the Federal Government's initial commitment of resources to assist in the rebuilding of the Liberty City and other riot-torn areas of Miami, Fla. Gene Eidenberg, Assistant to the President for Intergovernmental Affairs, and Frank N. Jones, Chairman of the Federal Interagency Task Force on Miami, announced a 7-agency program at Miami City Hall.

The program of Federal aid focuses on both short-term and long-term employment. It includes both new and reprogramed moneys to the Miami-Dade area. In making the announcement, Eidenberg emphasized that, "This announcement reaffirms President Carter's promise that the Federal Government would play a role in the rebuilding of the Liberty City community. However, as the President emphasized in his meeting with community leaders on June 9, the Federal Government cannot solve the problems that caused the riot by itself. The State and local governments, and particularly the private sector, must play the lead role in addressing the complex issues facing Miami."

The 7-agency program includes:

—$4.280 million for U.S. Department of Labor training and job programs;
—$5 million for both short- and long-term economic development from the

Economic Development Administration;
—$17.3 million of expedited Urban Mass Transportation Administration funds to provide jobs for black contractors;
—$40 million for small businesses impacted by the civil disturbances from the Small Business Administration;
—$1.3 million for anticrime efforts in public housing projects in Liberty City;
—$2 million of Law Enforcement Assistance Administration reprogramed to the area for criminal justice programs;
—$1,250,000 for health and human service efforts in the impacted areas from the Department of Health and Human Services.

Frank Jones announced that he has submitted his interagency report on the riot in Miami to the White House. The report is being reviewed by White House staff.

The report includes a number of specific recommendations to revitalize the impacted areas, emphasizing economic development, in general, and the specific needs of the black-owned businesses. The Task Force recommends that the President appoint a Federal coordinator in order to ensure that Federal agencies continue to work in a coordinated manner in the Miami rebuilding effort.

The report noted the efforts being made by State and local governmental agencies, by the business sector, and by community organizations to find jobs for those who are unemployed due to the disturbances.

It praises the cooperation between the area's three chambers of commerce, representing the white, black, and Latin business sectors in the post-riot. The Federal Government will continue to work with all the parties at the State, local, and private sector levels to ensure the success of these initiatives.

Agricultural Trade Development

Executive Order 12220.   June 27, 1980

By the authority vested in me as President of the United States of America by the Agricultural Trade Development and Assistance Act of 1954, as amended (7 U.S.C. 1691, *et seq.*) and Section 301 of Title 3 of the United States Code, and in order to provide for the delegation of certain functions to the United States International Development Cooperation Agency and to revise existing delegations, it is hereby ordered as follows:

1–1. Department of Agriculture.

1–101. Except as otherwise provided in this Order, the following functions vested in the President by the Agricultural Trade Development and Assistance Act of 1954, as amended (hereinafter referred to as the Act), are delegated to the Secretary of Agriculture: Titles I and IV (7 U.S.C. 1701, *et seq.*, and 1731, *et seq.*).

1–102. The Secretary of Agriculture shall transmit the reports required by the provisions of paragraph 5 of the Act of August 13, 1957 (71 Stat. 345; 7 U.S.C. 1704a).

1–103. The Secretary of Agriculture, after consultation with the Secretary of State, the Secretary of the Treasury, the Director of the United States International Development Cooperation Agency, the Chairman of the Council of Economic Advisers, the Director of the Office of Management and Budget, and the Assistant to the President for National Security Affairs, shall transmit to the Congress all reports required by Section 408 of the Act (7 U.S.C. 1736b).

1–2. United States International Development Cooperation Agency.

1–201. Administration of Title II. The functions vested in the President by Title II of the Act (7 U.S.C. 1721, *et seq.*) are delegated to the Director of the United States International Development Cooperation Agency.

1–202. Other functions.

(a) The functions vested in the President by the Act of negotiating and entering into agreements with friendly countries are delegated to the Director of the United States International Development Cooperation Agency. Such functions shall be exercised in accord with Section 112b of Title I of the United States Code and applicable regulations and procedures of the Department of State.

(b) The functions delegated to the Director of the United States International Development Cooperation Agency by subsection (a) of this section are exclusive of any functions under Section 104 of the Act (7 U.S.C. 1704) that are delegated to any other agency by this Order and of functions under Section 310 of the Act (7 U.S.C. 1692).

(c) The functions delegated by this Order to the Director of the United States International Development Cooperation Agency may be redelegated to the head of any other Executive agency.

1–3. Department of State.

1–301. The Secretary of State shall perform the function of determining which countries are friendly countries within the meaning of Section 103(d) of the Act (7 U.S.C. 1703(d)).

1–302. The functions delegated by this Order to the Secretary of State may be redelegated to the head of any Executive agency.

1–4. Foreign Currencies.

1–401. (a) Foreign currencies which accrue under Title I of the Act (7 U.S.C.

1701, *et seq.*) may be used for the purposes set forth in Section 104 of the Act (7 U.S.C. 1704) in amounts consistent with applicable provisions of law, sales agreements and loan assessments. Except as may be inconsistent with such law or agreements, priority shall be accorded to the sale of such currencies to appropriations or to their sale otherwise for dollars. The Director of the Office of Management and Budget shall fix the amounts of such currencies to be used for the purpose set forth in Section 104 of the Act. The Director of the Office of Management and Budget shall notify the Secretary of the Treasury with respect to any amounts so fixed.

(b) The function vested in the President by the penultimate proviso of Section 104 of the Act (7 U.S.C. 1704) of waiving the applicability of Section 1415 of the Supplemental Appropriation Act of 1953 (31 U.S.C. 724) is delegated to the Director of the United States International Development Cooperation Agency with respect to Section 104(e) of the Act and to the Director of the Office of Management and Budget in all other respects.

1-402. The Secretary of the Treasury shall issue regulations governing the purchase, custody, deposit, transfer and sale of foreign currencies received under the Act.

1-403. The provisions of Sections 1-401 and 1-402 of this Order shall not limit Sections 1-202 and 1-3 of this Order. The provisions of Section 1-402 of this Order shall not limit Section 1-401 of this Order.

1-404. The purposes of the following paragraphs of Section 104 of the Act (7 U.S.C. 1704) shall be carried out as follows:

(a) Those under paragraph (a) by the agencies with authority to pay the United States' obligations abroad.

(b) Those under paragraph (b)(1) by the Department of Agriculture.

(c) Those under paragraph (b)(2) by the agencies with responsibility for such functions.

(d) Those under paragraph (b)(3) of the Act as follows:

(1) Those with respect to collecting, collating, translating, abstracting, and disseminating scientific and technological information by the Director of the National Science Foundation and the head of such other agency or agencies as the Director of the Office of Management and Budget may designate after appropriate consultation;

(2) Those with respect to programs of culture and educational development, health, nutrition, and sanitation by the Director of the International Communications Agency, the Department of State, and the head of any other appropriate agency;

(3) All others by such agency or agencies as the Director of the Office of Management and Budget may designate after appropriate consultation.

(4) The term "appropriate consultation" shall include consultation with the Secretary of State, the Director of the National Science Foundation, and the head of any other appropriate agency.

(e) Those under paragraph (b)(4) by the Department of State and any other agency or agencies designated by the Secretary of State.

(f) Those under paragraph (b)(5) by the Librarian of Congress.

(g) Those under paragraphs (d), (e), (f), (g), and (h) by the United States International Development Cooperation Agency.

(h) Those under paragraph (j) by the Department of the Treasury in consultation with the Department of State.

1–405. The functions vested in the President by Section 104 of the Act (7 U.S.C. 1704) are delegated as follows:

(a) Those under paragraph (f) of determining the manner in which the loans provided for in that paragraph shall be made to the Director of the United States International Development Cooperation Agency.

(b) Those under paragraph (j) of prescribing terms and conditions to the Secretary of the Treasury in consultation with the Secretary of State.

1–406. In negotiating international agreements pursuant to the Act, the Secretary of State shall avoid restrictions which would limit the application of normal budgetary and appropriation controls to the use of foreign currencies accruing under Title I of the Act (7 U.S.C. 1701, *et seq.*) which are available for operations of the United States Government.

1–5. Revocations.

1–501. Executive Order No. 10900 of January 5, 1961, as amended, is revoked.

1–502. The following Executive Orders which have previously been superseded, at least in part, are revoked:

(a) Executive Order No. 10560 of September 9, 1954;

(b) Executive Order No. 10685 of October 27, 1956;

(c) Executive Order No. 10708 of May 6, 1957;

(d) Executive Order No. 10746 of December 12, 1957;

(e) Executive Order No. 10799 of January 15, 1959;

(f) Executive Order No. 10827 of June 25, 1959;

(g) Executive Order No. 10884 of August 17, 1960; and

(h) Executive Order No. 10893, as amended, except Section 201 thereof.

JIMMY CARTER

The White House,
June 27, 1980.

[Filed with the Office of the Federal Register, 4:43 p.m., June 27, 1980]

Improving Government Regulations

Executive Order 12221. **June 27, 1980**

By the authority vested in me as President of the United States of America, and in order to continue existing procedures for improving government regulations pending the enactment of regulatory reform legislation, Section 8 of Executive Order No. 12044 of March 23, 1978, is hereby amended to read, "Unless extended this Order expires on April 30, 1981.".

JIMMY CARTER

The White House,
June 27, 1980.

[Filed with the Office of the Federal Register, 4:44 p.m., June 27, 1980]

United States-Peru Agreement on Nuclear Energy

Message to the Congress Transmitting the Proposed Agreement. **June 27, 1980**

To the Congress of the United States:

I am pleased to transmit to the Congress, pursuant to Section 123 d of the Atomic Energy Act of 1954, as amended (42 U.S.C. 2153(d)), the text of the proposed agreement between the United

States and Peru Concerning Peaceful Uses of Nuclear Energy, with an accompanying agreed minute. The proposed agreement is accompanied by my written determination, approval, and authorization and the memorandum of the Director of the United States Arms Control and Disarmament Agency with the Nuclear Proliferation Assessment Statement concerning the agreement. The joint memorandum submitted to me by the Secretaries of State and Energy, which includes a summary analysis of the provisions of the agreement, and the views of the Director of the United States Arms Control and Disarmament Agency and of the Members of the Nuclear Regulatory Commission are also enclosed.

The Nuclear Non-Proliferation Act of 1978, which I signed into law on March 10, 1978, establishes certain requirements for new agreements for cooperation. In my judgment, the proposed agreement for cooperation between the United States and Peru, together with its agreed minute, meets all statutory requirements.

Peru has long supported the Treaty of Tlatelolco and the Non-Proliferation Treaty, having ratified the former on March 4, 1969, and the latter on March 3, 1970, and supports international non-proliferation efforts generally. The proposed agreement reflects the desire of the Government of the United States and the Government of Peru to broaden the scope of peaceful nuclear cooperation in a manner that recognizes the shared non-proliferation objectives of our two countries. The proposed agreement will, in my view, further the non-proliferation and other foreign policy interests of the United States.

I have considered the views and recommendations of the interested agencies in reviewing the proposed agreement and have determined that its performance will promote, and will not constitute an unreasonable risk to, the common defense and security. Accordingly, I have approved the agreement and authorized its execution, and urge that the Congress give it favorable consideration.

JIMMY CARTER

The White House,
    June 27, 1980.

Peace Corps Advisory Council

*Nomination of Sidney Suher To Be a Member.
June 27, 1980*

The President today announced his intention to nominate Sidney Suher, of Rochester, N.Y., to be a member of the Peace Corps Advisory Council. Suher has been a partner in the law firm of Suher & Heller since 1963.

He was born April 8, 1934, in Holyoke, Mass. He received a B.A. from Cornell University in 1957 and a J.D. from Boston University Law School in 1960.

Digest of Other White House Announcements

The following listing includes the President's public schedule and other items of general interest announced by the White House Press Office and not included elsewhere in this issue.

THE PRESIDENT'S TRIP TO EUROPE

June 19

After an early morning departure ceremony on the South Lawn of the White House, the President boarded Marine One and went to Andrews Air Force Base, Md., for the flight to Italy. (For departure remarks, see page 1135.)

Late in the evening, Air Force One arrived at Ciampino Airport, Rome. The President was greeted by Marcello Guidi, Chief of Protocol for the Italian Republic, Richard N. Gardner, U.S. Ambassador to Italy, and Paolo Pansa Cedronio, Italian Ambassador to the United States.

The President then boarded Marine One and went to the Quirinale Palace, the official residence of the President of the Italian Republic. He was welcomed by President Alessandro Pertini and other Italian Government officials.

Following the review of the Palace Guard (Corazzieri) in the Salone Dei Corazzieri, the President remained overnight at the Palace.

June 20

In the morning, the President and Mrs. Carter met privately with President Pertini in the Sala D'Ercola at the Palace. The President and President Pertini then held expanded talks with members of the U.S. and Italian delegations.

Later in the morning, the President boarded Marine One enroute to the Villa Madama. After a short motorcade from the helipad, the President arrived at the Villa and was greeted by Prime Minister Francesco Cossiga. Following a private meeting, the President and Prime Minister joined members of the U.S. and Italian delegations for expanded talks and a working luncheon.

Following the luncheon, the President went by motorcade to the Victor Emmanuel Monument, where he inspected the honor guard of various services and participated in a wreath-laying ceremony at the Tomb of the Unknown Soldier, which is marked by an equestrian statue at the summit of the monument.

Immediately following the ceremony, the President, Mrs. Carter, and Amy began a tour of the Colosseum, conducted by Professor John D'Arms, Director of the American Academy of Rome. The First Family then toured the ruins of the Roman Forum.

In the late afternoon and early evening, the President held three separate meetings at the Quirinale Palace.

The first meeting was attended by members of Italian political parties of the coalition government: President Orlando Forlani and Secretary Flaminio Piccoli of the Christian Democratic Party; President Bruno Visentini and Secretary Giovanni Spadolini of the Republican Party; and Secretary Bettino Craxi of the Italian Socialist Party.

Participants in the second meeting were: Secretary Valerio Zanone of the Liberal Party and Secretary Pietro Longo and President Giuseppe Saragat of the Social Democratic Party.

At the third meeting, the President talked with Amintore Fanfani, President of the Italian Senate.

In the evening, the President and Mrs. Carter were guests at a state dinner hosted by President Pertini in the Salon Delle Feste at the Quirinale Palace. Following the dinner, the President remained overnight at the Palace.

A joint press statement was issued at the conclusion of the President's state visit to Italy.

June 21

Following a morning departure ceremony in the courtyard of the Quirinale Palace, the President went by motorcade to the memorial which marks the spot where former Prime Minister Aldo Moro's body was found in 1978 after he was assassinated by members of the Red Brigade. A wreath from the President and people of the United States had been placed near the bronze plaque commemorating the former Prime Minister.

The President visited the American Embassy in Rome and addressed members of the staff and the American community at a gathering in the courtyard.

Following his visit to the Embassy, the President went by motorcade to the Villa Borghese Park helipad, where he boarded Marine One for the flight to Vatican City. Upon arrival at the Vatican helipad, the President was greeted by Ambassador Robert Wagner, Envoy of the President to the Vatican, and representatives of the Vatican.

The President arrived by motorcade at the San Damaso Courtyard of the Vatican and proceeded inside to the Papal Study, where he was met by Pope John Paul II. The President and the Pope held a private meeting before being joined by Mrs. Carter and Amy. The President then introduced members of the U.S. delegation to His Holiness, and following the introductions, the President and the Pope exchanged remarks.

The President and the Pope went to the Clementine Room and addressed a group of American pilgrims who had traveled to the Vatican for the ceremony marking the beatification of Kateri Takakwitha, an Indian maiden who died in 1680.

Following the remarks in the Clementine Room, the President, Mrs. Carter, and Amy were given an hour-long tour of the Vatican. The President then went by motorcade to the helipad atop Vatican Hill, boarded Marine One, and flew to the Piazza di Siena helipad at the Villa Borghese Park. He then traveled by motorcade

to the Villa Taverna, residence of the U.S. Ambassador to Italy.

Late in the afternoon, the President departed Villa Taverna via motorcade, enroute to the Piazza di Siena helipad at the Villa Borghese Park. There he boarded Marine One and flew to Ciampino Airport, where he boarded Air Force One for the trip to Venice.

A group of national and city officials greeted the President upon his arrival at Marco Polo Airport, Venice, early in the evening. After reviewing the honor guard at the airport, the President boarded Marine One. Upon arrival at the Morosini Naval College, where he was met by Commandant Vittorio Valente, the President boarded a boat and went to the Cipriani Hotel where the First Family stayed during their visit in Venice.

Shortly after arriving at the Cipriani Hotel, the President met with Chancellor Helmut Schmidt of the Federal Republic of Germany. The two leaders were joined in their discussions by Secretary of State Edmund S. Muskie and Minister of Foreign Affairs Hans-Dietrich Genscher. At the conclusion of the meeting, the President and the Chancellor answered reporters' questions outside the hotel.

Later in the evening, the President, Mrs. Carter, and Amy took a 45-minute boat tour of Venice which included a cruise along the Grand Canal. They then returned to the Cipriani Hotel.

June 22

Early in the morning, the First Family went by boat to the Church of St. Eufemia for Mass. Following the service, the President went by boat to the Cini Foundation, the site of the economic summit conference.

Prime Minister Francesco Cossiga of Italy, Chairman of the Conference, greeted the President upon his arrival at the Cini Foundation for breakfast with the other summit participants.

Shortly after breakfast, the first session of the economic summit was held in the Longhena Library.

At the conclusion of the first session, the summit participants walked to the Church of San Giorgio Maggiore for a short tour.

Following the tour of the monastery, the summit participants returned to the Cini Foundation for a working luncheon.

The second session of the economic summit was held in the afternoon in the Longhena Library. Statements on Afghanistan, refugees, diplomatic hostages, and hijacking were issued by Prime Minister Cossiga.

At the conclusion of the second session, the President met privately with President Valéry Giscard d'Estaing of France at the Cini Foundation.

Upon his return to the Cipriani Hotel, the President debarked and went to the terrace outside the hotel restaurant where he answered reporters' questions.

In the evening, the President went to the Doges Palace, the former residence of the rulers of the Venetian State. After a reception in the courtyard, a private dinner for the summit participants was held in the Sala Erizzo at the Palace.

Following the dinner, the President returned to the Cipriani Hotel.

June 23

Early in the morning, the President went to the Church of San Giorgio Maggiore where he had breakfast with a group of Benedictine monks.

Following breakfast, the President re- turned to the Cipriani Hotel for a meeting with Prime Minister Pierre Elliott Trudeau of Canada.

The President then went to the Cini Foundation, where he met with Prime Minister Margaret Thatcher of the United Kingdom prior to attending the third session of the economic summit in the Longhena Library.

Following the third session, the summit participants held a working luncheon.

In the afternoon, the summit participants made concluding statements to the press in the Sala Degli Arazzi at the Cini Foundation and the declaration of the summit conference was issued.

At the conclusion of the conference, the President went by boat to the Cipriani Hotel, where he was interviewed by reporters.

In the evening, Ambassador and Mrs. Gardner joined the President, Mrs. Carter, and Amy for dinner at the Locanda Montin, a Venetian restaurant. Following the dinner, the First Family returned to the Cipriani Hotel.

June 24

In the morning, the President went by boat to the Morosini Naval College, where he boarded Marine One enroute to Marco Polo Airport. Upon arrival at the airport, the President boarded Air Force One for the trip to Yugoslavia.

The President arrived at Surcin Airport, Belgrade, and was greeted by President and Mrs. Cvijetin Mijatovic, Ambassador Ranko Vilus, Chief of Protocol of Yugoslavia, and Lawrence S. Eagleburger, U.S. Ambassador to Yugoslavia. After the welcoming ceremony, the two Presidents went by motorcade to Dedinje Palace, the former residence of the Court of the Serbian royal family, where the First Family stayed during their visit to Belgrade.

Later in the morning, the President, Mrs. Carter, and Amy went by motorcade to the tomb of former President Tito, which lies in a pavilion-greenhouse on the grounds of his Belgrade residence. The President placed a wreath on the tomb.

Following the visit to the Tito gravesite, the President went by motorcade to the Palace of the Federation, where he met with President Mijatovic and other Yugoslav Government officials.

In the afternoon, the President and Mrs. Carter had lunch at an outdoor restaurant called Milosev Konak, and then returned to the Dedinje Palace.

Late in the afternoon, the President, Mrs. Carter, and Amy went by motorcade to Friendship Park, the site of a grove of trees dedicated to lasting friendship among nations. They were greeted by the Mayor of Belgrade, Zivorad Kovacevic, and following a tradition established by President Tito for visiting foreign leaders, took part in a tree-planting ceremony. After planting a 4-foot-tall California Sequoia Gigantica, the President signed the Golden Book of Belgrade.

The President, Mrs. Carter, and Amy then went by motorcade to Kalemegdan Park, located on a bluff at the juncture of the Danube and Sava Rivers. Following a tour of the park, the First Family was entertained by a group of dancers, wearing costumes representative of the country's regions, who performed local dances called *kolos*. Following the performance, the First Family returned by motorcade to the Dedinje Palace.

In the evening, the President and Mrs. Carter were guests at a state dinner hosted by President Mijatovic in the Federal Hall at the Palace of the Federation.

Following the dinner, the President and Mrs. Carter returned to the Dedinje Palace.

June 25

In the morning, the President had breakfast with a group of Yugoslav officials at the Dedinje Palace and then went by motorcade to Surcin Airport.

Following the departure ceremony at the airport, the President boarded Air Force One for the trip to Spain.

A joint statement was issued at the conclusion of the President's visit to Yugoslavia.

The President arrived at Barajas International Airport, Madrid, and was greeted by King Juan Carlos I and Queen Sofia, Prime Minister Adolfo Suárez, Terence A. Todman, U.S. Ambassador to Spain, Jose Llado, Spanish Ambassador to the United States, and other Spanish officials. Following the welcoming ceremony, the President, accompanied by the King, went by motorcade to the Royal Palace.

At the Royal Palace, the President and Mrs. Carter and the King and Queen greeted luncheon guests in the Throne Room prior to attending the state luncheon.

Following the luncheon, the President held a meeting with King Juan Carlos I in the Papal Envoy Room at the Palace.

In the afternoon, the President, Mrs. Carter, and Amy went by motorcade to the Prado, where they toured the museum with Director Jose Manuel Pita Andrade and several American and Spanish officials.

Following the tour, the President went to Ambassador Todman's residence, where he met with Felipe Gonzalez, head of the Spanish Socialist Workers' Party.

In the evening, the President went to

the Palace of La Moncloa, the residence of the Prime Minister, for a meeting with Prime Minister Suárez. Following the meeting in the Prime Minister's office, the President attended a working dinner with the Prime Minister and Spanish and American officials.

At the conclusion of the dinner, the President returned by motorcade to Ambassador Todman's residence, where he remained overnight.

June 26

In the morning, the President visited the Chancery at the American Embassy and addressed members of the staff and American community. He then returned to Ambassador Todman's residence, boarded the motorcade, and departed enroute to Barajas International Airport.

Upon arrival at the airport, the President was greeted by King Juan Carlos I and Queen Sofia, and the President and the King held a short meeting inside the Pabellon de Estado (VIP Building).

A departure ceremony followed the President's meeting with the King. The President then boarded Air Force One for the trip to Portugal.

A press statement was issued at the conclusion of the President's visit to Spain.

Later in the morning, the President arrived at Portela Airport, Lisbon, and was greeted by President António dos Sanos Ramalho Eanes, Prime Minister Francisco Sá Carneiro, Richard J. Bloomfield, U.S. Ambassador to Portugal, Joao Hall Themido, Portuguese Ambassador to the United States, and other Portuguese officials. Following the welcoming ceremony, the two Presidents went by motorcade to Jeronimos Mosteiro.

The President, Mrs. Carter, and Amy toured the monastery, and the President placed wreaths on the tombs of Portuguese epic poet Luis Vaz de Camoes and explorer Vasco de Gama.

The President left the monastery and went by motorcade to the Ajuda Palace, the royal residence of the last three Portuguese rulers, where he met with Prime Minister Sá Carneiro in the Diplomats Room.

Following the meeting, the President met with Socialist Party leader Mario Soares, former Prime Minister of Portugal, in the Diplomats Room.

In the afternoon, the President went by motorcade to Belem Palace, where he met with President Eanes in the Portuguese President's office. Following a walk in the Palace Garden, the Presidents went by motorcade to the Ajuda Palace.

The President and Mrs. Carter were guests at a state luncheon hosted by President Eanes in the Dining Room at the Palace.

After the luncheon, the President and President Eanes went to Portela Airport. Following the departure ceremony, the President boarded Air Force One for the flight to the United States.

A joint statement was issued on the President's visit to Portugal.

The President arrived at Andrews Air Force Base, Md., early in the evening and then boarded Marine One. He flew by helicopter to Camp David, Md., for a weekend stay.

NOMINATIONS SUBMITTED TO THE SENATE

The following list does not include promotions of members of the Uniformed Services, nominations to the Service Academies, or nominations of Foreign Service officers.

NOMINATIONS—Continued

Submitted June 23, 1980

WALTER C. CARRINGTON, of New York, to be Ambassador Extraordinary of the United States of America to the Republic of Senegal.

The following-named persons to be members of the Board of Directors of the Legal Services Corporation for terms expiring July 13, 1983:

STEVEN L. ENGELBERG, of Maryland (reappointment).

CECILIA DENOGEAN ESQUER, of Arizona (reappointment).

HILLARY DIANE RODHAM, of Arkansas (reappointment).

RICHARD ALLAN TRUDELL, of California (reappointment).

JOSEPHINE MARIE WORTHY, of Massachusetts (reappointment).

The following-named persons to be members of the National Science Board, National Science Foundation, for terms expiring May 10, 1986:

MARY LOWE GOOD, of Louisiana, vice L. Donald Shields, term expired.

PETER T. FLAWN, of Texas, vice Grover E. Murray, term expired.

PETER DAVID LAX, of New York, vice Saunders Mac Lane, term expired.

HOMER A. NEAL, of Indiana, vice Norman Hackerman, term expired.

MARY JANE OSBORN, of Connecticut, vice William Neill Hubbard, Jr., term expired.

DONALD B. RICE, of California (reappointment).

STUART A. RICE, of Illinois, vice James H. Zumberge, term expired.

Submitted June 26, 1980

THOMAS R. DONAHUE, of the District of Columbia, to be a member of the board of directors of the Communications Satellite Corporation until the date of the annual meeting of the Corporation in 1981, vice George Meany.

Submitted June 27, 1980

JOHN DAVID HUGHES, of Texas, to be a member of the Federal Energy Regulatory Commission for the term expiring October 20, 1983, vice Don Sanders Smith, resigned.

CHECKLIST OF WHITE HOUSE PRESS RELEASES

The following listing contains releases of the White House Press Office which are not included in this issue.

Released June 20, 1980

News conference: on the President's state visit to Italy—by Press Secretary Jody Powell

Advance text: toast at the state dinner in Rome, Italy

Released June 22, 1980

Transcript: question-and-answer session on Soviet troops in Afghanistan—by Zbigniew Brzezinski, Assistant to the President for National Security Affairs

News conference: on the Venice Economic Summit Conference—by Mr. Powell

Released June 24, 1980

Announcement: President's trip to Jacksonville and Hollywood, Fla., on July 17

Transcript: interview of Dr. Brzezinski on the President's trip to Europe—by John Chancellor of NBC News

Transcript: interview of Dr. Brzezinski on the President's trip to Europe—by Daniel Schorr of the Cable News Network

Advance text: toast at the state dinner in Belgrade, Yugoslavia

Released June 25, 1980

Advance text: remarks on arrival in Lisbon, Portugal

Released June 26, 1980

Advance text: toast at the state luncheon in Lisbon, Portugal

ACTS APPROVED BY THE PRESIDENT

Approved June 27, 1980

H.J. Res. 521_____ Public Law 96-282
A joint resolution making additional funds available by transfer for the fiscal year ending September 30, 1980, for the Selective Service System.

Customs Valuation Code of the General Agreement on Tariffs and Trade

Proclamation 4768.   June 28, 1980

PROCLAMATION TO CARRY OUT THE AGREEMENT ON IMPLEMENTATION OF ARTICLE VII OF THE GENERAL AGREEMENT ON TARIFFS AND TRADE (THE CUSTOMS VALUATION CODE) AND FOR OTHER PURPOSES

By the President of the United States of America

A Proclamation

1. Pursuant to Section 204(a)(2) of the Trade Agreements Act of 1979 (93 Stat. 203) in order to implement, beginning on July 1, 1980, the new customs valuation standards as provided in Title II of that Act, and for other purposes, I make the following determinations, and do proclaim as hereinafter set forth.

2. Section 225 of the Trade Agreements Act of 1979 (93 Stat. 235), Sections 131, 132, 133, 134, 135, and 161(b) of the Trade Act of 1974 (19 U.S.C. 2151, 2152, 2153, 2154, 2155, and 2211(b)) and Section 4(c) of Executive Order No. 11846 of March 27, 1975, (3 CFR 1971–1975 Comp. 974), have been complied with.

3. Pursuant to Section 101(a) of the Trade Act of 1974 (19 U.S.C. 2111(a)) and having made the determinations required by that section with regard to the following trade agreements, I, through my duly empowered representative, (1)

on July 11, 1979, entered into a trade agreement with other contracting parties to the General Agreement on Tariffs and Trade (61 Stat. (pts. 5 and 6)), as amended (the General Agreement), with countries seeking to accede to the General Agreement, and the European Communities, which agreement consists of the Geneva (1979) Protocol to the General Agreement, including a schedule of United States concessions annexed thereto (hereinafter referred to as "Schedule XX (Geneva—1979)"), (2) on December 18, 1979, entered into a trade agreement with Switzerland, which agreement consists of an exchange of letters, a copy of which is annexed to this proclamation as Part 2 of Annex I, (3) on December 21 and 27, 1979, and on January 2, 1980, entered into trade agreements with the European Communities, which agreements consist of joint memoranda, copies of which are annexed to this proclamation as Part 3 of Annex I, (4) on January 2, 1980, entered into a trade agreement with the Dominican Republic, which agreement consists of an exchange of letters, a copy of which is annexed to this proclamation as Part 4 of Annex I, and (5) on December 29, 1979, entered into a trade agreement with Indonesia, which agreement consists of a memorandum and an exchange of letters, copies of which are annexed to this proclamation as Part 5 of Annex I.

4. After having complied with Section 102 of the Trade Act of 1974 (19 U.S.C. 2112), and having made the required determinations, I notified Congress of my intention to enter into the Agreement on Implementation of Article VII of the

General Agreement on Tariffs and Trade (a copy of which is annexed to this proclamation as Part 1 of Annex I); and an implementing bill, approving the agreement and the proposed administrative action, has been enacted into law (Section 2(a) of the Trade Agreements Act of 1979 (93 Stat. 147)).

5. (a) Pursuant to Section 2(b)(3) of the Trade Agreements Act of 1979 (93 Stat. 147), I determine (1) that each major industrial country, as defined therein, with the exception of Canada, is accepting the Agreement on Implementation of Article VII of the General Agreement on Tariffs and Trade, (2) that the acceptance of this Agreement by Canada is not essential to the effective operation of the Agreement, (3) that a significant portion of United States trade will benefit from the Agreement, notwithstanding such nonacceptance, and (4) that it is in the national interest of the United States to accept the Agreement (and have so reported to the Congress);

(b) Pursuant to Section 204(a)(2)(A) and (B) of the Trade Agreements Act of 1979 (93 Stat. 203), I determine that the European Communities (including the European Economic Community) have accepted the obligations of the Agreement on Implementation of Article VII of the General Agreement on Tariffs and Trade with respect to the United States and each of the member states of the European Communities has implemented the Agreement under its laws (effective July 1, 1980);

(c) Pursuant to Section 503(a)(1) of the Trade Agreements Act of 1979 (93 Stat. 251), I determine, after interested parties were provided an opportunity to comment, that the articles classifiable in the following new items of the Tariff Schedules of the United States (TSUS) (19 U.S.C. 1202), added thereto by An-

nex II to this proclamation, were not imported into the United States before January 1, 1978, and were not produced in the United States before May 1, 1978:

402.54	405.70	409.76	411.74
402.82	405.82	409.84	411.86
403.14	406.09	409.92	411.96
403.59	406.42	410.02	412.04
403.66	406.58	410.10	412.12
404.30	406.63	410.18	412.36
404.38	407.07	410.22	412.40
404.47	408.23	410.34	412.50
404.90	408.29	411.10	412.66
405.09	408.38	411.42	412.70
405.34	409.28	411.50	413.30;
405.62	409.68	411.58	

(d) Pursuant to Section 503(a)(2)(A) of the Trade Agreements Act of 1979 (93 Stat. 251), I determine, after providing interested parties an opportunity to comment, that each article identified in Annex IV to this proclamation is not import sensitive.

6. Each modification of existing duty proclaimed herein which provides with respect to an article for a decrease in duty below the limitation specified in Sections 101(b)(1) or 109(a) of the Trade Act of 1974 (19 U.S.C. 2111(b)(1) or 2119 (a)), and each modification of any other import restriction or tariff provision so proclaimed is authorized by one or more of the following provisions or statutes:

(a) Section 101(b)(2) of the Trade Act of 1974 (19 U.S.C. 2111(b)(2)), by virtue of the fact that the rate of duty existing on January 1, 1975, applicable to the article was not more than 5 percent ad valorem (or ad valorem equivalent);

(b) Section 109(b) of the Trade Act of 1974 (19 U.S.C. 2119(b)), by virtue of the fact that I have determined, pursuant to that section, that the decrease authorized by that section will simplify the computation of the amount of duty imposed with respect to the article; and

(c) The Trade Agreements Act of 1979 (93 Stat. 144 *et seq.*) including, but not limited to, Sections 503(a)(1), (2)(A) and (6) (93 Stat. 251 and 252) by virtue of the fact that they permit departures from the staging provisions of Section 109(a) of the Trade Act of 1974 (19 U.S.C. 2119(a)).

7. In the case of each decrease in duty, including those of the type specified in clause (a) or (b) of the sixth recital of this proclamation, which involves the determination of the ad valorem equivalent of a specific or compound rate of duty, and in the case of each modification in the form of an import duty, the United States International Trade Commission has determined, pursuant to Section 601(4) of the Trade Act of 1974 (19 U.S.C. 2481 (4)), in accordance with Section 4(e) of Executive Order No. 11846 of March 27, 1975 (3 CFR 1971–1975 Comp. 973), and at my direction, the ad valorem equivalent of the specific or compound rate, on the basis of the value of imports of the article concerned during a period determined by it to be representative, utilizing, to the extent practicable, the standards of valuation contained in Sections 402 and 402a of the Tariff Act of 1930 (19 U.S.C. 1401a and 1402) applicable to the article during such representative period.

8. Pursuant to the Trade Act of 1974 and the Trade Agreements Act of 1979, I determine that each modification or continuance of existing duties or other import restrictions and each continuance of existing duty-free or excise treatment hereinafter proclaimed is required or appropriate to carry out the trade agreements identified in the third recital of this proclamation or the Agreement on Implementation of Article VII of the General Agreement on Tariffs and Trade.

Now, Therefore, I, Jimmy Carter,

President of the United States of America, acting under the authority vested in me by the Constitution and the statutes, including but not limited to Title I and Section 604 of the Trade Act of 1974, Section 2 and Titles II and V of the Trade Agreements Act of 1979, and Section 301 of Title 3 of the United States Code, do proclaim that:

(1)(a) The valuation standards amendments made by Title II of the Trade Agreements Act of 1979 (93 Stat. 194 *et seq.*) to Sections 402 and 402a of the Tariff Act of 1930 (19 U.S.C. 1401a and 1402), and,

(b) subject to the provisions of the General Agreement, of the Geneva (1979) Protocol, of other agreements supplemental to the General Agreement, of the other agreements identified in recitals 3 and 4, and of United States law (including but not limited to provisions for more favorable treatment),—

(i) the modification or continuance of existing duties or other import restrictions, and

(ii) the continuance of existing duty-free or excise treatment provided for in these agreements and in trade agreements legislation,

shall become effective on or after July 1, 1980, as provided for herein.

(2) To this end—

(a) The amendments made by Title II of the Trade Agreements Act of 1979 (93 Stat. 194 *et seq.*), except amendments made by section 223(b), shall be effective with respect to articles exported to the United States on and after July 1, 1980;

(b) The TSUS is modified as provided in Annexes II, III and IV of this proclamation;

(c) The modifications to the TSUS made by Sections A and C of Annex II, and Section A of Annex III, of this proclamation shall be effective with respect to articles exported to the United States on and after the effective dates specified in those annexes;

(d) The modifications to the TSUS made by Sections B, D and E of Annex II, Section B of Annex III, and Sections A and B of Annex IV, of this proclamation shall be effective with respect to articles entered, or withdrawn from warehouse for consumption, on and after the effective dates specified in those annexes;

(e) The United States Trade Representative shall make the necessary determinations relevant to the designation of the effective dates of the modifications of the TSUS made by Sections F and G of Annex II and Section C of Annex III to this proclamation, and shall publish in the FEDERAL REGISTER the effective date with respect to each of the modifications made by these sections; such modifications shall apply to articles entered, or withdrawn from warehouse for consumption, on and after such effective date;

(f) With respect to the modifications to the TSUS made by Annex IV to this proclamation and Annex IV to Presidential Proclamation 4707 of December 11, 1979, relating to special treatment for the least developed developing countries (LDDC's), whenever the rate of duty specified in the column numbered 1 for any TSUS item is reduced to the same level as the corresponding rate of duty specified in the column entitled "LDDC" for such item, or to a lower level, the rate of duty in the column entitled "LDDC" shall be deleted from the TSUS;

(g) Annexes III and IV of Presidential Proclamation 4707 of December 11, 1979, are superseded to the extent inconsistent with this proclamation.

IN WITNESS WHEREOF, I have hereunto set my hand this 28th day of June,

in the year of our Lord nineteen hundred and eighty, and of the Independence of the United States of America the two hundred and fourth.

JIMMY CARTER

[Filed with the Office of the Federal Register, 3:57 p.m., June 30, 1980]

NOTE: The annexes to the proclamation are printed in the FEDERAL REGISTER of July 2, 1980.

The text of the proclamation was released on June 30.

Generalized System of Preferences for Developing Countries
Executive Order 12222.   June 28, 1980

AMENDING THE GENERALIZED SYSTEM OF PREFERENCES

By virtue of the authority vested in me by the Constitution and statutes of the United States of America, including Title V of the Trade Act of 1974 (19 U.S.C. 2461 *et seq.*), as amended by Section 1111 of the Trade Agreements Act of 1979 (93 Stat. 315), and Section 604 of the Trade Act of 1974 (19 U.S.C. 2483), and as President of the United States of America, in order to provide for the continuation, to the greatest extent possible, of preferential treatment under the Generalized System of Preferences (GSP) for articles which are currently eligible for such treatment from countries designated as beneficiary developing countries, notwithstanding the numerous changes to the Tariff Schedules of the United States (TSUS) (19 U.S.C. 1202) which have resulted from the enactment of Title II of the Trade Agreements Act of 1979 (93 Stat. 194 *et seq.*) and Proclamation 4768 to Carry Out the Agreement on Implementation of Article VII of the General Agreement on Tariffs and Trade (the Customs Valuation Code) and for Other Purposes, to make technical corrections to Executive Order No. 11888, of November 24, 1975, as amended, and to make conforming modifications to the TSUS, it is hereby ordered as follows:

SECTION 1. Annex II of Executive Order No. 11888, as amended, listing articles that are eligible for benefits of the GSP when imported from any designated beneficiary developing country, is further amended as provided in the Annex to this Order, attached hereto and made a part hereof.

SEC. 2. Annex III of Executive Order No. 11888, as amended, listing articles that are eligible for benefits of the GSP when imported from all designated beneficiary countries except those specified in General Headnote 3(c)(iii) of the TSUS, is further amended by deleting items 114.05 and 315.55 therefrom, and adding items 114.04 and 114.06 thereto.

SEC. 3. General Headnote 3(c)(iii) of the TSUS, listing articles that are eligible for benefits of the GSP except when imported from the beneficiary countries listed opposite those articles, is modified by deleting therefrom the following:

"114.05_____ Thailand
315.55_____ Philippines";
and by adding thereto, in numerical sequence, the following:
"114.04_____ Thailand
114.06_____ Thailand".

SEC. 4. The amendments made with respect to items 315.55, 470.57, 772.69, 772.70, and 772.71 by Sections 1, 2, and 3 of this Order shall be effective as to articles that are both (1) imported on or after January 1, 1976, and (2) entered, or withdrawn from warehouse for consumption, on or after July 1, 1980.

SEC. 5. The amendments made by Sections 1, 2, and 3 of this Order, with the exception of those listed in Section 4 above, shall be effective as to articles that are exported to the United States on and after July 1, 1980.

JIMMY CARTER

The White House,
June 28, 1980.

[Filed with the Office of the Federal Register, 3:58 p.m., June 30, 1980]

NOTE: The annex to the Executive order is printed in the FEDERAL REGISTER of July 2, 1980.

The text of the Executive order was released on June 30.

Uniformed Services Health Professionals Special Pay Act of 1980

Statement on Signing S. 2460 Into Law.
June 30, 1980

I am pleased to sign into law S. 2460, the Uniformed Services Health Professionals Special Pay Act of 1980. In recent years, the Department of Defense has experienced severe difficulty in retaining its physicians, particularly those in critical specialties. This bill will improve the health care system of the Department of Defense through more efficient use of special pay for health professionals.

Earlier this year Congress passed a bill, H.R. 5235, that sought to deal with the needs of the Department of Defense. Unfortunately, that bill contained provisions unnecessarily expanding the scope and cost of Uniformed Services health professionals pay to such an extent that I found it unacceptable and returned it without my approval. In my veto message of March 11, 1980, I urged the Congress to reconsider the legislation in light of my objections. I am very pleased that Congress has now done so.

The bill I have signed has been narrowed to address the key problem—the shortage of physicians in our Armed Forces—while providing adequately for the other health professionals covered by the legislation.

With respect to Public Health Service (PHS) Commissioned Corps physicians, S. 2460 maintains the existing bonus payments and also improves PHS recruitment and retention capabilities by authorizing the Secretary of Health and Human Services to award additional discretionary bonuses of up to $8,000 annually for hardship locations and medical shortage specialties. In signing S. 2460, I want to reiterate my appreciation of the special role and responsibilities of the PHS Commissioned Corps. I also appreciate congressional efforts to address the needs of the PHS independently.

S. 2460 recognizes the importance of tailoring Federal compensation policies to meet the specific needs of each agency to attract and retain qualified health personnel. Accordingly, I am pleased to sign S. 2460 into law.

NOTE: As enacted, S. 2460 is Public Law 96–284, approved June 30.

Energy Security Act

Remarks on Signing S. 932 Into Law.
June 30, 1980

THE PRESIDENT. I had to take a minute to speak to my heroes. [*Laughter*]

Senator Scoop Jackson, who's representing Bob Byrd—Bob is on the floor now on one of the important appropriations bills—Majority Leader Jim Wright in the House, other Members of Congress, and distinguished Americans, who are here *because you are deeply concerned about the energy security of our country:*

This is a proud day for America. The keystone of a national energy policy is finally being put into place.

Our intolerable dependence on foreign oil threatens our economic security and also threatens our national security. And America's energy security is the key to both, because all three of those—economic, national, and energy—are links in the same chain of America's security.

From the very moment of assuming office, I've maintained that the energy problem is a clear and present danger to our lives and to our livelihood, both as individuals and also as a nation. Just as foreign oil drives our cars, so foreign high prices of oil drives America's inflation. And with that inflation comes unemployment and also declining productivity in this country and scarcity and poverty, economic deprivation, even approaching chaos, among the less developed countries of the world.

These are the hard facts, and it's been very difficult for Americans to face these facts. But during the last 12 months, Americans in all walks of life and at all levels of government have shown our determination that this country will produce more, discover more, create more and conserve more energy and that we will use American knowledge and American resources and American labor to do it.

Passage of the Energy Security Act is the highlight of our efforts to develop and implement a comprehensive national energy policy—a policy that meets our energy problems, a policy that sets out a program for Americans to follow in the future, a policy that gives us weapons to wage and to win the energy war. Our legislative and executive accomplishments already are unprecedented in this area, and our joint effort is already producing impressive results. This has not been an easy achievement. But I'd like to outline for you very briefly what Americans have already done to make me so proud.

We've cut imports since 1977 by more than 1½ million barrels of oil per day. Prior to that time, there had been a steady upward trend in the amount of oil from overseas that we were buying. So far this year, imports are down 12.9 percent below what they were the same months of 1979. Gasoline consumption is down 8 percent, and total oil consumption has dropped more than 9 percent.

We've reversed the decline in domestic crude oil production, and we're mining more American coal, our most abundant natural resource. Coal is being produced now at more than 16 percent higher than it was the same period a year ago.

This new Energy Security Act will help the American people to conserve more energy than I've already outlined and will help industry of all kinds in the energy field to produce more energy than they are today.

This legislation will also help to create more than 70,000 new jobs a year, to design, to build, to operate, and to supply resources for synthetic fuels plants and for production of alcohol and other biomass fuels. Thousands of other jobs will be created in the conservation field and in the production of solar energy, and indirect employment, not included in these figures, will be generated by all these efforts.

This bill establishes a corporation to encourage production of 2 million barrels a day of synthetic fuels by the year 1992, by converting coal to synthetic oil and gas and by extracting oil from shale and from tar sands and by other means. The Solar Energy and the Energy Conservation Bank will provide over $3 billion in direct subsidies to homes and to industries to conserve energy and to use renewable supplies of energy, helping us to reach our goal of deriving 20 percent of all the energy we use by the end of this century directly from the Sun. This act will also provide over $1 billion to help produce biomass energy, such as gasohol. This year alone, in 1980, we will quadruple our capacity to produce gasohol.

The act also recognizes that energy and environmental problems are closely interrelated, both very serious problems. Under the provisions of this act, we will complete a comprehensive study of the problem of acid rain and the other impacts of fossil fuel consumption on our environment, our economy, and on our society.

In sum, the Energy Security Act will launch this decade with the greatest outpouring of capital investment, technology, manpower, and resources since the space program. Its scope, in fact, is so great that it will dwarf the combined efforts expended to put Americans on the Moon and to build the entire Interstate Highway System of our country. This tremendous commitment will make the 1980's a time of national resolve and also a brave and exciting achievement.

In the past, when we switched from wood to coal, there was a great amount of fear and trepidation, and then when we switched from coal to oil, there was also uncertainty about the future. But those changes, as we well know, brought only better things to Americans—a better lifestyle, more leisure time, more essentials, like electricity and heat. Now, as we switch from foreign oil to American fuels, again we stand only to gain for our economy, our security, and our confidence.

Our accomplishments are historic, but our work is not yet complete. Last year the energy mobilization board was recommitted to conference—a serious disappointment and a major setback. I urge the leaders of the Congress to reconvene the energy mobilization board conference committee, to produce an effective board which will expedite the process of project approval and which respects environmental protection as well. Utility oil backout legislation, which will let us replace the consumption of oil and natural gas in utility plants with more plentiful supplies of energy like coal, should be passed also without delay. Only the last few days, the Senate had a major victory in the passage of this important legislation.

I would like to point out that the fight for energy security is not a partisan fight. I ask the members of both parties to complete our energy agenda in the same spirit of cooperation that has brought us the success which we are celebrating today. The battle for America's energy security has been joined; there will be no retreat. We must recognize our energy problem for what it truly is: our Nation's greatest opportunity in a lifetime.

We are the same Americans who, just 10 years ago, put a man on the Moon. We're the generation that dedicated our society to change, social change, to provide equality of opportunity and equality under the law for all Americans, and to end generations of discrimination, to provide human rights and justice. We have the knowledge, the wisdom, and the skill derived from more than two centuries of overcoming obstacles. We have the will and the power of a mature nation, and we have the vision and the determination of a young people.

In just a few days we will celebrate the birthday of our declaration of political independence. I can think of no more fitting birthday present than this declaration of energy security or energy independence, which I'm very proud to sign now with all of you present today. Thank you very much. It's a great day for America.

[*At this point, the President signed the bill.*]

It would really be appropriate to call on every one of these distinguished Members of the Congress on the stage, but I will call on two—one to represent the fine work that was done in the Senate and one to represent the work that was done in the House.

First, I'd like to call on the Chairman of a committee responsible for this legislation in the Senate, Senator Scoop Jackson. Scoop.

SENATOR JACKSON. Thank you, Mr. President. First off, I want to express to you, to the administration, Secretary Duncan, our appreciation for the support, all-out support that we had in this long fight.

Energy legislation represents contentious legislation. There isn't anything you do that can make people totally happy, but it brings out the worst in all of us. And any alternative source that you suggest, people object. Even out in my country, we're putting up windmills, but we're getting objections on the ground that it results in noise pollution and interferes with television reception. And so, there isn't any alternative source that you do not have trouble.

This program is a result of many years of effort. On the platform is Senator Randolph, who, with Senator O'Manney, started the ball rolling in 1944. The present legislation is a result of 12 years of effort. The man in the Senate who really led the charge is Senator Johnston of Louisiana, and I want him to stand. He deserves all the credit, Mr. President, on the Senate side. I simply delegated my responsibility to him, and he did a terrific job.

Mr. President, as you mentioned, it was a bipartisan effort. Senator Hatfield, on the Republican side, the ranking minority member, backed up Senator Domenici, did a terrific job, made possible the movement of this legislation through the Senate in short order. I want both of them to stand.

Senator Ford, of course, has no interest in coal. [*Laughter*] Stand up. He worked around the clock. And even Hawaii has tremendous interest in this sort of thing; Senator Matsunaga, please stand. And way out west—Senator Church, who did a great job in helping all of us on the committee.

As the President has mentioned, the bill was more than just a synthetic fuels program, but it covered some eight or nine additional titles involving everything from gasohol to, shall we say, conservation. And so we have here representatives of the other committee: Senator Sarbanes of Maryland, Senator Riegle. They're all modest; I guess none of them are running. [*Laughter*] Senator Tsongas—Ron here? I know that Herman Talmadge will stand up. And you're not running. And so, Mr. President, have I left anyone out?

THE PRESIDENT. Bradley?

SENATOR JACKSON. Senator Bradley? Here you are. Get up. And Senator Stewart. Stand up. One of them is running.

Mr. President, we again want to thank you. Again, I would mention that this is the largest—it's not spending—this is the largest investment program ever undertaken by the Government of the United States to prosecute a single project except in time of war. We're talking about $100 billion in round numbers, and we're all very proud of this noble beginning.

Thank you very much.

THE PRESIDENT. This bill actually started as a very small proposal, with profound significance, by Congressman Bill Moorhead, but it was adopted by the House, sent to the Senate, and then, as part of the bill, incorporated many titles which will transform the life and the attitude and the security of our whole country.

To speak for the House, I'd like to call now on Majority Leader Jim Wright of Texas, who played such a crucial role in this legislation. Jim Wright.

REPRESENTATIVE WRIGHT. Mr. President, as I approached this moment and watched your signing of this monumental piece of legislation, I thought of those words from Kipling: "If you can wait, and not be tired by waiting, or being lied about, don't deal in lies, or being hated, don't give way to hating, and yet don't look too good nor talk too wise." We have waited for this energy legislation, and we haven't looked too good. And so, I suppose Kipling is pleased with us. [*Laughter*]

For three decades, ever since the Paley Commission warned us that our voracious thirst for power would eat its way inexorably through the finite resources of oil and gas that it took nature some 6 million years to lay beneath the Earth and that we'd be wise if we began immediately to find replacements for oil and gas and particularly in our abundant supplies of coal, of which we have approximately one-third the world's known reserves, we have waited.

During those three decades, a combination of timidity, lethargy, and parochialism have kept us from doing those things that we needed to do. And it remained until this year, under the inspiration and leadership of President Carter, that a heterogeneous collection of opinionated individualists, each of us an energy expert in his own right, from four separate House committees came together to give life and breath to this skeleton outline that had been laid before us three decades ago.

Bill Moorhead has already been mentioned. And it was he, as Chairman of that subcommittee and the banking and currency and housing committee of the House, along with his associate on the Republican side, Stuart McKinney from Connecticut, who began this long process. And on the commerce committee, we had Republicans and Democrats working together. We had John Dingell and Jim Broyhill, a Democrat from Michigan and a Republican from North Carolina. I would like for those four I've already mentioned to stand, because I want the public to recognize the importance of your contributions.

And the Chairman of the science committee of the House, Don Fuqua, had a major role in the shaping of this legislation, as did Chalmers Wylie of Ohio.

There are so many that I want you to see the breadth of ideological and geographical spread that came together to produce this legislation: Jim Blanchard of Michigan, Bruce Vento of Minnesota, please stand and let them acknowledge you; Stu McKinney and Don Fuqua, I've mentioned; John Dingell, I've mentioned; but Phil Sharp of Indiana, a truly creative Member of the House; and with him, Albert Gore of Tennessee, who worked diligently on the conservation sections of this bill; along with John Wydler and with Stephen Neal of North Carolina; and with Ken Kramer and Dick Ottinger and Toby Moffett, who worked together with Bob Edgar of Pennsylvania and Berkley Goodell of Iowa; and Phil Gramm of Texas, my colleague and neighbor; and Austin Murphy of Pennsylvania; and Tom Daschle of South Dakota.

And if I have left anybody—oh, the main one I wanted to mention last— [*laughter*]—Mary Rose Oakar of Ohio. Is Harley here? Of course, the chairman of them all, the *papacito* of the commerce committee, interstate and foreign, Harley Staggers of West Virginia. I hope I haven't neglected to mention anyone else.

This bill is a monumental piece of legislation. I think it is in the American tradition. It doesn't set out to do it all by government nor by tax dollars. It sets out instead to let government be the catalyst to perform the role that government best can perform in this free society of ours, to create the climate that will be conducive to the investment on the private sector that will make real the development of a commercial synthetic fuels industry capable of making this country energy sufficient again. It will unleash the dynamics of the American enterprise system.

And I think that this day ranks with that day in the beginning of the 1940's when, with the United States cut off from sources of raw rubber by the Japanese invasions of Asia, Franklin D. Roosevelt called together Bernard Baruch and Bill Jeffers and gave them the challenge to create in this country a synthetic rubber industry. Nobody knew exactly how it should be done. But 4 years later when the Allies rolled into Berlin, they rolled triumphantly on rubber tires made by an indigenous American synthetic rubber industry. We made the commitment, and we fulfilled the promise.

And then two decades later, at the beginning of the 1960's, John F. Kennedy came before the Congress of the United States and promised that we would have a man on the Moon by 1970. To put yourself back into the frame of mind of 1961, you'd have to recall the sheer audacity of that promise. Nobody knew that it could be done; scarcely any of us dared to believe that there were those who knew how to do it. But we gave it the commitment and the priority that it deserved, and we made the promise into a reality.

No less fatefully significant is this day, when President Jimmy Carter, signing this landmark legislation, promises that in this decade upon which we now have embarked, we're going to make America energy independent again. Our presence here bespeaks our commitment to that goal, and we enlist with you, Mr. President, behind that banner.

THE PRESIDENT. I'd like to ask all the Congressmen to stand up at one time and Mrs. Oakar and let the audience express, in closing, our deep appreciation to them for their farsighted leadership and for their investment and confidence in America. Our country will be greater, happier, have a better quality of life, a better environment, utilize our resources more efficiently, and be more secure because of their action and this legislation.

Bob Byrd just sent me word that he was sorry he couldn't be here. He was a ringleader, as you know, in the passage of this historic legislation.

Thank you all very much. Let's give the Congressmen and women a round of applause.

NOTE: The President spoke at 4:04 p.m. on the South Lawn of the White House.

As enacted, S. 932 is Public Law 96–294, approved June 30.

Nuclear Regulatory Commission Authorization Bill

Statement on Signing S. 562 Into Law.
June 30, 1980

I am pleased to sign S. 562, authorizing appropriations to the Nuclear Regulatory Commission for fiscal year 1980. This important bill, enacted under the leadership of Senator Hart and Congressman Udall, is a vital step in ensuring the safe operation of America's nuclear plants. It provides the necessary funding and authority for many of the recommendations of the Kemeny Commission concerning the regulation of nuclear reactors, the inspection of facilities and enforcement of regulations, the development of safety and environmental standards and contingency plans, and the conduct of nuclear regulatory research.

S. 562 also authorizes the Nuclear Regulatory Commission to promulgate regulations to withhold safeguards information from the public. I expect that the Nuclear Regulatory Commission will cooperate with other Federal agencies to ensure that its exercise of this authority is carried out in a manner consistent with the responsibilities exercised by other agencies dealing with national security information and restricted data.

NOTE: As enacted, S. 562 is Public Law 96–295, approved June 30.

Color Television Receiver Imports

Proclamation 4769.   June 30, 1980

EXTENSION OF THE ORDERLY MARKETING AGREEMENTS AND TEMPORARY QUANTITATIVE LIMITATIONS ON THE IMPORTATION INTO THE UNITED STATES OF COLOR TELEVISION RECEIVERS AND CERTAIN SUBASSEMBLIES THEREOF

By the President of the United States of America

A Proclamation

1. By Proclamation 4634 of January 26, 1979, the President proclaimed, under the authority of the Constitution and the

statutes of the United States, including sections 203(a)(5), (e)(3) and (g)(2) of the Trade Act of 1974 (19 U.S.C. 2253(a)(5), (e)(3) and (g)(2)) (the Trade Act), the implementation of the orderly marketing agreements entered into with Taiwan and with the Republic of Korea which imposed quantitative restrictions on imports from Taiwan and Korea of color television receivers and certain subassemblies thereof. The limitations applied to covered articles entered, or withdrawn from warehouse for consumption, on or after February 1, 1979, and were to continue through June 30, 1980, unless earlier modified or terminated. Proclamation 4759 of May 15, 1980, modified Proclamation 4634. The limitations currently in effect, applicable to articles provided for in items 923.74 through 923.83, inclusive of the Tariff Schedules of the United States (TSUS) (19 U.S.C. 1202), will terminate at the close of June 30, 1980, unless extended by the President under section 203(h)(3) of the Trade Act (19 U.S.C. 2253(h) (3)).

2. On May 16, 1980, the United States International Trade Commission (USITC), in accordance with sections 203(i)(3) and (5) of the Trade Act (19 U.S.C. 2253(i)(3) and (5)), reported the results of its investigation under section 203(i)(3) of the Trade Act (19 U.S.C. 2253(i)(3)) to the President (USITC Publication 1068). The USITC advised the President that termination of the import relief currently in effect with respect to certain color television receivers and subassemblies thereof will have an adverse effect on the domestic industry producing like or directly competitive products.

3. Section 203(h)(3) and (5) of the Trade Act (19 U.S.C. 2253(h)(3) and (5)) provides that any import relief in-

stituted under the authority of section 203 may be extended by the President at a level no greater than that in effect at the time of extension if the President determines, after considering the advice of the USITC and the factors indicated in section 202(c) of the Trade Act (19 U.S.C. 2252(c)), that such extension is in the national interest.

4. In accordance with section 203(h) (3) of the Trade Act (19 U.S.C. 2253(h) (3)), I have determined that the level of import relief hereinafter proclaimed extends import relief at a level no greater than that in effect for the period of February 1, 1979 through June 30, 1980, and, having considered the advice given by the USITC in its report to the President and the factors indicated in section 202(c) of the Trade Act (19 U.S.C. 2252(c)), I have determined that the extension of the orderly marketing agreements with the Coordinating Council for North American Affairs and the Republic of Korea, covering certain color television receivers and subassemblies thereof as provided in the Annex to this proclamation, is in the national interest.

Now, THEREFORE, I, JIMMY CARTER, President of the United States of America, acting under the authority vested in me in the Constitution and the statutes of the United States, including section 203 of the Trade Act (19 U.S.C. 2253), section 604 of the Trade Act (19 U.S.C. 2483), section 301 of Title 3 of the United States Code, and sections 4(b)(2) and 6(b) of the Taiwan Relations Act (22 U.S.C. 3303(b)(2) and 3305(b)), and in accordance with Article XIX of the General Agreement on Tariffs and Trade (GATT) (61 Stat. (pt. 5) A58; 8 UST (pt. 2) 1786), do proclaim that—

(1) Orderly marketing agreements, with respect to trade in certain color television receivers and subassemblies thereof,

extending in part those currently in effect, were initialled June 28, 1980 by the Government of the United States of America and the Government of the Republic of Korea, and on June 28, 1980 by the American Institute in Taiwan and the Coordinating Council for North American Affairs. Both agreements will be signed in the near future.

These agreements, which will be made effective July 1, 1980, are to be implemented according to their terms and by the quantitative restrictions as directed in this proclamation, including the Annex.

(2) The Tariff Schedules of the United States (19 U.S.C. 1202) are modified as set forth in the Annex to this proclamation.

(3) The authority of the President under section 203(e)(2) of the Trade Act (19 U.S.C. 2253(e)(2)) to negotiate orderly marketing agreements with other foreign country suppliers of articles subject to this proclamation after any import relief proclaimed pursuant to section 203 (a) (1), (2), (3) or (5) of the Trade Act (19 U.S.C. 2253(a) (1), (2), (3) or (5)) takes effect is delegated to the United States Trade Representative (Trade Representative). The authority of the President, under section 203(e)(3) of the Trade Act (19 U.S.C. 2253(e)(3)) to determine that any agreement negotiated pursuant to section 203(a)(4) or (5) or 203(e)(2) of the Trade Act (19 U.S.C. 2253(a)(4) or (5) or 2253(e)(2)) is no longer effective, is delegated to the Trade Representative, to be exercised after consultation with representatives of the member agencies of the Trade Policy Committee. In the event of such a determination, the Trade Representative shall submit to the President a proclamation to implement import relief authorized by section 203(e)(3) of the Trade Act (19 U.S.C. 2253(e)(3)).

(4) The authority of the President in section 203(g)(1) and (2) of the Trade Act (19 U.S.C. 2253(g)(1) and (2)), having been delegated to the Secretary of the Treasury under section 5(b) of Executive Order No. 11846, shall be exercised by the Secretary of the Treasury, upon direction by the Trade Representative, in consultation with representatives of the member agencies of the Trade Policy Committee.

(5) In exercising the authority delegated in paragraphs (3) and (4) above, the Trade Representative shall, in addition to other necessary actions, institute the following actions:

(a) Statistics on imports of articles covered by the agreements shall be collected on a monthly basis.

(b) If, for two years beginning on July 1, 1980, the quantity of imports of the articles covered by the agreements from sources other than those covered by the agreements described in paragraph (1) appears likely to disrupt the effectiveness of the provisions of the orderly marketing agreements described in paragraph (1) above, the Trade Representative may initiate consultations with those countries and may exercise the authority under 203 (g)(2) of the Trade Act (19 U.S.C. 2253 (g)(2)) to prevent further entry of such articles for the remainder of that restraint period or otherwise moderate or restrict imports of such articles from such countries. Before exercising this authority, the Trade Representative shall consult with representatives of the member agencies of the Trade Policy Committee.

(c) Should the Trade Representative, under the authority of this proclamation, determine to institute import restrictions on articles entered, or withdrawn from warehouse for consumption, from sources other than those covered by the agreements described in paragraph (1) that action shall be effective not less than eight days after the publication in the FEDERAL REGISTER of the determination and any necessary changes in the TSUS.

(6) The Trade Representative shall take those actions and perform those functions for the United States which may be necessary concerning the administration, implementation, modification, amendment or termination of the agreements described in paragraph (1) of this proclamation, and any actions and functions necessary to implement paragraphs (3), (4) and (5) of this proclamation. In carrying out his responsibilities under this paragraph, the Trade Representative is authorized to delegate, to appropriate officials or agencies of the United States, authority to perform any functions necessary for the administration and implementation of the agreements or actions. The Trade Representative is authorized to make any changes in the TSUS which may be necessary to carry out the agreements or actions. Any changes in the agreements shall be effective not less than 8 days following their publication in the FEDERAL REGISTER.

(7) The Commissioner of Customs shall take those actions which the Trade Representative determines are necessary to carry out the agreements described in paragraph (1) of this proclamation and to implement any import relief under the authority of paragraphs (3), (4) and (5) of this proclamation, or any modification of it, with respect to the entry, or withdrawal from warehouse for consumption, into the United States of products covered by the agreements or by other import relief authorized above.

(8) The USITC shall issue reports and conduct the following surveys with respect to the certain color television receivers, and subassemblies thereof the subject of this proclamation:

(a) *Quarterly* surveys by calendar quarter to obtain from producers in the United States monthly data on production, shipments, inventories, employment, man-hours, prices, and other economic factors indicative of conditions in the U.S. industry. The initial surveys shall cover the second quarter of 1980. Subsequent surveys shall cover individual quarters with the last such survey covering the quarter which ends not less than 60 days prior to the termination of the import relief. The USITC shall publish the results of the surveys within 45 days after the end of the surveyed quarter.

(b) *Annual.* Annual surveys to obtain data from producers in the United States by calendar quarter on profits, capacity, and annual data on capital expenditures and research and development expenditures; and to obtain from importers data by calendar quarter on prices, orders, and inventories. The initial surveys shall cover the calendar year 1980, and the results shall be published by March 31, 1981. The results of subsequent surveys shall be published by March 31 of each year thereafter so long as the import relief is in effect.

(9) This proclamation shall be effective as of July 1, 1980, and shall continue in force through June 30, 1982, unless the period of its effectiveness is earlier expressly modified or terminated.

IN WITNESS WHEREOF, I have hereunto set my hand this thirtieth day of June, in the year of our Lord nineteen hundred and eighty, and of the Independence of the United States of America the two hundred and fourth.

JIMMY CARTER

[Filed with the Office of the Federal Register, 10:32 a.m., July 1, 1980]

NOTE: The annex to the proclamation is printed in the FEDERAL REGISTER of July 2, 1980.

Occupational Safety and Health Programs for Federal Employees

Executive Order 12223.　June 30, 1980

By the authority vested in me as President by the Constitution and statutes of the United States of America, including Section 7902(c) of Title 5 of the United States Code, and in accord with Section 19 of the Occupational Safety and Health Act of 1970, as amended (29 U.S.C. 668), and in order to provide sufficient time for the development of adequate implementing instructions which will govern the new occupational safety and health programs for Federal employees, Section 1–704 of Executive Order No. 12196 of February 26, 1980, is hereby amended to read, "This Order is effective October 1, 1980.".

JIMMY CARTER

The White House,
　June 30, 1980.

[Filed with the Office of the Federal Register, 10:31 a.m., July 1, 1980]

NOTE: The text of the Executive order was released on July 1.

Motor Carrier Act of 1980

Remarks on Signing S. 2245 Into Law. July 1, 1980

THE PRESIDENT. These are my heroes back here, and I'm very grateful for what they've done for the country.

Yesterday we signed on the South Lawn an historic piece of legislation that will literally transform the lives of the American public in the years ahead. The Energy Security Corporation was established, an ability to finance the change from overdependence on foreign oil to a much more heavy dependence on conservation, first of all, and the production

of energy from American sources. There's not a family whose lives will not be changed beneficially by that legislation. It was difficult, but it was necessary.

Today we continue on a major effort, in addition to that, which will benefit American lives, help to control inflation, and give us an opportunity to use the free enterprise system of our country in its most effective form.

We've had notable success with this Congress during the last 3½ years in getting the Federal Government's nose out of the private lives of American people and the private enterprise system. Deregulation and the reduction in paperwork has been a major commitment of us all.

The deregulation of the airline industry, according to the CAB's own figures, has already saved the American citizens more than $5 billion. It's made the airline industry more competitive, more profitable, and more efficient. Earlier this year, we signed the deregulation bill for the financial institutions of our country, again to enhance competition and to give Americans a better life. We have also cut paperwork already by 15 percent, caused by the Federal Government, and that effort is continuing.

We are now approaching the final decision on rail deregulation, which will remove unnecessary Government restraint on competition in the rail industry and let that industry benefit from the system of competition on which our Nation was founded and on which it rests its economic freedom.

A year ago, at the White House, I proposed broad changes in the regulations that deal with the trucking industry. People then said that it was impossible to pass a trucking deregulation bill because of the powerful political forces involved and the controversial nature of this kind of legislation. That I'm signing this bill into law today, almost exactly 1 year later, is a tremendous credit to all those who've worked so closely with me in devising and in passing this legislation.

Senate Commerce Committee Chairman Howard Cannon has done yeoman work in preparing a basis for a better understanding not only of the consumers and the shippers of our country but also the trucking industry itself and the American public. Senator Bob Packwood worked very closely with him. And it's particularly gratifying to me to welcome Senator Kennedy to the Rose Garden today, because he's done such a tremendous job, too, in helping the whole Nation understand the advantages to be derived from this trucking deregulation bill.

I think it's important that consumers are being protected well, and at the same time, the trucking industry, who have been involved in the process in a very constructive way, will also be benefited in the future.

We have, on the House side, Bizz Johnson and Jim Howard, subcommittee chairman—Bizz Johnson is the committee chairman—who have met with me several times in the Oval Office as progress was being made, sometimes in times of discouragement and despair, sometimes in an attitude of hopefulness and determination. Congressmen Bill Harsha, Bud Shuster, and others have done a very fine job in representing both consumers, businesses of all kinds, farmers, and the truckers themselves.

This is historic legislation. There is no other nation on Earth that depends so heavily upon motor transportation for its economic life's blood. We are a nation addicted to broad spaces, which we love, and the necessity in a vital economy to transport goods and equipment and services rapidly and efficiently.

In the past—for the past 45 years, as a matter of fact—this freedom of the use of the highways has been constrained by excessive Government restriction. The Motor Carrier Act of 1980 will eliminate the redtape and the senseless overregulation that have hampered the free growth and the development of the American trucking industry. It will be highly anti-inflationary in effect, reducing consumer costs by as much as $8 billion a year, by ending wasteful practices and enhancing the essence of competition. It will save literally hundreds of millions of gallons of gasoline every year, because wasteful trucking practices will no longer be required by Federal law and Federal regulation.

The heart of this legislation is more efficiency. No longer will trucks have to travel empty because of rules that absurdly limit the kind of goods they can carry. No longer will trucks be forced literally hundreds of miles out of the direct route for no logical reason at all or prohibited pointlessly from stopping at points on their routes to pick up and deliver goods as is necessary to serve their customers.

This act will bring the trucking industry into the free market system where it belongs. It will encourage new truckers and expansion of existing firms. It will also ensure the dealing fairly with trucking firms owned by minorities and by women. And consumers, of course, will benefit from lower prices. Labor will benefit, because we'll have new jobs. And finally, the trucking industry itself, a strong, vital, profitable, well-organized industry, will benefit, because it will have greater flexibility and more opportunity for innovation.

Well, this act is important in its own right. It's important for the American people, and it's a great tribute in its effectiveness and its incisiveness to the men standing behind me this morning. Again, on behalf of the people of our country, I want to express my deep appreciation and admiration to the Members of Congress who have acted so courageously and so effectively in passing this legislation.

And now, it's with a great deal of pleasure that I sign into law the Motor Carriers Act of 1980. Thank you very much.

[*At this point, the President signed the bill.*]

I'd like to ask Senator Howard Cannon to come say just a word, if he will.

SENATOR CANNON. Thank you very much, Mr. President.

This legislation demonstrates that we can effectively reduce Government regulation and that the two major political parties can work together effectively to solve problems of major significance. I'm very proud that this bill originated in and received the strong support of the Senate. During that process, there were many people who were vital in assuring passage of such a strong bill. I can't possibly imagine how it could have been done without Bob Packwood's leadership among the Republicans. I've rarely seen a more effective individual effort. Among the other members of the committee, two in particular deserve special attention: Adlai Stevenson and Jack Schmitt. And of course, the House public works committee, under the leadership of Bizz Johnson and Jim Howard, should be commended for their efforts.

Above all, however, I want to recognize Ted Kennedy for his initial efforts on this issue and the consistent work he did on the trucking legislation over the past 3 years. This bill demonstrates how effective the Senator can be in developing a controversial issue and working with his colleagues in the Congress in implementing comprehensive and effective legislation. I look forward to our two committees con-

tinuing this partnership on legislation of mutual interest.

Of course, the issue depended on more than the strong support of a few Members of Congress. In great part this victory belongs to a unique coalition of consumers, shippers, industries, and public interest groups that worked hard to promote and achieve this legislation. And while they covered the entire political and economic spectrum, they all shared the belief that less regulation and more competition are essential to the future development of a sound transportation system in this country.

And finally Mr. President, I want to say that this bill demonstrates how effective this administration and you personally can be in supporting and promoting controversial legislation throughout the legislative process. In the days shortly before Senate consideration of the bill, Secretary Neil Goldschmidt, Stu Eizenstat, Fred Kahn, and their staffs spent so much time working the hallways in the Senate Office Buildings, working on the issue, that on one or two occasions they even had to eat in the Senate cafeteria, which is just about the strongest test of dedication that I'm aware of. [*Laughter*]

Thank you very much, Mr. President, and thanks again for your great help.

THE PRESIDENT. I'd like to ask Chairman Bizz Johnson to say a word, if he will. Mr. Chairman.

REPRESENTATIVE JOHNSON. Thank you, Mr. President.

This has been a long, long period of time in putting this bill together. When we first started out over a year ago, I doubted whether we'd ever get a bill to you. When the date was set of June 1, we didn't quite make it. But we worked very hard with all of your people, the Senate, our committee. Jim Howard, Bud Shuster, Bill Harsha did a lot of yeoman's work in putting this bill together. I want to commend Jim Howard, Bud Shuster, Bill Harsha here today.

We met with all segments of the trucking industry. We met with all segments of the consumer groups. And we finally brought it down to where we had a hard-working coalition of our staff, the White House, the trucking industry, the consumer groups, shippers. The last, I would say, was labor coming into the picture. We worked out our problems.

I just hope we have a good bill, the bill will do what we think it will do: benefit the consumer, the industry, which is a very, very large segment of our private enterprise. The trucking industry includes a good many people throughout the United States, and to get all of those people to say, "Yes, we support the bill"— Mr. President, you are to be commended.

THE PRESIDENT. Thank you very much.

Although the coalition which was finally successful in passing the bill was really organized effectively about a year ago, as Howard Cannon has pointed out, there was one Senator who worked on this legislation for at least 2 years or more prior to that, sometimes alone, sometimes facing discouragement, but never giving up on the concept. I'd like to ask Senator Kennedy to say a word if he will.

SENATOR KENNEDY. Well, there's no debate on trucking deregulation. [*Laughter*]

I want to commend the President and the administration for the very special effort that they have made in achieving this moment here today and to also single out those that have been previously recognized: the leader in the United States Senate, Howard Cannon, who has worked so hard with this administration and previous administrations on the truck deregulation and also in airline deregulation, and

Bizz Johnson, Glenn Anderson, and to Jim Howard, who worked so hard, as well, on the whole area of truck deregulation.

The number one concern of the American people is the state of our economy. I don't believe that there'll be a piece of legislation that'll be passed during this Congress that will have a greater impact in dampening the fires of inflation as the truck deregulation legislation. As we have seen from the Congressional Budget Office, the savings to consumers and the dampening effect that this legislation will have on inflation will be even greater than the budget cuts which have been proposed in the Congress and Senate of the United States.

It will offer new opportunities for competition. It'll get the heavy hand of the Federal Government out of the area of the private sector. It'll mean new opportunities, new jobs. And I believe that there are other areas in which we can work, work closely together, to dampen inflation and also see the restoration of the vitality of the American economy.

Also, when we talk about deregulation, I think Mr. President would agree that we have Fred Kahn here, who is one of those in the very early days, when we first started the hearings some 6 years ago in the Senate Judiciary Committee, who came down and made one of the very eloquent statements and comments about how the economy could be served and how the consumer could be served and American industry served. And he has been one of the really great figures, I think, in both this administration and in our country, in trying to ensure that the forces of competition and the reinvigoration of our American industry will be well served. And it's nice to see you here today.

Thank you, Mr. President.

THE PRESIDENT. It would be good to

call on everyone here, but I would particularly like to call on Jim Howard, who in times of great duress stood courageously and, with a great political sensitivity, was able to bring together disparate groups, who had widely ranging attitudes toward this legislation, successfully. Jim, would you come and say just a word?

REPRESENTATIVE HOWARD. Thank you very much.

As you know, this was not an easy task. And 1 year ago, to think that we might be able to get the consumers, the shippers, the Teamsters, the marketers, everyone together on a piece of legislation for the national good looked almost impossible. But the big thing about it is that everyone cooperated. Everyone gave a little bit in order to get a good overall bill.

Besides the people mentioned here thus far, we couldn't be where we are today without the tremendous help that we got on both sides of the Capitol from the valuable staff members that we have, who kept negotiations going, who talked when we weren't available. And although there are too many of them to mention, they're symbolized by the head of the House negotiating staff team, Jack Friar. And I think that we owe an awful lot to our staffs.

I'm very, very grateful to all the groups who gave so much to get such a good bill. And, Mr. President, I'm mostly grateful that it's all behind us now. [*Laughter*]

THE PRESIDENT. In closing, let me say that you have participated in a momentous occasion for our country. I'm very grateful that you were here. This legislation will have a great beneficial impact on those that you care about and those that you help to lead. Thank you very much for being here.

And again, thanks to all the Members of Congress who were successful in passing this controversial, crucial, important, fine legislation. Thanks again.

NOTE: The President spoke at 9:31 a.m. in the Rose Garden at the White House.

As enacted, S. 2245 is Public Law 96–296, approved July 1.

Motor Carrier Act of 1980

Statement on Signing S. 2245 Into Law.
July 1, 1980

I have today signed into law S. 2245, the Motor Carrier Act of 1980. This is historic legislation. It will remove 45 years of excessive and inflationary Government restrictions and redtape. It will have a powerful anti-inflationary effect, reducing consumer costs by as much as $8 billion each year. And by ending wasteful practices, it will conserve annually hundreds of millions of gallons of precious fuel.

All the citizens of our Nation will benefit from this legislation. Consumers will benefit, because almost every product we purchase has been shipped by truck, and outmoded regulations have inflated the prices that each one of us must pay. The shippers who use trucking will benefit as new service and price options appear. Labor will benefit from increased job opportunities. And the trucking industry itself will benefit from greater flexibility and new opportunities for innovation.

The heart of the Motor Carrier Act of 1980 is its call for prompt and sweeping change of the regulations that have insulated the trucking industry from competition since 1935. No longer will trucks travel empty because of rules absurdly limiting the kinds of goods a truck may carry. No longer will trucks be forced to travel hundreds of miles out of their way for no reason or prohibited senselessly from stopping to pick up and deliver goods at points along their routes.

The Motor Carrier Act of 1980 will bring the trucking industry into the free enterprise system, where it belongs. It will create a strong presumption in favor of entry by new truckers and expanded service by existing firms. It will build upon progress the Interstate Commerce Commission has begun to make in opening opportunities for minorities, for women, and for all truckers who are eager to provide good service at a competitive price.

It will phase out most of the antitrust immunity that has allowed rate bureaus to fix prices. It will eliminate redtape and encourage price competition by allowing trucking companies to price their goods within a zone of reasonableness not subject to ICC review, and it immediately ends antitrust immunity for all rates set through that zone. The premise of the rate-zone provision is that increased competition between truckers will prevent abuses of this pricing freedom. I expect the ICC to implement this legislation effectively and promptly to ensure the vigorous competition needed to make greater pricing freedom work in the interest of shippers and consumers.

The bill broadens the list of agricultural commodities that are completely exempt from regulation and provides greatly eased entry with an absolute minimum of redtape for independent owner-operators who carry processed food. While not as broad as the complete exemption for processed food we had proposed, this provision is still an important procompetitive force in helping to hold down the price of food.

I am also particularly pleased that the bill will improve truck service to small communities and enhance business opportunities for independent truckers.

In brief, the purpose of the legislation is clear. Protective and wasteful regulations are to be replaced wherever possible by competition and the discipline of the free market. These changes will work to the benefit of all consumers.

The Motor Carrier Act of 1980 is important in its own right. It should also be seen in context, as a key part of this administration's sweeping program of regulatory reform. We have done far more than any other administration in history to eliminate excessive or outmoded regulation and to manage more productively the regulations that remain essential.

We fought successfully for domestic and international airline deregulation. As a result, the Civil Aeronautics Board estimates that air travelers saved $2.8 billion in 1978 alone and that the productivity increases that produced those reductions continued throughout 1979, for overall savings in excess of $5 billion. I proposed and have now signed into law reform legislation to remove regulatory barriers that for years prevented more competition and better service in the banking industry. I proposed and Congress is nearing final passage of legislation to remove archaic and superfluous regulation of the railroads.

Where regulations cannot be eliminated, we have established a program to reform the way they are produced and reviewed. By Executive order, we have established a requirement that regulators carefully and publicly analyze the costs of major proposals, which had never been done before. We have required that interested members of the public be given greater opportunity to participate in the regulatory process. We have established a sunset review program for all major new regulations. We have cut Federal paperwork by 15 percent and will cut it further. And we are making real progress in eliminating inconsistent regulations and developing and encouraging innovative regulatory techniques—techniques that are already saving hundreds of millions of dollars while still meeting important statutory goals.

Our comprehensive program of regulatory reform is a major accomplishment, and the trucking bill ranks high among its elements. A year ago, when I proposed trucking reform legislation, many people said that real trucking reform could not be accomplished. That I am signing this bill into law only 1 year later is a tremendous credit to all who worked with me to achieve reform.

I am deeply grateful to those key Members of Congress who worked tirelessly for this legislation. Senate Commerce Committee Chairman Howard Cannon and Senator Bob Packwood exercised superb leadership in developing a comprehensive record of the need to change the present system and in consistently pressing for expeditious reform. Senator Kennedy has been a steady and important supporter of trucking reform and helped to shape our original joint proposal. In the House, the crucial efforts on this proconsumer legislation were made by Public Works and Transportation Committee Chairman Bizz Johnson, Subcommittee Chairman Jim Howard, Chairman Peter Rodino of the Judiciary Committee, Congressman Bill Harsha, and Congressman Bud Shuster.

Tremendous credit is also due to the large number of people outside the Congress, representing consumers, businesses of all sizes, farmers, independent and regulated truckers, and others interested in working toward genuine reform.

Finally, I want to commend Chairman Gaskins and the members of the Interstate Commerce Commission for their support and encouragement of this reform effort. I know I can count on the Commission to take prompt and effective action to bring to the public the benefits of greater competition, greater productivity, and lower prices that this law will provide.

NOTE: As enacted, S. 2245 is Public Law 96–296, approved July 1.

Airlift of Military Equipment to Thailand

Announcement of the Airlift.   July 1, 1980

President Carter today approved an immediate U.S. airlift of military equipment to Thailand, involving the shipment of small arms and artillery on U.S. military aircraft from Army arsenals in the United States directly to Bangkok. The President's determination, about which the appropriate committees of the Congress have been informed, was taken under section 506(a) of the Foreign Assistance Act.

The decision was made in the wake of last week's Vietnamese attack across the Thai/Kampuchean border on refugee concentrations and Thai villages. The airlift responds to urgent Thai requests for accelerated delivery of equipment items purchased by Thailand under the foreign military sales (FMS) program. The airlift, which is expected to cost roughly $1 million, will transport M–16 rifles, 106mm recoilless rifles, and 105mm howitzers.

The United States will also begin expediting surface shipments to Thailand of needed small arms and artillery ammunition and is making arrangements to accelerate the delivery by sea of 35 M48–A5 tanks, following completion of the required 30-day congressional review period on July 23, 1980.

Vietnam Veterans Memorial Bill

*Remarks on Signing S.J. Res. 119
Into Law.   July 1, 1980*

THE PRESIDENT. Since I've been living in the White House and working in the Oval Office, I've known of very few unanimous resolutions or actions by the United States Senate. But it's especially fitting that this resolution and the effort to provide a suitable memorial for those who fought and died for our Nation during the Vietnam war, should have such broad and bipartisan support.

My wife, Rosalynn, for instance, has joined as one of the cochairpersons, with many others, on the sponsoring committee of the Vietnam Memorial Fund.

I particularly want to acknowledge the dedication of Jan Scruggs who began this effort formally, after years of preliminary work, in April of 1979, and the leadership of Senator Mathias, Senator Warner, Congressmen Bonior and Daschle and Chairman Bumpers and Chairman Nedzi and Congressman Hammerschmidt and many others who led the legislation successfully through the Congress.

I also want to congratulate and thank Secretary Cecil Andrus, who couldn't be here today, but whose agency supported and whose department will be responsible for the management and the maintenance of this monument; and for the Veterans Administration, Max Cleland, who will speak to us in a few minutes, whose service to his country has continued since that war through today, and who joyfully celebrates his own "alive day" each year, because he knows better than most of us what it means to sacrifice and to serve and to suffer and to survive.

A long and a painful process has brought us to this moment today. Our Nation, as you all know, was divided by this war. For too long we tried to put that division behind us by forgetting the Vietnam war and, in the process, we ignored those who bravely answered their Nation's call, adding to their pain the additional burden of our Nation's own inner conflict.

Over the last 3½ years, I have encouraged and I have been heartened to witness an enormous change in the attitude of Americans toward those who served in Vietnam. A Nation healing and reconciliation is a good sight to behold from the viewpoint of the Presidency, and we are ready at least to acknowledge more deeply and also more publicly the debt which we can never fully pay to those who served.

The word "honor" has been used so often and sometimes so carelessly—especially in public ceremonies—that there's a danger that it might lose its meaning. More importantly, we might forget what its true meaning is and, with it, the concept of duty and a standard of behavior and sense of humility that's precious and also irreplaceable. And when I say today that I am honored to be able to sign this resolution into law, I use that word with great care.

This is an important step toward the establishment of a permanent memorial for the young men and women who died in the service of our country in Vietnam; for those who, despite all our efforts, are still missing in Southeast Asia; and for all those who served and returned. We are honored to have a small part in offering this overdue recognition. They honored us and their country with their service, and no delay in recognizing them can lessen the value of their personal sacrifice.

Perhaps even more than those who served, our Nation needs this memorial as a reminder of what happened in the past, what was lost, and our need to learn from our experience. We need it also as a physical place where we can pay tribute to those young lives, what they meant, to kind of place apart, to recall the meaning of the word "honor", so that the word can retain all its simple and austere grandeur.

In honoring those who answered the call of duty, we do not honor war. But we honor the peace they sought, the freedoms that they fought to preserve, and the hope that they held out to a world that's still struggling to learn how to settle differences among people and among nations without resorting to violence.

All of us must be willing to sacrifice to protect freedom and to protect justice, but we are not called upon to sacrifice equally. In every war there are some who are called on to make the ultimate sacrifice of their own lives. Some come home with bodies that must bear daily pain for the rest of their lives. A tragically large number were still missing when the war in Vietnam was over, and we'll continue to exert the fullest possible effort to account for all those who are still missing.

It's a pointless act of inhumanity and cruelty to prolong the vigil of those who love, waiting for those for so many years, and it's a vigil that's shared not just among the families directly, but shared by all Americans.

At the time of our White House reception in honor of Vietnam veterans last year, Phil Caputo, the author of "A Rumor of War", permitted me to read from his book. I was greatly moved by this passage, as were the others at the time, and I feel it even more appropriate to read here today the same words, what Caputo wrote in 1976, I believe, about the death of one of his close friends named Walter Levy, who was killed in Vietnam trying to save a fellow soldier, and I quote:

"So much was lost with you, so much talent and intelligence and decency. You were the first from our class of 1964 to die. There were others, but you were the first and more: you embodied the best that was in us. You were a part of us, and a part of us died with you, the small part that was still young, that had not yet grown cynical, grown bitter and old with death. Your courage was an example to us, and whatever the rights or wrongs of the war, nothing can diminish the rightness of what you tried to do. Yours was the greater love. You died for the man you tried to save, and you died *pro patria*. It was not altogether sweet and fitting, your death, but I am sure you died believing it was *pro patria*. You were faithful."

To die for one's country is a sacrifice that should never be forgotten.

Caputo goes on to say that our country has not matched the faithfulness of that war hero, because our country tried to forget the war; that 11 years after his friend's death, Caputo wrote, there were no monuments, no statues, no plaques, no memorials, because such symbols would make it harder to forget.

I didn't read that part aloud last year. Now, we'll build a memorial to the Walter Levys who died on the other side of the world, sacrificing themselves for others, . sacrificing themselves for us and for our children and for our children's children. With this memorial we will say with Caputo: "We loved you for what you were and what you stood for." We will prove with this monument that we care, and that we will always remember.

I'd now like to ask Max Cleland, the director [Administrator] of our Veterans Administration, one of the finest men I know, a long-time personal friend of mine, to say a few words.

Max Cleland.

MR. CLELAND. Mr. President, thank you very much. Those words of Caputo have a special meaning for me. I consider myself fortunate to have survived Vietnam and survived the aftermath back in this country. It's a special honor to be here on a day of celebration and a day of recognition. As a Vietnam veteran myself, I want to thank those who have made this day possible, those citizens, those Members of the Congress, and you, Mr. President, for this recognition.

I think it does say that we do honor those who have honored us. And I'd like to invite all of you to get better acquainted with Constitution Gardens, on behalf of Cecil Andrus and myself. We look forward to that as a site for a memorial that will say to all Vietnam veterans and their families: This Nation cares, and we remember.

Thank you very much.

THE PRESIDENT. And now I will sign the resolution into law, following which, without further introduction, I'd like to ask Senator Mac Mathias to speak to us, and also then Congressman Nedzi.

[At this point, the President signed the bill.]

SENATOR MATHIAS. Thank you very much, Mr. President, for the act you have just performed, and for your very touching words. The President has been very generous in giving credit for the passage of this act. I want you to know that as far as the United States Senate is concerned, the labor and the honor has been very equally divided in 101 different parts. I say, Mr. President, 101, because not only did every single Member of the Senate cosponsor this legislation, which is unusual in itself, but we've had the untiring help and assistance of the Secretary of the Senate, Sam Kimmett, who has been a very big part of the passage of the legislation.

I believe the President's signature on this legislation, and the votes of approval, the unanimous votes of approval in the Congress, are an outward and visible sign of the reconciliation of this great country after a difficult war; an outward and visible sign that we now have the perspective on Vietnam which makes it possible for us to resolve the differences that divided us during that war.

I undertook the initial sponsorship of this legislation because of the obvious sincerity, the moving dedication, of the Vietnam veterans who first came to see me about it, and because of the sense of debt that I felt for those who, as a great man who lived in this house once said, "gave the last full measure of devotion." But it's a cause in which so many people can participate, not just those who originally thought of the idea, not just those who helped to get the bill through Congress, not those of us who are limited by the confines of this garden, but all Americans can play a role, can participate, can play a part. And this is the time when we invite everyone to become a part of this living Vietnam memorial.

Thank you.

REPRESENTATIVE NEDZI. *Mr. President, my colleagues in the Congress, Vietnam veterans and their friends—and I know that includes everybody here:*

It's truly an honor for me to represent the House of Representatives at this signing. I recognize that the moving force— as Senator Mathias has so eloquently stated—behind this resolution was the Vietnam Veterans Memorial Fund, Incorporated. However, many Members of the House and the Senate also worked very diligently on it. The House Memorial Subcommittee, which I chair, happened by legislative chance to have a role to play, and we were very, very pleased to play it.

A former President once said: "Doing the right thing is easy. Knowing what the right thing is is hard." All Members of the House, I am sure, want to do the right thing in regard to Vietnam veterans. And while many of us realize that we will probably be unable to fully groove on the attitudes and experience of the Vietnam-era veteran, we do want to try. And I believe the Capital and the Nation will be well served by the initiative and the creativity of the Vietnam Veterans Memorial Fund, particularly the tone in which this whole enterprise was undertaken. Thanks largely to them, a harmonious and unifying memorial will arise out of what was a generally disharmonious period of our national history.

The memorial is a creative, finely honed, high-minded, and encompassing idea. It is sensitive to the individual dignity of the men and women who served, and to the very American impulses of kinship, conscience, love, hope, and faith. When fully realized, and it will be fully realized, this memorial will serve as an enduring beacon of national appreciation and national reconciliation.

Thank you.

THE PRESIDENT. In closing this ceremony, let me say that this is a wonderful occasion for us all: a time of sober reflection and a time of the realization of the blessings that we share; a time of hope and expectation about the future, with a united and a strong America, realizing the true meaning of honor, the true meaning of bravery, and the true meaning of sacrifice.

As requested by the Vietnam veterans themselves, this memorial will not be financed by Federal funds; it'll be financed by contributions from all Americans. After it is completed, the Federal Government, of course, will operate it, under the Interior Department. And it will be designed for all Americans to come to express our gratitude for what our Na-

tion is and our deep thanks and appreciation for the courage and the sacrifice of those who have given their lives on occasion, but offered their lives even when they weren't lost, for the preservation of liberty and hope.

Thank you very much. God bless you all.

NOTE: The President spoke at 2:05 p.m. at the ceremony in the Rose Garden at the White House. In his remarks, he referred to Vietnam veteran Jan C. Scruggs, a founding member and president/director of the Vietnam Veterans Memorial Fund, Inc., a nonprofit, charitable organization which is gathering contributions for the building of the memorial.

As enacted, S.J. Res. 119 is Public Law 96–297, approved July 1.

Implementation of the International Sugar Agreement

Executive Order 12224.   July 1, 1980

By the authority vested in me as President of the United States of America by an Act providing for the Implementation of the International Sugar Agreement, 1977, and for Other Purposes (P.L. 96–236; 94 Stat. 336) and Section 301 of Title 3 of the United States Code, it is hereby ordered as follows:

1–101. The functions vested in the President by Public Law 96–236 (94 Stat. 336) are delegated to the United States Trade Representative.

1–102. In carrying out the functions delegated to him, the United States Trade Representative shall consult with the Secretary of Agriculture and the Secretary of State. The United States Trade Representative may, with the consent of the head of another Executive agency, redelegate some or all of those functions to the head of such agency.

1–103. This Order is effective July 1, 1980.

JIMMY CARTER

The White House,
    July 1, 1980.

[Filed with the Office of the Federal Register,
    11:22 a.m., July 1, 1980]

Sugar, Sirup, and Molasses Imports

Proclamation 4770.   July 1, 1980

AMENDMENT OF PROCLAMATION No. 4663 REGARDING THE ALLOCATION OF QUOTAS ON CERTAIN SUGARS, SIRUPS, AND MOLASSES

By the President of the United States of America

A Proclamation

1. Proclamation No. 4663 of May 24, 1979, modified Headnote 3 of Subpart A, Part 10, Schedule 1 of the Tariff Schedules of the United States (TSUS) (19 U.S.C. 1202), authorizing the Secretary of State to allocate the sugar import quota among supplying countries or areas to the extent necessary to conform with the International Sugar Agreement, 1977, which the United States then was applying provisionally.

2. The United States signed the International Sugar Agreement on January 2, 1980. The International Sugar Agreement 1977, Implementation Act (P.L. 96–236; 94 Stat. 336) (the Act) enacted on April 22, 1980, authorized full implementation of United States rights and obligations under that agreement.

3. In order to carry out and enforce the International Sugar Agreement, the Act authorizes the President to limit the entry into the United States of sugar, as defined in the Agreement, which is the product of foreign countries, territories or areas not members of the International Sugar Agreement, to take other action and to issue and enforce rules and regulations necessary or appropriate to enforce U.S. rights and obligations under the Agreement. The President also is authorized to designate agencies or offices of the United States which will exercise the powers and functions conferred by the Act.

4. Reorganization Plan Number 3 of 1979, transferred to the United States Trade Representative the functions of the Secretary of State with respect to commodity agreements. Executive Order No. 12224 of July 1, 1980, delegated the powers and duties of the President to the United States Trade Representative.

5. To reflect the developments described in paragraphs 2, 3, and 4, Proclamation 4663 must be amended. The actions proclaimed below conform with the International Sugar Agreement, 1977, and give due consideration, as required by Headnote 2, of Subpart A, Part 10, Schedule 1 of the TSUS, to the interests of domestic producers of sugar in the United States and of affected contracting parties to the General Agreement on Tariffs and Trade.

Now, THEREFORE, I, JIMMY CARTER, President of the United States of America, acting under the authority vested in me by the Constitution and statutes of the United States, including the International Sugar Agreement 1977, Implementation Act (P.L. 96–236; 94 Stat. 336) and in conformity with Headnote 2 of Subpart A, Part 10, Schedule 1 of TSUS, do hereby proclaim:

(1) The first paragraph of Headnote 3 of Subpart A, Part 10, Schedule 1 of the TSUS is modified by substituting for the second and third sentences of that paragraph the following:

"The U.S. Trade Representative or his designee may allocate this quantity among supplying countries or areas, and may prescribe further rules, regulations, limitations or prohibitions on the entry of sugar in accordance with the International Sugar Agreement, 1977, and Public Law 96–236. The U.S. Trade Representative or his designee shall inform the Commissioner of Customs of any such action regarding the importation of sugar, and shall publish notice thereof in the FEDERAL REGISTER".

(2) The provisions of this proclamation are effective July 1, 1980.

IN WITNESS WHEREOF, I have hereunto set my hand this first day of July in the year of our Lord nineteen hundred and eighty, and of the Independence of the United States of America the two hundred and fourth.

JIMMY CARTER

[Filed with the Office of the Federal Register, 11:23 a.m., July 1, 1980]

Federal Juvenile Delinquency Programs

Message to the Congress Transmitting a Report.   July 1, 1980

To the Congress of the United States:

I have reviewed the report entitled "The Fourth Analysis and Evaluation of Federal Juvenile Delinquency Programs" submitted to me and the Congress by the Office of Juvenile Justice and Delinquency Prevention, the Law Enforcement Assistance Administration, Department of Justice.

I concur with the recommendations in the report that I: (1) assure that the statutory members of the Coordinating Council on Juvenile Justice and Delinquency Prevention designate individuals to attend Council meetings who have significant decision-making authority; (2) encourage each Federal agency which administers a Federal Juvenile Delinquency program to cooperate with the Coordinating Council and the Office of Juvenile Justice and Delinquency Prevention in the Development of the Annual Analysis and Evaluation of Federal juvenile delinquency programs; (3) encourage statutory members of the Coordinating Council to provide adequate staff support for the Council; and (4) reaffirm the importance of a concentration of Federal effort for all Federal juvenile delinquency programs and activities.

I am deeply committed to the goals and objectives of the Juvenile Justice and Delinquency Prevention Act and strongly support its reauthorization. To fully realize their potential, it is crucial that there be a maximum coordination between all Federal programs directed at troubled youth. In this time of budget austerity, it becomes even more critical that the Federal government maximize the potential of its scarce resources.

The Coordinating Council on Juvenile Justice and Delinquency Prevention has made much progress in having agencies work together. Joint programs are underway with the Office of Juvenile Justice, Department of Labor, Department of Housing and Urban Development, Department of Education, Department of Health and Human Services and the Department of Agriculture. I applaud this kind of cooperation and strongly urge that it be continued and broadened.

I have asked the Director of the Office of Management and Budget, acting on my behalf, to take all necessary steps to implement fully the first three recommendations.

This report is submitted pursuant to Section 204(c) of the Juvenile Justice and Delinquency Prevention Act of 1974, as amended (42 U.S.C. 5614(c)).

JIMMY CARTER

The White House,
   July 1, 1980.

Registration Under the Military Selective Service Act

Remarks on Signing Proclamation 4771.
July 2, 1980

Congresswoman Holt asked me how I knew all the names. I know a lot more about you all than you think I do. [*Laughter*] This morning I'll be signing a proclamation to implement the terms of the registration act that the Congress recently passed. I would like to say at the beginning that this is a very wise decision that the Congress has made. And I would like to emphasize that the registration act—which has now been passed and will go into effect—is not to threaten war, but is to preserve peace.

The action taken by our country and almost all other nations in the democratic world is designed to preserve peace. We are deeply concerned about the unwarranted and vicious invasion of Afghanistan by the Soviet Union and occupation by them of this innocent and defenseless country, which is completely unwarranted.

We have taken a series of steps—economic, diplomatic, political, military steps—in order to convince the Soviet

Union that their action is ill advised and, of course, encouraging them to withdraw their troops from Afghanistan and also to prevent further aggression if they should be tempted to do so. All of the action we have taken is peaceful in nature, and we will stay committed to a peaceful resolution of disputes.

The freedom-fighters in Afghanistan, who are striving for the liberation of their country, deserve the admiration of the entire world, and their courage and persistence in fighting for freedom is the greatest single deterrent to the Soviet aggression being successful.

I would like to emphasize that the registration act is not a draft; I am not in favor of a peacetime draft. This registration act will do a great deal to marshal our own Nation's resistance to succumbing to temptation which might lead to war, and therefore lead to a mandatory draft. The only time that I envision a mandatory draft law being advocated to the Congress would be in time of war or in time of national emergency, and in a case of that kind, when our Nation's security is threatened, separate legal action would be required by Congress, a separate law, to initiate a draft under those circumstances.

I might say that we will continue to rely on voluntary enlistment by the military forces to defend our country. As a matter of fact, in the 1981 budget and through legislation initiated by some of the Members of Congress behind me, and by us, we will add approximately $1 billion to the military budget, to encourage additional enlistment of highly qualified young men and women, and also to make retention of those highly trained military personnel more effective.

In closing, let me say that following the signing of this proclamation, young men who were born in 1960 and in 1961 will be required to register at the post offices in their local communities. This will not mean that they are being drafted. It means that we are expediting the process by which, if our Nation enters a time of emergency or a threat to our national security or a time of war in the future, the marshaling of our defense mechanisms can be expedited. It's a precautionary measure; it's designed to make our country strong and to maintain peace.

I would like to ask the support of all Americans for this move: Americans in the age that will be registered and Americans of all ages who believe in a strong country, who believe in patriotism, who believe in maintaining peace through strength.

At this time I'd like to sign the proclamation that will implement the registration act.

[*At this point, the President signed the proclamation.*]

And I'd like to express my thanks to the Members of Congress who have wisely and courageously passed this law. Thank you very much.

NOTE: The President spoke at 9:33 a.m. in the Cabinet Room at the White House.

Registration Under the Military Selective Service Act

Proclamation 4771. July 2, 1980

By the President of the United States of America

A Proclamation

Section 3 of the Military Selective Service Act, as amended (50 U.S.C. App. 453), provides that male citizens of the United States and other male persons residing in the United States who are be-

tween the ages of 18 and 26, except those exempted by Sections 3 and 6(a) of the Military Selective Service Act, must present themselves for registration at such time or times and place or places, and in such manner as determined by the President. Section 6(k) provides that such exceptions shall not continue after the cause for the exemption ceases to exist.

The Congress of the United States has made available the funds (H.J. Res. 521, approved by me on June 27, 1980), which are needed to initiate this registration, beginning with those born on or after January 1, 1960.

Now, THEREFORE, I, JIMMY CARTER, President of the United States of America, by the authority vested in me by the Military Selective Service Act, as amended (50 U.S.C. App. 451 *et seq.*), do hereby proclaim as follows:

1–1. *Persons to be Registered and Days of Registration.*

1–101. Male citizens of the United States and other males residing in the United States, unless exempted by the Military Selective Service Act, as amended, who were born on or after January 1, 1960, and who have attained their eighteenth birthday, shall present themselves for registration in the manner and at the time and places as hereinafter provided.

1–102. Persons born in calendar year 1960 shall present themselves for registration on any of the six days beginning Monday, July 21, 1980.

1–103. Persons born in calendar year 1961 shall present themselves for registration on any of the six days beginning Monday, July 28, 1980.

1–104. Persons born in calendar year 1962 shall present themselves for registration on any of the six days beginning Monday, January 5, 1981.

1–105. Persons born on or after January 1, 1963, shall present themselves for registration on the day they attain the 18th anniversary of their birth or on any day within the period of 60 days beginning 30 days before such date; however, in no event shall such persons present themselves for registration prior to January 5, 1981.

1–106. Aliens who would be required to present themselves for registration pursuant to Sections 1–101 to 1–105, but who are in processing centers on the dates fixed for registration, shall present themselves for registration within 30 days after their release from such centers.

1–107. Aliens and noncitizen nationals of the United States who reside in the United States, but who are absent from the United States on the days fixed for their registration, shall present themselves for registration within 30 days after their return to the United States.

1–108. Aliens and noncitizen nationals of the United States who, on or after July 1, 1980, come into and reside in the United States shall present themselves for registration in accordance with Sections 1–101 to 1–105 or within 30 days after coming into the United States, whichever is later.

1–109. Persons who would have been required to present themselves for registration pursuant to Sections 1–101 to 1–108 but for an exemption pursuant to Section 3 or 6(a) of the Military Selective Service Act, as amended, or but for some condition beyond their control such as hospitalization or incarceration, shall present themselves for registration within 30 days after the cause for their exempt status ceases to exist or within 30 days after the termination of the condition which was beyond their control.

1–2. *Places and Times for Registration.*

1–201. Persons who are required to be registered and who are in the United States on any day fixed herein for their registration, shall present themselves for registration before a duly designated employee in any classified United States Post Office.

1–202. Citizens of the United States who are required to be registered and who are not in the United States on any of the days set aside for their registration, shall present themselves at a United States Embassy or Consulate for registration before a diplomatic or consular officer of the United States or before a registrar duly appointed by a diplomatic or consular officer of the United States.

1–203. The hours for registration in United States Post Offices shall be the business hours during the days of operation of the particular United States Post Office. The hours for registration in United States Embassies and Consulates shall be those prescribed by the United States Embassies and Consulates.

1–3. *Manner of Registration.*

1–301. Persons who are required to be registered shall comply with the registration procedures and other rules and regulations prescribed by the Director of Selective Service.

1–302. When reporting for registration each person shall present for inspection reasonable evidence of his identity. After registration, each person shall keep the Selective Service System informed of his current address.

Having proclaimed these requirements for registration, I urge everyone, including employers in the private and public sectors, to cooperate with and assist those persons who are required to be registered in order to ensure a timely and complete registration. Also, I direct the heads of Executive agencies, when requested by the Director of Selective Service and to the extent permitted by law, to cooperate and assist in carrying out the purposes of this Proclamation.

IN WITNESS WHEREOF, I have hereunto set my hand this second day of July in the year of our Lord nineteen hundred and eighty, and of the Independence of the United States of America the two hundred and fourth.

JIMMY CARTER

[Filed with the Office of the Federal Register, 11:44 a.m., July 2, 1980]

National Porcelain Art Month

Proclamation 4772. July 2, 1980

By the President of the United States of America

A Proclamation

The art of painting on porcelain has been recognized as a fine art by all the world's great civilizations and has enriched museums in many countries for hundreds of years.

This art form, requiring great skill, training, and talent, has been enthusiastically adopted and enhanced by thousands of talented Americans whose labors will awe and delight generations yet to come.

The Congress, by Senate Joint Resolution 115, has requested the President to proclaim the month of July 1980 as National Porcelain Art Month.

Now, THEREFORE, I, JIMMY CARTER, President of the United States of America, do hereby proclaim the month of July 1980 as National Porcelain Art Month, and I call upon the people of the United States to observe the month with appropriate ceremonies and activities.

IN WITNESS WHEREOF, I have hereunto set my hand this second day of July in the year of our Lord nineteen hundred and eighty, and of the Independence of the United States of America the two hundred and fourth.

JIMMY CARTER

[Filed with the Office of the Federal Register, 11:45 a.m., July 2, 1980]

Energy-Expo '82

Nomination of Charles E. Fraser To Be Commissioner General of the U.S. Government. July 2, 1980

The President today announced that he will nominate Charles E. Fraser, of Hilton Head Island, S.C., to be Commissioner General of the United States Government for Energy-Expo 1982.

Fraser, 51, is chairman and founder of Sea Pines Co. and chairman of Hilton Head Management Services. He is a trustee of the Southern Center for International Studies and has previously served as chairman of the board of trustees of the National Recreation and Park Association and as a member of the South Carolina Parks, Recreation, and Tourism Commission.

Small Business Administration Authorization Bill

Remarks on Signing S. 2698 Into Law. July 2, 1980

THE PRESIDENT. I'm very pleased to be here with this group of distinguished Members of the House and Senate and also interested Americans who want to see a strong small business community in our country and recognize it as a bulwark of our free enterprise system and also the economic progress that we expect to have now and in the future.

The small business development act of 1980 has been finally passed as a result of a year, almost 2 years of negotiations and consultation. I think it makes a major step toward resolving some of the problems that have existed in the past.

It restructures the aid program for farms and for small businesses who suffer disasters, and it concentrates primarily the responsibility for this action in the Farm Home Administration for farmers. In addition, the legislation will reduce delays in the approval of assistance for farmers and for small business people when they suffer a disaster and, in addition to that, will simplify the paperwork in the application forms for small business loans.

There is a provision here which would authorize the Small Business Administration to guarantee the financing of business enterprises through the issuing of bonds by local and State governments.

And finally, I'd like to say that this legislation is completely in accordance with the recommendations made by the White House Conference on Small Business that convened early this year through the leadership of those who are assembled here behind me.

It's with a great deal of pleasure now that I sign Senate bill 2698, the small business development act of 1980, with my thanks to the Members of Congress and all who are responsible for this major step forward in strengthening agriculture and small business in our great country.

[*At this point, the President signed the bill.*]

A lot of people are responsible for this progress, but I'd like to call on two who have been most instrumental in it; representing the House and the Senate, Gaylord Nelson and then Congressman Neal Smith. Gaylord, would you say just a word?

Senator Nelson. Well, Mr. President, this culminates, as you said, 2 years of efforts. We passed this measure five times in the United States Senate. We finally negotiated the appropriate compromises with the House and with your representatives.

It does contain four recommendations of the White House Conference, which you called—the most important conference involving independent enterprise in this country, I think, in history. I think it's a great accomplishment. And the Small Business Development Centers will be a very useful consulting, advising instrumentality for small businesses all around the country. My State now has outlets on 11 campuses; it's working very well.

I want to congratulate you and your staff and all those who participated in making this a success.

The President. Thank you. I might point out that Gaylord Nelson and Neal Smith are two very tough negotiators—[*laughter*]—and also, I might say, successful ones.

Neal, would you say a word, please?

Representative Smith. Well, thank you, Mr. President.

I want to say, first of all, as you have indicated, it's a very extensive and comprehensive bill. It could have been broken into about 40 bills; perhaps that's the reason it took so long. It also covers more than $30 billion in loans and guarantees.

But more important than that, I think, is something that you said. You indicated that it is an indication that we're going to have a partnership between government and small business. And in a number of ways, this can be done. We have a number of other bills out of committee that we hope will be down here before we adjourn this year, the innovation bill, access to justice, attorneys' fees bill, a couple of other bills. And we just hope that this hour in the Cabinet Room will lead to a day in the sun for small business.

THE PRESIDENT. Well, thank you very much.

Dee, would you like to say a word?

SENATOR HUDDLESTON. Well, Mr. President, I've been very pleased to have been part of this process. And it has been a long process, and I think we've accomplished a great deal. I was particularly interested in the aspects of the bill dealing with disaster loans, and I think we've made a substantial improvement there both for the farmers and for the small business people in the country. And I appreciate the work that Congressman Neal Smith and our chairman on the Senate side, Gaylord Nelson, put into this effort, and also your staff. We've had a number of meetings negotiating out the final details of the bill, and I think we have a product that we can all be proud of.

THE PRESIDENT. I would like to say that the House and Senate are both in session now. It would not be well to pass this opportunity to point out that Tom Foley and Senator Talmadge, representing the agriculture committees as chairmen in both Houses, played a crucial role in this legislation, as did Sam Nunn and others. On occasion I would ask them to come down to the Cabinet Room or the White House Oval Office to meet with me to try to iron out differences that did exist and the perspectives from small businesses, from agriculture, from the departments involved. And their help, along with Neal Smith, Gaylord Nelson, and

Dee Huddleston and others, has been crucial.

And again, let me thank all of those who are not in the Congress or in the administration who, through their own leadership and intense interest, made this final product possible. Now the Small Business Administration can take over and do its job, and the Farm Home Administration will do the same.

Thank you all very much for making this a good day.

NOTE: The President spoke at 2:06 p.m. in the Cabinet Room at the White House.

As enacted, S. 2698 is Public Law 96–302, approved July 2.

Citizenship Day and Constitution Week, 1980

Proclamation 4773. July 2, 1980

By the President of the United States of America

A Proclamation

On September 17, 1980 the Constitution of the United States will be 193 years old. Yet, it is as forceful and dynamic today as on that day in 1787 when it was signed by our Forefathers. Not only has this hallowed document endured, it has grown stronger in the nearly two centuries since its adoption and continues to increase in vitality with each succeeding generation. Today, as ever, it stands as a beacon for those dedicated to the principles of government by and for the people.

By joint resolution of February 29, 1952 (36 U.S.C. 153), the Congress designated September 17 as Citizenship Day, in commemoration of the formation and signing of the Constitution and in recognition of all who have attained the status of citizenship. The resolution authorized the President to issue annually a proclamation calling upon officials of the Government to display the flag on all Government buildings on that day. By a joint resolution of August 2, 1956 (36 U.S.C. 159), Congress authorized the President to designate the period beginning September 17 and ending September 23 of each year as Constitution Week and to issue a proclamation calling for observance of that week.

Now, THEREFORE, I, JIMMY CARTER, President of the United States of America, call upon appropriate Government officials to display the flag of the United States on all Government buildings on Citizenship Day, September 17, 1980. I urge Federal, State and local officials, as well as leaders of civic, educational and religious organizations to conduct meaningful ceremonies and programs on that day.

I also designate as Constitution Week the period beginning September 17 and ending September 23, 1980, and urge all Americans to observe that week with meaningful ceremonies and activities in their schools, churches and in other suitable places in order to foster a better understanding of the Constitution, and of the rights and duties of United States citizens.

IN WITNESS WHEREOF, I have hereunto set my hand this second day of July, in the year of our Lord nineteen hundred and eighty, and of the Independence of the United States of America the two hundred and fourth.

JIMMY CARTER

[Filed with the Office of the Federal Register, 4:47 p.m., July 2, 1980]

Public Works Contracts for Minority Businesses
White House Statement on a Supreme Court Decision. July 2, 1980

The President strongly applauds the Supreme Court's decision upholding the constitutionality of the minority business set-aside provision in the 1977 Local Public Works Act. The Court's decision substantially strengthens Federal efforts to increase participation of minorities in our Nation's free enterprise system. Moreover, the Court's decision once again approves the use of affirmative action as a proper tool to remedy past acts of discrimination.

The set-aside provision in question required that 10 percent of the contracts let under the $4 billion Local Public Works Act of 1977 be made with minority business firms. When the set-aside was first proposed by U.S. Representative Parren Mitchell, D-Md., critics doubted whether minority businesses had the capacity to handle the $400 million in public works contracts involved in implementing this provision. Congressman Mitchell, this administration, and other supporters of minority business knew that such a goal could and would be met.

Department of Commerce records show that the 10-percent goal has been met and exceeded. Indeed, over 15 percent of the contracts entered into thus far, more than $600 million, have been with minority-run firms. The records further indicate that these contracts have all been or will be successfully completed.

The Court's decision firmly establishes that Government efforts to assist minority businesses in obtaining economic equality are on solid constitutional ground. This administration will proceed vigorously with its set-aside program as well as other efforts to support minority business.

This administration will continue to work to increase minority participation in Federal procurement at the prime and subcontract levels, strengthen minority banks, and increase minority ownership of broadcast properties. With the assistance of advocates like Congressman Mitchell, Joe Addabbo, the National Business League, NAACP, and other leaders in this fight, we will continue to increase the Federal role in assisting minority businesses become more productive.

This administration will also work aggressively with organizations like the Business Roundtable, the Chamber of Commerce, Minority Purchasing Council, and others to see that the private sector does its share toward making the promise and potential of the free enterprise system a reality for all Americans, regardless of race, color, sex, or national origin. Such efforts increase competition and productivity, help produce stronger and more viable businesses, create more employment opportunities for our people, and help improve the quality of our lives.

United States-Indonesia Agreement on Nuclear Energy

Message to the Congress Transmitting the Proposed Agreement. July 2, 1980

To the Congress of the United States:

I am pleased to transmit to the Congress, pursuant to Section 123 d of the Atomic Energy Act of 1954, as amended (42 U.S.C. 2153(d)), the text of the proposed Agreement for Cooperation between the Government of the United States of America and the Government of the Republic of Indonesia Concerning Peaceful Uses of Nuclear Energy with accompanying agreed minute; my written approval, authorization and determination concerning the agreement; and the memorandum of the Director of the United States Arms Control and Disarmament Agency with the Nuclear Proliferation Assessment Statement concerning the agreement. The joint memorandum submitted to me by the Secretaries of State and Energy, which includes a summary analysis of the provisions of the agreement, and the views of the Members of the Nuclear Regulatory Commission and the Director of the United States Arms Control and Disarmament Agency are also enclosed.

The Nuclear Non-Proliferation Act of 1978, which I signed into law on March 10, 1978, calls upon me to renegotiate existing peaceful nuclear cooperation agreements in order to obtain the new provisions set forth in that Act. In my judgment, the proposed agreement for cooperation between the United States and Indonesia, together with its agreed minute, meets all statutory requirements.

I am particularly pleased to note in this connection that Indonesia deposited its instrument of accession to the Treaty on the Non-Proliferation of Nuclear Weapons on July 12, 1979, thereby becoming the 109th Party to that landmark treaty and cornerstone of international non-proliferation efforts. This action reflected Indonesia's commitment to international non-proliferation efforts, and marks a notable step toward the ultimate goal of universal acceptance of the objectives of the NPT.

The proposed bilateral agreement between us reflects the desire of the Government of the United States and the Government of Indonesia to update the framework for peaceful nuclear cooperation between our two countries in a manner that recognizes both the shared non-proliferation objectives and the close relationship between the United States and Indonesia. The proposed agreement will, in my view, further the non-proliferation and other foreign policy interests of the United States.

I have considered the views and recommendations of the interested agencies in reviewing the proposed agreement and have determined that its performance will promote, and will not constitute an unreasonable risk to, the common defense and security. Accordingly, I have approved the agreement and authorized its execution, and urge that the Congress give it favorable consideration.

JIMMY CARTER

The White House,
July 2, 1980.

National P.O.W.-M.I.A. Recognition Day, 1980

Proclamation 4774. July 2, 1980

By the President of the United States of America

A Proclamation

In each of America's wars our prisoners of war have been called upon to make uncommon sacrifices. Upon them has fallen the arduous responsibility of defending American ideals under the absolute control of the enemy. Extremely difficult at best, this responsibility becomes magnified almost beyond comprehension when men and women are treated inhumanely—in violation of ordinary human compassion, fundamental moral standards, and basic international obligations.

The Congress has by Joint Resolution designated July 18, 1980 as "National P.O.W.-M.I.A. Recognition Day."

All Americans should recognize the special debt we owe our fellow citizens who, as prisoners during wartime, sacrificed their freedom that we might enjoy the blessings of peace and liberty. Likewise, we must remember the unresolved casualties of war—our soldiers who are still missing. The pain and bitterness of war endures for their families, relatives, and friends.

Our Nation will continue to seek answers to the many questions that remain about their fate.

Now, THEREFORE, I, JIMMY CARTER, President of the United States of America, do hereby designate Friday, July 18, 1980, as National P.O.W.-M.I.A. Recognition Day, a day dedicated to all former American prisoners of war, to those still missing, and to their families. I call on all Americans to join in honoring those who made the uncommon sacrifice of being held captive in war, and their loved ones.

And I call on State and local officials and private organizations to observe this day with appropriate ceremonies and activities.

IN WITNESS WHEREOF, I have hereunto set my hand this second day of July in the year of our Lord nineteen hundred and eighty, and of the Independence of the United States of America the two hundred and fourth.

JIMMY CARTER

[Filed with the Office of the Federal Register, 11:41 a.m., July 3, 1980]

Credit Control Revocation

Announcement of Actions by the President and the Federal Reserve System. July 3, 1980

The Federal Reserve acted today to remove the special restraints on credit initiated last March as part of the President's anti-inflation program. President Carter is heartened by the success of the selective credit restraints in rapidly bringing about conditions in financial markets helping to reduce inflationary pressures and lower interest rates.

Speculative activities in financial and commodity markets have moderated substantially, signaling an easing of credit demands and a reversal of inflationary expectations. Business use of credit has declined. Households generally have cut back on credit-financed spending and increased the proportion of their income going into savings. Interest rates have fallen dramatically, thus sharply reducing costs of credit for productive investment. These shifts in financial trends have occurred in an environment of continued moderation in growth of the money stock that is essential to the longrun task of restraining inflation.

The President is today removing the authority granted the Federal Reserve last March under the Credit Control Act, except for the continued authorization necessary for an orderly termination of the program.

The action of the Federal Reserve to remove the selective constraints on consumer credit has been made possible precisely because those controls have accomplished their purpose. Consumer and other forms of credit are no longer being used excessively.

The removal of the controls, however, should not be taken as a signal for the resumption of a profligate use of credit by consumers or by business. The President retains his authority under the Credit Control Act of 1969. The administration will monitor credit developments carefully, and should an excessive use of credit reemerge under circumstances

which again call for the use of that authority, the President is prepared to invoke it.

Credit Control Revocation
Executive Order 12225. July 3, 1980

By the authority vested in me as President of the United States of America by Sections 205 and 206 of the Credit Control Act (12 U.S.C. 1904, 1905), and for the purpose of phasing-out in an orderly fashion the credit controls authorized by Executive Order No. 12201, it is hereby ordered as follows:

1–101. Section 1–101 of Executive Order No. 12201 is amended effective July 28, 1980, to read as follows:

"The Board of Governors of the Federal Reserve System is authorized to exercise authority under the Credit Control Act (12 U.S.C. 1901 *et seq.*) to establish uniform requirements for changes in terms in open-end credit accounts for consumer credit; provided however, such authorization is revoked as of October 31, 1980.".

1–102. The authorizations granted by Section 1–102 of Executive Order No. 12201 is revoked as of August 11, 1980.

1–103. The authorization granted by Sections 1–103 and 1–104 of Executive Order No. 12201 are revoked as of July 28, 1980.

1–104. Section 1–105 of Executive Order No. 12201 shall be amended, effective July 28, 1980, to read as follows:

"For purposes of this Order 'consumer credit' and 'open-end credit' shall have such meaning as may be reasonably prescribed by the regulations of the Board of Governors of the Federal Reserve System.".

1–105. Section 1–106 of Executive Order No. 12201 is revoked.

JIMMY CARTER

The White House,
July 3, 1980.

[Filed with the Office of the Federal Register, 11:42 a.m., July 3, 1980]

Deep Seabed Hard Mineral Resources Act

White House Statement on H.R. 2759. July 3, 1980

The Deep Seabed Hard Mineral Resources Act, signed by the President on June 28, 1980, reaffirms this Nation's commitment to both a law of the sea treaty and orderly development of a United States ocean mining capability. Our Nation needs assured access to the nickel, copper, cobalt, and manganese—metals important in steelmaking, high performance alloys, and many other industrial uses—found in seabed nodules. This legislation will further these domestic and international aims. The act establishes an interim regulatory procedure for ocean mining activities conducted by U.S. nationals that will be superseded when a law of the sea treaty enters into force for the United States.

Since 1974 many nations have been working through the U.N. Conference on the Law of the Sea to design rules governing the entire range of uses of the oceans. Arrangements for mining deep ocean minerals have constituted the greatest challenge to the Conference. Both developed and developing nations see the opportunities for exploring new avenues of international cooperation and decision-making. The International Seabed Authority being considered could become the

first international organization with authority to manage a major natural resource.

The United States Government has been working with other nations at the Conference to fashion a treaty acceptable to the world community and serving the best interests of the United States. We hope that substantive negotiations on the treaty can be concluded this year.

The Deep Seabed Hard Mineral Resources Act will serve as a steppingstone to this broader, long-term international goal. It will fill the gap created by the pace of technological development and our need for minerals on the one hand and the slow, deliberate process of international lawmaking on the other. Without the national ocean mining legislation that we are enacting, the deep seabed provisions of the law of the sea treaty would be hollow, since private industry would not be able to deliver benefits to this Nation and the world for many years.

In enacting this legislation, the Congress displayed the bipartisan cooperation necessary to strike a judicious balance between American domestic and international interests. This legislation has been continuously revised and improved since its original introduction in 1971. During the past 18 months, it was considered and reported by four House and six Senate committees and numerous subcommittees and was unanimously passed by both Houses. The Chairmen and members of those various committees and subcommittees deserve praise for their patient leadership in shepherding this complex legislation to its final enactment. The cooperation and support of the mining industry and labor unions were instrumental in reaching this valuable result.

This act will serve three purposes. First, it will ensure that when a law of the sea treaty is implemented, there will, in fact, be a viable ocean mining industry. Second, it will subject ocean mining operations conducted in the interim to stringent domestic regulation to ensure protection of the marine environment, safety of life and property at sea, prevention of unreasonable interference with other uses of the high seas, and conservation of mineral resources. Third, it will encourage nations that embark on ocean mining ventures before the treaty is in force to manage the activities of their nationals in a similar fashion and to respect licenses and permits issued under this and other national legislation.

Moreover, the act is drafted to be compatible with the work of the Law of the Sea Conference. It recognizes that the resources of the seabed are common heritage of mankind. It requires that revenues from commercial production be set aside for developing countries. No sovereign jurisdiction is asserted over areas of the international seabed. No license will be issued for exploration to be conducted before July 1, 1981, and more importantly, no permit for commercial recovery will be effective sooner than January 1, 1988.

Under this timetable, the Law of the Sea Conference will have ample time to complete its work and to prepare for implementation of the treaty before commercial recovery under American law would actually take place. At the same time, potential ocean miners are assured that they may continue the orderly progress of their work without fear that delays in the international process will cause unanticipated and costly interruptions in their development programs.

The act authorizes reciprocal agreements with any foreign nation that regulates the conduct of its citizens in a manner compatible with this legislation, recognizes the licenses, permits, and priorities of right granted under it, and provides an interim framework for ocean mining that respects other nations' freedom of the high seas. Responsible cooperation among the early ocean mining nations can set the stage for successful implementation of a law of the sea treaty.

Ocean mining holds great promise for meeting the strategic mineral needs of this Nation. With the Deep Seabed Hard Mineral Resources Act, we can look forward to an era in which ocean resources benefit all mankind and the institutions overseeing these resources set a new standard for international cooperation.

NOTE: As enacted, H.R. 2759 is Public Law 96–283, approved June 28.

United States-Israel Convention on Income Taxes

Message to the Senate Transmitting a Protocol Amending the Convention. July 3, 1980

To the Senate of the United States:

I transmit herewith, for Senate advice and consent to ratification, a Protocol Amending the Convention between the Government of the United States of America and the Government of Israel with Respect to Taxes on Income, signed at Washington on November 20, 1975. The Protocol was signed at Washington on May 30, 1980. I also transmit three related exchanges of notes and the report of the Department of State with respect to the Protocol.

Consideration of the Convention by the Senate has been delayed pending the correction of certain technical problems in its text. The Protocol accomplishes this by making certain amendments to the Convention. For example, Article 10 (Grants) is modified to conform more closely to United States and Israeli law with regard to the treatment of Israeli grants to United States investors.

The Protocol also modifies the withholding rates applicable to dividends paid by a subsidiary to a parent corporation and adds a new article dealing with charitable contributions.

It is most desirable that this Protocol, together with the Convention, be considered by the Senate as soon as possible and that the Senate give advice and consent to ratification of both instruments.

JIMMY CARTER

The White House,
    July 3, 1980.

United States Participation in the United Nations

Message to the Congress Transmitting a Report.   July 3, 1980

To the Congress of the United States:

I am pleased to transmit to the Congress this report of the activities of the United States Government in the United Nations and its affiliated agencies during calendar year 1978.

This 33rd annual report covers the second year of my Administration, and I believe it confirms our conviction that the United Nations is of vital and growing importance to the conduct of U.S. foreign relations.

The year 1978 revealed some of the strengths of the UN system. Among the actions taken during 1978 by the United Nations that best exemplify its strength were the rapid establishment of the United Nations Interim Force in Lebanon (UNIFIL) and the development of a UN plan to ensure the early independence of Namibia through free and fair elections. The UN plan for Namibia includes the authorized establishment of a United Nations Transition Assistance Group (UNTAG) to assist the Secretary General's Special Representative for Nambia. Formation of UNTAG still awaits final agreement on the implementation of a Namibia settlement.

The establishment of UNIFIL was particularly important for the development of the UN's peacekeeping operations. UNIFIL is a test of the UN's ability to gain the cooperation of the parties concerned because, unlike other peacekeeping operations, it operates without a precise agreement between opposing parties. In an area where there has been little or no exercise of legitimate civil authority, the Force is attempting to maintain peace within the territory of a sovereign country where there are indigenous, rebellious armed groups supported from outside. The technique of peacekeeping is among the most innovative activities of the United Nations, and one of the most successful.

The year 1978 also witnessed small but growing third world interest in UN human rights initiatives, and the Special Session on Disarmament, which set forth goals and priorities for disarmament negotiations. The United Nations also began to become closely involved in efforts to alleviate the human tragedy in Kampuchea.

The continuing difficulties of the United Nations in dealing with general economic issues were demonstrated by the year-long impasse over the mandate of the Committee of the Whole. In contrast, the decision to convene a Conference on New and Renewable Sources of Energy, which we strongly support, and the reconvening of the negotiating conference on the Common Fund for Commodities, which has since made substantial progress, are solid evidence of the UN's growing ability to deal effectively with specific international economic problems.

The United States remains deeply concerned about the budgetary growth in the UN system, and in 1978 voted against the UN budget for the first time because it failed to exercise the necessary financial restraint. We are continuing to monitor closely UN expenditures, programs, and personnel practices.

It is my hope that this report will contribute to knowledge of and support for the UN as an institution, and to continued active and constructive U.S. participation.

JIMMY CARTER

The White House,
July 3, 1980.

NOTE: The 309-page report is entitled "United States Participation in the UN—Report by the President to the Congress for the Year 1978."

National Science Foundation

Message to the Congress Transmitting a Report. July 3, 1980

To the Congress of the United States:

I have, on many occasions, stressed my belief that our Nation's future—in particular its economic health—is tied to the vitality and advances of science and technology. For that reason I am pleased to transmit this annual report for Fiscal Year 1979 of the National Science Foundation. The National Science Foundation's primary responsibility—unique among Federal agencies—is to assure that we continue to generate broad scientific knowledge and to draw on the collective expertise of the scientific community to identify the most important problems and best opportunities for Federal support.

As this annual report shows, National Science Foundation-supported research continues to produce promising and far-reaching results. If we look at a variety of developments important to today's world—such as advances in agriculture, medical science, communications, alternative energy supplies and conservation, computers, or industrial processes—we can trace threads back through the years to the basic research, often supported by the National Science Foundation, that made them possible. Likewise, we can be assured that many of the results being reported now will, eventually, similarly enhance our daily lives and well-being.

Our success in continuing this process of nurturing and speeding the generation of knowledge is not an intellectual luxury but is critical to our future. At a time of increasing constraints on the availability of material resources throughout the world, our national research capability is a particularly valuable resource to enable us to devise innovative approaches to difficult problems. The National Science Foundation is important to the development and maintenance of that resource, and I hope you will take the opportunity to review its recent activities described in this report.

JIMMY CARTER

The White House,
July 3, 1980.

NOTE: The report is entitled "National Science Foundation—Twenty-Ninth Annual Report for Fiscal Year 1979" (Government Printing Office, 138 pages).

Windfall Profits Tax Revenues

Letter to the Speaker of the House and the President of the Senate Transmitting an Allocation Proposal. July 3, 1980

Dear Mr. Speaker: (Dear Mr. President:)

Pursuant to Section 102(d) of the Crude Oil Windfall Profit Tax Act of

1980, I am submitting this proposal for an allocation of the net revenues expected from the Act during fiscal year 1981.

The allocation which I propose is, of course, consistent with my recommendations on the budget for 1981. It also reflects congressional action on the 1981 budget.

As I stated when I signed the Act into law, expenditure of the funds raised by the windfall profit tax requires specific authorization and appropriation by the Congress through the normal legislative process. This provides both the Administration and the Congress with the flexibility needed from year to year to determine how these funds will be used in the best interests of the country.

At present our highest priorities are fighting inflation and disciplining public spending. In meeting these goals, spending for low income assistance, for transportation, and for energy objectives must continue. Although enactment of tax reductions for 1981 may be appropriate in the next Congress, it is impossible at this time to allocate funds between tax reductions and deficit reductions. The enclosed allocation shows these two purposes combined.

Sincerely,

JIMMY CARTER

NOTE: This is the text of identical letters addressed to Thomas P. O'Neill, Jr., Speaker of the House of Representatives, and Walter F. Mondale, President of the Senate. Both letters included the enclosure printed below.

ALLOCATION OF WINDFALL PROFIT TAX REVENUES FOR FY 1981

[In millions of dollars]

	Sec. 102 Formula [1]	President's Budget
Total net revenues available _____	16,242	16,242
Proposed disposition		
Low income assistance _____	4,294	4,294 [2]
Energy and transportation programs __	2,015	2,015 [3]
Income tax reductions _____	9,933 ⎫	9,933 [4]
Deficit reduction _____	0 ⎭	
TOTAL _____	16,242	16,242

[1] Derived from basic net revenues except as follows. $2,806 million of additional net revenues are included in total net revenues available. This represents the amount of revenues beyond the level assumed in the Conference Report on the Act. These additional net revenues are distributed to low income assistance ($935 million) and income tax reductions ($1,871 million).

[2] FY 1981 outlays proposed in the President's budget (revised in March 1980) are $39,536 million for the total public assistance subfunction (604).

[3] FY 1981 outlays proposed in the President's budget (revised in March 1980) are $19,689 million for all energy and transportation programs in the energy function (270) and the ground transportation subfunction (401).

[4] As noted in the Conference Report on the Act, amounts not otherwise allocated to and appropriated for the uses shown would reduce the deficit. Although enactment of tax reductions for 1981 may be appropriate in the next Congress, it is impossible at this time to allocate funds between tax reductions and deficit reductions. The allocation therefore shows these two purposes combined.

Senior Executive Service

Statement on Congressional Action on the Performance Bonus System.   *July 3, 1980*

Within the last several days, there have been serious efforts in the Congress to put severe limitations on the performance bonus system for the Senior Executive Service.

While the Congress has not approved the full implementation of the Senior Executive Service bonus system, I am pleased that we were able to develop a reasonable compromise under which up to 25 percent of Senior Executive Service members may receive full awards this year. The action of the Congress is especially important, because it reaffirms a central principle of civil service reform— that pay should be linked to performance.

The Senior Executive Service is one of the keys to improving the efficiency and effectiveness of the Federal Government. Because that effort depends in large measure on the motivation and leadership of top Federal managers, I am very appreciative of the support and assistance Senior Executive Service members have provided in making civil service reform a reality.

National Science Foundation

Nomination of John B. Slaughter To Be Director.   *July 3, 1980*

The President today announced that he will nominate John B. Slaughter, of Pullman, Wash., to be Director of the National Science Foundation (NSF). He would replace Richard C. Atkinson, resigned. Slaughter is academic vice president and provost of Washington State University and is a former assistant director of NSF.

He was born March 16, 1934, in Topeka, Kans. He received a B.S. from Kansas State University in 1956, an M.S. from the University of California at Los Angeles in 1961, and a Ph. D. in engineering science from the University of California at San Diego in 1971.

Slaughter was an engineer at Convair Division of General Dynamics Corp. from 1956 to 1960 and was physical science administrator of information systems at the Naval Electronics Laboratory Center from 1961 to 1975. From 1975 to 1977, he was director of the Applied Physics Laboratory at the University of Washington. From 1977 to 1979, he was Assistant Director of NSF for Astronomical, Atmospheric, Earth, and Ocean Sciences.

United States Ambassador to Mauritania

Nomination of Henry Precht.   *July 3, 1980*

The President today announced that he will nominate Henry Precht, of Savannah, Ga., to be Ambassador Extraordinary and Plenipotentiary of the United States to the Islamic Republic of Mauritania. He would replace E. Gregory Kryza, who is being assigned to the State Department.

Precht has been Director of Iranian Affairs at the State Department since 1978.

He was born June 15, 1932, in Savannah. He received a B.A. from Emory University in 1951 and an M.A. from Fletcher School of Law and Diplomacy in 1970. He served in the U.S. Navy from 1953 to 1957.

From 1958 to 1961, Precht was a management intern, then analyst, with the Labor Department. He joined the Foreign Service in 1962 and was posted in

Rome and Alexandria, on detail at the National Aeronautics and Space Administration, and at the State Department.

In 1969–70 Precht attended Fletcher School of Law and Diplomacy. He was Deputy Chief of Mission in Port Louis from 1970 to 1972. From 1972 to 1976, he was posted in Tehran as political officer, then counselor for political-military affairs. In 1976 and 1977, he was a political-military affairs officer at the State Department. From 1977 to 1978, he was Deputy Director of the Office of Security Assistance and Sales.

United States Ambassador to Paraguay

Nomination of Lyle Franklin Lane.
July 3, 1980

The President today announced that he will nominate Lyle Franklin Lane, of Tacoma, Wash., to be Ambassador Extraordinary and Plenipotentiary of the United States to Paraguay. He would replace Robert E. White, who has been appointed Ambassador to El Salvador.

Lane has been Ambassador to Uruguay since 1979.

He was born September 19, 1926, in Tacoma. He received a B.A. from the University of Washington in 1950 and an M.S. from George Washington University in 1969. He served in the U.S. Army from 1946 to 1947.

Lane joined the Foreign Service in 1952 and served in Guayaquil, Madrid, and at the State Department. He took advanced economic studies at the University of California at Berkeley in 1961–62. From 1962 to 1966, he was Principal Officer in Cebu.

From 1966 to 1968, Lane was detailed to the Agency for International Develop-

ment and served as political adviser, then Deputy Director for Development Planning, in Guatemala. From 1968 to 1969, he attended the Naval War College.

From 1969 to 1971, Lane was Administrative Officer at the Bureau of Inter-American Affairs at State. From 1971 to 1972, he was Deputy Director, then Acting Director, of the National Security Council Interdepartmental Group for Inter-American Affairs. From 1972 to 1973, he was Deputy Executive Director of the Office of Management at the Bureau of Inter-American Affairs.

Lane was Deputy Chief of Mission in San Jose from 1973 to 1976, and in Lima from 1976 to 1977. From 1977 to 1979, he was Principal Officer in the U.S. Interests Section in Havana.

Department of Justice

Nomination of Harry Alan Scarr To Be Director of the Bureau of Justice Statistics.
July 3, 1980

The President today announced that he will nominate Harry Alan Scarr, of Bluemont, Va., to be Director of the Bureau of Justice Statistics, a new position.

Scarr has been with th Justice Department since 1972 and is currently Administrator of the Federal Justice Research Program, Office for Improvements in the Administration of Justice.

He was born May 4, 1934, in Massilon, Ohio. He received an A.B. from the University of Michigan in 1956 and a Ph. D. from Harvard University in 1963.

From 1961 to 1963, Scarr was an assistant research sociologist with Harvard University Health Services. He was a staff fellow at the National Institute of Mental Health Laboratory of Socio-environmental Studies from 1963 to 1966. From 1966 to 1969, he was an assistant professor of sociology at the University of Pennsylvania.

From 1970 to 1972, Scarr was a research scientist with Human Sciences Research. He joined the Justice Department in 1972 as a social scientist with the National Institute of Law Enforcement and Criminal Justice, and then served as Acting Assistant Administrator of that Institute. In 1973 and 1974 he was a social scientist with the Office of Criminal Justice, and from 1974 to 1977, he was with the Office of Policy and Planning as Supervisory Social Scientist, then Assistant Director.

Farm Credit Administration

Nomination of Two Members of the Federal Farm Credit Board.   July 3, 1980

The President today announced that he will nominate two persons to be members of the Federal Farm Credit Board. They are:

RALPH RAIKES, of Ashland, Nebr., who raises corn, soybeans, and milo, and livestock. He served as director of Farm Credit Banks of Omaha for 26 years.

WILLIAM D. WAMPLER, of Dayton, Va., who raises poultry and cattle and serves as vice president of Wampler Foods, Inc.

Digest of Other White House Announcements

The following listing includes the President's public schedule and other items of general interest announced by the White House Press Office and not included elsewhere in this issue.

June 30

The President returned to the White House from Camp David, Md.

The President met at the White House with:

—Frank B. Moore, Assistant to the President for Congressional Liaison;
—Secretary of State Edmund S. Muskie.

July 1

The President met at the White House with:

—Zbigniew Brzezinski, Assistant to the President for National Security Affairs;
—the Democratic congressional leadership;
—Mr. Moore.

The President announced that $96 million will be made available to provide additional jobs this summer and fall in selected cities. The funds are expected to generate 32,000 jobs in 31 cities with very serious unemployment and poverty problems. In addition, almost $260 million of projects will be accelerated in the selected cities, providing more than 5,000 jobs more quickly. No new budget requests will be required to fund these programs.

The President transmitted to the Congress the fiscal year 1978 annual report of the Office of Alien Property, Department of Justice, and the 1979 annual report of the Federal Council on the Aging.

July 2

The President met at the White House with:

—Dr. Brzezinski;
—Mr. Moore;
—President Gaafar Mohamed Nimeiri of the Sudan;
—Foreign Minister Hans-Dietrich Genscher of the Federal Republic of Germany;

—Foreign Minister Kamal Hasan 'Ali of Egypt and Interior Minister Yosef Burg of Israel.

The President announced the appointment of Secretary of State Edmund S. Muskie as a member of the board of governors of the American Red Cross.

The President announced that he has designated S. B. Pranger, Associate Director for Agency Relations of the Office of Personnel Management, as Chairman of the Government Red Cross Blood Program for the Washington area.

The President announced the appointment of Herta Lande Seidman, Assistant Secretary of Commerce for Trade Development, as a member of the Commission on Security and Cooperation in Europe.

The President announced the appointment of William A. Borders, Jr., of Washington, D.C., as a member of the District of Columbia Judicial Nominating Commission. Borders is in private practice in Washington and is president-elect of the National Bar Association.

July 3

The President transmitted to the Congress the 1979 annual report of the Federal Prevailing Rate Advisory Committee.

The President announced the appointment of Harold Amos, of Boston, Mass., as a member of the President's Cancer Panel. Amos is a professor of bacteriology and immunology at Harvard Medical School.

The President announced the appointment of Rear Adm. Gerald J. Thompson as a member of the Committee for Purchase From the Blind and Other Severely Handicapped. Thompson is Deputy Director of the Defense Logistics Agency for Contract Administration Services.

The White House announced that the President has designated Calvin W. Carter as Vice Chairman of the Advisory Council on Historic Preservation.

The President left the White House for a trip to California and Florida, followed by a visit to Plains, Ga. Releases and announcements issued on the trip begin on page 1295.

NOMINATIONS SUBMITTED TO THE SENATE

The following list does not include promotions of members of the Uniformed Services, nominations to the Service Academies, or nominations of Foreign Service officers.

Submitted July 2, 1980

CHARLES E. FRASER, of South Carolina, to be Commissioner General of the United States Government for Energy-Expo 82 (new position).

MATT GARCIA, of Texas, to be Commissioner of Immigration and Naturalization, vice Leonel J. Castillo, resigned.

BRIAN P. JOFFRION, of Louisiana, to be United States Marshal for the Western District of Louisiana for the term of 4 years, vice Emmett G. Wyche, term expired.

Submitted July 3, 1980

JOHN BROOKS SLAUGHTER, of Washington, to be Director of the National Science Foundation for a term of 6 years, vice Richard C. Atkinson, resigned.

CHECKLIST OF WHITE HOUSE PRESS RELEASES

The following listing contains releases of the White House Press Office which are not included in this issue.

Released June 30, 1980

Advance text: remarks on signing S. 932, the Energy Security Act

Fact sheet: S. 932, the Energy Security Act

Fact sheet: energy programs and accomplishments

Released July 2, 1980

Announcement: nomination of Brian P. Joffrion to be United States Marshal for the Western District of Louisiana

Fact sheet: Small Business Administration authorization bill

ACTS APPROVED BY THE PRESIDENT

Approved June 28, 1980

H.R. 2759_____ Public Law 96–283
Deep Seabed Hard Mineral Resources Act.

S. 2460_____ Public Law 96–284
Uniformed Services Health Professionals Special Pay Act of 1980.

H.R. 6022_____ Public Law 96–285
An act to establish the Tensas River National Wildlife Refuge.

H.J. Res. 569_____ Public Law 96–286
A joint resolution to provide for a temporary increase in the public debt limit.

H.R. 5926_____ Public Law 96–287
An act to establish the Biscayne National Park, to improve the administration of the Fort Jefferson National Monument, to enlarge the Valley Forge National Historical Park, and for other purposes.

H.R. 6169_____ Public Law 96–288
An act to establish the Bogue Chitto National Wildlife Refuge.

H.R. 6614_____ Public Law 96–289
An act to authorize appropriations to carry out the national sea grant program for fiscal years 1981, 1982, and 1983, and for other purposes.

H.R. 4887_____ Public Law 96–290
An act to authorize appropriations for the San Francisco Bay National Wildlife Refuge, and for other purposes.

H.R. 4889_____ Public Law 96–291
An act to extend the authorization period for the Great Dismal Swamp National Wildlife Refuge.

H.R. 5259_____ Public Law 96–292
An act to name a certain Federal building in Santa Fe, New Mexico, the "Joseph M. Montoya Federal Building and U.S. Courthouse".

Approved June 30, 1980

H.R. 7685_____ Public Law 96–293
An act to amend title IV of the Employee Retirement Income Security Act of 1974 to postpone for one month the date on which the corporation must pay benefits under terminated multiemployer plans.

S. 932_____ Public Law 96–294
Energy Security Act.

ACTS APPROVED—Continued

Approved June 30—Continued

S. 562_____ Public Law 96–295
An act to authorize appropriations to the Nuclear Regulatory Commission in accordance with section 261 of the Atomic Energy Act of 1954, as amended, and section 305 of the Energy Reorganization Act of 1974, as amended, and for other purposes.

Approved July 1, 1980

S. 2245_____ Public Law 96–296
Motor Carrier Act of 1980.

S.J. Res. 119_____ Public Law 96–297
A joint resolution to authorize the Vietnam Veterans Memorial Fund, Inc., to establish a memorial.

H.R. 7477_____ Public Law 96–298
An act to amend the Internal Revenue Code of 1954 to provide a three-month extension of the taxes which are transferred to the Airport and Airway Trust Fund.

Approved July 2, 1980

S.J. Res. 115_____ Public Law 96–299
A joint resolution designating July 1980 as "National Porcelain Art Month".

S.J. Res. 188_____ Public Law 96–300
A joint resolution extending the reporting date of the National Commission on Air Quality.

H.R. 5751_____ Public Law 96–301
An act to more adequately protect archeological resources in southwestern Colorado.

S. 2698_____ Public Law 96–302
An act to provide authorizations for the Small Business Administration, and for other purposes.

H.R. 2475_____ Private Law 96–54
An act for the relief of Isaac David Cosson.

H.R. 3818_____ Private Law 96–55
An act for the relief of Clarence S. Lyons.

H.R. 5156_____ Private Law 96–56
An act for the relief of certain employees of the Naval Ordnance Systems Command.

Approved July 3, 1980

H.R. 5997_____ Public Law 96–303
An act to provide for the display of the Code of Ethics for Government Service.

H.R. 2148_____ Private Law 96–57
An act for the relief of Colonel (doctor) Paul A. Kelly.

Los Angeles, California

Remarks to the National Education Association. July 3, 1980

President McGuire, Vice President Freitag, Secretary/Treasurer McGarigal, Terry Herndon, my good friend ex-President John Ryor, distinguished members of the selection committee—who I think did a very good job and whom I want to thank personally:

What a tremendous crowd this is. [*Applause*] Thank you very much. I might say that it's also a very fine experience for me to be here with my good partners. It's a tribute to the strength of NEA that this is one of the few places in the whole Nation that's big enough to hold you. And I would like to bring to you the good wishes of another excellent friend of NEA. You know him well; you've heard him speak many times; you've even shown the extra exhibition of friendship by laughing at his jokes—I'm talking about one of the finest Vice Presidents this Nation has ever seen, Fritz Mondale.

I might say something that you already know, and that is that both the President and the Vice President of our great country consider that we are part of the NEA, and I'm very deeply proud to accept the "Friend of Education" award. It's remarkable that someone who has served 3½ years as President, and before that served 7 years on a local school board, could have this much support from teachers, and I deeply appreciate that as well.

I'm also proud because you represent America at its very best. The heart of our democracy, as you well know, is universal, strong, free, public education, and the heart of that system—[*applause*]—and the heart of that education system is the teacher. The simple truth is that the more complex and difficult our national issues become, the more valuable to America is an educated public.

When we began our partnership in 1977—as a matter of fact, we actually began our partnership about a year earlier—we had gone through two administrations that were hostile to the American education programs that you worked so hard over the last number of years to enact. The result of this was an actual decline, in real terms, in support of education, during 8 years of serious and growing need.

A quick look at the record will be very helpful to us. I would like to look at the facts with you. Working together, you and I have reversed that downward trend. Compared to the budget proposal which I inherited when I was inaugurated as President in 1977—and which I immediately changed—the 1981 budget will have increased Federal funds for education by 73 percent. We've had some good administrations in Washington in the past, but this is the greatest increase in any such period in the history of our Nation, and we're not through yet.

And equally important, and as you also know, we have concentrated our efforts on those who are most in need, those who are not often treated fairly or equitably because of economic or social problems, at the lower levels of government.

We've increased title I by 55 percent. For the handicapped Americans, we have trippled State grants. For bilingual education, we have doubled funding. And

1295

throughout the country, we've established centers where teachers can upgrade their skills. With expanded college aid for middle-income families, as well as for impoverished students, overall student aid has more than doubled. And now for the first time in the history of our Nation, there is no need for any young person in America to miss a college education because of financial reasons.

And as Willard McGuire has already mentioned, there is now a chair in the Cabinet Room next to the Oval Office, and it's marked on it, "Secretary of Education." And we have a distinguished Californian who sits there, Secretary Shirley Hufstedler. Later on she'll be addressing this convention, and she'll go into more detail about specific programs on which we will be cooperating in the months and years ahead. But from now on, education will have a strong voice at every Cabinet meeting. The children, the parents, and the teachers of America will be well represented, and you can depend on that.

You and I have worked as partners in the full knowledge that if we fail, so does the basic ideal of our country—the ideal of equal opportunity and the ideal of enlightened democracy. In the last decade schools have reeked the whirlwind of public discontent and social unrest. Many people blame teachers for this discontent and unrest, and they expect the schools to solve problems where sometimes all other institutions have failed.

In the most important, constructive social change of our lifetimes, the elimination of legal and de facto discrimination in our schools, the churches failed, the courts failed, the Congress failed, local and State officials failed, the communities failed, and who succeeded?—the teachers of this country, and I thank you for it.

At the same time, all our people in this country, including you and me, are rightly concerned that many of our children do not yet learn to read and write, that schools and classrooms are sometimes disorderly, that good teachers are becoming disenchanted, and that administration of our schools is often haphazard and wasteful. Whatever the reasons—[*applause*]— I was interested in seeing when you would applaud on that line. [*Laughter*] Whatever the reasons for these acknowledged problems, the answer does not lie in dismantling Federal programs, in taxpayer revolts, or in chastising the teachers in the classroom. The answer lies in more and better education, not only as a commitment to our children but as a commitment to our Nation.

We've heard many times, "A mind is a terrible thing to waste." No nation can afford this waste, and the United States, as powerful as it is, is no exception to this rule. We must meld together more closely the classroom and a life's career, and particularly among the poor and the destitute and the deprived and the ignored and the suffering and those who suffer discrimination, the young Americans as they approach adulthood.

That's why I've submitted to the Congress this year a $2-billion drive to establish a permanent youth employment program. This will bring the total to $6 billion for an effort that enlists educators and others in providing basic skills and jobs to the disadvantaged young people. That legislation is making good progress, but I need the help of every member of NEA and all friends of education in getting it passed through the Congress.

We are also preparing for the reauthorization of the Vocational Education Act in the next Congress.

As we look further into the decade, we must prepare our children for a world that is barely imaginable today, for a world changing so rapidly that it will tax the best trained minds and the most courageous and daring people.

We face great challenges—not yet easy to understand or predict—in energy, in health, in agriculture, in national security, in science, in the quest for peace, in economic innovation, in productivity, and we will face even greater challenges in the next century.

It's surprising to realize that children born this year will come of age in the 21st century. A child will not be ready for life if there is no chance to learn the eternal truths of science, history, the humanities, how to relate to other human beings in the same community.

It's possible that our country may not be ready. I'm concerned, for example, that almost one-sixth of our high school students are all that take courses necessary to pursue science and engineering degrees in college; the other five-sixths do not. Only half ever go beyond the 10th grade geometry or biology in high school. Every year, fewer and fewer students learn a foreign language. At the same time that our farms, factories, and national defense require an increasingly sophisticated knowledge of these skills, our children get even less training in those technical subjects. That not only forecloses tremendous opportunities for them in the future, it also weakens the economic and the international status and the security of our Nation.

Equally important, in a world that is increasingly interdependent and when exports have become so critical to our economic health, our young people have less foreign language capacity than they did 10 years ago. Our schools are deemphasizing foreign language studies. All of these trends must be reversed.

I'm also concerned about working conditions for teachers, and I'm concerned about the fundamental role of collective bargaining. As I've said before, and I'd like to repeat, the quality of education depends first and foremost on the morale and the effectiveness of the classroom teacher.

I've authorized an interagency study, that will report to me, of how teachers' salaries and conditions affect the quality of education and what governments can do in a proper and legitimate way, at all levels, so that we can have constructive alternatives to strikes and to work stoppages by meeting the legitimate needs and requirements of the teachers of this country.

I'm also determined that in a special way, our Nation will give outstanding classroom teachers recognition for their long struggle, often unrecognized, to educate our children. I'm sending to the Congress a small bill, legislation that will create the national distinguished teachers fellowships. They'll be rewarded, a few teachers, with an award going to one elementary teacher and one high school teacher in each one of our States and territories, to reward excellence in teaching.

In summary, I'd like to say that for the last 3½ years we've worked for education programs to give even the poorest child the chance to learn, a chance to dream, a chance to succeed. We've worked for programs that prepare our young people and our Nation for the great challenges that we face in this century and in the century not too far away.

The 1980's will be a decade of fundamental choices. Our partnership on national issues will be even more important in the future than it has been in the past. For example, it's a tragedy that after 2 years—two centuries of struggle for more democracy in our country, we have not guaranteed the equal rights of one half the citizens of this Nation. More than any other single organization in this country, the NEA, year after year, has championed that simple matter of equity. And I renew my pledge to you that we will keep the faith, and we will ratify the equal rights amendment for this country.

It's obvious that we do stand together for the ERA as we have stood together for many other vital issues. When I needed your help on energy legislation, you were with me, and we finally turned the corner on the energy problem. Oil imports are down 1 million barrels per day below what they were a year ago, and they're down a million and a half barrels a day compared to when I took office. In the past we had had a constant upward trend, and the importance of this change is hard to overestimate. We now have a place on the law books of our country being filled with the first energy policy for our Nation that can guarantee our Nation's security in energy.

When I needed your help on the SALT treaty, you were there; for consumers, you were there; for the poor and the elderly and for better communities, for stronger families, you were there; for civil service reform, you were there; for fairer housing legislation, you were there. On issue after issue, win, sometimes lose, you were with me. In every case, the NEA was on the side of hope. The NEA was on the side of progress. The NEA was on the side of human rights. The NEA was on the side of peace.

You've made it possible for this country under the most difficult possible circumstances to face up to the challenges that have been pushed aside for so many years. And as we have faced up to the present, to the world as it is, we are resolute in the realization that you and I, together, all the teachers of this land, are building a better country for the future.

We've not always looked at the future. We've rightly looked at the past for traditional values in our family and personal life. But we cannot allow nostalgia built on an incorrect memory to blind us to what life was like when government did nothing to protect minorities, the working people, or the poor; when disease and ignorance and prejudice took a fearful toll; when only 70 years ago, only half of America's school-age children had a chance to go to school. We still face difficult times together. We cannot wish away or promise away America's problems.

The most recent example of the simplistic approach to serious issues, one that I'm having to fight every day in Washington, is the effort now in Congress to stick onto totally unrelated bills, without any public hearings, proposals which would lead to a 30-percent across-the-board tax cut over the next 3 years. By 1985, this would cost us $280 billion annually. It would reward the wealthy. It would mean a wholesale retreat from the painful progress that we've made over the last several months to reduce inflation and reduce interest rates. It is sheer deception to promise the American people that we can have this enormously expensive and unfair tax cut, that we can dramatically increase defense expenditures even above and beyond the substantial levels I've recommended, and that we can sustain our programs in education, employment, health, and other areas, and that we can exercise budget restraint at the same time.

You all know that this kind of hasty offer can only be called by one word, and that's irresponsible. And we will not stand for it. It's a classic offer in a political year of a free lunch, something for nothing. The American people know better. They know, as Walter Lippmann reminded us, that there is nothing for nothing any longer. The American people know that our challenges are not simple; they are complex. The American people know that the solutions are not simple or painless or easy. The American people will support honest, constructive ideas, steady commitments, and hard work to achieve social and economic justice for our country. It's the only way we have ever made progress, it's by determination and tenacity and courage and hard work and unity and cooperation and telling the truth.

And I call on you today to reaffirm our joint commitment to the realization of our principles, which we share in action. We must choose in this decade a new partnership of government and the private sector that builds for the future. We can only do this if we invest heavily in our most precious possession, our human capital, through education.

In you, the members of NEA, I see the spirit of building, the spirit of pulling together. I see a renewal of our dedication to children and to their education. I see our capacity and the opportunity for lasting solutions to even our most serious and difficult problems. When later generations look back, I want them to see us, you and me, as the people who did build for the future and who left as a legacy, a strong education system in a strong and great nation. Together, we will realize that dream.

Thank you very much.

NOTE: The President spoke at 10:44 a.m. at the opening session of the 118th annual meeting of the association which was held at the Los Angeles Convention Center.

Prior to his remarks, the President accepted the 1980 Friend of Education award, which consists of a specially designed pair of cuff links and an inscribed plaque, from Willard McGuire, president, on behalf of the NEA.

Earlier in the day, the President left the White House and went by motorcade to Andrews Air Force Base, Md., where he boarded Air Force One for the flight to California.

Upon arrival at the Los Angeles International Airport, the President was greeted by Gov. Edmund G. "Jerry" Brown, Jr., State Treasurer Jess Unruh, and Mayor Thomas Bradley of Los Angeles.

The President went by motorcade from the airport to the convention center, where he was met by Terry Herndon, executive director, Ken Melley, director of political affairs, Bernard Freitag, vice president, and John T. McGarigal, secretary/treasurer, of the National Education Association.

Oakland, California

Remarks at a Reception for East Bay Area Community and Civic Leaders.   July 3, 1980

When I asked Mayor Wilson who was going to be at this meeting, he said, "Just a few city officials." [*Laughter*] I think there are almost as many officials in the East Bay/Oakland area as there are around the Oval Office in Washington. [*Laughter*]

I know, however, that there have been a good many other community leaders to join us this afternoon, and I'm very delighted to be the first President, really since 1904, to come here to Oakland on an official visit and to meet with people who are important to this community and to make a few brief remarks. A couple of other Presidents have kind of passed through, but I don't see how they could possibly have passed through this place and not stopped and stayed and meet the wonderful people who are here.

It's an exciting thing to see and to know and to learn about what has happened in this tremendous, fast-growing, dynamic, beautiful area. Three and a half years ago when I became President of our great country, the thing that I was determined to do was to form a partnership between your government in Washington, your government in Sacramento, and your government here in the Oakland/Bay area. We've been successful, far beyond what we ever thought. And what I have seen this afternoon and what I've learned this afternoon is a vivid demonstration of what I mean.

In the last 3½ years, we have had a net increase of 110,000 jobs in the bay area. This is good progress. And although we are now suffering from economic adversity and problems which are very serious, the unemployment rate in January of 1977 was 60 percent higher than it was the last figures we had for May 1980. This is a great tribute to you and to the forceful attitude and the forward-looking attitude that's typical of this region of our country.

There've been a lot of reasons for it. First of all, is a better partnership, a close consultation, which is a vivid reminder to me that every one of the constituents of Lionel Wilson is also a constituent of mine. And I'm determined to sustain this growth and the progress that you have made, not by interference in your affairs but by mutual consultation on how we can work together to meet common problems and to take advantage of common opportunities.

We wrote and passed into law not many months ago a remarkable trade bill, an historic occasion when we agreed with foreign countries to minimize protectionism and to increase trade among our countries. This has been good for our whole Nation, and it's also, of course, been good for American workers, because it's provided a lot of new jobs.

Oakland and your port, which I've just had a chance to visit, has demonstrated this in a remarkable way. Containerized shipping is something relatively new. You have been in the forefront in developing

this means by which American products could be transported efficiently and quickly to foreign markets. This helps everybody in Iowa and everybody in Nevada who's interested in the production of goods that are attractive to foreign buyers.

We've had a remarkable increase in total export shipping from the west coast because of that landmark legislation, and also from the fact that we have now formed diplomatic relationships with the People's Republic of China, comprising in their population one-fourth of the total people who live on Earth.

It's been good already to see this change made, but the prospects for the future are exciting indeed. There are a group, as you know, of port managers here, observing how well you perform your shipping duties, from the People's Republic of China. And in this process, which was a highly sensitive and controversial decision that I had to make a little more than a year and a half ago, we have also increased dramatically our trade with Taiwan and the people who live there.

In the entire west coast area, as a matter of fact, exports the first quarter of this year were 32 percent higher than they were last year, and in the bay area, I'm sure it won't surprise you, it was 39 percent, more even than the tremendous growth on the west coast. I want to see this kind of progress continue not only in trade and exports but also in the revitalization of communities which you're so eager to help yourselves.

I was looking down the list at some of the things that EDA has done and the UDAG program has done. This UDAG program, for instance, is designed to have minimal paperwork, quick return—if a proper request is made—and a maximum input of private investment and private capital and local initiative and local control, with just a little bit of Federal seed money. And it's worked far beyond what we had ever thought. The mayors proposed it; the Federal Government decided to do it after the Congress acted.

The Oakland downtown revitalization program is one example of what can be done with this kind of cooperation. The Judson Steel Company has been really a remarkable project, with private and government cooperation, the Richmond Marina—and the Stewart Street Project in San Francisco is another example. The EDA program has been in effect now for 15 years; it started in 1965. But over 60 percent of the total EDA funds used for the benefit of the American people have been expended in the last 3½ years, because the local people now feel that when they make an application, it will be addressed and approved—if it's worthy—without delay and with a maximum amount of partnership and cooperation.

We have made good progress in the last few months in dealing with the high inflation and the high interest rates. The prime rate now is exactly the same as it was 12 months ago, and I hope and I believe that the inflation rate is going to continue to drop throughout this summer. It's still going to be too high. We have been getting discouraging news on unemployment. This time it did level off a little compared to last month, but the problems are not over. But I'm determined that we will focus the very highly tuned job opportunity programs on communities like yours as we see these high unemployment figures come in. The bay area will get about 1,600 new jobs, for instance, in the next few weeks, to help compensate for the loss of jobs because of the adverse effect of excessive oil imports and the extremely high inflation rate and interest rates that we experienced earlier this year.

This year, for instance, we will send to foreign countries to pay for their oil $90 billion of American money, money that could be used to make investments in facilities like yours, to make our communities better, to build American factories, to put American people back to work. And when we import that much money [oil], we also import inflation and unemployment. It's hard to imagine what $90 billion amounts to, but what it amounts to is this: $400 for every man, woman, and child in the United States of America goes to pay for oil bought from foreign countries. That's what we've worked on for the last 3½ years, to try to get a comprehensive energy policy for our Nation that can let us save energy in this Nation and not waste it, and at the same time produce more energy from all sources in our country so we can keep the money and the jobs here at home and to help to control inflation.

Well, I feel good about this country; I feel good about the future. My prime responsibility is to keep our Nation at peace, at peace through strength—military strength, economic strength, political strength and, I pray God, moral and ethical strength based on principles that never change. That's not an easy thing to do in a time of world turmoil, and the close interrelationship among nations, and the violation of the international spirit brought about the Soviet invasion of Afghanistan, and the unwarranted and inhumane capture and holding of 53 innocent Americans in Iran. But all of us need to look to the future with determination, with a maximum degree of unity, and with confidence.

We've got the greatest nation on Earth, and I don't have any doubt that in the future, with your help, it's going to be even greater.

Thank you very much for letting me be with you.

NOTE: The President spoke at 4:35 p.m. in Goodman's Hall, after an introduction by Mayor Lionel Wilson of Oakland, who hosted the reception.

Earlier in the day, Mayor Wilson greeted the President upon his arrival at the Oakland International Airport.

The President then went to Berth #10 at the Port of Oakland, where he was met by Walter Abernathy, executive director of the Oakland Port Authority, and boarded a boat for a tour of Oakland Harbor.

Portola Valley, California

Remarks at a Democratic National Committee Fundraising Dinner.   July 3, 1980

How many of you think that we can whip the Republicans from the top to the bottom in California in November? [*Applause*] Well, so do I.

It's a great pleasure for me to be here tonight with Walter Shorenstein and with Phyllis, with Dick O'Neill, and all of the others who've come here tonight to express your support for some of the most important factors in the lives of free people throughout the Earth and particularly, of course, in our great Nation.

I don't have a prepared text, but I would like to say a few things about the responsibilities that we share. This is the first time under the election laws when funds that are raised at an event like this can be shared between the Democratic National Committee and the Democrats in California. In 1976 when I first ran for President, we could not do this. There could not be an interrelationship in the campaigns between myself and a congressman or between the funds that were raised. But I think over this last 4 years all of us have realized, along with the Federal Election Commission, that Democrats at the local, State, and Federal level share a great responsibility.

The biggest responsibility on my shoulders, as President, is to keep our Nation at peace, a peace through strength—military strength, which I pray will never have to be used, economic strength, political strength, diplomatic strength, moral and ethical strength, based upon the principles on which our Nation was founded and which have never changed.

We have a country that is strong. And our strength is recognized by our allies; it's recognized by those nations which are genuinely nonaligned; it's recognized by nations struggling for a sustained existence and for progress; it's recognized by potential adversaries. This must be maintained, and an important element of it is a degree of unity and common commitment which, on occasion, has been lacking in this country, because our Government itself was not open and because it was not trusted.

It's almost impossible to think back 4 years ago, or 5 years ago, or perhaps 6 years ago, when our Nation was embarrassed, when our Nation was going through torture because of Vietnam, because of Watergate, because of the embarrassments of the CIA revelations, when things in Washington were done in secret and, when revealed, brought shame to the White House, to the Oval Office, and to every American.

That has changed. No one denies that every human being is fallible, and no one denies that we have made mistakes. But they have been mistakes based on good intention and based on determined progress, and the mistakes have been minimal. We've made notable progress. In California, when I came here to campaign first in '75 and '76, the unemployment rate was 10 percent or more. The unemployment rate in January of 1977, when I was inaugurated, was 60 percent higher than it was in May of 1980, the last data which we have.

We have not only kept our country at peace, but we have struggled, as you well know, to bring peace to others. In the Mideast, we haven't made sustained progress, but we've had two notable achievements which have reversed a 30-year history of hatred and distrust and division and bloodshed. And now, as Walter pointed out so well, the major Arab nation on Earth, the major focal point of military strength which brought war to Israel, is now Israel's friend, with open borders, and diplomatic recognition, and Ambassadors in the capital cities, and planes flying back and forth between Jerusalem and Tel Aviv on one side, and Cairo and Alexandria on the other.

Yesterday afternoon I had a private meeting with Mr. Burg, Dr. Burg, representing Israel, and General 'Ali representing Egypt. When I asked them if they would recommence the peace negotiations immediately, Mr. Burg said his instructions were to do so.

General 'Ali said he had to have a private conversation with me first, so we went into the Oval Office, and he said, "President Sadat wants to know what you want, Mr. President." I said, "I want the negotiations to start." And he said, "Would you give me time to make a call to Egypt?" And I said, "Yes." And in about 30 minutes he came back and said that negotiations will start again.

So, we're making progress. And the progress will be sustained only to the extent that those two nations trust the United States. When we lose that trust and that faith in me, as President, and in our country as a fair and objective, conciliatory element, then the prospects for further progress toward peace in the Middle East will be gone, maybe for a long time, maybe forever. I pray not.

But we are determined to continue to make progress. We cannot give up simply because we have a temporary setback, because we have to realize that we are dealing with two sovereign nations—Israel, as democratic a nation as there is on Earth, with a cabinet and a Knesset and a populace highly motivated, deeply committed to principles that don't change, desperately concerned about the maintenance of their security now and forever.

And we recognize that in a democratic country there cannot be the imposition of a decision, either by an elected leader, the Prime Minister, and certainly not by the President of a distant country, even as powerful as the United States. So it must be tedious and it must be slow, but it must be consistent.

We've also had to face some longstanding needs in our country. This year we will send to foreign nations $90 billion to buy oil to use here. It's a lot of money. It's hard to envision what $90 billion is, but what it is amounts to $400 for every man, woman, and child who lives in the United States, to buy oil from foreign countries. And that $90 billion could be used for investments and better productivity and more jobs and a better life and more economic security for our country. And we've been struggling, as you well know, for 3½ years under the most difficult possible circumstances, to bring about the kinds of change that would give our Nation energy and economic security, because along with oil we import inflation and we import unemployment.

We are now making some progress because of the sound judgment and deep commitment and the patriotism of the American people. As you well know, up until 1977 we had a constant escalation, always upward, in the amount of oil that we were buying from overseas. Today we are buying 1½ million barrels less every day than we did 3½ years ago. This is good progress. It's good progress, but it's not enough.

Walter also mentioned the great prospect that we have in the future from our new relationship with the People's Republic of China. I just was blessed with the opportunity to inspect the port facilities in the bay area, San Francisco and Oakland. On the west coast of our country, in the first quarter of this year, export trade was up 32 percent in the bay area, up 39 percent compared to last year. We've done this just because we've opened a crack in the door of dealing with a billion new friends, and in the process we have not injured our trade relationship with the people of Taiwan, because trade with Taiwan is up even more, more than 40 percent. So this opening of American hands and American arms and American hearts to receive a better relationship with those who in the past were not our friends is an historic and a major achievement.

This progress must continue. It can't be aborted and it can't be restrained, and we cannot undo what we have struggled so hard to achieve. The economic problems on our country are severe. They're severe throughout the world. But it's very gratifying to me to know that our major allies in Venice last week committed ourselves unanimously to economic progress based on a common approach to inflation, unemployment, and energy consumption restraints.

At the same time, we recognized the threats to peace that have been foisted upon the world by the unwarranted Soviet invasion of Afghanistan, when an innocent, nonaligned, deeply religious, courageous nation was invaded and is now occupied by Soviet military forces. And we expressed our admiration for those freedom-fighters who are struggling for their national liberation. The world, as you know, through the United Nations, condemned with 104 votes, the Soviet's invasion of that country and called for the withdrawal of their forces.

I might say that we are eager to get along well with the Soviet Union. We are eager to see that détente [is] not weakened but strengthened. And we are eager to control nuclear weapons, to reduce our dependence on them, and ultimately to eliminate nuclear weapons as a factor from the face of the Earth. This is our ultimate goal. And as soon as we can achieve a clear indication from the Soviet Union that they are ending their occupation of this neighboring country which threatened no one, that progress will be recommenced with the fullest enthusiasm on our part.

But that is a prospect that will be terminated if the Republicans are successful in November, because they have announced that SALT agreements to restrain the escalation in nuclear weapons that can destroy the Earth are not a part of their agenda. They would oppose the ratification of a carefully negotiated treaty, negotiated not just under myself, but even under two previous Republican Presidents.

The final thing I want to say is that the Democratic Party is committed to strength, to peace, to better relations with all peoples, to the controlling of nuclear weapons, to sound judgment in management of our economy and the energy question, but we are also committed to caring for those less fortunate than are we—the deprived, the poor, the inarticulate. Those who've suffered from discrimination of all kinds have always been at the forefront of the consideration of our party, and they still will be. And we've been trying to bring into the consciousness of America and the governing of America those who have been too long excluded.

I have been able to make some appointments to the courts. I've appointed more women, more Spanish-speaking Americans, more blacks, than all the other Presidents who ever served in this country. And we intend to continue that progress.

And the last thing I want to say is this: The progress has not been total. We've still got difficult problems. There are no simplistic, easy answers for them. Our country has never made progress the easy way. We've done it by courage, by determination, by insight, by sensitivity, by trusting one another, by determination, by tenacity, by idealism, by compassion, by concern, by competence, and by unity. And I hope that we'll see a unified Democratic Party guided to victory in November, because we share those commitments and we share those principles that have made our Nation great and, with your help, will make it even greater in the future.

Thank you very much. God bless you all.

NOTE: The President spoke at 8:31 p.m. after being introduced by Walter Shorenstein, who hosted the fundraising event at his Portola Valley residence, "The Meadows."

Earlier in the evening, the President met with Gov. Edmund G. "Jerry" Brown, Jr., at the Airport Travelodge Motel near the Oakland International Airport. Mayor Diane Feinstein of San Francisco then joined the President on Marine One for an aerial tour of San Francisco enroute to Portola Valley.

Following the fundraising event, the President returned to the Oakland International Airport on Marine One, and proceeded by motorcade to Mayor Wilson's residence where he remained overnight.

Merced, California

Remarks and a Question-and-Answer Session at a Town Meeting.   July 4, 1980

THE PRESIDENT. Before we start with the questions, let me say first of all that I deeply appreciate the welcome that I've received ever since I landed at Castle Air Force Base. Mayor Bob Hart has made me feel at home. And the people along the way and those outside when the helicopter landed who couldn't get in, and all of you have really warmed my heart. I also would like to say that you have one of the finest Members of Congress who ever served in Washington, Tony Coelho.

You don't know how it makes a farmer feel—[*laughter*]—who's been in Washington now for 3½ years, to fly in a helicopter over this beautiful country. Not only do you have the Sierra Nevada Mountains in the background all during your lives, the gateway to Yosemite, and some of the most beautiful earth that was ever created, but the productive land that you have here is also an inspiration to me as a President and also one of the greatest natural resources that we have.

AMERICAN ACHIEVEMENTS AND STRENGTHS

I'm glad to come here, too, on a special day, the birthday of our country. It's a time to remember the spirit of those who first came to this region to settle it, pioneers facing danger, facing challenges, facing uncertain times ahead, sometimes families divided by death or by attacks. The times that they had—much more challenging, much more dangerous than the ones we face today, but we still have that same basic commitment to principles of freedom, innovation, pioneer spirit, courage, unity, patriotism in our country.

And we do face serious problems, serious challenges.

The whole world looks to us for leadership, in human rights, in freedom, in the innovative spirit, that can attack the future that they don't quite understand, not with fear and trepidation and cowardice, but with a calm assurance in our own ability, in the strength of our Nation, and in the unity that binds us together and always has bound us together when our Nation was threatened from any source.

I'm deeply honored, as we look back on the 204 years since the Declaration of Independence was signed, we do pay homage and we remember those who came before us, who fought in the Revolution, who fought in the War Between the States to keep our country united, who fought in the Second World War and the First World War, the Korean war, who represented our country in Vietnam, who went through social change, that literally shocked this country and the world, to give equal opportunity to those who in the past have been deprived of that opportunity because of their own color or their own race.

And we remember in times of pressure that this is a country of immigrants, it's a country of refugees, who have come here for religious freedom or for personal freedom or for a better chance in life. And unless there are some native Indians here, every family represented came here earlier as immigrants, maybe 2 years ago, maybe 200 years ago. But we've never been weakened because we opened our arms to receive those who have been persecuted and in danger. This is a difficult thing for us to assimilate when we get here and enjoy all the advantages of full American citizenship and wealth and freedom, to say, "Let's keep it the way it is." I'm glad that folks didn't feel that way when my folks got ready to come over here a long time ago.

But in closing, let me say this: Ours is a generation that put the first man on the Moon. And ours is the generation that fought for civil rights in the South and transformed the attitudes of Americans one toward another. And ours is the generation that's been able, in the last few years, to accommodate the divisiveness of the Vietnam war and the divisiveness and embarrassment of Watergate and the embarrassment of the revelations about the CIA. And we've survived. And it may be that our country is even stronger than it was in the past.

We've got a long way to go, in energy, inflation, unemployment, the marketing of our products, but we're making good progress. We've not got a dismal, downhearted attitude justified by the future of Americans; we've got a great, glorious, exciting, challenging future that we can meet if we are united, and we are.

And one final sentence: What has let our Nation make this progress is the same thing that's important on this Fourth of July here in Merced, and that's the partnership that exists between people and government. And there's no better way to celebrate our birthday, in my opinion, than a direct relationship between the people of this great community and the President of the United States. I'm thankful to you.

And now we'll have the first question from microphone number one.

QUESTIONS

SOLAR ENERGY

Q. Mr. President, my name is Laurie Hays, and I live here in Merced when I'm home from college. And I would like to ask you a short question. Would you favor a bill that would allow a tax break for homeowners who use solar energy to help meet their families' energy needs?

THE PRESIDENT. Yes. And we have already passed such a bill, with Tony Coelho's help, and I'll tell you how it works. If a family does invest in energy-saving devices in the home, like solar power, then the following year when you file your income tax returns for that particular year, you can take credit for it. I'm not sure about the exact details, but I believe it's up to $2,000. So, we've got that already on the books. And this is one of the things that we've done the last couple of years, and that is to pass new laws in our country that do two things to reduce our excessive dependence on foreign oil.

This year we'll send overseas to buy foreign oil $90 billion, kind of robbing ourselves in order to use too much oil from overseas. That's $400 for every man, woman, and child who lives in this country.

There are only two things you can do about it. One is to save energy, not to waste energy, to be very careful about what we use, and the other thing is to produce more American energy. We've got the energy. Solar is a wonderful way to go about it. And by the year 2000, we hope and believe that when we put all these laws into effect that the Congress is now passing that we'll have 20 percent of the total energy used in this country coming directly from the Sun.

We've made progress. When I came into office 3½ years ago, we were constantly going up every year in how much oil we bought from overseas. Today we're using 1½ million barrels less oil every day from overseas than we did just that short time ago. So, we're making good progress and going to keep it up.

Q. Thank you very much.

STANISLAUS RIVER; SOVIET INVASION OF AFGHANISTAN

Q. Good morning, Mr. President.

THE PRESIDENT. Good morning.

Q. I am the wife of an American farmer, and naturally my question will be related to agriculture. My name is Eileen Dagson, and I'm from Winton, California. If a bill should reach your desk which designates the Stanislaus River as wild and scenic and prohibits the building of the new Melones Dam, would you approve that bill, or would you veto it?

And also, we approve of your effort to chastise the Russians in Afghanistan, but we feel that it has been at some expense to the American farmer with the grain embargo. When will you lift the grain embargo?

THE PRESIDENT. All right. Those are two difficult questions. And before I answer them, I think I'll take off my coat, okay? [*Laughter*] It's kind of hot up here.

As you know, on the Stanislaus River, the new Melones Dam, we have to go by what the law says and also how the courts interpret the law. We are now at the point where the Secretary of Interior, with my approval, has authorized the filling of the lake to the 818-foot level. And I believe in the wild river concept. And I think the Stanislaus River is one of the most beautiful rivers on Earth.

The Secretary of the Interior has informed the Congress in the last few weeks, accurately, that the upper part of the Stanislaus River was suitable for a wild river designation. I don't know yet what the Congress will decide. It'll be decided by all 535 of them in the House and Senate.

My guess is, my present prediction is that if the bill gets to my desk, otherwise acceptable and with that in it, then I would sign it, to answer your first question. Ordinarily legislation of this kind is extremely complicated, and it has literally hundreds, sometimes thousands of individual items in them. So, I think I've answered your first question—that if the Congress decides this, then I would sign the bill.

On the second point, I believe that it's important for our Nation to make sacrifice, if necessary, in order to stop aggression overseas. The Soviets have invaded Afghanistan in a completely unwarranted action. They now have approximately 85,000 heavily armed troops inside of this small, relatively defenseless, formerly non-aligned country, highly and deeply religious, committed to freedom. The freedom-fighters in Afghanistan are literally offering their lives every day to fight for the liberation of their own country.

There are very few things that we have that we can do short of actual war. We can take political action, and we've done that in the United Nations when 104 countries condemned the Soviet invasion and demanded that they withdraw. Subsequent to that, I think 34 Moslem countries—Afghanistan happens to be a Moslem country, basically—demanded that the Soviets get their troops out of Afghanistan.

We have also imposed some economic restraints on the Soviet Union. One is that we've prevented Soviet ships from fishing within 200 miles of American coastlines. Another thing that we've done is to restrict the kinds of materials that we sell to the Soviet Union if it might contribute to a better and more effective Soviet military force or economic force that can be fed in to the military. And the other thing that we've done is to restrain the shipments of feed grains to the Soviet Union.

This year we are shipping the Soviets 8 million tons of food and feed grains in accordance with a treaty or an agreement signed between the two Governments. But we have cut down on extra sales of grain to the Soviet Union, while they are suffering through this year of intense shortages themselves. They have replaced some of that grain that we did not sell them, but they still are suffering now about a 10 or 11 million ton shortage in the Soviet Union, which, in my opinion, impresses on every Soviet citizen that not only are they suffering because the world is basically boycotting the Moscow Olympics in August but they're also suffering because they're not producing as much poultry and red meat as they would otherwise.

So, I am not going to lift the farm restraints on the Soviet Union in the foreseeable future unless the Soviets make some tangible and demonstrable move to stop their invasion of Afghanistan, but we will continue to sell the 8 million tons of grain to the Soviets which we have never interrupted. I think we ought to punish the Soviet Union for their invasion and convince them that aggression in this world does not pay. And I would like to remind you that everything we have done against the Soviets is effective, but it's peaceful in nature.

And I would like to say one other thing. The most important responsibility on any President, no matter who it is, is to keep our Nation strong and at peace, and I don't believe that we can keep our Nation at peace, which I thank God we have done so far, without our Nation being strong—militarily, economically, politically, diplomatically, and, I believe, morally and ethically. And the only way you can keep that moral and ethical strength is to condemn aggression and the persecution of innocent people and to enhance human rights in accordance with the principles that have made our Nation strong.

So, I will continue to punish the Soviet Union— [*applause*].

USE OF CRUISE MISSILES AGAINST SOVIET
UNION

Q. Mr. President, my name is Samson Clare, and I live in Livingston, California. I was wondering if your administration is presently reconsidering deploying the B-1 bomber, and if so deployed, will it be based at Castle Air Force Base?

THE PRESIDENT. We have decided not to build the B-1 bomber itself. I think it was a wise decision, and let me tell you why.

The Soviet defense capability within their own country against penetrating aircraft has been the subject of about $100 billion investment on their part, with radar installations, fighter aircraft, and so forth. We don't need and don't have a similar air defense capability, because the Soviets cannot attack the continental United States of our country with conventional aircraft.

What they have built up over the last few years and can build up in the future would be very effective against any bomber, obviously the B-52, even the B-1, that penetrated their air space over Soviet land to make an attack. So therefore, I don't think it's a good investment to put so much money into that kind of penetrating bomber, and the Congress has agreed and the military has also agreed.

But we will need a way to penetrate the Soviet Union in lieu of sending our own manned bomber planes over the Soviets if war should come. We decided to go with the cruise missiles, primarily the air-launched cruise missiles, relatively small, relatively inexpensive, highly mobile, almost invisible to radar, and which can pack a real wallop when they land. So, what we will do is to develop a new kind of carrier for these air-launched cruise missiles, which will be designed without delay, so that each one of these carriers, which is an airplane, like a bomber, can carry about 20 of them. And they would stand off the shores of the Soviet Union, like maybe a thousand miles, launch their war attack, if necessary—and I pray God we'll never have to do it, but if we do, we want to be ready—and then let those cruise missiles, 20 of them simultaneously from each plane, penetrate the Soviet Union much more effectively. It saves money, it's almost impossible to defend against them, and it's much more effective in the long run.

I have no doubt, however, that the Castle Air Force Base, no matter what kind of bombers or cruise missile carriers we have in the future, will be an important element in the defense mechanism of our country. And as Commander in Chief, I was just as thrilled to land at Castle and see what you've got there, which I have already known in that role, as I was to see the beautiful land where you grow food.

I might say, in closing, this: The best way not to spend American lives in war and the best way to have weapons that are never used to kill other human beings is to have fighting men and women that are ready and to have weapons that will be effective if they are needed. That's the best way to keep the Soviets in a mood to keep peace.

Q. Thank you, Mr. President.
THE PRESIDENT. Thank you.

SUPPORT FOR THE PRESIDENT; WELFARE
AND HEALTH CARE PROGRAMS

Q. Mr. President, my name is Clifford Childers; I live in Atwater, California. I have a two-part question. First, I would like for you to remember in the next 3 years those who failed to give you any support and what have you for the next 3 years coming up, and treat them accordingly. And I think you know what I mean. [*Laughter*]

My question, Mr. President, is this: The rich are getting richer; 51 percent are taking a free ride, are freeloaders—medical and food. And people like the audience of this 2,000 people here are footing the bill, and I don't think it's right.

THE PRESIDENT. I understand. Clifford, let me respond. I guess you want me to respond to those comments.

An election year is, in a way, a difficult time for a country and obviously for those of us who hold public office. However, in many ways it's the best year of all, because it gives us a chance to confront difficult issues and to let the people be more deeply involved in shaping our country for the future. I learn a lot in a campaign, and I learn a lot in a meeting like this— what's on your mind, what your concerns are, what your doubts are, what your confidences are, what your hopes are.

And people that support me politically, I deeply appreciate it, and I won't ever forget them. And those that don't support me, I'll try to forget. [*Laughter*] I'm a human being though, and sometimes my memory is better than I want it to be. [*Laughter*]

Q. Good for that.

THE PRESIDENT [*laughing*]. Right.

And this other part about your question is an interesting one. What I've tried to do since I've been in office is to take programs like welfare and health care, which are quite expensive, and modify them so that they are more efficient and are preventive in nature.

The welfare proposals that I have put to the Congress, for instance, are designed so that able-bodied Americans will be even encouraged or required to work——

Q. Good.

THE PRESIDENT.——because of two reasons: I don't believe in the Government financing somebody's livelihood if a job's available to that person, and secondly, with the limited amount of funds available for welfare programs, those funds ought to be concentrated on the people that can't work.

Secondly, health—our Nation needs a comprehensive health program designed for several things: first of all, to cut down on the expense of it; secondly, to prevent illness. It's very inexpensive to keep a child from getting a serious disease or illness that would incapacitate that person for the rest of their life and maybe cost 20 or 30 thousand dollars a year to take care of them, when, if they were given adequate examinations, adequate dental care, adequate immunization shots as a young child, they could be healthy the rest of their lives.

Also, we need to make sure that we don't destroy the personal relationship that ought to exist, in my opinion, between a family and the medical doctors and personnel that treat them.

And I've worked hard—the last point— to cut down on hospital costs. The hospitals are overcharging the American people for health care. The reason they are doing it is this—[*applause*]—one reason is that they give people services that they don't need, and the other is that there's not much competition in the hospital care field, because quite often, as Tony Coelho well knows, in recent years the amount of increase in hospital costs has been almost twice as much as the inflation rate. There are several reasons. In many cases a community is served by one hospital—which is okay; you don't want too many hospital beds, because the folks that are in the beds have to pay for the empty beds—but secondly, medical doctors quite often have a great deal of control over or even an investment in the profits of the hospital.

So, we'll try to hold down hospital costs, make sure we don't have excessive hospital beds in the country that sick people have to pay for when those beds are empty, prevent disease by giving health care for young people, and in the welfare program, encourage able-bodied people to work, so that can be the focus of our attention on those that cannot work. Those are the kind of approaches, I think, that would partially address the question that you just raised, and I believe that's the best approach for the American Government to take. And we'll continue to work on it with those goals in mind.

Q. Thank you.

AMERICAN HOSTAGES IN IRAN

Q. Good morning, Mr. President.

THE PRESIDENT. Good morning.

Q. For one thing, my name is John Sells, and I'd like to welcome you to Merced.

THE PRESIDENT. Thank you.

Q. This question has been asked very many times. Do you have any idea when the hostages in Iran will be released?

THE PRESIDENT. John, if there's one subject that literally never leaves my mind, it's the 53 innocent Americans that have been held so long by the kidnapers and international terrorists in Iran, supported by and condoned by the Iranian Government. I have probably put more time and more prayer on that one subject than any other that I've faced as President.

In the last few hours, as a matter of fact, I have been in touch with the State Department and with others that I can't name publicly in trying to have an avenue to the Iranian leaders to get our hostages released. As you know, we tried a rescue mission, which failed tragically; which, if it could have gone forward, would have been successful. We've tried diplomatic means. We've been to the world court. We've been to the United Nations.

We've got two considerations in mind today that we've had since the very first day of this tragedy. One is to protect the lives and the safety of the hostages. And so far as we know, although they suffer from imprisonment, their lives and their safety have been protected. Secondly, we've upheld the principles of our Nation. There are some things that I could not do in order to secure the release of the hostages if it meant embarrassing our country or apologizing for something which we have not done or bringing our Nation to its knees to beg those terrorists to do what they ought to do under international law and in the realm of human compassion.

I can't tell you when the hostages will be released. The problem has always been that there is no one in the Government of Iran who has either the courage or the leadership capability or the authority to make that decision. We're trying now to work with the President of Iran, Bani-Sadr, the Foreign Minister of Iran, Ghotzbadeh. We have very little access directly to Ayatollah Khomeini. We're working with the opposition mullahs who have opposed Bani-Sadr and Ghotzbadeh when they announced they would return the hostages.

But we obviously are doing everything we can. I do not know what else we can do without endangering the lives of the hostages themselves. But every day, all day, by every possible means to reach the Iranian people, we are trying to induce them to release the hostages.

The last thing I want to say is this: We are punishing Iran severely for holding the hostages. It's costing them literally millions of dollars every day in lost revenue, lost trade, a poorer quality of life for their people. Their Government is divided, they're in chaos politically, because they're holding these hostages. But they are fanatics, some of them; they're terrorists, some of them; they're irresponsible, a large number of them.

And how to get the hostages home I've not yet discovered. But I hope that every American, every day, will remember those 53 hostages, remember them in our prayers. And I believe that they will be coming home safely.

I would like just to add one other point, because it is the Fourth of July. It's not a sign of weakness that a great nation like ours has been so deeply concerned about this issue. Many countries in the world would forget about 53 people. They're not famous people; they're not great people, as far as their past accomplishments are concerned. They're just common, ordinary, good, dedicated, patriotic Americans. We have never forgotten them. And when 220 million Americans are deeply obsessed with the lives and safety of just 53 people for months, to me that's a sign of greatness.

MINORITIES

Q. *Bienvenido, Señor Presidente.* [Welcome, Mr. President.]

THE PRESIDENT. *Gracias, Señor.*

Q. *Me llamo José Lada.* [My name is José Lada.]

THE PRESIDENT. *Gracias.*

Q. I'm a bilingual teacher in the Merced city school district. As you may know, there is a high percentage of Hispanics in California. And my question is——

THE PRESIDENT. Yes, I've heard about this. [*Laughter*]

Q. —— if you are reelected, what will you do to see that the Federal programs designed to help the minorities of this country will be protected and strengthened?

THE PRESIDENT. I will continue to do what we have done for this first 3½ years.

There is no doubt that in the past 204 years of our Nation's history since the Declaration of Independence was signed, there has been a gross discrimination against many minority groups—discrimination against the blacks, discrimination against those from Ireland, discrimination against those who happen to be Jews, discrimination against those from Eastern Europe, discrimination against Asians, discrimination against those who don't speak English well, the Hispanics. But the important thing is that our Nation has made steady progress in accommodating differences among people, letting them preserve their heritage and their commitment and their religious beliefs and the closeness of their families, and at the same time letting them enjoy the benefits of American society. I think our country has got a good record in dealing with minority groups.

The latest, of course, problem that we have is the excessive number of refugees who've been forced out of Southeast Asia and Communist countries at the danger of their lives. Another very serious problem that we have faced is the large number of Hispanic people who've come here not because they were under persecution politically, like from Mexico, but because they wanted a better life in our country. We're doing the best we can to accommodate those groups. It's not easy.

I believe, however, that we have had a rigid enforcement of the equal employment opportunity laws. And also, in my appointments to major positions, I've tried to bring in as advisers to me those who were especially knowledgeable about and especially sensitive to the needs of particular minority groups. And to make the answer to your question brief, I'll just give you one example.

In the Federal district courts and circuit courts, where policy is made and where the service is for life, I've tried to correct past discrimination in appointments to those positions that we all recognize now. And I've only been in office 3½ years, but I've appointed more women judges, I've appointed more black judges, I've appointed more Hispanic judges than all the other Presidents combined since this Nation was formed. So, I'll continue that.

I'd like to add one other point. As each one of these groups have become more closely assimilated or absorbed in our society, keeping their own special characteristics as a matter of pride, they've become better and better Americans, and they have stood on their own feet. And they have started dealing with other groups, who might come later, with the same degree of concern and compassion that the Irish and the Eastern Europeans now exert toward Hispanics and those who come from Southeast Asia.

So, I see the time coming very rapidly when the status of Hispanic Americans is absolutely assured, when discrimination against them has been eliminated, when they are playing a major role in elective office, appointive office, making decisions, setting the policy and the character of our country, and being responsible, which you already are becoming, for dealing with other groups who might be more newcomers than you are.

So, this is the way our Nation grows, and I'll be sure and commit to you that that progress will continue.

Thank you very much.

Q. Thank you.

IMMIGRANTS TO THE UNITED STATES

Q. Mr. President, my name is Les McCabe, from Merced. Agriculture has the need for a large labor force, especially during the harvest time. Mexico is the nearest source of large numbers of people able and willing to work in the agricultural industry. Recent TV news stories showing the fence between the United States and Mexico and, later in the same broadcast, showing boatloads of people coming into the country seemed to portray a contradiction. Would you comment on the policy which seemingly excludes people able and willing to work, yet permits others to come into the country who in some cases will never work?

THE PRESIDENT. Les, I'll answer your question, but I can't agree with the premise of it, because I'm the one that has to deal with this question as the President, as you know, and I think I'm fairly familiar with it.

When I was sworn in as President by the Chief Justice of the Supreme Court, I took an oath, a solemn oath, to uphold the Constitution of our country and to enforce its laws. A part of those laws are the immigration and naturalization laws, and it's my responsibility, at the Mexican border, the Canadian border, or the shorelines of our country, to restrict as much as possible illegal entry of persons to our country.

We are blessed in this country by having friends to the north in Canada and to the south in Mexico. It's a great blessing. We also have a large influx of Mexican citizens who come into our country, many of them without being documented, and they provide good work. A remarkable number of them voluntarily go back to Mexico even if they haven't come here originally with the adequate certification from the Government. That will probably continue, and my guess is that the number of Spanish-speaking people in this country will continue to grow.

I would not want to see our Nation, coincidentally, or parenthetically, become a two-language nation. You've seen what happened in Canada between the French- and British-speaking people. And my hope and my expectation and my policy as President is to provide bilingual education, but to assure within the bounds of my authority and my influence that the Spanish-speaking people who come into our country ultimately learn how to speak English and become American citizens the same as everyone else. I might say that I hope that their families will also continue to know how to speak Spanish. My wife and I study Spanish, and we encourage our children to learn Spanish, because it is becoming a very important language throughout the world.

The other part of your question concerns the refugees who come by boat. We have an absolute, effective effort being made now to keep those illegal Cuban refugees from coming to our country. We have Navy ships between Cuba and the south coast of Florida. We keep Castro informed that we will not permit any further Cuban refugees come into our country unless they are first processed in accordance with American law. There was a massive influx of people who came from Cuba to our country back in the previous weeks; that's been stopped.

The people coming to our country from Southeast Asia, primarily again because the Communist government has failed and

people are escaping persecution and for freedom, are processed very carefully. They go into a country like Malaysia or the Philippines or Thailand, they are processed there by American representatives, officials, and if they are qualified to come here under American law, then they are permitted to come.

The difficulty of Cuba, of course, is it's only 90 miles away, and there's a constant stream of boats coming from the Cuban coast. But we've got that pretty well under control. And I'll continue to do this as best I can, to make sure that those who do come into our country to work, to have a better life, to escape persecution are treated fairly.

There's a special provision in the law that we ought to remember, and that is that if people come here to escape Communist persecution, they have a slightly different status. But my responsibility is to enforce the law.

The last thing I'd like to say—and I'm going to disagree with you again on this— I gather from your question that you don't believe that the boat people from Southeast Asia and from Cuba come here to work. I don't guess there's ever been a better—did I misunderstand you?

Q. Yes, sir.

THE PRESIDENT. Well, explain what you meant by that.

Q. I'm a farmer also, part-time, and we once had a *bracero* program that made it easy to get workers during harvest time. Your immigration service has taken my picking crew several times. [*Laughter*]

THE PRESIDENT. I understand. Well, okay. I might say it's your immigration service too, right? [*Laughter*]

Q. I'll tell them to leave next time. [*Laughter*]

THE PRESIDENT [*laughing*]. No, they'll

have to do their duty. [*Laughter*] They'll have have to do their duty.

But the point is, in my opinion, almost all of the people who come here from any foreign country are looking for a better life, and our record with those people has been remarkably good. It was good when my family came here from Ireland and England. I don't know where your family came here [from], but they came here to work and have a better life.

I think if you went into the Miami area, just as an example—I won't belabor this point any more—you would find that the Cubans who came here to escape Communist persecution, they came here, and they went to work, and they went to college, and they learned, and they have made darn good citizens. And I believe that that experience has been the same basically ever since our Nation was first founded. There are loafers in my own family; I hate to admit it—[*laughter*]—maybe even in yours, maybe even in your family.

Q. I don't talk about my in-laws. [*Laughter*]

THE PRESIDENT. Les said he doesn't talk about his in-laws. [*Laughter*]

But anyway, in general our country has benefited, and we'll try to enforce the law under difficult circumstances. The point we have to remember is that when almost any other nation has people leaving their country, there's one place they want to come: the United States of America. And I can understand why, can't you?

Q. Thank you.

THE PRESIDENT. Thank you, Les. Les, how's your crop this year—a good crop?

Q. Very good. I grow persimmons, incidentally. [*Laughter*]

THE PRESIDENT. Oh, very fine. We grow wild persimmons on my farm in Georgia. [*Laughter*] I've eaten them all my life.

Thank you. Over here.

1980 SUMMER OLYMPICS

Q. Mr. President, I'm Joy Basie, and I'm from Merced. And I was wondering if we're going to have Olympic games this year in Moscow.

THE PRESIDENT. Okay. How old are you, Joy?

Q. Eleven.

THE PRESIDENT. Eleven years old; Amy is twelve. You'll have to come see her sometime. [*Laughter*]

There will be Olympic games in Moscow. The United States will not participate. I'd like to add one other thing, Joy. I'm sorry this happened, but there are times when our country must stand for principle and for what is right.

The Olympic games are supposed to be to enhance peace and brotherhood and friendship. When the Soviet Union, just before the Olympic games were scheduled, invades an innocent country and kills literally thousands of men, women, and children who have done them no harm and then professes with a great propaganda effort that they are *the* peace-loving nation on Earth and that the Olympic games were actually assigned to Moscow because their foreign policy and their principles were right, it's time for other nations to let them know that they cannot get away with that false claim and propaganda.

We are encouraging the Olympic athletes in our own country, who are superb, as you know, to be recognized in every possible way. I've asked the Congress—and Tony Coelho helped—to award a special medal to every single American athlete who's going to be competing with one another and who finally wins a place on what would have been the Olympic team to go to Moscow. They'll be brought into Washington. They'll be honored at Kennedy Center. They'll be honored by the Congress with a special medal. They'll be honored by me.

And I intend to go to some of the Olympic trials myself this year to let the athletes know that we appreciate their sacrifice in not going to the Olympic games, but we also appreciate their willingness, as determined by the American Olympic Committee and the Congress and the people and myself, that we'll not condone aggression by the use of our athletes. So, we won't go, but we'll be honoring our athletes in every possible way as well. And I am grateful to them for the sacrifice they are making for our country. It's worth it.

Thank you.

Q. Thank you.

AMERICAN IMAGE AND STRENGTH

THE PRESIDENT. Good morning.

Q. Good morning. My name is Lee Wright, and I live in Merced. Today is so patriotic, I kind of hate to ask this question, but——

THE PRESIDENT. It's all right. Go ahead.

Q. It seems that recently the American people and our allies are suffering from a lack of faith in our Government's ability to support its policies and respond to international crises such as Iran and Afghanistan. How do you explain this, and how do you intend to change this image which, surprisingly to many of us, is weaker politically, economically, and militarily than we are accustomed to knowing it?

THE PRESIDENT. Lee, I'll try to answer your question. It's a good question, and it's a good day to ask it.

There are two superpowers on Earth, recognized by almost everyone: One is the Soviet Union; the other is the United States of America. Our country stands for openness, for debate, for the expression of opinion without restraint. We have the right to criticize our Government. We have the right to air publicly our disappointments, our grievances, our frustrations, our fears, our concerns, our doubts. And when we deal with other nations on Earth, like Canada or Mexico or Great Britain or Germany or France or Japan, they are free countries as well. And when somebody expresses a concern about the Chancellor of Germany, it's in the newspaper. And when somebody doesn't like what the Prime Minister of Great Britain did or said, it's top headlines in the paper, and it's on the evening television.

In open democracies, where freedom is important and where human beings are respected, any slight differences are the news. The strength of our country, the production of our land, the commitment to principles, the unity that binds us together, our success economically, what we're doing about energy, the strength of our Armed Forces, that doesn't make headlines in our country, because the Government doesn't control what the people hear or see or read.

In Russia the people only hear or see or read what the Government wants them to read. If there are sharp differences of opinion between the members of the Politburo about their invasion of Afghanistan or about the desire of literally tens of thousands of people to escape the Soviet Union for freedom, the people in Russia don't know about it. You don't read the Russian newspaper about how folks are dissatisfied with President Brezhnev.

And when you look at the refugee situation around the world, there are literally 3 or 4 million refugees who are starving and who are deprived. They're not escaping from the democracies. I've been to Berlin, and I've seen a horrible looking wall. That wall's not built there to keep people out of East Germany; it's built to keep people in East Germany who want to escape to the kind of society that we have, as exemplified in West Germany.

And you don't see boatloads of Americans trying to escape to Cuba, right? [*Laughter*]

Q. Right.

THE PRESIDENT. No, you don't. And in Kampuchea, which was formerly Cambodia, the Vietnamese invaded it and now literally hundreds of thousands of people are escaping for their lives. In Ethiopia, a Communist country with Soviet and Cuban presence there, hundreds of thousands of people have left Ethiopia, willing to starve, just to seek freedom. Afghanistan—there are 800,000 refugees who have left their homes in Afghanistan to go into Pakistan looking for freedom.

So, there is a difference of opinion quite often among us. I guarantee you, knowing the facts, that these differences as reported in the press are exaggerated, greatly exaggerated. But that's the way our system ought to work, because there's no reason to have on the evening news that Germany and the United States agree on something, but when we disagree on something, it is news. If we disagreed all the time, then when we disagree, it wouldn't be news, right?

Q. Right.

THE PRESIDENT. Okay. So, there's no sign of weakness here when there's slight differences between us and France or us and Germany or us and Japan about trade matters or agriculture matters or defense matters, because we are acting in concert to a maximum degree possible.

The final thing I'd like to say to you is this: The United States of America is the strongest nation on Earth militarily; the United States of America is the strongest nation on Earth politically; the United States of America is the strongest nation on Earth economically; and the United States of America is the strongest nation on Earth, I'm convinced, morally and ethically. And those are the strengths, to me, that are important. And it's crucial that you as a young man and I as a President and all the people here and the ones who might listen to our voice realize that the differences among us are part of our strength, and the fact that we bring those differences to the surface, and get embarrassed by them sometimes, that means that we are facing them frankly.

We've never made progress in this country in the last 204 years by weakness or cowardice or by avoiding an issue just because it was difficult. And when we face the energy problem and when we try to do something about high interest rates and we try to do something about inflation or unemployment or trade, that's not a sign of weakness; it's a sign of strength.

So, don't be concerned about the United States of America. We're the greatest nation on Earth now, and when you get old enough to run for President, it's going to be even greater.

Q. Thank you.

THE PRESIDENT. This will probably be the last question. I'm sorry. Go ahead; I want yours.

ENERGY

Q. Boy, am I lucky. [*Laughter*] Mr. President, I'd like to welcome you.

THE PRESIDENT. Thank you.

Q. My name is Kathy Brent; I'm from Merced. My question is quite short. I've read in magazines about the synfuel project.

THE PRESIDENT. Yes.

Q. My question is: How much is it going to save us at the pumps if it's so expensive to make?

THE PRESIDENT. Okay. I signed last week the synfuels bill to which Kathy is referring. We had the biggest crowd on the South Lawn of the White House we have ever had to sign legislation into law, because the people assembled there knew the importance of this. That bill that we passed, Kathy, will probably change the life of Americans in the future and indeed the entire world.

We will now begin to produce other kinds of energy in addition to oil and natural gas and also conserve energy. It's all wrapped up into that one bill. To produce synthetic fuels or heavy oil, clean-burning gas and oil out of coal, out of shale, or solar energy, to take growing crops like corn and make gasoline out of it or gasohol, to take trees that were formerly just wasted or parts of trees that were not harvested to make lumber and plywood and so forth and make fuel out of it that we can burn in our cars or burn in our homes—that's what's included in that bill.

The size of it is unbelievable. It's a greater program than the Marshall Plan that rebuilt all of Europe after the Second World War plus the total space program, including putting a man on the Moon, plus the total Interstate Highway System in our country. That's how big the synthetic fuels conservation program, gasohol program, solar power program is going to be.

And in this next 10 years, we'll be devoting American ingenuity and American money derived from taxing the oil companies with a windfall profits tax to let America be energy secure, so that we won't be vulnerable with a 12,000-mile pipeline coming out of a troubled Perisan Gulf–Middle East area, to give us the lifeblood that creates jobs and a better life and warm homes and so forth for us. So, the synthetic fuels bill will be a major step forward.

Energy, to answer the last part of your question, is not going to be cheaper in the future; it's going to be more expensive. The cheap energy comes from two places. One is what you save. When you don't use a barrel of oil, that's cheap and inexpensive. When you drive carefully, when you have five or six people in a car instead of one going to and from work regularly, when your home is well insulated, when you walk instead of ride, that's cheap energy. And the other thing is the energy that comes from the Sun.

In this marvelous agricultural region, for instance, I think in the future we'll see much less cultivation of crops. Minimum tillage is already a very important element of the life of some agricultural communities, and the other thing is in the drying of crops. Instead of using natural gas or oil heat, more and more we'll use the Sun, so that farmers can still produce better crops, better quality, and use the Sun more.

So, there are so many ways that we can change our lives, not going downhill, but going uphill. It'll be an exciting challenge to give Americans a better life at the same time we correct our overdependence on foreign oil. That's what the synthetic fuels bill will do. And we'll undoubtedly find ways in the future to produce energy that we haven't even dreamed of yet. So, in your lifetime you're going to see some wonderful, glorious, fine things happen in the energy field. Now it's kind of a depressing thing—energy. But in the future it's going to be a great, wonderful, glorious opportunity to show that Americans, a superpower, are still on the cutting edge of progress.

And when times change, with our ingenuity and with our human freedom we have always been able to accommodate those changes, not to give us a worse life, but to give us a better life. And I have no doubt that that's what we're going to do in the field of energy. And I'm very grateful that our country has that kind of characteristic, not only in the government, not only in our laws but in the hearts and minds of people who comprise its greatness.

I'm very deeply honored to be here in Merced this morning. You've made me feel at home. I hope that God will bless every one of you.

NOTE: The President spoke at 9:04 a.m. in the Merced College Gymnasium.

Earlier in the morning, the President left Mayor Wilson's residence and departed from Oakland International Airport on Air Force One.

Upon arrival at Castle Air Force Base, Atwater, Calif., the President was greeted by Lt. Col. Leo W. Smith, Wing Commander, and Mayor Greg Olzack of Atwater. He then boarded Marine One for the flight to Merced College.

Modesto, California

Remarks at a Democratic National Committee Fundraising Brunch.
July 4, 1980

I'm overwhelmed at this moment with a lot of feelings. First of all, my thanks to Frank and Ludie for making it possible for us to meet in this beautiful place on such a delightful day, the birthday of the greatest nation on Earth.

Secondly, I feel a sense of intense patriotism, as I've flown over these beautiful lands that God has used to bless us with and for which we are charged with stewardship; for great public servants like Pat Brown and Tony Coelho, who not only serves this district and California well but is a great Representative in the Congress; for our entire Nation; for all of you who have confidence in our country, who've been willing to come here at some financial sacrifice, but to be amply rewarded with the knowledge that you're participating in shaping the future of your own families and your own friends; the people that I've had meet me.

I flew over one field about 4 or 5 miles outside of town. And a farmer had used a lot of limestone or something, but there was a great big sign in the middle of the field that we could see from the airplane that said, "Hello, Jimmy. Welcome, Jimmy." [*Laughter*] But that was great. I don't know who did it, but I thank him.

And of course, we just came from Merced, where we had one of the most exciting townhall meetings that I've ever had. This was my 19th one. And the electricity that went through that crowd and the intensity of feeling for one another, the respect for the Presidency itself, love of our country was indeed an overwhelming sense of common purpose and common commitment toward the future.

So, it's a good day for us. And I'm very grateful to all of you for having come here to help us see how we can shape our country to be even better than it is today. I won't make a long speech, because I would like to spend the time I have with you shaking hands and thanking you individually and personally for the role that you play in making our country better. But I would like to say that we have a lot to be thankful for.

The biggest single responsibility on the shoulders of any President is to keep our Nation strong and at peace. God has blessed us, as you know, the last few years with peace, and I pray that I can go out of the office, having completed my service as President, with our Nation having stayed at peace. But I know that we can only do it if we are strong militarily, which we will be and are, if we stay strong economically, if we stay strong politically, diplomatically, and don't forget the moral and ethical standards of our country, which have been the source of our strength now for the 204 years since the Declaration of Independence was signed.

I have a great confidence in our country. One of the most stimulating questions that I got a few minutes ago in Merced was from a young man who said: How can we claim our country is great when there's so much difference between us within this Nation and between us and our friends and allies around the world, and all you read in the newspapers, all you see on television about those differences? And I pointed out to him that the sign of those differences is the sign of strength, that if we didn't have a lot in common, if we were always disagreeing, then it wouldn't be news, first of all, and the freedom that we share to express ourselves, to probe for better ways to live, to expose differences and failures and correct our mistakes, that's what makes the news. And that's a sign of dynamism and growth and strength that has been the source of progress in our country since it first began.

We had quite a discussion about immigrants. This crowd is a very blessed, affluent crowd. I look around at the faces and the characteristics and the features, and I would guess that every person here is part of an immigrant family. I don't see any native Indians here; there may be a few. But there has always been a tendency, as you well know, once our families got here—[*inaudible*]—to say, that's it, you know, let's don't go any further. When my family came over from England and Ireland, I would guess that some of them back in those days said, "We don't want to let the poor Irish come in, and we don't want to let folks from Eastern Europe come in, because they don't speak English very well," and so forth. And then later, of course, we had other people come.

Well, our Nation can assimilate this as long as we do it in accordance with the law and in accordance with a searching out, once people arrive here, of the true responsibilities of citizenship—hard work, dedication, struggling at first to learn a new language and to be part of a societal structure that's not a blend where we lose our religion and we lose our history and we lose the values that we brought here, but where we fit in like a beautiful mosaic with different parts, putting it together and making a country that's the best country on Earth.

And I mentioned briefly the refugees. There are 3 or 4 million refugees, hundreds of thousands trying to escape communism in Kampuchea, in Vietnam. Hundreds of thousands, over 10 percent of the population of Cuba want to get out. A lot of you have probably been to Berlin. You've seen the wall. It wasn't designed to keep people out of East Germany. It was designed to keep people in East Germany that want to escape from communism. We've got 800 or 900 thousand people that have left Afghanistan because the Soviet communism has been placed on those people, just wanting to get away from it.

And our country is so attractive that when people are refugees, there's one place they want to go. It's just like the promised land, just like it was to my folks several hundred years ago, another family 20 years ago or 2 years ago.

And our Nation is protected, because God has blessed us with great natural resources. But the main thing He's blessed us with are our human resources. It gives me power and authority and influence as President, because in our Nation we have people that relate to every other country on Earth, not just because of interest but also blood kinship. And we can understand not only people in foreign countries but one another better.

Another thing I'd like to say is that we've got problems. God knows that we've got problems. All Americans know that we've got problems, We've always had them. 204 years ago there were some people that signed the Declaration of Independence, put their names on the line— 56 of them. Mayor Hart's great-grandfather in Merced was one of the signers of the Declaration of Independence. And those people suffered. After they signed the Declaration of Independence, a lot of them went bankrupt, including Thomas Jefferson. Their wives died in the war, one wife trying to escape British soldiers. Seven of them, I believe, fought in battle. Eight or ten of them were captured and served as prisoners. They faced bankruptcy. But they didn't lose their honor, and they didn't lose their principles and their morality and their commitment to freedom.

And then later on we had the War Between the States, then the First World War, the Second World War, the Great Depression, the Korean war, the Vietnam war, very divisive; the changing of social mores in this country so that black people were treated equally for the first time— that was not easy; it was tough times, tore people apart one from another—and then the embarrassment of Watergate; the

Vietnam war tore us apart; the CIA embarrassments. Those kind of things afflicted our Nation much worse than the problems we face today.

But our country is a superpower because we've always been able to accommodate change with courage and with unity. We've never whined. We've never failed to face difficult issues. We've never failed to admit our mistakes. We've never failed, I know very well, to criticize our own Government. [*Laughter*] That's good, that's good, because when I'm criticized, I listen and I try to do better, and so does Tony Coelho, so did Pat Brown when he was in the Governor's office. This is part of the strength of America.

The last point I want to make is this: We've got struggles going on among us— environmental considerations versus economic progress. We've got struggles going on among us between the production of energy and conservation; the use of sunshine and the use of oil, imported oil, that energy produced in our own country. We've got movements of population, highly mobile population. The average person now stays in one place only about 5 years. It used to be, when I was a boy, that people very seldom moved, at least where I lived. We've got agriculture facing times of decreasing use of pesticides, decreasing use of cultivation, increasing use of solar power to produce better and better crops.

We are opening up areas of friendship between ourselves and new people around the world. In the last 2 years, we have made new friends of one-fourth of all the people who live on Earth, just when we recognized the People's Republic of China. This year out of the bay area so far, in spite of some economic depression, for instance, we have shipped American exports, American jobs, and so forth 39 percent more than we did last year. And at the same time we've reached out our hand of friendship to China, we have not lost the friendship and the trade that benefits us with the people of Taiwan.

So, we've explored for peace, explored and kept our strength, faced our problems, don't ignore them, don't deny them. But I can tell you that our country is today the greatest on Earth, strongest on Earth, and it's going to stay that way and it's going to be greater in the future.

And I think the part of it all that's overwhelming is the people and the partnership that we've formed. We have never failed to unite ourselves in a common effort when we recognized a challenge or a danger or a threat to our country. And I'm very grateful that on this Fourth of July we can kind of dramatize that partnership and that relationship, when the President of the United States can come to Modesto to shake hands with fine Americans and thank you individually for all you mean to this country.

Thank you very much. God bless you.

NOTE: The President spoke at approximately 11 a.m. at the residence of Attorney Frank Dambrell, who hosted the brunch.

Following the brunch, the President boarded Marine One at the Christine Sipherd School and returned to Castle Air Force Base where he boarded Air Force One for the flight to Miami, Fla.

Miami, Florida

***Remarks to the National Association for the Advancement of Colored People.** July 4, 1980*

Let me say first of all that it's great to be here. As you can see, I did not have any trouble accepting my invitation to come to the NAACP convention. And the reason for that is that I know what NAACP stands for, and I also know what the NAACP organization in the last 80 years has meant to this Nation and has meant to my life as an American. It's important for me as President to extend my congratulations and my support to this organization, because you still mean so much to our country.

While I'm here, I want to add my voice to yours to help assure a very strong, vital, well-financed, well-supported NAACP in the future years. And I'm eager to help you. You will have a friend in the Oval Office, and you can depend on that.

I want to thank you, Kelly Alexander, and Margaret Bush Wilson, my good friend, Dr. Montague Cobb, Dr. Benjamin Hooks, members and friends of the NAACP.

I've tried as much as I could as President to consult with people from all walks of life on important issues, and for that reason I have especially valued Benjamin Hooks' opinions, because they save me a lot of time. I get the views of all walks of life, of a preacher, a lawyer, a judge, an FCC Commissioner, a civil rights leader all at the same time from one man. And I might say I get this opinion very often and very strong—[*laughter*]—and so you can depend on his voice being well expressed in Washington, in the Oval Office, for you.

As you all know, 204 years ago today America declared its independence with a truth that still sets people free throughout a troubled world, that all people are endowed with rights that cannot be bought or sold, rights that no power on Earth can justly deny. But the Declaration that we celebrate unfortunately avoided another truth. When Jefferson's condemnation of the King of England for refusing to end the slave trade was struck from the final draft, Thomas Jefferson said, "I tremble for my country when I reflect that God is just." All of us know how violent were the wounds that this contradiction caused; 200 years later we're still working to heal them.

America's first great moral struggle was to free the slaves, and it took nearly 90 years, but our Nation won. And the next great moral struggle took almost a hundred years—to end legalized segregation. That's the basic reason the NAACP was formed, and you were in the forefront of that fight. You fought for progress through long years of crucial legal procedures and historic legislative battles. You held us to our Nation's highest principles. And again America won, because of you.

Today we're in the midst of America's third great moral campaign—fighting to extend equal justice and equal opportunity to every human being in this society. This is my responsibility as President, and it's also your responsibility as leaders. We must not and we will not fail in this effort.

I wish I could come here to you tonight, as President of the greatest country of all, to say that this battle for moral justice was over, but it's not, not while groups such as the Ku Klux Klan and the self-proclaimed Nazis and others still encourage racial hatred and religious hatred, not when minorities still fear police harassment, when children are not getting the education or the health care they need, when too many young people cannot find jobs, when too many mothers and fathers cannot support their families, and when too many people are still afraid, in the greatest country on Earth—too many people are still afraid of the present and of the future.

I'm not here to tell you that we've reached the promised land. We cannot undo 30 decades, 300 years of discrimination in 3 or 4 years. But we're on the right road, and we'll stay on the right road until we reach the promised land, the goal that God set for us. To lose sight of that promised land is to lose our sense of direction. But we have had some victories, and it's a mistake for the NAACP to deny itself credit for those victories, because to deny ourselves the sustenance and the encouragement of what we have done is to deny the inspiration and the support required to continue the struggle.

Everything in this Nation is not black and poor. Many people obviously are black and poor, but we've got a future ahead of us and a present life that's the envy and the admiration of almost all other people on Earth.

The walls built around totalitarian countries are not designed to keep free people out. I've been in Berlin, and I've seen the wall. It's designed to keep the people in East Berlin, under communism, prisoners. And you don't see boats trying to leave this country going to Southeast Asia or to Cuba. And you don't see people trying to get into Afghanistan so they can suffer under totalitarian subjugation. Our country is still the admiration of the world, and it's a mistake for us when we only look at the gloomy side of what we are and what we have done.

In the last few years we've looked at the real needs of our urban centers, and we've provided more than $25 billion for State and local governments. We've not yet revitalized every city in the United States, but we are succeeding in ways that would have been undreamed of 3½ years ago. When you go to a meeting now of local officials, mayors, or county officials and talk to them, you see a new hope and a new expectation and a new sense of accomplishment that was not there just a few short years ago.

Unemployment, and particularly black unemployment and particularly black young unemployment, is far, far too high. But we've created more new jobs in the last 3½ years than at any other time in history, even including the years of war.

One million more black Americans hold jobs today than they did in January 1977. Employment, even among black teenagers, has risen dramatically, and in the spring of this year, for the first time in 7 years, black teenage unemployment even went down.

We don't say that to minimize the challenge and the problem that we face, but the fact is that because of your good work, joined by many others who share the same goals with you, our existence, your existence is worthwhile. And if every American knew what you have been able to accomplish, working through government, working with the private sector, your rolls and your contributions would be growing by leaps and bounds, and I urge you not to hide your light under a bushel.

Economic justice means more than just jobs for minorities; it also means a chance to build minority-owned businesses. With the support of the NAACP, we are making progress. In the last 3 years, for instance, Federal deposits in banks owned by minority Americans have more than doubled. And as Benjamin Hooks knows so well, communications, especially radio and television, are critically important in our society. But when the radio and the television licenses were handed out, not many blacks were in any position to apply. Because of initiatives over the last 2 years, there are now exactly twice as many minority-owned radio and television stations as there were 2 years ago.

We've already tripled the dollar amount of Federal contracts with minority businesses, something unheard of in the past. When Congressman Parren Mitchell first proposed a 10-percent mandatory set-aside for Federal contracts to go to businesses that were owned by minority groups, nobody thought that there would even be enough minority-owned businesses that could qualify for that much business. But they were quickly proven wrong, and

we've far exceeded that by 50 percent above what was ever thought about as being possible.

And the Supreme Court decision this week upholds this law requiring that 10 percent of all Federal contract money goes to minority-owned businesses, and at the same time, as you know—and the issue has been in doubt—the Supreme Court approved affirmative action to eliminate the results of past discrimination. This is the third time we've acted together, my administration and you, to defend major affirmative action programs before the Supreme Court, and we've won—Bakke, in higher education; Weber, in employment; and now this case involving minority business.

We've targeted economic aid to encourage private sector jobs for the hardcore unemployed. Resources for youth employment in the last 3½ years have increased from 2½ billion to 4 billion dollars, and this year the major domestic program that we've put before the Congress, that I believe will be passed, is to add $2 billion more for permanent youth employment and training programs. This is above and beyond the 1 million summer jobs that will be provided for unemployed youth and all the youth programs that presently exist on the books and which are being fully financed. Fighting to create these new jobs is my responsibility as President, but it's also your responsibility. And together, if we work together, we can win this fight as we've won so many others.

With your help, since I became President funding for teaching basic skills to disadvantaged children has more than doubled; Job Corps is up 157 percent; CETA programs, up 115 percent; food stamps, up 99 percent, and no longer do poor people have to pay for food stamps with cash money. Funding for women's, infants', and children's programs is three times as great as it was in 1976. Despite our continuing effort to control inflation, we are protecting such programs that are important to you as social security, Aid for Families with Dependent Children, and we're greatly increasing subsidized Government housing and programs like Head Start.

As you know from your long struggles on civil rights, one of the most important powers of any President is the power of appointment. Presidents come and go, but those appointments quite often stay on, and they determine the policies of our Nation that affect the lives of everyone, not just Cabinet, administrative officials, as crucial as they might be, but U.S. attorneys, members of regulatory boards, and Federal judges.

I have appointed people like Drew Days and Eleanor Holmes Norton to administer the laws that enforce civil rights. I have put black people on regulatory boards of all kinds, and I've also always insisted on affirmative action. The results speak for themselves. I won't quote the statistics, in order to save time.

I've only served 3½ years as President, but I have already appointed more blacks, more women, and more Hispanics to the Federal bench as judges than all other Presidents in the 200-year history of this country. And I'm not through yet. And I might say I've done it in such a way, with your help, that we have brought credit to the Federal bench. I have proved, with your help, that you don't have to lower the standards on the judicial bench when you fulfill the obligations to the black citizens of our Nation that had been deprived for so many years.

If you don't listen to anything else I say tonight, I want you to hear the next few words: These Federal judges serve for life. They will be interpreting your rights, the rights of our children, and the

rights of our children's children into the next century. Young people born this year will become adults in the 21st century. And I want you to consider very carefully and very seriously how this Nation's future will be affected by the appointment of the next three or four Justices of the United States Supreme Court.

Just stop a few moments and think about it, because you know, in looking back over the previous years, that when local school boards and mayors, State legislatures and Governors, Presidents and the Congress have not been willing to give the rights to Americans that had been withheld, the United States Supreme Court has been the final bulwark of freedom.

We'd been through 8 years, before I came in office, of appointments to the Supreme Court. The Republican administration under Richard Nixon made a profound impact on the attitude and tone of that court. It's still a good court, because we got a good ruling this week. But you just think about what will happen with another three or four appointments.

We're waging important battles right now, today, in the Congress that affect your lives, for the confirmation of Federal judges that I have sent to the Hill that have not yet been approved, for welfare reform, for fair housing legislation, to make sure that we take the '68 act, which was good and which has never been enforced, and have enforcement powers. We got that bill to the legislature, to the Congress and the House, with your help, and now we're struggling to get it out of the Judiciary Committee in the United States Senate. And then we might face a filibuster in the Senate.

This will be the most important civil rights legislation of the last 10 years, and I'm very grateful to have the NAACP at my shoulder as we fight this battle over the next few weeks. It's my responsibility and it's your responsibility to see that discrimination in housing, which exists today throughout our country, joins other outmoded concepts, like separate but equal schools, as just a notation in the old, dusty history books of our country.

As Dr. Martin Luther King, Jr., said, "Every crisis has both its dangers and its opportunities. The ultimate measure of a man is not where he stands in moments of comfort and convenience, but where he stands in moments of challenge and controversy." And that's true not only for a man; it's true for an organization like yours, and it's true for a nation.

This is a decade of decision. It's our responsibility to defeat those forces which threaten the progress that we have made and cloud our hopes for the future. There's a general acknowledgement that the battles that we have won in recent months and recent years have been very difficult. Anybody who looks at the attitude and tone of the Congress knows that this is true.

We cannot solve any of our problems by pretending that they are not there, and we also cannot solve any of our problems by pretending they're so great that they can't be solved. If the NAACP had given up 50 years ago just because people were discouraged, you would not be sitting here tonight, and I would not be talking to you. But we've seen the unfortunate results of that kind of an approach in past administrations in Washington, in blocking equal opportunity and equal justice.

This week I signed into law a bill which you may not have noticed much, but which will affect your lives—the largest peacetime program in the history of our country, the Energy Security Act, to develop alternative forms of energy and to end our dangerous dependence on foreign oil and, in the process, to give tens of

thousands of new jobs in an exciting new opportunity for progress in our country in the years ahead.

It's been hard for our people to understand that when we talk about energy problems, we're not just talking about the price of gasoline, we're not just talking about the price of heating our own homes; we're talking about the price of food, and we're talking about running our industries, we're talking about expanding our economy, we're talking about financing our schools, we're talking about providing jobs and careers for Americans and decent standards of living everywhere, and we're also talking about peace in the world, and we're talking about the security of our country.

The security of our economy is my responsibility, and it's also yours. I've taken the dangerous and the difficult steps to control inflation and to cut down interest rates, and these measures are working. This will increase buying by you and by others, and then producing those products that are going to be bought and employing people to do that production, to put our factories back to work.

We have programs in place and also in the works in Congress to help ease the burden when serious problems do arise in a family's life, but we must remember no matter what I do or what any President could do, no matter what you might do, that five out of six jobs in this country are in the private sector. Inflation has been eating up the dollars needed to create those jobs, but most of all, inflation has been robbing the poor, the elderly, the young, and others who already suffer from discrimination, who have to trade at the corner grocery store, where the prices are probably twice as high as they are in a supermarket out near the beltway or the circumferential highway. The poor are the ones who can't buy things wholesale, and the poor are the ones that can't move to another distant location, and the poor are quite often the ones that are not educated enough to shop around for different kinds of jobs.

Those are the ones that have suffered most from the ravages of inflation, and we cannot reignite the fuse of inflation. The current politically inspired efforts in the Congress, that you've read so much about lately, to tack what amounts to a 30-percent tax cut over the next 3 years on totally unrelated bills in the Congress, so they won't have to have public hearings, would do just that. You need to understand what this could mean to you if the effort is successful.

By the year 1985 it would cost us $280 billion per year. It would set off a new round of inflation that would quickly erase any benefits to taxpayers. And that disaster would come at the expense of the poor, the elderly, the sick and disadvantaged, our cities, jobs, the kinds of things that the NAACP has struggled to achieve during the last 80 years of your life. Programs designed for social programs would have to be robbed more than $200 billion worth. And the proposal, as you can well imagine looking at the origin of it, certainly won't make the rich lose. Those making more than $200,000 a year would get a tax cut 80 times bigger than the family making less than $10,000 a year.

Just as we must not abandon our efforts to regain control of our economic destiny, we cannot abandon our fight for fundamental human rights and for peace around the world.

In Zimbabwe we stood firm for majority rule. We had tough battles in the Congress, as you well know, to maintain that position, and NAACP was in there fighting tooth and toenail. And because we had the courage to hold out, others had the courage to continue. And I was glad

to send Andy Young to represent me and you and all Americans at the celebration of the true independence in that long-troubled African nation. Zimbabwe is now free, democratic, and independent.

We are struggling against international terrorism in Iran. And it's good on an Independence Day celebration to remember 53 Americans who are not free. They are innocent. They are kidnap victims by terrorists who have the support of their own government.

And because we're standing up against the Soviet Union, who have taken away the freedom of those who live in Afghanistan—and we'll continue that struggle— we're determined to prove to the Soviets that it does not pay to deprive freedom from people. Those freedom-fighters there have our admiration. They're struggling for national liberation. Over 800,000 of them have crossed the borders into Pakistan, another 100 or 200 thousand into Iran. If anyone on Earth understands what it means to lose that kind of freedom and the importance of struggling to restore it, it would be those in this room who are assembled here tonight.

We must continue to uphold for people and for nations and to work for peaceful solutions throughout the world. I cannot promise you everything will be better from this moment forward, that there will be no more sacrifice, because there will; no more delay in meeting treasured goals, because there's going to be delay. And I will not lie to you and say that all is right in the world, because it's not, or alright in our Nation, because it's not.

And I will not pretend to you that we can work miracles with mirrors to create full employment without a competitive economic base, because we cannot; or that we can force peace on an unwilling world, because we can't; or establish equal justice without further cost and without further sacrifice, because we cannot. We have never acquired an additional element of fairness and equity and freedom and justice without struggle and without sacrifice, and we'll never do it.

So, I just want to tell it to you straight. This is a time of controversy. This is a time of impatience. This is a time of pain. This is a time of struggle. But most of all, this is a time of making decisions.

Our hard-won gains face the most severe counterattack since the time of *Brown* versus *the Board of Education*. It's time to stand firm against any national retreat to dreams of a remembered rosy past, because you and I know the past was not always rosy. It's no time for selective amnesia. [*Laughter*]

And I'm not just giving you idle talk, because there are those who say that the way to solve our energy problem is for the Government to just leave us to the tender mercies and the humanitarian impulses of the oil companies. [*Laughter*] And there are those who look at youngsters who cannot read, and they tell you it's just the parents' fault, that Government can't do anything, that the best way to solve our education problems is to abolish the Department of Education. But they're looking at the bottom line for the rich instead of looking at the needs and hopes of those who have been too long at the bottom of the economic heap.

The directions that we choose this year will determine not only what happens in the next few years but for the rest of this century. This is no time for our courage to waver. This is no time to endanger a good, solid, common commitment and a partnership. At critical times such as this, the NAACP has always been in the forefront of every fight for freedom and for justice and for opportunity.

I cannot think of any more fitting group for the President of this country to join in celebrating the Fourth of July than the NAACP. Throughout this century—and you were formed at the beginning of this century—you fought to extend the principles of the Declaration of Independence to all of our people, in courtrooms across the land, in legislative chambers in the State capitols and also in Washington, and in day-by-day living, seeking always to uphold the original idea of our Nation, even when many more advantaged than you forgot or would not face the fact of what our Nation ought to be, that the purpose of government is to protect the inalienable rights of all its citizens.

The fight for justice must be renewed with each new day, with each new law, with each law enforcement action, with each ruling in the State and Federal courts, and with each dealing with an individual human being. On this 204th birthday of our Nation, let us rededicate ourselves to fight until victory is won. You've got a friend in the Oval Office who will join that fight with you.

Thank you very much, and God bless you all.

NOTE: The President spoke at 8:37 p.m. at the 71st annual convention-Freedom Fund awards banquet of the NAACP, which was held in the Grand Ballroom of the Fontainebleau Hotel.

Earlier in the evening, the President arrived at Miami International Airport following the flight from California and was greeted by U.S. Trade Representative Reubin O'D. Askew, Representatives Claude Pepper and Dante Fascell of Florida, Mayor Maurice Ferre of Miami, Mayor Stephen Clark of Dade County, and Rev. Theodore Gibson, Miami city commissioner.

Following the banquet, the President returned to Miami International Airport and boarded Air Force One enroute to Georgia. After a short stop at Robins Air Force Base, Warner Robins, Ga., the President boarded Marine One for the flight to Plains, where he stayed until Tuesday, July 8.

Detroit, Michigan

Remarks to Reporters Following a Meeting With Automobile Industry Representatives. July 8, 1980

Good morning, everybody. I think it's obvious to those who are interested in the American economy and particularly interested in the automobile industry that this is indeed an historic meeting. Eight weeks ago, we invited the leaders of the different American manufacturing companies for automobiles, plus Doug Fraser and representatives of the UAW, to come to the Cabinet Room to discuss what we might do to help the American automobile industry make the transition phase over to accommodate the changed consumer preferences brought about by unanticipated increases in energy price.

As you know, we've now been working for 8 weeks, literally day and night, with the industry and labor leaders to prepare a package of proposals that would help this industry. I'm deeply concerned about the adverse impact on communities where the automobile industry is a major factor in employment. I'm particularly grieved and concerned about the very high unemployment rate in the industry now.

We want to move as rapidly as we possibly can to correct any problems that can be corrected through Government action and joint action with the industry itself. We will make changes in prospective regulations that would add about $500 million to the cash flow of the American automobile manufacturers. We will also provide about $50 million or so, perhaps more than that, in special assistance for communities that have high unemployment rates brought about by the changes being made in the automobile industry. Through the Small Business Administration we'll provide whatever is necessary— between $200 million and $400 million— for dealers, in guaranteed loans which might be necessary for them to keep their stock and trade adequate.

Later on this year, perhaps in the next few weeks, I'll be visiting personally some of the manufacturing plants that produce the extremely high quality, fuel-efficient automobiles brought about by the rapid retooling that is taking place in the American automobile industry. The Treasury Department will help by taking cognizance of the fact that because of rapidly changing consumer preferences, there is an economic obsolescence in some of the tools and equipment being used to manufacture automobiles. In other words, there will be a faster depreciation permitted, which is completely proper under the law for this purpose.

In addition to that, when economic conditions do permit, in the future when we show an adequate self-discipline by restraining Federal expenditures, and when we work out a proposal that can be anti-inflationary in nature, and propose to the Congress a general tax reduction plan, the automobile industry will obviously have consideration to meet its special needs.

I might point out that perhaps the most important thing to remember today is that this package of proposals—that has been worked out jointly with the industry and with the UAW and with the Federal Government—is just a first step. We will set up an automobile industry committee that will continue to provide some assistance, which is completely proper, compatible with the free enterprise system that we cherish, conducive to high competitiveness within the industry, and we will not in any way violate our commitment to high air standards, air quality standards, nor to efficiency.

It's obvious that the competitive nature of the international automobile industry is much more restrictive in this respect now than any Government regulations.

But we will be very cautious in the future in implementing new regulations to make sure that they are conducive to a strong, vital automobile industry in our country and not derogate in any way the air quality standards nor the efficiency standards that are necessary.

And finally, let me say that I have asked, or will ask, the ITC, Trade Commission, for an expedited ruling on whether or not imports of automobiles into this country have adversely affected or improperly affected the industry in our country. This does not prejudge what their finding might be, and it does not prejudge what action I will take when I get a recommendation from them. But because of the importance of this industry and the needs at this time, it's important to me, as President, to have a quick ruling, after adequate time is given for the hearings and investigation, from the ITC.

We have formed, in effect, a very close-knit, permanent partnership, within the bounds of propriety for our free enterprise system, between the Government itself and the automobile industry—representing labor, manufacturing, perhaps automobile parts, and perhaps even the dealers. And I believe that this will be a major step forward in providing for the American consumer the extremely high quality, fuel-efficient automobile which will be required in the months and the years ahead.

I would like to express my thanks to the representatives of all the automobile manufacturing plants who are here—the chairmen of the board and the presidents of all of them are present—to Doug Fraser and his vice presidents who've assembled with us, and to the leaders of our Transportation Department, the Treasury Department, our Special Trade Representative, and those others who are associated with me representing the Federal Government.

The mayor of Detroit is here, Coleman Young. The Michigan delegation is here; I think en masse. And I'm deeply grateful that they would get up this early in the morning on such an important consideration. We're all in it together, and I have great hopes and expectations that the automobile industry of our country will make strides in the future that will be pleasing to all of us. We are now producing in our country roughly 1½ million of the small, fuel-efficient automobiles. It's anticipated that by 1983, a very short time in the future, we'll be producing in the neighborhood of 7½ million of these automobiles that will be required by the American consumer. This is a major goal. It's one that we will meet, I believe, with this kind of cooperation guaranteed among us.

Thank you very much for being with us this morning. It's an important day in the life of our country. Thank you very much.

NOTE: The President spoke at 7:52 a.m. in the lounge of the Michael Berry International Terminal at the Detroit International Airport following the meeting which was also held in the terminal.

After his remarks, the President boarded Air Force One for the flight to Japan, with a short stop in Anchorage, Alaska.

Domestic Automobile Industry

Letter to the Chairman of the U.S. International Trade Commission. July 9, 1980

To Chairman Alberger

You are now beginning an investigation under Section 201 of the Trade Act of 1974 to determine whether domestic producers of passenger cars, light trucks, vans, and general utility vehicles are being seriously injured, or threatened with serious injury, substantially caused by increased imports.

Given the widespread attention in this country to recent developments in the automotive sector, this investigation (TA–201–44) has become a matter of great national and international importance. I urge you to conduct your work as expeditiously as is practicable (pursuant to Section 201(d)(2)), so that all of those involved will not be burdened for a period of 6 to 8 months with the uncertainty such a case creates. This case touches so many businesses, workers, and consumers in this country that an investigation of normal length could cause major uncertainties which could significantly affect automobile trade and production. At the same time, of course, it is critical that all parties have a full opportunity to be heard and to submit information and arguments that must be considered in your deliberations.

The Commission faces a challenging task and carries a great responsibility in this investigation. I recognize that your current workload is substantial, but I would deeply appreciate your efforts to accelerate your schedule on this important case.

My Administration stands ready to assist the Commission in whatever manner you feel would be appropriate.

Sincerely,

JIMMY CARTER

[The Honorable Bill Alberger, Chairman, U.S. International Trade Commission, Suite 274, 701 E Street, N.W., Washington, D.C. 20436]

NOTE: The text of the letter was made available by the White House Press Office.

Nuclear Regulatory Commission

Nomination of Albert Carnesale To Be a Member. July 9, 1980

The President today announced his intention to nominate Albert Carnesale, of Lexington, Mass., to be a member of the Nuclear Regulatory Commission. Upon confirmation by the Senate, he will be designated Chairman.

Carnesale was born July 2, 1936, the Bronx, N.Y. He received a B.M.E. from The Cooper Union in 1957, an M.S. from Drexel Institute in 1962, and a Ph. D. from North Carolina State University in 1966.

From 1957 to 1962, he was senior engineer for the nuclear division of the Martin Marietta Corp., in Baltimore, Md. Carnesale was Chief of the Defensive Weapons Systems Division of the U.S. Arms Control and Disarmament Agency from 1969 to 1972. From 1972 to 1974, he was professor and head of the division of university studies and university coordinator for environmental studies at North Carolina State University. Since 1974 Carnesale has been professor of public policy in the John F. Kennedy School of Government and associate director of the Center for Science and International Affairs.

Nuclear Regulatory Commission

Statement on the Designation of Albert Carnesale as Chairman. July 9, 1980

The Three Mile Island accident and the Kemeny Commission report have underlined the need for strong, concerned leadership at the Nuclear Regulatory Commission. I am appointing Dr. Carnesale because I know he can and will provide that kind of leadership. I also know that he will be especially sensitive to the overriding importance of safety and environmental protection in the development of our nuclear power resources.

I am confident that under Dr. Carnesale's direction, the NRC will work to enhance its efforts to ensure that the Kemeny Commission recommendations are fully implemented and that public safety and health are protected in our Nation's nuclear powerplants.

National Cancer Institute

Appointment of Vincent T. DeVita, Jr., as Director.   July 9, 1980

The President today announced the appointment of Vincent T. DeVita, Jr., of Bethesda, Md., as Director of the National Cancer Institute (NCI). He replaces Arthur C. Upton, who has resigned.

DeVita has been Acting Director of NCI since the beginning of this year.

He was born March 7, 1935, in the Bronx, N.Y. He received a B.S. from the College of William and Mary in 1957 and graduated from George Washington University School of Medicine in 1961.

DeVita joined NCI in 1963 as a clinical associate in the Laboratory of Clinical Pharmacology, leaving in 1965 to complete his advanced training in medicine at Yale-New Haven Medical Center. He returned to NCI in 1966, and has served consecutively as a Senior Investigator in the Solid Tumor Service, Head of the Solid Tumor Service, Chief of the Medicine Branch, and Director of the Division of Cancer Treatment. Since 1975 he has also held the post of Clinical Director, NCI.

DeVita has been an associate editor of the Journal of the National Cancer Institute and is the author of numerous scientific papers. He has received many awards and honors.

National Endowment for the Humanities

Nomination of Nine Members of the National Council on the Humanities.   July 9, 1980

The President today announced nine persons whom he will nominate to be members of the National Council on the Humanities. They are:

MARCUS COHN, of Chevy Chase, Md., a partner in the firm of Cohn and Marks and a professional lecturer in law at George Washington University's Graduate School of Public Law;

SAMUEL DUBOIS COOK, of New Orleans, president of Dillard University;

ROLAND PAUL DILLE, of Moorhead, Minn., president and professor of English at Moorhead State University;

A. BARTLETT GIAMATTI, president of Yale University;

GEORGE ALEXANDER KENNEDY, of Chapel Hill, N.C., Paddison professor of classics at the University of North Carolina at Chapel Hill and chairman of the board of governors of the University of North Carolina Press;

LOUISE AÑO NUEVO KERR, of Evanston, Ill., an assistant professor of history at Loyola University of Chicago;

FRANCES DODSON RHOME, of Bloomington, Ind., an associate professor of English at Indiana University and director of university affirmative action there;

PHILIP A. SCHAEFER, of Belvedere, Calif., a stockbroker and vice president of Bear, Stearns & Co., who is active in civic and political affairs;

ANITA SILVERS, of San Francisco, professor of philosophy at San Francisco State University.

President's Commission on Executive Exchange

Appointment of Three Members.   July 9, 1980

The President today announced the appointment of three persons as members of the President's Commission on Executive Exchange. They are:

THOMAS HSIEH, of San Francisco, Calif., president of the architectural firm Thomas Hsieh, AIA, and active in civic affairs;

DAVID T. KEARNS, president and chief operating officer of Xerox Corp.;

MENO TRUMAN LAKE, of Hidden Hills, Calif., president and chief executive officer of Occidental Life of California.

Vice President Mondale's Trip to Senegal, Niger, and Nigeria

Statement by the President.   *July 10, 1980*

Vice President Mondale will head the U.S. delegation to the upcoming round of the U.S.-Nigerian bilateral talks and has accepted invitations to visit Senegal and Niger. The Vice President will also make a brief stop in the Cape Verde Islands. The visit will take place during July 17–23, 1980.

I have asked the Vice President to serve as my personal representative during these visits.

During his visit to Nigeria, the Vice President will serve as Chairman of the U.S. delegation to the next round of formal bilateral consultations, scheduled to begin July 22, to review U.S.-Nigerian cooperation in the fields of trade and investment, science and technology, agriculture and energy.

Close and cordial relations with these nations and with the nations of Africa are very important to us, and the Vice President's visit will reinforce them.

During the course of these visits, the Vice President will review our excellent bilateral relations, current developments in Africa, and other international issues of mutual interest.

NOTE: The White House announced that Mrs. Joan Mondale will accompany the Vice President on the trip.

Supplemental Appropriations and Rescission Act, 1980

White House Statement on the Food for Peace Program Provisions of the Act.   *July 10, 1980*

President Carter signed, during his trip to Tokyo, a supplemental appropriation bill which provides an additional $143 million for the Food for Peace (P.L. 480) program during the fiscal year which ends September 30, 1980. The additional funding is expected to purchase approximately 530,000 metric tons of food commodities, primarily wheat and wheat flour, corn and vegetable oil.

A substantial part of this food will go to countries in East Africa which are experiencing serious drought problems and increasing numbers of refugees. The funds also will provide additional food assistance to meet acute refugee needs in other areas of the world, particularly Kampuchea and Pakistan. This cooperative action by the Congress and the executive branch thus will help to meet important humanitarian needs on a global basis.

Approximately $123 million will be used in the title II program, which provides grant food assistance through the World Food Program, Government-to-Government programs, and private voluntary agencies. Through this title, U.S. religious and other private groups play a vital role in averting starvation. The remaining $20 million will be used in the title I program, which provides food assistance through concessional loans to the developing countries for purchase in the United States of the needed commodities.

NOTE: As enacted, H.R. 7542 is Public Law 96–304, approved July 8.

Soft Drink Interbrand Competition Act

Statement on Signing S. 598 Into Law.
July 10, 1980

I have signed into law S. 598, the "Soft Drink Interbrand Competition Act." The purpose of this legislation is to "clarify the circumstances under which territorial provisions in licenses to manufacture, distribute, and sell trademarked soft drink products are lawful under the antitrust laws."

Since 1971, soft drink bottlers have been faced with the uncertainty created by pending legal proceedings challenging the legality of territorial provisions in their franchise agreements. As the report of the Committee on the Judiciary of the House of Representatives explains, this legislation is intended simply to eliminate that uncertainty by reaffirming legislatively the rule of reason approach followed by the Supreme Court in *Continental T.V. Inc.* v. *GTE Sylvania, Inc.,* 433 U.S. 36 (1977). While I have had misgivings about the language of earlier versions of this bill, I believe that the amendments adopted by the House of Representatives, and agreed to by the Senate, have met the objective of eliminating that uncertainty. The House report emphasizes that the act "does not grant antitrust immunities." Under these circumstances, I do not believe that the bill establishes a special antitrust exemption or permits otherwise illegal restrictions on competition.

NOTE: As enacted, S. 598 is Public Law 96–308, approved July 9.

United States Ambassador to Malaysia

Nomination of Barbara M. Watson.
July 10, 1980

The President today announced that he will nominate Barbara M. Watson, of the District of Columbia, to be Ambassador Extraordinary and Plenipotentiary of the United States to Malaysia. She would replace Robert H. Miller, resigned.

Watson has been Assistant Secretary of State for Consular Affairs since 1977.

She was born November 5, 1918, in New York City. Watson received an A.B. in 1943 from Barnard College and an LL. B. in 1962 from New York Law School.

From 1943 to 1946, she was an interviewer with the United Seamen's Service of New York. Watson was owner and executive director of Barbara Watson Models from 1946 to 1956 and a clerk with The Christophers of New York from 1956 to 1957. From 1958 to 1959, she was coordinator of student activities and foreign student adviser at Hampton Institute. Watson was a statutory aide with the Board of Statutory Consolidation of New York from 1962 to 1963 and assistant attorney with the law department for New York City from 1963 to 1964. From 1964 to 1966, she was executive director of the New York City Commission to the United Nations.

She served as special assistant to the Deputy Under Secretary of State for Administration in 1966 and as Deputy and Acting Administrator of the Bureau of Security and Consular Affairs from 1966 to 1968. From 1968 to 1974, she was Administrator of the Bureau of Security and Consular Affairs. From 1975 to 1976, she was a lecturer to colleges and universities in the United States and from 1976 to 1977, she was legal consultant with Triangle Publications, Inc.

United States Ambassador to Uruguay

Nomination of Robert S. Gershenson.
July 10, 1980

The President today announced that he will nominate Robert S. Gershenson, of Potomac, Md., to be Ambassador Extraordinary and Plenipotentiary of the United States to Uruguay. He would replace Lyle Franklin Lane, who has been appointed Ambassador to Paraguay.

Gershenson has been Deputy Assistant Secretary of State for Personnel since 1978.

He was born August 17, 1928, in Philadelphia, Pa. Gershenson received a B.A. from Temple University in 1956 and served in the U.S. Army from 1951 to 1953.

Gershenson joined the Foreign Service in 1957 and served in Mexico, Brazil, Costa Rica, and Ecuador. From 1968 to 1970, he was counselor for administrative affairs in Uruguay. He attended the Industrial College of the Armed Forces from 1970 to 1971.

From 1971 to 1972, he was personnel officer at State and special assistant to the Assistant Secretary for Administration from 1972 to 1974. He was counselor for administrative affairs in Brussels from 1974 to 1976. From 1976 to 1978, Gershenson was Executive Director for Inter-American Affairs at State.

National Institute of Education

Nomination of Four Members of the National Council on Educational Research.
July 10, 1980

The President today announced four persons whom he will nominate to be members of the National Council on Educational Research. They are:

MARIA B. CERDA, of Chicago, executive director and founder of the Latino Institute, who is active in numerous civic activities, including groups concerned with multicultural education.

JOSEPH J. DAVIES, JR., of Arabi, La., a member of the Louisiana State Board of Trustees for Colleges and Universities and chairman of its Academic Affairs Committee. He was superintendent of schools for St. Bernard Parish for 18 years.

TIMOTHY S. HEALY, S.J., president and professor of English at Georgetown University.

JOHN S. SHIPP, JR., of Marianna, Fla., director of administration of the Florida State Department of Agriculture and Consumer Services, and a former associate State commissioner of education for administration.

Advisory Commission on Intergovernmental Relations

Reappointment of Three Members.
July 10, 1980

The President today announced the reappointment of three members of the Advisory Commission on Intergovernmental Relations. They are:

LYNN G. CUTLER, a member of the board of supervisors of Black Hawk County, Iowa, and a member of the board of directors of the National Association of Counties;

JAMES T. MCINTYRE, JR., Director of the Office of Management and Budget;

RICHARD A. SNELLING, Governor of Vermont.

World Conference for the United Nations Decade for Women

Statement on the U.S. Delegation's Departure for Copenhagen.   July 11, 1980

As President of the United States, I extend my best wishes to the U.S. delegation which departs tonight for Copenhagen to represent our Government at the World Conference for the United Nations Decade for Women. This delegation of distinguished women and men reflects the wide diversity of our society and is ably led by Ambassador Donald McHenry and Presidential Assistant Sarah Weddington.

The Conference will provide a constructive opportunity to review the progress of women throughout the world during the past 5 years and to establish a meaningful plan of specific actions to benefit women for the coming 5 years. The work of this Conference to improve the conditions of women's lives everywhere in the world can make a major contribution to the enhancement of human rights, a goal which has been a vital element of my administration's policy. The United States is deeply committed to eliminating all forms of discrimination and will continue to work for equal rights at home and abroad.

I am proud to authorize Sarah Weddington to sign, on behalf of the United States, the Convention on the Elimination of All Forms of Discrimination Against Women. Following the signing ceremony in Copenhagen on July 17, the Convention will be subjected to the normal constitutional processes of the United States.

I am confident that this delegation will contribute to international understanding and cooperation on these vital issues and will reflect great credit on our country.

Digest of Other White House Announcements

The following listing includes the President's public schedule and other items of general interest announced by the White House Press Office and not included elsewhere in this issue.

July 8

The President left Detroit, Mich., for visits to Tokyo, Japan, Anchorage, Alaska, Sapelo Island, Ga., and Jacksonville and Hollywood, Fla. Releases and announcements issued on the trip begin on page 1339.

NOMINATIONS SUBMITTED TO THE SENATE

The following list does not include promotions of members of the Uniformed Services, nominations to the Service Academies, or nominations of Foreign Service officers.

Submitted July 7, 1980

LYLE FRANKLIN LANE, of Washington, a Foreign Service officer of Class one, to be Ambassador Extraordinary and Plenipotentiary of the United States of America to Paraguay.

HENRY PRECHT, of Georgia, a Foreign Service officer of Class two, to be Ambassador Extraordinary and Plenipotentiary of the United States of America to the Islamic Republic of Mauritania.

HARRY ALAN SCARR, of Virginia, to be Director of the Bureau of Justice Statistics (new position).

The following-named persons to be members of the Federal Farm Credit Board, Farm Credit Administration, for terms expiring March 31, 1986:

RALPH RAIKES, of Nebraska, vice Dennis S. Lundsgaard, term expired.

WILLIAM D. WAMPLER, of Virginia, vice Galen B. Brubaker, term expired.

Submitted July 10, 1980

ROBERT S. GERSHENSON, of Pennsylvania, a Foreign Service officer of Class one, to be Ambassador Extraordinary and Plenipotentiary of the United States of America to Uruguay.

BARBARA M. WATSON, of New York, to be Ambassador Extraordinary and Plenipotentiary of the United States of America to Malaysia.

The following-named persons to be members of the National Council on Educational Research for the terms indicated:

NOMINATIONS—Continued

Submitted July 10—Continued

For the remainder of the term expiring September 30, 1980

María B. Cerda, of Illinois, vice Frederick Henry Schultz, resigned.

For terms expiring September 30, 1982

Joseph J. Davies, Jr., of Louisiana, vice Carl H. Pforzheimer, Jr., term expired.

Timothy S. Healy, of the District of Columbia, vice Jewel Lafontant, term expired.

John S. Shipp, Jr., of Florida, vice Wilson C. Riles, term expired.

For a term expiring September 30, 1983

María B. Cerda, of Illinois (reappointment).

The following-named persons to be members of the National Council on the Humanities for terms expiring January 26, 1986:

Marcus Cohn, of Maryland, vice Luis A. Ferre, resigned.

Samuel DuBois Cook, of Louisiana, vice Robert B. Hollander, Jr., term expired.

Roland Paul Dille, of Minnesota, vice Robert Nisbet, resigned.

A. Bartlett Giamatti, of Connecticut, vice Caroline Ahmanson, term expired.

George Alexander Kennedy, of North Carolina, vice Kay Howe, term expired.

Louise Ano Nuevo Kerr, of Illinois, vice Ted Ashley, term expired.

Frances Dodson Rhome, of Indiana, vice Truman G. Madsen, term expired.

Philip Aaron Schaefer, of California, vice Blanchette Rockefeller, term expired.

Anita Silvers, of California, vice William A. Hewitt, term expired.

CHECKLIST OF WHITE HOUSE PRESS RELEASES

The following listing contains releases of the White House Press Office which are not included in this issue.

CHECKLIST—Continued

Released July 7, 1980

Announcement: the President's trip to Hendersonville, Ky., and Dallas, Tex., on July 21

Released July 8, 1980

Fact sheet: automobile industry assistance program

News conference: on the automobile industry assistance program—by Vice President Walter F. Mondale, Secretary of Transportation Neil Goldschmidt, Secretary of the Treasury G. William Miller, and automobile industry representatives

Released July 11, 1980

Announcement: designation of Sarah C. Weddington, Assistant to the President, and Donald F. McHenry, U.S. Representative to the United Nations, as Cochairpersons of the U.S. delegation to the World Conference for the United Nations Decade for Women

---

ACTS APPROVED BY THE PRESIDENT

Approved July 8, 1980

H.R. 7542_____ Public Law 95–304
Supplemental Appropriations and Rescission Act, 1980.

S. 751_____ Public Law 96–305
Navajo and Hopi Indian Relocation Amendments Act of 1980.

H.R. 7482_____ Public Law 96–306
An act to authorize the President of the United States to present on behalf of Congress a specially struck gold-plated medal to the United States Summer Olympic Team of 1980.

S.J. Res. 168_____ Public Law 96–307
A joint resolution designating July 18, 1980, as "National POW–MIA Recognition Day".

Approved July 9, 1980

S. 598_____ Public Law 96–308
Soft Drink Interbrand Competition Act.

S. 2546_____ Public Law 96–309
An act to authorize the Secretary of the Interior to design and construct a gunite lining on certain reaches of the Bessemer Ditch in the vicinity of Pueblo, Colorado, to prevent or reduce seepage damage on adjacent properties, and for other purposes.

Tokyo, Japan

Remarks on Arrival at Haneda International Airport. July 9, 1980

As President of the United States, I am both honored and saddened to return to Japan on this solemn occasion. Prime Minister Ohira was a good friend and a wise counselor. I valued his advice, and I admired his statesmanship. All Americans deeply appreciated his cooperation, and particularly in recent months as we have worked together to meet difficult challenges to world stability and peace.

I have come to Japan to convey my personal condolences to Mrs. Ohira and her family, to the Prime Minister's friends and colleagues, and to the people of Japan. I hope that my visit will also be understood as an expression of the deep friendship and respect felt by the American people for your great nation.

Prime Minister Ohira and I always believed that our personal friendship was a symbol of the firm bonds between our two nations. We worked together to strengthen our peoples' enduring ties of mutual respect, common interests throughout the world, and of shared values of democracy and freedom for individuals and for nations. Prime Minister Ohira's leadership will be sorely missed, but because of his many contributions, the relationship between the United States and Japan will continue to grow.

When Prime Minister Ohira visited the United States last year he said, and I quote his words, "I am eager to work to make the American-Japanese partnership a more powerful and productive force for the progress of the world community toward a more stable peace and a more widely shared prosperity for all." With these words, he spoke for both of us and for both our peoples.

In this spirit, I bring to Japan today my personal condolences and the sincere respect of the United States of America.

Thank you very much.

NOTE: The President spoke at 12:18 p.m. He then went to the residence of Michael J. Mansfield, U.S. Ambassabor to Japan, where he stayed during his visit in Tokyo.

Later in the afternoon, the President attended a memorial service for former Prime Minister Masayoshi Ohira at the Budokan. Following the service, he met with Emperor Hirohito at the Imperial Palace and, later, with Acting Prime Minister Masayoshi Ito at the Akasaka Palace. While at the Akasaka Palace, the President also attended a reception for the foreign dignitaries who had attended the memorial service.

In the evening, the President met with Mrs. Ohira and members of her family at their home in Tokyo.

Tokyo, Japan

Interview With Japanese Reporters. July 10, 1980

MEMORIAL SERVICE FOR PRIME MINISTER
OHIRA

Q. Let me begin, Mr. President, by asking your impressions of the memorial service for the late Prime Minister Ohira yesterday. What were the thoughts which came across your mind while attending the service?

THE PRESIDENT. Well, the most profound thoughts that I had were of my personal friendship with Prime Minister Ohira and the closeness that had developed between my family and his. We had been together often in some historic moments.

And I thought the funeral service, the commemorative service was very impressive, very solemn, but it expressed the genuine outpouring of respect that was felt for Prime Minister Ohira from throughout the world. Someone told me that 108 nations were represented there——

Q. That's right.

THE PRESIDENT.——at the services. And this is not only a sign of respect for him and his leadership during troubled times but also a respect for the greatness of Japan and its growing leadership throughout the world, not only economically but also politically and diplomatically.

And finally, I was reminded of the closeness of our two countries, which I think is unprecedented and which was exemplified by my closeness to him personally.

UNITED STATES-JAPANESE RELATIONS

Q. Mr. President, in a relationship so broad and complex like the relationship between Japan and the United States, there are bound to be some problems from time to time.

THE PRESIDENT. Yes.

Q. How do you see the United States dealing with current issues, including trade and defense?

THE PRESIDENT. Well, all nations in this modern world have problems, and particularly those that are in the role of a leader, as is the case with both Japan and the United States. With the skyrocketing price of energy, economic problems are a responsibility for all leaders now, but the thing to remember is not those problems, but the resolution that we have to resolve the problems, working together.

We have so much in common in the challenges and the approach to them that these common approaches and common commitments far outweigh any differences that might exist between us. We both represent dynamic, aggressive societies where people are very confident about the future, where we set the pace for other nations, and where we have never feared the meeting of a challenge with courage and conviction.

Economically, trade, we have unprecedented benefits to both our nations from the rapidly growing volume of trade. And of course, on defense our mutual security treaty is a foundation for our own ability and commitment in the Western Pacific to maintain stability and to maintain peace for all people.

We believe that this good relationship between our two countries in a competitive spirit is going to grow and that the 1980's will show even greater progress than we've seen in the 1970's, because of the common purpose of our countries, in progress and also in freedom, and our commitment to democracy and to peace. We believe, finally, that the good relationship between our two countries is very beneficial to other nations and that we have set an example of the kind of growth that can benefit both peoples in a rapidly changing technological world if those peoples share those common commitments, which I've already mentioned.

Q. Mr. President, in regard to what you are saying now, what kind of contribution would you like to have from the Japanese side to strengthen the tie of both countries?

THE PRESIDENT. With regard to what? With regard to——

Q. What kind of contribution would you like to have?

THE PRESIDENT. Oh, yes. Well, I don't have any fear of Japan pursuing its own goals and the United States pursuing its independent goals, because we have so much in common that this pursuit is mutually supportive and not contradictory. We want stability and peace throughout Asia, and our commitment to a strong defense, at some sacrifice to us, is supportive of the Japanese commitment to defend your own area and your own people. There is no problem between us in that respect.

Similarly, in the development of technology, science, research, development, education, dealing with the energy problem, meeting the challenges of Soviet aggression in Afghanistan, international terrorism exemplified by the holding of American hostages in Iran, the growth of the strength of the ASEAN group, which is a very encouraging development, the opening up of China, a vast country very important to us both, with new opportunities for trade and exchange of ideas and a common purpose, the sharing of strategic matters—all of these elements of the life of Americans is identical with the importance in the life of Japanese.

So, as we pursue our own individual goals, sharing all these problems and all these opportunities for the future, I have great confidence that the relationship between our people will be better, even, in the future than it has been in the past and that we can solve these problems together with gratification to the people of both nations.

PEOPLE'S REPUBLIC OF CHINA

Q. Mr. President, now you are about to have talks with Premier Hua Guofeng of the People's Republic of China. Can you tell us at this time what you expect out of this meeting and, also, how the closer relations between the United States and China would affect Japan and the rest of the world——

THE PRESIDENT. Good.

Q. ——specifically the Soviet Union?

THE PRESIDENT. Well, I don't think it would be appropriate to outline all of the subjects that we're going to discuss with Premier Hua, but I'll be seeing him in just a few minutes, as you know, across the street.

In the first place, this last 18 months since I decided to normalize relations between our country and the People's Republic of China has been one of exciting progress between our two great nations, and of course, this is a similar experience to what has been the case between Japan and the People's Republic of China.

We believe that this new development is conducive to peace and stability and progress throughout the Asian region of the world. We also see it as a means by which we can share our long-range strategic concerns to minimize the threat of the Soviet military buildup, which is exemplified most vividly by their unwarranted invasion of Afghanistan and their support of the Vietnamese invasion of Kampuchea.

We believe that this new relationship, however, should not be used by either our country or Japan, with China, against the Soviet Union. We should not combine our efforts against another nation, but we should combine our efforts to maintain peace and the freedom of each country to make its own decisions free of outside

1341

interference and certainly free of an invasion.

So, I believe in every respect the new peaceful relationship between our two countries on the one hand and China on the other is better for us all, in the matter of peace and trade and an improved, better life for our people. My guess is that 50 or 100 years from now, as historians look back on this last few years, the turning of China outward to friendship with Japan and the United States will be a major development in the lives of all people.

Q. Thank you very much, Mr. President.

THE PRESIDENT. Thank you. It's a pleasure to be with you.

NOTE: The interview began at 7:40 a.m. in the Okura Hotel. It was broadcast live on Japanese television.

Following the interview, the President met in the hotel's south wing with Premier Hua Guofeng of the People's Republic of China. He then returned to Haneda International Airport and boarded Air Force One enroute to Elmendorf Air Force Base, Alaska.

Elmendorf Air Force Base, Alaska

Exchange With Reporters on Departure From Anchorage. July 10, 1980

Q. Mr. President, it seems Iran is going to release one of the hostages. What does that mean, sir?

THE PRESIDENT. Well, I had the message on the helicopter, coming back a few minutes ago, from the national security adviser. The press reports were that a young man named Richard Queen, I believe, from Maine, has been announced as being released by the terrorists in Iran, because he was seriously ill and could not

be adequately treated in Tehran. We don't yet have a confirmation of this report. If it is true and if the young man is well after adequate treatment, of course we'll be very thankful.

Obviously, the proper thing for the terrorists to do is to release all of the hostages who are being held, because they are innocent and they deserve to be with their families as well as those who are too ill to be treated. So, until we get a firm report on whether the young man has been released, I think it would be inappropriate for me to comment any further.

Q. Well, why do they have any humanitarian concern for one hostage if they don't for the rest?

THE PRESIDENT. Well, as I said, the humanitarian thing to do would be to release all the hostages immediately. They should have done this long ago. But I think it would be better for me not to comment on Mr. Queen, because we don't want to say anything that might interfere with his release.

Well, I would like to say additionally that I had a very delightful and a very successful fishing trip. This is some of the most beautiful country in the world, and we were well hosted by Rupe Andrews [1] and also by the Governor of Alaska, Jay Hammond, who were very gracious to us. We had a chance to fish for about 5 hours and to travel about an hour and a half in and back and really thoroughly enjoyed the brief vacation. It reminds us again of the beauty of Alaska and the wonderful gifts that God has given our country, and I'm very grateful for this chance to see part of it.

Thank you very much. Yes, one more question maybe.

---

[1] Rupert E. Andrews, Director of the Alaska State Division of Sport Fishing.

Q. Mr. President, Senator Mike Gravel is running for reelection, with a large part of his platform being the Alaska lands issue. Senator Gravel maintains that no bill is better than either one of the bills currently in Congress. If no bill passes this session, do you anticipate Executive withdrawals of more lands?

THE PRESIDENT. My presumption is and my hope is that we will have an adequate D–2 lands bill passed that would preserve the beauty of Alaska and allow for an appropriate economic development now and in the future. I think it's much superior if we do have legislation approved by the Congress than if any further Executive action is necessary. So, we're going to work hard to get an acceptable legislative bill through.

Thank you all very much. I've enjoyed being here.

NOTE: The exchange began at 1 p.m. The President then boarded Air Force One enroute to Georgia. After a short stop at Glynco Jetport, Brunswick, Ga., he boarded Marine One for the flight to Sapelo Island.

Sale of Trident I Missiles to the United Kingdom

Exchange of Letters Between the President and Prime Minister Margaret Thatcher of the United Kingdom. July 14, 1980

Dear Madame Prime Minister:

In reply to your letter of July 10, 1980, I am pleased to confirm that the United States attaches significant importance to the nuclear deterrent capability of the United Kingdom and to close cooperation between our two Governments in maintaining and modernizing that capability. To further that objective, the United

States is prepared to supply the United Kingdom TRIDENT I missiles, equipment and supporting services, as you propose in your letter, subject to and in accordance with applicable United States laws and procedures.

I view as important your statements that the POLARIS successor force will be assigned to NATO and that your objective is to take advantage of the economies made possible by our nuclear cooperation to reinforce your efforts to upgrade the United Kingdom's conventional forces. As you know, I regard the strengthening of NATO's conventional and nuclear forces as of highest priority for Western security.

I agree that as the next step in implementing these agreed arrangements, our two Governments should initiate the technical and financial negotiations which you propose.

Sincerely,

JIMMY CARTER

[The Right Honorable Margaret R. Thatcher, M.P., Prime Minister, London]

———

10 July 1980

Dear Mr. President,

As you are aware the United Kingdom Government attaches great importance to the maintenance of a nuclear deterrent capability. It will be necessary to replace the present Polaris force in the early 1990s, and having reviewed the options, the Government has concluded that the Trident I weapon system best meets the need to maintain a viable nuclear deterrent capability into the 21st century. I write therefore to ask you whether the United States Government would be prepared, in continuation of the cooperation which has existed between our Governments in this field since the Polaris Sales Agreement of 6 April 1963, to supply on a continuing basis, Trident I missiles, equipment and supporting services, in a manner generally similar to that in which Polaris was supplied.

The United Kingdom Government would wish to purchase sufficient missiles, complete with multiple independently targettable re-entry vehicles and less only the warheads themselves, together with equipment and supporting services, on a continuing basis to introduce and maintain a force of 4 British submarines (or 5 if the United Kingdom Government so prefer), close coordination being maintained between the Executive Agencies of the two Governments in order to assure compatibility of equipment.

The successor to the Polaris force will be assigned to the North Atlantic Treaty Organisation, like the Polaris force; and except where the United Kingdom Government may decide that supreme national interests are at stake, the successor force will be used for the purposes of international defence of the Western alliance in all circumstances. It is my understanding that cooperation in the modernisation of the United Kingdom nuclear deterrent in this way would be consistent with the present and prospective international obligations of both parties.

In particular, I would like to assure you that the United Kingdom Government continues to give whole-hearted support to the NATO Long-Term Defence Programme and to other strengthening of conventional forces. The United Kingdom Government has substantially increased its defence spending, in accordance with NATO's collective policy, and plans to make further such increases in the future in order to improve the effectiveness of its all-round contribution to Allied deterrence and defence. In this

regard the objective of the United Kingdom Government is to take advantage of the economies made possible by the cooperation of the United States in making the Trident I missile system available in order to reinforce its efforts to upgrade its conventional forces.

If the United States Government is prepared to meet this request, I hope that as the next step the United States Government will be prepared to receive technical and financial missions to pursue these matters, using the framework of the Polaris Sales Agreement where appropriate.

Yours sincerely

MARGARET THATCHER

[The President of the United States of America]

NOTE: The text of the letters was released on July 15. The White House press release also includes the letters exchanged by Secretary of Defense Harold Brown and Secretary of State Francis Pym of the United Kingdom.

Sale of Trident I Missiles to the United Kingdom

White House Statement. July 15, 1980

Today in London, the British Government is informing the House of Commons of its decision to modernize the British strategic nuclear deterrent force. In this connection, the British Government has requested that the United States sell the United Kingdom U.S. Trident I missiles. The Trident I missiles would be carried in new submarines built in Britain and would replace the existing British Polaris sea-based strategic missile force in the early 1990's. This request was formally conveyed in a letter from Prime Minister Thatcher to the President on July 10, 1980. In a letter sent to the Prime Minister yesterday, the President agreed that the United States will sell Trident I missiles to the United Kingdom.

Since the Second World War, the United States has cooperated intimately with the United Kingdom on nuclear matters. In President Roosevelt's administration, American and British scientists began working together on the development of nuclear weapons. In 1962 at Nassau, President Kennedy agreed to assist the British in the development of their strategic nuclear forces by selling Polaris missiles to the United Kingdom.

Today's announcement of Anglo-American cooperation on a modernized British Trident missile force signals a continuation of this longstanding cooperation, which is a central element in the close cooperation between the United States and the United Kingdom. This cooperation is, of course, not limited to the nuclear field and includes a strong U.K. conventional commitment to NATO, which Britain also intends to strengthen.

The administration believes the independent British strategic nuclear force which is assigned to NATO makes an important contribution to the ability of the North Atlantic Alliance to deter Soviet aggression. For this reason, the President decided to assist the United Kingdom in the maintenance of a modernized, independent British deterrent force into the 21st century.

This joint step by the United States and United Kingdom is part of the broader pattern of efforts by this administration and our allies in Europe to strengthen NATO defense capabilities—3-percent real growth in defense budgets, the NATO long-term defense program, and the NATO decision to modernize theater nuclear forces. It is a sign of our determination to strengthen close cooperation with our allies on sensitive security matters.

Heat and Drought Conditions in the United States

Announcement of Federal Assistance Actions. July 15, 1980

In response to the extreme heat conditions now affecting many parts of the United States, the President has directed the Community Services Administration (CSA), the Federal Government's antipoverty agency, to make available $6.725 million to assist low-income individuals, especially the elderly, who are facing life-threatening situations.

The funds will be made available through CSA's network of Community Action Agencies. Eligible activities include transportation to local- and State-operated heat relief centers, purchase or rental of low-cost appliances, such as fans and window air-conditioning units, to reduce heat, payment of utility bills, as well as the provision of other supportive services which will reduce the potential hazard to the health of low-income persons resulting from extreme heat. To receive assistance with these funds, a household must demonstrate that it has a total income at or below 125 percent of the Federal poverty guidelines, which is approximately $9,300 for a family of four.

The States earmarked to receive funds immediately are Texas, Arkansas, Oklahoma, Missouri, Kansas, and Louisiana. The amount of assistance to be provided to each State is: Texas, $2.5 million; Arkansas and Oklahoma, $1 million each; Louisiana and Kansas will receive $500,000; and Missouri will receive $1.25 million. These funds are being allocated on the basis of the number of elderly poor in the respective States and the counties to be served.

1345

The President has also directed Secretary of Agriculture Bob Bergland to report to him on the effects of the drought on agriculture and on those measures being taken to provide economic relief. The current weather conditions have had a particularly severe impact on the agriculture of that region. A variety of assistance is available, including emergency livestock feed assistance, conservation assistance, disaster payments, emergency loans, and crop insurance. The President directed the Secretary to ensure that this assistance is made available in a timely and effective manner.

Finally, the President has directed John Macy, Director of the Federal Emergency Management Agency (FEMA), to coordinate the Federal response to this situation and to meet with representatives of State government in the affected regions to ensure that Federal assistance is closely coordinated with that from other units of government. Meetings will be held later this week in Dallas, Kansas City, and Denver for this purpose.

Pennsylvania Avenue Development Corporation

Appointment of Max N. Berry as a Member and Chairman of the Board of Directors. July 15, 1980

The President today announced the intention to appoint as a member and Chairman Max N. Berry, of Washington, D.C., to the Pennsylvania Avenue Development Corporation.

Berry was born December 29, 1935, in Cushing, Okla. He received a B.A. in 1958 and an LL.B. in 1960 from the University of Oklahoma. Berry received an LL.M. from Georgetown Law Center in 1963. He served in the United States Army from 1960 to 1963.

From 1963 to 1967, he served in the Office of the General Counsel at the Department of the Treasury. Since 1967, Berry has specialized in the private practice of administrative law, dealing with various Federal Government agencies as well as with the Members and committees of Congress. Berry has been a senior partner with Berry, Epstein, Sandstrom & Blatchford since 1967.

United States Attorney Herman Sillas, Jr.

White House Statement. July 15, 1980

The matter of Herman Sillas' continued service as United States attorney in Sacramento is now under review by the President's Counsel. The Counsel is proceeding to evaluate Department of Justice recommendations regarding Mr. Sillas' case and after full evaluation will make a recommendation to the President.

The primary concerns of the President's Counsel, since beginning his evaluation of the Sillas case, have been to protect the integrity and public reputation of the office of the United States attorney, while at the same time affording Mr. Sillas and his own legal counsel a fair opportunity to present his side of the matter. In the circumstances, it would be inappropriate for the White House to respond to Mr. Sillas' remarks at his press conference today.

Republican Presidential Candidate

Telegram to Gov. Ronald Reagan on His Nomination by the Republican Party. July 17, 1980

Dear Governor:

Rosalynn joins me in sincere congratulations to you on your nomination as the Presidential candidate of the Republican Party. I know you share with me an appreciation for the challenges our country faces and the serious choices before the American people this fall and in the years ahead. So that these alternatives can be clearly delineated, I suggest that we meet in a series of debates in the various regions of our nation. I would hope that at least three or four debates can be scheduled so that we can thoroughly discuss issues of national concern and of interest to the people of particular sections of our nation.

I look forward to a hard-fought and thoughtful campaign that will help to inform the American people about the complex and important issues which face the nation we both love and seek to serve.

Sincerely,

JIMMY CARTER

[The Honorable Ronald Reagan, c/o Detroit Plaza Hotel, Detroit, Michigan]

NOTE: On the same day, Deputy Press Secretary Rex L. Granum announced during a news conference that the President telephoned Governor Reagan at 9:30 a.m. to offer his congratulations and suggest a series of debates.

Jacksonville, Florida

Remarks at a Public Reception. July 17, 1980

Governor Bob Graham, Mayor Jake Godbold, distinguished officials of the State of Florida and the city of Jacksonville and surrounding communities, and my friends who have come out to greet me on this beautiful day in the most wonderful, free, strong, dynamic, aggressive, competent, united nation on Earth:

Thank you very much.

In the last few weeks I've been a lot of places on Earth. I've been to Italy and to Yugoslavia. I've been to Portugal, and I've been to Spain. I've been halfway around the world to Japan. I've been to California. I came back from Japan through Alaska. But if I had my choices of all the places I'd want to be in the world right now at this minute, it would be right here with you in Jacksonville, Florida, and there are some special reasons for it.

In traveling overseas, the President of the United States represents his country in searching for peace, in demonstrating our strength and our influence, in working to pull together our allies and friends to stand with us in times of trial and uncertainty, in times of rapid change in the world. There are some things that do not change: the hunger in people's souls for liberty or for freedom, the commitment to democratic principles, the right of a human being to stand on his or her own feet, to make one's own decisions, to face the future with confidence, to join hands together. Those things don't change. And that's what a President does—to demonstrate those commitments and those principles—in travels in countries afar and throughout this Nation.

Jacksonville was named after Andrew Jackson. Historians have said that Andrew Jackson was probably the most American of all Americans, and I would say that among all the cities in our Nation, Jacksonville is one of the most American of all American cities.

I'm not going to speak long, because I think it's a little bit warmer than Mayor Godbold just indicated—[*laughter*]—not as hot as it has been the last few days, but still hot enough. But I would like to say a few things about Andrew Jackson and about Jacksonville and about our Nation very briefly.

First of all, he and you and I believe in peace through strength, and I'm very grateful for what this community and the surrounding area mean to our Nation's defense. It's important that a nation have a strong defense. In the last 3½ years, our commitment to a strong defense has been increasing every year, following 8 years of a strong downward trend. We have done this already. And for the next 5 years, I guarantee you, if I'm the leader of this Nation, our commitment to defense will continue to increase year by year.

Just a few minutes ago—less than an hour, as a matter of fact—we flew over King's Bay. It happens to be in Georgia, but it's awful close to Jacksonville. It'll be a tremendous boon to this country and also to your community. It's another indication of our commitment to a future for the United States of America, in its military strength, will be second to none. That's the way it is now, and that's the way our Nation will be in the years ahead. But your commitment to a strong defense establishment has been proven down through the years ever since the lifetime of Andrew Jackson.

There's another thing that you believe in, and that is confidence in ourselves. We've had difficult times. There's no doubt about that. We've had challenges; we've had troubles; we've had, sometimes, causes for disunity. But we struggle with one another for some advantage. We've been through a Great Depression; we came out strong. We've been through the First World War, the Second World War; we came out stronger. We've been through the Korean war and even the Vietnam war, which divided our Nation one from another; but in the end, we've come out stronger. We've been through the embarrassment of Watergate that shook the confidence of the American people in the Oval Office itself; but because of your strength in your commitment, we came out stronger.

The problems that we face today are great ones—I don't want to mislead you about it—and there are no easy answers. They are complex problems. They are not simple problems. But we've faced much more difficult ones in the past. And with a strong America, confident in ourselves, united shoulder to shoulder, we can meet those challenges, overcome those problems, answer those difficult questions, and in the end we'll come out stronger even than we are today. That's another characteristic of the namesake for your great city.

The final point I want to make is this: Andrew Jackson and I and you believe in hard work. We don't believe in a free lunch. We believe that one of the freedoms of Americans is to make our own decisions, but to do it in a constructive way, without taking direction from anyone else, knowing that we cannot get a handout if we are able to stand on our own feet, bear our own load, and make our own decisions. Americans have proved this in recent years.

We have faced the energy question with courage, with conviction, with confidence in ourselves, and with growing success. Year after year after year after year, we did nothing about the horrible increase in imported oil. Year by year, we bought more oil from overseas than we did the year before. But beginning 3½ years ago, when I became President, with the commitment of the American people, we reversed that trend. And today we imported 1½ million fewer barrels of oil from overseas than we did the first day of January 1977. This is because Americans, when they are faced with a problem and recognize it and become united, have never failed.

This community, in spite of economic problems, the first day of January 1977 had had 63 percent more unemployment that day than the last day of June 1980. That's a tremendous increase in the number of people at work. That's the kind of progress that quite often goes unrecognized. But you see in the strength of your own community what can be done.

Finally, let me say that this progress has been made not because of Washington, not because of the Federal Government alone, but because of a partnership that has been formed. With the Federal, State, and local governments working with private industry, working with private labor, working with the home leaders, we have made our country proven to be stronger. The future is going to be even better than it has been in the past.

I'm very proud of Jacksonville. I'm very proud of Florida. You've always been friends of mine. The first time I ever left Georgia to go into a foreign State, it was to go to Jacksonville and Jacksonville Beach. I did it every year. And it let me see what the outside world was like, and I liked what I saw. And I would guess, when I was 8 or 10 years old, if I hadn't come down here to see how you lived, I might have been satisfied and still been plowing with a mule in Sumter County, Georgia, growing peanuts. So, I thank you for broadening my perspective.

I want to thank you for coming out to give me this tremendous welcome. And

I want to pledge to you that if we continue the partnership we've had in the past, we will make, together, the greatest nation on Earth even greater in the future. That's what I want to do. With your help, we'll do it.

Thank you very much. God bless you all.

NOTE: The President spoke at 12:54 p.m. during a reception sponsored by Mayor Jake Godbold at the Daniel State Office Building.

Earlier in the afternoon, the President left Sapelo Island, Ga., aboard Marine One. Upon arrival at the Gator Bowl parking lot in Jacksonville, he was greeted by Florida State Governor Bob Graham and Mayor Godbold.

Jacksonville, Florida

Remarks and a Question-and-Answer Session With Community and Civic Leaders.
July 17, 1980

THE PRESIDENT. It's good to be in Jake Godbold's city and mine, too. I might say that all of his constituents or Bob Graham's constituents and all of their constituents are my constituents. [*Laughter*] I think this is typical of the attitude that has problems with their leadership in the Nation has struggled to overcome the embarrassment and disappointments of the past and to carry out the principles and the ideals on which our Nation was founded.

I will be going to Hollywood right after I leave Jacksonville. Miami is a city that has problems with their leadership in the black community and the relationship, as you know, between the blacks and the Cubans and also the white leaders of that city. We have other places around our Nation that face these difficult problems.

Sometimes they anticipate them, they cooperate, the leadership works together, they prevent disturbances and hardships and divisiveness before it happens. And I'm very grateful to be in Jacksonville, because of that as well.

I'm not here to brag about the Federal Government nor to brag about what we have done in the last 3½ years. I am here to brag about what you have done. There's a great demonstration of confidence in the future of your own great city, and in my earlier remarks outside in a tremendous welcoming event, I contrasted the attitude of Andrew Jackson, the namesake of your city, Jacksonville—confidence in one another, a commitment to hard work, recognizing our potential, and doing everything we could at the local scene, with private and government effort combined, to realize the great potential of our own free lives in the greatest of all democracies on Earth.

You are making good progress. I've been very pleased at the progress made in your public transportation system, the EDA grants that have been forthcoming to you, the new energy project on Blount Island, I flew over just a few minutes ago, the good progress that has been made with development of the private sector here in Jacksonville, and the harmony that prevails in your city.

I think another thing that you exemplify, for which I'm very grateful as President, is the good working relationship between those of us who have different backgrounds in religion, in the color of our skin, in our heritage, and even in our place of birth. It's a sign of courage and a sign of dedication, a sign of faith when people who are different can work together in a spirit of unity. And this is particularly gratifying in a time in our history when the future is uncertain, when many parts of the world are torn by strife and death and hatred, to see a community like this bound together in a spirit of brotherly love.

It's also a pleasure for me as President to see the greatness of our Nation exemplified by a strong defense commitment. Around your area, as you know, our Nation has a major investment in a strong defense. That investment is growing rapidly, because we not only have confidence in this region of our country, but also the people who are here share the belief that a nation can remain at peace only if it is strong—strong militarily, yes; but also strong economically, strong morally, strong ethically, and strong politically.

This is an election year, as you well know. It's not a time for us to be torn apart one from another. It's a time to put our record on the line, to let the American people, the people of Florida look at what we have done and judge whether or not we've been good stewards of the high office at the local, State, and Federal level in the democratic system.

I would like to say, in closing, before I answer a few questions, that you also believe in hard work. The unemployment rate 3½ years ago in January was 63 percent higher for the Jacksonville area than it is now, and that shows that in spite of difficulties with the economy, you have continued to make progress. And I think that your great mayor and the people who support him here are the root of that confidence and that progress.

So, thank you for this good welcome for me. And I'm deeply grateful as President to be here in a place that makes me proud to serve the greatest nation on Earth.

And now I'd like to answer a few questions if you don't mind. Yes, sir?

QUESTIONS

THE ECONOMY

Q. [*Inaudible*]—we have talked about a tax cut. We are somewhat opposed to a tax cut at this time. We feel that it would be inflationary. And we would like to have your comments on—put people back to work, make them a taxpayer instead of this system of welfare. And I would like to have your comments on inflation, particularly.

THE PRESIDENT. I was pleased yesterday to get some good news on the housing starts in this country. Compared to the previous month, they were up 30 percent. This is part of a general response to the rapid fall in recent months of the interest rates, first of all, and secondly and following that very rapidly, a drop in the inflation rate. This will do a lot to give people more money in their own pocket; with the inflation rate being lower, able to purchase homes, automobiles, consumer goods. And when they purchase a home or an automobile or a refrigerator or a stove, then people who make those products can go back to work. So, I believe that the corrective action is built in.

We will stand firm, hold a steady course on economics. It is not easy in an election year, because it is so easy to promise magic answers from massive tax cuts. This has been proposed by some, but I will not do that until I'm sure that we're in control of inflation. And until I'm sure that the Federal Government has exercised proper discipline in setting an example for the rest of the Nation, I see no reason for moving ahead on a tax cut.

My belief is that in 1981 we will be prepared to take steps, including a tax cut, to hurry along a little bit the economic recovery. We don't want to stimulate the economy too much, because we don't want to rekindle the fires of inflation. That's what we've tried to do.

And also in the last few years, since I've been in office, we've tried to focus our attention on those kind of things that would provide long-term benefits for our people. I won't go into any detail about it. But one thing is that we've focused Federal help for education by a 73-percent increase in Federal funds, but leaving control of the schools at the local level of government. And we've also made it possible now so that virtually every child in the United States can get a college education regardless of the economic status of the family involved. That's the kind of progress that we've tried to make in just one of those services.

So, investments in energy, as you say, is going to be an exciting, stimulating, dynamic, wonderful opportunity for Americans in the future, something that we have never experienced before. How to do two things to cut down on oil imports: One is to save energy, with all kinds of conservation measures that would give us a better life, not a worse life; and the other one, to produce energy of all kinds other than to buy oil from overseas. This year we will send overseas $9 [90] billion of American money to buy foreign oil. It's hard for me to visualize what a billion dollars is, but what that amounts to is every man, woman, and child in the United States will, in effect, send $400 overseas, money that could be invested here. We've made the first steps toward a great investment in America's future, not only a better life for us but better security as well.

I thank you for what you said.

FEDERAL PROGRAMS FOR MINORITIES

Q. Mr. President, Edward Dawkins, president of the local chapter of the NAACP. Mr. President, what plans do you have to eradicate the inequality that blacks experience in employment, or in other words, what is your formula for the proper mix of economic, manpower, education, equal opportunity, and affirmative action to achieve equality in employment for blacks?

THE PRESIDENT. Thank you very much.

One thing that we have done, that's only now being felt in the country, is to require by law that in all the public works projects financed by the Federal Government, which is your tax money to require that 10 percent of that money goes to firms owned by minority citizens of our country. This was a proposal that was first scorned and laughed at by even some Members of the Congress, but it passed and we've been protecting the legality of that commitment in the Federal court.

Only a week or so ago, as you may remember, Ed, the Supreme Court ruled that this was indeed both a constitutional and legal requirement that when we have major public works projects, 10 percent of that commitment should go to minority-owned firms. As a matter of fact, we will do more than 10 percent; that's a minimum. We'll probably meet a goal of about 15 percent.

We've more than tripled already the investment of Federal funds—after they are collected, before they are spent—in minority-owned banks. And in the last 2 years, we have tripled the number of radio and TV stations that are owned by minority American citizens.

I have put in control, in the executive branch of Government, of the administration of the Equal Employment Opportunity Commission and other agencies the same civil rights workers that risked their lives, as a matter of fact, to eliminate segregation in this country. This is one of the best things that ever happened to the South—to Florida, to Georgia, to other parts of the South—and also one of the best things that ever happened to our Nation. And I have put people who are dedicated—with their lives, if necessary—to achieve equality, to make sure that under the present laws that those laws are carried out fairly.

The other thing that I've tried to do is to remember that even though all of the white people in this room might be deeply dedicated to fairness and to justice under the law, it takes people who are black and who have been deprived and who have seen their families suffer from discrimination to understand the long-range effect of just simple decisions that are made in the city council or made in the Federal Communications Commission or made in the Federal Trade Commission or, particularly, made in the Federal courts.

I don't want to make my answer too long, because I want to answer several other questions. But I have been able, since I've been President—only 3½ years, as you know—to appoint more women Federal judges, more Spanish-speaking Federal judges, and more black Federal judges than all the other Presidents who have served our Nation in almost 200 years, and I am not through yet.

Thank you, Ed.

HAZARDOUS CHEMICAL WASTES

Q. I'm Julia Buckingham, president of the League of Women Voters of Jacksonville. Mr. President, a rash of recent incidents resulting from improper disposal of hazardous waste has made it clear that hazardous waste management practices, both past and present, represent a threat to the environment and to public health. The creation of a superfund to pay the cost to clean up and containment of releases of hazardous materials has been a major environmental priority for your administration. With this session of Congress drawing to a close, what are your plans to ensure passage of good, strong superfund legislation?

THE PRESIDENT. When I was Governor and when I served on local governments as well and when I campaigned around this Nation, it became increasingly evident to me that because Americans had not faced up to this problem in past years, that it had reached almost crisis size.

The Love Canal incident in New York State has been highly publicized, because there was, in effect, a garbage dump for chemical wastes for generations. And now, all of a sudden, people started dying; they have something wrong with their blood. The reports are that some of them might be seriously injured in the future. We don't know for sure yet about the permanent consequences. But we've had to move 700 families out of that region, because they had built their homes in a place they thought was safe.

We have about 50,000 places potentially like that in this country, where hazardous chemical wastes have in the past been dumped, and the people who lived there didn't really know it. As a matter of fact, the people who dumped the waste didn't know about the long-term effects of some of those chemicals. It would cost the Federal Government an unbelievable amount of money if the taxpayers of the Nation had to pay all of the damages that have been caused and to clean up those dump sites and to determine who is legally responsible.

So, what we thought we would do, after literally almost 2 years of hard work, was

to set up a kind of insurance fund; we call it the super fund. It doesn't involve very much public money—a little bit of taxpayers' money to administer the program. But what it will do is this—to oversimplify a complicated thing. It will require chemical manufacturers to add a very tiny percent to the cost of their product, and the people who buy those chemicals will pay a little bit more, not enough to really hurt. Out of that small amount that's withheld, we will create, in effect, an insurance fund to help over a long period to clean up those dump sites and also help to pay for damages once those damages are revealed.

The Congress has responded well to this proposal, and it's making good progress in the House and has strong support in the Senate. It's one of the five or six top-priority bills of my administration. I think that I can predict to you that because of widespread support from the League of Women Voters and many others—and not opposed, by the way, by the chemical industry or others—that this is the proper way to go about correcting this longstanding problem. I believe we will be successful. And when we are successful, it'll help every community in the Nation.

THE ECONOMY

Q. Do you feel, Mr. President, that you can continue your anti-inflationary efforts and avoid a severe depression that we appear to be sliding toward?

THE PRESIDENT. Yes, I think so. The reason I say that without too much hesitation is that our Nation is inherently so strong, with natural resources, with human resources, people eager to work, with a free enterprise system that brings out the best in industries and in workers, and with an accommodation by the American people of rapidly changing circumstances. Our country has always been on the cutting edge of change. We have an ability, because of the freedom in this Nation, when something does come up that we did not anticipate, a new circumstance, like a shortage of energy, to correct past mistakes and to make plans for the future to accommodate those new problems that face us. We have done this in the last 3½ years, with the Congress passing, finally, legislation to set up a national energy policy.

We have been through, in 1979 and the first part of 1980, an unprecedented increase in oil prices. OPEC raised the price of oil in 12 months more than the price of oil had gone up since the first day it was discovered back in the 1800's. So, the whole world has suffered from a shock of that highly increased price of oil. Americans have cut down on their consumption, which has helped. But it created inflation that is all over the world. Israel has an inflation rate over 200 percent per year. Ours is too high.

As you know, both the interest rate and the inflation rate were approaching 20 percent before our economy adjusted to take care of this shock of OPEC oil prices and some others. But since March, when I announced my anti-inflation package, you've seen the interest rates drop very rapidly. As a matter of fact, the prime rate was dropping about 1 percent per week, and now most interest rates are lower today than they were 12 months ago. The inflation rate is coming down also very rapidly, and I predict to you that later on in the summer you'll see the inflation rate reach fairly low levels.

We've still got a basic rate that's too high, but I don't believe that we ought to panic. And if I took corrective action now, like a very massive tax reduction—I think Governor Reagan has proposed a 30-per-cent cut in Federal income taxes over a 3-year period; that's $280 billion by the year 1985—the shock of that and all that flood of extra money coming into the economy, I think, would restimulate the inflationary spiral in a devastating way.

So, my commitment, in spite of pressures in an election year, is to hold firm and let our economy continue to progress—the inflation rate, the interest rates, now lower; housing starts, much better than they were before; the American people, confident in ourselves. And we'll have a massive stimulation, in effect, from the new investment that we will make in better ways to conserve energy, to weatherize homes, to produce synthetic fuels. I think here in Jacksonville, in Blount Island, you'll have a mixture of coal and oil, that I think we've just given, I think, a million dollar grant for. But I see a bright future for this Nation.

I want to close my answers by saying I don't want to paint too rosy a picture for you. I don't think it would be good to mislead the American people. But we're not suffering severely yet. I don't believe that we will suffer severely. We are much better able to take care of those who are temporarily unemployed than we were back in 1973 or 1974, when we had a recession then. A family that has an unemployed person in it, however, is suffering severely, and we want to make sure that that family realizes that the corrective actions are built in, and if the economy should get worse than I think it is, I would not hesitate to take additional action. But now I believe a steady course, probably a tax reduction and other stimulating efforts in 1981, is the best course to follow. I don't want to revitalize, though, the inflationary spiral.

Q. Mr. President, I would like to, first of all, thank you for the call, the phone call I received from you at the White House.

THE PRESIDENT. Thank you, Ed.

Q. Also, I would like to, with your approval, get with three or four people from this group, look over our needs, community needs, clear them through the mayor's office, and make them known to the proper agency at the Washington level, with your permission.

THE PRESIDENT. Nothing would suit me better. I called Ed Pope, because like many of you, he's a long-time friend of mine. And I'm really glad to see you so well and here today.

CHILD WELFARE AND HEALTH CARE

Q. Mr. President. I'm Carol Lormer, representing the Junior League of Jacksonville. In the area of child action, we would like to thank you for your quick action on the child welfare reform legislation, but we urge you to work actively for an appropriation to fund this bill. What do you see as the outlook for the child health legislation?

THE PRESIDENT. I think it's fairly good. The new child welfare bill that was passed was long overdue. It was really landmark legislation, and it didn't get very much publicity. But I think that this will change, literally, the attitude of American people toward children who come from a divided home and who don't have permanent parents. In the past we've done too much to provide Government redtape to prevent people who hunger for parents and to prevent parents who hunger for children, if they can't have children of their own, from getting together.

Also, our commitment to women, infants', and children health care has already been more than tripled since I've been in office. The CHAMPUS program,

which is primarily—for those of you who are not so well familiar with it—a preventive health program for little children. It gives Federal funds to examine a child at a very early life, beginning really at a prenatal stage, and then when a child is an infant, to see if they've got any congenital defects or any potential defects in the child that might be very costly as an adult to society if they are not corrected. We've made great progress on immunization programs as well.

My own philosophy of government is if you can prevent a person from being dependent on society by doing corrective action quite early in a person's life to prevent an unnecessary illness or to let a person develop their full potential that God has given them, it's a very, very good investment. I believe that we will see these programs adequately financed, and we have asked, as you know, in spite of a very stringent budget for 1981, to triple the funds for that particular project.

Yes, sir?

BLACK COLLEGES

Q. Mr. President, I'm Bishop Morris of the AME Church and chairman of the Black Leadership Council of Jacksonville. As the chairman of the board of trustees of Edward Waters College, I have a very serious concern about the survival of the historical black colleges. We appreciate your directive in January 1979, directing the Federal agencies to give greater support to the black colleges. And in connection with that, you established an office, a black college initiative office, in order to ensure compliance. Since the creation of the new Department of Education, however, it appears that that office is being phased out. I understand that the director has resigned and that many of the staff have left.

Now, my question is, what is the status of that office? Is it being phased out, and if so, what assurance can you give that your initiative is going to be followed through in the matter of the support of these historical black colleges?

THE PRESIDENT. I'll have to find out the answer to the first part of your question, because I'm not familiar with the fact that the special office on the black colleges is being phased out.

When I became President, and having been the Governor of Georgia, where the Atlanta University complex was so significant for changing the social structure of our Nation, I became familiar with the importance of a predominantly black college in the societal structure of our whole country. When I got there, I found that the black colleges were being neglected. And I asked you and some others, Benjamin Hays from Atlanta and others, to come up to see me, to meet with me in the Cabinet Room, and you all brought to me a list of things that you thought ought to be done to revitalize the black colleges. I think we did almost everything that you asked for.

I also sent a directive—I think it was early in '79, as you pointed out—to all of the agencies in the Federal Government, whether they dealt directly with education or not, and asked them, in the allocation of research funds, in the allocation of Government grants, and so forth, not to forget the importance of strengthening the black colleges in our country. Since then, we've continued that effort, and I believe that we are well on the way now to preventing the deterioration of the predominantly black colleges in our country. Again, in spite of a very stringent 1981 fiscal year budget to control inflation, I advocated the $15 million increase in

money to go specifically for the strengthening of the black colleges.

But, Bishop Morris, if you will let me, I will find out about the particular office to which you refer, talk to Secretary Shirley Hufstedler about it. I think in the new Department of Education, one of the last things I want to see is the black colleges forgotten. So, I'll be back in touch with you within a day or two about the status of that office.

Yes, sir? Mr. Brown?

WINDFALL PROFITS TAX

Q. I would like to ask you about the windfall profits tax. It is my understanding that it will generate roughly $50 billion over the next 2 years, according to the present legislation. But there is no money earmarked for human resource services. Would you consider the inclusion of a human resource support out of that money?

THE PRESIDENT. Well, the money will actually amount to roughly $227 billion over a period of 10 years. As you know, this is a tax on the excess profits of the oil companies, brought about by increasing oil prices. Eighty-eight billion dollars of that, roughly, will go to provide new sources of energy, and I think 15 percent of the total will go to help the poor people. It's not designed for social services, but it is designed to help families both heat and cool their homes. We've increased this amount every year in the last 3 years.

I don't believe that I would recommend, I don't believe that Congress would go along with just putting that money in a general fund, because when they did pass it, they specified certain things for which it can be used. One, by the way, is to reduce taxes—I don't think that's a prospect now, but sometime in the future. Another one is to conserve energy by helping, particularly, poor people weatherize their homes, so that they can use less energy. Another one is to send cash payments to someone who has an increased fuel oil bill or heating gas bill. And, of course, others are to generate, as I said, new jobs with synthetic fuels.

But I don't think that it's possible, under that particular money, to spread it out and make it a general fund allocation. We now have about a third of our total Federal budget that goes for caring for elderly people; I would guess that that ratio will probably continue. But I don't believe I want to take the windfall profit tax money and broaden it any further than the Congress has already passed. It was hard enough for me to get that tax passed. [*Laughter*] And I don't want to open up a door any more to let the oil companies escape through it, while I'm trying to help the poor folks.

FEDERAL GOVERNMENT RESPONSIBILITIES

Q. [*Inaudible*] What have been some of the achievements of the last 4 years of your administration in meeting that problem? And do you think that big government can ever be eliminated in American democracy?

THE PRESIDENT. I doubt that big government can be eliminated, because the Federal Government is responsible for the defense of our Nation; the Federal Government is responsible for handling money that is paid in through a lifetime by a working person so that they can have security after they retire, with social security, for instance; the Federal Government also collects tax money and, in effect, turns around and gives it right back for Medicare and Medicaid, to give good health for

our people, to prevent infant diseases, as I described; and it is responsible for some elements of the highway system, like the Interstate Highway System, and parts of the secondary roads.

The Federal Government is becoming increasingly responsible for the operation of some of the railroads, not the strong, well-managed, profitable railroads in the Southeast, but some are on the verge of collapse. [*Laughter*] And if we had the same kind of management all over the Nation, we could keep the Federal Government out. But there are some roles that the Federal Government is required to play because of the failure of the nongovernmental sector, and there are some other roles, like national defense, that the Federal Government has to carry out.

We've made good progress, I think, on zero-base budgeting. Every item of the Federal Government is now scrubbed every year, and we put the old programs on the same basis as the brand new programs in the allocation of funds. Several other States have done that; I started that program, as you may know, in Georgia. We've tried to hold down the Federal Government employment rolls. We have 20,000 fewer Federal Government employees, or did the first of March, than we had the day I came in office, in spite of substantial increases in Federal expenditures. And we set a goal for ourselves, by hiring restraint, that by the end of this fiscal year, the first day of October, to reduce that by 20,000 more. At the same time, we've greatly increased the allocation of funds for defense, with a steady growth in real terms.

I think the important thing, also, is that we have cut paperwork by 15 percent, and we've begun a long effort to deregulate private industry. We've been successful in deregulating the airlines. We have been successful now in deregulating the trucking industry to a major degree. We have already deregulated investment institutions, banks, savings and loans, and so forth; I signed that bill earlier this year. We're working on rail deregulation now, which I hope will be successful. We're trying to deregulate to a major degree the communication industry.

So, we're trying to get Government's nose out of the private lives of our citizens and out of the private enterprise system as much as possible. But there are some roles that the Federal Government must continue to play. And I would say that the Federal Government is going to continue year by year to get a little bit larger, but to restrict its role to just those things that private citizens and State and local government cannot do.

My own belief is that whenever government must function, it can function better in a local community, and when a role can be carried out by a private citizen or group of citizens on a fair and equal basis under the American Constitution, that it ought to be done without government involvement at all. That's what I've been working for. I think we're making good progress.

Maybe one more question. Yes?

URBAN DEVELOPMENT ACTION GRANTS

Q. Mr. President, I represent a group of businessmen in the redevelopment of our downtown. We've been somewhat frustrated, because under our consolidated form of government, we don't qualify for UDAG funds for downtown development.

THE PRESIDENT. I know.

Q. I wonder if you have any plans to broaden the eligibility requirement to enable communities like Jacksonville to qualify.

THE PRESIDENT. Well, there are two things that you'd have to do to qualify: One is to have more people out of work, and the other one, to be poorer. [*Laughter*] I don't believe there's much likelihood to broaden the definition of the requirements, but I would like to point out that you more than compensate for it with the dynamism and the growth and the strength of your community. I'll just give you a couple of examples.

Last year, for instance, I believe you got in excess of $10 million for local public transportation. This is more than three times as much as you got in 1976. It's because the community got together, presented a workable plan to the Federal Government agencies, primarily the Department of Transportation, and then in competition with other communities around the Nation, you won, because you were better prepared, knew what you wanted, and moved forward on it. I think the revitalization of your downtown area has been one of the remarkable success stories of the entire country.

And the new project that we just announced on Blount Island, I think the Federal Government ought to put a million dollars in it. This would be something that would be beneficial to you in the future, and nobody knows what the ultimate size or growth of that might be.

I think you just had more than a half-million dollars allocated to revitalize, I think, nine of your public parks, primarily in the poorer sections of the community.

And when we've increased Federal funds for public education, I think more than 70 percent in the last 3 years, Jacksonville has more than gotten its share. We have now a situation in our country where every child, as I said earlier, no matter what the economic condition of their family might be, has a chance to go to college. If they are qualified academically, they can go to college with loans or grants or work-study programs.

We have, I think, got a good record on EDA grants for Jacksonville. And, as you know, on your people mover, we are now trying to figure out, with my personal help, how Jacksonville can qualify, although you are more prosperous and your unemployment rate is very low, less than 5 percent in Jacksonville. We're trying to find some way under the law so that you can qualify, because you've done such a good job in other respects.

But I don't want to apologize for you, because you've done such a good job in keeping your people at work. But a lot of those programs, in order for the Congress to pass them, are earmarked for communities that are in much worse shape economically than is Jacksonville and Duval County. I have a great admiration for what you've done here, and within the bounds of the law, you've got a friend in the Oval Office who will help you get your share of the tax money that you pay.

Let me say, in closing, that I've really enjoyed this session. I don't claim to know all the answers. The Federal Government is enormously complicated, and there are literally thousands of bills in the Congress every year. I try to stay up with them as much as I can. But these are challenging times. And my whole belief is that the partnership that presently exists under our urban policy between local, State, and the Federal Government is unprecedented in its effectiveness. It was designed by mayors and by county officials, with the help of Governors. And when it was finally put together, then I adopted as my own as President, and it was passed through the Congress. And I think it's worked remarkably well.

When I ran for President the first time in 1976, everywhere I went the picture was of America's cities going down the drain. It was not only New York City, but it was Philadelphia and Detroit and San Francisco, all over this Nation. Now there's a different spirit and a different attitude and a different level of achievement. We haven't solved all the problems; that's true. But it would be hard for you to go into a community where the mayor was nonpartisan, Democrat, or Republican and not have that mayor say that we have really made a lot of progress in the last 3 years in solving the problems of our cities and our communities and facing the future with confidence and the American commitment to realizing a dream of a better life for all our citizens, not just a few.

Thank you.

Q. Thank you very much for being here. Mr. President, I can't tell you how proud we are of the job you're doing and how we respect the job and the office. And we know that you carry burdens everywhere you go. I'm glad you had a little time off to—he's been telling me about fly fishing. He's an expert now. [*Laughter*]

Let me tell you one story. He's got to get out, but I've got to tell you. He was telling me that he was up in Alaska fishing. And everybody around him wasn't doing a thing, and he was catching fish left and right. And they finally went over to one of the Secret Service and said, "How does he do that?" And they said, "He makes his own flies." And so they all came over and borrowed his flies, and then they started catching some fish. [*Laughter*]

THE PRESIDENT. I have enjoyed fishing lately. I also caught some sea trout on a fly rod. [*Laughter*]

But I'm glad to see you all again. And it makes me a lot more confident about my ability to do a good job as President, knowing I've got partners like you.

Thank you very much.

NOTE: The President spoke at 2:20 p.m. in the employees' lounge at the Independent Life Building.

Prior to the meeting, the President attended a Democratic National Committee fundraiser in the River Club at the Independent Life Building.

Jacksonville, Florida

Exchange With Reporters. July 17, 1980

Q. Mr. President, can I ask you a few questions?

THE PRESIDENT. All right.

Q. What are your thoughts, Mr. President, about the ticket? What about the ticket? Did you watch last night on television and see the convention?

THE PRESIDENT. No, I didn't watch it. But I think they have got a very good ticket. I called Governor Reagan this morning when he woke up and congratulated him on his nomination. I told him I was sure that the convention would go along with his recommendation for Vice President. I pointed out that it would be good for us both if we could have a series of debates around different sections of the country, I think at least three or four, and let our views be expressed clearly to the American people. And he said that sounded like a good idea to him. I sent him an official telegram of congratulations. And I think the ticket they've chosen will be formidable, but I'm confident and look forward to the election in November.

Q. Mr. President, do you think it's an easier ticket to beat than would Reagan/Ford have been?

THE PRESIDENT. I don't know. I have mixed emotions about it. That's a choice for the Republicans to make. But I would like to debate—[*inaudible*].

Q. Let me ask you about your brother, Billy, Mr. President. Do you feel that it was proper for him to have taken all that money from the Libyan Government?

THE PRESIDENT. Well, I'm not going to comment on that part of it. I think it was a regrettable thing that happened. As you know, Billy leads a life of his own. I didn't know about it. He conducted those activities privately. I just hope that he doesn't get hurt too badly, that's all.

Q. Did you talk to him again today?

THE PRESIDENT. No, except that a few days ago, I recommended to him to go ahead and make a complete revelation of what had been done—[*inaudible*]. And he thought it over for awhile, and he decided to do that. But I did not—[*inaudible*].

Q. You didn't know about the money that he had received?

THE PRESIDENT. No, not at all.

Q. Mr. President, it looks like a tough combination to beat, a moderate and a conservative.

THE PRESIDENT. I think we can handle them okay.

Q. Thank you, Mr. President.

NOTE: The exchange began at approximately 3 p.m. outside the Independent Life Building. The President then went to Jacksonville International Airport, where he boarded Air Force One enroute to Fort Lauderdale, Fla.

As printed above, this item follows the text of the White House press release.

Hollywood, Florida

Remarks at the Annual Congress of the International Transport Workers Federation. July 17, 1980

President Fritz Prechtl, who would have no problem getting a job as English instructor in any of our schools in this country, Secretary-General Lewis, the North American host committee, who have been honored, along with me and all Americans, by your presence here, and delegates to the 33d International Congress of the Transport Workers Federation:

I've come here to meet with this distinguished group, because as the President of our country I am very proud and honored that you have chosen this site for your 33d convention. This Congress has honored us.

I, as a leader of one of the great nations of the world, recognize with admiration and appreciation what you stand for, the breadth of your knowledge and experience in matters that bind nations together, and also because I share with you, as President Prechtl has said, a deep commitment to human rights. You represent, perhaps among all labor organizations, a perspective and an ability to understand international relationships, to see the differences that exist among nations and among peoples, and also to make sound judgments on how those differences can be eliminated or minimized or overcome.

I'm convinced, looking at the perspective of history, that a free labor movement is a pillar of democracy and is absolutely necessary for freedom and for democracy to survive. And I'm filled with admiration, because not only do you represent your millions of members throughout the world but collectively you have espoused, you have supported, sometimes you have even been willing to endanger your own lives or freedom for the human rights of others. You have been in the forefront of this long and continuing, not yet completely successful struggle.

I know, prior to myself, a great American leader, Lane Kirkland, has spoken to you—one of your own, a maritime union member who understands that human rights has a breadth of meaning not completely encompassed in its political connotations. Human rights means

the right of an able-bodied man or woman to have a job, to use whatever talent or ability a person might possess to a useful purpose, to support one's own family, to realize one's own personal ambitions, to strengthen one's own community, and to enhance the freedom and a better life for those who live around him.

Human rights also means the granting of justice to those less fortunate, less influential, perhaps weaker, less articulate than are we. Fairness, equality, the honoring of the principles of justice, the elimination of persecution wherever it exists is of course a part of human rights. Political freedom, as President Prechtl pointed out, has not yet been won in many communities and nations around the world. But the struggle for this freedom is indeed a noble one, one that challenges the finest commitments of human beings and sometimes requires the greatest degree of courage.

We also know that part of human rights for an individual or a national community is peace, the absence of war, the absence of hatred, the absence of death. Peace is the noblest purpose of a statesman, but we also recognize that peace can only be achieved through strength, because confidence comes from strength.

With strength, a nation need not prove that it is strong. With strength, a nation can take care of its own needs and seek peace for others. With strength, a nation can be bound together in a sense of unity, without fear of the future, and can assess ways to improve the interrelationship among nations which are not inherently compatible with one another.

You realize, perhaps more than any other group on Earth, the personal economic benefits to be brought to all of us through peace among nations: the opening up of opportunities for trade, commerce, tourism, exchange of ideas, better education, better homes, a better life, a better way to accommodate rapid, unpredictable change. This comes necessarily through the peaceful interrelationship among nations and among people.

A great labor leader, perhaps the greatest who ever lived in our Nation, President George Meany, said international relations are too important to be left to diplomats—[*laughter*]—or prime ministers or chancellors or presidents or kings. International relations are best understood and best shaped by people like you, who have your primary responsibility in your own home, in your own community, among those who look to you for leadership in dealing with their own human needs, but who see the advantages of a good relationship among nations.

I'm grateful that you've come here to our country, to a beautiful seacoast in a land that is free. I can't tell you that the United States of America is perfect, and I cannot tell you that those who have achieved complete freedom and a complete element of political democracy in their lives will lead a perfect life. The challenges still exist for us all. The questions are difficult to answer. The obstacles are not easily overcome. Courage is still a requisite. Strength is still mandatory. Unity in the face of challenge is required. An ability to accommodate change, when change is inevitable, is a characteristic that must be present among free people. And finally, I think confidence in oneself, in principles and beliefs that never change provide a stabilizing factor in our lives that tide us over the most difficult of times.

These are characteristics of a great nation. These are characteristics of a great labor organization. These are the characteristics of the International Transport Workers Federation, whose Congress here in Hollywood, Florida, in my own Nation, which is so dear to all of us who live here, has honored the people of my country.

So, from the bottom of my heart, let me say congratulations on your great achievement, welcome to a great country, and my best wishes for a more peaceful, more prosperous, and a more free world, where human rights in its broadest possible definition will be honored by all men and women throughout the world.

Thank you, and may God bless you in the future.

NOTE: The President spoke at 5:32 p.m. in the Convention Center at the Diplomat Hotel.

Hollywood, Florida

Remarks at a Democratic National Committee Fundraising Dinner.
July 17, 1980

Senator [Congressman] Pepper, Governor Graham, Ambassador Askew, Congressman Lehman, Congressman Stack, Attorney General Smith, Secretary of State George Firestone, my good friend, Chairman Charlie Whitehead, and particularly Joe Cantor, who has done so much this evening to make this a resounding success:

I'd like to start out by asking a question of this group. How many of you believe that in Florida and throughout the Nation we can whip the Republicans in November? [*Applause*]

I've been observing the situation in Detroit, as has Senator Pepper, and I have just one comment to make about it. I'm very glad to be down here in Florida, in Hollywood with you. I come representing an administration and a party that's well organized. We took off from near Sapelo Island a few minutes, this morning, before noon, and we landed in Hollywood, Florida, at the right airport. And we're very grateful for that. A lot of the planes coming out here lately have not done so in the past. [*Laughter*] It just shows how much farther advanced the Democratic Party is than some others that I won't mention.

We've got in prospect for us a good year. The Democratic Party is well organized. The Democratic Party National Committee, for the first time in history under the U.S. laws, can now join with the State and local Democratic Parties to share funding campaign efforts between local, State, congressional, and the Presidential campaigns. This opens up a vista of cooperation and common purpose that will be very significant, and I think that the extraordinary and, I might say, unpredicted success of this banquet this evening is a testimony to that.

I want to talk to you very briefly and, from the bottom of my heart, to say that in order for the Democrats to be elected in November, we must deserve victory. We will have to stand on our record, and we will also have to present the vision of a future that will be attractive and exciting, significant and acceptable to the American people. We must be a party—and this is difficult—with some degree of humility, recognizing that we don't know all the answers, recognizing that there have been mistakes made under Democratic administrations, no matter how enlightened or how dedicated or how honest they have been.

Beginning in 1932, when Franklin Roosevelt ran for President in the depths of a debilitating and disheartening depression, the Democratic stamp has been on the Government of the United States. We have not betrayed that trust, and we are not now betraying that trust placed in us by the American people.

I like Florida. You've been good to me. Every time I've run for office, we have surprised people in Florida. And I also like Florida because of the climate. The weather, of course, is good, but I like the fact that the political climate here is conducive to good will and to progress. You've got a Democratic Governor, a Democratic cabinet, a Democratic congressional delegation, a Democratic legislature, Democratic local officials, and a strong Democratic Party here in Florida that accurately exemplifies the hopes and ambitions of the Florida people. You've not betrayed that trust, and that's why we have been so successful in your great State.

Let's look very briefly at what the Democratic Party has meant and means to this country. I think first and foremost, ours is a party of peace. We believe that nations should be at peace with one another. We believe that differences should be resolved without bloodshed. We believe that peace can only be maintained through strength, because with strength comes a certain aura or element of confidence. We don't have to prove our strength by combat. We don't have to prove our strength by pushing small nations like Panama around. And with a degree of confidence within our hearts and within our souls, we are able and eager to reach our hands out to others and to provide the hope for peace to them.

One of the most significant developments in the last few years has been the bringing of the prospects for peace to the nation of Israel, a troubled, young, aggressive, strong, dedicated democracy, crucial to the strategic future of our own country. In the last 32 years our Nation has provided Israel with 22 billions of dollars in aid. I'm glad to say that since I've been President, a very short time, about half that amount of money has been requested from the Congress, about $11 billion. This is not a handout from us to a people, no matter how worthy or how much they are in need of a strong defense capability; it's a real paying investment in our own future, in our democratic principles, and in our own strength and security.

We are committed to certain principles that have never varied since I've occupied the White House. We have never threatened Israel with a withdrawal of funds or the withholding of armaments that they needed to defend themselves in a time of crisis, as was the case, as many of you remember, under the administration that preceded mine. We have recognized the worth of the ambitions of the Egyptian people. We've also known that Egypt, as the strongest, most dynamic, most influential Arab country, was the key to progress toward peace for Israel. And because of the courage of President Sadat and the deep commitment and courage of Prime Minister Menahem Begin, we have so far made good progress.

The avenue toward peace for the Middle East has not been one that's smooth. It's not always predictable. It doesn't always move as rapidly as I would like. But the commitment there by our Nation has indeed paid rich dividends for us all. We could not possibly do this if our own Nation's defense was not assured, if we were not strong militarily. We are now strengthening our own Nation's defenses. For 8 years, under the preceding Republican administrations, our commitment to defense went down in real dollars. Since I have been in office, there has been a steady, sustained, predictable, efficient growth in our commitment to our own defense capability. That's one of the reasons that I look forward to the future of a country, our country, able to maintain peace.

This is a troubled world; it's an unpredictable world; it's a complex world. It's almost impossible to understand. We cannot dominate others; that's not the American way. But we can provide them with a vision of the future and an assurance of their own security and a realization of the hopes and dreams of people who live under subjugation that provides some glimpse of how we can work together in the years ahead.

We have seen gross violations of the peace—the Soviet invasion of Afghanistan, a powerful nation attacking free, deeply religious, committed people, who were no threat to anyone, and now who persecute them, as you well know, with military force, brutally brought to bear on the small villages and towns of that troubled country.

In Iran we've seen the grossest example of the violation of human rights, through international terrorism condoned and supported by the Government of that country. We have no quarrel with the people of Iran; we have no quarrel with the results of their revolution. We do not want to interfere in their internal affairs. In the future we would like to see a good working relationship in trade and commerce with them. We want to see an Iran that is united, secure, stable, and at peace with its neighbors. That's our hope.

But as long as 52 Americans, innocent Americans, are held against their will, I as President can never rest. And it's heartening to me to see 220 million people in this great Nation almost completely obsessed with the safety and the freedom of just 52 Americans, who are not rich, not famous, not wealthy, but who belong to us. That's an example, I think, of the greatness of our country.

We're a nation that believes in compassion, and we're a party that represents a compassionate attitude to those not quite so fortunate as we. We've been the party of civil rights, and we are the party of human rights, not only in our own country but around the world. I just met a few minutes ago and made a speech to the International Transport Workers Congress, a very broad-based group of labor organizations. This is their 33d annual congress. They have never before met in North America. In addition to taking care of their own members, their prime commitment over the years has been for human rights. That's been one of the top priorities of my own administration and compatible, again, with the principles of the Democratic Party.

We are also a party of courage. We've not tried to avoid controversial issues when they might have been costly in a political sense. It was not politically advisable, after 14 years of delay, to have a Panama Canal treaty signed and to fight that battle in the Senate, ultimately to get it ratified. But I have no doubt that history will show that it prevented violence, it treated a small nation fairly, and it provided for the security and continued use of a vital waterway joining the two oceans that span our shores.

It was not politically advisable to move toward evolving a national energy policy. When I spoke to the Nation in April of 1977, I predicted that I would lose 15 percentage points in the public opinion poll when I presented an energy policy to our Nation. I underestimated the loss; I dropped a lot more than 15 percent. But as the Members of Congress here well know, that has been a successful struggle that will provide our country with a dynamic and exciting future as we develop new forms of energy and we break our ties and dependence on a 12,000-mile uncertain pipeline that goes into one of the most troubled areas of the whole world.

It will also provide us with an opportunity to conserve energy, a new approach to natural resources by this great country, because we've never had, in the past, to face the prospect of limits on us. And I predict to you that this facing of the prospect of limitations on the use and waste and importing of energy will open up a new future as exciting as anything we've ever seen. In the next 10 years we'll have $128 billion in income from the windfall profits tax passed by Congress; $88 billion of that, roughly, will go to develop new kinds of energy. And we'll have, indeed, new jobs, new industry, a new complex of life that we cannot possibly envision even today.

In addition, we are a nation that believes and a party that believes in hard work. We believe that part of that hard work and the human rights is that each person able to hold a job ought to have a job. We've provided in the last 3 years a net increase of 8½ million new jobs in this country, something never before done even in time of war. The commitment is sound. It's one that's compatible with the hopes and aspirations of American people. It particularly addresses the yearnings of those who've suffered in the past from discrimination of all kinds.

And we opened up vistas of the nourishment of human capability, given to each person by God, through a better educational system. We've increased expenditures in 3 years for Federal aid to education by 73 percent, at the same time letting local people control the school system. And now, for the first time in the history of this Nation, there is no reason for any child to be deprived of a college education because of economic limitations of that child's family.

Additionally, we've moved in areas to bring local, State, and Federal Government entities together. With an urban policy, we've transformed the attitude of people in New York, Philadelphia, cities in the South that formerly were deeply discouraged about the future. This is a part of binding our Nation's wounds and bringing our country together.

And finally, let me say, in talking about the Democratic Party, that we are one that believes in competence. We have been able to deregulate American private industry and let the free enterprise system begin to work as it was originally conceived during the early years of our history. We've also been able to cut paperwork by 15 percent. We've reduced Federal employees at the same time we've greatly enhanced the allocation of Federal services to the American people. We've been the party of progress, and we've been the party of the enhancement of civil rights.

I've only been in office now 3½ years, not nearly long enough. But I've had a chance in this brief time to appoint more women Federal judges, more Spanish-speaking Federal judges, more black Federal judges—one of whom is sitting on my left here, Judge Hastings—than all previous Presidents who've ever served in the White House combined, and we're not through yet. We've got a long way to go.

In contrast, we'll be running in this election this year against a party almost exactly opposite from us, a party that opposed social security, a party that opposed the rural free delivery of mail, a party that opposed the minimum wage, even when Democrats were trying to set a goal of 25 cents an hour, a party that opposed

Medicaid, a party that opposed Medicare, a party that brought us the disgrace of Watergate, a party that failed to provide for an energy policy of this Nation, even after the embargo of 1973, a party with a narrow vision, a party afraid of the future, a party whose leaders are inclined to shoot from the hip, a party that never has been willing to put its investment in human beings who were below them in the economic and social status; in this country of freedom and equality, a party that is going to be defeated in November if the Democrats, in an honest way, present our case to the American people, never fail to tell the truth, even when it hurts, never offer simplistic answers to complicated questions, never fail to point out the difficulty of obstacles that we have not yet surmounted, if we never lose confidence in the people who put us in positions of leadership, a nation that never deviates from a commitment to peace, a nation that never forgets the principles that have made this the greatest and the oldest political party on Earth.

That is not an easy task. It's not even an easy task just to tell the truth and to let the American people make an honest and fair judgment. I'm convinced that we can do so, with inspiration, with unity, with commitment, with compassion, with confidence, with courage, with moral and ethical commitments that never change. That's why I'm proud to be President of a great country; that's why I'm proud to be part of the Democratic Party.

If we work together in a spirit of unity, then we will not fail, and November will answer the question that you answered, at the beginning of my talk, successfully, and we will whip the Republicans all over Florida and all over this great Nation of ours again. And that's what the Nation needs, that's what the Republicans need, and that's what the Democrats need as well.

Thank you very much.

NOTE: The President spoke at 6:49 p.m. in the Cafe Cristal Room at the Diplomat Hotel.

Following his remarks, the President returned to the Fort Lauderdale/Hollywood International Airport, where he boarded Air Force One for the flight to Washington, D.C.

Alaska Natural Gas Transportation System

Letter to Prime Minister Pierre Elliott Trudeau of Canada.   July 17, 1980

Dear Mr. Prime Minister:

Since you last wrote to me in March, the United States Government has taken a number of major steps to ensure that the Alaska Natural Gas Transportation System is completed expeditiously.

Most significantly, the Department of Energy has acted to expedite the Alaskan project. The North Slope Producers and Alaskan segment Sponsors have signed a joint statement of intention on financing and a cooperative agreement to manage and fund continued design and engineering of the pipeline and conditioning plant. The Federal Energy Regulatory Commission recently has certified the Eastern and Western legs of the System.

The United States also stands ready to take appropriate additional steps necessary for completion of the ANGTS. For example, I recognize the reasonable concern of Canadian project sponsors that they be assured recovery of their investment in a timely manner if, once project construction is commenced, they proceed in good faith with completion of the Canadian portions of the project and the Alaskan segment is delayed. In this respect, they have asked that they be given confidence that they will be able to recover their cost from U.S. shippers once Canadian regulatory certification that the entire pipeline in Canada is prepared to commence service is secured. I accept the view of your government that such assurances are materially important to insure the financing of the Canadian portion of the system.

Existing U.S. law and regulatory practices may cast doubt on this matter. For this reason, and because I remain steadfastly of the view that the expeditious construction of the project remains in the mutual interests of both our countries, I would be prepared at the appropriate time to initiate action before the U.S. Congress to remove any impediment as may exist under present law to providing that desired confidence for the Canadian portion of the line.

Our government also appreciates the timely way in which you and Canada have taken steps to advance your side of this vital energy project. In view of this progress, I can assure you that the U.S. government not only remains committed to the project; I am able to state with confidence that the U.S. government now is satisfied that the entire Alaska Natural Gas Transportation System will be completed. The United States' energy requirements and the current unacceptable level of dependence on oil imports require that the project be completed without delay. Accordingly, I will take appropriate action directed at meeting the objective of completing the project by the end of 1985. I trust these recent actions on our part provide your government with the assurances you need from us to enable you to complete the procedures in Canada that are required before commencement of construction on the prebuild sections of the pipeline.

In this time of growing uncertainty over energy supplies, the U.S. must tap its substantial Alaska gas reserves as soon as possible. The 26 trillion cubic feet of natural gas in Prudhoe Bay represent more than ten percent of the United States' total proven reserves of natural gas. Our governments agreed in 1977 that the Alaska Natural Gas Transportation System was the most environmentally sound and mutually beneficial means for moving this resource to market. Access to gas from the Arctic regions of both countries is even more critical today as a means of reducing our dependence on imported petroleum.

Successful completion of this project will underscore once again the special character of cooperation on a broad range of issues that highlights the U.S./Candian relationship.

I look forward to continuing to work with you to make this vital energy system a reality.

Sincerely,

JIMMY CARTER

[The Right Honorable Pierre Trudeau, Prime Minister of Canada]
NOTE: The text of the letter was released on July 18.

Alaska Natural Gas Transportation System

Statement by the President. July 18, 1980

My administration's energy policy has always recognized that the energy problem is not unique to our country. The energy burden of the 1980's is shared by all the industrialized nations and by the lesser developed nations as well. Just as the energy burden is shared by all nations, so must the solution be borne by all in a cooperative spirit.

Just last month in Venice, I met with the heads of six other leading nations of the industrialized world to establish specific goals and a series of comprehensive commitments to conservation and the development of new energy supplies. At the time, we pledged increased international cooperation among ourselves and with other countries to help achieve these objectives.

When I met with Prime Minister Trudeau of Canada in Venice, we agreed that one of the potential cooperative projects—one that could be most meaningful to both our countries—was the Alaska Natural Gas Transportation System. I am very pleased that today the Canadian Government has announced its willingness to move forward on this vast project by approving the construction of the first major segment of what is intended eventually to be a 4,800-mile pipeline from Prudhoe Bay in Alaska through British Columbia and Alberta to the heartland of the United States.

This first segment, approved today by the Canadian Government, will enable U.S. consumers in 33 States to begin receiving additional natural gas from Canada by 1981, replacing 200,000 barrels a day of crude oil, even before the Alaskan and northern Canadian portions of the pipeline are completed. Eventually, too, Canadian natural gas from the north will be able to flow to consumers in Canada.

The entire project, which I approved in 1977, is intended to be completed in 1985 and will bring about 2.4 billion cubic feet of Alaskan natural gas to U.S. consumers each day, replacing more than 400,000 barrels of foreign oil. Prudhoe Bay natural gas represents 10 percent of our Nation's reserves.

I have today sent a letter to Prime Minister Trudeau expressing our confidence that this project will be carried forward to completion and become an example to the world of how international cooperation can serve the common energy needs of both partners. Both Houses of Congress have recently passed resolutions of support for the Alaska Pipeline, and I have been able to provide several specific assurances to Prime Minister Trudeau on our commitment as a nation to this joint project.

The pipeline is one of the most complex and demanding energy ventures ever undertaken. When completed, it will be a major element in our transition to a more diversified and secure energy economy.

Girls Nation

Remarks to Delegates Attending the Annual Meeting. July 18, 1980

THE PRESIDENT. I think this is the prettiest the Rose Garden has looked all year. [*Laughter*]

First of all, I want to thank you all for coming here. One of the best things that ever happened to our country was that 42 years ago, because of the support of the Auxiliary of the American Legion, girls' State organizations were formed and young women of our country began to learn about government through personal experience. And I understand that by the end of this year, more than 590,000 American girls will have learned about government in that way.

And this is the 34th annual convention, I believe, of Girls Nation. And I want to congratulate, first of all, your new presi-

dent, who happens to be from Tennessee, Lenora Mosley, Vice President Tamara Madison, and to thank President Agnes Kennedy and Director Margaret Yankovich for bringing you here.

Have you all already seen the White House? Have you already been through the White House?

DELEGATE. Yes.

THE PRESIDENT. Well, I hope you liked the White House. [*Laughter*] And I'm glad none of you are 35 years old. How many of you are governors or have been governors? Former governors and governors. I've heard a lot lately about former governors, and I—[*laughter*].

This is a wonderful country in which we live. It's blessed by God with unbelievable natural benefits for us. The resources that we have in rich land and forests and trees and mineral deposits, access to the oceans, space, beauty are unmatched anywhere on Earth. And, of course, the benefits that we've been given through our forefathers and through the commitment of courageous people, men and women, in the past to be free: free to speak as we please, free to criticize our own government, free to change it through legal processes, free to shape its future, free to be different, free to take whatever talent and ability God has given us and develop it to the utmost, depending on our own ambition and commitment and ability to work hard—these are the kinds of benefits that many people on Earth don't share with us.

It's not any accident that people throughout the world struggle to come to the United States to live. I would guess, unless there are a few native Indians among you, that all your families have been immigrants, sometimes refugees, seeking a better life here in the United States. Maybe some of you have come here as immigrants, maybe some of your parents or grandparents. But it's because our country is so blessed that people want to live among us.

We hear a lot, I'd say particularly in Washington, about the negative side of American life. The criticisms, the differences, the debates, the condemnations, the moaning and complaining are always part of a political process, and in that process—highly publicized, because that's where the news is—we tend to forget about the good things, not only in the past and the present but particularly about the future.

You've had a chance to be in Washington now and learn a little bit in a brief period of time about how the Federal Government works; its problems—we don't know all the answers; the difficulties—we have sometimes apparently insurmountable obstacles to overcome; the divisions, because each person has a right to speak and express differences of opinion. Those things create the semblance of confusion, and sometimes there's an adequate amount of actual confusion here, in State governments, even in private homes.

I've had a chance now to be President for 3½ years. Before that, I was a candidate for a long time, traveling around our country in every State, and prior to that I was a Governor. Prior to that, I was an unsuccessful candidate for Governor, and before that, I served in the State senate for two terms, and before that, I served in local government. So, I've had a chance as a private citizen, a father, a husband, and now grandfather, and also as a President to see our country from the different points of view.

Let me say that I'm glad you're here, because the messages you take back to your homes and to your communities, to others who've chosen you as their leader will be a very important message—to express to them the complexity of life in a rapidly changing world, to express to them confidence in our system of government and the flexibility with which it can deal with change.

Many nations on Earth who are even democracies and who have a modicum at least of freedom have difficulty in accommodating change. The future is uncertain. No one knows what's going to happen next year or the next 10 years in even the field of energy alone, much less transportation, commerce, trade, peace, the search for accommodation of human rights throughout the world. Nobody can predict the future.

But our Nation, with its, first of all, freedom of expression and study and exploration and debate, is able to make its way through changing times and benefit from those changes. And secondly, the diversity of our Nation gives us a tremendous resource. We've got people who live here whose allegiance is to the United States Constitution and our country, who represent every nation on Earth, who've come from those countries or whose families have come from those countries, who have blood ties there and pride in one's own heritage, whether it be Eastern Europe or Western Europe or Asia or Latin America or Africa, and who can bring to our country the consensus and the understanding and even genuine personal love that will help to bridge the political obstacles that sometimes arise at the international boundaries.

The last thing I want to say is that you will yourself have to face controversial issues. One example of that, and I won't dwell on it, is the growth of our country in the last 200 years toward full freedom and equality for our people. It took us 90 years after the Declaration of Independence before we eliminated legal slavery in the United States. It took us another hundred years before the American law and the rulings of the Supreme Court eliminated legal discrimination against people because they were black; 190 years to make those changes. We have now embedded in our Constitution and laws guaranteed equality for every person in the Nation except one group, and that's women.

There is an amendment proposed to the Constitution—highly controversial, distorted in its explanation to the American people—which must be decided. The wording is very simple; I've written it down here. And my suggestion to you is that no matter whether you support the equal rights amendment or not that you make up your own mind. These are the simple words: "Equality of rights under the law shall not be denied or abridged by the United States or by any state on account of sex." What that means is that the United States Government cannot deny you a right or abridge or reduce your rights because you're a woman, and neither can any State pass a law abridging or denying your rights because you're a woman. That's all the amendment says. It prohibits discrimination because you're a woman.

I think the equal rights amendment ought to be ratified, and I hope that it will be ratified. As you know, 35 States have decided that it should be, and an overwhelming majority of the Congress has decided twice that the equal rights amendment should be ratified. This will be the last legal step toward granting equality, not only for those in our country who speak Spanish, not only for all adults above the age of 18, not only among those who are black but, finally and after great difficulty, even for those who are female. Well, that's one of the controversial, divisive issues that must finally be addressed not by government exactly, but by private citizens who bring their influence to bear on government.

In closing, let me say that it's an honor for me to have you all here. It's inspiring to a President to see new leadership coming along with idealism and hope and expectation and confidence and happiness and pleasure and appreciation of freedom, but also with the sober realization that in just a few years you'll have to take on the responsibilities of a family or a community or perhaps an entire State, as a Governor, or perhaps a nation.

And maybe someday, after Amy serves as the first woman President, maybe—[*laughter*]—or maybe she could follow one of you—you'll see that this office is open to women, as well. I don't have any doubt that before too long we will have our first woman President. It'll be a great step foward for our country, and will prove to the world that we are indeed a nation of equality and hope and freedom.

Thank you for letting me be honored. I love every one of you.

NOTE: The President spoke at 9:50 a.m. in the Rose Garden at the White House. In his remarks, the President referred to Lenora Mosley, president, Tamara Madison, vice president, and Margaret Yankovich, director, Girls Nation; and Agnes Kennedy, national president of the American Legion Auxiliary, sponsor of Girls Nation.

Great Plains Coal Gasification

Remarks Announcing Federal Loan Guarantee for Plant To Be Built in North Dakota. July 18, 1980

THE PRESIDENT. This is one of those rare historic moments in the history of a nation and its interrelationship between government and the private sector of our economy to launch a new vista for improvements and for a better quality of life for all Americans.

The Canadian Government has just announced that they have approved the construction of the first leg of the 4,800-mile natural gas pipeline from Prudhoe Bay down to the heartland of America. We are very pleased with this. This will be the biggest single private contract operation in the history of the world. And by 1985 it will be completed and will provide about 2½ billion cubic feet of natural gas per day, equivalent to about 400,-000 barrels of imported oil that we won't have to buy.

This project here, which is a very rapid-moving project, since we only signed the Energy Security Act 3 weeks ago—less than 3 weeks ago—is another example of the progress that is being made toward making our Nation energy secure.

I would like to announce this morning and deliver to these assembled leaders the approval by the Federal Government of a $250 million loan guarantee for the construction of this coal-to-natural gas conversion plant to be built in North Dakota. I would particularly like to thank Governor Art Link and Senator Quentin Burdick for the leadership role they have played in coordinating the Government effort. And Mr. Seder, on my left, represents a consortium of five energy-producing industries in our Nation that will be responsible for the design, the construction, and the operation of the plant.

This plant will be the first commercial coal-to-gas plant ever built in our Nation. There have been other pilot models built of a relatively small size, but this will be a full-scale commercial plant. We expect it to produce the equivalent of 9 million barrels of oil per year, and this will mean, during the construction phase, the hiring of about 3,000 workers and the permanent hiring of about 500 to operate the plant, highly advanced in its design, in the forefront of engineering technology of the modern age throughout the world.

This is a very good example of how the Government, through its own action in devising an energy policy, can provide for the private enterprise sector of our economy the means by which their tremendous resources can be tapped for the benefit of our Nation.

I would also like to express my thanks that President J. Turner is here this morning and President Jack Lyons. I understand that President Bob Georgine will be coming in a few minutes. And there are representatives, behind, of the other companies involved in the private consortium.

It's with a great deal of pleasure that I deliver to Mr. Seder this conditional commitment to guarantee the $250 million in loans from which a great deal more money can be derived from private sources for the construction of this remarkable plant. We'll be observing its progress with great interest and anticipation, and the entire Nation will be benefited by this project.

Mr. Seder, congratulations to you, and it's a pleasure to have you with us.

MR. SEDER. Thank you very much, Mr. President.

THE PRESIDENT. Art, would you like to comment, you and Senator Burdick?

GOVERNOR LINK. I want, first of all, President Carter, to thank you and the Department of Energy for this support for the construction of the first coal gasification plant in the Nation. I want to commend and congratulate you, Mr. Seder, on behalf of the consortium, my colleague, formerly in the Congress and now is working in the U.S. Senate in very close cooperation, for this very important historic moment in the energy industry.

There's a significance connected with this that we should also note, that it's being built on the same ground and in conjunction with an electric coal-fired generating facility operated by Basin Electric. And they have a close working relationship that will put into effect a great many economical, innovative procedures, both from the economic and utilization of the fuel and also from the environmental impact effects of this kind of development.

And so, Mr. President, all of us in North Dakota and those who have worked very closely, particularly in promoting this plant, are deeply grateful to you, the Department of Energy, and to your foresight and support and encouragement in the progress that we've made in getting this project off the ground as we are this morning. I think we'd certainly want to hear from Mr. Seder and from Senator Burdick. And I want to thank you personally.

THE PRESIDENT. Senator Burdick?

SENATOR BURDICK. Mr. President, this is indeed a moment in history. It means that we are going ahead, determined to secure energy independence in this country. This is a project that will save, as the President said, millions of gallons of oil, and it will be a key in our development of energy independence.

And I want to thank the President and all those who had anything to do with this development. It's much needed, and I think our country will go forward with it.

THE PRESIDENT. Thank you very much, Senator Burdick.

One of the things that's interesting, also to the coal industry is that, I believe, this plant will use about 22,000 tons of coal per day. Is that correct?

MR. SEDER. Yes, that's correct.

THE PRESIDENT. That's good news, too, because as all of you know, our most plentiful supply of energy is in coal, and we're very grateful that this project will go forward.

I'd like to ask Mr. Seder to comment if he would.

MR. SEDER. Mr. President, apropos of your last remark, I think it's significant that this plant will take the 22,000 tons of low-grade lignite coal, which otherwise can't be properly utilized, will convert it to natural gas, which has a very high end use, as you know, and will transport it to homes and businesses throughout the country. I think it's also important to note that this plant will be located only a few miles from that Alaskan gas pipeline, or the U.S. segment of it, so that at the time this plant is completed, we hope that segment of the Alaskan pipeline will also be completed so that we can use joint facilities.

Mr. President, I want to thank you for taking time to be with us and to announce this commitment this morning. For the project, of course, it's a very important day. We've been working on this project for nearly 8 years, so it's been a long time in coming, but certainly is worth it.

I think it's important, as you suggested, for the Nation, too, that this plant be constructed and that it get underway at this particular time. It will produce a significant amount of energy, the equivalent of 20,000 barrels of oil a day, or 9 million barrels a year, as you suggested. But that's only the beginning. I think that this plant will be the prototype of many additional plants to come. And so, within the next decade and certainly beyond, synthetic fuels made from coal will provide a very important part of our Nation's energy mix.

So, I want to thank you and to say that we have enjoyed tremendous cooperation from the Department of Energy. And I want to say just one word for Governor Link. I think when these outlanders from Detroit first came up to North Dakota, he wasn't entirely sure what it was we were proposing. But he took the time to analyze the project, its environmental consequences, its capacity to provide energy for the country and for North Dakota, and once he was convinced that it was a desirable project, he's been a tremendous bulwark of support. And Senator Burdick in the Senate has helped us over several very rough periods. So, I want to thank them and especially to commend the Department of Energy for their role in this.

THE PRESIDENT. Thank you. Let me ask you a question. Where is the pilot plant located, and what size is it, on which this design is predicated?

MR. SEDER. Well, actually, Mr. President, there isn't a pilot plant, because we already have the prototype of this plant several places, most particularly in South Africa, where, within a few years, over 60 percent of that country's petroleum needs will be provided by plants of exactly this kind. So, we are working on the basis of a design and a concept that has been proven commercially, but it has never been done in this country. And what this plant will do will be to provide the proof of the economics, the environmental consequences, the desirability of the plant generally, so that then this can be the prototype for many more to come.

GOVERNOR LINK. Art, you might mention the amount of coal that you shipped there from the source.

MR. SEDER. Yes, Governor. Before going forward with the design of this plant, we shipped an entire boatload, 12,000 tons of coal, from North Dakota down to South Africa to be run through those plants to be sure that the process worked with the North Dakota coal. So, it's a proven process. But there's still a lot to be learned, and this project will provide the basis on which that learning process can go on.

THE PRESIDENT. Is it your thought that in the future this would be kind of a standard size plant, or would they be a good bit larger? Or can you multiply what's basically here and have a higher production?

MR. SEDER. This is only phase one of a multiple-phase plant that has already been projected.

THE PRESIDENT. For the same site?

MR. SEDER. For the same site. We will have certainly a phase two of comparable size, and then there are other sites in North Dakota and elsewhere where plants of this general design can be replicated. So, this is a very large plant. It will cost in the neighborhood of a billion and a half dollars when it's completed in 1983, so it's by no means a small plant. Nevertheless, it's capable of being duplicated continually.

So, as I say, we're looking forward much beyond this project. If there were only this in the offing, why, it wouldn't be worth going forward, but certainly this must be an important part of the Nation's energy mix as we go forward and reduce our dependence on foreign sources of energy.

THE PRESIDENT. And you anticipate the environmental problems to be pretty well solved?

MR. SEDER. Yes. That was one of the concerns that the Governor raised at the very outset—what would be its environmental effects. And much of the process, the conversion of coal to gas, takes place within contained systems, so that the emissions are less than for an electric generating plant, for example, and the sulfur is removed within these contained systems. And so far as the mining of the coal is concerned, North Dakota, I think, is probably in the forefront of reclamation requirements, which we're quite prepared to meet. And I think the people, Governor, are reasonably well reassured that the land can be returned to its original state or even better, and that is our intent and our goal.

THE PRESIDENT. Thank you.

Did Bob Georgine ever come in?

PARTICIPANT. No, I didn't notice, sir.

THE PRESIDENT. Well, I know the construction workers, the iron workers, and others are very happy to see these kinds of plants get started in our country. And this is the first one of many that will be now supported and aided by the Federal Government through the windfall profits tax funds. But the emphasis ought to be placed, I think, by the news media and the understanding of the American people that these are private enterprise projects. The Government will not design, build, nor operate this plant. We will provide the facilities by which the initial commitment can be made, but it's completely within the private enterprise system of our Nation. That's the way I prefer to have it.

Good luck. Thank you very much.

NOTE: The President spoke at 11:30 a.m. in the Cabinet Room at the White House. Arthur Seder is president of American Natural Resources Co., Detroit, Mich.

Ocean Thermal Energy Conversion Research, Development, and Demonstration Act

Statement on Signing H.R. 7474 Into Law. July 18, 1980

I have signed H.R. 7474, the Ocean Thermal Energy Conversion Research, Development, and Demonstration Act, a bill to establish within the Department of Energy an accelerated research and development program to foster the early use of ocean thermal energy conversion (OTEC) facilities. Senator Matsunaga and Representative Fuqua are to be commended for recognizing the potential contribution that renewable energy resources can make in meeting our Nation's long-term energy needs.

The bill establishes a long-term national goal of 10,000 megawatts of electrical capacity or energy product equivalent from OTEC systems by the year 1999. In order to achieve this goal as well as intermediate goals and to facilitate the development of an industrial base for OTEC technology, this bill authorizes the Secretary of Energy to design, construct, and operate two OTEC demonstration facilities on a cost-sharing basis.

In implementing the provisions of this bill, the Department will carry out a measured program for the development of OTEC technology consistent with technological developments and sound fiscal policy. A major commitment by the private sector will be indispensable to the successful development of OTEC technology, and the Department of Energy will seek significant cost-sharing by the private sector for these demonstration facilities.

NOTE: As enacted, H.R. 7474 is Public Law 96–310, approved July 17.

Board for International Broadcasting

Nomination of John A. Gronouski To Be a Member and Designation as Chairman. July 18, 1980

The President today announced his intention to nominate John A. Gronouski for reappointment as a member of the Board for International Broadcasting. On confirmation by the Senate, Gronouski will be redesignated Chairman of this Board. Gronouski, 60, was appointed a member and Chairman of the Board for International Broadcasting in 1977.

He was previously professor of economics and public affairs at the Lyndon B. Johnson School of Public Affairs of the University of Texas at Austin. He organized this school in 1969 and served as its dean until 1974. He was a member of the 1972–73 Milton Eisenhower Commission, whose recommendations led to the establishment of the Board for International Broadcasting.

Digest of Other White House Announcements

The following listing includes the President's public schedule and other items of general interest announced by the White House Press Office and not included elsewhere in this issue.

July 11

While on Sapelo Island, Ga., the President and Mrs. Carter telephoned Richard Queen, the American hostage released by his captors in Iran, who was recuperating in a hospital in Zurich, Switzerland.

July 13

The President met on Sapelo Island with his economic advisers.

July 17

The President returned to the White House following his trip to Jacksonville and Hollywood, Fla.

The White House announced that the President has designated Donald F. McHenry, the Permanent Representative of the United States to the United Nations, to lead a U.S. delegation to ceremonies commemorating the first anniversary of the Nicaraguan Revolution, in Managua, July 19. The delegation's attendance at the ceremonies will reaffirm U.S. interest in pluralistic and democratic development in Nicaragua.

July 18

The President met at the White House with:

—Zbigniew Brzezinski, Assistant to the President for National Security Affairs;

—Secretary of Defense Harold Brown, Secretary of State Edmund S. Muskie, Deputy Secretary of State Warren M. Christopher, Hedley W. Donovan, Senior Adviser to the President, Jack H. Watson, Jr., Assistant to the President, and Dr. Brzezinski;

—Frank B. Moore, Assistant to the President for Congressional Liaison.

NOMINATIONS SUBMITTED TO THE SENATE

The following list does not include promotions of members of the Uniformed Services, nominations to the Service Academies, or nominations of Foreign Service officers.

Submitted July 18, 1980

ALBERT CARNESALE, of Massachusetts, to be a member of the Nuclear Regulatory Commission for the term expiring June 30, 1985, vice Richard T. Kennedy, term expired.

CHECKLIST OF WHITE HOUSE PRESS RELEASES

The following listing contains releases of the White House Press Office which are not included in this issue.

Released July 10, 1980

News conference: on the President's meeting in Tokyo, Japan, with Premier Hua Guofeng of the People's Republic of China—by Press Secretary Jody Powell

Released July 17, 1980

Transcript: statement and news conference on the President's telephone conversation with and telegram to Gov. Ronald Reagan—by Deputy Press Secretary Rex L. Granum

CHECKLIST—Continued

Released July 18, 1980

News conference: on the Alaska Natural Gas Transportation System—by Stuart E. Eizenstat, Assistant to the President for Domestic Affairs and Policy, John C. Sawhill, Deputy Secretary of Energy, and Leslie J. Goldman, Assistant Secretary of Energy for International Affairs

News conference: on the administration's record and Governor Reagan's proposals concerning the Federal work force—by Alan K. Campbell, Director, and John P. White, Deputy Director, Office of Management and Budget

ACTS APPROVED BY THE PRESIDENT

Approved July 17, 1980

H.R. 7474_____ Public Law 96–310 Ocean Thermal Energy Conversion Research, Development, and Demonstration Act.

H.R. 7573_____ Public Law 96–311 An act to provide an extension of the timeframe for nomination of a selection pool under the Cook Inlet land exchange.

Congressional Medal of Honor

Remarks on Presenting the Medal to Lt. Col. Matt Urban, U.S. Army, Retired. July 19, 1980

Secretary Alexander, General Meyer, General Craig, Colonel Kingley, Colonel and Mrs. Urban, men of the 9th Division and the wives that stand beside you:

I can't get over how young you look. [*Laughter*] It's a special pleasure to be with the men whose service in World War II—in Sicily, in Africa, France—was responsible for the 9th Division being known ever after as the "Old Reliables."

We are here today to honor a hero. Unfortunately, he has had to wait almost 36 years for official recognition from the Government of his special act of heroism. But as the eye witness accounts testify and as the documents prepared at that time testify and as those of you who served with him know, Matt Urban is truly a hero of this great Nation.

Matt Urban becomes the sixth of the "Old Reliables" to be awarded the Medal of Honor for World War II service. His conduct throughout the period from June the 14th until September the 3d, 1944, was an outstanding example of the bold, courageous, inspired, and heroic action which this medal was established to honor.

We also have a special picture of the kind of leadership that sets Matt Urban apart. He galvanized his men, and he led them to success while repeatedly risking his life to save others and to break his troops out of positions when they were pinned down, in sometimes apparently hopeless circumstances, by punishing enemy fire. He was wounded several times.

I notice that he wears the Purple Heart with six oak-leaf clusters. But he always kept coming back, and each time his presence brought something extra to his men when they needed it most. He was always willing to give the last ounce of his strength and the last full measure of courage and devotion to his comrades and to his Nation.

War is a terrible thing, wasting the young before they have a chance to reach their full potential. But there are moments, terrible in their danger and devastation, that can also bring out unimaginable courage and leadership that cannot be fully described; but once seen and felt, can never be forgotten.

It is of such soldiers like Lieutenant Colonel Urban and many of you that victory is made, not just in individual battles but in the ultimate conflict between the champions of justice and liberty and all those forces that are marshaled against them. Such men not only draw the full measure of capability from within themselves but call forth the best from those around them, inspiring in others the courage and the tenacity to go beyond the limits of endurance and sometimes even beyond the limits of hope, and to succeed in doing what, just a moment before, seemed to be impossible.

I deeply regret the delay of this ceremony for so many years, but I'm grateful, as President and as Commander in Chief, for the privilege of presenting the Medal of Honor to Lieutenant Colonel Urban. I'm grateful, too, for this reminder, so many years later, to our Nation of what freedom means, what it has cost us in the past, what really is at stake when we talk about the spirit of America, what might be demanded of us in the future to protect our Nation's honor and to preserve peace through strength.

As a people we need heroes, real heroes, who when tested excel and in doing so inspire others to reach for greatness within themselves. We need heroes not just for the victories that they make possible on the battlefield but in later days to remind us of what America at its best can be now and in the future—the greatest nation on Earth.

Thank you very much.

NOTE: The President spoke at 9:31 a.m. at a ceremony in the Regency Ballroom at the Shoreham Hotel.

Carter/Mondale Presidential Campaign

Remarks at a White House Reception for Delegates to the Democratic National Convention. July 19, 1980

How many of you think we're going to win in November? [*Applause*] This is going to be a very good year for Democrats, and it's because of people like you. This has been a good day for me, as well as, I know, it's been instructive for you, coming here to learn about our party and our platform, our administration, and the future of our Nation.

This morning I went over to one of the nearby hotels to give a Congressional Medal of Honor to a lieutenant colonel who served in 1944 in Europe, in Sicily, in Normandy. He had not received his medal because, although the recommendation was made at the time, the records had been misplaced. And a few months ago, they were discovered. And in front of the 9th Division, which are called the

"Old Reliables," we heard read out the record of his heroism.

He was wounded as a captain, commander of a company. He kept on fighting and eventually prevailed, saved the lives of several of his men; was transferred back to a hospital in England, with a shattered leg. He heard over the radio that all the senior officers in his company had been lost and his company was still in combat. He eased out of the hospital at night, hitchhiked across part of England, caught a ride to France, found his company as it went into battle again. It was losing with a tank attack. He asked a lieutenant and a sergeant to join him in getting the tanks going again; both of them were killed on the way to their tank. He mounted it and prevailed again, saved some of his men; was returned again to the hospital; and later on, in November, went out and fought as a wounded veteran of two major battles.

When I first met him, he was very thrilled to meet a President. I was even more thrilled to meet him. He was wearing the Purple Heart with six oak-leaf clusters. And the emotion of that recognition of true heroism and true courage, when the freedom of our country was challenged, inspired the entire audience in that hotel.

Later this morning, I met a young man named Richard Queen, who spent about an hour with me and Rosalynn—[*applause*]. He spent about an hour with me and Rosalynn. I won't tell you the entire conversation. But his prime concern was not for himself, although he has been found to have multiple sclerosis; his prime concern was not to do or say anything other than what would contribute to the release of the 52 other Americans who have suffered now since last November from unwarranted imprisonment in Iran.

He told about weeks of being locked up in what he called "the tomb," in a place in a basement with no light or fresh air. And he was finally moved at night, blindfolded, to another building. They had the windows sealed up, but there was a small crack between two bricks in the wall. And he talked about the intense excitement he had the first morning, when day broke, to see a little glimpse of sunlight between two bricks. And eventually he heard two little girls talking in the streets outside the compound as they went to school one day, and even heard, he said, some birds sing.

This is the kind of experience that a President has, not every day, but often, that are true reminders of the greatness of a nation—220 million people brought to their knees, not in submission, but in prayer that 52 or 53 Americans can be free again. It reminds us of what our Nation is. It reminds us also of what our party stands for.

This has been a long, difficult, challenging primary and caucus season. You've all won your elections. I congratulate you. Now it's up to you to make sure Fritz and I win ours. [*Laughter*]

I didn't take the time to watch the Republican Convention. I read about it. [*Laughter*] I read about it, heard some of the things about what happened. And I was concerned about the attitude of that convention and the nominee of the Republican Party and the debacle that occurred when the loss of the realization of what the Presidency means became apparent during the choice of a Vice President. The Oval Office is not something to be traded in a hurried fashion in the middle of the night, where part of the responsibilities of a President under the Constitution can be granted to another person.

And there has been a great deal made about the harmony and the lack of debate, the lack of division, in the convention in Detroit. My guess is that ours will be different in New York, but that's not something that's entirely to be avoided nor about which we need be concerned.

We will be debating how we can grant full rights under the Constitution of the United States to women and under the laws of the United States to women. We'll have 50 percent of our delegates or more there who are women. And we'll be debating about how we can carry out the commitments to minority Americans, because about 25 percent of all the delegates in New York will represent minority Americans. Only about 3 percent did this in Detroit.

There was no controversy, because there was no issue; there was no deep commitment. But we have the commitment and the issue, and we'll be debating how we can carry out the principles of the Democratic Party, as has been done in conventions gone by. This has not been an easy thing for us, but the Democratic Party has been on the cutting edge of the progress of this Nation.

I mentioned the other night in California about some of the ancient differences we'll be talking about in the fall as I campaign actively around this country with Fritz Mondale and others—about modern differences.

My first job after I finished high school was at the minimum wage, which at that time was the highest salary I had ever made. It was in 1941; the minimum wage was 40 cents an hour. The Republicans opposed the increase from 25 cents to 40 cents. They also opposed the granting of a 25-cent minimum wage. They are still opposing increases in the future in the minimum wage.

The Republicans opposed the rural free delivery of mail. I happened to live on a rural route—[*laughter*]—and I appreciated the fact that we got it, The Republicans opposed Medicaid and Medicare and social security and all the advancements that have been made to give basic rights and a better life to American people.

We are a party of compassion and understanding and sensitivity, and we believe in the true worth of an individual human being, the right to stand on one's own feet, to take what talent God gives us and develop it and utilize it on the basis of equality. And we believe in reaching a helping hand to those who have suffered from discrimination of all kinds and deprivation, because we believe that a human being who is healthy and well educated and employed and blessed with justice will be a full, self-supporting, strong, dynamic American that helps shape the future of this country.

The Republicans had very little debate about helping those who are economically deprived. The average medium income of the Republican delegates was about $50,000 a year. They don't worry too much about deprivation. They do worry a lot about a 30-percent reduction in income taxes over the next few years, which will either give us enormous deficits or a debilitated Federal Government.

So, when we debate issues at the convention, it's not a sign that the Democratic Party is weak. It's also not a sign that the Democratic Party will be divided when election day comes in November, because those things about which we do debate among ourselves in the convention and in the primary and caucus season are the very things that bind us together with a common purpose when we face the Republican challenge in the general election.

It's not an accident that we have a President in the White House who's a Democrat. It's not an accident that two-thirds, roughly, of the Members of the House of Representatives are Democrats. It's not an accident that two-thirds of the Senators are Democrats. The fact is that the Democratic Party has been tested in the forge of performance, under the scrutiny of American voters. And they have decided, "These are the leaders that I am going to support, that will give me a better life in the future."

Ours is a strong country. We have our faults. We've had our failures. The United States of America is not a perfect nation. The Democratic Party is not a perfect political party. My administration, along with Fritz Mondale, is not a perfect administration. But our faults are obvious, and they are brought about because sometimes we strive for too much, not because we strive for too little. And they are brought about in the public eye, because we do not avoid the tough issues which sometimes bring about political sacrifice, where we lose votes dealing with them. But the fact is that we look to the future with anticipation, confidence, unity, courage, commitment, never failing to tie closely together the principles on which our Nation was founded, which are the exact same principles that have been the lifeblood and the backbone of the Democratic Party.

So, your first answer to my question when I began my talk is the one that will prevail in my mind. We will beat the Republicans badly in November, with your help.

Just another word. Rosalynn reminded me that we'll have refreshments in the other end of the hall.

And I would like to tell you this: We still have some political struggle, perhaps at the convention itself. But I'm convinced that as you sit by and talk to and perhaps debate with the delegates that are committed to Senator Kennedy, that you have to remember that although we might be debating against them in New York, we'll be working with all of them throughout the country in November. So, keep that in mind. We'll all win together as friends.

NOTE: The President spoke at 4:34 p.m. in the East Room at the White House.

50th Anniversary of the Veterans Administration

Remarks During a Program Celebrating the Anniversary. July 19, 1980

Max Cleland, Administrator of the Veterans Administration, Harold Brown, Secretary of Defense, members of the Joint Chiefs of Staff, other Cabinet Secretaries, Members of Congress, and particularly those representatives of the Veterans Administration who work with Max, who've been so instrumental in giving a new life and new hope to literally millions of Americans who have offered their lives for the freedom and for the service of our country:

Fifty years ago the Veterans Administration was formally organized, but of course, this was not the first time our Nation had paid homage to and provided services for those who were willing to give their lives for freedom and for our Nation. Even while the Revolutionary War was actually in progress, the Continental Congress provided those services necessary for veterans who had suffered during that war and for the widows and orphans who were left by them.

In his second inaugural address, President Abraham Lincoln said these words, which have now been adopted as a motto for the Veterans Administration, and I quote: "It's purpose is to care for him

who shall have borne the battle, and for his widow, and his orphan." Very simple words, but deep with significance and with meaning for all of us who hear them and contemplate on them, and particularly a deep meaning for those who receive those benefits, who have suffered, and who need a helping hand.

Since the Veterans Administration was formed, three wars and 50 years of an uneasy peace have indeed created tremendous opportunities for service and also tremendous responsibilities to those who were willing to serve. We now have 30 million veterans, six times more than were present in our country in 1930, when the Veterans Administration was formed. And at this time, about 90 million Americans—about 40 percent of our total population—are theoretically qualified for Veterans Administration services. This is a tremendous commitment to our Nation and also a wonderful opportunity for our Nation to repay their sacrifice.

Each generation, I'm sure, particularly 50 years ago, it was hoped that the First World War was the last war, that there would be no more veterans coming back who were wounded or who left their lives overseas and left widows and orphans here. But we've not been yet so fortunate. It has been necessary for men and women to be strong, to be courageous, to be heroes, to be willing to offer themselves to preserve peace, through the strength of a mighty nation and through the strength of offered and sometimes granted personal sacrifice.

It would be difficult and mistaken for us to look upon the Veterans Administration service as just a negative kind of investment to repay those who've suffered deeply and to repair the ravages of war. In October of 1943, Franklin Roosevelt, in building a new program for the rehabilitation of all veterans and offering them a new life, by giving education and home benefits, pointed out the advantages to our country in investment in the future, in new prosperity for the entire Nation, in new happiness within homes where the suffering had not been personally deep, but where the sacrifice offered had been equally great.

One major element of the Veterans Administration service growing quite rapidly is that of hospitals. There's been an increase, of course, more than three-fold, in the last 50 years in the number of hospitals provided for veterans. And the outpatient services have grown by leaps and bounds, because we have recognized, particularly under Max Cleland's leadership, the advantage of quick treatment, outpatient if possible, relatively inexpensive, and also designed to prevent further suffering instead of just trying to treat suffering after it occurs.

Research has benefited veterans, of course, in the treatment of medical afflictions, also in rehabilitation, but it has provided untold benefits for millions of people all over the Earth who have not been directly related to our important and highly skilled medical services in the Veterans Administration. By joining with others, we've learned through the Veterans Administration how best to treat and prevent tuberculosis. The heart pacer was developed, the process for kidney transplants was assisted by Veterans Administration research. The laser-beam walking cane for blind veterans is now available to all who need it. The prevention of sickle cell anemia, particularly in our minority groups, was a major project of the Veterans Administration. And the psychotropic drugs have given new life and new hope to many who suffer from mental health problems.

I'm completely committed to a high-quality, independent health care system for veterans in this Nation. And I'm particularly grateful to Max Cleland, who, under his leadership, was able to prevail in Congress after 10 years of effort in setting up a new psychological readjustment service. This program, which operates in a very inexpensive way—most of the time in storefronts—has been one of the finest and best-received and most deeply appreciated programs we have ever seen in this country. Already, after just a few months, we have treated 15,000 veterans by giving them a way to overcome psychological problems.

We now provide for dependents and for survivors of veterans—to 5 million in our country—increased compensation each year. I'm glad to say that since I've been in office, we've increased that compensation substantially each year so far. This is money deeply needed, deeply appreciated, and also an excellent investment for our Nation's future.

It would be good for us to remember the rapidly aging group of veterans served. The doughboys who served in 1918 are now in their eighties, and of course, those of us who went to the military service early in the forties are rapidly approaching our sixties or have already reached that time. When I was Governor, and still, I was surprised to know that we still provide services for dependents and widows of those who served in the War Between the States and a larger number, of course, who served in the Spanish-American War. Along with that is the service of those who have recently offered their lives in Vietnam.

There would hardly be a family here, perhaps no families here, which has not felt directly the effect of service in the military. My own father was a first lieutenant in the First World War. He was fortunate. But when I grew up in Plains, it was a common thing along the streets of my little town to know those people intimately who had been in combat in Europe during that war. They suffered permanent disability, diseases that were inevitably producing an early death for them, and long pain and also an early death from gas and other poisons.

My mother's youngest brother, Tom Gordy, was a radioman in the Second World War, on Guam, and less than a week after the war began, after Pearl Harbor, he was captured. After a few months, we were notified that he was dead. At the end of the war, he was found alive. He weighed less than a hundred pounds. He had been in prison in Japan since the early days of the war. He came home as one who had been missing in action, who had been reported dead. He led a good life until his death recently.

This is a vivid reminder to me of those who are still listed as missing in action and the suffering of families who still look toward Southeast Asia for a word of truth and certainty about the whereabouts or the status of their loved ones. And no one in this country can rest until those answers come to families still waiting with a question in their hearts.

My oldest son volunteered and served in Vietnam, and he, along with millions of other young men, including Max Cleland, again offered their lives under the most difficult of circumstances. They suffered the pain and anguish of danger and suffering in Vietnam, and in addition, they had an additional burden to bear, because our Nation was divided about that war. And the deep love and appreciation, the outpouring and the expressions of care when other veterans returned quite often were not available to Max Cleland, to my oldest son, and to many others.

In all this time, and for all these veterans, when the Nation forgot in a time of certainty and stability and peace, the Veterans Administration was there, hour after hour, day after day, week after week, year after year, providing love, care, attention, sometimes publicity when the Nation turned its head the other way, struggling in the Congress, struggling in the home communities to provide for those who had offered everything for us. The Veterans Administration bound their wounds, provided new limbs for those who'd lost them, made new lives for widows, provided jobs, provided college education, provided homes, provided new happiness.

Some day we hope that there will be no war, that there will be no threat of war, no need to call Americans to duty in a time of peace in order to preserve that peace. That time has not yet come. It is still necessary for our Nation to have a strong defense. It is still necessary for young men and women to demonstrate patriotism in a time of peace in order to prevent war and to prevent death. George Washington, our first President, said, "To be prepared for war is one of the most effectual means of preserving peace."

We will continue to have new veterans; I'm thankful for that. But we do not want them to be joining more than 1 million other veterans who died in war for our Nation during the last 204 years. We want them to serve without death, without firing their weapons in anger, to preserve our Nation as it is—at peace, strong, secure, united, confident, filled with courage and conviction—to preserve the principles which have made us great, so that our veterans can now continue to come home to families, to safety, to respect and appreciation, to health, to a full life, enjoying the peace they helped to preserve with the courage that they exhibited in their commitment to freedom.

This is the kind of life, the kind of commitment the Veterans Administration helps to provide. And I'm very deeply grateful to those of you assembled here who represent that wonderful organization, many of you that I see who received the benefits directly from that organization, and to Max Cleland, a wonderful leader of the Veterans Administration, who will now speak to us.

Max Cleland, God bless you and all those who work with you.

NOTE: The President spoke at 9:07 p.m. on the South Lawn of the White House.

Prior to the program, the President and Mrs. Carter hosted a reception on the State Floor of the White House.

Alaska Lands Legislation

Remarks During a White House Briefing.
July 21, 1980

Senator Tsongas, other Members of the Congress, Senator Mathias:

I mention them, because their amendments are going to be up very shortly—[*laughter*]—and they're our allies and friends and coworkers and cofighters for one of the most important decisions that the Congress will ever make and undoubtedly the most important decision on conservation matters that the Congress will face in this century.

I'm deeply grateful to Cecil Andrus for the good work he's been doing and will do in the next few days. And I want to thank you, Mardy, for honoring me, in memory of your distinguished husband, Olaus Murie, who did so much for the Alaskan wilderness. And I want to thank John Denver and Tom Crum and Sally Ranney and Gary Herbert for this splendid bear. I've been standing right outside the door while John Denver talked, ad-

miring it. And I want to guarantee you that we will provide a good home for it here in Washington and, also, we'll provide a good home for the other bear and wildlife throughout Alaska in the years and the centuries ahead.

It's important for me to point out to you, as the President of a great nation, how much your hard work and deep dedication and sometimes sacrificial effort have all meant to the present and future of our country. On behalf of all Americans who care about progress, who care about beauty, who care about wilderness, I want to express my thanks. As I've said before, preserving the priceless heritage of Alaska's natural resources is my own number one environment priority.

We've worked on this project to get good legislation for Alaska even before I was inaugurated as President. It's been the top effort of my administration in environmental subjects, and this goal that we have sought so avidly now seems to be within reach. The Alaska proposals that we espouse, joined by you in a remarkable show of unity, are the result of many years of careful drafting, intense negotiation, thorough debate, and close consultation.

The proposals that we support are balanced. They will close less than 10 percent of Alaska, as you know, to sport hunting. They will allow for a timber program which is adequate to maintain jobs and to provide for economic growth for that wonderful and beautiful State. Our proposal will also provide for American energy security by permitting 100 percent of the offshore areas of Alaska to be open for exploration and 95 percent in the promising land areas. Those areas that are restricted to oil and natural gas exploration are highly sensitive areas that must be preserved during the years ahead.

Unfortunately, the Senate bill, as passed by the [Energy and Natural

Resources] Committee, will upset the delicate balance between economic growth and progress on the one hand and protection and preservation on the other. It would actually reduce the overall wilderness and natural park area and the wildlife refuge acreage which is now protected. It would allow mining and sport hunting in the fragile gates of the Arctic and the Wrangell Mountain areas. It would compromise the natural forests of southeast Alaska. It would threaten the integrity of the Admiralty Islands and the Misty Fiords National Monuments, which I moved by Executive action to establish in 1978. It would endanger the William O. Douglas Arctic Wildlife Range.

We must correct these deficiencies in the Senate committee bill. That's our task during the next few days. It will not be an easy task. It will require, again, dedicated, courageous, tenacious effort and a high degree of accuracy and persistence in presenting our arguments to the Senators, many of whom have not yet deeply studied the issues involved. During this weekend and again early this morning, I have been calling individual Members of the Senate. Many of them say they will seek advice and counsel, as the debates and the votes progress this week, on what decisions they themselves will make on the five key amendments, which will restore integrity and balance to the legislation now proposed.

As you know, the House passed a good bill. But if we are to prevail, all of us must marshal our efforts to strengthen the bill in the battle before the Senate today and later on this week. Through the hard work of many of you here, through Senator Tsongas and his colleagues who are co-sponsoring the five amendments which we are supporting, we need to establish these improvements. I will continue to do my utmost to this end. I will guarantee that we will marshal the full effort of all the members of my own administration, but your active commitment in the next few days—you and all those organizations and enlightened Americans whom you represent—will be the key factor.

The significance of this struggle goes far beyond the specific proposals that will be debated and decided this week. The underlying question is this: Beyond the immense beauty and the value of the State of Alaska, will we as a Nation have the foresight to safeguard now, and to prepare perhaps for additional developments in the future, as circumstances permit, for the benefit of all Americans and for the security of our own Nation, these valuable treasures in Alaska? That's a very important question, one that you and I must help to answer successfully.

Alaska's beauty and Alaska's diversity, Alaska's resources are, in a word, absolutely irreplaceable. Preserving them will require a special courage on the part of Congress, the administration, and all Americans. Many of you here were involved in this fight, in this effort, in this analysis, in this preparation long before I was elected President. Now we must join forces as a unified, dedicated team.

We simply cannot afford to be shortsighted. We owe our children and our country so much more. We owe our children and their children and our Nation our best. All of us should make and must make a unified effort to achieve economic development and progress for Alaska; that is not in doubt. But we must at the same time preserve the precious beauty and the valuable treasures of the United States of America, so vividly and specifically exemplified in the parts of Alaska that we are trying to protect.

You have a strong ally in the Oval Office. You can depend on me, and I, in turn, will depend on you for a successful effort this week and in the weeks ahead.

Thank you very much. God bless you all.

NOTE: The President spoke at 10:49 a.m. in the East Room at the White House to representatives of environmental groups and others who have been active in preserving Alaskan lands.

In his remarks, the President referred to Secretary of the Interior Cecil D. Andrus; Mardy Murie, a member of the board of directors of the Wilderness Society; singer John Denver, who is active in environmental issues; Tom Crum, executive director of the Windstar Foundation; Sally Ranney, president of the American Wilderness Alliance; and Gary Herbert, sculptor of the bronze grizzly bear that was presented to the President.

Robards, Kentucky

Remarks at a Democratic National Committee Fundraising Luncheon.
July 21, 1980

It's hard to follow a speech by John Y. Brown. It was just wonderful and a fine reminder to us of what we have, what we have to be thankful for in the past, present, and even more exciting, in the future.

It's also good to be with two friends. Dale and Margaret Ann took me in, in 1975, when I didn't have very many friends in Kentucky. I didn't have very many friends in the Nation, as a matter of fact. I came and spent the night here. I was hoping for a bed; I got a couch. [*Laughter*] But I think it was the best night's sleep and the best introduction to a wonderful family and to a wonderful community and to a wonderful State that I've ever had.

I'm honored that Dee Huddleston is here and Wendell Ford, Carroll Hubbard, and Carl Perkins, Lieutenant Governor Collins, and other distinguished elected officials of Kentucky. It shows your sound judgment in putting good Democrats in office and keeping them there to serve you and to serve our Nation well. And I thank you from the bottom of my heart for that.

In a few minutes, after I leave here, I'm going to Dallas, Texas. John White, former commissioner of agriculture in Texas, is now our wonderful national party chairman. I've come here to Henderson not to raise money for my campaign, but to raise money for the Democratic National Committee, for Democrats in Kentucky and throughout the Nation, because I believe not only in our country and what it stands for but the complete compatibility between what has made America great and what the Democratic Party stands for.

We're a party that knows history. We're the oldest political party on Earth. We're a party with competence and also a party with compassion. We're a party that believes in peace. And I thank God that during this term of mine, we've not had a single young American lose his life in combat, and I pray God that when I go out of office in the White House, we'll keep that record intact.

A President has a lot of responsibilities—some of them quite burdensome; some, like this, very pleasant. But the most important single responsibility of a President, whether it was George Washington, Abraham Lincoln, or now in this modern time, is to keep our Nation strong, and only through strength can we maintain peace.

Saturday night at the White House, we had a commemoration service for the 50th anniversary of the Veterans Administration. We looked back on the history of our Nation that night, from Colonial times all the way up through the Vietnam war. I thought back on the fact that my own father was in the First World War as a first lieutenant and the horrible devastation to the people who lived in the little town of Plains, when you walk down the street and see veterans there crippled permanently with poison gas, whose lungs wouldn't quite function. And of course, the Second World War, the Korean war, the Vietnam war, tore our Nation literally apart in the Vietnam war—it's been put back together. Watergate, a deep embarrassment to our country, to the Oval Office itself—our country has healed those wounds.

We have a responsibility in government at all levels to make sure that people of this country realize that those who are in office have one obligation, and one only—to those who put them in office and to maintaining not only our Nation's present and future but also preserving the principles of the past.

You have a special opportunity in Kentucky, in the future, for another aspect of our Nation's security; that is, energy security. We've become overly vulnerable to a heavy dependence on foreign oil. This year we will import $90 billion worth of oil from overseas. That's a lot of money, hard to understand. It amounts to $400 per man, woman, and child throughout the United States. I want to depend not on foreign oil at the end of a 12,000-mile uncertain pipeline into a doubtful area of the world, but in the future I want to depend on Kentucky coal.

There are no easy answers to any of the questions that confront me in the Oval Office or that confront you in your own lives, and we don't claim to cut corners or to find simplistic answers to difficult questions or easy ways to resolve insurmountable problems. But America, as John Y. pointed out, has always been willing and always been able, without fail when we've recognized an obstacle or a problem and when our country was united, not to fail.

We have already cut back our importa-

tion of foreign oil in this short 3½ years by 1½ million barrels of oil every day, and we've just scratched the surface. We're beginning to broaden our effort—in the conservation, coal use, hydropower, solar power, geothermal, dependence on the integrity and the innovation of American free enterprise, American courage, American spirit, American competence—to resolve those questions.

The other point I want to make is that we've not abandoned our commitment to human beings. This Nation cares, our party cares about giving those among us who are afflicted in any way a helping hand, to remove permanent dependence on government, and to let each human being, regardless of race, religion, or color or past history, stand on one's own feet, make one's own decision, take what talent or abilities God might have given them, and use it in a beneficial way. That's a characteristic of our party—compassion, not dependence, belief in human beings.

Along with peace for our own country, we've not forgotten peace for others. In the Middle East, ancient enemies are now bargaining across the table, sometimes slowly, sometimes in a disappointing way. God only knows how difficult it has been to get those who have hated each other with a burning passion to sit down as potential friends, to search for peace together, an integral part in the future security of our Nation.

We've faced disappointments—the Soviet invasion of Afghanistan, the taking away of the freedom of people in a small country which harmed no one, a threat to no one, deeply religious, fiercely independent. The Soviets' attempts to subjugate them have been of deep concern to our country.

Our country has an ability to survive any challenge, and our country and our party is bound together in a common purpose. I don't have any doubt that together we'll prevail again, not only in those crucial issues that have made our Nation great now and greater in the future, but I have no doubt that in November we will have an ability together, as Democrats, to whip the Republicans right and left. That's what I'm committed to do. With your help, we will not fail.

Thank you very much. God bless you all.

NOTE: The President spoke at 1:25 p.m. at the residence of Dale and Margaret Ann Sights. He was introduced by Gov. John Y. Brown of Kentucky.

In his opening remarks, the President referred to Senators Walter D. Huddleston and Wendell H. Ford, Representatives Carroll Hubbard, Jr., and Carl P. Perkins, and Lieutenant Governor Martha Layne Collins of Kentucky.

Prior to the luncheon, the President rode in a parade through Henderson, Ky.

Justin, Texas

Remarks Following a Tour of a Field Damaged by Heat and Drought. July 21, 1980

THE PRESIDENT. [Inaudible]—Commissioner Brown and others:

I've directed the Federal Emergency Management Agency—[inaudible]—intense heat wave that has covered a large part of our Nation in the last few weeks. It's been now 4 weeks in this area when the temperatures have been at or above 100 degrees every day, and we've had, up through yesterday, more than 1,150 Americans who've died with the heat wave itself. Missouri, for instance, had 283 people die, and now 98, up through yesterday, have died in Texas alone.

This field, which I wanted to come and visit because it is typical, shows the differ-

ence between what has occurred with this drought and the normal production of milo, which is used on this farm as a feed for hogs. And this particular head of milo was brought in from about 50 miles east, where they happen to have gotten adequate rainfall.

We are directing emergency loans. I think more than 20 counties in Texas now get emergency feed allocations. But of course, hay is difficult to find, and the price has gone up 50 or 60 percent in the last few weeks alone. We're giving, also, direct disaster aid and conservation payments. But this is the kind of thing that is afflicting farmers in a large part of our Nation.

Just north of Texas, in Oklahoma and Kansas, they have had a cold or cool front come through now, and they've had a good bit of relief. And Mr. Range, I tried to send a nice shower—[laughter]—but just a little relief for this visit. But my heart goes out to you. And I wanted to come here to dramatize for the rest of the Nation the practical effect of the intense heat wave that has stricken most of Texas and also a large part of the West and also down in the Southeast. But we're trying to do everything we can with the commissioner of agriculture, with Bob Bergland, and with the Federal Emergency Management Agency to help out as best we can.

Good luck. God bless. We'll be praying for rain and cooler weather in the future. Good luck to you.

MRS. RANGE. We enjoyed having you.

THE PRESIDENT. Thank you very much. I appreciate your letting me come here and see you this way.

Can I take these with me?

MR. RANGE. Yes, sir.

MRS. RANGE. Sure. Sure thing.

THE PRESIDENT. Thank you. I'd better

leave you this one. You can feed the hogs with it. [*Laughter*]

NOTE: The President spoke at approximately 5 p.m. at the edge of a field on the farm owned by Olen and Mertie Helen Range. In his opening remarks, he referred to Reagan V. Brown, the Texas State Commissioner of Agriculture.

As printed above, this item follows the text of the White House press release.

Dallas, Texas

Remarks at a Dallas County Democratic Committee Voter Registration Rally.
July 21, 1980

Senator Bentsen, Lieutenant Governor Hobby, Congressman Jim Mattox, Congressman Martin Frost—I see a lot of campaigners in here for him—Chairman Billy Goldberg, Commissioner Ray Orr, Chairman David Carlock, who's done such a good job in preparing for this event, Chairman Estil Vance, and many other great Democrats:

I want to ask you one question. How many of you believe we're going to whip the Republicans in November? [*Applause*] Right on. Absolutely. And the reason for that is that the Democratic Party—what we have done, what we are doing, what we will do—is compatible with the finest ideals of the American Nation of which we are so proud.

The Democratic Party believes that our Nation ought to stay at peace through strength. Our Nation will stay strong. I know how Texans feel and what you believe in and what your commitments are, and I know the depth of your patriotism and the height of your aspirations for our country.

Ours is a nation that has always believed in a strong defense, and for 8 years, before I was elected President with your help, we saw a steady downward trend in our Nation's commitment to defense. Our Nation must be strong in its ability to preserve freedom, because that is the best way for us to stay at peace—for all those who believe in us, our allies and our own people, and all those who might want to challenge us to know that any challenge would be doomed to failure, because America is so unified and so strong. And that's the way the Democrats are going to keep this country.

I might point out that we have dealt with some very difficult issues. We've not only been satisfied with peace for ourselves; we've tried to strengthen NATO, we've tried to bring in the Middle East two nations and their people, who have hated each other for more than 30 years, to sit down in a spirit of friendship and cooperation around the bargaining table and work out their apparently insurmountable differences between them.

We've opened up new friendships with more than a fourth of the total population on Earth—the People's Republic of China. At the same time, we have kept our trade going and building and our friendships firm with the people of Taiwan. We've had good relationships to the north with Canada and to the south with Mexico. We've treated the Latin American countries as our equals, because they are.

And we've respected the rights of all people throughout the world. Our commitment to human rights will never change, and that's what we believe in.

And I would like to point out to you that with the exception of eight brave Americans who gave their lives in an accident in the desert of Iran, we have not had a single American life lost in combat since I've been President, and I pray God we'll keep it that way.

Let me point out, too, that my ancestors and your ancestors have always been willing to invest themselves in peace. Today is the first day of registration for our young men, to make sure that in the future, if we are challenged, we will be able to defend ourselves. We do not anticipate departing from a full-volunteer military force. We are registering today just in case we are challenged in the future. But that's the best way to make sure that we will be strong.

Our Nation is not only strong militarily; we are strong economically. As a matter of fact, all of you know that our country is the strongest nation militarily, economically, politically, and I believe, morally and ethically as well. We believe in and fight for our principles, and they'll never change.

As you know, we had an OPEC oil embargo against us beginning in 1973, and all the way through until 1977, the previous Republican administration did absolutely nothing to protect our Nation from its overly dependent posture and vulnerability about a 12,000-mile uncertain pipeline from one of the most troubled areas of the world. Under the leadership of men like Martin Frost, Jim Mattox, Lloyd Bentsen, the Congress has now put into effect a sound energy policy for our country. And already, in just a short 3 years, we have reduced the amount of foreign oil that we import every day by 1½ million barrels. We're making progress. We're going to continue, with the help of Texas.

I think the American people—even including the Communist Workers Party, who is shouting back here in the audience—recognize that our Nation is one that believes in human beings. We make our major investment in people, because we are a party not only of competence and commitment but we are also a party of compassion. We believe that when God makes a human being and gives that person a certain amount of talent and ability, that that talent and ability ought to be nourished and improved and each citizen of this great country ought to have a chance to stand on one's own feet, to make one's own judgments, and to bear part of the responsibilities of full citizenship. We don't believe in permanent dependence on the Federal Government. We believe in helping people, with a hand, to stand on their own feet.

And the last thing I would like to say to you is this: The Democratic Party, in the finest sense of the word, believes in people. We don't forget who put us in office, and we don't forget who can take us out of office if we don't measure up to your expectations. As you all remember, 5, 6, 7, 8 years ago, our Nation was embarrassed by divisive war; we were embarrassed in the Oval Office itself by Watergate. The people felt that they could not trust public officials. The truth was not always told to you even by the highest officials in our own Government. That time has changed.

I don't claim to you that the Democratic Party is perfect; I don't claim to you even that the United States of America is perfect. But we always strive to face issues without fear. We are not afraid of open debate. We are not afraid to let differences be aired. We are not afraid to analyze our own thoughts and our own failures and our own troubles, and we are never afraid to strive to overcome those obstacles and overcome those difficulties and answer those tough questions, together as a united people. As a matter of fact, at this time, even though we do face problems with unemployment and inflation and sometimes energy shortages, compared to previous people, generations before us, even compared to some previous years in our own lives, we are blessed far beyond any other people on Earth.

I've been to Berlin, and I've seen the Berlin Wall. On one side are Communists in East Berlin. The wall was not built to keep people from going into East Germany; the wall was built by the East Germans as a prison for their own people, because they want to escape from communism and come to the United States.

And there's also a Communist government not very far from our own shores in Cuba. You don't see a bunch of boats lined up in the United States for people trying to escape to Cuba, right? And there's a Communist government in Southeast Asia, the Vietnamese, occupying Kampuchea—hundreds of thousands of people trying to escape from communism to freedom.

And the same applies in Afghanistan, where the Soviet Union has invaded a small, relatively defenseless, deeply religious country that was no challenge to anyone. Nine hundred thousand freedom-loving people have escaped Afghanistan into Pakistan and Iran. They're escaping from communism to freedom, not from freedom to communism.

So, in spite of the fact that we are not a perfect nation, we've got a lot to be thankful for. And as we read in the newspapers and watch the television and listen to the radio, we hear about the arguments and the debates; we hear about the temporary inconveniences; we hear about the disappointments; we hear about the questions that haven't yet been answered; we hear about the problems that we've not yet solved; and we hear about the obstacles that we've not yet overcome. But our Nation has never failed to answer a question, to solve a problem, or to overcome an obstacle when our American people were united and when we saw the obstacle clearly and the goals we wanted to reach.

We live in the greatest nation on Earth. And with your help and all those who believe in the principles of our Nation and our Democratic Party, we're going to be an even greater nation in the future with a tremendous victory in November.

Thank you very much. God bless you all. Thank you.

NOTE: The President spoke at 5:53 p.m. in the Grand Hall at Union Station.

In addition to Members of Congress from Texas, the President referred in his opening remarks to Lieutenant Governor William Hobby, Billy Goldberg, chairman of the Texas State Democratic Party, Ray Orr, Dallas County commissioner, David Carlock, chair of the Dallas County Democratic Party, and Estil Vance, chairman of the Tarrant County Democratic Party.

Dallas, Texas

Remarks at a Democratic National Committee Fundraiser. *July 21, 1980*

Instead of repeating all of the names that have just been called, even the distinguished United States Senators and Governors and others, I'd like to address my formal remarks to all of you collectively, but especially to Jess Hay and to Betty Jo, who've made this such a wonderful evening for all of us. And I deeply appreciate what you've done for us, Jess.

I didn't come here at all concerning my own campaign. That's against the law at this time. I came here to help the Democratic National Committee. I came here to help the Texas Democratic Committee and all the members of it. But primarily I came to Dallas to find out confidentially who shot J. R.[1]—[*laughter*]—and if any of you could let me know that, I could finance the whole campaign this fall.

It's a wonderful thing for us to be able to get together. I've had a good day. I was in Kentucky earlier, briefly in Indiana, and then went by Justin, Texas, to visit

---

[1] A character on the television show "Dallas."

one of the homes of the farm families that have been devastated by the drought, and then to have a great rally at the station here in Dallas, and then to come out to Jess Hay's home.

It's a wonderful opportunity for a President to see the strength of our Nation, the unity that we share, the confidence in ourselves, the blessings which God has given all of us, and the opportunity for an even greater America in the future. When we look at the current headlines and television and listen to the radio, the prime impression we get is one of disappointment, failure, difference, debate, weakness, fear, doubt, trepidation, and lack of confidence. That's not at all the America that you know and the America that I know as President.

We're a nation that has maintained peace, because we are strong. And we are a nation that has never failed to measure up to responsibilities when they are placed on our shoulders. And we are a nation that will never fail in the future. We will stay strong. We will stay at peace. We are not a country that's trying to dominate others. We are not a nation that is willing to open up a new vista of a cold war. Within the process of keeping our own selves at the full measure of our economic, military strength, we can keep peace for ourselves and for many others who look to us for leadership.

The Democratic Party is one that has never forgotten the principles on which our Nation was originally founded. The Declaration of Independence was signed 204 years ago. We have made steady progress. The Democratic Party is almost that old; it's the oldest political party on Earth. It's one that believes in competence; it's one that believes in the strongest government being the closest to the people. It's the government and a party which has shared in the last 3½ years some of the most intense, focused problems and responsibilities of the entire world in peacetime history. We've not failed to measure up to that responsibility.

We have extended our hand of friendship to literally hundreds of millions of people around the Earth who, in the past, looked upon us as enemies or potential enemies. We've kept our Nation at peace. With the exception of eight servicemen who were lost in the desert in Iran, in an accident, on a humanitarian mission, we've not had a single American serviceman or woman killed since I've been privileged to serve in the White House. And I pray to God that I can go out of office with that same record intact.

We've recognized not only the military strength but political strength of our Nation. Others look to us for leadership. In Europe we have strengthened NATO—its spirit, its military commitment, its unity—far beyond anything it has seen since NATO was originally founded. When I meet with the leaders of Europe and of Japan, they recognize that the bulwark of liberty and freedom, of stability in a troubled world is our own great Nation.

This country, because of its innovative spirit, because of the free enterprise system, which we cherish, has always been on the cutting edge of change. We've never feared change. Sometimes we face the future, which is uncertain, with some degree of trepidation, some degree of caution. But as we see a problem that has not yet been answered, as we see an obstacle which has not yet been overcome, the natural tendency of Americans is to bind ourselves together in a spirit of unity and common commitment, of drawing closer to the principles that are precious and never change, and a facing of the future with an accommodation for technology and for changing political circumstances, which we absolutely do not fear.

We now have entered an era which will change the lifestyle of Americans, an energy period when we have first had to recognize that the natural resources with which we have been blessed have some limit. We've not flinched from that responsibility.

As you all know, in 1973 we had our Nation's security threatened. Our Nation was almost brought to its knees economically and, indeed, threatened militarily when our lifeline of oil, 12,000 miles to a troubled area of the Middle East, was endangered by an embargo. Unfortunately, the Republican administration then in power in Washington did nothing, and we have not had until just recently, with a courageous Congress, a fine energy policy for our country. Everything in that policy couldn't suit the people of Georgia or the people of New York or the people of Texas, but we've set our hand to a plow that will set a furrow that will get the Federal Government and its nose out of the private affairs of American citizens and out of the free enterprise system and let our Nation be strong.

As we stand on our own feet and make our own decisions in an independent manner, there are two ways that we can stop our overdependence on foreign oil: One is through conservation, to save energy, to stop wasting energy; and the other one is to produce more energy in this country. We are doing both. And the next 10 years will see us spend, for the benefit of our Nation, in those areas more than $227 billion for a new life for our people, a life that will not constrain our style of living or the quality of our existence, but will give us an exciting, dynamic, challenging opportunity again to prove that we live in the greatest nation on Earth.

And, finally, I'd like to say that as President of this country I never forget that my party is one that has never forgotten the individual human being. We are competent, we are consistent, we are concerted in our effort; but we are also compassionate. We look upon those who are less fortunate than we, who have suffered from some affliction or some discrimination, with a great deal of understanding, recognizing that if they are able to take whatever talent or ability God might have given them and to use that talent to a useful purpose, they will sever their dependence on government to sustain themselves and become productive and aggressive citizens, joining in with us.

And now to close my speech, I would say this morning, when I started to come to Texas, I asked [Senator] Lloyd Bentsen, "What do you need more than anything else—a fine long speech from the President?" And he said, "No, Mr. President. What we need is rain." And I said, "Okay, we'll have rain." So, in appreciation to the rain God has given us, let's harness our efforts and whip the Republicans in November and keep our country strong.

Thank you very much.

NOTE: The President spoke at 7:34 p.m. at the residence of Jess and Betty Jo Hay.

Following the fundraiser, the President returned to the White House.

National Cystic Fibrosis Week
Proclamation 4775.   July 22, 1980

By the President of the United States of America

A Proclamation

Cystic fibrosis is the most common fatal genetic disease afflicting American children today. An inherited disorder of unknown cause, cystic fibrosis affects approximately 20,000 to 30,000 infants, children, and young adults. While the cost of medical treatment reaches into the millions of dollars, the costs of cystic fibrosis in terms of human suffering are inestimable.

Through biomedical research, the outlook for cystic fibrosis patients has become brighter over the years. Long considered fatal in childhood, cystic fibrosis has begun to yield to the efforts of science. The life expectancy of cystic fibrosis victims has increased well into the teens, twenties and beyond. Moreover, improved methods of treatment have enhanced the quality of patients' lives. Despite this progress, however, the basic cause of cystic fibrosis, as well as its cure, continues to elude investigators.

The Department of Health and Human Services, in cooperation with private, voluntary agencies, is meeting the challenge of cystic fibrosis with an intensified research program. Through the National Institutes of Health, the Department's biomedical research arm, studies are now under way to identify the causes—and consequences—of the disease, and to develop improved methods of detection, treatment, and, eventually, prevention.

In recognition of the progress that has been made, and of the many research questions that still remain to be answered, the Congress has by House Joint Resolution 445 designated the week of September 21, 1980, "National Cystic Fibrosis Week", a time to highlight the hope for the future that this Nation shares with cystic fibrosis victims and their families.

Now, THEREFORE, I, JIMMY CARTER, President of the United States of America, do hereby proclaim the week beginning September 21, 1980, as "National Cystic Fibrosis Week."

IN WITNESS WHEREOF, I have hereunto set my hand this twenty-second day of July, in the year of our Lord nineteen hundred and eighty, and of the Independence of the United States of America the two hundred and fifth.

JIMMY CARTER

[Filed with the Office of the Federal Register, 11:33 a.m., July 23, 1980]

Administration of Foreign Assistance

Executive Order 12226.   July 22, 1980

By the authority vested in me as President of the United States of America by Section 640B of the Foreign Assistance Act of 1961, as amended (22 U.S.C. 2399c), and in order to add the Peace Corps to membership on the Development Coordination Committee, it is hereby ordered that Section 1–506(a) of Executive Order No. 12163 is amended by adding "the Director of the Peace Corps;" after "the President of the Export-Import Bank of the United States;".

JIMMY CARTER

The White House,
   July 22, 1980.

[Filed with the Office of the Federal Register, 11:34 a.m., July 23, 1980]

United States Sinai Support Mission

Executive Order 12227.   July 22, 1980

By the authority vested in me as President by the Constitution and statutes of the United States of America, including Chapter 6 of Part II of the Foreign Assistance Act of 1961, as amended (22 U.S.C. 2348, 2348a.–2348c.), Sections 1(b) and 1(c) of Executive Order No.

11896 of January 13, 1976, as amended, are hereby further amended to read as follows:

"(b) The Mission shall, in accordance with the Foreign Assistance Act of 1961, as amended, including Part II, Chapter 6 thereof, the Joint Resolution of October 13, 1975 (Public Law 94–110, 89 Stat. 572, 22 U.S.C. 2441 note), and the provisions of this Order, assist in the implementation of the provisions of Annex I and the Appendix to Annex I of the Treaty of Peace between the Arab Republic of Egypt and the State of Israel, signed March 26, 1979. The Mission shall assist by (i) verifying Zones A and B and the provisions of Annex I of the Treaty relating to force levels, fortifications, and installations by on the ground inspections and reconnaissance flights, (ii) verifying the technical installations within the Interim Buffer Zone as provided in Article V(3)(c) of the Appendix to Annex I of the Treaty, and (iii) conducting other assigned tasks in order to further the implementation of the Treaty of Peace. Such assistance shall be subject to broad policy guidance received through the Assistant to the President for National Security Affairs, and the continuous supervision and general direction of the Secretary of State pursuant to Section 622(c) of the Foreign Assistance Act of 1961, as amended (22 U.S.C. 2382))."

"(c) It shall be the duty and responsibility of the Mission to ensure that the United States role enhances the prospect of compliance in good faith with the terms of the Egyptian-Israeli agreement and thereby promotes the cause of peace."

JIMMY CARTER

The White House,
July 22, 1980.

[Filed with the Office of the Federal Register, 11:35 a.m., July 23, 1980]

The Cyprus Conflict

Letter to the Speaker of the House and the Chairman of the Senate Foreign Relations Committee. July 22, 1980

Dear Mr. Speaker: (Dear Mr. Chairman:)

In accordance with the provisions of Public Law 95–384, I am submitting the following report on progress made during the past 60 days toward conclusion of a negotiated solution of the Cyprus problem.

The intercommunal talks remain recessed despite persistent efforts by UN Secretary General Waldheim and his staff to bring the two parties back to the conference table. Ambassador Hugo Cobbi, the new Special Representative of the Secretary General, arrived in Cyprus in May and immediately began working with the two sides in an effort to overcome the remaining difficulties. As the UN efforts intensified, the Secretary General also dispatched Under Secretary General Perez de Cuellar to Cyprus. Mr. Perez de Cuellar presented the two parties with a compromise formula under which they might resume the intercommunal talks. Early on June 7, the Greek Cypriots informed the Under Secretary General that they would accept the proposal. Later that day, the Turkish Cypriots told Mr. Perez de Cuellar that they had given the UN formula serious consideration but felt unable to accept it.

It is encouraging to note, however, that the Perez de Cuellar mission succeeded in narrowing somewhat the gap between the positions of the two parties, and Ambassador Cobbi is continuing to consult with the two sides in an attempt to reach a compromise. The Secretary General's June 13 statement to the Security Council on Mr. Perez de Cuellar's mission is attached.

I am pleased to report that the United Nations Security Council voted on June 13 to extend the mandate of the UN Peacekeeping Forces in Cyprus (UNFICYP) for another six months. The calm that prevails on the island today is due to the professionalism and dedication of the men of UNFICYP. Without the stability provided by the peacekeeping troops, there would be little hope for eventually achieving a negotiated Cyprus settlement. (The Secretary General's report to the Security Council on UNFICYP is also attached.)

Secretary of State Muskie recently returned from Ankara where he discussed the Cyprus problem with Turkish Prime Minister Demirel. In a productive exchange of views, Secretary Muskie stressed the continuing interest of the United States in seeing the Cyprus dispute resolved. During his meeting with the Turkish Prime Minister as well as in his discussions with Greek Foreign Minister Mitsotakis, the Secretary of State reaffirmed our faith in Secretary General Waldheim's efforts as the best hope for achieving an early resumption of the intercommunal talks.

Other members of the Executive Branch have also been active in support of the Secretary General's efforts. On June 23, for example, while in Athens, Under Secretary of State Nimetz took the opportunity offered by the presence of Cyprus Foreign Minister Rolandis to arrange an informal but useful meeting on the Cyprus problem.

The United States Government will continue to use every opportunity to emphasize to all concerned parties that cooperation with the efforts of UN Secretary General Waldheim offers the best chance for a resumption of the intercommunal talks. The Secretary General has pledged

to persevere in his mission, and the two parties on Cyprus have renewed their commitment to reach a negotiated settlement. The roots of the Cyprus problem are deep, and a solution will not easily be found. I am convinced, however, that if the two communities on Cyprus are seriously committed to resolve their differences, a settlement will eventually be achieved. I urge both sides to return to the negotiating table and begin the process of searching for a just and lasting solution that will meet the needs of all people of Cyprus.

Sincerely,

JIMMY CARTER

NOTE: This is the text of identical letters addressed to Thomas P. O'Neill, Jr., Speaker of the House of Representatives, and Frank Church, chairman of the Senate Foreign Relations Committee.

Department of State

Nomination of Diego C. Asencio To Be Assistant Secretary for Consular Affairs.
July 22, 1980

The President today announced that he will nominate Diego C. Asencio, of Port St. Lucie, Fla., to be Assistant Secretary of State for Consular Affairs. He would replace Barbara M. Watson, who is being appointed to another post. Asencio has been Ambassador to Colombia since 1977 and a Foreign Service officer since 1957.

He was born July 15, 1931, in Nijar, Almeria, Spain. He received a B.S.F.S. from Georgetown University in 1952. He served in the U.S. Army from 1955 to 1957.

Asencio joined the Foreign Service in 1957 and was posted in Mexico City, Panama, and at the State Department.

From 1965 to 1967, he was special assistant to the Assistant Secretary of State for Inter-American Affairs. From 1967 to 1972, he was posted in Lisbon as political officer, then Deputy Chief of Mission.

From 1972 to 1975, Asencio was Counselor for Political Affairs in Brasilia. From 1975 to 1977, he was Deputy Chief of Mission in Caracas.

Advisory Committee on Federal Pay

Appointment of Eva Robins as a Member.
July 22, 1980

The President today announced the appointment of Eva Robins, of New York City, as a member of the Advisory Committee on Federal Pay.

Robins is an arbitrator and mediator in labor disputes in the private and public sectors. She is president of the National Academy of Arbitrators. She is a former deputy chairman and executive director of New York City's Office of Collective Bargaining.

National Energy Efficiency Program

Remarks at a Ceremony To Announce the Program's Second Phase and Present Transportation Efficiency Awards.
July 22, 1980

I'm very grateful to have this second major meeting on how we can save energy in our Nation by the concerted effort of leaders like yourselves and those who are eager, I believe, as patriotic citizens to increase our Nation's security through reducing our dependence, unwarranted and excessive dependence, on imported oil.

Today we have formed a council for energy efficiency, and we have the panel members here, the award winners, whom we'll recognize in a few minutes, and community leaders, and I want to thank all of you for being present.

As you know, millions of our citizens now recognize vividly, as they didn't perhaps just 12 months ago, how vital it is for each one of us to join in reducing imports. There are only two ways to do it, as I've said many times: one is to eliminate the waste of energy, which has never been an integral part of Americans' lives; and secondly, to produce more energy ourselves. The cheapest, most efficient approach between those two, obviously, is to reduce our own consumption of energy, which I believe we can do, as has been proved by many of you already, without reducing the quality of our own lives.

For the past 3½ years I and many of you here, all the members of my own administration, almost every Member of the Congress, has fought for and has finally achieved the basic framework of a comprehensive energy policy for our country, something that we've never had before and something which is already paying rich dividends for us.

We now import, the first half of this year, almost 15 percent less oil than we did the same 6 months in 1979. That's a remarkable achievement, particularly in view of the fact that in the years preceding this year we had had a steady upward trend in the amount of oil that we had bought from overseas. We've still not reached our goals. And as you know, by 1990 we have set as a goal for ourselves a slashing in half of the actual amount that we import and a reduction by more than two-thirds of the amount that we would have imported had we not put into effect these conservation measures.

We have today, this day, imported about 1½ million less barrels than we did an equivalent day 12 months ago. This is a very fine achievement, thanks to many of you. We've got to keep this progress going. We've still got much to do, and we've made good progress already.

We've got two basic approaches, as you well know from the briefing you've had and from the discussion today. One is in the area of transportation, and we'll recognize some that have achieved superior performance already. And we also are launching, with as effective a program as possible throughout our Nation, a means by which we conserve energy within individual homes. And we think that each home, on the average, can save 25 percent of the energy it has been consuming. This can be done through tax credits to encourage the weatherization of homes, the installation of devices like thermostats, that are timed by day, to prevent excessive air conditioning or heating loads when they are not needed, because somebody might be absent-minded and not change the thermostat when they could have changed it, and of course, the installation of solar heating devices of all kinds.

We have received from the transportation industry about 190 different specific commitments derived from the previous meeting that we've had here. So, that is an achievement already. The homes will be the second achievement and a third one that we're working for is in the field of agriculture.

I've been a farmer almost all my life, except when I've been in government service. All of my people before me for many generations have been full-time farmers, and I know from practical experience that, in my earlier days, we had much less dependence upon bought fuels for the heating or drying of crops and for cultivation and, as any farm agent knows

and as any superior farmer knows, minimum tillage can be an advantage and not a disadvantage. And the sun-drying of our crops, instead of using imported oil or natural gas or butane, can be a very efficient way to do an equally superior job.

We anticipate that if the farmers can save only 5 percent of the energy they use compared to a year ago and if homeowners can reduce, by an amount that I've already described, that we can cut our oil imports at a $32 per barrel price by roughly $20 billion each year.

We have, finally, a need to expand the public awareness of what can be done. A lot of people have feared energy conservation because it's new to them, and they have assumed, incorrectly, that to save energy in their own lives, in their homes, on their farms, in their businesses, in their transportation, would cause them to lead an inferior quality of life compared to what they had been using, to which they had been accustomed. This is not the fact. I think that this can be the means by which safety can be enhanced—with strict enforcement of driver habits, speed limits, more efficient automobiles, more efficient homes, more attention to sharing rides, the location of buildings in a proper fashion, and the orientation in business of a much more efficient operation with the production of goods—with a minimum amount of energy expended.

In closing, let me say that we shared this kind of discussion in Venice, recently, among the leaders of the seven major democratic industrialized nations. This is not a unique problem with America. As a matter of fact, of all the nations represented there, ours perhaps is the most blessed with the broadest range of energy availability. France, Italy, Japan, in particular, are heavily dependent on imported fuels. Great Britain, with the North Sea deposits, has now become relatively self-sufficient. Of course, we know that Canada has certain forms of energy, not nearly so much and so diverse as do we. But all of the nations are now moving toward a more careful approach to the consumption of energy.

I'd like to ask Neil Goldschmidt now to come forward to give the awards for outstanding energy efficiency in the transportation sector, and later on, in a subsequent ceremony, after the contests and the competition has been observed and analyzed, we'll have similar awards made for conservation in homes and on the farms. And we'll be asking all those who are directly involved, including farm co-ops, the TVA, major utility companies, to participate in special ways to inform their customers and their members about what they can indeed do in their own homes and on their own farms to enhance the conservation of energy in our Nation.

This is important to the well-being of our people; it's important to the security of our country. And I'm deeply grateful for the partnership that you have formed with us in this worthwhile pursuit. Secretary Goldschmidt.

NOTE: The President spoke at 4:03 p.m. in the East Room at the White House.

President's Award for Energy Efficiency

Announcement of 25 Award Recipients in the Field of Transportation.   July 22, 1980

The President today presented the first 25 of the President's Awards for Energy Efficiency. Those receiving awards at a White House ceremony were honored for outstanding energy conservation efforts in the field of transportation. Among the award winners were small business firms, large corporations, professional and trade associations, State police and transportation departments, one city, one Federal agency, and an Air Force base.

Additional transportation awards will be presented later this year, as well as Presidential awards for energy conservation achievements in agriculture and in the residential sector.

The President's Energy Efficiency Awards Program was announced on April 29, 1980. The awards program is part of a long-term Federal initiative to encourage citizen participation in the national drive toward greater energy efficiency.

Prominently featured on the President's award certificate is a "double-E" energy efficiency emblem. This emblem will appear on all Federal publications and advertisements promoting energy conservation. Award winners have earned the right to reproduce the emblem as demonstration of their exceptional contributions to the national conservation effort.

Many of today's award winners have developed ridesharing and driver efficiency training programs for their employees. The first phase of the President's long-term conservation initiative stressed the promotion of such programs by businesses and trade associations.

The award winners announced today are:

Atlantic Richfield Co., Los Angeles, Calif. Sixty-seven percent of the company's 3,050 Los Angeles-based employees commute to work by sharing rides or using public transportation. The company began subsidizing bus fares for employees in 1973, and in 1976 Atlantic Richfield collaborated with other private and public organizations to create a Los Angeles-area vanpool program, which has become a model program for other companies across the Nation.

Central Freight Lines, Waco, Tex. Central Freight Lines pursues an aggressive fuel conservation program involving training of drivers in fuel efficiency techniques and the use of innovative fuel-saving devices in fleet vehicles.

Champion Spark Plug Co., Toledo, Ohio. Champion technicians have tested more than 30,000 vehicles as part of the company's Mobile Proving Ground test program, which began in 1975. Vehicles have been tested to determine the impact of engine conditions on fuel consumption and environmental emissions. Tests have been conducted in 30 locations in the United States, Western Europe, and Mexico.

The City of Portland, Oreg. Portland serves as a model to other urban areas on how comprehensive transportation planning can contribute to energy efficiency goals. Transportation improvements made in the last 10 years include a downtown "transit mall," a citywide ridesharing program, and the incorporation of transportation planning into a broader urban development policy. A light-rail transit system for Portland is in the planning stages.

Coats and Clark, Inc., Atlanta, Ga. Coats and Clark stresses the importance of fuel efficiency in its company-owned trucks by hiring drivers on a conditional basis until they attain certain fuel economy goals. Monthly reports are compiled indicating each driver's average mileage per gallon and cost per mile.

Coleman/Goff, Inc., St. Paul, Minn. This advertising and public relations firm called attention to fuel economy techniques for truck operators by conducting a 3-day demonstration of specially equipped test trucks. The Minnesota legislature adjourned its session to view the demonstration, which attracted much attention by the media and the general public. The firm is involved in other energy conservation promotional campaigns in St. Paul and in San Francisco.

Connecticut Department of Transportation, Wethersfield, Conn. Since 1973, the department has provided, free of charge, carpool matching and consultation services to 102 private employers representing nearly 170,000 employees. This program has resulted in a 20-percent increase in ridesharing by employees of participating companies. The State of Connecticut has taken a number of other steps to encourage greater ridesharing by residents.

Energy Conservation Study Group, Maintenance Council of the American Trucking Associations, Greenwich, Conn. The study group holds three meetings annually, at which maintenance and operational executives of hundreds of major trucking firms share information about the means toward low-cost, efficient operation of trucking fleets.

Evergone, Inc., Federal Way, Wash. This small firm, a United States Postal Service contractor, has installed sophisticated fuel-economy devices on its fleet of three trucks, significantly boosting fuel economy.

Golden Gate Bridge Highway and Transportation District, San Francisco, Calif. An extensive ridesharing promotional campaign, begun in 1970, has increased by 10,000 daily the number of commuters who cross the Golden Gate Bridge, with virtually no increase in the number of vehicles crossing. Currently, 65 percent of the nearly 41,000 bridge commuters are in public transit vehicles, carpools, vanpools, or club buses.

Hallmark Cards, Inc., Kansas City, Mo. Hallmark has promoted ridesharing and the use of public transit by offering a computerized matching system for potential ridesharers, by allowing employees to purchase public transit passes through payroll deductions, and by supporting the operation of 50 vanpools for Hallmark workers. By the end of 1980, one-third of Hallmark's employees will be sharing rides or using buses.

Institute of Industrial Launderers, Washington, D.C. At least 150 member laundry companies have sent representatives to a route alignment training course offered by the institute. This course emphasizes the fuel-efficiency advantages of careful route planning for laundry delivery trucks.

Maryland State Police Department, Pikesville, Md. The Maryland State Police Department was the first State police department in the country to send staff members to the Department of Energy's Driver Energy Conservation Awareness Training (DECAT) program. As a result of the department's DECAT participation, it has trained 1,400 fleet drivers and sponsored training sessions for fleet operators of other organizations.

McDonnell Douglas Aircraft, St. Louis, Mo. McDonnell Douglas St. Louis-area employees are sharing rides and taking public transit because of company-encouraged ridesharing efforts. About one-third of the company's employees are commuting to work on buses, in vans, and in carpools.

Michigan Department of Transportation, Lansing, Mich. The department operates the largest State employee vanpool program in the county, serving 1,300 State workers with 118 vans and saving about 900,000 gallons of gasoline each year. In addition, the department recently allocated over $500,000 to fund 20 statewide ridesharing planning offices, which will provide advice to private and public employers.

Montana Department of Highways,

Helena, Mont. The Montana Department of Highways has successfully established a driver efficiency training program for State employees.

National Bureau of Standards, U.S. Department of Commerce, Gaithersburg, Md. This Federal agency reduced by nearly 40 percent its consumption of gasoline between April 1, 1979, and March 31, 1980, over the previous 1-year period. The reduction was accomplished without curtailing any of the Bureau's official responsibilities.

The Prudential Insurance Co. of America, Newark, N.J. Prudential operates one of the largest vanpool programs in the United States, and its employees in the Newark area are using it to great advantage. The company estimates that only 10 percent of its Newark work force are single drivers, about 50 percent of the employees ride in carpools or vanpools, and the remaining 40 percent use public transit.

Reynolds Electric and Engineering Co., Las Vegas, Nev. The Reynolds Electric and Engineering Co. funds a driver efficiency training program, which so far has reached 3,000 drivers in Nevada and nearly 100 driving instructors there.

Seattle First National Bank, Seattle, Wash. The bank will spend up to $600,000 in 1980 to support its popular "Bus With Us" program, which subsidizes public transit passes for over 40 percent of its 7,500 employees statewide. Seattle First National estimates that during its first year the program will eliminate 12 million miles which would have been driven by employees and could save as much as 750,000 gallons of gasoline. "Bus With Us" began in November of 1979.

Shemya Air Force Base, United States Air Force, Shemya AFB, Alaska. Shemya Air Force Base is located on Shemya Island, a 4.5 mile by 2.5 mile island near the tip of the Aleutian Chain. Base personnel reduced gasoline consumption by nearly 25 percent between April 1, 1979, and March 31, 1980, over the previous year. They are walking more, consolidating trips when they must drive, and becoming accustomed to the fact that energy efficiency is not a temporary goal but a way of life on tiny Shemya Island.

Southern New England Telephone Co., Hartford, Conn. Southern New England Telephone Co. has been promoting alternate means of commuting since 1971, and the effort has paid off: Thirty-seven percent of its employees now use public transit, carpools, and vanpools.

Texas Medical Center, Houston, Tex. More than 40,000 people work at the Texas Medical Center, a complex which houses a number of different medical facilities. A multiemployer transportation program was begun there in June of 1978, promoting vanpooling, providing a carpool matching program by computer, supplying discounts for public transit passes, and taking other steps to assure easy access to the formerly congested, crowded parking facilities and roadways serving the center.

3M Company, St. Paul, Minn. Largely through the efforts of 3M senior transportation engineer Robert D. Owens, the company's model vanpooling program has grown from 6 vans in 1973 to 135 vans currently in operation. Owens is regarded as the "father of vanpooling," and his work in conjunction with 3M has revolutionized commuter transportation worldwide.

Truck and Bus Fuel Economy Advisory Committee, Society of Automotive Engineers, Euclid, Ohio. Made up of 40 individuals from the truck and bus manufacturing industry, the committee develops fuel-economy test procedures for new devices and concepts.

President's Council for Energy Efficiency

Appointment of the Membership.
July 22, 1980

The President today announced the appointment of the President's Council for Energy Efficiency. Members of the Council will serve in an honorary capacity. They will help encourage citizen participation in the national effort to achieve greater energy efficiency. The President's Council is one component of an overall Federal program to involve individual Americans in low-cost and no-cost energy conservation efforts at home, on the road, and on the farm.

The President announced the formation of the Council on April 29, 1980. The members appointed today are:

ANSEL ADAMS, of Carmel, Calif., photographer;

EDWARD AVILA, of Washington, D.C., executive director of the National Association of Elected Officials;

JOSE BAHAMONDE, of Miami, television producer;

BOBBY BARE, of Hendersonville, Tenn., country singer;

WILLIAM BEEBE, of Atlanta, chairman of the board, Delta Airlines;

ERMA BOMBECK, of Paradise Valley, Ariz., humorist and author;

DAVID BURWELL, of Washington, D.C., assistant director of public works, National Wildlife Federation;

WILLIAM CLINTON, of Fayetteville, Ark., Governor of Arkansas;

SAM CHURCH, JR., of Washington, D.C., president of the United Mine Workers;

ROBERT S. COLODZIN, of Stamford, Conn., vice president, Champion International Corp.;

JAMES D. CRAIG, of Northeaston, Mass., Olympic gold medalist;

JAMES B. CREAL, of Arlington, Va., president, American Automobile Association;

ANDRAE CROUCH, of Woodland Hills, Calif., gospel singer;

PAM DAWBER, of Los Angeles, actress;

JAMES PORTER DEAN, of Alcorn County, Miss., chairman, National Internal Affairs Committee, the American Legion;

CHARLES J. DI BONA, of Washington, D.C., president, American Petroleum Institute;

KIRK DOUGLAS, of Beverly Hills, Calif., actor;

ERIK ESTRADA, of Studio City, Calif., actor;

WILLIAM C. FRANCE, of Daytona Beach, Fla., president, National Association of Stock Car Auto Racing, Inc.;

DONALD C. FRISBEE, of Portland, Oreg., chairman, Pacific Power and Light Co.;

JOSEPH GARRAHY, of Narragansett, R.I., Governor of Rhode Island;

JOSE GOMEZ, of Washington, D.C., chairman, National Economic Development Association;

MARGARET L. GOVER, of Albuquerque, N. Mex., project director, Americans for Indian Opportunity;

ROOSEVELT GRIER, of Los Angeles, former football player;

EARL HINES, of Oakland, Calif., jazz musician;

DON HO, of Kailua, Hawaii, entertainer;

C. C. HOPE, JR., of Charlotte, N.C., president, American Bankers Association;

MAYNARD JACKSON, of Atlanta, Ga., mayor of Atlanta;

JOHN H. JOHNSON, of Chicago, Ill., publisher;

OLAF J. KAASA, of Washington, D.C., president, American Association of Retired Persons;

ROBERT P. KEIM, of New York City, president, the Advertising Council;

ROBERT KIRBY, of Pittsburgh, Pa., chairman of the board, Westinghouse Electric Corp.;

LANE KIRKLAND, of Washington, D.C., president, AFL–CIO;

GEORGE LATIMER, of St. Paul, Minn., mayor of St. Paul;

DAVID LEVINSON, of Middletown, Del., president, Levinson Corp.;

ARTHUR LEVITT, JR., of New York City, chairman, American Stock Exchange;

NANCY LOPEZ, of Mason, Ohio, professional golfer;

JAMES LOW, of Washington, D.C., president, American Society of Association Executives;

ALBERT L. MCDERMOTT, of Washington, D.C., Washington representative, American Hotel and Motel Association;

MARSHALL MCDONALD, of Miami, Fla., chairman of the board, Florida Power and Light Co.;

SANFORD NOYES MCDONNELL, of St. Louis, Mo., president, McDonnell Douglas Corp.;

MARY TYLER MOORE, of Los Angeles, Calif., actress;

ROBERT PARTRIDGE, of Washington, D.C., general manager, National Rural Electric Cooperative Association;

LINUS PAULING, of Portola Valley, Calif., scientist;

MARTHA V. PENNINO, of Vienna, Va., Fairfax County (Virginia) supervisor;

TIMATHA S. PIERCE, of New York City, president, American Women in Television and Radio;

MARY ELIZABETH POWERS, of New York City, senior editor for consumer affairs, Good Housekeeping magazine;

LEONTYNE PRICE, of New York City, opera singer;

DAN RANKOW, of Coral Gables, Fla., secretary-general, Jaycees International;

WILLIAM KANE REILLY, of Washington, D.C., president, Conservation Foundation;

BURT REYNOLDS, of Jupiter, Fla., actor;

CHARLES MCKINLEY REYNOLDS, JR., of Virginia Beach, Va., president, National Bankers Association;

DAVID M. RODERICK, of Pittsburgh, Pa., chairman, United States Steel Corp.;

CHARLES T. ROYER, of Seattle, Wash., mayor of Seattle;

WILLIAM RUDER, of New York City, president, Ruder and Finn;

HARVEY RUVIN, of Miami Beach, Fla., Dade County commissioner;

DR. JONAS SALK, of La Jolla, Calif., scientist;

NEIL SIMON, of Los Angeles, Calif., playwright;

STEPHEN STILLS, of Beverly Hills, Calif., singer;

DR. GEORGE C. SZEGO, of Warrenton, Va., president, Intertechnology Corp. and Solar Corp. of America;

CHERYL TIEGS, of Los Angeles, Calif., model;

WILLIAM D. TOOHEY, of Washington, D.C., president, Travel Industry Association;

ALEXANDER TROWBRIDGE, of Washington, D.C., president, National Association of Manufacturers;

TED TURNER, of Marietta, Ga., businessman and sportsman;

JACK VALENTI, of Washington, D.C., president, Motion Picture Association of America, Inc.;

SARAH VAUGHN, of Hidden Hills, Calif., singer;

ABRAHAM S. VENABLE, of Detroit, Mich., director of urban affairs, General Motors Corp.;

EDWARD VILELLA, of New York City, dancer;
ISABELLE P. WEBER, of Washington, D.C., director, energy department, League of Women Voters;
CALE YARBOROUGH, of Olanta, S.C., race car driver.

Billy Carter's Activities With the Libyan Government

White House Statement on the Investigation by the Department of Justice.   July 22, 1980

The White House has, of course, been aware of press reports, running back over many months, that the Department of Justice was conducting an investigation into the question of whether Billy Carter was legally obliged to make a filing under the Foreign Agents Registration Act with respect to activities on behalf of the Government of Libya. At no time, however, has there been any contact in either direction between the White House and the Department of Justice concerning the conduct of this investigation, except for the FBI interviews with Mr. Phillip Wise and the call to him mentioned below.

On June 10, 1980, Billy Carter requested a meeting with the President's national security adviser, Dr. Brzezinski, and the meeting was held on June 11. When Dr. Brzezinski heard the subject of the meeting, he asked the White House Counsel, Lloyd Cutler, to join the discussion.

Billy Carter said he had been interviewed that morning by Justice Department investigators and asked to describe any discussions with White House officials relating to Libya. He inquired whether there was any national security reason why he could not disclose a prior meeting, which occurred on November 27, 1979, with Dr. Brzezinski and a Libyan official, which Billy Carter arranged at Dr. Brzezinski's request, to explore the possibility of

seeking Libyan Government support in urging the release of the American hostages in Iran. This was 3 weeks after the seizure of the hostages, and the United States was exploring every possible avenue of contact with the Iranian leaders. Billy Carter was asked to arrange the meeting on short notice, because of the cool official relations then existing between the United States and Libya.

Dr. Brzezinski and Mr. Cutler advised Billy Carter that there was no national security objection to informing the Department of Justice investigators about this meeting, and Mr. Cutler added that Billy Carter had a legal obligation to respond fully to the Department's questions.

In the course of the meeting, Mr. Cutler learned that Billy Carter had attended the interview without the participation or advice of legal counsel. Mr. Cutler urged Billy Carter that he should promptly obtain counsel to advise him of his rights and duties and represent him before the Department. At Billy Carter's request to suggest a qualified counsel in Washington, Mr. Cutler recommended several lawyers, including Steven J. Pollak, Esq., and Henry Ruth, Esq., of the firm of Shea & Gardner. At Billy Carter's request, Mr. Cutler introduced him to Mr. Pollak over the telephone.

Thereafter, at Mr. Cutler's request, Mr. Pollak and Mr. Ruth informed Mr. Cutler that Dr. Brzezinski's meeting with a Libyan official and Billy Carter concerning the hostages had been reported to the Justice Department. They also informed him that Billy Carter was considering the prompt filing of a registration statement reporting his activities. Mr. Cutler reported this information to the President. On July 1, the President telephoned Billy Carter and urged him to file the registration statement and make a full disclosure.

Until July 11, Mr. Cutler received no information about the particulars of Billy

Carter's activities or about the financial aspects of this relationship. On July 11, Mr. Pollak and Mr. Ruth informed Mr. Cutler that the Department was about to file a civil complaint and that the parties were in negotiation about the simultaneous filing of a registration statement and a consent judgment. On July 14, they advised Mr. Cutler that the complaint, registration statement, and consent judgment had been filed. In these conversations they informed Mr. Cutler of a few of the particulars of the reported activities and financial transactions, and, after the court filing, delivered to him copies of the filed papers.

OTHER CONTACTS WITH THE WHITE HOUSE STAFF

During the course of the Department's investigation, on March 14 and June 4, 1980, the FBI interviewed Mr. Phillip Wise, Appointments Secretary to the President, to inquire about calls from Billy Carter to Mr. Wise concerning Libya in 1978 and January 1979. On July 1, 1980, Mr. Wise also received a telephone inquiry from a Department lawyer about such a conversation. Mr. Wise responded that he has no record or independent recollection of any such call or conversation.

In 1978, before traveling to Libya, Mr. Henry R. Coleman, an associate of Billy Carter's, had telephone conversations with Karl F. Inderfurth and William E. Quandt, then on the NSC staff, for a general briefing about U.S. policy toward Libya. Billy Carter participated briefly in one of these conversations. After leaving the NSC staff, Quandt and Inderfurth were questioned about these conversations by Department of Justice investigators.

Last March, Dr. Brzezinski noted an intelligence report that Billy Carter was attempting to assist an oil company in obtaining an increased allocation of Libyan oil and telephoned Billy Carter to advise him that he should not engage in any activity that could cause embarrassment to the administration. Dr. Brzezinski subsequently informed the President of this conversation. Neither the President nor Dr. Brzezinski had any other information, at any time before the news accounts of the filing of the court papers on July 14, concerning the financial transactions between Billy Carter and the Government of Libya.

Billy Carter's Activities With the Libyan Government

Statement by the President.   July 22, 1980

I do not believe it is appropriate for a close relative of the President to undertake any assignment on behalf of a foreign government. Facts relating to the existence of any relationship should be fully and publicly disclosed.

When my Counsel informed me that according to my brother's attorneys he was considering whether to register under the Foreign Agents Registration Act and report his activities, I urged him to register and make a full disclosure. I note from the registration that he is not presently engaged in any activities on behalf of Libya and has no activities on its behalf under consideration.

Central Idaho Wilderness Act of 1980

Remarks on Signing S. 2009 Into Law. July 23, 1980

THE PRESIDENT. *Senator Frank Church and Governor John Evans, Secretary Cecil Andrus, distinguished members of the leadership in Idaho and throughout the country who believes in the beauty of our Nation and who have sound judgment in coordinating adequate development of our natural resources with the preservation of that beauty:*

It is indeed a pleasure for me to be with you.

A few minutes ago I was talking to my own staff members and to Senator Church and to Cecil Andrus. I think if I had to pick out the three or four best days of my life in politics, it was the time I spent going down the Salmon River by raft two summers ago. This was a delightful trip. Not only was it restful and filled with beauty, but also we had good companionship with me and Cecil Andrus. And I might add that my raft caught more trout than his raft did—[*laughter*]—at least that's the official Government position. [*Laughter*]

The River of No Return, encompassing the Middle Fork of the Salmon River, is indeed one of our Nation's treasures. This legislation, introduced, sponsored by Senator Frank Church, is the largest single contribution to the wilderness area in the lower 48 States, and I think is a major step forward toward preserving what we have as a precious treasure for this generation and for our children's children as well.

There are special provisions in it which are innovative in nature. A small region of the area will have special attention given to cobalt mining, for instance, designed very carefully not to disturb the beauty of the rest of the region. There's been a careful balance between the prospect of harvesting of timber and the preservation of these wonderful areas surrounding the wilderness area itself.

When I was first elected President, I sent to the Congress in 1977 an environmental message, which has been the guideline for our administration and which has been remarkably successful in its own implementation. I called for a substantial increase in the wilderness areas, and since then we have added 4.7 million acres of wilderness area to be preserved and protected for the benefit of American citizens. This is a 48-percent increase in the total wilderness area in just the last 3 years.

We now face another, even more important—and I say that very cautiously, knowing my audience—a more important decision as we face the Alaska lands legislation. Within this century there hardly can be a more important decision for the Congress to make than how to treat the preservation of the Alaska lands, that are so vital, and also the proper utilization of natural resources in that new State of our country.

But this morning I am grateful to sign into law Senate bill 2009, sponsored by, promoted by, and sustained by Senator Frank Church, with the strong support of Governor Evans, Cecil Andrus, also Secretary Bob Bergland, and the Agricultural Committee, and of course many Members of the Congress. And it's with a great deal of gratitude to them and to all of you who've been responsible for this success that I sign this bill into law.

Following my signature, I would like to ask Senator Frank Church if he would make comments concerning the significance of this legislation to his own State and to our country.

[*At this point, the President signed the bill.*]

SENATOR CHURCH. *Mr. President, Secretary Andrus, Governor Evans, ladies and gentlemen:*

First of all, Mr. President, I congratulate you on your catch on the Salmon.

THE PRESIDENT. We released them all, by the way. [*Laughter*]

SENATOR CHURCH. We trained those fish very carefully. [*Laughter*]

THE PRESIDENT. If you're going to say that, I'll say we released almost all of them. [*Laughter*]

SENATOR CHURCH. This is a great moment for Idaho. And I know I speak on behalf of Governor John Evans, who's long been a strong advocate of this wilderness, and Cecil Andrus, who as Governor promoted it and has continued to give it his consistent and sustained support, when I say how grateful we are to you for signing into law this morning a bill that will create the finest wilderness in the American West, outside of Alaska.

This bill, Mr. President, has been 2 years in genesis. We held hearings in Idaho last year at which more than 650 witnesses testified, which is indicative of the intense interest of the State in the preservation of this magnificent back country of Idaho. The bill brings to a close 15 years of controversy as we classify this beautiful area. And I think that we have done it in a way, Mr. President, that will assure no impediment to the Idaho economy. The mining activity, the national need for cobalt and molybdenum has been taken into full consideration in the delineation of the borders, and there has been no trespass upon the working forests of our State. So, it is, I think, a piece of legislation which will serve our people well, both the people of Idaho and the people of the Nation.

And so, Mr. President, we thank you for this culmination today, by your signature, creating the River of No Return Wilderness, which will serve Idaho and the Nation for many years to come.

Thank you very much.

SECRETARY ANDRUS. Mr. President, it may be raining in your Rose Garden, but it's a great day for Idaho. As Senator Church has pointed out, it's been a long time coming to this, to where we can have that pristine area that you visited and caught and released many of our trout. We invite you to come back in your second term of office and enjoy it again, or after you complete the second term in '85, maybe we can——

THE PRESIDENT. We will. Thank you. [*Laughter*]

SECRETARY ANDRUS. You're welcome. It might be a possibility.

But we sincerely appreciate you helping us bring to a close the 8 years that I've been involved in this, and the appreciation of Idaho goes to you, sir. Thank you.

THE PRESIDENT. Thank you very much.

I very quickly realized, as we started down the river on adjoining rafts, that my invitation from Cecil to go down this area was not entirely altruistic in nature—[*laughter*]—because by the time we ended our 3- or 4-day trip, I was well versed in all the arguments, pro and con, and I became an avid supporter of this legislation.

John Evans, I would like to have you comment.

GOVERNOR EVANS. Thank you very much, Mr. President.

You know, over a lifetime of public service, we look at things that we've taken part in, and there's nothing more exciting for me, as Governor of the State of Idaho at this time in our history, to have been a part of the development, the support, the outlining of the Central Idaho Wilderness Area, the River of No Return.

I want to particularly thank Senator Frank Church for the outstanding leadership that he provided to secure the passage of this legislation not only through the Senate but through the House of Representatives. He had tremendous opposition from some of our citizens in Idaho, but he had the strength of conviction to move ahead and do what was right, what was right for not only Idaho but for the entire Nation.

And I look on this wilderness area as something we've set aside for the future of this country, for the children of this country. So, it's a great pleasure of mine, as Governor of Idaho, to participate in this ceremony. And, Mr. President, once again, on behalf of the people of Idaho and the people of America, thank you very much for your part in setting aside the River of No Return Wilderness Area.

Thank you.

THE PRESIDENT. Good luck to you. Thank you all very much.

I'd like to ask you all to move to the Hill now and help us with Alaska— [*inaudible*]. [*Laughter*]

NOTE: The President spoke at 9:55 a.m. in Room 450 of the Old Executive Office Building.

As enacted, S. 2009 is Public Law 96–312, approved July 23.

Central Idaho Wilderness Act of 1980

Statement on Signing S. 2009 Into Law.
July 23, 1980

I am today signing the Central Idaho Wilderness Act of 1980. This act is important as a major expansion of the National Wilderness Preservation System for Idaho and the Nation. It creates the largest single wilderness in the lower 48 States—the River of No Return Wilderness. I recall vividly my trip down the Middle Fork of the Salmon River in the middle of this huge and primitive heartland of Idaho. I hope it will be the first of several major wilderness enactments by the 96th Congress.

Shortly after entering office, in my May 1977 environmental message to the Congress, I urged prompt expansion of the National Wilderness Preservation System. On February 24, 1978, I had the privilege of signing the Endangered American Wilderness Act of 1978, which added about 1.3 million acres in 10 western States to the National Wilderness Preservation System. That was the largest single addition to the wilderness areas of this country since the original enactment of the Wilderness Act in 1964. On October 21, 1978, I again had the privilege of signing into law the Boundary Waters Canoe Area Wilderness Act, which expanded and perfected that area's designation. In addition, I have approved other legislation which added about 3.4 million acres to the Wilderness System. Thus, prior to the Central Idaho Wilderness Act, a total of 4.7 million acres has been added to the Wilderness System in the last 3 years.

On May 2, 1979, as a result of the roadless area review and evaluation, I recommended to the Congress wilderness designations for an additional 15.4 million acres of roadless areas on the National Forest System lands, consisting of 5.5 million acres in Alaska and 9.9 million acres in 35 other States and the Commonwealth of Puerto Rico.

The Central Idaho Wilderness Act will add more than 2.3 million acres to the Wilderness System and will designate 125 miles of the Salmon River in Idaho as a Wild and Scenic River. This wilderness designation brings the total acreage in the National Wilderness Preservation System to 21.4 million acres, an increase of about 48 percent during this administration. I want to express especially my appreciation to the Members of Congress, their staff, and those in the administration for their untiring efforts in working out the many details of the legislation.

We are a privileged nation to have the opportunity to protect the primitive lands and natural resources represented in this act and in all of the other areas included in my May 2, 1979, recommendations. In preserving these lands we protect irreplaceable parts of our national heritage that will be enjoyed by the American people and generations to come.

I look forward with anticipation to the completion by the Congress of other acts providing wilderness designation. In particular, I urge Congress to complete action on the Alaska lands legislation. This will add areas of major national significance to the National Park, National Wildlife Refuge, National Forest, and National Wilderness Preservation Systems.

NOTE: As enacted, S. 2009 is Public Law 96–312, approved July 23.

United States Ambassador to Guinea-Bissau and Cape Verde

Nomination of Peter Jon de Vos.
July 23, 1980

The President today announced that he will nominate Peter Jon de Vos, of North Key Largo, Fla., to be Ambassador Extraordinary and Plenipotentiary of the United States to the Republic of Guinea-Bissau and to the Republic of Cape Verde. He would replace Edward Marks, who is being assigned to another post.

De Vos has been Deputy Director of Southern African Affairs at the State Department since 1979 and has been a Foreign Service officer since 1962.

He was born December 24, 1938, in San Diego, Calif. He received a B.A. from Princeton University in 1960 and an M.A. from Johns Hopkins University in 1962.

De Vos joined the Foreign Service in 1962 and was posted in Recife, Naples, Luanda, and at the State Department. He was political officer in Sao Paulo from 1970 to 1971 and in Brasilia from 1971 to 1973.

From 1973 to 1975, he was Special Assistant to the Assistant Secretary of State for Inter-American Affairs. From 1975 to 1978, he was political officer in Athens. In 1978–79 he attended the National War College.

United States Parole Commission

Nomination of Leslie R. Green To Be a
Commissioner. July 23, 1980

The President today announced that he will nominate Leslie R. Green, of St. Cloud, Minn., to be a Commissioner of the U.S. Parole Commission. He would replace William Amos, Jr., whose term is expiring.

Green has been chairman of the Minnesota Corrections Board since 1979. He was born February 10, 1943, in Minneapolis, Minn. He received a B.S. from St. Cloud State University in 1972.

From 1969 to 1972, Green was a counselor at St. Cloud Children's Home, where he worked with emotionally disturbed teenagers. In 1972 he was an instructor in the teacher education department at St. Cloud University.

From 1972 to 1974, Green was an instructor in the integrated studies and criminal justice counseling programs at the College of St. Benedict. From 1974 to 1979, he was vice chairman of the Minnesota Corrections Board.

National Capital Planning Commission

Appointment of T. Eugene Smith as a Member.   July 23, 1980

The President today announced the appointment of T. Eugene Smith, of McLean, Va., to be a member of the National Capital Planning Commission.

Smith is president of the National Bank of Fairfax and serves as a consultant on real estate and real estate finance to investment trusts, investment bankers, and small business investment companies. He is a former chairman of the Planning Commission of Fairfax County.

Commission on Executive, Legislative, and Judicial Salaries

Appointment of Three Members and Designation of Chairman.   July 23, 1980

The President today announced the appointment of three persons as members of the Commission on Executive, Legislative, and Judicial Salaries. They are:

THOMAS R. DONAHUE, of Washington, D.C., secretary-treasurer of the AFL–CIO and former executive assistant to AFL–CIO President George Meany.

MARTHA W. GRIFFITHS, of Romeo, Mich., former Member of Congress and now a partner in the law firm of Griffiths & Griffiths.

JOSEPH H. McCONNELL, of Del Ray Beach, Fla., now retired, formerly chairman of Communications Satellite Corp., president of Reynolds Metals Co., and president of the National Broadcasting Company. McConnell has been designated Chairman of this Commission.

United States Attorney Herman Sillas, Jr.

White House Statement.   July 23, 1980

The matter of the continued service of the prosecutor referred to in the annual report of the Office of Professional Responsibility continues to be under review by the Counsel to the President. After fully evaluating Department of Justice recommendations concerning the prosecutor, the Counsel will make a recommendation to the President. We have been evaluating the Department of Justice's recommendations in light of materials submitted by the counsel to the prosecutor and the Department's responses to those submissions.

The issues involved in this matter are difficult and complex. Primary concerns of the President's Counsel, since beginning his evaluation of this case, have been to protect the integrity and public reputation of the office of the United States attorney, while at the same time affording the prosecutor and his own legal counsel a fair opportunity to present his side of the matter.

Everything we have done in connection with this matter has been in consultation with the office of the Deputy Attorney General. The process is still underway, although we expect it to be completed shortly. It would be inappropriate to make any further remarks on this matter at this time.

Boys Nation

Remarks to Delegates Attending the Annual Meeting.   July 24, 1980

THE PRESIDENT. Good morning, everybody. It's good to have you here. I know it's a relief to you to have your presidential election over. And you made a very wise choice. I'm just glad that none of you are 35 years old.

One of the most intense personal feelings that I have, as we're assembled here on the White House grounds in the Rose Garden, is gratitude to the American Legion for the wonderful work that has been done over the last number of decades, even generations, in helping to promote the interest of young men, at the present time in their lives, in the future of our Nation. I'm very grateful that Bob Spanogle is here and Bob Kruse, both representing that distinguished organization.

As you know, the Boys State effort was begun, I think, in 1934 and the Boys Nation in 1946, and literally hundreds of thousands of young Americans have been acquainted with the role of government, the problems, the challenges, the difficulties, the complexities of government during that long interval of time.

Our Nation has changed a lot since then. We've been through a major world war, through a very severe depression of the thirties and early forties, the Korean war, the Vietnam war, the intense, shocking social changes as we struggle to eliminate racial discrimination from the legal aspects of our country. Americans have always been strong enough and courageous enough to face those difficult challenges and to face changing times without fear and without trepidation and without timidity. My belief is that an integral part of that ability of Americans to meet changing times as a cutting edge of world society has been the intense interest of young people like yourselves in government and in the future of the Nation which you yourselves will lead in the years ahead.

There is no easy answer to the complex question that faces our Nation in any of the areas that you've discussed in the last few days, even here in Washington. Energy, national security, the role of government—how to do it efficiently and at the same time humanely—in meeting the needs of our people are very difficult questions. Those that I receive on my desk in the Oval Office are issues and questions that cannot be resolved, even with the best intention and the most careful focusing of attention, at the county courthouse or the city hall or the State capitol or the State legislatures of our country.

Those issues that I and the Congress share, in trying to deal with them on an enlightened basis for the best interest of our country, are indeed complex. But that doesn't meant that we need to despair, because in every test of our Nation, in every crisis which our Nation has ever faced, in every time of uncertainty that's come about historically—much more difficult, much more challenging, much more disconcerting in the past than at the present time—our Nation has never failed. When we could understand a question, when we could see clearly a problem or discern an obstacle, when our Nation united, we have never failed to answer the question, to resolve the problem, or to overcome the obstacle. That's the case now.

We've made remarkable progress in energy, which you've discussed recently. In the last 3½ years, the Congress has forged, along with me, a policy that will guide our Nation to the future very well. We've already slashed our dependence on foreign oil, which is vital to our Nation's own military security as well as economic security. We've had remarkable success among the American citizens, who've rallied to this cause in a very sacrificial and patriotic way.

I won't go into detail on the other elements of government, because you know them quite well. One of the most controversial which you've had to face and will face shortly is registration.

Our country is challenged in its commitment to freedom and peace by the unwarranted Soviet invasion of Afghanistan. A small nation, no threat to anyone, deeply religious, fiercely committed to freedom for themselves, has been invaded in an unwarranted fashion by the Soviet Union with powerful, overwhelming military forces. The Soviets have not been successful in subjugating these courageous freedom-fighters, who are struggling for their own nation's liberation.

And the need for our young people to be registered—not to be drafted, we don't anticipate any need for a draft; but to be registered, to expedite the process if and when it is needed—is something that I have proposed and which I support and which I will carry out regardless of any obstacle that might arise in this country. And I need your help and your support in that respect.

Our people in this country, generation after generation after generation, have been willing to lay down their very lives, if necessary, to defend this country and the principles on which our Nation was based. We are asking a very minor demonstration of commitment and patriotism from Americans to strengthen our own country and its role in international affairs and the preservation of peace and for the enhancement of freedom. And I would like to have you leaders help me with this particular issue.

So far this week, we've had remarkable success in the post offices in the communities of our Nation, in young men coming forward and saying, "I am perfectly willing to register," and if necessary in the future—and God knows I pray as deeply and frequently as anyone on Earth that we will have continued peace—if it should become necessary, to offer your services. In my judgment it will not become necessary. And one of the best ways to prevent

a mandatory draft, one of the best ways to prevent any military action in which our Nation must be involved, is a demonstration of unity and commitment to our country. So, I call on you to help me in that respect.

In closing, let me say that I want to congratulate Jonathan Shapiro, your new president, and also Kiernan Conway for their election. If I had the time, Id like to consult with them privately on the secret of their success.

I think this election year will give our Nation a chance to pursue an open, helpful debate on the controversial issues that afflict our country, which we can handle very well, and to carve out for you and for others a remarkable good life in the rest of this century and in the century ahead.

Thank you very much. Congratulations, Mr. President.

MR. SHAPIRO. Mr. President, we are so appreciative of you taking time out from your schedule to meet with the leaders of today and the young leaders of tomorrow. We'd like to also wish you the best in leading our country, in the great responsibility that it is. We'd like to present you with this pin of Boys Nation, a pin that we all wear proudly and we hope will let you remember us and what we stand for.

THE PRESIDENT. Thank you very much.

MR. CONWAY. Mr. President, I am honored on behalf of the Boys Nation to present you today this honorary pen and pencil set on behalf of the entire Boys Nation and the American Legion program.

THE PRESIDENT. Thank you very much.

MR. SHAPIRO. And finally, Mr. President, we understand that you are a rather avid runner. And we'd like to present you with this duffel bag with the Boys Nation insignia for your Presidential runs, sir.

THE PRESIDENT. Thank you. Good luck. And I'll use it. Thank you.

Before I leave I'd like to come around, if you don't mind, and shake hands with everybody and thank you and congratulate you on your own choice as leaders of our country.

NOTE: The President spoke at 9:52 a.m. in the Rose Garden at the White House.

Bob Spanogle is executive director of the Washington, D.C., headquarters of the American Legion; Bob Kruse is director of Boys Nation; Jonathan Shapiro and Kiernan Conway are the 1980 president and vice president of Boys Nation.

Global 2000 Study

Statement on the Report to the President.
July 24, 1980

Shortly after assuming office in 1977, I directed the Council on Environmental Quality, the Department of State, and other Government agencies to study the profound changes that may take place in our world's population, natural resources, and environment through the end of the century. Never before had our government or any government attempted to take such a comprehensive, long-range look at interrelated global issues such as world population, agriculture, water resources, forest resources, energy needs, and the overall environmental quality of the Earth we live on.

The Global 2000 study is now complete. Its report projects global conditions which could develop by the end of this century, assuming that present trends and patterns around the world continue. Many of the report's findings must be of great concern to all of us. These findings point to de-

velopments related to the world's peoples and resources that our prompt attention can begin to alleviate. We will make use of the information from the Global 2000 report in carrying out public policy wherever possible. In addition, we must continue to analyze the serious issues it raises.

It is important to understand that the conditions the report projects are by no means inevitable. In fact, its projections can and should be timely warnings which will alert the nations of the world to the need for vigorous, determined action at both the national and international levels.

The United States is not alone in responding to global population, natural resource, and environmental issues. The recent Venice summit declaration committed the Western industrial nations to cooperate with developing countries in addressing global food, energy, and population problems. The summit nations agreed on the need for a better understanding of the implications of resource availability and population growth for economic development. In the United Nations many of the key issues raised in the Global 2000 report are being included in the formulation of a new international development strategy.

A number of U.S. and international responses to critical global issues are already underway. For example, since the United Nations Conference on the Human Environment in 1972, our Government has contributed actively to a series of world conferences on these issues, and to followup actions.

Nonetheless, given the importance, scope, and complexity of the challenges set forth in the report, I believe America must provide special leadership in addressing global conditions. I am therefore today appointing a Presidential Task Force on Global Resources and Environment, to be chaired by the Chairman of the Council on Environmental Quality and to include the Secretary of State, the Assistant to the President for Domestic Affairs and Policy, the Director of the Office of Science and Technology Policy, and the Director of the Office of Management and Budget. The Task Force will report to me as soon as possible with recommendations for action in problem areas needing priority attention. I am directing other Federal agencies to cooperate with and support the Task Force's efforts.

I am also directing the State Department to raise the issues and problems identified in the Global 2000 report in all appropriate international meetings, and I myself will raise them as well. For example, in my second environmental message last August, I expressed my concern about the loss of tropical forests. For immediate action on this critical problem, I am directing all relevant Federal agencies to respond within 60 days to the Interagency Task Force Report on Tropical Forests, which was submitted to me last month. In their responses, agencies will detail the steps they will take to carry out the report's recommendations. In receiving these reports, the Interagency Task Force on Tropical Forests will operate as an arm of the Presidential Task Force on Global Resources and the Environment. Finally, I am requesting the Commission of the Eighties to give careful attention to these global issues.

There are less than 20 years left in our 20th century. The time to look forward to the world we want to have in the year 2000 and leave to succeeding generations is now. It is my firm belief that we can build a future in which all people lead full, decent lives in harmony with a healthy and habitable planet. And I believe that the skills, experience, vision, and

courage of the American people today make the United States a natural leader in charting and guiding humanity's course towards a better world tomorrow.

NOTE: The report is entitled "The Global Report to the President: Entering the Twenty-First Century" (Government Printing Office, 3 volumes—Volume One, The Summary Report; Volume Two, The Technical Report; Volume Three, The Government's Global Model).

Task Force on Global Resources and Environment

Memorandums From the President.
July 24, 1980

Memorandum for the Secretary of State, Director, Office of Management and Budget, Chairman, Council on Environmental Quality, Assistant to the President for Domestic Affairs and Policy, Director, Office of Science and Technology Policy

Among the most urgent and complex challenges before the world today is the projected deterioration of the global environmental and resource base. Unless nations of the world take prompt, decisive action to halt the current trends, the next 20 years may see a continuation of serious food and population problems, steady loss of croplands, forests, plant and animal species, fisheries, and degradation of the earth's water and atmosphere.

To increase our capability to respond to these problems, I am establishing a Presidential Task Force on Global Resources and Enivronment. I am asking you to serve as members of this Task Force and am asking the Chairman of the Council on Environmental Quality to serve as Chairman.

The objectives of this Task Force will be:

- to ensure that high priority attention is given to important global resource, population, and environment problems;
- to assess the effectiveness of Federal efforts in these areas; and
- to assess ways to improve the Federal government's ability to project and analyze long-term resource, population, and environment trends.

The Task Force will report to me as soon as possible with recommendations for problem areas needing priority attention by the Task Force. It will report to me within six months and periodically thereafter on its progress and on ways in which Federal programs in these areas can be strengthened and improved.

The Task Force will carry out its responsibilities in consultation with and with the assistance of the Department of Agriculture, the Department of Commerce, the Department of Defense, the Department of Energy, the Department of Health and Human Services, the Department of the Interior, the Department of Transportation, the Department of Justice, the Central Intelligence Agency, the International Development Cooperation Agency, the National Science Foundation, the Environmental Protection Agency, the National Aeronautics and Space Administration, and my Assistant for National Security Affairs.

JIMMY CARTER

Memorandum for the Secretary of Agriculture, the Secretary of Commerce, the Secretary of Defense, the Secretary of Energy, the Secretary of Health and Human Services, the Secretary of the Interior, the Secretary of Transportation, the Attorney General, Department of Justice, the Director, Central Intelligence Agency, the Director, International Development Cooperation Agency, the Director, National Science Foundation, the Administrator, Environmental Protection Agency, the Administrator, National Aeronautics and Space Administration, the Assistant to the President for National Security Affairs

Among the most urgent and complex challenges before the world today is the projected deterioration of the global environmental and resource base. Unless nations of the world take prompt, decisive action to halt the current trends, the next 20 years may see a continuation of serious food and population problems, steady loss of croplands, forests, plant and animal species, fisheries, and degradation of the earth's water and atmosphere.

To increase our capability to respond to these problems, I have established a Task Force on Global Resources and Environment consisting of the Chairman of the Council on Environmental Quality as chair, the Secretary of State, the Director of the Office of Management and Budget, the Assistant to the President for Domestic Affairs and Policy, and the Director of the Office of Science and Technology Policy.

I have directed the Task Force to work closely with you in carrying out its responsibilities, which will be:

- to ensure that high priority attention is given to important global resource, population, and environment problems;
- to assess the effectiveness of federal efforts in these areas; and
- to assess ways to improve the federal government's ability to project and analyze long-term resource, population, and environment trends.

Each of your agencies shall cooperate with and support this important Task Force. The Task Force will report to me as soon as possible with recommendations for problem areas needing priority attention by the Task Force. It will report to me within six months and periodically thereafter on its progress and on ways in which federal programs in these areas can be strengthened and improved.

JIMMY CARTER

Saint Lawrence Seaway Development Corporation

Message to the Congress Transmitting a Report. July 24, 1980

To the Congress of the United States:

I transmit herewith the Saint Lawrence Seaway Development Corporation's Annual Report for 1979. The Corporation, an agency of the Department of Transportation that is financed by income received from tolls and other charges, earned $11 million in 1979, up from $9.9 million in 1978. It is responsible for the operations and maintenance of that part of the Seaway within the territorial limits of the United States, and for vessel traffic regulation and other safety-related maritime activities. This report has been prepared in accordance with Section 10 of the Saint Lawrence Seaway Act of May 13, 1954, and covers the period January 1, 1979 through December 31, 1979.

In 1979 the Saint Lawrence Seaway, jointly operated by the United States and Canada, celebrated the twentieth anniversary of its opening to deep-draft navigation with the Seaway's third highest cargo tonnage year. Overall, 848 million metric tons of cargo have moved through

the Seaway since it was opened in 1959. This waterway is one of the most important commercial routes for the shipment of agricultural and industrial cargoes between North America and major overseas ports. It is a proud example of effective international cooperation.

JIMMY CARTER

The White House,
July 24, 1980.

Department of the Interior

Nomination of Wallace O. Green To Be an Assistant Secretary. July 24, 1980

The President today announced that he will nominate Wallace O. Green, of Washington, D.C., to be an Assistant Secretary of the Interior. He would replace John Henry Kyl, resigned, and his area of responsibility would be territorial and international affairs. Green has been serving in this position in an acting capacity since earlier this year.

He was born March 26, 1948, in Washington, D.C. He received an A.B. from Morgan State University in 1970 and an M.S. from Boston University in 1971.

Green was a political and public relations consultant from 1971 to 1973 and an advertising executive from 1973 to 1974. From 1975 to 1976, he was staff director of the House District Subcommittee on Bicentennial Affairs, the Environment, and International Community.

From 1976 to 1977, Green was staff director of the congressional Joint Committee on Arrangements for Commemoration of the Bicentennial. He joined the Interior Department in 1977 as Executive Assistant to the Under Secretary and then served as

Deputy Under Secretary from 1978 until February 1980.

Civil Aeronautics Board

Nomination of James Robert Smith To Be a Member. July 24, 1980

The President today announced that he will nominate James Robert Smith, of Bradenton, Fla., to be a member of the Civil Aeronautics Board. He would replace Richard J. O'Melia, who has resigned, and be appointed to an additional term expiring in 1986. Smith has been airport manager for the Sarasota-Bradenton Airport since 1979.

He was born May 9, 1945, in Auburn, Ala. He received a B.A. in aviation management from Auburn University in 1967 and an M.A. in transportation from the University of South Carolina in 1974.

From 1967 to 1970, Smith was administrative assistant to the airport manager at Norfolk (Virginia) Regional Airport. From 1970 to 1975, he was assistant airport director at Columbia (South Carolina) Metropolitan Airport. He was operations manager of Portland (Oregon) International Airport from 1975 to 1977 and deputy director of aviation for the city of Philadelphia, Pa., from 1977 to 1979.

Federal Council on the Aging

Nomination of Jacob Clayman To Be a Member. July 24, 1980

The President today announced that he will nominate Jacob Clayman, of Bethesda, Md., to be a member of the Federal Council on the Aging. He would replace Nelson Cruikshank, whose term has expired.

Clayman, 75, has been president of the National Council of Senior Citizens since 1979. He was with the Industrial Union Department of the AFL–CIO for almost 20 years and served as president and secretary-treasurer from 1977 to 1979.

National Consumer Cooperative Bank

Nomination of Wayman D. Palmer To Be Director of the Office of Self-Help Development and Technical Assistance. July 24, 1980

The President today announced that he will nominate Wayman D. Palmer, of Toledo, Ohio, to be Director of the Office of Self-Help Development and Technical Assistance of the National Consumer Cooperative Bank, a new position. Palmer has been director of the Department of Community Development of the city of Toledo since 1973.

He was born February 28, 1927, in Paris, Tenn. He received a B.S. from Ohio State University in 1950 and an M.Ed. from the University of Toledo in 1970. He served in the U.S. Army from 1945 to 1946.

From 1950 to 1966, Palmer was a classroom teacher, first in Columbia, S.C., then in Toledo. From 1966 to 1967, he was director of the Neighborhood Youth Corps for Toledo's Board of Community Relations.

Palmer was with the Economic Opportunity Planning Association of Greater Toledo from 1967 to 1972, first as assistant director, then as executive director.

From 1972 to 1973, he was assistant director of the Toledo Department of Community Development.

Presidential Advisory Board on Ambassadorial Appointments

Appointment of Jerry Apodaca as a Member.
July 24, 1980

The President today announced the appointment of Jerry Apodaca, of Santa Fe, N. Mex., as a member of the Presidential Advisory Board on Ambassadorial Appointments. He replaces Donald Stewart, who has resigned.

Apodaca was Governor of New Mexico from 1975 to 1979. He is currently president of Jerry Apodaca and Associates, a consulting firm, and serves as chairman of the board and chief executive officer of Texas Racquetball, Inc. and New Mexico Court Clubs.

Billy Carter's Activities With the Libyan Government

White House Statement on the Senate
Judiciary Committee Inquiry.   July 24, 1980

The President will instruct all members of the White House staff to cooperate fully with the special subcommittee of the Senate Judiciary Committee as to requests for information about the relationship between Billy Carter and the Government of Libya, as well as about any contacts between any member of the White House staff with Billy Carter or with the Department of Justice relating to Billy Carter.

The President does not expect to assert claims of executive privilege with respect to these matters. Members of the White House staff will be instructed to respond fully to such inquiries from the subcommittee and to testify if the subcommittee determines that oral testimony is necessary. To the extent that such inquiries from the subcommittee relate to classified information, the President expects that appropriate safeguards can be worked out to protect the security of the information to be provided.

The President himself will also respond fully to the subcommittee's inquiries relating to these matters, in accordance with mutually agreeable procedures consistent with the responsibilities and time constraints of his office.

NOTE: Press Secretary Jody Powell read the statement to reporters assembled in the Briefing Room at the White House.

Allowances for Personnel on Foreign Duty

Executive Order 12228.   July 24, 1980

By the authority vested in me as President of the United States of America by Sections 7 and 8 of the Defense Department Overseas Teachers Pay and Personnel Practices Act of 1959, as amended (20 U.S.C. 905–906), Section 235 of Title 38 of the United States Code, and Section 301 of Title 3 of the United States Code, and in order to delegate authority with respect to allowances for Veterans Administration personnel and to update existing authorities, it is hereby ordered as follows:

1–101. Payment of the additional compensation authorized by Section 8(a)(2) of the Defense Department Overseas Teachers Pay and Personnel Practices Act of 1959, as amended, shall be governed by the regulations contained in Executive Order No. 10000, as amended, which govern the payment of additional compensation in foreign areas (referred to as foreign post differential), subject to the provisions of Section 8(b) of that Act (20 U.S.C. 906(a)(2) and (b)).

1–102. The following functions vested in the President are delegated to the Secretary of State:

(a) That part of the functions in Section 7(a) of the Defense Department Overseas Teachers Pay and Personnel Practices Act which consists of the authority to prescribe regulations relating to quarters and quarters allowances (20 U.S.C. 905(a)).

(b) The authority in Section 8(a)(1) of the Defense Department Overseas Teachers Pay and Personnel Practices Act to prescribe regulations relating to cost of living allowances (20 U.S.C. 906(a)(1)).

(c) The following authority in Section 235 of Title 38 of the United States Code to prescribe rules and regulations:

(1) Section 235(2), except as that section pertains to an allowance similar to that provided for in Section 911(9) of the Foreign Service Act of 1946, as amended (22 U.S.C. 1136(9)).

(2) Section 235(3);

(3) Section 235(5);

(4) Section 235(6); and

(5) Section 235(7).

1–103. The following functions vested in the President by Section 235 of Title 38 of the United States Code are delegated to the Administrator of the Veterans Administration. The authority with respect to the allowances or benefits of paragraphs (1) and (4) of Section 235 which are similar to the benefits and allowances provided in the sections of the Foreign Service Act of 1946, as amended, designated in those paragraphs.

1–104. Executive Order No. 10853, as amended, is revoked. The rules and regulations which were prescribed by the Sec-

retary of State or the Administrator of the Veterans Administration pursuant to Executive Order No. 10853, as amended, and which would be valid if issued pursuant to this Order, shall be deemed to have been issued under this Order.

JIMMY CARTER

The White House,
   July 24, 1980.

[Filed with the Office of the Federal Register, 10:47 a.m., July 25, 1980]

Heat and Drought Conditions in the United States

Announcement of Federal Assistance Actions. July 25, 1980

The White House today announced several additional measures the administration is taking to provide assistance to low-income and elderly persons and to farmers affected by the extreme heat and drought that have plagued large parts of the Nation over the past few weeks. These actions are a followup to those taken on July 15, when $6.725 million was allocated to the States of Texas, Arkansas, Missouri, Louisiana, Oklahoma, and Kansas by the Community Services Administration (CSA). Although rain and falling temperatures have brought relief in parts of the Nation, other areas continue to suffer from above-normal temperatures and lack of rain.

Following congressional approval, the President will direct CSA and the Department of Health and Human Services to reprogram up to $21 million of last winter's Energy Crisis Assistance Program funds for use in areas currently affected by the heat. These funds represent unspent money that States would otherwise return to the Treasury at the end of the fiscal year. This administration initiative is consistent with the legislative efforts initiated by Congressman Mario Biaggi and supported by numerous members of both the Senate and the House of Representatives earlier this week.

The reprogramed funds will be made available, through CSA's network of Community Action Agencies, to those States most severely affected by the continuing heat wave. CSA Director Richard Rios announced that in addition to the original six States, eligibility has been extended today to Illinois, Kentucky, Tennessee, Mississippi, Alabama, and Georgia.

The estimated amount of assistance to be provided to each of these States immediately is as follows: Illinois, $1.8 million; Kentucky, $0.8 million; Tennessee, $1.6 million; Mississippi, $1.6 million; Alabama, $1.5 million; Georgia, $1.8 million. Approximately $4.9 million is being allocated to the six States which received assistance last week. The additional amounts tentatively earmarked for each State are: Texas, $2 million; Missouri, $0.75 million; Oklahoma and Arkansas, $0.5 million each; Louisiana, $1 million; Kansas, $0.2 million. The remaining $7 million to be reprogramed is being set aside on a contingency basis to assist other States should the need arise.

Assistance is being allocated on the basis of several factors, including the number of elderly poor and the severity of the weather experienced. Eligible activities include the provision of transportation to heat relief centers, purchase and rental of fans and coolers, rental or lease of small air-conditioners when medically necessary, and payment of utility bills in life- or health-threatening situations. To receive assistance, a household must demonstrate that it has a total income at or below 125 percent of the Federal poverty guideline, which is approximately $9,300 for a family of four.

The White House also announced that State and area agencies on aging are taking special steps to alleviate or minimize the impact of the heat wave on the elderly. This includes 24-hour information and referral services for providing fans, provision of cooling facilities at nutrition sites and senior centers, free transportation to cooled facilities, additional funds to increase meal services, and expanded outreach services to the elderly for medical attention and food. These services are being provided to the nonambulatory poor elderly on a priority basis.

In response to the President's July 15 directive to accelerate needed help to farmers, Agriculture Secretary Bob Bergland has implemented several important drought assistance programs, principally emergency livestock feed, natural disaster payments, and emergency loans.

Emergency livestock feed assistance is being provided to livestock producers whose feed production has been reduced by at least 40 percent. This aid is now available in over 400 counties in 20 States.

Disaster payments will be made to those farmers who either were prevented from planting their crop at all or suffered a crop loss of at least 40 percent. The extent of damage will be assessed by the county Agricultural Stabilization and Conservation Service committees.

The Farmers Home Administration is providing emergency loans at 5 percent interest to farmers whose production has been cut by at least 20 percent and who cannot obtain credit elsewhere. These loans have already been made available in 324 drought-affected counties in 10 States.

Finally, the President commended local communities and voluntary organizations for the swift and effective measures they have taken to reach out to those in need during this unusual situation. He also appealed to the Governors of the affected States to work closely with their public utility commissions in establishing deferred payment plans for low-income and elderly persons, because of the difficulty such persons might encounter in paying their increased utility bills associated with the heat wave.

Heat and Drought Conditions in the United States

Telegram Sent to Governors of 12 States. July 25, 1980

I want to commend you for the swift and effective actions you have taken in [State] to ease the impacts of the continuing heat wave on our citizens. I am certain that your actions have minimized both the loss of life and various health hazards associated with the extreme heat conditions.

I pledge to you the continuing support of the federal government during this unusual situation. I have already directed John Macy, director of the Federal Emergency Management Agency (FEMA), to coordinate the federal government's response. I have also directed the heads of other federal agencies, including the Community Services Administration and the departments of Agriculture and Health and Human Services, to work with state and local officials in assessing the impacts of the heat wave on our people and the agricultural sector, and to provide needed assistance through existing federal programs.

Finally, it has been brought to my attention by FEMA and by state and local officials that life and health threatening situations associated with the heat wave have resulted in large part because of low income and elderly persons' fears about their ability to pay higher than usual utility bills. In such instances, some of these economically disadvantaged persons have decided not to use various cooling appliances. If you have not already done so, I urge you to work with the state's public utility commission in establishing deferred utility payment plans for low income and elderly persons because of the difficulty that such persons might encounter in paying their increased utility bills.

Thank you for your assistance.

Sincerely,

JIMMY CARTER

NOTE: This is the text of identical telegrams sent to the following Governors: Forrest H. James, Jr., of Alabama; Bill Clinton of Arkansas; George Busbee of Georgia; James R. Thompson of Illinois; John Carlin of Kansas; John Y. Brown, Jr., of Kentucky; David C. Treen of Louisiana; William F. Winter of Mississippi; Joseph P. Teasdale of Missouri; George Nigh of Oklahoma; Lamar Alexander of Tennessee; and William P. Clements, Jr., of Texas.

Community Services Administration

Nomination of Harold Lafayette Thomas To Be an Assistant Director. July 25, 1980

The President today announced that he will nominate Harold Lafayette Thomas, of Washington, D.C., to be an Assistant Director of the Community Services Administration. He would replace John Gabusi, resigned. Thomas has been Director of Administration at the Legal Services Corporation since 1977.

He was born February 5, 1939, in Birmingham, Ala. He received a B.S. from Talladega College in 1960 and a J.D.

from Howard University School of Law in 1970.

From 1970 to 1971, Thomas was with the Baltimore, Md., Legal Aid Program, where he worked primarily in the area of housing law. From 1971 to 1973, he was legal adviser to the National Tenants Organization, where he served as liaison between that organization and legal services attorneys representing low-income tenants around the country. He also held the Reginald Heber Smith Community Law Fellowship from 1970 to 1973.

In 1973 Thomas was a consumer protection specialist with the Movement for Economic Justice. From 1973 to 1975, he was a management analyst with the Fairfax County (Virginia) Government. He was Special Assistant to the Executive Vice President of the Legal Services Corporation from 1975 to 1977.

National Historical Publications and Records Commission

Appointment of Norbert Brockman as a Member. July 25, 1980

The President today announced the appointment of Norbert Brockman, of Dayton, Ohio, as a member of the National Historical Publications and Records Commission.

Brockman, 46, has been a member of the Society of Mary (Marianists) since 1952 and was ordained a priest in 1973. He is director of the Marianist Training Network, a training group that provides educational and renewal services and consulting to religious and non-profit organizations.

Brockman directs an annual training program for religious archivists. In 1979 he organized the first national meeting of

Catholic church archivists, and he has brought this group into affiliation with the Society of American Archivists.

Carter/Mondale Presidential Campaign

Remarks at a White House Reception for Delegates to the Democratic National Convention. July 25, 1980

You've had a full day of very careful briefing and consideration, a chance to ask your questions and to think about the future of our Nation and our party. And I want to ask you one question: How many of you are convinced we're going to whip the Republicans in November? [*Applause*] I think you've got the political situation sized up very accurately—[*laughter*]—which shows your sound judgment, because this time 8 months ago, if most of you had said you're going to run as a Carter delegate, the chances are folks would have said, "Ah, you'll never win." [*Laughter*] And you've all won, right?

There are several reasons why the American people, the first week in November, will make the right judgment. One of the most important reasons that I will be reelected as President is because I have carefully chosen Fritz Mondale to be my running-mate. And I might say that, as was the case in New York in 1976, Fritz Mondale is my first choice.

No one can possibly look forward to the New York convention without the prospect of sharp divisions, heated debates, issues thoroughly discussed, sometimes dissensions, sometimes disagreement, sometimes maybe even hard feelings for a transient moment. But those characteristics of Democrats are exactly the characteristics that make our party the strongest and the oldest party on Earth. They're also the characteristics that have made our Nation strong.

We are a nation of diversity. We're a nation comprised of people who are different. And we're a nation and a party comprised of people who are outspoken, who have deep beliefs and are not ashamed to put them forward. Right? We're a party of immigrants. And when you look around this room and when I stood in the receiving line and when I meet with any group of Americans, almost every time, a constant impression is one of different kinds of people, different beliefs, different religion, different color, different ethnic backgrounds, different communities, different commitments, different hopes, dreams, ideas, fears, concerns, trepidation, competence.

But when we Americans, when we Democrats in an election year are faced with a difficult question or a complicated problem or a serious obstacle, if we can see it clearly and unite to meet a threat to our Nation, we have never failed. And when we meet in New York and see clearly the question to be answered by the American people, the problem to be resolved in the threat of a Republican takeover of the White House, and an obstacle to be overcome in winning the election, we Democrats, united, will not fail.

I look forward, actively, constantly, aggressively, to being out there with you as the Democratic candidate. And that's one reason, also, that we are not going to fail; we're going to win.

There's another point that I'd like to make. Our Nation, with its freedom, with its free enterprise system, with its tremendous advantages, and with the success that we've had with the innovative spirit that fills the heart and minds of Americans, have always been on the cutting edge of change. Democrats are not afraid of change. Democrats are not afraid of challenge. Democrats are not afraid to address difficult issues. We've never hidden our heads in the sand and just hoped that someone else would finally take the responsibility to resolve a question like excessive energy dependence or civil service reform or setting up a new Department of Education or giving our people a better chance in life. We've never been afraid of those things.

I have to admit to you that opening up some of those questions is not always politically advantageous in the short run, because people see the debate and the divisions; they see the disappointments in a subcommittee vote; they see some setbacks when you advocate a perfect program and you get 95 percent of it, because they always are reminded of the 5 percent you didn't get. But the progress that this Nation makes is because of that courage and commitment and unity of Democrats. Republicans have always been just the opposite.

I grew up on a farm. The Republicans were opposed to rural free delivery of mail. The Republicans were opposed to social security. The Republicans were opposed to Medicaid; they were opposed to Medicare. The Republicans have always been opposed to those very programs that are so dear to Americans who have suffered from poverty and alienation and discrimination, but who, when they're given a chance to stand on their own feet, to make their own judgments, have become our finest citizens. And those finest citizens that I'm describing to you are the kind of delegates that are going to be in New York to give me the nomination and to give us an advantage.

We're probably going to have some arguments about minority rights at the convention, and the arguments will be designed on how we can carry out even better our commitment to give minority

Americans full opportunities to overcome discrimination from which they've suffered in the past. The Republicans didn't have an argument. They didn't have any minorities in Detroit—3 percent; we've got 25 percent. And I don't have any doubt that we'll be arguing about women's issues in New York, because we're going to have at least 50 percent of the Democratic delegates in New York female.

And we're not going to be arguing about whether to help our ailing cities. We don't argue about whether to help people; it's how can we help those to whom we are deeply committed. And the reason we're committed to the poor, to the elderly, to those searching for a chance in life, to those looking for a better education, to those looking for a better neighborhood, is because those people are we; they're us. We're talking about our own problems and the ones we've helped to overcome. So, we understand, because the Democratic Party is the party of the people.

And I want to make one other point. We're a nation of strength. This country, in spite of all our arguments and debates and temporary disappointments and sometimes slight inconveniences, is the strongest nation on Earth. We're the strongest politically. Our influence throughout the world is beneficial, pervasive, and growing. This country is the strongest on Earth economically. What we do here in developing new ideas, new concepts, new goods, new services helps us, yes; but it's destined inevitably to help people all over the world. This Nation is the strongest militarily, the strongest on Earth. And my judgment is that this Nation is also the strongest morally and ethically.

We believe in principles that do not change. And the fact that Democrats are so sure of ourselves in dealing to change in the technological world, to dealing with change in the educational world, to deal-ing in change in the business and financial world, in dealing with change in the sociological world—the reason we don't fear those changes is because there are things in our own heart and in our own mind and in our own consciousness and in our own commitment which do not change. And those kinds of principles that have always guided our party gives us that reassurance that in spite of our diversity and difference of approach and difference of perspective, that we can unify ourselves and our effort to carry out those high principles on which our Nation and our party are founded.

We are the majority party. It's not an accident. The fact that the Democrats have about a two-to-one majority in the House and Senate, the fact that the Democrats have a President in the White House is a tribute to the sound political judgment of the American people, and I don't believe they're going to lose that sound judgment this fall.

And I don't want to forget to point out to you that we are a nation at peace. We're at peace because we are strong. And if we are going to maintain peace in the future, we've got to keep that strength of all kinds that I described to you a few minutes ago. We lost eight brave servicemen in the desert in Iran in an accident, on not a warlike but a humanitarian mission. And except for them, since I've been in this White House we have never had a single American soldier killed in combat. And I hope and pray that I'll go out of office at the end of my second term with that record still intact.

So, with you help in New York, I trust that I will be making an acceptance speech there to you, and as I do and in preparation for that moment, please remember that we have strong, good Democratic Americans who support Senator Kennedy for President. Give them respect and a hand of friendship and the right to express themselves. That's part of the Democratic process; I do not fear it. And remember that after the convention is over, if things go the way we want them and expect them to go, they will not be our political adversaries; they will be our political allies, fighting the same battle to make sure that your prediction that we'll whip the Republicans in November will come true.

Thank you very much.

NOTE: The President spoke at 6:03 p.m. in the East Room at the White House.

Digest of Other White House Announcements

The following listing includes the President's public schedule and other items of general interest announced by the White House Press Office and not included elsewhere in this issue.

July 19

The President met at the White House with:

—Zbigniew Brzezinski, Assistant to the President for National Security Affairs;

—Richard Queen, recently released as a hostage in Iran, members of Mr. Queen's family, and Deputy Secretary of State Warren M. Christopher.

July 21

The President met at the White House with Dr. Brzezinski.

July 22

The President met at the White House with:

—Dr. Brzezinski;

—Frank B. Moore, Assistant to the President for Congressional Liaison;

—the Democratic congressional leadership;

—Representative Jim Wright and community and civic leaders from Fort Worth, Tex.

The President transmitted an interim report on the Labor Surplus Area Procurement Program to the chairmen of the House and Senate Committees on Armed Services, the House Committee on Small Business, and the Senate Select Committee on Small Business.

The President announced that he has designated Attorney General Benjamin R. Civiletti as a member of the Council on Wage and Price Stability.

July 23

The President met at the White House with:

—Dr. Brzezinski;

—Senator Herman E. Talmadge of Georgia and Representative Thomas S. Foley of Washington, chairmen of the Senate and House agriculture committees, and Secretary of Agriculture Bob Bergland, to discuss farm and agriculture policies;

—Mr. Moore;

—Secretary of State Edmund S. Muskie, Stansfield Turner, Director of Central Intelligence, Jack H. Watson, Jr., Assistant to the President, and Dr. Brzezinski;

—Arthur Burns, former Chairman of the Board of Governors of the Federal Reserve System, to discuss anti-inflation measures.

The President sent memorandums to Secretary of Education Shirley M. Hufstedler and John W. Macy, Jr., Director of the Federal Emergency Management Agency, asking them to ensure their agencies' participation in the Regulatory Council, beginning with the designation of representatives to the Council.

July 24

The President met at the White House with:

—Dr. Brzezinski;

—Mr. Moore;

—Vice President Walter F. Mondale.

The President transmitted to the Congress the fiscal year 1979 annual report of the National Endowment for the Arts and the National Council on the Arts.

The President declared a major disaster for the State of Wisconsin as a result of severe storms and flooding beginning on or about July 15, which caused extensive property damage.

July 25

The President met at the White House with:

—Dr. Brzezinski;

—Vice President Mondale, Secretary of Defense Harold Brown, Secretary Muskie, Dr. Brzezinski, and Mr. Watson;

—Mr. Moore;

—Edward Andersen, master of the National Grange;

—Representative John Hutchinson of West Virginia;

—Mr. and Mrs. Edward Keiser, recipients of Sertoma International's Humanitarian Award;

—a group of his advisers for a budget review session.

The President announced that he has accorded the personal rank of Ambassador to Herbert B. Thompson while he heads the U.S. delegation to the meetings of the Inter-American Council for Education and Culture and the Inter-American Economic and Social Council. Thompson is Deputy United States Permanent Representative to the Organization of American States.

The President left the White House for a weekend stay at Camp David, Md.

NOMINATIONS SUBMITTED TO THE SENATE

The following list does not include promotions of members of the Uniformed Services, nominations to the Service Academies, or nominations of Foreign Service officers.

Submitted July 23, 1980

WILLIAM JENNINGS DYESS, of Alabama, a Foreign Service officer of Class one, to be an Assistant Secretary of State.

DIEGO C. ASENCIO, of Florida, a Foreign Service officer of Class one, to be Assistant Secretary of State for Consular Affairs.

PETER JON DE VOS, of Florida, a Foreign Service officer of Class three, to be Ambassador Extraordinary and Plenipotentiary of the United States of America to the Republic of Guinea-Bissau and to serve concurrently and without additional compensation as Ambassador Extraordinary and Plenipotentiary of the United States of America to the Republic of Cape Verde.

Submitted July 24, 1980

LESLIE R. GREEN, of Minnesota, to be a Commissioner of the United States Parole Commission for a term of 6 years, vice William E. Amos, term expiring.

Submitted July 25, 1980

WALLACE ORPHESUS GREEN, of the District of Columbia, to be an Assistant Secretary of the Interior, vice John Henry Kyl, resigned.

NORMAN P. RAMSEY, of Maryland, to be United States District Judge for the District of Maryland, vice J. Stanley Blair, deceased.

JAMES ROBERT SMITH, of Florida, to be a member of the Civil Aeronautics Board for the remainder of the term expiring December 31, 1980, vice Richard Joseph O'Melia, resigned.

JAMES ROBERT SMITH, of Florida, to be a member of the Civil Aeronautics Board for the term of 6 years expiring December 31, 1986 (reappointment).

JACOB CLAYMAN, of Maryland, to be a member of the Federal Council on the Aging for a term expiring December 19, 1982, vice Nelson Cruikshank, term expired.

WAYMAN D. PALMER, of Ohio, to be Director of the Office of Self-Help Development and Technical Assistance, National Consumer Cooperative Bank (new position).

CHECKLIST OF WHITE HOUSE PRESS RELEASES

The following listing contains releases of the White House Press Office which are not included in this issue.

Released July 21, 1980

News conference: on the administration's midsession review of the fiscal year 1981 budget—by Charles L. Schultze, Chairman of the Council of Economic Advisers, and James T. McIntyre, Jr., Director of the Office of Management and Budget

Released July 22, 1980

News conference: on the national energy efficiency program—by Anne Wexler and Alonzo L. McDonald, Jr., Assistants to the President, Thomas E. Stelson, Assistant Secretary of Energy for Conservation and Solar Applications, and Kitty Schirmer, Associate Director for Energy and Natural Resources, Domestic Policy Staff

Fact sheet: national energy efficiency program

CHECKLIST—Continued

Released July 24, 1980

News conference: on contacts by the President, Zbigniew Brzezinski, Assistant to the President for National Security Affairs, and Billy Carter with Ali El Houdari of the People's Bureau of the Libyan Diplomatic Mission in Washington, D.C.—by Press Secretary Jody Powell

Announcement: nomination of Norman P. Ramsey to be United States District Judge for the District of Maryland

Released July 25, 1980

Announcement: contract between the Department of Agriculture and the National Rural Water Association to provide assistance to rural water systems

---

ACTS APPROVED BY THE PRESIDENT

Approved July 23, 1980

S. 2009_____ Public Law 96–312
Central Idaho Wilderness Act of 1980.

Tinicum National Environmental Center and Sailors' Snug Harbor

Statement on Signing S. 2382 Into Law. July 26, 1980

I have signed S. 2382, a bill "to provide for additional authorization for appropriations for the Tinicum National Environmental Center."

This bill authorizes additional appropriations of $8.4 million for needed land acquisition and development projects at the Tinicum National Environmental Center near Philadelphia. The administration supports this increased authorization in order to permit completion of land acquisition at the Center and to construct appropriate visitor facilities. I would especially like to thank Congressman Bob Edgar of Pennsylvania for his efforts on behalf of this important wildlife area.

The bill also establishes Federal management of an 80-acre site on Staten Island in New York known as Sailors' Snug Harbor. Upon donation of the property to the United States by the City of New York and conclusion of a cooperative agreement between the Secretary of the Interior and the Snug Harbor Cultural Center, Inc., regarding operation and maintenance of the site, the Secretary is directed to manage the area as a National Wildlife Refuge. Within 2 years of enactment, the Secretary must determine whether the area should be permanently managed as a National Wildlife Refuge by the United States Fish and Wildlife Service or transferred to a more appropriate agency of the Interior Department. The bill authorizes appropriations of $1,750,000 through 1983 for operation and maintenance of the area.

In signing this bill, I must note my concerns over this Snug Harbor provision. As a policy, we must select only the highest priority areas for inclusion in our national recreation and conservation systems. Given the large existing backlog of authorized but unacquired Federal parks, refuges, and other recreation areas, it is especially important that we maintain high standards for selection of these areas.

Sailors' Snug Harbor is an area of primarily local interest, whose use by wildlife is insignificant. It is already owned by a public body, the City of New York, which can administer Snug Harbor for recreation or wildlife purposes as it sees fit. I believe it is not the best policy for the Federal Government to assume responsibility for local recreation areas which are now managed by other units of government. This simply increases Federal budget costs and does not add to the recreation opportunities available to our citizens.

Although I have these concerns about Snug Harbor, I have signed S. 2382 because of the overriding importance of the Tinicum National Environmental Center. I am hopeful, though, that in future deliberations of potential wildlife refuges, the Congress will seriously weigh all of the relevant factors before establishing Federal areas that do not meet the test of national interest.

NOTE: As enacted, S. 2382 is Public Law 96–315, approved July 25.

National Oceanic and Atmospheric Administration and Mississippi River Commission

Nomination of Herbert R. Lippold, Jr., To Be Director of the National Ocean Survey and a Member of the Commission. July 28, 1980

The President today announced that he will nominate Rear Adm. Herbert R. Lippold, Jr., of Atkinson, N.H., to be Director of the National Ocean Survey of the National Oceanic and Atmospheric Administration and to be a member of the Mississippi River Commission. In both positions he would replace Rear Adm. Allan Powell, who has retired. Lippold is currently Acting Director of the National Ocean Survey.

He was born April 9, 1926, in Methuen, Mass. He received a B.S. from New England College in 1949 and a bachelor of civil engineering from the University of New Hampshire in 1950. He served in the U.S. Army Air Corps from 1944 to 1946.

Lippold has been with the National Ocean Survey and its predecessor agency, the Coast and Geodetic Survey, since 1950. He has done research and surveying on land and sea and spent 9 years of sea duty on eight vessels, three of which he commanded. He established a satellite triangulation worldwide network. He has served as Director of the National Ocean Survey Pacific Marine Center and as associate director of the Office of Fleet Operations.

Intergovernmental Advisory Council on Education

Appointment of 20 Members. July 28, 1980

The President today announced the appointment of 20 persons as members of the Intergovernmental Advisory Council on Education. The Council, established by the Department of Education Organization Act, will be responsible for advising the President, the Secretary of Education, and the Congress on intergovernmental policies and relations in education. Those being appointed are:

FRANK BOWE, of Woodmere, N.Y., director of the American Coalition of Citizens with Disabilities.

GENE A. BUDIG, president of West Virginia University and professor of educational administration and journalism.

HENRY STEELE COMMAGER, professor of history at Amherst College and author of numerous books.

RAMON C. CORTINES, superintendent of schools for the Pasadena (California) Unified School District.

RICHARD CARLETON GILMAN, of Los Angeles, president of Occidental College.

ROBERT GRAHAM, Governor of Florida and president-elect of the Education Commission of the States. He will serve as Chairman of this Council.

ROBERT L. HARDESTY, vice chancellor for administration of the University of Texas system.

RICHARD HATCHER, mayor of Gary, Ind.

SANDRA KAY LUCAS, of Pembroke, N.C., who will enter Brigham Young University Law School this fall. She is a member of the National Indian Education Association's executive board.

LUCILLE MAURER, of Silver Spring, Md., a member of the Maryland House of Delegates. She is a member of the Education Commission of the States and is on the executive committee of the National Conference of State Legislatures' Education Committee.

WENDA MOORE, chair of the University of Minnesota Board of Regents.

JUDITH M. OWENS, of Ocean, N.J., a high school mathematics teacher and member of the executive committee of the National Education Association.

CRAIG PHILLIPS, of Raleigh, N.C., North Carolina State superintendent of public instruction.

JESSIE MENIFIELD RATTLEY, a member of the Newport News (Virginia) City Council and president of the National League of Cities.

J. GLENN SCHNEIDER, of Napierville, Ill., a member of the Illinois House of Representatives and chairman of its Elementary and Secondary Education Committee. He is also a high school instructor in history and American government.

Jose E. Serrano, New York State assemblyman from the Bronx. He was a member of the New York Board of Education from 1969 to 1974.

William A. Shea, of New York City, a partner in the law firm of Shea, Gould, Climenko & Casey. He was director of the New York World's Fair Corp., in 1964 and 1965 and is very active in civic affairs.

Abraham Shemtov, of Philadelphia, Pa., director of American Friends of Lubavitch, which coordinates the national public activities of the Lubavitch movement's 60 educational centers.

Daisy W. Thaler, of Louisville, Ky., president of DWT Corp., an investment and management company. She is a former teacher and reading specialist and was a Kentucky State senator for 4 years.

Hiroshi Yamashita, of Honolulu, president of the National School Boards Association and a member of the Hawaii State Board of Education.

White House Coal Advisory Council

Executive Order 12229. July 29, 1980

By the authority vested in me as President by the Constitution of the United States of America and in order to establish, in accordance with the provisions of the Federal Advisory Committee Act, as amended (5 U.S.C. App. I), an advisory committee on matters relating to the use of coal in meeting energy demand in the United States, it is hereby ordered as follows:

1-1. Establishment.

1-101. There is established the White House Coal Advisory Council.

1-102. The Council shall be composed of nine members appointed by the President, none of whom shall be an officer or a full-time employee of the United States Government. The President shall designate one of the members to Chair the Council.

1-2. Functions.

1-201. Whenever requested by the President or the Secretary of Labor, the Council shall advise the President and the Secretary of Labor on matters pertaining to labor-management relations in the coal industry, to mine safety, and to productivity in the coal industry.

1-202. The Council shall, from time to time, advise the President or the Secretary of Labor on other issues when the President or the Secretary specifically request the advice of the Council on a particular matter.

1-3. Administration.

1-301. The Secretary of Labor shall, to the extent permitted by law and subject to the availability of funds, provide the Council with such administrative services, funds, facilities, staff, and other support as may be necessary for the effective performance of its functions.

1-302. Members of the Council shall serve without compensation. While engaged in the work of the Council, members may receive travel expenses, including per diem in lieu of subsistence, as authorized by law (5 U.S.C. 5702 and 5703).

1-4. General Provisions.

1-401. Notwithstanding the provisions of any other Executive order, the functions of the President under the Federal Advisory Committee Act, as amended, (5 U.S.C. App. I), except that of reporting annually to the Congress, which are applicable to the Council, shall be performed by the Secretary of Labor in accordance with the guidelines and procedures established by the Administrator of General Services.

1–402. The Council shall terminate one year from the date of this Order.

JIMMY CARTER

The White House,
July 29, 1980.

[Filed with the Office of the Federal Register, 4:11 p.m., July 29, 1980]

Securities and Exchange Commission

Nomination of Barbara S. Thomas To Be a Member. July 29, 1980

The President today announced that he will nominate Barbara S. Thomas, of New York City, to be a member of the Securities and Exchange Commission for a term expiring June 5, 1985. She would replace Irving Pollack, whose term has expired. Thomas is in general corporate and securities law practice as a partner with the New York firm of Kaye, Scholer, Fierman, Hays & Handler.

She was born December 28, 1946, in New York City. She received a B.A. from the University of Pennsylvania in 1966 and a J.D. from New York University School of Law in 1969.

From 1969 to 1973, Thomas was an associate with the firm of Paul, Weiss, Rifkind, Wharton & Garrison. She joined Kaye, Scholer, Fierman, Hays & Handler as an associate in 1973 and became a partner in 1978.

Thomas is chair of the Corporation Law Committee of the New York City Bar Association and a member of the Committee on Federal Regulation of Securities of the American Bar Association and the Securities Regulation Committee of the New York State Bar Association.

Conference on Security and Cooperation in Europe

Remarks at a Ceremony Commemorating the Fifth Anniversary of the Signing of the Final Act in Helsinki. July 29, 1980

I know Griffin Bell, and I know what a taskmaster he is, so I'm sure you've had a full day already and also a very gratifying day with Secretary Muskie and with Arthur Goldberg, with the distinguished Members of Congress, and with Max Kampelman and your new Chairman, Judge Griffin Bell.

This event which will take place in Madrid is one of the most important of 1980. I'm very pleased that all of you could come to Washington today to meet with the leaders of the delegation. Our public members, about 30 of you, are here in the audience, and you've had a chance to review both the purpose of the Helsinki accords and what we hope to accomplish, working with the other nations, in November of 1980. We will have to rely on you very heavily, not only to represent our Nation and the principles on which it's founded but also, in an evocative way, a clear way, to present our beliefs and our commitments, our principles and our ideals to the rest of the world.

There is opposition abroad, as you well know, to the pursuit of the principles espoused by the 35 nations at Helsinki, and there is some skepticism here at home from others who don't understand the fundamental truth that peace on the one hand and the pursuit of human rights on the other are irrevocably interrelated. Peace and the pursuit of human rights cannot be strengthened one without the other; they cannot be successfully advanced independently of one another. That belief, which we all share, is above party, as the history of the Helsinki process proves. A Republican administration signed the accords, and now a Democratic administration is deeply committed to carrying out those agreements.

The accords embody goals and values in which Americans believe, as human beings who are struggling to build a more decent and a more humane world. The pledges given by the 35 signatories at Helsinki 5 years ago were not lightly undertaken, and they cannot be lightly abandoned or ignored. The document that was signed there, even though it was called the Final Act, was not the end of our work. It was just a fresh start on work that commenced in this Nation more than 200 years ago.

The Madrid meeting this year is designed to assess what progress has been made and, if possible, to speed its pace and to widen the scope of that progress. Like the Belgrade meeting in 1977, attended by some of you, Madrid is an opportunity to look carefully backward and also to permit us to push forward vigorously.

Some have said that we should stay away from Madrid, that we ought to drop out of the Helsinki process. Such ideas spring from ignorance of the meaning of Madrid. Some have even compared the meeting in Madrid to the Moscow Olympics, suggesting that since American athletes chose not to go to Moscow, that American diplomats and citizens should not go to Madrid. This reasoning, of course, is very confused.

As host to the Olympics, the Soviet Union sought to enjoy both the fruits of aggression in Afghanistan and the prestige and the propaganda value of being the host of the Olympics at the same time. American athletes and those of 50 other nations rejected that equation as indecent

and unacceptable. I commend them. They stayed at home, at great sacrifice to themselves, and without them, the Moscow spectacular has become a pathetic spectacle.

But Madrid will not be an aggressor's propaganda festival. The Spanish are the hosts, not the Soviets. The Soviet Union will be there, as the other 34 states will be there—to give an account of the manner in which the commitments at Helsinki have been fulfilled or not fulfilled is the undertaking of the meeting at Madrid. It would certainly please those who are most guilty of violation of the principles of Helsinki, including human rights, to be freed of their obligation to account for their actions before world opinion, which will be focused upon the meeting in Madrid.

There will be no medals awarded in Madrid. It's not a wrestling match or a gymnastic tournament among diplomats. What it will test is the progress made on the international agenda of security and cooperation and the firmness of the principles by which the 35 participants agreed to be bound.

In pursuing the cause of human rights, through the Helsinki accords, there are no shortcuts. The road that we're on is the right one. As the Belgrade meeting was ending, Dante Fascell, who was our congressional chairman at the time, said, and I quote from him: "Advocacy of human rights is not a quick fix. It holds no promise of easy victories." We know that all too well. But this advocacy of human rights, no matter how difficult it might be at times and how much it is scorned at times, must be pursued. And at Madrid it will be pursued, aggressively, persistently, and with the full focus on it of world opinion.

When I became President, as a matter of fact even in my acceptance speech almost exactly a year [4 years] ago, I emphasized our commitment as a nation to human rights as a fundamental tenet on which our foreign policy was based. That commitment of mine is as deep and as important to me today as it was then. It's as central to America's interests now as when our Nation was first born. Then, as now, our commitment to human rights persists in our own country and also worldwide. Beyond Europe, we've sought in Africa, Asia, Latin America to stand behind basic principles of respect for each individual person, for fair trials, for political liberty, and for economic and for social justice. We've made it clear that the United States believes that torture cannot be tolerated under any circumstances and that officially sanctioned, so-called "disappearances" are abhorrent in any society. As we've insisted on the right of free movement everywhere, so we've worked hard to give aid to the world's refugees, compelled to flee from oppression and hardship.

As we have maintained these policies as a government, sometimes they have not had the full support of American citizens. I have often had people come to me and say, "Drop this human rights posture. It's damaging our relationship with such-and-such a dictatorship, where people are being imprisoned and where they are being hidden or where they are being killed." We have maintained our position and will continue to do so.

We pursue these policies because we recognize that both our country and our world are more secure when basic human rights are respected internationally. In pursuing our values, we enhance our own security. Let no one doubt that our words and actions have left their mark on the rest of the world. Many governments have released their political prisoners. Others have lifted states of siege, curtailed indiscriminate arrests, and reduced the use

of torture. We've seen several dictatorships, some of them in this hemisphere, change into democracies, where their present leaders were freely elected by people who did not fear any further political persecution because they expressed themselves as human beings.

And because of our leadership, the defense of human rights now has its rightful place on the world agenda for everyone to see. I doubt that there is a leader on Earth who is frequently not reminded of the human rights of the citizens of that particular country and of the human rights performance of that country's neighbors or others associated with it in other parts of the world. Those who seek to deny individual rights must now answer for their actions, at least among these 35 nations. Those brave men and women struggling for liberty, often against great odds, are no longer alone. In the past, because our Nation turned its head away, they were frequently alone.

In working with the 35 Helsinki states, in North America and in Eastern Europe and in Western Europe, we pursue the same values with great vigor. The Helsinki accords commit the signatories to ease military threats and to ease international tensions, to promote progress and to respect human rights, fundamental freedoms, and the self-determination of peoples. We have never expected an uninterrupted record of progress. The behavior of the Soviet Union, in particular, has dishonored the principles of the Helsinki accords, both inside and outside its own borders.

The Soviet invasion of Afghanistan and the increasingly brutal occupation of that once free nation can no more be reconciled with the Helsinki pledges than it can be reconciled with the Charter of the United Nations. For invading a neighbor, the Soviet Union already stands condemned before the world. A hundred and four members of the United Nations condemned the Soviet Union and demanded the immediate withdrawal of its occupying troops. If they are still there at the time of the Madrid conference, we will continue the pressure for the withdrawal of those Soviet troops.

As many of you know vividly, because of the experiences of your own family and those people whom you love, Soviet authorities have also intensified at home their repression of the freedoms which they pledged at Helsinki. To promote the banishment into internal exile of Andre Sakharov, a great scientist and a great humanist, is the best known, but sadly not the only instance of such violations of the Helsinki commitment made by the Soviet Union.

More than 40 courageous men and women are now in prison or in exile just because they worked in private groups to promote the Helsinki agreement and to encourage the Soviet Union to live up to its pledges. Now they are silenced, but in Madrid, no one can silence their cause. And we will make sure—[*applause*].

Although I do have importunities from some of our own citizens to lessen our commitment and our public posture concerning human rights, I have had from those who are in exile or who are persecuted in foreign countries unanimous messages, sometimes of a highly secret nature: "Mr. President, do not abandon us; do not abandon the commitment of the United States to protect our rights."

Madrid will be a sober meeting. The talk will be frank and straightforward, but we hope without polemics. We will be seeking progress, not propaganda. There is some progress, of course, which we can welcome, and we will be glad to do so. Some confidence-building measures have been implemented.

The Helsinki accords have given some impetus to the long-term process of breaking down East-West barriers [relations] [1] and easing the flow of people and the flow of ideas across frontiers that were once almost completely closed. For example, thousands of people emigrated to the West last year from East European countries, in accord with the Helsinki undertakings. There have been recent efforts by a number of states to resolve outstanding family reunification problems with us, and we welcome those also.

The Helsinki provisions have also helped Soviet Jews to emigrate, although the encouraging record level set in 1979 is being reduced this year. At Madrid, we will seek an explanation for that decline and a commitment by the Soviet Union to reverse it.

I might say now, as I approach the close of my remarks to you, that on all these issues at Madrid we can count on the support of the great majority of participants. This is not always the United States position in international fora. The others share the basic philosophy of international relations that underly the Helsinki accords. Indeed, the effort to negotiate the accords originally, and now to assure their implementation, has made Western Europe and the United States recognize all the more vividly how much we share political and moral values and interests, in a time when there is so much glib talk, most of it ill advised and erroneous, about Western disharmony. The Madrid meeting can give a clear expression to our unity on fundamental values and on fundamental goals, and with that support, we can continue at Madrid to pursue the aims to which we committed ourselves at Helsinki.

---

[1] White House correction.

We want to encourage progress in human rights performance by the Soviet Union and its allies, and we have no hesitation about submitting our own record to examination by others at Madrid. We are not perfect; we don't claim that the United States is perfect. But we're making a strong and continuing effort to improve, because preserving and extending human rights is the heart and soul of our whole system in this country.

At Madrid, we will use the CSCE process to break down even more the barriers to human contacts between the East and the West, to help with the reunification of families, to help with the movement of people and ideas and the resolution of immigration issues.

We'll try, as part of a balanced result, to achieve practical progress in the military security field.

The Helsinki session should not become primarily an arms control forum at Madrid, but the United States is prepared to test the possibility of achieving significant, verifiable, and comprehensive confidence-building measures relating directly or indirectly to weaponry, which can help and to enhance mutual security desired in East and West Europe. Madrid gives us an important opportunity to restate both our genuine desire for better East-West relations and our firm belief that the principles of reciprocity and mutual restraint are there, on which workable ties can be built.

There will be sharp differences at Madrid between the values we espouse and those which the Communist nations will seek to advance, but we will not go to Madrid looking for conflict. We approach that meeting, instead, eager for progress, determined not to abandon our principles in any instance, determined to put our views forward in the most forceful possible manner, and committed to only one contest—the struggle to advance freedom and, through freedom, mutual security.

The Helsinki accords, to us, hold a promise of a freer, more humane, and thus a more secure Europe, based not just on superpower accommodation but on the fundamental principles of international conduct. These principles require that states earn the respect of their neighbors by treating their citizens with full respect for their rights and dignity as persons. My own faith in the ultimate outcome of this struggle is undimmed. Our Nation's role must never be in doubt.

One of the best ways to express this commitment, I'd like to say in closing, is to quote from the words of Archibald MacLeish: "There are those who will say that the liberation of humanity, the freedom of man and mind, is nothing but a dream. They are right. It is. It's the American dream."

NOTE: The President spoke at 2:30 p.m. to representatives of ethnic and human rights organizations in the East Room at the White House.

In his opening remarks, the President referred to Arthur J. Goldberg, Chairman of the U.S. delegation to the 1977 Belgrade meeting of the Conference, and to Chairman Griffin B. Bell and Cochairman Max M. Kampelman of the U.S. delegation to the Conference review meeting to be held in Madrid.

On the same day, the White House announced that the following persons will serve as the public members of the U.S. delegation to the review meeting in Madrid:

MRS. OWANAH ANDERSON, Wichita Falls, Tex.;
LOUIS BAKER, Los Angeles, Calif.;
REV. IMRE BARTALAN, New Brunswick, N.J.;
WILLIAM BORDERS, Washington, D.C.;
HONORABLE CLIFFORD CASE, Washington, D.C.;
SOL CHAIKIN, New York, N.Y.;
RAY CHESONIS, Cinnaminson, N.J.;
BEN EPSTEIN, New York, N.Y.;
MAYOR DIANNE FEINSTEIN, San Francisco, Calif.;
MRS. ROBERT TRENT JONES, Woodside, Calif.;
NORMAN KEE, New York, N.Y.;
AMBASSADOR LOU LERNER, Chicago, Ill.;

STANLEY LOWELL, New York, N.Y.;
THEODORE MANN, Philadelphia, Pa.;
EDWARD MARDIGIAN, Birmingham, Mich.;
PROFESSOR ALBERT A. MAVRINACK, Waterville,
  Maine;
ALOYSIUS A. MAZEWSKI, Chicago, Ill.;
JULIUS MICHAELSON, Providence, R.I.;
MRS. BETKA PAPANEK, Scarsdale, N.Y.;
HONORABLE VAL PHILLIPS, Madison, Wis.;
DR. DAVID PREUS, Minneapolis, Minn.;
ED ROMERO, Albuquerque, N. Mex.;
ORVILLE SCHELL, New York, N.Y.;
MARILYN SMITH, Miami, Fla.;
MYROSLAW SMORODSKY, Rutherford, N.J.;
M. D. "LITA" TARACIDO, New York, N.Y.;
HENRY TAUB, Tenafly, N.J.;
BEN WATTENBERG, Washington, D.C.;
MRS. ADDIE WYATT, Washington, D.C.;
MRS. ROSALIND WYMAN, Los Angeles, Calif.

Billy Carter's Activities With the Libyan Government

Remarks Concerning the Disclosure of Administration Actions. July 29, 1980

THE PRESIDENT. The American people deserve complete answers to questions that have been raised about my actions with regard to my brother's relationship with Libya. The concern which any such relationship might arouse is heightened in this case by the frequent and sharp differences in policy between the Government of Libya and the Government of the United States. I'm eager to use whatever legitimate forum is available at the earliest opportunity to answer any questions and to lay all those concerns to rest.

I've instructed those who work with me in the Government to cooperate fully in presenting a full and complete description of the actions of our administration in this matter. I have insisted for the last 2 weeks that relevant facts be made public as soon as possible, even when those facts might prove embarrassing or might re-

quire clarification of incomplete information already distributed.

I will complete and present to the Senate subcommittee by early next week the report which it has requested. I'm willing to respond and I'm eager to respond in person to further questions from members of that subcommittee, in a manner consistent with the responsibilities of my office, at any time in the future—the sooner the better. I will also present that report to the public and respond to questions from the press on its contents.

I have no doubt that complete disclosure of the facts will clearly demonstrate that at no time did my brother influence me in my decisions toward Libya or the policies of this Government concerning Libya. And I'm convinced that the facts will make clear that neither I nor anyone acting in my behalf ever sought to influence or to interfere in the investigation of my brother by the Department of Justice.

Thank you.

REPORTER. Mr. President, are you content to wait until after the convention to make your personal appearance at a hearing?

THE PRESIDENT. I'll be eager to answer those questions next week, and Jody [Powell] will follow up shortly.

NOTE: The President spoke at 4:46 p.m. to reporters assembled in the Briefing Room at the White House.

National Endowment for the Arts

Appointment of Seven Members to the National Council on the Arts. July 29, 1980

The President today announced seven persons whom he will nominate to be members of the National Council on the Arts. They are:

KURT HERBERT ADLER, general director of the San Francisco Opera and founder and artistic supervisor of Western Opera Theater, Spring Opera of San Francisco, and Brown Bag Opera;

MARGO ALBERT, a member of the board of directors of the Music Center, Los Angeles, and of Plaza de la Raza, East Los Angeles Chicano Educational and Cultural Center;

ROBERT JOFFREY, founder and artistic director of the City Center Joffrey Ballet;

ERICH LEINSDORF, retired conductor, who was music director of the Boston Symphony Orchestra from 1962 to 1969 and director of the Metropolitan Opera from 1957 to 1962;

TONI MORRISON, author of "Song of Solomon" and other books and a part-time editor with Random House;

I. M. PEI, award-winning architect;

LIDA ROGERS, executive director of the Mississippi Arts Commission and chairman of the Southern Arts Federation.

President's Council on Physical Fitness and Sports

Designation of Alfred J. McGuire as Chairman.   July 29, 1980

The President today announced that he has designated Alfred J. McGuire as Chairman of the President's Council on Physical Fitness and Sports. McGuire has been a member of this Council since 1978.

He is a college basketball commentator for NBC. He was head basketball coach for Marquette University from 1964 to 1977 and athletic director from 1973 to 1977. He played for the New York Knicks from 1951 to 1954.

Budget Deferrals

Message to the Congress.   July 30, 1980

To the Congress of the United States:

In accordance with the Impoundment Control Act of 1974, I herewith report two revisions to previously transmitted deferrals increasing the amount deferred by $137 thousand. These items affect programs in the Department of Defense and the International Communication Agency.

The details of the deferrals are contained in the attached reports.

JIMMY CARTER

The White House,
    July 30, 1980.

NOTE: The attachments detailing the deferrals are printed in the FEDERAL REGISTER of August 1, 1980.

Strategy Council on Drug Abuse

Appointment of Two Members.   July 30, 1980

The President today announced the appointment of two persons as members of the Strategy Council, an advisory body on drug abuse. They are:

THOMAS B. KIRKPATRICK, JR., of Oak Park, Ill., executive director of the Illinois Dangerous Drugs Commission and a former coordinator of criminal justice programs for the Drug Abuse Council;

CLAUDE H. REESE, of New Orleans, director of the City of New Orleans Bureau of Drug Affairs.

United States Summer Olympic Team

Remarks at the Medal Presentation Ceremony.   July 30, 1980

Mr. Speaker, Senator Byrd, members of the U.S. Olympic Committee, distinguished American visitors, and particularly the members of the United States Olympic team:

The members of the team and I will be seeing more of each other this afternoon in an informal way at the White House itself, but I came here to express by appreciation and my respect in an official and more formal way.

As President I have had the opportunity to recognize outstanding athletic ability. A few minutes ago I welcomed to the White House, to honor, two beautiful young women, Miss U.S.A. and Miss Universe. I've recognized other men and women of outstanding scholastic achievement, and I've recognized Americans of great heroism, those who have demonstrated their love of country through acts of nobility and determination and of courage.

The recognition for excellence of achievement, for nobility, patriotism, and courage are an exciting part of a President's life. Today I have a unique ability and an opportunity to honor Americans who qualify in all these categories—the United States Olympic Team.

The medals that you will receive today recognizes a notable achievement—your selection as a member of the United States Olympic team. This achievement would be commendable under any circumstance, but the congressional medal will have a special meaning. It is a sign for all time, not just of your athletic excellence, but also of the dignity and the resilience that you've demonstrated under extraordinary and difficult circumstances. It's a sign of your courage in the face of adversity. Ernest Hemingway once defined courage as "grace under pressure." You, the members of the U.S. Olympic team, have displayed this kind of courage.

Some people live their whole lives without ever devoting themselves to one major attempt, one chance for outstanding achievement. It's hard for that kind of person to appreciate what it means to endure pain and exhaustion and personal sacrifice through years of intense training and to give not just your time and your energy but your entire self to achieving a great goal. To go through all that and then to suffer defeat in athletic competition is one thing, but to have your chances dashed by a brutal act of aggression and a threat to world peace, something that really has nothing to do with your own efforts, can be an even harder blow.

The overwhelming call by the Congress for a strong response and the decision of the United States Olympic Committee and by 50 other nations not to participate in the Moscow Olympics was a vital and indispensable reaction to the Soviet invasion of Afghanistan. It was the only correct course of action for our Nation.

If our Olympic team had been in Moscow these past days, with all the pageantry and spectacle, it would have been impossible for us credibly to maintain our leadership on the world scale in our continuing effort to seek freedom in Afghanistan. No matter what else we had done, no matter what other step we had taken, our participation would have sent an unmistakable message to the Soviet Government, the Soviet people, and to people all over the world. That message would have been this: The United States might not like the idea of aggression and the deprivation of freedom for people, but when it really comes down to it, we are willing to join the parade as if nothing had happened. For the sake of world peace, we cannot and could not allow such a message to be conveyed.

I know that some Olympic athletes disagree with the decision not to compete. You have disagreed with grace and with dignity and, I believe, with credit to yourselves. All of you have maintained arduous training. You've won your place on the U.S. Olympic team against high-caliber competition. You've come here to accept not simply the applause but the gratitude of a nation for what you've done and for the course that you have set for your lives.

All of you, in your own way, have been willing, eager to look to the future, to new challenges. Today I want to join you in looking to the future.

The Soviet invasion and its embarrassing consequences have had an unexpected byproduct. Major national attention has been focused on the importance of the Olympics, on amateur athletics, on the challenges confronting the amateur athletes, and on commensurate human freedom. We're taking advantage of this increased public concern. Congress has appropriated, as you well know, a substantial matching grant for the Olympic Committee to support the amateur sports movement in this country and to prepare for the 1984 Olympic games.

As I did when our Winter Olympic team came back to the White House, today I urge Americans again, from all walks of life, from all parts of our Nation, to demonstrate your appreciation for what you represent in this team by supporting and contributing to the United States Olympic Committee. I know that many of you on the team will lend your talents to make these efforts successful. No other nation on Earth has so many gifted and dedicated athletes and coaches, able to give so much to the growth of physical fitness and sports programs throughout the world, as do we here in the United States.

In closing, I would like to say a personal thing to the members of the team itself. For your excellence in competition, for your personal courage, for your demonstrated love of country, and for your enhancement of freedom throughout the world, I commend you. It is no exaggeration to say that you have done more to uphold the Olympic ideal than any other group of athletes in our history. That is very important, yet the meaning of your action goes far beyond even that.

Future generations of Americans will know what you did, not just from the record books but from the history books. They will know that in the year 1980 you did as much as any other group on Earth, large or small, in any nation, to hold high the banner of liberty and peace. I salute you for it, and the American people salute you for it also.

Thank you from the bottom of my heart. God bless every one of you.

NOTE: The President spoke at 12:02 p.m. on the steps of the Capitol.

United States Ambassador to Honduras

Nomination of Jack Robert Binns.
July 30, 1980

The President today announced that he will nominate Jack Robert Binns, of Spokane, Wash., to be Ambassador Extraordinary and Plenipotentiary of the United States to Honduras. He would replace Mari-Luci Jaramillo, who is being appointed Deputy Assistant Secretary of State for Inter-American Affairs. Binns has been Deputy Chief of Mission in San José, Costa Rica, since 1979.

He was born May 13, 1933, in Eugene, Oreg. He received a B.S. from the U.S. Naval Academy in 1956. He served in the U.S. Navy from 1952 to 1962.

Binns joined the Foreign Service in 1962 and was posted in Guatemala, La Paz, and at the State Department. He was a labor trainee at Harvard University in 1966–67. He was posted in San Salvador from 1967 to 1971, as labor officer, then political officer.

From 1971 to 1974, Binns was an international relations officer at the State Department. From 1974 to 1979, he was political officer in London.

United States Metric Board

Nomination of Four Members.
July 30, 1980

The President today announced that he will nominate four persons to be members of the United States Metric Board. They are:

ALFREDO A. CANTU, of Denver, Colo., owner of Cantu Advertising and Graphics;

BRUCE PAUL JOHNSON, of Reno, Nev., chairman of the electrical engineering department at the University of Nevada (reappointment);

JAMES M. ROSSER, of Bradbury, Calif., president of California State University at Los Angeles and a professor of health care management there;

DENNIS R. SMITH, of Middleboro, Mass., a high school mathematics teacher and metric coordinator for the Middleboro Public Schools (reappointment).

Drug Enforcement Administration

Executive Order 12230.   July 30, 1980

COMPETITIVE STATUS FOR SPECIAL AGENTS OF THE DRUG ENFORCEMENT ADMINISTRATION

By the authority vested in me as President of the United States of America by Sections 3301 and 3302 of Title 5 and Section 301 of Title 3 of the United States Code, it is hereby ordered as follows:

1–101. Criminal investigators of the Drug Enforcement Administration, Department of Justice, who have Schedule A or B appointments and who have completed three years of fully satisfactory service may be converted noncompetitively to career or career-conditional appointments, if they meet qualifications and other requirements established by the

Director of the Office of Personnel Management.

1–102. The Director of the Office of Personnel Management shall prescribe such regulations as may be necessary to implement this Order.

JIMMY CARTER

The White House,
　July 30, 1980.

[Filed with the Office of the Federal Register, 8:45 a.m., July 31, 1980]

Billy Carter's Activities With the Libyan Government

White House Statement.   July 30, 1980

We have noted the press reports that, according to FBI memoranda delivered by the Justice Department to the House Committees on the Judiciary and Foreign Affairs, Billy Carter told the FBI that the President had shown Billy Carter State Department cables concerning Libya and that Billy Carter has possession of such cables. We have not seen the FBI reports referred to and cannot comment on the accuracy of press reports concerning them.

The President's best recollection is that the only State Department cables he has ever discussed with Billy Carter are low classification cables from our Embassy in Libya, reporting on Billy Carter's first trip to Libya in September 1978 and indicating that the trip had gone well from the Embassy's point of view. The President does not now recall whether he saw the texts of these cables himself or heard about them from others. He does not now recall showing the texts to Billy Carter or giving him copies.

NOTE: C. Ray Jenkins, Special Assistant to the President, read the statement to reporters assembled in the Press Secretary's office at the White House.

United States Summer Olympic Team

Remarks at a White House Reception for Members of the Team.   July 30, 1980

If I could have everybody's attention for just a moment, the first thing I would like to do is to ask Mr. Walter Haas, who's head of Levi Strauss, to come up here so everybody can thank him for his generosity—Is he here?—and also Mrs. Haas. While they are coming up, I would like to say that the uniforms they've given out are just beautiful.

All of you are standing in front of one of the world's symbols of freedom and democracy, and that's our White House, on my left. Every President of this Nation has lived here except George Washington, and it was built before the second President left office.

All of you are part of a great team, assembled here together, but we know that your achievements in the past, present, and future are because of your own individual courage, commitment, and initiative. You'll be going from here to compete in international competition in the future. I know, because of your own excellence and commitment, that you'll do well and continue to represent our Nation in the finest possible way.

I want to say again that this has been a day of opportunity for me, as President of our great Nation, and for the Members of Congress, representing the legislative branch, to pay our tribute to you on behalf of more than 220 million Americans, who share with you a deep commitment to individuality, to freedom, to personal achievement, and to liberty not only for ourselves but for others around the world.

You have honored me by letting me shake your hand, and you have honored the White House and all it stands for by representing our Nation so well. God bless you. I love every one of you.

Thank you very much.

Here's Mr. Haas, who's been so nice to all of you. And I think you might want to just express your pleasure and your thanks to him.

Rosalynn asked me to announce that the White House is open, if you'd like to visit it. In the meantime, of course, we have refreshments and things for you and your parents and your friends.

Thank you very much.

If the employees of Levi Strauss would come to the stage, we'd like to see you just a moment. The employees of Levi Strauss, who came into Washington to help with the fittings of the uniforms and the clothing—if you'd just come to the stage for a moment, we'd appreciate it.

NOTE: The President spoke at 5:46 p.m. on the South Lawn of the White House.

Later in the evening, the President and Mrs. Carter attended a benefit at the Kennedy Center for the athletes.

Commission on Presidential Scholars

Appointment of Four Members.   July 31, 1980

The President today announced the appointment of four persons as members of the Commission on Presidential Scholars. They are:

BEVERLY JOYCE BIMES, of St. Louis, Mo., an English teacher at Hazelwood East High School, who was named Teacher of the Year for 1980.

FRANCES SNOW LEE, of Wichita, Kans., who is currently in a masters degree program in education at Wichita State University. She was a television teacher and production supervisor of "Romper Room School" on KAKE television for 12 years and is active in civic affairs.

SCOTT D. THOMSON, of Reston, Va., executive director of the National Association of Secondary School Principals, who has also served as superintendent of a school district and as a university lecturer in school administration.

RAFAEL RIVERA GARCIA, director of the Office of Cultural Affairs, La Fortaleza, San Juan, Puerto Rico, and a former assistant director of the University of Puerto Rico Museum.

National Commission on Libraries and Information Science

Nomination of Three Members and Designation of Chairman.　July 31, 1980

The President today announced that he will nominate three persons to be members of the National Commission on Libraries and Information Science. They are:

CHARLES W. BENTON, of Evanston, Ill., chairman and chief executive officer of Films, Inc., a subsidiary of Encyclopaedia Britannica Films which distributes 16-millimeter films, and president of Public Media, Inc. (reappointment). On confirmation by the Senate, Benton will be redesignated Chairman.

GORDON M. AMBACH, of Newtonville, N.Y., president of the University of the State of New York and commissioner of education.

PAULETTE H. HOLAHAN, of New Orleans, La., chairman of the board of directors of the New Orleans Public Library, a member of the Louisiana State Library Commission and the board of directors of the National Urban Libraries Council, and national vice president of the American Library Trustee Association.

Uniformed Services University of the Health Sciences

Nomination of Five Members of the Board of Regents.　July 31, 1980

The President today announced that he will nominate five persons to be members of the Board of Regents of the Uniformed Services University of the Health Sciences. They are:

LAURO F. CAVAZOS, president of Texas Tech University, former dean and professor of anatomy at Tufts University School of Medicine;

ROBERT H. EBERT, president of the Milbank Memorial Fund, former dean of Harvard Medical School, and president of the Harvard Medical Center;

EUGENE M. FARBER, of Portola Valley, Calif., professor of dermatology and chairman of the department of dermatology at Stanford University School of Medicine;

CARO E. LUHRS, of Washington, D.C., a private practitioner of medicine, owner of a health care consulting firm, and former medical adviser to the Secretary of Agriculture;

WILLIAM R. ROY, of Topeka, Kans., a private practitioner in obstetrics and gynecology, former Member of Congress, and a member of the Institute of Medicine of the National Academy of Sciences.

United States Advisory Commission on Public Diplomacy

Nomination of Leonard Silverstein To Be a Member.　July 31, 1980

The President today announced that he will nominate Leonard Silverstein, of Bethesda, Md., for reappointment as a member of the United States Advisory Commission on Public Diplomacy.

Silverstein is senior partner in the Washington law firm of Silverstein and Mullens. He is executive director of the Commission on Private Philanthropy and Public Needs and serves as chairman of the advisory board and chief editor for "Tax Management."

Council on Wage and Price Stability

Message to the Congress Transmitting a Report. July 31, 1980

To the Congress of the United States:

In accordance with Section 5 of the Council on Wage and Price Stability Act, as amended, I hereby transmit to the Congress the twenty-first quarterly report of the Council on Wage and Price Stability. The report contains a description of the Council's activities during the fourth quarter of 1979 in monitoring both prices and wages in the private sector and various Federal Government activities that may lead to higher costs and prices without creating commensurate benefits. It discusses Council reports, analyses, and filings before Federal regulatory agencies. It also describes the Council's activities of monitoring wages and prices as part of the anti-inflation program.

The Council on Wage and Price Stability will continue to play an important role in supplementing fiscal and monetary policies by calling public attention to wage, price and other developments that could be of concern to American consumers.

JIMMY CARTER

The White House,
July 31, 1980.

Inter-American Foundation

Nomination of Four Members of the Board of Directors. July 31, 1980

The President today announced that he will nominate four persons to be members of the Board of Directors of the Inter-American Foundation. They are:

GUY FELIZ ERB, of San Francisco, Calif., Deputy Director of the U.S. International Development Cooperation Agency (IDCA). Erb was on the National Security Council staff before being appointed to IDCA earlier this year.

DORIS B. HOLLEB, of Chicago, Ill., director of the University of Chicago's Metropolitan Institute, senior research associate at its Center for Urban Studies, and associate professorial lecturer in the College. She is an economist and urban affairs consultant.

LUIS GUERRERO NOGALES, of Northridge, Calif., senior vice president of Golden West Broadcasters. He is a former White House Fellow and was chairman of the board of directors of the Mexican-American Legal Defense Fund in 1979–80.

PAULA STERN, of Washington, D.C., a Commissioner of the U.S. International Trade Commission (ITC). She was with the Carnegie Endowment for International Peace before being appointed to the ITC in 1978.

Overseas Private Investment Corporation

Nomination of E. G. Koury To Be a Member of the Board of Directors. July 31, 1980

The President today announced that he will nominate E. G. Koury, of Lorain, Ohio, to be a member of the Board of Directors of the Overseas Private Investment Corporation. He would replace Wallace Bennett, whose term has expired, and would be appointed to an additional term expiring in 1983. Koury has practiced law in Lorain since 1955.

He was born August 1, 1928, in Lorain. He received a B.S. in commerce from Ohio University in 1950 and an LL.B. from the University of Cincinnati College of Law in 1953. He served in the U.S. Army from 1953 to 1955.

Koury has served as special counsel in Lorain County to the attorney general of Ohio. He is active in civic affairs.

Advisory Committee on Trade Negotiations

Appointment of 10 Members. July 31, 1980

The President today announced the appointment of 10 persons as members of the the Advisory Committee on Trade Negotiations. They are:

ROBERT B. DELANO, of Warsaw, Va., president of the American Farm Bureau Federation.

FRANK DROZAK, acting president of the Seafarers International Union and president of the AFL–CIO Maritimes Trades Department.

JACK FELGENHAUER, of Spokane, Wash., president of the National Association of Wheat Growers.

RUSSELL L. HANLIN, of Pasadena, Calif., president and chief executive officer of Sunkist Growers, Inc., an agricultural marketing cooperative representing 6,500 citrus growers.

RICHARD R. RIVERS, of Chevy Chase, Md., a member of the law firm of Akin, Gump, Hauer, and Feld, who served for 2 years as General Counsel of the Office of the Special Representative for Trade Negotiations and headed the U.S. team that negotiated the Agreement on Subsidies and Countervailing Measures in the Tokyo round of multilateral trade negotiations.

EDWARD L. ROMERO, of Albuquerque, N. Mex., president and founder of Solar America, Inc., and ELR Enterprises. Solar America designs, manufactures, and installs alternative energy systems; ELR provides consultant services in the areas of marketing and public relations.

ELSPETH ROSTOW, dean of the Lyndon B. Johnson School of Public Affairs at the University of Texas and professor of government (reappointment).

J. STANFORD SMITH, of Greenwich, Conn., chairman and chief executive officer of the International Paper Co. (reappointment).

GEORGE W. STONE, of Choctaw, Okla., president of the National Farmers Union and chairman of Green Thumb, Inc., which employs elderly rural citizens to carry out beautification and environmental programs.

ALAN WM. WOLFF, of Washington, D.C., a partner in the Washington law firm of Verner, Liipfert, Bernhard and McPherson. He served as deputy special representative for trade negotiations from 1977 to 1979. He was the first chairman of the 20-nation International Steel Committee of the Organization for Economic Cooperation and Development.

International Solvent Refined Coal II Agreement

Remarks on Signing the Agreement. July 31, 1980

THE PRESIDENT. *Ambassador Hermes, Ambassador Okawara, Senator Byrd, Senator Randolph, Governor Rockefeller, Congressman Staggers, Mr. Chairman and other Members of the West Virginia delegation, distinguished members of our own American community who have been so instrumental in making the progress which we commemorate today with a very important and significant event in the history of energy security for our country:*

I'm extremely proud to come before you today to participate in the signing of documents between three great nations— the United States of America, the Federal Republic of Germany, and the great nation of Japan. This event continues the spirit of the economic summits—which have been conducted primarily in Tokyo last year and in Venice this year—indicating the awareness among the industrialized and developed countries of our world, energy-consuming nations, of the importance of dealing with the energy problem on two basic levels.

One is to enhance conservation, to eliminate the waste of energy, to be more economical in the use of all forms of energy. I've just seen this morning the data on the first 5 months of this year: American imports of foreign oil are down 15 percent compared to the same 5 months of 1979. This is an extraordinary conservation achievement; with no derogation to our guests from other countries, much better, I might say, than any other consuming nation. It's because of the concerted effort of many Americans, and it's because of the fact that in the past we had not made adequate progress in conservation.

The other element of reducing imports is to develop additional forms of energy which can be derived from untapped natural resources in our country. This event this morning will commemorate the production of clean-burning fuel from high-sulphur coal, a major plant to be located in the State of West Virginia. Later, after the signing ceremony, I will introduce Senator Byrd, who has been so instrumental in making possible this event. I might say that synthetic fuels programs, the use of solar power, the production of gasohol and other forms of energy from growing plants, and geothermal supplies, shale, coal, will be greatly enhanced in the future as a source of energy for our country.

We are blessed in the United States by having very large reserve supplies of energy, unlike even some of our close allies and friends. Last week we signed an agreement to help guarantee a loan for the Great Plains Coal Liquefaction Plant in North Dakota. This will produce, as a matter of fact, gas from very low quality lignite, similar to but quite distinct from the production plant in West Virginia, which will use high sulphur coal to produce liquid fuels.

These are the kinds of new projects that can stimulate the American economy, provide large numbers of jobs for our people, and give us the excitement and the prospect of a notable technological and economic achievement. The plant in West Virginia, which will be organized and financed jointly by our three nations represented here this morning, will produce the equivalent of 7 million barrels of oil each year—that's 7 million barrels fewer that we will have to import from overseas in oil.

It will also create a lot of jobs—thirty-five hundred direct construction jobs in West Virginia alone. This does not include those who will operate the plant permanently. And of course, it will also use 2 million tons of coal each year in an environmentally acceptable way, I might add, and this also of course means many more jobs for the coal mining industry.

This is a precursor of wonderful things to come. It's part of our National Energy Program of which we're very proud. It includes the Energy Security Act which I signed on the South Lawn of the White House grounds not too long ago. It requires cooperation from all those in our own Nation who are involved in the production and consumption of energy, and that includes almost every single American citizen. And of course, this opportunity to share the responsibilities and the benefits with the great nations of Germany and Japan adds an excitement and the prospects of further progress to an already wonderful occasion.

Again, I want to express my thanks not only to the Government representatives of

Germany and Japan, but to the business representatives and the scientists and others who will benefit directly from this project. This means a commitment to make more fuel and to face the future, a troubled, sometimes uncertain future, with a reassurance in our own capability and the resources with which God has blessed us, and also with a reassurance of a close alliance, not only political and military to guarantee our security in those areas, but economic alliance to guarantee the economic security of our countries.

I want to express also my total confidence in the skill and the resources and the courage of the citizens of our nations who look to the future not with doubt and trepidation and fear, but with courage and with confidence that we'll have a better life, a brighter life, a more exciting life for all our citizens in the years to come.

Thank you very much.

[At this point, the President, Ambassador Peter Hermes, and Ambassador Yoshio Okawara signed the agreement.]

I'd like to ask the Ambassador of the Federal Republic of Germany to say a few remarks if he will.

AMBASSADOR HERMES. *Mr. President, distinguished guests:*

Today is an important day for trilateral cooperation between the Federal Republic of Germany, the United States of America, and Japan. Our signing today of a number of agreements in connection with the SRC–II Project is a symbolic act. It stands for the great efforts our three countries are making individually, as well as jointly, to drastically change our energy policies.

The main thrust of this policy is to substantially decrease our dependence on the import of foreign oil. You, Mr. President, have been successful in your continuous efforts to obtain the necessary legislation for the implementation of these policies. My own Government and the Government of Japan have been pursuing the same aim in a similar fashion.

The SRC–II Project is a project designed to demonstrate the feasibility of coal liquefaction technology by jointly establishing and jointly operating a large facility in this country with important scientific, technical, and financial contributions by all three participating countries.

I'm happy to note that my country was among the first, if not the first, to successfully use the coal conversion technology more than a generation ago. Today, the Federal Republic of Germany is pursuing research and development for the use of coal conversion technology on a much broader scale. At the present time, we have 10 pilot plants for coal conversion under construction or in operation and as many as 14 additional coal conversion projects in the planning stage. Of these, the SRC–II Project is by far the largest one. It has been termed the most ambitious international energy project ever to be undertaken, and my Government is committed, together with our American and Japanese partners, to making it a full success benefiting all three countries.

Thank you very much.

THE PRESIDENT. Now I'd like to call on the Ambassador of Japan to make a few remarks.

AMBASSADOR OKAWARA. *Mr. President, distinguished guests, ladies and gentlemen:*

It is my great pleasure and honor to have signed with you, Mr. President, the agreement between the Government of Japan and the Government of the United States of America on cooperation in coal liquefaction using the SRC–II process. The SRC–II Project is a most important one in the field of coal conversion, in which the initial emphasis has been placed along with fusion under the Japan-United States energy R&D cooperation agreement.

The 1980's will be an epoch-making decade when the industrialized countries take firm steps towards ending their excessive dependence on oil and thus strengthening the foundation of the economies. In this new challenge it is indeed significant that the United States, the Federal Republic of Germany, and Japan will cooperate with the utmost advanced technologies in the largest coal liquefaction project in the world.

When the project proceeds satisfactorily as expected, Japan will come to import coal-derived liquid fuels converted from the abundant coal resources of the United States. This will bring about the situation to be welcomed by the U.S. coal industry over the long run, and from the long-term point of view will contribute to enhancing the U.S.-Japan trade relations.

Furthermore, it is anticipated that the technology developed through this project could be applied to the rich coal resources in such countries as Australia and China. Such future development would expand the present tripartite initiative into broader international cooperation.

We may be confronted by some technological and other unforeseeable difficulties when we proceed on the long-term project of this giant scale. However, the special cooperation that unifies us together in this project will no doubt allow us to surmount such difficulties. It is now clearly recognized in forums like the economic summit or the International Energy Agency that the present difficult energy situation can be greatly improved by concerted effort in the promotion of alternative energy development and the acceleration of new energy technologies, as was clearly stated in the recent economic summit declaration. I am convinced that this project will prove successful with such international endorsement and blessings.

In closing, on behalf of all the people and institutions in Japan involved in this imaginative venture, I wish to express my sincere respect for your initiative, Mr. President, and for your tremendous effort taken toward the realization of this project.

Thank you very much.

THE PRESIDENT. Before I introduce Senator Byrd, I'd like to ask Senator Jennings Randolph to please stand, and Congressmen Staggers and Nick Joe Rahall and Congressman Hutchinson— Is he here? [*Applause*] Thank you.

I might say that if all the citizens of our country who recognize the value of coal and the value of American employment were as enthusiastic as this group that I've just introduced, plus our Majority Leader, we wouldn't have any unemployment in the coal industry, and we would have long been much more, further along our way toward energy independence than we are now. I'm deeply grateful to all of you for what you have done in the past and are doing at the present time to give our Nation energy security leading towards a better future for us all.

Now, it's a great pleasure for me as President to introduce not only the Democratic Majority Leader of the Senate, but a true leader on a nonpartisan basis of our Nation. He is a man who has been in the forefront of the national energy policy development for many years, and he early recognized, along with his colleagues from West Virginia, the value of coal and its role in history toward energy security for our country.

Over the last 20 years, he has made remarkable contributions to the coal industry—not only in West Virginia, but to our entire Nation. He was the original sponsor of the Coal Research Act of 1960, which established the Office of Coal Research under the Department of the Interior. In fact, he helped to obtain the first $1 million to fund coal research. I share his satisfaction at how far we have come.

And before he approaches the podium, I'd like to say that with the full cooperation and recommendation of the West Virginia delegation, I asked a couple of years ago, their Governor, Jay Rockefeller, to head up a commission to study the opportunities for the further use of coal in our Nation. The Governor, the congressional delegation of West Virginia, are to be congratulated on all the fine work they've done to make this possible.

And now I would like to ask the leader in our Senate and a leader in the coal promotion industry and a leader in the evolution of our Nation's energy policy to come say a few words. Representing West Virginia and our country and the Congress—Senator Robert Byrd.

SENATOR BYRD. *Mr. President, Governor Rockefeller, distinguished Ambassadors, members of the House delegation from West Virginia, my senior colleague, Jennings Randolph, ladies and gentlemen:*

We have worked a long time to see this day arrive, and I wish to express my gratitude and the gratitude of the delegation from the State of West Virginia and the people of West Virginia, if I may, to the distinguished representatives of Japan and Germany who are joining with this country in this important project development. The fact that they are becoming partners with us in this project indicates that this problem of energy is a world problem, and I hope that this event today marks only the beginning of this partnership which will allow the free world to achieve energy independence.

We are, Mr. President, as it were, entering into a new energy era. And in essence, we're looking backward into the past to find our energy future, because it was coal that allowed our forefathers to launch the power and the might that became the Industrial Revolution. And it was coal that fueled the growth of America. And coal has been the basis of the industrial strength of this country from which has flowed the overall might and power of America.

The technological wizardry which will enable, through this project, the flowing of millions of barrels of synthetic fuels into the energy pipeline of this country, is going to make for human betterment. It will allow the American people to control their energy destiny and, as the Ambassador from the Federal Republic of Germany said, it will be symbolic of the determination on the part of these countries to deal with our energy problems as the world's innovative leaders. And as innovators, we must recognize that in order to make a better world we must dare to try the untried and dare to attempt the new.

Brooks Atkinson, the drama critic, focused on the spirit of America when he said that there has been a calculated risk in every stage of American development. This Nation was built by men who took risks: pioneers who were not afraid of the future, scientists who were not afraid of the truth, thinkers who were not afraid of progress, and dreamers who were not afraid of action.

Mr. President, this is the spirit in which we have joined together in signing this agreement today, and it is a proud moment. May I say, on behalf of Governor Rockefeller, who has done an extraordinary job in heading up the President's Coal Commission about which the President spoke, and on behalf of Jennings Randolph, who has done an extraordinary job in serving on that commission, and on behalf of Mr. Staggers and the others, it is a proud moment for us, a proud moment for West Virginia, and a proud moment for our country.

THE PRESIDENT. Before we adjourn, I'd like to ask, first of all, Ambassador Peter Hermes to stand and let us express our appreciation to the Federal Republic of Germany, to him personally, by a round of applause. [*Applause*]

And Ambassador Okawara from Japan, we are deeply grateful to you and to the people of your great country. [*Applause*]

Now let's all go to work.

NOTE: The President spoke at 9:32 a.m. in the Rose Garden at the White House.

President's Award for Energy Efficiency

Remarks on Presenting the Award to the Future Farmers of America. July 31, 1980

THE PRESIDENT. *National Adviser Byron Rawls and National President Doug Rinker, distinguished fellow members of the Future Farmers of America:*

As a lifetime member myself, I vividly recall that the first organization I ever joined was the Baptist Church, and the second organization I joined was the Future Farmers of America. I never made president of the Plains chapter; I was secretary. But I know how to give the reports. And it's a very vivid part of my own background and my own pleasant memory.

I've also had a chance to come to you at your national convention on several occasions, to speak not only as one of the former leaders and interested Governors involved in the Future Farmers of America movement but also as a President, representing our great country. I

hope that all of my policies and statements as President have been compatible not only with the principles of the FFA but in the best interest of the American farm and ranch families.

Today is very special to me. At last year's meeting of the State presidents, when I was asked ahead of time, "What is the most important single issue that faces our Nation on which the Future Farmers of America can be helpful?", I told them that it was energy conservation. This is a request that was honored very well. As you know, throughout the Nation more than 2,000 chapters have responded, and although I always expect a lot from the FFA, you have done even more than I expected a year ago.

Energy is a critical factor in every family's life, but it's especially critical in a farm family's life. As you know, oil prices, that are set by exporting nations completely beyond our control and with the minimal influence that we can exert, are the single most important factor in causing inflation and the presently existing recession. For over a 12-month period, during most of 1979, we had a 10-percent increase in the price of oil every month. Oil prices increased more in a 12-month period than had been the case since the first day oil was discovered in the late 1800's. Our economy has had to accommodate that shock, along with the economies of other nations throughout the world who are our trading partners, our allies, and our friends.

The American people have responded well. You may remember a television broadcast that I gave July the 15th last year, when I said that our Nation needed to have its confidence in the future restored and the spirit of America held up as a guide for us all, and called upon the American people, as a sacrificial, patriotic gesture, to cut back on oil consumption. The results, again, have been far beyond what I expected. The first 5 months of this year we have had a 15-percent reduction in the amount of oil that we have imported from overseas compared to the first 5 months of 1979.

This is a good indication of what we can have for the future. We don't anticipate the maintenance of that rate of reduction over a long, extended period of time. That would be expecting too much. But Americans have responded, and I'm very grateful, as an FFA member, that you have been in the forefront of that enormous progress. If we continue this progress, then in the long run we can help to ensure the economic security of our Nation.

I'm very grateful this morning to announce that the national winner of the energy challenge is Alamosa, Colorado, chapter. My congratulations go to Kirk Goble, to Shannon Selvidge, to Shawn Woods and all the members. And I would like to read the amazing accomplishments of this chapter.

First of all, you organized numerous workshops and presentations that affected the entire community. You conducted a comprehensive energy audit throughout the community. You built projects that included a solar greenhouse, 10 solar panels, 3 solar food dryers, and a model distillery for alcohol—fuel, I presume. [*Laughter*] And I might point out that all this took place in just 1 year, and the total membership of this chapter is only 43. That is a notable achievement. It's outstanding.

But there were some close competitors, and 2,000 chapters helped in a similar fashion. I would particularly like to congratulate the regional winners—the Woodland chapter of Woodburn, Indiana, the Richdale chapter of Morrow, Ohio, and the Madison-Gary chapter of Madison, Florida.

These combined projects, not only the winners but all the others, have had a big contribution to the well-being and the security of our Nation that we love so much. I think more importantly, though, you have shown every American family and every American citizen that each person can contribute to improving our Nation's status in the world and the future good life of Americans, not in a depressing, sacrificial way, but in an exciting, dynamic, patriotic, unified way.

I would guess that the people of the communities of those who've won these prizes or awards have not suffered. My guess is that the communities have been brought closer together, that families have a better future, that the quality of their life has been enhanced, that houses are better insulated, heat bills are down, families have been drawn closer together, waste in transportation has been reduced, and the excitement of millions of new jobs in the future, brought about from solar power and other elements that have been explored, give our American people more hope and expectation of an even greater life in the years ahead.

We'll be sending each one of the chapters a commemorative award, a certificate of award, but I want to show my special appreciation, as an effort by the President, in making this next presentation. If Byron Rawls and Doug Rinker will step forward, I want to read the award.

This first award is for all of you and for all FFA members throughout the Nation who couldn't be here this morning. "The President's Award for Energy Efficiency is awarded to the Future Farmers of America in recognition of outstanding contribution to America's economic and national security through exemplary leadership in the national effort to achieve energy efficiency." Signed, Jimmy Carter, the White House, July 31, 1980.

And the representatives of the Alamosa FFA chapter, please. Shannon, congratulations. Shawn, good luck to you. Thank you very much. I'd like to read this award, too.

I might say that these awards are in competition with the major corporations of our Nation, the universities of our Nation, States of our Nation, and other major entities—none any more major or any more important than Future Farmers of America.

I'd like to read: "The President's Award for Energy Efficiency is awarded to the Alamosa FFA chapter, Alamosa, Colorado, in recognition of outstanding contribution to America's economic and national security through exemplary leadership in the national effort to achieve energy efficiency." Signed, Jimmy Carter, the White House, July 31, 1980.

And now in closing, let me say that in addition to the excitement of the awards, on behalf of the people of our country, I want to thank you. A lot of this work that has been done by the award chapters and by all others has been difficult. I know how serious an effort must be expended to marshal 43 or 200 FFA members to work in a consistent policy and then to recruit parents, teachers, leaders of the community, mayors, county officials, and others to join in to make a successful community effort.

This first year, I hope, will be just a beginning, and I hope that every chapter that has received an award will try to do even better in the second year. And if there are FFA chapters in the Nation who have not yet participated, I hope they'll be recruited. This is one award where the recognition is important, but where every person in our country benefits and where the greatest nation on Earth, as you know, becomes even greater because of your efforts.

God bless you. Thank you again, on behalf of us all.

MR. RINKER. Mr. President, not only do you have a belief in young people but you also have a belief in America's number one industry, agriculture and agribusiness; our sincere appreciation, because of the efforts that you've shown to the Future Farmers of America and almost 500,000 young people in all 50 States, Puerto Rico, and the Virgin Islands, who believe in themselves and believe in a future in agriculture. And it's people like you, Mr. President, who provide for that future.

This plaque reads: "To President Jimmy Carter, in sincere appreciation for meeting with the State presidents of the Future Farmers of America and giving the 500,000 FFA members and advisers the opportunity to participate in your efforts to make our Nation energy secure. Presented July 31, 1980."

Mr. President, thank you very much.

THE PRESIDENT. Thank you, Doug.

I want to thank Doug and all of you. I think the indication from these mutual awards is that we're all in it together to make our country even greater. And I'm especially grateful for the fact that while I was speaking, you sat down and while your own president spoke, you stood up. [*Laughter.*] But I feel like Doug is my president, too, as I am his.

God bless you all. Thank you again.

NOTE: The President spoke at 10:48 a.m. in the Rose Garden at the White House to participants in the State President's Conference of the Future Farmers of America.

Commission on Wartime Relocation and Internment of Civilians Act

Remarks on Signing S. 1647 Into Law. July 31, 1980

THE PRESIDENT. Senate bill 1647 establishes a seven-person commission that will work during the next 18 months to look into one of the disappointing and sometimes embarrassing occurrences in the history of our Nation.

In February of 1942, the President signed a proclamation setting aside certain areas of our country from which American citizens could be excluded and within which American citizens and resident aliens could be interned. This was in a time of war, but no German American citizens or aliens were incarcerated and no Italian Americans were interned either. The only ones who were interned in these camps were the Japanese Americans. There were about 120,000 of them, during the wartime period, who were interned.

In addition, about a thousand residents of Pribilof Island and the Aleutian Islands were removed from their homelands and brought to the mainland, because of the claim, which may have been completely legitimate, that those islands were subject to attack because of their exposed position. Later, some attempts were made for addressing these grievances for the thousand residents of the Aleutian Islands and the Pribilofs, for instance. Ten thousand dollars was set aside, a total. That's $10 per person to attempt some compensation for their inconvenience and their suffering. And as a matter of fact, some lives were lost.

I believe it'll be very helpful for this Commission to assess this episode in American history, to see if adequate compen-sation has been awarded under previous efforts, which were more generous in the case of the Japanese Americans, and also to reconfirm our Nation's commitment to basic human rights.

I'm grateful that Danny Inouye has taken the leadership in this legislation; Sparky Matsunaga, the other Senator from Hawaii, has also been instrumental in this; Senator Hayakawa from California—all of Japanese descent—and Ted Stevens, representing the citizens of the islands off the Alaska coast. We also, of course, have Congressman Mineta, Congressman Matsui, of Japanese descent, and others representing the citizens who are involved. Senator [Representative] Bob McClory is here, as well. The Japanese-American Citizens League has kept this issue alive, along with the Aleutian-Pribilof Island Association. And we have representatives from those groups here with us.

And it's with a great deal of pleasure that I sign this legislation into law. This Commission study will be adequately funded. It's not designed as a witch hunt. It's designed to expose clearly what has happened in a period of war in our Nation when many loyal American citizens of Japanese descent were embarrassed during that crucial time in our Nation's history. I don't believe anyone would doubt that injustices were done, and I don't think anyone would doubt that it is advisable now for us to have a clear understanding, as Americans, of this episode in the history of our country.

Now I'll sign the legislation into law.

[*At this point, the President signed the bill.*]

And I'd like to ask Senator Inouye if he has a comment, right, since he was the author of the bill.

SENATOR INOUYE. Mr. President, this has been a day awaited by many American citizens. I don't suppose that by this action we can set aside and rest, because we demonstrated that in a great democracy such as ours we can make mistakes. I just hope that we can maintain our vigilance so it will not happen again, sir.

THE PRESIDENT. Thank you, Danny, very much.

Sparky, would you like to make a comment?

SENATOR MATSUNAGA. I wish to thank you, Mr. President, for signing a bill which has been waited for for many, many years. I think it proves that this Nation of ours is great enough to recognize its mistakes where it has made mistakes, and I think the Commission's investigation will show that we, indeed, did make a mistake in dealing with a large segment of our population. And I am sure I speak in behalf of all Americans of Japanese ancestry in the United States when I say thank you, Mr. President.

THE PRESIDENT. Thank you, Sparky.

Ted Stevens represents the Aleutians and Pribilof Island citizens, some of whom are here. Ted, would you like to——

SENATOR STEVENS. Thank you very much, Mr. President.

I was delighted when the Senators from Hawaii were willing to accept the amendment that places the Aleut people under the same study, and I join with them in welcoming an opportunity to make the record for history and thank you for your administration accepting this initiative. I think it will be an interesting one, and I think it should lead to some actions to right some very old wrongs. I appreciate it very much.

THE PRESIDENT. Okay. Norm Mineta?

REPRESENTATIVE MINETA. Thank you, Mr. President.

Having been one of the 120,000, as a 10½-year-old boy, being evacuated and interned, this to me is a very significant day, and I'm just very thankful to you for your leadership that you've shown in making sure that the Department of Justice was also supportive of our efforts in getting this bill passed. And I just feel that the facts that will come out of this Commission study will, as Senator Inouye says, guarantee that an incident like this shall never happen to anyone else.

THE PRESIDENT. I'd like to point out that all of the agencies of the Federal Government recommended that this legislation be signed.

REPRESENTATIVE MINETA. That's correct.

THE PRESIDENT. This is not always the case with legislation that comes to my desk. [*Laughter*]

Bob?

REPRESENTATIVE MCCLORY. Yes, I'd like to, Mr. President.

I'm very proud and happy that I had an opportunity to conduct the hearings and the markup of the bill amending it into the present form and also to manage it on the floor of the House, not only because of my long friendship with Spark and Dan and Norm and others who worked on the bill but because I have the honor of representing a district which probably has more Japanese Americans than any other district in the Congress.

Mr. President, I, all of us, have had some kind of an intimate experience with one part or the other of the work that is being undertaken by this Commission. And I know that we each individually have great expectations that this legislation can clear the air, it can improve the quality of life in our country and, as others have said, to assure that we do not have a recurrence of the experience that we had in World War II.

Thank you.

THE PRESIDENT. Thank you.

One of the things that I should have said earlier and overlooked is that following this episode, our Government did make an honest attempt to give the Japanese American citizens a chance to express their grievances and to estimate their losses. The fact is that we want to be sure that those efforts were adequate, which will be judged by this Commission in its recommendation to me and to the Congress, and also, we want to make sure that their recommendations will prevent any recurrence of this abuse of the basic human rights of American citizens and also resident aliens, who enjoy the privileges of the protection not only of American law but of American principles and ideals.

Again, I want to thank the representatives of the Japanese American community who are not yet in Congress.

NOTE: The President spoke at 12:02 p.m. in the Cabinet Room at the White House.

As enacted, S. 1647 is Public Law 96–317, approved July 31.

Ceremony Honoring Hispanic Americans

Remarks at the Swearing-In Ceremony for Richard J. Rios as Director of the Community Services Administration and the Signing of a Proclamation. July 31, 1980

THE PRESIDENT. *Congressman Kika de la Garza, Congressman Ken Hance, Congressman Corrada, Senator [Representative] Claude Pepper, and other distinguished representatives of areas of our Nation where many Hispanic citizens are living:*

Bienvenidos a la Casa Blanca. Es un gran placer para nosotros tener tantas de mis amistades aquí en este importante celebración. [Welcome to the White House. It's a great pleasure for us to have so many of my friends at this important celebration.]

As a President here on the South Lawn of the White House, the symbol of freedom, the symbol of a nation which has always clasped to its breast immigrants and sometimes refugees, I'm thrilled by this ceremony. It is indeed a pleasure to have you here today representing more than 12 million Americans all around this country with Hispanic backgrounds. We even have three Georgians here who are struggling against our non-Hispanic background to learn your beautiful language, so that we can participate even more closely in matters that concern you and the people that you represent as leaders of this great and growing community.

This Nation was founded on a common belief in freedom, in justice, in equality of opportunity, in hope, in progress, confidence in one another, and a spirit of unity whenever our Nation was threatened with great challenge, great doubt, or great concerns. We're a nation with a vast common geography and a diversity of history, a diversity of language, a diversity of cultural background. We're made up of people from all over the world. It's one of our great strengths, because when our Nation faces an international problem, we have people here who are loyal Americans in the fullest sense of the word, who have ties of knowledge and blood kin and understanding to every one of those individual nations.

We've come here for betterment of our own lives and to guarantee a better life for our children and for their children. This aspect of American culture is just as important today as it was 200 years ago or 300 years ago. Newly arrived Hispanics, who may have been here only a few weeks or a few years, join generations who, as you well know, were here generations before the Pilgrims landed at

1457

Plymouth Rock. Had the history books we studied been written in Spanish instead of English, we would know that much more clearly.

When I visited the river area of my own State of Georgia or when we vacationed recently on the coastal islands of Georgia, we were reminded of this proud Spanish heritage, Latin heritage, by the ancient buildings there and the culture that still remains. At Pensacola, St. Augustine, in the Midwest and Far West of our Nation, we still have viable communities, growing, that have never forgotten this great Spanish heritage.

I think I know well, much better than 3½ years ago, the special problems of those who don't speak English well when they first come to this country. Our Nation has experience that well qualifies us to deal with that new evolution in the life of a person seeking a better life. And I'm also aware of the great contributions in science, art, culture, education, medicine, politics, the Nobel Prize winners, who represent the Hispanic culture so well.

And I'm also aware of the unrecognized contributions of thousands or even millions of average Hispanic citizens, going about their duties, carrying out their responsibilities as citizens, and having an exemplary record in keeping the family structure so closely bound together and so strong, which is the foundation of any nation, and particularly a democracy. In these citizens, who embody the deepest and best characteristics of our heritage, we join today to celebrate.

As President, as you know, I'm called on to make hundreds of difficult decisions every week. The Oval Office, just to my left, and the desk within it is where problems arise that cannot be solved in a family's home, in a county courthouse, in a city hall, in a State legislature, or among the business and labor and other leaders of our country. These are the problems that are most difficult. And the decisions that I make, along with those of the Members of the Congress, are the ones that shape the present and future lives of Americans, particularly those troubled Americans and those relatively new Americans who are being assimilated into our culture as have the ancestors of almost everyone who's assembled here.

When I came into this office, I was determined that there would be nothing from the Oval Office or in the decisions that I made that perpetuated any degree of discrimination because of race or language or cultural background or economic or social status. We have not yet fully won this battle in our Nation for complete equality of opportunity. There are still some elements of discrimination left, some perhaps deliberate on a small community basis, others inadvertent when deprivations and needs are overlooked by public officials at all levels of government. But we are determined that no man or woman shall lack a job or a job opportunity because of that background, and I think this special time to recognize our Hispanic community, which I will commemorate in a few minutes with my personal signature, brings this vividly to the minds of us all.

I'm determined that every child in every family and every community of this Nation will have a chance to take whatever talent or ability that child might have been given by God and develop it to the greatest, whether that child ultimately will be a great business leader or a doctor or a teacher or political leader or a carpenter or a scientist or common laborer, who joins together to make our Nation even greater. That's why in 3 years we have increased our Head Start program by more than 70 percent.

The Congress, along with me, has increased the allocation of Federal funds for education in just a short period of 3 years by 73 percent. We've now been able to form a new Department of Education that can focus special attention, undeviating attention on the special needs of those who are searching to broaden their minds and to open their hearts. Our Secretary of Education is here today, Shirley Hufstedler, who's particularly eager to see special programs enhanced. We've already increased bilingual education funds, for instance, by 117 percent. And we're not through yet.

Part of the role that I have as President is constantly to expand those programs specially designed for American citizens who need them most. The powerful, the influential are not the ones who suffer when a Federal program does not work well; it's the person who is struggling for a better life and a better opportunity, so that that particular person can, in the future, bear the responsibilities, the enjoyments, and perhaps even the burdens of leadership in our society.

Next week we'll send to the FEDERAL REGISTER new regulations on bilingual education dealing with a sensitive issue. Those regulations will be published in the FEDERAL REGISTER, and we want all of you to participate, along with Secretary Hufstedler, in evolving them in a better way for your own families and your friends and those whom you represent.

I won't go into detail about all the progress that we have made, because we've got a long way to go. We know that. But in Job Corps and in minority-owned businesses, we've tried to focus the advantages to those who had formerly been excluded.

In contracts for the carrying out of major public works programs, for instance, we've put a mandatory provision that at least 10 percent of those contracts would have to be awarded to businesses with minority ownership. Many said we couldn't do it; the Congress passed it. Many said we couldn't implement it; we have more than met the 10 percent—almost 15 percent. This program has been challenged all the way to the Supreme Court, and as you know, within the last few weeks the Supreme Court ruled that this was indeed a legitimate exercise of congressional and Presidential authority. And we will continue this program to guarantee that when your Federal tax moneys are spent that minority-owned businesses will get their fair share for the first time in the history of this country.

I've been fortunate to have good advice from those who have a special interest in you. We have brought in to the Government many great Hispanic Americans to lead agencies which were crucial to the lives of those about whom you care so deeply. We have increased Hispanic employment greatly, although our overall Federal employment has actually dropped in the last 3½ years. For instance, before the new Education Department was split off from Health and Human Services, we had increased Hispanic employment by 37 percent, and in the Labor Department, primarily responsible for jobs, we had increased Hispanic employment 100 percent. This is not enough. We are still making progress, but as you know, it's very difficult to overcome literally generations of discrimination. With your help, we will continue to make this progress.

And I have also been particularly sensitive to the special needs of Spanish-speaking citizens in the administration of justice. For that reason, I have put a lot of time locating and appointing distinguished jurists from the Hispanic community as Federal judges. I have already, in a short period of not much more than 3 years, appointed more Spanish-speaking Federal judges than all other Presidents combined who've ever served our Nation.

As you know, those judges will be interpreting the law and protecting your rights and the rights of your children far beyond the end of this century.

And I think that one of the most complex and difficult issues which I face is that of immigration. Ours is a nation so great that it's attractive to those in foreign countries for various reasons: in some communist nations, just to escape personal prosecution and to find human freedom; in others, to join loved ones who've already come here; in other cases, to find a better life and a better opporunity economically. How to assimilate this influx of would-be American citizens and those who come here on a temporary basis and intend to return to their former home is a very difficult question, indeed.

But I've had two fine men to serve with me, and I'm very grateful to Leonel Castillo and now Matt Garcia, who will be heading up the Immigration and Naturalization Service.

Our Nation is at peace because we are strong and because we are united and because we don't deviate in our commitment to basic principles. Part of our responsibility is to make sure our Armed Forces are strong and that they are free of discrimination, as well. And I'm very proud to have as Secretary of the Navy Mr. Hidalgo, who's in the second row here. And I want to express my deep appreciation to you for serving with us.

This Monday we had a Cabinet meeting, and Victor Marrero, who's the Undersecretary of HUD, was sitting in the Secretary's seat, one of the few times in the history of our country. Is Victor here? I think all of you know that HUD is the agency responsible for the revitalization of communities and for the repair of damage that has been done when economic circumstances afflict the lives of people who live in those communities. And to have Victor there in the top position in that great department is indeed of value to me.

I would now like to sign the proclamation, authorized, indeed directed, by Congress, and I know that these Members of Congress sitting on the front row are indeed proud to participate with me. I'd like to ask them to come and join me now as I sign this proclamation. And then following that, we will have a ceremony to administer the oath of office to a new and great Hispanic leader who will perform his duties subsequent to this meeting.

Would the Members of Congress please come and join me for this next part of the ceremony?

This is a very brief proclamation, but I'd like to read it, if you don't mind.

[At this point, the President read and then signed the proclamation.]

I'd now like to ask Richard Rios and his family to come forward and those who will participate in the oath of office ceremony.

I spoke earlier of the many talented Hispanics I have been able to bring into the Government. Richard Rios, the new Director of the Community Services Administration, is typical of those concerned and dedicated and capable public servants. He follows another outstanding administrator in that same post managing this major agency, Graciela Olivarez.

Before assuming his new duties, he was director of the California State Office of Economic Opportunity and his background ranges from working with juvenile offenders to employment development to multicultural and educational programs at the college level.

Richard, I want you to understand something from the very beginning. I've not appointed you to manage antipoverty programs. I've appointed you to lead people out of poverty. Your job is to make programs work for people and to let people help themselves by working when they're able. For that reason, I'm pleased to witness your formal oath of office here at the White House lawn before this distinguished gathering of Hispanic Americans and to call upon everyone here today to help you in this fight to bring economic opportunity not only to Hispanics but to all Americans.

And now we'll have the oath of office, following which our new Director of this major department will say a few words.

[*At this point, Judge Lucian Perkins administered the oath of office.*]

Mr. Rios. *Mr. President, Mrs. Carter, honored guests:*

I feel privileged and honored to have been chosen as the Director of the Community Services Administration.

In choosing a former community action agency director, you have once again made visible your continuing commitment to the poor. This opportunity to serve will permit me to serve, will permit me to focus on assisting our administration to more adequately meet the needs of all low-income citizens, who, as you know, are both young and old, male and female, and include all races. Once again, let me say how proud I am to be able to represent this vital national effort and your critical concern.

It is fitting that this swearing-in ceremony takes place before my family, my *amigos,* and my peers on such an historic occasion, the signing of the proclamation designating September 14th through the 20th as Hispanic Heritage Week. Our coming together reflects the desire of this administration to serve all people throughout America. We look forward to your signing of a similar proclamation for the next 4 years, during which time we

will continue to strengthen the programs and policies serving the poor.

Thank you very much for this honor.

THE PRESIDENT. Esteban? Abelardo? Come on. I just want to call a couple of my good advisers up. They help to keep me straight. If you have any problems with me, see them and they'll get me straight.

In closing, let me say that to have a major White House adviser constantly at my elbow in times of crisis and difficult decisions is very valuable to me and to you. And of course, when we have any foreign visitor come to our Nation, the one who is responsible is the director of protocol, with the title of Assistant Secretary of State. And of course, if he has a beautiful wife, that makes us get two noted achievements and services for the price of one. Won't you stand up just a moment?

Again, you've honored me and Rosalynn—and I see Amy came in—by being with us. Thank you all. *Vaya con Dios.* [May God be with you.]

Thank you.

NOTE: The President spoke at 7:06 p.m. on the South Grounds at the White House.

In his closing remarks, the President referred to Esteban E. Torres, Special Assistant to the President for Hispanic Affairs, and Abelardo L. Valdez, Chief of Protocol, Department of State.

National Hispanic Heritage Week
Proclamation 4776. July 31, 1980

By the President of the United States of America

A Proclamation

Hispanic peoples have played a distinguished role in the history of our Nation.

They founded settlements in Florida and Georgia half a century before the Pilgrims landed in Massachusetts, and were homesteading in New Mexico more than 150 years before the War of Independence. The names of scores of American cities and towns—such as Los Angeles, Albuquerque, San Antonio, and Saint Augustine—remind us that many of the explorers and settlers who opened our frontiers were of Hispanic origin.

The Hispanic community has given us generals, admirals, philosophers, statesmen, musicians, athletes, and Noble Prizewinning scientists. Hispanic Americans have contributed gallantly to the defense of our Nation, and many have received the highest decoration our country can bestow—the Congressional Medal of Honor.

Outstanding Hispanic men and women add daily to our Nation's accomplishments in science, technology, the arts, and politics. And Hispanic citizens contribute daily to the quality of our lives. Hispanics exhibit an eminent pride in our American heritage, a passionate love of family, a profound devotion to religion, and an energetic commitment to hard work.

As we enter the 1980s, it is fitting that we pause to recognize and celebrate our Hispanic heritage.

Now, THEREFORE, I, JIMMY CARTER, President of the United States of America, do hereby proclaim the week beginning September 14, 1980, as National Hispanic Heritage Week. I call upon Federal, State, and local officials to observe this week with appropriate activities and to search out innovative ways for government to work in partnership with the Hispanic community. Hispanic immigrants were among the earliest and are now among the most recent to arrive in this haven of liberty and human rights, and I urge all Americans to reflect on the invaluable contribution they have made to the greatness, the diversity, and the strength of this Nation.

IN WITNESS WHEREOF, I have hereunto set my hand this thirty-first day of July in the year of our Lord nineteen hundred and eighty, and of the Independence of the United States of America the two hundred and fifth.

JIMMY CARTER

[Filed with the Office of the Federal Register, 11:20 a.m., August 1, 1980]

Privacy Act of 1974

Letter to the Speaker of the House and the President of the Senate Transmitting a Report. August 1, 1980

Dear Mr. Speaker: (Dear Mr. President:)

I am herewith forwarding the Fifth Annual Report of executive branch activities implementing the Privacy Act of 1974.

The report shows that Federal agencies have successfully incorporated the Act's requirements into their daily activities and made the Federal workforce sensitive to privacy concerns.

With the success of these efforts in mind, I urge the Congress to proceed with its consideration of the Administration's legislative privacy proposals. Together, we have done much to identify and protect the privacy rights of our citizens, but our task is not yet finished.

Sincerely,

JIMMY CARTER

NOTE: This is the text of identical letters addressed to Thomas P. O'Neill, Jr., Speaker of the House of Representatives, and Walter F. Mondale, President of the Senate.

Customs Valuation Agreement

*Message to the Congress Transmitting a
Protocol Amending the Agreement.
August 1, 1980*

To the Congress of the United States:

I am today transmitting to the Congress, pursuant to Section 102 of the Trade Act of 1974, the text of a trade agreement negotiated in the Tokyo Round of the Multilateral Trade Negotiations and entered into in Geneva, Switzerland on May 28, 1980. This agreement is a protocol which will make a minor amendment to the Agreement on Implementation of Article VII of the General Agreement on Tariffs and Trade, known as the Customs Valuation Agreement. The Customs Valuation Agreement was approved by Congress in the Trade Agreements Act of 1979.

The new agreement will amend the Customs Valuation Agreement to eliminate one of the four tests under that agreement by which related parties can establish a transaction value for customs purposes. This amendment will have little impact on United States law but will greatly facilitate acceptance of the Customs Valuation Agreement by a significant number of developing countries. All of the developed country signatories to the Customs Valuation Agreement support the protocol.

I am also transmitting to Congress, as is required by section 102 of the Trade Act of 1974, an implementing bill and a statement of Administrative Action. This bill approves the protocol and makes changes in our customs valuation law which are necessary or appropriate to implement the protocol. The legislation will also make certain technical amendments to Title II of the Trade Agreements Act of 1979, relating to customs valuation.

I urge the early approval and implementation of the protocol to the Customs Valuation Agreement by the Congress.

JIMMY CARTER

The White House,
August 1, 1980.

Carter/Mondale Presidential Campaign

Remarks at a White House Reception for Delegates to the Democratic National Convention.   August 1, 1980

AUDIENCE. [*Chanting*] "We want Jimmy."

THE PRESIDENT. [*Laughing*] Okay; you got me. Thank you very much.

AUDIENCE. [*Chanting*] "Four more years."

THE PRESIDENT. Right on. Thank you very much.

Well, as Rosalynn and I stood in the receiving line and shook hands with hundreds of you this afternoon it was obvious to me that the spirit of the Democratic Party and the commitment of the delegates who are committed to me and Fritz Mondale will guarantee that we'll win the nomination in New York and win the election in November.

I know a lot of you can think back 9 or 10 months ago when you were making up your mind whether or not to run as a Carter delegate, and all the predictions were that anybody who ran for a Carter/Mondale delegate would surely lose, and that we didn't have a chance to win. And now all of you have won. Now it's my time, right? [*Applause*]

I'm not going to list all the reasons we're going to win, but I would like to mention one reason that you had with you this morning, and that is that I've got the best partner and the best Vice President this country has ever seen. And I might add that in 1976 and in 1980, Fritz Mondale is my first choice.

I hope this has been a good day for you. As you all know, who are familiar with political history in this Nation, the few days prior to a Democratic Convention and, quite often, a Republican Convention, are filled with tension, with debate, with anticipation, with some degree of trepidation, with controversy. That's what makes our party great, and I believe that at the convention in New York we will have sharp differences, we will have debates, we will have thorough discussion of issues, but we will come out of that convention with Fritz Mondale and me at the head of a ticket and with a united party determined to whip the Republicans in New York.

And with that determination in New York, as a unified convention, with a fine platform and the issues clearly on our side, I have no doubt that we'll go through every State in this Nation, and we'll put up a major battle in the fall and come out victorious in November. This is important to us and important for our country.

Don't be afraid of controversy. Don't be afraid of change. The Democratic Party has always been fhe party where differences of opinion were freely expressed. And we'll be at the convention talking about issues, not whether or not we will help the cities, not whether or not we'll be a staunch friend of farmers, not whether or not we'll be the champion of the working families of this country, not whether or not we'll give equality of opportunity to minority groups, not whether or not women will be treated as equals in every possible respect, not whether or not our Nation will be kept at peace and kept strong, but how we'll carry out these commitments is the only argument among us, not whether we'll do it.

The Republicans didn't have to worry about how to deal with the troubles of labor organization members at Detroit, the center of organized labor for major industries of our country—out of 2,000 delegates, I think 4 represented labor unions. And they didn't have to worry about minorities. We'll have about 25 percent of all the delegates at the Democratic Convention who represent minority citizens in this country.

The Republicans have 3 or 4 percent——

AUDIENCE MEMBER. One!

THE PRESIDENT. One? I try to be careful not to exaggerate, but I'll take your figure, 1 percent. They had to import one to speak, as you know—*[laughter]*—for minorities. And I am very grateful to say that at the Democratic Convention, 50 percent of our delegates will be women, working for——

AUDIENCE MEMBER. It is enough for the men.

THE PRESIDENT. Absolutely. Working finally in the Constitution of the United States to give women full equality under the laws of our Nation. That's important to us.

We are willing to meet every challenge. The Democratic Party has always been on the cutting edge of progress. The Nation is troubled. The world is in a state of flux and challenge. But we know that we represent a party that is the oldest political party on Earth. It's a party whose principles and commitments and ideals have never changed. They are the same principles and commitments and ideals which have made our Nation the greatest nation on Earth. And that guiding light for us, that undeviating guiding light has stood us in good stead and helped us to weather differences that have arisen among us, as we struggle for that progress so precious to people who in the past did not have equality of opportunity.

Ours is a nation of immigrants. I often say we are a nation of refugees—people who have come here literally from every nation on Earth, either us or our parents or grandparents, seeking a better life. And almost every influx of people from foreign countries, when they got here, didn't have influence. They didn't have a place to express their desires and their hopes and their yearnings and their aspirations and their commitments and their ambitions. And when they found themselves isolated from the mainstream of political influence, they very quickly found it, to the extent that they committed themselves to the Democratic Party and formed partnerships there.

That's the element which has given us strength. It's not an accident that about two-thirds of the Members of the House of Representatives in the Congress are Democrats. It's not an accident that two-thirds of the Senators are Democrats. It just shows the sound political judgment of the people to keep a Democrat in the White House and a Democratic Congress. And that principle is not going to change.

I just want to say two other things. We're also the party that's willing to tell the American people the truth. Our Nation was almost brought to its knees in embarrassment and disappointment and the alienation of well-meaning, dedicated, patriotic American citizens—even from the Oval Office of the White House, in recent years—by Watergate and by some of the things that have happened under the leadership of the Republican Party. It's not necessary for us to revive that on a daily basis as we campaign throughout the country, but we should have learned a lesson from it: that the truth that has always permeated the Democratic Party commitments in telling the American people the facts—sometimes unvarnished facts, sometimes unpopular facts—have stood us in good stead.

We cannot afford to deviate from that commitment during the campaign this year by providing easy answers or simplistic solutions to problems that are indeed difficult and which cannot be resolved overnight. That'll be the responsibility of me and Fritz Mondale, yes, of Rosalynn and my family, all the Cabinet, yes. But it's also your responsibility to make sure that every time you meet with a single person or a small group, that you tell the truth and, in the process, meld together a unified America. Because our Nation has never failed in a time of crisis or challenge or trouble or difficulty—when we recognized that crisis or that obstacle or understood the question—to unite and to prevail. We have never failed, and we're not going to fail in the future.

Ours is a country at peace. We've had rare administrations that have gone 4 years with our Nation at peace. And I always pray to God that when I go out of this office, that I can look back and say, "We kept our Nation at peace for 8 solid years."

You've probably discussed today the convention rules. [*Laughter*] And I know you've heard the statements, perhaps on both sides—maybe there is some division among you, I'm not sure about that——

AUDIENCE. No!

THE PRESIDENT. Right on.

Then I will agree with you that it's almost incomprehensible how a brokered, horse-traded, smoke-filled room convention could be labeled open, and the decision made by 20 million Democrats in the open primaries and the open caucuses could be called closed.

These rules, as you know, that we are defending were initiated back as far as 1964, 1968, 1972, under people like Harold Hughes, George McGovern, and also

Barbara Mikulski, [Morley] Winograd. You know the names of the commissions that have said, "Let's don't let the political bosses control our party any longer. Let's give to the people of our Nation who profess to be Democrats the right to decide who the nominee of the party will be."

These rules were established, clearly understood, by all the candidates or potential candidates 18 months or more before the first caucuses were held in Iowa. And we will have an open convention, as every delegate has a right to debate these rules, to vote on the rules, to decide on the platform, to establish credentials— [*inaudible*]—to set the changes in the charter if we want to, to set the rules for the 1984 convention. What I want to be sure is that when a voter goes to the ballot box in Plains, Georgia, or Chicago, Illinois, or Schenectady, New York, or Newport News, Virginia, and says this is what we want, is the decision to choose the nominee of our party, and then later, the delegates are chosen to carry out the will of millions of Democrats, that that decision—made by the grassroots, by Democrats who have their faith in you, confirmed by an oath by the delegates to carry out that charge, made openly and freely, in conformity with 42 States' laws—is carried out. To violate that commitment and that oath and that promise would be a travesty, in my opinion, of honesty.

I might close by saying I have absolutely no doubt that no matter what rule is chosen that Fritz Mondale and I will be nominated at the convention. That is not the point. The point is what I've been talking about earlier: honesty, truth, principle. That's what's been our guiding light, and that's what's going to bring us to victory and our Nation to victory and per- manent peace, through strength, after the election in November. Thank you all. God bless every one of you.

THE FIRST LADY. I am so glad to see you here this afternoon, and I thank you for all of your help and what you mean to Jimmy and to me, personally, and for what you mean as active Democrats to our country. It's wonderful to have you.

We'll be leaving from the South Lawn in the helicopter. We invite you to come down the steps and out to watch us leave—be careful because you might get blown away—and then come back in the House, into the State Dining Room for some refreshments.

Thank you all.

NOTE: The President spoke at 5:41 p.m. in the East Room at the White House. As printed above, the First Lady's remarks follow the text of the White House press release.

Billy Carter's Activities With the Libyan Government

Statement by the White House Press Secretary. August 1, 1980

Late this afternoon, after extensive effort, we determined that Billy Carter did receive a copy of one of the cables which we released to you yesterday and which was released under F.O.I.A. [Freedom of Information Act] in May of last year. We've also determined that he received a copy by mail from the President.

First, let me tell you how it came about, and then I'll describe to you how we determined how it came about.

On or about October the 11th, 1978, Susan Clough, the President's secretary, received a note from Tom Beard, with the cable attached. Mr. Beard, as you know, conducts liaison between the White House and the State Deparment on nonpolicy matters and, as you also know, was the person who relayed White House instructions to the State Department that Billy Carter's 1978 trip be considered nonofficial and that Billy be cautioned again on the sensitivity of the U.S.-Libyan relationship when he arrived in Tripoli.

Susan gave the cable and the note to the President, presumably because the note contained a comment about the President's mother, and the cable contained, as you know, a favorable report on Billy's visit to Tripoli. The President penned a brief note to Billy on the cable and had it mailed to him.

Neither the President, Miss Clough, nor Mr. Beard remembered the incident or the existence of the note prior to this afternoon. We determined that Billy had received a copy of the cable and that the President had sent it to him, through inquiries from Mr. Alfred Moses, who, as you know, is working on this matter with the White House Counsel's Office, to Billy Carter's attorneys, Mr. Ruth and Mr. Pollak. Once questions were raised on the Hill Wednesday about cables and whether Billy Carter did or did not have cables— you will remember that the first we knew about the cable question was when it was raised on the Hill—Mr. Moses called Mr. Ruth and Mr. Pollak that day to seek any assistance they could properly give us in resolving these questions.

Mr. Moses spoke with them by telephone again Thursday and once more this morning. In response to those calls, the White House received a copy of the cable from Billy's attorneys this afternoon about 5:30. The attorneys had felt it appropriate to check with the Department of Justice before providing the cable to us since they had sent a copy to Justice this morning, pursuant to a Department of Justice

request. They were informed this afternoon that the Department of Justice had no objection to the White House receiving a copy.

Mr. Cutler [Lloyd N. Cutler, Counsel to the President] and I presented this information to the President this evening, shortly before his departure for Camp David. The President instructed us to prepare a statement for release as soon as possible today, and to clear it with him after he had reached Camp David.

That's the end of my statement.

NOTE: Press Secretary Jody Powell read the statement in the Briefing Room at the White House during a news briefing for reporters which began at 8:15 p.m.

On Thursday, July 31, the White House made available copies of seven cables concerning Billy Carter's 1978 trip to Libya.

Corporation for Public Broadcasting

Nomination of Four Members of the Board of Directors. August 1, 1980

The President today announced that he will nominate four persons to be members of the Board of Directors of the Corporation for Public Broadcasting for terms expiring in 1986. They are:

REUBEN W. ASKANASE, of Houston, Tex., president and director of Hou-Tex Corp. and a director of several other companies. He is a director of the Houston Foundation and the Houston Symphony Society and is active in civic affairs and the arts.

DIANA LADY DOUGAN, of Salt Lake City, Utah, for reappointment. She has been a member of this Board since 1976. She is president of Dougan & Associates, a public relations consulting firm, and chairman of the board of directors of Friends of KUED (Utah's PBS station).

LILLIE E. HERNDON, of Columbia, S.C., for reappointment. She has been a member and Chairman of this Board since 1976. She is a member and former chairman of the South Carolina State Board of Education and former vice president of the National Association of State Boards of Education.

HOWARD A. WHITE, of New York City, senior vice president and general counsel of ITT World Communications, Inc., and executive director of the Legal and Regulatory Administration Department.

Digest of Other White House Announcements

The following listing includes the President's public schedule and other items of general interest announced by the White House Press Office and not included elsewhere in this issue.

July 26

The White House announced that the President has received letters from Chairmen Peter W. Rodino, Jr., of the House Judiciary Committee and Clement J. Zablocki of the House Foreign Affairs Committee, requesting comments and information on a resolution of inquiry that was introduced in the House of Representatives on July 22 and contains nine areas of inquiry relating to Billy Carter. With the exception of the last two inquiries, which have been directed by the committee chairmen to the Department of Justice for response, the President intends not only to comment fully but also to provide detailed responses that will supply substantially all of the information requested, subject to appropriate safeguards to protect the security of any classified information.

July 27

The President returned to the White House from Camp David, Md.

July 28

The President met at the White House with:

—Zbigniew Brzezinski, Assistant to the President for National Security Affairs;

—the Cabinet;

—Frank B. Moore, Assistant to the President for Congressional Liaison;

—representatives of farm organizations and Members of Congress, to discuss farm policy.

The President announced that he will nominate Charles F. Meissner for the rank of Ambassador. Meissner is United States Special Negotiator for Economic Matters.

July 29

The President met at the White House with:

—the Democratic congressional leadership;

—Dr. Brzezinski;

—Mr. Moore;

—Dr. Eugene Fanta, of Kinnelon, N.J., the 1980 Family Doctor of the Year;

—Paul Oei and Gretchen Alspach, winners of the first National Student Exposition on Energy Resources, and representatives of the National Energy Foundation;

—the Democratic members of the 95th Congressional Caucus, to discuss foreign and domestic policy.

July 30

The President met at the White House with:

—Dr. Brzezinski;

—Mr. Moore;

—Shawn Weatherly, Miss Universe, and Jineane Ford, Miss U.S.A.;

—a group of his advisers for a budget review session.

The President transmitted to the Congress the fourth report on Title VI of the Housing and Community Development Act of 1974 (Mobile Home Standards).

The White House announced that Florida Governor Bob Graham will deliver the nominating speech for the President at the 1980 Democratic National Convention and that Coretta Scott King and Sol Chick Chaikin will deliver the seconding speeches.

July 31

The President met at the White House with:

—David L. Aaron, Deputy Assistant for National Security Affairs;

—Vice President Walter F. Mondale, Secretary of the Treasury G. William Miller, James T. McIntyre, Jr., Director of the Office of Management and Budget, Charles L. Schultze, Chairman of the Council of Economic Advisers, R. Robert Russell, Director of the Council on Wage and Price Stability, Alfred E. Kahn, Advisor to the President on Inflation, Stuart E. Eizenstat, Assistant to the President for Domestic Affairs and Policy, and Alonzo L. McDonald, Jr., Assistant to the President;

—Mr. Moore.

The President announced that he will withdraw the nomination of David Bronheim to be a member of the Board of Directors of the Inter-American Foundation. Bronheim is resigning his position as Associate Director of the U.S. International Development Cooperation Agency. He had been nominated to the Inter-American Foundation Board as a Government member; his nomination is now being withdrawn since he will no longer be in Government service.

In the evening, the President attended a reception at the Washington bureau of the Los Angeles Times.

August 1

The President met at the White House with:

—Dr. Brzezinski;

—Vice President Mondale, Secretary of Defense Harold Brown, Secretary of State Edmund S. Muskie, Deputy Secretary of State Warren M. Christopher, Lloyd N. Cutler, Counsel to the President, Hedley W. Donovan, Senior Adviser to the President, Jack H. Watson, Jr., Assistant to the President, and Dr. Brzezinski;

—Mr. Moore;

—Democratic Members of the House of Representatives;

—Representatives Charles B. Rangel of New York, Mickey Leland of Texas, William H. Gray III of Pennsylvania, and Bennett M. Stewart of Illinois, members of the Congressional Black Caucus.

The President left the White House for a weekend stay at Camp David.

NOMINATIONS SUBMITTED TO THE SENATE

The following list does not include promotions of members of the Uniformed Services, nominations to the Service Academies, or nominations of Foreign Service officers.

Submitted July 28, 1980

HAROLD LAFAYETTE THOMAS, of the District of Columbia, to be an Assistant Director of the Community Services Administration, vice John B. Gabusi, resigned.

NOMINATIONS—Continued

Submitted July 29, 1980

CHARLES F. MEISSNER, of Maryland, for the rank of Ambassador during his tenure of service as United States Special Negotiator for Economic Matters.

REAR ADM. HERBERT R. LIPPOLD, JR., NOAA, to be Director of the National Ocean Survey, National Oceanic and Atmospheric Administration, vice Rear Adm. Allen L. Powell, retired.

REAR ADM. HERBERT R. LIPPOLD, JR., National Oceanic and Atmospheric Administration, subject to qualifications provided by law, for appointment as a member of the Mississippi River Commission.

BARBARA S. THOMAS, of New York, to be a member of the Securities and Exchange Commission for a term expiring June 5, 1985, vice Irving M. Pollack, resigned.

LESLIE G. FOSCHIO, of New York, to be United States Attorney for the Western District of New York for a term of 4 years, vice Richard J. Arcara, term expired.

Submitted July 30, 1980

HOWARD F. SACHS, of Missouri, to be United States Circuit Judge for the Eighth Circuit, vice Floyd R. Gibson, retired.

The following-named persons to be members of the National Council on the Arts for terms expiring September 3, 1986:

KURT HERBERT ADLER, of California, vice Leonard L. Farber, term expiring.

MARGO ALBERT, of California, vice Sandra J. Hale, term expiring.

ROBERT JOFFREY, of New York, vice Harry M. Weese, term expiring.

TONI MORRISON, of New York, vice Dolores Wharton, term expiring.

IEOH MING PEI, of New York, vice James E. Barnett, term expiring.

LIDA ROGERS, of Mississippi, vice Harvey Lavan Cliburn, Jr., term expiring.

ERICH LEINSDORF, of Massachusetts, to be a member of the National Council on the Arts for the term expiring September 3, 1986, vice George Crossan Seybolt, term expiring.

Submitted July 31, 1980

JACK ROBERT BINNS, of Washington, a Foreign Service officer of Class three, to be Ambassador Extraordinary and Plenipotentiary of the United States of America to Honduras.

The following-named persons to be members of the United States Metric Board for the terms indicated:

NOMINATIONS—Continued

Submitted July 31—Continued

For the remainder of the term expiring June 14, 1982

BRUCE PAUL JOHNSON, of Nevada, vice Paul Block, Jr., resigned.

For a term expiring March 23, 1986

ALFREDO A. CANTU, of Colorado, vice Carl A. Beck, term expired.

For terms expiring June 14, 1986

JAMES M. ROSSER, of California, vice Bruce Paul Johnson, term expired.

DENNIS R. SMITH, of Massachusetts (reappointment).

MIGUEL A. GIMENEZ-MUNOZ, of Puerto Rico, to be United States District Judge for the District of Puerto Rico, vice a new position created by P.L. 95–486, approved October 20, 1978.

The following-named persons to be members of the Board of Regents of the Uniformed Services University of the Health Sciences for the terms indicated:

For terms expiring June 20, 1983

ROBERT HIGGINS EBERT, of New York, vice Joseph D. Matarazzo, term expired.

EUGENE M. FARBER, of California, vice Charles E. Odegaard, term expired.

For terms expiring June 20, 1985

LAURO F. CAVAZOS, of Texas, vice Alfred A. Marquez, term expired.

CARO ELISE LUHRS, of the District of Columbia, vice H. Ashton Thomas, term expired.

WILLIAM R. ROY, of Kansas, vice Durward G. Hall, term expired.

The following-named persons to be members of the National Commission on Libraries and Information Science for terms expiring July 19, 1985:

CHARLES WILLIAM BENTON, of Illinois (reappointment).

GORDON M. AMBACH, of New York, vice Marian Pollensky Leith, term expired.

PAULETTE H. HOLAHAN, of Louisiana, vice Mildred E. Younger, term expired.

LEONARD SILVERSTEIN, of Maryland, to be a member of the United States Advisory Commission on Public Diplomacy for a term expiring July 1, 1983 (reappointment).

CHECKLIST OF WHITE HOUSE PRESS RELEASES

The following listing contains releases of the White House Press Office which are not included in this issue.

Released July 29, 1980

Advance text: remarks at a ceremony commemorating the fifth anniversary of the signing of the Final Act of the Conference on Security and Cooperation in Europe

Announcement: nomination of Leslie G. Foschio to be United States Attorney for the Western District of New York

Announcement: nomination of Howard F. Sachs to be United States Circuit Judge for the Eighth Circuit

Released July 30, 1980

Announcement: selection of Gov. Bob Graham of Florida, Coretta Scott King, and Sol Chick Chaikin to deliver nominating and seconding speeches for the President at the Democratic National Convention; biographies of the speakers

Advance text: remarks at the medal presentation ceremony for members of the United States Olympic team

Transcript: White House statement on Billy Carter's activities with the Libyan Government, as read by C. Ray Jenkins, Special Assistant to the President, and news conference by Mr. Jenkins

Released July 31, 1980

Fact sheet: International Solvent Refined Coal II Agreement

Announcement: nomination of Miguel A. Gimenez-Munoz to be United States District Judge for the District of Puerto Rico

Transcript: announcement on postponing the President's planned trip to Cleveland, Ohio, on August 4 and news conference on Billy Carter's activities with the Libyan Government—by Press Secretary Jody Powell

ACTS APPROVED BY THE PRESIDENT

Approved July 25, 1980

S.J. Res. 180_____ Public Law 96–313
A joint resolution to provide for the reappointment of William A. M. Burden as a citizen regent of the Board of Regents of the Smithsonian Institution.

S.J. Res. 181_____ Public Law 96–314
A joint resolution to provide for the reappointment of Murray Gell-Mann as a citizen regent of the Board of Regents of the Smithsonian Institution.

S. 2382_____ Public Law 96–315
An act to provide for additional authorization for appropriations for the Tinicum National Environmental Center.

Approved July 30, 1980

S. 2240_____ Public Law 96–316
National Aeronautics and Space Administration Authorization Act, 1981.

Approved July 31, 1980

S. 1647_____ Public Law 96–317
Commission on Wartime Relocation and Internment of Civilians Act.

Approved August 1, 1980

S. 1466_____ Public Law 96–318
An act to provide for the distribution of certain funds appropriated to pay judgments in favor of the Delaware Tribe of Indians and the absentee Delaware Tribe of Western Oklahoma in Indian Claims Commission dockets 27–A and 241, 289, and 27–B and 338, and for other purposes.

S. 2508_____ Public Law 96–319
An act to provide for the disposition of the Gila River Pima-Maricopa Indian Community judgment funds awarded in dockets 236–A, 236–B, and 236–E before the Indian Claims Commission and the United States Court of Claims, and for other purposes.

Ocean Thermal Energy Conversion Act of 1980

Statement on Signing S. 2492 Into Law. August 4, 1980

I have signed into law S. 2492, the Ocean Thermal Energy Conversion Act of 1980, sponsored by Senator Daniel Inouye. This bill establishes a licensing and permitting program within the National Oceanic and Atmospheric Administration for the ocean thermal energy conversion industry and authorizes use of the Maritime Administration's loan guarantee authority for the construction of ocean energy facilities, once this technology has been successfully demonstrated.

Ocean thermal energy conversion (OTEC) is a new energy technology that, when developed, could contribute greatly to our goal of meeting 20 percent of U.S. energy needs from solar and renewable sources by the year 2000. Just 2 weeks ago, I signed into law the Ocean Thermal Energy Conversion Research, Development, and Demonstration Act. That law authorizes an ambitious program of research and development of OTEC technology. S. 2492 is another early step in the process of bringing OTEC technology into the mainstream of our energy marketplace.

OTEC technology is still in its infancy. Therefore, we must be careful to ensure that the loan guarantees for commercialization activities provided by S. 2492 are made only if they are necessary and appropriate, and only after this technology has been demonstrated. S. 2492 recognizes the need for such prudence by requiring that the authority for a loan guarantee be conditional on certification by the Secretary of Energy that the OTEC technology to be used in the facility in question has been successfully demonstrated on a scale sufficient to establish the likelihood of economic success. Furthermore, the guarantee authority provided by S. 2492 is discretionary. If events indicate that financial assistance is not needed, or that another form of Federal financial assistance is more appropriate than loan guarantees for commercializing OTEC technology, S. 2492 does not foreclose the proper course of action.

The Nation's energy security demands that we pursue renewable energy sources that are secure from foreign interdiction. S. 2492 provides a licensing program and a financing tool that may be of substantial assistance in applying OTEC technology after it has been demonstrated in the years ahead. It is with pleasure that I sign this bill into law.

NOTE: As enacted, S. 2492 is Public Law 96–320, approved August 3.

United States Ambassador to Haiti

Nomination of Henry L. Kimelman. August 4, 1980

The President today announced that he will nominate Henry L. Kimelman, of St. Thomas, Virgin Islands, to be Ambassador Extraordinary and Plenipotentiary of the United States to Haiti. He would replace William B. Jones, who is being assigned to Hampton Institute as diplomat in residence.

Kimelman is chairman of the board and president of WICORP, Inc. (West Indies Corporation) in St. Thomas. He was born January 21, 1921, in New York City. He received a B.S. from New York University in 1943. He served in the U.S. Navy from 1943 to 1946.

From 1949 to 1960, Kimelman was president and treasurer of Virgin Isle Hotel, Inc., and Virgin Islands Realty Corp. From 1961 to 1964, he was commissioner of commerce for the Virgin Islands, chairman of the Virgin Islands Economic Development Board, and administrator for the Virgin Islands of the United States Area Redevelopment Administration.

From 1964 to 1967, Kimelman was chairman of the board of Island Block Corp. and Henry Elliot, Ltd. From 1967 to 1969, he was assistant to the Secretary of the Interior, and from 1968 to 1972, he was director of the U.S. National Park Foundation. From 1969 to 1971, he was president of Overview Corp., in Washington, D.C. He has been chairman and president of WICORP since 1969.

Kimelman is chairman of the Development Advisory Board, Child Development Associate Consortium. He is a member of the Advisory Committee on the Arts of the John F. Kennedy Center for the Performing Arts, and the World Business Council.

Labor Day, 1980

Message of the President.　August 4, 1980

My best wishes and thanks go to you on this 99th annual Labor Day. This is a time for us all to acknowledge the achievements of American workers.

The United States has the world's most productive work force. With your dedication and skills, you have built the world's highest standard of living. Our world leadership for freedom and peace would not be possible without your economic achievements.

Yet serious challenges jeopardize those achievements. Despite eight million new jobs created in our economy since 1976, unemployment has risen again. Inflation and declining productivity have sapped our economic strength.

Our first priority must be to keep in the United States the capital needed to create American jobs, capital which now flows overseas to pay for oil. In three years, we have already made a dramatic reversal of our growing dependence on imported oil. Our energy policy, the first in our history, will reduce that dependence more in this decade.

Next, we must rebuild our aging industrial base. We must save and invest more in new tools and factories and new jobs for American workers. We must rebuild our transportation networks. We must restore our competitive edge in world trade and expand exports. We must invest in our human capital by providing workers with needed skills.

But most important, we must do all this in a way that expands economic and social justice in our country. We must protect the health and safety of workers. We must sustain aid to the poor, the ill, and the elderly. We need a new and enduring partnership of businesses, government, and labor, building from the National Accord begun a year ago.

These are more than economic challenges. They challenge our ability to pull together as a people, to look honestly at problems, to build for our long-term needs, and to look beyond quick-fix solutions and simple slogans.

Our history is one of a people diverse in backgrounds but united in common values, facing one serious challenge after another. We have faced depressions, wars, injustice, and prevailed each time. We will prevail again and, with your help, meet fully the challenges of our time.

On this day, let us give thanks for our blessings and rededicate ourselves to making this great country of ours even greater.

JIMMY CARTER

International Convention Against the Taking of Hostages

Message to the Senate Transmitting the Convention. August 4, 1980

To the Senate of the United States:

With a view to receiving the advice and consent of the Senate to ratification, I transmit herewith a copy of the International Convention Against the Taking of Hostages, adopted by the United Nations General Assembly on December 17, 1979 and signed on behalf of the United States of America on December 21, 1979. The report of the Department of State with respect to the Convention is also transmitted for the information of the Senate.

In recent years, we have witnessed an unprecedented and intolerable increase in acts of terrorism involving the taking of hostages in various parts of the world. Events have clearly demonstrated that no country or region is exempt from the human tragedy and immense costs which almost invariably result from such criminal acts. Consequently, the urgent need to take positive action against these manifestations of international terrorism has become readily apparent. Although the penal codes of most States contain provisions proscribing assault, extortion, kid-

napping, and other serious crimes inherent in hostage-taking incidents, an international framework for cooperation among States directed toward prevention of such incidents and ensuring punishment of offenders, wherever found, has not previously existed.

The Convention creates a legal mechanism whereby persons alleged to have committed offenses under the Convention will be prosecuted or extradited if apprehended within the jurisdiction of a State Party, wherever the offense was committed. In essence, the Convention imposes binding legal obligations upon States Parties either to submit for prosecution or to extradite any person within their jurisdiction who commits an act of hostage-taking (as defined in Article 1), attempts to commit such an act, or participates as an accomplice of anyone who commits or attempts to commit such an act. A State Party is subject to these obligations without regard to the place where the alleged act covered by Article 1 was committed.

Article 1 of the Convention declares that the act or offense of taking of hostages is committed by any person who seizes or detains and threatens to kill, injure, or continue to detain another person (the "hostage") in order to compel a third party (a State, an international intergovernmental organization, a natural or juridical person, or a group of persons) to do or abstain from doing any act as an explicit or implicit condition for the release of the hostage. States Parties to the Convention will also be obligated to cooperate in preventing hostage-taking offenses by means of internal preventive measures, exchange of information, and coordination of enforcement activities.

This Convention is a vitally important new element in the campaign against the scourge of international terrorism in general and the heinous crime of hostage-taking in particular. I hope that all States will become Parties to this Convention, and that it will be applied universally. I recommend, therefore, that the Senate give early and favorable consideration to this Convention.

JIMMY CARTER

The White House,
    August 4, 1980.

United States-Jamaica Convention on Taxation and Fiscal Evasion

Message to the Senate Transmitting the Convention. August 4, 1980

To the Senate of the United States:

I transmit herewith, for the advice and consent of the Senate to ratification, a Convention between the Government of the United States of America and the Government of Jamaica for the Avoidance of Double Taxation and the Prevention of Fiscal Evasion with Respect to Taxes on Income (the Convention), together with a related exchange of notes, signed at Kingston on May 21, 1980. I also transmit the report of the Department of State with respect to the Convention.

In general, the Convention follows the pattern of the United States model income tax convention, although there are some accommodations to Jamaica's status as a developing country. For example, business profits of an enterprise of one country, as in the model convention, may be taxed by the other only if they are attributable to a permanent establishment in the other country. In the proposed Convention, however, the definition of a permanent establishment is more broadly drawn. Similarly, in the United States model, an individual who is a resident of one State may be taxed by the other on income from

personal services performed in the other State only if certain thresholds are passed, but in the proposed Convention, the time threshold is shorter for independent services and a dollar threshold has been added.

The exchange of notes sets forth certain understandings between the two Governments. It deals, among other matters, with the conditions under which the United States would allow a foreign tax credit for Jamaican income taxes on bauxite profits. The exchange of notes also confirms the fact that the Convention has been designed to cover a substitute tax which may be imposed by Jamaica "in lieu of" the corporate income tax on such profits if such substitute tax meets the requirement of section 903 of the Internal Revenue Code.

I recommend that the Senate give early and favorable consideration to the Convention and its advice and consent to ratification.

JIMMY CARTER

The White House,
    August 4, 1980.

Strategic Petroleum Reserve

Executive Order 12231.   August 4, 1980

By the authority vested in me as President of the United States of America by Title VIII of the Energy Security Act (Public Law 96–294) and by Section 301 of Title 3 of the United States Code, and in order to meet the goals and requirements for the strategic petroleum reserve, it is hereby ordered as follows:

1–101.   The functions vested in the President by Section 160(c) of the Energy Policy and Conservation Act, as amended, are delegated to the Secretary of

Energy (42 U.S.C. 6240(c); see Section 801 of the Energy Security Act).

1–102. The functions vested in the President by Section 7430(k) of Title 10 of the United States Code are delegated to the Secretary of Energy (see Section 804(b) of the Energy Security Act).

1–103. The functions vested in the President by Section 805(a) of the Energy Security Act are, consistent with Section 2 of Executive Order No. 11790, as amended, delegated to the Secretary of Energy.

JIMMY CARTER

The White House,
  August 4, 1980.

[Filed with the Office of the Federal Register, 11:58 a.m., August 5, 1980]

THE PRESIDENT'S NEWS CONFERENCE OF AUGUST 4, 1980

THE PRESIDENT. This evening we will extend the press conference time to a full hour to give me an adequate opportunity to present a statement and then to answer more questions than would ordinarily be the case.

BILLY CARTER'S ACTIVITIES WITH LIBYAN GOVERNMENT

In 1976, as a candidate, I made a commitment that explains why now as a President I want to make this statement to the American people this evening. Four years ago our country was deeply shaken by an administration that had betrayed its high trust and had tried to hide the truth from public judgment. I was asked then how Americans' lives would be changed if I was elected President. I answered that I would work to restore the confidence of the American people in the integrity of their Government. Integrity has been and will continue to be a cornerstone of my administration. When questions of propriety are raised, I want to make sure they're answered fully. When the questions concern me, I want to answer them myself.

Questions have now been raised concerning my actions and those of my administration regarding my brother Billy Carter and the Government of Libya. We have made as thorough an investigation as possible, and the facts are available for the committees of Congress and for the public to examine. They will show that neither I nor any member of my administration has violated any law or committed any impropriety. I've today filed a full report with the Congress. I cannot read it all to you tonight, but here are the main points.

Let me first say a word about the U.S. policy toward the nation of Libya.

There are few governments in the world with which we have more sharp and frequent policy disagreements. Libya has steadfastly opposed our efforts to reach and to carry out the Camp David accords to bring peace to the Middle East. Our two governments have strongly different opinions and attitudes toward the PLO and toward international terrorism. Within OPEC, Libya has promoted sharply higher prices of oil and, on occasion, has advocated the interruption of oil supplies to the United States and to other Western nations.

On the other hand, we have substantial trade with Libya. Libya is one of our major oil suppliers, and its high-quality crude oil is important to our east coast refineries. Libya has publicly and privately opposed Iran's seizure and holding of our hostages, and for a time, Libya joined with other Moslem countries in opposing the Soviet invasion of Afghanistan.

So for many years, our policies and actions toward Libya have therefore mixed firmness with caution.

And now I'd like to say a word about my brother's relations with Libya. As all of you know by now, Billy is a colorful personality. We are personally close. I love him, and he loves me. Billy is extremely independent. On occasion he has said, "I don't tell Jimmy how to run the country, and he doesn't tell me how to run my life." When I was elected President, Billy was thrust into the public limelight. Media attention made him an instant celebrity. He was asked to make a number of television and other speaking engagements, and he even put his name on a new brand of beer.

And in the summer of 1978, Billy was invited to visit Libya with a group of businessmen and State officials from Georgia. This highly publicized trip occurred late in September 1978. I was not aware that he was planning the trip until after he had left the United States and shortly before he arrived in Libya. When I heard about it, I was deeply concerned that there might be some serious or unpleasant incident while he was there.

Shortly after he returned from Libya, in October 1978, I saw a message from our chargé in Tripoli reporting on the positive nature of the visit. I was greatly relieved, and I sent a copy of that message to Billy. This message contained no sensitive information, was never encoded, and in fact, more than a year ago it was made publicly available by the State Department to a news columnist.

Early in 1979 a Libyan trade mission came to the United States, visited several localities in our country. Billy visited with the Libyans and made a number of controversial statements, which were roundly

criticized both by the press and also by the American public. I publicly deplored, in a news conference, some of those comments myself.

As a result of Billy's remarks and his new association with the Libyans, almost all of his scheduled television and other appearances were canceled. His income from these public appearances almost totally disappeared, while his financial obligations continued to mount.

I shared the general concern about Billy's relationship with Libya, and the members of our family were also concerned about some of his personal problems. During this period, Billy entered the hospital for medical treatment. On one occasion while he was hospitalized, he discussed with me the possibility of another trip to Libya, and I urged him not to go, partly because of his health and partly because of the adverse effect it could have on our Middle East negotiations, which were at a critical stage at that time.

By the late summer of 1979, Billy had successfully completed his medical treatment, and despite my advice he made a second trip to Libya. There was relatively little publicity about this trip.

I am not aware of any effort by Billy to affect this Government's policies or actions concerning Libya. I am certain that he made no such effort with me. The only occasion on which Billy was involved, to my knowledge, in any matter between Libya and the United States was his participation, with my full approval, in our efforts to seek Libyan help for the return of our hostages from Iran. Let me discuss this incident briefly.

On November the 4th, 1979, our hostages were seized in Tehran. In the weeks that followed, we explored every possible avenue to bring about their release. We increased our military presence in the

Persian Gulf, we stopped all oil imports from Iran, and we seized the assets of that country. We appealed to the United Nations Security Council and to the World Court. We asked other governments, and particularly Moslem governments, including Libya, to support our position. As is still the case, we explored every official and unofficial avenue of contact we could find to encourage the Iranians to release the American hostages.

Public statements coming out of Libya at that time were not supportive and indicated that our diplomatic efforts to secure their assistance had not been successful. During the third week in November, it occurred to us that Billy might be able to get the Libyans to help to induce the Iranians to release the American hostages. As requested, he talked to the Libyans about our hostages and arranged a meeting with a Libyan diplomat at the White House. I did not attend that meeting, and so far as I'm aware, Billy played no further role in these discussions with the Libyans.

As matters turned out, the Libyan foreign office announced that the hostages should be released, and the leader of Libya, Colonel Qadhafi, also made the direct private appeal to Ayatollah Khomeini that we requested. At least in this respect, the approach to the Libyans was successful; whether it would have been successful if Billy had not participated is a question that no one can answer with certainty.

I made this decision in good faith, with the best interests of the hostages and our Nation in mind. Billy merely responded to our request for assistance, and I believe his only motive in this effort was to seek release of the American hostages from Iran.

And now, concerning Billy's alleged Government contacts on behalf of Libya:

There have been many press reports that Billy may have tried to influence U.S. policy on licensing aircraft to Libya or on other matters. I can state categorically that my brother Billy had no influence or effect on my decisions or on any U.S. Government policy or action concerning Libya. Billy has never asked me to take any step that would affect any of these actions or policies. And so far as we have been able to determine after long and extensive investigation, Billy has not made any such effort with anybody in my administration.

Concerning the Department of Justice investigation, let me say this: Under the President's supervision, law enforcement responsibility is delegated to the Attorney General. The President's power of supervision of the Justice Department was abused in the Watergate scandal, as none of us can ever forget.

When I took office, I instructed the Attorney General, Griffin Bell, that neither I nor any White House official would ever attempt to influence the Department of Justice investigations concerning any charges of law violation. When possible conflict-of-interest issues arise, as in the case of a member of the President's official family or his personal family, we take extra precautions to prevent improper interference.

This policy was followed strictly in the present case from the time the investigation began until the final papers were filed on July the 14th. There was no contact in either direction between the Department of Justice and the White House concerning the conduct of this investigation. On July 22d, the White House issued a public statement to this effect.

Two days later, I found a reference in my notes to brief comments which I had exchanged with Attorney General Civiletti about 6 weeks earlier at the conclusion of a long meeting concerning judicial appointments and other matters. I had not remembered these comments, and I decided that they should be made public. While the July 22d statement was technically correct, it clearly required amplification to disclose these brief comments.

To me, integrity does not mean that a mistake is never made; integrity means that when a mistake is made, even though it's highly technical in nature and was inadvertent, it ought to be disclosed. And that's exactly what we did.

In this brief exchange between myself and the Attorney General, which lasted just—less than a minute, I would guess, the Attorney General did not inform me of any detail as to the conduct of the investigation. He told me only about the Department's insistence that Billy file a registration statement and about the Department's standard enforcement policy.

On June 26th, after I returned from the Venice summit conference, my Counsel notified me that Billy's lawyers hoped to resolve this matter by his filing the registration statement, and I called Billy to encourage him to work harmoniously with his lawyers. He said that his lawyers were in negotiation with the Department of Justice, but that he personally did not think that he needed to file a registration statement. On July the 1st, just a few days later, I called Billy again to urge him to accede to the Department's request and to follow his lawyers' advice and make a full disclosure. He did so on July 14th.

It was not until July the 15th that I knew of the two large payments or loans of money from Libya to my brother. So far as we have been able to determine, no one in the White House had any information about the payments or about any evidence relating to such payments until Billy Carter's lawyers informed my Counsel about them on July the 11th, when

the court papers were about to be filed. No one in the White House furnished information about the investigation to Billy or to anyone associated with him at any time.

Finally, there's one more rumor that I would like to lay to rest. No payments or transfers of this money have been made to me, and no such payments or transfers have been made to Carter's Warehouse. And I will also see to it that no direct or indirect benefit of any kind will ever flow to me in the future.

To summarize, Billy has had no influence or effect on my decisions or any U.S. Government policy or on any action concerning Libya. Neither I nor anyone in the White House has ever tried to influence or to affect the Justice Department's actions or decisions. Neither I nor anyone in the White House informed Billy of any leads or evidence obtained by the Department. Everything that I and the White House staff did with respect to this case was designed to serve the interests of law enforcement and justice.

I am deeply concerned that Billy has received funds from Libya and that he may be under obligation to Libya. These facts will have to govern my own relationships with my brother Billy. Billy has had no influence on U.S. policies or actions concerning Libya in the past, and he will have no influence in the future.

Our political history is full of stories about Presidential families and relatives whom other people have tried to use in order to gain favor with incumbent administrations. In most such cases, the appearance of favoritism has been much worse than the reality. My brother Billy's case is one of many such examples. To keep this problem from recurring, I've asked my Counsel to draft a rule that will bar any employee of the executive branch from dealing with any member of the

President's family under any circumstances that create either the reality or the appearance of improper favor or influence.

Now I'd be glad to answer questions, if you have them.

QUESTIONS

BILLY CARTER

Q. Mr. President, on the question of propriety, do you think that it was proper for the Attorney General to tell you to urge Billy to register as a foreign agent and to tell you that he would not be prosecuted if he did so? And also, on the question of the money, you told us where the money didn't go. Do you know where the Libyan payments did go and how Billy used the money?

THE PRESIDENT. No, I don't know where the money went or where it might go. Billy can answer that question, and I understand he's prepared to answer any questions.

I don't think there's any impropriety at all in the conversation that I had with the Attorney General. He did not ask me to take any action. I did not ask him to take any action. He simply informed me— I believe I can quote his words from my notes—that Billy was foolish not to comply with the Department insistence that he file the registration papers. And he said that if he filed these papers truthfully that the normal procedure of the Department was not to punish or to prosecute a person in that category.

DEMOCRATIC NATIONAL CONVENTION

Q. Mr. President, a number of prominent Democrats, Senator Byrd and Mayor Koch of New York among them, have suggested that you might release your convention delegates to vote their preference on the first Presidential ballot. Are there any circumstances under which you would do this, and do you fear that doing so might hurt your chances of getting the nomination?

THE PRESIDENT. I have no plans to do this. I ran in all the primaries, all the caucuses. In that intense political competition, I won about 60 percent of the commitments of the delegates in accordance with the decisions that were made by the 19 million Democrats who participated actively in the primaries and the caucuses. These are not my delegates; they are the Democratic voters' delegates.

This so-called open convention, which is a phrase that's been used by Senator Kennedy and others and picked up broadly by the press, is a gross misnomer. What they actually are calling for is a brokered convention, to induce those delegates to violate their signed pledge or oath that they would go to the convention and vote in accordance with the way the voters cast their ballots back home.

There is a requirement throughout this entire electoral process, a decision made by the Democratic National Committee, unanimously, 18 months before the first caucuses, which were in Iowa, that this is the way the rule would be imposed. All the candidates agreed to it and understood it. And also, there was a requirement that in the States there be a line for uncommitted delegates, who did not want to express their preference. Some uncommitted delegates were chosen. That line was put there to give them that option.

What Senator Kennedy and others are now asking for is for those candidates who are elected by the people who wanted me to be the nominee violate their oath and that all the delegates in effect be uncommitted. This puts back 10 years of progress that the Democratic Party has made to democratize a process and to remove control of the convention from the power-brokers and put it in the hands of people who go to the polls and vote on primary day or go to the caucuses and select delegates. That's the issue at stake. It's a very simple, clear issue.

My position is that the convention ought not to be a brokered convention, but that the delegates should vote the way the voters back home told them to vote. Others who have lost in the primaries now want to change the rules, after the primaries and caucuses are all over, to go back to the old brokered-type convention.

BILLY CARTER

Q. Mr. President, I've been around a long time, but there are still some questions of a personal nature that are painful to ask. And yet, I feel there is one that must be asked.

THE PRESIDENT. I'll be happy to answer any question.

Q. Accepting your statement that you did not know until mid-July that your brother Billy was getting money——

THE PRESIDENT. Yes.

Q.——you say that you are personally very close to him; you love him, and he loves you; and you know him very well. Having known since September 1978 that he was involved in some way doing some work for the Libyan Government, having known more recently through an intelligence report that he was trying to get oil allocations for an oil company in the United States, did it never occur to you, knowing his penchant for get-rich-quick schemes and making money—did it never occur to you that he might be seeking financial gain from that relationship?

Mr. PRESIDENT. Yes, it occurred to me—not as early as you described.

We have several hundred—I think more than 2,000 Americans who live in Libya. As I said, we have major trade relationships with Libya. It's not a completely outcast nation. There are people who go from this country to Libya on a daily basis.

Billy did go to Libya without my knowledge or approval. I think it was in September of 1978. At that time, I don't believe from what I know now that Billy had any idea of becoming anything as a representative for or a special friend of Libya. He went there with some businessmen from Georgia and some members of the State legislature—not secretly, unfortunately; it was a highly publicized trip.

The first special relationship Billy had with Libya was when a Libyan trade delegation came to the United States, in effect to reciprocate that visit by the Georgians. They came to Atlanta; they came to Washington and some other places. Billy, in effect, acted as their host in Georgia. This was an extremely highly publicized and controversial time, and Billy was severely castigated in the press and by many American citizens, as I said, including myself in one news conference, for some of the remarks he made.

Following that, I tried to encourage Billy not to go to Libya. In the documents that I filed with the congressional committees this afternoon, there's one letter that I wrote to Billy while he was in the hospital in California—the letter is a matter of record—encouraging him not to go to Libya. Obviously, I was concerned. But I don't have authority to order Billy to do something. It's not illegal for him to make a trip to Libya, for instance. I had no knowledge at all of any payment that was made to Billy. But of course, I was concerned about his relationship with Libya, wish he never had any relationship with Libya.

So, I can't condone what he has done. I'm not trying to make excuses. Anyone who knows Billy knows that no one can push him around. And I think that we used an adequate amount of personal persuasion, when I had the opportunity, then the telephone call from Dr. Brzezinski, warning Billy not that his action was illegal, as known, but that he might cause embarrassment to our country and embarrassment to me. I don't believe that there's anything further that I could have done that would have been effective.

Q. Mr. President, you said just a few minutes ago, sir, in your opening remarks, that neither you nor any member of your administration had violated any law or committed any impropriety.

THE PRESIDENT. That is correct.

Q. But, sir, don't you think that by using your brother, Billy Carter, at least as an emissary to make a contact with a foreign government—don't you feel that perhaps it might have been better judgment to have used a trained diplomat in that capacity?

THE PRESIDENT. No, not in that particular instance concerning the hostages. We were using trained diplomats. Immediately after the hostages were seized, this became an absolute, total obsession of mine, to get those hostages released. We inventoried every possibility of influence on the Iranians to induce them to release our hostages, safely and immediately. We sent messages—and had our diplomats in those countries and contacted their diplomats in Washington—to almost every nation on Earth, every one that we thought might have the slightest semblance of influence with Iran. We especially thought that the Moslem countries, believing in the Koran, having the same religion as the Ayatollah Khomeini, might have a special influence.

We had tried through diplomatic means to get Libya to give us some support in condemning the Iranian action and calling for the release of the hostages. Up through the 18th of November, the public statements coming out of Libya—and these are documented in Dr. Brzezinski's report—had been negative, against our position, in effect supporting the holding of the hostages. Some private comments from Libyan diplomats to our diplomats in the United Nations, for instance, had said, "We would like to help you," but the public comments, which were the important ones, were contrary to that.

Under those circumstances, I decided to use Billy to see if he could have some special influence to get the Libyans to help. I had no reticence about it.

That was the same day that the religious fanatics attacked the mosque in Saudi Arabia. It was the same day, I believe, that Khomeini announced that the hostages, American hostages, would be tried and, if convicted, Khomeini said, "Jimmy Carter knows what's going to happen to them." We thought that the hostages' lives were directly in danger.

I saw then and see now nothing wrong with asking Billy and other private citizens to try to help if it's appropriate and legal. The only thing Billy did was to contact the Libyans, whom he knew personally—he does not know Qadhafi, but he did know the chargé in Washington—and say, "We would like very much to have your help in having the hostages released. Will you meet with Dr. Brzezinski at the White House," a week from then, which was the 27th day of November.

Billy then met a week later with Dr. Brzezinski and the chargé, and we believe that some progress was made. As I said in my opening statement, I cannot say for sure that Billy had anything in the world to do with the progress that was made. But 2 days after Billy contacted the chargé, they made a public announcement for the first time, Libya did, calling for the release of the hostages. After that meeting, Colonel Qadhafi himself sent a personal emissary to Khomeini, asking Khomeini for the first time to release our hostages, and then he sent me word that he had done so.

I'm not trying to claim great things from that small involvement of Billy. But Billy came up to Washington, so far as I know, at his own expense on two occasions. He went back to Plains. He never told anybody publicly that he had done it. He never bragged about it. And I have enough judgment to know that that may have enhanced Billy's stature in the minds of the Libyans. That's the only down side to it that I can understand. And that may have been bad judgment, but I was the one that made the judgment. I did what I thought was best for our country and best for the hostages, and I believe that that's exactly what Billy was doing.

COMPETENCE OF ADMINISTRATION

Q. Aside from the questions of legality and propriety, some of your critics say that this Billy Carter case is another example of a general aura of incompetence that hangs over your Presidency—the fits and starts with which the case came out, the corrections, the records, the recollections that had to be refreshed. Do you recognize that there is this charge of incompetence that settles over you, and if so, what are you going to do about it?

THE PRESIDENT. I've heard you mention that on television a few times, but I don't agree with it. No, I think the historic record of this administration, years looking back, will show that it was a competent administration, that it accurately represented the ideals of the American people and had many notable achievements. I need not enumerate those now.

But I don't believe that this is a comedy of errors or that we have made many errors—a few, yes. We've made some mistakes, because we were in a hurry to get all the information out. It was much better to have the information come out as we determined it than it would be if we had withheld all information and, in effect, stonewalled the question for 2 or 3 weeks.

It might very well be that in the future we discover some new fact or someone comes up and makes a statement that we didn't know about. If so, we will immediately make that information available to you and the other news media. But I think that's the best way to handle it, and I don't have any concern about having acted other than competently in this case.

PRESIDENT'S REELECTION CAMPAIGN

Q. Next week you go before the Democratic Convention to seek renomination, as we all know.

THE PRESIDENT. I remember. [*Laughter*]

Q. Not only given the state of the press conference tonight but looking ahead to such matters as the economy, inflation, growing unemployment, recession, troubles abroad, will you offer yourself to the delegates of the Democratic Convention as a man proposing changes or will you simply say the country should have 4 more years of the same?

THE PRESIDENT. Four more years of the same President, with changes and progress to be achieved during those 4 years.

We have economic problems. I think every nation on Earth has them—some much worse than we. We've made some progress. We've never had as many jobs added, for instance, in the first 3½ years, in any period of our history as we have since I've been in office. Lately we've seen a substantial lowering of interest rates and inflation rate. I think we'll see some more progress made on inflation in the next few months. I believe that we have established a very good working relationship between our country and other nations, opened up new friendships, maintained this country at peace, and so forth. I need not enumerate what I think we've done that is good.

But I believe that the most important part of an election year is to give the American people an opportunity to hear the issues debated, the record assessed for the incumbent, and then to let the American people choose: Do we want the Nation for the next 4 years to be led by the Republicans, or do we want it led by the Democrats? And specifically, do we want it led by Ronald Reagan, or do we want it to be led by the Democratic nominee? And I am expecting it to be myself. And in that process, with, I hope, numerous debates between me and Ronald Reagan on all the issues that are important to the American people, the American people will make a judgment.

This is the way I've always run for office, the way I ran in 1976. I think we have an excellent record to take to the American people and an excellent prospect for an even better life in this country in the years ahead.

BILLY CARTER

Q. Mr. President, you say you and your brother Billy are close. Have you had any conversations with him since the July 1 phone call, when you urged him to register, and can you characterize those conversations?

THE PRESIDENT. I have not had any conversations with Billy since July the 1st except in a crowd of people at a softball game in Plains, and I went into his service station one day to invite him to play softball the following day. I've never discussed this case or Libya or government or anything of that kind and have not spoken a word to Billy in private since July the 1st, the conversation that I've described to you.

You can ask a followup question, if you like.

Q. Mr. President, do you think you should be discussing it with him?

THE PRESIDENT. No. I think it's improper for me now to be having a direct conversation with Billy. There have been some communications between us through our attorneys, through my Counsel in the White House and through his attorneys. But they've been completely proper, and records have been maintained of them. And I believe that's the best way to handle this matter until it is resolved.

As I said in the closing part of my statement, even in the future, regardless of the outcome of this occurrence, I will not accept any benefit from the funds that Billy has received. And also, as long as I have the slightest suspicion that Billy is still involved with Libya, I will exclude any sort of relationship between myself and Billy that relates to government matters that could possibly impact on Libya.

Q. Mr. President, I have talked to hundreds of Democrats, and I think that in the White House you have more fear of this affair than there is need for. All people tell me that they have great confidence in you, although they might consider that you had a little bit more heart for your brother than for the Presidency. In your own assessment, did you act as a President or as a brother?

THE PRESIDENT. I think Billy would say that I acted more as a President than a brother, and I think I have.

My responsibility, uniquely, is to the

Presidency and the upholding of the principles of our Nation, and I'm sworn by oath to uphold the Constitution of the United States and the laws of our Nation. If any member of my family should violate those laws, then I'm charged with the responsibility, which I would not avoid, to see that the law is carried out, no matter if my own family members should suffer. And this is the process that is presently ongoing: an investigation and the decision to be made by the Justice Department, without my involvement.

I have not promoted this incident; in fact, I wish that it had never been promoted by the press and by the interest of the American people. But since it has become a burning issue in the minds of many people, with headlines and evening news stories, sometimes even dominating the day's news events, my commitment has been, the last 2 or 3 weeks, to search out all the facts that I could find and lay them before the American people in two ways: one, through the investigating committees in the Congress, House and Senate; and secondly, here, with a brief statement telling the facts and then to answer your questions. But this group is at liberty to ask me questions about other matters as well as this.

Q. Mr. President, regarding your mention of your responsibility to enforce the laws, since your adviser, Dr. Peter Bourne,[1] was never prosecuted for his phony drug prescription taken across the State line, how can you expect the Justice Department to be taken seriously by Billy, regarding admitting he's an agent and telling the truth about the money they gave him?

THE PRESIDENT. I think you could ask

---

[1] Former Special Assistant to the President for Health Issues and Director of the Office of Drug Abuse Policy.

Billy whether or not he takes the Justice Department seriously. My belief is that he does. And I don't think anyone in this Nation who has any confidence in our country's laws and the enforcement of them would take the Justice Department any way but seriously. It's a serious matter, and it'll be handled accordingly.

PRESIDENT'S FINANCES

Q. Mr. President, you referred to rumors about some of this money going to you——

THE PRESIDENT. Yes, I've read that in the paper, and allegations have been made by Members of the Congress. That's why I wanted to answer it.

Q. Do you have any joint economic investments with Billy? I think of the Carter trust or what's left of the warehouse holdings or property. Have you tried to help Billy financially through the blind-trust arrangement, through Mr. Kirbo, and the blind-trust arrangement in—I think he's got tax liens on his house that sort of thing?

THE PRESIDENT. When I became President, I announced to the American people that I was putting my financial affairs into a trust, under a trustee. Legally, it's not a blind trust, because it's impossible for me, as President, not to read news stories and other reports that come from Plains and from the warehouse affairs. But to the best of my ability, I've stayed aloof from that. I've not made any decisions, and they've been handled in accordance with the law, sometimes publicly by my trustee. Also, I pledged myself, as President, annually to release my income tax return, which is prepared by other people—but I have to sign it—and also my financial statement, which I've done each time.

But within that boundary, I have not

been involved in financial affairs of the warehouse. There is still a relationship between Billy and the warehouse and myself and the warehouse. That Carter's Warehouse has been rented out now ever since the first year I was in office, and I have had absolutely nothing to do with it or its financial condition.

BILLY CARTER

Q. Mr. President, you have answered our questions very openly. You have said that there were no instances in this matter of illegality, wrongdoing, impropriety. You told one of my colleagues that this was really not a question of bad judgment. You told another colleague it's not a question of incompetence. Given all of that, simply put, how do you think you got into this big mess?

THE PRESIDENT. Well, I think the American press and the public will have to judge how big a mess it is. It's been a highly publicized affair. But if the facts, as I have given them to you, are confirmed, if no one in my administration—and if I myself—have committed any illegal act or impropriety, then I think that's been an investigation and a report that's served itself well.

The Justice Department is investigating still. There have been literally dozens and dozens of people who have searched their telephone records and appointment records and their memoranda of conversations. And the Congress is going to investigate it. So, I believe that this is a good way to go about resolving a question once it's raised.

I do not approve of the fact that my brother has gotten involved in a controversial relationship with an extremely unpopular government. He has, still, certain legal and constitutional rights. If he is found to have violated the law, my belief is and my hope is that he will be treated properly in accordance with the law—punished if he's guilty, exonerated if he's innocent.

But I have seen these things sweep across this Nation every now and then, with highly publicized allegations that prove not to be true. And you and others have participated in the raising of these questions. One incident that comes to mind is Hamilton Jordan, where people, later found to have lied, told stories about Hamilton Jordan, and a thorough investigation, absolutely independently of me, with a special prosecutor involved from the Justice Department, found that the allegations were not true. But for a time it was a highly publicized case, which damaged Hamilton Jordan quite a lot.

I don't know what the outcome of this case will be. But I can tell you that no one in my administration—and I have not been guilty of an illegality or an impropriety in any way, and I believe that the facts in the future will determine that to be the case.

ROLE OF PRESIDENT'S FAMILY

Q. Mr. President, you said in the report that you issued tonight—you confirmed the fact that your wife, Rosalynn Carter, was the first person to initiate the idea of using your brother Billy as the contact regarding the Iranian hostages——

THE PRESIDENT. Yes, that's correct.

Q. ——that she called him directly and then informed you later, and you asked Dr. Brzezinski to pursue the matter. I want to ask you what you think that says about her role in this administration and what the public should conclude about it? And secondly, given this regulation that you have asked your Counsel to draft on members of the family and the staff——

THE PRESIDENT. Yes.

Q. ——whether you have any second thoughts in hindsight about family diplomacy and the virtues of that, and members of the President's family going to represent him or the country abroad at ceremonies and the like?

THE PRESIDENT. No, I don't have any trepidation about continuing the policy that I have pursued in that respect.

I think it's completely appropriate for Rosalynn to have thought about how we could get the hostages released and to have called Billy to see if he thought he could possibly help. When he said that he might be able to help, she informed me of that idea. I considered it. I'm the one that made the decision, not my wife or Dr. Brzezinski or anyone else. And I decided that it was a good idea. And I told Dr. Brzezinski to call Billy and pursue it, which he did. That was the limit of her role in the entire process.

But I think it's very important that my mother on occasion, my sons on occasion, my wife on occasion participate in international affairs. When Golda Meir, former Prime Minister of Israel, died, my mother went to represent me at her funeral. She also went to the funeral of Marshal Tito, President Tito, and so forth.

So, this is the kind of thing that a President's family legitimately ought to be able to do. With many cultures in the world, many countries in the world, a President's family member plays an extremely important role in demonstrating an important personal relationship, particularly in the inauguration of a new President if I cannot go, for instance, or the death of a prominent member of that national community. I think these kinds of things are completely appropriate.

What I want the Counsel to draft is a rule that would bar any employee of the executive branch from dealing with any member of my family under any circumstances that create either the reality or the appearance of improper favor or influence. That doesn't mean that all the members of my family have to be locked up in a closet and never appear in public, because they play a very useful role. But I believe that their appearances have been proper, when Rosalynn or my mother have attended these kinds of state affairs. And I expect that they will continue to do so.

SECRETARY OF STATE EDMUND S. MUSKIE

Q. Mr. President, Edward Bennett Williams, as you know, is taking a leading role in seeking to undo the faithful delegate rule. Mr. Williams is a close personal associate of the Secretary of State. And we see now signs of the draft Muskie movement—bumper stickers. I wonder whether this has caused some kind of strain between you and the Secretary of State.

THE PRESIDENT. No, it has not. Secretary Muskie has actively attempted to stop this effort to subvert the rules of the Democratic Party and to violate the oath or the promise or the pledge that the delegates have made to follow the mandates expressed in the primaries and caucuses. He has not promoted himself; he's tried to discourage that. He's issued a public statement on the subject. And I have no doubt that this effort is not only independent of him but I doubt whether they are genuinely interested in the promotion of Secretary Muskie. They are probably interested in the promotion of someone else.

BILLY CARTER

Q. Mr. President, on June 17th, Mr. President, which was 15 days after Attorney General Civiletti found out about the payments and a month before you say you found out about the payments to your brother, you have said tonight that the Attorney General told you, informed you of the seriousness of the possible charges against your brother and told you that it would be foolish, in your own words, foolish for him not to file papers. Was he, do you not——

THE PRESIDENT. That's not exactly what he said, but go ahead.

Q. Well, let me just ask the question.

THE PRESIDENT. Okay.

Q. Do you not see an impropriety there, in the sense of your being told between the lines, even if you weren't told directly about the money, that your brother was in trouble and unless somebody got the word to him to come in voluntarily and file, there could be serious charges filed against him? Is that not the impropriety here?

THE PRESIDENT. No, there is no impropriety. That's not what the Attorney General told me, by the way, exactly. He said, first of all, that he could not reveal to me and would not reveal to me any detail or any facts about the investigation that was ongoing. Secondly, he said he thought that Billy was foolish not to comply with the registration act, and third, he said that if Billy did not comply truthfully, then he would not be prosecutable or, I think I jotted down in my notes, punished.

At that time, my understanding is—and this should be confirmed by you from other sources—at that time, my understanding now is that the Justice Department was already relaying this exact same information to Billy's attorneys and therefore to him. I never revealed the conversation to anyone. As a matter of fact, it was a very brief conversation—I have said probably less than a minute in all—at the end of a long meeting with the Attorney General, and several other items were taken up in the privacy of that meeting. But I didn't think about it until days later, and I never revealed any of that information to anyone else and never acted on any information I got.

Q. So if the Justice Department was informing Billy at the same time that you were learning of this from the Justice Department, you're saying, in effect, that there was no need, even, for anyone in the White House to let Billy know that he should come in and voluntarily admit that he was an agent?

THE PRESIDENT. Well, I'm not sure—I don't know of any allegation that hasn't been refuted. Nobody in the White House, myself or anyone else, ever gave Billy any information that related to his case, any evidence, or any leads or anything else. So, that question didn't cross my mind.

But from what I know now, looking back on it, after we've investigated thoroughly and I have seen the order of events that did take place, I can tell you that the Attorney General was telling me the same thing, in effect—I've just outlined to you the totality of the conversation, according to my notes—that they were telling the lawyers of my brother prior to that time. I think Billy got those lawyers the 11th or 12th, which was about a week before this conversation took place.

Q. It didn't occur to you that the Attorney General was saying to you between the lines, "Your brother has taken a lot of money," or maybe——

THE PRESIDENT. No. No, I never had any indication that Billy was taking any money until I read about it in the newspaper on July the 15th. And the first person, so far as I know, in the entire White House that knew about any money payments was my Counsel, who was informed on the 11th of July, just before those official papers were completed for filing with the Justice Department.

AMERICAN HOSTAGES IN IRAN

Q. Mr. President, you said that you were obsessed with the hostages and that's why you called your brother in. Do you have any new ideas for freeing the hostages now?

THE PRESIDENT. No, we are pursuing the same kind of degree of effort that we were then.

I think I tried to point out, as best I could remember, a couple of things that were happening at that time—the threat by Khomeini that the hostages might be killed and the fact that the Grand Mosque in Jidda was—in Mecca, I think—was attacked by radical believers in the Moslem faith. Those were the kind of things that were causing me great concern.

The approach to Libya, although now it has taken on great significance, here, 9 or 10 months later, was one of a broad pattern of things that I was doing, the National Security Council was doing, everyone in the State Department assigned to this task was doing, and many private citizens were doing. And there was nothing extraordinary about it. It was just one of a broad gamut of things that we were attempting to do in every possible way to get word to Khomeini that it was better for Iran to release those hostages.

BILLY CARTER

Q. Mr. President, were you aware, sir, of the arrangement with the Charter Oil Company that would have given your brother a commission on oil imported—that he got imported from Libya, when you talked with his friend, Jack McGregor, in the Oval Office?

THE PRESIDENT. No, I was not. The only information I had about Jack McGregor was I talked to Billy in the hospital; he told me that his former commanding officer in the Marine Corps was scheduled to come to the White House for a briefing on hospital cost containment. There were about 400 business leaders who had been chosen by my staff without my participation at all.

McGregor, on that hospital cost containment briefing day, came by the Oval Office, had an appointment for a stand-up photograph. We never sat down, even. We stood over by my desk. The records show that he was there a total of 9 minutes. We discussed some of his and Billy's experiences in the Marine Corps, and we discussed Billy's illness and how he was responding well to treatment in the hospital. And McGregor mentioned Billy's financial problems and said he hoped that he would be successful in working out of them. No reference was ever made to anything concerning oil companies or anything of that nature.

AMERICAN HOSTAGES IN IRAN

Q. Mr. President, your spokesman, Mr. Powell, has said, in defending your use of your brother as an intermediary—and you have alluded to this as well—that we'd be very surprised some day when we hear of some of the other unorthodox emissaries you've used, channels to other countries to try and secure the release of the hostages. Can you surprise us a little and tell us who they are, who some of them might be? And might we be embarrassed by the revelations of any of their names?

THE PRESIDENT. No, you wouldn't be embarrassed, but I think maybe the surprise ought to come later.

DEMOCRATIC PRESIDENTIAL NOMINEE

Q. Mr. President, you have about 300 more delegates than are required for the nomination. And so for another candidate to get the Democratic Presidential nomination, he would need to attract some of these delegates.

THE PRESIDENT. Yes.

Q. Yet you've said if someone did that, they would be subverting the rules of the Democratic Party. And you said last week——

THE PRESIDENT. Yes, they would.

Q.——that it would be a travesty if any of these delegates wandered away. So, if someone else is nominated at the convention in New York, would you be able to support that nominee, or would you only be able to support yourself?

THE PRESIDENT. I have always pledged, since the very beginning of my effort, to support the nominee of the Democratic Party if it should not be myself.

BILLY CARTER

Q. Mr. President, in going back to the conversation with Attorney General Civiletti on June the 17th, you said that the knowledge of—let me say, Justice Department policy in handling foreign agents was general knowledge. Why then, sir, did you need to inquire of the Attorney General whether your brother would be prosecuted if he went ahead and registered as a foreign agent?

THE PRESIDENT. I didn't say it was general knowledge. I was not familiar then with the exact policy that the Attorney Generals down through history had followed.

I think this Foreign Registration Act was passed in the 1930's. I noticed an article in one of the Washington papers not too long ago that said that since the 1960's there had been no criminal prosecutions under that act. Ordinarily, what the Department does, I now know, is to confront a person who is suspected or believed to be an agent of a foreign country, present them with the alternatives if they do not file, and require them to file. And that's what Billy's lawyers finally advised him to do, was to file as an agent—I don't know if my brother ever admitted it or acknowledged that he was an agent— but to file as an agent and if he had extenuating remarks to make, to put those remarks in the registration papers. That's what Billy did.

At the time the Attorney General talked to me, I did not know what I have just described to you as a standard policy of the Department in handling these kinds of cases.

Q. Mr. President, what kind of information did our intelligence agencies gather about Billy's activities trying to set up the oil deal with Libya? And specifically, were they concerned that Billy was part of a wide-ranging and massive effort by the Libyans to influence the public opinion and the Government here?

THE PRESIDENT. That intelligence information has been delivered to the Senate intelligence committee. It's of a highly sensitive nature, and I'm not at liberty to reveal it in public.

PRO-KHOMEINI TERRORISTS

Q. Mr. President, you have some more trouble coming, I'm sorry.

THE PRESIDENT. I'm sure I do. [*Laughter*]

Q. [*Inaudible*]—this week with that Bayh committee over there. It's been told to about a half-dozen Senators by an intelligence organization from New York

City that you and the State Department——

THE PRESIDENT. Yes.

Q. ——and Brzezinski are conniving with Nazarian, the rug dealer, to let pro-Khomeini people come in here and engage in certain terrorist activities in exchange for getting the hostages home. Any truth to that?

THE PRESIDENT. No, ma'am.

DEMOCRATIC NATIONAL CONVENTION

Q. Mr. President, if you were to look at the convention from a slightly different point of view, and you were a delegate heading up to New York next week and you had an incumbent President who's as low as you are in the polls and has the difficulty of a congressional investigation facing him, how would you feel about the prospect of renominating that same President?

THE PRESIDENT. I would feel okay. [*Laughter*] I would take my written pledge to be very seriously binding on me. If I was from Plains, Georgia, and the voters who went to the ballot box in Plains had voted for a candidate, candidate A, and I was later chosen as their delegate, then I would feel bound to go and cast my vote at the convention in accordance with the way people had voted in Plains, regardless of whether I personally thought at that moment that the candidate I was chosen to support was above the Republicans in the public opinion polls.

I think this time 4 years ago, I was much further ahead of President Ford than I am behind, as I saw in a Newsweek poll, today. But polls go up and down. And when President Ford wound up the campaign, he was very close to me. Also, I think you'll remember that last October the polls showed that I was three or four

to one behind Senator Kennedy and if he ran, the almost sure prospect was that he would win the nomination. That has not proven to be the case.

So, the polls ought not to be the deciding factor. The pledge on a written document that a delegate will comply with the votes cast in his own district or area is important. Also, the fact that the Democratic Party, through its national committee, unanimously voted to institute these rules before the primary season even started is also a very important factor. That's what we're trying to protect.

MINORITIES

Q. Thank you, sir.

Mr. President, the problem of oppression of blacks in this country is extremely serious. We've had riots in Miami; we've had riots in Chattanooga. Is there any way that you can begin to address this problem? If you think Billy has problems, you'd better be glad he's not black. But the real issue becomes one of, is there something that you, as President of this country, would do to begin to address these problems before it blows up?

THE PRESIDENT. Yes. In the Miami case, I went to Miami, as you know, met with the leaders in Liberty City, and helped to put together a package, working with those black leaders there, that would give them some economic assistance. Through the Community Services Agency and others, we provided food, for instance, at about 35-percent less cost than the supermarket charges. And we've tried to provide jobs. And we've tried to work also—I have personally—with the white and Cuban leaders in Miami, to make sure that there was harmony between the three races.

In addition to that, I sent the Attorney General to Miami to make sure that the apparent absence of complete application of justice for highly publicized cases concerning black citizens was corrected. And the Attorney General directed his people to go into Miami and to make sure that the trials involved were fair.

In addition to that, on a much more broad basis, I have tried to put black citizens in my administration to administer those areas of the Federal Government that were particularly important to a black or minority citizen. We have required by law, with the help of the Congress, that a certain portion of all Federal contracts and the deposit of Federal funds in banks and the allocation of charters for new radio stations and so forth, that have long been withheld from blacks and other minorities, be assigned to them. I've also tried to appoint black Federal judges, who will be here long after I'm gone, to administer justice, to make sure that we didn't have a further deprivation of our black citizens.

So, on a broad range of issues, I've tried to do the best I can and will continue to do the best I can to eliminate any discrimination or any injustice in this country for minority citizens.

Thank you all very much.

NOTE: The President's fifty-eighth news conference began at 9 p.m. in the East Room at the White House. It was broadcast live on radio and television.

United States Olympic Swim Team

Remarks at a Medal Presentation Ceremony. August 5, 1980

Joel Ferrell and Ross Wales, all the coaches and trainers, and particularly the members of the greatest swimming team in the whole world:

I'm glad to have you here. This is a time of great excitement for our Nation— great pride in what you are and what you have done, great appreciation for your attitude toward a very difficult situation, and also great admiration for the achievements that you reached in the competition for the U.S. Olympic team. The breaking of American records, world records, Olympic records, and the comparison between the times was very exciting for all of us who are interested in you and interested in this great sport.

It was indeed a thrill for me as President to see how your times and your record and your achievements compared to those of yourselves in the past, other Americans and athletes who would compete with you throughout the world. I know some of you are going from here to Honolulu and to China. I appreciate your stopping by Washington on the way. And this is, I believe, a good send-off for you, to let you know how I, as the President of our great country, and the Members of the Congress, the legislative leaders of our great country, look on you and on your achievements.

I think it's not necessary to talk particularly about the great sacrifice that you all have made. The decision by the Congress was not easy. It was a very difficult decision by the U.S. Olympic Committee. I know it's even more difficult for you. I don't know of any other sport where the intensity of training and the great personal sacrifice exceeds that which you've been willing to offer in your own young lives.

You've represented our Nation well already, and I have no doubt that in your life in the future you'll continue to bring credit to yourselves and to the United States of America.

I would like to say in closing that you've honored me by coming here. As I look in your young faces and see the beautiful medal on your chests, I realize again that you have been unique in the history of amateur sports in our country. What you have accomplished is not only notable for the athletic record books, but what you have accomplished is going to be notable in world history books.

The contribution that you've made personally is notable, but also what you've done for freedom and for justice is also to be remembered for generations to come. I know that some of you did not agree with the action taken by the U.S. Olympic Committee. In your expressions of disagreement, you have been mature and you have been, I think, very reticent and, I think, constructive. In every action that you have taken, every achievement that you have reached, every exemplification of your own character, you've brought credit on yourself and on our country. And for this I thank you and congratulate you. You're wonderful diplomats, and I have no doubt that in your travels to Hawaii and to China that you'll additionally bring credit on our country.

Thank you everyone. God bless you now and in the future years of your lives. Thank you again.

NOTE: The President spoke at 9:51 a.m. in the State Dining Room at the White House. Prior to the President's remarks, Joel Ferrell, Jr., Vice President of the U.S. Olympic Committee presented medals, which were authorized by Congress, to the athletes and coaches.

Department of Health and Human Services

Nomination of Richard B. Lowe III To Be Inspector General.   August 5, 1980

The President today announced that he will nominate Richard B. Lowe III, of New York City, to be Inspector General of the Department of Health and Human Services. He would replace Thomas D. Morris, resigned. Lowe has been Acting Inspector General since 1979 and was Deputy Inspector General earlier in 1979.

He was born July 26, 1941, in New York City. He received a B.S. from the University of Wisconsin in 1964 and a J.D. from St. John's University in 1967.

Lowe was with the New York County district attorney's office from 1967 to 1979. He served as a trial attorney and as chief of the major felony program, the complaint bureau, the early case assessment bureau, and the trial bureau. From 1976 to 1979, he was chief of the trials division.

He has been a lecturer at Fordham, St. John's, Hofstra, and Cornell University Law Schools and also served as a faculty member for the homicide investigator's course of the New York City Police Department.

National Labor Relations Board

Nomination of John C. Truesdale To Be a Member.   August 5, 1980

The President today announced that he will nominate John C. Truesdale, of Bethesda, Md., for reappointment as a member of the National Labor Relations Board (NLRB). Truesdale has been a member of the NLRB since 1977.

He was born July 17, 1921, in Grand Rapids, Mich. He received an A.B. from Grinnell College in 1942, an M.S. in industrial and labor relations from Cornell University in 1948, and a J.D. from Georgetown University Law Center in 1972.

Truesdale worked for the NLRB from 1948 to 1957, serving as a field examiner, then administrative analyst. From 1957 to 1963, he was with the National Academy of Sciences, serving as Deputy Director, then Director, of Information for the International Geophysical Year.

In 1963 Truesdale returned to the NLRB, where he served as Associate Executive Secretary until 1968, Deputy Executive Secretary from 1968 to 1972, and Executive Secretary from 1972 to 1977.

Ceremony Honoring Simon Wiesenthal

Remarks on Presenting a Special Gold Medal to Mr. Wiesenthal on Behalf of the Congress. August 5, 1980

THE PRESIDENT. *Senator McGovern, Senator Boschwitz, Senator Warner, distinguished guests and visitors in this home, including several members of my own Cabinet:*

Many historic events have occurred in this particular room and in this historic house, events that have transformed our Nation and the future, events which have been inspirational, events which have reminded us of troubled times, events which have brought to our minds the memory of heroism and great achievement, events which have also reminded us of tragedy and the fallibility of human beings. Today with this commemoration of the achievement of one single human being, who sometimes was lonely, sometimes unrecognized, we combined all those emotions which have filled this room in years gone by into one notable event.

We're here today to honor a man of incomparable courage and conviction—Simon Wiesenthal. Last November, the Congress passed a bill authorizing this medal on my right to be given in recognition of Mr. Wiesenthal's contributions to international justice. Some might think we're here to honor him, but, as a matter of fact, his presence here honors us and honors this home and the principles for which it stands.

Simply his presence here is an exciting thing for me. I met him earlier, in 1976. As a matter of fact, he gave me his good wishes and we exchanged in just a few minutes some memorable thoughts between two men who encountered each other on life's way. That's an insignificant fact in his life.

Why we're here today is to talk about what has occurred during the last 42 years, because that long ago, in 1938, Simon Wiesenthal was a young architect, the holder of a university degree, the proud owner of his new business. At the age of 30, he had all the eagerness and all the potential and all the ambition and all the imagination of youth, yet no one could have imagined the situation in which he would find himself just 4 years later. No one could have guessed the scope of the injustice which swept over his life. Because he was Jewish, he was denied all opportunity, he was denied all freedoms. Under the Nazis, Simon Wiesenthal and many other Jews did not even have the right to exist.

Simon Wiesenthal defied the Nazis. For 4 years he fought for his own life and tried to protect those others who were with him. He was one of only 34 prisoners to survive out of an original group of 149,000, and then after his survival he carried on for those who could not. He vowed to build justice before he would return to building houses. He set up the Jewish Documentation Center in Vienna, Austria, and from there for more than three decades, he's led the search for the Nazi war criminals. Persistently, tirelessly, courageously, sometimes almost alone, he's coordinated the pursuit of those who terrorized and took the lives of so many European men and women and children.

His goal has not just been to see justice done, not just to see criminals punished. His motive has not only been to seek revenge but to remember and to make certain that never again will such a crime against decency and civility and humanity be committed—never.

It's up to all of us to harness the outrage of our memories to banish all human oppression. We must recognize that when any fellow human being is stripped of humanity, when any person is turned into an object of torture or is defiled or is victimized by terrorism or prejudice or racism, that all human beings are victims. Simon Wiesenthal has devoted his life to preventing genocide. We must join him.

There are generations today who were born and raised and who are raising their own children now, who know the Holocaust only as history, if they know it at all. What we tell them they will pass on not just to our grandchildren but to the descendants that we will never see. We owe these generations something more than just the legacy of a lawlessness that they will never be able to fathom, a crime that they will never be able to comprehend. They must understand that Nazis were human beings who went awry. They must realize that human beings are capable of unspeakable, unbelievable atrocities. Human beings. But they must also understand that people can only be molded in the image of evil when they have no principles of their own to uphold, that people are moved to violence only when they are not convinced of the strength of peace.

We must convince our children of the strength of peace by dedicating ourselves to the pursuit of peace. We must instill in them an undying commitment to human rights by demonstrating our commitment to human rights.

We saw what happened when human rights were violated and trod upon with violence. Eleven million people were slaughtered, 6 million of them Jews. Even today the survivors are not spared the savagery which they escaped physically, because they only have to close their own eyes now, still to see it. We have to open our own eyes and keep them open. We need to be forever wary of force, forever cautious of excessive power. Our conscience must never waver. Our memory must never die.

Simon Wiesenthal has helped to teach us that. He's a unique example of all those who value the pursuit of peace and who work to strengthen human rights. Yet, no matter how eloquent any of us try to be about Simon Wiesenthal, he explains himself best, and I particularly like this quote. When my secretary handed me this typed card with the quote on it, she had tears in her eyes, and she said, "Mr. President, I like that man." This is what he had to say: "I believe in God and in the world to come. When each of us comes before the 6 million, we will be asked what we did with our lives. One will say that he became a watch-maker and another will say that he became a tailor . . . but I will say, 'I did not forget you.' " Nor, Simon Wisenthal, will the world ever forget you.

MR. WIESENTHAL. *Mr. President, Mrs. Carter, excellencies, distinguished ladies and gentlemen:*

It was a long way from the shacks in the Mauthausen concentration camp to where I stand today. It took 35 years from the 5th of May, 1945. That 5th of May, we were 900 prisoners in block six, in the dead block, and there seemed little chance of survival for any of us. Life expectancy was not more than a few days, a few weeks at most, a few hours for many among us. We in the dead block were already too weak to work, even by SS standards. The little food we were given was cheaper than a bullet. Those who were still strong enough to walk around were keeping us informed about the progress of the German retreat.

As the American troops approached, our guards fled in panic, leaving us to our fate. Our doctor came running into our hut shouting, "The Americans are coming." The cry made us gather whatever strength was left in us. Those who could move at all staggered and crawled out of the shacks. I was among them that made it. A bright sun helped us to celebrate the moment of liberation. American tanks had entered the camp, and every prisoner struggled to get to them. I was about 150 yards from the first tank. The soldiers who had come with it were surrounded by prisoners, sinking into their arms, crying and laughing at the same time, exalted beyond any ordinary feeling.

I covered the first hundred yards but then collapsed on the ground. I was lying there trying to get up again, panting and staring, fascinated at the American flag.

In the times of suffering we were all looking for symbols to cling to, and in this moment of liberation I was seeing the stars on the flag as symbols not only for the States of the Union but for all the things we had lost in the Nazi Holocaust. Every star had acquired a meaning of its own. One was the star of hope; one of justice, of tolerance, of friendship, of brotherly love, of understanding, and so on. I cannot remember to how many stars I gave a name, how many I called by something beautiful, something desirable for the future, which we have rebuilt. And in the stripes I saw the roads to freedom. I don't know how long I sat there staring at the flag, daydreaming. At that moment I understood those who gave their lives for defense of their flag.

Then suddenly, two strong hands picked me up and carried me back to the hut. I don't know whose hands they were, but they put me down gently and I sat beside the other prisoners on the steps of the dead block, warming myself in the midday sun. A little later I saw prisoners from other blocks marching by—Czechs, Poles, Italians, and others—each group carrying their nation's flag. They had secretly made them for the day of liberation. I looked around me. We were all Jews, and I became aware that only we Jews had no flag. I was longing for such a symbol of liberty and national dignity. One of us had a faded blue shirt; I had one which had once been white. We took them off. Another prisoner managed to make them into something like a blue and white flag. We were much too weak to attempt a parade like the other groups, and so we just sat there in the sun holding and waving our makeshift flag.

Jews from other blocks came over and cried. Some of them kissed our flag, a symbol of hope amidst dead and dying. At that moment I felt instinctively that my future life would be determined by these two flags, the American flag as a symbol of our liberation—for which I will always be grateful—and of the promise that we would be able to go on living as free men, the Jewish flag as a symbol of people resurrected from the ashes of destruction. There was never a problem of double loyalty for me. On the contrary, it was a symbiosis—liberty for us and for the world through the United States, and dignity for the Jews as a nation through Israel. These notions have become the pillars of my own life and my work ever since.

I found that it was impossible to resume my life as an architect, which had been brutally interrupted, as if nothing had happened. You know what I have fought for in these 35 years. I don't have to tell you the story of my life. It strived for justice. And this fight for justice was so easy for me because I am not a hater, and the word "revenge" has no meaning for me.

Looking back on these 35 years that have since passed, there is one thing I can say. Having survived through nothing less than a miracle, I am reminded of those who suffered with me, their last thoughts, their hopes, and their fears. They have become my own.

I have done all I could to help to prevent a recurrence of this Holocaust for us and also for all other peoples. Unfortunately, there is no denying that Hitler and Stalin are alive today, not necessarily in the same countries, but under new and different guises. Their successors have adapted themselves and their style to their respective situations. They are waiting for us to forget, because this is what makes their resurrection possible. Sad to say, evil has not disappeared with the physical death of these two monsters, Hitler and Stalin.

The fight is too dangerous to mankind. It's a great responsibility for which everybody who is willing should devote himself.

Whenever I am a guest in your beautiful country, I am reminded of the fact that it was the U.S. Army, American soldiers, who 35 years ago gave me a second lease on my life. It is something I will never forget. The great idea of liberty behind the American flag is still a strong force in this divided world of ours. It gives the freedom-loving people in many different countries the strength to resist those who want to enslave them. And the flag we once made from two crumpled shirts in front of the dead block, which at that time was just a symbol of survival, in the meantime has become the proud flag of Israel, a country whose very existence ensures us against a recurrence of the Holocaust.

Mr. President, the honor you and the Congress have conferred upon me today I accept in the name of those for whom, I hope, through the work of my life, I have earned the right to speak. I am only their trustee. In reality you are honoring them who cannot be with us today.

Mr. President, I thank you.

NOTE: The President spoke at 2:05 p.m. in the East Room at the White House.

Disturbances at Indiantown Gap, Pennsylvania

Statement by the White House Press Secretary. August 5, 1980

The President has received a report on disturbances today at Indiantown Gap. In his opinion, the Federal Protective Service and backup military personnel acted properly in moving quickly and firmly to quell the disturbances and restore order.

He has been assured by the Department of Defense and the Department of Justice that any repeat of today's disturbances will also be met by firm and appropriate action. He's also been informed that in this case, none of those involved in the disturbances left the base.

The President wishes to emphasize that the hospitality of the American people does not include toleration of violent and illegal action against the personnel or property of the American Government. He also wishes to emphasize that the small minority who engage in such acts are by no means representative of the Cuban Americans who already live in this country or of the vast majority of those who have recently fled Cuba in search of freedom.

NOTE: Press Secretary Jody Powell read the statement to reporters during his regular news briefing, which began at 3:07 p.m. in the Briefing Room at the White House.

New York City, New York

Remarks at the Annual Conference of the National Urban League. August 6, 1980

Chairman Coy Eklund and John Jacob— I think Jake has done a tremendous job lately in the absence of Vernon Jordan— members of the Urban League:

I'm very delighted to be with you.

Just a few moments ago, I had a talk with Vernon Jordan. He and I were reminiscing about a meeting that we had in the corner of a private home at a party more than 10 years ago, when he and Andy Young and I shared with each other our secret ambitions about the future. Andy Young said, "I just want to stay in Atlanta, be quiet, avoid publicity, and avoid controversy." [*Laughter*] And I told Vernon and Andy my ultimate ambition was to be Governor of Georgia. And Vernon said, "All I want in life is to be the Congressman from the 5th District of Georgia."

Well, as you know, none of us wound up the way that we planned. But I think all of you would agree that among the three of us that Vernon got the best job. Right?

It's a joy for me to be here with my personal friends and with dedicated leaders, who have been my partners in so many fights and with whom I share so many basic beliefs that are important to our country and important to those who look to you for leadership.

I want to salute you, first of all, for 70 solid years of leadership and service to all the citizens of this Nation. Yours is not a narrow responsibility. The breadth of what you do and what you have done and what you will do in the future is indeed impressive in our analysis of the Urban League.

And I want to thank you for the counsel and the support that you've given me over the years, the frequent, constructive criticisms that I've received from you— [*laughter*]—and from your leader, as we have pressed forward toward common goals down a common road. We've stood together for what was right, and we have often prevailed under very difficult circumstances.

With your help, in the 3½ years since I became President, funding for teaching basic skills, for instance, to the disadvantaged of our Nation has more than doubled; Job Corps, up 157 percent; CETA programs, up 115 percent; food stamps, up 99 percent. And we removed the requirement that poor people have to pay cash for food stamps. Our funding for women and children's programs and for infants is three times what it was in 1976. Despite our continuing effort to control inflation, we're protecting the programs that are most important to you, like Aid for Families with Dependent Children, social security, subsidized Government housing, and programs like Head Start. As a matter of fact, about 35 percent of our next year's budget will be allocated to giving the elderly citizens of this country a better life.

I want to express my personal appreciation to your leader, who's been such a strong advocate of all these causes and, quite often ahead of me or anyone else, has been in the forefront of economic and social progress. You can really afford to be proud of Vernon Jordan, who's a fighter. He's watching now on television. He has his mother and others with him. I'll be going from here to visit him in his hospital room, to pay my personal respects, and to wish him again a speedy recovery.

[At this point, the President was interrupted by a person in the audience, later identified as a member of the Communist Workers Party.]

As I was saying before the Communist speaker captured the audience, I'm going to stop by his room, pay my personal respects, wish him a speedy recovery, and I'm going to assure Vernon that I'm the last Presidential candidate that he'll have to entertain this week. *[Laughter]*

Today is a special day. Does anybody know what it is? It's the 15th anniversary of the Voting Rights Act. And together with the Civil Rights Act of 1964, these two new laws, passed with your support and with your courageous conviction, opened up a new and vastly improved era of American life for many citizens who had been deprived. These measures paved the way for new levels of opportunity.

Who would have dreamed, for instance, back in those days that we would see the election of people like Dick Arrington and Maynard Jackson in the South? Who would have dreamed that one day the mayors of Atlanta and Birmingham would be prominent, respected, national leaders who were black?

I've been proud, as President, fighting for a more just and equitable and prosperous society, to have had at my side in this fight such good friends, old friends from those early days like Vernon and Andy Young and Coretta King and many others many of you, who've contributed so much to making civil rights an integral part of the American conscience. All of your children now enjoy a life that's fun-

damentally changed from the one that you knew. You and I know that the struggle is far from over.

This is a sober time, a time to think about where we have been, where we are, and where we might go in the future. You and I know that our struggle is far from over. I'm here today to renew my permanent pledge to you, that I will never relent in our joint pursuit of equal rights, equal opportunity, and equal dignity for everyone who lives in America.

I'm not here to tell you we've reached the promised land. You cannot undo 30 decades, 300 years of discrimination in just 3 or 4 years. But we're on the right road, and we're going to stay on the right road until we do reach the promised land, the goal that God set for all of us, black and white together. For us to lose sight of that promised land is to lose our sense of direction, for we have had some victories. And it's a mistake for the Urban League or anyone else who's been involved in this fight to deny itself credit for the victories that we have achieved, because to deny ourselves the sustenance and the encouragement of what we have done is to deny the inspiration and the support required to continue this struggle together.

For more than 200 years, our Nation has groped as a country, sometimes slowly, sometimes painfully, to stretch its moral horizons and to fulfill its moral promise. First it was the elimination of slavery; this took 90 years. And then it was the elimination of legalized segregation and the beginning of integration; that took a hundred more years. Today we are still challenged to reach the brightest of all horizons—the extension of equal justice and full economic opportunity to every human being in our society.

I wish I could celebrate with you here this morning the end of the age of racial antagonism, but as you know so well, the days of racial violence are not all behind us, not while groups such as the Ku Klux Klan and the reemergence of that group to stir up racial and religious hatred is seen in our country and not while so many citizens of all races are afraid for their personal safety and not while the code words of bigotry are still heard in the political arena and even in the legislative halls in Washington and in State capitols.

It's the sworn duty, for instance, of every police official throughout our country to protect the life and liberties of every citizen in a nondiscriminatory manner, regardless of race. By and large, our law enforcement officials do just that, but there's still some distrust and some fear between minority citizens and the police. Where we have found lapses, as recently in Miami, for instance, where we have found any officials victimizing any citizens, our Justice Department has acted.

Every American should know that the President of the United States, the chief law enforcement officer of our country, is absolutely determined that the liberties and well-being of every citizen will be protected to the full extent of the law. All Americans must know that the Government of the United States is on their side. The person in the Justice Department responsible for carrying out that commitment that I've just made to you is Drew Days, and I'm very delighted that I've appointed people like him and Eleanor Holmes Norton to administer the laws that enforce civil rights.

I've put black people on regulatory boards of all kinds, and I've always insisted on affirmative action. The results speak for themselves. In order to save time, I'm not going to quote to you statistics.

But I've served 3½ years as President, and I've already appointed more blacks,

more women, and more Hispanics to the Federal bench as judges than all other Presidents combined in the 200-year history of our country. Three other comments: One, I'm not through yet; second, the quality of these appointments is a credit to the judicial system of our Nation; and third, remember that these Federal judges serve for life. Their influence extends far beyond any single Presidential administration, even though it might be 8 years in length. Don't forget that these judges will be interpreting your rights and the rights of your children and the rights of your children's children on into the next century.

This administration has been committed to strict enforcement of civil rights here at home, but we've also been equally aggressive in advancing human rights abroad. We've been successful, thanks in part to the wonderful efforts of people like——

[*At this point, the President was interrupted again by a member of the Communist Workers Party.*]

It's a nation of free speech. Some people don't even need a microphone. That's what always surprises me. [*Laughter*]

As I was saying before the second intermission—[*laughter*]—our extension of civil rights here at home, in the human rights throughout the world has been made, thanks in part to the wonderful efforts of Andy Young and Don McHenry, who've enhanced our relationships with the developing people of the world, and particularly those who live in Africa. Our greatest single success has been to help in the peaceful transition in Zimbabwe, of a nation which is now free and independent and democratic. And I am really proud of that.

A couple of years ago I visited, and 2 weeks ago Vice President Mondale visited west Africa. He went on my behalf to celebrate another advance, important to you and to all those who love freedom and democracy throughout the world. He took with him our best wishes to the people of Nigeria, the largest, perhaps the most influential, certainly the strongest economically of all the predominantly black nations on Earth. He took my best wishes and your best wishes on their return to a complete democracy, where their leaders were chosen by the freely expressed will of the people who live there.

He repeated once more our clear-cut policy toward South Africa: The relations between our two countries will depend on its progress toward full human rights and full political participation in that country by everyone who lives in South Africa.

I've often been asked why our country should play such a strong role in Africa and pay so much attention to it, because previous administrations before I became President did not do so. I believe an answer to that is fundamental to what Americans believe. It's best described in a letter written by Dr. Martin Luther King, Jr., during the height of his nonviolent battle for desegregation, in which he said: "Injustice anywhere is a threat to justice everywhere."

In order for us to build an America of full social justice, we must do more than just to protect basic civil liberties. We must move toward much broader, moral Americans.

We all know that discrimination in employment still remains an all too frequent part of American life. When job bias is compounded, when job discrimination is compounded by a painful period of slow economic growth in our country, a disproportionate share of blacks become caught up by the brutal phrase, "Last hired; first fired."

With your help, the Federal Government has acted. With the help of Weldon Rougeau,[1] we are putting heat on Government contractors. A number of major U.S. corporations have found out the hard way that the Federal Government means business when it says, "no job discrimination."

And within the Federal Government, we're pursuing a vigorous, unprecedented affirmative action program in Federal procurement, never attempted before. We're moving to triple the amount of Federal business going to minority-owned contractors. And as you know, a couple of weeks ago, the Supreme Court has now finally ruled that the requirement for a 10-percent set-aside for minority businesses is constitutional. I might say this is not just a law that's on the shelves gathering dust. In public works we have already reached not 10 percent, but 18 percent. And that's not the limit of what we're going to do.

I'd like to mention a very important issue to you. We need this same kind of muscle in our fair housing laws. We've got a bill already that has passed the House of Representatives, with the help of Charlie Rangel, Bob Garcia, and others here, Pete Peyser, that will put teeth, for the first time, in the 1968 Fair Housing Act, which has never been enforced. It's the most important civil rights legislation in the last 10 years. It now only needs Senate approval. We can make it possible for the first time ever, if you will help get the Senate to pass this legislation, for people who want jobs to find homes where the jobs are. That's what we need to do.

Another very important problem for our Nation that has not been resolved is the problem of youth unemployment. Since taking office we've hammered away persistently on this urgent problem of minority youth unemployment. We've al-

---

[1] Director, Office of Federal Contract Compliance Programs, Department of Labor.

ready almost doubled funding from 2½ to 4 billion dollars a year, but that is not enough.

Last year I asked Vice President Mondale to head a special youth employment task force. Working with Vernon Jordan and others in the Urban League and other community-based organizations, we developed a major youth employment bill, which is now before the Congress. It will increase our commitment to youth employment from 4½ up to 6 billion dollars and open new career opportunities to 2 million young people. We do not need to wait for new promises or new plans. Talk is cheap. Here is work that we can be doing right now. I hope you'll get behind this measure with me, and we can meet head on the challenge of youth without jobs.

These two measures, the fair housing bill and the youth act, are not pie-in-the-sky or future dreams. They're an agenda for today, and they're in their final stages of congressional consideration at this very moment. Every Member of the Congress, on this first row, will agree with this: No group should dare play politics with them. They are vital strides forward for our country, and they require no more debate. They open a vast array of economic doors for minority Americans, and we need these bills to be passed without another moment's delay. And I believe that we can rally our efforts and unite in this cause, that before the Congress adjourns this year, we'll have this legislation on the books and we'll have a major stride forward toward the end of discrimination in housing and putting our young people back to work. That's what we must do together.

Once the doors of equal opportunity are opened, we've got to make sure that there's some genuine economic opportunity behind those doors. And to do that

right, and to do it permanently, our Nation's great economic foundation must be rebuilt, so that every American can have a decent, productive job without all Americans losing their income through inflation. I pledge to you that this Government is going to meet that challenge successfully. We have a strong base on which to build.

This might surprise you, but our economy is the most productive on Earth. If you read the newspaper headlines, you would not know that. We produce more per worker than any other country in the world. And in the last 3½ years, we've added more than 9 million men and women to the American work force, the largest increase in war or peace in the Nation's history. One million more black Americans now have full-time jobs than they did in January of 1977.

We are making progress, but for years some of our basic industries have been losing their competitive edge. They've not been modernizing as rapidly as those same industries in other countries. Our human and our technical investments have been inadequate, and our growth in productivity has come to a halt. That's one cause of persistent inflation that has damaged the life of every American—black or white, young or old—and undermined the ability of government and industry to generate all the jobs and the services that we need.

Another major cause of crippling inflation is the soaring price of imported oil. That's why I've worked literally every day for the last 3½ years to give our Nation, finally, an energy policy.

We've made rapid progress in reducing imports, with your help. The first 200 days of this year, we imported 15 percent less oil than we did at the beginning of 1979. That's a reduction every day of a million and a half barrels of oil below the same days a year ago.

However, we still suffer, because the price of oil imposed on the world by the OPEC nations increased more in 1979 than in all the years since oil was first discovered. That's been a blow to the world's economy. And we have poured out billions and billions and billions of dollars out of the pockets of American consumers into the pockets of those who produce oil in the OPEC nations. This takes away domestic jobs. It creates inflation. And that inflation has been so dangerous early this year, as you remember, that I had to take steps to protect the American economy and our Nation's security itself.

Because we faced the truth then, we have cut inflation sharply, and you will see, this month and the next month and the next, the inflation rate continuing to go down. Interest rates have dropped quicker the last few weeks than ever before in history. We have laid the foundation for a sustained period of economic recovery and economic growth, based on lower inflation and interest rates.

I'll shortly present to the American people an economic renewal program, carefully designed, based on the following principles. And I'll be very brief.

It will put American people to work, not in make-work jobs, but in modernizing our American industries, improving their ability to compete, and expanding our exports.

[*At this point, the President was interrupted again by members of the Communist Workers Party.*]

You know, we have a lot of people trying to escape out of communist countries and come to our Nation. You don't see many boats trying to escape from Key West and going to Cuba, though. [*Laughter*]

This new program will put people to work, also, not with massive programs that hide inflationary time bombs, but with carefully designed measures that will also make possible continued reductions in inflation, to put our people back to work without reigniting inflation.

It'll put people to work building the facilities that we need to conserve more energy, change the way we use energy, and produce more energy. You know how massive the program was that our Government instituted for the entire space program to put the first men on the moon. You know how massive the program was after the Second World War to rebuild Europe under the Marshall Plan. You know how massive the program has been in our country, throughout this Nation, to build the whole Interstate Highway System. If you put all those together, what we are going to spend the next 10 years to take care of our energy program will be even greater.

It will put millions and millions and millions of people back to work in new jobs, exciting jobs, stimulating jobs, to make our Nation greater, stronger, and more secure. It's an exciting time, an exciting prospect to rebuild these facilities and to give us a new life, a better life, based on the technology and the commitment and the courage and the unity and the innovative spirit of American people that have always made our Nation so great.

It'll put people back to work, also, with special programs of distressed areas, to focus attention on those communities in America where the unemployed workers are there and have marketable skills. And if they don't have marketable skills, a major part of our program to revitalize America will be to give them those skills that will let them take whatever talent or ability God might have given them and use it to their own advantage, to the advantage of those they love, and for the betterment of our country.

Under this economic renewal program, we'll modernize our industrial capabilities, we'll stimulate more research and development, we'll build new facilities for alternative energy sources, things we may not have ever dreamed about so far, and we will replace billions of dollars worth of older facilities, made obsolete by higher energy costs. We'll weatherize our buildings, private homes and public buildings, improve our facilities for exporting coal. We'll expand mass transit and many other things that I don't have time enough to enunciate to you now. We'll channel investment into areas where industry has been declining and where unemployment is especially high. Literally millions of jobs will be created as we make America's industry more vital and deal with our energy problems.

In the next few weeks I'll be working with you, with your leaders, with other leaders in government and private industry, and I'll set forth an economic renewal program to restore growth and to reduce unemployment without fanning the fires of inflation, which we've so successfully dampened the last few months.

We have in our country energy far beyond what the OPEC countries have, technology, education, dedicated people, freedom to have new ideas. We've always been on the cutting edge of change. We've never feared change. We're the leaders in the world. Other countries look to us. What is the United States going to do about this new worldwide problem that's been brought about as the price of oil has gone up from $2 a barrel to $35 a barrel? It has almost wiped out the economy of many nations. It's hurt us, with inflation and unemployment. But I have absolutely

no doubt the strength of our Nation will be successful in meeting it.

We'll have the 1980's be a decade of sound growth for America. This is a sound approach, a considered approach, a workable approach to our economic challenges.

But I'd like to mention briefly an idea that is not sound. It's ill considered and unworkable. Be on your guard against it. A bill has been introduced in Congress, and it is endorsed by major political candidates, that would cut Federal income taxes 30 percent in the next 3 years. That sounds nice. But I mean to tell you the truth about the so-called Kemp-Roth proposal. It may well be the most inflationary piece of legislation ever introduced and considered seriously by the United States Congress.

Kemp-Roth offers rebates to the rich and fierce inflation and deprivation for other Americans who are particularly vulnerable. It substitutes a fantasy of instant gratification instead of a realistic vision of a better future. It's even worse than a free lunch. It's sugar-coated poison. And I'm not exaggerating.

The same people who are pushing this tax also promise massive increases in the defense budget, and they also promise to balance the budget. Whom are they trying to fool? If they're serious about these problems—and they say they are—would they cut all Federal help for all other programs? We have done an analysis of this. If this proposal is put into effect, if moderate increases are made in the defense budget, if the social security program is just protected, not improved, and the budget is balanced, every other agency and department and program in the Federal Government would have to be eliminated 100 percent.

Would they cut out all the Federal programs for all these other vital services? Or would they run the money printing presses, so we had inflation that was uncontrollable? Why can't they tell us which programs are cut out? Maybe later this year, we'll make these questions be answered. Where would the massive budget cuts come from? What are they afraid of—the truth?

It's not surprising that many of those who propose this Kemp-Roth massive tax cut are the same ones that have opposed every form of social progress of the past generation. This is a "soak the poor" tax. Its backers serve as Robin Hoods in reverse, taking money from those social programs that benefit the poor and the elderly and the sick and the disadvantaged, and delivering the proceeds to the rich. It would be extremely regressive in nature, providing a person making $200,000 a year 35 times more than a family that makes $20,000 a year.

As long as I am President of the United States, there will be no "trickle down economics" in the United States of America. This is not an idle threat by those who propose this tax and this economic program; it is a very serious threat. We will strengthen the private sector, which is the heart of our economic system, and we will also rebuild our cities and educate and train our people, for those who for too long have been the victims of discrimination. We ensure a future that promises the full right to participate in the achievement of American prosperity and to share its benefits.

Franklin Delano Roosevelt has been quoted recently. I would like to quote him in the true context of his life. This is what he said about government: "Let us not be afraid to help each other. Let us never forget that government is ourselves and not some alien power over us."

I believe in our country, in the generosity and the good sense of the American people. I believe in our Government and what it can achieve. I believe in a true partnership between the American people and your own Government, and I believe that that partnership holds the key to the future and to our hopes for this country. These have been my beliefs in my life and throughout my Presidency. They've been your beliefs as individuals and as leaders within the Urban League.

We've never acquired an additional element—*never* acquired an additional element—of fairness or equity or freedom or justice without struggle and without sacrifice, and we never will. In a society like ours, that's open and free, there is no way to make progress by looking for an easy answer or by avoiding the truth or by being afraid or by creating disunity among those who are on the cutting edge of progress and compassion and love.

I look forward to continuing our fight, together, to make all our beliefs a reality for all Americans.

Thank you very much, and God bless you.

NOTE: The President spoke at 9:15 a.m. in the Grand Ballroom at the New York Hilton Hotel. In his opening remarks, he referred to Coy Eklund, chairman of the board of trustees, Vernon E. Jordan, Jr., president, and John Jacob, vice president, National Urban League.

New York City, New York

Remarks to Reporters Following a Visit With Vernon E. Jordan, Jr.   August 6, 1980

I just have a word to say about my brief visit with Vernon Jordan. I repeated my promise to him that I would be the last politician to visit him this week, and he's now going to get more rest.

I had a good talk with his doctors. They gave me a fine report on Vernon's recovery, the progress that he has made. And they expect, within a reasonable and predictable period of time, that Vernon will be released from the hospital completely cured.

We had a long talk about our past relationships. We've been personal friends for many years. And I told Vernon that at the time of his injury, the attack on him, that the entire Nation was concerned about his health, not just for what it meant to him personally but for what his life has meant to this country in the past and what it can mean in the future.

So, he's in very good spirits, and he's recovering well. And I'm very proud of what Vernon's life has meant, not only in the Urban League but for all those in this country who believe in justice and truth and progress and an end to hatred and an end to discrimination.

Thank you very much.

NOTE: The President spoke at 10:24 a.m. at the New York Hospital/Cornell University after visiting Mr. Jordan in his hospital room.

Following his remarks, the President returned to the White House.

Presidential Management Improvement Award

Announcement of the 1979 Award Recipients. August 6, 1980

The President today announced the winners of the 1979 Presidential Management Improvement Awards. The awards recognize Federal personnel who have made the year's most exceptional contributions to management improvement. James T. McIntyre, Jr., Director of the Office of Management and Budget, and Alan K. Campbell, Director of the Office of Personnel Management, will present the awards in a ceremony in Room 450, Old Executive Office Building, at 2 p.m. today.

Efforts of the 13 winners of nine awards—seven individuals and two groups—contributed more than $27 million in measurable benefits to taxpayers. They also contributed benefits such as strengthening national defense, improving communications and operations, and providing better service to students and veterans.

Established in 1970, the Presidential Management Improvement Awards program was expanded in 1977 to permit Presidential recognition in the form of congratulatory letters to Federal employees whose suggestions, inventions, or other special achievements resulted in tangible benefits to the Government of $5,000 or more. To date, the President has sent approximately 6,000 such letters. Total measurable benefits of the contributions recognized by the President exceed $697 million.

Recipients of the 1979 awards are:

Charlotte N. Anderson, a plastics worker at Tinker Air Force Base, Okla., who developed new procedures for repairing metal braces on TF–30 aircraft engine fiberglass duct fairings that resulted in measurable benefits to the Government of more than $1 million.

Nicholas Bournias, auditor with the Office of the Inspector General, Audit Agency, Department of Health, Education, and Welfare (now Health and Human Services), Washington, D.C., who contributed to reduction of fraud, abuse, and errors in the Medicaid program by developing a method for auditing billions of dollars spent under the program. His efforts are expected to result in annual benefits of more than $6 million to the Government.

Clayton T. Boyle, communications management specialist, Naval Communications Area Master Station, Eastern Pacific, Honolulu, Hawaii, who devised an alternate, less expensive means of handling intercontinental telephone calls. His concept made it possible to close the switchboard facility at Kunia, Hawaii, and resulted in first-year benefits to the Government of more than $1 million.

Thomas J. Creswell, Director, Aeronautical Center, Federal Aviation Administration, Oklahoma City, Okla., who improved operations at the Mike Monroney Aeronautical Center. Staff reductions with no loss in production, cost savings and increased energy conservation through controlled use of Government vehicles, reduced printing, reproduction, and telephone costs, and efficiencies in the purchase order distribution system resulted in first-year savings of more than $250,000.

Jakie Muscar, Jr., contract specialist, Division of Contract and Grant Operations, HEW (now HHS), Washington, D.C., who conducted recompetition for a contract to carry out data processing and systems support requirements for the guaranteed student loan program. The contract he negotiated will result in benefits to the Government of $15 million over the next 5 years.

Gayton Silvestro, production assurance engineer, U.S. Army Materiel Development and Readiness Command, Dover, N.J., who made significant improvements in the technology of propellant usage that have potential future application to all artillery and tank-fired munitions programs. He developed specific procedures for an extensive renovation program for 150-mm tank ammunition that resulted in measurable benefits to the Government of more than $2.3 million by rendering usable 1.8 million pounds of stockpiled propellants.

Danny A. Wright, Pershing missile repairman, who, as a member of the 579 Ordnance Company, U.S. Army, New Ulm, West Germany, solved a longstanding problem by designing a special tool to be used during a critical alignment phase of missile jet vane assemblies. The tool he designed reduces damage and time spent in maintenance of missile systems throughout the world.

Yeongchi Wu, physician, and Harold J. Krick, corrective therapist, Department of Medicine and Surgery, Veterans Administration, Chicago, Ill., who developed an improved method for treating below-the-knee amputations. Before development of their method, postsurgery complications resulted in painful recovery and extended hospital stays. With their method, treatment and recovery have been greatly improved.

Robert S. Flum, Sr., systems analyst, and Lionel L. Woolston, Roland G. Daudelin, and Bob Norris, supervisory engineers, Headquarters, Naval Materiel Command, Antisubmarine Warfare Systems Project, Washington, D.C., who pioneered development of the submarine rocket. Their technical advancements transformed a weapons system concept into an operational nuclear missile and fire control system of vital importance to national security.

Small Business Regulatory Flexibility Legislation

Statement on Senate Approval of the Legislation. August 6, 1980

Earlier today the Senate passed and sent to the House of Representatives the small business regulatory flexibility act, S. 299. The bill was a major recommendation of the White House Conference on Small Business and has been a high priority of this administration.

I would like to express my personal thanks to Senator John Culver and Senator Gaylord Nelson as well as to Senator Paul Laxalt for their hard work in securing Senate passage of this bill. Senator Culver and Senator Nelson have worked closely with the administration, with House leaders, including Congressman Andy Ireland and Congressman Neal Smith, and with the leaders of various small business groups in developing this legislation.

I am confident that with the support of Congressmen Ireland and Smith and others who are concerned about small business, the House will pass this legislation soon after the Democratic Convention recess and that the bill will promptly be signed into law.

Leif Erikson Day, 1980

Proclamation 4777. August 7, 1980

By the President of the United States of America

A Proclamation

The name of Leif Erikson symbolizes the triumph of the human spirit. A thousand years ago, he and his crew of Norsemen conquered the North Atlantic in an open boat and set a permanent standard of fearlessness, fortitude and endurance. His example will always be an example to men and women of daring and imagination.

In commemorating his life, we also salute the achievements of the Scandinavian people, whose voyages at the dawn of the Middle Ages pushed back the frontiers of human geographical knowledge in many parts of the world, and whose accomplishments have enriched Western man from that era to our own.

As a mark of respect to the courage of Leif Erikson and his Norse followers, the Congress of the United States, by joint resolution approved September 2, 1964 (78 Stat. 849, 36 U.S.C. 169c), authorized the President to proclaim October 9 in each year as Leif Erikson Day.

Now, THEREFORE, I, JIMMY CARTER, President of the United States of America, do hereby designate Thursday, October 9, 1980 as Leif Erikson Day and I direct the appropriate Government officials to display the flag of the United States on all Government buildings that day.

I also invite the people of the United States to honor the memory of Leif Erikson on that day by holding appropriate exercises and ceremonies in suitable places throughout the land.

IN WITNESS WHEREOF, I have hereunto set my hand this seventh day of August, in the year of our Lord nineteen hundred and eighty, and of the Independence of the United States of America the two hundred and fifth.

JIMMY CARTER

[Filed with the Office of the Federal Register, 2:35 p.m., August 7, 1980]

Senior Adviser to the President

Announcement of the Resignation of Hedley W. Donovan. August 7, 1980

The White House announced today that Senior Adviser to the President Hedley Donovan has resigned, effective August 15, to return to private life.

In his letter of resignation, Mr. Donovan noted that by August 15 he will have completed 1 year's service in the White House and that he will have completed the specific assignments given him by the President, including the appointment and general organization of the President's Commission for a National Agenda for the Eighties. Mr. Donovan also said that for personal reasons he wished to return to the New York area. Mr. Donovan said that as a private citizen he would be honored to continue to offer his advice and counsel to the President whenever the President thought it would be helpful.

In his letter of resignation, Mr. Donovan also said, "Thank you again for a most interesting year, made especially pleasant by your own thoughtfulness and good humor, and the warm hospitality you and Rosalynn have shown me."

In his acceptance of Mr. Donovan's resignation, the President said he looked forward to receiving Mr. Donovan's counsel in the future and praised him for his "sound judgment and advice." The President also said, "You have been very helpful to me and to our White House deliberations during some important and trying times for our nation."

United Steelworkers of America

Remarks by Telephone to Delegates Attending the Union's Convention in Los Angeles, California. August 7, 1980

THE PRESIDENT. Hello, Lloyd McBride?

MR. MCBRIDE. Yes, Mr. President.

THE PRESIDENT. You got anybody there with you?

MR. MCBRIDE. We're all here, and we're anxious to hear from you. Our convention has overwhelmingly endorsed the candidacy of you and Vice President Mondale, and we are going to work awfully hard to see that you get elected. Our delegates are assembled, and they'll be most happy to hear from you.

THE PRESIDENT. Lloyd, that's some of the best news we've had lately. In fact, the news has swept Washington, and all of the White House staff and all my Cabinet members are very grateful. I want to say, first of all, to all the members of the Steelworkers of America and also to our friends from Canada how deeply grateful I am and how proud I am to have your almost unanimous, maybe unanimous, endorsement for me and Fritz Mondale. We've got a big job to do together this fall, and I don't have any doubt that we'll be successful.

I know that Ed Muskie has talked to you about the critical absence in the Republican commitments to a balanced program on foreign affairs. Ray Marshall has outlined to you, also, what the Democrat and Republican Parties stand for and the differences between them. And of course, Pat Harris discussed several things with you, I think, including some endorsements as well.

This is a critical election. It's more than just a choice between two men. In fact, it's more than just a choice between two parties, as important as that is. This election in 1980 can determine, and probably will determine, what our Nation will be the rest of this century. Together, Fritz Mondale and I, in an active, day-by-day way, will get out and fight, and we will win this election.

We're going to talk sense to the American people. We're going to tell them the truth. We're not going to underestimate the intelligence of those who will be observing the candidates this fall. We're not going to underestimate the courage of

Americans. And in the process, we're going to make the Republicans stand up and show their true colors.

If you think I've had a few things to explain this week in the press conference, take a good look at the Republican platform and the Republican statements of their candidates for the last few years. They really have a lot of explaining to do, and they'll never be able to do it to the satisfaction of the working people of the United States of America. Before this campaign is over, we're going to make sure that this country knows what the Republicans do stand for, or either we're going to make them admit that they don't really stand for much of anything that's important to the future of this country.

I remember early this year, when I had very difficult decisions to make, sitting here in the Oval Office, where I am now, after the Soviet Union military forces invaded Afghanistan. I remember, too, that the steelworkers stood with me. Where were the Republicans that now want to lead this country? They stood foursquare for some kind of tough response just so long as nothing about it was controversial and as long as they didn't lose any votes. They were against the trade embargo. The Republicans were against the Olympic boycott. The Republican leaders were against draft registration. I think they underestimate American young people. They underestimate American athletes. They underestimate American farmers and American workers and the American public.

Where do the Republicans stand on the economy? That's important to every one of you listening to my voice. They talk different now, just before the elections, just as they always do every 4 years. But I'll tell you what they're for. They're for the Reagan-Kemp-Roth tax plan, perhaps the most inflationary piece of legislation ever to be seriously considered by the U.S. Congress.

This is a program to rob working people and reward the rich. Someone who makes $200,000 a year, in the Reagan-Kemp-Roth plan, would get 35 times more benefit than someone that makes $20,000 a year. And they ask the American people to believe that they're going to balance the budget, have massive increases in defense spending, and cut taxes by hundreds of billions of dollars all at the same time. That's nonsense. You know it, and I know it. And together, you and Fritz Mondale and I this fall will make sure that the American people know what the Republicans are trying to do.

We have paid a terrible price recently with unemployment and inflation, because the tough decisions were not made while the Republicans spent 8 years in this office. The American people were not told the truth. Nothing was done to prepare us for the energy crisis that we've had to face during this last 12 months. We're still paying that price, but we are making some progress.

Our energy program is just about ready. The Democratic Party has made courageous decisions. We will have intact a comprehensive national energy program or policy for the first time. As you all know, the inflation rate is turning down, interest rates have dropped sharply, home construction is turning up, automobile sales, turning up. We've reached a time where we can begin to build upon the difficult, controversial, sometimes painful decisions that we've had to make during these last 3 years.

We're going to present to the American people not an election-year economic gimmick, but a well-considered, workable economic renewal program—a program to put Americans to work without reigniting the inflation fires that we've been fighting so hard against the last few months, a program to put Americans to work to modernize our industrial capabilities in all kinds of industries throughout our country, a program which will put Americans to work by stimulating research and development, a program to put Americans to work by expanding and modernizing our transportation system, and a program to put Americans to work by building the facilities that conserve or save energy and to develop alternative sources of energy.

You and your leadership, particularly you, Lloyd, will have to play an important role in the next few weeks, as we make these final decisions on this enormous, beneficial program to millions of Americans. You'll play an equally important role in helping me to present this program to the American people this fall and to the Congress next year. And the American steel industry will play an even more important role in implementing that plan in the years to come.

This is an exciting, challenging, wonderful time for Americans to face in the 1980's. We've never failed to meet every challenge presented to us since this Nation was formed, if we could understand the problem and unite ourselves in a common commitment.

I deeply appreciate the help and support you've given me in the past. I thank you for your vote of confidence and support today, and I look forward with determination and confidence to what we will do together in the future. This next few months is going to bring a tremendous victory to the Democratic Party, to Fritz Mondale and me, to the Steelworkers of America, and to the entire Nation. We're partners. We're in it together. We will not lose.

Thank you. Good evening, and God bless all of you.

MR. McBRIDE. Thank you, Mr. President, and good luck to you.

THE PRESIDENT. Thank you, Lloyd.

NOTE: The President spoke at 6:30 p.m. from the Oval Office at the White House.

Lloyd McBride is president of the United Steelworkers of America.

White House Barbecue for Georgians

Remarks to the Guests.   August 7, 1980

THE PRESIDENT. I see we have a lot of barbecue lovers here tonight. [*Laughter*]

AUDIENCE MEMBER. And Jimmy Carter lovers.

THE PRESIDENT. And Jimmy—thank you. That's right on. And Jimmy Carter lovers. I appreciate that.

I'd like to, first of all, recognize about 250 people from Laurens County, Georgia, who put together this delicious supper for us and who really are our hosts. Would everybody from Laurens County hold up your hands?

Well, I'm really grateful to you. When I was running for Governor in 1970, nobody thought I had a chance to win. And I went down to Laurens County—and the Atlanta newspapers were against me, as you probably remember—and they took a poll among all the people that came to Laurens County, to eat barbecue and some other things. [*Laughter*] And I came out about 6 to 1 ahead of former Governor Carl Sanders. And they couldn't hide it; they couldn't hide it. It turned the tides on the Governor's election, and I became Governor of Georgia in January of 1971 and went on to be elected President, with your help.

I told some of the news people this morning that having this crowd here was good for me in three different ways. First of all, as a President, it helps me to be a better leader of this great country to have a close relationship with people like you, the pride of our Nation, where the strength and the character and the unity and the ideals and the hopes and aspirations of America are concentrated. Just to be able to talk to you and listen to you and shake your hands and look in your face helps me to be a better President.

The second way it helps me to have you here is as a politician. I don't like to lose elections, and I don't intend to lose this year. And you're going to make sure I don't.

And the third reason that it's important for me to have you here is the deep personal friendship that I have with so many of you. When I didn't have many friends, you were my friends. And when things looked difficult for us politically in the past, you were there, in your own communities, within your own States, traveling to foreign States, just to talk about me, talk about Fritz Mondale, and give us a helping hand. And that personal relationship, based on love and friendship, is the third thing that makes it dear to me to have so many folks gathered here on the South Lawn of this historic White House.

We've had a lot of people here. We've had some of the greatest opera singers. We've had some of the finest dancers. We've had jazz musicians, we've had country-music singers, and we've had gospel singers. We've had all kinds of wonderful performers, people from Broadway. This is the first time, however, we've had a special program of bluegrass music, and I figured it's a night for guitars and banjos and fiddles.

And there's a special character, as you know, to this crowd, and there's a special character to bluegrass music. It's ancient music; came here from England and Scotland and Wales and Ireland and other parts of the world; concentrated, even before this country was a nation, in the mountains of the southeastern part of the United States. It's based on country-church gospel songs. It's based on love; it's based on disappointment; it's based on sorrow; it's based on hope; it's based on happiness. Country music has been a part of the life of this Nation.

Although this is the first time we've had a special program of bluegrass music, we've got people here tonight that are no newcomers to bluegrass. How many of you have ever heard on the radio, before we ever had television, Bill Monroe and the Bluegrass Boys? Well, you're going to have him tonight in person. And this afternoon I had a chance also to hear Doc Watson and his crowd playing beautiful music that went to the heart not only of all those assembled here cooking barbecue but all those over here in the West Wing trying to work at the same time. [*Laughter*]

And we have a special group, as well, tonight from Laurens County—down-to-earth music that lifts the spirits high as we enjoy wonderful cooking from those people. The Lee Jessup Country Band from Laurens County has been playing for you, and they'll be back. This crowd is really moonlighting on the South Lawn of the White House tonight. One of them is a school teacher; one of them is a farmer; one of them is a mayor. And we have a lot to be thankful for from Laurens County.

After I leave this stand, after expressing my heartfelt thanks to all of you for coming, Ralph Rinzler, who's one of the most noted folk historians in this country and responsible for the very successful and historic Smithsonian Institute capturing for history country music and bluegrass music, will come here and tell you about folk festivals and about the groups that are going to sing and play for us. He's helping me tonight, and he's going to give you a special presentation about each individual group that plays.

So, to welcome Mr. Rinzler and to welcome a wonderful evening of bluegrass music, let's give them all a round of applause.

Thank you. I love you all.

THE FIRST LADY. While they're coming on the stage, I want to thank you, too, for all that you do for us. It's just been wonderful to walk through the crowds and see old friends, and it's reminded me of all the things we've been through together. We've had good times and bad times; we've had disappointments; we've worked hard. But in the end, we've always won together, and it's because we have friends like you who are willing to do anything to help us. And I just wanted you to know how much we thank you and how much we love you.

Thank you all for being here.

NOTE: The President spoke at 7:55 p.m. on the South Lawn of the White House. Guests at the barbecue included Presidential primary campaign volunteers, members of the President's and Mrs. Carter's high school graduating classes, and Democratic Members of Congress from Georgia.

Ralph C. Rinzler is Director of the Folklife Unit of the Smithsonian Institution.

Historically Black Colleges and Universities

Remarks on Signing Executive Order 12232.
August 8, 1980

THE PRESIDENT. *Secretary Hufstedler, my good and old friend, Dr. Benjamin Mays, President Charles Lyons, who represents the presidents of the predominantly black colleges, and my friends:*

I just had a private exchange with Benjamin Mays. He said, "Have you got my little personal note?" I said, "Yes, sir." He said, "Did you read it?" I said, "Yes, sir." "Did you agree with it?" "Yes, sir." [*Laughter*] That's been going on a long time in my life. That's one of the reasons that I was able to be elected and serve as Governor and one of the reasons I've been elected and served as President—is because of the advice of Dr. Benjamin Mays and others like him who have the sound experience and the idealism and the realization of the worth of this Nation and its values and has never let those capabilities in his own life be concealed or hidden, even at times when it took great courage for him to be a forceful spokesman for all the finest elements that you represent here this morning.

I've heard him say that a mind is a terrible thing to waste, and especially when it's keen and curious, when it's eager to serve, eager to succeed, a mind which has been aware of deprivation and discrimination, a mind struggling to excel above and beyond the limits that were permitted the parents of the possessor of that young mind. One of the most important things that we can do to let young people like this realize their potential is to support the institutions that support them.

In Georgia I saw the tremendous impact and the change in consciousness in my own region and throughout the world brought about by the private institutions in Atlanta that have predominately had majority black student bodies. This was not easy in those times, in the forties and fifties and sixties, but there was never any wavering of that commitment. Five colleges there, others throughout the State, 100 now throughout our Nation have predominately black student bodies. They are preservers of a heritage, precious to us all, black or white. And although they only comprise about 5 percent of the total number of colleges and universities, they provide 38 percent of all the baccalaureate degrees granted to black students. This shows the importance of them.

But just as the students and their parents have been deprived by discrimination from an adequate opportunity in life, so have the predominately black colleges and universities been deprived of an opportunity in the economic life of the academic community in this Nation up till this moment. Very early in my own Presidential term, many of you came—I think Dr. Mays was a spokesman—and said something must be done. We have added a modest increase in the allocation of Federal resources to the black colleges of our country. We've not done enough.

I issued a memorandum to all the departments, I think the first of 1979, asking that they increase the participation by black colleges and universities in the Federal programs that we have. I think we've increased about $30 million since I've been in office. I've not been satisfied with that progress.

I want a person specifically charged with the responsibility of searching out every possible way that your colleges can participate more fully in Federal programs, not just for education but in all Federal programs, to strengthen what you do, to give you a more sound economic status, and to give your students a better life in the years to come. That's what I want. That's what we're going to get. We must encourage those who have been most discouraged, and we must help those who have been most deprived.

Dr. Shirley Hufstedler is here with us. She'll speak in just a moment. But I'm going to issue today an official Executive order, directing her to pursue these goals

that I've just outlined to you so briefly, give me a written annual report and requiring every department of the Government—in Labor, in HUD, in Health and Human Services, in State, in Defense—all the programs in the Federal Government will have within each department a high official who will explore every possibility for the strengthening of programs in the predominantly black colleges and universities of this country and report to her, and she to me, on an annual basis so that we can monitor the progress and make sure that we take advantage of every opportunity.

I look on this not just as a way to help your colleges, I look on this as a way to help our country, because what we share in the process, in better research, better development, innovation, better social consciousness within all Government structures, fed back by you through experience on a daily basis among these eager students, through the professors and administrators, through Shirley Hufstedler and all the departments and agencies, back up to me will be very helpful to me as a President. I think it'll strengthen our whole college and university system throughout the country, black and white, private or public, and that's what I hope to derive from this Executive order.

Let me say, in closing, that as I sign this order I'd like to ask you to be particularly vigilant in the months and the years ahead, to detect those ways where you can strengthen us and vice versa. I want you to get to know Dr. Hufstedler, who has been a great jurist and who's now head of this new department, set up, among many reasons, to give you a better voice, because when the commitment to education was, in effect, buried underneath Health and Welfare, it was hard for its voice to be heard. But now there's a chair in that Cabinet Room, just on your left, "Secretary of Education," and there's a voice there to be heard, not just in squabbles between the Federal Government and a local school board on a legal matter but to make sure that the quality of education is enhanced.

I believe this is a wonderful opportunity for me as President, for you as distinguished educators, for the students and parents whom you represent, and for our entire Nation. And now I would like to sign the Executive order, following which Shirley Hufstedler, Secretary of Education, will speak. And if Dr. Mays is not too timid, I would like for him to say a few words, in closing.

Thank you very much.

[*At this point, the President signed the Executive order.*]

SECRETARY HUFSTEDLER. Thank you very much, Mr. President.

We in the Department of Education are not only pleased, we're exceedingly proud of our responsibility for overseeing implementation of the Executive order you have signed this day to increase Federal support at all levels for the historically black colleges and universities.

This President's commitment to quality education was made known to me from the very first time we met, when he gave me the honor of inviting me to undertake this job. The first time I met with at least some of the leadership of black colleges and universities was sitting in my temporary office, and that leadership of NAFEO was there when my confirmation as Secretary of Education was received by me. It was only a very brief time thereafter that the President once again told me about his commitment to the preservation and the increasing achievement of black universities and colleges. I welcome that kind of wonderful joint venturing in quality achievement for black Americans.

I do not for a moment suggest that black colleges and universities are feeble institutions. They are not. They are extraordinarily tenacious, strong, and dedicated. That kind of dedication and courage has been shown each and every day of the more than 100 years of history of black universities and colleges in the United States.

It is those universities and colleges, as everyone here knows, the worthy institutions that created, that educated the backbone of black leadership in the United States. It was from those institutions that were created in a national way, in a real, personal way, the kind of spirit of leadership epitomized by Dr. Benjamin Mays and by the extraordinary leaders who sat at his feet as they were learning what it meant to become an educated black American in the United States. Some of those very people are with us today. Some of them are not with us today, but are with us always in spirit. I do not name them all; I only mention Dr. Martin Luther King, Jr.

We have to find ways to not only preserve but to escalate the quality of the kind of education that black Americans and other minority students are receiving all over this country. But we know that one of the ways to make that happen is to work with what we already know succeeds, and that's the black institutions of higher learning in the United States.

It is, of course, not enough that youngsters have an opportunity to go to college. It is not enough that talented young black boys and girls can go to black universities and colleges. But the black universities and colleges have to have more help in order to prepare those young people to go to postgraduate institutions all over this country. We are going to do our level best to see that those young people, with your help, get the help they need.

In working in the Department to bring to complete fruition the implementation of the President's order and of the memorandum, which has been prepared in the White House, to help us do that, I have the enormously able assistance of my Under Secretary, Steve Minter, who will identify himself, if I just beg him to—there he is—of Herman Coleman, whose dedication to the cause of black education has been absolutely unflagging—Herman? And, there he is—of course, always in cooperation with Louis Martin, whose aid to the whole cause has been wonderful, to Deputy Undersecretary Margaret McKenna, who has worked constantly on the project, and to the black leadership, constantly represented in the Department by a very distinguished advisory council.

It gives me the greatest pleasure not only to say welcome to each and every one of you but welcome to a new engagement for excellence, a new engagement of support, a new engagement of faith in the direction of great achievement for historically black universities and colleges.

Thank you. [*Applause*] You know, the wrong people are applauding. I am the one—and each of you know the person to be applauded, in addition to the President of the United States, is Dr. Benjamin Mays.

DR. MAYS. *Mr. President, Secretary of Education, Mrs. Hufstedler, ladies and gentlemen:*

I feel highly honored to be here this noon, not only because the President of the United States invited me to come and because the Secretary of Education is participating but because I have been interested in the United Negro College Fund since its inception in 1944 or '45, when President Patterson of Tuskegee Institute approached me as one of the first persons to talk about the United Negro College Fund. The first time I wasn't quite sure, but when Patterson got through, there was no doubt in my mind.

So, I'm very happy to be here. I'm happy to be here, because it is my considered judgment that President Jimmy Carter has done more for black people and for the Nation in his appointment of Federal judges, Ambassadors, Attorney Generals, generals in the Army, Cabinet members. And I think the President promises to do more.

In the great Georgian series, President Carter was one of the persons interviewed, and he made statements about me in a commendable manner. He had been a friend to the black people. It is my considered judgment that he's done more for the black people and for the United States of America than any President in the history of the United States, and that includes Lincoln. He's followed in the footsteps of Truman and Lyndon Johnson.

And it may be that since God moves in a mysterious way his wonders to perform—it may be that God has called Jimmy Carter out of Plains, Georgia, out of Georgia—a nation that did its share of discriminating and lynching Negroes. It may be that God has called him to be the one to show the American people how to implement the Declaration of Independence, how to implement the words of Abraham Lincoln, and how to implement all of the important things that we need to make America the kind of democracy which I believe God has called upon us to do.

It is for this reason that I'm happy and honored to represent my colleagues in the United Negro College Fund and all the people interested in education throughout the length and breadth of this land.

Thank you very much.

THE PRESIDENT. Thank you, everybody. Let's all go to work. Thank you very much.

NOTE: The President spoke at 11:45 a.m. in the Rose Garden at the White House.

Historically Black Colleges and Universities

Executive Order 12232.   August 8, 1980

By the authority vested in me as President by the Constitution of the United States of America, and in order to overcome the effects of discriminatory treatment and to strengthen and expand the capacity of historically Black colleges and universities to provide quality education, it is hereby ordered as follows:

1-101. The Secretary of Education shall implement a Federal initiative designed to achieve a significant increase in the participation by historically Black colleges and universities in Federally sponsored programs. This initiative shall seek to identify, reduce, and eliminate barriers which may have unfairly resulted in reduced participation in, and reduced benefits from, Federally sponsored programs.

1-102. The Secretary of Education shall, in consultation with the Director of the Office of Management and Budget and the heads of the other Executive agencies, establish annual goals for each agency. The purpose of these goals shall be to increase the ability of historically Black colleges and universities to participate in Federally sponsored programs.

1-103. Executive agencies shall review their programs to determine the extent to which historically Black colleges and universities are unfairly precluded from participation in Federally sponsored programs.

1-104. Executive agencies shall identify the statutory authorities under which they can provide relief from specific inequities and disadvantages identified and documented in the agency programs.

1-105. Each Executive agency shall review its current programs and practices and initiate new efforts to increase the participation of historically Black colleges and universities in the programs of the agency. Particular attention should be given to identifying and eliminating unintended regulatory barriers. Procedural barriers, including those which result in such colleges and universities not receiving notice of the availability of Federally sponsored programs, should also be eliminated.

1-106. The head of each Executive agency shall designate an immediate subordinate who will be responsible for implementing the agency responsibilities set forth in this Order. In each Executive agency there shall be an agency liaison to the Secretary of Education for implementing this Order.

1-107. (a) The Secretary of Education shall ensure that an immediate subordinate is responsible for implementing the provisions of this Order.

(b) The Secretary shall ensure that each President of a historically Black college or university is given the opportunity to comment on the implementation of the initiative established by this Order.

1-108. The Secretary of Education shall submit an annual report to the President. The report shall include the levels of participation by historically Black colleges and universities in the programs of each Executive agency. The report will also include any appropriate recommendations for improving the Federal response directed by this Order.

JIMMY CARTER

The White House,
August 8, 1980.

[Filed with the Office of the Federal Register,
2:14 p.m., August 8, 1980]

American Enterprise Day, 1980

Proclamation 4778.   *August 8, 1980*

*By the President of the United States
of America*

A Proclamation

The American free enterprise system, the cornerstone of our Nation's economy, has endured and flourished for more than 200 years. It provides us with one of the highest standards of living in the world, and guarantees freedom of choice in a way that sets us apart among nations.

It is a system that depends upon and rewards initiative and innovation, a system that offers opportunities to Americans from all walks of life, a system whose benefits accrue to each of us.

Today, our free enterprise system is buffeted by changes both at home and abroad. Inflation, the energy crisis, growing competition in world markets—all challenge our resourcefulness. To preserve the health of our system and our position in the international economy, we must work together to increase productivity by developing and implementing new techniques for the more effective use of raw materials, energy, machines, and our own labor. In the process, we will reaffirm our confidence in the American future.

In recognition of the importance of our enterprise system, the Congress in Senate Joint Resolution 109 has requested the proclamation of October 3, 1980, as American Enterprise Day.

Now, THEREFORE, I, JIMMY CARTER, President of the United States of America, do hereby proclaim October 3, 1980, as American Enterprise Day, and I urge business, labor, agricultural, educational, professional, consumer and civic groups, as well as the people of the United States generally, to observe American Enterprise Day with appropriate activities that promote appreciation of the American free enterprise system and its benefits.

IN WITNESS WHEREOF, I have hereunto set my hand this eighth day of August, in the year of our Lord nineteen hundred and eighty, and of the Independence of the United States of America the two hundred and fifth.

JIMMY CARTER

[Filed with the Office of the Federal Register,
8:55 a.m., August 11, 1980]

National Diabetes Week, 1980

Proclamation 4779.   *August 8, 1980*

*By the President of the United States
of America*

A Proclamation

Diabetes, a disorder in which the body is unable properly to convert nutrients into energy, affects approximately 10 million Americans. As the fifth leading cause of death by disease, it has become a serious and widespread public health problem. Diabetes is a major contributing factor to heart attacks, stroke, kidney failure and blood vessel disease, and the number of diabetics is increasing in all age groups. The medical cost of diabetes is also on the rise, approaching $7 billion annually—and that does not even take into account the complications of the disease. But the highest price of all is paid in terms of the quality of its victims' lives.

Not since the discovery of insulin over half a century ago, however, has the outlook for advances in the treatment, cure and ultimate prevention of diabetes been as promising as it is today. In recent years, research has yielded new and exciting information about the causes and treatment of diabetes and its complications.

The National Diabetes Mellitus Research and Education Act of 1974 provided the impetus for the intensified research effort now under way in hospitals and medical centers around the country. The Federal Government, in cooperation with private voluntary organizations, is leading the research challenge with a multiagency attack on the disease. This continuing coordinated approach is expected to lead not only to more effective methods of diabetes control but eventually to a reduction in the impact of this disease on the people and economy of this Nation.

By Joint Resolution enacted April 2, 1980 (Public Law 96–224), the Congress has designated the week beginning October 5, 1980, as National Diabetes Week.

Now, THEREFORE, I, JIMMY CARTER, President of the United States of America, do hereby proclaim the week beginning October 5 through October 11, 1980 as National Diabetes Week and I call upon the people of the United States to observe that week with appropriate ceremonies and activities.

IN WITNESS WHEREOF, I have hereunto set my hand this eighth day of August, in the year of our Lord nineteen hundred and eighty, and of the Independence of the United States of America the two hundred and fifth.

JIMMY CARTER

[Filed with the Office of the Federal Register, 8:56 a.m., August 11, 1980]

Child Health Day, 1980
Proclamation 4780.   August 8, 1980

By the President of the United States of America

A Proclamation

All the wealth in the world, in its various forms, and all the progress that man has ever achieved would be meaningless were it not for the children who will some day receive it as a legacy. Our children give our lives continuity and meaning, and it is imperative that we do our utmost to give them, in return, the chance to live rich, vigorous and rewarding lives.

The infant mortality rate in the United States has steadily decreased during this century and is now the lowest in our history—but it is not low enough. Statistically, a child born in this country today can expect 73.2 years of healthy and productive living, but many of our children still die in childhood or infancy.

The health of our children and our posterity requires unfailing vigilance and dedication. Accordingly, I have proposed to the Congress this year a Child Health Assurance Plan to help ensure adequate health care for all American children.

Now, THEREFORE, I, JIMMY CARTER, President of the United States of America, do hereby proclaim Monday, October 6, 1980, as Child Health Day.

I urge all Americans to join me in the task of planning, promoting and providing for the physical, environmental and mental health needs of our children.

IN WITNESS WHEREOF, I have hereunto set my hand this eighth day of August, in the year of our Lord nineteen hundred and eighty, and of the Independence of the United States of America the two hundred and fifth.

JIMMY CARTER

[Filed with the Office of the Federal Register, 8:57 a.m., August 11, 1980]

National Farm-City Week, 1980

Proclamation 4781.   August 8, 1980

By the President of the United States of America

A Proclamation

The Nation's most basic resources are the food and fiber produced on American farms. As these supplies are used, they are renewed each growing season. Without food and fiber, all else would cease.

The production of our food and fiber is the most common example of the use of solar energy. Plants, through interaction with the sun's rays, capture solar energy and package it in the usable form of food and fiber.

These actions are so taken for granted that we may overlook the phenomena of interdependence between sun and plants that is so basic to our well-being. Without plants, the earth would be a barren planet, incapable of sustaining life; and without energy from the sun, the earth would be an uninhabitable globe whirling in space.

We may also take our national food and fiber abundance so much for granted that we overlook the interdependence of farms, which produce our food and fiber, and cities, which process the food and fiber and distribute it within easy reach of each of us. Without farms, cities would be barren monuments of concrete, and without cities, farms would be primitive forms of economic life.

To achieve a better appreciation of the contributions and cooperation of farms and cities, the Nation has set aside a week in November as National Farm-City Week. The theme is "Farm and City, Partners in Progress—Key to the Future."

Now, THEREFORE, I, JIMMY CARTER, President of the United States of America, do hereby designate the period November 21 through November 27, 1980, as National Farm-City Week.

IN WITNESS WHEREOF, I have hereunto set my hand this eighth day of August, in the year of our Lord nineteen hundred and eighty, and of the Independence of the United States of America the two hundred and fifth.

JIMMY CARTER

[Filed with the Office of the Federal Register, 8:58 a.m., August 11, 1980]

Demarcation Lines Dividing the High Seas and Inland Waters

Statement on Signing H.R. 1198 Into Law. August 8, 1980

Today I am signing into law H.R. 1198, a bill "to clarify the authority to establish lines of demarcation dividing the high seas and inland waters." H.R. 1198 provides that the Secretary of Transportation shall establish identifiable lines dividing the high seas and inland waters for certain navigational and safety purposes.

The establishment of any line dividing the seas raises the possibility that arguments will be made using the lines to justify positions for which they are not intended and, consequently, may have both domestic and international implications for the location and measurement of territorial seas. The legislative report on H.R. 1198 clearly states that the lines called for by this bill relate solely to safety and are not intended to be used for any other purpose. To emphasize this legislative intent, I am directing the Secretary of Transportation to consult with the Secretary of State and the Attorney General prior to each establishment of a line under H.R. 1198. This procedure will ensure that the firmly established Federal positions regarding the location and measurement of the territorial seas are not prejudiced. In addition, it is my understanding that the lines established under H.R. 1198 are not to be deemed determinative of territorial jurisdiction under international law.

Any powers of the United States relating to the Panama Canal are, pursuant to the Panama Canal treaties, to be exercised exclusively by the Panama Canal Commission. Therefore, inclusion of the "Canal Zone" in the definition of "United States" in H.R. 1198 cannot be read to override our treaty obligations and will not be applied by the administration to override those obligations. To clarify this point, the administration will seek an amendment to remove "Canal Zone" from the definition of "United States."

The administration plans to seek additional technical amendments to H.R. 1198 in the next session of Congress to correct certain deficiencies in the bill. An amendment should be made to subparagraph (b) to ensure that no false impression is created with regard to territorial jurisdiction. I have clearly stated that the United States will not claim jurisdiction out to 12 nautical miles from the base line before conclusion of a comprehensive Law of the Sea Treaty. Other changes may be needed as well.

NOTE: As enacted, H.R. 1198 is Public Law 96–324, approved August 8.

Legislation Amending the Foreign Assistance Act

Statement on Signing S. 1916 Into Law. August 8, 1980

The Congress has acted wisely in passing legislation amending the Foreign Assistance Act to authorize the Overseas Private Investment Corporation (OPIC) to operate in the People's Republic of China.

The establishment of diplomatic relations between the United States and the PRC in January 1979 opened a new era based on equality, common interest, and mutual respect. In order to develop this mutually beneficial relationship, we have made agreements covering scientific and technological cooperation, consular affairs, claims settlement, and bilateral trade. The PRC has now adopted a new law on joint ventures, making it possible for private American business to participate in the economic modernization and growth of the PRC.

Over the past 10 years, OPIC has written more than $10 billion in political risk insurance, covering long-term American investments in nearly 70 developing countries. By facilitating this flow of private investment OPIC and our private investors carry out an important part of U.S. foreign economic policy. Now, private U.S. investors and contractors insured by

OPIC can serve the interests of both the United States and China.

OPIC is selective, supporting only those investments that contribute to the development of the host country and that do not harm the U.S. economy. The investments and contracts supported by OPIC open up new markets for U.S. industrial goods and agricultural products.

This legislation will permit negotiation of an agreement to initiate OPIC services in the People's Republic of China. It is a further step in establishing mutually beneficial economic relations between the largest nation and the largest economy in the world.

NOTE: As enacted, S. 1916 is Public Law 96–327, approved August 8.

Digest of Other White House Announcements

The following listing includes the President's public schedule and other items of general interest announced by the White House Press Office and not included elsewhere in this issue.

August 3

The President returned to the White House from Camp David, Md.

August 4

The President met at the White House with:

—Zbigniew Brzezinski, Assistant to the President for National Security Affairs;

—Frank B. Moore, Assistant to the President for Congressional Liaison.

The President transmitted to the subcommittee of the Senate Judiciary Committee his report on administration actions relating to Billy Carter's activities with the Libyan Government.

August 5

The President met at the White House with:

—Dr. Brzezinski;

—Mr. Moore;

—Lt. Gov. Ted Schwinden of Montana;

—Vice President Walter F. Mondale.

August 6

The President met at the White House with Senator Thomas F. Eagleton of Missouri, Senator Lloyd Bentsen of Texas, and Representative Mario Biaggi of New York, to discuss heat and drought conditions in the United States.

August 7

The President met at the White House with:

—Dr. Brzezinski;

—Mr. Moore;

—Matthews Saad Muhammed, the World Boxing Council Light Heavyweight Champion;

—Mrs. Carter, for lunch.

The President signed a determination authorizing the use of an additional $10 million from the U.S. Emergency Refugee and Migration Assistance Fund to finance assistance for Cuban and Haitian refugees.

August 8

The President met at the White House with:

—Dr. Brzezinski;

—Vice President Mondale, Secretary of Defense Harold Brown, Deputy Secretary of State Warren M. Christopher, Hedley W. Donovan, Senior Adviser to the President, Jack H. Watson, Jr., Assistant to the President, and Dr. Brzezinski;

—singer Roberta Flack.

The President left the White House for a stay at Camp David.

NOMINATIONS SUBMITTED TO THE SENATE

The following list does not include promotions of members of the Uniformed Services, nominations to the Service Academies, or nominations of Foreign Service officers.

Submitted August 1, 1980

The following-named persons to be members of the Board of Directors of the Inter-American Foundation for the terms indicated:

For the remainder of the term expiring September 20, 1982

GUY FELIZ ERB, of California, vice Carolyn R. Payton, resigned.

For the term expiring October 6, 1984

DORIS B. HOLLEB, of Illinois, vice Charles A. Meyer, term expired.

For the term expiring September 20, 1986

PAULA STERN, of the District of Columbia, vice Arnold Nachmanoff, term expiring.

For the term expiring October 6, 1986

LUIS GUERRERO NOGALES, of California, vice Manuel R. Caldera, term expiring.

The following-named persons to be members of the Board of Directors of the Corporation for Public Broadcasting for terms expiring March 26, 1986:

REUBEN W. ASKANASE, of Texas, vice Donald E. Santarelli, term expired.

DIANA LADY DOUGAN, of Utah (reappointment).

LILLIE E. HERNDON, of South Carolina (reappointment).

HOWARD A. WHITE, of New York (reappointment).

Withdrawn August 1, 1980

DAVID BRONHEIM, of Connecticut, to be a member of the Board of Directors of the Inter-American Foundation for the remainder of the term expiring September 20, 1982, vice Carolyn R. Payton, resigned, which was sent to the Senate on March 20, 1980.

NOMINATIONS—Continued

Submitted August 4, 1980

HENRY L. KIMELMAN, of the Virgin Islands, to be Ambassador Extraordinary and Plenipotentiary of the United States of America to Haiti.

Submitted August 5, 1980

JOHN C. TRUESDALE, of Maryland, to be a member of the National Labor Relations Board for the term of 5 years expiring August 27, 1985 (reappointment).

RICHARD BRYANT LOWE III, of New York, to be Inspector General, Department of Health and Human Services, vice Thomas D. Morris, resigned.

CHECKLIST OF WHITE HOUSE PRESS RELEASES

The following listing contains releases of the White House Press Office which are not included in this issue.

Released August 6, 1980

Advance text: remarks at the annual conference of the National Urban League in New York City, N.Y.

Released August 7, 1980

News conference: on current issues—by Press Secretary Jody Powell

ACTS APPROVED BY THE PRESIDENT

Approved August 3, 1980

S. 2492_____ Public Law 96–320 Ocean Thermal Energy Conversion Act of 1980.

Approved August 4, 1980

S. 2995_____ Public Law 96–321 An act to allow the transfer of certain funds to fund the heat crisis program.

H.R. 6666_____ Public Law 96–322 An act to revise the laws relating to the Coast Guard Reserve.

H.R. 5580_____ Public Law 96–323 North Atlantic Treaty Organization Mutual Support Act of 1979.

ACTS APPROVED—Continued

Approved August 8, 1980

H.R. 1198_____ Public Law 96–324
An act to clarify the authority to establish lines of demarcation dividing the high seas and inland waters.

H.R. 6613_____ Public Law 96–325
Maritime Labor Agreements Act of 1980.

H.R. 827_____ Public Law 96–326
An act to establish dispute resolution procedures to settle disputes between supervisors and the United States Postal Service.

ACTS APPROVED—Continued

Approved August 8—Continued

S. 1916_____ Public Law 96–327
An act to authorize operations by the Overseas Private Investment Corporation (OPIC) in the People's Republic of China.

H.R. 5748_____ Public Law 96–328
An act to amend title 32, United States Code, to modify the system of accountability and responsibility for property of the United States issued to the National Guard.

Id-al-Fitr

Message of the President.   August 11, 1980

As the month of Ramadan draws to a close, Rosalynn and I send our warmest greetings and good wishes to our fellow Americans of the Moslem faith.

Strict adherence to your religious beliefs during this time of fasting has built discipline and character. It has inspired the true surrender to God which the word Moslem implies. And it has brought about a cleansing of the soul in preparation of the joyous celebration of the holiday of Id-al-Fitr.

We hope you will look back on this period of self-denial with the satisfaction of knowing that your prayers and fasting have strengthened your faith and expanded its positive influence as a force for good in modern life.

JIMMY CARTER

New York, New York

Remarks at a Reception for Democratic National Convention Delegates, Volunteers, and Supporters.   August 13, 1980

I want to say first of all that I'm very proud of Mayor Ed Koch and New York and all the people who live here. My heart goes out in thanksgiving to the delegates who did such a wonderful job Monday night in protecting the integrity of the primary system and in honoring the votes of 19 million Democrats who expressed their will this year. And I also wanted to point out that last night, after one of the greatest speeches I have ever heard, I called Senator Kennedy and told him how much I appreciated it.

Ours is a nation, ours is a party, well represented by thousands of people like you who believe in the greatness of the United States and who believe in openness, debate, controversy, courage, conviction, and who believe in the future and are not afraid to express your will in the most open, democratic, and greatest party on earth. I'm grateful to you for that.

And I'm also grateful for a party which, at the end of this convention, will be united and ready to face the Republicans no matter what comes. And I have absolutely no doubt that Fritz Mondale and I will be ready to serve 4 more years beginning in January.

And finally, let me say to you that throughout this year and throughout the last 4 years you've shown your confidence in me. We have faced formidable odds in the past. We have never been defeated on any major issues and any major campaigns, and I have no doubt that together we'll be victorious not only for ourselves, but for our country.

I want you to have a good evening on Wednesday night, tonight. Don't forget how you're going to vote. [*Laughter*] And then I hope you'll honor my request for the greatest Vice President this Nation has ever seen to be renominated. Fritz said that's obviously a very successful line in my speech, and I ought to use it more often. [*Laughter*] I look forward to seeing you tomorrow night, Thursday night, and I'll make the decision about accepting your nomination at that time.

I now want to keep you in suspense, so good day, work hard tonight and tomorrow. I'll see you Thursday evening. God bless you.

NOTE: The President spoke at 9:38 a.m. in the Albert Hall at the Sheraton Centre Hotel, the hotel where he stayed during his visit to New York City.

New York, New York

Remarks at a Reception for State and Local Officials. August 13, 1980

Let me say first of all, that for a President of our great country to walk into this room and look into the faces and shake the hands of friends who've meant so much to me in 1976 and throughout my entire administration so far, who helped to guide the policies of this Nation, who've let your voices be heard, who've bound together in a true spirit of federalism in local, State, and Federal Government, who've represented so many millions of Americans who want a better life, who want our Nation to be free and strong— I'm deeply grateful to you. And I'm looking forward to 4 more years in the same kind of relationship.

I've been observing the convention with a great deal of attention and personal interest, as you can well imagine. [*Laughter*] I've been particularly excited to see the reception which the people of New York City have given to the delegates from all over the Nation.

I was also pleased with the vote Monday night when the Democratic conventioneers reconfirmed legally our rec-

ognition that the ultimate voice and the ultimate base for the authority of the Democratic Party were the 19 million Democrats who went to the polls and voted this year. And I was also pleased last night, and I called Senator Kennedy to tell him that that was one of the greatest political speeches I have ever heard, and I think it'll go a long way toward unifying our Nation and guaranteeing a victory in November.

And finally let me say that I could not have a better partner than Fritz Mondale to serve with me during this next administration, as he has so well for the last 3½ years. We will have an opportunity in the next, I think, 83 days, to let the American people clearly see the sharp, stark difference between the Republican Party today and what it stands for and the Democratic Party today and what it stands for, between two men who represent such a brutal difference in their concept of America now and the concept of our future, and to let the Republicans try to explain some of the ridiculous attitudes they've already assumed and the promises that they've made to the American people that can never by carried out and, even worse, the promises that they've made to the American people that you and I will see will never be carried out, because they'll never serve in this White House the next 4 years.

And finally, let me say that I'll be with you tomorrow night at the convention. I want to have some good votes today on the platform issues and a good vote tonight on the nominations. Don't forget us and I won't forget you.

Thank you very much. God bless you.

NOTE: The President spoke at 10:07 a.m. in the Georgian Ballroom B at the Sheraton Centre Hotel.

New York, New York

Remarks at the Democratic Congressional Campaign Committee Victory Luncheon. August 14, 1980

You're getting me in the mood for tonight. Thank you very much.

Speaker O'Neill, Majority Leader Byrd, Majority Leader Jim Wright, Jim Corman, Mayor Koch, Joan Mondale and the Mondale family, all of my friends who have been so remarkable in supporting me during this last 4 years and also, particularly, during the last 2 or 3 days:

In my judgment this has been one of the best Democratic conventions that I have ever seen, and I believe it's not just because I was nominated last night but because we've had a superb presiding officer who has kept things going upward, upward, upward all the way.

Everyone says we Democrats have put on a better show than the Republicans. It's probably because that ours is a convention that didn't have to suffer from the actors' strike. [*Laughter*] We're going to have some problems this year with actors, but I don't think too much. They're quick to learn, and they need to learn new lines.

I noticed some of the posters in the convention that said, "What is parity and who is Giscard d'Estaing?" Fritz was pointing out to me just before I came over that if a catastrophe should befall our country and if the Democrats should lose in November, at the next economic summit conference people will have to walk around with labels on their chest saying, "Hello, my name is Helmut Schmidt. I am from Germany," and so forth. [*Laughter*] We're going to try to avoid that kind of embarrassment to our country by waging one of the most united, concerted, sharply defined campaigns in the history of this country.

The issues are deep between us. Our Nation will make a fundamental decision in November to set the course of this country for the rest of this century. Once that decision is made, the first week in November, it won't be possible to repeal it or to reverse it. The decision will affect the life of every person in this land and the lives of every person on Earth. We Democrats are ready for the fight. I am really looking forward to it.

This week has been stimulating to me and also very gratifying. I've had several telephone calls to and from Senator Ted Kennedy. We've kept a close, amicable, constructive relationship. There have been some differences between us on issues affecting our economy and affecting the progress of the campaign during this spring, but those issues have been resolved compatible with the principles of the Democratic Party and compatible with the procedures in the Democratic Party—open, thorough, public debate. And the judgment ultimately being made for the power of our party lies among the average, good, enlightened, working families of this Nation and those who reach out a hand, not for a handout, but for help upward to a better life, a more constructive life, a safer life, and a life that typifies the principles of the United States of America, which are exactly the same as the principles of the Democratic Party, which represents us and which we're going to represent so well in November with a great victory.

It's important for everyone in this room, including myself, to make sure the Nation knows what the Republicans stand for, or at least we're going to make them admit that they don't stand for much of anything that's valuable to the American people.

There's a unique character of the Presidency, and there's a unique character of responsibility among the majority Members of the House and the Senate. You have to be more responsible, you have to consider the results of your decisions. The minority party can be irresponsible, and they have well fulfilled that role. Vote after vote after vote in the Congress have been contrary to the best interests of this Nation, yielding on almost every instance to powerful special interest groups. And when those votes are analyzed there is no doubt in my mind that the sharp distinction between me and Governor Ronald Reagan will be mirrored accurately and to our benefit by the sharp distinction to be drawn by Democratic candidates for Congress who are going to be reelected, the new Democrats who are going to come to Congress to replace Republicans that ought not to be there, and we'll have a victory together in November.

This has not been an easy time for me or for the Democratic Congress or for our country. We've been tested, because we inherited in January of 1977 a mess, and we've been dealing with it ever since. We've made great progress. We've met the challenge of keeping our country at peace. We've dealt with that issue in the most complicated, complex, rapidly changing world that human beings have seen. And we've dealt with difficult issues like energy, which had been avoided, literally for generations. In spite of the efforts made by past leaders all the way since Harry Truman, those tough, difficult issues had not been successfully resolved.

Now we've been successful. In the last 3½ years there's been a remarkable degree of harmony and support between me and the White House and the Congress on the Hill. That record has not been clearly described to the American people and has not yet been understood by the news media and those who listen to and watch the news media for a description of the economic and political health and achievements of our Nation. There has not been a President in modern history, including Franklin Delano Roosevelt and including Lyndon Baines Johnson, who has had a better record of support from the Democratic Congress than has Jimmy Carter, and I am deeply grateful to the Congress for that support.

And the decisions uniquely the responsibility of the President have been difficult. When the invasion of Afghanistan came, the world was watching. What would the United States do? We had all the options available to me, political options, economic options, military options. We responded forcefully and effectively. We've marshaled the support of 104 members of the United Nations to condemn Soviet aggression—and that condemnation still stands—and to demand that the Soviets withdraw their troops from Afghanistan—that demand still stands. And it's spread throughout the Moslem world and the less developed countries of the world, who were formerly allies and sometimes dependent upon, sometimes subservient to the Soviet Union. And we imposed a trade embargo, and we called for draft registration, and we asked the other nations to join us in stopping participation in the Moscow Olympics.

None of those decisions was easy. None of them was particularly politically popular, but the Democratic Congress stood staunch vote after vote and the Republican nominee and the Republican Members of Congress yielded to the temptation of weakness. They were against the boycott, against registration, against not going to the Olympics. But they underestimated American young people and they underestimated the American farmer, they underestimated American athletes, they underestimated American workers, and they underestimated the American public. And I believe that they'll see that that underestimation of the voters in November will bring grief and black wreaths to the Republican convention and campaign halls on the night of November 4.

Every 4 years the Republicans are tempted to put on overalls and start talking about jobs. [*Laughter*] But they've not changed underneath. Instead of talking about progress and fairness and equity and employment and a better, enlightened life for Americans, they talk about Reagan-Kemp-Roth, perhaps the most inflationary piece of legislation that's ever been introduced in the Congress for serious consideration. It is serious, because the Republicans have marshaled not only the voices of Members of Congress and the candidate behind it but the strength and the power of the Republican propaganda machine and the Republican convention platform.

It's not something to be taken lightly. It's a proposal that would be catastrophic if it was imposed. I'll talk about it a little more tonight.

But those are the kinds of things about which our Nation needs to be cautious and concerned and aware as they make a decision about 83 or 84 days from now. There is no way they could carry out those promises, and I'm determined that they won't have a chance to try.

The last point I want to make is this— because I have another speech to make this evening—I'll try to do a good job in expressing the perspective of our Nation as I uniquely can see it from the position of a President. But I believe that what we have done this last 3½ years since we got the Republicans out of the Oval Office has been momentous, not only the addition of 9 million new jobs—a million for black people alone, a million more new jobs for those who speak Spanish in this country alone—but for what we are prepared to do in the future.

We have laid a foundation or a basis for one of the brightest, most dynamic, successful, exciting decades in the history of our Nation. Americans' lives are going to be transformed for the better, because we now have an organizational structure in government and because we now have a better relationship between government and industry and because we now have the prospect of having more energy produced and more energy discovered and new kinds of energy produced and a new change in the homes and automobiles and the way of life of American people. All of this will be the most massive single opportunity to improve the economic health of our country with American labor and American brilliance and American knowledge and American innovation and American spirit and American competence and American unity that the world has ever seen. The prospect of that if understood clearly by the American public can transform the electorate and prove to you who are my partners that the election of a Democratic Congress and the election of a Democratic President will be not only one of the greatest achievements of all times, but will bring the greatest benefits of all times to Americans and to those about whom we care throughout the world.

It is going to be a great decade. And now let's all go to work, right? [*Applause*]

NOTE: The President spoke at 1:52 p.m. in the Grand Ballroom at the Plaza Hotel.

New York, New York

Remarks Accepting the Presidential Nomination at the 1980 Democratic National Convention.   August 14, 1980

Fellow Democrats, fellow citizens:

I thank you for the nomination you've offered me, and I especially thank you for choosing as my running mate the best partner any President ever had, Fritz Mondale.

With gratitude and with determination I accept your nomination, and I am proud to run on the progressive and sound platform that you have hammered out at this convention.

Fritz and I will mount a campaign that defines the real issues, a campaign that responds to the intelligence of the American people, a campaign that talks sense. And we're going to beat the Republicans in November.

We'll win because we are the party of a great President who knew how to get reelected—Franklin Delano Roosevelt. And we are the party of a courageous fighter who knew how to give 'em hell—Harry Truman. And as Truman said, he just told the truth and they thought it was hell. And we're the party of a gallant man of spirit—John Fitzgerald Kennedy. And we're the party of a great leader of compassion—Lyndon Baines Johnson, and the party of a great man who should have been President, who would have been one of the greatest Presidents in history—Hubert Horatio Hornblower—Humphrey. I have appreciated what this convention has said about Senator Humphrey, a great man who epitomized the spirit of the Democratic Party. And I would like to say that we are also the party of Governor Jerry Brown and Senator Edward Kennedy.

I'd like to say a personal word to Senator Kennedy. Ted, you're a tough competitor and a superb campaigner, and I can attest to that. Your speech before this convention was a magnificent statement of what the Democratic Party is and what it means to the people of this country and why a Democratic victory is so important this year. I reach out to you tonight, and I reach out to all those who supported you in your valiant and passionate campaign. Ted, your party needs and I need you. And I need your idealism and your dedication working for us. There is no doubt that even greater service lies ahead of you, and we are grateful to you and to have your strong partnership now in a larger cause to which your own life has been dedicated.

I thank you for your support; we'll make great partners this fall in whipping the Republicans. We are Democrats and we've had our differences, but we share a bright vision of America's future—a vision of a good life for all our people, a vision of a secure nation, a just society, a peaceful world, a strong America—confident and proud and united. And we have a memory of Franklin Roosevelt, 40 years ago, when he said that there are times in our history when concerns over our personal lives are overshadowed by our concern over "what will happen to the county we have known." This is such a time, and I can tell you that the choice to be made this year can transform our own personal lives and the life of our country as well.

During the last Presidential campaign, I crisscrossed this country and I listened to thousands and thousands of people—housewives and farmers, teachers and small business leaders, workers and students, the elderly and the poor, people of every race and every background and every walk of life. It was a powerful experience—a total immersion in the human reality of America.

And I have now had another kind of total immersion—being President of the United States of America. Let me talk for a moment about what that job is like and what I've learned from it.

I've learned that only the most complex and difficult task comes before me in the Oval Office. No easy answers are found there, because no easy questions come there.

I've learned that for a President, experience is the best guide to the right decisions. I'm wiser tonight than I was 4 years ago.

And I have learned that the Presidency is a place of compassion. My own heart is burdened for the troubled Americans. The poor and the jobless and the afflicted—they've become part of me. My thoughts and my prayers for our hostages in Iran are as though they were my own sons and daughters.

The life of every human being on Earth can depend on the experience and judgment and vigilance of the person in the Oval Office. The President's power for building and his power for destruction are awesome. And the power's greatest exactly where the stakes are highest—in matters of war and peace.

And I've learned something else, something that I have come to see with extraordinary clarity: Above all, I must look ahead, because the President of the United States is the steward of the Nation's destiny. He must protect our children and the children they will have and the children of generations to follow. He must speak and act for them. That is his burden and his glory.

And that is why a President cannot yield to the shortsighted demands, no matter how rich or powerful the special interests might be that make those demands. And that's why the President cannot bend to the passions of the moment, however popular they might be. That's why the President must sometimes ask for sacrifice when his listeners would rather hear the promise of comfort.

The President is a servant of today, but his true constituency is the future. That's why the election of 1980 is so important.

Some have said it makes no difference who wins this election. They are wrong. This election is a stark choice between two men, two parties, two sharply different pictures of what America is and what the world is, but it's more than that—it's a choice between two futures.

The year 2000 is just less than 20 years away, just four Presidential elections after this one. Children born this year will come of age in the 21st century. The time to shape the world of the year 2000 is now. The decisions of the next few years will set our course, perhaps an irreversible course, and the most important of all choices will be made by the American people at the polls less than 3 months from tonight.

The choice could not be more clear nor the consequences more crucial. In one of the futures we can choose, the future that you and I have been building together, I see security and justice and peace.

I see a future of economic security—security that will come from tapping our own great resources of oil and gas, coal and sunlight, and from building the tools and technology and factories for a revitalized economy based on jobs and stable prices for everyone.

I see a future of justice—the justice of good jobs, decent health care, quality education, a full opportunity for all people regardless of color or language or religion; the simple human justice of equal rights for all men and for all women, guaranteed equal rights at last under the Constitution of the United States of America.

And I see a future of peace—a peace born of wisdom and based on a fairness toward all countries of the world, a peace guaranteed both by American military strength and by American moral strength as well.

That is the future I want for all people, a future of confidence and hope and a good life. It's the future America must choose, and with your help and with your commitment, it is the future America will choose.

But there is another possible future. In that other future I see despair—despair of millions who would struggle for equal opportunity and a better life and struggle alone. And I see surrender—the surrender of our energy future to the merchants of oil, the surrender of our economic future to a bizarre program of massive tax cuts for the rich, service cuts for the poor, and massive inflation for everyone. And I see risk—the risk of international confrontation, the risk of an uncontrollable, unaffordable, and unwinnable nuclear arms race.

No one, Democrat or Republican either, consciously seeks such a future, and I do not claim that my opponent does. But I do question the disturbing commitments and policies already made by him and by those with him who have now captured control of the Republican Party. The consequences of those commitments and policies would drive us down the wrong road. It's up to all of us to make sure America rejects this alarming and even perilous destiny.

The only way to build a better future is to start with the realities of the present.

But while we Democrats grapple with the real challenges of a real world, others talk about a world of tinsel and make-believe.

Let's look for a moment at their make-believe world.

In their fantasy America, inner-city people and farm workers and laborers do not exist. Women, like children, are to be seen but not heard. The problems of working women are simply ignored. The elderly do not need Medicare. The young do not need more help in getting a better education. Workers do not require the guarantee of a healthy and a safe place to work. In their fantasy world, all the complex global changes of the world since World War II have never happened. In their fantasy America, all problems have simple solutions—simple and wrong.

It's a make-believe world, a world of good guys and bad guys, where some politicians shoot first and ask questions later. No hard choices, no sacrifice, no tough decisions—it sounds too good to be true, and it is.

The path of fantasy leads to irresponsibility. The path of reality leads to hope and peace. The two paths could not be more different, nor could the futures to which they lead. Let's take a hard look at the consequences of our choice.

You and I have been working toward a more secure future by rebuilding our military strength—steadily, carefully, and responsibly. The Republicans talk about military strength, but they were in office for 8 out of the last 11 years, and in the face of a growing Soviet threat they steadily cut real defense spending by more than a third.

We've reversed the Republican decline in defense. Every year since I've been President we've had real increases in our commitment to a stronger Nation, increases which are prudent and rational.

There is no doubt that the United States of America can meet any threat from the Soviet Union. Our modernized strategic forces, a revitalized NATO, the Trident submarine, the Cruise missile, the Rapid Deployment Force—all these guarantee that we will never be second to any nation. Deeds, not words; fact, not fiction. We must and we will continue to build our own defenses. We must and we will continue to seek balanced reductions in nuclear arms.

The new leaders of the Republican Party, in order to close the gap between their rhetoric and their record, have now promised to launch an all-out nuclear arms race. This would negate any further effort to negotiate a strategic arms limitation agreement. There can be no winners in such an arms race, and all the people of the Earth can be the losers.

The Republican nominee advocates abandoning arms control policies which have been important and supported by every Democratic President since Harry Truman, and also by every Republican President since Dwight D. Eisenhower. This radical and irresponsible course would threaten our security and could put the whole world in peril. You and I must never let this come to pass.

It's simple to call for a new arms race, but when armed aggression threatens world peace, tough-sounding talk like that is not enough. A President must act responsibly.

When Soviet troops invaded Afghanistan, we moved quickly to take action. I suspended some grain sales to the Soviet Union; I called for draft registration; and I joined wholeheartedly with the Congress and with the U.S. Olympic Committee and led more than 60 other nations in boycotting the big propaganda show in Russia—the Moscow Olympics.

The Republican leader opposed two of these forceful but peaceful actions, and he waffled on the third. But when we asked him what he would do about aggression in Southwest Asia, he suggested blockading Cuba. [*Laughter*] Even his running mate wouldn't go along with that. He doesn't seem to know what to do with the Russians. He's not sure if he wants to feed them or play with them or fight with them.

As I look back at my first term, I'm grateful that we've had a country for the full 4 years of peace. And that's what we're going to have for the next 4 years—peace.

It's only common sense that if America is to stay secure and at peace, we must encourage others to be peaceful as well.

As you know, we've helped in Zimbabwe-Rhodesia where we've stood firm for racial justice and democracy. And we have also helped in the Middle East.

Some have criticized the Camp David accords and they've criticized some delays in the implementation of the Middle East peace treaty. Well, before I became President there was no Camp David accords and there was no Middle East peace treaty. Before Camp David, Israel and Egypt were poised across barbed wire, confronting each other with guns and tanks and planes. But afterward, they talked face-to-face with each other across a peace table, and they also communicated through their own Ambassadors in Cairo and Tel Aviv.

Now that's the kind of future we're offering—of peace to the Middle East if the Democrats are reelected in the fall.

I am very proud that nearly half the aid that our country has ever given to Israel in the 32 years of her existence has come during my administration. Unlike our Republican predecessors, we have never stopped nor slowed that aid to Israel. And as long as I am President, we will never do so. Our commitment is clear: security and peace for Israel; peace for all the peoples of the Middle East.

But if the world is to have a future of freedom as well as peace, America must continue to defend human rights.

Now listen to this: The new Republican leaders oppose our human rights policy. They want to scrap it. They seem to think it's naïve for America to stand up for freedom and democracy. Just what do they think we should stand up for?

Ask the former political prisoners who now live in freedom if we should abandon our stand on human rights. Ask the dissidents in the Soviet Union about our commitment to human rights. Ask the Hungarian Americans, ask the Polish Americans, listen to Pope John Paul II. Ask those who are suffering for the sake of justice and liberty around the world. Ask the millions who've fled tyranny if America should stop speaking out for human principles. Ask the American people. I tell you that as long as I am President, we will hold high the banner of human rights, and you can depend on it.

Here at home the choice between the two futures is equally important.

In the long run, nothing is more crucial to the future of America than energy; nothing was so disastrously neglected in the past. Long after the 1973 Arab oil embargo, the Republicans in the White House had still done nothing to meet the threat to the national security of our Nation. Then, as now, their policy was dictated by the big oil companies.

We Democrats fought hard to rally our Nation behind a comprehensive energy policy and a good program, a new foundation for challenging and exciting progress. Now, after 3 years of struggle, we have

that program. The battle to secure America's energy future has been fully and finally joined. Americans have cooperated with dramatic results. We've reversed decades of dangerous and growing dependence on foreign oil. We are now importing 20 percent less oil—that is 1½ million barrels of oil every day less than the day I took office.

And with our new energy policy now in place, we can discover more, produce more, create more, and conserve more energy, and we will use American resources, American technology, and millions of American workers to do it with.

Now, what do the Republicans propose? Basically, their energy program has two parts. The first part is to get rid of almost everything that we've done for the American public in the last 3 years. They want to reduce or abolish the synthetic fuels program. They want to slash the solar energy incentives, the conservation programs, aid to mass transit, aid to elderly Americans to help pay their fuel bills. They want to eliminate the 55-mile speed limit. And while they are at it, the Republicans would like to gut the Clean Air Act. They never liked it to begin with.

That's one part of their program; the other part is worse. To replace what we have built, this is what they propose: to destroy the windfall profits tax and to "unleash" the oil companies and let them solve the energy problem for us. That's it. That is it. That's their whole program. There is no more. Can this Nation accept such an outrageous program?

AUDIENCE. No!

THE PRESIDENT. No! We Democrats will fight it every step of the way, and we'll begin tomorrow morning with a campaign for reelection in November.

When I took office, I inherited a heavy load of serious economic problems besides energy, and we've met them all head-on. We've slashed Government regulations and put free enterprise back into the airlines, the trucking and the financial systems of our country, and we're now doing the same thing for the railroads. This is the greatest change in the relationship between Government and business since the New Deal. We've increased our exports dramatically. We've reversed the decline in the basic research and development, and we have created more than 8 million new jobs—the biggest increase in the history of our country.

But the road is bumpy, and last year's skyrocketing OPEC price increases have helped to trigger a worldwide inflation crisis. We took forceful action, and interest rates have now fallen, the dollar is stable and, although we still have a battle on our hands, we're struggling to bring inflation under control.

We are now at the critical point, a turning point in our economic history of our country. But because we made the hard decisions, because we have guided our Nation and its economy through a rough but essential period of transition, we've laid the groundwork for a new economic age.

Our economic renewal program for the 1980's will meet our immediate need for jobs and attack the very same, long-range problem that caused unemployment and inflation in the first place. It'll move America simultaneously towards our five great economic goals—lower inflation, better productivity, revitalization of American industry, energy security, and jobs.

It's time to put all America back to work—but not in make-work, in real work. And there is real work in modernizing American industries and creating new industries for America as well.

Here are just a few things we'll rebuild together and build together:

— new industries to turn our own coal and shale and farm products into fuel for our cars and trucks and to turn the light of the sun into heat and electricity for our homes;

— a modern transportation system of railbeds and ports to make American coal into a powerful rival of OPEC oil;

— industries that will provide the convenience of futuristic computer technology and communications to serve millions of American homes and offices and factories;

— job training for workers displaced by economic changes;

— new investment pinpointed in regions and communities where jobs are needed most;

— better mass transit in our cities and in between cities;

— and a whole new generation of American jobs to make homes and vehicles and buildings that will house us and move us in comfort with a lot less energy.

This is important, too: I have no doubt that the ingenuity and dedication of the American people can make every single one of these things happen. We are talking about the United States of America, and those who count this country out as an economic superpower are going to find out just how wrong they are. We're going to share in the exciting enterprise of making the 1980's a time of growth for America.

The Republican alternative is the biggest tax giveaway in history. They call it Reagan-Kemp-Roth; I call it a free lunch that Americans cannot afford. The Republican tax program offers rebates to the rich, deprivation for the poor, and fierce inflation for all of us. Their party's own Vice Presidential nominee said that Reagan-Kemp-Roth would result in an inflation rate of more than 30 percent. He called it "voodoo economics". He suddenly changed his mind toward the end of the Republican Convention, but he was right the first time.

Along with this gigantic tax cut, the new Republican leaders promise to protect retirement and health programs and to have massive increases in defense spending—and they claim they can balance the budget. If they are serious about these promises, and they say they are, then a close analysis shows that the entire rest of the Government would have to be abolished, everything from education to farm programs, from the G.I. bill to the night watchman at the Lincoln Memorial—and their budget would still be in the red. The only alternative would be to build more printing presses to print cheap money. Either way, the American people lose. But the American people will not stand for it.

The Democratic Party has always embodied the hope of our people for justice, opportunity, and a better life, and we've worked in every way possible to strengthen the American family, to encourage self-reliance, and to follow the Old Testament admonition: "Defend the poor and the fatherless; give justice to the afflicted and needy." We've struggled to assure that no child in America ever goes to bed hungry, that no elderly couple in America has to live in a substandard home, and that no young person in America is excluded from college because the family is poor.

But what have the Republicans proposed?—just an attack on everything that we've done in the achievement of social justice and decency that we've won in the last 50 years, ever since Franklin Delano Roosevelt's first term. They would make

social security voluntary. They would reverse our progress on the minimum wage, full employment laws, safety in the work place, and a healthy environment.

Lately, as you know, the Republicans have been quoting Democratic Presidents. But who can blame them? Would you rather quote Herbert Hoover or Franklin Delano Roosevelt? Would you rather quote Richard Nixon or John Fitzgerald Kennedy?

The Republicans have always been the party of privilege, but this year their leaders have gone even further. In their platform, they have repudiated the best traditions of their own party. Where is the conscience of Lincoln in the party of Lincoln? What's become of their traditional Republican commitment to fiscal responsibility? What's happened to their commitment to a safe and sane arms control?

Now, I don't claim perfection for the Democratic Party. I don't claim that every decision that we have made has been right or popular; certainly, they've not all been easy. But I will say this: We've been tested under fire. We've neither ducked nor hidden, and we've tackled the great central issues of our time, the historic challenges of peace and energy, which have been ignored for years. We've made tough decisions, and we've taken the heat for them. We've made mistakes, and we've learned from them. But we have built the foundation now for a better future.

We've done something else, perhaps even more important. In good times and bad, in the valleys and on the peaks, we've told people the truth, the hard truth, the truth that sometimes hurts.

One truth that we Americans have learned is that our dream has been earned for progress and for peace. Look what our land has been through within our own memory—a great depression, a world war, a technological explosion, the civil rights revolution, the bitterness of Vietnam, the shame of Watergate, the twilight peace of nuclear terror.

Through each of these momentous experiences we've learned the hard way about the world and about ourselves. But we've matured and we've grown as a nation and we've grown stronger.

We've learned the uses and the limitations of power. We've learned the beauty and responsibility of freedom. We've learned the value and the obligation of justice. And we have learned the necessity of peace.

Some would argue that to master these lessons is somehow to limit our potential. That is not so. A nation which knows its true strengths, which sees its true challenges, which understands legitimate constraints, that nation—our nation—is far stronger than one which takes refuge in wishful thinking or nostalgia. The Democratic Party—the American people—have understood these fundamental truths.

All of us can sympathize with the desire for easy answers. There's often the temptation to substitute idle dreams for hard reality. The new Republican leaders are hoping that our Nation will succumb to that temptation this year, but they profoundly misunderstand and underestimate the character of the American people.

Three weeks after Pearl Harbor, Winston Churchill came to North America and he said, "We have not journeyed all this way across the centuries, across the oceans, across the mountains, across the prairies, because we are made of sugar candy." We Americans have courage. Americans have always been on the cut-

ting edge of change. We've always looked forward with anticipation and confidence.

I still want the same thing that all of you want—a self-reliant neighborhood, strong families, work for the able-bodied and good medical care for the sick, opportunity for our youth and dignity for our old, equal rights and justice for all people.

I want teachers eager to explain what a civilization really is, and I want students to understand their own needs and their own aims, but also the needs and yearnings of their neighbors.

I want women free to pursue without limit the full life of what they want for themselves.

I want our farmers growing crops to feed our Nation and the world, secure in the knowledge that the family farm will thrive and with a fair return on the good work they do for all of us.

I want workers to see meaning in the labor they perform and work enough to guarantee a job for every worker in this country.

And I want the people in business free to pursue with boldness and freedom new ideas.

And I want minority citizens fully to join the mainstream of American life. And I want from the bottom of my heart to remove the blight of racial and other discrimination from the face of our Nation, and I'm determined to do it.

I need for all of you to join me in fulfilling that vision. The choice, the choice between the two futures, could not be more clear. If we succumb to a dream world then we'll wake up to a nightmare. But if we start with reality and fight to make our dreams a reality, then Americans will have a good life, a life of meaning and purpose in a nation that's strong and secure.

Above all, I want us to be what the Founders of our Nation meant us to become—the land of freedom, the land of peace, and the land of hope.

Thank you very much.

NOTE: The President spoke at 10:28 p.m. at Madison Square Garden. His remarks were broadcast live on radio and television.

New York, New York

Informal Exchange With Reporters Following a Meeting With Black Delegates to the Democratic National Convention. August 15, 1980

Q. Mr. President, could you give us your impressions of the meeting?

THE PRESIDENT. Well, it was an outstanding meeting. The fact is that the minority American—the blacks and the Spanish and others—have perhaps more at stake in this election than they've had in my lifetime, because the course of this country in the future—about equality and opportunity, the elimination of discrimination, the provision of jobs, the services for the old and the afflicted people—depend on who wins in November. And regardless of whether these delegates here supported Senator Kennedy or me—and they were fairly well divided—we are absolutely united in making sure the Democratic Party wins in the fall, because I think the future of this country, particularly for minority Americans and their rights, is at stake.

Q. Mr. President, do you have any reason to think that you won't get as much of the black vote this year than you did in 1976?

THE PRESIDENT. No. I think I'll get at least as much or more.

REPORTER. Thank you.

NOTE: The exchange began at 8:05 a.m. at the Sheraton Centre Hotel.

As printed above, the item follows the text of the White House press release.

New York, New York

Informal Exchange With Reporters Following a Visit to the Picasso Exhibit at the Museum of Modern Art. August 15, 1980

Q. Mr. President, can you tell us how you enjoyed last night? Do you think that Kennedy was conciliatory enough?

THE PRESIDENT. Oh, yes. I think it was fine. Last night was good, and I think the convention, although it may have started out doubtful and kind of rocky and somewhat divided, there was a steady buildup both of enthusiasm and unity. My belief is that it's been a major step forward for the Democratic Party and I think, therefore, for the Nation.

Q. Do you think it gave you the boost in the polls? Do you think it will give you the boost in the polls your campaign advisers want?

THE PRESIDENT. I don't know. I never have worried too much about polls.

Q. Were you saying last night that Ronald Reagan was not qualified to be President?

THE PRESIDENT. Well, I was just saying that I and the Democratic Party are better qualified to run this Nation the next 4 years.

Q. Didn't you think that Senator Kennedy was a little cool?

THE PRESIDENT. I thought it was a very gracious thing for him to come.

Q. But no traditional handclasp. Why not?

THE PRESIDENT. We shook hands several times.

Q. What do you think of Picasso?

THE PRESIDENT. Great.

NOTE: The exchange began at approximately 9:30 a.m. outside the museum.

Following the exchange, the President went to the Grand Ballroom at the Plaza Hotel to attend a meeting of the Democratic National Committee Finance Council.

As printed above, the item follows the text of the White House press release.

New York, New York

Remarks at a Meeting of the Democratic National Committee. August 15, 1980

One of the most remarkable characteristics of my own campaign in 1976 and again in the primary season this year and, I think I'll predict, in the coming weeks of the general election, has been that we've had two or three secret weapons. One was the intense outpouring and commitment of the minority citizens of our country for me and for Fritz Mondale as expressed this morning by a collection of Kennedy and Carter delegates, now all Carter delegates, with whom I met to represent black America. The press and the public have never understood this feeling of compatibility and support that has always exemplified itself, even in the primary season, when I had a very formidable opponent.

The other secret weapon that I've had has been my own family, Rosalynn and Chip and all of my family, my mother. And I think perhaps the most significant of all, without minimizing the former two, has been Fritz Mondale.

Whenever a group of Democrats who comprise the so-called Roosevelt coalition have had doubts, sometimes legitimate doubts, about me, not knowing me very

well before, they've always looked and said, "Well, if we can't completely trust Jimmy Carter to do what we think is best for our constituency group, labor or educators and others, we can trust Fritz Mondale to make sure that our desires and our hopes and ambitions are not frustrated." To me he represents the finest aspect of Hubert Humphrey Democratic commitments, and I'm grateful to him for that. We make a good team, and I have no doubt that the dedicated Democrats of this Nation, my family and Fritz Mondale and all of you, will make a winning team in November, no doubt whatsoever.

I like to influence elections, sometimes successfully; sometimes my efforts are unsuccessful. But I'd like to try a little bit of influence on you. I don't think that we could possibly have a better group of National Democratic Committee officers than the ones who are on the platform with me this morning, and my own hope is that you would see fit to give them an extension of time. I know how important 4 more years can be to me to do everything I've set out to do, and if you would give them the same opportunity that would certainly be compatible with my own desires.

John White and Coleman Young, Carmela Lacaya, have been just great in putting together a coalition of Democrats to make this convention a success, and of course, Dorothy Bush, there's no way to improve on Dorothy Bush. As you know, Peter Kelley and Chuck Manatt have done an unprecedented job in raising funds and keeping us sound and solvent. And they've had a good team with them. I've just come from the Finance Council meeting and they're in an exuberant spirit.

I'd like to say a few other things, just kind of some private thoughts that I have had during this last few days. This convention, in my judgment, in retrospect, could not have been better. It started out in a spirit of doubt with some real possibility of disunity, an almost certain prospect that a powerful Democratic constituency group or more would, in a spirit of frustration or misunderstanding, depart from the convention floor. And as you know there was always the speculation, sometimes enhanced by the questions presented by the electronic news media in particular. There was a prospect of our coming out of the convention disunited and with an absence of spirit. There was also a remote prospect that very early in the week all of the doubt would be removed and the convention would lose its life and lose its interest for the public and for the media as well.

None of those concerns materialized. There was enough tension and enough interrelationship, enough debate, enough concern expressed so that the American people, as Fritz said, had an accurate picture of a dynamic party, a party of diversity, a party of deep commitment, a party of strong beliefs, of strong hopes and anticipations that in the past have not been adequately realized, a concern about jobs and a concern about inflation and a concern about peace and a concern about minority rights. Those things were expressed so vividly in the tense interrelationship within that convention that it worked up to a climax of unity and achievement and purpose that I believe it guarantees that we have turned the corner and that now America sees a real prospect, which we are not going to let them be disappointed with, that Democrats will be in the White House and the Congress overwhelmingly in the next 4 years and our country will be benefited from it.

Last night in my remarks I tried to make three points clearly, and as you go back to your own communities, I hope you will pursue these goals and these thoughts that have been so vivid in my own mind. And Fritz and I very carefully coordinated our two speeches so they were mutually supportive. We repeated a few things in both speeches for emphasis.

One is that there is a sharp, maybe an unprecedented difference between the Democratic Party of today and the Republican Party of today—and the Democratic candidate of today and the Republican candidate of today. With a possible exception of Goldwater versus Johnson, there has never been a sharper distinction about what this election can mean. That's one point we ought to make.

Secondly, the seriousness of the choice. It's not just for an election year, and it's not even just for the next 4 years. Because of international and national events and circumstances, we are genuinely setting the course for our Nation and therefore the world for the next 20 years— to the end of this century—to the start of a new millenium. And it's close to us. So, the choice is going to be sharp, but the consequences are going to be profound.

It's not a frivolous thing. As you all know, in a primary season, quite often the votes are frivolous. There are massive changes back and forth in public opinion in just 2 or 3 days, because if a candidate is almost defeated, there's a natural inclination in the press on the side of the public to keep the contest going. And there's never that sober consideration in a primary season as there will be on November 4: "How will the life of my child be affected 20 years from now? How will we make a choice in this Nation between progress and retrogression? How will we fulfill the basic commitment to human rights and civil rights and equality and opportunity for downtrodden and afflicted people in this next generation? Will my son die in war, or will we continue an era of peace?"

Those kinds of questions will be on the minds and the hearts of American voters as we approach the general election. And it's important to us as Democratic leaders to make sure that that sober, careful consideration is a part of American consciousness as this campaign season comes to a close in November.

And the other thing that's important to us is to make sure that every American realizes a personal responsibility for the future of our country. We need to expand registration and make sure that those people, who are quite often inarticulate and perhaps uneducated and perhaps even unemployed and alienated from society, are brought into the mainstream of the political process by hard work during this next 80 or 82 days, between now and November. And I'm going to try to marshal every single constituency group and also every mayor and Governor and other official, every Congress Member, to assure a massive turnout of Americans once we convince them about the sharp difference and the profound consequences of the election.

You're the mainstay of the Democratic Party; you've held it together during troubled times, and you are the ones who are responsible for the success of this convention—and it's been notable, far beyond what I ever anticipated a week or a month ago. And as you go back to your own communities I do not want you to underestimate your potential or your own responsibility.

Joan and Fritz, Rosalynn and I, and all of our people will do the best we can to realize a victory, but there is not a single person here, as I told the Financial Council members, who cannot expand your own influence 50-fold or a hundredfold among your own circle of friends and acquaintances, to marshal them to a spirit of dynamic commitment to achieving the goals which we understand so clearly. We need leaders recruited by you leaders. It's not enough to have the honor of membership on the Democratic National Committee. It is an honor, but you have a responsibility commensurate with that honor. And if you ever do anything in the future for the Democratic Party, expand your influence greatly in this next few weeks, not called and urged and begged or cajoled by me or by John White or by Fritz, but on your own initiative. Let each one of you be a nucleus of, in effect, a new Democratic Party organization.

Bring in a few business acquaintances or religious leaders or educational leaders or labor leaders or professional leaders or your own social friends, who may not be very active in politics in the past, and let them be the Democratic leaders, the stalwarts of the future, and let that future be very near to us. So, be recruiters, and if you will do that as you have performed so superbly these last few years, changing the structure and nature and commitment of the Democratic Party to the advantage of our Nation, then I have no doubt that on November 4 we will celebrate a tremendous victory for me and Fritz, for the Democratic Party, for this Nation and, I believe, the entire world.

Thank you very much.

NOTE: The President spoke at 10:28 a.m. in the Terrace Ballroom at the New York Statler Hotel.

Digest of Other White House Announcements

The following listing includes the President's public schedule and other items of general interest announced by the White House Press Office and not included elsewhere in this issue.

August 9

The President, expressing concern over the potential impact of Hurricane Allen on portions of America's Southwest, dispatched John W. Macy, Jr., Director of the Federal Emergency Management Agency (FEMA), to Texas to serve as his personal representative on the scene. If requested, FEMA and other agencies are ready to move immediately to assist State and local governments in their ongoing recovery efforts. Federal personnel are enroute to duty stations in the threatened areas.

August 11

The President declared a major disaster for portions of the State of Texas as a result of Hurricane Allen, beginning on or about August 10, which caused extensive property damage.

August 12

The President returned to the White House from Camp David, Md.

August 13

The President left the White House for the trip to New York City.

August 15

The President left New York City for a stay at Camp David.

NOMINATIONS SUBMITTED TO THE SENATE

NOTE: No nominations were submitted to the Senate during the period covered by this issue.

CHECKLIST OF WHITE HOUSE PRESS RELEASES

The following listing contains releases of the White House Press Office which are not included in this issue.

Released August 14, 1980

News conference: on matters concerning the Democratic National Convention—by Robert S. Strauss, chairman of the Carter/Mondale Presidential Committee

Advance text: remarks accepting the Presidential nomination of the Democratic National Convention

---

ACTS APPROVED BY THE PRESIDENT

H.R. 7786_____ Public Law 96–329
An act to amend Public Law 90–331 to provide for personal protection of the spouses of major Presidential and Vice Presidential candidates during the 120-day period before a general Presidential election.

Security in the Persian Gulf Area

White House Statement in Response to a Newspaper Column. August 16, 1980

The suggestion that this or any other administration would start a war for political benefit is grotesque and totally irresponsible. The allegation made by Jack Anderson is absolutely false. With respect to the Persian Gulf, the President has said that we consider this region an area of vital interest. Therefore, while it is necessary to have plans for dealing with any external threats to countries of the region, we have no intention whatever of initiating any conflict ourselves, and neither the President nor any other responsible official has expressed any intention to take such an action either in October or at any other time.

Erroneous and totally irresponsible reports such as the Anderson column increase the danger to the American hostages in Iran, impede efforts to obtain their release peacefully, and jeopardize American interests in the area generally.

Trade Agreements Program for 1979

Message to the Congress Transmitting a Report. August 18, 1980

To the Congress of the United States:

In accordance with Section 163 of the Trade Act of 1974, I am pleased to submit herewith the Twenty-Fourth Annual Report on the Trade Agreements Program—1979. This Report also complies with provisions of Section 135(i) of the 1974 Act, as well as Section 304d(3) of the Trade Agreements Act of 1979.

The highlights of last year's activities were the conclusion of the Tokyo Round of Multilateral Trade Negotiations (MTN); the passage by the Congress of the Trade Agreements Act of 1979, which implemented the MTN agreements for the United States; and the reorganization of governmental trade responsibilities. In arriving at a successful completion of these negotiations, we benefitted from the interest and cooperation of many Members and committees of Congress, as well as of advisors from the private sector.

The Tokyo Round agreements establish strict new codes covering international trade, reductions of barriers to agricultural trade, and tariff reductions on industrial goods. These actions achieve our principal objective—a fairer and more open trading system that will benefit U.S. citizens.

By adopting these new codes, our major trading partners have agreed to limit the use of major nontariff measures that distort international trade. The negotiated agreements that deal with subsidies, dumping, product standards, customs valuation, licensing and government procurement will open up foreign markets to our domestic industries and exporters.

Additional agreements were negotiated in the areas of agricultural trade, industrial tariffs, and civil aircraft, providing important future economic benefits to the United States through expanded exports. Also of great value are the modernized procedures for handling trade disputes under the General Agreement on Tariffs and Trade that were negotiated in the Tokyo Round.

Most agreements entered into force at the beginning of 1980. The rest will become effective by January 1, 1981. The initial reductions in tariff rates made by the United States and its trade partners took effect on January 1, 1980. The full tariff reductions will be phased in over an eight-year period. Our tariff reductions will benefit consumers and have a desirable anti-inflationary impact, while the reductions by our trade partners will benefit our workers, farmers and businesses.

As a result of the successful conclusion of the most far-reaching and comprehensive multilateral trade negotiations ever held, the United States enters the decade of the 1980s with greatly expanded opportunities to strengthen its international trade performance. In order to take full advantage of these opportunities and to strengthen U.S. export performance, I have restructured Executive Branch responsibilities for international trade activities. This reorganization consolidates trade policy leadership and all trade negotiation responsibilities in the Office of the United States Trade Representative, formerly the Special Representative for Trade Negotiations. The reorganization also places the responsibility for the administration of trade programs, including export promotion, in the Department of Commerce.

I have instituted these changes in order to meet our current and future global economic and trade challenges. My Administration places a high priority on assuring that the full trade potential of the U.S. is realized, in order to maintain and improve the economic health of our nation. Approximately 17 percent of all goods produced in this country are exported. The agricultural produce of one out of every three acres of U.S. farmland is shipped to foreign countries, and approximately one out of every eight manufacturing jobs is directly or indirectly related to U.S. exports.

We made great progress in improving our international trade position last year. Our merchandise exports grew by 26 percent in 1979, our trade balance in manufactures improved by more than $10 billion, and our traditional agricultural surplus grew by 24 percent to more than $18 billion. Our trade deficit was reduced by almost $4 billion despite rapidly rising oil prices that substantially increased the value of our petroleum imports.

Further enhancement of United States exports is a prime objective of my Administration and I will continue my efforts to ensure that government programs help achieve that end. I look forward in the coming year to working with Congress in strengthening our foreign trade performance, and to reporting to you further successes in our international trade program.

JIMMY CARTER

The White House,
   August 18, 1980.

NOTE: The report is entitled "Twenty-Fourth Annual Report of the President of the United States on the Trade Agreements Program— 1979" (Government Printing Office, 191 pages).

Railroad Retirement System

Message to the Congress Transmitting a Report. August 18, 1980

To the Congress of the United States:

I hereby transmit the Annual Report of the Railroad Retirement Board for Fiscal Year 1979.

This report includes the 14th triennial actuarial valuation of the railroad retirement system, which was completed in August 1979. It is the first Board analysis to project the fund's future income and outgo under five sets of economic and legislative assumptions. This approach, involving alternate sets of assumptions, more thoroughly takes into account the variable factors which can significantly affect the system in the coming years, and provides more information for an examination of the system's financial condition. The general conclusion is that the railroad industry retirement system has an acute short-term financial problem as well as long-term financial problems, and corrective legislation is needed to assure sound financing of benefits by the railroad sector.

The 1979 14th valuation projected a cash shortfall under all but the most optimistic set of assumptions. Chairman Adams has advised me that the situation has become markedly worse and that funds will be inadequate to pay rail industry benefits by 1983. The latest projections, based on the economic assumptions used in the March 1980 revisions to the Budget, indicate that the railroad retirement trust fund will exhaust its balance during fiscal year 1983, and could run out of cash in fiscal year 1982.

As discussed by Chairman Adams in the report, the Administration has proposed legislation to protect current and future railroad beneficiaries by sponsoring a fair and evenhanded method for sound financing of the rail industry pension without additional subsidies from general tax revenues. A financially sound rail industry pension is vital to the one million annuitants now receiving benefits, and to the half-million workers now qualified for benefits in the future. The Administration invited, for the second year, a rail management and labor proposal to restore solvency to the rail industry pension without additional general revenue subsidies. Resolution of the system's financial problems is a serious, pressing concern for rail workers, the rail industry, and the million rail pension beneficiaries.

JIMMY CARTER

The White House,
    August 18, 1980.

NOTE: The 149-page report is entitled "Railroad Retirement Board 1979 Annual Report for Fiscal Year Ending September 30."

United States Sinai Support Mission

Appointment of Frank E. Maestrone as Special Representative and Director. August 19, 1980

The President today announced the appointment of Frank E. Maestrone, of Manchester, Conn., as Special Representative and Director of the U.S. Sinai Support Mission. He replaces C. William Kontos, who has been appointed Ambassador to the Democratic Republic of the Sudan.

Maestrone was diplomat in residence at the University of California at San Diego in 1979–80 and has been a Foreign Service officer since 1948.

He was born December 20, 1922, in Springfield, Mass. He received a B.A. from Yale University in 1942. He served in the U.S. Army from 1942 to 1946.

Maestrone joined the Foreign Service in 1948 and was posted in Vienna, Hamburg, Salzburg, Khorramshahr, and at the State Department. He attended the Naval War College in 1962–63. He was political adviser on the International Staff, Paris/NATO from 1963 to 1965.

From 1965 to 1966, Maestrone was Chief of the Regional Affairs Division, Office of Research-Analysis for Western Europe. From 1966 to 1968, he was Deputy Director of the Office of Research-Analysis for Western Europe. He was political officer at Brussels/NATO from 1968 to 1971 and counselor for political affairs in Manila from 1971 to 1973.

In 1973–74 Maestrone was a faculty adviser at the Naval War College. He was Deputy Chief of Mission in Cairo from 1974 to 1976 and Ambassador to the State of Kuwait from 1976 to 1979.

Alaska Lands Legislation

Statement on Senate Approval of the Legislation. August 19, 1980

I am pleased by today's action in the Senate on the Alaska lands bill. The full Senate overwhelmingly approved legislation that guarantees essential protection for the nationally significant natural resources in Alaska, allows for needed development of Alaska's valuable energy potential, and provides opportunities for economic growth for all the citizens of that State. In significant measure, this bill closely resembles the proposals I sent to the Congress more than 3 years ago. It is a victory in the long struggle to resolve this issue.

The bill designates more than 43 million acres of National Park System lands, 54 million acres of National Wildlife Refuges, 56 million acres of wilderness, and 1.3 million acres of National Wild and Scenic Rivers. In essence, the "crown jewels" of the Alaskan natural wonders are afforded protection. At the same time, the bill provides for development of Alaska's oil, gas, mineral, and timber resources while conveying to the State and native communities lands of interest to them.

The resolution of the Alaska lands question is the most important conservation measure to come before any Congress or any President in this century. It has been my highest environmental priority since taking office, and I want to congratulate the Senate for its perseverance and patience in taking this historic step today.

Passage of this bill has taken the hard work and leadership of Senators Jackson and Tsongas and the help of many of their colleagues, including Senators Cranston, Hart, Nelson, Culver, Levin, McGovern, Randolph, Church, Chafee, Roth, Hatfield, Proxmire, Eagleton, and Mathias. The Senate has now greatly increased the chances that we will have an Alaska lands bill passed in this session of Congress. The House has already passed a strong Alaska lands bill, and I am hopeful that the House and Senate will be able to reach agreement on a final bill that I will be proud to sign.

Boston, Massachusetts

Remarks on Arrival. August 21, 1980

SENATOR EDWARD M. KENNEDY. Well, it's a pleasure to welcome Jimmy Carter to Boston, Massachusetts, as the President of the United States and also as the nominee of the Democratic Party.

During the early days of last summer, Mr. Carter was behind Mr. Reagan in the polls, but there is no authority like myself in the country that can say with greater authority than I can, in the crucial times when the time comes to vote, that Mr. Carter is successful. And I am confident that he'll be successful in November, and I'm determined that he'll be reelected as the President of the United States.

Mr. President, the early Founding Fathers of this country said that Massachusetts should lead the way, and over the period of the last five Presidential elections, this State has voted for the Democratic nominee. And I think all of those who have gathered out here to greet you in Boston are ready and willing to put their shoulder to the wheel and make sure that you're reelected as the next President of the United States.

Welcome to Boston and welcome to Massachusetts.

THE PRESIDENT. First of all, let me say to Senator Kennedy that I'm grateful to be on the platform with him twice in less than a week. Both times he's been very generous, and the expression of support that he's given me is very gratifying to one who's met him, who's had a chance to debate the issues, who's seen much more compatibility between us on important issues to the American people than any differences that have separated us, and I'm very deeply grateful for the words that he just said.

To Senator Paul Tsongas, to the Governor of your great State, to the members of the congressional delegation, I want to express my thanks to all of you who've come out to be with me today. This campaign in the fall will be one of extremely sharp differences between myself and the Republican nominee, between the Democratic Party and the Republican Party, and will affect the future lives of all Americans.

I have confidence that we will win together. And one of the major factors that gives me that confidence is the assurance that Senator Kennedy and all those Americans who supported him during the primary and caucus season will be on my side, helping me to lead the Democratic Party to a great victory.

Senator, thank you again. Tell the members of the AFT, Teachers Federation, that I'll be following you out there tomorrow. And I know you'll prepare the way for me, and I'll try to follow you up well. Thank you again. God bless you. It's good to have you as a friend and an ally.

NOTE: The exchange of remarks began at 10:20 a.m. at Logan International Airport.

Boston, Massachusetts

Remarks at the Annual Convention of the American Legion. August 21, 1980

National Commander Frank Hamilton, fellow Legionnaires, fellow Americans:

It's a real honor to address this wonderful convention representing more than 2.7 million American veterans. The American Legion, of which my father was also a member, having helped organize American Legion Post II in Americus, is a very important organization to me and a very proud and rapidly growing organization.

As I was preparing my remarks, I tried to think of the difference between my father's attendance at American Legion conventions and my own coming here to make a speech. One obvious difference is that my father used to have a lot more fun at the conventions than I do these days. [*Laughter*]

Yours is one of the proudest organizations and rightly so. The American Legion embodies the traditions of the citizen-soldier, the ideals of patriotic service equally dedicated to the duties of war and to the challenges of peace—both extremely difficult tasks for patriotic and enlightened Americans.

As President, I'm conscious of your service, and I'm conscious of our Nation's debt to veterans, and I have full confidence in Max Cleland, the director of the Veterans Administration, to serve you well. He and I have worked hard to meet the needs of veterans. Pension benefits, as well as compensation for veterans who are disabled in the service of our country, will increase by more than a third during my first term. I noticed that Max said that for disabled veterans the increases will approach 40 percent in the short period of time.

The Veterans Administration continues to provide more and better health services, particularly in the critical areas of out-patient and long-term care. And we've initiated a psychological counseling program for Vietnam era veterans. We already have 91 centers under this program all across the country. They are well attended, growing, being used, reaching thousands of young veterans who, until now, have felt that they had no place to turn. Also, the Veterans Administration and the Department of Labor are concentrating their work to increase employment among veterans, particularly through the Disabled Veterans Outreach program, which has successfully helped thousands of disabled Vietnam era veterans to find jobs.

Max Cleland has especially dedicated his effort to helping disabled veterans, and we have not had to lower standards at all to match their performance in their new jobs. And I can promise you that we'll continue to improve the services rendered to veterans throughout this country.

Today, as in the past, America needs your service, your commitment, your courage, and your common sense. While our country demands these qualities from all of us, you veterans who have offered your lives for our Nation's honor and survival in the past have an extra incentive to fight to secure peace for Americans today and peace for Americans in the future.

The surest guarantee of that peace today is an American military force strong enough for now and for tomorrow. All of us—myself, the American Congress, you, and other citizens—are making the hard and sometimes costly choices that ensure that American strength remains not only unsurpassed for the present but equal to all our needs in the future.

This morning, as Commander in Chief, I want to talk to you very briefly and very frankly about some of the problems that we face, some of the achievements that we've had, some of the uncertainties about the future, and how you can help. As Commander in Chief of America's Armed Forces, working with the Congress, I have the final responsibility for making those difficult choices. They are critical choices. They are far from simple. I need your support and your understanding based on experience in the Armed Forces in understanding the real choices that we face in defense and in the broader realm of national security policy.

Our goals, simple but profound: security, honor, and peace. Those are the victories we seek for ourselves, for our children, and for our children's children. These victories can be won, but not by nostalgic nor wishful thinking, and not by bravado. They cannot be won by a futile effort either to run the world or to run away from the world. Both of these are dangerous myths that cannot be the foundation for any responsible national policy.

America requires the authority and the strength—and the moral force—to protect ourselves, to provide for the defense of our friends, and to promote the values of human dignity and well-being that have made our own Nation strong at home and respected abroad. To this end, our national security policy has four specific objectives.

First, to prevent war, through the assurance of our Nation's strength and our Nation's will. In this we will not fail.

Second, to share with our friends and allies the protection of industrial democracies of Europe and Asia. In this we will not fail.

Third, to safeguard and to strengthen our vital links to the nations and the resources of the Middle East. In this we will not fail.

And fourth, to defend America's vital interests if they are threatened anywhere in the world. And in this we will not fail.

All of these objectives require America's great military strength. But arms alone cannot provide the security within which our values and our interests can flourish. Our foreign policy must be directed toward greater international stability, without which there is no real prospect for a lasting peace. Thus, our strength in arms—very important—must be matched by creative, responsible, and courageous diplomacy.

We have as a nation that strength and that courage now to present clearly to potential adversaries as well as to our allies. We must continue to build wisely for a future when our patience and persistence will be taxed by challenges perhaps even more diverse and even more dangerous than those that we've seen in recent years. In planning for that future we must have the foresight to accept the reality of change. Americans have never feared change. We must prepare for what we cannot completely predict—there is no way for any nation or any person to know what might happen next—and to know with certainty the objectives that we intend to reach and to hold.

For the sake of all humanity, we must prevent nuclear war. To do so requires the most modern strategic forces based on America's superior technology. Our country has always been in the forefront of new developments, new ideas, new technology, new systems for defense. The decisions that we make today, some of them highly secret, will affect the risks of nuclear war well into the next century.

Like our weapons, our diplomacy must also be aimed at enhancing strategic stability. Thus far in my administration we've strengthened every single element of our strategic deterrent, and we have also worked to enhance strategic stability through world peace and through negotiation of mutual and balanced limits on strategic arms. And I'm thankful to the American Legion for your support of that effort to control nuclear weapons.

We could have spent more money on our strategic forces, but we would not have spent it as wisely. We could have placed our chips on the B-1 bomber, which would have been in service quickly, and obsolete almost as quickly. In order to capitalize on advanced American technology and to deal with predictable improvements in Soviet air defense capabilities, I decided instead, after close consultation with the Secretary of Defense and the Joint Chiefs of Staff, to accelerate the development of cruise missiles.

Four years ago there was no program for long-range air-launched cruise missiles. This year, in a very quick period of time, we will actually begin production of those kinds of missiles. Because of their accuracy and because of their ability to penetrate Soviet air defense systems, they represent a far more effective deterrent than would have the B–1 bomber. We needed the right answer for the long run, and Soviet air defense capabilities, as known today, and U.S. technological developments, as known today, have proven this answer to be the right one.

Similarly, we could have decided, and some still propose, to resume production of land-based intercontinental missiles and simply build more vertical silos to house them. But that solution would not have increased our strategic strength, because the new missiles in fixed silos would have been just as vulnerable as the old ones to the predictable improvement in the accuracy of Soviet missile systems. Instead, we conducted a searching evaluation of our real and responsible choices, and I chose to go forward with the MX missile program.

Four years ago, there was no known solution to the increasing vulnerability of fixed silos. Today, we've devised a mobile system for basing these missiles that will really shelter them from attack. The MX will be ready to strengthen our strategic defenses just when we need that added strength. And I might point out to you that the total area covered by the MX system from which civilians, newsmen and others, would be excluded, only would comprise 25 square miles, a block of land in our whole country just 5 miles on a side. And the total cost of the MX mobile missile system, in constant dollars, would be less than the B–52 bomber system, less than the Minuteman missile system, and less than the combined cost of the Poseidon and the Polaris submarine-launched missile systems.

At sea, as well, we've altered the wayward course that we were steering in 1977. We've put the Trident missile system and the Trident submarine programs back on track. The U.S.S. *Ohio,* the first Trident submarine, is about to begin sea trials. Its sister ship, the U.S.S. *Michigan,* is ready to be launched, and five more Tridents are under construction.

And finally, in this combined system, let me mention that we've made steady progress in a less visible and less dramatic but crucially important area of our strategic forces, and that is the system of command and control to ensure that they and the communications associated with them can survive a crisis, a peremptory, unexpected attack or a major conflict. This has been an area of our defense system which has been too long overlooked and neglected in the past.

All these steps add up to a prudent and a forward-looking program for enhancing our strategic forces and the credibility of our deterrent. In order to keep those forces adequate for the future, we continue to work on new aircraft and on new technology and weapons of all kinds that will be equal to any threats that may arise in the next decade or beyond.

Our strategy, now modernized to take advantage of Soviet planning and Soviet attitudes, must leave them no room for the illusion that they can obtain any advantage over the United States of America by the use of their force. And we will keep our forces that strong and that clearly dominant.

Recently there's been a great deal of press and public attention paid to a Presidential directive that I have issued, known as PD–59. As a new President charged with great responsibilities for the defense of this Nation, I decided that our Nation must have flexibility in responding to a possible nuclear attack—in *responding* to a possible nuclear attack. Beginning very early in my term, working with the Secretaries of State and Defense and with my own national security advisers, we have been evolving such an improved capability. It's been recently revealed to the public in outline form by Secretary of Defense Harold Brown. It's a carefully considered, logical, and evolutionary improvement in our Nation's defense capability and will contribute to the prevention of a nuclear conflict.

No potential enemy of the United States should anticipate for one moment a successful use of military power against our vital interest. This decision will make that prohibition and that cautionary message even more clear. In order to ensure that no adversary is even tempted, however, we must have a range of responses to potential threats or crises and an integrated plan for their use.

Equally vital for our strategic purposes is the pursuit of nuclear arms control and balanced reduction of nuclear arsenals in the world. Just as we build strategic forces equal to our needs, we seek through negotiated agreements to keep unnecessary competition from carrying us into a purposeless and dangerous nuclear arms race to the detriment of our Nation's security and to the detriment of the adequate strength of our conventional and other forces. We will continue to make every responsible effort to bring our forces and those of any potential foe under strict, balanced, and verifiable controls, both in the quantity of strategic arms and in their quality.

I want to make clear that if an unlimited nuclear arms race should be forced upon us, we will compete and compete successfully. Let no one doubt that for a moment. But to initiate such a dangerous and costly race, abandoning our efforts for nuclear weapons control, would be totally irresponsible on our part.

The destructive power of the world's nuclear arsenals is already adequate for total devastation. It does no good to increase that destructive power in search of a temporary edge or in pursuit of an illusion of absolute nuclear superiority. To limit strategic nuclear weapons, as the SALT treaties do, is not to reduce our strength, but to reduce the danger that misunderstanding and miscalculation could lead to a global catastrophe. This is a course that has been pursued by the last six Presidents, both Democratic and Republican. To go beyond the reductions that were outlined in SALT II treaty, as I firmly intend to do, is to advance the stability on which genuine peace can be built.

Stability in the strategic area, however, leaves us still to meet serious challenges now and in the future in Europe, in the Far East, the Middle East, and in Southwest Asia. We must understand those challenges in order to deal with them prudently and responsibly. We do not need massive standing armies in place everywhere in the world to defend our friends and our interests. But we do need and we and our allies are acquiring the skilled, modernized, specially equipped conventional forces that can respond fast and effectively to crises and threats before they engulf us in larger conflicts.

With NATO in Europe, for example, we do not need overwhelming tank forces. We and our allies do not plan to start a war on the European continent. What we do need and what we will maintain are the weapons to repulse any force that seeks or threatens the domination of Europe. After years of neglect during the Vietnam war, we have led NATO's commitment to the deterrent levels of strength it actually needs. The Long-Term Defense Program to which we are now all committed, a 15-year program, will add $85 billion to NATO's fighting strength over the next decade or so and will permit the Alliance to meet any real threat to Europe's security and to our own. This is a major step forward in the closer coordination among ourselves and our allies and a restoration of the spirit of NATO that is crucial to the defense of Europe and to the security of our own country. It must be continued, and it will be continued.

Reversing a long, downward trend in real defense expenditures, above and beyond inflation, we have had real growth for the last 4 years, and we will continue this commitment during the years ahead. That is a promise that I make to you, and that is a promise that the Congress of the United States has also confirmed. We will not permit us to take a downward trend, as was the case during the 8 years before I became President.

A very significant development was the NATO decision last December to modernize theater nuclear forces in Europe, a direct response to the Warsaw Pact build-up of the last 10 years with their SS-20 medium-range missile and others similar to it. This is a vital part of our commitment. It was very difficult politically for some of the European nations to agree to take this major step. The Soviets used every possible propaganda that they could marshal. But our efforts and those of our allies were successful.

In the Pacific and in East Asia, our alliances and our military strengths are firm and they're adequate. We have the military presence on land and at sea to ensure that no would-be aggressor can profit at the expense of ourselves or our friends from any upheaval in that region. Sustained, normal relations with China are very important and improve the prospects for a stable and a peaceful future in Asia.

You of the American Legion have pledged at this convention to the cause of Cambodian relief. It's important that we Americans show the world the strength of American compassion and concern. I applaud your decision to alleviate human suffering and to help the cause of peace in Southeast Asia.

In the most volatile and vital area to our security, the Persian Gulf and Southwest Asia, we're taking additional steps to protect our vital interests. The security of the region and the crucial energy that it supplies to us and other nations are both now exposed to the new threat of Soviet forces in Afghanistan, which have turned that country from its former status as a buffer state into a wedge pointed at the sealanes of the Persian Gulf and to the rich oil deposits. To deter any further encroachment of Soviet power in this region, we must help to strengthen the resolve and the defenses of the countries there.

We are continuing to build up our own forces in the Indian Ocean and in the adjacent areas and to arrange to use facilities on land which we might need to aid our friends in the region in case of conflict and primarily to prevent the need for conflict. We've speeded up formation of a mobile force of up to 100,000 personnel that could be rapidly deployed to any area where sudden trouble loomed and needed to be met. We've arranged to put supplies and equipment for such a force in place ahead of time so they will be there when and if they're needed.

Most of all, in the Middle East, we've pursued the arduous, difficult, frustrating but absolutely essential cause of peace between Israel and its Arab neighbors. The real security of that crucial area of the world depend heavily on the force with which we promote stability and political compromise to avoid the outbreak of conflict. It's crucial that our Nation use all its influence to prevent a fifth Middle East war. The Camp David accords and the Egyptian-Israeli peace treaties that followed them were two extraordinary steps on a long road that until 1978 no one had been able to travel.

In the real world we know that we cannot expect miracles on the Middle East peace negotiations. The issues are too emotional. The difficulties are too great. The obstacles sometimes appear to be insurmountable. But I'm convinced that Israel wants peace, and I'm convinced that the Egyptians want peace, and I'm equally as convinced that those who live in Jordan, Syria, Lebanon, and the Palestinians all want peace. We know that our own future peace makes this work

very important, and it's work that must be continued.

At home, over intense opposition, as you know, but with great help from the American Legion, we have won the fight for peacetime draft registration. We need the ability to mobilize quickly and effectively, and we have shown our resolve to both friend and foe alike.

It should be clear to everyone who studies national security or defense that our work to keep America the strongest nation in the world is not finished. There are no laurels on which to rest. There are no victories which are final. There are no challenges which have disappeared magically. But we've resumed a firm and steady course of diplomacy and defense preparedness to lead our allies and our friends and ourselves with confidence toward the challenges facing the world of today and the world of tomorrow.

The independence, the security, and the development of the countries of the Third World, the small nations, the new nations, the developing nations, the nonaligned nations, are also very important to our national security. Violence and radical revolution thrive in an atmosphere of political repression, economic want, massive unemployment, and hunger. Our interest is served when the countries of the developing world are able to meet the needs and aspirations of their people peacefully, democratically, and through cooperation with the United States of America and the other Western nations.

In helping them to achieve these objectives, we are encouraging democracy, yes, but we are also strengthening our ability to compete effectively with the Soviet Union. Those who are most concerned about Soviet activism in the world should be the strongest supporters of our foreign aid programs designed to help the moderate transition from repressive tyranny to democratic development and to bolster the strength and independence of our friends.

We've revived in this administration the policy that gives added purpose to our Nation's strength: our whole-hearted, national commitment to promote the universal standards of human rights. Freedom for ourselves is not enough. Americans want to see other people enjoy freedom also. It's an unswerving commitment of our Nation, and as long as I'm in the White House, it'll be a major part of our international policy.

We do not maintain our power in order to seize power from others. Our goal is to strengthen our own freedom and the freedom of others, to advance the dignity of the individual and the right of all people to justice, to a good life, and to a future secure from tyranny. In choosing our course in the world, America's strength must be used to serve America's values.

The choices ahead are every bit as demanding as the ones we've already made. Facing them takes a clear understanding of where we are and where we want to go as a nation. Responding to dangers that might menace our future security also will measure America's common sense and courage, just as previous history has measured America's common sense and courage.

I've known America's courage by seeing it tested. I've seen it in the men who went to Iran to attempt so valiantly in an isolated desert to rescue their fellow Americans who are still held hostage there. I saw it in the families of the men who died in that effort, and I've seen it in the families with whom I've met as

frequently as possible of the citizens who are still held captive in Iran. What a nation we are to produce such men and women. All Americans are thankful to them.

And finally let me say that our country also has the courage to reject the easy illusions of something for nothing, the fantasy goals of strength without sacrifice, the irresponsible advocacy of shortcut economics and quick-fix defense policy. There are no magic answers. Easy solutions are very difficult to find. Courage, sometimes quiet courage, unpublicized courage, is the most to be appreciated.

I see this kind of courage in you, as veterans who have served and sacrificed already, but who still work continuously for the sake of service, not for recognition or reward. Your example strengthens my faith in our Nation and in the future of our Nation. With your help and with your courage and with your common sense, I know America will continue to to be a nation of unmatched strength, a nation that faces the world as it is today and works with realism to bring to the world of the future freedom, peace, and justice.

Thank you very much.

NOTE: The President spoke at 11 a.m. at the John B. Hynes Veterans Auditorium.

Detroit, Michigan

Remarks at the Annual Conference of the American Federation of Teachers.
August 22, 1980

President Al Shanker, members of the executive committee, visitors from foreign lands, members of the American Federation of Teachers:

I see the signs around, *"Buena Suerte,"* *"Shalom,"* and I see another one over here that says, "Hi, you all." [*Laughter*] It makes me feel good to come here.

I have always been aware of the fact that Lane Kirkland's and Mr. Meany's [1] window was looking down on the White House. And there have been a few times when White House binoculars were trained on that window as well. [*Laughter*]

We share a lot of concerns, and we share a lot of hopes, and we share a lot of dreams. The progress that our Nation has made has been, to a large degree, predicated on the good relationship between the men and women who work in this Nation and those leaders like you who represent them and an enlightened Democratic leadership in the White House who is just as visionary, just as dedicated, to service as anyone in the labor movement. It's a good partnership. It's a partnership that ought to be preserved. It's a partnership that I'm eager to honor and your confidence I'm determined to prevail.

I'm proud to be the first President to address your annual convention. The other Presidents don't know what they've missed. I hope you'll let me come back to your convention, but I hope for the next 4 or 5 years no other different person will come as President.

As proud as I am of that honor, I'm even prouder to have your endorsement as candidate for President, and I'll do the best I can not to betray your trust and not to disappoint you during the campaign this fall—which I intend to be successful—nor in the administration that's going to follow that for the next 4 years. And I'm also grateful and pleased to have the

support of the AFL–CIO executive council. Together we're going to make this election a victory, not just for myself and Fritz Mondale but for all teachers and students and for all the working men and women of our country. That's my commitment, and I'm not going to betray you.

I might say that, speaking of teachers and students, I learned a lesson this year about the value of an AFT endorsement. It's inscribed very clearly on my mind the classrooms where I was taught, places like New York and Rhode Island and Pennsylvania. [*Laughter*] I really learned it pays to have the AFT with you, and I'm so glad that we are once again, as we were in 1976, on the same side politically. And I'd like to say something now about a mutual friend who was part of this year's education process: a great man, Senator Ted Kennedy.

Yesterday morning, just before he left Boston to come and be with you, he welcomed me to his home city. It was a warm, genuine, deeply appreciated welcome, and it reminded us both of last October when he and I were together, also in Boston, at the dedication of the John F. Kennedy Library. It was a day full of memory and a day full of promise. I made a speech on that day that was challenging to write but an honor to deliver, and I said then that despite all the changes that have taken place since the early 1960's the spirit of dedication and the spirit of idealism that marked John Kennedy's life is even more urgent today than perhaps it was then.

Ted Kennedy personifies to me that spirit, and I'm glad to be working with him and also with all the others that he inspired to join him and now to join me in a common cause.

I don't want to overlook an opportunity to say that I'm also very pleased and it's

---

[1] President and past president, AFL–CIO.

good for me to have on my ticket a man who shares this spirit in full measure and throughout his entire life of dedication to human concerns and dedication to better education in our Nation—and that's Fritz Mondale. I doubt very seriously that in the last 200 years there has been a closer partnership, both personal and political, than exists between me and my Vice President. Our country couldn't have a finer man.

And I would also like to say a word about one other person, another dedicated American, because this is a time when, as was just mentioned, human beings around the world in a highly publicized way are reaching out for freedom—we see this in the world headlines today—and also reaching out for the true principles of trade unionism. The combination is free trade unionism, and I'm glad to stand together, once again, with a man who has dedicated his life to these principles, your president and my friend, Al Shanker.

Almost every time there's a quiet, confidential discussion about the AFT, you're always characterized as a fighting union, a union of classroom teachers. And I have a special feeling for those who fight for principle and those who represent the finest element of education in our country. This feeling comes from my lifelong concern with education, but it's also because of a special nature of responsibilities which you and I share. Harry Truman's old motto "The buck stops here" applies just as much to teachers as it does to Presidents. In any system of education, the teacher's the one who finally does the difficult job, or else the job just doesn't get done.

As you well know, teachers and Presidents have to take a lot of heat— [*laughter*]—for problems in our society that we don't originate. I can't think of a better story than one of my favorites, which I'm sure you may have heard, about the man that was brought before the judge. The judge said, "You've been accused of getting drunk and setting the bed on fire." And the man says, "Judge, I plead guilty to getting drunk but the bed was on fire when I got in it." [*Laughter*] This is exactly the situation when a new President walks into the Oval Office or when a new teacher walks into a classroom. But I don't know of a better place to put the responsibility for difficult changes that must take place in any society, and particularly in a democracy, where we're on the cutting edge of change and progress.

Both of us have a day-in-day-out, full-time responsibility to do all we can to alleviate the human costs of society's problems, and in our jobs we know that there are no shortcuts, there are no substitutes for hard and dedicated work. But the deepest bond between us, in your work as teachers and in my work as President, is that we are both concerned above all with the future. The people you teach not only represent the future, they are the future, and the seeds of knowledge and understanding, of independent thought that you plant often bear their sweetest fruit many years after you finish your job with that person.

As President, I too have a responsibility for the future, knowing that the hard decisions that I make today—and there are no easy ones—will shape the kind of world that we pass on to future generations. So, as we meet today, not just as a candidate and voters and leaders, but as comrades in arms for a better, more humane, and more decent future, the election of 1980 will determine whether your struggle and mine is successful.

Seldom in electoral history has the choice been so clear. The only possible other election in my lifetime when the choice was so clear was in 1964 between Barry Goldwater and Lyndon Johnson. Seldom has the views and the commitments of the candidates been so profoundly different. The American people will be choosing not just between two men, not even just between two political parties, but between two paths that lead to two quite different futures for ourselves, our families, and for all those about whom we're concerned.

I'm convinced that the American people will choose wisely, because I respect the character and intelligence of our people. And when the general election time comes and individual Americans go in that voting booth to think about the future of their family and their children and their Nation, with allies like you, I believe that we can and will be successful, because we believe as Americans that united, in spite of difficulties that we face and acknowledge, that we can shape the future as we want it to be.

Other nations, other people, are fearful about years to come, and they are fearful about changes that they don't quite understand. But Americans have shared some of that concern, but, in effect, we have thrived on it, because Americans are committed to individual human beings who are free and to a free enterprise system that encourages innovation, that can accommodate change, where we're not frozen because we are fearful to speak and where open debate quite often leads to the best decision. We're not afraid of differences among us, and we don't try to discipline the human minds to the extent that it's not constantly probing for even difficult and unpleasant truths.

An election year is a good time in a democracy for sober assessment of our past achievements and our past failures, for our challenges, and also for our opportunities. I look forward this year to several debates with the Republican nominee in different parts of the country. And I'm also willing to debate other candidates, any candidate who might even have a theoretical chance to be elected President.

I'm eager to let the issues be made clear and to let the people decide. The thing I want most of all though is a clear, two-man debate between myself and Ronald Reagan. That is where the people can decide most clearly how these two paths to the future might affect the lives of all of us.

The truth and the facts are important. There's no place in American life for a "pie in the sky," but there's a new math that's being propounded in different proposals. One of them is that in this election year there are claims being made that there can be some massive tax cuts for the rich equivalent to a trillion dollars in the years ahead; that we can at the same time have a massive increase in defense commitments, including the reinstitution of a nuclear arms race; that we can balance the budget at the same time and still provide social services, adequate education, and other needs of the American people. This is obviously a fallacy, and the American people are too intelligent to fall for it. But the facts must be presented in order for the American people to understand the fallacious nature of this kind of proposal.

Our country has gone through difficult times, which I need not enumerate here now. But we've also gone through some successful times quite recently. One is a national process of education on one of the most important domestic and international issues of our lifetime, and that is energy.

We now know, as Americans, something we didn't know even 12 months ago, or many would not acknowledge, and that is that we must cut down our dependence on foreign oil. It's crucial to our Nation's security. It's also crucial to the security of our country, and it also removes the chance of blackmail that might be imposed on us and other nations of the world if that excessive dependence is continued.

The American people have acted. There's been a dramatic cut in the amount of oil we import already. Today, we imported 1½ million barrels less, in 1 day, than we did a year ago. And that same record has been continued ever since the beginning of 1980. We've not succeeded completely yet in this effort, but we've laid a good foundation, and now we're ready to build on it. This gives us a new and exciting way to change American life for the better, not with a decrease in our quality of life, but an increase in the quality of our life.

Within the next week, I intend to outline to the Nation a practical and aggressive new strategy for renewing our economic and our industrial base, part of it predicated upon the inevitable changes brought about by energy independence and a commitment that our Nation's made. This will create literally hundreds of thousands of new jobs and can be accomplished at the same time with even more stable prices for all. This will not be an easy task, but I'm determined to succeed. And along with energy, our rededication to American education is crucial to that strategy and to the future.

Before I became President, the Federal commitment to education was constantly declining in real terms. Together we've reversed that trend. During a time of necessary budget restraint in order to meet the challenge of international inflationary pressures invoked on us by OPEC, we've increased spending for education more than 73 percent in just a little over 3 years.

It's important to me to protect public education. We've fought together successfully against a proposal that would undermine public education, and that is tuition tax credits, and we're going to continue that fight. Universal, free, quality education for all Americans is part of the greatness of our future as well as our past, and we do not want it endangered, and if you'll stick with me, we will not permit it to be endangered. And we're also seeking better working conditions for teachers, because we know that the education of our children depends on the morale and the commitment of classroom teachers.

Along with you and your executive committee and your president, I'm concerned about the fundamental role of collective bargaining. We need to remove difficult, discouraging, unrewarding circumstances that teachers have to face. I've authorized an interagency study to report to me on how teachers' salaries and working conditions affect the quality of education. I'll honor the prerogatives and the authority of local and State officials, but I want all of us to understand what government at every level can do to offer constructive alternatives to work stoppages by meeting the real needs of the teachers of this country.

In the humane future that we all want, there must be a self-fulfilling and a gratifying place for young Americans. A mind is a terrible thing to waste—we've all heard this compelling appeal by the United

Negro College Fund. We've all seen the television portrayal of a young man sitting alone, listening helplessly to the sounds of the city outside, a world in which he cannot hope to compete and within which he cannot hope to take the talent or ability given to him, given by God, and use that talent or ability productively.

So far in my administration, we've increased funding for youth employment and for training almost 100 percent, but we've not yet done enough and we're determined to do more without further delay. That's why, with your help, with the active participation of Al and many of you, we've developed the most far-reaching youth measure ever proposed to the Congress. We call it the youth bill.

It bolsters basic education and job training, and it offers the kind of part-time work that's linked to the learning which is going on in the classroom. It encourages those who would otherwise drop out of school to stay there, and it ties much more closely to educational process with a chance for a successful career after the classroom work is completed. The measure will add $2 billion in more muscle into our existing $4 billion commitment to youth programs. That's a lot of money, but it's the kind of money that we cannot afford not to spend.

Investing in education, investing in youth is one of the essential ways that we can provide for a better future. That's why I wanted to elevate education to a top level of government, and that's why we are fighting to improve education programs from Title I, to education for the handicapped, to teacher centers, where teachers themselves can help to shape programs that will give us a better approach to education. That's why we'll continue to cut redtape and paperwork and let teachers get on with the job of teaching for a change. It's important to me that the AFT and your leaders play an integral role with me as President, with Secretary Shirley Hufstedler, and with others, including of course the Congress, as you've done so well, as we make these kinds of decisions. I won't try to enumerate all the things that are going on in the Congress and in the administration and in your own lives concerning education.

I speak about these concerns not only as President but also as a parent. My sons were all educated in the public schools and also in the public colleges. And my daughter, Amy, is now beginning her fourth year in the Washington, D.C., public schools, where I've been able to see firsthand the skill and the dedication of members of Local Number Six. [*Laughter*] I might add that Amy's looking forward to more years of—[*laughter*]—quality education in Washington, D.C., at least 4 more years to be exact.

And while I'm on the subject, I want Amy to have something else. When she grows up I want Amy to have the same rights that her brothers have now, and I want those rights as a woman guaranteed where they belong, in the Constitution of the United States of America.

In the great national debate over the future direction of our country, there is no doubt where you and I stand. We stand for civil rights, strictly enforced. We stand for vigorous protection of the lives and safety of every worker, guaranteed by the Government. We stand for reform of the labor laws, and we're going to fight for it again next year and win. And we stand for human things like pure air and pure water that you can drink. We stand for revitalizing our cities, which is very important to me, and we will not abandon our cities. And we stand for a strong America, and we stand for world peace.

For the last 3½ years our Nation has been at peace. We've secured that peace by enhancing our strength, both our military strength and our moral strength. It's been a long time, more than 50 years, since a President has served a complete term or terms in the White House without having combat troops lose their lives in war.

We've pursued peace not only for ourselves but for others. In the Middle East Israel no longer confronts her most powerful Arab neighbor across barbed wire. Instead, they talk together; with difficulty, yes; sometimes with delays that are very frustrating to me and to Prime Minister Begin and to President Sadat. But they talk and they exchange ideas not only across the peace table but through Ambassadors of their own nations in the other nation—in Tel Aviv and in Cairo—about the right road to permanent peace.

Three years ago, who would have dreamed that such a thing would be possible? Who would have dreamed that planes would be flying between Jerusalem or Tel Aviv and Cairo and Alexandria, that tourists would cross the border to make friends on the other side, that full diplomatic relations would exist, and that we could have a prospect of perpetual peace there? My total personal effort, in spite of every obstacle, this year and in the future, will be devoted to the realization of the commitments made in the Camp David accords so clearly and so solemnly by all three of our nations: a peaceful and secure Israel, peace and justice for all people in the Middle East. When the history books are written about my administration, that is my fondest hope, that that will be included.

To meet the Soviet challenge we've strengthened our defense capabilities while at the same time we have sought mutual limits on nuclear arms. A peaceful future includes both strength and control of nuclear arms. We must prevent nuclear war.

We've heard the word "noble" used. We must recognize the nobility of an honorable peace, and I'm very proud that our country is again the champion of human rights around the world. We take that stand, because we are Americans and the love of liberty is the very soul of our people and of our Republic. And as long as I'm President, no matter what the temptations might be to the contrary for temporary diplomatic advantage, you can be sure that our Nation, your Nation, will go on struggling for human rights.

Let me say in closing that the work you do as teachers is very much a part of all these commitments, and many that I haven't taken the time to enumerate. What you do is important, not just because it adds to the skills of our labor force or the size of our gross national product, but because it strengthens democracy and freedom itself. We often place too heavy a load on the schools and on the men and women who teach in them, but the fact remains that your classrooms are the place where society is able to speak to itself, where young Americans take new strength from the American past and from the whole common experience of humanity. You help America develop the intellectual and the moral tools to master the future.

Building the future is the essence of your life and mine. It's also the essence of America. In his memorable novel "You Can't Go Home Again" Thomas Wolfe wrote these stirring words, and I quote from his book: "I think the true discovery of America is before us. I think the true fulfillment of our spirit, of our people, of our mighty and immortal land is yet to come. I think the true discovery of our democracy is still before us. I think that all these things are as certain as the morning, as inevitable as noon. Our America is here, is now, and beckons us, and this glorious assurance is not only our living hope but our dream to be accomplished." A beautiful quote.

In the year 1980 America still beckons us toward that same hope and that same dream, but it's not going to come automatically nor easily. We must fight for it, and I'm glad we're fighting for it together side by side, and together you and I will be victorious.

Thank you very much.

NOTE: The President spoke at 11:27 a.m. in the Renaissance Ballroom at the Detroit Plaza Hotel.

Veterans Administration Health Care Legislation

Message to the House of Representatives Returning H.R. 7102 Without Approval. August 22, 1980

To the House of Representatives:

I am returning without my signature H.R. 7102, the Veterans Administration Health Care Amendments of 1980, because this bill would provide $80 million a year to Veterans Administration ("VA") physicians in unwarranted salary bonuses rather than target that amount on veterans themselves.

As President, I have worked with the VA to ensure that the health care provided to our veterans is the finest in the world. Toward that goal, during the last three years, I have supported and signed legislation to expand and improve the treatment of all veterans who need to receive care from the Veterans Adminis-

tration. Clearly, much more remains to be done for our veterans, and it is essential that we direct additional funds to those most in need.

What is *not* essential, and what does *not* further our goal of directly helping sick and disabled veterans, is spending a large sum of money to give VA physicians currently earning an average of $55,000 a year up to 38% bonuses, making them by far the highest paid medical personnel in the entire government. Indeed, so generous are the bonuses provided in this bill that mid-career VA physicians could earn 30% more ($76,200 vs $58,700) than the maximum authorized annual salary for Armed Forces physicians. The Defense Department has recommended a veto of this bill because this differential in pay may adversely affect its ability to solve the current physician recruitment and retention problems in the military.

I am concerned about attracting and retaining excellent VA physicians. But the current salary and benefits are more than sufficient to do that. At the same time, the current level of health care is not, in all areas, sufficient. Therefore, rather than spend $80 million on unneeded bonuses for a relatively few physicians, I would prefer that the Congress target funds more directly on improving health care benefits and treatment for veterans.

I therefore urge the Congress to pass a bill which meets the other goals of H.R. 7102, including the Veterans Administration real and specific needs for certain physician specialists, while providing— from the money that would have been projected for excessive bonuses—for improved health care treatment of veterans.

JIMMY CARTER

The White House,
August 22, 1980.

Digest of Other White House Announcements

The following listing includes the President's public schedule and other items of general interest announced by the White House Press Office and not included elsewhere in this issue.

August 16

The President declared a major disaster for the State of West Virginia as a result of severe storms and flooding, beginning on or about August 4, which caused extensive property damage.

August 18

The President transmitted to the House Committee on Foreign Affairs and the House Committee on the Judiciary his report on administration actions relating to Billy Carter's activities with the Libyan Government.

August 19

The President declared a major disaster for the Commonwealth of Pennsylvania as a result of severe storms and flooding, beginning on or about August 14, which caused extensive property damage.

The President returned to the White House from Camp David, Md.

August 20

The President met at the White House with:

—David L. Aaron, Deputy Assistant for National Security Affairs;

—Frank B. Moore, Assistant to the President for Congressional Liaison;

—Vice President Walter F. Mondale, Secretary of the Treasury G. William Miller, Jack H. Watson, Jr., Assistant to the President, James T. McIntyre, Jr., Director of the Office of Management and Budget, Charles L. Schultze, Chairman of the Council of Economic Advisers, Alfred E. Kahn,

Advisor to the President on Inflation, Stuart E. Eizenstat, Assistant to the President for Domestic Affairs and Policy, and Alonzo L. McDonald, Jr., Assistant to the President.

August 21

The President met at the White House with:

—Mr. Aaron;

—Swiss Ambassador to the United States Raymond Probst.

The White House announced that the President will meet President Ziaur Rahman of Bangladesh in Washington on August 27. The President of Bangladesh will be in the United States to address the United Nations General Assembly Special Session on Global Economic Issues.

August 22

The President met at the White House with:

—Zbigniew Brzezinski, Assistant to the President for National Security Affairs;

—Vice President Mondale, Secretary of State Edmund S. Muskie, Secretary of Defense Harold Brown, Deputy Secretary of State Warren M. Christopher, Mr. Watson, and Dr. Brzezinski.

In an Oval Office ceremony, the President received diplomatic credentials from Ambassadors Don Carmelo Nvono Nca Menene Oluy of Equatorial Guinea, Abdelkader Braik al-Ameri of Qatar, Prok Amaranand of Thailand, Juan Jose Amado of Panama, Aboubacar Bokoko of the Gabonese Republic, and Jose Luis Fernandes Lopes of Cape Verde.

NOMINATIONS SUBMITTED TO THE SENATE

NOTE: Only nominations for promotions of members of the Uniformed Services were submitted to the Senate during the period covered by this issue.

CHECKLIST OF WHITE HOUSE PRESS RELEASES

The following listing contains releases of the White House Press Office which are not included in this issue.

Released August 19, 1980

Announcement: the administration's initiative to prevent the influx of Southwest Asian heroin into the United States

Released August 21, 1980

Advance text: remarks at the annual convention of the American Legion in Boston, Mass.

CHECKLIST—Continued

Released August 22, 1980

Announcement: President's approval of Congressional Medal of Honor award to former Cpl. Anthony Casamento, USMC

ACTS APPROVED BY THE PRESIDENT

NOTE: No acts approved by the President were received by the Office of the Federal Register during the period covered by this issue.

Fire Prevention Week, 1980

Proclamation 4782.   August 25, 1980

By the President of the United States of America

A Proclamation

Fire causes more loss of life and property in the United States than all other natural catastrophes combined. Fire is the second most frequent cause of accidental death in the home.

The human costs of fire are borne disproportionately by career and volunteer firefighters. Their profession is one of America's most hazardous.

Each year approximately 8,500 Americans die; another 300,000 are injured in fires and $5 billion worth of property is destroyed. America loses more to fire than most other countries in the industrialized world.

In an effort to alter this tragic situation, the Administration has implemented a Reorganization Plan, placing the United States Fire Administration's fire programs in the Federal Emergency Management Agency. This agency now coordinates America's disaster preparedness and response efforts, and, within it, the fire service still stands as the First Responder, with the capability and mission to contain, mitigate or resolve emergencies.

Yet the Federal government alone cannot reduce America's fire losses. The public and private sector must do their part. Together, working as a team, we can lessen the unnecessary, life-threatening destruction caused by fire.

Now, THEREFORE, I, JIMMY CARTER, President of the United States of America, do designate the week of October 5 through 11 as Fire Prevention Week.

Because fire deaths most often occur in homes, I call upon American families and other property owners to install smoke detectors, to practice exit drills, and to be especially vigilant in guarding against fires. I further urge all citizens already possessing smoke detectors to use this week to test their devices to ensure their operational status.

I support and encourage the cooperative efforts of private enterprise and government in developing low cost residential sprinkler systems that may revolutionize fire safety in the home.

I encourage the fire service, police, prosecutors, the insurance industry and governmental agencies to continue to work together to improve arson prevention and control measures. Arson remains America's fastest growing crime and we need total commitment to combat it.

I call upon every fire department in the country to improve the delivery of emergency medical services and to teach citizens the fundamentals of basic life support and cardio-pulmonary resuscitation.

I urge the fire service to open their profession fully to women.

I encourage the fire service to take full advantage of the National Fire Academy.

I acknowledge the National Fire Protection Association and its affiliate, the Fire Marshals Association of North America, for their sponsorship of this week's international observance.

Finally, I call upon members of the Joint Council of National Fire Service Organizations, members of the International Association of Fire Fighters, members of the International Association of Fire Chiefs, all other organizations concerned with fire safety, and the United States Fire Administration to provide the leadership, planning and innovation necessary for an effective national fire prevention and control effort.

IN WITNESS WHEREOF, I have hereunto set my hand this twenty-fifth day of August, in the year of our Lord nineteen hundred and eighty, and of the Independence of the United States of America the two hundred and fifth.

JIMMY CARTER

[Filed with the Office of the Federal Register, 3:16 p.m., August 25, 1980]

White Cane Safety Day, 1980

Proclamation 4783.   August 25, 1980

By the President of the United States of America

A Proclamation

In every activity of daily life, most of us depend upon our sight. We take for granted the ability to wend our way through the woods, dodge children and bicycles on the sidewalk, and navigate around cars at busy intersections. As a result, we rarely stop to consider that these everyday activities can be hazardous to the six million Americans who are blind or partially sighted.

Fortunately, visually handicapped people have a distinctive tool available to them which can help in these potentially dangerous situations. That tool is a white cane.

Using the cane as an extension of the body, a sightless person can explore unfamiliar environments, locate landmarks, and find a path free of obstacles. Thanks to this simple aid, millions of visually handicapped persons are able to move about their communities with a degree of independence that would otherwise be denied them.

As valuable as the white cane is, however, it cannot warn its user of hazards more than a few feet away. It cannot detect rapidly moving vehicles, joggers, and young people on roller skates. Therefore, we must all be alert to the needs of people who carry the white cane. Often a gesture as simple as yielding the right-of-way to a visually handicapped person, or offering assistance when it seems to be needed, can make the difference between a safe journey and a hazardous one. In this way, we can help visually handicapped people overcome the difficulties that threaten to limit the freedom of movement that all of us value so highly.

To heighten public awareness of the importance of the white cane to the independence and safety of blind and partially sighted Americans, the Congress, by a joint resolution approved October 6, 1964 (78 Stat. 1003; 36 U.S.C. 169d) has authorized the President to proclaim October 15 of each year as White Cane Safety Day.

NOW, THEREFORE, I, JIMMY CARTER, President of the United States of America, do hereby proclaim October 15, 1980, as White Cane Safety Day.

I urge all Americans to observe this day by reflecting on the accomplishments of the blind and visually handicapped, by showing sensitivity to the rights and needs of all handicapped citizens, and by resolving to aid them in their continuing struggle for independence.

IN WITNESS WHEREOF, I have hereunto set my hand this twenty-fifth day of August, in the year of our Lord nineteen hundred and eighty, and of the Independence of the United States of America the two hundred and fifth.

JIMMY CARTER

[Filed with the Office of the Federal Register, 3:17 p.m., August 25, 1980]

Office of Personnel Management

Message to the Congress Transmitting a Report.   August 25, 1980

To the Congress of the United States:

I am pleased to transmit herewith the First Annual Report of the Office of Personnel Management for the Fiscal Year ended September 30, 1979, in accordance with the Civil Service Reform Act of 1978 (P.L. 95–454, Sec. 906(a) (5 U.S.C. 1308(a)).

The report discusses the first year of operations under the comprehensive Civil Service Reform Act. The results are encouraging. The Senior Executive Service program has been overwhelmingly accepted by Federal managers and morale is high. The exchange of people, ideas and information between the Federal government and State and local governments has increased tremendously. The division of functions among the Office of Personnel Management, the Merit Systems Protection Board and the Federal Labor Relations Authority is working effectively.

I am proud of the performance of thousands of dedicated civil servants, and of the leadership of the Office of Personnel Management and its Director, Alan Campbell.

I encourage you to review this report,

as we look ahead to the full implementation of the Act in the coming years.

JIMMY CARTER

The White House,
  August 25, 1980.

NOTE: The 125-page report is entitled "The Annual Report of the Office of Personnel Management, 1979—1st Annual Report."

National Advisory Council on Women's Educational Programs

Nomination of Anne Thorsen Truax To Be a Member.   August 25, 1980

The President today announced that he will nominate Anne Thorsen Truax, of Minneapolis, to be a member of the National Advisory Council on Women's Educational Programs. She would replace Jon Fuller, whose term has expired.

Truax, 55, is an adjunct instructor of family social science and an instructor in the women's studies program at the University of Minnesota. She is director of the Minnesota Women's Center and is active in community and professional organizations.

Interagency Committee on Women's Business Enterprise

Appointment of Rilla Moran Woods as Chairperson.   August 25, 1980

The President today announced the appointment of Rilla Moran Woods, of Nashville, Tenn., as Chairperson of the Interagency Committee on Women's Business Enterprise.

Woods, 55, is Deputy Commissioner of the Transportation and Public Utilities Service of the General Services Administration. She has been a member of this Committee since last year.

President's Export Council

Appointment of Two Members.
August 25, 1980

The President today announced the appointment of two persons as members of the President's Export Council. They are:

EDWARD M. LEE, 44, of Englewood, Colo., president of Information Handling Services and a member of the Colorado District Export Council.

RICHARD SUISMAN, 49, of Hartford, Conn. Suisman, formerly part owner-operator of a scrap iron and metal dealership with customers in this country and overseas, is currently working with a small group in Hartford to start a second daily newspaper. He is a former member of the Hartford City Council.

Dinner for Retiring Members of Congress

Remarks at the White House Dinner.
August 25, 1980

If I could have your attention a minute. As I was standing in the receiving line with Rosalynn, looking into the faces of the great Members of Congress who are here tonight, I thought about my own campaign for the Congress back in 1966 after I had been State Senator for two terms. I almost had the race won when I changed my mind and ran for Governor. And I was just thinking, if I had only stayed in the congressional race— [laughter]—I'd be a seven-term veteran instead of just a freshman President. [Laughter] As a matter of fact, it has been a wonderful experience to be a freshman President. The only thing that I could

think of that would be better would be a sophomore President—[laughter]—which we're working on now.

This is an election year, as you may have remembered. I know it's a very fine thing for you to be looking at the election with smiles on your faces and complete relaxation. I never have seen such a happy crowd, I think, at the White House. [Laughter] I've been enjoying the debate today. I watched the news before I came up, the debate between two major candidates on the China policy. [Laughter]

I know how bored you can get talking about politics when you're not involved in it yourself, and I don't want to bore you very long tonight, but this is a time of thanksgiving on my part as a President for what you've contributed to our country. It's an honor for me and Rosalynn to have you in the White House. You represent 500 years of service to our Nation, a tremendous contribution in human terms to giving life to a government.

Obviously this Capital City is beautiful. It's an exciting place to live. It's a challenging life in the interrelationship among Americans as concentrated here, not only in the Oval Office for me but at the Capitol for you, over a long period of time. I know some of the people at my table here have served for 16 terms, and this is a matter of great pride, not only to you individually and to your whole family but also to the family that you represented back in your States or in your districts.

The beauty of a capital or the beauty of even a capitol building is part of a democracy, of course, because it exemplifies that it belongs to the people. But the most important aspect is the one represented by you, and that is the human dimension, which truly gives a democracy its life. And you've given your lives, at least a portion of them, to public service, quite often without recognition, without credit for your tremendous accomplishments, with a great deal of criticism and sometimes castigation, sometimes disappointment, I know, sometimes a sense of frustration. But the holding together of the finest nation on Earth and its Government in the midst of the closest possible public scrutiny and to make steady progress, with an absence of partisanship as the Congress decides the major issues of the day and of the century, must be extremely gratifying to you—it is to me—to observe in your faces the finest elements of public service.

I believe that all of you leave here with a recognition that your lives have been meaningful so far, but, without exception, I know that you're looking forward to continuing an active life, capitalizing on the great experience that your own constituents have given you. It's a two-way street, of course. Not only have you honored your district and your State, but you've been honored by being permitted to serve, as I'm being honored by being permitted to serve.

I know that in the future you'll watch our Government with the greatest attention, perhaps with a more quizzical expression, perhaps a little more critical attitude now that you'll be on the outside looking at us. And I hope that you'll give me the same kind of continued on-the-job training that you have done so well in providing for me the last 3½ years. I know what a chore this has been for you. I know how dear you hold your other congressional peers, and I know you wouldn't want to put another chore like this on them in January of 1981. [*Laughter*]

So, in a nonpartisan way I would like to close by quoting a Democrat. I tried to find a quote that would exemplify your own comments in the future, and the best one I could find was when Harry Truman got back to his home city in 1953, after a distinguished career, as you know, in local government, as a United States Senator, as a Vice President, and then as President of our Nation.

One of the newsmen asked him—and I'll read it, to be accurate—if he would analyze his public career. Truman stood there frustrated, having had too many questions like this from the news people, and finally he replied, and I quote, "I did my damnedest, and that's all there is to say about it." [*Laughter*] And Truman turned around and walked away.

I think that statement is a good one, and I know that in addition to the superb achievements that you have contributed to our country, which gives you so much gratification, all of you have done your damnedest to make your own lives meaningful and to make our Nation the greatest nation on Earth. And because of that I thank you, on behalf of the American people, from the bottom of my heart. Thank you. God bless you all.

If you'll permit me, I'd like to offer a toast: To those Members of the Congress represented here, to all of your families, whom you have filled with pride, and to the people of our Nation, whom you have served so well. God bless you all.

NOTE: The President spoke at 7:25 p.m. in the State Dining Room at the White House.

National Employ the Handicapped Week, 1980

Proclamation 4784.   August 26, 1980

By the President of the United States of America

A Proclamation

Our Nation is moving strongly toward greater equality for people with physical and mental disabilities.

The United Nations has designated next year as the International Year of Disabled Persons. As President, I not only reaffirm this country's commitment to equality for handicapped individuals, I intend to make every effort to see that the coming decade is one in which their aspirations are fulfilled.

We must do all we can to give the handicapped maximum independence, full access to our society, and the opportunity to develop and use their talents and skills. This must be done case by case, event by event, and program by program. Working together, we can make certain that disabled people at last enter completely into the mainstream of our great society.

To affirm our commitment to independence for handicapped individuals, the Congress, by joint resolution of August 11, 1945, as amended (36 U.S.C. 155), has called for the designation of the first full week in October each year as National Employ the Handicapped Week.

Now, THEREFORE, I, JIMMY CARTER, President of the United States of America, do hereby designate the week beginning October 5, 1980, as National Employ the Handicapped Week. I urge all Governors, Mayors, other public officials, leaders in business and labor, and private citizens at all levels of responsibility to help remove the barriers to equal opportunity for handicapped individuals and to help them in their search for productive employment.

IN WITNESS WHEREOF, I have hereunto set my hand this twenty-sixth day of August, in the year of our Lord nineteen hundred and eighty, and of the Independence of the United States of America the two hundred and fifth.

JIMMY CARTER

[Filed with the Office of the Federal Register, 3:50 p.m., August 26, 1980]

International Atomic Energy Agency

Nomination of U.S. Representative and Alternate Representatives to the 24th Session of the General Conference. August 26, 1980

The President today announced the persons whom he will nominate as Representative and Alternate Representatives of the United States to the 24th Session of the General Conference of the International Atomic Energy Agency, to be held September 22–26 in Vienna, Austria. They are:

Representative

JOHN C. SAWHILL, Deputy Secretary of Energy;

Alternate Representatives

GERARD C. SMITH, Ambassador at Large and U.S. Special Representative for Non-Proliferation Matters, and Representative of the United States to the International Atomic Energy Agency;

ROGER KIRK, Deputy Representative of the United States to the International Atomic Energy Agency, with the rank of Ambassador.

Women's Equality Day, 1980

Remarks on Signing Proclamation 4785. August 26, 1980

I've been asked to sign the proclamation first and then make my remarks, but I'll use the Presidential prerogative and make my remarks first—[*laughter*]—because I would like to put into context the importance of this day.

It's obvious that the banners aligned behind me here represent a great deal of courage, a great deal of conviction, a great deal of American history, a great deal of persecution and frustration, temporary failure. We're here to celebrate the 60th anniversary of the ratification and the implementation of the 19th amendment to the U.S. Constitution, the amendment that gave women the right to vote.

I'm very pleased that, I believe, we have three Members of Congress here—Cardiss Collins, Geraldine Ferraro, and Pat Schroeder—who represent part of the ultimate culmination of women's right to vote—full participation in the political process; advancement, not only for women but for all Americans. And we are here also to dedicate ourselves to the attainment of full equality for women in every single aspect of American life.

Looking back 60 years, women did not win the right to vote easily or quickly. More than 72 years elapsed, as a matter of fact, between the women's rights convention assembled in Seneca Falls, New York, and the time when the adoption of the 19th amendment signified that great victory, years in which literally generations of courageous women continued their crusade in spite of the powerful opposition of economic and political forces and in spite of repeated disappointments that would have caused an end to the effort of lesser human beings. Women were fighting not only for their own rights but for the rights of all who were excluded from or mistreated in the American society. They set an example of dedication to justice, to liberty, and to opportunity that inspires and strengthens us here six decades later as we seek to complete the victory which they initiated.

I share that commitment, and as President of all Americans, I'm not waiting until women enjoy a full equality in all the areas of American life before doing all I can to help women enjoy the full responsibilities of participation in the Federal Government.

We've got a long way to go. In my first 3 years as President, I've appointed as many women to Cabinet positions as were appointed in the previous 200 years.

Women have headed the Departments of Education; Health and Human Services, whose budget is the third biggest in the world—the only two budgets larger are the United States Government in its entirety and the Government of the Soviet Union—Commerce; Housing and Urban Development. And they also, of course, have served and do serve in high-level positions in agencies like Agriculture, Defense, Transportation, mine safety, workers safety and health, management and budget, in every area of Government life. It's not enough, I recognize that.

There are now 43 Federal judges who are women. I appointed 38 of them. And among the 38 that I've appointed, their qualifications have been superb. We have never been tempted even to lower the standards of professional capability nor judicial temperament in order to find women to serve. That's not enough. I don't say it to brag. These judges, as you know, will be interpreting all rights in this generation, for our children and also for our children's children.

To eliminate discrimination in employment in the Federal Government and discrimination in promotion and also to improve our Goverment at the same time, I fought for and won with your help a complete revision of civil service, the first reform in a hundred years. And just in the recent months, since that reform took place, the impact of it is beginning to be felt. The number of women in the highest ranks of the civil service have already increased by 45 percent. That's not enough, because the original base was so small, but the reforms that we have implemented are now taking effect. We now have in the mid-level grades, where women were formerly largely excluded as you well know, women holding 3 out of every 10 jobs. Since I've been in office, because of reorganization and other changes, we have had a decrease in the total number of Federal employees, but the number of women workers in the Federal Government has increased by 66,000. We're making some progress—still a long way to go.

We've set high standards for every Federal agency and department to increase the prime contracts for goods and services to be awarded to businesses that are owned and managed by women. We've exceeded all those goals. Many of those goals were set by those of you who advised me on what our Nation should strive to attain. You didn't set the goals quite high enough. I know you'll correct that in the near future.

We've consolidated 19 Government units involved in equal employment opportunity under Eleanor Holmes Norton into one agency, at the Equal Employment Opportunity Commission. Cases that once languished for years are now resolved almost immediately. When I was elected and took office, we had 30,000 back cases involving discrimination against minorities and women. Now that backlog has been almost completely eliminated, and a lot of the examples that have been set in the successful prosecution of those cases has prevented further discrimination that would have led to additional backlogs of thousands of cases.

In all these areas of opportunity—and I won't belabor the point—we simply must do more. Equality for women, as you know, is not just limited to jobs nor to business sales nor to involvement in the Federal Government or the free enterprise system of our country. It involves education and advancement and full participation in every single aspect of our society.

Women have not been deprived in one area, and that is the burden of hard work and labor. Women comprise 43 percent of our total workforce. What they have been deprived of is equal pay, equal opportunity, equal chances for promotion. The average working woman earns only 59 percent as the average working man in our country. The results are costly to our Nation, yes, but they are cruel to the families that must depend on the income of that woman to meet the family's needs. One-fourth of all the American families are headed by a woman, but one-half of all the families below the poverty level are headed by a woman.

Some sociologists say that the dramatic movement of women into the mainstream of society, especially into the labor market, is the most significant social revolution in history. You may or may not agree with that assessment, because civil rights is also a major change in societal structure, but the two are so closely interrelated that it's almost impossible to separate the one from another.

The U.S. Congress has voted overwhelmingly to eliminate discrimination under the laws that still exist, to the embarrassment of our Nation. Women's rights vary from State to State. Not only the U.S. Congress but the majority of State legislatures, 35 of them as a matter of fact, have voted to end this injustice. The majority of the American people in poll after poll have declared their desire to end this injustice. Every President who has lived in this house and served in this office since Franklin D. Roosevelt has supported the equal rights amendment. Both the Democratic and Republican Party platforms have supported the equal rights amendment in every Presidential election for the last 40 years—until this year, when the Republicans repudiated it.

The issue has not changed; the injustice against women has not changed; the position of State legislatures and the Congress have not changed; the position of the majority of Americans has not changed. All that has changed is the strength and the organization and the financing of the opposition—and the Republican Party's rejection of their own historic support of equal rights for women. Now they say that equal rights for women are acceptable in principle, but not in the Constitution of the United States. If they know in their hearts it's right, why don't they want it in the laws?

It's not enough for the new Republican leaders to give this emphasis in their own hearts. Women need equality in their paychecks and in their opportunities to get an education, and to get a job, and to enter a profession, and to get a loan, and to own a house, and to care for a family, and to get a promotion, and to start a business of their own. Well, that's why we are going to see, working together, that the principle of equal rights for women is not left to the faint hearts of those who took it out of a party platform. But we're going to make sure that before June of 1982 that equal rights for women are guaranteed in the Constitution of the United States.

I'd like to read a proclamation that I'll sign in just a moment. It's entitled "Women's Equality Day, 1980."

[*At this point, the President read the proclamation.*]

"In witness whereof, I have hereunto set my hand" this date—and at this time, I would like to sign this proclamation and ask all of you who observed to join in with me in a total commitment, yourselves and all those who look to you for leadership, in making sure that the purposes of this proclamation and the ratification of the equal rights amendment is a culmination that will be enjoyed, not just by women but by all those who love freedom in this country and around the world.

Thank you very much.

NOTE: The President spoke at 1:32 p.m. at the ceremony in the Rose Garden at the White House.

Women's Equality Day, 1980
Proclamation 4785.   August 26, 1980

By the President of the United States of America

A Proclamation

America struck a blow for justice on August 26, 1920, when the 19th Amendment, granting women the right to vote, became law. On this 60th anniversary, American women and men recall how far we have come on the road toward equal opportunity for all Americans and reaffirm our commitment to full equality for women. We celebrate today the achievements of the past, but even more we celebrate our dream for a future in which all Americans share equally in the rights and responsibilities of this land.

Social and political change is never easy, as we know by the sacrifices of the early Suffragists. Courageous and high-principled, these women wrote, marched and argued for their cause through long years of delay and disappointment, but they never accepted defeat. Only a few weeks before her death at 86, Susan B. Anthony addressed a convention on the theme, "Failure is impossible!" They knew the rightness of their cause, and found the will and courage to create a climate of change. We can best honor their memory today by continuing their crusade.

In the intervening years women have faithfully carried out responsibilities at all levels of government, in every area of employment and education, and in the nurturing of families and children. Yet many of the rights that should accompany those responsibilities are missing. Despite our hard-won progress, the rights of women vary from state to state. The Equal Rights Amendment to the Constitution, which would set a clear national standard outlawing discrimination against women, is still an unfulfilled promise. Thanks to the efforts of millions of women and men, 35 states have ratified the Equal Rights Amendment. We have until June, 1982, to complete the ratification process in three more states and make the principle of equality a Constitutional guarantee.

Today, I reaffirm my own commitment to make the Equal Rights Amendment part of our Constitution. I urge all Americans to rekindle the spirit of early Suffragists, to use their energies, their wisdom and their compassion to achieve full equality for women. To advance the cause of women's rights is to advance the cause of human rights.

Now, THEREFORE, I, JIMMY CARTER, President of the United States of America, do hereby proclaim August 26, 1980 as Women's Equality Day.

IN WITNESS WHEREOF, I have hereunto set my hand this twenty-sixth day of August, in the year of our Lord nineteen hundred and eighty, and of the Independence of the United States of America the two hundred and fifth.

JIMMY CARTER

[Filed with the Office of the Federal Register, 8:45 a.m., August 27, 1980]

Presidential Campaign Debates of 1980

Telegram to the Chairman of the Board of Governors of the National Press Club. August 26, 1980

Dear Seth:

I am pleased to accept your invitation to a one-on-one debate with Governor Reagan at the National Press Club. I believe that the earliest possible date would be preferable so that the maximum number of debates can be scheduled.

Members of my campaign staff are ready to discuss format and timing immediately. I look forward to this debate as the beginning of a constructive cross-examination of the candidates by members of the press.

Sincerely,

JIMMY CARTER

[Mr. Seth T. Payne, Chairman, Board of Governors, National Press Club, Room 809, National Press Building, Washington, D.C.] Attention: Mr. Peter A. Holmes

NOTE: The text of the President's telegram was made available by the White House Press Office.

Veterans Administration Health Care Amendments

Statement on the Congressional Override of the Veto. August 26, 1980

I am disappointed at the decision by the Congress to override my veto of H.R. 7102, the Veterans Administration Health Care Amendments of 1980. I vetoed that bill because it would provide $80 million a year to VA physicians in unwarranted bonuses rather than to provide that amount on improved health care treatment for veterans themselves. I continue to believe that H.R. 7102 is an unsound piece of legislation.

H.R. 7102 provides excessive and inequitable bonuses to attract and retain physicians and dentists in VA's health care system. The VA currently enjoys an excellent recruitment and retention record, especially compared to other Federal medical systems. Further, this legislation would create an unfortunate disparity between the pay scale provided for VA physicians and that for the Armed Services and Public Health Service medical personnel. I am very concerned that, with the passage of this legislation into law, recruitment of needed physicians to non-

VA health care systems will be adversely affected. The Defense Department was so concerned about this adverse effect on its health care system that it recommended a veto of H.R. 7102.

My administration is committed to providing quality health care for our Nation's veterans. As President, I have worked with the VA and the Congress to ensure that this care is the finest in the world. I would have preferred that Congress rewrite and improve this legislation by targeting money from the excessive bonuses to more concrete and tangible improvements in the veterans' health care system. I regret that this was not done.

NOTE: The President vetoed the legislation on August 22.

United States Ambassador to Madagascar

Nomination of Fernando E. Rondon. August 27, 1980

The President today announced that he will nominate Fernando E. Rondon, of Alexandria, Va., to be Ambassador Extraordinary and Plenipotentiary of the United States to the Democratic Republic of Madagascar. He would be the first U.S. Ambassador to that country since the departure of Joseph A. Mendenhall in 1975.

Rondon has been Deputy Chief of Mission in Tegucigalpa since 1978 and a Foreign Service officer since 1961.

He was born May 6, 1936, in Los Angeles, Calif. He received a B.S. from the University of California at Berkeley in 1960.

After joining the Foreign Service in 1961, Rondon was posted in Tehran, Tangier, Constantine, and Antananarivo and studied French and Arabic. From 1970 to

1973, he was detailed to the National Security Council.

From 1973 to 1975, Rondon was political officer in Lima. He attended the National War College in 1975–76. From 1976 to 1978, he was alternate director of the Office of East Coast Affairs at the State Department.

Budget Deferrals

Message to the Congress.   August 27, 1980

To the Congress of the United States:

In accordance with the Impoundment Control Act of 1974, I herewith report a new Department of Commerce deferral of $15.8 million in funds for the International Energy Exposition in Knoxville, Tennessee. In addition, I am reporting a revision to a previously transmitted deferral for the National Oceanic and Atmospheric Administration's Coastal energy impact fund increasing the amount deferred by $0.5 million.

The details of each deferral are contained in the attached reports.

JIMMY CARTER

The White House,
    August 27, 1980.

NOTE: The attachments detailing the deferrals are printed in the FEDERAL REGISTER of September 4, 1980.

Meeting With President Ziaur Rahman of Bangladesh

Remarks Following the Meeting. August 27, 1980

PRESIDENT CARTER. It's a great pleasure for me this afternoon to welcome to the White House and to our Nation, President Ziaur, the very fine leader of Bangladesh. Since their war of independence in 1971, tremendous progress has been made under his leadership. And with the courage and determination of the people of his great country, with a population of about 90 million, and with tremendous opportunities for economic improvement, President Ziaur has been in the forefront of making the lives of the Bangladesh citizens better each year.

The world suffered along with Bangladesh in recent years because of extreme hunger and deprivation among the citizens there, but President Ziaur and I have been discussing, in the last few minutes, the possibility—he says the inevitability—that Bangladesh will in the near future be self-sufficient in food production—perhaps even able to export food to other countries.

We also had a chance to discuss the advantages of democratization of the Bangladesh political system. The open and free election process which resulted in the election of President Ziaur has been an inspiration to the world. Also we have been very grateful at the leadership that President Ziaur has played personally, not only among the Moslem nations and the community there but indeed throughout the entire world community.

As a member of the United Nations Security Council, Bangladesh played a very important and statesmanlike role during the difficult months just past. We are deeply grateful that President Ziaur has come here. We observe with great interest his statement to the United Nations General Assembly, where he called upon the OPEC nations to provide oil to the poor and developing countries of the world at lower prices and also encouraged the OPEC nations with their tremendous influx of capital to invest in the developing nations, like Bangladesh, to

provide a better life and employment for the people there.

President Ziaur, we're delighted to have you with us. It's an honor for our country to have you here, and we share with you the basic principles in a completely compatible way as we face the future together. And I'm very honored that you would come here to pay me this visit.

PRESIDENT ZIAUR. Mr. President, it has been a great honor for me and my delegation to have the opportunity to meet you at a time when you are so very busy for the election and you have so much work at hand.

Mr. President, let me tell you how grateful the people of our country are to the people of your great country for the moral support that was rendered to us, in fact, support in all possible manner. Those were rendered to us during our war of independence in 1971, and the massive economic aid that we received from you, from your great country thereafter to meet the many necessities, which otherwise would have, if not met, would have created tremendous problems for us.

We are very grateful indeed, Mr. President, for your special interest for the development, the economic development, in Bangladesh, for which, during your period, we have received full support, and specially in the food sector the support that you have given us, I can assure you that our people are grateful to the American people and to you, Mr. President.

In the short meeting that we had a few minutes ago, we had discussed all possible aspects of our relationship, and we discussed some of the important problems facing the world, both economic and political. And I must say how happy I am that in these cases our views are identical.

Mr. President, the important role that your great country has played—the people of the United States and yourself—

to uphold the charter of the United Nations for maintenance of peace and stability in the world, is something that we praise you for and especially your value that you attach to the question of human rights and human dignity is something that all of us, the whole world could be proud of.

Mr. President, I wish you success. I wish the American people success and stride in the future.

Thank you very much.

NOTE: President Carter spoke at 2:13 p.m. to reporters assembled on the South Grounds of the White House.

Meeting With President Ziaur of Bangladesh

Joint Statement.   August 27, 1980

President Carter and President Ziaur Rahman of Bangladesh met for one hour today. The two Presidents held a wide-ranging discussion on bilateral and international matters. Others participating in the talks included Foreign Minister Shamsul Huq, Agriculture Minister Nurul Islam, Information Consultant Daud Khan Majlis, Ambassador Tabarak Husain and Additional Foreign Secretary Ataul Karim for Bangladesh and, for the United States, Edmund Muskie, Secretary of State; Zbigniew Brzezinski, Assistant to the President for National Security Affairs; Thomas Ehrlich, Director of the International Development Cooperation Agency; and David Schneider, Ambassador to Bangladesh.

The two Presidents reviewed bilateral relations and discussed regional and international issues of mutual concern. They agreed to work for upholding the principles of the United Nations Charter and expressed opposition to foreign armed intervention or interference of any kind in the internal affairs of any country and called for the immediate withdrawal of all foreign troops from Afghanistan and Kampuchea. They also discussed the Middle East problem and stressed the need for a comprehensive and peaceful settlement of this problem at an early date.

President Ziaur Rahman thanked President Carter for the meaningful role played by the U.S. in economic cooperation with Bangladesh. He described the various measures adopted for social, political and economic development in Bangladesh including restoration of democracy and also the launching of the new Five Year Plan. President Carter expressed his personal admiration for the economic and political progress Bangladesh has made under President Ziaur Rahman's leadership and assured him of all possible cooperation in the successful implementation of the second Five Year Plan.

Both Presidents noted with satisfaction the excellent state of relations between the two countries and agreed to work to further improve the friendship and understanding which already exist.

Meeting With Prime Minister Robert Mugabe of Zimbabwe

Remarks at a White House Reception. August 27, 1980

THE PRESIDENT. *Mr. Prime Minister, Ambassador McHenry, former Ambassador Andrew Young, distinguished leaders of our Nation and of the new Republic of Zimbabwe, and friends of Zimbabwe from throughout the United States:*

This is an exciting time in our country's history and the history of the world, and we're delighted to have you, Mr. Prime Minister, here with us.

On all too rare occasions, there is achieved a result which thrills the entire world, based on decency, based on freedom, based on independence, based on equality, and based on human courage. The independence of Zimbabwe is the result of all those factors. And the small role that our Nation played in the support of these efforts for freedom and independence and for equality and for elimination of racial discrimination is indeed gratifying to me and to the 240 million people that I represent.

In the past few months and years, the leadership of people like Andy Young and Don McHenry in our country has helped to shape and to change opinion among the American populace in support of this notable achievement. And the admiration, Mr. Prime Minister, for your courage over long and sometimes lonely years under the most difficult possible circumstances is a feeling which I share with millions of Americans who admire you very deeply.

I want to congratulate you on the acceptance of Zimbabwe as a new member of the United Nations, on your tremendous speech on that occasion which exemplified the principles and ideals of your own life and also of proving already that you are the leader not only of a great new republic but a notable world leader exemplifying the finest aspects of humanity.

I might say that you have also been invited here, because I want to observe very closely the techniques that you have used in your successful political effort. [*Laughter*] I think we underdogs have to stick together. [*Laughter*] And I have been observing, as a matter of fact, your progress in the brief time you've spent in our own country.

You have accepted membership in the United Nations. You've made a notable address to the U.N. General Assembly. You had a remarkable political rally in Harlem. [*Laughter*] You've already been on "The MacNeil/Lehrer Report." [*Laughter*] You've had a notable performance on "Meet the Press." I've seen very favorable and supportive editorials in the New York Times, the Christian Science Monitor, the Washington Post— [*laughter*]—building up additional political and economic support for your country from our Nation, and you've also dined with some of the major business leaders in our country. You had congressional leaders there, particularly the Black Caucus, and you had lunch with Secretary Muskie. Before I had a chance to meet with you, you had already marshaled all the support on your side so that it was impossible for us to find very many differences between us. [*Laughter*]

This is a very fine opportunity for our Nation to get to know you better and to let you know how deeply we share your pride in what has been accomplished. But we have come to expect this kind of dynamism, this kind of sensitivity, this kind of leadership, this kind of political acumen from Prime Minister Mugabe.

You're the kind of person who rejects orthodoxy when the maintenance of the status quo is an obstacle to progress. You're a leader who has probed other nations and other societies for new ideas and new concepts that might provide the basis for good investments, for a better life for your own people. You've already become a leader among other African leaders, struggling for great things among the people of that continent and for the end of discrimination and apartheid and the enhancement of independence among all the nations of Africa.

We know that the road to liberation has been very difficult for the people of

Zimbabwe. There has been too much bloodshed. There has been too much division. There's been too much economic deprivation. The first 140 days of your own administration has been a notable example of the alleviation of tension, the assuaging of unwarranted fears, and a description of a possible future for the people of your country which inspires confidence, unity, and hope.

Your nation has been blessed by very fine national resources; mineral deposits not even yet explored, certainly not exploited; productive land, the potential of which has not nearly been reached; eager, well-trained, highly motivated people who want to work in a sense of peace for future progress. But I think perhaps one of the greatest assets is the wisdom and the courage and the knowledge of the people which you express in your own character and in your own commitments.

I think the greatness of any nation is measured not just in material things, not even what it possesses, but what it stands for. And I'm very proud as an American to realize that the principles and ideals of our two countries, as exemplified by you and your new government, are very similar, perhaps even identical.

In this sense, there are strong parallels between our two countries. We've both learned that the path to social justice is not an easy one. Our Nation had been in existence for many generations before we finally were able to eliminate the legal discrimination against the black people of our country. That was not an easy path to follow. And some of those, even on the platform with me, who were instrumental in that major breakthrough in human decency and equality were also not coincidentally involved in the breakthrough toward decency and equality in your own new nation.

We've also learned that a nation faced with great challenges, if united, can prevail and that justice can indeed be established. We've learned that the best road to progress is through peace, through the respecting of different views and different concerns, and the forging in a common effort of a future based on principles and ideals which, in a changing world, do not change.

Some have asked me as President, "Why do you take such an interest in Africa? Your predecessors never did." I believe this is one of the great opportunities for our Nation, not only to beneficially affect the lives of many others who've been deprived too long but to give a new depth and a new dimension to the lives of Americans and a new pride in the beneficial extension of the principles of which I'm so proud in our country. A deeper answer perhaps, or one equivalent, can be found in the words of Dr. Martin Luther King, Jr., written by him during our own struggle for civil rights. "Injustice anywhere," he said, "is a threat to justice everywhere."

The peaceful transition of Zimbabwe to popular majority rule is the strongest affirmation of our own human rights policy. Human rights is not an idle concept. It's not a dormant concept. It's not one that ever sleeps. It's a burning, vital issue, not only in governments but in the hearts and minds of human beings throughout the world. It's a testament to hard work, and it involves the courage of great men. And I would say that the essence of human rights, as exemplified by our own country, has been expressed in the recent careers, in fact the longstanding careers, of two men behind me on this platform, and that is Andrew Young and Don McHenry.

In closing, let me say that they never let me forget—[*laughter*]—your struggle, Mr. Prime Minister, and they never let the Members of Congress forget the burning issues involved. It required some political courage on the part of many Members of our Congress to make votes which were quite often contrary to the majority opinion of the American people, but because of the courage of Andy Young and Don McHenry and the Congress, the opinion of the American people changed and became extremely supportive of the effort that finally resulted in success.

We stood with the sanctions against the former oppressive government; we stood with the forces of liberation and justice. And today we stand with Zimbabwe's efforts toward economic development and toward stability in your own country and the realization of the legitimate hopes and dreams of the people whom you lead.

I had not had a chance to meet with Prime Minister Mugabe until today, but I feel that we have been, in the past and will be for many years, on the same road. We've begun to chart an equally hopeful course for our future mutual relationships and for the realization of the dreams and the hopes and the ideals of all our people.

After Prime Minister Mugabe responds, he would like to stand in the Blue Room and to have all of you come by, and you can express on behalf of the people of our country the same sentiments that I have expressed as the leader of our country.

Mr. Prime Minister, we would be delighted to hear from you.

THE PRIME MINISTER. *Mr. President, Lady Carter, ladies and gentlemen:*

This is a moment when I feel I must make reference to one ancient fighter, but reverse him, for he fought for imperialism. I indeed came, I saw, I was conquered. [*Laughter*]

I feel really conquered, overwhelmed by the support that I've received the whole way through since my arrival in the

United States, support from all quarters. At every stage when I've had occasion to meet the people of the United States, this spontaneous welcome that I've enjoyed, the words of praise and the warmth of friendship have indeed been overwhelming. Mr. President, may I thank you, as I thank your people, for the support given me and given my newly independent Republic of Zimbabwe.

When we decided to take up arms in order to bring about change in our country, we were doing so out of a commitment to definite principles, which principles you had fought for, established, and consolidated in the United States: the principle of a democratic society, the principle of nonracialism and equality, the principle that a society which divides itself into groups of people on the basis of race is anathema to humanity. And these principles you had enshrined in your own Constitution. We fought, therefore, to overthrow an evil system based on racialism. It was a colonial system, one which had been imposed by history on us, and one which had brought about a great deal of suffering amongst our people.

When we took to arms it was not because we wanted to see blood flowing in our streets. We did so because there was no alternative, and as I said yesterday in my address to the General Assembly of the United Nations, we had to resort to war in order to bring about peace, using war as a means for achieving peace. You had done it here with pride, and we felt we could do it with pride and emerge at the end of it with a democratic society.

We have done it; not alone, Mr. President, but with the help that came from all quarters of the international community. And here may I also, in the same way as you paid tribute to me and to the people of Zimbabwe, pay equal tribute to your administration, Mr. President, and to the people of the United States who in our hour of need came to our support. It may not have been obvious to the rest of the world, but it was quite obvious to some of us that in your administration here we had a true friend.

The bitterest period of our war was indeed the last 3 years. It was during this period that we had massacres of all kinds, that we had the frontline states being harrassed and bombed and their populations suffering as much as our people were suffering. These were the very bitter years of our struggle.

It was during that period we relied on you to continue to argue for sanctions against the settler regime of Ian Smith to continue. It was upon you we relied to effectively block the internal settlement which had started brewing in Salisbury, and in partnership with you we tried to negotiate against the internal settlement for a constitutional agreement which would have brought about the independence that we now enjoy.

I remember those days when, with Andy Young and Don McHenry here and later with Cyrus Vance in Dar-es-Salaam, we battled to reach agreement, to get a compromise between the British side and our side. It was not possible at the time to conclude the discussion, because there wasn't, in Britain, the presence of an authority which would have effected a decision in Salisbury. But you did your best. You couldn't have gone to the extent of assuming the authority of an administering power and thereby usurping the authority of Britain in order to bring about change.

We admire you for the efforts that you showed, and we admire you for the stand that you took, which was, as we saw it, a kind of solo effort in a situation which threatened to reverse the good work that the United States had done when, last

year, there was the threat in the Senate to lift the ban on sanctions which, I take it, would have led to the recognition of the internal settlement in the country. But the President stood firm, stood firm on a matter of principle, and I think today those who would have reversed the decision must be men who admire him as much as we admire him.

Mr. President, ladies and gentlemen, as an independent Republic of Zimbabwe we cannot say that we have achieved every goal that we set about to achieve. We have achieved only some of our primary goals. The goal of independence has been achieved, but we view our independence now as a process which is destined to lead us to attainment of the socio-economic goals we have set ourselves.

We have established the theme of reconciliation in the context of this independence in order to enhance that independence, rather than detract from it. We believe, as you have believed for years, that after civil strife, after the loss of many lives, men must agree to achieve peace; that once peace has been attained there is no longer any need to be vindictive, because the peace has been achieved; and that peace then becomes an instrument that enables us to harness the totality of our population, regardless of race, color, or creed, in a new phase that is aimed at achieving the goals that our people expect us to work for.

And so, today we say even to Ian Smith, who, as you are aware, caused so much suffering, even to Ian Smith, who was capable of so much illegality—we called it treason at the time—[*laughter*]—that he too is acceptable to us. He too is free to choose to live with us, but live with us as a friend who has learned from history, as a man of peace, not a man of war. And reconciliation to us therefore means that there is a preparedness on the part of those who have been victorious, a magnanimity to accept those who stand defeated and have lost in the battle for justice which we fought for, that there is need on the part of those who fought for an unjust society, for the maintenance of the racial society, to accept the objectives of the new government. If there is that responsiveness from their side to the magnanimity that the new government offers, then there is the necessary rapport between us of the nature that can unite us into one nation with a single loyalty.

This is our belief. It was your belief yesterday. We would want to believe that we also enjoy that belief because you, having established a democratic society, have made it impossible [possible][1] to learn from you some of the golden ideals that go into creating a truly humanitarian entity in our society.

Mr. Chairman—Mr. President— [*laughter*]—let me once again repeat how touched I am by the warmth of friendship that I've found in the United States. I'll return home in full belief that here in the United States we have friends and allies who can assist us in consolidating our independence in the same way as they have assisted us in achieving that independence; that our hand of friendship, which we have extended to the people of the United States, is in response to the hand of friendship they have extended to us during the years of our bitter struggle; and that between our two countries and our two peoples there is true amity, there is that depth of feeling which makes us true allies.

It is this admiration we have of the people of the United States and of you personally, Mr. President, which leads me to wish you well in the race you are running.

---

[1] White House correction.

Ladies and gentlemen, the race he's running is, unfortunately, in the United States. I'm sure if he was running it in our territory he would be assured of victory.

He asked for a tip. [*Laughter*] I didn't have a tip. I had a crowing cock. [*Laughter*] I don't know whether you would want us to give you that emblem, for indeed you are the cock of the United States. [*Laughter*]

Once again, ladies and gentlemen, may I say thank you for all the support you have given us. May I say, Mr. President, thank you for all the support that I have received since my arrival here, which really is a continuation of the support you have given us all along.

We are one people, bound together by our common ideals and our need to improve the lot of our people. We believe in the same democratic principles. May these continue to tie us together. But more than that, may the friendship that we have established hitherto continue to exist.

Thank you.

NOTE: The President spoke at 3:52 p.m. in the East Room at the White House.

Meeting With Prime Minister Mugabe of Zimbabwe
White House Statement. August 27, 1980

The President met with Prime Minister Robert Mugabe of Zimbabwe today for a 45-minute discussion. Accompanying the Prime Minister were Bernard Chidzero, Minister of Economic Planning, and Dr. Elleck K. Mashingaidze, Zimbabwe's Ambassador to the United Nations and Ambassador-designate to the United States. With the President were Deputy Secretary of State Warren Christopher, Assistant to the President for National Security Affairs

Zbigniew Brzezinski, Assistant Secretary of State for African Affairs Richard Moose, Ambassador Donald McHenry, and Assistant to the President Louis Martin.

In the course of a cordial, constructive talk, the President and the Prime Minister discussed the situation in southern Africa, relations between the United States and Zimbabwe, and the prospects for a peaceful settlement in Namibia. They discussed in some depth Zimbabwe's immediate reconstruction and development needs. Following the meeting in the Oval Office, the President escorted Prime Minister Mugabe to a reception in his honor in the East Room.

Youth Employment Legislation

Statement on House of Representatives Approval of the Legislation.   August 27, 1980

The President expressed his deep appreciation to Speaker O'Neill and Members of the House today for their overwhelming support of H.R. 6711, the Youth Act of 1980. The President has stated that youth employment legislation is one of his top domestic priorities, and he is extremely pleased with the broad, bipartisan endorsement that the bill received. The President especially praised Chairman Carl Perkins and Gus Hawkins and Congressmen Jim Jeffords and Bill Goodling for their support of the legislation.

The President believes this $2 billion initiative to provide job skills and basic education to more than 1 million disadvantaged and unemployed young people is the key to lowering the unacceptably high rates of youth unemployment. He is hopeful that the Senate will soon take up this legislation and that a bill can be enacted before the October recess.

Economic Renewal Program

Remarks Announcing the Program. August 28, 1980

I'm very delighted to have the Speaker here and distinguished Members of the House and Senate, the Governor of New York, Governor of New Jersey, and others who represent State and local government, members of my Cabinet, and distinguished Americans who've come here representing business and labor, the professions, other elements of life of the greatest nation on Earth.

This is a time of economic testing for our Nation. Inflation has fallen sharply. The recession is near bottom, and we'll recover.

This is no time for an excessive stimulus program, nor is it a time for inflationary tax reductions. We must be responsible, and we must make careful investments in American productivity. We can build in a progressive way a future which America will see that will be creative and will grow more vigorously in this next decade than perhaps any other time since our first industrial revolution over a hundred years ago.

According to a well-known proverb, a journey of a thousand miles begins with one step. We began before now, but each step is important, and the steps that I describe this afternoon will continue that journey toward a more productive and more competitive and a more prosperous American economy. The new steps will put people back to work, reduce taxes, increase public and private investment in the future, and constrain inflation all at the same time. But such progress will be possible only if we regard the past not as a refuge within which we can hide, but a treasury of lessons from which we can learn.

I'd like to consider for a moment a few of those lessons: First, we cannot treat the symptoms of inflation and ignore the underlying causes. Second, inflation and recession augment one another. Third, the longer we ignore our decline in productivity, the more likely we Americans are to live with hard times. The fourth lesson, and it may be the most important of all, is that if a solution is politically attractive it's often economically wrong.

Now, in the heat of an election year, is not the time to seek votes with ill-considered tax cuts that would simply steal back in inflation in the future the few dollars that the average American taxpayer might get. America needs to build muscle, not fat, and I will not accept a preelection bill to cut taxes.

All of us know, who've served in government or in other areas of American life, that there are no simple or easy solutions to serious problems that build up over a long period of time. But there are responsible ways to create productive jobs, and there are responsible ways to restore our technological and competitive lead over all other nations on Earth, and there are responsible ways to strengthen our economy enough to guarantee opportunity and security for every American citizen.

The fundamental challenge to our economy in the 1980's is a difficult combination but one which this program addresses successfully: full employment, stable prices, and real growth, with jobs that attack our declining productivity and our energy dependence, the major causes of inflation and of the recession in the first place. The detailed program which will be explained to all of you after my speech sets forth measures which I will ask the Congress to enact next year.

There are four major goals which I'd like to discuss briefly. First, increase private and public investment to revitalize America's economy. Second, create a forward-looking partnership between government and the private sector to deal with national problems which can only be solved through that cooperation. Third, to help people and communities overcome the effects of industrial dislocations. And fourth, to help to offset the rising individual tax burdens in ways which do not rekindle inflation.

These new proposals will add almost a half-million jobs in the coming year and a total of 1 million jobs by the end of 1982. These are in addition to those that will result from normal recovery and also in addition to the jobs that will result from the new programs already in effect or already on the Hill in existing proposals. We expect to add with these new proposals 2-percent growth to the gross national product of our Nation, increase real investment by 10 percent, and help to hold down inflation at the same time.

We must now build on the progress that we've made already in many vital areas. In the last 3½ years we have added more than 8 million new jobs for workers to America's job rolls. This is more than any other similar period in our Nation or the world's history, in peacetime or in war. Exports have grown substantially. Balance-of-trade figures are very encouraging, and with the 1981 budget we will have cut in half the real annual growth in Federal spending.

We are reducing the anticompetitive regulation of the airlines, trucking, rail, banking, and the communications industries. This is the most fundamental restructuring of the interrelationship between government and the private sector that's taken place since the days of Franklin D. Roosevelt's New Deal.

Above all, after vigorous and painful debate and political decisions, we've put in place now a national energy policy that has already helped to reduce oil imports by 20 percent and has encouraged more drilling to discover new oil and new gas than at any time in the last quarter of a century. And the program, as you well know, has only recently been passed by Congress and is not even yet fully implemented. But we must not just be proud of what has been done. We must continue to build. Our task is nothing less than to revitalize America's economy.

Increasing productivity is the foremost economic challenge of the 1980's. From management we need innovation and more long-range planning. From labor we must have more participation in making the basic decisions, dedicated work, and the skills to take advantage of the most modern tools and technology. From government we must have sound judgment and political courage. And from all Americans there must be a commitment, deep commitment, and also the use of common sense.

We will meet the challenge of a more productive America as if our economic life depended on it—because it does—and this is how we're going to do it. How will we increase private and public investment to revitalize America's economy? The first important step we can take to revitalize America's economy is to provide incentives for greater private investment.

We need a major increase in depreciation allowances to promote investment in modern plants and equipment, and we need dramatic simplification of the tax code so that not only large businesses but also small businesses of our country can benefit.

The investment tax credit, which has been hailed as a bonanza by some, is now of no help to new firms or to distressed industries, because they have no earnings and therefore they pay no taxes and investment tax credits do not help them.

Therefore, part of the investment tax credit must be refundable. This is a profound change in concept in American tax policy and will help immediately the small businesses and the new industries, an important source of both technological progress and employment, as you well know, and will also be of special help to those industries which are in distress, such as those which now produce steel and automobiles.

We'll also, of course, implement many of the recommendations that were made earlier this year by the White House Conference on Small Business. To complement the benefits derived from tax changes for the private sector, we must also expand public investment, especially in crucial areas like energy, technology, transportation, and exports. I'd like to comment on each one of those briefly.

Our energy program already approved for the 1980's, what we've already got planned and committed, is the most massive peacetime undertaking in American history. Its impact will be immense, perhaps greater than any of us at the present time can even envision, ranging from hundreds of thousands who will work in synthetic fuel plants to the millions of individuals who are weatherizing their homes, using solar power, or building our new and fuel-efficient automobiles.

Since I took office we've enacted tax credits and have more than doubled direct spending in order to stimulate energy production and conservation. In addition, we'll create a vast new synthetic fuels industry, and we are seeking new authority to convert utilities from oil to coal and other sources of energy. We need to add substantially more funds for work on energy conservation projects that will help us to fight inflation and to achieve energy security.

Energy, of course, is important. The second thing is technology. Technological advance has provided much of the productive growth of the United States in this last century. We can create literally millions of jobs with new technology in the years ahead. In addition to tax incentives for investment in the latest technology, I favor substantial real growth in Federal support of basic research, and particularly in the great research centers of our colleges and universities.

Mark Twain once defined an American as a person who does things because they haven't been done before. The exciting possibilities for Americans in the 1980's range from lasers for surgery to super-alloys that never rust, from exotic energy technologies to microchips that can make computers as common as radios and as compact as wristwatches. These kinds of advances in technology and in science can well exceed anything that we have seen in this century so far.

The next item is transportation, which is vital to our country. The difference between a healthy transportation network and a broken down highway or a dying railroad is the difference between jobs and joblessness for tens of thousands of Americans, and it's between strength and weakness for our entire Nation. My proposals for major improvements in mass transit, air transportation, and railroad assistance programs are already pending before the Congress. These should be enacted and should be funded without delay, and I'll propose a further significant increase for surface transportation programs. There is simply no more essential investment or element in America's future than a viable, modern, efficient transportation system.

The last item I'd like to mention from the public sector is exports. Americans don't live and breathe exports like some of our European allies and others do. When I took office, exports accounted for 6½ percent of our gross national product. Now, that figure has jumped to 9 percent. This increase has been an essential source of American jobs. One out of every seven jobs in our country now is directly related to producing goods for exports. One out of every three acres of land cultivated in the United States produces food and fibre for exports. Thirty percent of all industrial profits are derived from exports. And we have a great potential for even more growth in jobs and exports in our vast reserves of coal.

We must begin immediately to upgrade our transportation and our port facilities for coal exports. I think you all read the article in the paper Sunday that showed that ships now stand off Norfolk and Hampton Roads and wait 20 or 30 days before they can come there and load their valuable cargo of American coal which is so crucial as a replacement for OPEC oil. Through tax modifications and through a new concept of export trading companies we'll even further expand American exports of both goods and services. This investment in America is important.

The second question is: How can we create a forward-looking partnership between government and the private sector to deal with those kinds of national problems which require that cooperation? To help us revitalize American industry, business, labor, and the government must form a new and a vital partnership. We're all in this together, and the sooner we start acting like it, the better off our Nation will be.

In some areas, such as national security, as you all know, government must play the dominant role. But where government is involved in the economic sphere it will function best not as a boss, but to assist or to cooperate with business and labor only as it's necessary. This can be done. We are cooperating properly now in dealing with coal, steel, and the automobile industries, as well as in many aspects, particularly the new ones, involving our energy program.

The time has now come to extend this experience in cooperation. And this again will be a major change in economic policy for our country. I will establish an Economic Revitalization Board composed of some of the best leaders from American labor, industry, and the public. Cochairmen of this Board will be Irving Shapiro, the chief executive officer of du Pont, and Lane Kirkland, the president of AFL–CIO.

This will be a small group of distinguished Americans, and I'll ask that Board to develop specific recommendations for me, for the Congress, and for the public for an industrial development authority to mobilize both public and private resources, including capital from private markets and from pension funds, to help revitalize American industry in areas most affected by economic dislocations or by industrial bottlenecks. This Board will also consider the integration of industrial development activities now carried out in all the various government agencies, and—this is particularly important—they will address the long-range problems of balancing regulatory costs against the benefits of regulation.

Any project receiving financial assistance must meet tough standards of economic viability. Only a commitment that promotes progress and not obsolescence will be truly in the interests of business, labor, and the American people.

The third question to answer is: How can we help people and communities overcome the effects of industrial dislocations? As we work together on the problems and

the intricate issues of economic renewal, we must never forget that we're talking about real people in real places.

Change is inevitable if we are to grow. But as we cope with change, it's my responsibility as President to safeguard communities which are a vital part of our national life and the individual lives of the men, women, and children who are America. That's the whole thrust of one of the most important programs of my Presidency with which almost all of you have helped, that is, economic development in distressed areas. A community cannot exist where there is no work.

We can be proud that direct support of our economic development has increased by over 70 percent just in the last 3 years. We've instituted effective urban and rural programs to stimulate private investment in distressed areas. Funding for programs to promote small business has more than doubled. The Congress now has before it my proposals for substantial increases in economic development financing. But we must do more.

I'll propose a large additional annual increase in funding for economic development for 1981 and for 1982 to create permanent jobs, productive jobs in industries and in regions which are hard hit by industrial change. We also need a special targeted investment tax credit to provide strong incentives for American businesses to invest and to create jobs in those areas which are threatened by economic decline.

These kinds of measures stimulate business, but it cannot help a community when it's already in financial distress. When a community cannot maintain police, fire, education, sanitation services, it loses both its old industry, and it cannot hope to get new industry. In order to help communities like this maintain the services necessary to promote development,

I'll propose countercyclical revenue-sharing at a level of $1 billion in 1981.

I'd like to point out that my major domestic program which was new this year is a jobs and training program to help young Americans look forward to a future of hope, not to a life of waste. This is the one action we can take now that will make a difference in the lives of a whole generation of Americans.

I'm also asking the Congress to provide 13 additional weeks of unemployment compensation for eligible workers in high unemployment States. That, by the way, is the only specific recommendation that I intend to send to the Congress at the present time. The other proposals will be made to the Congress for action in the coming year.

And the final question I'd like to answer is: How will we offset the rising individual tax burdens in ways that do not rekindle inflation?

Tax burdens are now scheduled to rise in ways that both increase inflation and slow down our economic recovery. Therefore, I'll ask Congress for three measures next year to deal with this problem in addition to those tax measures designed to stimulate industry.

To help offset the social security tax increases scheduled to take effect in 1981, a social security tax credit for employers and for workers. In addition, the earned income tax credit for working families, those who have income but who have a low income, this to be expanded. And a special tax deduction to counter the inequity that presently exists when a husband and wife both work and who typically have to pay more taxes than two single individuals making the same amount.

All of these policies that I've described to you can be carried out within a responsible budget, so that we can simultaneously promote economic recovery and reduce the pressures of inflation.

To make still further progress we'll consult with business, with labor and other groups about how to improve our voluntary wage and price policies. Because inflation is such a stubborn problem we must design future tax reductions, earned by continued control of Federal spending, in ways that contribute to moderating wage and price increases. For any nation's economy the severe problems come in times of great change. For our Nation this is one of those times. If we keep firmly to our path and attack our problems with courage and responsibility, the result will be an exciting future for our economy and for our Nation.

Let us not forget that this country of ours still has the most productive workforce on Earth. Our standard of living is the highest in the world. Our industrial base is the strongest in world history. We have the greatest human and physical resources of any nation that exists, but we cannot continue to draw them down forever. We must renew those human and natural resources, and we will. That's the basis of the proposal that I'm outlining this afternoon.

Let's don't forget the breadth of what we are discussing. We are embarking on a course to build a major synthetic fuels industry, to double our production and to expand our exports of American coal, to retool our automobile industry in order to produce more fuel-efficient cars and to meet any competition from overseas, to modernize our basic industries like steel, to make our houses and our buildings and our factories more energy efficient, to shift our electric power production from dependence on oil to the use of coal and other fuels, to create a whole new industry, to produce solar and other renewable energy systems, to rebuild our cities and our towns, to continue progress toward a cleaner and a healthier and a safer environment, to expand and to modernize our entire public transportation system, to provide our workforce with skills and jobs to meet a rapidly changing, technological world, to ease the burdens of change and the fear of the future, and to continue to build the homes and produce the goods and the services needed by a growing America.

Our difficult struggle toward economic renewal will be waged in many ways, but we are united in our purpose. We'll put Americans to work fighting the major long-term causes of inflation itself, our declining productivity and our excessive dependence on foreign oil. We'll fight for full employment, at the same time stable prices, at the same time healthy growth. We'll overcome the problems of today together by building for a better future, a better life, for everyone who lives in America.

Thank you very much.

NOTE: The President spoke at 2:08 p.m. in the East Room at the White House.

Veterans Federal Coordinating Committee

Appointment of Executive Director and Deputy Director. August 28, 1980

The White House today announced the appointment of Dennis K. Rhoades as Executive Director of the Veterans Federal Coordinating Committee and Paul Weston as Deputy Director.

The Committee was established by the President in 1978 after an interagency policy review of Federal programs affecting veterans of the Vietnam war era. It is charged with improving coordination among Government programs affecting veterans and targeting benefits and services to disadvantaged veterans, particularly those of the Vietnam era. The Committee is chaired by Stuart Eizenstat, Assistant to the President for Domestic Affairs and Policy, and Eugene Eidenberg, Assistant to the President for Intergovernmental Affairs and Secretary to the Cabinet. It includes representatives of nine Federal agencies that provide services and benefits for veterans.

Dennis Rhoades, 36, was previously head of the Veterans Employment Service at the Labor Department. He also served as Assistant Director of the Veterans Federal Coordinating Committee, where he worked on designing and implementing the Veterans Outreach and Community Services program. He worked on drafting the Presidential review memorandum on the status of Vietnam veterans in 1978, developed the Disabled Veterans Outreach program in 1977, and was assistant State director for veterans employment in his native California between 1974 and 1976. Rhoades is an Army veteran and served for 18 months in Southeast Asia between 1967 and 1969.

Paul Weston, 34, was previously Special Assistant to Veterans Administration (VA) Administrator Max Cleland. He was White House project director for Vietnam Veterans Week in 1979, and was the VA's liaison to veterans and military organizations in 1978–79. A Vietnam era Air Force veteran, Weston has also worked with the President's Committee on Employment of the Handicapped, ACTION, and VA's Voluntary Service program. Weston served as chairman of the Commission on Volunteerism in his native Georgia before coming to Washington in 1977.

Marine Protection, Research, and Sanctuaries Appropriations Bill

Statement on Signing S. 1140 Into Law. August 29, 1980

I have today signed into law S. 1140, a bill authorizing 1981 appropriations of $2,250,000 to the Department of Commerce to carry out title III of the Marine Protection, Research, and Sanctuaries Act of 1972. Title III of that act authorizes the Secretary of Commerce, upon obtaining the President's approval, to designate marine sanctuaries for preservation or restoration of ocean, coastal, and Great Lakes waters that have conservation, recreational, ecological, or esthetic value.

In approving this legislation, I reaffirm my commitment to environmental protection and, in particular, to the protection of the ocean and the living marine resources in those areas deserving special status as protected marine sanctuaries.

Nevertheless, I am signing S. 1140 reluctantly, as I have serious reservations about the constitutionality of its legislative veto provision. Section 2, which purports to confer authority on Congress to disapprove—by concurrent resolutions not to be presented to the President—certain designations of marine sanctuaries, violates the presentation clauses of the Constitution, Art. I, Section 7, cls. 2 and 3, and violates the separation of powers doctrine by interfering with the discretion of the executive branch in the administration of an ongoing program. Pursuant to my message to Congress dated July 21, 1978, I will treat the legislative veto provision as a "report-and-wait" provision. If Congress adopts a resolution under its authority, the resolution will be given serious consideration but, under my

reading of the Constitution, will not be considered binding.

NOTE: As enacted, S. 1140 is Public Law 96–332, approved August 29.

Working Mothers' Day, 1980

Proclamation 4786.   August 29, 1980

By the President of the United States of America

A Proclamation

In greater numbers than ever before, American mothers are taking on important job responsibilities outside the home. In workplaces across our Nation and in every occupation, more than 16 million employed mothers are contributing their valuable skills to the labor force. In fact, more than half of all the mothers in this country have taken on jobs outside the home, and it is estimated that by 1990, 75% of all two-parent families will have both parents in the work force.

On the job and in the home, working mothers are making a vital contribution to the national economy and to the strength of the American family. Working mothers do not shed homemaking and parental responsibilities; they merely add the demands of a job to those of wife and mother. As we recognize the hard work and dedication of these women, we also acknowledge the many special problems they confront in meeting their dual responsibilities. We have an obligation to reinforce and support them in their endeavors.

To give special recognition to working mothers for fulfilling their exceptional responsibilities in the home and in the world of commerce, the House of Representatives (House Joint Resolution 379) has requested that I designate August 31, 1980, as Working Mothers' Day. I fully support this Resolution.

Now, THEREFORE, I, JIMMY CARTER, President of the United States of America, do hereby designate August 31, 1980, as Working Mothers' Day and call upon families, individual citizens, labor and civic organizations, and the business community to recognize publicly the unique contributions of mothers currently in the work force, and to honor former generations of working mothers for their important role in building American society.

IN WITNESS WHEREOF, I have hereunto set my hand this twenty-ninth day of August, in the year of our Lord nineteen hundred and eighty, and of the Independence of the United States of America the two hundred and fifth.

JIMMY CARTER

[Filed with the Office of the Federal Register, 4:15 p.m., August 29, 1980]

General Pulaski's Memorial Day, 1980

Proclamation 4787. August 29, 1980

By the President of the United States of America

A Proclamation

Each year on the eleventh of October, the American people pay tribute to the memory of General Casimir Pulaski. In doing so they not only honor this great Polish champion of American freedom but also give recognition to the ties between our two nations, to the contributions of millions of other Polish-Americans to the birth and development of this country, and to the indivisibility of freedom everywhere.

By giving his life on the battlefield of our revolution, General Pulaski has provided inspiration to generations of his countrymen—in the United States and in Poland.

Now, THEREFORE, I, JIMMY CARTER, President of the United States of America, do hereby designate Saturday, October 11, 1980, as General Pulaski's Memorial Day, and I direct the appropriate Government officials to display the flag of the United States on all Government buildings on that day.

I also invite the people of the United States to honor the memory of General Pulaski by holding appropriate exercises and ceremonies in suitable places throughout our land.

IN WITNESS WHEREOF, I have hereunto set my hand this twenty-ninth day of August, in the year of our Lord nineteen hundred and eighty, and of the Independence of the United States of America the two hundred and fifth.

JIMMY CARTER

[Filed with the Office of the Federal Register, 4:16 p.m., August 29, 1980]

Columbus Day, 1980

Proclamation 4788. August 29, 1980

By the President of the United States of America

A Proclamation

On October 12, 1492, an Italian sea captain and his crew, having sailed into the western void in three fragile craft, touched land and revealed a New World to the astonished eyes of the old.

The Genoese Christopher Columbus, sailing for his royal Spanish patrons in search of fortune, glory and the validation of his dream, found these and more.

Today, almost five centuries later, we still honor Columbus for the stout heart and tenacity of purpose that sustained his exploits. He inspired an age of exploration and a continuing era of victory over the forces of complacency and ignorance.

As we prepare to commemorate the four hundred eighty-eighth anniversary of Columbus's historic landfall, we of the New World can pay no greater tribute to his memory than to keep alive that spark of hope and nerve that never failed him and has never failed us.

In tribute to the achievement of Columbus, the Congress of the United States of America, by joint resolution approved April 30, 1934 (48 Stat. 657), as modified by the Act of June 28, 1968 (82 Stat. 250), requested the President to proclaim the second Monday in October of each year as Columbus Day.

Now, THEREFORE, I, JIMMY CARTER, President of the United States of America, do hereby designate Monday, October 13, 1980, as Columbus Day; and I invite the people of this Nation to observe that day in schools, churches, and other suitable places with appropriate ceremonies in his honor.

I also direct that the flag of the United States of America be displayed on all public buildings on the appointed day in memory of Christopher Columbus.

IN WITNESS WHEREOF, I have hereunto set my hand this twenty-ninth day of August, in the year of our Lord nineteen hundred and eighty, and of the Independence of the United States of America the two hundred and fifth.

JIMMY CARTER

[Filed with the Office of the Federal Register, 4:17 p.m., August 29, 1980]

United Nations Day, 1980
Proclamation 4789.   August 29, 1980

By the President of the United States of America

A Proclamation

This year marks the 35th Anniversary of the founding of the United Nations, an organization dedicated to maintaining international peace and security, developing friendly relations among nations, and achieving international cooperation in solving global problems. Today 153 nations work within the United Nations framework to resolve some of the most crucial problems of our time.

Never has the United Nations been more important to the United States and to the world than it is today. The past year has seen momentous international events. Many have not yet run their full course but have already changed the way we see the world around us. We have become more conscious of the risks of war and more aware of the urgent tasks of peace.

Today, peace is threatened in many ways. There are the visible threats like the invasion by a super power of an innocent, defenseless land. And, there are the more subtle threats of hunger, spiraling inflation, inadequate health care, and depleted natural and monetary resources. These threats have filled the United Nations with a strong sense of the urgency of creating an international system based on active and equitable, social and economic cooperation among the countries of the North and South.

The United Nations, through the work of its specialized agencies and programs, its regional organizations and international conferences, has become an indispensable frontline defense against the events and forces that threaten world stability. It has played a central role in setting the pace and direction for international cooperation in an interdependent world.

The United States has always been an active and dedicated supporter of the United Nations. As President, I have been proud to carry on and expand this tradition. My Administration continues to be firmly committed to a strong United Nations system.

Now, THEREFORE, I, JIMMY CARTER, President of the United States of America, do hereby designate Friday, October 24, 1980, as United Nations Day. I urge all Americans to use this day as an opportunity to better acquaint themselves with the activities and accomplishments of the United Nations.

I have appointed Mr. Charles L. Brown to serve as 1980 United States National Chairman for United Nations Day, and the United Nations Association of the United States of America to work with him in celebrating this special day. I invite all the American people, and people everywhere, to join me in expressing sincere and steadfast support for the United Nations on its thirty-fifth anniversary. It is only through multilateral institutions like the United Nations that the solutions to our ever more urgent global problems will be found.

IN WITNESS WHEREOF, I have hereunto set my hand this twenty-ninth day of August, in the year of our Lord nineteen hundred and eighty, and of the Independence of the United States of America the two hundred and fifth.

JIMMY CARTER

[Filed with the Office of the Federal Register, 4:18 p.m., August 29, 1980]

National Institute of Building Sciences

Nomination of Six Members.
August 29, 1980

The President today announced that he will nominate six persons to be members of the National Institute of Building Sciences. They are:

RALPH M. BALL, of Oklahoma City, an architect, chairman and chief executive officer of HTB, Inc., an architectural firm.

ROBERT A. GEORGINE, of Silver Spring, Md., president of the Building and Construction Trades Department of the AFL–CIO (reappointment).

BENNIE S. GOODEN, of Clarksdale, Miss., vice president of Southland Management Corp. and president of Elderly Housing, Inc.

ALBERT J. HOFSTEDE, of Minneapolis, an urban consultant and former mayor of Minneapolis.

BERT D. LEE, of East Lansing, Mich., secretary-treasurer of the Southeastern Michigan Building and Construction Trades Council.

VIVIENNE S. THOMSON, of Jamaica Plain, Mass., handicapped services specialist with the Boston Housing Authority. She is president of the Massachusetts Council of Organizations of the Handicapped and the Massachusetts Association of Paraplegics. She is a member of the Boston Indian Council.

Foreign Claims Settlement Commission

Nomination of Francis Leon Jung To Be a Member. August 29, 1980

The President today announced that he will nominate Francis Leon Jung, of Woodbridge, Va., for reappointment as a member of the Foreign Claims Settlement Commission of the United States.

Jung, 32, is a Washington attorney specializing in international trade matters. He was appointed to this Commission earlier this year.

National Council on the Handicapped

Nomination of Carl V. Granger To Be a Member. August 29, 1980

The President today announced that he will nominate Carl V. Granger, of Rehoboth, Mass., to be a member of the National Council on the Handicapped for a 2-year term.

Granger, 51, is director of the Institute for Rehabilitative and Restorative Care at Brown University. He is also a professor of community health at Brown and director of the Department of Physical Medicine and Rehabilitation at the Memorial Hospital, Pawtucket, R.I.

American Battle Monuments Commission

Appointment of J. Glennon Travis as a Member. August 29, 1980

The President today announced the appointment of J. Glennon Travis, of St. Louis, Mo., as a member of the American Battle Monuments Commission. He replaces the late Charles Potter.

Travis is president of Wentzway Corp. He is a World War II veteran and a former lieutenant commander in the U.S. Naval Reserve.

Federal Civilian Pay Increases

Message to the Congress Transmitting the Federal Pay Comparability Alternative Plan. August 29, 1980

To the Congress of the United States:

An adjustment in Federal white collar pay is required on October 1 under the Pay Comparability Act of 1970.

As specified in that Act, my Pay Agent and the statutory Advisory Committee on Federal Pay have made their report to me on comparability findings for the next fiscal year.

Current law provides that the annual increase for the military be the same as the average of the civilian increase. The Department of Defense Authorization Act, 1981, which has passed both Houses of Congress provides for a larger military pay adjustment this year. The larger increases proposed under that Act will supersede the increases military personnel otherwise would receive under the Alternative Plan.

A decision on pay comparability for Federal civilian employees necessarily must be made in the broader context of the present economic situation in this country. Inflation is a continuing threat to the economy, and consequently we still have anti-inflationary pay standards for all pay increases, public or private. For the past two years, I have looked to those standards in determining the Federal pay adjustment just as I expected other employers to do in formulating increases for their workers. I have continued that approach for this year's Federal increase.

The Pay Act gives me authority to propose an alternative adjustment to full comparability if deemed appropriate in light of economic conditions. Under that authority, I have decided upon an alternative pay plan consisting of an across-the-board 9.1 percent increase, and a partial exemption from the full effect of that limitation for the lowest paid civilian employees. That increase is fully within the range of the current national pay standards.

A President must balance economic

PHOTOGRAPHIC
PORTFOLIO

President Jimmy Carter

Overleaf: At the Democratic Congressional Campaign Committee victory luncheon in New York City, August 14. *Above left:* With Western and Japanese leaders at the conclusion of the Venice Economic Summit Conference, Italy, June 23. *Above right:* Dancing in Kalemegdan Park, Yugoslavia, June 24. *Below right:* With Pope John Paul II at the Vatican, June 21.

Above left: Signing ceremony for the Energy Security Act on the South Lawn of the White House, June 30.
Below left: Greeting freed American hostage Richard Queen and his mother in the Oval Office, July 19.
Above right: Speaking from the Oval Office to members of the United Steelworkers of America, August 7.
Below right: With Vice Premier Geng Biao of the People's Republic of China in the Roosevelt Room, May 28.

Left: Preparing the Presidential
nomination acceptance speech at
Camp David in Maryland, August 11.
Right and below: At the Democratic
National Convention in New York
City, August 14. *Overleaf:* Speaking to
servicemen on board the U.S.S.
Nimitz, May 26.

considerations against the fact that Federal employees face the same kinds of problems with inflation as other citizens. In so doing, I have concluded that the dedication of these loyal public servants deserves no less relief than we would allow for other workers.

For those reasons, I urge the Congress to support the Alternative Plan submitted with this message.

JIMMY CARTER

The White House,
   August 29, 1980.

FEDERAL PAY COMPARABILITY ALTERNATIVE PLAN

Because of economic conditions affecting the general welfare, I hereby transmit to Congress the following Alternative Plan, in accordance with 5 U.S.C. 5305(c)(1):

The adjustment in rates of pay of each Federal statutory pay system to become effective on the first day of the first applicable pay period that begins on or after October 1, 1980, shall be limited to a 9.1 percent increase at each grade in lieu of the adjustment determined under the comparability procedure set forth in 5 U.S.C. 5305(a)–(b); Provided, however, that the full adjustment determined under the comparability procedure shall take effect to the extent it does not increase any rate of pay to an amount of more than $9,069 per year.

Accordingly, the overall percentage of the adjustment in the rates of pay under the General Schedule will be a 9.12 percent increase. The overall percentage of the adjustment in the rates of pay under the other statutory pay systems (Foreign Service and the Department of Medicine and Surgery of the Veterans Administration) will be slightly less, a 9.1 percent

increase, because all salaries under those systems are higher than the $9,069 per year limit which would permit comparability increases.

In accordance with 5 U.S.C. 5382(c) the following rates of basic pay for the Senior Executive Service shall become effective on the first day of the first applicable pay period that begins on or after October 1, 1980:

ES–1	49,198
ES–2	51,461
ES–3	53,827
ES–4	56,303
ES–5	58,892
ES–6	61,600

Digest of Other White House Announcements

The following listing includes the President's public schedule and other items of general interest announced by the White House Press Office and not included elsewhere in this issue.

August 23

The President met at the White House with Zbigniew Brzezinski, Assistant to the President for National Security Affairs.

August 25

The President met at the White House with:

—Dr. Brzezinski;

—Secretary of the Treasury G. William Miller, James T. McIntyre, Jr., Director of the Office of Management and Budget, Charles L. Schultze, Chairman of the Council of Economic Advisers, and Stuart E. Eizenstat, Assistant to the President for Domestic Affairs and Policy;

—Senator Edward M. Kennedy of Massachusetts.

August 26

The President met at the White House with:

—Dr. Brzezinski;
—the Democratic congressional leadership;
—Frank B. Moore, **Assistant to the President for Congressional Liaison**;
—Vice President Walter F. Mondale;
—Representatives James J. Florio of New Jersey, Edward R. Madigan of Illinois, James T. Broyhill of North Carolina, and Harley O. Staggers and Nick Joe Rahall II of West Virginia;
—the executive board of the International Union, United Automobile, Aerospace & Agricultural Implement Workers of America.

The White House announced that the President has approved the award of the Medal of Freedom, the Nation's highest civilian honor, to Horace Marden Albright. The award ceremony will take place at a later date. Mr. Albright was the cofounder of the National Park Service, which was established in 1916, and was its second director. Mr. Albright, who is 90, lives in Studio City, Calif.

August 27

The President met at the White House with:

—Dr. Brzezinski;
—a bipartisan group of Members of the House of Representatives.

The President announced that he has designated Arthur Levitt, Jr., to advise the administration on its response to the recommendations of the White House Conference on Small Business. Mr. Levitt, chairman and chief executive officer of the American Stock Exchange, was Chairman of the Small Business Conference Commission.

August 28

The President met at the White House with:

—David L. Aaron, Deputy Assistant for National Security Affairs;
—a bipartisan group of Members of the House of Representatives;
—Mr. Moore;
—Stansfield Turner, Director of Central Intelligence.

August 29

The President met at the White House with:

—Dr. Brzezinski;
—Secretary of State Edmund S. Muskie, Secretary of Defense Harold Brown, Deputy Secretary of State Warren M. Christopher, Jack H. Watson, Jr., Assistant to the President, Lloyd N. Cutler, Counsel to the President, and Dr. Brzezinski.

In an Oval Office ceremony, the President received diplomatic credentials from Ambassadors Filipe Nagera Bole of Fiji, Mohamed Warsame Ali of the Somali Democratic Republic, Bhekh Bahadur Thapa of Nepal, Frank Gill of New Zealand, Jan Hendrik Lubbers of the Netherlands, Anton Hegner of Switzerland, Joseph Kingsley Baffour-Senkyire of Ghana, and Elleck K. Mashingaidze of Zimbabwe.

The President left the White House for a weekend stay at Camp David, Md.

NOMINATIONS SUBMITTED TO THE SENATE

The following list does not include promotions of members of the Uniformed Services, nominations to the Service Academies, or nominations of Foreign Service officers.

Submitted August 26, 1980

S. GERALD ARNOLD, of North Carolina, to be United States District Judge for the Eastern District of North Carolina, vice a new position created by P.L. 95–486, approved October 20, 1978.

NOMINATIONS—Continued

Withdrawn August 26, 1980

CHARLES B. WINBERRY, JR., of North Carolina, to be United States District Judge for the Eastern District of North Carolina, vice a new position created by P.L. 95–486, approved October 20, 1978, which was sent to the Senate on March 29, 1979.

Submitted August 28, 1980

FERNANDO E. RONDON, of Virginia, a Foreign Service officer of Class two, to be Ambassador Extraordinary and Plenipotentiary of the United States of America to the Democratic Republic of Madagascar.

EUGENE H. NICKERSON, of New York, to be United States Circuit Judge for the Second Circuit, vice Murray I. Gurfein, deceased.

GERALD B. LACKEY, of Ohio, to be United States District Judge for the Northern District of Ohio, vice Don J. Young, retired.

PETER M. LOWRY, of Texas, to be United States District Judge for the Western District of Texas, vice Jack Roberts, retired.

DAVID G. ROBERTS, of Maine, to be United States District Judge for the District of Maine, vice George J. Mitchell, resigned.

Submitted August 29, 1980

CARL V. GRANGER, of Massachusetts, to be a member of the National Council on the Handicapped for a term of 2 years (new position).

FRANCIS LEON JUNG, of Virginia, to be a member of the Foreign Claims Settlement Commission of the United States for the term of 3 years expiring September 30, 1983 (reappointment).

The following-named persons to be members of the Board of Directors of the National Institute of Building Sciences for the terms indicated:

For terms expiring September 7, 1981

ALFRED JOHN HOFSTEDE, of Minnesota, vice S. Peter Volpe, term expired.

BENNIE S. GOODEN, of Mississippi, vice Jasper S. Hawkins, term expired.

For terms expiring September 7, 1982

RALPH M. BALL, of Oklahoma, vice O. M. Mader, term expired.

ROBERT A. GEORGINE, of Maryland (reappointment).

BERT D. LEE, of Michigan, vice David S. Miller, term expired.

VIVIENNE S. THOMSON, of Massachusetts, vice Glen R. Swenson, term expired.

CHECKLIST OF WHITE HOUSE PRESS RELEASES

The following listing contains releases of the White House Press Office which are not included in this issue.

Released August 26, 1980

Advance text: remarks on signing Proclamation 4785, Women's Equality Day, 1980

Announcement: withdrawal of nomination of Charles B. Winberry, Jr., to be United States District Judge for the Eastern District of North Carolina

Announcement: nomination of S. Gerald Arnold to be United States District Judge for the Eastern District of North Carolina

Released August 28, 1980

Announcement: nomination of Eugene H. Nickerson to be United States Circuit Judge for the Second Circuit

Announcement: nomination of David G. Roberts to be United States District Judge for the District of Maine

Announcement: nomination of Gerald B. Lackey to be United States District Judge for the Northern District of Ohio

Announcement: nomination of Peter M. Lowry to be United States District Judge for the Western District of Texas

Advance text: remarks announcing the economic renewal program

Fact sheets: the economic renewal program (2 releases)

White paper: economic growth for the 1980's

ACTS APPROVED BY THE PRESIDENT

Approved August 26, 1980

EDITOR'S NOTE: The following bill became law over the President's veto of August 22 (see page 1563).

H.R. 7102_____ Public Law 96–330
Veterans' Administration Health-Care Amendments of 1980.

Approved August 28, 1980

S. 1863_____ Public Law 96–331
An act to authorize the Secretary of Commerce to charter the nuclear ship *Savannah* to Patriots Point Development Authority, an agency of the State of South Carolina.

ACTS APPROVED—Continued

Approved August 29, 1980

S. 1140_____ Public Law 96–332
An act to amend title III of the Marine Protection, Research, and Sanctuaries Act of
1972, as amended, to authorize appropriations for such title for fiscal years 1980 and
1981, and for other purposes.

S. 1730_____ Public Law 96–333
An act to declare that title to certain lands
in the State of New Mexico are held in trust
by the United States for the Ramah Band of
the Navajo Tribe.

ACTS APPROVED—Continued

Approved August 29—Continued

H.J. Res. 589_____ Public Law 96–334
A joint resolution providing additional program authority for the Export-Import Bank.

S. 659_____ Private Law 96–58
An act for the relief of the Black Hills Area
Council of the Boy Scouts of America.

S. 1626_____ Private Law 96–59
An act for the relief of H. F. Mulholland and
the estate of John Oakason.

Tuscumbia, Alabama

Remarks at a Campaign Rally at Spring Park.   September 1, 1980

Senator Stewart, Senator Heflin, Senator Sasser, Senator Sparkman, Senator Eastland, Senator Gore, Governor James, Governor Winter, Governor George Wallace, Congressman Bevill, Congressman Flippo, whose district this is, Congressman Shelby, Lieutenant Governor McMillan, Speaker McCorquodale, President Bradford, and my friends and Americans and fellow Southerners:

I'm glad to be here.

We also have Congressmen Jones and Elliot and Raines, and a lot of people here from this great State, from Tennessee, Mississippi, a few from Georgia, a few from the Carolinas, and also we've got some wonderful entertainment. And before I begin my remarks, I'd like to say thank you first of all to the Speer Family, the first family of gospel music—the Speer Family; and to Larry Gatlin, a longtime friend of mine—he's nominated this year for four country music awards; and also to Charlie Daniels—who rode down on the plane with me—from Hartford, Connecticut. His song, "In America" has swept the country, as you know, and "The Devil Went Down to Georgia" was voted the best song of 1979.

Not long ago I saw Charlie Daniels when he was on the way up north to give a concert tour, and I said, "Charlie, when you had three fundraising events for me back in 1976 not many people knew who you were, and now you're world famous."

He said, "Mr. President, when I gave those three fundraisers for you in '76, a lot more people knew who I was than knew who you were." [*Laughter*]

It's good for me to be at home. It's been a long time since I've been to a good, old-fashioned Alabama picnic like this, and I want to let you know I love it.

In the last few years, particularly the last 4 years, I've been to a lot of places and I've seen a lot of people, but I just want to say how great it is to be with folks who don't talk with an accent.

On a good day like this it's good to be out in the country. Thanks to all of you, I've got a job in the city now—[*laughter*]—I'd like to keep it for about 4 more years. But I won't ever forget, as a farmboy myself, that the greatness of America lies in its land. The land typifies the values which are dear to us—hard work, self-reliance, trust in our families, trust in our neighbors, and trust in our God. And I pray to God that we in the South and the people of this Nation will never get away from those values which do not change.

I know what you feel for this Nation. I know the pride and the love for this country that's in your hearts, and I know the hopes that you have in your hearts for the future. Our region, the Southland, has been through a lot of pain and a lot of change, but we came out all right in the end because of our determination to move ahead and to face our problems together.

There are still a few in the South, indeed around the country, some I heard from today, who practice cowardice and who counsel fear and hatred. They marched around the State Capitol in Atlanta when I was Governor. They said we ought to be afraid of each other, that whites ought to hate and be afraid of blacks and that blacks ought to hate and be afraid of whites. And they would persecute those who worshiped in a different way from most of us. As a Southerner, it makes me feel angry when I see them with a Confederate battle flag because I remember Judah P. Benjamin who was Secretary of State of the Confederacy; he was a Jew. And I remember General Pat Cleburne of Arkansas who died in battle not very far from this very spot, and General Beauregard of Louisiana, brave men. Both were Catholics, and so were many others who served under that flag. And sometimes I see the raising of a cross and I remember that the One who was crucified taught us to have faith, to hope, and not to hate but to love one another.

As the first man from the Deep South in 140 years to be President of this Nation, I say that these people in white sheets do not understand our region and what it's been through, they do not understand what our country stands for, they do not understand that the South and all of America must move forward. Our past is a rich source of inspiration. We've had lessons that we learned with a great deal of pain. But the past is not a place to live. We must go forward in the South, and we will.

You people here have the same background, the same families, the same upbringing that I have—people from Alabama, Mississippi, Tennessee, Georgia, the Carolinas, Virginia, Florida. You share my past and my values, yes, but you also share my love of this country. It was you who put me on the road to the greatest honor that any American can possibly have, to serve as your President, and today I've come back home.

I've come back to the part of this Nation that will always be my home, to ask you to join me once again in a great and noble campaign that, with your help, will lead to victory in November. This will be a campaign for a secure peace. This will be a campaign for jobs. This will be a campaign for stable prices, a campaign of confidence and unity, but most of all it'll be a campaign for the future of this richly blessed and beloved country.

This is a day of celebration, not long speeches, so I'm just going to talk about two things. The first is our economic future, our bread and butter.

Everybody here knows what a full day of hard work is all about, on the farm or in the factory. If there's anybody here who doesn't know what a full day's work is all about, raise your hand. Just a few don't know. You know what others might forget: that the true strength of our country does not lie in the big corporations, it does not lie in big government, but in the sweat and the muscle and the nimble hands and the brains of working men and women. You're the ones that built America, and you're the ones that will continue to build and to rebuild America to meet the challenges of the future.

The working families of this country do not want handouts for the able-bodied. None of us do. That is not the American way. We want opportunities; we want equal opportunities. We want a chance to provide for our families, to bring up our children, and to do what the Declaration of Independence says we have a right to do—to live in liberty and to pursue happiness for ourselves and for those we love.

These aspirations, which have always burned in the hearts of Americans, are now within our grasp. We can have the future we want. We can make our dreams for this country come true. The choice is ours to make, and part of that choice will be made the first Tuesday in November.

We must uphold our American tradition of self-reliance, and we must lick the energy challenge. We have to use the billions and billions of American dollars we now send overseas for foreign oil to create new energy and new jobs here at home. I need not remind you this is not the first time we've taken on an energy problem in the South. You know that our country undertook a great energy program once before. They called it TVA.

I grew up on a Georgia farm, and I remember what TVA and the rural electrification program meant to people. I was 13 years old when the lights came on in our house. If you're too young to remember, ask your parents about it. Ask them what Franklin D. Roosevelt and the Democratic Party and the Tennessee Valley Authority did for this valley. There were a lot who opposed it. The Republicans opposed it. But the TVA and the REA didn't just create energy; it opened up new opportunities of all kinds; it allowed farms to prosper, businesses to prosper; it created jobs where there were no jobs; it gave us a better life.

TVA met the energy challenge of the 1930's, and now we are meeting the energy challenge of the 1980's. The energy program that we've established—after 3 years of struggle—is the biggest enterprise ever undertaken in peacetime America. It's bigger than our total space program and the interstate highway program combined. It's working already.

We're now importing 20 percent less oil from overseas—that's 1½ million barrels every day less than when I took office. And at the same time, we're drilling more oil wells and more gas wells in the United States today than we have in the last 25 years. And we're going to do even better. We're going to run our homes and our cars and our factories on American indus-

try, American energy, American coal, American solar power, American synthetic fuels, American gasohol. And we're going to use American technology and American resources and last, but not least, millions of American workers to do it.

We have finally laid a good energy foundation, and now we can revitalize the entire economy of our Nation. I want to make sure that we replace OPEC oil in international trade with American coal. And we need to modernize our steel industry, retool our automobile industry, and meet and defeat foreign competition for American workers. Furthermore, as all of you know, now and in the years ahead, the most treasured natural possession of any nation on Earth is not the oil of Saudi Arabia, it's the soil of the United States of America.

I'll save time by just telling you that we can use our many blessings that God's given us for an even greater tomorrow, but remind you again, that the choice of the two paths to the future will be made in November. The Democratic Party has always been the party of progress, and Democratic leadership, along with American ingenuity and American dedication, offers the brightest economic future for all the people of the United States.

And the other thing I want to mention to you is even more important, and that's peace—a secure peace based on American strength.

I'm grateful that I can look back on my first term and see 4 years of peace, and that's what we want for the next 4 years is peace. But I'd like to remind you that the peace we enjoy is based on American military strength and American moral strength.

After years of decline under Republicans before I took office, this last 4 years we have steadily rebuilt our military capabilities. I wouldn't be a true southerner if

I hadn't done that in the White House, and I promise you that as long as I'm in the White House we'll keep our Nation strong militarily.

And I'd also like to point out to you that America is now the peacemaker of the world and that, too, will continue as long as I'm President, because the role as peacemaker comes right out of our own history and our own heritage.

Let me tell you a brief true story that may bring this home to you so you can remember it. Two years ago this month, I was at Camp David with President Sadat and Prime Minister Begin. We were trying to find a way to bring those two nations together. They had been at war for 30 years, four different times. I wanted them to settle their differences in peace. After several days of hard negotiating, it got so that Prime Minister Begin and President Sadat were not even talking to one another. There was a deadlock. We weren't getting anywhere. So, I said to the two men, "Let's take a day off," and I took them across the border, the Maryland-Pennsylvania border, to Gettysburg. I had been there a little before with a southern historian, Shelby Foote, so I knew pretty well what to expect when we arrived. I wanted to show these two men that we Americans know something about war, and we know about neighbors fighting against neighbors.

The three of us walked through the valleys and hills where more than 40,000 young Americans fell in battle—Cemetery Hill, Seminary Ridge, Little Round Top, Devil's Den. I thought then of the 14th Volunteer Regiment from Clarksville, Tennessee, as they marched toward Gettysburg the second day of July of 1863. There were 400 men in the 14th Tennessee Regiment. As the sun rose 2 days later, on July the 4th, 1863, of the 400 men there were left only 60. And when the Sun set on that terrible day, there were only three men left.

As we looked across the fields, standing on the same place where General Robert E. Lee stood, I thought of General MacArthur's farewell address to the cadets at West Point. General MacArthur said, "The soldier above all people prays for peace, [for] he must suffer and bear the deepest wounds . . . of war."

I remembered that in all our Nation's wars, every war, young men from the South have led the rolls of volunteers and also led the rolls of casualties. We Southerners believe in the nobility of courage on the battlefield, and because we understand the cost of war, we also believe in the nobility of peace.

After that day at Gettysburg we went back to Camp David, and you know the rest. We hammered out a peace agreement between Egypt and Israel. We Americans work for peace not just to do a favor to others but because we want our own children and our own grandchildren to live in peace. That's why we must keep America strong, and that's why we must work for arms control, to stop and prevent a nuclear war that might mean the end of ourselves and all we love. And that's why we've opened full diplomatic relationships with the largest nation on Earth, China; and that's why we fought for democracy and for justice in Africa; and that's why we struggle to make our Nation energy independent, so that no nation might be tempted to risk the peace by trying to blackmail the United States of America.

In closing, let me say that as long as I'm President, we'll remain strong and America will continue to work for peace. We'll struggle for a strong and secure and a just society here at home, and as long as I'm President, America will hold high the banner of human rights.

There are those who say we ought not to do it. Some say it's naive for America to stand up for freedom and democracy in other lands. But they are wrong. But don't take my word for it. Ask those who are suffering under tyranny around the world about human rights. Ask them if America should stop fighting and speaking out for American principles, and ask the American people. We'll go on defending human rights for our own country and for people throughout the world.

And I'd like to mention briefly the situation in Poland. Celebrating our own labor holiday today, Americans look with pleasure and with admiration on the workers of Poland. We have been inspired and gratified by the peaceful determination with which they've acted under the most difficult possible circumstances. By their discipline, their tenacity, and their courage, the working men and women of Poland have set an example for all those who cherish freedom and human dignity. They have shown the world not just how to win a victory for labor, but that the hunger for human rights is everywhere. And they've accomplished this by themselves, without any interference from anywhere, and they and the Government of Poland have shown how a society which deals frankly with its problems can strengthen itself in the process. We are pleased at what has happened in Poland, and we wish them Godspeed and a future of prosperity, peace, and freedom.

For us in the last 200 years, even in the last 20 years, many things have changed, but our belief in America has remained the same. We still have our same dreams. We're determined that America shall redeem its destiny as the land of hope, of freedom, and of peace.

A great Southern author, Thomas Wolfe, once wrote these stirring words: "The true discovery of America is before

us. The true fulfillment of our spirit, of our people, of our mighty and immortal land, is yet to come. Our America is here, is now, and it beckons us, and this glorious assurance is not only our living hope but our dream to be accomplished."

In the year 1980, America still beckons us toward that hope and that dream, but it will not be easy. We have never had nor expected anything of value to be easy. We must fight for it, and as we choose the path this year to America's future, I ask for your help and support. If we fight [for] our future side-by-side, then together we will be victorious, our Nation will be strong, united, and free, and we will have a better life for all Americans.

God bless you. Stick with me, and we'll win.

NOTE: The President spoke at 1:26 p.m. at the annual Quad-Cities' Labor Day picnic. He was introduced by O. G. Bradford, president of the Tri-City Central Labor Union.

Prior to the picnic-rally, the President attended a Democratic reception at Mr. C's Restaurant at Muscle Shoals, Ala.

Labor Day

Remarks at a White House Picnic for Representatives of Organized Labor. September 1, 1980

THE PRESIDENT. We just got back from Tuscumbia, Alabama. It was kind of warm down in Alabama. [*Laughter*] I hope it stayed cool here in our Nation's Capital today.

The first thing I want to do on behalf of myself and Rosalynn is to welcome you to the White House. As you all know, Labor Day is a uniquely American celebration, designed to let the world know the history and the contributions of working people of our great country. But that's not all that Labor Day is about. Labor

Day is also about freedom. It's almost impossible to separate the trade union movement of this world from freedom. It's also about a struggle of American workers to organize and to demand for themselves, legitimately, better working conditions and at the same time to extend democracy for all Americans.

I'd like to say a special word about Poland. Celebrating our own labor holiday, Americans can look with gratitude and admiration at what the working people of Poland have accomplished. We're inspired and we are gratified by the peaceful determination with which they acted, by their discipline, their tenacity, and their personal courage. The working men and women of Poland have set an example for all those who cherish freedom and honor human dignity. They've shown the world at least two things: one, how to win a victory for labor, and the other one is that the hunger for human rights covers the entire world.

I'm particularly grateful that the workers of Poland accomplished this by themselves, without outside interference, but with quiet prayer that their struggle for freedom would be successful. We've seen how a society that deals frankly with its problems can strengthen itself in the process. We pray for the well-being of the people of Poland, for the independence of their nation, for the freedom of their people, and for their future prosperity.

I think it's important for us to know that in our own country, as manifold as our blessings are, and despite steady progress, many of our own goals are still not fully realized. But we share an unshakable commitment to a more humane and a more decent future.

We've had a chance for the last 3½ years to work together. We've accomplished a lot. We've cut our dependence on foreign oil drastically in just a short period of time. We now import 20 percent less oil than we did when I first took office. This is 1½ million barrels every day that we do not import which we formerly bought from overseas. And now these billions of American dollars can be used to create American industry, American energy, American jobs for millions of American workers, and to give us a stronger nation in the process, and to remove the temptation from any nation on Earth that might think they can blackmail the United States of America.

Almost everyone on this lawn has been involved in this struggle. And you know how difficult it has been to finance this tremendous program of conservation and energy production from the windfall profits tax on the unearned earnings of the big oil companies. It's not been easy. But now with that new energy base of a permanent national policy, we can afford to look forward to the future with a great deal more confidence that an exciting, dynamic, bright, productive life can be possible for all Americans.

We can create new energy industries. The scope of this commitment is far beyond anything that the world has ever seen—much bigger than the total space program, the Interstate Highway System, and even the Marshall plan all combined. What this can do to give Americans a better life, a more secure life, a more productive life can not even yet be fully imagined. We also will be able now to improve our entire public transportation system. And I'm particularly eager to take the first strong moves to replace the world's excessive dependence on OPEC oil with the purchase of American coal.

We have now laid a foundation, and we're ready to build on it to renew the industrial strength of this Nation. For too long we've expected American workers to produce more with machinery that each year was less efficient. After close consultations with labor, and with a firm urging from Lane Kirkland,[1] I set forth last week an economic renewal program to rebuild our industrial might. We're going to restore the competitive edge in world markets by encouraging new industries and by revitalizing our most basic ones like steel and automobiles. In 2 years, above and beyond what we already encompass, with programs on the Hill and just put into effect, and above and beyond what normal economic recovery will bring us, this program will create more than a million new jobs for American workers—productive careers in strong and growing industries. We bring business and labor and government together as equals, an unprecedented commitment in the history of our Nation. And we'll be able, now, to combine public with private investments, including the use of employee pension funds in revitalization projects to give us better communities throughout our Nation.

Also in the next 4 years, we'll continue our urban policy, which has reversed the decline of many of our cities. And I want to enact new welfare reform proposals, as well as to expand our youth employment programs, and I stand ready with you to fully implement a national health insurance program for the people of the United States.

I just want to mention two more things. I hope that the labor movement has not given up and that you will join with me in achieving, next year, labor law reform. I believe that in any progressive industrial policy that fair labor laws are essential. And my hope is that this new working partnership, with increased trust, increased communication, increased understanding of one another will help to alleviate a major portion of the unwarranted business opposition to labor law reform that let us lose by one vote in the Senate when we tried so hard before. But I'm determined, no matter what the obstacles might be, to work with you toward success and a victory with labor law reform in the coming year.

And finally, I want the United States, through its strength, military and moral strength both, to continue to stand for peace in the world. With your help, we strengthened our defenses. We negotiated a successful SALT II agreement. We ratified the Panama Canal treaties. We helped to bring peace between Egypt and Israel. We've sustained a level of foreign aid, and we've relighted and kept bright the beacon of human rights. In all these elements of an enlightened American foreign policy, designed for peace abroad and for peace here at home, your support has been invaluable. The American labor movement was built on realism and persistence and our future depends on these same qualities, combined with the idealism which keeps hope alive in the human breast. I look forward to working with you to make our dreams for the future come true.

Let me conclude by noting that this is our first Labor Day in many years without the presence of President George Meany. We all owe him a great debt, and we miss him greatly. He symbolized the heart and spirit of American labor. At my request, in tribute to his memory and to the achievements of American labor, the United States Postal Service is issuing today a special commemorative stamp.

I want to introduce Postmaster General Bill Bolger and Lane Kirkland to make a few remarks at this time about this stamp. Bill and Lane.

---

[1] President, AFL–CIO, and Cochairman of the Economic Revitalization Board.

POSTMASTER GENERAL BOLGER. Thank you, Mr. President.

Ladies and gentlemen, it's an honor and a pleasure to be here today for this auspicious occasion. We have come together to dedicate a postage stamp which honors not only the American labor movement but also George Meany, who championed the development of trade unionism in the United States.

Under longstanding postal policy, memorial stamps for other than Presidents may not be issued sooner than 10 years after an individual's death. However, I believe there's every reason to recognize George Meany's influence on all levels of American life by hereby honoring all of organized labor in his name. I was therefore happy to respond favorably to you, Mr. President, when you asked me to issue this stamp that is being dedicated today.

Under Mr. Meany's leadership, the labor movement was and continues to be a force for freedom and democracy. Mr. Meany's dedication to and support of the working man earned respect, dignity, and security for millions of his countrymen. In an effort to incorporate those high ideals in the design of the stamp, we chose our national symbol, the American eagle for the central design element. The eagle, of course, symbolizes democracy, individual liberty, social justice, and human rights—goals shared by organized labor. The image is purposely strong and bold, and the message beneath it is unequivocable—organized labor, proud and free.

While the Postal Service's primary role is to move the mail, we welcome our related opportunity to mark significant events in American history and life and to honor distinguished individuals through our stamp issuance program. I hope that the millions of copies of this stamp flowing throughout the mailstreams of the world will remind everyone of the high value America places on the singular role of organized labor, a role reinforced by the 500,000 or so men and women who belong to American postal unions and who do move the mail.

And now it gives me great pleasure to present a souvenir album containing a sheet of the new stamps to the President of the United States—by tradition always gets the first album. Mr. President.

And the second one to Secretary of Labor Ray Marshall. Mr. Secretary.

Thank you very much, Mr. President.

THE PRESIDENT. Thank you, Bill, for those remarks. And, Lane, I'd like very much for you to make your remarks now, and I want to present you a special edition of the stamp.

MR. KIRKLAND. Mr. President and Mrs. Carter, on behalf of the AFL–CIO I want to thank you for your gracious hospitality. We look forward to returning to celebrate Labor Day here with you for the next 4 years if I am reelected. [*Laughter*]

I also want to thank Postmaster General Bolger and the Postal Service for issuing the stamp honoring organized labor in memory of George Meany. He was our strength and inspiration, and we are honored that others have drawn similar inspiration from a man that we revered. We appreciate the fact that the free trade union movement of America is honored by its Nation through this stamp and by the President through his kind invitation to celebrate this holiday at his house, the Nation's house.

We do not take for granted the rights and liberties enjoyed by American workers. Those rights and liberties are both precious and fragile. Just how precious they are is sharply revealed by the courage shown by workers in other countries, particularly today those in Poland. Their fragility is obvious from the measures totalitarian regimes have used to deny working people the free trade unions so necessary to enforce their rights and to realize their aims. Our thoughts and prayers on this day are with those workers in Poland who have shown such valor and self-sacrifice in placing their lives and safety on the line for the rights of all workers—the rights that all workers need and must have to be truly free.

If George Meany were here, I believe that he would declare that the fighting eagle on the stamp honoring our labor movement is for now a Polish eagle, a stirring emblem of the desire of all workers for freedom. Long live the free workers of Poland. Long live the cause of free trade unionism everywhere.

Thank you.

THE PRESIDENT. I'm very delighted that we have with us also one of the daughters of President George Meany, Eileen Meany Lee. I'd like to ask her to come forward now. And I want to present her with a special edition of this stamp, and to give Eileen with two other editions for her sisters, who could not attend today, Genevieve Meany Lutz and Regina Meany Mayer. Eileen, this is for you and for your sisters.

The memories of Mr. George Meany flood my mind and heart. I didn't know him as long as many of you, but the last time I was with him, the next to the last time I was with him at a public event, was on this South Lawn when Pope John Paul II was here. The Pope made his speech from over near the White House. Mr. Meany was in the front row, and afterwards the Pope went down and shook hands with Mr. Meany, pointed out that he was a famous man, because worldwide he had always stood for human rights and for basic freedoms. It was one of the thrilling moments of my life as tears came into Mr. Meany's eyes, and the emotion of the

moment also filled the face of Pope John Paul II.

Now, I would like to point out to you that as you leave this evening, you'll receive one of a limited edition of a lithograph depicting Americans at work. There's a small reproduction of it on the back of the program. This lithograph evokes the spirit of Labor Day, and Rosalynn and I hope that it will be a reminder of the fellowship and the good spirits of this day for many years to come.

I'd like to introduce the artist, Jacob Lawrence, professor of art at the University of Washington. Mr. Lawrence. And I would also like to thank Ken Brown, president of the Graphic Arts International Union, and all his members who donated their labor and printed this beautiful poster as a souvenir of this day. Ken, why don't you stand and let us all thank you, too.

And finally, there's one other person here whom I've come to know and to respect as a friend and trusted ally. I don't believe America has ever had a Secretary of Labor who worked harder on behalf of working people or one who cared more deeply about people who need their help than Ray Marshall.

Ray, I want to present this copy of Jacob Lawrence's poster to you, and if you don't mind, when you get it unwrapped, I'd like to share the inscription on it with all of your friends who are here. That shows the nimble fingers of the Secretary of Labor. [*Laughter*] And it's inscribed at the bottom, "With appreciation to Ray Marshall for being a great leader for the working people of America," and it's signed "Jimmy Carter."

And now with happiness on your faces, you'll be glad to hear that we come to the music, which to me is the highlight of this evening.

We often overlook the rich heritage of songs that the American labor movement has given our country. It's one of the purest forms of folkmusic, but it's folkmusic with a serious purpose. The songs often come out of the bitterest periods of our history. The first songs I ever heard, maybe outside of Sunday school, were the ones I heard in the cottonfields and the peanutfields of south Georgia. They evoke from working people the inevitable triumph of human aspirations, that enduring idealism and optimism of American working men and women.

I know you will enjoy the musicians here tonight. You already have. To introduce each act, which we now have a chance to enjoy, we have with us one of our Nation's leading labor folklorists, a member of the United Brotherhood of Carpenters and Joiners, and a personal friend to many of us, Dr. Archie Green.

Dr. Green, please come and take over.

NOTE: The President spoke at 6:13 p.m. on the South Lawn of the White House.

Kansas City, Missouri

Informal Exchange With Reporters on Arrival.   September 2, 1980

Q. Mr. President, yesterday Governor Reagan complained that you opened the campaign in the home of the Ku Klux Klan. Why would he say that?

THE PRESIDENT. I wasn't going to answer any questions, but I will respond to that one.

I resent very deeply what Ronald Reagan said about the South and about Alabama and about Tuscumbia when he pointed out erroneously that I opened my campaign in the home of the Ku Klux Klan. Anybody who resorts to slurs and to innuendo against a whole region of the country, based on a false statement and a false premise, is not doing the South or our Nation a good service.

This is not the time for a candidate, trying to get some political advantage, to try to divide one region of the country from another by alleging that the Ku Klux Klan is representative of the South or Alabama or Tuscumbia, Alabama.

Q. Do you think it was a low blow?

THE PRESIDENT. I think it was uncalled for. I think it was inaccurate, and I think it was something that all southerners will resent. As an American and a southerner I resent it.

NOTE: The exchange began at approximately 9:30 a.m. at the Kansas City Municipal Airport.

Independence, Missouri

Remarks and a Question-and-Answer Session at a Townhall Meeting.   September 2, 1980

THE PRESIDENT. *Senator Eagleton, Governor Teasdale, Congressman Bolling, Congressman Gephardt, Congressman Skelton, friends from Jackson County, Independence, Kansas City:*

It's really fine for me to be in the home of Bess and Harry Truman, the Kansas City Royals, and George Brett.

How many of you think Harry Truman was a great President? [*Applause*] How many of you think the Royals are going all the way? [*Applause*] How many of you think George Brett's going to bat .400 this year? [*Applause*] I'm just as eager to see him do it as you are. He and I have a quiet arrangement that we made as I stepped off Air Force One at the airport a few minutes ago. He's not going to run for President this year—[*laughter*]—and I have promised not to support anybody against him for President in the future, okay? [*Laughter*]

Immediately before I came here I stopped by a famous place in our Nation to visit with Bess Truman, and she asked me as I come to the Truman School to express her love to all of you, her appreciation for your many kindnesses. And I'm particularly grateful that this wonderful school was named by the people in Independence not just for Harry Truman but for Bess and the Truman family. It's a pleasure for me to be here in one of the finest schools with one of the finest names in the United States of America.

And I'm also glad to be here with a fine and decent man, a friend of mine, a tireless worker for our Nation, Tom Eagleton, one of the greatest Senators I've ever known. As you may know, next year Tom Eagleton will become the chairman of the extremely important Government Operations Committee in the Senate. He'll be the first Missourian since Harry Truman to become chairman of a major committee.

President Harry S. Truman

I'm here today to answer your questions, not to give a long speech. But before we get started I want to say just a few things about Harry Truman, because as President I have a unique perspective of him, what he was, and what he meant to our country.

He's been an inspiration to a lot of Americans, but especially to Presidents. Once he was asked by a student if he would classify himself as one of the great Presidents of our Nation. He said he wasn't one of the great Presidents, but he had a good time trying to be one. [*Laughter*] I agree with almost everything Harry Truman said. That's one thing with which I disagree. He was indeed one of

our great Presidents, and more and more people, particularly since he went out of office, are beginning to agree that of the very few among the 39 in total, he was one of the top leaders of our Nation, in the same class as Washington and Lincoln and Jefferson in my opinion.

Today our Nation faces some very difficult questions, challenges, opportunities. They were difficult when he was President; different, but difficult. And what's important to me is not the nature of the times when Truman served as President, but the nature of the man when he served for President. He set a tough standard for all those who've come after him to serve in the White House. Fortunately, that standard is a very fine example of what a President ought to be.

And as he had a good time trying to be a great President, so I've had a good time trying to be a President like Harry Truman. He had common sense; he was able to see a problem for what it was. He had the honesty not to mislead the American people at times when the truth hurt and when the truth was not popular. He did what he thought was right. No matter what anyone said he had to make a lot of hard decisions, and in the process quite often his public opinion poll ratings went down. But when he was criticized he responded, and I'll quote from him: "Any President who makes decisions on the basis of public opinion polls is not worthy to hold the office."

Harry Truman was a common man, some say an uncommon man, who spoke up for the common men and women of this country. He understood us, he spoke for us, and he said that it was important for a President to stand up against the lobbyists and against the special interests who sometimes seemed to fill the city of Washington, D.C. He said, quite often you had to be well-organized or very rich to have a lobbyist in Washington. But the President, he says, has to be the lobbyist for the people.

He was a courageous champion of social justice and fair play. His daughter, Margaret, wrote about an incident that took place in 1924, the year she was born, the year I was born. Her father was running for reelection as a county judge. And some members of the Ku Klux Klan threatened his life. Judge Truman astonished the Klansmen by going into one of their meetings. He marched right up on the stage and called them a bunch of "cheap, un-American fakers." That was dangerous and it was a lot more difficult to do in 1924 than it is in 1980.

He lost the election that year because he let the people know where he stood, but he won a lot of elections after that— because he let the people know where he stood. And what counted most, in 1948, although he didn't have much of a chance to win, he told the people the truth and he got his message across to the American people and he won the election. And I can't deny that that's one reason I wanted to talk to Ms. Bess Truman this morning—to find out some of his secrets.

When I have to make a tough decision now, which is often in the Oval Office, I think about the tough decisions he had to make. And when I take a step that's not very popular, I think of the unpopularity that Harry Truman had to suffer before he was finally vindicated. When I'm criticized in the media, I think about the much more severe criticism that he had to bear, and when I look at the public opinion polls, I remember how bad they were for him in 1948.

When I give a speech to a group like this, I recall that Harry Truman said that he was not a great orator, but he did know how to talk with people. And he also said, "I know of no better way of communicating with the people of this Nation in the shortest period of time than a question-and-answer method." I agree with President Harry Truman.

Now let's have the first question.

QUESTIONS

PRESIDENT'S PERSONAL FAITH

Q. My dear Mr. President, it is a great pleasure to meet you face to face——

THE PRESIDENT. That's a wonderful question. Thank you very much. [*Laughter*]

Q. I just want you to know that my husband, Bill, and I are wholehearted supporters of yours and we are praying for you all the time.

THE PRESIDENT. Thank you very much.

Q. Here's my question. We know that you are a born-again Christian. Do you feel that your spiritual life has suffered because of the incredible pressures of your job?

THE PRESIDENT. No. I believe very deeply as a Baptist and a Christian that there ought to be a proper separation of the church and the state, and I've never let my beliefs interfere in my administration of the duties as President. But I've never found any incompatibility. I pray more than I did when I was not President, because the burdens on my shoulders are much greater than they were when I was a Governor or when I didn't hold public office.

This Nation is one that's been acknowledged by our Founding Fathers since the first days of the idea to be founded under God. "In God We Trust" is on our coins. It's not a bad thing for Americans to believe deeply in God, but the fact is that the Constitution gives us a right to worship God or to worship as we choose. And the

Congress cannot pass any law respecting the establishment of religion.

But my own personal faith and my personal belief is stronger now than it's ever been before. I pray more than I did, and I don't find any incompatibility between being a Christian, on the one hand, and being President of this country, on the other.

EMPLOYMENT

Q. Mr. President, welcome to Independence.

THE PRESIDENT. Thank you. Tell me what your name is.

Q. I'm Don Pennel.

THE PRESIDENT. Don, thank you.

Q. What level of unemployment do you feel is healthy for our economy, and what plans do you have to reach this level of unemployment?

THE PRESIDENT. What I have as a goal is that every able-bodied person in our Nation would have a job available to them. Now the unemployment rate is between 7 and 8 percent, a little bit under 8 percent. For the last 6 weeks we've had a decrease in the unemployment compensation claims filed by Americans, and we've had a chance to go through a very serious ordeal where the price of oil on a nationwide, worldwide basis increased 120 percent just since the beginning of 1979. This has created unemployment and high inflation all over the world.

One of the proudest things of my own administration so far has been that in the first 3 years I was President, in spite of these shocks to the economic system of the world, we increased the net numbers of jobs in this country by more than 8 million. This is the biggest and fastest increase in employment that our Nation has ever experienced or any nation in the world has ever had, even in time of war.

At the same time, as people got new jobs, a lot of their discouraged neighbors, like young teenagers, saw "My neighbor got a job, now put my name on the job rolls." So, we've had a great increase in the number of people seeking jobs. I think this is very healthy, but I would like to continue my effort to get the unemployment rate down so that every able-bodied American who wants a job can find one.

I might say one other thing. We cannot abandon the struggle against inflation. It's a temptation, as you well know, in a Presidential election year, to offer people something for nothing, enormous tax decreases, gifts to people of maybe a few dollars on their income tax payment, but that would, in effect, mean that inflation in the future was going to rob back more than they got with a massive tax reduction in an election year.

So, what I've planned for our Nation is a steady growth in economic recovery, carefully targeted programs to create jobs, not in government jobs or handout jobs or temporary jobs, but in permanent jobs, and to bring the unemployment rate down that way. So, we'll continue to work in that respect, putting our basic steel industry, our automobile industry, back on its feet, competitive with any foreign imports, and I believe that's the best way to approach it. We'll continue to work until the unemployment rate goes down to meet the goal that I described to you.

Thank you very much, Don.

THE MIDDLE EAST

Q. Hello. As a host sister to an Egyptian student who's here in the local area studying year-long, I would like to ask, are there any indications of change in America's policy with Egypt and the Middle East in the near future?

THE PRESIDENT. We will not change our policy in the Middle East anytime in the foreseeable future.

It's easy for us to get discouraged about the faltering, sometimes excessive delays in the peace process that was initiated at Camp David exactly 2 years ago. Before we went there, with myself and Prime Minister Begin and President Sadat, nobody thought we'd be successful. I had serious doubts, and of course, I think Begin and Sadat had even more serious doubts that we could bring peace between two nations whose whole existence the last 30 years had been based on the prospective war and sometimes intense hatred among their people. In 30 years at that time four different wars had broken out between Israel and Egypt.

We were successful at Camp David. There is now a peace treaty between Egypt and Israel, and we're working with great determination to continue that process and to bring a comprehensive peace to the Middle East with security for Israel and with the realization of the legitimate aims of the Palestinian people. This is something that Begin, Sadat, and I have all agreed to do.

We've had some setbacks lately. The peace process is still alive. President Sadat has called for another summit conference sometime later on this year. I'm sure that when the invitations are extended for that summit conference that Prime Minister Begin would also respond affirmatively. I have just sent, last Friday night, Sol Linowitz, my chief negotiator, back to see Prime Minister Begin. So far, tomorrow he'll go to Egypt to talk to President Sadat. When he comes back we'll have a clearer picture of what are the prospects for immediate progress.

But I think it would be a mistake for the American people to give up hope and to be discouraged because of transient obstacles that are foreseeable. I think if you talk to President Sadat or Prime Minister Begin, you would find that they are very gratified at what's taken place so far. And when I see Egyptian Ambassadors in Tel Aviv and Israeli Ambassadors in Cairo, when I see the borders open, airplane flights now back and forth between Alexandria and Tel Aviv and Jerusalem and Cairo, tourists going back and forth, it really thrills my heart.

In the last week there have been a series of top Israeli officials who have been over to visit Sadat. Prime Minister Begin has not visited with him lately. But the peace prospect is still alive, and this is an important thing, not only for Israel, Egypt, Jordan, Syria, and Lebanon, but it's also extremely important for our country.

I'm glad that our Nation is strong; I'm glad that for the last 4 years we have been at peace. I pray God that when I go out of office—hopefully the end of the next 4 years—we will have been at peace for 8 years. And I'm also proud that peace in the Middle East has brought our own Nation additional security. Our policy with the Middle East has not changed and is not going to change.

THE NATION'S ECONOMY

Q. Mr. President, we're very pleased and honored to have you here in Independence.

Most economic indicators point toward a serious decline in national productivity. My question is two-fold: Can the administration affect this downward spiral, and if so, what solutions do you, as President, propose? Thank you.

THE PRESIDENT. Last month's economic indicators, as you know, showed the greatest improvement in the history of the economic indicator, and also last month, for the first time in 13 years, showed that the inflation rate was zero. I don't expect that extremely good month to continue in the future. It would be hoping for too much.

I see in our own Nation the same kind of challenge in the 1980's that we faced in the 1930's, when Roosevelt, with the New Deal, followed by President Truman, continuing those programs, put our Nation back on its economic feet.

We have for too long had the American workers expected to constantly increase their productivity with an industrial plant and with machinery that was not constantly modernized. After World War II, because of the Marshall plan which was initiated by President Truman, the nations that we had defeated in the war had nothing to start with, but they built all new plants—Japan and Germany are the two best examples of that. It's now time for us to rebuild the American industrial machinery when it's needed. Steel is one example; automobiles is another but different example.

We have now completed in the first 3 years of my own term a comprehensive energy policy to take cognizance of and take advantage of the most profound economic challenge to the world, that is, an enormous increase in the price of oil. We've got to do two things—hold down American waste of energy, by having strong conservation programs, and secondly, produce more energy in our own country.

We're making good progress. We have now cut back oil imports by 20 percent or more this year compared to the first year I was in office. Every day like today, we import 1½ million barrels of oil less than we did in 1977—very good progress.

On that new base, we are now ready to move forward to deal with the energy question and to revitalize American industry simultaneously. The new energy policy financed by the windfall profits tax on the unearned profits of the oil companies will give us a better investment program than we had with the Interstate Highway System, the space program, and the Marshall plan all combined.

This can give us an exciting, dynamic, growing chance in America to take advantage of our natural resources and also to take advantage of our human resources and our ingenuity and our good education system and our free enterprise system to move forward. So, I think now is the time to take advantage of these opportunities.

This past week I outlined to the Nation my proposals to move our Nation forward, which would mean, in effect, that business would be encouraged to put investments in new plants, private and public money would be used, productivity would be greatly improved for American workers—and I might add parenthetically something that people don't know, the highest productivity in the world among workers is right here in the United States. We are still far more productive, American workers on the average, than any other nation. The problem is that we haven't been growing as fast in productivity lately.

So, with that combination of tax incentives, narrowly targeted programs to help communities make those changes, we can expect a much brighter future than we have had in the past.

Two things that you ought to remember. One is we talk about the great strategic advantage of oil in Saudi Arabia. We have a much greater strategic advantage in the soil of the United States. And secondly, we think that the OPEC nations have all the reserves of energy. All the Arab countries combined have about 6 percent of the world's energy reserves, 6 percent. The United States has 24 percent. So, we need to change our style of living for the better, invest in the future, and I believe we'll have a better life with higher productivity for Americans in the years ahead.

VIEWS ON THE PRESIDENCY

Q. Mr. President?

THE PRESIDENT. Yes.

Q. Welcome to the home of a great President.

THE PRESIDENT. I'm glad to be here.

Q. And with the thoughts that you put forward here today I would like for you to answer one question.

THE PRESIDENT. All right.

Q. Why in the hell could Reagan, do you think Reagan would want to be President, and why do you think you want your job? [*Laughter*]

THE PRESIDENT. I can't speak for Governor Reagan. But I will say that although the Presidency is the most difficult job, maybe, on Earth, because it's complex, complicated, and all the hard decisions come to the Oval Office to be made, at the same time it's one of the most exciting and gratifying jobs on Earth, because the President can be kind of a spokesman for and a representative of the 240 million people who live in the greatest Nation on Earth.

And I remember when Harry Truman learned that Franklin Roosevelt was dead. He said he felt as though the Moon and the Sun and all the stars had fallen on him. I don't believe that anyone is completely qualified to be President, certainly not if you try to stand alone. But with prayer, with faith, with a knowledge of our Nation, with support from people like you who are unselfish and patriotic, with the democratic system where the President is not alone, but who represents the will and the strength and the courage and the commitment and the idealism and the hope of 240 million strong and free people, it makes the job a lot easier.

Our country does face problems, and we do face difficulties, and we do make mistakes on occasion. But in spite of all that, the President still leads the greatest nation on Earth. This is proven by the fact that when people are displaced from their own homes or when they want to find freedom or find better opportunity, or when they want to worship in their own way or join a dynamic, exciting prospect for the future, where do they want to come? They want to come to the United States. And you don't see any boats lined up at Key West getting filled up with Americans trying to escape to Cuba, right? And they didn't build the Berlin Wall to keep you from going into Communist Germany. So, people want freedom, they want democracy, they want an opportunity in life.

I don't have any doubt that as the people assess myself, with good experience and a proven record, representing the Democratic Party, having kept our Nation at peace, having helped to unite our country, compared to Governor Reagan and what he has to offer and what the Republicans have to offer, that the people will make the right decision.

This year will be the sharpest difference in the voters' choice that I remember in my lifetime that the Americans have had to make. Reagan is different from me in almost every basic element of commitment and experience and promise to the American people, and the Republican Party now is sharply different from what the Democratic Party is. And I might add parenthetically that the Republican Party now is sharply different under Reagan from what it was under Gerald Ford and Presidents all the way back to Eisenhower.

I believe in peace, I believe in arms control, I believe in controlling nuclear weapons, I believe in the rights of working people of this country, I believe in looking forward and not backward. I don't believe the Nation ought to be divided one region from another. In all these respects Governor Reagan is different from me, and I have confidence that when November 4 comes that the people will make the right decision as they did in November of 1948.

HYDROGEN ENERGY

Q. Mr. President, I'd like to direct a question towards the energy program. Recently a hydrogen firm has located here in Independence, and I want to know if you think that hydrogen energy is a viable alternative and what role does it have in the energy program.

THE PRESIDENT. Yes I do. In my opinion our Nation is just approaching the threshold of not only wonderful job opportunities that will come from the massive energy commitment that our Nation's making, but it's also the threshold of wonderful, scientific and technological discoveries. Obviously, hydrogen itself and the products that can be produced from it as a fuel are one of those kinds of opportunities that we need to explore further. It would be a serious mistake for us to discount the opportunities that exist in hydrogen or the other fuels that we're presently exploring.

We have now an opportunity not only to turn to hydrogen, as well as methanol derived from growing crops, liquid fuels and gaseous fuels from shale and from coal, but also solar power to a major degree. But I think that now with the new energy program intact, which these Members of the Congress have helped to initiate, and with masssive financial resources

that can be used primarily by the private sector but also by the public sector that we've got vast areas of scientific and technological job opportunities to explore. Hydrogen is obviously one of those that holds great promise.

AUTOMOBILE INDUSTRY

Q. Mr. President, my name is Karen Garrison, and I'm a teacher here at Truman High School, and I have the opportunity to work with young debaters. And I feel like the debaters are a vital part of America's future. And our topic this year is on consumer product safety. This question is on that topic and in behalf of my debaters.

According to a Department of Transportation ruling, all cars must be equipped with passive passenger restraints by 1983. How will this ruling be enforced on foreign car imports, and would this be a possible way of lowering our high import level?

THE PRESIDENT. I believe in debates too, and I'm looking forward to a chance to debate Governor Reagan. We've already accepted three invitations, and I'm looking forward to a chance to carry that commitment that you described on.

The passive restraints basically apply to seatbelts that are automatically in place when the door is closed and also with the air bags, depending upon the choice of the automobile manufacturers and also the purchasers of those cars. Any requirements for safety that fall upon the American manufactured cars that are sold here apply in an equally stringent way to imports that are sold in the American market.

I think you all noticed in the news a couple of weeks ago—it was on television quite frequently—the tests of the American small cars compared to the foreign small cars as it related to the safety of the person involved in a head-on collision. The American small cars, equally efficient and equally clean in their operation, were much safer in the tests that I saw described on television. So, we will require with equal stringency the same safety equipment on imports as we require on the American cars themselves.

I would like to add that I'm very proud of the transition that is now taking place in the automobile industry of our country. We have been caught in the last few months with a very quick change in the buying preferences of American consumers who wanted the small and efficient automobiles because of the rapid increase of worldwide oil prices.

The Germans, the Japanese, and other foreign manufacturers have always had gasoline prices in the neighborhood of $2 to $2.50 a gallon, while we were enjoying gasoline much cheaper than that, less than a dollar a gallon. They had to build those small cars in their own countries because of that, so they had a headstart on American manufacturers. But as you know, Chrysler, Ford, General Motors and others, American Motors, are all shifting very quickly to the small and efficient cars that will permanently be the preference of American consumers, and I have no doubt that we'll see a quick rebuilding of the American automobile industry and a quick transfer by the American consumers of their preferences toward American produced cars.

But we'll keep the same standards on the foreign cars as we require on American cars, making them constantly more efficient, cleaner burning to save our air quality, and also more safe. All three of these things can be done, they are being done on foreign and domestic cars as well.

REPUBLIC OF KOREA

Q. Mr. President, I'd like to ask you a question in the area of foreign policy. What improvements in Korea do you expect from the new Korean President, President Chun Doo Hwan?

THE PRESIDENT. We have enjoyed historically a very close relationship with the Republic of Korea. Ever since the war there, when President Truman, working with the United Nations, went in to preserve the freedom of the South Korean people, we've enjoyed that good relationship.

There have been ups and downs in the relationship as there have been between ourselves and all our allies. We believe that the Government of Korea should move faster for complete freedom of the people, on expression to the news media, to eliminate any imprisonment of political opponents by the incumbent leaders, and should move more rapidly toward complete democracy in their form of government than the Koreans so far have been able to do.

Our views are clear. They are well known by new President Chun and were known by President Park, with whom I met. We hope that the present commitments of the Korean leaders to have a new constitution which will move Korea toward more freedom of political expression and also more democracy will come true.

We'll continue to use our influence to bring about this desired goal, which I believe is the goal of most citizens of Korea as well, and in the meantime we will maintain our close relationships with the people of Korea and our shared security arrangements, which help to stabilize the whole northern part of the Asian Continent on the eastern coast.

Thank you very much for a good question.

PROGRAMS IN SECOND TERM

Q. I'm Dorothy Stoeger of Platte County. Mr. President, is there any one thing that you would like to achieve during your second term that you were not able to accomplish during your first?

THE PRESIDENT. Yes. There are several.

The most important thing to me or to any President is to keep our Nation strong and secure and at peace. So far—and I thank God for it—I've been able to do that, and that's my highest hope. There are some needs, however, that have not yet had that degree of success.

One is, I want to continue the peace process in the Middle East and bring it to a firm conclusion. Secondly, I want to set the tone for the rest of this century by revitalizing American industry and accommodating the inevitable change that has been forced on the world by the energy problems brought about by OPEC.

So far, this has been kind of a negative development in the minds of Americans. It's caused us a little bit of concern, and we've been a little too doubtful about the future. I see it, after having been deeply involved in it now for more than 3 years, not as a problem for Americans to face, that causes us trepidation and concern, but as a wonderful opportunity to do some things in American industry that we should have done a long time ago: to modernize our steel industry; to retool our automobile industry; to provide new opportunities for farmers, for instance, to develop their land, to have better conservation practices, to be more productive, to have more storage on farms, and to produce crops at a much lower cost because they save energy in different cultural practices. So, the opportunities for

us to move forward and take advantage of the energy problem are very fine.

I want to see a comprehensive nationwide health program for Americans with the emphasis on prevention of disease. And I also want to see our welfare system reformed to make sure that every ablebodied American who wants to work is encouraged to work. That's important to me. And finally, not to make too long an answer, I want to continue our peaceful relationships with other nations on Earth.

One of the things that I have done that history might see as most significant is opening up full diplomatic relationships with the People's Republic of China, with a fourth of the people on Earth, and that constant probing for better ways to get along with people of other nations is important to me. I would like to see our relationships with the Soviet Union improved, but I will not base that improvement on the invasion by the Soviet Union of Afghanistan and their ignoring of the principle of human rights. So, I would like to see our commitment to human rights continued as we continue peace.

Those are a few things that come to mind immediately. Some have been done fairly well. Some we still have a long way to go.

STRATEGIC ARMS LIMITATION

Q. Mr. President, welcome to Missouri.

THE PRESIDENT. I feel welcome.

Q. My question is pertaining to the SALT II treaty. When do you think this treaty will be ratified?

THE PRESIDENT. In my opinion, the SALT II treaty is very good for the United States of America. It puts balanced limits on the nuclear weaponry of ourselves and the Soviet Union. It would result, when implemented by the Senate through ratification, in a 10-percent cut in the number of missiles that the Soviet Union presently has. It would not cut our nuclear arsenal at all. It would prevent the development of future missiles and future weapons that might destabilize the international relationship and cause some movements toward a nuclear war.

The SALT II treaty also puts stringent limits on what the Soviets can do secretly. It requires them to develop and to test any permitted nuclear weapons so that we can observe and monitor what the Soviets do. If we don't have a SALT treaty they can act in secret.

So, these are the reasons why the SALT II treaty ought to be implemented. Another very important reason is that going into SALT III with much greater reductions in nuclear weapons, which would be to our advantage as well as to that of all nations on Earth, is pretty well dependent on how well we do with SALT II.

When we see positive movement by the Soviets to withdraw their occupying troops from Afghanistan—at that point, I believe the Senate will then be ready to consider again the ratification of SALT II. When that time comes I'll be devoting my full time, working with Tom Eagleton, and with other Members of the Senate, to get SALT II treaty ratified, because it's best for our country and it's best for the entire world.

TAX RATES FOR MARRIED COUPLES

Q. Mr. President, I would like to have you explain your recent proposal to ease the marriage penalty tax and whether or not you think this would have an opportunity of passing through Congress.

THE PRESIDENT. All right. To me the stability of American families is crucial to the survival and the improvement of American society in general. Now we have a situation in our tax laws so that if a man and woman, both are employed—maybe one making a lot of money, the other one not making much money—and they live together as husband and wife, they pay a much higher income tax bill than if they live together and are not married. This is not right.

And so what we are asking the Congress to do—and I hope they'll start on it immediately after January 1—is to remove that penalty that's presently imposed against married couples. It would let the partner who has the lowest income get a credit for part of that income so that there would not be any more a penalty because the couple is married. It would move toward an equal opportunity for them to pay the same kind of income tax that they would pay if they were not married, whether or not they were living together.

So, this is something, in my opinion, that's long overdue. It will not mean that there would be an additional penalty placed on people who are single and who are not married, but it would just remove an inequitable circumstance in the income tax laws that have been there for a long time.

SPACE PROGRAM

Q. I want to know if you're going to send any more rockets into outer space?

THE PRESIDENT. Yes. The answer is yes. It's extremely important to us to have a good space program.

Our next major move, as you know, is a space shuttle, where we can send up a space rocket, you might say, that can travel around and around the world a long time with people in it and with valuable cargoes in it, with telescopes in it to look into outer space further. And then we can bring that same thing that looks like a airplane back home, reload it, and fire it again. It'll be a wonderful new step for us.

In addition to that we will have explorations going beyond the Earth's atmosphere, past the Sun, out among the planets and even further, to take close looks at them and also to assess what is taking place in radio waves, to learn more about the universe and therefore about us. As you know, we've had very good luck with this, not only in landing a man on the Moon, and then followed by other Americans on the Moon, but also in taking a very close look at some of the planets further out than the Earth that we never had seen well before.

But we'll continue a good space program, the space shuttle in our own orbit around the Earth and exploration far beyond the Earth and the planets, even out among the stars eventually. So, the answer is yes.

That's a good question. What's your name?

Q. J. B.

THE PRESIDENT. J. B. what?

Q. Martin.

THE PRESIDENT. I'm glad to meet you, J. B. Martin. Thanks a lot.

PRAYER IN SCHOOLS

Q. We want to welcome you to Independence, Missouri, Mr. President. And my name is Abdul Muamin Khalifah, and I'm a member of that great religious movement here in America, the American Muslim Mission, led by a great leader, Imam Warith Deen Muhammad. And I'd like to say before I get into my question that myself, as all of America, we're praying for our safe return of our hostages——

THE PRESIDENT. Yes.

Q. ——and I'm sure that Allah willingly will return, and I pray constantly

that you will win the reelection, because I believe that Mr. Reagan has an unhealthy fixation on a time and an era gone by.

My question is that I hope that you would use the powers of your office to help restore prayer or some form of prayer back in our American schools, because I find it sort of ironic or almost hypocritical to where our children can't say prayer in our public schools, but we teach them to say grace when they eat, to pray before they go to bed, and then when our children rise from grade school and ascend to the highest office in our land, which is the President, and at your Inauguration, then we invoke the blessings of God, of Allah, through prayer. And so, I know you just stated that the Congress can't do anything or pass any legislation about religion, but if you would just relook that issue over.

Thank you.

THE PRESIDENT. Thank you very much. Let me respond to your question.

I think there is a place for prayer in the home, in the Oval Office, and in school. I don't believe that our Government should ever interfere in the right of an American citizen to worship and to worship as they see fit.

I believe that there ought to be a place and a time in school for voluntary prayer. The thing that I'm against, as President— and as a Baptist, coincidentally—is the Government telling people they have to worship at a certain time and in a certain way. To me that violates the constitutional separation of church and state. I would not want the Government to tell my children that they would have to worship in a Muslim way, and you would not want the Government to tell your children that they would have to worship just like a Southern Baptist.

But as long as the Government stays out of it and permits people to worship as we see fit, including in the schools, that's what I want. But I am not in favor of the Government telling a child, "You've got to worship a certain god in a certain way in the classroom." That's where I draw the line.

DEFENSE SPENDING

Q. Mr. President?

THE PRESIDENT. Yes, sir?

Q. My name is Henry Stoever. I approve of your stances on protecting human rights, boycotting the Olympics, the grain embargo, mediating at Camp David between Egypt and Israel, and defending civil rights. I favor drastic cuts in defense spending. Presently defense spending is at an alltime high. I believe that you have said that you are willing to increase defense spending.

THE PRESIDENT. Yes.

Q. I think that we can possibly learn a lesson from the Polish strikers, who won major concessions without the intervention of a Western military power, without guns or armed conflict. Their nonviolent action paralyzed their country, the military, and I believe that their courage, ethics, religious convictions, and determination would have made Mahatma Gandhi or Martin Luther King proud of their actions.

Now, my question to you is, how do you differ from Mr. Reagan on defense spending? It seems both of you want to increase it.

THE PRESIDENT. Good. As I said earlier, above all other responsibilities of a President, the security of our Nation comes first. And only if our Nation is strong can we maintain peace. The best soldier that our Nation has is one who does not have to die in battle, and the best weapon that a nation can have is one that is never fired to kill others. But the fact that our Nation is strong and the fact that other nations know that we are going to stay strong, in my judgment, is the best thing to preserve peace for our Nation and for other countries around the world who look to us for leadership and who look to us to protect their basic freedoms, either directly or indirectly.

We now spend roughly 5 percent of our gross national product on defense. It's about the lowest level that we've ever experienced in modern times. I believe that that's a good investment. We also have encouraged our allies in Europe, also in Japan, New Zealand, Australia, Korea, at least to invest enough of their national product to protect their own countries and to protect the world from blackmail or forcible control over them by Communists or other nations who have a much heavier investment in defense.

I'm determined that our Nation will never be second to any, certainly the Soviet Union, in defense capability. As long as the Soviets know that, then they will not be tempted to commit suicide for themselves by attacking the United States of America. And I believe that most Americans believe that we've got to have a calm, steady, determined, unwavering commitment to maintaining strong defense forces.

At the same time I'm committed to the negotiation for balanced reductions in the expenditure for nuclear weapons, and I pursued that in an aggressive way. There lies one of the sharpest possible differences between myself and Governor Reagan. President Eisenhower, Truman, and all the Presidents who have served since them have been deeply committed to the principle of controlling nuclear weapons and not launching a nuclear arms race against the Soviet Union which no one could win. Ronald Reagan is the first one to depart from that commitment.

He has announced that if he's elected

President, that he will initiate a massive nuclear arms race against the Soviet Union. This would mean that if he did that, then there would be no reason for the United States and the Soviet Union to try to negotiate an arms control treaty.

I consider this one of the most serious threats to the safety and the security and the peace of our Nation and the world that is being dramatized in this 1980 election. And therein lies the major difference. I think we ought to have a predictable, steady, slow but determined growth in defense capability right on up for the next 5 years—and that's what I intend to maintain. But at the same time, searching for peace and using our military strength, not only to keep our Nation secure but to keep us out of war, not in a war.

Do you have a followup?

Q. Mr. President, we have limited resources, and we have to make a decision whether we want to rebuild the inner cities, revitalize American industry—and it appears that you're going to spend dollar per dollar the amount that Ronald Reagan will spend on defense. Is that correct?

THE PRESIDENT. No. I don't know what his defense figures are. All of the proposals that I have made for defense spending, not only this year and in 1981 but all the way through 1985, have now been made public in my proposals to the Congress. That's what I intend to do.

DEPARTMENT OF ENERGY

Q. Hello, Mr. President. My name is Scott Berry, and I welcome you to the Independence area and Kansas City, Missouri, area.

THE PRESIDENT. Thank you, Scott.

Q. It's been said the United States spends 30 percent more energy than any other country in the world, and it's also been said of independent candidate John Anderson—which I'm a supporter for—that he's gone farther on a little bit of innovative thinking than any other candidate. You're an engineer yourself and have taken courses in nuclear energy. And Mr. Anderson has been—14 years sat on the board of the Nuclear Regulatory Commission. And have you heard of Dr. Edward Teller? I'd like to quote from him.

He says in a true energy crash the only help that can come from energy conservation—we will have to cut our energy consumption in half. And my question is, what does the Department of Energy do, whose annual budget is greater in the after-tax profits of all major oil companies combined?

THE PRESIDENT. Well, what we've done so far is to try to change the attitude of American people, compared to what it was 3 years ago or even a year ago, to convince not only Americans but the rest of the world that we have to conserve energy and not waste it any longer, and secondly, produce more energy ourselves.

As you know, the Congress was quite reluctant to put into effect the energy proposals that I made to it in April of 1977. It's taken almost 3 years to get it done. But the results have been dramatic already.

I mentioned a little earlier this morning that we have had a 20-percent reduction this year in oil imports, compared to when I became President, first year, and also that we've cut oil purchases from overseas by 1½ million barrels every day. That's part of it. The other part is that we now have more exploration going on for both new oil wells and new gas wells in the United States than we've had for the last 25 years. So, if we do two things—produce more American energy, which gives American technology, American jobs, American innovation a way to benefit Americans' lives; at the same time conserve energy—that's the best combination. That's the purpose of the Department of Energy.

The Department of Energy also has other responsibilities. Part of the responsibility for developing nuclear power and fusion power, solar power, utilizing coal, the development of ways to export more coal, the shift toward the use of more hydroelectric power, in making it more efficient, the development of new kinds of electric motors and the use of shale oil— all those responsibilities and many others come under the aegis of the Department of Energy.

Most of the budget of the Department, by the way, is used to be invested in a better life for Americans. That not only applies to the development of new kinds of energy, which I've outlined, but also the weatherization of private homes and the making of public buildings more efficient. And of course the Department of Energy works very closely with the Department of Transportation to make sure that automobiles and buses, trains, and other parts of our transportation system are more efficient as well.

So, those are some of the things the Department does. We've made good progress in the last 3 years, and I don't have any doubt that if we elect the right President, we'll make even more progress in the future.

I have time for one more question, and I'd be glad to hear from you.

PALESTINIAN SELF-DETERMINATION

Q. Okay. My name is Mohammed Madani. I'm from Jordan, and I'm a student here. Mr. President, you are the only American President so far who mentioned about the Palestinian people homeland, they should have——

THE PRESIDENT. Yes.

Q. So, my question is, American Government has 99 percent of the Palestinian problem solution in its hand, so why until now are you still ignoring the Palestinian people rights and you don't solve their problem? As you can see, President Sadat gave Israel a full chance to do justice, but Israel refused. And remember, Mr. President, if the Palestinian people lost faith in the past American Government, and they still have faith in you.

Thank you.

THE PRESIDENT. Thank you very much. Let me try to answer your question very briefly.

I don't know if you've had a chance to read the text of the Camp David accords. It's only a few pages, and if you'll give one of my aides here your name and address we'll send you a copy of it. It's a very interesting document, which points out that Prime Minister Begin, speaking for Israel, and President Sadat, speaking for Egypt, and myself committed ourselves to the resolving of the Palestinian issue in all its aspects, and it gives the Palestinian people—the Israelis say "Palestinian Arab people"—a voice in the determination of their own future.

For a long time, certainly since—in the last two or three decades we have had practically no progress made toward bringing peace between Israel and her neighbors nor recognizing the problem with the refugees and the Palestinians themselves. I don't claim that we've done enough yet, but we have laid a groundwork now, a basis for future progress. There is no reason for the Palestinian people to deny the good will that President Sadat has expressed in the Camp David accords and that I have expressed with my signature on the Camp David accords. The basic problem is still how to deal with the security of Israel being preserved and the peace between Israel and her neighbors, and the resolution of the Palestinian question in all its complicated aspects and the giving of the Palestinian people a voice in the determination of their own future. That is a complicated series of questions to resolve, but the fact is that for the first time in the history of the Mideast, Israel, Egypt, and the United States are committed to doing exactly what I've just outlined to you so briefly.

We cannot forget the Palestinian issue. It's foremost in the minds of the leaders of Israel and Egypt and the United States, along with the security of Israel, the unity of the city of Jerusalem, free access to the city of Jerusalem for the worship by all people. I hope that when the history books are written about my own administration, that a small paragraph at least will say that President Jimmy Carter was able to contribute to a comprehensive peace in the Middle East when Israel stayed secure, when Jerusalem was honored by those of all faiths, and the Palestinian people had a voice in the determination of their own future and the issue was solved in all its aspects. That's what I'm going to work for continuously.

Let me say in closing just a brief remark. I know that you were invited to come here not because you were supporters of mine but you came on a first come, first served basis, and I know there are supporters here of all the candidates who are running for President this year. I would like before I leave, though, to ask you for your understanding and your support, and I'd like to let you know again how crucial to our Nation the decision will be that you'll make this year. Nothing could be more important. And I would like to close by quoting from a favorite politician of mine, who's been mentioned before today, and that's Harry Truman. He said, "It's not the hand that signs the laws that holds the destiny of America.

It's the hand that casts the ballot on election day."

Thank you very much.

NOTE: The President spoke at 10:38 a.m. in the Truman High School gymnasium.

Following the meeting, the President visited the Harry S. Truman Library and the gravesite of the former President.

United States-Cook Islands Maritime Boundary Treaty

Message to the Senate Transmitting the Treaty. September 2, 1980

To the Senate of the United States:

I transmit herewith, for the advice and consent of the Senate, the Treaty between the United States of America and the Cook Islands on Friendship and Delimitation of the Maritime Boundary between the United States of America and the Cook Islands. Also transmitted for the information of the Senate is the report of the Department of State with respect to the Convention.

This treaty is necessary to delimit the continental shelf and overlapping claims of jurisdiction resulting from the establishment of a 200 nautical mile fishery conservation zone off the coasts of American Samoa in accordance with the Fishery Conservation and Management Act of 1976, and the establishment of a 200 nautical mile zone by the Cook Islands.

In this connection, the status of four islands has also been resolved.

The treaty satisfies the interest of the people of the Cook Islands that their claim to sovereignty over these four islands, inhabited by citizens of the Cook Islands and represented in the legislative and administrative branches of the Cook Islands Government, will not be encumbered by a conflicting and largely unsupported claim by the United States. The

1625

treaty meets the United States interest in securing a maritime boundary in accordance with equitable principles. It furthers United States foreign policy interests in the area by establishing a basis for friendly relations with the Cook Islands and by furthering our interest in a peaceful, secure, and stable South Pacific.

I am transmitting for the information of the Senate a diplomatic note from the Government of New Zealand confirming that the Cook Islands has the competence to enter into this treaty and that New Zealand has no objection to its doing so and a separate exchange of letters between the United States and the Cook Islands, signed on June 11, 1980, setting forth the understanding of each side that United States flag fishing vessels and foreign vessels supplying the canneries in American Samoa will not be barred on a discriminatory basis from seeking licenses to fish in the Cook Islands' 200 mile zone.

I recommend that the Senate give early consideration to the treaty and give its advice and consent to ratification.

JIMMY CARTER

The White House,
   September 2, 1980.

Amendments to the Manual for Courts-Martial, United States, 1969 (Revised Edition)

Executive Order 12233.   September 1, 1980

By the authority vested in me as President of the United States of America by Chapter 47 of Title 10 of the United States Code (the Uniform Code of Military Justice), and in order to make some clarifying and technical amendments to the Manual for Courts-Martial, United States, 1969 (Revised edition), prescribed

by Executive Order No. 11476, as amended by Executive Order No. 11835, Executive Order No. 12018, and Executive Order No. 12198, it is hereby ordered that Executive Order No. 12198 is amended as follows:

1-101. Rule 506(j) in the Table of Contents to the Military Rules of Evidence is amended by deleting "claim or privilege" and substituting therefor "claim of privilege" in the first line.

1-102. Rule 302 of the Military Rules of Evidence is amended by changing paragraph (b)(2) to read as follows:

"An expert witness for the prosecution may testify as to the reasons for the expert's conclusions and the reasons therefor as to the mental state of the accused if expert testimony offered by the defense as to the mental condition of the accused has been received in evidence, but such testimony may not extend to statements of the accused except as provided in (1).".

1-103. Rule 304(b) of the Military Rules of Evidence is amended by deleting the reference "under rule 305(d)–(e)" and substituting therefor the reference "under rules 305(d), 305(e), and 305(g)".

1-104. Rule 305 of the Military Rules of Evidence is amended by changing the last sentence of paragraph (h)(2) to read as follows:

"An interrogation is not "participated in" by military personnel or their agents or by the officials or agents listed in subdivision (h)(1) merely because such a person was present at an interrogation conducted in a foreign nation by officials of a foreign government or their agents, or because such a person acted as an interpreter or took steps to mitigate damage to property or physical harm during the foreign interrogation.".

1-105. Rule 317(b) of the Military Rules of Evidence is amended by deleting at the end thereof "for purposes of enforcing the Uniform Code of Military Justice" and substituting therefor "for purposes of obtaining evidence concerning the offenses enumerated in section 2516(1) of title 18, United States Code, to the extent such offenses are punishable under the Uniform Code of Military Justice".

1–106. Rule 317(c) of the Military Rules of Evidence is amended to read as follows:

"(c) *Regulations.* Notwithstanding any other provision of these rules, members of the armed forces or their agents may not intercept wire or oral communications for law enforcement purposes unless such interception:

"(1) takes place in the United States and is authorized under subdivision (b);

"(2) takes place outside the United States and is authorized under regulations issued by the Secretary of Defense or the Secretary concerned; or

"(3) is authorized under regulations issued by the Secretary of Defense or the Secretary concerned and is not unlawful under section 2511 of title 18, United States Code.".

1–107. Rule 321(b)(2)(B) of the Military Rules of Evidence is amended by deleting the reference "(1)" and substituting therefor the reference "(A)".

1–108. Rule 403 of the Military Rules of Evidence is amended by correcting "exluded" to read "excluded" in the first clause of that rule.

1–109. Rule 408 of the Military Rules of Evidence is amended by correcting "purposes" to read "purpose" in the last sentence of that rule.

1–110. Rule 506(f) of the Military Rules of Evidence is amended by deleting "classified information" and substituting therefor "government information" in the last sentence of that rule.

1–111. Rule 507(a) of the Military Rules of Evidence is amended by deleting "information resulting in an investigation" and substituting therefor "information relating to or assisting in an investigation" in the second sentence of that rule.

1–112. Rule 1101(b) of the Military Rules of Evidence is amended by deleting the reference "Section V" and substituting therefor the reference "Sections III and V".

1–113. Section 12 of Part B, which provided for amendments to paragraph 127*c*(1) of Chapter XXV of the Manual, is amended by adding thereto the following:

"Paragraph 127*c*(1) is also amended by deleting "or the Code of the District of Columbia, whichever prescribed punishment is the lesser,". Further, paragraph 127*c*(1) is amended by deleting "or the Code of the District of Columbia and the respective Code" and substituting therefor "and the United States Code.".

JIMMY CARTER

The White House,
    September 1, 1980.

[Filed with the Office of the Federal Register, 10:59 a.m., September 3, 1980]

NOTE: The Executive order was announced by the White House Press Office on September 3.

Enforcement of the Convention for the Safety of Life at Sea

Executive Order 12234. September 3, 1980

By the authority vested in me as President by the Constitution and the laws of the United States of America, and in order to implement the International Convention for the Safety of Life at Sea, 1974, it is hereby ordered as follows:

1–101. The International Convention for the Safety of Life at Sea, 1974, signed at London on November 1, 1974, and proclaimed by the President of the United States on January 28, 1980 (TIAS 9700), entered into force for the United States on May 25, 1980.

1–102. The Secretary of State, the Secretary of the Department in which the Coast Guard is operating, the Secretary of Commerce, and the Federal Communications Commission shall (a) perform those functions prescribed in the Convention that are within their respective areas of responsibility, and (b) cooperate and assist each other in carrying out those functions.

1–103. (a) The Secretary of the Department in which the Coast Guard is operating, or the head of any other Executive agency authorized by law, shall be responsible for the issuance of certificates as required by the Convention. (b) If a certificate is to include matter that pertains to functions vested by law in another Executive agency, the issuing agency shall first ascertain from the other Executive agency the decision regarding that matter. The decision of that agency shall be final and binding on the issuing agency.

1–104. The Secretary of the Department in which the Coast Guard is operating may use the services of the American Bureau of Shipping as long as that Bureau is operated in compliance with Section 25 of the Act of June 5, 1920, as amended (46 U.S.C. 881), to perform the functions under the Convention. The Secretary may also use the services of the National Cargo Bureau to perform functions under Chapter VI (Carriage of Grain) of the Convention.

1–105. The Secretary of the Department in which the Coast Guard is operating shall promulgate regulations necessary to implement the provisions of the Convention.

1–106. To the extent that the International Convention for the Safety of Life at Sea, 1974, replaces and abrogates the International Convention for the Safety of Life at Sea, 1960 (TIAS 5780), this Order supersedes Executive Order No. 11239 of July 31, 1965, entitled "Enforcement of the Convention for the Safety of Life at Sea, 1960."

1–107. Executive Order No. 10402 of October 30, 1952, entitled "Enforcement of the Convention for the Safety of Life at Sea, 1948," is revoked.

JIMMY CARTER

The White House,
    September 3, 1980.

[Filed with the Office of the Federal Register,
    2:45 p.m., September 3, 1980]

Management of Natural Gas Supply Emergencies

Executive Order 12235. September 3, 1980

By the authority vested in me as President by the Constitution and statutes of the United States of America, including Section 304(d) of the Natural Gas Policy Act of 1978 (92 Stat. 3387; 15 U.S.C. 3364(d)) and Section 301 of Title 3 of the United States Code, and in order to assign management responsibility in case of a natural gas supply emergency, it is hereby ordered as follows:

1–101. The functions vested in the President by Sections 301 through 304 (c) of the Natural Gas Policy Act of 1978 (92 Stat. 3381–3387; 15 U.S.C. 3361–3364(c)) are delegated to the Secretary of Energy; except for the authority to declare, extend, and terminate a natural gas supply emergency pursuant to Section 301 thereof (15 U.S.C. 3361).

1–102. The functions vested in the President by Section 607 of the Public

Utility Regulatory Policies Act of 1978 (92 Stat. 3171; 15 U.S.C. 717z) are delegated to the Secretary of Energy; except for the authority to declare, extend, and terminate a natural gas supply emergency pursuant to Section 607 (a) and (b) thereof (15 U.S.C. 717z (a) and (b)).

1–103. The Secretary shall consult with the Administrator of the Environmental Protection Agency, the Director of the Federal Emergency Management Agency, and the heads of other Executive agencies in exercising the functions delegated to him by this Order.

1–104. All functions delegated to the Secretary by this Order may be redelegated, in whole or in part, to the head of any other agency.

1–105. All Executive agencies shall, to the extent permitted by law, cooperate with and assist the Secretary in carrying out the functions delegated to him by this Order.

JIMMY CARTER

The White House,
   September 3, 1980.

[Filed with the Office of the Federal Register, 2:46 p.m., September 3, 1980]

Philadelphia, Pennsylvania

Remarks at the Zion Baptist Church.
September 3, 1980

Thank you very much, Congressman Bill Gray. I'm very proud to have you as an assistant pastor today. [*Laughter*] I noticed Leon Sullivan said "copastor," but I'm sure he meant "assistant." [*Laughter*]

It's an honor for me to stand here in this pulpit in a church that's literally known around the world—a church with a heart, a church which has reached its hand to help others, to many nations on Earth, a church which gives its support to Leon Sullivan and to his fine work.

I'm also very glad to have with us today Mayor Bill Green, State Auditor Al Benedict—[*applause*]—go ahead and applaud for him—Representative Leroy Ervis and particularly Grace Sullivan, and many other distinguished leaders on the State and on the local basis, and distinguished clergy here. You mean so much to me in my private and religious life and who also mean so much to us in making our Nation a greater place to live—and particularly the members of the Zion Baptist Church.

It's great for me to be back home in Philadelphia. When I first got married, my wife and I came to Philadelphia to live for awhile. I was a young naval officer assigned to study radar at the Philadelphia Navy Yard, and we learned here first that Philadelphia truly deserved its name of the City of Brotherly Love. We also learned some other firsts—how to like scrapple and soft pretzels. And since then, of course, we've seen that Philadelphia has kept alive the finest elements of belief and hope and courage expressed here when our Nation was founded more than 200 years ago.

It is good to be in Zion Church. And I want to say to you that I first met your permanent pastor in Georgia when I was Governor. I hate to miss having Leon here with me today, but I learned a long time ago that it's dangerous to get in the same pulpit with a Baptist preacher when he's filled with the spirit. [*Laughter*] As you know, Leon Sullivan [1] always seems to be filled with the spirit. [*Laughter*]

Reverend Sullivan said at a public event not too long ago that it was nice to have a President who knew all the

---

[1] Reverend Sullivan is also president of the Opportunities Industrialization Centers of America.

words to "Amazing Grace." [*Laughter*] Well, I'm not sure that everybody—that anybody knows all the words to "Amazing Grace," because every now and then, kind of quietly, I compose a new verse just for myself. [*Laughter*] And I think that Leon probably composed the third verse. He says, as you know, "Through many dangers, toils and shares [snares] I have already come . . . ."[*Laughter*] You know what comes next: " 'Tis Grace that brought me safe this far and Grace will lead me home." [*Laughter*] So, I told Leon to just leave me and Grace here and to go on to South Africa and that we would take care of things while he was gone. [*Laughter*]

I know that his beloved wife shares in all his good works, but she also has her own work as well, programs that are helping not just individuals in this immediate community but that helps the entire city. Today as I was riding in from the airport, Mayor Bill Green and I were talking about the common effort that they have made on the Miniversity Program, that brings together policemen and community leaders to establish better avenues of understanding among people and better avenues of communications. That's where peace is maintained without inhibiting progress. That's where people can understand how to correct the defects in a community, to resolve problems before they become crises, and to pull people together in a common effort.

I'm very proud that your new mayor is reaching out to unite this great city. And he works with me in Washington, and he works with Congressmen like Bill Gray and Bob Edgar to try to bring this city into the forefront of progress and leadership. There's a strong partnership that I have with mayors throughout this country that we've forged in the last 3½ years. I'm glad that in the brief months

that Bill Green has been in the mayor's office that we've restored already Philadelphia's eligibility for housing and urban development grants, and already his leadership is bringing new jobs and new hope to this community. And I'm thankful for the support that you give him.

In Philadelphia, no President could come without being reminded that this Nation has not always lived up to the ideals expressed here when our Nation was founded 200 years ago or more. For generations—this congregation, this audience knows it better than most—for generations many people have seemed to be blind to injustice, blind to the lack of freedom, and blind to the denial of opportunity in our midst. As in the old hymn, we were blind but now we see. And having seen, we've begun to make good progress. But we still have a long way to go before we've realized all our hopes.

Sometimes we get so burdened down with our journey that we can't see or understand the past immediate dangers, toils, and snares. It's important to remember at those times how far we have come and to see how we are·on the right road in this Nation. It's important, because there are a lot of people out there who think we've come far enough. They want to turn back, but the American people are going to choose the path to progress when they go to the polls on November 4. And I believe that.

I need your help in this election, because I remember very clearly that we had a fine man running for President in 1968, Hubert Humphrey. He put his confidence in the people of this Nation. He put his confidence in the Democrats of this Nation. And the Nation let him down, and Richard Nixon was elected. It wasn't because people like you and me had anything against Hubert Humphrey; it's because Democrats throughout this Nation didn't know what the issues were at stake.

And the great strides that had been made in civil rights under Lyndon Johnson and under John Kennedy came to a screeching halt. And we heard code words like "States' rights" again become the vocabulary of the administration in Washington. And we heard a so-called southern strategy that to me was an insult to the South. But it sent a message that slowed this Nation down in its progress, and it was a threat to all those who sought equal treatment and justice and opportunity. The poor of all races and particularly those who are poor and members of minority races, working people, city dwellers all suffered under the Republicans for 8 solid years. We cannot afford to let that happen again in 1980, and if you'll help me we won't. But I tell you it could happen.

We're now making progress on bringing our party and our Nation back together. A few minutes ago, about 2 minutes before I came into this auditorium, I had a call from out in the Midwest from Senator Ted Kennedy. He wanted to wish me well, and he wanted me to express his hope to you that the Democratic Party will be united in November and fervent in our work between now and then.

I don't remember any progress that this Nation has ever made that didn't require prayer, hard work, sometimes frustration, sometimes fear, and required a lot of courage. We absolutely must look to the future, not just to enhance basic legal rights and equality of opportunity of minority groups but to give our Nation a new economic base for a new day in America. We've made a lot of progress in the last 3½ years. We've now laid a groundwork or a basis or a foundation for more progress. I've talked about this with Leon Sullivan at the annual convention. I talked to him about the 100,000 new

jobs to which we are jointly committed for young people, 90 percent of which will be permanent jobs, in private industry, in private commerce.

The Zion Baptist Church has been doing what you can on a local basis, in your 1036 Club enterprises. That's not an easy thing either, to try to save $10 a month for 36 months. That's particularly difficult for a poor person, whose income is not very great. But you've recognized quite early that to save that much money and invest it in a common effort can create better life, more enjoyment, stronger families, better communities, more jobs for everyone, and that's what I want to do with my new economic program on a nationwide basis, just what you've done with the 1036 program here under the leadership of Grace and Leon Sullivan.

We want to help the basic industries like steel and the rapidly changing industries like the automobile manufacturers and assembly plants. We want to help communities who might suffer from change—and change cannot be prevented—and make sure that when a factory does close down because what they make is no longer to be sold, that new opportunities come along so people don't have to move from one community to another. This is the kind of careful planning that must be implemented during these next few years.

When there is Government aid to be given it needs to be focused or targeted where the aid is most important. And as we put all these programs together, to move to the future to provide jobs, to rebuild communities, to give people a better life, we do it all in such a way that we do not reignite inflation, because inflation robs the poor more than any other group in this country.

The program I outlined last week, in addition to all the programs that we've already got approved, in addition to normal recovery that's going to take place anyhow, in addition to all of the programs that are now before the Congress to be approved, the new ones will provide a million jobs in the next 2 years. This will be very important to us. We need to put our people to work doing jobs that need to be done—solving energy problems, rebuilding our railroads and bridges, making sure our ports can handle the tremendous exports to foreign countries, improving our mass transit systems and other transit systems. We cannot rely on the solutions of the past to solve today's problems. But that does not mean that we have to abandon vital programs that were so precious in the past and carved out with much difficulty in order to move forward in the future.

For instance, millions and millions of our people depend upon social security. It was a program put into effect by Democrats. It was opposed almost unanimously by the Republicans. Elderly people, disabled people who've worked all their lives depend upon social security. As you know, the Republican candidate had suggested that participation in social security not be required for all those who work anymore, but it be voluntary. That would destroy the social security system. Millions of Americans who've worked so hard to build up this program and who now depend on it and who've paid their share would suffer. Retired Americans have not volunteered for that kind of suffering, and if we make the right decision in November, which I'm sure we will, we won't ask them to suffer in the years ahead.

I wish I could stand here as a President, as a Baptist, and tell you we've reached the promised land—[*laughter*]—but I can't do it. I'd like to tell you that no child in America was coming out of school ill-prepared, but I can't do it yet.

I'd like to tell you that no mothers and fathers would have to struggle to find a job or work in order to feed their families. I can't tell you that anymore [either].[2] We're making progress. And that's what I can tell you.

Inflation has fallen sharply. Last month, for the first time in 13 years, the inflation rate was zero. I don't predict that's going to continue to happen, but it is a sign of progress. Last month the economic indicators showing how well our Nation was progressing—it was the highest it's ever been since the records were kept. I can't tell you that's going to continue, but it's a good sign. For the last 6 weeks, unemployment compensation claims have been going down. I can't promise you that they're going to keep on going down, but it's a good sign. Housing starts are going up. The number of laid-off workers in the automobile industry dropped last week. General Motors announced that almost 20,000 workers were already scheduled to go back to work. But we still face serious problems here at home and overseas as well.

But the point is we're moving down the right road, we know where we want to go, we're united now, and we can't change course, and we can't change leadership. In order to get where we want to go, I've been listening to some good advice. I hear from Leon Sullivan often.

And we've been making some good investments for the future: Federal funds for economic development—up 70 percent. For education—up 73 percent. Youth employment and training has tripled. We're putting more money in equal employment opportunity enforcement—Eleanor Holmes Norton, in charge of it—subsidized housing, child nutrition programs. In addition, we've

---

[2] White House correction.

got an urban policy that targets Federal aid where it's most needed. Every Federal decision now has to be made on the basis of how can we spend American taxpayers' money and get the most benefits back from it.

Let me give you just a couple of examples that apply to your own lives here in the Philadelphia area. Bob Edgar, Bill Gray, two fine Congressmen, working with your mayor, Bill Green, were able to announce last week that Philadelphia will not lose the Defense Contract Administration, but will gain jobs instead. The last time I was in Philadelphia that question came up.

And these men know how hard we had to work for me to make this next statement, which you already know about. The U.S.S. *Saratoga* will come to the Philadelphia Naval Shipyard later this month for refitting. That will not only save between 8,500 and 9,000 jobs, but it'll bring in an additional 2,600 jobs, not handouts, not makework jobs, but important jobs that will add 15 years of service to the life of this great ship, jobs that will build a stronger and a better and a more safe future for the country that we love. And I might add that the *Forrestal,* another great ship, will also be refitted here, and that's going to mean even more jobs than I said before.

In 1944 Franklin Roosevelt said he was not going to campaign, but he wanted to take the opportunity whenever it presented itself to set the record straight. And I intend to keep the record set straight. [*Laughter*] The record is that we have faced up to America's energy problems. We've cut our oil imports already by 20 percent below the day when I came in office. This day we bought from overseas 1½ million less barrels of oil than we did in a day in January of 1977. We're embarking on the greatest peacetime program to produce more energy in our country and to save more energy in our country than this Nation has ever seen. It's bigger all put together than the Marshall plan that rebuilt Europe, plus the entire Interstate Highway System, plus the entire space program. That's how much it will mean to you. And to weatherize homes and to produce American energy and to have more efficient and better automobiles produced in America will give us a life whose quality we can't even yet understand.

We also have a record of which I'm proud in the area that means a lot to you, and that's the new jobs created. In the first 3 years I was President we added more than 8 million new jobs, about a million of which, coincidentally, are held by black Americans. Those are new jobs.

Just briefly let me say that I understand the importance of having minority leaders administer Government programs. And what I have tried to do is to take people who marched in the forefront of the civil rights movement, along with some of you, and let them run the programs that were put into effect in the Federal Government.

I've appointed more blacks and more women and other minorities to top Government jobs than any other President in history, and I've appointed more black judges to the Federal courts than all the other Presidents in history that ever served. And two other things: The first one is I'm not through yet, and secondly, I have never had to lower the standards of quality and ethics and training in order to fill those vacancies. One example is Judge Jim Giles here in Philadelphia. We'll be having the benefits of those kinds of appointments long after I have quit being President at the end of 4 more years and also even into the end of this century.

I don't want to belabor the point, but I'd like to name just a few people with whom you're familiar that have faced the dangers and the toils of trying to solve the problems of inequality and prejudice and the lack of opportunity—people like Pat Harris. Pat Harris now runs the Department of Health and Human Services. It's the biggest budget in the world except for two. One of them is the entire United States Government, and the other one is the entire Government of the Soviet Union. Her budget though in that Department that she runs is bigger than the budgets of every other nation on Earth.

Another one is a man who doesn't like to speak out very much, but when he speaks, people listen, and that's Andy Young. I've already mentioned Eleanor Holmes Norton, Don McHenry; people like Drew Days. I understand Drew Days has an uncle here, doesn't he, Senator Freeman Hankers? Senator Hankers, right. Drew Days is the chief law enforcement officer of our country. He's the one that decides when a case should be prosecuted, and it's important to me to have a man like this, who happens to be black, who knows the background of inequality in the administration of justice, is now in charge of the whole thing. And I've got Sadie Alexander, whose husband was a member of this church, to help me with the problems of the old people. And we've got a new Department of Education, and the Assistant Secretary of Education is a former deputy school superintendent of Philadelphia, Thomas Minter.

I don't want to go any further about naming the things that we've done in the past, but I'd like to close by saying just a few more things.

I've tried to be a President that would restore to America its rightful role as champion of human dignity and freedom, not just for our own Nation but for other countries as well. Not everything is right, and everything that's right can't be accomplished overnight. I had hoped for settlement in Rhodesia-Zimbabwe the first year I was in office. Andy Young worked on this problem almost full time, trying to bring together the groups that had been fighting with each other for years and see final success. But we all had to learn a little patience, but we never yielded on our principles. I knew that only the people of that troubled land could reach a just settlement. We held out for what was right, and last week, new Prime Minister Mugabe, chosen in a free election by majority rule, came to visit me in the White House. It was an exciting thing. His presence there was testimony that America is most influential when we stand up for our highest principles. And the experience that we have had here, in America, is of great benefit to others who have been suffering in the past from deprivation and persecution and are now reaching for freedom. Leon Sullivan is now in South Africa. One of the things that he and I have discussed many times is the hope that the next nation that becomes a free democracy, with majority rule, will be the nation of Namibia. And we also want to see apartheid eliminated completely from South Africa.

We don't want to be too patient, but often our fondest dreams take longer than we imagined. We've already come through many dangers and toils and snares, too many to lose our faith that right will ultimately prevail. The next 4 years can be a time of great progress, a time when we at last let old prejudices go by the board, as we put our people, all our people, to work, building a better America, economically strong, but strong also in our faith in one another, strong in our commitment to freedom, our commitment to justice, our commitment to opportunity. I ask you for your help and your prayers, that together we might make this Nation the promised land for all our people, not just a few of them.

Thank you very much. God bless you.

NOTE: The President spoke at approximately 2 p.m.

Earlier in the day, the President visited the South Philadelphia Community Center and a street market in the Italian American section of the city.

Philadelphia, Pennsylvania

Interview With Correspondents of WPIV–TV. September 3, 1980

JIM GARDNER. Good afternoon and welcome to Action News Issues and Answers for this Wednesday evening, a special edition. Our guest today is the President of the United States, Jimmy Carter, who has been on a campaign swing through south and north Philadelphia today. And we are going to be talking about the campaign and the major issues at hand. Our panelists today include Jim O'Brien and Vernon Odum and Mark Howard, all from Channel Six, Action News.

SUPPORT FOR THE PRESIDENT

Mr. President, I was at Madison Square Garden and witnessed your acceptance speech, the night of your acceptance speech, and it seemed that even among your delegates, reactions to your speech and your renomination failed to produce the outpouring of enthusiasm that we normally associate with such events. The same day I asked a New York City cabdriver, "Whom are you voting for?", and he said, "Carter." And I asked him why, and he said, "Because Reagan is even worse."

It seems that some people, or perhaps

many people, who intend to vote for you perceive you as the lesser of evils, as opposed to the better of candidates. Do you agree with that evaluation, and if that's true, do you think that can cause problems in your efforts to govern and lead effectively even after the election?

THE PRESIDENT. Well, I agree with part of it. When a President is in office or a mayor or a Governor and there is not a campaign going on, then the likelihood is that that incumbent will be compared to perfection. And whenever anything goes wrong or doesn't quite measure up to the hopes or expectations of a voter, they say that the President or the mayor is at fault.

During the primary season, also, the voters tend to express their displeasure about circumstances in the world by voting against an incumbent, particularly a President. And in the general election there is a hard choice that the voters make, sometimes a pleasant choice, between the two candidates who are running who have a chance to win—the Democratic and the Republican nominee.

So, there will be people who say, "I don't like everything about Jimmy Carter but I think he's the better of the two men," and there are those who say, "I like what he's done, and I want to support him because I have absolute confidence in him." I'll be glad to take the votes either way.

But I've seen, since the convention, a remarkable coalescing of unity within the Democratic Party. I had a call this afternoon, for instance, from Senator Kennedy, who was in the Midwest speaking for me at the Machinists convention, just to wish me well here and to give the Philadelphia people his best regards. So, I think that the Party is coming back together.

The sharp choice that the American people will make this year is perhaps between two men and two current party philosophies that are in as much disagreement as we have ever seen, certainly in my lifetime. So, this, of course, is going to be a good one.

DIFFERENCES IN THE CANDIDATES

Q. Economically, it seems that you're pretty much what I guess you'd call conservative, in the sense that neither one of you is advocating any tremendous Government expenditures. You both want to hold down expenses. You both basically talk in spending more on defense, which tends to be conservative.

How—what would it matter to a voter? What's the difference to me or anybody who's watching this program which of you becomes President as far as our daily lives are concerned?

THE PRESIDENT. Well, I think the two things that are important are, one, a better domestic life—what will bring a family together, what will give American people jobs, what will let us look to the future with confidence, what will honor the basic civil rights and human needs of American people, how we will have better education, better welfare programs, and a better relationship between the Federal Government and the local and State government. That's one domestic issue. The other one is how do we keep our Nation strong and at peace; at the same time make sure that we don't have the prospect of the possibility of a nuclear war.

Q. Could you give us one example of where you really are different, where if he's elected it'll be one way and you're the other way?

THE PRESIDENT. Sure. Well, one difference is in the basic structure of the tax program. Reagan has advocated the Reagan-Kemp-Roth proposal, which will cut taxes in this country roughly a trillion dollars between now and 1987, which means that almost every ongoing Federal program would have to be eliminated in order to meet that target that he has. He also wants to increase Federal spending and claims he can balance the budget. This is obviously a fallacious thing.

In addition to that, for a comparison between my tax proposal and his, mine is a careful program designed to revitalize American industry, and it's highly progressive in nature in that it'll give the average working family in this country a much greater proportion of the tax savings. For instance, for a family making $200,000 a year Reagan's proposal would give that family about 50 times more in tax cuts than would my own proposal. My program is designed to revitalize our Nation's economy, to keep people at work, and to give a balanced benefit from any tax reductions.

JOHN B. ANDERSON

Q. Mr. President, the Anderson factor—he seems to be slipping or not moving at all in the polls. If this trend continues, how long before you're ready to declare him not a serious enough candidate to be considered for debates or even in the November election?

THE PRESIDENT. Well, it's not up to me to decide, you know, who is serious and who isn't. I look on all of the people who are running for President—and there are probably a hundred of them, four or five who are well known—as being significant and important. Some of them represent a political philosophy that's important, like Barry Commoner, with his emphasis on the quality of the environment. Another one, Mr. Clark, is a libertarian who wants to remove the Federal Government and all government, as a matter of fact, from the daily lives of Americans, I think to the detriment of our society.

John Anderson is a Republican. He ran, as you know, as a Republican candidate. He never won a primary. He never won a State caucus campaign, even in his own home State, and after he lost out, then he decided to run as an independent. But he's still basically a Republican, and for me to run against two Republicans is something that I don't want to avoid, but I don't particularly want to promote it.

The basic choice that the American people will have to make is among those who have a chance to win. And I am convinced at this time—and I don't see anything to change my mind in the future—that the choice is between myself and Governor Reagan.

But the fact is that when public opinion polls are run, either by myself or the ones that have been made public, whenever Reagan [Anderson] picks up seven votes at my expense, he only picks up one vote at Governor Reagan's expense. So, as Anderson goes down in the polls it does help me. But I'm perfectly willing to face any candidate that runs, and I'll run it on my own record, not against them.

THE NATION'S ECONOMY

Q. Mr. President, let's get back to the economic sector for just a minute. Last week you introduced your seventh economic program since becoming President. You say that it will fight unemployment, that it will encourage investment and productivity without fueling the fires of inflation.

THE PRESIDENT. Yes.

Q. Why should the voters, why should our viewers have faith that this program will work, when the current state of the economy would suggest that the six that came before it did not?

THE PRESIDENT. Well, you can't have an economy frozen in concrete that will last year after year after year. Circumstances change. In 1979 alone we had the price of oil on a worldwide basis go up more than the price of oil had gone up since it was first discovered in the 1800's, and this was a shock to the international economic system. So, the first part of March I had to put some restraint on budget spending, and 85 percent of those budget restraints are still intact. I had to put some restraints on credit and also try to bring down the interest rates, and they've dropped precipitously, and inflation rates, and they've dropped, too.

I don't want to pick out one month as being typical, but last month we had the first time in 13 years that the inflation rate has been zero. I don't expect it to be zero in August, but the fact is that was a good indication. Last month, in July, we had the highest increase in economic indicators in this country of any month since the indicators were first started being kept or recorded. I don't expect that to continue.

For six straight weeks now we've had a decrease each week in unemployment compensation claims. And it's obvious that the American automobile industry is beginning to rejuvenate itself as the Ford, General Motors, Chrysler, and others produce the kind of small, efficient cars that the American consumers want. So, I see some indications that are favorable— housing starts, the last indications are very good; business investment plans, very good. I think we've bottomed out on the recession rates.

The fact is that the commitment I made back in March to keep a tight restraint on spending and to keep the dollar strong and to keep an emphasis on controlling inflation has not changed.

AUTOMOBILE INDUSTRY

Q. I think we have a tendency, Mr. President, to look to you and the White House as being sort of a Pandora's Box that you open up and everything comes flying out okay. In the area of the automobile industry, that seems to be a pivotal point for you fellows these days as you try to win votes and win union support and what have you. And the general trend comes to us that when you're there they're going "yea," and when Reagan's there they're going "yea" but booing a little bit and what have you. But it seems to me like you said not long ago that you tried to get the automobile industry a couple of years back to realize——

THE PRESIDENT. Three years ago.

Q. ——right—that there needed to be some changes made as far as producing these fuel-efficient, smaller compact type cars, rather than getting mad at Japan or mad at Germany for sending them over here. Why didn't the automobile industry listen to you then? Why couldn't you get their attention? Why couldn't you make the point at that time from your executive position to make this vast industry take notice and make the changes then that should have been made, rather than get into this critical situation we're in now?

THE PRESIDENT. I made a speech on television—maybe you heard it—in April of 1977. And I called the energy crisis the moral equivalent of war——

Q. Use that all the time myself.

THE PRESIDENT.——and it was, at that time at least, ridiculed. There was a lot of fun made of it. As a matter of fact, my prediction that the world supply of oil would be matched by world demand in

1985 was more optimistic than what actually occurred.

We had a meeting then—I had personally a meeting then—with all the leaders, the presidents and the chief executive officers, of the major automobile manufacturing companies and told them that they had to change their model styles to comply with environmental standards and also to comply with efficiency and safety standards. They pointed out to me then that they could not do it. And I said, "Well, they're doing it in Sweden, they're doing it in Germany, they're doing it in Japan." And they said, "Yes, but the gasoline over there's already $2.40 a gallon. The American consumer will not buy that small, efficient automobile." Well, the fact is had they changed then they would have been in much better shape now.

But American buyers are now demanding that kind of automobile. And I'm very grateful that with a tremendous investment of money and with great confidence in the future the automobile workers themselves and the American manufacturers are now producing that kind of automobile that will be very attractive in the future to the American consumer. At the same time it's efficient and clean-burning, it's more safe, as proven by recent tests, than are the foreign imports.

So, I think that the American manufactured cars are going to be in a good competitive position from now on.

ENERGY PRICES

Q. What about the bottom 20 or 25 percent, though, of our population that really can't afford to spend $1.30 a gallon for gas? So far nobody's come up with any way to help them or some kind of a cushion there to put under the poor people who can't pay that price.

THE PRESIDENT. Well, we've had a

major investment in recent years in the rapid transit systems. As a matter of fact, the community of Philadelphia has benefited greatly since I've been in office.

In addition, out of the windfall profits tax, which is a tax that'll be taken away from the oil companies, away from their unearned income, we'll have about $13 billion in the next 10 years, above and beyond what was already scheduled for rapid transit, to put into public transportation systems of all kinds, some buses, some rail, and some intercity transit systems. At the same time we're trying to rebuild our railroad system, improve the repair of our highway system, and improve our ports and waterways.

One of the tremendous, untapped opportunities that we have in this country is to export American coal and let it replace OPEC oil as a growing energy source, not only in this country but around the world. But we don't yet have the adequate rail and highway and port facilities to handle it fast enough. That will be a major part of this new program that I've put forward.

Q. That's long run, though, but in the short run, basically the people who live in the suburbs of Philadelphia, in a sense you're telling them, "You just can't go into town to shop" or "You can't go to the shore, because you can't spend that money on gas." Is that really what you're saying?

THE PRESIDENT. No, that's not what I'm saying. There's a limit to what government can do, and one limit that I've put on myself is not to lie to people. There is no way in the foreseeable future that the price of gasoline and the price of oil internationally is going to go down, and we've got to change some of our habits, we've got to share more transportation or, if we own automobiles, carpool more, use public transportation more and sometimes just not travel as much. But in my judg-

ment this can be the basis for a better life for American people as we live more efficiently, as we insulate our homes better, as we have more efficient automobiles, as we bring our families closer together. Take a little more physical exercise. There might be more walking and jogging and a little bit more bicycle riding than in the past, and there might be an inclination for families not to travel so far when they go on vacation.

But I don't see that the quality of life of Americans will be damaged as we face this tremendous new opportunity through the next decade to take advantage of the change that's been forced on us and carve out a new program for Americans' lives.

I'd like to add one other point.

In this next 10 years, we'll have more Government money derived from the windfall profits tax and the oil companies to spend on conservation, transit systems, and to help poor people heat their homes and also to produce more energy than the total of the Marshall plan that rebuilt Europe, the total space program, and the total Interstate Highway System. And to invest those billions and billions of American dollars into American technology, with American know-how, American education, American innovation and to create American jobs can give us a much better life even though we've had——

Q. Thirty-cent dollars, I think.

Q. I was going to say——

Q. Yes, inflated dollars.

Q. ——some cynic might wonder whether that's a measure of commitment or a measure of inflation.

THE PRESIDENT. That's a measure of commitment. And in the process we'll cut down inflation. In fact, the entire economic program that I described last week is noninflationary in nature, a sharp difference, that I didn't point out before, between what the Republicans have put forth, which is highly inflationary. As a matter of fact, the Republican Vice-Presidential candidate, Mr. Bush, said that the Ronald Reagan-Kemp-Roth tax proposal would increase inflation in this country more than 30 percent, and I think he's right.

FOREIGN RELATIONS

Q. Mr. President, we see a lot of headlines these days: Soviets are number one; America, a country in decline; the allies lose respect for America and for Jimmy Carter. Does this country still have the clout, still have the ability to stand up to the Russians if push comes to shove?

THE PRESIDENT. Yes. This country is not second to the Soviet Union in military strength nor in political influence nor in economic strength nor in moral strength.

Q. What about your relationship with the allies?

THE PRESIDENT. I think it's better now than it's been in the last 20 years. The NATO Alliance has been strengthened. We have a common commitment to theater nuclear force, to building up our cooperation and consultation. We've strengthened our military presence in the Persian Gulf and Indian Ocean area. In every way I think we're better off, and what's becoming more obvious to people all over the world is that our policy on human rights works.

You don't see any boats lining up in Key West with Americans trying to get in those boats to escape to Cuba. And I think people are beginning to realize, more and more, that the wall that's been built in Berlin is not to keep people out of Communist Germany, it's to keep people from coming to freedom.

What our country has to offer, in strength and stability and a brighter future, is much better than the Communist world. And one of the reasons the Soviets went into Afghanistan—and they should not have done it—is because their own system failed. There is not a single other nation on Earth that's trying to build their own government now patterned after Communist Soviet Government.

KU KLUX KLAN

Q. Mr. President, if I could go back to domestic situations for one moment. There has been a lot of talk in the past several days about the Ku Klux Klan, based on Mr. Reagan's remarks in Michigan the other day. But aside from that, there has been a militant revival, it seems to me, of Klan and Nazi offshoot party activity in this country in recent years. What special is the Justice Department doing to handle that situation?

THE PRESIDENT. Well, as you know, the top law enforcement officer under the Attorney General is Drew Days, who is a very knowledgeable civil rights worker who happens to be black, who's very eager to eliminate any element of racial harassment or racial division in our country.

We have a standard operating procedure now that as soon as a racist act takes place in a community, the Justice Department and the FBI offer their services. If it's obvious that the local and State officials can care for that situation and if the State courts are going to proceed in accordance with the Constitution, then that's where the first responsibility lies. But my commitment and the Attorney General's and Drew Days' is all to prevent that kind of resurgence that you described.

I've grown up in the South, and I can tell you that compared to when I was a younger man, the Ku Klux Klan is practically insignificant. When I spoke in Tuscumbia, Alabama, Monday, when I realized that there were Klansmen there, and I lashed out at them as being un-

American and not understanding the South or our Nation, it was the biggest round of applause I got among those tens of thousands of people there—and they were all southerners, from Mississippi, Alabama, Tennessee, with a few from the Carolinas and Georgia. But that shows that there's a new attitude in our country of condemnation of those cowards who hide behind white sheets and who besmirch the flags and who also besmirch the cross where a crucified savior said we need to love one another and not hate.

AMERICAN HOSTAGES IN IRAN

Q. I hate to bring this up, Mr. President, but we've got to talk about something that's very much on the minds of most people these days, and that's Iran, the situation over there.

THE PRESIDENT. Yes.

Q. It's gone past 300 days now, and we hesitate to bring it up mainly because we sort of feel like we're getting into a touchy area because you're doing everything you possibly can. We can't blow any secrets, and we know we can't let the cats out of the bags and what have you as far as what you're really planning on doing somewhere in the future. But somehow or other the people, I think, need to know what the difference between then, when you were in the White House for 6 months without really moving, because you were so absorbed in this thing, and now, where you can be out campaigning for President, because that's what you've got to do to get your next 4 years in the White House and see this thing through.

How do we stand with the Iranian situation, with the hostages?

THE PRESIDENT. I don't have much good to report about the immediate prospects for release of our hostages. It's a problem that's always with me as President. As I said in my acceptance speech

in New York, it's as though those hostages were members of my own family, my own sons and daughters.

We stay in close touch with the families of the hostages, and we have a constant effort ongoing, some through public means, some through private diplomatic channels, some through emissaries who are not part of government, to try to induce the Iranians to release those hostages as something that's humane in nature but also something that would remove a tremendous burden politically, economically, and financially from Iran itself. There is a serious problem in Iran brought about to a major degree because those hostages are being held.

In the past there has been no government with whom we could deal. Last week their Prime Minister was finally chosen. He's not yet been approved by their parliament. The parliament has now been elected, a speaker has been chosen, and a President has been chosen. So, we finally have, just in the last few days, a government in Iran that's still in the formative stages, and this week Secretary Muskie sent to the new Prime Minister an outline of our hopes that the hostages would be released and the circumstances under which we would cooperate with Iran after that had been accomplished.

HUMAN RIGHTS

Q. Do you think that this constant reference of yours to human rights, in other words, I think you've attacked the whole Iran problem in that area of it's only right that these people be released; they're innocent. You're constantly referring to that whether it be with regard to Cuba or the Jews in the Soviet Union or the strikers in Poland or whatever it is. Every now and then that almost places you in a bit of a posture as being weak, because you're constantly talking about human rights.

We all want human rights, but every now and then this country in its history has had to sort of rear up on its hind legs and fight for human rights or stand up strongly, and yet you never seem to take that posture. You always seem to slowly go along talking about human rights because it's right and because it's good.

Do you really believe the rest of the world looks at human rights like that and can absorb that from you, or can we lead in that way?

THE PRESIDENT. Yes. The best way to enhance human rights around the world is not to go to war and to kill people; it's to keep constantly before the leaders and the people of this world the possibility of freedom, of liberty, of democratic processes, of equality of opportunity. We've seen several military dictatorships in this hemisphere since I've been in office change into true democracies, with new leaders chosen by the people, compatible with the people, and responsible to the people. I think we've seen this happen in Africa too, where for the first time our Nation is playing a major role in that large continent.

We have helped greatly to bring about the realization of human rights in Zimbabwe, formerly Rhodesia, and now we have a democracy there with an elected leader, who was over here to visit us the other night. We have, in Namibia, a chance for that country to become free and to establish human rights based on democratic principles. We hope to eliminate apartheid in South Africa as well.

But our country's position is staunch and strong. We've sent a clear signal to the people that are behind the Iron Curtain, dominated in the past, sometimes without recognition, by a totalitarian government. The dissidents who are held in

the Soviet Union send me messages frequently, "Mr. President, please do not yield in your demand for the realization of human rights."

In November we'll be going to Madrid, Spain, to make the Soviets and others answer for any deprivation of human rights among the people who live in their countries. This is an agreement that was worked out, and we'll be having a preliminary conference on that in September.

And I think that, although we did not interfere at all, we stayed completely aloof from it, the recent demand by the Polish workers for free labor unions and freedom of the press and the right for religious services to be telecast throughout Poland was a realization of the pent-up desire for human rights. It's not something that I'm responsible for. It's not something that I get up and wave a flag for by myself. It's in the hearts and minds of people all over this world who have not had freedom in the past and who demand it, and for our country, that epitomizes human rights, to keep high that banner and not let people forget about it, I think, is a legitimate and responsible role for a President.

MAYOR WILLIAM GREEN

Q. Mr. President, two quick questions; we have 2 minutes left.

Mayor Green was a staunch supporter of Senator Kennedy. Senator Kennedy lost; you won. If you win the general election in November, is there any penalty coming to Philadelphia as a result of Mr. Green's allegiance with the Senator?

THE PRESIDENT. No. I think Bill Green is one of the finest mayors in this Nation, and ever since he's been in office, he and I have had a very close and good and proper working relationship. He's had a longstanding friendship with the Kennedy family. Before he ever endorsed Senator Kennedy in the primaries, he told me his reasons for it. I understood it completely. And after the Pennsylvania primary was over and before the other primaries had been completed, I came to Philadelphia, as you may remember. Bill Green pledged his support to me then.

I don't have any doubt that he'll do everything he can to help the Democratic ticket win in November, and regardless of whether I win or lose in Philadelphia or Pennsylvania in November, I represent the people of Philadelphia just as much as the mayor does.

SUPPORT FOR THE PRESIDENT

Q. One final question. When you open a newspaper and you see that 78 percent of the people polled in a Gallup Poll or a Harris Poll do not think that you're doing a very good job—a 22-percent approval rating—do you insist to yourself that nobody quite understands what you're up against, or do you sometimes think that when you're by yourself and engaging the same fears and apprehensions as every other American, that perhaps they have some justification for thinking that you're not doing a good enough job?

THE PRESIDENT. Look, the only poll that matters in politics is the poll that the people conduct on election day. If I went back 5 years ago, nobody would know who I was and nobody thought I would win, even in early '76. I won. Ten months ago, when the prospects were that Senator Kennedy would announce for President, most people thought that I would just resign and not even run for reelection.

Q. Some were seriously asking the question?

THE PRESIDENT. Yes, seriously asking. I won. The people, I think in the judgment, said that they had at least adequate confidence in me.

I'll do the best I can in the next few weeks, and when the people go to the polls in November to decide about the future of this Nation, I'll trust their judgment. And I think that's the poll that counts. But obviously, if you ask somebody, "Are you very pleased or satisfied or do you think he's doing a fair job or a good job with inflation or foreign affairs," the answer could be, "He's not doing a good job" or "I think he's doing a fair job"—or I think very few say, "He's doing an outstanding job." That doesn't bother me a bit.

Q. Okay. President Carter, thank you for being with us on Action News Issues and Answers. Our thanks to Jim O'Brien, Vernon Odum, and Mark Howard. For Action News Issues and Answers, I'm Jim Gardner. Good night.

NOTE: The interview began at 3 p.m. at the WPIV–TV studios. It was taped for broadcast later the same day.

White House Coal Advisory Council

Appointment of Nine Members and Designation of Chairman.
September 3, 1980

The President today announced the appointment of nine persons as members of the White House Coal Advisory Council.

The Council was established by Executive Order 12229 on July 29, 1980, to advise the President and the Secretary of Labor on matters pertaining to labor-management relations in the coal industry, to mine safety, and to productivity in the coal industry. The President announced that this Council would be created on March 14, when he received the recommendations of the President's Commission on Coal.

The members are:

KENNETH V. BUZBEE, of Carbondale, Ill., chairman of the Illinois Energy Resources Commission and chairman of the Interstate Coal Task Force, a group of State legislative and energy department officials.

NICHOLAS THOMAS CAMICIA, of Greenwich, Conn., chairman, president, and chief executive officer of the Pittston Co. He is chairman of the Coal Industry Advisory Board of the International Energy Agency and has served as chairman of the Bituminous Coal Operators' Association and the National Coal Association.

SAM CHURCH, JR., of Springfield, Va., president of the United Mine Workers (UMW), a former miner and UMW local president.

JOHN M. ELLIOTT, of Philadelphia, Pa., senior partner and chairman of the litigation department of the Philadelphia firm of Dilworth, Paxson, Kalish and Levy. He is chief counsel to the Pennsylvania Coal Mining Association and counsel to several coal companies. He is a member of the Pennsylvania Environmental Quality Board.

ROGER A. MARKLE, of Oil City, Pa., president and chief executive officer of the Valley Camp Coal Co., and director of Quaker State Oil Refining Corp. He is a former Director of the U.S. Bureau of Mines and has served as vice chairman of Utah's Energy Conservation and Development Council.

GERALD H. PATRICK, of Leawood, Kans., president and chief operating officer of Arch Mineral Corp., and an advocate in the coal industry of strong land reclamation policies.

JOHN D. ROCKEFELLER IV, of Charleston, W. Va., Governor of West Virginia. He was Chairman of the President's Commission on Coal and will serve as Chairman of this Council.

J. C. TURNER, of Washington, D.C., general president of the International Union of Operating Engineers and a vice president of the AFL–CIO Executive Council. He has represented the United States at International Labor Organization conferences and has undertaken international missions for the AFL–CIO.

JAMES C. WILSON, of Longmont, Colo., president of Rocky Mountain Energy Co., a mining subsidiary of Union Pacific Corp. He is president of the Colorado School of Mines Foundation and is on the board of directors of the Rocky Mountain Center on Environment.

The President also announced that the Federal Cochairman of the Appalachian Regional Commission, Albert P. Smith, Jr., and the Assistant Secretary of Labor for Labor-Management Relations, William B. Hobgood, will serve as *ex officio* members of this Council.

High Holy Days

Message of the President. **September 4, 1980**

On the occasion of the High Holy Days, Rosalynn and I welcome the opportunity to greet our fellow Americans of the Jewish faith.

The New Year is a time of self-examination and moral rededication. The traditional commitments you make on Rosh Hashanah and Yom Kippur are an important contribution to the strength and vitality of our nation. The New Year is also a time to reaffirm those common, cherished, ethical principles and values which form the foundation of our democratic society.

We pray with you as you seek sustenance and as you set out refreshed and recommitted to our common effort to defend peace and protect the lives and human rights of all our fellows on this globe. We face a formidable task, but as the great Jewish sages remind us, while we are not required to complete our task, neither are we free to shrink from it. Therefore, let us continue in the pursuit of that which is right for our nation and for people throughout the world.

Rosalynn and I trust you will find personal renewal in these Holy Days and that your prayers and acts will advance our shared hopes for a just and peaceful world.

JIMMY CARTER

Executive Schedule

Executive Order 12236. September 4, 1980

LEVELS IV AND V OF THE EXECUTIVE SCHEDULE

By the authority vested in me as President of the United States of America by Section 5317 of Title 5 of the United States Code, in order to delete two positions from and add one position to level IV of the Executive Schedule, Section 1–101 of Executive Order No. 12154, as amended, is hereby further amended as follows:

1–101. In subsection (a) delete "Senior Adviser to the Secretary, Department of State" and substitute therefor "Counselor to the Secretary, Department of the Treasury".

1–102. In subsection (d) delete "Special Assistant to the Special Representative for Trade Negotiations, Office of the Special Representative for Trade Negotiations."

JIMMY CARTER

The White House,
 September 3, 1980.

[Filed with the Office of the Federal Register,
 10:59 a.m., September 4, 1980]

Executive Schedule

Executive Order 12237. September 4, 1980

LEVELS IV AND V OF THE EXECUTIVE SCHEDULE

By the authority vested in me as President of the United States of America by Section 5317 of Title 5 of the United States Code, in order to place two new Deputy Under Secretary positions in level V of the Executive Schedule, Section 1–102 of Executive Order No. 12154, as

amended, is further amended by adding thereto the following new subsections:

"(e) Deputy Under Secretary for Education, Department of Education."

"(f) Deputy Under Secretary for Education, Department of Education.".

JIMMY CARTER

The White House,
 September 3, 1980.

[Filed with the Office of the Federal Register,
 11 a.m., September 4, 1980]

National Forest Products Week, 1980

Proclamation 4790. September 4, 1980

*By the President of the United States
of America*

A Proclamation

The vast, unforgettable forests of America have always been one of our most precious treasures. Today, we have some 740 million acres of woodland—roughly one-third of the Nation's land area. This vast resource provides many of the products we depend upon—lumber for our homes, paper for recording our thoughts, fuel for heating and cooking, and the basic elements of thousands of other products.

Seventy-five years ago, the Forest Service was created within the United States Department of Agriculture to help conserve and protect America's forestlands. The dedicated men and women of this agency can be proud of their accomplishments. The science of forestry has made great strides. Today, researchers are finding ways to speed the growth of trees; discovering new methods for protecting forests from fire, insects, and disease; and developing production methods for more fully utilizing our wood resources. New methods for extracting energy from wood are also under development to help solve the Nation's energy problems.

Progress is also being made in the effort to ensure that adequate areas of our forests are preserved in their natural state for the enjoyment and benefits of Americans both now and in the future. Congress is now considering my recommendations for classifying an additional 15.4 million acres as wilderness within the National Forest System. These lands, in addition to the wilderness already created by Congress, will preserve the pristine quality of more than 30 million acres of National Forest.

While our forests continue to meet our demands for wood and recreation today, careful management is needed if they are to continue to do so in the future. All of us need to become more aware of the role woodlands play, directly and indirectly, in our lives. We must strive to improve our small woodlots as well as our large, professionally managed, public and private forests.

In order to promote awareness and to recognize the efforts of the thousands of men and women who have devoted their lives to managing this valuable resource, the Congress has designated the third week in October as National Forest Products Week.

Now, THEREFORE, I, JIMMY CARTER, President of the United States of America, do hereby proclaim the week of October 19 through October 25, 1980, as National Forest Products Week and ask all Americans to demonstrate their appreciation of the value of forests through suitable activities.

IN WITNESS WHEREOF, I have hereunto set my hand this fourth day of September, in the year of our Lord nineteen hundred and eighty, and of the Independence of the United States of America the two hundred and fifth.

JIMMY CARTER

[Filed with the Office of the Federal Register, 4:14 p.m., September 4, 1980]

United States-Denmark Convention on Taxation and Fiscal Evasion

Message to the Senate Transmitting the Convention.   September 4, 1980

To the Senate of the United States:

I transmit herewith, for Senate advice and consent to ratification, a Convention between the Government of the United States of America and the Government of the Kingdom of Denmark for the Avoidance of Double Taxation and the Prevention of Fiscal Evasion with Respect to Taxes on Income (the Convention), together with a related exchange of notes, signed at Washington on June 17, 1980. I also transmit the report of the Department of State with respect to the Convention.

The Convention will replace the existing convention between the United States and Denmark, which has been in effect since 1948. It is similar to the United States model income tax convention published in May 1977, which takes into account the modernization of tax laws and conventions, but it retains certain provisions of the existing convention. For example, interest from investment and royalties continues to be exempt from withholding of tax at source.

In the new Convention, Denmark agrees to extend to United States shareholders in Danish corporations a dividend tax credit similar to that available to

Danish shareholders; Denmark regards this as a major concession, in that the United States does not grant an analogous reciprocal credit.

In addition, the Convention contains a provision, at the request of the United States, that allows either country to tax capital gains derived by residents of the other country from the sale of real property located in the first country.

An exchange of notes clarifies some technical points.

I recommend that the Senate give early and favorable consideration to the Convention and its advice and consent to ratification.

JIMMY CARTER

The White House,
    September 4, 1980.

Federal Labor Relations Authority

Message to the Congress Transmitting a Report.   September 4, 1980

To the Congress of the United States:

I am transmitting herewith the First Annual Report of the Federal Labor Relations Authority for the Fiscal Year ended September 30, 1979, in accordance with the Civil Service Reform Act of 1978 (P.L. 95–454, Sec. 701) (5 U.S.C. 7104(e)).

As the independent agency set up to resolve union-management disputes in the Federal sector, the Authority oversees the creation of bargaining units, supervises elections, rules on the scope of negotiations, hears complaints of unfair labor practices, and interprets the labor-management statute. These activities have greatly enhanced the credibility and ef-

fectiveness of the Federal personnel system in resolving union-management disputes.

JIMMY CARTER

The White House,
    September 4, 1980.

NOTE: The report is entitled "First Annual Report of the Federal Labor Relations Authority and the Federal Service Impasses Panel for the Fiscal Period January 1–September 30, 1979" (Government Printing Office, 55 pages).

American Federation of Labor-Congress of Industrial Organizations

Remarks at the Organization's General Board Meeting.   September 4, 1980

First of all, let me thank you, President Lane Kirkland, for the introduction and also for the good news.[1]

I'm very glad to have with me a man who I believe has never been exceeded as Secretary of Labor in his commitment to the working people of this Nation, Ray Marshall. He makes a good partner and a good teacher, and I've been a good student and a good partner of his and of yours.

It's an honor for me to be here. I've gotten to know a lot of you personally, and I've also benefited not only from Ray Marshall's advice but also from yours. For instance, one board member advised me, "Mr. President, the best way to get your point across is to be soft-spoken. That makes a greater impression than raising your voice." And Jerry Wurf, I want to thank you for that advice. [*Laughter*]

---

[1] Earlier the General Board had voted to endorse the President for reelection.

Another board member, by the way, advised me, "Mr. President, don't ever be inflexible, be accommodating, work out matters among the people who are in dispute; the best approach is compromise." And I want to thank Teddy Gleason for that advice. [*Laughter*]

Another board member said, "Mr. President, remember that you set an example for the whole Nation; always watch your language very carefully." George Hardy, I appreciate that. [*Laughter*] That's not the only good advice I've gotten from you all, but I think that's about as far as I ought to go in public. [*Laughter*]

As you may remember, almost exactly 4 years ago to the day, I met with this General Board, and soon after that Fritz Mondale and I were elected as Vice President and as President of the greatest nation on Earth. And I can tell you without any fear of being contradicted that we would not have been elected without your endorsement and your support in 1976, and we know it.

We'll always be grateful, but I looked on that endorsement and that support not as a gift, but as an obligation on my part to be a good President for the working people of this country. I believe in renewing good contracts, and with your help we're going to renew that contract on November 4 for another 4 years.

An election can make a great difference, and enthusiasm can also have a profound effect on the history of a nation. Twelve years ago, in 1968, our country made a serious mistake in not adequately supporting Hubert Humphrey; Richard Nixon was elected. Four years ago with your help we had a change of guard in the White House, and we ended 8 years of Republican neglect of our Nation's most complex problems. Instead, we began to face up to those problems, to tell the American people the truth, and began to build lasting solutions. These last 3½ years have not been easy ones for me nor for you nor for our Nation nor for the world. But for us they've been creative years, and today we can face the future much better prepared than we were when that change of guard took place in January of 1977.

A changing of the guard of a different kind has taken place in the labor movement. We all miss President George Meany deeply and profoundly and personally; for a quarter of a century he embodied the American labor movement. As President of our country I recognized that he was the spirit and the strength of working America. The torch has now been passed to the able hands of Lane Kirkland and Tom Donahue, and it's fallen to them and to you to carry on the great unfinished work of American labor.

Change has also come to your executive council. I share with you the loss of a man who was among my closest friends in this entire board, and that was Paul Hall. It was a time of sadness for me when he passed away. He gave me encouragement when even many of you did not know who I was. And I share your pride in knowing again that the torch has been passed to some worthy people. And I'd like to congratulate your newest executive council members, Bill Konyha and John Sweeney and Joyce Miller. You might be interested in knowing that I set history 5 minutes ago by riding here in a White House limousine driven by the first female Secret Service agent who ever drove a President. And I felt perfectly safe. [*Laughter*]

And I've been pleased to see the growing leadership that the labor movement has set in establishing bonds among us, because as leaders we share not only a commitment to specific programs and the winning of elections, but you and I share the responsibility for something even more important, and that's the future. All of us know that there are no shortcuts; there are not any substitutes for hard work in the struggle for a humane and more decent world that we can pass on to our children. This country has never made progress the easy way.

The November election will decide whether or not our struggle is successful. Seldom in the political history of this country has the choice been more clear. Not just between two men, not just between two parties, but, as I said in New York a few weeks ago, between two futures. I believe that America must once again choose a future of thoughtful change, because change is inevitable, and human progress, because human beings are our responsibility. We've got to get on with the job we've begun.

In recent days our country has drawn inspiration from the courageous workers of Poland. We've been inspired by their discipline, by their tenacity, by their courage under the most difficult possible circumstances. They've shown the world not just how to win a victory for labor but also that the hunger for human rights is still alive worldwide. They and the Government of Poland have shown how a society that deals frankly with its problems free from interference by foreign powers can strengthen itself. And we are pleased at what's happened in Poland, and we wish them Godspeed toward a future of prosperity, peace, and freedom.

And I'd like to add this: In our country, some people who've raised the Polish workers strike and praised it seem to be a lot more supportive of strong trade unions overseas than they are here at home. To me there's only one standard: free trade unions for working people everywhere.

The Polish workers have demonstrated

something that you and I have known for a long time, that free trade unions are a basic instrument of democracy and that human rights and labor rights are indistinguishable. The Polish Government and the workers have hammered out this achievement by themselves in the best interest of their own people and their own nation. I cannot but believe that the resolve of the Polish workers was strengthened by the solidarity of trade unions—free trade unions around the world, including of course the AFL–CIO. You all have been an inspiration to people in this country and to workers all over the world, and I thank you for it on behalf of all Americans.

At home, the AFL–CIO has helped lead this country through a half century of unprecedented social and economic progress. Every advance in this half century—social security, civil rights, Medicare, aid to education—one after another came with the support and the leadership, not just the support, but leadership of American labor. You've represented all the people, not just your own members. You've been the voice of forgotten people everywhere.

Thirty-two years ago Harry Truman said, "It's time that all Americans realize that the place of labor is side by side with the businessman and the farmer and not one degree lower." We can no longer ignore this advice. The economic stakes are too high. It's time for our country to accept labor as an equal partner in our economic life and in our political life.

In the last 3½ years we've begun to establish this goal bit by bit—such a partnership of government, labor, and business. We expanded Construction Coordinating Councils to ease local problems in that key industry. We brought labor into international negotiations in a very meaningful way. We established the Coal Commission, the Steel Tripartite Advisory Committee, and the Automobile Industry Committee to help chart the future in these areas. To fight inflation we established the national accord and the Pay Advisory Committee to seek lasting equitable solutions. And last week we took another step forward with what can be central to rebuilding our Nation's industrial base—the President's Economic Revitalization Board, composed of leaders from American labor, industry, and the public. Heading the Board will be Irving Shapiro of du Pont and Lane Kirkland, your president, and I'm now in the process of choosing the other board members to work with those two fine leaders.

It would be a mistake for you to underestimate the profound consequence of that decision which I made. For the first time, we can build a consensus for our economic future—a consensus. The Board will advise me on a full range of issues. It will recommend the outlines of an industrial development authority to help mobilize both public and private capital, including employee pension funds, to restore and to create jobs in areas affected by economic dislocation.

We're involved in nothing less than the redefinition of the way labor, business, and government work together. It will not be easy, because we are plowing new ground. But you and I realize that it's absolutely essential to have creative ideas from all segments of our country, to iron out differences as much as we can, preserving our own integrity and our own autonomy and to approach the very difficult challenges which face our Nation in a cooperative spirit.

I see rich dividends coming from this, not only in the relatively narrowly defined revitalization of American industry but in other elements of life of working people, who have better understanding before legislation is presented to the Congress and before decisions are made among labor, business, and governmental leaders. This consensus building must mean that once and for all we recognize the legitimate rights of labor to be full participants in shaping the future of our country. I want to continue this relationship that we've enjoyed the first 3½ years.

I'm still with you for passage of common situs legislation. And I will veto any attempt to repeal Davis-Bacon. And I will continue to resist any sort of effort to weaken minimum wage or occupational safety and health protection and I believe and am convinced that this country needs, and I support, labor law reform, and I'll stand with you until we get it passed.

That would be good for our country. We missed by one vote in the Senate in getting cloture the past time we tried. The Senate leadership is still with us; the House is still committed to this legislation. And as soon as the November 4 elections are over and we see the makeup of the Congress, it's important that we start working together then to get the assured votes to pass this bill.

As I've faced the immense economic problems of the last 3½ years, I can't forget the great help that labor has been to me. You've helped to forge our Nation's first energy policy, something that was long overdue. As a nation we've learned that we absolutely must reduce our dangerous overdependence on foreign oil. We have been remarkably successful, although we were delayed 3 years because of political considerations in the need to educate our Nation in the final passage of important bills to establish this policy.

We've already been able to cut oil imports this year, compared to last year and 1977, by more than 20 percent—24 percent to be exact. And every day in 1980 we import 1½ million barrels of oil less than we did when I took over as President of this country. This is a good sign for the future.

There are two ways to cut imports. One is to have good, sound conservation measures, which help every family in this country, and the other way is to produce more American oil, gas, coal, shale, solar power, synthetic fuels, gasohol, and other matters that can be used to address a very serious threat to our country.

We will have with the new-found legislation, including the windfall profits tax, a tax on the unearned income of oil companies—the most massive peacetime commitment that the world has ever seen. It's greater in its totality than the entire Interstate Highway System, the entire space program, and the entire cost of the Marshall plan that rebuilt Europe combined. If we address this opportunity carefully and successfully in a spirit of cooperation and commitment, the energy crisis that we've experienced since 1973 can turn into a great and exciting new life for the American people, because we not only are embarking on saving energy and being more cautious about removing the potential blackmail of our Nation, but we're going to create an entire new synthetic fuels program, a new industry for our country using American resources, American ingenuity, American education, American free-enterprise system commitments, American capital, and creating in the process millions of exciting new American jobs.

When the history of these years is written, it'll be said that on energy we fundamentally altered for the better our Nation's future. And I believe it will also be said that we began a fundamental rebuilding of our Nation's industrial base. The program that I announced last week, which you helped to write, will continue to fight inflation and, in addition to the

ongoing programs that we have already on the books, those that already have been presented to the Congress, and normal recovery benefits, will add an additional 1 million new jobs in the next 2 years for our country's benefit.

More important—we'll put new and more efficient tools in the hands of American workers. We'll provide jobs in growing and competitive industries which can meet and turn back foreign competition. I have no doubt that American workers can compete with any in the world if we give them the tools and the technology to do the job, and together that's exactly what I intend to do.

We'll direct investments to communities and industries which have been hard hit by economic change. I'd like to point out to you that the economic change is inevitable. We'll help to retool the automobile industry. That's moving forward very well, to produce the fuel-efficient cars that American consumers want now and will want in the future. We'll help to modernize our basic industries like steel and encourage the new high-technology industries, some of which we've not even yet been able to encompass in our mind. We'll help to rebuild our cities and towns with job-producing investments. And we'll rebuild our transportation system both to carry goods and to improve public transit. Finally, we'll invest heavily in our human resources. We'll provide new training and new skills to workers which have been hit by sudden economic change. We'll strengthen existing programs for those who lack the skills to face the future.

Two years ago we passed the Humphrey-Hawkins act to reaffirm our commitment to the goal of full employment. This year we're laying the foundation for reaching that goal; a foundation of secure energy supplies, greater productivity, steady economic growth and stable prices. In the next few years we'll also continue our urban policy. It has begun to reverse the decline of many cities.

When I campaigned around this country 4 years ago that was the greatest crying need. The sense of discouragement and despair in the hearts and minds of mayors and other local officials was sobering indeed. And I believe that any broadscale conversation with the same officials now would show that the spirit and confidence about the future has been changed drastically.

We must gain passage of our welfare reform proposals that would lift 1½ million more families out of poverty, emphasize work for able-bodied people, and reduce the financial burden on local and State governments. And we must enact our proposed expansion of the youth employment programs to provide skills and jobs for hundreds of thousands of young people.

And I stand ready to implement with you national health insurance. This is long overdue. But I believe we've put forward now to the Congress a carefully planned, carefully costed national health insurance program that will go into effect with an emphasis on cost control, with an emphasis on the prevention of disease, and the emphasis on fairness and equity to give American families adequate health care.

We must strengthen the maritime industry, both for our own economic security and our military security. And finally, I want the United States to stand for peace in the world. We've been at peace for the last 3½ years; a peace based on our military strength and on America's will and our moral strength. With your help we have reversed an 8-year steady decline in defense spending under the previous Republican administrations. Our military power is unsurpassed today, and

it will stay that way as long as I'm President. And I believe that you and the Congress will support me in that commitment.

A nation's strength gives us confidence to carry out our purposes well. That strength allowed us to negotiate the SALT II arms control treaties successfully. I look forward to further negotiations in the future on a balanced and equitable way to remove a threat of nuclear destruction from the world. With your help we ratified the Panama Canal treaties, which has brought a new atmosphere in this entire Western Hemisphere. We've sustained our foreign aid programs, the best way peacefully to compete with alien philosophies different from our own.

We've helped to bring two ancient enemies, the people of Egypt and Israel, who no longer face each other across barbed wire, but now are willing to face each other across the negotiating table and through their Ambassadors in Tel Aviv and in Cairo. Three years ago few people dreamed that such a thing would be possible, that the Jerusalem Post would be sold on the streets of Cairo and that tourists would be going back and forth across the borders between those countries.

A few minutes ago I got a call from Prime Minister Begin, who expressed his deep satisfaction with the success of Sol Linowitz' present trip into the Mideast to get the negotiations started again and to lay the groundwork for a future summit meeting which Prime Minister Begin and I discussed this morning.

And we can be proud that the United States once again stands up in defense of human rights, including trade union rights throughout the world. And let me add that we must expand human rights here at home also by ratifying the equal rights amendment to give our women an equal opportunity.

Well, to summarize, let me say that we've accomplished a lot, often against great odds. In some cases the achievements would not have been deemed possible 4 years ago, when I first met with you. We've had to take the heat on many occasions for unpopular decisions, but we've spoken the truth, and it has not always been welcome.

We've faced our problems squarely because we've faced them together. As you know, as union leaders, above all, solidarity is important. I can think of no finer recent example of solidarity than your support for the tough measures that I took in response to the Soviet invasion of Afghanistan. Our solidarity helped to strengthen the will of the Nation, to marshal support of other nations around the world for our position, and to make sure that we had in our own country a commitment to preserve peace through strength.

I got a report this morning from the Director of the Selective Service System, who informed me that 93 percent of our young men have registered for the draft during the first month. This is a much greater percentage of participation than we've had in draft registration in the past. And I expect this number to rise very rapidly in the future. These young men, like the membership of the AFL–CIO, contradict those who say that America lacks the courage to face the future. We're meeting the Soviet challenge despite controversy and despite political opposition as a free democratic society first by facing the facts and by acting together.

The American labor movement was built on realism, on persistence, and on democratic values. Our Nation's future depends on those same qualities exactly,

qualities which today are still abundant in the American people. More remains for us to do. We must fight for progress. It will not be easy, but we're fighting for it the way the labor movement has always fought for progress—shoulder to shoulder. And as has been the case with the labor movement in this country and increasingly around the world, we fight to win. And I do not intend to lose along with your help.

Thank you.

NOTE: The President spoke at 11:46 a.m. in the Cotillion Ballroom at the Sheraton-Washington Hotel.

Community Services Administration

Nomination of Laird F. Harris To Be an Assistant Director.   September 4, 1980

The President today announced that he will nominate Laird F. Harris, of Ann Arbor, Mich., to be an Assistant Director of the Community Services Administration. He would replace Frank Jones, resigned. Harris has been Director of Regional Operations for the Community Services Administration since 1977.

He was born October 15, 1942, in Cleveland, Ohio. He received a B.A. from Wesleyan University in 1964 and an M.A. from the University of Michigan in 1971. He served in the U.S. Naval Reserve from 1966 to 1969.

From 1973 to 1976, Harris was an administrative officer with the Washtenaw County (Mich.) Sheriff's Department. He was executive director of the Democratic National Convention in 1976 and Midwest field director for the Democratic National Committee during the 1976 campaign.

Harris joined the Community Services Administration in 1977 as Special Assistant to the Director and assumed his current position in August 1977.

Federal Mine Safety and Health Review Commission

Nomination of Dennis Dale Clark To Be a Member.   September 4, 1980

The President today announced that he will nominate Dennis Dale Clark, of Greenbelt, Md., to be a member of the Federal Mine Safety and Health Review Commission. He would replace Jerome R. Waldie, who has resigned, and he will be nominated for an additional term expiring in 1986. Clark has been General Counsel of this Commission since 1979.

He was born December 31, 1944, in Detroit, Mich. He received a B.A. from Ohio Wesleyan University in 1967 and a J.D. from University of Michigan Law School in 1970.

From 1970 to 1976, Clark was an associate attorney with the Washington firm of Bredhoff, Cushman, Gottesman & Cohen. From 1976 to 1977, he was associate attorney with the Washington firm of Lichtman, Abeles, Anker & Nagle. From 1977 to 1979, he was Deputy Associate Solicitor with the Fair Labor Standards Division of the U.S. Department of Labor.

B'nai B'rith International

Remarks at the Closing Banquet of the Biennial Convention.   September 4, 1980

President Spitzer, President Day, Ambassador Evron, Senator Carl Levin, Secretary Klutznick, Secretary Goldschmidt, members and friends of B'nai B'rith International, ladies and gentlemen:

My wife made me promise that at the beginning of my speech I would recognize the presence of Mr. Shalom Doron, who's the chairman of the board of the B'nai B'rith Women Children's Home in Israel, one of the finest places that I have ever known about, where Rosalynn was privileged to visit when we were in Jerusalem last year.

This is a home, as you women certainly know, for children who are severely emotionally disturbed. They have a remarkable 70-percent recovery rate among those children. They give no drugs, and as Mr. Doron says, the therapy is love. My wife is one of the experts on mental health, says it's one of the most successful programs and schools that she has ever seen in her life, and you're to be congratulated for it.

I come before you at a special time in our Nation's history, a dynamic period of controlled turmoil known as election time. [*Laughter*] It's a time when good friends can find themselves in total disagreement. It's a time when parents are very likely to find themselves at odds with their own sons and daughters. It's a time when liberals ask the candidates if they'll do enough and conservatives ask the candidates not to do too much. It's a time when mere discussions become sharp debates and when debates turn into heated arguments. I understand it's a lot like hiring a new rabbi for the synagogue. [*Laughter*]

Speaking of elections, I'm told that Jack Spitzer was a shoo-in for reelection as your president this year. I find that a good omen as I appear before you. [*Laughter*]

Well, I'm delighted to be back with you again. I remember distinctly the excitement of my attendance at your banquet in 1976. And I'm delighted to be here, because, well, I think you know why. The B'nai B'rith and the Democratic Party have stood together for progressive causes for almost 50 years—from social security to strong trade unions, from civil rights at home to human rights abroad. We've made progress because we've worked together, and we've worked together because we've had shared goals, shared ideals, shared commitments.

People sometimes say that the old Democratic coalition no longer exists. But I say that all those who care about economic justice and personal dignity and civil liberties and pluralism have a living record of achievement that keeps that coalition alive. If anyone doubts that it's alive today, let them look tonight at the people and the ideals and the achievements of B'nai B'rith International. The whole world looks to you with admiration and with appreciation.

Like you, I believe both in progress and also in the preservation of tradition. Progress is the very essence of the American dream, the conviction that each generation through hard work can give its children a better life than we ourselves enjoy. But we do not want reckless change. We value political traditions, we value our cultural diversity, and we treasure them as guideposts for the future.

This will be a decade of change, perhaps even more rapid change, perhaps even more disturbing change than we experienced in the 1970's. But it's also a decade of challenge; it's a decade of hope. Our country is on the right road to the right future, and we will stay the course. The election is not about the past. I've called it a choice between two futures, and I believe that Americans want a future of justice for our society, strength and security for our Nation. And I believe that Americans want a future of peace for the entire world. We're on the right road in building a just society.

We're not a perfect nation but we're making good progress.

B'nai B'rith has always recognized the universality of that effort for justice and for basic civil or human rights. That's why you seek ratification of the equal rights amendment, and so do I. Our Nation is more than 200 years old, and it's time for the rights of all Americans, women and men, to be guaranteed in the Constitution of the United States.

You want to preserve the separation of church and state, a policy that's served us so well for 200 years, and so do I. And you want a competent and an independent judiciary, and so do I. I want America to stay on the road that we've set for ourself in the past and which we insist upon following in the future. We're on the right road to the right future in bringing peace to the Middle East, and we'll stay the course, no matter how difficult it might be, in our commitment to justice and peace and to the security and the well-being of Israel.

I hope that when the history books are written about my own administration, that one of the paragraphs there will be that President Jimmy Carter, representing the United States, helped the leaders and the people of Israel and Egypt to find a permanent peace. This is most important for us. Ever since President Truman recognized Israel's independence the very day it was proclaimed in Israel, our two nations have had a special relationship based on a common heritage and a common commitment to ethical and Democratic values. It's in the strategic and the moral interest of the United States of America to have peace in the Mideast and a secure and a peaceful Israel. It's in our interest as well as those of the people of Israel.

We've not been completely successful yet, but our course in the Middle East has brought the first real peace that that region has known in the 32 years of Israel's existence. There is no turning back. The brave vision of Prime Minister Begin and President Anwar Sadat has been vindicated. The proof is in the almost unbelievable present circumstance, for Ambassadors are exchanged between nations, in meetings between the leaders of those nations in Cairo, Tel Aviv, Jerusalem, and also in Alexandria, in airline flights between the two countries on a routine basis, and even the fact that now Israeli visitors or tourists can buy the Jerusalem Post at newsstands in Cairo.

Normalization has begun. It can and it must proceed further. When I went to Jerusalem and to Cairo and to Alexandria, the excitement of the hundreds of thousands of people on the streets were the most vivid testimony to me of the hunger in the hearts and minds of the people of those two great nations for a lasting peace and for justice.

The United States of America is a full partner with Israel and Egypt in the task of extending that peace—extending a genuine peace between Israel and all her neighbors. And I'm also convinced that the people of Jordan and Syria and Lebanon and the other nations in the Middle East who are Arab want peace as deeply as do the people of Israel and of Egypt. Some leaders have not yet been convinced, but I'm convinced that the people there want peace.

Together we're engaged in the only negotiation that has ever addressed both Israel's security and the political status of the West Bank and Gaza at the same time on the same agenda. And I'd like to remind you that this was an agenda set by the leaders of the two nations—Israel and Egypt—even before we began the three-way talks that led to Camp David accords and the peace treaty itself. Prime Minister Begin has assured me that he wants this from the bottom of his heart.

The road will not be easy. I cannot assure you that our country will always agree with every position taken by the Government of Israel. But whatever differences arise, they will never affect our commitment to a secure Israel. There will be no so-called reassessment of support for Israel in a Carter administration.

As Ambassador Evron pointed out to you, when he spoke recently, we have never threatened to slow down or cut off aid to Israel, and I can assure you that we never will. I know from experience and from long and extended negotiations and discussion with the leaders of those two countries that without security for Israel there can be no peace. President Sadat understands this just as clearly, as do I, or as Prime Minister Begin understands it. That's why we moved so quickly in the first few months of my own Presidency to enact a strong antiboycott law.

Such a law, as you know, has been blocked under the Republicans by the Secretaries of State and Treasury. They were afraid it would hurt our relationships, diplomatic and trade relationships with the Arab world. I thought about this. But I decided to go ahead despite these risks, because I knew it was the right thing to do. Now foreigners no longer tell American business leaders where they can do business and with whom. And Secretary Phil Klutznick, the Secretary of Commerce, is making sure that we're going to keep it that way.

The United States Government and myself personally are committed to United Nations Resolution 242, and we will oppose any attempt to change it. The United States Government and I personally oppose an independent Palestinian state, and unless and until they recognize Israel's right to exist and accept Resolution

242 as a basis for peace, we will neither recognize nor negotiate with the PLO. As I have repeatedly stated, it is long past time for an end to terrorism.

Also I know, and have known since my early childhood, the importance of Jerusalem in Jewish history. From the time King David first united the nation of Israel and proclaimed the ancient city of Jerusalem its capital, the Jewish people have drawn inspiration from Jerusalem. I sensed that special feeling myself last year when I stood as President of the United States before the Knesset in Jerusalem. I was there searching for peace in the city of peace. My prayers were answered in the Egyptian-Israeli peace treaty.

We're still pursuing with Israel and Egypt the larger peace that all of us seek. In such a peace, Jerusalem should remain forever undivided, with free access to the holy places, and we will make certain that the future of Jerusalem can only be determined through agreement with the full concurrence of Israel.

It's important for me to point out to you—because we share an intense interest in this subject—that President Sadat understands perfectly that my positions have been, are now, and will be those that I have just described to you.

I believe in keeping Israel strong, and I'm proud that in the 32 years of Israel's existence, one half the total economic and military aid has been delivered to that great democracy during the brief time that I have been President of the United States. I don't look on this as being kind to Israel, nor as a handout; I look upon it as President of our country as an investment in the security of America.

Ultimately, as all of you know, there is no other path to peace in the Middle East except through negotiation, and those negotiations are difficult, tedious, some-times contentious. Sometimes there is a delay in progress that causes us all to be frustrated, sometimes almost discouraged. No one who cherishes the goal of peace can allow that course to founder. This is the policy that I will always follow. There will not be one policy for election year and another policy after the election. Exactly the same policy that led to the Camp David accords and to the peace treaty between Israel and Egypt and an uninterrupted supply of military and economic aid to Israel will continue as long as I am President of the United States.

I shared a common problem with Prime Minister Begin and with President Sadat. As was the case with them, my personal involvement in the Camp David process carried high political risks. No politician likes to have a highly publicized effort for a great achievement and fail. There was certainly no guarantee of success. The differences seemed almost insurmountable. Neither was there any guarantee of success in Jerusalem or Cairo when I went there to remove the obstacles to a peace treaty. I have been personally involved in the peace process because in conscience there is really no choice for me. We simply must continue to move away from war and stalemate to peace and to progress for the people of Israel and for the people of Egypt.

Our efforts were successful in 1978. Our efforts were successful in 1979. If we stay the course, they will be successful in the future. This is a time not for despair, but for a renewed commitment.

This week my personal representative to the peace negotiations, Ambassador Sol Linowitz, has been in the Middle East again, meeting with Prime Minister Begin and then with President Sadat. Once again we've found a way to move towards peace. The talks will resume. And again I will personally join in the search for peace, if necessary in a summit meeting, which Prime Minister Begin and I discussed on the phone when he called me this morning. He called to express his personal gratitude at the success of the Linowitz mission to the Middle East, and also to express his gratitude at the renewed prospects for progress. As you know, President Sadat has already publicly agreed with this idea of a a summit meeting if necessary to ensure success.

We are on the right road in working for peace and in helping to keep Israel secure, and we'll stay on that road in close partnership with our Israeli friends as long as I'm President.

The Mideast peace effort cannot be isolated as an international affair. Closely related to it—and I hope that you will mark my words—we are on the right road also in moving toward energy security in the future. We had to fight for 3 years, as Senator Carl Levin knows, who helped me with this effort, to enact a comprehensive energy program. It's only just begun to work, because the legislation has only just recently been passed. But the benefits are already clear. We're now importing 24 percent less foreign oil than we were when I became President. The first year, 1977, that I was in office, we averaged importing about 8½ million barrels of oil every day. This year we expect that average to have dropped to about 6½ million barrels per day, which means that's a 2 million barrel less purchase of foreign oil every day, because we've moved on energy. But this progress is not a sure thing for the future. The success of this effort depends on the outcome of the election this year.

The new Republican leaders sneer at energy conservation. They say we should do away with the 55-mile speed limit. They say we should do away with the synthetic fuel program. They say we should abolish the windfall profits tax, a tax on the unearned profits of the big oil companies. And they would like to let the big oil companies keep the money, money that we will use to spur solar energy, coal use, gasohol and to help the poor and the aged pay for the higher cost of fuel to heat their homes.

As an alternative, all they offer is the wan hope that if we just give the oil companies enough money, they'll solve the energy problem for us and maybe help to shape our foreign policy at the same time. We must be very careful about this. The new Republican leaders do not seem to recognize the cost of foreign oil dependence—not just the financial cost, not just the cost in joblessness and inflation, but the foreign policy cost and the national security costs as well. To abandon conservation, to abandon our energy program could be to take the destiny of our Nation out of our own hands and put it in the hands of OPEC. We must not permit that. You should consider very carefully who might be Secretary of Energy or Secretary of State in a different administration next year.

We're on the right road also in rebuilding the cities of America. We've built a tough-minded working partnership between American mayors and the Federal Government and also private industry. You can see and feel the result in cities all over America—a renewed sense of pride and accomplishment and confidence.

When I campaigned for President in 1976 and went into almost any city in this country and talked to the local officials there in the counties and the city governments, there was a sense of discouragement, alienation, and despair. We've not yet been completely successful, but we have started rebuilding the spirit of accomplishment and confidence in our cities. We still have a long way to go and this program—so successful so far—is not a sure thing for the future. It depends on the outcome of this election.

A gigantic, election-year tax cut promised—Reagan-Kemp-Roth—would deprive us of over a trillion dollars between now and 1987—the financial tools to finish this job, not only in the cities but to meet the social needs of America. The scheme would deal our cities a great blow and would set them back a generation. We simply cannot permit this to happen.

Now our country is ready to build on these kinds of foundations. The economic renewal plan that I announced last week will help us do just that. We will retool American industry and make it more competitive and more innovative and more productive. The results will be more jobs and more stable prices for all the people of our country.

The alternative presented by the new Republican leaders would reignite inflation just as we're beginning to get it under control. The Republican nominee for Vice President once estimated that the scheme that he now advocates, Reagan-Kemp-Roth, would mean an inflation rate of more than 30 percent. This is one free lunch that America simply cannot afford.

We're also on the right road to the right future in meeting challenges from abroad. Before I took office, our military strength slid steadily downward for 8 straight years. We have reversed that trend, to ensure that we'll continue to have the modern conventional forces and the modern strategic forces needed to deter war, to keep our Nation at peace through strength.

We are now moving decisively to increase our security—and also that of our friends—in NATO and in the critical Indian Ocean, and in the Persian Gulf area we are building American strength. The brutal Soviet invasion of Afghanistan shows how important these efforts are. We're determined to respect the independence of the nations of that area, and we are determined to meet any threats to our vital interests.

At the same time, we will stand by our commitments to control nuclear arms. As long as I'm President, the United States will not initiate a pointless and a dangerous nuclear arms race. We'll continue to work for the control of nuclear weapons. Mutual and balanced nuclear arms control is not some sentimental act of charity. It's not a favor we're doing for some other nation. It's essential to our own national security.

And we're on the right road to promoting human rights. I'll not be swayed from that course. We'll stand firm for human rights at the Review Conference on European Security and Cooperation in Madrid this fall to make sure that the Helsinki agreements are carried out. We'll be fighting for human rights as we did in Belgrade under Secretary Goldberg at the last session.

Because of our strong efforts and the focus of world attention, more than 50,000 Soviet Jews moved last year to freedom in Israel and to the United States. As you know this was the greatest number in history. They found freedom to worship, freedom to rejoice in the cultural and religious traditions of centuries. But in July, last month, less than 2,500 were permitted to emigrate—an annual rate of 30,000—and the rate of new approvals was even lower. This makes our cause more urgent, our resolve more certain, and we will continue to communicate that resolve very clearly to the Soviet leaders.

In closing, let me say that, as President of our country, I try to represent its people. The American people believe in peace, for ourselves and for our allies whom we love. The American people believe that in order to have peace we must be strong, strong militarily, and we're second to no nation in the world in military strength; that we must be strong politically; that our influence must be extended to others in a benevolent and acceptable way; strong morally, that we do not ever yield from a commitment to the unchanging principles and goals and ideals on which our Nation was founded—a nation committed to freedom and to pride in the future and to the worth of an individual human being, a nation committed to the principle that every person can worship as he or she chooses, and that in diversity, in the plurality of our economy and our social structure, lies not weakness, but strength.

I represent a nation that believes in truth, and sometimes the truth hurts. Sometimes it's a temptation for a political leader in a democracy like ours or like Israel's to mislead the people, because most people want to hear good things. But Americans and Israelis are not afraid to face the facts, and that's part of the strength of our society.

And I represent a people who believe in democracy and openness in letting government differences be exposed, in letting the people of our nations be involved in the debates. We're not afraid of those differences and those debates. We're not afraid to strip away the bark and let people understand the reasons why decisions are made.

Part of our strength as a country is that a President or a Prime Minister—we're not alone. When we speak, we speak for the people, not in spite of the people. And I also represent a country that believes in the future. A country that's not afraid. A country that realizes that we have never made progress the easy way. A country

that knows that we can't find simple solutions to difficult questions and that we cannot waver in our commitment. And that the country must be united. It must be bound together with confidence in our own strength, recognizing the blessings that God's given us, thankful for them and willing to use them for the benefit not only of ourselves but of others.

We would never have been successful in Camp David had it not been for our attention to the future. The last few hours we were there were hours of despair, because we felt that we had failed. As we prepared to leave Camp David Prime Minister Begin sent over a stack of photographs of me and him and President Sadat and asked me if I would simply sign my name. He wanted to give them to his grandchildren. And I had my secretary go and find out from some of the other members of the Israeli delegation the personal names of every one of his grandchildren. And I took a little extra time, and I wrote each name on the photograph and signed it myself. And instead of sending it back to Prime Minister Begin by messenger, I carried it over myself.

We were both discouraged men, because we had reached what seemed to be an impasse. And we stood there on the porch of one of those little cabins at Camp David, and he began to go through the photographs—they were all just alike but had different names—and he told me about each one of his grandchildren and which one he loved the most and which one was closest to him and which one got in trouble, which one was the best student. And I told him about my grandchildren, too. And we began to think about the future and the fact that what we did at Camp David was not just to be looked upon as a political achievement that might bring accolades or congratulations to us. It was not just an investment in peace for our own generation; it was an investment in the future.

We share a lot, Prime Minister Begin and I. The people of the democratic world share a lot—a common faith in our own country and its principles and a faith in the worth of other human beings all over the world, even those quite different from us. We believe that there's the same yearning in the hearts of people in every land for freedom, for self-realization, a better life for their children, and a future of peace and security and hope. That's what I want for our country and for the countries that are so important to us, like Israel.

Thank you very much.

NOTE: The President spoke at 9:53 p.m. in the Sheraton Ballroom at the Sheraton-Washington Hotel. In his opening remarks, he referred to Jack J. Spitzer, president of B'nai B'rith International, Grace Day, president of B'nai B'rith Women, and Israeli Ambassador to the United States Ephraim Evron.

Confederated Tribes of the Siletz Indians of Oregon

Statement on Signing S. 2055 Into Law.
September 5, 1980

I am pleased to sign into law S. 2055, an act to establish a reservation for the Confederated Tribes of the Siletz Indians of Oregon.

Early in my administration I signed into law the Siletz Indian Restoration Act of 1977, restoring Federal acknowledgment of the Confederated Tribes of Siletz Indians of Oregon and making them eligible for the special programs and services provided by the United States for Indians. Section 7 of that act provided for the establishment of a reservation for the tribe and required the administration to submit to the Congress

within 2 years a plan for the establishment of the reservation.

S. 2055 reflects this administration's plan and strikes a balance among the interests of the tribe and those of the local community, the State of Oregon, and the Federal Government. Most of the lands to be conveyed to the tribe under the act are timberlands. They also include an important area which would permit the tribe to centralize its facilities and activities in a place to which the tribe has strong historical, cultural, and emotional ties.

All parties involved—officials of the administration, of the tribe, and of the State and local governments of Oregon are to be commended for their fine spirit of cooperation. I want to specially commend Congressman Les AuCoin and Senator Mark Hatfield for their leadership in this endeavor.

It is with pleasure that I sign S. 2055.

NOTE: As enacted, S. 2055 is Public Law 96–340, approved September 5.

United States Attorney Herman Sillas, Jr.

White House Statement. **September 5, 1980**

There have been a number of press reports about the Department of Justice's recommendations to the President concerning Mr. Herman Sillas, the United States Attorney for the Eastern District of California. The President's Counsel, Lloyd N. Cutler, has reviewed these recommendations and, together with the Department of Justice, has afforded Mr. Sillas and his counsel a full opportunity to examine the record and submit their comments.

Mr. Cutler has presented his report to the President, who has reviewed and approved it. It concludes that the allegation against Mr. Sillas has not been proven. An unproven allegation, of course, should not damage Mr. Sillas' good reputation. However, the report also concludes that because of the course of the investigation and the events connected with it, the necessary relationship of mutual trust and confidence between the Department of Justice and Mr. Sillas, as a United States attorney, has been impaired to the point where either or both may wish to discontinue the relationship. Mr. Cutler has therefore called upon Mr. Sillas to examine his position in the light of these conclusions, before Mr. Cutler advises the President further concerning the matter.

Digest of Other White House Announcements

The following listing includes the President's public schedule and other items of general interest announced by the White House Press Office and not included elsewhere in this issue.

August 31

The President returned to the White House from Camp David, Md.

September 2

The President met at the White House with Zbigniew Brzezinski, Assistant to the President for National Security Affairs.

The President transmitted to the Congress the annual report of the Commodity Credit Corporation for the fiscal year ending September 30, 1979.

September 3

The President met at the White House with:
—Dr. Brzezinski;
—the executive board of the American Federation of State, County, and Municipal Employees.

September 4

The President met at the White House with:
—Dr. Brzezinski;
—Representative Geraldine A. Ferraro of New York;
—Frank B. Moore, Assistant to the President for Congressional Liaison;
—Alfred J. McGuire, Chairman of the President's Council on Physical Fitness and Sports;
—leaders of the National Conference on Soviet Jewry.

September 5

The President met at the White House with:
—Dr. Brzezinski;
—Secretary of State Edmund S. Muskie, Secretary of Defense Harold Brown, Deputy Secretary of State Warren M. Christopher, Jack H. Watson, Jr., Assistant to the President, Lloyd N. Cutler, Counsel to the President, and Dr. Brzezinski;
—the executive committee of the U.S. Conference of Mayors, and Stuart E. Eizenstat, Assistant to the President for Domestic Affairs and Policy, Anne Wexler, Assistant to the President, Eugene Eidenberg, Assistant to the President for Intergovernmental Affairs, and James T. McIntyre, Jr., Director of the Office of Management and Budget.

The President left the White House for a weekend stay at Camp David.

NOMINATIONS SUBMITTED TO THE SENATE

NOTE: Only nominations for promotions of members of the Uniformed Services were submitted to the Senate during the period covered by this issue.

CHECKLIST OF WHITE HOUSE PRESS RELEASES

The following listing contains releases of the White House Press Office which are not included in this issue.

Released September 1, 1980

Advance text: remarks at the Quad-Cities picnic-rally in Tuscumbia, Ala.

Released September 2, 1980

Advance text: opening remarks at the town meeting in Independence, Mo.

Released September 3, 1980

Advance text: remarks at the Zion Baptist Church in Philadelphia, Pa.

Released September 4, 1980

Advance text: remarks at the B'nai B'rith International convention closing banquet

Advance text: remarks at the AFL–CIO general board meeting

ACTS APPROVED BY THE PRESIDENT

Approved September 4, 1980

H.R. 507_____ Public Law 96–335
An act to authorize Federal participation in stream rectification, Trinity River Division, Central Valley project, California, and for other purposes.

S. 496_____ Public Law 96–336
An act to increase the appropriations ceiling for title I of the Colorado River Basin Salinity Control Act (the Act of June 24, 1974; 88 Stat. 266), to increase the appropriations authorization for the Small Reclamation Projects Act of 1956 (70 Stat. 1044), and for other purposes.

S.J. Res. 83_____ Public Law 96–337
A joint resolution to authorize the Camp Fire Girls of Cundys Harbor, Maine, to erect a memorial in the District of Columbia.

S. 1998_____ Public Law 96–338
An act to provide for the United States to hold in trust for the Tule River Indian Tribe certain public domain lands formerly removed from the Tule River Indian Reservation.

S. 2549_____ Public Law 96–339
An act to authorize appropriations for fiscal years 1981, 1982, and 1983 for the Atlantic Tunas Convention Act of 1975, and for other purposes.

S. 2055_____ Public Law 96–340
An act to establish a reservation for the Confederated Tribes of Siletz Indians of Oregon.

Military Personnel and Compensation Amendments of 1980

Remarks on Signing H.R. 5168 Into Law. September 8, 1980

THE PRESIDENT. *Chairman Stennis, Chairman Price, Senator Nunn, Secretary Brown, members of the Joint Chiefs of Staff, distinguished citizen, civilian leaders of the Department of Defense, and others who are interested in a strong America and a fine Armed Forces that will keep our Nation strong:*

I'm very pleased to be signing into law today this very important legislation, the military personnel management and compensation bill that was sponsored primarily by Senators Nunn and Warner. This legislation will increase the compensation for the men and women of the Armed Forces and will help greatly to keep our Nation secure because of an improvement in the recruitment and retention of qualified members of the Armed Forces.

With the support of the Congress in recent years we have made great progress in strengthening our Nation's defense. Our sustained real increases in defense spending have encouraged, as well, increases by our own allies, particularly those in the Western European theater. The 5-year defense plan that I put to the Congress will increase real defense spending by over $100 billion between now and 1985. But we know that dollars alone cannot enhance nor preserve our American security. People, the men and women of our military forces, are the heart and soul of America's military strength. Their work,

their sacrifice, their dedication to duty are the keys to military power in the United States.

Through this legislation our Nation reaffirms its strong support and our appreciation to these men and women who serve us all so well. It authorizes $700 million in increased benefits that will alleviate financial hardship and sacrifice that have both been too onerous on the shoulders of the men and women who serve us so well. This will help those people in the Armed Forces with several different elements of financial burden. Together with the military pay raise which I just signed into law this morning and the rest of my legislative and budget proposals on military compensation, total pay and benefits during this fiscal year, 1981, will go up more than $4 billion. This is the biggest single increase in the history of our Nation in either war or peace.

To supplement the higher pay this legislation will make important changes in military benefits. For people in high-cost areas, we are raising the housing allowance. Reimbursement for travel and transportation, which many military men and women now have to pay out of their own pockets, will now be much higher. Special pay and bonuses for career military personnel who serve at sea will be raised, who have flight duty will be raised, and also for those who serve in critical skills.

I want to acknowledge the strong leadership and the hard work of many Members of Congress, especially of course Senator Sam Nunn and Senator John Warner, Bill Nichols in the House, and the chairmen of the committees in the House and Senate.

History records the heroism and the sacrifice of those who served in battle, but there are many different kinds of heroism, many kinds of sacrifice for the benefit of our own Nation. The dedication and effectiveness of those who serve in times of peace to prevent war are less often recognized, but just as important.

On the first day of May, I went to the U.S.S. *Nimitz* to point out to them how much our Nation appreciates what they and others have done for our country. I said to the crew on Memorial Day that the pay or benefits or privileges that are given to them, however much they might be raised, could never fully reward those who put their lives on the line in the service of our country, but it's important that those who do so must be adequately compensated. This is important, not only for reasons of fairness but also for reasons of national security. It's a great loss to our country to have a well-trained military person who, because of excessive financial burdens on the family, have to resign from the military to seek a way to sustain their own loved ones.

This legislation goes a long way toward achieving the goal of expressing our Nation's indebtedness to the courageous men and women of the Armed Forces and to enhancing our Nation's security. And I'm deeply grateful to the men and women standing behind me for the leadership they've shown in the passage of this forward legislation.

I'd now like to sign the bill, and I'll call on two or three of our distinguished visitors to say a word.

[*At this point, the President signed the bill.*]

Thank you very much.

SENATOR STENNIS. Well, Mr. President, I think you've stated the facts well, and I appreciate your attitude and all of those that have worked in our committees very vigorously.

You went at the hard thing, not just pitch in a raise, but a raise and a supplement at the critical points, and that's what this bill really covers. It took weeks and months, and I'm very glad to see it become law. I think it carries strength. Strength is what it'll mean, and it's needed. I feel that we could even go as far as sacrificing some manpower to get the money put the right place, the same money put to the right place.

Thank you.

THE PRESIDENT. We'll try not to have to do either.

Thank you.

REPRESENTATIVE PRICE. Mr. President, I of course join Senator Stennis in his response to your statement. The House Armed Services Committee followed good leadership, and I doubt if there was a vote—I'd have to check the record—but I doubt if there was a vote against this legislation in the committee.

THE PRESIDENT. I think that's right.

REPRESENTATIVE PRICE. Having been elected to Congress when I was a corporal I know what this means to the enlisted man. [*Laughter*]

I think that we may have waited a little longer than we should have in bringing about these pay reforms and benefit reforms, and I hope that both the House and the Senate committees keep their interest in this particular phase of military life so that the people in the service know that they will never be forgotten.

Thank you.

THE PRESIDENT. Thank you, Mr. Chairman.

Well, as a President and Commander in Chief of our military forces and also as a former professional military officer I recognize excellent work when I see it. All of us are here to join in the occasion and to express our appreciation for what has been done. But there's one man here who had the special insight and knowledge and commitment to do the detailed work of making sure that these hundreds of millions of dollars are an excellent investment in our Nation's future, who understands the details of the personnel problems in the military, and who joined with Senator John Warner, who can't be here this afternoon, in sponsoring this legislation. This is a very fine birthday present for Senator Sam Nunn, and I'd like to call on him to say a word if you would.

Sam, congratulations to you.

SENATOR NUNN. Mr. President, this is a great day, and it's a great birthday present for me, but more importantly for the men and women who serve our Nation. You know, this bill is sort of unprecedented in the sense that, as one of the coauthors, I call it the Warner-Nunn bill and John Warner calls it the Nunn-Warner bill and to those people in the military who are so grateful for this bill it's known as the Warner-Nunn bill. To those on Wall Street who are concerned about fiscal responsibility and the inflation rate it's known as the Nunn bill. [*Laughter*]

But, nevertheless, it is a bipartisan effort; it is started as a bipartisan effort; it is continued as one. We had the complete cooperation of Congressman Nichols and his counterpart on the Republican side on the House. We had the total backing of the chairmen, Chairman Stennis and Chairman Price. The Joint Chiefs played a major role in this. The civilian Secretaries played a major role, Secretary of Defense, and Robin Perry played a major role. George Travers, on my staff, who does all the work for me, has done a tremendous amount. George, I wish you would hold up your hand. And Hugh Evans in the Legislative Counsel's Office, who's been drafting bills for years and years, and this is his first signing ceremony. Hugh, hold up your hand and let people see you, because you drafted this legislation.

So, to all of you I say thank you, who have played a role in this. And I think the gratifying thing about it, Mr. President, with your cooperation and your enthusiastic support, we are signing into law today, and you've signed into law, a measure that will not only help the young men and women who serve in our military forces, but most importantly, it will help contribute to the protection of our national security. So, I say thank you to you, Mr. President.

THE PRESIDENT. Thank you, Sam.

GENERAL JONES. Mr. President, on behalf of the millions of men and women who wear the uniform in the armed services, we'd like to thank you and the Members of Congress for this recognition of the heavy burden. You can be assured of the dedication and the courage of the people who wear the uniform, and this gives us an opportunity to keep many of the well-trained, experienced personnel with us. Thanks to all of you.

THE PRESIDENT. Thank you, Dave.

Thank you all very much.

NOTE: The President spoke at 2:17 p.m. at the ceremony in the Cabinet Room at the White House.

As enacted, H.R. 5168 is Public Law 96–343, approved September 8.

Department of Defense Authorization Act, 1981

Statement on Signing H.R. 6974 Into Law. September 8, 1980

I have today signed into law H.R. 6974, the Department of Defense Authorization Act, 1981. This bill authorizes appropriations of nearly $53 billion for defense procurement, research and development, civil defense, and military pay and benefits. I am pleased that this bill is fundamentally in agreement with my national security policy. I remain committed to a policy of continuing real growth in the defense budget.

I fully support the military pay and benefits authorized by this bill, for I share with the Congress its concern for assuring a level of compensation for our service men and women commensurate with their considerable contribution and sacrifice.

I am seriously concerned, however, over the unrequested additions in procurement and research and development contained in this bill. My 1981 budget proposals carefully balanced the need for a strong national defense against other competing foreign and domestic requirements. As I have previously indicated, the administration will be working with the Appropriations Committees to bring the defense budget more in line with my original request, thus restoring this budget balance.

Finally, in signing H.R. 6974, I must comment upon section 302(b) which provides that when a determination is made by the Secretary of Defense that certain limitations on enlistments should be waived for national security reasons, it shall be effective only if "the Congress adopts a concurrent resolution stating in substance that it approved the proposed waivers."

I must reiterate my opposition to such provisions which violate the fundamental doctrine of separation of powers. Accordingly, I intend to treat this unconstitutional provision as a "report-and-wait" provision and am directing the Secretary of Defense to notify the Congress of any determination to waive the applicable limitations when reasons of national security so require.

NOTE: As enacted, H.R. 6974 is Public Law 96–342, approved September 8.

Wind Energy Systems Act of 1980

Statement on Signing H.R. 5892 Into Law. September 8, 1980

I have today signed H.R. 5892, the Wind Energy Systems Act of 1980, a bill authorizing a wind energy research, development, and demonstration program. The bill's purpose is to accelerate the widespread utilization of wind energy, which can play an important role in reaching the national goal I set last year of providing 20 percent of U.S. energy needs from solar and renewable sources by the year 2000. Senators Jackson and Matsunaga, Congressmen Mineta and Fuqua, and the numerous sponsors of this legislation are to be commended for their foresight in obtaining the enactment of H.R. 5892.

H.R. 5892 establishes specific objectives for wind-powered electric generating capacity and wind systems costs by 1988 and authorizes financial assistance, including Federal procurements of wind energy systems, to help achieve these ends. The bill also wisely permits discretion in selecting the types of financial assistance best suited to promoting the act's objectives. The Department of Energy will exercise this discretion to promote wind energy systems that are commercially viable and economically competitive. The Department will also seek significant cost-sharing from the private sector in order to reduce wind energy systems costs and to improve the prospects for commercialization.

My approval of H.R. 5892, along with my recent approval of tax credits for wind energy systems, clearly demonstrates this administration's continued commitment to renewable energy resources. The programs established by H.R. 5892 can make an important contribution to the administration's ongoing wind energy program, and it is with pleasure that I sign this bill into law.

NOTE: As enacted, H.R. 5892 is Public Law 96–345, approved September 8.

National Advisory Council on Extension and Continuing Education

Appointment of Three Members. September 8, 1980

The President today announced the appointment of three persons as members of the National Advisory Council on Extension and Continuing Education. They are:

Dagmar I. Celeste, of Delaware, Ohio, an education specialist who is active in community affairs. She has been a program coordinator with the Academy for Contemporary Problems in Columbus, Ohio, and a trustee of PACE Association (Plan of Action for Cleveland's Education).

John B. Ervin, of University City, Mo., vice president of the Danforth Foundation (reappointment). He was previously dean of the School of Continuing Education and the summer school at Washington University.

James C. Summers, of Morgantown, W. Va., an extension specialist in research and program evaluation at West Virginia University's Center for Extension and Continuing Education, and an associate professor of industrial relations in the College of Business and Economics at West Virginia University.

Auto Industry Committee

Appointment of 14 Members to the Executive Committee. September 8, 1980

The President today announced the appointment of 14 business, labor, and Government leaders to the Executive Committee of the President's Auto Industry Committee.

The Auto Industry Committee is being created as part of the President's program to help revitalize the domestic auto industry. The Committee will be responsible for developing an ongoing Government-business-labor partnership to expand employment, productivity, and sales in the domestic auto industry. The Committee will be chaired by Neil Goldschmidt, Secretary of Transportation.

The Executive Committee will act as the focal point for a continuing review of issues fundamental to the health and vitality of the U.S. industry. It will set the agenda for the Auto Industry Committee, develop specific proposals to strengthen the domestic auto industry, and make recommendations for action to the President's Economic Policy Group.

The Auto Industry Committee also will have task forces to consider proposals in areas such as plant location, worker adjustment, and community impact; international competitiveness; regulations; capital needs; investment incentives and tax policy; research and technology; and trade. The Auto Industry Committee also will work regularly with a bipartisan congressional consultative committee.

The members of the Executive Committee will hold an organizational meeting in Detroit on Wednesday, September 10, 1980. The first meeting of the Executive Committee will be scheduled later this month.

The members of the Executive Committee named by the President are:

NEIL GOLDSCHMIDT, Secretary of Transportation (Chairman);

JAMES BERE, chairman of the board, Borg-Warner;

PETER BOMMARITO, international president, United Rubber Workers;

PHILIP CALDWELL, chairman of the board, Ford Motor Co.;

DOUGLAS FRASER, president, United Auto Workers;

LEE IACOCCA, chairman of the board, Chrysler Corp.;

GEORGE IRVIN, president, National Automobile Dealers Association;

PHILIP KLUTZNICK, Secretary of Commerce (*ex officio*);

RAY MARSHALL, Secretary of Labor (*ex officio*);

LLOYD MCBRIDE, international president, United Steel Workers;

JAMES W. MCLERNON, president and chief executive officer, Volkswagen of America;

GERALD MEYERS, chairman of the board, American Motors;

THOMAS A. MURPHY, chairman of the board, General Motors;

ESTHER PETERSON, Special Assistant to the President for Consumer Affairs (*ex officio*).

Rosh Hashanah

Interview With Dan Raviv of Israel Television.   September 8, 1980

THE PRESIDENT. I'm very pleased to speak with the people of Israel on the joyous occasion of Rosh Hashanah, the Jewish New Year 5741. It's a time both to recall the past and to look forward to the future. Rosh Hashanah falls this year on an historic anniversary: It's been 2 years since Prime Minister Begin, President Sadat, and I met at Camp David.

For 13 days and nights we worked there together, seeking one overriding objective, a secure and lasting peace in the Middle East. All the hopes of many generations came together at that time. We succeeded, largely because of the courage and vision of your Prime Minister and of the President of Egypt. Then, for the first time since Israel's rebirth as a modern state, peace came—a real peace between Israel and Egypt. The people of America joined our friends in Israel in rejoicing.

Now my country is working as a full partner with Israel and Egypt to complete the process so hopefully begun at Camp David. For the past 16 months, we've labored together to make possible the next great step toward our vital goals. Much remains to be done. Progress may be slow. Yet, as we learned at Camp David, we must never relent; we must never yield in the face of temporary difficulties. We must persevere just as we did last week in mutually arranging for Israel and Egypt to resume the autonomy negotiations.

The commitment of all three parties is clear. And to that I add my personal commitment to do all that I can to make possible the realization of the ancient dream of the Jewish people—security and peace in the land of your fathers.

As this New Year begins, I reaffirm the commitment of the American Nation and its Government to the indestructible ties of friendship between us and the people of Israel. Together we share a special relationship, a unique indelible relationship based on deep devotion to the same moral and democratic ideals. The United States is now and forever committed to a secure and free Israel, an Israel whose security and well-being are fundamental to our own strategic, political, and moral concerns. And to this I add my own personal commitment as President of the United States. This policy will not change.

So, I join you at this New Year in looking to a future of hope and promise. May this be the year of the next great steps towards a permanent and lasting peace.

MR. RAVIV. Mr. President, if I may ask you, this is an election year, and the Jewish vote might be decisive—but I don't have to tell you about it. There is a theory, Mr. President, that after the election, without the fear of the voters, you'll come down on Israel as strongly as you came over disputable topics between your administration and the Israeli Government, like settlements, Jerusalem, Palestinians. Would you please comment on that?

THE PRESIDENT. Yes. As I said to the B'nai B'rith annual meeting this past week, there will not be one policy or attitude toward Israel before the election and a different policy or attitude after the election.

I've been in office now for 3½ years, and our American position, which is clearly understood by Prime Minister Begin and also by President Sadat and the American public, is sound, undeviating, and I think it's conducive to the full realization of the hopes that all of us have for peace. There is no possibility that the American public or the American Government would change its basic attitude toward Israel—that of insisting upon a secure Israel, an independent and free Israel, an Israel which is able to live in peace with all her neighbors, and an Israel which is given a full voice in any agreement that might be hammered out in the careful and sometimes tedious negotiations that are ahead of us.

I have also a need to make clear one other thing. My positions toward the settlements, toward the West Bank, toward the security of Israel, toward the intimate ties that bind our two countries together, toward the mutual benefits that are derived from this strategic interrelationship, our commitment to aid for Israel, economic and military aid, are clearly understood by President Sadat, and they're clearly understood by other Arab leaders in the area. I had a recent meeting with King Hussein. I have nothing to conceal and no inclination to change. We are deeply committed to the peace process, and it would be devastating to me as a mediator, a full partner in the negotiations, if I changed my position in any material way.

What I want to do is to work closely with the leaders of Israel and the leaders of Egypt to find a secure peace for all, understanding that both nations individually and other nations in the future would have to agree to a comprehensive peace settlement when it is devised through negotiations.

MR. RAVIV. Mr. President, on behalf of the Israel television, thank you very much.

THE PRESIDENT. Thank you. My best wishes to all the people of your great country.

NOTE: The interview began at 9:50 a.m. in the Library at the White House. It was taped for broadcast in Israel on September 9.

United States Advertising in Foreign Broadcasting Industries

Message to the Congress on Proposed Legislation. September 9, 1980

To the Congress of the United States

I have determined that the provision of Canadian tax law which denies a deduction for the cost of advertising placed with a foreign broadcaster and directed primarily at the Canadian market is an unreasonable practice which burdens U.S. commerce within the meaning of section 301(a)(2)(B) of the Trade Act of 1974 (19 U.S.C. 2411). The Canadian law was intended to strengthen the Canadian broadcast industry as an aspect of Canadian culture. However, the law places the cost of attaining its objectives on U.S.

companies and thus unreasonably and unnecessarily burdens U.S. commerce. It is estimated that U.S. broadcasters have lost access to more than $20 million in advertising revenues annually as a result of this law.

Therefore, I am proposing legislation which would amend the Internal Revenue Code to deny a deduction, otherwise allowable under the Code, for expenses of an advertisement placed with a foreign broadcast station and directed primarily to a market in the United States if a similar deduction is denied to advertisers, in the country in which such station is located, for the costs of advertising directed primarily to a market in that country when placed with a U.S. broadcast station. The effective date of the proposed amendment would be for taxable years beginning after December 31, 1981.

This legislation will establish a disincentive for the transfer of U.S. advertising revenues to foreign broadcasters only if the laws of the country in which such broadcasters are located create a similar disincentive vis-a-vis U.S. broadcasters. Thus, if Canada should repeal its law, this amendment will cease to apply to Canada.

I urge the early passage of this legislation.

JIMMY CARTER

The White House,
September 9, 1980.

Government Printing Office

Nomination of Gerald R. Dillon To Be Public Printer. September 9, 1980

The President today announced that he will nominate Gerald R. Dillon, of Minneapolis, to be the Public Printer, Government Printing Office. He would replace John Boyle, resigned.

Dillon has been in the printing business in Minneapolis since 1949 and is president of Meyers Printing Co. and an officer in Dillon Press.

He was born February 23, 1920, in Minneapolis. He received a B.A. from the University of Minnesota in 1942. He served in the U.S. Army Air Force during World War II.

Meyers Printing Co., which began with one employee in 1949, now employs about 165 persons and does business of more than $10 million. The company does offset lithography, letterpress, electronic and other typesetting, and other printing processes, and does business in all 50 States and overseas.

Dillon is a member of the Citizens' League of Hennepin County and has served on its board of directors. He is former president of the Minnesota Planning Association and is active in numerous other civic activities.

Perth Amboy, New Jersey

Remarks at Dedication Ceremonies for the Raritan River Steel Company Plant. September 9, 1980

First of all let me thank Brendan Byrne for that fine introduction. It's a pleasure to be with President Shields and Chairman Heflin, who's down here for a meeting with his entire company leaders to see at firsthand what modern technology can do for the well-being of our Nation and our people. Senator Bradley and Mayor Otlowski, Congressman Ed Patten, I'm really delighted to be with all of you as well.

I'm especially thankful for those kind words that Bill Bradley said about me. As you know, he and I have some deep philosophical differences: He believes in basketball; I'm more of a softball player myself. [*Laughter*] He's got a lot to learn. He's learning fast. Whenever he gets one of his bills through the Senate he still refers to it as a slam dunk. [*Laughter*] But I might tell you that your junior Senator has now acquired a strong leadership role although he's only been there just a few years, and there is no doubt in my mind that Brendan Byrne's prediction about a bright, wide future for Bill Bradley is going to come true.

I'm also glad to be with Brendan Byrne. It's always a pleasure to come to New Jersey and find him passing through his home State. [*Laughter*] This is the only State in the Nation where I can come and say, "Welcome back, Governor." But I might point out to you that when he's outside of New Jersey he's working for you.

I was checking some figures this morning on the way up here on Air Force One. Since January of 1977 the unemployment rate in New Jersey has dropped 29 percent. There have been a total of 478,000 new jobs added just in New Jersey alone. That shows that when Brendan's out of town he's working for his home State. And I might say that Bill Bradley, Ed Patten, and others have done a good job for you in Washington as well.

Federal funds for mass transit have totaled more than $400 million. This is more than all the previous years combined in Federal allocation of funds for improving the transportation systems that take you to and from work. Economic development aid in the last 3 years, it has comprised two-thirds of all the economic development aid coming to New Jersey from the Federal Government since 1965. And urban parks to make your life more pleasant—there's only one State in the Nation that's got more Federal funds for urban parks than New Jersey, and New Jersey's rapidly creeping up on that State.

So, all in all, I think in the last few years with the leadership standing behind me on this stage, New Jersey's come out very well.

This morning I want to pay particular tribute to Eddie Patten. As you know, he was mayor of Perth Amboy before he went to the Congress. He's now served 18 years, 18 years of very quiet public service. You don't hear much from him, as you know, but he does his work for the folks back home. He has a congressional career that has specialized in serving what you might call "forgotten people," the people that don't have a strong voice or a lawyer or a lobbyist in Washington working for you. Eddie Patten serves that role, and I want to thank him publicly as President of our great country and wish him Godspeed in his voluntary political retirement in the years ahead.

And Mayor Otlowski was telling me about the slogan that he's pursued, "Pride in Perth Amboy." Looking around, I can see under his leadership why that's such a proud slogan and why you're carrying it out.

I'd like to say a few words about this steel plant, not just looking at Perth Amboy or even New Jersey but looking at what it means to this Nation and, indeed, to the entire world. It does mean 450 present jobs for this community. It means a kind of core around which past, present, and future other businesses will come to your community. It means that for the first time, really, the modern technology of a quality environment can be combined with a very rapid production of steel. I want to congratulate the management of this new mill, the investors, the suppliers, the designers, the workers, the mayor and the people of Perth Amboy for making it possible. The county and city officials worked very closely with the State officials and with me in making this a real success story.

My understanding is that this mill is the most advanced in this country and is unexcelled anywhere in the world. This mill will produce more steel per worker than any mill anywhere. Your president just told me that each worker, including the president, on an average produced 1,349 tons of steel a year. Is that right? Almost correct—1,339 tons of steel per year. That's unbelievable, and it's a record that's not equaled anywhere in the world.

The steelrods produced here, as you know, will compete head-on with imported rods from anywhere. As a matter of fact, about 50 percent of the present production of steelrods from this plant goes to Mainland China, the People's Republic of China. And we can produce steel in this plant, ship it halfway around the world, and still compete and beat the high competition from Japan—just a short distance from the People's Republic of China.

As you know, the northeastern part of the United States imports a tremendous amount of steelrods. This plant alone, if it was devoted exclusively for domestic consumption, could cut our imports of steelrods from overseas in the northeastern part of the United States by 25 percent alone.

I'm particularly grateful, too, in this time of energy shortage that this plant produces steelrods only using about 30 percent of the energy that's ordinarily expended in the open-hearth process. And I'm particularly pleased at the care for human beings, the respect to historical buildings in this community, the environmental quality. There is no air pollution from this plant, there is no water pollution from this plant, and this plant is a model that I'm sure that other modern plants can use for their development in the fu-

ture. I know it's important to you who live here, to make sure there's a good relationship betwen the job that you hold, the pride in doing a good job, and the quality of life that a factory presents for you and for your families, now and in the future.

This plant is also a part of something very special and important that's taking place in America, and that is the rebuilding of America's industrial base. As your president pointed out, early in this century, we were ahead of all the nations on Earth in steel production and also the technology of it. Now it's time for us to come back. We've had some very difficult problems in recent years with the energy crisis. It's taken the Congress about 3 years to come out with an effective national energy policy. Now we are embarked on a two-pronged policy: one, to conserve energy, which this plant is doing and which all of you are doing so well, and the other one is, to produce more energy in our own country.

This base gives us an opportunity now to utilize the tremendous innovative spirit of American people, the free enterprise system of which we are so proud, and the dynamic and aggressive attitude to build a better future for us all. It's very important for us to realize too that a careful, planned industrialization or modernization program for economics is important.

The so-called Reagan-Kemp-Roth tax cut is a very, very serious mistake. It means tremendous tax cuts for the rich, and it means a devastating blow to the American economy and high inflation for the average working family in this country. It is so bad that my prediction to you is that the Republican candidate for President and other Republicans will soon be abandoning their own Kemp-Roth proposal and looking for something even more reasonable than that.

What we need is a carefully planned, targeted, workable revitalization program for America that will increase investment, that will offset social security income tax increases now scheduled for next year, that'll help those parts of the Nation that need it most, and, at the same time, all that's being done to hold down inflation. That's exactly what our plan is going to do for this country.

There is no need for me to mislead you, and there is no need for me to try to gain some political benefit from a very fast-moving, ill-advised tax cut here just before the November election. We have, as you know, in this country made the right choice in many ways. We have a lot of lessons to learn, a lot of basics to which we must return. We now have the highest productivity per worker of any nation on Earth, the highest in the world. But some of the other countries have been catching up with us, because our productivity per worker on the average in this Nation has not been increasing. That's what we've got to change. We must stay competitive.

I want you to tell your grandchildren and I want to be able to tell my grandchildren that we were able to face the future with confidence, that we had confidence in our Nation and in ourselves, that we didn't flinch from tough decisions, that we made those decisions with confidence in ourselves and in one another, that it was not easy, it was not simple, we knew there were no magic answers, we knew we couldn't make changes overnight. But change can't take place just in one spot—Perth Amboy—but must be broadscale, all across our Nation, with business and labor working with a new sense of partnership and cooperation. But once we got started, the American productivity system out-produced, out-built, and out-competed that of any other nation on Earth.

There are some cynics in this country that say that our country, being more than 200 years old, is already over the hill, that somehow we're on the decline, that our productivity and our ingenuity and our way of life and our quality of life are headed downhill. Don't you believe them.

The same kinds of people said 4 years ago, that because the Republicans had failed, that there was no way for America to face, successfully, the tremendous challenge of the energy problem that's been foisted on us by OPEC. Well, since then our oil imports are down 24 percent.

The first year I was in office, we imported 8½ million barrels of oil from overseas every day. We have now cut that on the average in 1980 by 2 million barrels of oil per day that we do not buy overseas. At the same time, we are now drilling more oil wells and more natural gas wells than in any time during the last 25 years. That's the subject of a whole speech, and I won't go into it. But I would like to say that we've turned around that serious problem that we faced 3½ years ago, and now we've made it the basis for a tremendous and exciting future, when every family in our country can have a better life, a more exciting life, a more challenging life, and a happier life with more leisure and more pride in what we're doing.

The cooperation that you've seen here, with a relatively small $12 million investment or loan guarantee from the Government, has been expanded into an investment total of more than $140 million. That's the kind of cooperation that we need between Government and private industry, with the Government providing the help that it can, removing obstacles, working in a cooperative way, but the primary emphasis being and primary responsibility being on the shoulders of the private enterprise system. We don't want the Government to stick its nose in the lives of American people or the lives of American free enterprise system.

I just have a couple more remarks to make. The economic system that I described just 2 weeks ago, to revitalize America, building on the energy success, will add a net total of more than a million jobs in the next 2 years. This is above and beyond what we expect from normal economic recovery and from the programs already proposed to the Congress. But more importantly, it'll put new and efficient tools in the hands of the efficient American workers. This is something we've not done adequately in the past. We've got to give the tools and technology to you to do the job, and that's exactly what we're going to do.

The direct investment in communities and in industries hard hit by economic change are important. We'll welcome foreign investments. Foreign investments in the automobile manufacturing business are good, and the foreign investment from Canada here in Perth Amboy in this plant is very good for our country.

We need to retool the automobile industry to produce the fuel-efficient cars that Americans want. Steel is a major and basic industry, and this kind of modern technology will put us back in a competitive position so that we can meet any competition anywhere on Earth. The steel industry throughout our country is now benefiting from $550 million in aid programs begun 2 years ago by my own administration. We've liberalized the tax provisions to provide more capital. We'll do that more in the future, and at the same time we have not abandoned the strict requirements on air quality and on water quality.

We'll also have an unprecedented use of high technology and an unprecedented emphasis on research and development to keep the new ideas coming along, to keep America competitive and to keep Americans working. And out of the windfall profits tax we're building a better transportation system for our Nation. This not only concerns railways and highways but also the seaports and other facilities to ship our products overseas.

And finally I'd like to say that we must invest very heavily in our human resources. As change takes place—and there's no way for us to stop change; we don't want to stop change—we've got to make sure that workers who are displaced from an old or obsolescent industry have a chance without moving their families to get training and preparation for the new jobs that will move into that same locality to provide employment for those people. And for young people coming along out of high school, we've got to have training jobs to prepare them for a prominent and productive career. These are the kinds of programs to which I'm deeply dedicated and with which your fine congressional delegation and your Governor have helped so much.

We have, in our country, the finest opportunities in the world. The politicians sometimes tend to take credit for the progress we're making. The credit goes to people like you who are willing to work hard, to get along well with your neighbors, to keep your pride in stable families, to hold your communities together, to prepare for the future, to accommodate change, to have vision and courage, not to be fearful and to be proud of our country. Those are the characteristics of the American spirit that haven't changed since our Nation was first conceived in 1776, not far from this place.

Our country thanks you for what's been done here in Perth Amboy, for the tremendous advancements that you yourselves have made, and the demonstrated ability of Americans to meet any competition and to keep our Nation, which is already the best on Earth, the best on Earth throughout our lives and the lives of our children and our grandchildren.

God bless you, thank you, congratulations.

NOTE: The President spoke at 11:41 a.m. outside the plant. Prior to his remarks, he was given a tour of the facilities by plant executives.

Perth Amboy, New Jersey

Remarks at a Reception for Civic and Community Leaders.   September 9, 1980

Let me express my thanks both to Bill Bradley and to Eddie Patten for those fine introductions.

Washington's not going to be the same without Congressman Eddie Patten there. For 18 years he's served this area and our Nation so well that I can't pass by an opportunity to say that on behalf of 240 million Americans we express our deep thanks to him for what he's meant and still will mean in the future to our great country.

And I also want to thank a bright and shining new star in the political firmament of our country, and that's Bill Bradley. He has a wonderful future. I know for a fact that he works more than 2 hours a day. [*Laughter*]

As a matter of fact, it seems that the most popular job around New Jersey is not Bill Bradley's. I'd like to remind you that there are only 54 days left for the Presidential election campaign, and then you can devote yourself to the serious political task in New Jersey, and that's choosing a new Governor. [*Laughter*] I'm told that the next Governor of New Jersey might very well be in this room. But

I was told that the room was not big enough to hold all the candidates so—[*laughter*]—Brendan Byrne said they've already decided, the Democratic chairman, Chairman Coffee back here, has said that there won't be room enough on the ballot for names, you'll just have to be given numbers as you qualify to run for Governor.

I'm very grateful that you would come here and meet me. I recognize that this audience, as Brendan Byrne has pointed out, comprises the leadership of New Jersey. And I have no doubt that when the election returns come in on November the 4th that the Democrats who are running for reelection to the Congress and Fritz Mondale and myself will have a tremendous victory racked up in your wonderful State.

I came here 2 or 3 years ago when Brendan Byrne didn't look too well in the public opinion polls. His election after that fairly dismal start for reelection has been an inspiration to me this year. I came here to help him, and my heart was in it. I look on Brendan Byrne as being a Governor in the same mold as Hughes, Woodrow Wilson, and others who have brought credit to this State and to the Nation—a man of great personal courage who has represented your State so well and also a man who's a personal friend of mine.

I'm not going to make a speech to you this morning—this afternoon now. I would like to say that I was able to visit one of the technological achievements of our country, located here in Perth Amboy. The Raritan River Steel Plant is indeed a credit to you, to the foresight of your leadership, and also a forerunner of what will be a tremendous achievement in our country as we revitalize American industry.

At the first of this century, as you know, we were in the leadership in the entire world—in modern technological advancement in the production of steel and also in our other basic industries. We have suffered since then in some ways. Of course, we still have the greatest nation on Earth.

The American worker, at this moment, is the most productive worker in the world. Our productivity per person has not been increasing as rapidly as some of the other nations on Earth, particularly those that were destroyed by us in the Second World War—like Japan and West Germany. But we now have reached a point in the evolutionary development of our country when we have a tremendous and exciting opportunity looking to the years ahead.

Three or four years ago there was a dismal feeling in this country that we could not possibly deal with the complexities of a rapidly growing crisis in energy. We were at the political mercy and the economic mercy of the OPEC oil-producing nations. And when I made a speech in April of 1977, saying that the energy crisis was the moral equivalent of war, a lot of the press and a lot of the people in this country discounted it as an idle threat designed for political purposes. It's proven to be true.

But in that 3-year period, the Congress has courageously addressed this issue that we've now prepared ourselves to save energy in this country—to stop wasting energy, to have strong conservation commitments individually and collectively, at the same time produce more energy for America. This will mean that we have an opportunity now to have a brighter, more exciting ability to capitalize on America's natural resources and our human resources.

The OPEC nations, the Arab countries all put together, have about 6 percent of the world's total energy reserves—6 percent. The United States has 24 percent, and ours is not just oil and natural gas alone; ours is oil and natural gas, but it's also a broad range of energy reserve supplies that we've not yet even considered an adequate way to tap. This is why we now face the opportunity to rebuild the American industrial system, to care for communities where changes take place and lives are disrupted, to retrain human beings to go back on the job in new and exciting and innovative kinds of opportunities; at the same time to have deep research in technology and research and development, to revitalize our transportation system, to build our ports, to increase our exports.

At the steelplant, the Raritan River Steel Plant, I was told that 50 percent of the total production is going to the People's Republic of China. This is a nation of about a billion people. One-fourth of the human beings on Earth live in the People's Republic of China. Two years ago we had no diplomatic relationships and no trade relationships with China at all. We have, through good sound judgments made by myself and the Congress and supported by the American people, opened up this opportunity for a new relationship of great benefit to us all. That cannot be endangered. We have got to keep those ties of friendship and trade and export to give Americans ourselves a better life.

I'm very grateful that I've had a chance to come here to New Jersey today to open the campaign. I would like to say one other thing. You all are vitally committed, loyal, and effective Democrats. We've been through a tough primary season. Senator Kennedy was a formidable opponent. I still have the political scars to prove that statement is true. But since the convention has been over, Senator Kennedy and his supporters have rallied generously and effectively to reunite the country. I couldn't have a better proof of that than the man who's traveling with me this morning, and that's Jerry Doherty.

Jerry Doherty is a long-time friend of the Kennedy family. In 1976, when I ran for President, he volunteered to help me in New York State, and although we didn't have very good prospects at the beginning, we carried New York State because of his leadership and his sensitivity and his knowledge about politics. Now he'll be helping us in New Jersey.

And I'd like to introduce to you Jerry Doherty, a good friend of Senator Kennedy, a good friend of mine, a good friend of yours, and one of the finest political and most knowledgeable and effective people I have ever worked with. Jerry Doherty, would you raise your hand?

We've got a lot of work carved out for us. A disunited or divided Democratic Party, which we did face several weeks ago, was catastrophic for us and for our Nation in 1968, when Democrats either took for granted or did not support the candidacy of Hubert Humphrey. It was a personal calamity for all of us and also a deep embarrassment and a calamity for our Nation in later months. We don't want the same thing to happen. We need to have a secure nation, a strong defense, jobs, a good secure energy policy, a strong full-employment economy, a united society, free of discrimination, compassion for the sick, the elderly, and the poor, and where workers have a right to organize and to work safely. And, as you know, we've just seen that wonderful thing happen in Poland, and we're very proud of that.

As a matter of fact, this is a time in our country's history, too, when a lot of people are claiming their ancestors came from

Poland, and I'm not sure they did—[*laughter*]—but it's a bright and shining day for the workers of the world to see this tremendous demonstration of courage.

Finally, let me say this: We've got a lot at stake. We're making a choice, as we did in 1968, between two futures for America. I can't win without you, but with you we'll win together.

Thank you very much.

NOTE: The President spoke at 12:27 p.m. at the Olive Street Community Center.

Perth Amboy, New Jersey

Question-and-Answer Session With New Jersey News Editors. September 9, 1980

THE PRESIDENT. Well, I would like to say, first of all, that I'm very glad to be back in New Jersey. We've had a delightful and exciting visit to the Raritan River Steel Plant, which is a new technological development. It's very beneficial to our country. And this is my first visit here after I got through with the convention and got the nomination. I'm intending to carry New Jersey in November. And I'm here as President and as a candidate to answer any questions that you might have.

SUPPORT FOR THE PRESIDENT

Q. Mr. President—[*inaudible*]—in what you're doing in winning over the strong support Senator Kennedy had here, and how hard do you think that's going to be and how far have you progressed?

THE PRESIDENT. Well, the entire convention was a unifying effort. When we came out of the convention, the party was, I think, remarkably committed to common goals. And the very slight differences between myself and Senator Kennedy on emphasis—on public service jobs, for instance, within government rather than private industry jobs—was the main difference.

Since then, Senator Kennedy has been very gracious and helpful. He's let it be known publicly, both at the convention and particularly when I visited Massachusetts, that he was strongly for me. He went out to the American Federation of Teachers convention and spoke for me, went to the Machinists convention and spoke for me. And he's done that on several occasions. He and I intend to appear jointly at a Democratic National Committee fundraising effort in Los Angeles— I think September 22.

A lot of Senator Kennedy's supporters—labor unions and other leading Democrats—have also endorsed me since the convention was over. Recently, this weekend, for instance, the Farm Workers in California and the UAW—I think I got about 89½ percent of all the 17 regional meetings in the UAW. So, those are the kinds of things that have happened since then that have brought a natural consistency back toward a unified position.

Jerry Doherty, who will be heading up my campaign in New Jersey, is a longtime family friend of Senator Kennedy's. He helped in this year's election in the primary season in a leading role. Jerry also happens to have run my own campaign in New York State in 1976, and now he'll be helping me again.

So, those are a melding of effort among Democrats that's the result of some of those elements that I mentioned.

POLISH WORKERS' STRIKES

Q. I just heard you say that you've just seen that wonderful thing in Poland and we're proud of that. [*Inaudible*]—are you confident that the changes in Poland will be—[*inaudible*]—leadership?

THE PRESIDENT. Well, so far the changes in Poland have survived the change of government. Mr. Kania, as you know, in his first public statement said that he would honor the agreement worked out with the Polish workers. There are still a few labor disturbances in Poland as local party officials don't recognize the right of the Polish workers to have independent unions in their particular locality, but that's the only aftermath that I know of that's creating any publicized problem.

I believe that the depth of the commitment of the Polish workers was demonstrated by their courage and their tenacity during recent weeks, and had it not been extant, their success would not have been so significant. In addition to that, the Polish Government, in making its changes, had an opportunity to reverse the agreements and decided otherwise.

So, my judgment is that barring some unforeseen developments over which I have no control and don't want to have any influence, that the changes will be permanent and that both the workers and the government will carefully pursue the agreement that has been hammered out.

NORTHEASTERN REGION

Q. There's a widespread perception in this region that the so-called snowbelt States are suffering from an economic imbalance with respect to the rest of the country—we're losing population, productivity is lagging—[*inaudible*]—tax base. Do you agree that such an imbalance exists, and if so, what can a second Carter administration do to correct it?

THE PRESIDENT. I agree that it did exist. But it's important to point out the achievements of my first 3½ years working with Bill Bradley, with Brendan Byrne and others. I mentioned a few of the statistics in my statement at the steel plant.

There has been a net increase of 478,000 jobs in New Jersey. The unemployment rate's dropped from 11.4 percent down to 8.1, which is still too high, but that's a 30-percent reduction. In mass transit in this 3½ years New Jersey has gotten more than $400 million, which is more than all the previous years of Federal support of mass transit in history put together. In economic development aid there's been a program for the last 15 years. Two-thirds of the total that New Jersey has received has been in the last 3½ years. Only one State, Ohio, has gotten more Federal funds for urban parks systems. This is the kind of change that's taken place.

And I believe that with the changes in formulae approved by the Congress for the allocation of Federal assistance funds in things like education, housing, transportation, urban parks, economic development, that there has been a basic improvement of the lot of the so-called snowbelt in the last few years since I've been in office.

The new economic development program that I outlined week before last will help even more, because with the special emphasis on changing technology and the ability of industry to establish new plants where highly skilled workers already exist—certainly that applies to New England and the snowbelt, as you call it. And also the ability to revitalize obsolescent industry with tax benefits, that will help your region of the country as well.

The other element of the program has been the strong urbanization program that we've had, the urban policy. We've worked it out on a nonpartisan basis with the mayors and local officials, both Democrats and Republicans. And I think it would be hard for you to find a mayor around the country who doesn't say that this new emphasis on the revitalization of our deteriorating central city areas has

been a positive development. I would see this trend as being positive so far and improving even more in the future.

OIL IMPORTS

Q. New Jersey is very dependent, and still, on imported oil. Could you comment on how the Syrian-Libyan unification talks are apt to affect our Mideast policies and our oil supplies?

THE PRESIDENT. As you know, Libya and their policies are unpredictable. We import about 10 percent of our oil from Libya, a much less amount from most of the other countries, and none from Syria. Syria is an oil-importing nation. I don't think this will affect the amount of oil supplies on the international market.

Now, as you know, because of strict conservation measures taken here and in other industrialized, consuming countries like Japan, Germany, France, and so forth, the demand for oil is now approximately equal to the supply so that the spotmarket prices are at or below the OPEC established prices, quite different from what it was just a few months ago. We and the other countries have committed ourselves to a long-term change in efficiency of energy consumption; that is, we expect to reduce by 40 percent the amount of energy it takes to produce a given level of gross national product.

We're already making great strides on that. Secretary Duncan announced that our oil imports now was 37 percent less than it was just a year ago in this past month, and we expect to import this year, every day, an average of 2 million barrels less than we did a year ago. That means that we're not nearly so subject to damage or to attempted blackmail by an individual OPEC nation that wants to try to force us to act in a certain way as was the case back in 1973 and 1974. We're doing this through conservation—which I've already mentioned—and more efficient use of energy, and secondly, to increasing our own production of energy, both oil and gas on the one hand and also derivative energy sources, synthetic fuels from shale, coal, and also from solar power and others. You might be interested in knowing too that we have a higher level of exploration now for oil and natural gas than we have had in the last 25 years.

So, we're making good progress with a brand new energy policy. What will happen in the years ahead is hard to predict, but I would guess that this will be an uninterrupted progression of more efficient use of energy and more production of energy at home. It'll make us less subject to damage from interruptions of supplies and less subject to blackmail or an attempt by foreign countries to orchestrate our foreign policy.

ADMINISTRATION'S ACCOMPLISHMENTS

Q. You've stressed aid to the snowbelt States—[*inaudible*]. Are you saying that the American people in general are better off today than they were when you took office, and if so—[*inaudible*]?

THE PRESIDENT. I think so. We have more than 8 million additional people with jobs now than we did when I took office. As I said earlier—I just looked up the figure this morning—478,000 of those new jobs are in New Jersey.

I think our country is more united than it was. I think there's a greater respect for the Government and its integrity than existed in the aftermath of the Vietnam war and the CIA revelations and the Watergate scandals which took place shortly before I was elected. In my opinion, there's a major achievement in tone or confidence in the future brought about by the evolution of a new energy policy. This was like a cloud hanging over our head when I was running for President.

The social security system has been stabilized and put back on a sound basis. We also have, I think, completely reversed the despair that existed among our older cities that was so apparent when I was a candidate back in 1976.

We have opened up new opportunities for trade and friendship with China, which is a major stabilizing force in Asia and also opens up new trade possibilities for us that we didn't previously enjoy. We've not interrupted our trade with Taiwan, at the same time. And we've had 3½ years of peace. And in addition to that, we've been able to bring peace to the Mideast. We've got a new policy toward Africa, where we now have an intense interest in the democratization of Africa and the building up of new trade opportunities there. So, in those areas we have improved in domestic affairs and also in international diplomacy.

And the other thing that we've improved has been the structure of our defense establishment. For the 8 years prior to my inauguration, we had a steady decrease in the amount of money spent for our military defenses in real dollars. Every year since I've been in office, with the help of Bill Bradley and others, we've had a steady increase in the amount of real dollars above and beyond inflation that we devote to a defense capability, and we have projected in the future and the Congress has endorsed for the next 5 years the continued increase in our Nation's commitment to a strong defense.

So, I think those are a few things that we've done well. I don't have time, unless you want to pursue it further, to accentuate civil rights and human rights and the ability of our young people to get better training and so forth, but there's a gamut of things that have been accomplished which can be described more clearly and also analyzed more thoroughly—criticized on occasion during a political campaign. I've just outlined to you some of those that come to mind in an off-hand way.

JOHN B. ANDERSON

Q. Mr. President, how do you assess the Anderson candidacy and the feeling that some observers have that it'll hurt you more than it'll hurt Ronald Reagan?

THE PRESIDENT. Well, there's no doubt that it hurts me more than it does Reagan. All the polls indicate that it's different, and particularly in States like California and New Jersey—California and New York—and I'm not sure about New Jersey.

I think Anderson is primarily a creation of the press. He's never won a primary, even in his own home State. He's never won a caucus contest in any State in the Nation. He ran as a Republican, and he's still a Republican. He hasn't had a convention; he doesn't have a party. He and his wife hand-picked his Vice-Presidential nominee. But Anderson being the third candidate in the race, who's given equal treatment on the evening news and in the newspapers with myself and the Republican nominee, is obviously the recipient of support from people who are disaffected with me or with Governor Reagan, and this makes him a very significant factor in the 1980 election contest.

We've had other third candidates running down through history, some with parties and some without parties. On occasion they've been highly publicized, as was the case with Theodore Roosevelt when he tried to run for reelection, and George Wallace when he ran. But I don't know what's going to come out later on.

It's still early in the season, and we are concerned about the fact that I've not been able to induce Governor Reagan to debate me, for instance, on a two-man basis. What he will do in the future is hard to discern, but as you know, a three-person debate format is more like a forum than it is a real debate.

But I've accommodated political uncertainties in the past and been fairly successful, and I have no aversion to making the same attempt in the next few weeks. I believe I'll be successful with it. It's hard to say what the final outcome will be, whether Anderson will be a significant factor or not. Right now I'd say he's a significant factor.

Q. You stand pat on the decision not to debate, not to just take—[*inaudible*].

THE PRESIDENT. I've never said that we wouldn't debate Anderson. What I've said was that we wanted to have two-man debates with Reagan assured and that I would be glad to debate Reagan, Anderson, or any other candidates in an open forum. I have no aversion to that at all.

TOXIC WASTE DISPOSAL

Q. Do you think that big business or the Government should bear most of the economic burden with the toxic waste problems, and do you think that the superfund is—that we're doing enough with the superfund to deal with that problem?

THE PRESIDENT. The superfund is a great idea that absolutely must be implemented. In my opinion, the superfund is better for the communities, for the people, for business, including those that produce toxic materials, and obviously is better for the Federal Government. It's kind of an insurance program where a very small amount of money is put in for each barrel of toxic material sold, into a fund. The name is probably not a very good one. And if in the future damage to a community is threatened or materializes or to a person is threatened or materializes then out of that insurance fund, so-called, the damages would be paid, and within very narrowly defined limits the Federal Government would coordinate this effort.

Bill Bradley has been one of the strongest supporters of the superfund idea. It'll be voted on within the next few days. And I deeply hope that the Congress will pass this legislation.

We have more than 50,000 potentially toxic dumpsites in this country, each one of which could become a very serious threat in the future. And unless we take some action now, I believe we're going to have a serious developing crisis in our country.

REGULATORY REFORM

Q. Mr. President, one of Ronald Reagan's main campaign themes has been less government intrusion in our lives. Some of your earlier initiatives tended somewhat in that direction, with attempts to reduce the Federal bureaucracy and deregulate in certain cases. We haven't heard much talk along these lines lately since Reagan's campaign has heated up. Does this indicate that the Republicans are able on that issue to dictate somewhat the force of your campaign, and what do you feel about that philosophical point itself, less government intrusion in our lives?

THE PRESIDENT. Well, the reason you don't hear much about it is because the Republicans don't want to raise that issue because we've done such a good job with it as Democrats. We've had a more profound change in the government-business relationship since I've been President of any time at least since the New Deal.

We have deregulated completely the CAB. We have deregulated the trucking industry. We're now on the verge of deregulating the rail industry. We have deregulated the financial institutions of this country, and we have an excellent prospect of deregulating the communication industry in the next few months. Nothing

like this has ever been done before, and I think it's a very major achievement.

I have the same basic philosophy about government intrusion in the private enterprise system as is exemplified by these actions that the Congress has taken with my full support and, in some cases, my leadership. I think it's absolutely important that we continue this deregulation process and reduce the amount of paperwork and the onerous burden of government intrusion into the free enterprise system. But I don't stand aside for anyone in acknowledging the importance of it, and I believe this is one of the notable achievements that we've had for our country in this 3½ years.

THE NATION'S ECONOMY

Q. Mr. President, Governor Reagan seems to be using the economy as an issue here in New Jersey and elsewhere as one way of wooing the blue-collar vote. What can you say to those blue-collar voters about the economy, about inflation, in order to convince them to vote for you in November?

THE PRESIDENT. The more people know about the absolutely ridiculous Reagan-Kemp-Roth tax proposal, the more they get frightened of it. This became an issue in 1978 in the congressional elections all over the country. The Republicans lost because of it, and toward the end of the congressional election season in '78 many of those who espoused it at the beginning were disavowing this ridiculous proposal.

Now Governor Reagan is saddled with the Reagan-Kemp-Roth proposal. He backed off a little bit, I understand, today in some of the productivity elements of it. This is highly inflationary. It doesn't do anything to help revitalize the American industrial system. It's not a carefully targeted, nonpolitical approach to taxation and to the economic revitalization like we've put forward. It would cost our economy about a trillion dollars between now and 1987, and an economic analysis of it shows that there is no way that you can have a Reagan-Kemp-Roth proposal intact, make an attempt to balance the budget, keep a strong defense, to which Governor Reagan professes to be committed, and even continue the routine programs that are designed to help the American people have a better life. It's just a ridiculous proposal, and any economist who studies it knows that.

Recently, I understand that former President Ford was given a briefing on the Reagan-Kemp-Roth proposal by, I think, Governor Reagan himself—at least in his presence—and announced that he could not support it. And I don't know of any qualified economist, except Mr. Laffer, who originated this concept, who is endorsing the Reagan economic program. And I don't know of any labor union, where they have highly qualified economists on occasion saying, "What is best for the workers who employ me and who pay me to give them advice?"—I don't know of any labor union that's endorsed Mr. Reagan or his proopsals, either one,

So, I don't believe he's going to be successful, but that's the challenge for me as a candidate to make sure these issues are clearly described to the American workers and then let them make a judgment on their own.

RELIGIOUS INFLUENCE ON POLITICS

Q. There's been a lot written in the press about an evangelical political movement, or the solidification of evangelicals as a political movement. Do you think that's a real phenomenon, and if so, how do you see it playing a part in the campaign?

THE PRESIDENT. Well, I think it's a real phenomenon. The new public attempt by the electronic media evangelicals to become politically organized and politically active—that to me is a new development. The leader of it—I noticed his photograph on the front of one of the news magazines this week—is Jerry Falwell. When I ran for President in 1976, I was a target of repeated attacks by Jerry Falwell at that time. So, his present support of Governor Reagan is no different development.

Of course, the word "evangelical" can be misinterpreted. I consider myself to be an evangelical, but I'm not part of the group that's been highly publicized recently as being directly involved in trying to shape political contests based on religious faith. I really don't believe that they will be as effective as has been alleged in some of the articles that I've read about recently. I noticed the Gallup Poll this week that said that a certain definition of evangelicals supported me in preference to Governor Reagan, but the organized groups that I've just referred to—the electronics group—have pretty well endorsed Reagan.

I don't think that over a long period of time, that kind of a religious intrusion into the political process will be significant.

MILITARY PREPAREDNESS

Q. The public seems to be very concerned about conflicting reports or opinions concerning the ability of our present-day volunteer Army to defend us adequately. There's been talk about, rumors about recalling retired Army personnel and rumors about our volunteer Army being unable to handle sophisticated equipment they're given. Do you think that our present-day volunteer Army could adequately defend us, with this kind of attitude? And as far as I know, everyone is very concerned about it.

THE PRESIDENT. Yes. The answer is yes. I don't want to go into detail now, because the Army Chief of Staff and the Secretary of Defense today are answering an article that was published in the New York Times this morning on the front page saying that some of our Army divisions were not prepared for combat or did not enjoy combat readiness.

We've added, including a bill I signed yesterday to increase the pay and benefits of military personnel, we've added about $4 billion since I've been in office to improve the quality of military persons, to improve the retention rate among vital trained petty officers primarily and also to help with recruitment.

We've had remarkable success that we did not anticipate really with the registration for the draft with about 93 percent of the young people who were eligible registering for the draft. About 15 percent of those who registered expressed a desire to know more about career opportunities in the military forces—there was a place on the form that they could check there—which I think will help us with recruitment in the future.

The spirit within the military is very good. They've had some onerous assignments that I've given them, for instance, the long-term stationing of aircraft carriers and the support ships in the north Indian Ocean. They've performed superbly in that respect. I visited a lot of the military bases. I happen to be a professional military man by training, and I've found them to be well trained. So, I would guess that our military forces are in good condition.

We've had—I started to say, I think, a rebirth of spirit of cooperation among the NATO Allies, where formerly there was a lack of trust and a lack of cooperation. Now the commitment is there on a long-term basis for 15 years in the future to constantly improve the quality. A very difficult political decision was made by the military allies in Europe for the theater nuclear force weapons to meet the Soviet threat from the SS–20 and others, a sharing of kinds of weapons among the different allies so that there'll be a more efficient expenditure of limited funds. These kinds of things bode well, I think, for our Nation's military preparedness.

In balance I'm pleased with that. And the new technological developments that our Nation enjoys help to reassure me as Commander in Chief that we will stay in the forefront of the evolution of weapons, which I hope we'll never have to use, that are crucial to our Nation's defense and the maintenance of peace.

Maybe one more question. Yes, sir.

STEALTH TECHNOLOGY

Q. I saw President Ford this morning talking about the present administration's playing fast and loose with defense secrets, particularly with regard to the Stealth bomber. I wonder if you had had any indications of unhappiness on the part of the NATO Allies on this point—on the use of security in U.S. politics.

THE PRESIDENT. That's never been done. Governor Reagan and a carefully orchestrated Republican coterie made an absolutely false and ridiculous allegation that the Stealth information was promulgated improperly and with some derogation to our Nation's security. That is absolutely not true and it's unwarranted and I resent it very much.

As a matter of fact, the existence of a Stealth program was not even classified when I became President. The program did exist in its embryonic stage; it was unclassified. Public testimony was given about the Stealth program, not in a closed session. A contract was let for the evolution of a Stealth-type airplane, and it was a public contract. In the 3 months after I became President we classified this program, Harold Brown did, the Secretary of Defense in April of—in the springtime of 1977, I don't know the exact month—and we began to move forward with a development of this very important, new technological advance.

It is a profound change in military capability. And since that time, the program has grown more than a hundredfold. It's now reached the stage where large numbers of people have to be involved in it. Literally thousands of workers have been involved in the so-called Stealth program, and we have had to brief several dozen House and Senate Members and the crucial members of their staffs, because we're getting ready now to move toward a greater commitment to this program. And you cannot keep something like this secret that long. It is amazing that we were able to keep it secret this long.

Nothing has been revealed about the Stealth program except that it exists. That's all. Nothing has been revealed about the technological developments on the details of this program. So, there has been no violation of our Nation's security. And as a matter of fact, the only thing that has been revealed, to repeat myself, the existence of the program was unclassified when I became President.

So, you can see how absolutely ridiculous this whole series of highly publicized Republican allegations have been. If it weren't for the political season, there would have been a unanimous accolade for our Nation for this tremendous achievement. But I can't sit mute nor quiescent as President of our country and as Commander in Chief of our military forces just because a political season takes place. I've got to continue to strengthen our defense. I've got to continue to try to be innovative. I've got to continue to deal with crises and problems. I've got to continue to work for peace here and in the Middle East. I can't just go into seclusion in a closet somewhere just because there's a political season. And I think it's contrary to the best interests of our country for Governor Reagan and the Republicans to make a big issue out of this as though we were violating our Nation's security when, as a matter of fact, we have strengthened our Nation's security and improved greatly the confidentiality of the program compared to what it was when I became President. I feel very deeply about it as you can probably tell.

And I wish I had time for more questions, but Jody tells me that we have to go.

Thank you very much.

NOTE: The President spoke at 12:44 p.m. in the Olive Street Community Center.

Perth Amboy, New Jersey

Informal Exchange With Reporters.
September 9, 1980

THE PRESIDENT. I had one question inside that I thought I'd better repeat to you all, because you're going to get it in the transcript. I was asked about the Republican allegations concerning whether we have revealed the information about the Stealth airplane improperly.

This is an absolutely irresponsible and false charge by Governor Reagan and by a carefully orchestrated group of Republicans. As a matter of fact, no impropriety has been committed. The only thing that has been revealed about the Stealth development, which is a major technological evolutionary development for our country, is the existence of the program itself.

When I became President in January of 1977 the existence of the Stealth program then was not even classified. It was unclassified. Public testimony had been given on it, and a contract to develop a Stealth device was done with an open and published contract. We classified the Stealth program in the springtime of 1977.

Since that time it has grown, because of its importance and the major nature of it, more than a hundredfold. Lately large numbers of people were involved in the knowledge of Stealth and also the development of it. Literally thousands of workers have been involved in this project, and we have had to brief several dozen Members of the House and Senate and the crucial members of their staffs in preparation for large expenditures of funds for this major technological improvement in our Nation's defense.

It's obvious that the Republicans have taken what is a major benefit to our country and tried to play cheap politics with it by alleging that we have violated our Nation's security. The fact is that we have enhanced our Nation's security, and we took an unclassified program under the previous Republican administration, classified it, and have been successful for 3 years in keeping the entire system secret.

Q. Would you cooperate with a congressional investigation of just exactly what you were discussing then?

THE PRESIDENT. What was the question?

Q. Would you cooperate with a congressional investigation, including turning over documents, of this very subject, whether in fact you had revealed it?

THE PRESIDENT. Yes. Harold Brown will. The fact is that Harold Brown was the one who classified the program in the spring of 1977, and at the present time

nothing has been revealed about the Stealth program except that it exists. No details about it, no technological elements of it, have been revealed.

The first time the Stealth program was ever revealed was in Aviation Week magazine. This is back the first part of August, and it was a critical article, not designed to help my administration or to make me look good, but to criticize the Defense Department on the B-1 bomber situation.

So, this is a campaign issue that the Republicans have created, which I think is completely ill-advised and based on an absolutely false series of statements by the Republican leaders.

Q. So, there were no politics entered into the fact that you've finally actually made a very public issue out of it?

THE PRESIDENT. No. The only public issue that has been made out of it is that the program itself exists. No details of the Stealth program have ever been revealed so far as I know.

Q. What is the advantage of having the Secretary of Defense make that announcement that he did?

THE PRESIDENT. Because there were a series of articles either in preparation, plus the one in Aviation Week magazine that had already been published, and in order to tell the American people the truth that there did exist a major development of this kind is something that's completely legitimate and which the American people have a right to know.

Q. Sir, would you now participate in a debate now that Anderson is in it, according to the League?

THE PRESIDENT. We'll decide about that and announce it later.

NOTE: The President spoke at 1:10 p.m. outside the Olive Street Community Center.

United States Export Promotion Policies

Message to the Congress Reporting on the Administration Policies. September 9, 1980

To the Congress of the United States:

In accordance with the requirements of Section 1110(a) of the Trade Agreements Act of 1979, I have had a review conducted of Executive Branch export promotion functions and of potential programmatic and regulatory disincentives to exports. I am submitting today my report on these matters along with the full text of the comprehensive review, which was prepared by the Secretary of Commerce and the U.S. Trade Representative. Their detailed review, while not a statement of Administration policy, reflects an extensive canvass of the views of our exporting community which should assist the Congress and the Executive Branch in the development of policies in this area. My report expresses this Administration's policies.

The expansion of U.S. exports has been, and continues to be, a high priority objective of my Administration. Global events have made international trade substantially more important to the United States than in earlier years, and a strong export position has become a matter of great significance to the economic strength and welfare of our Nation, to the strength of the dollar, and to employment. Exports now account for one in every eight jobs in America's factories, and one in every four on America's farms. I am pleased to be able to report that our recent export performance has been strong. The value of America's merchandise exports has grown 50 percent in the last two years. In the same period, the volume of U.S. merchandise exports has grown at an annual rate of 10 percent, compared to a 6 percent annual growth rate for world trade.

Largely because of this export growth, we achieved a virtual balance in our current account in 1979, despite huge increases in the price of oil imports. It is vitally important that our international accounts be kept in balance. That goal cannot be reached without strong export growth. Over the longer run, the United States has suffered a declining share of world trade and a rate of export growth that has not kept up with imports. Business, agriculture, labor and government must work together to ensure that this historical trend is reversed.

The successful conclusion of the Multilateral Trade Negotiations—the Trade Agreements Act was ratified by Congress in 1979—makes this effort all the more important. The MTN agreements pose challenges to some producers in the form of tougher import competition. But they also present dramatic new opportunities for U.S. exports through the reduction of foreign trade barriers. The average tariff rate for most developed countries will fall by about 30 percent over the coming seven years, and roughly $21 billion in foreign government purchasing will now be opened to international competition. Other countries are moving aggressively to take advantage of these new trade opportunities. We must do the same.

However, strong export growth depends on the competitiveness of the American economy. We need more innovation, faster growth in productivity, and greater investment in more efficient plant and equipment. And we must reduce the rate of inflation lest we price ourselves out of competition with foreign producers. Only when inflation is under control will our economy be on a sound footing to undertake greater investment. U.S. producers and labor must retain the ability to offer the world high quality goods and services at attractive prices.

Government policies also affect our export position. Improving incentives and reducing or eliminating unintentional disincentives to exports is a continuing and complex process, for policies to encourage exports sometimes conflict with other national goals—such as budgetary soundness, national security, nuclear nonproliferation, health and safety, human rights, discouraging aggression and maintaining respect for diplomatic immunity. Our task is to reduce negative effects on exports without weakening other national objectives.

In response to this challenge, my Administration announced a National Export Policy in September 1978. We assigned exports a higher priority within the Executive Branch, we called on business and labor to devote more effort to exporting, and we initiated a set of measures confirming our commitment to export growth.

In 1979, in order to strengthen and centralize the government's ability to address the export needs of the Nation, my Administration proposed and Congress agreed to a reorganization of trade functions in the Executive Branch. The authority of the United States Trade Representative was expanded to cover export policy and other trade-related policies for which responsibility had previously been scattered among various agencies. Responsibility for the operational aspects of international trade, for the day-to-day implementation of the MTN, and for other trade policy decisions regarding nonagricultural products was concentrated in the Commerce Department.

This reorganization—in effect only since January 1980—has already begun to produce solid results. We are beginning to pursue vigorously our rights and opportunities under the MTN. We have also begun to act more quickly and decisively on matters of export policy, as shown by the Administration's timely interaction with the Congress on the Export Trading Company proposal and on legislation to preserve the confidentiality of Shipper's Export Declarations. Within the interagency mechanisms of government decision-making, we are providing a stronger voice in support of actions to promote our export growth.

In charging the Secretary of Commerce and the U.S. Trade Representative to review export promotion and export disincentives, I asked them to consult with other agencies and with business and labor. I also asked the President's Export Council for its views.

The review, now completed, shows significant progress in combining our promotion programs with the implementation of the MTN agreements. For example, the Commerce Department has initiated programs to publicize the opportunities stemming from the MTN and to help U.S. companies take advantage of those opportunities. Promotion initiatives are being targeted to the U.S. industries with the greatest potential to expand their exports. The Agriculture Department's Foreign Agricultural Service is working to ensure that the agricultural sector benefits fully from concessions received in the MTN. The Office of the U.S. Trade Representative has set up a trade policy coordination mechanism to guard our rights under the MTN codes.

In the area of potential programmatic and regulatory disincentives, however, there is no question that certain government policies and programs are perceived as having a detrimental effect on the ability and willingness of U.S. companies to export. Our national interest requires that such policies and programs be reviewed.

In February 1980 I released an interim progress report on the reduction of export disincentives. That report announced certain procedural reforms to reduce further the burden of government requirements and stated that I would convey additional views on export promotion and disincentives to the Congress. On the basis of the review just completed, I have concluded that further actions are necessary to ensure a better balance beween our trade policy and other national objectives.

SMALL BUSINESS

The participation of small businesses in exporting must be increased. One hundred companies account for approximately 50 percent of our manufactured exports, and only 10 percent of the nearly 300 thousand U.S. manufacturing firms are exporters. Thousands more produce goods that could be exported but are not. All of the export promotion resources of the Small Business Administration and most of those of the Commerce Department are aimed at encouraging small and medium-sized companies to market their products abroad. But we must do more to encourage these companies to export.

For this reason, my Administration has worked with Congress to develop the Export Trading Company proposal, which would greatly increase the attractiveness of export marketing for thousands of small and medium-sized firms. Export trading companies buying and selling on their own account and offering one-stop service to exporters could materially increase our exports. The key features of this proposal are: (1) to provide U.S. firms limited anti-trust immunity in competing abroad, immunity that would not adversely affect competition within the United States; and (2) to permit U.S.

banks to invest in export trading company ventures, as foreign banks are allowed to do, bringing the vast international experience and financial resources of our banking industry more fully to bear on developing U.S. exports.

I believe this proposal is essential to the increased participation of small and medium-sized firms in export markets, and it has the full support of my Administration. I call on the Congress for speedy consideration and passage of this important legislation.

EXPORT FINANCING

Eximbank financing is the most important official incentive for U.S. exports, and my Administration has consistently supported an effective and adequately funded Eximbank. I asked Congress to increase Eximbank lending authority to $5.1 billion for FY 1980. This increase is made essential by present economic and competitive conditions and was approved by both the House and the Senate on August 18. However, while awaiting Congressional action on its authorization, Eximbank exhausted nearly all of its direct lending authority for this fiscal year, and many worthwhile requests for export support have had to be deferred. Congress and the Administration must work together to alleviate this kind of budgetary problem and to ensure adequate and reliable Eximbank financing in the future.

In addition to providing timely and adequate funds for Eximbank, my Administration seeks to reduce the financial subsidies given by our competitor nations and to move to a more market-related system of export credit interest rates. I pursued this matter vigorously at the Venice Economic Summit, and the six other major industrial nations agreed that a new international credit arrangement should be negotiated by December 1, 1980. Such an agreement would substantially lessen the difficulties now faced by many American exporters trying to cope with heavily subsidized foreign credits.

But we must also seek to avoid a recurrence of this year's shortfall. Accordingly, I will be working with Congressional leaders and members of my Administration this fall to determine how best to ensure adequate and reliable Eximbank financing in the years ahead, taking into account progress in international negotiations.

TAXATION OF AMERICANS ABROAD

The Internal Revenue Code (sections 911 and 913) provides special deductions for extraordinary living expenses incurred abroad, a deduction for hardship conditions, and an alternative $20,000 exclusion of foreign earnings for individuals living in camps in remote hardship areas. These provisions were enacted in November 1978, in the Foreign Earned Income Act of 1978.

Many U.S. companies have pointed out that the United States is the only major nation that taxes the earnings of its citizens abroad and have criticized the current rules as insufficiently generous, excessively complicated, and discouraging to exports.

The Secretary of Commerce and the U.S. Trade Representative have undertaken a review of this matter. They report an increasing tendency to replace Americans overseas with foreign nationals, since, in many cases, our tax laws make it more expensive for American firms to employ Americans than foreigners.

Most of our competitor nations exempt from tax all or many of their nationals who reside and work abroad. The tax liability of American citizens employed abroad makes it more costly to hire Amer-

icans wherever the local income tax is lower than the U.S. tax. Various segments of the exporting community argue that these additional costs have some or all of the following consequences:

1. U.S. companies are replacing many of their American personnel with foreign personnel.

2. When American companies engaged in engineering or construction work abroad hire Americans in spite of the greater cost—because the companies are more confident of the skills and reliability of American employees—the companies risk losing contracts for overseas projects as a result of the higher cost of employees, and U.S. exports are lost.

3. When companies hire the nationals of other countries instead of Americans, they may gain the contracts, but much of the valuable follow-up exports of supplies and equipment are lost because foreign nationals favor foreign suppliers who are more familiar to them.

4. Foreign operations by American companies tend to create exports from the United States and also to generate substantial earnings that benefit the U.S. balance of payments. Some companies feel they can conduct such operations more successfully if they are free to use American rather than foreign employees.

5. American companies operating abroad sometimes pick up or develop valuable technology in the course of their foreign operations. This technology is less likely to be lost with American employees than with foreign employees, who are more apt to move to foreign-owned companies when they change employment.

6. The present detriment to competitiveness has a snowballing effect on future competitiveness as foreign companies gain strength at our expense.

7. The special deductions allowed for foreign living costs and hardship condi-

tions under present law are insufficiently generous and too complicated.

The cornerstone of U.S. tax policy has always been that all citizens must share in the obligation to finance their government. This policy must not be set aside lightly. In addition, it is difficult to quantify the effect of U.S. tax policy on exports in the aggregate. Not all Americans working abroad have an effect on exports. Many pay high foreign taxes, and therefore pay little or no U.S. tax after the foreign tax credit. And of course other factors, such as increased foreign competition, affect the success of U.S. exports as well. Taxation of U.S. employees working abroad is not solely responsible for the difficulties exporters are encountering.

The U.S. tax is most likely to be significant where employees are in a position to influence exports, where the foreign tax is low (so the foreign tax credit does not eliminate the U.S. tax liability), where compensation is necessarily high to offset hardship conditions (so the tax bracket is also high), or where the industry in question is labor intensive (so the tax cost of U.S. personnel is a significant component of total costs). Various combinations of these and other factors can give the U.S. tax greater impact than it might otherwise have.

Clearly, those who single out the tax factor as a serious export disincentive are convinced that further tax relief for Americans overseas is desirable and important. It is also clear that the consequences of recent changes in the tax laws affecting overseas Americans are likely to vary with the taxpayer's situation. Americans subject to a high foreign tax can be expected to profit little from changes in sections 911 and 913, because their foreign income tax presently offsets most or all of their U.S. tax liability.

It is difficult to measure the aggregate effects of taxation with any precision. The attempts undertaken to date have been inconclusive. Political factors, such as the removal of the U.S. presence from Iran, and other economic factors such as marketing technology and quality control, complicate the picture. We do not yet have data on how the new tax provisions are operating. (Data will be available in the spring of 1981.)

Although we do not have answers to all the relevant questions, the evidence gathered in preparing this report does illustrate the importance that the export community attaches to this tax issue. U.S. taxes on the earned income of U.S. individuals abroad do clearly have an adverse effect on the ability of some U.S. exporters to compete in some markets. Accordingly, I will propose to the Congress, in my 1981 legislative program, revisions of the current law in order to deal with this problem.

FOREIGN CORRUPT PRACTICES ACT

The Foreign Corrupt Practices Act (FCPA) was passed unanimously by the Congress in the wake of disclosure of widespread illicit payments by many American companies. The Administration and the Congress have taken the unequivocal position that corruption in international business transactions is morally repugnant and economically unnecessary. I remain deeply committed to the principles of the Act and am steadfastly opposed to weakening the intent of the Act. Eliminating illicit payments in international business should be a matter of concern to all nations. My Administration has been pressing—unsuccessfully to date—for a multilateral agreement in the United Nations.

At the Venice Economic Summit meeting in June 1980 I urged that these seven industrial democracies renew efforts to work in the United Nations toward an agreement to prohibit illicit payments by their citizens to foreign government officials; and, if that effort falters, to seek an agreement among themselves, open to other nations, with the same objective. While we did not set a time by which an agreement should be reached in the United Nations, I believe that one further year of negotiation should be sufficient. Accordingly, if an agreement has not been obtained in the United Nations General Assembly, I intend to ask the other heads of government at the 1981 Economic Summit to direct the prompt negotiation of such an agreement among our seven nations, but open to others.

Some in the business community have expressed their uncertainty about what conduct is prohibited and what conduct is not prohibited by the FCPA. Because of this uncertainty, some businessmen say that they are acting with a degree of caution that is resulting in the needless loss of exports. In an effort to deal with the problem of uncertainty, I announced in February 1980 the Justice Department would begin providing guidance under the Act to inquiring companies on proposed international transactions. This guidance is now available through the FCPA Review Procedure, and I urge business to use that procedure.

I also announced in February that the effectiveness of this procedure would be examined by the Attorney General and the Secretary of Commerce after one year of operating experience. I believe that, until the review is completed, it is premature to judge the effectiveness of the Review Procedure. I am transmitting the review conducted by the Secretary of Commerce and the U.S. Trade Representative for the information of the Congress and not as a final judgment on the effectiveness of the Review Procedure.

I have directed that the Attorney General and the Secretary of Commerce report to me by March 1, 1981, not only their assessment of the first year of operation of the FCPA Review Procedure, but also their recommendations of whatever actions may then be necessary to remove any ambiguities in the Act. Uncertainties should not be allowed to hamper exports, but in no event will I propose nor will I support any amendments which would weaken the Act's proscription of bribery or which would result in loopholes for bribery of foreign government officials.

EXPORTS CONTROLS

Another key concern of exporters has to do with the use of export controls when the goods being controlled are available from other supplier nations. I addressed this concern in my February 27 statement on export disincentives. In considering new export controls to achieve foreign policy objectives and in reassessing current sanctions—except in the field of arms exports—my Administration would be highly selective in the use of controls where the affected country has access to alternative supply. I reaffirm that position today.

In addition, my Administration continues to confront the problem of the administrative costs and delays associated with export control licensing. Based on the present review, I have decided on a change in the licensing requirements for our national security export controls that will lessen the burden on business without weakening the effectiveness of our controls or our ability to protect vital national security interests. The change is that we will stop issuing a separate U.S. reexport license in cases where we have already approved reexport of the same product as part of the COCOM process (the multilateral review procedure which oversees exports of strategic commodities to certain communist countries). In such cases, the separate U.S. licensing procedure is redundant.

We will continue to examine the export control system to seek additional ways of streamlining the process while assuring that national security needs are met.

FUTURE ACTION

The just completed review of export promotion and potential disincentives to exports is the most comprehensive study of its kind ever undertaken by the U.S. government. It contains a considerable amount of information that must be weighed and examined, and will serve as a solid basis for future actions by the Federal government. I look forward to close cooperation with the Congress in this important process.

JIMMY CARTER

The White House,
   September 9, 1980.

NOTE: The review is entitled "Review of Executive Branch Export Promotion Functions and Potential Export Disincentives."

United States Competition in World Markets

Message to the Congress Transmitting a Study. September 9, 1980

To the Congress of the United States:

In accordance with the requirements of Section 1110(b) of the Trade Agreements Act of 1979, I hereby submit to the Congress a study of the factors bearing on the competitiveness of U.S. producers and the policies required to strengthen their relative competitive position in world markets. This study is submitted in conjunction with a report reviewing Executive Branch export promotion activities and potential programmatic and regulatory disincentives to exports, as called for in Section 1110(a) of the Trade Agreements Act. The greater part of the present study was prepared by the staff of the Department of Labor under the guidance of the Trade Policy Staff Committee, chaired by the Office of the United States Trade Representative. Contributions to this study were also made by several other agencies.

The study outlines the broad dimensions of various aspects of the competitiveness of U.S. producers in world markets. It also delineates our competitive position relative to our various competitors on a sectoral basis. Finally, the study directs attention toward the most important general areas for economic and trade policy formulation to strengthen our export competitiveness.

The study finds that during the past two decades there was an erosion in U.S. competitiveness in foreign and domestic markets. The increased international competition facing U.S. producers is in large part the result of increasing supplies of human and capital resources and expanding technological capabilities. Because of higher rates of growth in investment and expanded research activities in other countries, their competitive positions improved, and the United States experienced a relative decline in its trade performance even though the value of U.S. exports increased substantially, particularly in recent years. That decline has not affected all products, nor has it continued steadily. However, there remains much room for improvement in our competitive position through improvements in productivity.

Problems in our international competitiveness have combined with rapid increases in the cost of oil imports to create persistent merchandise trade deficits.

Despite the reduced U.S. role in world trade and our trade deficits, the United States remains the world's largest exporter. Approximately one dollar out of every five dollars worth of goods produced in the United States is now exported. Further, the United States continues to be competitive with other countries in a wide range of products. Record trade surpluses were recorded in our strongest export sectors in 1979: $18 billion in agriculture and $33 billion in industrial capital equipment.

The evidence presented in the study suggests the following three areas where policies should be considered to improve the competitive position of U.S. producers in world markets:

1. Expanded investment and innovation to enhance the productive capacity of the U.S. economy and raise the productivity of the labor force;

2. Strengthened programs to assist workers in adjusting their skills to shifts in the sectoral structure of the U.S. economy brought about by changes in trade;

3. New policies and programs to implement the Toyko Round agreements liberalizing access for U.S. exports and, further, identification of the significant remaining barriers to U.S. exports in certain sectors and negotiation to eliminate them.

I believe that export expansion is critical to the health of our economy. The policy emphasis that I have given to increasing exports has been demonstrated in three areas:

1. The National Export Policy that I announced on September 26, 1978;

2. The successful completion of the Tokyo Round of Trade Negotiations and signing of the Trade Agreement Act of 1979; and

3. The reorganization of the trade functions of the Executive Branch carried out earlier this year.

The National Export Policy articulated this Administration's intention to expand exports by increasing direct assistance to U.S. exporters, reducing domestic barriers to exports, and reducing foreign obstacles to our exports. The Tokyo Round agreements allow our exporters to take advantage of greater access to markets overseas through the liberalization of foreign nontariff restrictions and the reduction of foreign tariffs. The Executive Branch trade reorganization centralizes U.S. trade policy functions in the Office of the United States Trade Representative and places trade administration and export promotion functions in the Department of Commerce. This reorganization has greatly enhanced the ability of the Federal government to implement policies for meeting the competitive trade challenges of the 1980s.

This study is the most comprehensive and detailed analysis of the competitive position of the United States in world markets ever undertaken by the U.S. Government. Its findings will be of immediate assistance to me and, I believe, to the Congress as we consider both broad economic policies and special measures to encourage more vigorous gains in our industrial productivity and to improve our international competitive position. I expect to address these matters extensively in the months ahead.

JIMMY CARTER

The White House,
    September 9, 1980.

NOTE: The study is entitled "Study of U.S. Competitiveness—Study of Export Trade Policy as Mandated in Section 1110 of the Trade Agreements Act of 1979."

Regulatory Flexibility Legislation

Statement on House of Representatives
Approval of the Legislation.
September 9, 1980

I congratulate the House on passing the regulatory flexibility act. This bill, which has already passed the Senate, provides vital help for America's small businesses.

This bill recognizes that regulations need not be uniform to be effective. It requires all regulatory agencies to anticipate the impact on small business of their rules and paperwork requirements. Agencies must tailor their rules to the size of those affected whenever they can do so without sacrificing basic regulatory goals. This approach works. Last year I directed the executive agencies to use this process, and already dozens of rules have been adjusted.

The regulatory flexibility act adds another piece to the far-reaching regulatory reform record that we and Congress are building. Major reform legislation has been passed covering the airlines, banking, trucking, and natural gas. I urge Congress to continue this impressive record of progress in the next month by passing the railroad deregulation bill and other pending regulatory reform measures.

1980 Presidential Rank Awards for the Senior Executive Service

Remarks at the Awards Ceremony.
September 9, 1980

Scotty Campbell and fellow Government employees, it's a pleasure to be with you. Also, I hope all of us have long years of service in the future in Washington. [*Laughter*]

I've just come back from a very fine visit to New Jersey to see a new steelplant that is exciting for an engineer and a President to observe. This is the most modern steelplant in the world. Each employee produces 1,340 tons of steel per year, including all the executive management. This is the highest productivity per steelworker in the world. They use 30 percent as much energy as the former steelplants used. They make steelrod of the highest quality, and 50 percent of it, you might be interested in knowing, is sold at this time to the People's Republic of China, successfully competing in price half the world away with the Japanese steelplants that are much closer. The dynamism and competence of our own Nation and its free enterprise system, in my judgment, is equaled by the dynamism and confidence and the competence of the public servants like you, who represent the American people in our Federal Government.

I came to the Presidency determined to make my own administration and the Government in general more responsive to the American public and at the same time more efficient in the delivery of services to those who look to us for leadership and for service. Since taking office, I have seen repeatedly that the key to the more effective Government, which we all desire, has been our creation of a more productive, more dynamic, and more cost-conscious Federal workforce.

In 1978, with the help of many of you assembled here, I was able to sign into law a bill which completely overhauled the civil service system of the Federal Government for the first time in a hundred years. It was a landmark achievement. It was

Scotty Campbell's concept, which the Congress courageously passed for my signature. It was one of the most significant achievements of my own administration.

The Civil Service Reform Act gives Federal managers, like many of you, some of the same management incentives that have proved so effectively to make our private economy and its free enterprise system competitive and the pride of the entire world. It emphasizes performance, not just longevity. It lets us select individual public servants and reward them, and thereby in a positive way encourage others to excel.

Today's ceremony is unprecedented, and it's also long overdue, in my judgment. Too often we single out Federal managers only when there's been a problem. We focus attention only on the shortcomings of the Federal bureaucracy and our public servants. This is no way to run a government, nor any enterprise. Federal managers exert an enormous influence on us all. Your responsibilities are often staggering in their scope and complexity and difficulty. Some of you are the most important executives in America. Where we find excellence, we need to acknowledge and reward that excellence publicly.

I'm pleased to be present today for this distinguished executive awards ceremony to 49 men and women who've served our Nation so well. Let me say that your service to our country has been truly distinguished. You're the best of the Government's senior executives; in my opinion the best of the best. I know that the awards have already been issued to you, but I'd like to name just a few that have come to my attention personally and, I think, are representative of the entire group's achievements.

Harold Denton of the NRC has won wide praise for his performance following the Three Mile Island accident. I talked to Harold just a few hours after this accident occurred. When I went to the Three Mile Island plant the Sunday following the accident I went into the control room with Harold, and from then on I saw on television every night his calm, professional, reassuring voice letting the American people know that they need have no fear.

Chris Kraft of NASA made space travel the safest transportation in the world. He has directed, as you know, and was principal organizer of the Mission Control Center in Houston of Mercury, Gemini, and the Apollo space missions, one of the most notable technological achievements in history.

Claude Farinha saved the United States Air Force $28 million through better logistics management, an achievement which would ordinarily not go recognized to the American people.

Charles Swinburn of the Department of Transportation saved taxpayers $100 million by restructuring the Amtrak route system.

I could go on and on. I'm sure that Scotty Campbell has already recognized individually what you all have accomplished. But on behalf of 240 million Americans, I want to say from the bottom of my heart, as President, thank you for what you've meant to our country.

These awards today are a solid investment for our country. The millions of dollars that you 49 people have saved, saved the taxpayer, could fund the senior executive bonuses for many decades in the future, even generations. In honoring you I hope to encourage others, all public servants, to higher levels of accomplishment. And I also want to make your excellence known to your employers, the people of America.

Thank you very much. God bless every one of you.

NOTE: The President spoke at 3 p.m. in the Rose Garden at the White House. Alan K. Campbell, Director of the Office of Personnel Management, presided at the ceremony.

On the same day, the White House released an announcement on the awards for the 49 Distinguished Executives and 206 Meritorious Executives.

Railroad Deregulation Legislation

Statement on House of Representatives Approval of the Legislation.
September 10, 1980

The House last night passed the Harley O. Staggers Rail Act of 1980. I want to congratulate Congressman James Florio, Edward Madigan, Harley Staggers, James Broyhill, and Nick Rahall for their outstanding leadership on behalf of this bill.

The last several decades have seen a decline in the rail freight industry in this country. The average rate of return for the railroad industry as a whole has been far lower than for comparable industries. Equipment and service have continued to deteriorate.

A primary reason for this state of affairs has been overregulation by the Interstate Commerce Commission. The legislation passed by the House last night addresses this problem. By eliminating needless, burdensome rules, it will restore the industry's financial health. At the same time, the Staggers-Rahall compromise, which was incorporated into the bill, provides appropriate additional protection for "captive shippers"—those who have no choice but to use the services of a particular railroad. Thus, this compromise has had strong support from shippers who

depend upon railroads to deliver their goods.

I hope the conferees will delete the legislative veto provision which I believe is unconstitutional.

I urge the Congress to act promptly to send me this legislation for signature.

United States Ambassador to Mozambique

Nomination of David E. Simcox.
September 10, 1980

The President today announced that he will nominate David E. Simcox, of Frankfort, Ky., to be Ambassador Extraordinary and Plenipotentiary of the United States to the People's Republic of Mozambique. He would replace William A. De Pree, who is being assigned to the State Department.

Simcox has been Deputy Director of Management Operations at the State Department since 1979 and a Foreign Service officer since 1956.

He was born November 25, 1932, in Frankfort, Ky. He received a B.A. from the University of Kentucky in 1956 and and M.A. from American University in 1971. He served in the U.S. Marine Corps from 1952 to 1954.

Simcox joined the Foreign Service in 1956 and served in Mexico City, Panama, David, Santo Domingo, Accra, and at the State Department. He attended the National War College in 1971–72.

From 1972 to 1975, he was political officer in Madrid, and from 1975 to 1977, he was counselor for political affairs in Brasília. He was director of Mexican affairs at the State Department from 1977 to 1979.

United States Ambassador to the Central African Republic

Nomination of Arthur H. Woodruff.
September 10, 1980

The President today announced that he will nominate Arthur H. Woodruff, of St. Petersburg, Fla., to be Ambassador Extraordinary and Plenipotentiary of the United States to the Central African Republic. He would replace Goodwin Cooke, who is being assigned to the State Department.

Woodruff has been Deputy Director of the Office of Foreign Service Career Development and Assignments at the State Department since 1978 and a Foreign Service officer since 1956.

He was born September 26, 1928, in Philadelphia, Pa. He received a B.A. (1950) and M.P.A. (1960) from Harvard University. He served in the U.S. Marine Corps from 1950 to 1952.

Woodruff joined the Foreign Service in 1955 and served in Casablanca, Lubumbashi, London, and at the State Department. From 1968 to 1973, he was political-military officer at USNATO in Brussels. He was detailed to the Canadian Defense College in 1973–74.

From 1974 to 1977, Woodruff was with the Office of Policy Planning, Public and Congressional Affairs, as an international relations officer, then Deputy Director. From 1977 to 1978, he was a member of the Board of Examiners for the Foreign Service.

South Pacific Commission

Appointment of U.S. Representative and Alternate Representatives.
September 10, 1980

The President today announced the appointment of the United States Representative and two Alternate Representatives to the South Pacific Commission. They are:

Representative

WILLIAM BODDE, JR., U.S. Ambassador to Fiji, to the Kingdom of Tonga, and to Tuvalu.

Alternate Representatives

VERNON A. MUND, of Seattle, Wash., who retired in 1975 after 38 years as a professor of economics at the University of Washington (reappointment). Mund has been a consultant on economics to a number of Government agencies.

MYRON B. THOMPSON, of Honolulu, Hawaii, trustee of the Kamehameha Schools/Bishop Trust. He was previously director of the Department of Social Services and Housing of the State of Hawaii and is a member of the North Mariana Islands Commission on Federal Laws.

Synthetic Fuels Corporation

Remarks Announcing the Nomination of John C. Sawhill To Be Chairman of the Board of Directors.   September 10, 1980

THE PRESIDENT. I'm proud to announce today my choice for the chairmanship of the Synthetic Fuels Corporation.

This corporation for energy security is a cornerstone of our national energy policy. It's our main instrument in cutting down the intolerable overdependence of our Nation on imported oil from, primarily, the OPEC nations. This threatens our economic vitality and also our national security. The Corporation will use American resources, American knowledge, and American labor to encourage a production of 2 million barrels per day of synthetic fuels by 1992. It will create hundreds of thousands of jobs specifically to design and to build and to operate these plants, which will turn our coal and our shale, our tar sands and other resources into synthetic fuels.

The governing body of this Corporation, its Board of Directors, will be authorized to commit up to $88 billion to strengthen our country and literally to change the way Americans live. As I've said many times, the scope of this project, the amount of money to be expended, is greater than the sum total of the Interstate Highway System, the Marshall plan, and the space program all combined. I have, therefore, searched throughout the country over a number of weeks for the finest Chairman that I could find and also the best qualified six-person Board of Directors. I believe that I've succeeded in this goal.

I'm nominating John Sawhill as Chairman of the Board and the Chief Executive Officer of the Corporation. John has a deep knowledge of energy policy, having served under my administration and also a previous Republican administration. He's knowledgeable about technology, he's compiled a brilliant record of management, both in the private and the public sectors, and has an outstanding record as an educator, an administrator, and an economist.

He served this Nation well as Deputy Secretary of Energy since 1979. He came to this administration after an outstanding tenure as president of New York University. John Sawhill is vigorous and is totally dedicated to making the Corporation the spearhead of our drive to attain energy independence.

The six board members have also been selected by me. They will be announced as soon as proper notifications have been completed.

I'd like to add a comment about a very important matter as well. It's ironic that on a day when we are making an announcement like this, I again have the responsibility to set the record straight because of false allegations made by the Republican nominee for President, Governor Reagan.

Today in Cleveland, Governor Reagan, without one shred of supporting evidence,

charged that the policies of this administration, and I quote, ". . . discourage the discovery and production of energy in this country." Governor Reagan is wrong. He's again made an accusation without checking the facts. Let me tell you the truth.

Coal production in the United States this year is at an alltime high. We will produce more coal in the United States in 1980 than we have ever produced in any single year in the history of this country.

Second, crude oil production has increased this year. This is only the second time in a decade that this has occurred. More oil wells will be drilled in the United States this year, 1980, than in any other year in the entire history of this country, and some experts are predicting that next year we will again set an alltime high record.

As of Monday this week 75 percent more oil wells were being drilled in the United States than they were at the same time 4 years ago when the Republican Party controlled the White House and the executive branch. These are not my figures. They are figures from the oil and gas industry itself, and some of them were reported in the Wall Street Journal this very morning.

I do not intend to let my Republican opponent continue to misrepresent the facts about this administration or about an issue so important to our country as energy itself.

Those are the statements I had to make. Thank you very much.

REPORTER. Mr. President, do you think you'll change your mind about the League debates and take part in them if they had one-on-one after a multi-candidate debate for the first time?

THE PRESIDENT. My position has been clear. It's consistent, and I do not intend to change it. We have offered in an unprecedented way to debate both the

Republican nominees, Reagan and Anderson, and any other candidate for President who might have a theoretical chance to be nominated for President.

The League of Women Voters has done a good job. But they have refused, along with Governor Reagan, to consider so far in any serious way a debate one-on-one between myself as the Democratic nominee for President and Governor Reagan as the Republican nominee for President. This is what we want.

We have already accepted three different invitations to debate Governor Reagan in a two-man debate. It's obvious to me and I think to almost everyone else in this country that the two people who have a chance to be elected as President are the nominee of the Republican Party, Governor Reagan, and myself as the nominee of the Democratic Party. That is what I want. And if the other two of the many candidates decide to debate as a Republican duo, to debate each other, that's perfectly all right with me.

We still are eager to have as many debates as we can schedule between myself and Governor Reagan first and then to debate Governor Reagan, Congressman Anderson, and any others that the sponsors of the debate might bring together.

Q. Is there any prospect today of a one-on-one debate?

THE PRESIDENT. It's up to Governor Reagan. We are——

Q. Do you know what the outlook is now?

THE PRESIDENT. We're still working on it, and we hope we will be successful.

Q. Is the debate issue hurting you at this point?

THE PRESIDENT. I don't know. I don't think so.

NOTE: The President spoke at 4:16 p.m. to reporters assembled in the Oval Office at the White House.

Veterans Day 1980

Proclamation 4791.   September 10, 1980

By the President of the United States of America

A Proclamation

Each year we set aside a special day to thank America's veterans for their unselfish sacrifice and service.

On Veterans Day, 1980, we pay tribute to 30 million living and 14 million deceased patriots who served in our Armed Forces so that you and I might live in freedom. We must honor these men and women as they deserve, not only with special ceremonies, not only through our support of veterans' benefits and services, but also by committing ourselves anew to the task of ensuring that the freedoms they helped to preserve and the Nation they fought to defend will be safe and secure for future generations of Americans.

Now, THEREFORE, I, JIMMY CARTER, President of the United States of America, do hereby invite every citizen of our great country to join with me in observing Veterans Day on Tuesday, November 11, 1980, with appropriate ceremonies and activities.

I call upon all Americans to support the Veterans Day theme—"A Grateful Nation Remembers"—and I urge families, friends, neighbors and fellow citizens to show their gratitude by visiting ill and disabled veterans in Veterans Administration medical centers across the country.

I ask that Federal, State, and local government officials arrange for the display of the flag of the United States on this special day—the flag under which our veterans served with honor, pride, and distinction.

IN WITNESS WHEREOF, I have hereunto set my hand this tenth day of September, in the year of our Lord nineteen hundred and eighty, and of the Independence of the United States of America, the two hundred and fifth.

JIMMY CARTER

[Filed with the Office of the Federal Register, 10:44 a.m., September 11, 1980]

United States Ambassador to Poland

Nomination of Francis J. Meehan.
September 10, 1980

The President today announced that he will nominate Francis J. Meehan, of Washington, D.C., to be Ambassador Extraordinary and Plenipotentiary of the United States to Poland. He would replace William E. Schaufele, Jr., who is retiring from the Foreign Service.

Meehan has been Ambassador to the Czechoslovak Socialist Republic since 1979 and a Foreign Service officer since 1951.

He was born February 14, 1924, in East Orange, N.J. He received an M.A. from the University of Glasgow in 1945 and an M.P.A. from Harvard University in 1957. He served in the U.S. Army from 1945 to 1947.

Meehan joined the Foreign Service in 1951 and served in Frankfurt, Hamburg, Paris, Moscow, and at the State Department. From 1967 to 1968, he was Deputy Executive Secretary of the Department of State, and from 1968 to 1972, he was Deputy Chief of Mission in Budapest.

From 1972 to 1975, Meehan was counselor for political affairs in Bonn. He was Deputy Chief of Mission in Vienna from 1975 to 1977, and in Bonn from 1977 to 1979.

Telecommunications Minority Assistance Program

Remarks at a White House Reception for Participants in the Program.
September 11, 1980

Chairman Ferris and Mr. Geller, Darlene Palmer, ladies and gentlemen:

It's a real honor for me to be with you in this historic East Room and to discuss with you one of the most important elements of American societal life—the right of American citizens to have truth. Full facts about issues that are important to us is absolutely crucial in a democratic society, and that's part of your responsibility, and I share it with you.

I'm proud that we've made some progress in this first 3½ years that I've been in the White House, because in the past, because of racial discrimination and other factors, you have not had your constitutional rights honored in giving a large element of American society the truth or the facts.

As I look around the room I see old friends whom I've known in Atlanta and who have been here to be with me on many occasions when we had important announcements to make or important tasks to undertake. As President, I make many difficult decisions each day in the Oval Office and here in this room and in this building, and each time I ask two fundamental questions: What effect will my decision have on the individual lives of American citizens and what effect will the decision I make have on the future of our country? This was the kind of decision that had to be made in January of 1978, when I established the Minority Telecommunications Development Program.

At that time you and I recognized that we had a long way to go and that very little progress had been made because very few commitments had been made in the past by those who led our Nation in the Oval Office or in other levels of government. We set out a very ambitious program, and we've made the first steps to carry out that program. We've not reached our goals. We've not yet done enough. And I need not only your criticisms and your counsel but also your advice and support in the months ahead as we persist in making additional progress.

I knew that minorities who were attempting to enter the broadcasting business faced such obstacles as not having adequate financing, the lack of technical training because of discrimination and exclusion in the past, and a shortage of available stations to buy or to manage, because so many were assigned long ago when racial discrimination was both a *de facto* and a *de jure* part of the American societal life. I also knew that participation in broadcasting was essential to promoting progress among minorities and their ability to contribute to our Nation's future. This has been one of the roots of the slow progress in the elimination of discrimination and the enhancement of justice in our Nation in the past.

In my own region of the country, because of an absence of black participation, for instance, in the communications media, the churches had to be the focal point for the dissemination of information. They proved to be ultimately effective, but it was a slow, tedious, compartmentalized, local effort that had to be successful only after excessive delay. The same kinds of problems obviously affect those Hispanic citizens and other minority groups in our Nation. Therefore, we all agreed we had to help.

This program has been successful beyond, I believe, what anybody anticipated. I don't mean that we've reached our goal, but what we have accomplished in this short period of time has been extraordi-

nary, because the Nation was ready for it and because my influence and my weight was joined with yours in bringing about necessary changes. In the short period since I just mentioned, minority-owned and operated facilities have increased by a hundred percent, from 62 stations up to 124.

In making this progress we've learned about how we can make more progress in the future. We've sponsored, as you know, at the White House in July a successful commercial broadcasting and technology conference for minority women from across the Nation. We are going to accelerate this effort and this progress in the years ahead.

The FCC, under Chairman Ferris, is acting to create about a thousand new radio stations. This will help to alleviate the second part of the problem, that is, that the stations simply were not available because the licenses had been snapped up early in the development of radio in this country. And as you know, the FCC is now considering a substantial increase in the number of television station licenses that will be [than were][1] available in the past. Several hundreds might very well be available if the FCC makes this decision. And of course, many of these stations can be targeted specifically within the minority audience groups.

I think it's important for our country to have more diversity in programing and specifically to focus programs where they're needed most. We can continue this kind of progress if we work together and if I have the benefit, as I said before, of your criticisms but also your advice and support. We have no different goals. Your goals are my goals—to make sure that minority owners and managers, announcers, and performers have the technical

---

[1] White House correction.

ability, the access to the licenses and the financing assistance, to reach the goal that we've established among ourselves.

We've already doubled the amount of Federal business going to minority-owned businesses of all kinds outside the broadcasting industry, because I think the two go hand in hand. You can't just have progress in the broadcasting industry and ignore the other needs in the minority communities which you will be addressing, where you will be selling the products that you advertise, and which will comprise the support that will let your efforts be successful.

Although we have doubled Federal business going to minority-owned businesses, that's not enough. We intend to triple what we have done in the past. As you know, the Supreme Court has ruled that the requirements for a 10-percent set-aside in public works and others is constitutional. We have joined in through the Attorney General's office, Department of Justice, in protecting this very important element, new element that never had been extant before—of guaranteeing that the massive amounts of money spent by the Federal Government address the opportunities there which exist among the minority-owned businesses. I'm pleased to say that we're already well ahead of the Economic Development Administration programs, where 18 percent, not just 10 percent of this money, now goes to minority businesses.

We've established an apprenticeship program in Government-funded science and engineering, research projects, which allows 1,000 minority high school graduates this summer and 2,000 next summer to work in the fields of technology that are vital to our country and which are compatible with the talent and ability and interests of those minority students.

I could go down a whole list which

Louis and Ambassador Torres [2] have prepared for me—I don't want to bore you with statistics. The point I'm trying to make is that we have a common challenge. We can succeed if we work in partnership, and there must be no cessation of our effort.

I believe that this is a program in its entirety which will have not only the support of Congress but also the support of the American people, because it's obvious that for those who are not members of minority groups, this is beneficial to the lives of all Americans.

It's tough for you to get your message across if you don't have your own broadcasting station. I have often thought that the President ought to have at least one broadcasting station. [*Laughter*] And I think it's important too, to recognize that, on the regulatory commissions, like the FCC and the CAB and in the administration of justice, in the allocation of job programs, in the decisions concerning health and welfare and education and housing, transportation, that we must have a continuing increase in top-quality minority representatives to run those programs that are so important to you.

I said I was not going to quote statistics, and I'm not, but I have been blessed and our Nation has been benefited by the fact that I've appointed more black, Hispanic, and other minority representatives, more women, to those top management positions than any other President who's ever served in this house and more Federal judges than all the Presidents in history combined, and we're not through yet. I'm not going to rest on my laurels, because I think it's an effort that must continue. And I hope that you will be constantly arousing interest among those who speak

---

[2] Louis E. Martin, Special Assistant to the President, and Esteban E. Torres, Special Assistant to the President for Hispanic Affairs.

Spanish, those who happen to be black, those who've not been long in this country, those who are women, and all other Americans that have suffered from discrimination, to let them know that they have a stake in the future and they will have a voice in the future.

We've got legislation on the Hill now that's extremely important. The open housing legislation is one example—I need your help. We've got a youth bill that's now being considered by the Congress that's extremely important for the quality of secondary school education and also extremely important in melding together the Labor Department effort and the Education Department effort, to make sure that when children are graduated, or adults are graduated from our high schools, our vocational technical schools, our junior colleges, and our colleges, that their preparation is compatible with the career opportunities that are waiting for them. And this is important to me and to you as well. This will also mean new careers for 2½ million more young people.

We've got about a $4 billion a year program now. It's been greatly expanded since I was in office. This will add another $2 billion to an already good program and will accomplish the ancillary benefits that I've just described to you. It's important that you help me get this bill through the Senate. As you know, it's already passed the House.

Another and last point I want to make is this: Nothing that we undertake that's important is going to be easy. This Nation has never searched for the easy way. Americans are not cowards, we're not timid. We are ready to face obstacles and to overcome them, to address difficult questions and find the answers through commitment, confidence in ourselves, freedom and unity.

It wasn't long ago that I stood in this very spot with a new Prime Minister,

whose name is Mugabe. A year ago it seemed almost impossible that a new nation could be born in Africa based upon equality of opportunity, the end of racism, and democracy. Our Nation stood firm. We didn't yield to the ill-advised political pressures that existed on the Hill, in the Congress, or in the country. And to see the emergence of this new nation was, indeed, exciting to us.

It was an emotional experience in this room to witness this leader, who was courageous and who had been condemned in this country for many years, expressing his appreciation to Secretary of State Cyrus Vance and to Andrew Young and to Don McHenry and to me and to the American people for having confidence in and a commitment in the principles and ideals and the standards and the morals which our Nation professes to support.

And our emphasis on human rights is a significant factor in worlds overseas, but it's equally important here in our own country. We've got a long way to go in international matters, also here in our country. But I intend to be successful in eliminating discrimination, repairing the damage that has resulted among you and those you lead and represent as a result of that longstanding discrimination, in having a constantly growing society based on truth, based on equality of opportunity, a better life, freedom and confidence that the greatest nation on Earth, our Nation, will be even greater in the future.

Thank you very much for letting me be with you.

NOTE: The President spoke at 2:47 p.m. in the East Room at the White House. In his opening remarks he referred to Charles D. Ferris, Chairman of the Federal Communications Commission, and Henry Geller, Assistant Secretary for Communications and Information, and Darlene Palmer, Program Manager, Minority Telecommunications Development, National Telecommunications and Information Administration, Department of Commerce.

International Maritime Satellite Organization

Executive Order 12238.   September 12, 1980

PUBLIC INTERNATIONAL ORGANIZATIONS ENTITLED TO ENJOY PRIVILEGES, EXEMPTIONS, AND IMMUNITIES

By the authority vested in me by Section 1 of the International Organizations Immunities Act (59 Stat. 669; 22 U.S.C. 288), and having found that the United States participates in the International Maritime Satellite Organization pursuant to Title V of the Communications Satellite Act of 1962, as amended (47 U.S.C. 751 *et seq.*), the International Maritime Satellite Organization is hereby designated as a public international organization entitled to enjoy the privileges, exemptions, and immunities conferred by the International Organizations Immunities Act.

JIMMY CARTER

The White House,
   September 12, 1980.

[Filed with the Office of the Federal Register, 10:53 a.m., September 12, 1980]

Carter/Mondale Re-election Committee

Remarks at the Committee Headquarters. September 12, 1980

MR. STRAUSS. Mr. President, I was looking around waiting for a local politician, Mr. Timothy Kraft, and I don't see— there he is. [*Laughter*]

THE PRESIDENT. Come on up, Tim. I don't see how we lost him.

MR. STRAUSS. You know Mr. Kraft, a local politician.

Mr. President, I'm not going to take any of your time away from these people. [*Laughter*] You know you're a guest over

here—now you behave like one. [*Laughter*]

Mr. President, I don't think any person ever had better partners than you have in this great venture, and it's my pleasure to present them to you and you to them.

THE PRESIDENT. Thank you. Although they've already left, I want to first express my deep thanks to Tim Kraft and to Bob Strauss for the superb job that they did throughout the primary and are doing now. I might say, secondly, that we're doing very well, and I thank you for that; third, that the success of our campaign efforts, this next few weeks up to November 4, depends on you.

And I look upon you as full partners with me, not just in the narrowly defined conduct of a political campaign but in the shaping of our Nation's future—the accurate analysis of what our Nation is now, the achievements that we've realized in an unvarnished, extremely accurate fashion, the problems and opportunities that we face at this moment, and what we hope to contribute to our Nation's greatness in the years ahead.

I can do the best from the Oval Office of which I'm capable, but you can do even more. Collectively, you reach the entire Nation every day, and I only reach it, as you know, infrequently, through the public news media and through my ventures out into individual communities. But you are part of me in deciding the future of the United States of America.

The other point I want to make is this: I have to conduct the affairs of our country on a daily basis. I can't take a 3-month vacation from being President in order to run a campaign, to attack opponents, to criticize every defect in our societal life, and to make projections of what might happen in the future in an irresponsible fashion. I have to deal with economics, with defense, with international affairs, with peace, with human problems every day.

When we have failures and disappointments or delays, which are inevitable, those are going to be highly publicized by the Republicans, most often in a distorted and irresponsible fashion. When we have successes—and I think they are notable—in international matters, in defense matters, in domestic affairs, the Republicans are going to claim that we had those successes not for the benefit of our Nation, but just for some political benefit for us. So be it.

The American people have very sound judgment when the facts are presented. I've worked on this campaign, not with trepidation or displeasure or reluctance, but with anticipation and confidence. It gives us a chance in a legitimate democratic way within the constitutional provisions that were prescribed for our Nation more than 200 years ago, to present our case to the people. And if we do that well, I have no doubt that on November 4 we will have a tremendous victory for myself and Fritz Mondale—who I might add is the best Vice President this country has ever seen.

I had, earlier, thought that I would make an outline of basic issues and give you a description of this campaign from my own perspective, its progress and its challenges. I'm not going to do that. What I would rather do, if you will accommodate me, is to go out into the adjacent room, and I'd like to shake hands with every one of you individually and get a photograph so that I can remember, the rest of my life, the people that meant so much to me—and that's you.

Thank you very much.

NOTE: The President spoke at 11:42 a.m. Robert S. Strauss is chairman and Timothy E. Kraft is national campaign manager for the Carter/Mondale Re-election Committee.

The Medal of Honor

Remarks on Presenting the Award to Cpl. Anthony Casamento.
September 12, 1980

THE PRESIDENT. *Secretary Hidalgo, General Barrow, Mr. Anthony Casamento, beloved members of the Casamento family:*

This is indeed a pleasure and an honor for me, as President of our Nation and as Commander in Chief of the military forces of the United States of America. On August 19th, 1940, more than a year before Pearl Harbor, Anthony Casamento enlisted in the United States Marine Corps. By volunteering for service in the Marines, he proved himself to be a patriot. Two years later in the jungles of Guadalcanal, he proved himself to be a hero as well.

The deed which Anthony Casamento performed is the kind that makes legends. Because of men like him, the name of Guadalcanal has taken its place alongside the other great battles of history in the annals of military valor. On November 1st, 1942, in the course of an American attack, Corporal Casamento led his section to a ridgetop position, then during a series of fierce Japanese counterassaults, Corporal Casamento held firm. He fought on until all of his comrades had either been killed or were too seriously wounded to help. He fought on after he himself had been wounded, again and again. Manning a machine gun, he held out until reinforcements could reach him. He lost consciousness. He had protected more than his own position; he had secured the vulnerable flanks of the companies below his ridge, and in so doing, he made possible the success of the American attack.

Corporal Casamento went beyond the struggle of most fighting men to survive. He went beyond the call of duty. He heard the call of his country and the honor of the Marine Corps and he fought on. By the time he was found, unconscious, by his fellow Marines, Corporal Casamento had been wounded 14 times. Since that day, for 38 years, he has carried the disability of those wounds as courageously and indomitably as he faced the enemy in 1942.

Today, the men and women of the Armed Forces of the United States draw strength from the same tradition and the same degree of sacrifice and service—always potential for them—which was personified and is personified by Anthony Casamento. While less dramatic, the sacrifices they make are just as important to the security and to the liberty of our Nation. The kind of determination that Anthony Casamento has shown is what all of us need if we are to win the things for which we struggle—human rights for all, peace for our country and throughout the world. His valor reminds us of our Nation's reserves of determination and strength and courage, and his sufferings remind us of the horrors of war.

War is a terrible thing, wasting the young, destroying much that is timeless and beautiful and irreplaceable; yet it is our solemn duty to be prepared for war, because that preparation is essential to the prevention of war.

In World War II, when men like Anthony Casamento performed great acts, our soldiers fought for freedom for all people. Today, we're not in the trenches or the jungles of physical combat, and we thank God for it, but we're still fighting. We fight for those things for which American veterans have always fought. We are using peace to fight for peace. We are using our own human rights to gain human rights for others, and we're using the strength that created this country to make this country stronger still.

This recognition of Anthony Casamento has been a long time coming, but heroism such as his is never diminished by the passage of time. He has the gratitude of a nation to which he will always be an example and an inspiration. I'd like to ask now the Secretary of the Navy to read the citation for this heroic man, who has brought great credit to our Nation, gratitude from us, and admiration from all.

[*At this point, Secretary of the Navy Edward Hidalgo read the citation, the text of which follows:*

The President of the United States in the name of the Congress takes pleasure in presenting the MEDAL OF HONOR to

CORPORAL ANTHONY CASAMENTO
UNITED STATES MARINE CORPS

for service as set forth in the following

CITATION:

For conspicuous gallantry and intrepidity at the risk of his life above and beyond the call of duty while serving with Company "D," First Battalion, Fifth Marines, First Marine Division on Guadalcanal, British Solomon Islands, in action against the enemy Japanese forces on 1 November 1942. Serving as a leader of a machine gun section, Corporal Casamento directed his unit to advance along a ridge near the Matanikau River where they engaged the enemy. He positioned his section to provide covering fire for two flanking units and to provide direct support for the main force of his company which was behind him. During the course of this engagement, all members of his section were either killed or severely wounded and he himself suffered multiple, grievous wounds. Nonetheless, Corporal Casamento continued to provide critical supporting fire for the attack and in defense of his position. Following the loss of all effective personnel, he set up, loaded, and manned his unit's machine gun, tenaciously holding the enemy forces at bay. Corporal Casamento single-handedly engaged and destroyed one machine gun emplacement to his front and took under fire the other emplacement on the flank. Despite the heat and ferocity of the engagement, he continued to man his weapon and repeatedly repulsed multiple assaults by the enemy forces, thereby protecting the flanks of the adjoining companies and holding his position until the arrival of his main attacking force. Corporal Casamento's courageous fighting spirit, heroic conduct, and unwavering dedication to duty reflected great credit upon himself and were in keeping with the highest traditions of the Marine Corps and the United States Naval Service.

JIMMY CARTER]

NOTE: The President spoke at 2:31 p.m. at the ceremony in the Rose Garden at the White House. In his opening remarks he referred to Gen. Robert H. Barrow, Commandant of the Marine Corps.

United States Ambassador to Argentina

Nomination of Harry W. Schlaudeman.
September 12, 1980

The President today announced that he will nominate Harry W. Schlaudeman, of San Marino, Calif., to be Ambassador Extraordinary and Plenipotentiary of the United States to Argentina. He would replace Raul H. Castro, who has resigned.

Schlaudeman has been Ambassador to Peru since 1977 and a Foreign Service officer since 1954.

He was born May 17, 1926, in Los Angeles, Calif. He received a B.A. from Stanford University in 1952. He served in the U.S. Marine Corps from 1944 to 1946.

Schlaudeman joined the Foreign Service in 1954 and was posted in Barranquilla, Bogotá, Sofia, and Santo Domingo. From 1963 to 1965, he was chief of Dominican affairs at the State Department, and from 1965 to 1966, he was assistant director of the Office of Caribbean Affairs. He was in the senior seminar in foreign policy in 1966–67.

From 1967 to 1969, Schlaudeman was Special Assistant to the Secretary of State.

He was Deputy Chief of Mission in Santiago from 1969 to 1973, and Deputy Assistant Secretary of State for Inter-American Affairs from 1973 to 1975. From 1975 to 1976, he was Ambassador to Venezuela, and from 1976 to 1977, he was Assistant Secretary of State for Inter-American Affairs.

United States Ambassador to Colombia

Nomination of Thomas D. Boyatt.
September 12, 1980

The President today announced that he will nominate Thomas D. Boyatt, of Cincinnati, Ohio, to be Ambassador Extraordinary and Plenipotentiary of the United States to Colombia. He would replace Diego C. Asencio, who has been appointed Assistant Secretary of State for Consular Affairs.

Boyatt has been Ambassador to the Republic of Upper Volta since 1978 and a Foreign Service officer since 1960.

He was born March 4, 1933, in Cincinnati. He received a B.A. from Princeton University in 1955 and an M.A. from Fletcher School of Law and Diplomacy in 1956. He served in the U.S. Air Force from 1956 to 1959.

Boyatt joined the Foreign Service in 1960 and was posted in Antofagasta, Luxembourg, and Nicosia, and detailed to the Treasury Department. From 1970 to 1971, he was Special Assistant to the Assistant Secretary of State for Near Eastern and South Asian Affairs.

From 1972 to 1974, Boyatt was country director for Cyprus at the State Department. He took the senior seminar in foreign policy in 1974–75. From 1975 to

1978, he was Deputy Chief of Mission in Santiago.

United States Ambassador to Peru

*Nomination of Edwin Gharst Corr.
September 12, 1980*

The President today announced that he will nominate Edwin Gharst Corr, of Norman, Okla., to be Ambassador Extraordinary and Plenipotentiary of the United States to Peru. He would replace Harry W. Schlaudeman, who is being nominated to be Ambassador to Argentina.

Corr has been Deputy Assistant Secretary of State for International Narcotics Matters since 1979 and a Foreign Service officer since 1961.

He was born August 6, 1934, in Edmond, Okla. He received a B.A. (1957) and M.A. (1961) from the University of Oklahoma. He served in the U.S. Marine Corps from 1957 to 1960.

Corr joined the Foreign Service in 1961 and was posted in Mexico City and Cali. He took Latin American area studies at the University of Texas in 1968–69, and was an international relations officer in the Bureau of Inter-American Affairs from 1969 to 1971. From 1971 to 1972, he was a program officer at the Inter-American Social Development Institute.

From 1972 to 1975, Corr was a political officer in Bangkok. He was posted in Quito from 1975 to 1978, as counselor for political affairs, then Deputy Chief of Mission. From 1978 to 1979, he was an international relations officer in the Bureau of International Narcotics Matters.

Agricultural Commodity Credit Guarantees to Poland

*Remarks Announcing Approval of the
Commodity Credit Corporation
Guarantees.   September 12, 1980*

Good afternoon.

The Government and the people of the United States have watched with concern and with hope as events have unfolded in Poland in recent days. Our response has been careful, constructive, and prudent. All of us have sympathized with the aspirations of the Polish people. All of us are glad that a crisis in Poland's evolution appears to be on its way to a peaceful and constructive resolution.

These events touched the emotions of all who care about the rights and dignity of people. There was progress. There's also continued economic dislocations. Now there's a need, the most basic kind of need—the need for food. On behalf of the American people I'm acting on an urgent basis to help meet that need for food.

I've directed today the U.S. Department of Agriculture to extend $670 million in new credit guarantees to Poland for the purchase of agricultural commodities. In plain language this means that the American people and American farmers will guarantee loans to sell some 4 million tons of grain and other farm products to the people of Poland.

I'd like to say just a word about why we are doing this. In taking this action the Government of the United States is responding quickly and completely to a request from the Government and the people of Poland. But in a deeper sense we are responding to the moral obligation that's rooted in the fundamental beliefs of the people of the United States and the people of Poland.

This action is a significant proof of the solidarity between the American people and the Polish people. It's an expression of our admiration for the dignity with which the entire Polish nation—the workers, the Government, and the church—is conducting itself during this difficult time of evolution and change. It's a demonstration of our willingness to use our greatest material asset, the bounty of the American earth, for humanitarian and constructive reasons.

Finally, it's a manifestation of the undiminished belief that a central human reality, the yearning for basic human rights, that yearning is one of the most powerful and constructive forces in the world, and our support for it is more than just a matter of words.

Thank you very much.

REPORTER. Mr. President, does the Ayatollah's speech offer new hope in the hostage crisis?

THE PRESIDENT. Well, we've observed carefully what has been said in Iran, both today and in the days during the past week. We've learned to be very cautious about statements from Iran, but we'll be monitoring what is going on and analyzing the statement further.

NOTE: The President spoke at 4:23 p.m. to reporters assembled in the Briefing Room at the White House.

Economic Assistance to Nicaragua

Announcement of the President's Determination Under the Foreign Assistance Act. September 12, 1980

As required by Section 536(g) of the Foreign Assistance Act, the President is transmitting to the Congress a certification to release funds for aid to Nicaragua. The specific finding required by the law was that the Government of Nicaragua has "not cooperated with or harbors any international terrorist organization or is aiding, abetting or supporting acts of violence or terrorism in other countries."

The certification is based upon a careful consideration and evaluation of all the relevant evidence provided by the intelligence community and by our Embassies in the field. It also takes into account the Government of Nicaragua's repeated assurances that it is not involved with international terrorism or supporting violence or terrorism in other countries. Our intelligence agencies as well as our Embassies in Nicaragua and neighboring countries were fully consulted, and the diverse information and opinions from all sources were carefully weighed. The conclusion was that the available evidence permits the President to make the certification required by Section 536(g) of the Act.

This certification to the Congress permits the administration to proceed with disbursement of economic assistance urgently required to further U.S. national interests in this critical area. The administration does not intend to abandon the vital Central American region to Cuba and its radical Marxist allies. To the contrary, the assistance made available by the President's certification will enable us to give effective support to those moderate and democratic Nicaraguans who are struggling to preserve individual freedoms, political pluralism, the democratic process, and a strong, free enterprise participation in their economy. Sixty percent of the total $75 million in assistance will go to the private sector in Nicaragua.

United Nations Educational, Scientific and Cultural Organization

Nomination of U.S. Delegates and Alternates to the 21st General Conference. September 12, 1980

The President today announced that he will nominate five persons as Delegates and five as Alternates to serve on the U.S. Delegation to the 21st General Conference of the United Nations Educational, Scientific, and Cultural Organization (UNESCO), to be held in Belgrade, Yugoslavia, beginning September 23, 1980.

The General Conference is UNESCO's governing body and meets every 2 years. At this meeting, representatives of 149 member states will review and approve the UNESCO program and budget for 1981–83. The agenda also includes consideration of the report of the International Commission for the Study of Communication Problems (the MacBride Commission), a report on the progress made in reaching the goals of the U.N. Decade for Women, and the draft resolution concerning the status of the artist.

The Delegates and Alternates to be nominated are:

Delegates

ROBIN CHANDLER DUKE, who will serve as Chairman of the Delegation. She is active in numerous national and international humanitarian organizations. She is a former journalist and has devoted much of her career to surveying various problems in underdeveloped nations. On confirmation by the Senate, she will be accorded the rank of Ambassador.

BARBARA NEWELL, who will serve as Vice-Chairman of the Delegation. She is the U.S. Permanent Representative to UNESCO, with the rank of Ambassador. She was previously president of Wellesley College and a professor of economics there.

ELIE ABEL, the Harry and Norman Chandler Professor of Communications at Stanford University. He was the U.S. member of UNESCO's International Commission for the Study of Communication Problems.

JOHN E. FOBES, a visiting professor at the University of North Carolina and Duke University, chairman of the U.S. National Commission for UNESCO, and former Deputy Director-General of UNESCO. He was a member of the U.S. Delegation to the last UNESCO General Conference in 1978.

JOHN HOPE FRANKLIN, a prominent historian and expert on black history, recently retired from the University of Chicago, where he was a professor of American history. He was previously chairman of the Department of History at Brooklyn College and Pitt Professor of American History and Institutions at Cambridge University.

Alternates

JOSEPH D. DUFFEY, Chairman of the National Endowment for the Humanities, former Assistant Secretary of State for Educational and Cultural Affairs, and a member of the U.S. Delegation to the 1978 UNESCO General Conference.

SANDRA LOPEZ DE BIRD, Assistant Regional Director of the New York Regional Office of the Federal Trade Commission and chairperson of the board of the Puerto Rican Legal Defense and Education Fund.

KATHLEEN NOLAN, an actress in television, films, and theater, former president of the Screen Actors Guild, and a member of the Board of Directors of the Corporation for Public Broadcasting.

BEATRICE RANIS, chairman of the board of the Hawaiian State Foundation on Culture and the Arts and chairman of the Consortium for Pacific Arts and Culture.

ROGER REVELLE, a professor of science and public policy at the University of California at San Diego. He is the Richard Saltonstall Professor of Population Policy Emeritus at Harvard University, a former director of the Scripps Institute of Oceanography, and founder of the Intergovernmental Oceanographic Commission.

Digest of Other
White House Announcements

The following listing includes the President's public schedule and other items of general interest announced by the White House Press Office and not included elsewhere in this issue.

September 7

The President returned to the White House from Camp David, Md.

September 8

The President met at the White House with:
—Zbigniew Brzezinski, Assistant to the President for National Security Affairs;
—members of the Conference of Presidents of Major American Jewish Organizations;
—Frank B. Moore, Assistant to the President for Congressional Liaison;
—Vice President Walter F. Mondale;
—officers of the National Rural Electric Cooperative Association.

The President declared a major disaster for the State of Michigan as a result of severe thunderstorms and high winds, during the period July 15–20, which caused extensive property damage.

September 9

The President met at the White House with Dr. Brzezinski.

The President transmitted to the Congress the 15th annual report of the Department of Housing and Urban Development.

September 10

—Dr. Brzezinski;
—the Democratic congressional leadership;
—Mr. Moore;

—members of the New York Democratic congressional delegation;
—leaders of environmental groups and Secretary of the Interior Cecil D. Andrus, Douglas M. Costle, Administrator of the Environmental Protection Agency, and Gus Speth, Chairman of the Council on Environmental Quality;
—Felix Rohatyn, former chairman of the New York Municipal Assistance Corporation.

September 11

The President met at the White House with:
—Dr. Brzezinski;
—Archbishop Jean Jadot, who is returning to the Vatican after serving as the Apostolic Delegate to the United States;
—Mrs. Carter, for lunch.

September 12

The President met at the White House with:
—Dr. Brzezinski;
—Vice President Mondale, Secretary of State Edmund S. Muskie, Secretary of Defense Harold Brown, Jack H. Watson, Jr., Assistant to the President, and Dr. Brzezinski;
—Mr. Moore.

The President transmitted to the Congress the third annual reports on the status of health information and health promotion.

NOMINATIONS SUBMITTED
TO THE SENATE

The following list does not include promotions of members of the Uniformed Services, nominations to the Service Academies, or nominations of Foreign Service officers.

NOMINATIONS—Continued

Submitted September 8, 1980

LAIRD F. HARRIS, of Michigan, to be an Assistant Director of the Community Services Administration, vice Frank Jones, resigned.

Submitted September 9, 1980

GERALD R. DILLON, of Minnesota, to be Public Printer, vice John J. Boyle, resigned.

Submitted September 11, 1980

JOHN C. SAWHILL, of the District of Columbia, to be Chairman of the Board of Directors of the United States Synthetic Fuels Corporation for a term of 7 years (new position).

Submitted September 12, 1980

HARRY W. SHLAUDEMAN, of California, a Foreign Service officer of the Class of Career Minister, to be Ambassador Extraordinary and Plenipotentiary of the United States of America to Argentina.

THOMAS D. BOYATT, of Ohio, a Foreign Service officer of Class one, to be Ambassador Extraordinary and Plenipotentiary of the United States of America to Colombia.

EDWIN GHARST CORR, of Oklahoma, a Foreign Service officer of Class two, to be Ambassador Extraordinary and Plenipotentiary of the United States of America to Peru.

NICKOLAS P. GEEKER, of Florida, to be United States Attorney for the Northern District of Florida for the term of 4 years (reappointment).

JAMES LESLIE BLACKBURN, of North Carolina, to be United States Attorney for the Eastern District of North Carolina for the term of 4 years, vice George M. Anderson, resigned.

DENNIS D. CLARK, of Maryland, to be a member of the Federal Mine Safety and Health Review Commission for the term of 6 years expiring August 30, 1986, vice Jerome R. Waldie.

CHECKLIST OF WHITE HOUSE PRESS RELEASES

The following listing contains releases of the White House Press Office which are not included in this issue.

CHECKLIST—Continued

Released September 8, 1980

Fact sheet: Military Personnel and Compensation Amendments of 1980

Announcement: creation of the Scott Newman Drug Abuse Prevention Award

Released September 9, 1980

Advance text: remarks at dedication ceremonies for the Raritan River Steel Company Plant in Perth Amboy, N.J.

Announcement: 1980 Presidential Rank Awards for the Senior Executive Service

Released September 10, 1980

Announcement: nomination of Nicholas J. Bua to be United States Circuit Judge for the Seventh Circuit

Announcement: nomination of Raymond L. Finch to be United States District Judge for the District of the Virgin Islands

Announcement: nomination of Atlee W. Wampler III to be United States Attorney for the Southern District of Florida

Announcement: nomination of Mack A. Backhaus to be United States Marshal for the District of Nebraska

Released September 12, 1980

Announcement: nomination of Nickolas P. Geeker to be United States Attorney for the Northern District of Florida

Announcement: nomination of James Leslie Blackburn to be United States Attorney for the Eastern District of North Carolina

Fact sheet: agricultural commodity credit guarantees to Poland

ACTS APPROVED BY THE PRESIDENT

Approved September 8, 1980

H.R. 8010_____ Public Law 96–341
An act to amend the Comprehensive Employment and Training Act to designate a Job Corps Center as the "Earle C. Clements Job Corps Center".

H.R. 6974_____ Public Law 96–342
Department of Defense Authorization Act, 1981.

ACTS APPROVED—Continued

Approved September 8—Continued

H.R. 5168_____ Public Law 96–343
Military Personnel and Compensation
Amendments of 1980.

S. 2680_____ Public Law 96–344
An act to improve the administration of the
Historic Sites, Buildings and Antiquities Act
of 1935 (49 Stat. 666).

H.R. 5892_____ Public Law 96–345
Wind Energy Systems Act of 1980.

Approved September 10 , 1980

H.R. 7072_____ Public Law 96–346
An act to amend sections 5702 and 5704 of
title 5, United States Code, to increase the
maximum rates for per diem and actual subsistence expenses and mileage allowances of

ACTS APPROVED—Continued

Approved September 10—Continued

Government employees on official travel, and
for other purposes.

Approved September 12, 1980

H.R. 1781_____ Public Law 96–347
An act to amend title 5, United States Code,
to provide that civilian air traffic controllers
of the Department of Defense shall be
treated the same as air traffic controllers of
the Department of Transportation for purposes of retirement, and for other purposes.

H.R. 1967_____ Public Law 96–348
An act to modify the boundary of the White
River National Forest in the State of
Colorado.

S. 390_____ Public Law 96–349
Antitrust Procedural Improvements Act of
1980.

Week Ending Friday, September 19, 1980

Synthetic Fuels Corporation

*Statement on the Nomination of Six Persons
To Be Members of the Board of Directors.
September 13, 1980*

I am proud to announce today my nominees for the Board of the Synthetic Fuels Corporation.

The Synthetic Fuels Corporation is a cornerstone of our national energy policy. It is our main instrument in cutting the intolerable dependence on foreign oil which threatens our economic vitality and our national security.

The governing body of the Corporation, its Board of Directors, will be authorized to commit up to $88 billion to strengthen our country and literally to change the way we live. I have, therefore, searched throughout this country for six Board members of the very highest caliber. After an arduous search, I believe we have succeeded in this goal.

Lane Kirkland, the president of the AFL–CIO, will bring wise, thoughtful leadership to the Board. He understands fully the enormous job opportunities the Corporation's energy program represents. The AFL–CIO has been instrumental in helping devise and enact our Nation's energy program, and I know Lane Kirkland will be tremendously helpful in implementing this program.

Cecil Andrus, Secretary of Interior, will be an invaluable member of the Board. If confirmed, he will officially join the Board upon his resignation as Secretary of the Interior sometime after the November election. Cecil has indicated for some time

his intention to resign as Secretary after the first term. I have tried to change his mind, but he feels strongly that he should leave after 4 years. Cecil has been a superb Interior Secretary. I know he will bring a keen knowledge of the West and the problems and opportunities the synthetic fuels initiative poses for Western States and communities to the Board. He also will have an appreciation for the environmental impact of the Corporation's proposed actions. I expect that as a former Governor, Cecil will help forge strong relationships between the Corporation and State and local governments.

Frank Savage, the vice president and manager of Equitable Life Insurance's Investment Management Department, has an outstanding financial and investment background. He will bring sound business and financial experience to the Board. He has managed Equitable's extensive energy investment programs and will understand how the Corporation can effectively stimulate the development and marketing of synthetic fuels in the private sector.

Frank Cary, the chairman of IBM, is one of America's most successful and innovative business leaders. He is an excellent manager and fine planner. He will bring a great deal of knowledge about finance, technological development, and sophisticated management techniques to the Corporation. Frank Cary shares my desire to make certain the private sector develops the capacity to quickly produce large quantities of synthetic fuels.

Catherine Cleary is a highly respected financial and business executive. She is the

1717

former chairman of the First Wisconsin Trust Company of Milwaukee and now serves as an adjunct professor of the University of Wisconsin's School of Business Administration. Catherine Cleary will be a strong Board member.

John DeButts, the retired chairman and chief executive officer of AT&T has compiled an enviable record as a manager and innovator. I have relied on his advice on numerous issues and have always found him to be thoughtful and constructive. He will bring tremendous business, financial, and technological experience to the Board. He deservedly has been recognized by his peers as one of our finest business executives, and I'm certain he will make significant contributions to helping organize and operate the Corporation.

National Italian-American Foundation

Remarks at the Foundation's Third Biennial Tribute Dinner.   September 13, 1980

Vice President Mondale, whose parents came here from Italy, stopping temporarily in Norway—[laughter]*—mine stopped for a few years in England and Ireland on the way from Italy to this country—*[laughter]*—Archbishop Hickey; Chairman Jeno Paulucci, who's done such a tremendous job in organizing and promoting this historic event; Mayor Joe Alioto; my good friend whom I admire from the bottom of my heart, Peter Rodino; Frank Annunzio and the other 30 members of the Italian-American congressional delegation, which is rapidly growing and I hope will grow in the future for the well-being of our own Nation; other distinguished guests, ladies and gentlemen:*

I first of all want to thank Peter Rodino for that nice introduction. He treated me very gently; as a matter of fact, I noticed he did not say that I was an Italian. I'm glad he overlooked that serious flaw in my recent background.

I am delighted to be here. I had a memorable evening with you 4 years ago. Two years ago, I had been scheduled to come, but I was at Camp David with President Sadat and with Prime Minister Begin. But if you will help me arrange it, I want to be with you for the next 4 years at your other banquets.

Tonight I come to you as President, representing 240 million Americans who share my deep feelings that I will try to express very briefly. I want to congratulate my friend Jeno Paulucci again—the moving force behind the National Italian-American Foundation—for the great success he's made with this effort and especially this second annual international conference and the third biennial tribute dinner.

The first Italian came to this land a long time ago, so it's no wonder that you have such an outstanding foundation, having had almost 500 years to organize it—since 1492, Jeno. [*Laughter*]

And the honorees this year, the quality of them, are a tribute to what has been accomplished by you, by others who are being participants in this distinguished gathering, and by those who have been specially singled out this evening—Henry Fonda, Robert Georgine, Alexander Giacco, Bob Giaimo, Dr. Margaret Giannini, Vincent Marotta, Dr. Edmund Pellegrino, John Volpe. What a wonderful demonstration of the extraordinary breadth and depth of the Italian-American influence on our Nation. As President, I thank you all for this great contribution.

This conference is a model of how ethnicity works best in America. You have brought together some of our Nation's best minds to consider questions and problems that affect everyone in this country.

A long list of brilliant and experienced Americans of Italian ancestry have discussed, in the last few days, government, the economy, education, the family, social justice, and international relations. The messages were delivered by Italian Americans. But the messages themselves were of national and, indeed, universal significance.

This is American pluralism in action. While maintaining the integrity of your own cultural group—as Jeno pointed out, the largest cultural group in this country—with all its historical and modern strengths, you use that strength and that beauty to enhance our whole society. Our Nation at its best—and I'm sure you'll agree with this statement—is in this room.

What gives the United States its essential character, its unique character, is the diversity of our people, joined together in their various separate identities to form a united whole—stronger and more beautiful than any one of us or any of its parts separately. *E Pluribus Unum:* Out of Many, One.

Instead of asking people to abandon their cultures that produced them, in this country we've encouraged them to bring to the American reality all the best of a hundred different traditions.

In spite of imperfections, no nation is perfect. In spite of occasional strife and tension, there has never been anywhere, or at any time, a greater miracle of government than this magnificent amalgam of different people which we call America. And of all the people from all over the world who have created this beautiful mosaic, no one's contribution shines with greater lustre than does yours. So much of what we are as a nation began by being Italian, and we are a greater nation because of it.

The land of your ancestors is the product and the source of one of the most important cultures in human history.

I saw that vividly when I visited Italy, Rome and Venice, just 3 months ago, when Italy played host to the seven leaders of the democratic industrial nations.

All of us were thrilled. Just try to imagine our own cities without the influence of Roman architecture, or our music without Italian opera. Try to imagine how we would have been diminished if our American experience had been denied Dante and Cicero, Michelangelo and Verdi, Cellini and Leonardo da Vinci. And just think where we politicians would be without Machiavelli. [*Laughter*]

There's another aspect, as you well know, to the heritage of Italian Americans that's just as important. And I'm talking about the contribution that has been made by recent immigrant generations of the late 19th and the early 20th centuries; often they are forgotten. Millions of Italians came here during that period. A few came already financially secure and seeking to expand their opportunities, but most came because they had no opportunities to compare with those in this country.

I'm sure that everyone in this room tonight knows that there are hundreds of stories that you could tell about these recent generations—in your own families—generations memorialized so beautifully by Pietro di Donato in the classic, "Christ in Concrete."

Many came without money or property and often without friends. They were powerless, but they were proud and ambitious. Perhaps they were frightened by a society they did not know, but they were forceful in making their way in. And the families that received them added to their strength and derived strength from those new immigrants. And always they were driven by unrelenting Italian commitments and beliefs and Italian passion, the passion for the family, a willingness to sacrifice to make something better for one's own children. Their commitment to the future was very personal and very concrete.

They came and they left their mark, a mark that said: These are the strong and the brave; the builders, the growers, the makers of families and of cities. These are the new Americans that came from Italy.

How great a mark that has been. These valiant immigrant generations of recent times and their progeny represented in this room gave us Enrico Caruso and Mother Cabrini, Fermi and La Guardia, and the hundreds of distinguished Americans in this room who cannot be recognized by name this evening. They gave us even more than that. They gave us a precious set of values which you have not permitted to change. They taught us a selfless, unshakeable respect for family—a deeper sense of the obligation of children to parents and of parents to children. They taught us a proud, bold patriotism as they offered even their lives for their new country.

We are honored tonight by the presence of a man who personifies that patriotic spirit. Yesterday I had the privilege, an emotional privilege, of presenting him with the highest honor that our Nation can bestow for valor, the Congressional Medal of Honor. His name is Anthony Casamento.

Mr. Casamento, please stand. [*Applause*]

In the Rose Garden yesterday there was not a dry eye, including mine, when the "Star-Spangled Banner" was sung so beautifully, and Tony Casamento, who had sat there with full control over his emotions, broke down and wept to hear our national anthem. And I thank him from the bottom of my heart again for what he means to me and to our Nation and the traditions of Italian Americans.

The immigrants also taught us a reverence for the dignity of work, a recognition of the overriding importance of education, a deep religious conviction which is unshakeable, humble in the face of the Almighty. Most of all, they taught us love.

Our society still needs, more than ever, a commitment to the values that these generations of giants gave us out of the sweat and the prayers and the smiles and the tears that comprised their lives.

You should be very proud, as all Americans are grateful. Our Nation has benefited from your success. You've helped to create the growth and success of America.

You've come a long way, but there's still a long way to go. There are still too many of you who are punished unfairly by cruel stereotypes.

I recall that when I was with you 4 years ago, I pointed out that as a southerner, as a Georgian, I had been stigmatized because of the region of my birth. And I pointed out to you that if I should be elected in that year, that I would be the first President from my region of the country in 140 years to serve this Nation. Italians, Georgians, are good people. And I think we've made a fair, an excellent partnership this last 4 years.

We've had good success, but there's an even brighter future for Italian Americans, just as there's a brighter future for all those who live in our country.

We've made great strides over the last 4 years, but surely there's more to be accomplished.

We've created 8 million new jobs, but we are still working to reduce the ranks of the unemployed.

We've reduced our dependence upon foreign oil, and in so doing we've won a beachhead in our battle for energy security and against the main cause of inflation that was forced on us by the OPEC nations. We will drill more oil and gas wells this year than any other year in the history of the United States, and we'll produce more United States coal this year than any other year in history.

After a long, tough fight, we've passed a windfall profits tax to pay for our quest for energy security. Now we must build on our new energy base to revitalize the tremendous productive machine that is the American economy.

We've adopted the first urban policy in history, and now we've begun to rebuild our cities and our communities so precious to you.

We've made the greatest strides in education in history, and now we're improving, even further, the preparation of our young people for a productive life.

We've fought to provide for the elderly and the impaired and the infirm and give them the care they require, but now we need a national program to prevent disease and to ensure good medical care for all Americans.

And we've put the land of the free back on the side of freedom. The oppressed of the world are not longer alone; they know that America is with them. And as long as I'm President, our Nation will hold high the banner of human rights all around the world.

And the last point I want to make is this: We're grateful that despite instability and turmoil in many parts of the world, we've kept our Nation strong and, therefore, we have had 4 years of peace. But we must reduce further the threat to peace, especially the ultimate threat of a nuclear holocaust.

With every achievement, we strive even harder—typical of the character of Italian Americans and typical of our Nation's commitment, not just to the past and present but to the future.

Part of my job as President is to respond to the clamoring and often conflicting demands of the moment. But my most important duty is to serve the future, because the President of the United States must be the steward and the guardian of the future of the United States. I've described the election of 1980 as a choice between two futures. It's a clear and a crucial choice. And in closing, I want to leave you tonight with my brief summary of the vision of what I see as the kind of future I'm fighting for.

When I look forward I see a nation at peace; a nation strong enough to be secure in its pursuit of progress for all people; a nation in which everyone can be afforded the dignity of decent employment; a nation whose children are educated to their maximum potential, whose elderly are treated with the respect which they've earned, whose families are intact and secure.

I have a vision of a nation free enough to attract and strong enough to welcome those who seek freedom. That's what America has done for the rural people of the *mezzogiorno* [southern part of Italy], for the potato farmers of Ireland, for the Jews of Eastern Europe, for the oppressed who came here seeking the opportunities denied them in their homelands.

I want to pursue that vision with you and with all the others like you who have ensured this Nation's success. I'm honored to be with you tonight. I hope you'll invite me to be with you again—hopefully as President—as we work together for 4 more years to make this Nation greater still for all those who will follow us to a better life and to freedom.

Sempre avanti.

NOTE: The President spoke at 7:48 p.m. in the International Ballroom at the Washington Hilton Hotel.

American Hostages in Iran

Informal Exchange With Reporters.
September 13, 1980

REPORTER. What did you think about the concert?

THE PRESIDENT. I enjoyed it.

Q. What was your favorite song?

THE PRESIDENT. Well, I think "Georgia."

Q. Why?

Q. What did you think of the comment by Mr. Reagan tonight—that we should accept three of the four proposals from the Ayatollah?

THE PRESIDENT. Well, I think it's better not to get involved, in the political campaign, with the Iranian situation.

Q. Thank you very much.

NOTE: The exchange began at 11:08 p.m. at the South Portico at the White House, following the President's return from Columbia, Md., where he attended a concert by Willie Nelson and a Carter/Mondale reception.

As printed above, this item follows the text of the White House press release.

Illegal Drug Traffic on the High Seas

Statement on Signing H.R. 2538 Into Law.
September 15, 1980

Today I am signing into law H.R. 2538, a bill which will improve the Coast Guard's ability to enforce laws aimed at stopping illegal drug trafficking on the high seas. This legislation was introduced by Congressman Mario Biaggi (D-N.Y.), Chairman of the Subcommittee on the Coast Guard and Navigation.

The Coast Guard, the U.S. Customs Service, and the Drug Enforcement Administration have greatly increased their efforts to stop drug trafficking on the high seas, particularly in the Caribbean. In many instances, however, current law makes it difficult to prosecute drug traffickers once they are apprehended. By closing a loophole in our maritime enforcement laws, H.R. 2538 will improve the ability of our Federal enforcement agencies to reduce international drug trafficking. This legislation makes it a crime to illegally possess or distribute drugs on the high seas and applies to all United States citizens, to all persons aboard any United States vessel regardless of their nationality, to individuals who intend to unlawfully import a controlled substance into the United States, and to all persons aboard vessels within the 12-mile territorial limits.

I am particularly pleased to sign this bill which will help us control the possession and distribution of drugs on the high seas. It is an excellent example of close coordination and cooperation between the administration and the Congress who worked on this legislation. I especially want to thank Congressman Biaggi for his efforts in having this bill passed. I also welcome this opportunity to reiterate my strong personal commitment and that of this administration to stemming the flow of illicit drugs throughout the world and to reducing the health and social costs to the citizens of our country caused by drug abuse.

NOTE: As enacted, H.R. 2538 is Public Law 96–350, approved September 15.

Military Service for Citizens of the Northern Mariana Islands

Statement on Signing H.R. 4627 Into Law.
September 15, 1980

I am pleased to sign into law H.R. 4627, which will permit the people of the Northern Mariana Islands to enlist in our Armed Forces.

In approving the Covenant to establish their Commonwealth, the people of the Northern Mariana Islands freely and overwhelmingly chose to become Americans. They will become United States citizens when the Covenant takes effect upon termination of the Pacific Islands Trusteeship Agreement. Until that time, however, they are effectively blocked from military service.

The inability to serve their Nation during this period has been a source of severe disappointment to many young people in the Islands. This bill rectifies that situation by giving them the right to enlist during the remaining period of trusteeship.

I want to congratulate Senator J. Bennett Johnston, Jr., and Delegate Antonio B. Won Pat for guiding H.R. 4627 through the Congress. This new law is a symbol of the permanent political union between the United States and the Northern Mariana Islands. That it was enacted at the request of the people of the Islands, through Governor Carlos S. Camacho and Representative Edward DLG. Pangelinan, is a testament to the loyalty of the newest members of the American political family.

NOTE: As enacted, H.R. 4627 is Public Law 96–351, approved September 15.

President's Commission for the Study of Ethical Problems in Medicine and Biomedical and Behavioral Research

Appointment of Carolyn Antonides Williams To Be a Member. September 15, 1980

The President today announced the appointment of Carolyn Antonides Wil-

liams, of Durham, N.C., as a member of the President's Commission for the Study of Ethical Problems in Medicine and Biomedical and Behavioral Research.

Williams is an assistant professor of epidemiology in the School of Public Health of the University of North Carolina at Chapel Hill and an associate professor of nursing in the School of Nursing.

Tariff Concessions on Certain Lead Products

Proclamation 4792. September 15, 1980

PROCLAMATION TO SUSPEND IN PART THE TARIFF CONCESSIONS ON CERTAIN LEAD PRODUCTS AND TO CORRECT TECHNICAL ERRORS

By the President of the United States of America

A Proclamation

1. On October 31, 1979, under the authority of section 101(a)(1) of the Trade Act of 1974 (the Trade Act) (19 U.S.C. 2111(a)(1)), the United States entered into a trade agreement with the United Mexican States (Mexico) containing certain tariff concessions by the United States. These tariff concessions were implemented by Proclamation No. 4707 of December 11, 1979, beginning January 1, 1980. This agreement provides that, under certain circumstances which now exist, the United States may suspend or withdraw these concessions in whole or in part.

2. An expectation, which this agreement stated to be the basis for the United States concessions therein, has not materialized, and only partially equivalent

substitute concessions have been received from Mexico.

3. Section 125 of the Trade Act (19 U.S.C. 2135) authorizes the President, following public hearings, to withdraw, suspend, or modify the application of trade agreement obligations of the United States under certain circumstances, which now exist. Public hearings on possible modification or suspension of concessions to Mexico were held on June 12, 1980, by the Office of the United States Trade Representative.

4. I have decided, under the provision regarding suspension in the October 31, 1979 agreement and under section 125 of the Trade Act (19 U.S.C. 2135), to suspend in part, until otherwise proclaimed by the President, the tariff concessions which were granted to Mexico in the October 31, 1979 agreement because adequate substitute compensatory concessions have not been provided by Mexico at this time.

5. As a distinct matter, it has been determined that certain technical errors in Proclamation No. 4707 and Proclamation No. 4768, which proclamations made numerous changes to the provisions of the Tariff Schedules of the United States (TSUS) (19 U.S.C. 1202), require correction.

Now, THEREFORE, I, JIMMY CARTER, President of the United States of America, acting under the authority vested in me by the Constitution and the statutes of the United States, including sections 125 and 604 of the Trade Act (19 U.S.C. 2135 and 2483), do proclaim that:

(1) The tariff concession proclaimed by Proclamation No. 4707, on litharge, provided for in TSUS item 473.52, is suspended as set forth in Annex I of this proclamation.

(2) The TSUS is modified as provided in Annexes I, II, and III of this proclamation.

(3) Annex II of Proclamation No. 4768 is amended as provided in Annex II of this proclamation.

(4) Annex IV of Proclamation No. 4707 is amended as provided in Annex III of this proclamation.

(5) The suspension in part of the rates of duty on litharge, provided for in Annex I of this proclamation, shall be effective with respect to articles entered, or withdrawn from warehouse for consumption, on or after September 15, 1980.

(6) The amendment to Proclamation No. 4768 and the consequential changes to the TSUS made by Annex II of this proclamation shall be effective with respect to articles exported to the United States on and after July 1, 1980, and as to which the liquidations of the entries or withdrawals covering the subject merchandise have not become final and conclusive under section 514 of the Tariff Act of 1930 (19 U.S.C. 1514), by the date of this proclamation.

(7) The amendment to Proclamation No. 4707 and the consequential changes to the TSUS made by Annex III of this proclamation shall be effective on the date of publication of this proclamation in the FEDERAL REGISTER.

IN WITNESS WHEREOF, I have hereunto set my hand this fifteenth day of September, in the year of our Lord nineteen hundred and eighty, and of the Independence of the United States of America the two hundred and fifth.

JIMMY CARTER

[Filed with the Office of the Federal Register, 12:17 p.m., September 15, 1980]

NOTE: The annexes are printed in the FEDERAL REGISTER of September 16, 1980.

Corpus Christi, Texas

Remarks and a Question-and-Answer Session at a Townhall Meeting.   September 15, 1980

THE PRESIDENT. *Lieutenant Governor Bill Hobby, Congressman Joe Wyatt, State Senator Carlos Truan, State Senator Bill Patman, who will be with me in Washington next year, ladies and gentlemen:*

Es un gran placer para miestar aquí con ustedes, mis amigos, en el gran estado de Texas.

And for those of you who don't speak Georgia Spanish, let me say that— [*laughter*]—it's a great pleasure to be here with all my friends in the great State of Texas. First of all, I want to thank you for the warm hospitality. And before I begin taking questions, I'd like to make just two points: first of all concerns our Nation's military strength.

I've just come from the Naval Air Station—as an old Navy man this is very important to me—and as you know, the Naval Air Station in Corpus Christi is important to our Nation's strength. And I can tell you there is no plan to be moving the Naval Air Station away from Corpus Christi.

CAMPAIGN ISSUES

When I was elected President and took office there had been an 8-year decline in the commitment of our Nation's wealth to a strong defense. We reversed that downward trend with the Cruise missile, the MX missile, the Rapid Deployment Force, the Trident submarine, with a stronger alliance with our NATO Allies and with others around the world. And we will continue in the next few years to make sure we've got a strong America so that we can have an America at peace, and you can depend on that.

It's very important that no potential adversary underestimate either the strength or the will or the unity or the commitment of the American people. Next month we'll be celebrating the birthday of the United States Navy, and Secretary of the Navy Hidalgo will be down at Corpus Christi to celebrate this birthday with you.

And the second point I want to make is that 1980 will be a very decisive year for you, for your personal lives, for the lives of your families, and for the future of this Nation. Americans on November the 4th will be choosing not just between two men, not just between two parties, but between two futures. We'll decide whether we continue down the road of equality of opportunity and justice and fairness or whether we'll turn away from that long and important struggle. In my judgment, I'm in the right city to talk about this because, as was the case with my own area of the Nation in the Deep South, we've struggled to overcome racial prejudice. No one can forget that tragic day 30 years ago when a brave war veteran was denied burial here just because he was an Hispanic. We don't want that ever to happen in this country again.

As you know, Corpus Christi is the birthplace of the American G.I. Forum and the League of the United Latin-American Citizens—LULAC. You organized to carry on a struggle—that's now nationwide—that at times was lonely and sometimes unpopular. These struggles must continue to make sure that our Nation accurately represents what our Constitution says and the principles and ideals that live in Americans' hearts of all races. It's a constant struggle. It needs constant commitment and constant bravery.

We want to make sure that justice is practiced throughout our Nation so that every person has a chance to work, to be useful, to have a decent life. I'm very proud that now there are nearly 5 million Hispanics at work in the United States. One out of four of those jobs, by the way, has been created in the last 3½ years, since I've been in the White House, and we're going to continue that kind of progress in the next 4 years.

We've come a long way; we've got to keep going. It's time for us to modernize American industry, to increase the productivity of American workers—already the highest in the world—and to lay the basis for a full-employment economy based on the tremendous progress we've made in energy in the last 3½ years. But in doing that, we cannot lose sight of this desire for justice and for fairness.

You're going to hear this year that the only way to create new jobs is to give a massive tax cut to the rich and hope that some of the benefits trickle down to everybody else. That's not so. An efficient government and fair tax laws can help to revitalize our economy and provide a better life for us all. And we must never forget that the major advances for justice and fairness came about—some of them under a great Texan, President Lyndon Johnson—simply because people like you could mobilize our Nation to do away with injustice and get action from the government.

Civil rights is part of all that. The violation of federally protected human rights is a serious crime, no matter who the victim might be, no matter who the violator of the law might be. And as long as I'm President, the United States Government will fully enforce civil rights laws.

I'm committed to equal justice for all Americans. That's why we now have four times as many Hispanic Federal judges as we did 3½ years ago when I took office.

I'm committed to securing for all children in America an equal chance to learn and to excel. There's a saying in Spanish, *"Negar la educación a nuestros niños es la ruina de las naciónes."* [To deny education to our children is the ruin of nations.] And if we deny a good education to our children, it could bring about the ruin of the Nation we love. We've increased Federal support for education, leaving control of our schools at the local and State level where it ought to be. We've greatly increased bilingual education, more than double since I've been in office, because we know that too many children, as they learn English, must also be able to learn other subjects at the same time.

And finally let me say that beyond all these actions, and underlying them, is a commitment to the ideals of our country. The ideals of a nation do not change. The commitment of a people does not change. Principles, deep beliefs do not change. America is great not just because we have military strength and economic power, but because we remain committed to those ideals that have brought ourselves and our ancestors here. We must live up to them.

Our Nation must always remain the champion of human rights around the world. We cannot stop until we have realized a dream for our Nation—for every American to have a better life in freedom.

Thank you very much.

And now I'm looking forward to the questions.

QUESTIONS

EDUCATION FOR CHILDREN OF UNDOCUMENTED WORKERS

Q. Welcome to Corpus Christi.

THE PRESIDENT. I feel welcome.

Q. My name is Anna Contreras, and my question is: Mr. President, with the recent Federal ruling affecting all school districts in regard to the enrollment of alien children, what will the immigration department do with the information gathered by the school districts in regard to the residency of their parents?

THE PRESIDENT. As you know, the other border States at this time provide education for the undocumented alien children, undocumented worker-children. This is a matter that is in the Federal courts. It would not be proper for me as President, because of the separation between the Executive and the judiciary, to involve myself in it. The State government, which has a substantial surplus which we don't yet enjoy in the Federal Government, has maintained that impact aid should be given to the Texas schools. This is not legal and will not be done, because impact aid is designed for communities that have extra costs in their school systems because of military bases and other Federal installations, and not because the State government happens to disagree with the Federal Government on an issue.

So the responsibility as presently expressed by the Supreme Court of the United States is that education must be provided for the undocumented worker-children, and I don't believe there's any possibility for impact aid from the Federal Government. The other States are complying with this ruling, and I feel sure that Texas will do the same since the courts have ruled.

Thank you.

FEDERAL RETIREMENT SYSTEM

Q. Mr. President, I'm Leonard Luther from Mathis, Texas. I'm a Federal retired person on civil service annuity, and I understand there's been an attempt to change the cost-of-living adjustment to twice a year and possibly even skip one and, on top of that, possibly put this annuity into another type retirement. My question is: We Federal retirees would like

to know, if you are reelected, will you try to retain the cost-of-living adjustment to twice a year with no skips and not allow it to be joined to another retirement system?

THE PRESIDENT. I won't do anything to damage the integrity of the retirement system. We have not proposed that there be a merger between the Federal retirement system and any other, and I don't anticipate that. We did propose, however, that the cost-of-living adjustment be made annually instead of twice a year. The Congress will not do that, so your concerns about this change taking place this year— you can forget about that. The Congress has decided in the reconciliation bill in the House—and I feel sure that it will pass the Senate, too—that there will be no change in the biannual adjustment.

So, I don't have any plans to merge the two systems. We still are keeping alive the possibility of an annual adjustment, which I think would be fair, but we will not have a change in the foreseeable future because the Congress has already acted on it.

Thank you, sir.

U.S.-SOVIET RELATIONS

Q. Mr. President, my name is Danny Kucera, and my question is: Has the Olympic boycott and the grain embargo you imposed on the Russians had any effect and, after you are reelected, will you take further measures to pressure the Soviets to withdraw from Afghanistan?

THE PRESIDENT. The answer is that there has been a great effect on the Soviet Union by the Olympic boycott and also by the interruption of grain sales to the Soviet Union. More than 50 other nations joined us in deciding not to send any athletes to Moscow at all, which was a major propaganda victory over the Soviet Union. In addition to that, many other countries let a few athletes go—like Australia, France, Italy—but they only permitted a very small number.

In the grain sales, the Soviets have had, in a 6-month period, a loss of 6½ million tons of grain which they would have gotten in worldwide markets which they were not able to buy. In addition, when they have bought some grain to replace that that would have come from our country, they've had to buy it at a very high price. And the ships involved were very small ships, so the unloading was uncomfortable for them.

They've had a sharp reduction in meat production in the Soviet Union because of this interruption of feed grain supplies. As a matter of fact, in July alone meat production in the Soviet Union was 15 percent below what it was in July of 1979, and the meat production in the Soviet Union, in spite of increased population, is no higher than it was 5 years ago.

At the same time, we have made sure that American farmers have not suffered. We have increased grain exports from this country to reach an alltime record. One of the most important elements of that is that we now have three times as much trade of all kinds with Mexico as we did 4 years ago, and grain shipments to Mexico have now reached the 10 million metric ton mark. Our new opportunities in China, our increased sales all over the world have made darn sure that American farmers don't suffer. But the Soviets have suffered, and they're going to continue to suffer from these kinds of actions until they get their troops out of Afghanistan.

I might add parenthetically, since it's an election year—[*laughter*]—that my Republican opponent has been against the grain embargo. He's been on both sides of the Olympic boycott—first he was strongly for it, then later he was against it. And he's also been against draft registration, the things that we have taken as actions against the Soviet Union that were effective. He's been against them all. He did advocate a blockade of Cuba—which, as you know, is on the opposite side of the world from Afghanistan—for some reason. But I think we've taken responsible action, and in my judgment, it has been effective.

DRAFT REGISTRATION

Q. Hello. My name is Tony Martinez, and I'd like to welcome you to Foy Moody High School. Since I'll be turning 18 in a few months, I'd like to know from you what you plan to do about the draft.

THE PRESIDENT. Okay. I don't think there's any likelihood at all, Tony, of having a draft any time soon. I have been strongly in favor, as you know, of registration for the draft in case we do have to mobilize our forces in the future. We want to be ready to move rapidly, and this sends a clear signal to our allies and friends, to the American people, and to our potential opponents in the future that Americans are willing to take patriotic action for their country. We had a 93-percent signup for draft registration among 18- and 19-year olds. But our volunteer military forces are strong. You might be interested in knowing that 15 percent of the young people who registered during that 1-month period said they would like to have additional information about the military forces. So, I think this will help with recruitment on a voluntary basis.

So as long as our voluntary forces are adequate and strong and getting stronger, I see no prospect at all of going for a mandatory draft. So you need not worry.

Q. Thank you.

INCOME TAX LAWS

Q. Good morning, Mr. President. I'm Madalyn Cooke, and I have an economic question for you. Especially in terms of revising the personal income tax laws, what is the major difference between your economic plan and the plan being offered by the Republican candidate?

THE PRESIDENT. I'm glad you asked that question. [*Laughter*]

In the first place, the economic plan that we have proposed is designed to build on the energy progress we've made and to give Americans an exciting, progressive, better life throughout the 1980's, by revitalizing America's industry and creating new jobs that we've never foreseen in the past. We'll have enough money, for instance, to spend on improved conservation and production of American energy that would be greater in size than the total Interstate Highway System, the Marshall plan that rebuilt Europe after the Second World War, and the space program all put together. So this means that we've got a base on which to make further progress.

We've designed our economic plan to be noninflationary; it'll actually reduce the inflation rate instead of increasing it. The Republican plan, known as Reagan-Kemp-Roth, is an ill-advised plan that the business community has said would be, and I quote accurately, "a disaster," which is true because it would be highly inflationary in nature. It's designed primarily to give income tax reductions to rich individuals. For instance, under Mr. Reagan's plan somebody that made $200,000 a year in income would get 35 times more benefit than someone that made $20,000 a year.

Our plan is designed primarily to create faster investments in order to create jobs. We also included in our plan a proposal that would reduce income taxes enough so that as we increase social security taxes next year to keep the social security system sound, there would be no net increase for Americans.

We've also included in our plan a proposal that would reduce the so-called marriage penalty, to make sure that a man and wife living together, where both of them work, would not have to pay more income taxes than a man and a woman, both working, who were not married. That's something that to me is very important.

There's another element to it—and then I'll wind up my answer—and that is that we have a total tax reduction in the year 1985 of $60 billion. It'll cost the Federal Government about $60 billion in 1985 under my plan; under Mr. Reagan's plan, $280 billion, and by 1987 a total of $1 trillion—that's a thousand billion dollars that Mr. Reagan's plan will cost. Where that money's going to come from, nobody knows. He says he's going to cut Federal spending by $92 billion. In 1976 when he was running against President Ford, he said he was going to cut the Federal Government $90 billion. That's a mystery, because nobody's been able to pin him down yet and say, "What are you going to cut out of the Federal Government that amounts to $92 billion per year?"

So I think in all those elements our plan is sound, progressive, noninflationary, well balanced, helps the working families, revitalizes American industry. And the Republicans' proposal is just the opposite. Other than that, their proposal's okay.

Thank you, Madalyn.

WELFARE REFORM

Q. Mr. President, my name is Raul Vasquez, Jr., president of LULAC council number one. Corpus Christi has been privileged to receive over 14 million Federal dollars to demonstrate a method of reforming our welfare system through employment. What is your administration's current stance on welfare reform, and do you expect it to become a reality by 1982?

THE PRESIDENT. The answer to the second part of your question is yes, I do expect it to become a reality, because it's such a sound proposal. It's based on this: first of all, the elimination of the confusing Federal bureaucracy so there can be a clear policy, administered efficiently, to provide welfare for those who are not able to work and to give encouragement to work to those that are able. And the other part of it is to provide jobs, primarily in the private sector, not in make-work Federal jobs, for those that don't presently find employment but can physically and mentally qualify for a job. This will also mean a substantial transfer away from the local taxpayers in the financing of welfare to the Federal Government in those areas that are burdened down so heavily with local welfare costs.

So those are the basic elements—simplification, a focusing of welfare payments on those that are not able to work, the provision of jobs for those that are able to work, and financial encouragement through tax reductions to encourage them to get off of welfare and get a job.

Thank you, Raul.

EMPLOYMENT

Q. Mr. President, my name is Roxanna Gonzalez, and I'd like to know what you have, what you want, what you plan to do for the poor people without jobs.

THE PRESIDENT. Okay; that's a good question, Roxanna.

We've been able, in the last 3½ years, in spite of worldwide economic problems, as you know, to add 8.6 million jobs in this country. We've never had that many new jobs created in any similar period of time in the history of our Nation. We've also been able to focus those job opportunities outside the Government, into the private, free enterprise system where the jobs could be permanent. And we've had a special emphasis on minority citizens in providing jobs for them.

As a matter of fact, employment among Spanish-speaking Americans has gone up 22 percent—1 million total increase in jobs; and among black Americans has gone up, I think, 18 percent—1.3 million jobs. So, so far we've done a good job.

In addition to that, with the economic plan that I just outlined to Madalyn, over here on your left, we have a possibility of at least a million additional new jobs in the next 2 years, above and beyond what we'll get with our proposals that are already in Congress hands and already on the books, and also above and beyond what normal economic recovery would bring.

We'll have about 500,000 new jobs in 1981, another 500,000 jobs in 1982. We also have now in Congress—which has an excellent chance to pass—what we call a youth bill. This will add another $2 billion in training for young people about your age, at the junior and senior level in high school, for instance, for preparation for a career in private industry. And that's a good program, too.

What this will do is to let a young person find a job in private industry, and they may not be qualified yet, but to receive special training at the high school on how to hold a job, how to show up on time, how to keep records, and do things like that. And then as they become qualified in a job, working for an oil company or working for a department store or working for Coca Cola Company or something like that, then the Federal Government gets out of it, and the young person holds the job from then on permanently.

This program will tie together the Labor Department, that knows where the jobs are, and the Education Department, where the children are trained either in high school or vocational-technical school or junior college. So this will mean in the future we'll have a much closer relationship between what a graduate of a school knows how to do and the jobs available in that young person's own community. Those are some of the things, very briefly, that we are doing to increase or to improve an already good record on building new jobs in this country.

AMERICAN HOSTAGES IN IRAN

Q. Mr. President, I'm Maria Lopez. Mr. President, as the leader of this great Nation, when will you do something to actually bring our hostages home?

THE PRESIDENT. Thank you. From the very beginning, when the hostages were taken, we've had two commitments, Maria, that have been constantly on my mind and on my heart: first of all, is to protect the honor of our country and the integrity of our Nation and to let other nations join in with us in convincing Iran that they were making a serious mistake for themselves in holding these innocent Americans captive. That's the first point. The second point is, then, not do anything as a President that would endanger the safety or the lives of the hostages themselves. And we've been very careful in both these elements.

The problem has been, in Iran, that there has been no government there with

whom we could talk or negotiate or who could act. The terrorists, the militants, the students, whatever you want to call them, have been the ones making the decisions. Now, finally, there is an elected congress—or Majlis, they call it—in Iran. There is finally, just chosen last week, a Prime Minister. There's a speaker of the house, and there's a President. So, they are making statements in Iran that might very well lead to a resolution of this problem in the future.

The last thing that any political candidate ought to do, including an incumbent President, is to get into a negotiation with the Iranian authorities through public statements or through the news media. So, this is constantly on my mind. We're maintaining our position. We'll do everything to get our hostages home safe and to protect our own Nation's integrity and honor and, at the same time, not do anything that would endanger the independence and freedom, as a nation, of Iran. But I think it would be a serious mistake for me to make specific public statements about what I accept or do not accept; it's just not a good way to negotiate with a government, through the public news media. Thank you very much.

BUSING

Q. Hello, Mr. Carter. My name is Chris Raymond, and I'd like to talk to you about busing. When they're busing the gifted and talented students, they handpick the teachers, also. Why don't they leave those all over town to help the other kids as well as us?

THE PRESIDENT. Thank you, Chris. Chris, I'm going to be frank with you and say something that I might get in trouble about. Okay? I don't believe that busing is the way to solve the school problems, in general. I want to make it plain that I'm not familiar with the local situation; I've not studied it. And sometimes these disputes to make sure that children have an equal opportunity go into the Federal courts, and when they're in the Federal courts, it's not appropriate for a President or anyone else to comment on them publicly. So I'm not trying to interfere in a local situation.

What is needed in Los Angeles and Atlanta, in Houston, in Chicago, in New York and Boston, in Plains, Georgia, where I live, is a sense of common commitment among the parents of the black students and the Hispanic-American students and the Anglo students—the parents, working with the teachers and the State and local officials to make sure that every element of discrimination or lack of equality of opportunity is eliminated.

I come from the Deep South, as you may know, from deep south Georgia. When I first got on the local school board, which is the most difficult political job I ever had, counting President—[laughter]—tough job; pray for the school board members, everybody—but when I first got on the local school board, the white kids rode the buses to school; the black kids in my county had to walk. The white kids got the new books, and the black kids got the old books that the white kids had worn out. The white kids had good schools; the black kids were going to school in the basement of churches and in the backrooms of people's houses. That kind of thing almost makes you sick to think about it, right? [Applause]

So I think that you, as a bright young man, ought to do everything you can to make sure that there's equal opportunity for all the children, regardless of their race or how much their parents are worth in money, and that there's a good quality education for everybody and that people

have a maximum chance to do what they wish, to go to the school of their own choice.

If the Federal courts do issue an order, then, of course, the only alternative that a President has or your parents have is to obey that order. And I believe that the good will that I describe to you, among parents and students of all races, is the best way to resolve the issue. If they can do that, then the role of the Federal Government and mandatory busing can be reduced to a bare minimum. That's the best way to handle it.

That's a good question. Thank you.

1980 CAMPAIGN DEBATES

Q. Mr. President, my name is Eliseo Cantu, Jr. I'd like to welcome you to Corpus Christi. The last time I had the opportunity to see you was in Fayetteville, North Carolina, at your nephew's wedding.

THE PRESIDENT. Good to see you again.

Q. I'm disturbed by the rumors that I hear that you're not going to participate, at least in the first Anderson-Reagan-Carter debate. I think that the people realize that Anderson, whether we like it or not, is on the ballot to stay, and I think that you are making a mistake if you do not debate Reagan and Anderson in person. With your appeal here, I think that you would clobber them.

THE PRESIDENT. I have already accepted three debate invitations to meet Governor Reagan, who's the nominee of the Republican Party and the only other man, in my judgment, that has any chance in the world of being elected President. Governor Reagan has refused to accept these same invitations. One of them was by a major television network, CBS, I believe, another one was the National

Press Club in Washington, to have a debate format between me and him, and the other one was a major magazine. My preference is to have frequent debates with Governor Reagan. And I have also said, although no President's ever done this before, that after that is done I would be glad to debate the other candidates, any other candidate, including Governor Reagan, Congressman Anderson, and others, who had a theoretical chance to be elected President.

I presume that next weekend there will be a Republican debate between Reagan and Anderson. I will not be there. But as I've said from the very beginning, I am eager to debate Mr. Reagan, and after that I'll be just as eager to debate Congressman Anderson, Mr. Commoner, or anyone else, along with Governor Reagan, who has a chance to win.

WINDFALL PROFITS TAX

Q. Mr. President, I'm Sarah Hill, and I want to thank you first for my birthday card. I attended a meeting in Austin—on the windfall tax, in Austin, and there was something about politics for Reagan. But anyway, I didn't go there for that purpose. I wanted to know more about it. Now, would you give me your opinion on the windfall tax that the oil companies are fighting you about?

THE PRESIDENT. All right. Before I became President, Ms. Hill, there was no energy policy for our country. In 1976, we were importing from overseas 8½ million barrels of oil every day and sending the money for it out of the United States to those foreign countries. Oil and natural gas were regulated, which was discouraging American production, and there was no way to finance a better transportation system, conservation in our homes, in-creased production of American energy, or a way to help poor people pay their heat bills with the increasing cost of energy.

We have corrected all of those problems with our comprehensive energy policy. All the Republicans talked for years and years about deregulating oil and natural gas; they never did it. Now we have a law that deregulates oil and natural gas. It's paying rich dividends. We will have more oil and gas wells drilled this year, 1980, than any other year in the history of our country. We'll produce more American coal this year than ever before in the history of the United States.

We are seeing a rapid increase in the use of solar power in homes. We are now using 10 times more—homes—solar power than we were just 4 years ago. The windfall profits tax, which is on the unearned income of oil companies, will help to finance some of these programs. When we begin to collect this money, it'll be used fairly. The oil companies, in spite of the tax, are having and will continue to have the highest, greatest income in their history, and those who explore for oil and gas, as I said before, are having unprecedented commitments to increasing American oil and gas.

We've cut down the amount of oil we import tremendously, already, with the help of people like you. This day and every day this year, we're importing 2 million barrels of oil less than we did in 1977. So, this is a very good start.

And although the oil companies in general don't like the windfall profits tax by itself, the total program that I described to you, including the windfall profits tax, is one that in my judgment, they approve privately, even though they might not approve it during these election-year weeks.

So, I think it's a good program for our

country; I have no apology to make. It's one of the greatest achievements of our administration and of this country and will put us back on the road to energy security, based on conservation here at home and the protection of energy in the United States, not where we have to buy it from overseas.

BUSING

Q. Good morning, Mr. President.

THE PRESIDENT. Good morning.

Q. My name is Larry Reynolds and I have one question here. In view of the busing situation in the country today, does the Federal Government plan to subsidize those school districts that are forced to bus or are we, the respective school districts, to foot the bill for the entire cost, especially with the rising cost in fuel as it is?

THE PRESIDENT. There has been a law on the books for years, that if a school district was required by a Federal court to bus children and incur the additional expense, that the Federal Government would help pay that expense. This has been used for years in places like Boston and in the South, and it'll be used in your community if that should happen.

ECONOMIC RENEWAL PROGRAM

Q. Hello, Mr. President. My name is Phyllis Brown. I'm a single parent with two teenagers. I'm one of the hard-working——

THE PRESIDENT. I sympathize with you.

Q. ——average American workers who work for a salary, and with the help of my children's father, I fall in the range that the Internal Revenue says is middle-income people. There are 38.2 percent of middle income, according to the Internal Revenue Service, and we pay 60.1 percent of the taxes. And you've been talking about work programs for the people who don't hold jobs. What I want to know is, what are you going to do for us working people who pay this burden of taxes, year after year after year?

THE PRESIDENT. The major cause, lately, for increased unemployment in our country is among people just like you who had jobs in the steel industry, who had jobs in the automobile industry, and others like them that were caught up in a cycle of very high inflation and changing buying habits and the obsolescence of the American industrial system and the tools that workers have to keep them employed.

The entire program that we have is designed to provide new jobs in changing times for families, not in government but in the private sector—in the oil companies, in those that produce goods and services that we sell. At the same time, we've tried to increase the amount of American products that are sold overseas. We've got three times as much trade now as we did 4 years ago with Mexico, for instance. Mexico has now become our third largest trade partner. The only other two nations on Earth that we trade more with have been Canada and Japan.

So, to build up exports, to provide tax programs to create new jobs for people like yourself, and to make sure that we do have a modern industrial system as times change to keep from having unemployment among the steelworkers and automobile workers and people of that kind— that's what we're trying to do exactly. We also have tax reductions built in to this program, designed to accomplish the purposes that I've described to you. But there will not be placed on you, for instance, next year, an additional income tax burden in your withholding taxes to pay for social security. We'll give you an 8-percent refund on your income tax payment that will compensate you for the increase to keep the social security sound.

So the entire program, I think, would benefit you. There are a few programs that would benefit the poor and the unemployed—like the $2 billion youth jobs program I'm telling about—that might very well not benefit you personally, but will benefit your children when they reach working age.

Q. I hope he goes to college.

THE PRESIDENT. Well, I hope so, too. But there are a lot of people that graduate from college that can't get jobs, and I'm trying to make darned sure that when they—yes, go ahead.

Q. May I come up and shake your hand?

THE PRESIDENT. That would be a very great pleasure for me, yes. You see, there are some nice things about being President, too.

SUPPORT FOR PRIVATE SCHOOLS

Q. Mr. President, my name is Steve Dulaney, and I'm attending Carnettwood Academy High School, which is a local parochial school. Since parochial schools are educating a greater number of students each year, and they play a major part in the American education system, should the parents of these children attending these schools get special school tax breaks, and how could the Government help support these schools?

THE PRESIDENT. Good. As you know, a lot has been done by the Federal Government, both since I've been in office and before, to provide services for young people who do go to the parochial or the private schools. And in addition to that, we've done a great deal to make sure that any child in this Nation, regardless of the wealth of their parents, can go to college if that child or young person is qualified

to do the work. This has been a great achievement for us.

In addition to that, we will have in the future a constantly expanding commitment by the Federal Government to education, both private and public, with the new Department of Education. In the past, the education programs have been buried underneath welfare and health. There has not been a single person in Washington where your parents or a school board member or a Governor could go and say, "We've got a problem," with private or public education, preschool, grammar school, high school, or college. "What can you do about it?" Now, Secretary Shirley Hufstedler is the new Secretary of a brand new Department of Education.

I'm not in favor of Federal payments directly to the private school system. But I recognize the tremendous contribution made by the private schools, and we have made equal benefits to young people who go to private colleges and those who go to the public colleges. And I believe the new Department will be beneficial to both the public and private school systems of this country.

Yes, you can ask another question.

Q. There's one point. My parents are paying taxes for the schools in this city, the public schools. And I attend a school, and they're paying a considerable amount of money to send me to that school. And I don't know, since I'm not using—since most of the private students don't use the public school facilities, should they still be supporting them?

THE PRESIDENT. In my judgment, yes.

Q. Why should they support them?

THE PRESIDENT. Have you never been to a public school?

Q. Yes, I have, for 2 years, sir, and those 2 years were probably a dormant stage in my education.

THE PRESIDENT. I see. Well, that's a judgment that you make.

Q. That's a judgment. That's my personal opinion.

THE PRESIDENT. That's a judgment that you make, and you have a right to your opinion. I'm able to send my kids to a private school, too. I've got a good salary, and I've had a good income a large part of my life. Amy's in the public school systems, and I think—in Washington, D.C.—a lot of people who are Members of Congress and who have jobs in my government think the private school system's better. I have always thought it was important to have a strong public school system.

I hope that your parents—wait a minute, let me finish—I hope that your parents and you are always financially able to pay the extra money to go to the private schools. That's your privilege in our country. But if something should ever happen to you or to your children—suppose you graduated from high school and couldn't get a good job and couldn't pay the tuition for a private school—I want to make darned sure there's a good public school there for your children to use.

I might point out that Steve's raised a good point and——

Q. The only point I'd like to say——

THE PRESIDENT. Please do.

Q. If some people that weren't paying taxes for these public schools, they might be able to attend some private schools if they wished to get maybe a Christian education.

THE PRESIDENT. I know.

Q. Okay, I'm not knocking the public school system.

THE PRESIDENT. I know. You've got a right to your opinion. We just happen to disagree. Good luck to you, Steve. You're a fine young man. Steve, are you on the debating team? You ought to be. You ought to be if you're not. Good luck to you. Thank you.

SUPPORT FOR THE PRESIDENT

Q. President Carter, Betty Godfrey. I represent—as a volunteer—I work with G.I. Forum and LULAC and all those other organizations of the United States of America. I'm tired of hearing what you didn't do. I want to bring out some points you did do, and other people blundered them. We have the national flood insurance program going on right now. There are men coming out—they are independent adjusters representing the United States Government, saying they are Government men, which I found one guilty; he is not a Government man but an independent insurance adjuster. I have taken care of this. I'm tired of hearing you blamed as our President for things you have not done.

Also, before we get any further, I represent the educational—[*inaudible*]—of Indian affairs. Indian discrimination—[*inaudible*]—Indian, and I know it still stands in Indian schools and Indian hospitals. I stand for their chiefs, for the chiefs' document, with Dr. Hector P. Garcia, for the education of anybody that can't afford it. Forty percent Federal aided—[*inaudible*]—for the people of the United States of America. I believe that our President is for the people, all people, the poor. It doesn't make any difference.

I am tired of hearing about the bad things he did—[*inaudible*]—these programs that are being misused by people who are not civil service workers who say they are at your door. I had a deal made at my home and was invited to the motel—what about that, Mr. President?

THE PRESIDENT. Thank you very much. I appreciate it very much.

Q. What about that?

THE PRESIDENT. Thank you very much. Thank you.

ENERGY

Q. Good morning, Mr. President. My name is Dorr Lewright.

THE PRESIDENT. What's your first name?

Q. Dorr.

THE PRESIDENT. D-o-r-e?

Q. D-o-r-r. I want to ask you a question on energy. Regarding the new excess profits tax being levied on the petroleum industry, I feel that America would be far better served by allowing the private sector to develop the energy for our future needs through a plowback provision than to allow the inefficient Federal Government to consume this money. How would you compare the efficiency of free enterprise to big government in solving our energy problems?

THE PRESIDENT. I think the free enterprise system is more efficient, and that's what we've emphasized, Dorr, as a matter of fact. The Federal Government is not in the oil-producing business; we're not in the oil-refining business; we're not in the oil exploration business. We're not going to get into it.

What we are doing, however, is to try to protect the consumers and, at the same time, remove the shackles that have bound up the free enterprise system for too long. There's been an effort made to deregulate natural gas and oil ever since Harry Truman was President back in the late 1940's and early 1950's. We have finally passed a bill—it wasn't easy—to deregulate oil and natural gas, careful, phased, predictable, and that's what meant so much to the oil explorers who now have 2,800 rigs running, a number that's never been equaled in the history of this country.

Also, it's very important to me to make sure that over a period of time we produce new kinds of energy, to take shale, which has not yet been used in our country, tar sands, to use lignite, which is now becoming used, to take coal, and to change those materials into oil and natural gas forms that can be used as well.

We've not had good conservation in this country; we've been wasting too much energy. And for us to encourage, through tax credits, people to insulate their homes and to use growing crops to make gasohol, for instance, is a very good step forward. With some of this money we will encourage the production of synthetic fuels, gasohol, and so forth, with the Federal Government not doing anything in that these projects will be designed, built, operated by the private enterprise system. But we will have an Energy Security Corporation, made up primarily of distinguished business leaders, that will decide how we can provide the incentive for these companies to get started on their own.

So, I believe very much in the free enterprise system. Let me add one other thing. We have gotten the Government's nose out of the free enterprise system on trucking. We've gotten the Government's nose out of the free enterprise system on financial institutions. We've gotten the Government's nose out of the free enterprise system on the airlines. We've deregulated those industries as well as oil and natural gas.

So, I believe very strongly in what you said, that private enterprise can do a better job, that consumers must be protected, and in the past the Government has protected the bigshot business leaders and their corporations at the expense of the consumers. But now we'll have a better energy industry, we'll have a better airline industry, we'll have a better trucking industry, a better financial institutions industry than we've ever had before, by getting the Government's nose out of American people's business. That's what I believe.

I'm sorry, my staff tells me I can't take another question because we're out of time. Let me say in closing that I appreciate your being here and your letting me meet with you. It's very important to me as a President to have a chance to be cross-examined by you on subjects that are important to you. This is the 25th townhall meeting I've had since I've been President; it's the second one this month. This Thursday, I'll be having another press conference with the national press; I think it'll be the 59th press conference that I've had since I've been President. It's important for a President, it's important for anyone trying to be President, to have these kind of cross-examinations in public so their views can be known.

You've probably noticed that the campaign staff of my Republican opponent have put him under wraps. He's not having meetings like this. He's not having press conferences any more, because when he has spoken on his own the last few days, he's gotten himself in trouble. But this point is, well, the point is when you're in the White House, in the Oval Office, as President, that's where the most difficult questions come, perhaps to any human being on Earth, and you've got to be able to respond accurately, in a way that doesn't embarrass you personally and does not embarrass our Nation.

And I believe that this campaign season will be an excellent chance for the American people to size up the candidates and decide who can keep this Nation at peace, who can continue the progress that our Nation has made on civil rights and equality of opportunity that's so precious to us, who can make sure we have better relationships with other nations around the world, who can keep our country strong

militarily, and who can let people like you have a voice in shaping the policies of our Nation so that the great principles that have made our Nation strong in the past will make our Nation even stronger and greater in the future. That's what I want.

God bless you all.

NOTE: The President spoke at 10:37 a.m. in the Moody High School gymnasium.

Houston, Texas

Remarks at a Democratic National Committee Fundraising Luncheon.   September 15, 1980

As all of you know, this luncheon was organized just 2 weeks ago, and a crucial thing for a President or a candidate is to have friends on whom one can call for additional assistance on short notice, when it's crucial to the success of a common effort. I'm particularly grateful to Jim Calaway who rode in here with me from Corpus Christi and Jack Warren who came from Washington down to Corpus and here, also, and of course, Lou Flournoy who was with me in Corpus Christi and who has been very helpful, and to all of you. It would be hard for me to list the whole group.

I would like you to know that I'm aware of some of your pressing local problems, and I'm sure that Jack would agree that as soon as they get their timing down—Statler [Stabler] [1] and his receivers—they will be winning games every week and put Houston back in the top where you belong. The Oilers are a great team, Houston's a great city, and I'm very grateful to all of you.

I understand that tomorrow the Republican candidate will be standing on

---

[1] Ken Stabler, quarterback of the Houston Oilers.

this spot. This is the only place he'll be replacing me—[*laughter*]—because I have help and support from people like you.

I'm not going to take long, because I want to shake hands with everyone here individually and thank you personally and have a photograph made, if you'll give me that much of an honor. But I think I would like to say a few words about two things. One is the Presidency itself. And the other one is the future of our country.

There's no way to measure in human terms the way people feel in this Nation about the office of the President. It's the greatest elective office in the world, the leader of the greatest nation on Earth, and there is a respect for the Presidency and an acknowledgement of the importance of the Presidency in the life of every American family. The world's future is shaped to a major degree by the decisions and the actions and commitments of our Nation expressed by the chosen leader. I've been there now about 3½ years; I've seen the complexity of the problems that come to the Oval Office. There are no easy questions that come there. There are no easy decisions made in the Oval Office. If the questions or the decisions are easy ones, they're made somewhere else—in the county courthouse or city hall or in the State legislature or in a Governor's office or in a private business or home. But when they reach me, I am sure they're difficult, and the more vital they are and the more complex and the more difficult, the more sure I am that my own advisers will be divided almost equally in telling me what they think ought to be done. I'm the one that has to make the decision.

We've made some difficult decisions this last 3½ years that have affected the lives of all of you, of Texas, of our country, and, I think, most nations on Earth.

We've made good decisions—highly controversial, yes, but the right ones. A lot of people criticize the energy policy that we've hammered out together. But what they fail to point out is that before I became President, there was no energy policy; there was no assured path to the future that would help us conserve energy in our own country and produce more energy in or own country. The time has just been very short, as you know—a matter of months—since we got the basic elements of our policy enacted into law and clearly understood by the American people. The results have already been notable. We have more oil drilling rigs running now, this year, than any other year in history.

The 3 years before I became President, we increased oil imports from overseas 44 percent. In the 3 years since I've been in office, we've decreased oil imports by 24 percent. This year, every day, we will import 2 million barrels of oil less than we did the same date in 1977. That's a tremendous amount of money that we don't spend overseas, and that's a tremendous amount of inflation and unemployment that we don't import every time one of those large oil tankers ties up coming here from the Middle East or Persian Gulf region.

This is not all of it. We will produce more coal in the United States in 1980 than in any other year in this history of our country. A lot of people don't know that. A lot of that coal is now being exported, and my hope is that American coal, to a major degree in the worldwide markets on energy, will replace in the near future OPEC oil. We have tremendous reserves, and we're trying to find and to use them better.

Energy is obviously important. But that's not the only thing. You people in Texas, I know, are similar to those in

Georgia. You believe we ought to get the Federal Government's nose out of the business of private families and the private enterprise system and let free competition prevail. It's better for business, it's better for the workers, it's better for consumers. Ever since 1948, or a few years after that, there have been efforts made to deregulate major elements of American life, unsuccessful efforts. Even when you had a Republican President and a Republican Congress, the efforts were unsuccessful.

We've now put into law deregulation of natural gas, deregulation of oil, deregulation of the trucking industry, deregulation of the airline industry, deregulation of the financial institutions of this country, and this is the kind of move and the kind of philosophy that, in my judgment, will make our country greater and freer in the future. The consumers benefit; our whole Nation joins in that benefit.

I was faced, when I was elected President, of an 8-year history of constantly decreasing commitments to our Nation's defense. In real dollars, our defense expenditures had gone down 8 years. My profession is as a naval officer. My background is as a southerner, and I could see very clearly that our Nation, in order to stay at peace, had to be strong. We have had a steady increase every year since I've been in office in real defense expenditures, not wasted money.

Under Harold Brown, Charlie Duncan, and Graham Claytor we've made very careful plans. The Joint Chiefs of Staff have spent more time with me, perhaps, than the Joint Chiefs have spent with all the Presidents since the Department of Defense was organized, making sure that we could see things clearly in the future. And the Trident submarines and the missiles, the MX missiles, cruise missiles, strengthening of NATO, and the building up of our conventional forces have sent a clear signal to Americans and to foreign countries that our country was united, had the will, determination, and capability to stay so militarily strong that any attack on us or threat to us would be suicidal on their part. And we've used that military strength to keep our Nation at peace, but also to provide peace for others. And in a peaceful world, in Africa, in the Middle East, in Asia, the principles for which our Nation stands can be enhanced and expanded.

We now have friendship with a billion people in the People's Republic of China we'd never had before, and we have not lost our trade relationships and our friendly relationships with the people of Taiwan. I was in the most advanced steel plant, I guess, in the world in Perth Amboy in New Jersey last week. Fifty percent of their steel rods are being exported to China. Half way around the world, they can sell American-made steel rods, made up of scrap material that used to be sent overseas, to China with a competitive advantage over the same steel rods made a few hundred miles away in Japan. American workers in that one factory produce more steel per year than in any other steel plant in the world.

Now that we've got the energy situation embedded into a national policy, we're ready to build on that to revitalize the American industrial system, to give new jobs, not in government but in private industry, to have more technology, better tools, better factories, to keep Americans producing efficiently. As you know, American workers are the most productive in the world, but that productivity has not been increasing lately, and that's what we have as a next major goal. This is an extremely important commitment, and it is going to be a successful commitment, compatible with the philosophy and the best interests of the people of Texas and the people of our country.

And finally, let me say that there's no way that we can have this sort of material progress unless we retain our commitment to the ideals and the morals and commitments of our country, commitments of freedom, the importance of the individual person, equality of opportunity, the protection of civil rights, keeping high the banner of human rights, expanding the beneficial effect of democratic principles, majority rule. These kind of things put us in a good competitive role on a peaceful basis with any challenge that might be mounted to the United States in the future.

So, this election year is not just a choice between two men or two parties, it's a choice between two futures for our country. And if you study the principles that are espoused in the Republican and Democratic platforms, the statements that are made, before he was muzzled, by my opponent compared to my own, and what we stand for for America's future, then I believe that your coming to this luncheon today is a good investment.

I don't intend to lose this election. With your help we'll have a tremendous victory on November the 4th.

Thank you very much.

NOTE: The President spoke at 1:43 p.m. in the Regency Ballroom at the Hyatt Regency Hotel.

Houston, Texas

Remarks at a Rally for Carter/Mondale Volunteer Workers. September 15, 1980

To Chairman John White, to all of you, let me say that on election day on November 4th, there can be no more important State than Texas. And I'd like to ask

you a question: How many of you believe that Fritz Mondale and I are going to be re-elected on November 4th? [*Applause*]

That's a pretty good majority. How many of you believe we're going to carry Texas? [*Applause*] Right on. Well, what happens here in the biggest city in the biggest county in the biggest continental State of all will have a great deal to do with what happens in Texas and what happens throughout the country.

As you know, in the past crucial results have come from how Texas people voted. When the average working Texans who are interested in the principles on which our Nation was founded, who believe in equality and hard work and dedication, a better life for our children, strong military, peace, go out and vote, the Democrats always win.

As a matter of fact in 1960, if a few people in Illinois and about 28,000 Texans had changed their votes, then John Kennedy would never have been President. Lyndon Johnson would not have been Vice President and later President, and the future of our Nation would have been dramatically changed.

I know from experience how the people of this Nation look upon the office of President. Because what our Nation is, what our Nation can be, the vision of our Nation is shaped in the Oval Office. No easy decisions come there. No easy questions are answered there, because the easy questions and decisions are solved and answered somewhere else—in the county courthouse or the city hall or the State legislature, the Governor's office, in private businesses, private homes. But those questions that arrive in the Oval Office are complex, difficult, and profoundly important—for our people, individually and personally in a home, for our Nation, and indeed for the entire world.

There is no way to win against massive campaign treasuries as are being raised in Texas for my opponent and the influence of powerful people who don't have the best interests of this country at heart, except by dedicated work from volunteers who believe in the future of our country. And that's why I have confidence in you and the outcome of the election the first week in November.

If people know the facts, that's the most important single thing we can do. If the American people realize accurately the unvarnished truth about what we have achieved in the past and what we hope to achieve and expect to achieve in the future, there's no doubt in my mind about the outcome of this campaign.

We've faced some difficult, troubled times on a worldwide basis the last 3½ years, tremendous economic shocks that have actually brought down the governments of many foreign countries and created chaos in others. Our country has made steady progress. In the last 3½ years, we have added 8.6 million net new jobs for Americans: Hispanic Americans, the employment rate has gone up 22 percent; black Americans, the employment rate has gone up 18 percent. That kind of progress has been made, in spite of a tremendous increase in OPEC oil prices, in spite of tremendous increases in worldwide inflation.

And that kind of progress is going to be continued in the future. It's important to a family to have the right to a good education and the right to self-respect, the right to dignity and the right to a job— and as you know, the Democratic Party is the party of jobs and the Carter/Mondale administration is the administration of jobs—now and in the future.

There's another element, too, and it's basic human rights—civil rights—the self-respect that can come to someone whose family happens to be poor or who happens to be black, who happens not to speak English very well. When I took over as President there was not that kind of belief among the minorities and among the poor people of this country. The elderly were afraid that social security was going to go bankrupt. Everywhere I went mayors came to me and said: my city is going down the drain, Mr. President—at that time, Governor. We've put together programs that guarantee the honoring of civil rights.

We've added 73 percent to expenditures for better education. We have a good bilingual education program. And I think you all know that 4 or 500 delegates to the National—to the National—I started to say National Education Convention— to the Democratic Convention were teachers and educators, because they recognize that they share with me a responsibility for the Nation's future. It's important for a teacher or a school administrator to know that the future of education is bright in America. But it's even more important to a child or to a father or to a mother interested in their children having a better life. So, the Democratic Party is a party of better education. I might say this: There is not a child, a young person in this country now who will be deprived of a college education because of the poverty of a family. We've got a complete, comprehensive program intact that will take care of that need.

I just want to make two other points in order to be brief. One is it's important for us to keep our Nation militarily strong. My background is as a professional military officer. I went to Annapolis. I was a submariner. I spent 11 years in the Navy. When I became President I realized that for 8 years under the Republican administrations that the commitment in real dollars to our Nation's defense had been going down. Our country had lost the respect that should come from a commitment to military strength and to will, a respect for government and to national honor. The Vietnam war, the Watergate disgrace, combined with what I've just described to you, had weakened our country in international councils. The spirit of our Allies in NATO had been shaken. We've had a steady real increase, since I've been in office, in commitments to military strength, and also we've strengthened our alliances.

This has not been designed for war. It's been designed for peace. And the reason we've kept our country at peace for 4 years and are going to keep it at peace for 4 more years is because our Nation is strong, and we're going to stay strong.

And we've brought strength to other people as well, and we've brought peace to other people as well. In Israel, Egypt, Zimbabwe, China, Latin America, there's been a constant strengthening of the relationships between our country and those people and in the process an enhancement of freedom and democracy and a better life. We now have good relationships with a billion new friends in China. We've not lost our friendship and trade opportunities with Taiwan. Mexico, our neighbor to the south—we've increased this year trade with Mexico 60 percent. We'll sell them 10 million tons of American grain. We have tripled trade levels with Mexico in the last 4 years, and have a good relationship not only with Mexico but with Canada, Japan, and others.

This kind of thing, the raising of an American banner of decency and honor and strength, not only helps us internationally, but it helps every family in our country, because now we've built upon a good energy policy in order to provide for us a better future life.

Our economy has been deteriorating in the past. You can't expect American workers to be efficient with outmoded tools and factories. We are now getting ready to spend the 1980's building on the foundation that we have laid so tediously and with so much difficulty, to create millions and millions of jobs.

We have during the next few weeks a chance to tell an accurate story because one of the things that a President must do is tell the truth. Sometimes the truth is not popular, and sometimes the political consequences of it are severe. But a campaign in a democracy like ours is a time to explain, to inventory, to dream, and to describe those dreams when people have their ears attuned to hear. When the lever is pulled on November the 4th, that decides what kind of future our Nation will have and, more importantly, what kind of future that person will have. Will civil rights be honored? Will freedom be enhanced? Will the worth of a human be recognized? Will education be better? Will housing be better? Will we have a better transportation system? Will we have jobs? Will we have progress? Will we have peace? Will we have strength? Will our elderly be secure? Will we honor one another? Will our Nation be unified? Can we be proud that our Government is truthful and decent and honorable? Will there be adequate communication between people and the Government leaders? These are decisions we'll be making all at once on November the 4th when we vote. And if people will listen between now and then and think and assess where should our country be in the 1980's and the rest of this century and the future, I have no doubt that with your help we'll win a tremendous victory on November 4th.

God bless you. Thank you very much.

NOTE: The President spoke at 2:06 p.m. in the Imperial Ballroom at the Hyatt Regency Hotel.

Houston, Texas

Informal Exchange With Reporters on Departure. September 15, 1980

Q. Mr. President, could you talk to us just for a minute? We were wondering, Mr. President, do you feel that your campaign has been hurt at all by the drug investigation against Mr. Kraft in that situation and his leave of absence now?

THE PRESIDENT. Well, obviously I would prefer that Tim be able to stay on until the campaign is over and beyond that. He's been very good for me, and I have confidence in Tim.

I would like to point out that the fact that there is an investigation, as there has been of Carter's Warehouse and Hamilton Jordan and others, is no insinuation that he's guilty.

Tim has denied the charges and says he's completely innocent, and I think the investigation will show that that's the case. I'm not trying to prejudge it, but I do have confidence in him. I think he made the right decision to step down now rather than to stay on throughout the campaign because it could be a focus of controversy. And Tim, in his statement on his own initiative, said he didn't want to do anything to hurt me.

Q. But, sir, do you believe this might have an influence on your campaign, be detrimental to your chances for reelection?

THE PRESIDENT. No. I don't think so. That was the main reason for Tim's decision to go ahead and take a leave of absence, so that he could answer the charges, which he says are false, and so that they would not have a politically damaging effect on our own campaign.

Q. Why didn't Hamilton Jordan step down then, Mr. President?

THE PRESIDENT. Well, you'll have to ask Hamilton about that.

Q. Do you believe the charges are false?

THE PRESIDENT. I'm not trying to prejudge it, but I have confidence in Tim, and he says that they're false.

Q. Did you discuss this with him, Mr. President?

THE PRESIDENT. No. I didn't discuss any details about it at all. Tim made his decision about stepping down on his own.

Thank you.

REPORTER. Thank you.

NOTE: The exchange began at 2:45 p.m. at the William P. Hobby Airport.

Alpharetta, Georgia

Remarks at Dedication Ceremonies for Dolvin Elementary School. September 15, 1980

Senator Talmadge, Governor Busbee, Congressman Fowler, President Otis Jackson,[1] Sissy, Mamma, my fellow Georgians:

You can't imagine how delighted I am to be back in Georgia, to see my friends and to drive through this beautiful part of God's world, and how thrilled I was to ride up in front of this beautiful school and see my Uncle Dolvin's name on it. It means so much to me.

He first came here to serve the parents and the young people of this part of Georgia in 1930. He was a young man. The years were not good. Jobs were scarce as you well know, and he went to Mr. Ira Dodd's house in the middle of the night to ask for a job—woke him up—and the natural inclination was to be to turn him down. But Dolvin was so filled with a commitment to serve and a love of the educational process and a concern about young people that his fervor prevailed, and he was hired. And he went to work in elementary school as principal at Ocee, and he served there for a long time. Then

---

[1] Fulton County School Board chairman.

he went to Crabapple and served there, I believe, for 19 years. And then he went to Roswell Elementary and served there for 15 years. And then later North Roswell was built, and he served as principal of both schools.

I visited often, because Sissy was my favorite aunt and helped to guide me through my formative years. And as I got into politics and government, Sissy's and Dolvin's house was a good place for me to come, not only to receive love and friendship and support but also to learn, because Dolvin was a tough debater. He knew that as a new State senator and later as a Governor that I was eager to learn and to improve the educational system of our State, and he taught me just as he taught his students in elementary school.

Dolvin was interested in two things, as you know, in education. One was the students, and the other was the teachers. He was president of Fulton County Teacher's Association for 10 years, and the thing that he believed was that teachers ought to be treated fairly. He thought that black teachers ought to get the same pay as white teachers. And he thought that elementary teachers ought to get the same pay as those in high school. He thought that the pay ought to be based on the responsibilities and the quality and not the age of the students or race. This was quite a startling thing in those days, but he was so persistent and he felt so deeply about what his beliefs were that he ultimately prevailed.

He fought hard for pension benefits and security at retirement for teachers and achieved notable results, benefiting not just the teachers in this immediate area but throughout Fulton County and eventually, I think, joined with many others in having a better life, better salary, better retirement, better security for teachers throughout the State.

He was not the kind of person to brag on himself. He was forceful, but quiet, and a lot of the achievements that he realized for me as a formative politician and a State leader and for the teachers and the students and the parents have never been adequately acknowledged until now. Nothing could have pleased him more than to have a beautiful school named for him.

This is a memorial that's much better than a book or a statue or speeches by political leaders. This is where his heart was. And as you know, the Roswell School was built on part of the ground of the Presbyterian Church where he was an elder, and he felt that serving students and helping to form young minds and bringing parents closer together to one another and opening up the delights of learning—all those things were part of God's work. He never saw any incompatibility between his service in the church and his belief in God and his service in school and his belief in human beings.

He meant a lot to me. He served in the time of depression, a time of transition in our State, when ideas had to be changed and when the politicians in Atlanta, in Washington, and the county courthouses and the city halls and the business leaders and the church leaders were not willing to make those social changes so important to the South. The teachers had to do it. The teachers were the ones that had to bear the scars of those social changes that transformed our Nation. And I would not ever have been elected President, the first one from the Deep South in 140 years, had it not been for teachers and school administrators like Jasper Dolvin, who thought that the principles of the Constitution of our Nation ought to apply to all Americans the same.

To have modern schools with good facilities, pleasant surroundings, beauty, is very good, and as he struggled with those

Depression-year children and welcomed a flood of new residents into the north Fulton County area, his leadership was very significant. He believed in what St. Paul said in First Corinthians 13, in three great things: faith, hope, and love—faith in young people who some day would strive to let their life burgeon forth, to let their minds be stretched, their hearts be expanded to love more people, to learn about God's world. He had faith in them and in their love to do things and to learn things.

And he had hope that no matter how dismal their background might be, no matter how poverty stricken their family might be, no matter how lacking in education their parents' life might have been, that that hope for that child was just as bright in the United States of America as for the wealthiest kid in Georgia.

And then, of course, he had love, not just for people but for nature, for the beauty of a mathematical equation and the loveliness of a song, and the inspiration of a painting as well as for books. And I believe that the most exciting thing he had to work with were young minds, and he never underestimated what those young minds could do and how difficult a challenge they were able to overcome.

Now, when I look at my grandchildren—Jason and James and little Sarah—who live in Georgia and I see so much potential there and so much eagerness to learn and to let their own lives be meaningful, I envy what Dolvin stood for—and Sissy was a teacher too—and what all the educators face: a delightful opportunity to spend the days opening doors for other children just as eager and just as full of potential as my grandchildren are. And when I see Amy learning and discovering and probing and asking questions, I wonder how all of the teachers do it. It's a tough job. And sometimes parents may not appreciate it enough, and sometimes the State legislators and the Governor and Presidents may not appreciate enough what teachers mean.

I had a special uncle, Jasper Dolvin, who meant a lot to me as a teacher. I had a special teacher, Miss Julia Coleman, who noticed in me, as a country boy, some potential and who let me take full advantage of it. She never lived to see me as President, and Dolvin never lived to see me as President, but they would have been proud not just of me but for all those students who had a better life because of them, the excitement of learning and the joy of a teacher in joining in the responsibility to prepare a better future for our Nation.

As President I have that responsibility, a better economic life, a safer life, peace, strength, unity, commitment, compassion, confidence of a nation, but my responsibilities are exactly the same—a little bit different perspective—as a teacher or a parent who also has to look to the future and feel responsible for it. Teachers, parents hold a special sacred trust to make an investment in a better life for us all. They've never let us down, and I'm deeply grateful to them and to Jasper Dolvin, being a superb example of what educators mean to me, to our Nation, and to the world.

NOTE: The President spoke at 6:30 p.m. in the school cafetorium.

Following the ceremony, the President attended a Democratic National Committee fundraising reception at the home of Mrs. Dolvin.

Roswell, Georgia

Remarks at a Democratic National Committee Fundraising Reception. September 15, 1980

I've just made a quick decision to come home more often.

Governor Busbee, Senator Talmadge, Senator Nunn, distinguished members of the Georgia congressional delegation, members of the State legislature and other State officials, a lot of visitors from surrounding States—from Florida, the Carolinas, Kentucky, Alabama, Mississippi, Tennessee—we make all of you honorary Georgians for tonight:

I am amazed, and that's a truthful statement. I asked Charlie who was going to be here tonight. He said, "Well, I'm just having a few kinfolks drop by." Carol Channing—I'd like for her to be my kinfolks. Isn't she great?

I asked him if I could spend the night with him. He said, "I'm sorry, Mr. President, but all the rooms are taken. You'll have to find some other place to stay." So, since I'm not in a hurry to go anywhere else, I'd like to speak for about 3 or 4 minutes to you, my friends, and then if you would give me your time, I would like to stand right in front of this microphone and shake hands with every single one of you and thank you personally for being my friends and meaning so much to me and to my family for this country.

It is good to come home. As I said over at Sissy's house a few minutes ago, there's only one place I'd rather be the next 4 years than in Georgia—[*laughter*]—and with friends like you I'm going to be there. But after that, back to Georgia for me.

I just had two thoughts that I wanted to express to the people whom I addressed today. One is about the Presidency itself, and the other one is about the future of our country. And I'll be very brief.

There is no more important elective office in the world than the one I hold, than the one for which you're responsible that I was elected. Many of you had confidence in me when I didn't have many friends, when people outside my home State and outside the South had no idea who Jimmy Carter was. But you contributed money, you went to foreign States and made them home States for me. And you made it possible for me to serve in this office which Americans revere and which the entire world looks to as a source of a better life for them.

When our Nation is strong, the world is more secure. When our Nation is at peace, that peace can be expanded to benefit others. When our Nation is prosperous, the rest of the world is better off. When our education system and our research and development pays rich dividends with new ideas and new thoughts and new products, the whole world benefits from it. And when our Nation raises high the banner of human rights, the breath of freedom is expanded in the hearts of those who haven't known it in the past. And when they see us with a democratic system working, as it is now in this election season, it makes the attractions of democracy and freedom even more valuable to others. So, what happens in my office in Washington does indeed not only affect us but affect the world.

The job's a difficult one even though it's exciting and gratifying. It's filled with history, the history of Presidents who've suffered much worse than have I from castigations and criticisms and disappointments or from trials that affect our Nation. A lot of people think this is tough times. When I sit in that White House or walk down the hall and see those portraits or read those history books, I thank God has blessed us in this generation and in this administration.

We're a nation that's steadily growing stronger militarily. It's part of my upbringing, part of my training, because as you know, my own background is as a professional military officer. My father or none of his ancestors so far as I know for 300 years ever had a chance to finish high school—I finished high school—and from the time I was 5 years old my daddy wanted me to go and get an education. During depression years it was doubtful that the family could afford it. Later it turned out that they could have. So, I always wanted to go to Annapolis. And I got the training as an officer to keep our country strong, because I believe that the reason we have been at peace for these last 4 years and the reason we're going to be at peace for the next 4 years is because our Nation is militarily strong.

The best weapon is one that's never fired, and the best soldier is one that's never killed. And for our own people and our allies and our potential adversaries to know how strong America is is the best guarantee that America can stay at peace.

There are not any easy decisions that come to the Oval Office. As I said before, tonight, if the decisions are easy, if the questions can be answered, they're answered before they get to me. They're answered in a family's home or in a county courthouse or a city hall or in a State legislature or the Governor's office. If they are so difficult and so sharply divided that they can't be answered there, they arrive on my desk, and I share those responsibilities with the Members of Congress and with others and try to make the right decisions. And I've found from experience that the most difficult questions, the ones most controversial, the ones most vital to our Nation's future, are the ones on which my own advisers are split almost exactly fifty-fifty—so I'm the one that has to make those decisions.

And the reason I outline this to you is because I believe when I make a sound judgment it's because I remember my upbringing. I remember the principles that I learned in Sunday school and church and listening to my daddy and working in the field, serving on the school board in Sumter County when we were trying to wrestle with the problem of black versus white, to make it black plus white in a better future. Those were tough times, and we weathered those tough times. And now we've got a brighter, better Southland, because we had the courage—it came slow—we had the courage to address that issue and prepare for a better future. So, my background and my upbringing, what you all taught me, has stood me in good stead and I'm grateful to you.

Now our country has made some good decisions. When I went into office we didn't have an energy policy. The 3 years before I became President we increased oil that we bought from overseas 44 percent in 3 years. Since I've been in office it's decreased 24 percent. We've got more oil drilling rigs, natural gas drilling rigs running this year than any other year in the history of our country. And at the same time people are beginning to be more conscious of conservation and saving what God gave us, and we are producing more coal in the United States this year than any other year in history, and we're learning now how to produce gasohol from growing crops and trees and waste products. And we're using solar power. Ten times more homes use solar power now than they did just 4 years ago.

And we're increasing trade overseas so that the things we produce in this country can be sold. The trade with Mexico, for instance, has tripled in the last 4 years, and we now have a fourth of the people on Earth, in China, that were formerly our enemies; now they are ready customers. I visited a little steelplant in Perth Amboy, New Jersey, last week. Half of their product goes to China, and they are now making steel and shipping it halfway around the world cheaper than Japan can make steel and ship it a few hundred miles.

What we have is a nation so strong and

so blessed, and having made tough decisions on energy, we've built a foundation for a future that can be bright with hope and achievement and more freedom and more beneficial influence. And God's given us blessings that not many people yet realize. D. W. Brooks realizes it. But OPEC oil doesn't stand a comparison with United States soil. In the future that blessing will let us use our influence throughout the world in a very beneficial way, and at the same time, benefit us.

So, we can count our blessings, we look to the future with confidence, we can have a better government, more trust, more decency, more honesty, more openness, more communication with the people, more soundness, and we can pull our Nation together. That's what I want to see, so that you and I together in the years ahead can make the greatest nation on Earth even greater.

God bless you and thank you again.

One thing—postscript. There are about five or six hundred people here and some of you have a long way to go. I'm going to spend the night at the Governor's Mansion with George Busbee, so I don't have very far to go. As I look around the faces, I see people that I could spend a half an hour talking to about: "Do you remember so and so," and sometimes I'd say, "No, I don't remember it at all." [*Laughter*] But I won't have time to have a conversation with each one of you, so just to make sure that the line's not too long on you all, let's just let me shake hands, say God bless you and thank you, and then let me shake hands with the next one. It's not because I don't want to talk to you, I just want to get through tonight.

Thank you very much.

NOTE: The President spoke at 8:28 p.m. outside the home of Charles Kirbo.

Following the reception, the President went to the Governor's Residence in Atlanta, where he stayed overnight.

Atlanta, Georgia

Informal Exchange With Reporters.
September 16, 1980

Q. What do you think about the latest things happening in Tehran? Are you hopeful, or do you think, as was said yesterday, that maybe we're near settling that problem?

THE PRESIDENT. Well, I think Ed Muskie described it accurately. We don't have any reason to believe that the situation has been resolved at all. But there is at least a government now in Iran, and they haven't had anyone so far that could speak with authority. But now that they have in Iran a Majles, or a parliament, and a President and a Prime Minister and a speaker, at least there is an entity there with whom we might be able to work out the differences. But we don't have any prospect at this time for an early resolution of the issue.

Q. When you spoke at that town meeting yesterday, were you aware at that point that there had been a repetition of their demand for an apology?

THE PRESIDENT. No, but I'm not surprised that there was a repetition.

Thank you.

Q. Thank You.

THE PRESIDENT. Aubrey, I'm glad to see you again.

Q. Mr. President, I missed what you were saying there about the importance of this occasion.

THE PRESIDENT. Well, obviously it's important to me to have broad and enthusiastic support for reelection in the South. And coming here to Ebenezer Church is symbolic to me of the changes that have taken place in the South, where the black and white people now, instead of working against each other, work together. This has been the essence of what

I've tried to do as President. And I might say that I would not have been elected the first President from the Deep South in 140 years had it not been for Martin Luther King, Jr., and the social change that he made, and along with many others.

Q. One other question, Mr. President, on this effort to bring the Ku Klux Klan into this Presidential race, your view?

THE PRESIDENT. Well, obviously the Ku Klux Klan is an obnoxious blight on the American scene, and anyone who'd inject it into the campaign made a serious mistake. But now I think Governor Reagan has been, in effect, muzzled by his campaign workers. He's not talking about China or evolution or the Ku Klux Klan, and I don't believe that the Klan will be any significant factor in the future.

Q. Are you worried about keeping the White House?

THE PRESIDENT. No, I'm not worried.

REPORTER. Thank you.

NOTE: The exchange began at approximately 9:15 a.m. outside the Ebenezer Baptist Church.

Atlanta, Georgia

Remarks at a Meeting With Southern Black Leaders.   September 16, 1980

THE PRESIDENT. *Thank you, Andy and Mayor Jackson, Congressman Parren Mitchell, my friend, Cameron Alexander, Reverend Dr. Roberts, Coretta King, Daddy King:*

REVEREND KING. Right here. [*Laughter*]

THE PRESIDENT. I was going to describe to you in my opening remarks how far we've come, but I think Maynard Jackson did it better than anyone that I know when he, as a black mayor, referred to a white President as a Georgia boy.

[*Laughter*] I think he pretty well wrapped it up, don't you? [*Laughter*] And I can actually say it gave me a warm feeling to hear it.

As I was coming in the church a while ago, I was asked a question by a newsman about the importance of this meeting, and I've been thinking about it since I decided to come down here. Several mentioned this. I could not improve on the speeches that have been made so far, and I wish I could sit in on the speeches after I leave—[*laughter*]—because there are some things that are going to be said that I would really like to hear. But I'll depend on you all to give me a report.

If it hadn't been for Daddy King and his beloved wife, I would not be President. Had they not had their son, Martin Luther King, Jr., I would not be President. Had he not been a man of courage and vision and tenacity and faith, I would not be President. And had it not been for the people in this audience—I started to say congregation—I would not be President. You all had confidence in me in 1976, when very few people knew who I was, and there was an actual stigma attached to a southern white politician, a Georgia Governor, that you helped to remove.

I have had continual need for you. Once during the campaign I made a remark about ethnic purity, and it almost crippled me fatally. I didn't know what to do. I got a call from Andy, and I got a call from Daddy King; I got a call from many of you. And I decided to come home to Atlanta, had a rally in the downtown square. Four or five thousand people came. All I wanted to do was what happened. I got on the stage, in front of the TV cameras, and Daddy King held my hand. And the people all over the Nation saw it, and it healed the wound that I had done to myself. So, I'm aware of the importance of this meeting, and what was said at the very beginning by Jesse Hill is accurate.

This meeting this morning could very well decide the outcome of this election and, more importantly, but significantly, the future of this country. When my Presidency has not always satisfied every one of you—and I acknowledge that's a fact— my phone has been open to you and others that are not here this morning. And you have never failed to use it. I get quick telephone calls, and they're returned. But if my opponent should be elected, you're going to have a hard time getting a telephone call answered at the White House. And if my opponent is elected, I doubt that there will ever be a Martin Luther King, Jr., holiday. And there ought to be one in this country.

Daddy King is a great politician. He's a great preacher. He's a great family man. Now he's become a great author. He's just written an autobiography, and I hope you'll all buy it and read it. I was hoping he'd give me a copy; he hasn't done it yet. I'll have to buy one like you will. [*Laughter*] But in the end he says that, "I was put here, as the old folks say, on a purpose." Maybe I was elected President on a purpose. Our country was created on a purpose. Freedom was born in the human breast on a purpose. Courage was created among human beings on a purpose. And we have an obligation to carry out that purpose.

I know that Daddy King's son once said, "Man . . . is not very flotsam and jetsam in the river of life, but he's the child of God." And it's important that in this Nation at least, as an example for all the rest of the world, that politicians don't forget that. That worth of an individual human being in the eyes of God and in the eyes of one's fellow human beings—that's been forgotten in the past.

In this region for too long, politicians who hoped to be elected to the office of county commissioner or mayor or Governor or Congressman or Senator had to divide blacks from whites and had to blame the poverty that afflicted our Nation among white people on the black people and vice versa. But it wasn't necessary to talk to blacks much, because they didn't have the right to vote. And there are some people sitting here who helped pave the way for those rights, which must be protected and preserved—John Lewis, in the audience, Joe Lowry—I'm going to visit him right after I leave here at Martin's headquarters—and Daddy King.

Back in the early thirties, Daddy King decided, according to his book, that he needed to have the right to vote for President, because the President's decision affected his life and the life of people he loved. He went to the county courthouse here. There were two elevators: one for white folks, one for colored folks; had signs above them so you wouldn't make a mistake. One of them was working up to the registrar's office. I don't think you need to think long to figure out which one was working. So, Daddy King said, "Well, I'll just walk up the stairs." When he approached the stairs, there was a policeman standing there, and a sign was there, by the stairs, that said, "White Only." He kept going back time after time after time, day after day.

Eventually the "colored" elevator was working, and he was able to get to the registrar's office. The registrar told him about the poll tax. Daddy King was willing to pay the poll tax, but he found that you didn't have to pay it not just for only yourself but for all your ancestors who had lived in Georgia and hadn't paid their poll tax. And finally, that obstacle was removed by the Federal Government.

And Daddy King went back as a young man, and they explained that there were 30 questions he had to answer, questions that a political science professor at the University of Georgia could not answer. They were still on the books when I became State senator. That first speech I made in the State senate was to do away with those 30 questions. And in Daddy King's book, he said a lot of black people learned a lot about government trying to answer those 30 questions. It's paying off now.

He never dreamed that eventually his son would be a world hero and that we would have black mayors in Atlanta and Detroit, Los Angeles, many other great cities—Birmingham now—many other great cities around this country. He never dreamed that his granddaughter would be in the Georgia legislature, that his daughter-in-law would serve at the United Nations, that Andy Young would be the spokesman for this country, among more than 150 nations on Earth, and would spread the Gospel that was preached on this pulpit throughout the world and that politicians who lead other nations would listen and would say, "So that's what the United States is. I was getting the wrong impression when Richard Nixon was the President."

These changes have been made. We've come a long way. We haven't yet reached the Promised Land that was spelled out so clearly for us by Martin Luther King, Jr., and by many of you who were also very courageous and very tenacious in spite of the most difficult possible obstacles.

We're no longer divided, white from blacks. We no longer see so many of our babies die, black and white. We no longer see so many of our young people leave the South because there was no alternative, black and white. We no longer see the devastation of poverty and disease and discrimination sweep through our communities, both black and white. We've made progress. We still have a long way to go.

I've appointed all those people that Andy described, and I can tell you this: I have not had to lower the standards of quality and excellence and commitment in order to do it. I haven't done them a favor; they've done me a favor. And I'm not through yet. We've got a lot of other appointments to make.

We've had economic difficulties the last few years, as Andy pointed out. But in spite of those obstacles, we've added 8½ million new jobs to the American economy. Employment among black people has gone up 22 percent in the last 3½ years. 1.3 million of those new jobs are held by black people; another million by people who speak Spanish. We've focused those jobs on those that need them most, and the plans for the future are much greater than that. And our Nation hasn't suffered. These are not make-work jobs created in Government. These are permanent jobs, solid jobs, career jobs.

We've got a proposal in Congress now to add two more billion dollars to put our young people to work, because we've got so far to go in that respect—a way to tie together the high school graduates and the trade school graduates with the jobs available in that community and make sure they know how to hold a job when they get there and to help tide over that salary payment for those few months as they become qualified. It's going to meld together labor and education now, for a change, and we'll have a much brighter future because of it.

We've solved to a great degree the problem of not having an energy policy. And we'll have $88 billion in the future to have help for poor people to pay their energy bills and to have a better transportation system to get to and from work and to create new technology and an exciting life and a dynamic life for our country, to rebuild America's industry and to give our workers tools with which to be more productive. And we are opening up the world, now and in the future, for additional trade.

I was in a little steel mill last week in Perth Amboy, New Jersey, the most modern steel mill in the world. The workers there produce more steel per year, each worker, than any other place in the world, and they are selling steel rods to China cheaper, halfway around the world, than Japan can make them and ship them a couple of hundred miles across the China Sea. It's the kind of thing we can do.

That valuable relationship with a billion people in China and millions of people in Zimbabwe and other areas of the world that are now our friends is very valuable to everyone here. One of the most emotional meetings I have ever had was with Prime Minister Mugabe in the East Room of the White House just a few days ago—the new Prime Minister of Zimbabwe. This was a terrible political struggle—Parren Mitchell and Andy Young know it—because of tremendous pressures from an ill-informed American public, concentrated on me in the Oval Office, not to stand for democracy, not to stand for majority rule, not to stand for the elimination of racial discrimination all the way over in the dark continent of Africa. But with your help we stood firm, and now there's a freedom there and a democracy there and a majority rule there that's an inspiration to the entire world. And I'm proud that Andy Young was there to help us make this come true.

You've seen in this campaign the stirrings of hate and the rebirth of code words like "States rights" in a speech in Mississippi, in a campaign reference to the Ku Klux Klan, relating to the South. That is

a message that creates a cloud on the political horizon. Hatred has no place in this country. Racism has no place in this country. Daddy King says in his book, "Nothing that a man does makes him lower than when he allows himself to hate anyone. Hatred is not needed," he says, "to stamp out evil. Despite what some people have been taught, people can accomplish all things God wills in this world. Hate cannot."

Just briefly, let's look to the future. I see a future for this country to be strong, to be united, to be confident, to be inspired, to be even more free, to be employed in useful work, to be well educated, to be united, to be filled with love and compassion one from another. I see a future in this country where those that fought hard to achieve civil rights will continue, in the Federal Government and all other governments, to administer the very laws that they were willing to risk their lives to achieve.

I see a Federal court system that's filled not only with a desire for justice but a desire for understanding of the special deprivation of justice that still prevails in this country against those who are poor or inarticulate or not well organized or not well educated. We've got a long way to go in the Federal courts where, still, money available to have competent lawyers is an obstacle to true justice. But whenever I appoint a black judge or Hispanic judge or even a woman judge, I know that they not only have committed in their own hearts a vision of what this Nation ought to be but a special knowledge of the effects of past discrimination that are still there as a means to prevent equality of opportunity.

And I see an America where young people don't have to worry about employment. I don't know of anything that's more devastating to a nation than to have a 17- or an 18- or a 19- or a 20-year-old young person, having struggled through high school, sometimes at great sacrifice to the family, having been given talent and ability and ambition and hope by God, week after week after week not be able to find a way to use their talent or that ability—becomes a matter of loss of self-respect and then following that, discouragement and despair and then alienation and then a sense of lashing out at the system that deprived that young person of a chance to be useful in God's world. We've got to continue that effort, and that is still a question in doubt. We have a youth bill in the Congress right now, a $2 billion youth bill to create that kind of opportunity for many of our young people.

And we've got another bill in the Congress that hasn't yet been passed, that many of you have worked to achieve, to create fair housing implementation. We had a fair housing bill passed in 1968. It hasn't been implemented. It's passed the House; it's in doubt in the Senate. I had a long conservation with Senator Kennedy yesterday on Air Force One, coming back from Texas. He said, "Mr. President, we've got to work together to get that bill through the Senate. It's now come out of my committee, and we'll be marshaling our forces to get that fair housing bill passed." He and I agreed on the phone it's the greatest civil rights legislation in the last 10 years.

You've not yet been adequately marshaled to put those Senators on the record. And I'd like to ask you this morning, if you don't do anything else in the Congress, to help get that fair housing bill passed. It's important to the future of our country to eliminate the last legal impediment of the right of our people to have equal opportunity by choosing where they want to live. This is extremely important.

And the last point I want to make to you is this: Andy Young, Don McHenry, Pat Harris, Eleanor Holmes Norton, Drew Days, Clifford Alexander, many others are now working with me in the Federal Government. I consider all of you to be my partners, as well. I know the importance among those who look to you for leadership for your voice to be heard in shaping our Nation's future. The decision is going to be made on November the 4th about what kind of future we will have.

And I ask you to study the platform of the Republican Party. It's not going to be possible in my judgment, although I hope I'm wrong, for me to face head on in a public debate Governor Reagan, the Republican nominee. He's now been deprived by his staff of the opportunity to speak out on the issues. He didn't do too well with the Ku Klux Klan or China, as you know. [*Laughter*] He was making some progress on evolution, but he cut that off. But it's going to be hard for the people to understand what this election is all about unless you tell them. And collectively, this group in this room can remember what happened to Daddy King and his son and many of those you love as they struggled for the right to vote and how important it is for people to register and take advantage of that right, that cost so much, which is so easily ignored.

And I see a nation at peace. Peace is not something that comes to the timid or to the weak. Our Nation is strong—strongest on Earth. Militarily, economically, politically, morally, ethically, our Nation is the strongest on Earth. And if we are strong, the weak need not have so much fear. And if we are at peace, then the world has a much better chance to stay at peace.

If we abandon the commitment to control nuclear weapons—which has been a part of the administration of every President, Democratic or Republican, since the time of Eisenhower and Truman—as has been advocated by the Republican nominee, then the chances for the avoiding of a nuclear war in the future will be severely reduced. I'm not predicting war, but I tell you that it's very important for us to stay strong and at the same time search for peace with the Soviet Union and with every other union or nation on Earth that wants to avoid a nuclear holocaust.

I'll do my part. The Vice President could make the same speech to you that I've made this morning, and you would have confidence that he was speaking from the heart. You know that. And my Cabinet officers—Andy and all of you know them—have the same philosophy that I have, and those that I've appointed to major positions in the Federal courts, and otherwise, share my commitment that I've described to you so briefly this morning. And all of us will do our part. But I have to tell you that the most important factor is what you do and others like you who are not running for office—at least not running for President, thank goodness.

But you see the importance of the outcome of this election. We are indeed talking about two paths to the future. And I believe that our path, your path, is the one that must prevail, but it can very well not prevail, unless you do your share.

You remember 1968, how a divided Democratic Party deprived Hubert Humphrey of a chance to serve as President and put Richard Nixon in the White House. A few votes, a few more speeches, a few more radio tapes and TV advertisements could have prevented the Nixon administration taking place. That's what we face this year.

Our party has been remarkably unified since the convention. Senator Kennedy is campaigning for me and with me. We'll be together on the 22d in Los Angeles, raising money. But that unity is not enough,

unless there's an enthusiasm and a commitment and a sacrificial spirit to help me solve these difficult issues, for which there are no easy answers, now and in the next 4 years.

You've got a friend in the Oval Office, and if you'll help me, I'll be there as your friend for the next 4 years.

Thank you very much.

NOTE: The President spoke at 9:34 a.m. in the Ebenezer Baptist Church.

Atlanta, Georgia

Remarks at Dedication Ceremonies for the Hartsfield Atlanta International Airport. September 16, 1980

Thank you, Mayor Maynard Jackson and Governor George Busbee.

It is a distinguished gentleman who has come to visit us—Fritz Hollings. He's welcome as a friend and a neighbor and a great leader, but he's also welcome as the chairman of the Senate Budget Committee. A lot of people think Georgia has only 10 Congressmen. We actually have more than 10. Butler Derrick is with him. He serves just across the line in South Carolina. He's just as interested in the future of Georgia as he is in the future of South Carolina. Butler, I'm very proud to have you with us, too.

I see in the front row, also, some of the great men with whom I served in the State senate and a fine young man, one of the finest people I have ever known—Doc Davis, sitting in the front row. Doc, will you stand just a minute?

With people like this, the future of the South and the future of our Nation is ensured. But it hasn't always been that way.

When I was running for Governor and later serving as Governor, when I was running for President, I promised myself that one of the first things I would help with was the improvement of the Atlanta airport. I don't know if you know of where I learned patience and restraint and tenacity; it was in the old airport. And I don't know if you all know where I learned how to jog; it was in the airport.

And now with the tremendous leadership of Maynard Jackson, this has become a notable example of progress and faith and cooperation and decency and social progress and pride. And I'm very proud to be part of it and to be the first passenger to depart, in just a few minutes on Air Force One, en route to our sister State, South Carolina. I'm proud that all Atlantans and all Georgians and our neighboring States have joined in this tremendous effort, because Hartsfield Atlanta International Airport has meant and will mean so much to us all.

No city that I know has been more intimately identified with this airport than has Atlanta, and I think no airport symbolizes the spirit and the growth and the confidence in the future of a city than does this one. Mayor Hartsfield many years ago made a famous statement that Atlanta was a city too busy to hate. That was a time when there was indeed a lot of hatred, and it was a remark that swept through the South and made possible many of the achievements that have led to this great day. There's no better way to remember him and to characterize what he meant and what Ivan Allen meant and what Sam Massell meant and what Maynard Jackson means than to name this airport after him.

He would have been pleased that the project came in ahead of time and on budget. And I know Fritz Hollings is smiling, because he shares with me the hope that many more can learn from this great experience. You've added these splendid works of art, which show that there is no

incompatibility between efficiency and a functional commitment in a project, and beauty and an enlightening of the American human spirit.

And I think he would have been pleased, as am I, that about one-third of the total construction and concession contracts went to minority contractors. As a matter of fact, the minority contractors— I just rode out here with Herman Russell—but the minority contractors on this airport comprise 80 percent of all the minority contractors on all the airports in the United States combined. This is a good achievement, and the quality of the work proves that this is also a sound investment.

Well, I just finished touring this facility. It's beautiful, simple to operate, convenient, exciting. And I am very proud that the many years that went into this project have now come to fruition. I'm glad that some of the dreams that I had as Governor and as a State senator and as a candidate and now as President have come true.

It's hard for a politician to admit that he wasn't the best that served in the office. I thought I was a good Governor of Georgia until I've watched George Busbee. He's a much better Governor than I ever was. I admit it, and I admit it with pride.

I spent the night with him in my old house—[*laughter*]—and we had a chance to talk about the international aspects of this airport. We were blocked 4 years ago. We could not get through the administration in Washington a single approval for a single international flight out of Atlanta. That was one of my commitments. George Busbee, Maynard Jackson, many of you, have made that commitment easy for me to keep. And now there is a growing number of international flights from Atlanta to the major industrial and political centers of the entire world.

I'm very proud of this, because I think it's not only a true recognition of Atlanta but of the importance of this entire region and the diversity of the offerings and the quality of life that exists throughout our country. I'm very proud, too, that ambitious young people are now flooding back to the South. And I believe that this achievement is a forerunner of what is happening throughout our country.

We've had difficult times in the last few years, since I've been in the Oval Office, dealing with unanticipated increases in the price of oil and heavy dependence on foreign oil. Now we've got intact an energy policy on which we can build as a foundation an exciting American life, typified in my judgment by the design and construction and functional characteristics of this fine airport.

We've had many lessons to learn. You can't do something great quickly. It requires confidence, commitment, courage, unity, and the use of America's ingenuity and the free enterprise system with minimal interference from Washington. Those kind of things have been demonstrated here in this airport and throughout this region. And I think that our Nation now is ready to embark, in the 1980's, on an exciting decade of achievement, progress, and also the realization of the dreams on which this Nation was originally founded.

In closing, let me say that this did not happen in just one place. It's happening in the hearts and minds of Americans coast to coast, in large and small communities, in the sunbelt and in the snowbelt. But once we've gotten started in rebuilding our cities, our transportation system, our housing system, in deregulating airlines and trucks and financial institutions and, in a few days, rail and, later,

communication, these kinds of things have opened up an opportunity for us that will indeed inspire Americans again to reach for greatness.

There's no doubt in my mind that we can outproduce and outbuild and outcompete any nation on Earth. We still have the most productive workers in the world. The American worker produces more per hour or per year than any other workers on Earth. But that productivity has not been increasing lately, because our American workers now are saddled with tools and factories that have not kept pace with innovative developments in the use of research and development and technology. But now we are ready to embark on a tremendously improved industrial complex that will make use of America's characteristics that have been so beneficial to us in the past.

Let me say that I'm proud to be here. This is a great city in a great State in a great region in the greatest nation on Earth.

We'll invest heavily in the future in our human resources. We've got to make sure that our workers are able to accommodate inevitable change. Our country has never been afraid of change. And we've got to provide jobs and better education and better training for our young people as they approach maturity, because we want to remove the depressing element of a person ready to enter adult life who doesn't have a chance to use the ability and talent and the ambition with which God has blessed that young man or that young woman. We want each generation to be better than the ones before.

We want our Nation to be strong militarily. We want our Nation to stay at peace. We want our Nation to honor civil rights for ourselves, human rights throughout the world. We'll keep the banner raised high. And I would like to remind you that our Nation has been inordinately blessed with rich land, with natural resources, with freedom, with the cherishing of the worth of each individual human being, with equality of opportunity, with confidence and unity. And whenever we face a difficult question or an obstacle to be overcome or a problem to be solved, this Nation, if united, has never failed.

Now we face, sure, problems; obstacles, yes; questions, of course; but primarily opportunities. And I'm determined, along with you, using this tremendous airport as kind of a new inspiration, to make the greatest nation on Earth even greater in the years to come.

Thank you. God bless you all.

NOTE: The President spoke at 11:20 a.m. in the airport's main terminal. Prior to his remarks, he was given a tour of the airport facilities.

Startex, South Carolina

Remarks to Employees of Startex Mills.
September 16, 1980

Senator Hollings, Governor Riley, Congressman Derrick, Congressman Holland, Mitchell Allen:

It's good to be in—[*inaudible*].

I think all of you know that in this very mill behind me, a great American statesman and a very fine senator, Ollin D. Johnson, worked in the mill, and now his daughter, Senator Liz Patterson, represents you so well in the State legislature. I'm proud to be here under conditions like that.

It's been a pleasure for me to have a chance to go through this modern mill and to recognize that when anyone drives down I–85 that they know that this area is booming with industry, all kinds of new industry, and also that this is the center of

America's textile industry. And I say that even as a Georgian.

Since I've been President and during the campaign, when I worked with John West as fellow Governors, I've always heard a lot about the textile industry from your own leaders. Governor Dick Riley, Senator Fritz Hollings, Butler Derrick, Ken Holland, State Senator Liz Patterson have all made sure that when our Nation makes their decision on any matter concerning the textile industry that your voice is heard in Washington.

Mitch Allen tells me that your new card room here is the most modern equipment available anywhere in the world and that Spartan [Startex] Mills is constantly modernizing and improving productivity. I'm very impressed, too, that you were able to preserve the original building while renovating the inside with the most modern equipment that can be bought. I was also told that all the equipment used in this building is made in the United States of America. I like that. So, you've kept intact the traditions represented by Ollin D. Johnson and the building behind me, but you've also kept up with the times, putting together more efficient tools that can be used by the most productive workers in the world, the workers in America.

From my own experience as Governor and in Sumter County, Georgia, where I first started my own political career, I know the importance of textiles, and I know the political importance of people whose families have kept this textile industry so strong in America. It's not an accident that I came here to be with you. As a matter of fact, one out of eight of all manufacturing employees in the United States work in the textile and apparel industry. There are over 2 million jobs at stake, about 150,000 of those, maybe more, in South Carolina. But I also know from personal experience about the way of life that this mill represents.

Many of you come from farms. Many of you still farm part-time. I know, because I've seen a lot of pickup trucks parked around this mill, and I know they're used for making a living in other ways as well. Many of you come from families that have worked in the mills for two or three generations. You've seen them grow. You've seen times of prosperity; you've seen times of disappointment and despair. And I know you realize, as well as I do, that the economic health of a textile industry in a community like this determines the economic life or death of the community itself.

Modernizing, keeping up with competition everywhere in the world is part of the American character. We've never been afraid of change. We've never been afraid to meet competition. Freedom and the free enterprise system is important to us. And God-fearing, hard-working families can earn a bright future by hard work if investments are made back in the plants and factories where we have to earn our living in this generation and in generations of the future. It can mean whether or not young people can finish high school, go on to college, have a great career; whether they can make a decent living if they decide to stay here or whether they have to move out of a community and go somewhere else. That's why, when I went to Washington, I was determined to sustain and improve the textile and the apparel industries of our Nation.

In March 1979, after close consultations with both industry and labor, I announced a new comprehensive textile program. Senator Fritz Hollings, many leaders that you know in the textile industry— workers and management—were in the Roosevelt Room, next door to the Oval Office, when that white paper was decided

upon to make sure that the interests of the textile industry were honored in every decision made by the Federal Government. This has paid rich dividends. This comprehensive new textile industry has removed the cloud that hung over our heads for so many years prior to the time that your neighbor from Georgia became President of the United States. And in the last 2 years we've made good progress, with your help.

Fritz Hollings, Dick Riley, Senators Holland, Butler Derrick, and others have made sure that I never forget what I promised to do. And we've paid rich dividends to you in the last 2 years. Tomorrow, for instance, after difficult negotiations, we'll sign an orderly marketing agreement with the People's Republic of China. This has been part of our effort to increase American exports of textile goods overseas and at the same time to reduce foreign imports coming into our country. We have increased exports since 1978 alone by 70 percent. This means $2 billion worth of American textiles made in plants like this are now sold overseas. That's completely different from what it was before I became President. At the same time, we have reduced imports coming into this country by 800,000 square yards of material since 1978. That's the kind of trends that you've made possible.

Let me hasten to add, before you say it yourself, it's not my achievement; it's not even the achievement of your Governor and those who represent you in Congress. This is your achievement, because if it wasn't for the dedication and hard work and courage and confidence and the efficiency of American workers, with the intense competition from places like Taiwan, Japan, China, Korea, Sri Lanka, India, we couldn't do what I've just described to you. This is your achievement. And on behalf of all the people of the

United States, I want to say thank you for what you've done for our country.

I want to add one other word, because I think it's important to put it in perspective. We haven't had easy times the last 3½ years. With the tremendous pressure put on us by OPEC oil prices, we've had to hammer out, under difficult circumstances, a national energy policy. We were importing too much oil, buying oil from overseas. The last 3 years before I was inaugurated President, we increased oil imports by 44 percent. Since I've been President, with the help of these men on the stage with me, we have decreased imports by 24 percent. Today, and every day in 1980, we are buying 2 million barrels of oil less from foreign countries than we did the first year I was President. That's a great achievement, and we're proud of it.

The thing is that when we import oil, we not only import that product but also we import inflation and we import unemployment. And cutting down all we buy overseas and building up the productivity of American workers is a major responsibility that I have for the future. What's been happening behind me in the Startex plant—modernization—makes sure that American productivity stays competitive in the years ahead.

We've solved now, in my judgment, the problem of having an energy policy for our great country. That was done in the late 1970's. In the 1980's we have an equally good chance to solve that problem of keeping America's plants and factories competitive and keeping American workers employed, to give us a firmer family life, better opportunities for our young people, better education, better transportation, better quality of life for us all.

It's not going to be an easy time. There's no way for me to stand here and tell you that the problems are solved overnight.

You know it takes a while. But our country has never failed. When the American people could understand a question or a problem or an obstacle and we were united, in times of war or peace, depression or prosperity, the United States of America has never failed. And we will not fail to meet these dreams that I've described to you in the years ahead.

You might be interested in knowing that this year we have more oil wells being drilled in the United States, more gas wells being drilled in the United States than any other year in history, and we are producing more United States coal than any year in history. What I want to see is not just textiles but all the other elements of American production improve in the future. I want to see OPEC oil replaced on the energy markets of the world with United States coal. That's what I want to see done.

Well, I think I'll close my remarks by saying this: I could outline to you a lot of things of which I'm proud, but I think the thing that stays on my mind most—as I look in the faces of southerners—husbands and wives, mothers and fathers, young people—bright with hope, confident of what you've achieved, grateful for the opportunities in this world—I'm determined to keep our Nation at peace. We've been at peace now for 3½ years. If I'm reelected, we're going to stay a peaceful nation for the next 4 years.

The Southland has always been in the forefront of patriotism, courage, and dedication. When you look down the list of those honored for heroism, the South is at the top. When you look at the list of those who gave their lives in action to save our country and its freedom, the South is always in the front. We're the ones who know how important peace is, because I don't want my sons and my daughter or your sons and daughters to have to give their lives to defend our country.

But the most important way to make sure that we keep our Nation at peace is to keep our Nation militarily strong. It's something I learned at Annapolis. It's something that I learned in submarines as an officer. It's something that I've shared with Fritz Hollings and others. And I guarantee you that as long as I'm in the White House, our country's defense will be second to none in the United States.

The last point I want to make is this: I've talked pretty much about material things, and they're important—weapons capable, mills modernized, trade expanding, homes built for people to live in. But the most important thing is our human resources, human beings—how we relate to one another and what kind of life we have.

I've had a great admiration for what's been achieved in South Carolina. You led the way, and we followed because of great Governors like Fritz Hollings, Dick Riley, John West, and others, Bob McNair. We learned from you. You've had an ability to see the worth in your young people and prepare them for a productive career. Your education system, your training schools, educational television has just been remarkable, and other States throughout the Southeast and indeed throughout the Nation have learned from South Carolina.

And you've been able to see to the inevitability of change. And when a new plant comes into a community, you've had those workers there trained, ready to move into the new plant when it opened, at no expense, quite often, to the people that own and have invested in that new work opportunity. For that reason, foreign investors—and I hate to say this—when they were choosing between Georgia and

South Carolina, often came to South Carolina.

Now we know that the time has come for the entire country to do what South Carolina has done so well and what the Southland has done so well, and that is to rebuild the industrial base of our country, but to build it on the basis of a better life for human beings, better education, better training, better health care, better housing, better recreation opportunities, clean air, clean water, freedom, strength, peace. Those things are important to me as President, and they are important to you.

This is going to be a very important year, because the future of our Nation is at stake. You think back to the depression years and you think back to some of the changes that have taken place for you because Democratic candidates have been successful, with your help, in holding office and compare how you feel about the matters that concern you and your family, and you can see that the future of this Nation depends on what happens on November the 4th, 1980. I believe we'll have that bright future. I feel like I'm a partner with you, and I'm determined, with your help, to make the greatest nation on Earth even greater in the years to come.

God bless you all. Thank you very much, everybody.

NOTE: The President spoke at 1:40 p.m. outside Startex Mills. Prior to his remarks, he was given a tour of the mill's facilities.

Lyman, South Carolina

Remarks at a Barbecue for Carter/Mondale Workers.   September 16, 1980

THE PRESIDENT. I've got a question I want to ask you. Are we going to have a Democratic victory in South Carolina in November? [*Cheers*]

I'm not going to speak but just a few

minutes, because I want to spend as much time as I can shaking your hands and thanking you for your confidence in me and also, more importantly, for your confidence in the future of our Nation. This is the greatest country on Earth. We have never failed to meet any challenge or answer any question or solve any problem if the Nation was united and if Democrats were in the White House and holding the major positions in this country. Right? [*Cheers*]

Your county chairmen, State chairman, William Jennings Bryant Dorn, your great Governor, Dick Riley, Fritz Hollings—Senator Hollings, Congressman Holland, and also, of course, Butler Derrick, all of us are united in believing that with your help we can have an even better future for our Nation than we've had in the past, with jobs for our people, with the rebuilding of our industrial capacity, new tools for our workers—I just came from the new Startex Mill; it's beautiful—and also with a belief in human beings, that our young people should have a better education, we should have better transportation systems, better homes, strong nation militarily, a nation at peace. Those are the kinds of things that we Democrats are going to keep in this country for the next 4 years, with your help. Will you help us? [*Cheers*]

AUDIENCE [*Chanting*]. We want Jimmy.

THE PRESIDENT. Thank you very much. You've got me.

Just so I can shake as many hands as possible, let me say that you've got me and you're going to have me for 4 more years.

Thank you very much.

NOTE: The President spoke at 2:16 p.m. outside the Lyman Town Hall.

Following his appearance at the barbecue, the President attended a South Carolina Democratic Party fundraising reception at the home of State Senator Verne Smith in the town of Greer.

Cleveland, Ohio

*Remarks at a Cuyahoga County Democratic Party Reception.
September 16, 1980*

There are a lot of people that can't get in, but I hope they can hear.

Senator Howard Metzenbaum and Mary Rose Oakar, Charlie Vanik, Chairman Tim Hagan and, of course, our host and our hostess:

You've made it possible for us to come here to this exciting place.

How many of you believe, since you've heard the recent statements on this platform, that the Democratic Party in Cuyahoga County and throughout the State of Ohio is united and that we're going to have a tremendous victory on November 4? How many of you believe that? [*Applause*] Very good.

I think all of you realize that since the Democratic convention was concluded that one of my best and strongest and most effective supporters and campaigners has been Senator Ted Kennedy and I deeply appreciate that. And I also appreciate this show of support for me among some of his very strong supporters during the primary season. It was a time for discussing the issues that affect our Nation. Now is the time to bring ourselves together to think about the importance of what we've done together and to think about the importance of the future.

Ours is a nation which has been at peace now for 3½ years, and with your help the United States of America will stay at peace for 4 more years. That's important to me and to your families. Ours is a nation that in the last 3½ years has added 8.6 million new jobs. We've had the most difficult economic season in international affairs in recent memory. We've got a long way to go, but we have now achieved for the first time in our Nation's history a comprehensive energy policy.

This year our country will produce more coal than in any other year in the history of the United States. This year our country has more drill rigs running to find more oil and natural gas than at any other time in the history of the United States.

In the 3 years before I became President we increased imports of foreign oil 44 percent. Since I've been in the White House, with the help of Senator Metzenbaum, Mary Rose Oakar, Charlie Vanik, and others, we have decreased our dependence on foreign oil by 24 percent. Today and every day in 1980 we will import from overseas 2 million barrels of oil less than we did in the year 1977. That's a tremendous achievement, and I want to express my thanks to you for it.

It's not been easy. Today, my Republican opponent will raise $2½ million in one fundraiser among the oil executives in Houston, Texas. In my judgment, what the Congress has done in the last 3 years in hammering together an energy policy for our country—which we've never had before—is one of the great historic achievements of all time. And now we have a base or a foundation on which we can actually revitalize the entire American economy and make sure that the growth in jobs and opportunities and career chances for our young people and our old ones, for those communities that have suffered from the times of change, will have a bright future ahead in the 1980's— brighter and more exciting and more prosperous than we have ever seen before in the history of the country. That's what I believe we can have with a Democratic administration the next 4 years.

The human element is important, because we have to think about the families—the need for those families to be strong, to be united. The preservation of the quality of individual neighborhoods is crucial to us.

When I campaigned around this Na-tion, including Ohio, several times, in 1976, I had a constant message that came to me from two sources. One was the elderly people in our country—those who are approaching or already having reached the retirement age—"Do not let social security go into bankruptcy." Now I never have that question raised, because they know that if I'm elected President for 4 more years, the social security system will be sound; it will not be voluntary. We will continue with Medicare, we'll continue with Medicaid. We care about people and the people's future and the security of families. Those things will be preserved. But it wasn't sure 3½ years ago.

And the other message to me from almost every mayor, Democratic or Republican, was our cities are deteriorating so rapidly that we face a constant crisis. You yourselves have had a very serious trial in this city—in Cleveland, in this metropolitan area. The future can be very bright as we solve the problems of better tools and better factories for our steelworkers, meet foreign competition in automobiles, make sure that we increase the production of American energy of all kinds, including coal—these kinds of things are now in the future, ahead of us, if America can retain the same commitment that's made our country strong.

This Nation with all its breadth of diversity—people having moved here from every country on Earth, retaining our cultural commitments, but uniting in a common effort—no matter what we have faced in problems that seem to be insoluble, questions that apparently could not be answered, obstacles that many thought could not be overcome—this country, when united, has never failed. And we will not fail in the next 4 years if we have a Democratic administration.

Peace is important to us. It's particularly important to a President. Americans revere the office of Presidency. The Oval Office is a place where difficult questions come. There are no difficult questions that come to anyone in the Nation any more trying for a human being. I never see an easy question or problem come to the Oval Office. If they are easy they're solved somewhere else—[laughter]—in a private home or in a city hall or in a county courthouse, in a State legislature, in a Governor's office. If they can't be solved in all those other places after a tremendous effort's made, they come to the Oval Office. And the most difficult ones and the ones that are most vital to the future of our country and the entire world are the ones where my own advisers are almost exactly equally divided in the advice they give me. And I have to make a decision about prosperity and failure, about moving forward or moving backward, about peace and war, about fairness and equity and opportunity compared to the loss of those opportunities for those that might be poor or whose families don't speak good English or who don't have political influence. Those are the kinds of decisions that I have to make.

This year will be a time of decision for the future of our country. It's more important than just a contest between two men. The differences are vast. Perhaps there's never been a sharper difference between two men with the possible exception of when Goldwater ran against Johnson. The choice between the two parties is sharp.

My opponent has departed radically even from the past history of his own party. The Republican platform this year could be devastating to the average working family of this country. Every President since Harry Truman and Eisenhower, Democratic and Republican, has said our Nation must be at peace, must be strong. But in order to do that we've got to control nuclear weapons and not have a massive nuclear arms race with the Soviet Union. That philosophy, that commitment, has been changed.

Our Nation has stayed at peace because we are militarily strong, and we're going to stay strong. The 8 years before I became President, we had a steady decrease in real expenditures for our defense capability. Since I have been in office, with the help of these Members of Congress behind me from both Houses, we've had a steady increase in our commitment to defense. That is a good investment. And I'd like to point out to you that the best weapon is the one that's never fired, and the best soldier is one that's never killed. And I'm determined to keep this country at peace.

And finally, let me say this. I've talked a lot about me as President, I've talked a lot about your Senators, your Members of the House in Washington. The outcome of this election doesn't depend on us. I'll do the best I can. So will Fritz Mondale, who was here not long ago. So will the members of my Cabinet and the members of my family. So will supporters of mine who are chairmen of the county and State parties and in the Congress. But the results of this election will depend on you. And I hope that every one of you in these next few weeks will think about the differences in your own life, in the lives of your own family members in the next 4 years, throughout the 1980's to the end of this century if the decision that's made is the wrong decision.

In 1968 we had two men running for President. One was Hubert Humphrey. The other one was Richard Nixon. We came out of the Democratic convention in Chicago divided. I would guess that everyone in this room felt even then that Hubert Humphrey was the better of the two men. But many people didn't rally to his support. They didn't contribute $5 or $50 or more. They didn't call their neighbors and ask the Democrats to go and vote. And by a very narrow margin, as you know, in spite of heroic efforts on his part, Hubert Humphrey lost. Ed Muskie was his running mate, and Richard Nixon was in the White House, followed by Gerald Ford, for 8 long years.

The same thing happened in 1960 the other way, when 28,000 votes in Texas, if they had changed, and just a few votes in Illinois would have meant that John F. Kennedy would never have been President. Our country now is facing a similar choice, and what you do as an individual American citizen, patriotic, wanting peace, wanting better education, wanting better transportation, wanting better job opportunities, wanting a better life for your family, will make the difference.

Our country has raised high the banner of human rights. We now stand for something fine and decent and honest and open and inspiring. And what's happened lately in Poland, to me, is a good indication of the benevolent influence of what our country can mean around the world. I'm not trying to take credit for the United States, for the heroism and the tenacity of the Polish workers, but it's a good sign. And it means that if our country can be strong and united and keep our principles intact and put our faith in the good, solid families that have been the structure and strength of this country, then after November 4 we'll make sure that the greatest nation on Earth is even greater the next 4 years and the rest of this century.

Thank you. God bless you.

NOTE: The President spoke at 5:58 p.m. at Kiefer's Restaurant.

Cleveland, Ohio

Remarks at a Democratic National Committee Fundraising Reception. September 16, 1980

It's delightful for me and very gratifying for me to come back to this beautiful home of Milt's and Roslyn's. I've visited them in their other home in Austria. Rosalynn's been here, as you well know, and some of you have attended all three of these events, which have been very gratifying to us and very helpful to us.

We have had kind of a social problem with the Wolfs. We wanted to return their hospitality and have them to the White House. We didn't know if they were prepared for roughing it after living here in this community. [*Laughter*] But with their genuine sacrificial nature, they condescended to come and be with us at the White House, and that was indeed a delightful thing for us.

They've also been at the White House for some notable events, and we were with them for a notable event. Also I want to say that it's important to us to have strong support from many of you, and I hope that in this year 5741 [Jewish New Year] you'll help me be reelected President again.

I'm very glad that Dennis Eckart is here. It's hard to envision anyone taking Charlie Vanik's place, but when you have a bright, young, aggressive, successful, sensitive political leader on the horizon who can serve this district for many, many years in the future, I hope that you won't forgo an opportunity to give him every possible support in these next few weeks as well. Dennis, good luck to you.

I just came from Mary Rose Oakar's district. I always feel at home there. She is indeed one of the sterling leaders of our country. She's a person who represents, in my opinion, the essence of America. She's looked upon as being kind of a symbol of the heterogeneity of our society but still the unity of the different ethnic groups in our country that comprises a major element of our strength. We've never been afraid of differences among us. We've always been very proud of preserving the heritage that makes us individually unique, and at the same time we've been able to meld ourselves together in kind of a mosaic that's both beautiful and very strong. And I'm grateful for Mary Rose for being one of my good and close friends.

In her district, the best speech that was made was by Howard Metzenbaum. It really did reassure me that my judgment is sound. He pointed out to the audience that of all the United States Senators—and there are a hundred of them, as you know—that he had the highest percentage of support for the President's proposals of all the Senators. That shows my judgment is good, and, Howard, I'm grateful to you.

In 1976, when I was here before, Howard was with me and also John Glenn. I just got off the phone with John, coming in here. He gave me exactly the same message he gave Milt Wolf to show his staunchness and his integrity. He said he was sorry he couldn't be here. He missed being with me to show his support and being with his friends—all of you. And the next time I come to Ohio to campaign he'd be at my side to let everyone know that he was giving me his full support in my reelection campaign. So, I'm very grateful to the congressional delegation that you have now and to those that you will have in the future to work with me in Washington.

I'm just going to say two things tonight, and I'll be fairly brief. I'm concluding a 2-day campaign effort in Corpus Christi, Texas, and in Houston, in Atlanta and its environs, and also in Greenville, South Carolina, and that area, and now, here. And I'll be going back to Washington tonight to be with Rosalynn later on this evening.

It's been a very exciting trip, and I tried to make two points almost everywhere I've been. One is about the Presidency itself.

I have the highest elective office in the world and one that's most revered by the 240 million or so people who live in this country. We know that the shape of our Nation is decided to a major degree in the Oval Office, working with other leaders like those I've already acknowledged here who serve in the Congress. The decisions that come to the Oval Office are very difficult ones. The answers are not easy to find. The problems are the greatest of all in our country.

If the answers are easy or if the problems are soluble or if the obstacles can be overcome anywhere else, they never come to the Oval Office. They're solved in a person's own decision or within a family structure in a home or in a county courthouse or a city hall or State legislature or a Governor's office. They don't come to me. But the ones that get there are crucial.

This election in 1980 is a decision, not just between two men who have the sharpest possible differences in attitude toward major issues and basic political philosophy, two parties which are further apart now in their platforms than I remember since I've been alive—but also the Republican nominee and his philosophy, as expressed in the platform, is a radical departure from what the Republican Party has stood for in modern times.

I was at Milt and Roslyn's home, the Embassy in Austria, when we negotiated the SALT II treaty. Eisenhower was for nuclear arms control. All the Republican Presidents since then were for nuclear arms control. Every Democratic President since Truman have been for nuclear arms control. To give up the thought that we could have so-called nuclear superiority—because when you adopt a policy of nuclear superiority, it means that you cannot negotiate mutual and balanced restraints or reductions—and for us to abandon the hope or the prospect of having nuclear weapons controlled in our own country, in the Soviet Union, and particularly among those nations that don't have nuclear weapons yet, that is indeed a radical departure in the prospects for peace in the future.

I don't want to be misunderstood. I'm not insinuating that my opponent is for war and against peace. But it's important for Americans to make a judgment on whether we should have this departure become part of our Nation's philosophy and commitment. I think it would be a devastating change. A President has good advisers—the best. I can make my choices from anywhere on Earth. I would put my Cabinet choices up against any Cabinet that's ever served this country—men and women of sound judgment representing our Nation accurately. But I've also learned that the most difficult decisions, the ones of most vital consequence to our Nation's well-being are almost invariably those on which my advisers divide almost equally, some saying yes, almost an equal number saying no. The ultimate decision has to be made in the Oval Office and in a proposal made to the Congress that requires congressional action or an executive decision by me.

After the Camp David accords were hammered out, almost exactly 2 years ago, at Camp David, there was a delay in carrying out the mutual commitment by Begin and Sadat and myself that there would be a Mideast peace treaty. You remember this well. We met, a small group in the Oval Office. I told them that I had gotten up quite early that morning, and I had decided to go to Jerusalem and to Cairo to make one last effort to bring about a treaty between the two nations. I don't believe any of my advisers agreed at first, because it was such an obvious public thing, and the failure would be so highly publicized around the world. But I felt that it was crucial not just to Israel and to Egypt and to the Mideast neighbors but also crucial to our country to have stability there and to have, for the first time since Israel was founded, the strongest, most powerful, most influential Arab country certify a commitment to peace.

And now when I see tourists traveling back and forth between Cairo and Alexandria and Tel Aviv and Jerusalem and see the negotiations being carried on between Ambassadors assigned because those two nations recognize one another diplomatically, and see trade slowly building up, the Foreign Minister of Israel being wined and dined in Cairo just this week, and seeing that people facing each other across a negotiating table instead of across barbed wire, it sends a thrill through my heart, for the Presidency itself ultimately depends upon a person, with good advisers, including many of you in this room, who want to shape our Nation and what it is.

And the other thing I want to mention to you is the future, the Presidency and the future.

The future of this country will be decided on November 4. I don't say that in derogation of my opponent. It's a fact, because what happens the next few years, the next 4 years, with a possible reelection prospect in 1984, will shape the road that our Nation will follow for the rest of this century. Will we have a deep, continuing commitment to democracy, to freedom, to human rights, to civil rights, to the honoring of principles of compassion and concern among the people who've not been quite so fortunate as we? Will there be a choice of administrative officials, regulatory officials, justices on the Supreme Court, judges on the Federal bench, compatible with the principles and ideals that permeate your life or not? That judgment will be made on November 4.

Will we be able to build upon what we've accomplished in the last 3 years with Howard Metzenbaum's help and with Rose Oakar's help in energy or will we not?

Three years before I became President, our oil imports from the OPEC nations increased 44 percent. Since I've been in office, although we had some delay in passing all the legislation, oil imports have decreased 24 percent. Today and every day this year our country is importing from overseas 2 million barrels less of oil. We recognize the importance of this economically, because we not only import oil, we also import inflation and unemployment. But there's another strategic element here that ought not to be forgotten.

Who will be the next Secretary of Energy? Who will be the next Secretary of State? Who will be the next Secretary of the Treasury, to make those basic decisions about who will influence our Nation's foreign policy? Will the oil companies again have their fingers intimately entwined in the shaping of policy, or will the American consumer who has just recently found an equal voice in the Congress, as Howard Metzenbaum well knows, continue to shape the policy for our country? This is crucial to you and to every family in our Nation.

We have not damaged the energy industry in this country. This year, 1980, we will drill more oil and natural gas wells than any year in history, and you'll be surprised, perhaps, to know that this year we will produce more American coal than

any year in history. And we're just on the verge of taking advantage of this base or foundation that we've laid to completely revitalize the entire American economic system.

I have a philosophy that I believe that you, most of you, would share. I think the intrusion of the Federal Government into the free enterprise system of our country ought to be minimal. I believe in intense competition, and as I believe in the worth of an individual human being and the freedom for that individual, I also believe in the freedom of our competitive business and financial system.

We have made great strides. We've changed the relationship between Government and industry more in the last 3½ years than ever before since the early years of the New Deal. We've deregulated the airlines, deregulated trucking, deregulated the financial institutions. This is extremely important to us. And at the same time we now are ready, as we have been successful in the 1970's, in the late years, in having an energy policy evolve. We never had one before; now we are ready to devote the 1980's to building on that foundation, with economic and diplomatic freedom, yes, but also to make sure that the American workers have up-to-date, modern, efficient tools and factories with which to work. Nobody knows more vividly than do I, than the steel industry, the automobile industry, the coal industry, and others. We are suffering from change, which is inevitable, and we don't want to stop change. Americans have never been afraid of change. And now to take advantage of that change, which is inevitable, is part of the American character.

I've been in a couple of factories just recently, and I'll be brief about this. Last week I was in a little factory in Perth Amboy, New Jersey, a steelplant. The Federal Government helped to get it started, put up a $12 million guarantee on a loan. It won't cost us a nickel. The plant cost $140 million. We formerly shipped scrap iron and steel overseas. It was processed and made into steel rods and things, and we bought it back. They take scrap metal and make high quality steelrods. A ⅜-inch rod comes out of that mill 18,000 feet a minute. They bind it up into bundles that weigh about a ton each and sell it. Half the total product of that mill is now going to the People's Republic of China. Every worker in that plant, including the president, produces more steel per year than in any other steelplant on Earth. And we can take that American-produced steel and ship it halfway around the world to China cheaper than the Japanese with their most modern plant can produce steel and ship it a few hundred miles. That's the kind of thing that's the forerunner of what's going to happen here.

Coincidentally—not coincidentally—that plant produces every ton of steel with 30 percent of the energy used in most of the steelplants in our country. That's the kind of thing that can be done.

I went to a textile mill in South Carolina today. The same sort of modernization, using an old building by the way, is keeping Americans at work. The last 2 years—this is a strange thing, but interesting—the last 2 years with a new textile policy we have increased American exports—listen to this—of textiles $2 billion, and we now import 800,000 yards of textiles less than we did 2 years ago.

Tomorrow I'm going to sign a textile agreement with the People's Republic of China and three other agreements. We've got a billion new friends in China to whom we can sell American products and who will be our allies and friends in other matters, not military yet, not military perhaps in the future, but trying to keep sta-

bility in that part of the world. This is the kind of thing that portends a good future for Americans, if we have the competence and the unity and the commitment and the dynamism and the vision that's always been a characteristic of the people who live in this blessed country.

The OPEC nations all put together have 6 percent of the world's energy reserves. We've got 24 percent here waiting to be tapped. And some of the coal that can't be burned efficiently now without very expensive scrubbers will in the future be made into clean-burning oil and gas under a tremendous investment that will inevitably be made with the windfall tax funds in synthetic fuels. Ten times as many homes now use solar power as did just 4 years ago.

When I was in Corpus Christi, I pointed out that our trade with Mexico is three times as much now as it was 4 years ago—unbelievable statistics. We're selling them 10 million tons of American grain this year, just to one country, and it's growing. Mexico, you might be interested in knowing, is the third most important trade partner that we have now.

The last point I want to make is this: With this confidence and strength in our country we can extend the benefits overseas. For 8 years before I became President, the commitment to American defense in real dollars went down, down, down. Since I've been in office we've reversed that trend. Every year since I've been there we've increased in real dollars, above and beyond inflation, our investment in American defense. It's still very modest, about 5 percent of our gross national product. But it's paying dividends, because with that strength we have been able to maintain peace, and we've been able to extend that peace to others, including the Middle East, which I've already mentioned to you. That must continue.

But American strength does not depend just on defense budgets. The best weapon that a country can have is one that's never fired to kill another human being; and the best soldier that we can have is one that never dies in war. Our country is at peace, and to keep our Nation at peace, through strength, is important to me and you.

I remember 1968, when America had a decision to make: Nixon versus Humphrey. Humphrey ran a courageous campaign; I'm sure many of you helped him— not enough—and he narrowly lost. It was a turning point in our Nation's history. In 1960 if 28,000 people in Texas had voted the other way and just a few thousand in Illinois, John Kennedy would never have been President. This is another one of those crucial election years.

I'll do all I can. Fritz Mondale, who speaks for me, will do all he can. The Cabinet will work hard. My wife will work hard. My children will work hard. But the outcome of the election will depend on people like you who have been blessed with material benefits and great influence among your friends and neighbors, and with an insight into what our Nation is and what it has been and what it can be, that perhaps is well above average. And I hope that you will join me and Fritz Mondale in this next few weeks in bringing about a victory not because of a personal sense or desire of gratification for myself, but because I genuinely believe that our Nation is at a turning point. And I want it to turn or continue on the same good road toward strength, humanity, compassion, concern, progress, education, a better life, a better industrial commitment, more freedom, more unity, and a continuation of peace.

That's what's at stake, and that's why I'm so deeply grateful to all of you for joining in with me in shaping the future of the greatest nation on Earth.

NOTE: The President spoke at 7:02 p.m. outside the home of Ambassador Milton Wolf.

Advisory Commission on Intergovernmental Relations

Appointment of Roy Orr To Be a Member. September 17, 1980

The President today announced the appointment of Roy Orr, of DeSoto, Tex., as a member of the Advisory Commission on Intergovernmental Relations.

Orr is a vice president of the National Association of Counties and a commissioner of Dallas County, Tex. He is a former mayor of DeSoto, Tex.

Charges Against the President and Administration Officials by Admiral Elmo R. Zumwalt, Jr.

Statement by the White House Press Secretary. September 17, 1980

Admiral Zumwalt yesterday made serious charges against the President, the Secretary of Defense, and the Deputy Assistant for National Security Affairs, David Aaron. Those charges are false in their entirety.

To make such charges without offering one shred of proof is both outrageous and irresponsible. The Admiral's partisan zeal on behalf of Governor Reagan can be no excuse for such rash action.

Mr. Zumwalt yesterday claimed to have impeccable sources for his accusations. The peccability of his sources has now been exposed by this morning's Washington Post, in which George Wilson states that the Admiral's charge that David Aaron leaked the Stealth story to him is false.

The President and Secretary Brown categorically deny that they ordered such a leak by anyone to anyone.

If Mr. Zumwalt has one witness or one iota of evidence to support his charges, he has a duty to come forward. If he fails to do so, he owes an apology to the President and the other administration officials he has maligned.

We would also hope that Governor Reagan would take the first opportunity to disassociate himself and his campaign from the false statements made by one of his most well-known national security advisers.

NOTE: Press Secretary Jody Powell read the statement to reporters at approximately 12:45 p.m. at his regular news briefing in the Briefing Room at the White House.

Ronald Reagan's Position on Fair Housing

Statement by the White House Press Secretary. September 17, 1980

In light of Governor Reagan's statement yesterday that he would like to see our civil rights laws strengthened, and in light of the fact that he has announced a press conference for this afternoon, we again call upon him to state his position on and to support the fair housing bill which is now in the Senate. The legislation, the most significant piece of civil rights legislation in perhaps a decade, has already passed the House. The Governor's position is also relevant in light of his record as Governor of California, which shows that he advocated repeal of the California fair housing law known as the Rumford Act.

NOTE: Press Secretary Jody Powell read the statement to reporters at approximately 12:50 p.m. at his regular news briefing in the Briefing Room at the White House.

United States-People's Republic of China Agreements

Remarks at the Signing Ceremony. September 17, 1980

THE PRESIDENT. *Vice Premier Bo, Mr. Ambassador, distinguished guests and friends:*

I'm delighted to welcome you here to our country, Mr. Vice Premier, and also your delegation. You are among friends, as you know.

We are here today to share some good news with each other. With the four agreements that we are about to sign, the normalization of relations between the United States of America and the People's Republic of China is at last complete. That relationship is a new and vital force for peace and stability in the international scene. In addition it holds a promise of ever-increasing benefits in trade and other exchanges for both the United States and for the People's Republic of China.

I am personally committed, Mr. Vice Premier, to the proposition that our relationship will not be undermined, but will be strengthened. Both the United States and China have made firm and written commitments which form the basis of this relationship. These commitments have the support of the people of my country and of your country and therefore they will be honored.

What we have accomplished together since the beginning of diplomatic relations between our countries has been extraordinary. But, as I said to Vice Premier Deng Xiaoping when he was here in January 1979, our aim is to make these exchanges not extraordinary, but ordinary. In other words, to make the benefits of this new relationship a routine part of the everyday lives of the citizens of this country and of the People's Republic of China. That is exactly what these four agreements will do.

Let me say a brief word about each one of them.

First, the civil aviation agreement. This agreement will mean regularly scheduled direct flights between the United States and China, beginning in the very near future. I have instructed the Civil Aeronautics Board to move quickly to name the first of the two United States airlines which, along with the Chinese carriers, will fly the new routes. At the airports in New York or Los Angeles or San Francisco or Honolulu a few months from today, we will hear flights announced for Shanghai and for Peking as well as to London and Paris.

Second, the maritime agreement. For the first time in more than 30 years, all United States ports will be open to Chinese merchant ships and American ships will have access to all Chinese ports of call. This will mean a stronger American maritime industry. It will mean revenue for United States shippers from the growing Chinese market for American goods, and growing trade and commerce will benefit the people of both China and the United States.

Third, the textile agreement. By permitting orderly marketing in this country of Chinese textile products, this agreement will benefit American retailers and consumers without damaging our own textile industry, which was fully represented in these negotiations.

The fourth agreement is the consular convention. It spells out the duties of consular officers in providing services to citizens of both our countries. One immediate benefit is to ensure the protection of the rights and interests of American citizens in China.

We have two consulates in China already, and now we will open three more. These offices will promote trade, travel, and cultural and educational exchange. They will serve the needs of hundreds of thousands of Americans who will be visiting China in the next few years. On this side of the Pacific Ocean, China now has two consulates in the United States, one in San Francisco and one in Houston. Soon, thanks to this agreement, there will be new Chinese consulates in New York, Chicago, and Honolulu as well.

These agreements, as you well know, are the fruit of some very hard work. A year ago when Vice President Mondale visited China, both nations pledged an effort to complete the political and legal framework of normalization by the end of 1980. We have met that goal with 3½ months to spare. The negotiators on both sides deserve the thanks and the appreciation of us all.

I'm privileged to lead my great Nation in taking this step. I consider this to be one of the most important achievements of my administration, but it's an achievement with a bipartisan history. President Nixon concluded the Shanghai Communique of 1972, and President Ford accepted and supported the principles of that communique. My administration, working closely with the Congress, has taken the decisive steps which made that goal a reality.

One result has been the activity by private and public organizations on both sides to build human contacts between our peoples after 30 years of near-total, mutual isolation. Another was the establishment of the Joint Economic Committee, which is meeting here this week under the chairmanship of Vice President Bo and Secretary Miller. Our economic ties, like our cooperation in science and technology, grow broader and closer every day. Trade between the United States and China this year will be nearly four times what it was 2 years ago. China will buy some $3 billion worth of American goods. That means jobs for American workers and opportunities for American businesses. And it means help for China's efforts to modernize and to develop her economy.

Almost 700,000 American citizens trace their roots to China. There are strong bonds of blood kinship and history between the United States and China. Yet both countries have acted not out of sentiment, but out of mutual interest.

In a few moments, normalization between our two countries will be a fact. We're building something together—a broadly-based, consultative relationship that will enable us to expand our cooperation as the years go by. Both of us will gain from this relationship. So, I firmly believe, will the peace of the world. America and China, so recently at odds, will have shown the world something about the possibilities of peace and friendship. In a world that badly needs a good deal of both, this is an achievement, Mr. Vice Premier, of which we can all be proud.

Thank you very much.

[At this point, the President and Bo Yibo, Vice Premier of the State Council of the People's Republic of China, signed copies of the four agreements.]

THE VICE PREMIER. *Mr. President, ladies and gentlemen:*

Today, in the field of Sino-U.S. economic cooperation, President Carter and I have completed a task of major significance. Starting from today the economic relations between our two countries will have moved from ordinary exchanges to institutionalization.

Just as President Carter pointed out in his very warm message to the Chinese trade exhibition which opened in San Francisco a few days ago, the cornerstone of our relationship is the communique on the establishment of diplomatic relations between our two countries which was solemnly declared to the whole world by the heads of government of our two countries on December 15, 1978. Since that time the relations between our two countries in various fields have developed rapidly on the basis of both sides abiding by the obligations undertaken in the communique. It is our firm opinion that these friendly relations should continue to develop forward.

Here it is my pleasure to declare that with the signing of the consular convention, we'll be setting up three more general consulates in your country. This will give a further impetus to the friendly contacts and trade and economic cooperation between our two peoples. Facts have proven and will continue to prove that such relations are not only beneficial to the two peoples but also to the peace and stability of the world.

Not long ago we held the third session of the Fifth National Peoples' Congress. Our newly elected Premier, Zhao Ziyang, explicitly pointed out that we will continue to carry out unswervingly the domestic and foreign policies which we have set forth in recent years. Through this session of the Peoples' Congress, the whole series of the effective new policies which we have been carrying out have been or will shortly be fully legalized and institutionalized. All our people are with full confidence ·working hard to build our country into a highly democratic and civilized modern nation. For this purpose, we need peace; we need stability; we need friendship; we need cooperation.

It is my conviction that the American people too need peace, need stability, need friendship, need cooperation. Let our two great nations and two great peoples on both sides of the Pacific advance hand in hand and make common efforts for world peace and stability and for the prosperity and strength of our two peoples.

Thank you, ladies and gentlemen.

NOTE: The President spoke at 2:42 p.m. in the Rose Garden at the White House. The Vice Premier spoke in Chinese, and his remarks were translated by an interpreter.

United States-People's Republic of China Agreements

Civil Air Transport Agreement.
September 17, 1980

AGREEMENT BETWEEN THE GOVERNMENT OF THE UNITED STATES OF AMERICA AND THE GOVERNMENT OF THE PEOPLE'S REPUBLIC OF CHINA RELATING TO CIVIL AIR TRANSPORT

The Government of the United States of America and the Government of the People's Republic of China,

Desiring to develop mutual relations between their countries, to enhance friendship between their peoples, and to facilitate international air transport;

Acting in the spirit of the Joint Communique of December 15, 1978 on the Establishment of Diplomatic Relations between the United States of America and the People's Republic of China;

Observing the principles of mutual respect for independence and sovereignty, non-interference in each other's internal affairs, equality and mutual benefit and friendly cooperation;

Recognizing the importance of reasonable balance of rights and benefits between both Parties under this Agreement;

Being Parties to the Convention on International Civil Aviation opened for signature at Chicago on December 7, 1944;

Have agreed on the estabilshment and operation of air transportation involving their respective territories as follows:

ARTICLE 1

Definitions

For the purpose of this Agreement, the term:

(a) "Aeronautical authorities" means, in the case of the United States of America, the Civil Aeronautics Board or the Department of Transportation, whichever has jurisdiction, and in the case of the People's Republic of China, the General Administration of Civil Aviation of China, or in either case any other authority or agency empowered to perform the functions now exercised by the said authorities;

(b) "Agreement" means this Agreement, its annexes, and any amendments thereto;

(c) "Convention" means the Convention on International Civil Aviation, opened for signature at Chicago on December 7, 1944, including

• any amendment which has entered into force under Article 94(a) of the Convention and has been ratified by both Parties, and

• any annex or any amendment thereto adopted under Article 90 of the Convention, insofar as such annex or amendment is effective for both Parties;

(d) "Airline" means any air transport

enterprise offering or operating international air services;

(e) "Designated airline" means an airline designated and authorized in accordance with Article 3 of this Agreement;

(f) "Air service" means scheduled air service performed by aircraft for the public transport of passengers, baggage, cargo or mail, separately or in combination, for remuneration or hire;

(g) "International air service" means an air service which passes through the air space over the territory of more than one State;

(h) "Stop for non-traffic purposes" means a landing for any purpose other than taking on or discharging passengers, baggage, cargo or mail.

ARTICLE 2

Grant of Rights

(1) Each Party grants to the other Party the rights specified in this Agreement to enable its designated airline(s) to establish and operate scheduled air services on the route(s) specified in Annex I to this Agreement. Such route(s) and services shall hereinafter be referred to as "the specified route(s)" and "the agreed services" respectively.

(2) Subject to the provisions of the Agreement, the designated airline(s) of each Party, while operating the agreed services on the specified route(s), shall enjoy the following rights:

(a) to make stops at points on the specified route(s) in the territory of the other Party for the purpose of taking on board and discharging international traffic in passengers, baggage, cargo and mail; and

(b) subject to the approval of the aeronautical authorities of the other Party, to make stops for non-traffic purposes at

points on the specified route(s) in the territory of the other Party.

(3) Nothing in paragraph (2)(a) of this Article shall be deemed to confer on the designated airline(s) of one Party the right of taking on at one point in the territory of the other Party traffic in passengers, baggage, cargo or mail destined for another point in the territory of the other Party (stopover and cabotage traffic), except the non-revenue traffic in personnel of such airline(s), their families, baggage and household effects, articles used by the representative offices of such airline(s) and aircraft stores and spare parts of such airline(s) for use in the operation of the agreed services. Any exchange of rights between the Parties to allow the designated airline(s) of either Party to carry on-line stopover traffic between the points on the specified route(s) in the territory of the other Party shall be subject to consultations at an appropriate time in the future.

(4) The operation of the agreed services by the designated airline(s) on routes over third countries shall be conducted on routes available to the airlines of both Parties, unless otherwise agreed.

(5) Charter air transportation shall be governed by the provisions of Annex II.

ARTICLE 3

Designation and Authorization

(1) Each Party shall have the right to designate in writing through diplomatic channels to the other Party two airlines to operate the agreed services on the specified route(s), and to withdraw or alter such designations. In the operation of the agreed services, the designated airlines may operate combination or all-cargo service or both.

(2) Substantial ownership and effective control of an airline designated by

a Party shall be vested in such Party or its nationals.

(3) The aeronautical authorities of the other Party may require an airline designated by the first Party to satisfy them that it is qualified to fullfill the conditions prescribed under the laws and regulations normally applied to the operation of international air services by the said authorities.

(4) On receipt of such designation the other Party shall, subject to the provisions of paragraphs (2) and (3) of this Article and of Article 7, grant to the airline so designated the appropriate authorizations with minimum procedural delay.

(5) When an airline has been so designated and authorized it may commence operations on or after the date(s) specified in the appropriate authorizations.

ARTICLE 4

Revocation of Authorizations

(1) Each Party shall have the right to revoke, suspend, or to impose such conditions as it may deem necessary on the appropriate authorizations granted to a designated airline of the other Party where:

(a) it is not satisfied that substantial ownership and effective control of that airline are vested in the Party designating the airline or its nationals; or

(b) that airline fails to comply with the laws and regulations of the Party granting the rights specified in Article 2 of this Agreement; or

(c) that other Party or that airline otherwise fails to comply with the conditions as set forth under this Agreement.

(2) Unless immediate revocation, suspension or imposition of the conditions mentioned in paragraph (1) of this Article is essential to prevent further noncompliance with subparagraphs 1(b) or

(c) of this Article, such rights shall be exercised only after consultations with the other Party.

ARTICLE 5

Application of Laws

(1) The laws and regulations of each Party relating to the admission to, operation within and departure from its territory of aircraft engaged in the operation of international air service shall be complied with by the designated airline(s) of the other Party, while entering, within, and departing from the territory of the first Party.

(2) The laws and regulations of each Party relating to the admission to, presence within, and departure from its territory of passengers, crew, baggage, cargo and mail shall be applicable to the designated airline(s) of the other Party, and the passengers, crew, baggage, cargo and mail carried by such airline(s), while entering, within and departing from the territory of the first Party.

(3) Each Party shall promptly supply to the other Party at the latter's request the texts of the laws and regulations referred to in paragraphs (1) and (2) of this Article.

ARTICLE 6

Technical Services and Charges

(1) Each Party shall designate in its territory regular airports and alternate airports to be used by the designated airline(s) of the other Party for the operation of the agreed services, and shall provide the latter with such communications, navigational, meteorological and other auxiliary services in its territory as are required for the operation of the agreed services, as set forth in Annex III to this Agreement.

(2) The designated airline(s) of each Party shall be charged for the use of air-

ports, equipment and technical services of the other Party at fair and reasonable rates. Neither Party shall impose on the designated airline(s) of the other Party rates higher than those imposed on any other foreign airline operating international air service.

(3) All charges referred to in paragraph (2) of this Article imposed on the designated airline(s) of the other Party may reflect, but shall not exceed, an equitable portion of the full economic cost of providing the facilities or services in question. Facilities and services for which charges are levied shall be provided on an efficient and economic basis. Reasonable notice shall be given prior to changes in charges. Each Party shall encourage consultations between the competent charging authorities in its territory and the airline(s) using the services and facilities, and shall encourage the competent charging authorities and the airline(s) to exchange such information as may be necessary to permit an accurate review of the reasonableness of the charges.

ARTICLE 7

Safety

(1) Mutually acceptable aeronautical facilities and services shall be provided by each Party for the operation of the agreed services, which facilities and services shall at least equal the minimum standards which may be established pursuant to the Convention, to the extent that such minimum standards are applicable.

(2) Each Party shall recognize as valid, for the purpose of operating the agreed services, certificates of airworthiness, certificates of competency, and licenses issued or rendered valid by the other Party and still in force, provided that the requirements for such certificates or licenses at

least equal the minimum standards which may be established pursuant to the Convention. Each Party may, however, refuse to recognize as valid, for the purpose of flight above its own territory, certificates of competency and licenses granted to or rendered valid for its own nationals by the other Party.

(3) Each Party may request consultations concerning the safety and security standards maintained by the other Party relating to aeronautical facilities and services, crew, aircraft and operations of the designated airlines. If, following such consultations, one Party is of the view that the other Party does not effectively maintain and administer safety and security standards and requirements in these areas that at least equal the minimum standards which may be established pursuant to the Convention, to the extent that they are applicable, the other Party shall be informed of such views together with suggestions for appropriate action. Each Party reserves its rights under Article 4 of this Agreement.

ARTICLE 8

Aviation Security

The Parties reaffirm their grave concern about acts or threats against the security of aircraft, which jeopardize the safety of persons or property, adversely affect the operation of air services and undermine public confidence in the safety of civil aviation. The Parties agree to implement appropriate aviation security measures and to provide necessary aid to each other with a view to preventing hijackings and sabotage to aircraft, airports and air navigation facilities and threats to aviation security. When incidents or threats of hijackings or sabotage against aircraft, airports or air navigation facilities occur, the Parties shall assist each other by facilitating communications intended to terminate such incidents rapidly and safely. Each Party shall give sympathetic consideration to any request from the other Party for special security measures for its aircraft or passengers to meet a particular threat.

ARTICLE 9

Representative Offices

(1) For the operation of the agreed services on the specified route(s), the designated airline(s) of each Party shall have the right to set up representative offices at the points on the specified route(s) within the territory of the other Party. The staff of the representative offices referred to in this paragraph shall be subject to the laws and regulations in force in the country where such offices are located.

(2) Each Party shall to the maximum extent practicable ensure the safety of the representative offices and their staff members of the designated airline(s) of the other Party, as well as safeguard their aircraft, stores, and other properties in its territory for use in the operation of the agreed services.

(3) Each Party shall extend assistance and facilities to the representative offices and their staff members of the designated airline(s) of the other Party as necessary for the efficient operation of the agreed services.

(4) The designated airline(s) of each Party shall have the right to convert and remit to its country at any time on demand local revenues in excess of sums locally disbursed. Conversion and remittance shall be effected without restrictions at the prevailing rate of exchange in effect for current transactions and remittance and shall be exempt from taxation on the basis of reciprocity. Wherever the payments system between the Parties is gov-

erned by a special agreement, that special agreement shall apply.

ARTICLE 10

Personnel

(1) The crew members of the designated airline(s) of either Party on flights into and out of the territory of the other Party shall be nationals of the Party designating such airline(s). If a designated airline of either Party desires to employ crew members of any other nationality on flights into and out of the territory of the other Party, prior approval shall be obtained from that other Party.

(2) The staff of the representative offices of the designated airline(s) of each party in the territory of the other Party shall be nationals of either Party, unless otherwise agreed. The number of such staff shall be subject to the approval of the competent authorities of both Parties. Each designated airline shall be permitted such number of staff as is adequate to perform the functions described in this Agreement associated with the provision of the agreed services, and in no event shall be less than that permitted to any foreign airline performing comparable services. Each Party shall by diplomatic note notify the other Party of the authorities which shall be considered the competent authorities for purposes of this paragraph.

ARTICLE 11

Market Access

(1) Matters relating to ground handling pertaining to the operation of the agreed services may be agreed upon between the airlines of both Parties, subject to the approval of the aeronautical authorities of both Parties.

(2) The sale, in the territory of each Party, of air transportation on the agreed

services of the designated airline(s) of the other Party shall be effected through a general sales agent(s). The designated airline(s) of each Party shall serve as general sales agent(s) for the designated airline(s) of the other Party unless such airline(s) is offered and declines such agency. The terms and conditions of each general sales agency agreement shall be subject to the approval of the aeronautical authorities of both Parties. The Parties shall ensure that, if either Party designates a second airline for provision of the agreed services, both designated airlines shall be given the opportunity to act as general sales agents for the designated airline(s) of the other Party on the same terms and conditions.

(3) Notwithstanding paragraph (2) of this Article, the designated airline(s) of each Party, in its representative office(s) in the territory of the other Party, may sell air transportation on the agreed services and on all of its other services, directly or through the agents of its own appointment. Any person shall be free to purchase such transportation in the currency of that territory or, in accordance with applicable law, in foreign exchange certificates of freely convertible currencies. In addition the representative office(s) may be used for management, informational, and operational activities of the designated airline(s).

(4) The general sales agent for a designated airline appointed in accordance with paragraph (2) of this Article shall be responsive to the preferences expressed by the traveling and shipping public regarding airline selection, class of services and other related matters.

ARTICLE 1 2

Capacity and Carriage of Traffic

(1) The designated airlines of both Parties shall be permitted to provide ca-

pacity in operating the agreed services as agreed by the Parties and set forth in Annex V of the Agreement. Within two and one-half years after the commencement of any agreed service under this Agreement, the Parties shall consult with a view to reaching a new agreement which shall apply to the provision of capacity.

(2) In keeping with the principles set forth in the Preamble to this Agreement, each Party shall take all appropriate action to ensure that there exist fair and equal rights for the designated airlines of both Parties to operate the agreed services on the specified routes so as to achieve equality of opportunity, reasonable balance and mutual benefit.

(3) The agreed services to be operated by the designated airlines of the Parties shall have as their primary objective the provision of capacity adequate to meet the traffic requirements between the territories of the two Parties. The right to embark on or disembark from such services international traffic destined for or coming from points in third countries shall be subject to the general principle that capacity shall be related to:

(a) traffic requirements to and from the territory of the Party which has designated the airline and traffic requirements to and from the territory of the other Party;

(b) the requirements of through airline operation; and

(c) the traffic requirements of the area through which the airline passes after taking account of local and regional services.

(4) Each Party and its designated airline(s) shall take into consideration the interests of the other Party and its designated airline(s) so as not to affect unduly the services which the latter provides.

(5) If, after a reasonable period of operation, either Party believes that a service by a designated airline of the other

Party is not consonant with any provision of this Article, the Parties shall consult promptly to settle the matter in a spirit of friendly cooperation and mutual understanding.

(6) If, at any time, either Party is of the view that traffic is not reasonably balanced, that Party may request consultations with the other Party for the purpose of remedying the imbalanced situation in a spirit of friendly cooperation and equality and mutual benefit.

ARTICLE 13

Pricing

(1) Each Party may require the filing with its aeronautical authorities of fares to be charged for transportation of passengers to and from its territory. Such filing shall be made sixty (60) days prior to the date on which the fares are proposed to go into effect. In adddition, the aeronautical authorities of both Parties agree to give prompt and sympathetic consideration to short-notice filings. If the competent authorities of a Party are dissatisfied with a fare, they shall notify the competent authorities of the other Party as soon as possible, and in no event more than thirty (30) days after the date of receipt of the filing in question. The competent authorities of either Party may then request consultations which shall be held as soon as possible, and in no event more than thirty (30) days after the date of receipt of the request by the competent authorities of the other Party. If agreement is reached during consultations, the competent authorities of each Party shall ensure that no fare inconsistent with such agreement is put into effect. If agreement is not reached during consultations, the fare in question shall not go into effect,

and the fare previously in force shall remain effective until a new fare is established.

(2) If the competent authorities do not express dissatisfaction within thirty (30) days after the date of receipt of the filing of a fare made in accordance with paragraph (1) above, it shall be considered as approved.

(3) Notwithstanding paragraph (1) above, each Party shall permit any designated airline to file and institute promptly, using short-notice procedures, if necessary, a fare for scheduled passenger services between a point or points in the United States of America and a point or points in the People's Republic of China, provided that:

(a) the fare is subject to terms and conditions as agreed in Annex IV to this Agreement, and such fare would not be less than 70 percent of the lowest normal economy fare approved for sale by any designated airline for travel between the same point or points in the United States of America and the same point or points in the People's Republic of China; or

(b) the fare on the specified route(s) (hereinafter, the matching fare) represents a reduction of an approved fare but is not below any approved fare or any combination of fares, whether or not approved, for the provision of international air service between the United States of America and the People's Republic of China (hereinafter, the matched fare), and is subject to similar terms and conditions as the matched fare, except those conditions relating to routing, connections, or aircraft type, provided that:

(i) if the matched fare is for services provided in whole or in part by a designated airline over the specified route(s), the designated airline(s) of the other Party shall be permitted to institute a matching fare over the specified route(s);

(ii) if the matched fare is for services provided in whole or in part by a designated airline over a route(s) other than the specified route(s), the designated airline(s) of the other Party shall be permitted to institute a matching fare over the specified route(s) which is not less than 70 percent of the lowest comparable approved fare, excluding discount fares;

(iii) if the matched fare is offered solely by a non-designated airline(s) over the specified route(s), a designated airline shall be permitted to institute a matching fare over the specified route(s) which is not less than 70 percent of the lowest comparable approved fare, excluding discount fares; and,

(iv) if the matched fare is offered solely by a non-designated airline(s) over a route other than the specified route(s), a designated airline shall be permitted to institute a matching fare over the specified route(s) which is not less than 80 percent of the lowest comparable approved fare, excluding discount fares.

The Parties shall review the practice of matching of fares before the end of three years after commencement of any agreed service.

Each Party also agrees to apply subparagraph (b), *mutatis mutandis,* to fares of the designated airline(s) of the other Party for the provision of international air service between the territory of the first Party and a third country.

If, under the terms of subparagraph (b), a designated airline institutes a lower normal economy fare than the fare, or fares, put into effect pursuant to paragraph (1) of this Article, the normal economy fare for the purpose of establishing the 30 percent zone of pricing flexibility set forth in subparagraph (a) shall

remain unchanged absent mutual agreement of both Parties.

Nothing in subparagraph (a) or (b) shall be construed as requiring a designated airline to institute any specific fare.

(4) (a) Each Party may require the filing with its aeronautical authorities of rates to be charged for transportation of cargo to and from its territory by the designated airline(s) of the other Party. Such filing shall be made forty-five (45) days prior to the date on which the rates are proposed to go into effect. In addition, the aeronautical authorities of both Parties agree to give prompt and sympathetic consideration to short-notice filings of the designated airlines.

(b) The competent authorities of each Party shall have the right to disapprove cargo rates. Notices of disapproval shall be given within twenty-five (25) days after receipt of the filing. A rate which has been disapproved shall not go into effect, and the rate previously in force shall remain effective until a new rate is established.

(c) A Party shall not require the designated airline(s) of the other Party to charge rates different from those it authorizes for its own airline(s) or those of other countries.

(5) Notwithstanding the provisions of this Article, each Party shall permit any designated airline to file and institute promptly, using short-notice procedures, if necessary, a fare or rate identical to that offered by any other designated airline in accordance with the provisions of this Article for transportation between the same points and subject to comparable terms and conditions.

(6) Each Party shall by diplomatic note notify the other Party of the authorities which shall be considered the com-

petent authorities for purposes of this Article.

ARTICLE 14

Customs Duties and Taxes

(1) Aircraft of the designated airline(s) of either Party engaged in the operation of the agreed services, as well as their regular equipment, spare parts, fuel, oils (including hydraulic fluids), lubricants, aircraft stores (including food, beverages, liquor, tobacco and other products for sale to or use by passengers in limited quantities during the flight) and other items intended for or used solely in connection with the operation or servicing of the aircraft, which are retained on board such aircraft shall be exempt on the basis of reciprocity from all customs duties, inspection fees and other national charges on arrival in and departure from the territory of the other Party.

(2) The following shall also be exempt on the basis of reciprocity from all customs duties, inspection fees and other national charges, with the exception of charges based on the actual cost of the service provided:

(a) aircraft stores introduced into or supplied in the territory of a Party and taken on board, within reasonable limits, for use on aircraft of a designated airline of the other Party engaged in the operation of the agreed services, even when these stores are to be used on a part of the journey performed over the territory of the Party in which they are taken on board;

(b) ground equipment and spare parts including engines introduced into the territory of a Party for the servicing, maintenance or repair of aircraft of a designated airline of the other Party used in the operation of the agreed services; and

(c) fuel, lubricants and consumable technical supplies introduced into or sup-plied in the territory of a Party for use in an aircraft of a designated airline of the other Party engaged in the operation of the agreed services, even when these supplies are to be used on a part of the journey performed over the territory of the Party in which they are taken on board.

(3) Aircraft stores, equipment and supplies referred to in paragraph (1) of this Article retained on board the aircraft of the designated airline(s) of either Party engaged in the operation of the agreed services may be unloaded in the territory of the other Party with the approval of the customs authorities of that other Party. The aircraft stores, equipment and supplies unloaded, as well as aircraft stores, equipment and supplies introduced into the territory of the other Party referred to in paragraph (2) of this Article, shall be subject to the supervision or control of the said authorities, and if required to fair and reasonable storage charges, up to such time as they are re-exported or otherwise disposed of in accordance with the regulations of such authorities.

(4) The exemptions provided for by this Article shall also be available where a designated airline of one Party has contracted with another airline, which similarly enjoys such exemptions from the other Party, for the loan in the territory of the other Party of the items specified in paragraphs (1) and (2) of this Article. The treatment by a Party of a sale of any such item within its territory shall be determined by agreement of the Parties.

(5) Each Party shall use its best efforts to secure for the designated airline(s) of the other Party, on the basis of reciprocity, an exemption from taxes, charges and fees imposed by state or provincial, regional and local authorities on the items specified in paragraphs (1) and (2) of this Article, as well as an exemption from fuel through-put charges, in the circum-

stances designated in this Article, with the exception of charges based on the actual cost of the services provided.

ARTICLE 15

Provision of Statistics

The aeronautical authorities of both Parties will consult from time to time concerning, and will provide, as agreed, statistics of traffic carried on the agreed services between the two countries.

ARTICLE 16

Consultations

(1) The Parties shall ensure the correct implementation of, and satisfactory compliance with, the provisions of this Agreement in a spirit of close cooperation and mutual support. To this end, the aeronautical authorities of the Parties shall consult each other from time to time.

(2) Either Party may, at any time, request consultations relating to this Agreement. Such consultations shall begin at the earliest possible date, in no event later than sixty (60) days from the date the other Party receives the request unless otherwise agreed.

(3) If any dispute arises between the Parties relating to the interpretation or application of this Agreement, the Parties shall, in a spirit of friendly cooperation and mutual understanding, settle it by negotiation or, if the Parties so agree, by mediation, conciliation, or arbitration.

ARTICLE 17

Modification or Amendment

(1) If either of the Parties considers it desirable to modify or amend any provision of this Agreement or its annexes, it may at any time request consultations with the other Party, and such consultations shall begin within a period of ninety (90) days from the date of receipt of the request by the other Party unless both Parties agree to an extension of this period.

(2) Any modification or amendment to this Agreement or its annexes agreed upon as a result of the consultations referred to in paragraph (1) of this Article shall come into force when it has been confirmed by an exchange of notes through diplomatic channels.

ARTICLE 18

Entry into Force and Termination

This Agreement shall enter into force on the date of its signature and shall remain in force for three years. Thereafter, it shall continue in force but may be terminated by either Party by giving twelve months' written notice to the other Party of its intention to terminate.

DONE at Washington, this seventeenth day of September 1980 in duplicate, each copy in the English and Chinese languages, both texts being equally authentic.

For the Government of the United States of America:

JIMMY CARTER

For the Government of the People's Republic of China:

BO YIBO

ANNEX I

I. First Route

A. *For the United States of America:*

The first airline designated by the United States of America shall be entitled to operate the agreed services on the following route, in both directions:

New York, San Francisco, Los Angeles, Honolulu, Tokyo or another point in Japan, Shanghai, Beijing.

B. *For the People's Republic of China:*

The first airline designated by the People's Republic of China shall be entitled to operate the agreed services on the following route, in both directions:

Beijing, Shanghai, Tokyo or another point in Japan, Honolulu, Los Angeles, San Francisco, New York. Anchorage may be utilized as a technical stop in both directions on this route.

II. Second Route

The Parties shall consult during the first two years following the commencement of any agreed service to decide on a route for operation by the second designated airline of each Party. If the Parties have been unable to agree upon a second route by the end of the second year, the second designated airline of each Party shall be entitled to commence operation of the agreed services on the first route in both directions, and to operate such services thereafter until the Parties agree upon a second route. In such circumstances, the Parties shall continue to consult and to exercise their maximum effort to reach agreement upon a second route, it being understood that the establishment of a second route is a mutually shared objective of both Parties. In the meantime, the Parties shall take overall review of the specified routes.

III. Extra Section

In case any of the designated airline(s) of either Party desires to operate additional sections on its specified route(s), it shall submit application to the aeronautical authorities of the other Party three (3) days in advance of such operation, and the additional sections can be commenced only after approvals have been obtained therefrom.

Notes

(1) On or after the effective date of this Agreement, each Party is entitled to designate one airline for operation of the agreed services. Beginning two years after the commencement of any agreed service, a second designated airline of each Party may also commence the operation of the agreed services. If either Party does not designate a second airline, or if its second designated airline does not commence or ceases to operate any service, that Party may authorize its first designated airline to operate the agreed services in all respects as if it were also designated as a second airline.

(2) Each designated airline may at its option omit any point or points on the above routes on any or all flights in either or both directions, provided, however, that the agreed service it operates begins or terminates at a point on the specified route in the territory of the Party designating the airline.

(3) Before operation of service through another point in Japan, referred to in Section I of this Annex, that point shall be agreed upon by the Parties. If a designated airline of either Party desires to change the point served in Japan, that airline shall furnish six (6) months' notice to the aeronautical authorities of the other Party. Such change shall be subject to the concurrence of that other Party.

(4) Subject to the provisions of Annex V, the designated airline(s) of each Party may make a change of gauge in the territory of the other Party or at an intermediate point or points on the specified route(s) provided that:

(a) operation beyond the point of change of gauge shall be performed by an aircraft having capacity less, for outbound services, or more, for inbound services, than that of the arriving aircraft.

(b) aircraft for such operations shall be scheduled in coincidence with the outbound or inbound aircraft, as the case may be, and may have the same flight number; and

(c) if a flight is delayed by operational or mechanical problems, the onward flight may operate without regard to the conditions in subparagraph (b) of this paragraph.

Charter Air Transportation

(1) In addition to the operation of the agreed services by the designated airlines of the two Parties, any airline(s) of one Party may request permission to operate passenger and/or cargo (separately or in combination) charter flights between the territories of the Parties as well as between a third country and the territory of the Party to which the requests are addressed. Each Party may provide to the other Party by diplomatic note a list of airlines qualified under the laws of the first Party to provide charter air transportation.

(2) The application for charter flight(s) shall be filed with the aeronautical authorities of the other Party at least fifteen (15) days before the anticipated flight(s). The flight(s) can be operated only after permission has been obtained. Permission shall be granted without undue delay in the spirit of equality of opportunity for the airlines of both Parties to operate international charter air transportation, mutual benefit and friendly cooperation.

(3) The aeronautical authorities of each Party shall minimize the filing requirements and other administrative burdens applicable to charterers and airlines of the other Party. In this connection, the charterers and airline of a Party shall not be required by the other Party to submit more than the following information in support of a request for permission to operate a charter flight or series of flights:

(a) Purpose of flight;

(b) Nationality of registration, owner and operator of aircraft;

(c) Type of aircraft;

(d) Either (i) identification marks and call signs of the aircraft, or (ii) flight number;

(e) Name of captain and number of crew members;

(f) The proposed flight plan (the air route, date, hours and destination);

(g) The identity of the charterer or charterers;

(h) The number of passengers, and/or the weight of cargo, on board; and

(i) The price charged by the airline to each charterer.

The information contained in the application for charter flight(s) and required by subparagraphs (d), (e) and (h) may be changed, subject to notification prior to each flight. Such changes shall be contained in the flight plan.

(4) In the event that either Party should have reasons to disapprove a particular charter flight or series of charter flights, it shall, under normal circumstances, give timely notification of the reasons therefor, and the applicant may, where appropriate, resubmit an application for approval of the requested flight or flights.

(5) Neither Party shall require the filing by airlines of the other Party of prices charged to the public for charter transportation originating in the territory of the other Party, or a third country.

(6) The provisions of Articles 2(4), 4, 5, 6, 7, 8, 9(2) and (4), 10, 11(1), and 14 and Annex III of this Agreement shall

apply *mutatis mutandis,* to charter air transportation.

Technical Services

I. Airports for Scheduled Service

(1) In accordance with Article 6, paragraph (1) of this Agreement, airlines designated by the Government of the People's Republic of China are assigned the following regular and alternate airports in the United States:

Regular Airports

New York, New York:
   JFK International Airport
Los Angeles, California:
   Los Angeles International Airport
San Francisco, California:
   San Francisco International Airport
Honolulu, Hawaii:
   Honolulu International Airport
Anchorage, Alaska:
   Anchorage International Airport

Alternate Airports

Baltimore, Maryland:
   Baltimore-Washington International Airport
Boston, Massachusetts:
   Logan International Airport
Newark, New Jersey:
   Newark International Airport
Philadelphia, Pennsylvania:
   Philadelphia International Airport
Pittsburgh, Pennsylvania:
   Greater Pittsburgh Airport
Moses Lake, Washington:
   Grant County Airport
Oakland, California:
   Metropolitan Oakland International Airport
Ontario, California:
   Ontario International Airport

Stockton, California:
   Stockton Metropolitan Airport
Hilo, Hawaii:
   Hilo International/General Lyman Airport
Seattle, Washington:
   Sea-Tac International Airport
Kansas City, Kansas:
   Kansas City International Airport
Fairbanks, Alaska:
   Fairbanks International Airport
Washington, D.C.:
   Dulles International Airport

(2) In accordance with Article 6, paragraph (1) of this Agreement, airlines designated by the Government of the United States of America are assigned the following regular and alternate airports in China:

Regular Airports

Beijing:
   Capital Airport
Shanghai:
   Hongqiao Airport

Alternate Airports

Guangzhou:
   Baiyun Airport
Hangzhou:
   Jianqiao Airport
Tianjin:
   Zhangguizhuang Airport

II. Airports for Charter Air Transportation

Aircraft of the airline(s) of each Party engaged in the operation of charter air transportation approved by the aeronautical authorities of the other Party may utilize airports appropriately identified in the Aeronautical Information Publication of that other Party as available for international flights, and such other airports as may be approached by such aeronautical authorities.

III. Air Routes

All flight operations by aircraft of the designated airline(s) of one Party operated in the airspace of the other Party shall be over established airways/prescribed routes or as cleared by the appropriate air traffic control service. Each Party will make reasonable efforts to ensure that air routes entering and within their sovereign airspace are as direct as practicable in the interest of economy, efficiency and fuel conservation, including the establishment of arrangements with controlling authorities of adjacent airspace as appropriate.

IV. Aeronautical Information

(1) The aeronautical authorities of both Parties shall provide each other with their Aeronautical Information Publication.

(2) Amendments and additions to the Aeronautical Information Publication shall be sent promptly to the aeronautical authorities of the other Party.

(3) The International NOTAM Code shall be used in the transmission of Notices to Airmen (NOTAMs). When the NOTAM code is not suitable, plain English shall be used. Urgent NOTAMs shall be transmitted by the quickest available means to the aeronautical authorities of the other Party.

(4) Aeronautical information and NOTAMs shall be made available in the English language.

V. Meteorological Services

Mutually acceptable meteorological service shall be provided in accordance with standards and recommended practices, to the extent to which they are applicable, developed pursuant to the Convention of the World Meteorological Organization and International Civil Aviation Organization.

VI. Radio Navigation and Communication

(1) For the operation of agreed services on the specified routes, the Parties recognize the requirement for the establishment of point-to-point aeronautical communications between the two countries. The Parties shall hold consultations as to the measures and procedures for the establishment of such communications.

(2) The English language and internationally accepted codes and procedures in force shall be applied in air-ground and point-to-point communications.

ANNEX IV

Conditions of Discount Fares

Discount fares within the zone of pricing flexibility described in paragraph (3) of Article 13 of this Agreement shall be subject to conditions of the type generally applicable to same or similar fares in other international air transportation markets. Such discount fares shall be subject to conditions in not less than four of the following categories:

• Round trip requirements;
• Advance-purchase requirements;
• Minimum-Maximum length of stay requirements;
• Stopover restrictions;
• Stopover charges;
• Transfer limitations;
• Cancellation refund penalties;
• Group size restrictions;
• Return travel conditions;
• Ground package requirements.

ANNEX V

Capacity and Carriage of Traffic

(1) The Parties agree that each designated airline shall have the right to operate two frequencies per week. If a Party does not designate a second airline, its first

designated airline shall, upon the commencement of service by the second airline of the other Party or upon the passage of two years from the commencement of any agreed service, whichever is earlier, be entitled to add to its operation two frequencies per week. For purposes of this Agreement a frequency is: one (1) round trip flight of an aircraft having a maximum certificated take-off gross weight not less than 710,000 pounds but not more than 800,000 pounds; one and one-half (1½) round trip flights of an aircraft having a maximum certified take-off gross weight equal to or greater than 430,000 pounds but less than 710,000 pounds; and two (2) round trip flights of an aircraft having a maximum certificated take-off gross weight less than 430,000 pounds. If a designated airline uses only aircraft having a maximum certificated take-off gross weight of less than 710,000 pounds, it shall be entitled to one additional round trip flight of an all-freight configured aircraft having a maximum certificated take-off gross weight of less than 430,000 pounds for every two frequencies. All unused frequencies may be accumulated by a designated airline and used at its discretion at any time. Any increase in frequencies during the first three years after commencement of any agreed service in excess of the frequencies as mentioned above shall be subject to prior consultation and agreement between the Parties.

(2) With a view to realizing the objectives set forth in Article 12, paragraph (2), the Parties agree that there should be a reasonable balance of the traffic carried by their respective designated airline(s) on the specified route(s) in terms of number of passengers and tons of cargo taken up and put down in the territory of the other Party.

The consultations referred to in Article 12, paragraph (6) shall take place as soon as possible, and in no event later than thirty (30) days following the date of receipt of the request by the latter Party. The Parties shall undertake to reach agreement within thirty (30) days as to effective measures for remedying the imbalanced situation and fully implement such agreed measures. In considering the measures to be undertaken, the Parties shall take into account all relevant factors, including commercial decisions of the designated airlines, load factors and actions of third parties. In case the agreed measures fail to remedy the imbalance within three months after their implementation, the Parties shall meet together to look into the cause of such failure and agree upon measures for remedying the imbalanced situation. In case the Parties fail to reach agreement on effective remedial measures, they shall look into the cause of the imbalance and consider amendments to this Agreement which may be required to eliminate such cause.

(3) The provision of paragraph (2) of this Annex is valid for three years from the date of commencement of any service under this Agreement. Not later than six months prior to the end of this three-year period, the Parties shall consult with a view to agreeing to the means to achieve reasonable balance of traffic referred to in paragraph (2) of this Annex.

———

Beijing
September 8, 1980

Mr. Lin Zheng
Leader
Civil Aviation Delegation
   of the Government of China

Dear Mr. Lin:

I have the honor to refer to the Agreement between the Government of the United States of America and the Government of the People's Republic of China relating to Civil Air Transport initialed today by our two governments. During the course of negotiations leading to the initialing of the Agreement, both sides discussed questions relating to the conduct of business in the territory of the other Party and other operational matters of the designated airlines. I understand that agreement was reached that the designated airline(s) of each Party shall have, in the territory of the other Party, the rights and privileges as set forth below:

1. With respect to the representative offices(s) referred to in Article 11, paragraph (3) of the Agreement, the designated airline(s) of each Party shall have:

(a) the right to issue, reissue, reconfirm and exchange tickets for transportation on the agreed services, for connecting air services, and for transportation over any other route or routes outside of the agreed services which are operated by such airline(s); and

(b) the right to make, reconfirm, or change reservations for passengers wishing to travel over the routes of such airline(s) whether or not such reservations are for transportation on the agreed services.

2. The designated airline(s) of each Party shall also have the right to import, maintain, store, and distribute informational materials (including, but not limited to, time tables, schedules, brochures, sales and tour literature, calendars, displays, etc.) and to advertise in the same manner and through the same or similar media as the designated airline(s) of the other Party.

3. With respect to operational matters, the designated airline(s) of each Party shall have:

(a) the right to import, install, and operate telex, computer, VHF radio, and handheld radio sets (walkie talkie) and related equipment for reservations, load planning and management, and for other operational purposes, subject to the approval of the appropriate authorities, where necessary;

(b) the right to supervise load planning and actual loading and unloading of its aircraft through its own employees or representatives;

(c) the right to import company-owned vehicles and to operate such vehicles on airport roadways and aircraft servicing ramps, subject to the approval of the appropriate authorities, where necessary;

(d) the right to inspect fuel storage and fuel pumping equipment on a quarterly basis and take samples at each source for export and subsequent laboratory analysis; and

(e) the right to film, under whatever supervision is necessary, the aircraft approach view to the runways of all regular airports and alternate airports contemplated for the operation of the agreed services, for purposes of pilot training, subject to the approval of the appropriate authorities.

4. Each Party grants to the other Party the assurance that the following authorizations, permits, and information will be provided, on the basis of reciprocity, in a timely fashion to each airline designated to operate the agreed services:

(a) airport security permits for assigned foreign and locally employed company staff authorizing them to move freely beyond airport customs and immigration screens into the terminal loading areas and onto the airport ramp areas;

(b) written information on the procedures to be employed by the airport authorities at each regular airport and alternate airport contemplated for the operation of the agreed services in the event of an emergency such as a crash, a hijacking, or a bomb threat, establishing the order of action in a given situation for units responsible for tower control, firefighting, medical assistance and transportation, perimeter security and other emergency and security functions in effect; and

(c) written information on aeronautical laws, including the rules and regulations thereunder and amendments thereto, each designated airline is expected to follow.

5. The appropriate authorities of each Party shall use their best efforts to assist the designated airline(s) of the other Party to receive housing for the staff of such airline(s) comparable in cost and quality to the best obtained by or provided to other foreign airlines.

6. The designated airline(s) of each Party shall have the right to train the personnel of any appointed agent in the procedures of that airline for passenger, cargo, and aircraft handling and in procedures relating to reservations, ticketing, marketing, management, and sales promotion, subject to prior agreement.

This letter will be effective on the date the Civil Air Transport Agreement is signed.

I would be grateful for your confirmation that this is also your understanding of the agreement we have reached.

Sincerely,
B. BOYD HIGHT
Chairman
Civil Aviation Delegation
of the Government of the
United States

Attachment: Initialed Translation

Beijing
September 8, 1980

Mr. B. Boyd Hight
Chairman
Civil Aviation Delegation of
the Government of the United States

Dear Mr. Hight:

I have the honor to refer to the Civil Air Transport Agreement initialed today by our two governments and to your letter of today's date which reads as follows:*

I have the honor to confirm that the above constitutes an agreed understanding between our two governments concerning the rights of the designated airline(s) of each Party in the territory of the other Party.

This letter will be effective on the date the Civil Air Transport Agreement is signed.

Sincerely,
LIN ZHENG
Leader
Civil Aviation Delegation
of the Government of China

Beijing
September 8, 1980

Mr. B. Boyd Hight
Chairman
Civil Aviation Delegation
of the Government of the United States

Dear Mr. Hight:

I have the honor to refer to the Agreement between the Government of the People's Republic of China and the Government of the United States of America Relating to Civil Air Transport, initialed today by our two governments. During the course of negotiations leading to the initialing of the Agreement, both sides discussed questions relating to the utilization of full traffic rights at a point or points in Japan in the operation of the agreed services. It is my understanding that agreement was reached that the utilization of full traffic rights at Japan by the designated airlines of both sides shall be governed by the following terms:

---

*EDITORIAL NOTE: The text of the Chairman's letter is restated in full and is printed on page 1788.

(1) The first designated airline of each Party, unless otherwise agreed, shall be permitted to operate two frequencies [1] with full traffic rights at Japan immediately upon the commencement of the agreed services. Two years following the commencement of any agreed service, the second designated airline of each Party, unless otherwise agreed, shall be permitted to operate two frequencies with full traffic rights at Japan. These rights shall continue until otherwise agreed by the Parties.

(2) If, two years after the commencement of any agreed service, the United States does not designate a second airline, or if one of the United States' two designated airlines does not operate all of the Japan frequencies authorized by paragraph (1) above, the Parties shall consult with a view to agreeing on the utilization of the unused Japan frequencies by the United States.

(3) The designated airline(s) of the People's Republic of China shall operate more than two Japan frequencies only if, and to the same extent that, the designated airline(s) of the United States are operating singly or in combination more than two Japan frequencies.

(4) Not later than two and one-half years following the commencement of any agreed service, the Parties shall review their respective utilization of Japan frequencies. If, upon such review, the number of Japan frequencies operated by the U.S. designated airline(s) exceeds the number of Japan frequencies which the Government of the People's Republic of China and the Government of Japan have agreed upon for the Chinese designated airline(s), the Parties shall consult with a view to agreeing upon an alternative opportunity or opportunities for the Chinese designated airline(s).

(5) If, by 90 days prior to the end of the third year following the commencement of any agreed service, the Parties have not agreed upon an alternative opportunity or opportunities, the People's Republic of China shall be entitled to select point services [2] for operation in the fourth year and thereafter equal to the difference between the number of Japan frequencies operated by the U.S. designated airline(s) and the number of Japan frequencies authorized for the Chinese designated airline(s). The Chinese designated airline(s) shall be entitled to operate such point services at one or more intermediate and/or beyond points selected at the sole discretion of the People's Republic of China. A list of intermediate and/or beyond points so selected shall be furnished to the Government of the United States through diplomatic channels not later than 60 days prior to the commencement of operations. The number of point services operated by the Chinese designated airline(s) shall be reduced by one for each new Japan frequency which the Chinese designated airline(s) is authorized to operate subsequent to the selection of point services.

This letter will be effective on the date the Civil Air Transport Agreement is signed.

> Sincerely,
> Lin Zheng
> *Leader*
> *Civil Aivation Delegation of the Government of China*

---

[1] For the purposes of this understanding, "frequency" shall have the same meaning as that set forth in Annex V, paragraph (1) of the Agreement.

[2] The term "point service" means one weekly frequency with full traffic rights at a point.

Beijing
September 8, 1980

Mr. Lin Zheng
Leader,
Civil Aviation Delegation
of the Government of China

Dear Mr. Lin:

I am in receipt of your letter of today's date relating to the Agreement between the Government of the United States of America and the Government of the People's Republic of China Relating to Civil Air Transport initialed today by our two governments, and more particularly relating to the utilization of full traffic rights at a point or points in Japan in the operation of the agreed services. Your letter reads as follows: *

I have the honor to confirm that the above constitutes an agreed understanding.

This letter will be effective on the date the Civil Air Transport Agreement is signed.

Sincerely,
B. BOYD HIGHT
Chairman
Civil Aviation Delegation of the Government of the United States

Attachment: Initialed Translation

———

Beijing
September 8, 1980

Mr. Lin Zheng
Leader
Civil Aviation Delegation
of the Government of China

Dear Mr. Lin:

I have the honor to refer to the Civil Air Transport Agreement initialed today

———

*EDITORIAL NOTE: The text of the Leader's letter is restated in full and is printed on page 1790.

by our two governments. With respect to paragraph (1) of Annex V to the Agreement, it is my understanding that in case the first designated airline of the People's Republic of China does not operate more than two B–747SP aircraft per week during the period of one year following its commencement of the agreed services, for this same period the designated airline of the United States of America will limit its available capacity to an average of 120 tons of payload per week, measured quarterly. Payload will be measured by the actual tons of passenger, cargo and mail traffic, embarked or disembarked in the People's Republic of China quarterly.

This letter will be effective on the date the Civil Air Transport Agreement is signed.

Sincerely,
B. BOYD HIGHT
Chairman
Civil Aviation Delegation of the Government of the United States

Attachment: Initialed Translation

———

Beijing
September 8, 1980

Mr. B. Boyd Hight
Chairman
Civil Aviation Delegation of
the Government of the United States

Dear Mr. Hight:

I am in receipt of your letter of today's date relating to the Agreement between the Government of the United States of America and the Government of the People's Republic of China relating to Civil Air Transport initialed today by our two governments, and more particularly relating to Annex V (1) setting forth a capacity regime to govern the operations of the designated airline of each Party during the first year following the commencement of the agreed services by the first designated airline of the People's Republic of China. Your letter reads as follows: *

I have the honor to confirm that the above constitutes an agreed understanding.

This letter will be effective on the date the Civil Air Transport Agreement is signed.

> Sincerely,
> LIN ZHENG
> *Leader*
> *Civil Aviation Delegation of the Government of China*

——————

Beijing
September 8, 1980

Mr. B. Boyd Hight
Chairman
Civil Aviation Delegation of
the Government of the United States

Dear Mr. Hight:

With reference to Annex V, paragraph (2) of the Agreement between the Government of the People's Republic of China and the Government of the United States of America relating to Civil Air Transport initialed today, I have the honor to confirm, on behalf of my Government, the following discussion between the civil aviation delegations of our two countries in the course of their negotiations.

In the operation of the agreed services on the specified routes by the designated airlines of the Parties, it is deemed that traffic will no longer be reasonably balanced whenever, on a semi-annual basis, the traffic carried by the designated airline(s) of one Party shall exceed 56.25 percent of the total traffic carried by the designated airlines of the two Parties.

——————

* EDITORIAL NOTE: The text of the Chairman's letter is restated in full and is printed on page 1792.

This letter will be effective on the date the Civil Air Transport Agreement is signed.

> Sincerely,
> LIN ZHENG
> *Leader*
> *Civil Aviation Delegation of the Government of China*

——————

Beijing
September 8, 1980

Mr. Lin Zheng
Leader
Civil Aviation Delegation
of the Government of China

Dear Mr. Lin:

I am in receipt of your letter of today's date with respect to Annex V, paragraph (2) of the Civil Air Transport Agreement initialed today by our two governments, and acknowledge the contents therein.

This letter will be effective on the date the Civil Air Transport Agreement is signed.

> Sincerely,
> B. BOYD HIGHT
> *Chairman*
> *Civil Aviation Delegation of the Government of the United States*

Attachment: Initialed Translation

——————

September 17, 1980

Mr. Lin Zheng
Leader
Civil Aviation Delegation
of the Government of China

Dear Mr. Lin:

I have the honor to confirm that the Government of the United States of America is prepared, within its authority, to make clear in its official publications and statements that "China Airlines" is an airline from Taiwan and is not the national flag carrier of China.

Sincerely,

B. BOYD HIGHT
Chairman
Civil Aviation Delegation of the Government of the United States

NOTE: As printed above, the agreement, annexes, and letters follow the texts printed in Selected Documents No. 18, U.S.-China Agreements, September 17, 1980, United States Department of State, Bureau of Public Affairs.

United States-People's Republic of China Agreements

Textile Agreement.   September 17, 1980

AGREEMENT RELATING TO TRADE IN COTTON, WOOL, AND MAN-MADE FIBER TEXTILES AND TEXTILE PRODUCTS BETWEEN THE UNITED STATES OF AMERICA AND THE PEOPLE'S REPUBLIC OF CHINA

The Government of the United States of America and the Government of the People's Republic of China, as a result of discussions concerning exports to the United States of America of cotton, wool, and man-made fiber textiles and textile products manufactured in the People's Republic of China, agree to enter into the following Agreement relating to trade in cotton, wool, and man-made fiber textiles and textile products between the United States of America and the People's Republic of China (hereinafter referred to as "the Agreement"):

1. The two Governments reaffirm their commitments under the Agreement on Trade Relations between the United States of America and the People's Republic of China as the basis of their trade and economic relations.

2. The term of the Agreement shall be the three-year period from January 1, 1980 through December 31, 1982. Each "Agreement Year" shall be a calendar year.

3. (a) The system of categories and the rates of conversion into square yards equivalent listed in Annex A shall apply in implementing the Agreement.

(b) For purposes of the Agreement, categories 347, 348 and 645, 646 are merged and treated as single categories 347/348 and 645/646 respectively.

4. (a) Commencing with the first Agreement Year, and during the subsequent term of the Agreement, the Government of the People's Republic of China shall limit annual exports from China to the United States of America of cotton, wool, and man-made fiber textiles and textile products to the specific limits set out in Annex B, as such limits may be adjusted in accordance with paragraphs 5 and 7. The limits in Annex B include growth. Exports shall be charged to limits for the year in which exported. The limits set out in Annex B do not include any of the adjustments permitted under paragraphs 5 and 7.

(b) With respect to Category 340, 200,-000 dozens of the quantity exported in 1979 shall be charged against the Specific Limit for that Category for the first Agreement Year.

(c) With respect to Category 645/646, 48,000 dozens of the quantity exported in 1980 will be entered without charge.

5. (a) Any specific limit may be exceeded in any Agreement Year by not more than the following percentage of its square yards equivalent total listed in Annex B, provided that the amount of the increase is compensated for by an equiv-

alent SYE decrease in one or more other specific limits for that Agreement Year.

Category:	Percentage
331	6
339	5
340	5
341	5
347/348	5
645/646	6

(b) No limit may be decreased pursuant to sub-paragraph 5(a) to a level which is below the level of exports charged against that category limit for that Agreement Year.

(c) When informing the United States of adjustments under the provisions of this paragraph, the Government of the People's Republic of China shall indicate the category or categories to be increased and the category or categories to be decreased by commensurate quantities in square yards equivalent.

6. The Government of the People's Republic of China shall use its best efforts to space exports from China to the United States within each category evenly throughout each Agreement Year, taking into consideration normal seasonal factors. Exports from China in excess of authorized levels for each Agreement Year will, if allowed entry into the United States, be charged to the applicable level for the succeeding Agreement Year.

7. (a) In any Agreement Year, exports may exceed by a maximum of 11 percent any limit set out in Annex B by allocating to such limit for that Agreement Year an unused portion of the corresponding limit for the previous Agreement Year ("carryover") or a portion of the corresponding limit for the succeeding Agreement Year ("carryforward") subject to the following conditions:

(1) Carryover may be utilized as available up to 11 percent of the receiving Agreement Year's limits provided, however, that no carryover shall be available for application during the first Agreement Year;

(2) Carryforward may be utilized up to seven percent of the receiving Agreement Year's applicable limits and shall be charged against the immediately following Agreement Year's corresponding limits;

(3) The combination of carryover and carryforward shall not exceed 11 percent of the receiving Agreement Year's applicable limit in any Agreement Year;

(4) Carryover of shortfall (as defined in sub-paragraph 7(b)) shall not be applied to any limits until the Governments of the United States of America and the People's Republic of China have agreed upon the amounts of shortfall involved.

(b) For purposes of the Agreement, a shortfall occurs when exports of textiles or textile products from China to the United States of America during an Agreement Year are below any specific limit as set out in Annex B, (or, in the case of any limit decreased pursuant to paragraph 5, when such exports are below the limit as so decreased). In the Agreement Year following the shortfall, such exports from China to the United States of America may be permitted to exceed the applicable limits, subject to conditions of sub-paragraph 7(a), by carryover of shortfalls in the following manner:

(1) The carryover shall not exceed the amount of shortfall in any applicable limit;

(2) The shortfall shall be used in the category in which the shortfall occurred.

(c) The total adjustment permissible under paragraph 7 for the first Agreement Year shall be seven percent consisting solely of carryforward.

8. (a) In the event that the Government of the United States believes that

imports from the People's Republic of China classified in any category or categories not covered by Specific Limits are, due to market disruption, threatening to impede the orderly development of trade between the two countries, the Government of the United States may request consultations with the Government of the People's Republic of China with a view to avoiding such market disruption. The Government of the United States of America shall provide the Government of the People's Republic of China at the time of the request with a detailed factual statement of the reasons and justification for its request for consultation, with current data, which in the view of the Government of the United States of America shows ·

1) the existence or threat of market disruption, and

2) the contribution of exports from the People's Republic of China to that disruption.

(b) The Government of the People's Republic of China agrees to consult with the Government of the United States within 30 days of receipt of a request for consultations. Both sides agree to make every effort to reach agreement on a mutually satisfactory resolution of the issue within 90 days of the receipt of the request, unless this period is extended by mutual agreement.

(c) During the 90 day period, the Government of the People's Republic of China agrees to hold its exports to the United States of America in the category or categories subject to this consultation to a level no greater than 35 percent of the amount entered in the latest twelve month period for which data are available.

(d) If no mutually satisfactory solution is reached during these consultations, the People's Republic of China will limit its exports in the category or categories under this consultation for the succeeding twelve months to a level of 20 percent for man-made fiber and cotton product categories (and of 6 percent for wool product categories) above the level of imports entered during the first twelve of the most recent fourteen months preceding the date of the request for consultations.

9. To prevent inadvertent or fraudulent circumvention of the Agreement, to ensure accurate record keeping, and to facilitate proper entry into the United States of the products covered by the Agreement, a Visa System shall be established as soon as practicable as an administrative arrangement under the Agreement.

10. The Government of the United States of America shall promptly supply the Government of the People's Republic of China with monthly data on imports of textiles from China, and the Government of the People's Republic of China shall promptly supply the Government of the United States of America with quarterly data on exports of China's textiles to the United States in categories for which levels have been established. Each Government agrees to supply promptly any other pertinent and readily available statistical data requested by the other Government.

11. (a) Tops, yarns, piece goods, made-up articles, garments, and other textile manufactured products (being products which derive their chief characteristics from their textile components) of cotton, wool, man-made fibers, or blends thereof,

in which any or all of these fibers in combination represent either the chief value of the fibers or 50 percent or more by weight (or 17 percent or more by weight of wool) of the product, are subject to the Agreement.

(b) For purposes of the Agreement, textiles and textile products shall be classified as cotton, wool or man-made fiber textiles if wholly or in chief value of either of these fibers.

(c) Any product covered by subparagraph 11(a) but not in chief value of cotton, wool, or man-made fiber shall be classified as: (I) cotton textiles if containing 50 percent or more by weight of cotton or if the cotton component exceeds by weight the wool and the man-made fiber components; (II) wool textiles if not cotton and the wool equals or exceeds 17 percent by weight of all component fibers; (III) man-made fiber textiles if neither of the foregoing applies.

12. The Government of the United States of America and the Government of the People's Republic of China agree to consult on any question arising in the implementation of the Agreement.

13. Mutually satisfactory administrative arrangements or adjustments may be made to resolve minor problems arising in the implementation of this Agreement, including differences in points of procedure or operation.

14. If the Government of the People's Republic of China considers that, as a result of a limitation specified in this Agreement, China is being placed in an inequitable position vis-a-vis a third country or party, the Government of the People's Republic of China may request consultations with the Government of the United States of America with a view to taking appropriate remedial action such as reasonable modification of this Agreement and the Government of the United States of America shall agree to hold such consultations.

15. At the request of either Government, the two Governments will undertake a major review of the Agreement at the end of the second Agreement Year.

16. Each Government will take such measures as may be necessary to ensure that the Specific Limits established for any categories under this Agreement are not exceeded. Calculations will be based on the date of export from the People's Republic of China. Neither Government shall act to restrain the trade in textile products covered by the Agreement except in accordance with the terms of the Agreement.

17. Either Government may terminate the Agreement effective at the end of any Agreement Year by written notice to the other Government to be given at least 90 days prior to the end of such Agreement Year. Either Government may at any time propose revisions in the terms of the Agreement.

DONE at Washington, in duplicate, in the English and Chinese languages, both texts being equally authentic, this seventeenth day of September, 1980.

For the Government of the United States
  of America:

JIMMY CARTER

For the Government of the People's Republic of China:

BO YIBO

ANNEX A

M and B = Men's and Boys'
W, G, and I = Women's, Girls', and Infants
n.k. = not Knit

Category	Description	Conversion Factor	Unit of Measure
YARN			
Cotton			
300	Carded	4. 6	Lb.
301	Combed	4. 6	Lb.
Wool			
400	Tops and yarns	2. 0	Lb.
Man-made Fiber			
600	Textured	3. 5	Lb.
601	Cont. cellulosic	5. 2	Lb.
602	Cont. noncellulosic	11. 6	Lb.
603	Spun cellulosic	3. 4	Lb.
604	Spun noncellulosic	4. 1	Lb.
605	Other yarns	3. 5	Lb.
FABRIC			
Cotton			
310	Ginghams	1. 0	SYD
311	Velveteens	1. 0	SYD
312	Corduroy	1. 0	SYD
313	Sheeting	1. 0	SYD
314	Broadcloth	1. 0	SYD
315	Printcloths	1. 0	SYD
316	Shirtings	1. 0	SYD
317	Twills and Sateens	1. 0	SYD
318	Yarn-dyed	1. 0	SYD
319	Duck	1. 0	SYD
320	Other Fabrics, n.k.	1. 0	SYD
Wool			
410	Woolen and worsted	1. 0	SYD
411	Tapestries and upholstery	1. 0	SYD
425	Knit	2. 0	Lb.
429	Other Fabrics	1. 0	SYD
Man-Made fiber			
610	Cont. cellulosic, n.k.	1. 0	SYD
611	Spun cellulosic, n.k.	1. 0	SYD
612	Cont. noncellulosic, n.k.	1. 0	SYD
613	Spun noncellulosic, n.k.	1. 0	SYD
614	Other fabrics, n.k.	1. 0	SYD
625	Knit	7. 8	Lb.
626	Pile and tufted	1. 0	SYD
627	Specialty	7. 8	Lb.
APPAREL			
Cotton			
330	Handkerchiefs	1. 7	Dz.
331	Gloves	3. 5	DPR

ANNEX A—Continued

M and B=Men's and Boys'
W, G, and I=Women's, Girls', and Infants
n.k.=not Knit

Category	Description	Conversion Factor	Unit of Measure
APPAREL—Continued			
Cotton—Continued			
332	Hosiery	4. 6	DPR
333	Suit-type coats, M and B	36. 2	Dz.
334	Other coats, M and B	41. 3	Dz.
335	Coats, W, G, and I	41. 3	Dz.
336	Dresses (incl. uniforms)	45. 3	Dz.
337	Playsuits, Sunsuits, Washsuits, Creepers	25. 0	Dz.
338	Knit shirts, (incl. T-Shirts, other sweatshirts) M and B.	7. 2	Dz.
339	Knit shirts and blouses (incl. T-Shirts, other sweatshirts) W, G and I.	7. 2	Dz.
340	Shirts, n.k	24. 0	Dz.
341	Blouses, n.k	14. 5	Dz.
342	Skirts	17. 8	Dz.
345	Sweaters	36. 8	Dz.
347	Trousers, slacks, and shorts (outer) M and B. .	17. 8	Dz.
348	Trousers, slacks and shorts (outer) W, G and I.	17. 8	Dz.
349	Brassieres, etc.	4. 8	Dz.
350	Dressing gowns, incl. bathrobes, and beach house coats, and dusters.	51. 0	Dz.
351	Pajamas and other nightwear	52. 0	Dz.
352	Underwear (incl. union suits)	11. 0	Dz.
359	Other apparel	4. 6	Lb.
Wool			
431	Gloves	2. 1	DPR
432	Hosiery	2. 8	DPR
433	Suit-Type coats, M and B	36. 0	Dz.
434	Other Coats, M and B	54. 0	Dz.
435	Coats, W, G and I	54. 0	Dz.
436	Dresses	49. 2	Dz.
438	Knit Shirts and Blouses	15. 0	Dz.
440	Shirts and Blouses, n.k.	24. 0	Dz.
442	Skirts	18. 0	Dz.
443	Suits, M and B	54. 0	Dz.
444	Suits, W, G and I	54. 0	Dz.
445	Sweaters, M and B	14. 88	Dz.
446	Sweaters, W, G and I	14. 88	Dz.
447	Trousers, slacks and shorts (outer) M and B. .	18. 0	Dz.
448	Trousers, slacks and shorts (outer) W, G and I.	18. 0	Dz.
459	Other Wool Apparel	2. 0	Lb.

ANNEX A—Continued

M and B=Men's and Boy's
W, G, and I=Women's, Girls', and Infants
n.k.=not Knit

Category	Description	Conversion Factor	Unit of Measure
APPAREL—Continued			
Man-made fiber			
630.........	Handkerchiefs...........................	1.7	Dz.
631.........	Gloves.................................	3.5	DPR
632.........	Hosiery................................	4.6	DPR
633.........	Suit-type Coats, M and B..............	36.2	Dz.
634.........	Other Coats, M and B..................	41.3	Dz.
635.........	Coats, W, G and I.....................	41.3	Dz.
636.........	Dresses................................	45.3	Dz.
637.........	Playsuits, Sunsuits, Washsuits, etc..........	21.3	Dz.
638.........	Knit Shirts (incl. T-Shirts), M and B.....	18.0	Dz.
639.........	Knit Shirts and Blouses (incl. T-Shirts), W, G and I	15.0	Dz.
640.........	Shirts, n.k............................	24.0	Dz.
641.........	Blouses, n.k...........................	14.5	Dz.
642.........	Skirts.................................	17.8	Dz.
643.........	Suits, M and B........................	54.0	Dz.
644.........	Suits, W, G and I.....................	54.0	Dz.
645.........	Sweaters, M and B....................	36.8	Dz.
646.........	Sweaters, W, G and I.................	36.8	Dz.
647.........	Trousers, slacks and shorts (outer), M and B.	17.8	Dz.
648.........	Trousers, slacks and shorts (outer), W, G and I	17.8	Dz.
649.........	Brassieres, etc........................	4.8	Dz.
650.........	Dressing gowns, incl. bath and beach robes	51.0	Dz.
651.........	Pajamas and other nightwear..............	52.0	Dz.
652.........	Underwear.............................	16.0	Dz.
659.........	Other Apparel.........................	7.8	Lb.
MADE-UPS AND MISC.			
Cotton			
360.........	Pillowcases............................	1.1	No.
361.........	Sheets................................	6.2	No.
362.........	Bedspreads and Quilts..................	6.2	No.
363.........	Terry and other pile towels..............	0.5	No.
369.........	Other Cotton manufactures..............	4.6	Lb.
Wool			
464.........	Blankets and auto robes.................	1.3	Lb.
465.........	Floor Covering........................	0.1	SFT
469.........	Other Wool manufactures................	2.0	Lb.
Man-made Fiber			
665.........	Floor Coverings.......................	0.1	SFT
666.........	Other Furnishings......................	7.8	Lb.
669.........	Other man-made manufactures............	7.8	Lb.

ANNEX B

SPECIFIC LIMITS

Category	Brief Description	First Agreement Year	Second Agreement Year	Third Agreement Year
331..........	Cotton Gloves			
	Dozen pair....................	3, 213, 600	3, 310, 008	3, 409, 308
	SYE.........................	11, 247, 600	11, 585, 028	11, 932, 578
339..........	Knit Shirts & Blouses, W, G, & I			
	Dozen........................	720, 000	912, 000	865, 280
	SYE.........................	5, 184, 000	6, 566, 400	6, 230, 016
340..........	Shirts, M and B, not knit			
	Dozen........................	540, 000	561, 600	584, 064
	SYE.........................	12, 960, 000	13, 478, 400	14, 017, 536
341..........	Blouses, W, G, & I, not knit			
	Dozen........................	381, 300	455, 100	443, 456
	SYE.........................	5, 528, 850	6, 598, 950	6, 430, 112
347/348......	Trousers			
	Dozen........................	1, 440, 000	1, 824, 000	1, 730, 560
	SYE.........................	25, 632, 000	32, 467, 200	30, 803, 968
645/646......	Sweaters			
	Dozen........................	550, 000	566, 500	583, 495
	SYE.........................	20, 240, 000	20, 847, 200	21, 472, 616

NOTE: As printed above, the agreement and annexes follow the texts printed in Selected Documents No. 18, United States-China Agreements, September 17, 1980, United States Department of State, Bureau of Public Affairs.

United States-People's Republic of China Agreements

Maritime Transport Agreement.
September 17, 1980

AGREEMENT ON MARITIME TRANSPORT BETWEEN THE GOVERNMENT OF THE UNITED STATES OF AMERICA AND THE GOVERNMENT OF THE PEOPLE'S REPUBLIC OF CHINA

The Government of the United States of America and the Government of the People's Republic of China

In conformity with the spirit of the Joint Communique on the Establishment of Diplomatic Relations between the United States of America and the People's Republic of China of December 15, 1978; and

Recognizing the importance of maritime relations for both countries; and

In consideration of the significance of maritime transport in the development and facilitation of trade between both countries; and

For the purpose of strengthening their cooperation in the field of maritime transport; and

In accordance with the principle of equality and mutual benefit

Have agreed as follows:

ARTICLE 1

For purposes of this Agreement:

a. The term "vessel" shall mean any merchant ship engaged in commercial maritime shipping or merchant marine training. The term "vessel" shall not include warships; vessels carrying out any form of state function except for those mentioned in the preceding sentence; or fishing vessels; fishery research vessels or fishery support vessels.

b. The term "vessel of a Party" shall mean a vessel flying the national flag of and registered in the United States of America or the People's Republic of China respectively.

c. The term "member of the crew" shall mean a person working on board a vessel of a Party who actually performs duties or services connected with the operation or maintenance of the vessel, holding appropriate identity documents issued by the authorities of that Party as provided in Article 5, and whose name is included on the crew list of the vessel.

ARTICLE 2

a. The Parties agree that when vessels of either Party, for the purpose of transportation of passengers and cargo, enter into or depart from the ports, mooring places and waters of the other Party, the latter shall adopt all appropriate measures to provide favorable treatment to such vessels with regard to servicing of vessels, port operations, the simplification and expedition of administrative, customs and all required formalities. The conditions under which vessels of one Party may enter the ports of the other Party are set forth in letters, exchanged between the competent authorities, which accompany this Agreement.

b. Each Party undertakes to ensure that tonnage duties upon vessels of the other Party will be as favorable as the charges imposed in like situations with respect to vessels of any other country.

ARTICLE 3

This Agreement shall not apply to the vessels of one Party in the transportation of passengers and cargo between the ports of the other Party. However, the right of vessels of either Party to engage in commercial passenger and cargo services in accordance with Article 2 shall include the right to pick up or discharge passengers and cargo at more than one port of the other Party if such passengers and cargo are destined for or are proceeding from another country on the same vessel.

ARTICLE 4

a. Each Party shall recognize the nationality of the vessels which fly the national flag of the other Party and hold certificates of their nationality issued according to the laws and regulations of the other Party.

b. Each Party shall recognize the tonnage certificates and other ship's documents issued by the competent authorities of the other Party to the extent permitted by applicable laws and regulations.

c. Each Party shall inform the other Party of any changes in its system of tonnage measurements.

ARTICLE 5

Each Party shall recognize the identity documents of crew members issued by the competent authorities of the other Party. Those issued by the United States of America shall be the "U.S. Merchant Mariner's Document" while those issued by the People's Republic of China shall be the "Seaman's Book". Should any change in the identity document of a Party occur, such change shall be communicated to the other Party.

ARTICLE 6

a. Members of the crew of vessels of either Party shall be permitted to go ashore during the stay of their vessel in the ports of the other Party, in accordance with its applicable laws and regulations.

b. Each Party may deny entry into its territory of a member of the crew of a vessel of the other Party in accordance with its applicable laws and regulations.

c. Members of the crew of vessels of either Party requiring hospitalization shall be permitted to enter into and remain in the territory of the other Party for the period of time necessary for medical treatment, in accordance with applicable laws and regulations of that Party.

d. Members of the crew of vessels of either Party holding documents as stipulated in Article 5 of this Agreement may enter the territory or travel through the territory of the other Party for the purpose of joining national vessels, for repatriation or for any other reason acceptable to the competent authorities of the other Party, after complying with the applicable laws and regulations of that Party.

ARTICLE 7

a. Should a vessel of either Party be involved in a maritime accident or encounter any other danger in the ports, mooring places and waters of the other Party, the latter shall give friendly treatment and all possible assistance to the passengers, crew members, cargo and vessel.

b. When a vessel of one Party is involved in a maritime accident or encoun-

ters any other danger and its cargo and other property is removed therefrom and landed in the territory of the other Party, such cargo and other property shall not be subject to any customs duties by that Party, unless it enters into its domestic consumption. Storage charges incurred shall be just, reasonable and non-discriminatory.

c. Each Party shall promptly notify the consular officials or in their absence the diplomatic representatives, of the other Party when one of its vessels is in distress, and inform them of measures taken for the rescue and protection of the crew members, passengers, vessel, cargo and stores.

ARTICLE 8

a. Each Party recognizes the interest of the other Party in carrying a substantial part of its foreign trade in vessels of its own flag and both Parties intend that their national flag vessels will each carry equal and substantial shares of the bilateral trade between the two nations.

b. Each Party, where it directs the selection of the carrier of its export or import cargoes, shall provide to vessels under the flag of the other Party a general cargo share and a bulk share equal in each category to those vessels under its flag, and consistent with the intention of the Parties that their national flag vessels will carry not less than one-third of bilateral cargoes.

c. Whenever vessels under the flag of one Party are not available to carry cargo offered for carriage between ports served by such vessels with reasonable notice and upon reasonable terms and conditions of carriage, the offering Party shall be free to direct such cargo to its national flag or third flag vessels.

d. When bulk cargo is carried between the United States and the People's Republic of China such cargo shall be carried at a mutually acceptable rate. Each Party, where it has the power to select the carrier, shall offer such cargo to vessels of the other Party at rates, terms and conditions of carriage which are fair and reasonable for such vessels.

ARTICLE 9

Each Party recognizes the interest of the other, through domestic legislation or policy, in regulating the conduct of cross-traders in their respective foreign ocean commerce and agrees to respect each other's laws and policies in this regard.

ARTICLE 10

Payments for transportation services under this Agreement shall either be effected in freely convertible currencies mutually accepted by firms, companies and corporations and trading organizations of the two countries, or made otherwise in accordance with agreements signed by and between the two Parties to the transaction. Parties to such transactions may convert and remit to their country, on demand, local revenues in excess of sums locally disbursed. Conversion and remittance shall be permitted promptly without restrictions in respect thereof at the rate of exchange applicable to current transactions and remittances. Neither Party may impose restrictions on such payments except in time of declared national emergency.

ARTICLE 11

The Parties agree to enter into such technical personnel and information exchanges necessary to facilitate and accelerate the movement of cargo at sea and in ports and to promote cooperation between their respective merchant marines.

ARTICLE 12

a. For the implementation of this Agreement the competent authority of the United States of America shall be the Department of Commerce while that of the People's Republic of China shall be the Ministry of Communications. Each Party shall authorize its competent authority to take action under its laws and procedures, and in consultations with the competent authority of the other Party, to implement this Agreement.

b. The Parties agree that representatives of the competent authorities will meet annually for a comprehensive view of matters related to the Agreement as may be desirable. Such meetings will be held at a time and place agreeable to both Parties. The Parties also agree to engage in such consultations, exchange such information, and take such action as may be necessary to ensure effective operation of this Agreement.

ARTICLE 13

This Agreement shall be in force for three years from the date of signing and shall expire on September 17, 1983. This Agreement may be extended, subject to negotiations between the Parties prior to the expiration date. The Agreement may also be terminated by either Party on 90 days written notice.

DONE at Washington, this seventeenth day of September 1980 in duplicate, each copy in the English and Chinese languages, both texts being equally authentic.

For the Government of the United States of America:

JIMMY CARTER

For the Government of the People's Republic of China:

BO YIBO

ACCOMPANYING LETTERS

September 17, 1980

Mr. Dong Huamin
Director
Bureau of Foreign Affairs
Ministry of Communications
Beijing, People's Republic of China

Dear Mr. Dong:

In connection with the Agreement on Maritime Transport concluded on this date between the Government of the United States of America and the Government of the People's Republic of China, and, in particular, Article 2 of that Agreement, I have the honor to confirm that the following conditions apply to the entry of vessels of each Party into the ports of the other Party:

1. Vessels flying the flag of the United States of America may enter all ports of the People's Republic of China which are open to international merchant shipping listed in Annex A to this letter subject to seven days' advance notice of such entry to the appropriate authorities of the People's Republic of China in accordance with regulations concerning entry by foreign vessels to China.

2. Vessels flying the flag of the People's Republic of China may enter ports of the United States of America in accordance with regulations concerning entry by foreign vessels. Entry into ports listed in Annex B to this letter will be subject to four days' advance notice of such entry to the appropriate authorities of the United States of America. Regarding ports not included in this Annex B, appropriate authorities of the United States of America will be informed not less than seven working days prior to an intended entry into such ports. It is understood that entry into these ports will ordinarily be granted, but that authorities of the United States may deny such entry for reasons of national security.

3. It is further understood that, in view of the expectation of both our governments that the relations between our countries will continue to grow, the list of ports contained in the Annexes to this letter will be reviewed periodically during the term of the Agreement with a view toward increasing the number of ports on these lists.

I request that you confirm these proposed conditions.

Respectfully,

SAMUEL B. NEMIROW
Assistant Secretary
United States Department of
of Commerce

ANNEX A

List of Chinese Ports

1. Dalian
2. Qinhuangdao
3. Tianjin
4. Yantai
5. Qingdao
6. Lianyungang
7. Wenzhou
8. Shanghai
9. Ningbo
10. Fuzhou
11. Xiamen
12. Shantou
13. Shanwei
14. Huangpu
15. Guangzhou
16. Zhanjiang
17. Beihai
18. Haikou
19. Basuo
20. Shijiusuo (under construction)

ANNEX B

List of United States Ports

1. Portland, Maine
2. Boston, Massachusetts
3. Fall River, Massachusetts
4. New York (New York and New Jersey ports of the Port of New York Authority), New York
5. Albany, New York
6. Philadelphia, Pennsylvania (including Camden, New Jersey)
7. Wilmington, Delaware
8. Baltimore, Maryland
9. Richmond, Virginia
10. Morehead City, North Carolina
11. Wilmington, North Carolina
12. Georgetown, South Carolina
13. Savannah, Georgia
14. Boca Grande, Florida
15. Port Everglades, Florida
16. Ponce, Puerto Rico
17. Tampa, Florida
18. Mobile, Alabama
19. Gulfport, Mississippi
20. New Orleans, Louisiana
21. Burnside, Louisiana
22. Baton Rouge, Louisiana
23. Orange, Texas
24. Beaumont, Texas
25. Port Arthur, Texas
26. Galveston, Texas
27. Houston, Texas
28. Corpus Christi, Texas
29. Brownsville, Texas
30. Anchorage, Alaska
31. Skagway, Alaska
32. Ketchikan, Alaska
33. Seattle, Washington
34. Bellingham, Washington
35. Longview, Washington
36. Everett, Washington
37. Tacoma, Washington
38. Portland (including Vancouver, Washington), Oregon
39. Astoria, Oregon
40. Coos Bay (including North Bend), Oregon

41. Eureka, California
42. Stockton, California
43. San Francisco (including Alameda, Oakland, Berkeley, Richmond), California
44. Sacramento, California
45. Los Angeles (including San Pedro, Wilmington, Terminal Island), California
46. Long Beach, California
47. Honolulu, Hawaii
48. Erie, Pennsylvania
49. Cleveland, Ohio
50. Toledo, Ohio
51. Bay City, Michigan
52. Chicago, Illinois
53. Kenosha, Wisconsin
54. Milwaukee, Wisconsin
55. Duluth, Minnesota/Superior, Wisconsin

———

September 17, 1980

Mr. Samuel B. Nemirow
Assistant Secretary
United States Department of Commerce

Dear Mr. Nemirow:

I have the honor to acknowledge the receipt of your letter dated today, the contents of which follow:*

I confirm the above contents of your letter as correct.

With my highest considerations,
Respectfully,
DONG HUAMIN
Director
Bureau of Foreign Affairs
Ministry of Communications
People's Republic of China

NOTE: As printed above, the agreement, accompanying letters, and annexes follow the texts printed in Selected Documents No. 18, U.S.-China Agreements, September 17, 1980, United States Department of State, Bureau of Public Affairs.

———

*EDITORIAL NOTE: The text of the Assistant Secretary's letter is restated in full and is printed on page 1805.

United States-People's Republic of China Agreements

Consular Convention. September 17, 1980

CONSULAR CONVENTION BETWEEN THE
UNITED STATES OF AMERICA AND THE
PEOPLE'S REPUBLIC OF CHINA

The Government of the United States of America and the Government of the People's Republic of China,

Desiring to regulate and strengthen their consular relations, in order to promote the development of friendly and cooperative relations between the two countries, and thus to facilitate the protection of their national interests and the protection of the rights and interests of their nationals,

Have decided to conclude this Consular Convention and have appointed as their plenipotentiaries the following:

For the United States of America:
> Jimmy Carter, President

For the People's Republic of China:
> Bo Yibo, Vice Premier

Who, having examined and exchanged their respective full powers, which were found in good and due form, have agreed as follows:

ARTICLE 1

Definitions

For the purpose of the present Convention, the terms listed below shall have the following meanings:

1. "Consulate" means a consulate general, consulate, vice consulate, or consular agency;

2. "Consular district" means the area assigned to a consulate for the exercise of consular functions;

3. "Head of a consulate" means the consul general, consul, vice consul or consular agent who is charged by the sending State to head a consulate;

4. "Consular officer" means any person, including the head of a consulate, who is charged by the sending State with the performance of consular functions;

5. "Consular employee" means any person who performs administrative, technical, or service functions at a consulate;

6. "Member of a consulate" means any consular officer or consular employee;

7. "Members of the family" means the spouse, minor children and other relatives of a member of a consulate who form a part of his household;

8. "Consular premises" means buildings or parts of buildings, as well as the grounds ancillary thereto, used exclusively for the purposes of a consulate, regardless of ownership;

9. "Consular archives" means all correspondence, codes and ciphers, documents, records, files, tapes and books of a consulate, as well as any article of furniture intended for their storage or safekeeping;

10. "Vessel of the sending State" means any vessel sailing under the flag of the sending State, in accordance with the law of the sending State, excluding military vessels;

11. "Aircraft of the sending State" means any aircraft flying under the nationality and registration marks of the sending State, in accordance with the law of the sending State, excluding military aircraft;

12. "Law" means

• for the People's Republic of China, all national, provincial, municipal, autonomous region and local laws, ordinances, regulations and decisions having the force and effect of law;

• for the United States of America, all federal, state or local laws, ordinances, regulations and decisions having the force and effect of law.

ARTICLE 2

Opening of Consulates

1. A consulate may be established only through agreement between the sending and receiving States.

2. The determination of the seat of the consulate, its classification, and its consular district, as well as any changes pertaining thereto, shall be through agreement between the sending and receiving States.

ARTICLE 3

Appointment of the Head of a Consulate

1. The sending State shall forward to the receiving State through diplomatic channels a written notification of the appointment of the head of the consulate. This notification shall contain the full name, nationality, sex and rank of the head of the consulate, a brief biography, the date on which he will begin to exercise his functions, the classification and seat of the consulate, and the consular district.

2. Upon receiving notification of the appointment of the head of the consulate, the receiving State shall, if there is no objection, confirm it in writing without delay. The head of the consulate may enter upon the performance of his functions only after the receiving State has provided such confirmation.

3. The receiving State may permit the head of a consulate to exercise his functions on a provisional basis prior to his confirmation by the receiving State.

4. The receiving State shall, immediately after granting recognition, including provisional recognition, take all measures necessary to enable the head of the consulate to exercise his functions and to enjoy the rights, facilities, privileges and immunities granted under this Convention and under the law of the receiving State.

5. If for any reason the head of a consulate is unable to exercise his functions, or if the position of the head of consulate is vacant, the sending State may place its consulate under the temporary charge of a consular officer of the same or of another consulate in the receiving State or a member of the diplomatic staff of the diplomatic mission of the sending State in the receiving State. The sending State shall notify the receiving State in advance of the full name of the person appointed as acting head of a consulate.

6. A person appointed as acting head of a consulate shall enjoy the same rights, facilities, privileges and immunities enjoyed by a head of a consulate under this Convention.

7. Entrusting a member of the diplomatic staff of the diplomatic mission of the sending State with the functions of head of a consulate does not limit the privileges and immunities to which such person is entitled by virtue of diplomatic status, subject to the provisions of Article 33, paragraph 4 of this Convention.

ARTICLE 4

Appointment of Members of a Consulate

1. The sending State may staff its consulate with the number of members of a consulate it considers necessary. The receiving State may, however, require that the number of such members of a consulate be kept within the limits which it considers to be reasonable, having regard to existing circumstances and conditions in the consular district and the needs of a particular consulate.

2. Consular officers shall be nationals of the sending State only, and shall not be permanent residents of the receiving State.

3. The sending State shall communicate in advance, in writing, to the receiving State the full name, functions and class of each consular officer other than the head of the consulate, his arrival, final departure or termination of functions, as well as all other changes affecting the person's status while assigned to the consulate.

4. The sending State shall also notify the receiving State in writing of:

(a) the designation of all consular employees, their full name, nationality and functions, their arrival, their final departure or termination of their functions, as well as other changes affecting their status while assigned to the consulate;

(b) the arrival and final departure of members of the family of a member of a consulate and when any such individual becomes or ceases to be a member of the family;

(c) the employment or dismissal of a consular employee who is a national or permanent resident of the receiving State.

ARTICLE 5

Performance of Consular Functions by a Diplomatic Mission

1. The provisions of this Convention relating to consular functions, rights, facilities, privileges and immunities shall apply in the case of consular functions being performed by a diplomatic mission.

2. The names of the members of the diplomatic mission entrusted with the performance of consular functions shall be communicated to the receiving State.

3. The members of the diplomatic mission referred to in paragraph 2 of this Article shall continue to enjoy the privileges and immunities granted them by virtue of their diplomatic status, subject to the requirements of Article 33, paragraph 4, of this Convention.

ARTICLE 6

Terminating Functions of Members of a Consulate

1. The receiving State may at any time, and without having to explain its decision, notify the sending State through diplomatic channels that the head of a consulate is *persona non grata* or that any other member of a consulate is unacceptable. In such a case, the sending State shall recall such person or terminate his functions in the consulate.

2. If the sending State refuses or fails within a reasonable time to carry out the obligation contained in paragraph 1 of this Article, the receiving State may either withdraw recognition from the person concerned or refuse to consider him as a member of the consulate.

3. The functions of a member of a consulate shall come to an end, among other things, upon the:

(a) notification by the sending State to the receiving State that his functions have come to an end;

(b) withdrawal by the receiving State of recognition; or

(c) notification by the receiving State to the sending State that the receiving State has ceased to consider the person as a member of the consulate.

ARTICLE 7

Facilities for the Operation of a Consulate and Protection of Consular Officers

1. The receiving State shall take all necessary steps for the establishment of the proper conditions for the normal operation of a consulate and shall accord full facilities for the performance of the functions of the consulate.

2. The receiving State shall afford appropriate protection to consular officers to prevent any attack upon their person,

freedom or dignity and further shall take all measures necessary to ensure that consular officers are able to perform their functions and enjoy the rights, facilities, privileges and immunities provided them under this Convention.

ARTICLE 8

Acquisition of Consular Premises and Residences

1. The sending State or its representative shall be entitled to purchase, lease or acquire in any other way, land, consular premises and residences as appropriate for consular purposes, except residences for members of a consulate who are nationals or permanent residents of the receiving State, and to construct or improve buildings for such purposes.

2. In exercising the rights provided under paragraph 1 of this Article, the sending State shall comply with the law of the receiving State, including the law relating to land, construction, zoning and town planning.

3. The receiving State shall, in conformity with its law, facilitate a consulate of the sending State in the acquisition of suitable consular premises. When necessary, the receiving State shall assist the sending State in the acquisition of residences for members of a consulate.

ARTICLE 9

Use of the National Flag and Emblems

1. The sending State shall be entitled to display the national emblem and the designation of the consulate on the consular premises in the languages of the sending and of the receiving States.

2. The sending State shall be entitled to fly the flag of the sending State on the consular premises and on the residence of the head of the consulate, as well as on the means of transport of the head of the consulate used in the performance of his official duties.

3. In exercising the rights provided by this Article, the sending State shall observe the law and customs of the receiving State.

ARTICLE 10

Inviolability of Premises and Residences

1. The consular premises shall be inviolable. The authorities of the receiving State may not enter the consular premises without the consent of the head of the consulate or the head of the diplomatic mission of the sending State or a person designated by one of those persons.

2. The receiving State is under a special duty to take all steps necessary to protect the consular premises against any intrusion or damage and to prevent any disturbance of the peace of the consulate or impairment of its dignity.

3. The provisions of paragraph 1 of this Article shall apply likewise to the residences of consular officers.

ARTICLE 11

Inviolability of Archives

The consular archives shall be inviolable at all times and wherever they may be. Documents and objects of an unofficial character shall not be stored in the consular archives.

ARTICLE 12

Freedom of Communications

1. A consulate shall be entitled to exchange communications with its government, with diplomatic missions of the sending State and with other consulates of the sending State, wherever situated.

For this purpose, the consulate may employ all ordinary means of communication, including diplomatic and consular couriers, diplomatic and consular bags and codes and ciphers. The consulate may install and use a wireless transmitter only with the prior consent of the receiving State.

2. The official correspondence of a consulate, regardless of the means of communication employed, as well as sealed consular bags and other containers, provided they bear visible external marks of their official character, shall be inviolable. They may contain nothing other than official correspondence and articles intended exclusively for official use.

3. The authorities of the receiving State shall neither open nor detain the official correspondence of a consulate, including consular bags and other containers, as described in paragraph 2 of this Article.

4. The consular couriers of the sending State shall enjoy in the territory of the receiving State the same rights, privileges, facilities and immunities enjoyed by diplomatic couriers of the sending State.

5. If a master of a vessel or captain of a civil aircraft of the sending State is charged with an official consular bag, the master or captain shall be provided with an official document showing the number of containers forming the consular bag entrusted to him; he shall not, however, be considered to be a consular courier. By arrangements with the appropriate authorities of the receiving State, and in compliance with the safety regulations of the receiving State, the sending State may send a member of the consulate to take possession of the consular bag directly and freely from the master of the vessel or captain of the aircraft or to deliver such bag to him.

ARTICLE 13

Immunity of Members of a Consulate from the Jurisdiction of the Receiving State

1. Members of a consulate and their family members shall be immune from the criminal jurisdiction of the receiving State.

2. Members of a consulate and their family members shall be immune from the civil and administrative jurisdiction of the receiving State respecting any act performed by them in the exercise of consular functions.

3. The provisions of paragraph 2 of this Article shall not apply to civil procedures:

(a) resulting from contracts that were not concluded by a member of a consulate on behalf of the sending State;

(b) relating to succession in which a member of a consulate was involved as executor, administrator, heir or legatee in a private capacity;

(c) concerning a claim by a third party for damage caused by a vessel, vehicle or aircraft;

(d) concerning private immovable property in the jurisdiction of the receiving State, unless the member of a consulate is holding it on behalf of the sending State for the purposes of the consulate;

(e) relating to any private professional or commercial activities engaged in by a member of a consulate in the receiving State outside of his official functions.

4. No measures of execution shall be taken against any of the persons mentioned in this Article, except in the cases under paragraph 3(d) of this Article, and then under the condition that these measures shall not infringe upon the inviolability of their person or residence.

5. Members of a consulate and their family members may be called upon to at-

tend as witnesses in the course of judicial or administrative proceedings. In the event of the refusal of a consular officer or a member of the officer's family to give evidence, no coercive measure or penalty may be applied to such person. Consular employees and members of their families may not decline to give evidence except with respect to matters mentioned in paragraph 6 of this Article.

6. Members of a consulate are under no obligation to give evidence concerning matters relating to the exercise of their official functions or to produce official correspondence or documents. They are also entitled to decline to give evidence as expert witnesses with regard to the law of the sending State.

7. In taking testimony of members of a consulate, the authorities of the receiving State shall take all the appropriate measures to avoid hindering the performance of their official consular duties. Upon the request of the head of a consulate, such testimony may, when possible, be given orally or in writing at the consulate or at the residence of the person concerned.

ARTICLE 14

Waiver of Immunity

1. The sending State may waive the immunity from jurisdiction of members of a consulate and of members of their families provided in Article 13 of this Convention. Except as provided in paragraph 2 of this Article, such waiver shall always be express and in writing.

2. In the event a member of a consulate or a member of his family initiates legal proceedings, with respect to which he would enjoy immunity from jurisdiction under this Convention, no immunity may be invoked with regard to any counter-claim directly related to the principal claim.

3. Waiver of immunity from jurisdiction with respect to civil proceedings shall not be held to imply waiver of immunity with respect to the execution of judgment, for which a separate waiver shall be necessary.

ARTICLE 15

Exemption from Services and Obligations

Consular officers and consular employees and members of their families who are not nationals of the receiving State and who are not aliens lawfully admitted for permanent residence in the receiving State shall be exempt in the receiving State from obligations and services of a military nature, from any kind of compulsory services, and from any contributions that may be due in lieu thereof. They shall likewise be exempt from obligations relating to the registration of aliens, from obtaining permission to reside, and from compliance with other similar obligations applicable to aliens.

ARTICLE 16

Exemption of Real and Movable Property from Taxation

1. The sending State shall be exempt from all dues and taxes and similar charges of any kind in the receiving State, for which it otherwise would be liable, with respect to:

(a) the consular premises and residences of members of a consulate referred to in Article 8 of this Convention;

(b) transactions or documents relating to such immovable property.

2. The sending State shall be exempt from all dues and taxes and similar charges of any kind on movable property which is owned, held or leased or otherwise possessed by it and which is used exclusively for consular purposes, as well as dues and .taxes in connection with the

acquisition, possession or maintenance of such property.

3. The provisions of subparagraph 1(a) of this Article shall not apply to payment for specific services rendered.

4. The exemptions accorded by this Article shall not apply to such dues and taxes if under the law of the receiving State they are payable by a person contracting with the sending State or with a person acting on behalf of the sending State.

5. The provisions of this Article also apply to all immovable property used for the official purposes of the diplomatic mission of the sending State, including residences of diplomatic mission personnel.

ARTICLE 17

Exemption of Members of a Consulate from Taxation

1. Except as provided in paragraph 2 of this Article, a member of a consulate and members of his family shall be exempt from payment of all dues and taxes and similar charges of any kind.

2. The exemption provided by paragraph 1 of this Article shall not apply with respect to:

(a) indirect taxes of a kind normally included in the price of goods and services;

(b) dues and taxes imposed with respect to private immovable property located in the territory of the receiving State, unless an exemption is provided by Article 16 of this Convention;

(c) estate, succession and inheritance taxes and taxes on the transfer of property rights imposed by the receiving State, except as provided in paragraph 3 of this Article;

(d) dues and taxes on private income earned in the receiving State;

(e) charges for specific services rendered;

(f) dues and taxes on transactions or on documents relating to transactions, including fees of any kind collected by reason of such transactions, except for fees and charges exemption from which is provided in Article 16 of this Convention.

3. If a member of a consulate or a member of his family dies, no estate, succession or inheritance tax or any other tax or charge on the transfer of movable property at death shall be imposed by the receiving State with respect to that property, provided that the presence of the property was due solely to the presence of the deceased in the receiving State in the capacity of a member of a consulate or a member of his family.

ARTICLE 18

Exemptions from Customs Duties and Inspection

1. All articles, including motor vehicles, for the official use of a consulate, shall, in conformity with the law of the receiving State, be exempt from customs duties and other dues and taxes of any kind imposed upon or by reason of importation or exportation.

2. Consular officers and members of their families shall be exempt from customs duties and other charges imposed upon or by reason of importation or exportation of articles intended for their own personal use, including articles for the equipment of their households.

3. Consular employees and members of their families shall be exempt from customs duties and other charges imposed upon or by reason of the importation or exportation of articles for their own personal use, including articles for the equipment of their households, imported at time of first arrival at a consulate.

4. Articles designed for personal use shall not exceed the quantities required for direct use by the person accorded an exemption by this Article.

5. Personal baggage of consular officers and members of their families shall be exempt from customs inspection. It may be inspected only in cases where there is serious reason to believe that it contains articles other than those mentioned in paragraph 2 of this Article, or articles the importation or exportation of which is prohibited by the law of the receiving State or articles which are subject to the law of quarantine. Such inspection must be undertaken in the presence of the consular officer concerned or member of his family or his representative.

ARTICLE 19

Immunity from Requisition

Consular premises as well as the official means of transport of the consulate are not liable to any form of requisition. If for the needs of the national defense or other public purposes expropriation of consular premises, residences or means of transport becomes necessary, all possible measures must be taken by the receiving State to avoid interference with the performance of consular functions and promptly to pay appropriate and effective compensation to the sending State.

ARTICLE 20

Freedom of Movement

Subject to the law of the receiving State concerning zones, entry into which is prohibited or regulated for reasons of national security, the receiving State shall ensure freedom of movement and travel in its territory to members of a consulate and members of their families.

ARTICLE 21

Exclusion from the Enjoyment of Rights, Facilities, Privileges and Immunities

Members of a consulate and members of their families who are either nationals or permanent residents of the receiving State shall not enjoy the rights, facilities, privileges and immunities provided by this Convention, except immunity from the obligation to give evidence concerning matters relating to the exercise of their official functions as provided in paragraph 6 of Article 13 of this Convention.

ARTICLE 22

Functions of Consular Officers

1. The functions of a consular officer consist of:

(a) protecting the rights and interests of the sending State and of its nationals, including juridical persons;

(b) rendering assistance to and cooperating with nationals of the sending State, including juridical persons;

(c) contributing to the development of economic, commercial, cultural, scientific and tourist relations between the sending and the receiving States;

(d) promoting in various ways the development of friendly relations between the sending and the receiving States;

(e) ascertaining by all lawful means conditions and developments in the political, commercial, economic, cultural, educational and scientific-technological life of the receiving State, and reporting thereon to the government of the sending State.

2. A consular officer shall, if authorized by the sending State, be entitled to carry out the functions described in this Convention, as well as other consular functions which are not prohibited by the law of

the receiving State or to which the receiving State does not object.

ARTICLE 23

Execution of Consular Functions

1. A consular officer shall be entitled to execute his functions only within the consular district. A consular officer may execute his functions outside the limits of the consular district only with the advance consent of the receiving State given separately in each instance.

2. In executing his functions, a consular officer may approach orally or in writing:

(a) the competent local authorities in the consular district;

(b) the competent central authorities of the receiving State, if and to the extent allowed by the law and customs of the receiving State.

3. With the advance approval of the receiving State, the sending State may perform consular functions in the receiving State on behalf of a third State.

4. A consulate may levy in the territory of the receiving State consular fees authorized under the law of the sending State for consular acts. Any such sums levied shall be exempt from all dues and taxes in the receiving State.

ARTICLE 24

Representation Before the Authorities of the Receiving State

1. A consular officer shall be entitled, in accordance with the law of the receiving State, to take appropriate measures for the protection of the rights and interests of nationals of the sending State, including juridical persons, before the courts and other authorities of the receiving State, where, because they are not present in the receiving State or for any other reason,

these nationals are not in a position to undertake timely defense of their rights and interests.

2. The measures referred to in paragraph 1 of this Article shall cease as soon as the national appoints his own representative or the national assumes the defense of his rights and interests.

3. Nothing in this Article, however, shall be construed to authorize a consular officer to act as an attorney-at-law.

ARTICLE 25

Functions with Regard to Travel Documents

A consular officer shall be entitled to:

1. issue to nationals of the sending State passports or similar travel documents, as well as make amendments in them;

2. issue visas or other appropriate documents to persons wishing to travel to or through the sending State.

ARTICLE 26

Functions Regarding Citizenship and Civil Status

A consular officer shall be entitled to:

1. register nationals of the sending State;

2. accept applications and issue or deliver documents on matters of citizenship;

3. accept applications or declarations relating to civil status from nationals of the sending State;

4. register births and deaths of nationals of the sending State.

ARTICLE 27

Notarial Functions

A consular officer shall be entitled to:

1. receive and witness statements made

under oath or affirmation, and, in accordance with the law of the receiving State, to receive the testimony of any person for use in connection with a legal proceeding in the sending State;

2. draw up or authenticate any act or document, as well as copies or extracts thereof, of a national of the sending State, including a juridical person, for use outside the receiving State or of any person for use in the sending State, or perform other notarial functions;

3. authenticate documents issued by competent authorities of the receiving State for use in the sending State.

ARTICLE 28

Legal Force of Documents Prepared by a Consular Officer

The acts and documents certified or legalized by a consular officer of the sending State, as well as copies, extracts and translations of such acts and documents certified by him, shall be receivable in evidence in the receiving State as official or officially certified acts, documents, copies, translations or extracts, and shall have in the receiving State the same validity and effect as the documents certified or legalized by the competent authorities of the receiving State, provided they have been drawn and executed in conformity with the law of the receiving State and with the law of the country in which they are to be used.

ARTICLE 29

Serving Judicial and Other Legal Documents

A consular officer shall be entitled to serve judicial and other legal documents in accordance with international agreements in force between the sending and receiving States or, in the absence of such

agreements, to the extent permitted by the law of the receiving State.

ARTICLE 30

Notification on the Establishment of Guardianship or Trusteeship

1. The competent authorities of the receiving State shall notify the consulate in writing of instances in which it is necessary to establish a guardianship or trusteeship over a national of the sending State who is not of age or lacks full capacity to act on his own behalf, or over property of a national of the sending State when for whatever reason such property cannot be administered by the national of the sending State.

2. A consular officer of the sending State may, on matters mentioned in paragraph 1 of this Article, contact the appropriate authorities of the receiving State, and may propose appropriate persons to be appointed to act as guardians or trustees, in accordance with the law of the receiving State.

ARTICLE 31

Notification Regarding the Death of a National of the Sending State

Whenever the competent authorities of the receiving State learn that a national of the sending State has died in the receiving State, they shall immediately notify the appropriate consular officer of the sending State and, upon his request, send him a copy of the death certificate or other documentation confirming the death.

ARTICLE 32

Notification Regarding the Estate of a Deceased National

1. Whenever the appropriate local authorities of the receiving State learn of an

estate resulting from the death in the receiving State of a national of the sending State who leaves in the receiving State no known heir or testamentary executor, they shall as promptly as possible so inform a consular officer of the sending State.

2. Whenever the appropriate local authorities of the receiving State learn of an estate of a decedent, regardless of nationality, who has left in the receiving State an estate in which a national of the sending State residing outside the receiving State may have an interest under the will of the decedent or otherwise in accordance with the law of the receiving State, they shall as promptly as possible so inform a consular officer of the sending State.

ARTICLE 33

Functions Relating to Estates

1. A consular officer shall be entitled to take appropriate measures with respect to the protection and conservation of the property of a deceased national of the sending State left in the receiving State. In this connection he may approach the competent authorities of the receiving State with a view towards protecting the interests of a sending State national, not a permanent resident of the receiving State, unless such a national is otherwise represented. He may also request the competent authorities of the receiving State to permit him to be present at the inventorying and sealing and, in general, to take an interest in the proceedings.

2. A consular officer shall be entitled to safeguard the interests of a national of the sending State who has, or claims to have, a right to property left in the receiving State by a deceased person, irrespective of the latter's nationality, and if that interested national is not in the receiving State or does not have a representative there.

3. A consular officer of the sending State shall be entitled to receive for transmission to a national of the sending State who is not a permanent resident of the receiving State any money or other property in the receiving State to which such national is entitled as a consequence of the death of another person, including shares in an estate, payments made pursuant to employees' compensation law, pension and social benefits systems in general, and proceeds of insurance policies, unless the court, agency, or person making distribution directs that transmission be effected in a different manner. The court, agency, or person making distribution may require that a consular officer comply with conditions laid down with regard to:

(a) presenting a power of attorney or other authorization from such national residing outside the receiving State;

(b) furnishing reasonable evidence of the receipt of such money or other property by such national; and

(c) returning the money or other property in the event he is unable to furnish such evidence.

4. In exercising the rights provided by paragraphs 1 through 3 of this Article, the consular officer must comply with the law of the receiving State in the same manner and to the same extent as a national of the receiving State and, irrespective of the provisions of Article 13 of this Convention, shall be subject in this respect to the civil jurisdiction of the receiving State. Further, nothing in these Articles shall authorize a consular officer to act as an attorney-at-law.

ARTICLE 34

Provisional Custody of Money and Effects of a Deceased National of the Sending State

If a national of the sending State, not a permanent resident of the receiving State, dies during a temporary stay in or transit through the receiving State, and the deceased person did not leave a legal representative in the receiving State, the consular officer shall be entitled immediately to take provisional custody of the money, documents and personal effects that were in the national's possession for transfer to an heir, executor, or other person authorized to receive such property, to the extent permitted by the law of the receiving State.

ARTICLE 35

Communication with Nationals of the Sending State

1. A consular officer shall be entitled, in his consular district, to communicate and meet with any national of the sending State, and, when necessary, to arrange for legal assistance and an interpreter. The receiving State shall in no way restrict access between a consular officer and a national of the sending State.

2. If a national of the sending State is arrested or placed under any form of detention within the consular district, the competent authorities of the receiving State shall immediately, but no later than within four days from the date of arrest or detention, notify the consulate of the sending State. If it is not possible to notify the consulate of the sending State within four days because of communications difficulties, they should try to provide notification as soon as possible. Upon the request of a consular officer, he shall be informed of the reasons for which said national has been arrested or detained in any manner.

3. The competent authorities of the receiving State shall immediately inform the national of the sending State of the rights accorded to him by this Article to communicate with a consular officer.

4. A consular officer shall be entitled to visit a national of the sending State who has been arrested or placed under any form of detention, including such national who is in prison pursuant to a judgment, to converse and to exchange correspondence with him in the language of the sending State or the receiving State, and may assist in arranging for legal representation and an interpreter. These visits shall take place as soon as possible, but at the latest, shall not be refused after two days from the date on which the competent authorities notified the consulate that said national had been placed under any form of detention. The visits may be made on a recurring basis. No longer than one month shall be allowed to pass in between visits requested by the consular officer.

5. In the case of a trial of, or other legal proceeding against, a national of the sending State in the receiving State, the appropriate authorities shall, at the request of a consular officer, inform such officer of the charges against such national. A consular officer shall be permitted to attend the trial or other legal proceedings.

6. A consular officer is entitled to provide to a national to whom the provisions of this Article apply parcels containing food, clothing, medicaments and reading and writing materials.

7. A consular officer of the sending State may request the assistance of the authorities of the receiving State in ascertaining the whereabouts of a national of the sending State. The authorities of the receiving State shall do everything possible to provide all relevant and available information.

8. The rights contained in this Article shall be exercised in accordance with the law of the receiving State. Nevertheless, such law shall be applied so as to give full effect to the purposes for which these rights are intended.

ARTICLE 36

Rendering Assistance to Vessels

1. A consular officer shall be entitled to provide any type of assistance to vessels of the sending State which are in the territorial or inland waters, ports or other anchorages of the receiving State.

2. A consular officer may board a vessel of the sending State as soon as permission has been granted the vessel to make contact with the shore. On such occasions, he may be accompanied by members of the consulate.

3. The master and members of the crew may meet and communicate with the consular officer, observing, however, the law relating to the port and the law relating to crossing the border.

4. The consular officer may request the cooperation of the authorities of the receiving State in carrying out his functions with regard to vessels of the sending State and with regard to the master, members of the crew, passengers and cargo.

ARTICLE 37

Rendering Assistance to Master and Crew

1. In accordance with the law of the receiving State, the consular officer shall be entitled:

(a) to investigate any incident occurring aboard a vessel of the sending State, to question the master and any member of the crew with reference to these incidents, to inspect the vessel's papers, to receive information in connection with the voyage and destination of the vessel and also to render assistance in connection with the entry, stay and departure of a vessel of the sending State;

(b) to settle disputes between the master and a crew member, including disputes concerning wages and employment con-

tracts, to the extent that this action is authorized by the law of the sending State;

(c) to take steps connected with the signing on and the discharge of the master and of any crew member;

(d) to take steps for hospitalization for repatriation of the master or a member of the crew of the vessel;

(e) to receive, draw up or certify any declaration or other document provided for by the law of the sending State in regard to the vessel of the sending State or its cargo.

2. The consular officer may, if permitted by the law of the receiving State, appear together with the master or a crew member before the courts or other authorities of the receiving State in order to render them any assistance.

ARTICLE 38

Protection of Interests in Case of Investigations

1. When the courts or other competent authorities of the receiving State intend to take compulsory actions or to start an official investigation aboard a vessel of the sending State which is in the internal or territorial waters of the receiving State, or on the shore with regard to the master or member of the crew, those authorities must notify the appropriate consular officer of the sending State. If, because of the urgency of the matter, it has not been possible to inform the consular officer before initiation of the actions involved, and the consular officer or his representative has not been present when the actions were carried out, the competent authorities of the receiving State shall promptly provide him with the full relevant particulars of the actions taken.

2. Except at the request of the vessel's master or the consular officer, the judicial

or other competent authorities of the receiving State shall not interfere in the internal affairs of the vessel on questions of relations between the members of the crew, labor relations, discipline and other actvities of an internal character, when the peace and safety of the receiving State are not violated.

3. The provisions of paragraph 1 of this Article shall not be applied, however, to ordinary customs, passport and sanitary controls, or, in accordance with treaties in force between the two States, to the saving of human life at sea, prevention of pollution of the sea, or to other activities undertaken at the request of, or with the consent of, the master of the vessel.

ARTICLE 39

Assistance to Damaged Vessels

1. If a vessel of the sending State is wrecked or grounded, or suffers any other damage in the internal or territorial waters of the receiving State, the competent authorites of the receiving State shall inform the consulate as soon as possible and inform it of the measures taken for saving the passengers, the vessel, its crew and cargo.

2. A vessel which has suffered a misfortune and its cargo and provisions shall be subject to customs duties on the territory of the receiving State unless they are delivered for use in that State.

ARTICLE 40

Functions with Regard to Aircraft

The relevant provisions of Articles 36 through 39 of this Convention shall also apply to civil aircraft on the condition that such application is not contrary to the provisions of any bilateral or multi-

lateral agreement in force between the two States.

ARTICLE 41

Observing the Law of the Receiving State

1. All persons enjoying privileges and immunities under this Convention are obliged, without prejudice to their privileges and immunities, to observe the law of the receiving State, including traffic regulations, and to respect the customs of the receiving State, and may not interfere in the internal affairs of the receiving State.

2. Consular officers and consular employees who are nationals of the sending State may not carry on any profession or undertake any activity for personal profit on the territory of the receiving State other than their official duties.

3. All means of transportation of the consulate or of members of a consulate and their families shall be adequately insured against civil actions by third parties.

ARTICLE 42

Entry into Force and Renunciation

1. The present Convention shall be subject to ratification. The exchange of instruments of ratification shall take place as soon as possible at Beijing.

2. The present Convention shall enter into force after the expiration of thirty days following the date of the exchange of instruments of ratification.

3. The present Convention shall remain in force until the expiration of six months from the date on which one of the Contracting Parties gives to the other Contracting Party written notification of its intention to terminate the Convention.

DONE at Washington this seventeenth day of September, 1980, in duplicate in the English and Chinese languages, both texts being equally authentic.

For the Government of the United States of America:

JIMMY CARTER

For the Government of the People's Republic of China:

BO YIBO

_____

ACCOMPANYING LETTERS

September 17, 1980
His Excellency Chai Zemin
　　Ambassador of the
　　People's Republic of China

Excellency:

I have the honor to confirm on behalf of the Government of the United States of America that in the course of negotiating the Consular Convention between the United States of America and the People's Republic of China, the two sides reached agreement on the following questions:

1. The two governments agree to facilitate the reunion of families and will process all applications as quickly as possible under mutually agreed arrangements and in accordance with each side's laws and regulations.

2. The two governments agree to facilitate travel between their respective countries of persons who may have a claim simultaneously to the nationality of the United States of America and the People's Republic of China, but this does not imply that the governments of the two countries recognize dual nationality. Exit formalities and documentation shall be dealt with in accordance with the laws of the country in which such person resides. Entry formalities and documentation shall be dealt with in accordance with the laws of the country of destination.

3. All nationals of the sending State entering the receiving State on the basis of travel documents of the sending State containing properly executed entry and exit visas of the receiving State will, during the period for which their status has been accorded, and in accordance with the visa's period of validity, be considered nationals of the sending State by the appropriate authorities of the receiving State for the purpose of ensuring consular access and protection by the sending State as provided for in Article 35 of the Consular Convention between the United States of America and the People's Republic of China. If judicial or administrative proceedings prevent the above-mentioned persons from leaving the country within the visa's period of validity, they shall not lose the right of consular access and protection by the sending State. Such persons shall be permitted to leave the receiving State without the necessity of obtaining documentation from the receiving State other than the exit documentation normally required of departing aliens.

4. Both governments agree that persons residing in one country who are entitled to receive financial benefits from the other country shall receive their benefits under mutually agreed arrangements and in accordance with each country's laws and regulations.

If your Excellency confirms the above by a note in reply on behalf of the Government of the People's Republic of China, this note shall constitute an integral part of the above-mentioned Consular Convention and shall come into effect simultaneously with the Consular Convention. At that time, the Annex on Practical Arrangements to the Agreement Between the Government of the United States of America and the Government of the People's Republic of China on the Mutual

Establishment of Consular Relations and the Opening of Consulates-General, signed on January 31, 1979 will cease to be in effect. •

Accept, Excellency, the renewed assurances of my highest consideration.

EDMUND S. MUSKIE
Secretary of State

September 17, 1980
The Honorable Edmund S. Muskie
Secretary of State

Excellency:

I have today received a note from Your Excellency, which reads as follows:*

On behalf of the Government of the People's Republic of China, I have the honor to confirm the above contents.

Accept, Excellency, the renewed assurances of my highest consideration.

CHAI ZEMIN
Ambassador of the People's Republic of China

September 17, 1980
His Excellency Chai Zemin
Ambassador of the
People's Republic of China

Excellency:

I have the honor on behalf of the Government of the United States of America to confirm that during the course of negotiations concerning the Consular Convention between the United States of America and the People's Republic of China, both sides reached agreement on the following matter:

Aside from the consulates whose open-

---

*EDITORIAL NOTE: The text of the Secretary's letter is restated in full and printed on page 1821.

ing has already been agreed upon, the United States and Chinese Governments agree to the establishment of three additional consulates general in each other's territory.

If your Excellency by return note confirms the above on behalf of the Government of the People's Republic of China, this note and your Excellency's note in reply will constitute an agreement between the Government of the United States of America and the Government of the People's Republic of China which shall take effect from the date of the Embassy's note in reply.

Accept, Excellency, the renewed assurances of my highest consideration.

EDMUND S. MUSKIE
Secretary of State

September 17, 1980
The Honorable Edmund S. Muskie
Secretary of State

I have today received a note from your excellency, which reads as follows:*

On behalf of the Government of the People's Republic of China, I have the honor to confirm the above contents.

Accept, Excellency, the assurances of my highest consideration.

HIS EXCELLENCY CHAI ZEMIN,
Ambassador of the People's Republic of China

NOTE: As printed above, the agreement and accompanying letters follow the texts printed in Selected Documents No. 18, U.S.-China Agreements, September 17, 1980, United States Department of State, Bureau of Public Affairs.

---

*EDITORIAL NOTE: The text of the Secretary's letter is restated in full and printed preceding the Ambassador's letter.

President's Commission on White House Fellowships

Appointment of Two Members.
September 17, 1980

The President today announced the appointment of two persons as members of the President's Commission on White House Fellowships. They are:

Jose A. Cabranes, of North Haven, Conn., United States District Judge for the District of Connecticut. Before his appointment as a District Judge last year, Cabranes was counsel to Yale Law School.

Kenneth Young, of Silver Spring, Md., executive assistant to the president of the AFL–CIO and a former director of the AFL–CIO legislative department.

President's Council on Physical Fitness and Sports

Appointment of Tom J. Fatjo, Jr., To Be a
Member.   September 17, 1980

The President today announced the appointment of Tom J. Fatjo, Jr., of Houston, Tex., as a member of the President's Council on Physical Fitness and Sports.

Fatjo, 39, is founder and president of The Houstonian, Inc., a project including a fitness center, preventive medicine center, inn, and conference center.

National Railroad Passenger Corporation

Nomination of Two Members to the Board of
Directors.   September 17, 1980

The President today announced that he will nominate two persons to be mem-

bers of the Board of Directors of the National Railroad Passenger Corporation (Amtrak). They are:

William T. Cahill, of Haddonfield, N.J., who would replace Robert G. Dunlop, resigned. Cahill was Governor of New Jersey from 1969 to 1973 and is now senior partner in the Haddonfield law firm of Cahill, Wilinski & Cahill. He was a Member of the U.S. House of Representatives from 1958 to 1969.

W. Howard Fort, of Akron, Ohio, who would replace Harry Edwards, resigned. Fort is a partner in the Akron law firm of Schwab, Grosenbaugh, Fort & Seamon Co. He is former president of the Akron Area Chamber of Commerce and former chairman of the Akron City Planning Commission.

Superior Court of the District of Columbia

Nomination of Dorothy Sellers To Be an
Associate Judge.   September 17, 1980

The President today announced that he will nominate Dorothy Sellers, of Washington, D.C., to be an Associate Judge of the Superior Court of the District of Columbia for a 15-year term. She would replace the late Edmund Daly.

Sellers has been a partner in the firm of Melrod, Redman, Gartlan since 1977.

She was born May 7, 1943, in St. Louis, Mo. She received a B.A. from Stanford University in 1965 and a J.D. from George Washington Law School in 1969.

From 1969 to 1970, Sellers was a court law clerk for the U.S. Court of Appeals for the District of Columbia Circuit. She joined Melrod, Redman, Gartlan as an associate in 1970.

Superior Court of the District of Columbia

Nomination of Ricardo M. Urbina To Be an Associate Judge. September 17, 1980

The President today announced that he will nominate Ricardo M. Urbina, of Washington, D.C., to be an Associate Judge of the Superior Court of the District of Columbia for a 15-year term. He would replace Norma Holloway Johnson, who has been appointed a district judge.

Urbina has been a professor at Howard University Law School since 1974.

He was born January 31, 1946, in New York City. He received a B.A. from Georgetown University in 1967 and a J.D. from Georgetown University Law Center in 1970.

From 1970 to 1972, Urbina was an attorney with the Public Defender Service in the District of Columbia. He was in private law practice from 1972 to 1973.

United States Railway Association

Nomination of Two Members to the Board of Directors. September 18, 1980

The President today announced that he will nominate two persons to be members of the Board of Directors of the United States Railway Association. They are:

Franklin D. Raines, of Seattle, Wash. Raines, 31, has been a vice president in the New York investment banking firm of Lazard Freres & Co. since 1979. He is active in municipal finance, mergers and acquisitions, and Government-assisted corporate finance. He was previously Associate Director for Economics and Government in the Office of Management and Budget. In 1977 and 1978, he was As-

sistant Director of the White House Domestic Policy Staff.

Stanton P. Sender, of Washington, D.C. (reappointment). Sender, 47, has been transportation counsel of Sears, Roebuck and Co., since 1969 and is an expert on rail transportation. He is a member of the board of directors and executive committee of the National Industrial Traffic League and serves on the transportation committees of the American Retail Federation and National Retail Merchants Association. He is former chairman of the Transportation Council.

Duty Increase for Textile Articles From the European Communities

Proclamation 4793. September 18, 1980

INCREASE IN THE RATE OF DUTY FOR CERTAIN TEXTILE ARTICLES FROM THE EUROPEAN COMMUNITIES

By the President of the United States

A Proclamation

1. On February 20, 1980, the European Communities announced the imposition of quotas, under Article XIX of the General Agreement on Tariffs and Trade (GATT) (61 Stat. (pt. 5) A 58; 8 UST (pt. 2) 1786), on polyester filament yarn and polyamide (nylon) carpet yarn, imported into the United Kingdom on or after January 1, 1980. These quotas apply to exports from sources including the United States but exclude certain other countries.

2. On March 10, 1980, pursuant to Article XIX:2 of the GATT, the United States and the European Communities entered into consultations on this issue.

These consultations have been suspended. The United States took note of certain trade liberalizing measures taken by the European Communities. An understanding has also been reached between the United States and the European Communities concerning the impact on the trade of the United States of excluding the products of certain other countries from the quotas. The quotas imposed by the European Communities are scheduled to expire on December 31, 1980. The actions taken to date by the European Communities including the above-mentioned liberalizing measures and the understanding, would not constitute adequate compensation if the quotas are extended beyond December 31, 1980.

3. Section 125(d) of the Trade Act of 1974 (the Trade Act) (19 U.S.C. 2135 (d)) authorizes the President, following public hearings, to withdraw, suspend, or modify the application of trade agreement obligations of the United States which are substantially equivalent to those which have been withdrawn, suspended or modified by a foreign country or instrumentality, or to proclaim under section 125(c) of the Trade Act (19 U.S.C. 2135 (c)) such increased duties or other import restrictions as are appropriate to effect adequate compensation from that foreign country or instrumentality. Public hearings on possible modification or suspension of concessions to the European Communities were held on April 3, 1980, at the Office of the United States Trade Representative.

4. I have decided, pursuant to section 125(c) of the Trade Act to increase the duty on the textile articles listed in the Annex to this proclamation, the product of any member country of the European Communities, effective January 1, 1981, if the aforementioned import restrictions

are extended by the European Communities beyond December 31, 1980, without providing adequate compensation.

Now, THEREFORE, I, JIMMY CARTER, President of the United States of America, acting under the authority vested in me by the Constitution and the statutes of the United States, including sections 125 and 604 of the Trade Act (19 U.S.C. 2135 and 2483), and in accordance with Article XIX of the GATT do proclaim that:

(1) Subpart D, part 2 of the Appendix to the Tariff Schedules of the United States (TSUS) (19 U.S.C. 1202) is modified as set forth in the Annex to this proclamation.

(2) This proclamation shall be effective with respect to articles entered, or withdrawn from warehouse for consumption, on or after January 1, 1981, unless the United States Trade Representative (USTR) determines that the quotas imposed by the European Communities, the subject of this proclamation, have terminated or will terminate prior to January 1, 1981, or that adequate compensation has been provided by the European Communities. If the USTR makes such a determination (published in the FEDERAL REGISTER), the modifications to the TSUS made by this proclamation shall not take effect.

(3) Conforming modifications shall be made to Part I of Schedule XX to the GATT when the actions set forth in the Annex to this proclamation become effective.

(4) The TSUS, as modified by the Annex to this proclamation, shall be further modified as required by section C of Annex II to Proclamation No. 4707 of December 11, 1979, effective as to articles entered, or withdrawn from warehouse for consumption, on or after January 1, 1982.

IN WITNESS WHEREOF, I have hereunto set my hand this 17th day of September, in the year of our Lord nineteen hundred and eighty, and of the Independence of the United States of America the two hundred and fifth.

JIMMY CARTER

[Filed with the Office of the Federal Register, 11:37 a.m., September 18, 1980]

NOTE: The annex to the proclamation is printed in the FEDERAL REGISTER of September 19, 1980.

THE PRESIDENT'S NEWS CONFERENCE OF SEPTEMBER 18, 1980

ADMINISTRATION POLICIES

THE PRESIDENT. Although attention is naturally focused on domestic politics, events around the world and here at home still demand my attention and action in ways that affect the well-being of American citizens.

Yesterday we completed the normalization of relations with the People's Republic of China with four agreements—for trade, for consulates, for normal airline service, and for textiles. We've opened a new era of normal relationships now between our two great countries.

Also yesterday, the second anniversary of the signing of the Camp David accords, I met with Israeli Foreign Minister Shamir and Egyptian Foreign Minister Hassan Ali as efforts continue in our quest for a lasting peace in the Middle East, which is so important to the future of Americans and to the entire world. They have been, since that meeting with me, conducting negotiations or discussions with our own Ambassador responsible for the discussions for peace.

We're preparing now for preliminary exchanges with the Soviet Union on the control of theater nuclear weapons in Europe. These talks should begin next month, and Secretary Muskie will be addressing this important subject in his discussions with Foreign Minister Gromyko of the Soviet Union in New York in the near future.

We've also been concentrating on the slow, difficult, diplomatic effort to free our hostages in Iran.

Here at home there are some encouraging economic signs. The unemployment rate has been steady or slightly down for the last 4 straight months. Unemployment compensation claims, which is a weekly statistic that we receive, has been encouraging. In the last 2 months we've added some 470,000 new jobs. Housing starts are up now for the third month in a row. New orders for durable goods were up sharply in July, and for the past 90 days retail sales have also shown increases. But—and this is essential—while inflation has been dampened down, it's still a major, continuing concern.

I'm standing firm against any tax reduction in this preelection political climate. But I will press ahead to strengthen our economy, to increase productivity, to revitalize our American industrial system, and to create real jobs.

A tripartite automobile committee is now attacking this industry's problems on a continuing basis. A few hours ago Japanese Minister Tanaka made an encouraging statement in his estimate of Japanese exports of automobiles to this country for the remainder of this year. At the Venice summit conference we discussed with the Japanese the automobile situation, and they are sensitive to this transition period through which America is now going in changing consumer demand for the smaller and more efficient automobiles.

I'm also pleased to note that there are some initial recalls of steelworkers. And I look forward to receiving within just a few days a strong report from our tripartite committee on steel dealing with the pressing problems that face that basic industry so important to our country.

Finally, nowhere is America's progress more important than reducing energy dependence. The results so far have been excellent, far above what we had anticipated. Our imports of oil are down more than 20 percent below last year—about 1½ million barrels less oil imported each day this year. A record number of drilling rigs are in use. The number of oil and natural gas wells that will be drilled in 1980 will exceed any other previous year. American coal production in 1980 will be the highest in history, and we are now launching the most massive peacetime effort in our history to produce energy from shale, from coal, from the Sun, from farm products, geothermal sources, and many others.

Finally, I'm working with the Congress for the passage of critical bills. I think we will have a good legislative year—in dealing with youth employment, Alaska lands, toxic wastes, pay and incentives for military personnel, deregulation of the American free enterprise system, and the enhancement of civil rights.

In domestic and international affairs, the progress of America goes on.

I will now be pleased to answer any questions that you might have for me.

Ms. Santini [Maureen Santini, Associated Press].

QUESTIONS

RONALD REAGAN

Q. Mr. President, in Atlanta on Tuesday, you referred to Ronald Reagan's campaign statements about the Ku Klux Klan and States rights. And then you said that hatred and racism have no place in this country. Do you think that Reagan is running a campaign of hatred and racism, and how do you answer allegations that you are running a mean campaign?

THE PRESIDENT. No. I do not think he's running a campaign of racism or hatred, and I think my campaign is very moderate in its tone. I did not raise the issue of the Klan, nor did I raise the issue of States rights, and I believe that it's best to leave these words, which are code words to many people in our country who've suffered from discrimination in the past, out of the election this year.

I do not think that my opponent is a racist in any degree.

AMERICAN HOSTAGES IN IRAN

Q. Mr. President, earlier this week you raised expectations on the release of the hostages, and then you seemed to back off. What is today's prospect for an early release of the hostages, and aside from the Shah's assets, over which we have no control, are all of the latest Iranian demands negotiable?

THE PRESIDENT. I've not changed my position on the prospects for the hostages release. I do not predict an early resolution of the issue, because it's not in my hands, unilaterally. It has to be done through very careful negotiations with the Iranians and quite often because of unilateral decisions to be made by them.

One of the major obstacles to progress in the past has been the absence of any viable government in Iran. Only in recent weeks, in fact in some instances in the last few days, have they had a parliament or a speaker of the parliament who could speak for them, or a Prime Minister. They have had a President for a long time. The President himself, Bani-Sadr, has been consistently in favor of the hostages being released. Now that their government is intact and now that the Ayatollah Khomeini has made a public statement for the first time outlining to some degree the demands to be pursued by Iran, obviously the situation has improved.

Our position has been consistent. We have two goals in mind that have not changed since the first day the hostages were taken. One is to preserve the honor and integrity of our Nation and to protect its interests. That's never changed. And the second goal has also never changed, and that is not to do anything here in this country that would endanger the lives or safety of the hostages nor interfere with their earliest possible release back to freedom.

This is an issue that's been constantly on my mind and on the minds of the American people.

Q. Does an apology rule out the question of honor?

THE PRESIDENT. Yes. The United States is not going to apologize.

We have long said that there would be a legitimate forum provided for the Iranians, who consider themselves to be aggrieved in many ways, to present their case. We encouraged the United Nations mission to go to Iran, to investigate the situation there, to have hearings in Iran, and to let there be a public exploration of Iran's claims or complaints. At the time we filed our suit in the World Court in the Hague we also invited Iran to participate with us, not in a combative way, but in a friendly way, to give them that forum, which would have been well covered by the world press, to express their concerns or their complaints about us or others in the past. So, this is not a new development at all. Our position has been very consistent.

I cannot predict what will happen in the near future, but we are pursuing every possible legitimate avenue, as we have for many months, to reach some agreement with Iran, with those two constraints that I described to you concerning our Nation's honor and the safety of the hostages, to relieve this problem between us, which is obviously damaging to the United States and also very damaging to the people of Iran.

PRESIDENT'S CAMPAIGN STYLE

Q. I'd like to return to a portion of Miss Santini's question. There are people who say that in political campaigns you get mean; that you attempt to savage your opponents. They cite Hubert Humphrey, Edward Kennedy, and now Ronald Reagan. Will you tell us why you think this is not correct, and will you discuss your campaign style from that standpoint?

THE PRESIDENT. I have not raised these issues today in the press conference; it's been raised twice out of three questions. And obviously in the heat of a campaign there is give and take on both sides. An incumbent Governor or a President is almost always the subject of the most enthusiastic attacks by those who seek his office, and quite often those kinds of political verbal exchanges from those who seek to replace someone are either accepted as a normal course in a political campaign or ignored. If an incumbent, a Governor or a Congressman or a Senator or a President responds, that's immediately given the highest possible notice as an attack on one's challengers.

So, I try to keep a moderate tone; I try to discuss the issues. And I do not indulge in attacking personally the integrity of my opponents, and I hope that I never shall.

1980 CAMPAIGN DEBATES

Q. Mr. President, the big debate really concerns who will occupy this place next January 21. And since Presidential elections are now federally funded, I was just wondering whether you might consider, as President, inviting your chief opponent, Ronald Reagan, to a debate here in the White House?

THE PRESIDENT. I would be glad to have a debate with my Republican opponent either here at this very spot or in the East Room of the White House or any other forum anywhere in this Nation, and as frequently as possible. We have already accepted three invitations to debate on a one-to-one basis between the Democratic nominee, myself, and the Republican nominee. One of the networks invited us both on a man-to-man basis; I accepted. The National Press Club invited us both to attend the debate; I accepted it. And a women's magazine with its organization invited us both to meet on a one-to-one basis to debate, and I accepted these invitations. So far, Governor Reagan has not chosen to accept this one-on-one debate.

I am very eager to pursue this idea and have no concern at all about the location or the time except that I want it to be anywhere in this Nation and as frequently as possible.

PRESIDENT'S PERSONAL LOANS

Q. Mr. President, on July 22, you said that it was inappropriate for your brother, Billy, to serve as a foreign agent and to accept the $220,000 loan from the Libyans. Yet from January of 1978 until March of 1980 you were personally liable for $830,000 to a Saudi-controlled financial institution. And in fact in 1978, con-temporaneously with your decision to sell and advocacy of the sale of sixty F–15 jet fighters to Saudi Arabia, you accepted through Carter's Warehouse a loan accommodation from the Saudi-controlled bank which was worth $266,000 to you personally, free-tax dollars.

In light of your statement about the inappropriateness of your brother accepting a $220,000 loan accommodation, why do you think it was appropriate for you to accept what amounts to a $266,000 loan accommodation from a Saudi-controlled financial institution? And why do you think this does not represent an actual or potential conflict of interest, which you said you would rule out in your administration?

THE PRESIDENT. I have never accepted any loans from any organization——

Q. [*Inaudible*]—a loan accommodation——

THE PRESIDENT. Would you like for me to answer your question?

I've never accepted any loans from an organization that's owned or controlled by any foreign government or any foreign nationals. The only loans that I have gotten were loaned before I became President from American-owned banks in Atlanta, and I have so far paid those loans off as required by the bank itself.

Q. The bank was purchased by the Saudi citizen, and he now owns the bank, Mr. President——

NUCLEAR WARFARE

Q. Mr. President, in the context of your decisions about the MX missile and Presidential Directive 59, I'd like to ask if it's realistic for any American President to believe that he could limit his response to a Soviet nuclear first strike against U.S. missiles if that first strike incurred, let's say, 20 to 50 million casualties. Could you limit your response under those circumstances, or would you have to fire off everything that was left?

THE PRESIDENT. When anyone decides to run for President of our country with any expectation of being elected, the question of the use of atomic weapons has to be addressed, because it's crucial for our Nation, for our allies, and for our potential adversaries to know that, if necessary, atomic weapons would be used to defend our Nation. And that knowledge is the deterrent that would prevent a potential adversary from attacking our country and therefore destroying 100 million or more American lives.

I have done everything I possibly could as President not only to maintain peace—and I thank God we've been successful so far—but to lay the groundwork for continued maintenance of peace and the avoidance of ever having to use atomic weapons. There is a likelihood—I can't say how strong it might be; it's not an inevitability but it's certainly a likelihood—that if an atomic exchange of any kind should ever erupt that it might lead to a more massive exchange of intercontinental and highly destructive weapons that would result in tens of millions of lost lives on both sides. That very knowledge, which I have very clearly in my mind, is shared by the Soviet leaders, and I have discussed this common knowledge with President Brezhnev in Vienna when we signed the SALT II.

The policy of our two countries ever since President Eisenhower and President Truman were in office and everyone since then, Democratic or Republican, has been to try to reduce the dependence on atomic weapons and to have balanced atomic forces and, lately, to reduce constantly on an equal basis the arsenals that we have.

I cannot tell you what would happen if an exchange should take place. I would try to defend my Nation's integrity and its security and the integrity and security of our allies without resort to atomic weapons, but if necessary to defend the freedom and security of Western Europe and this country, then I would use atomic weapons. I pray to God that that time will never come, but it's important for our people, our allies, and the Soviet Union to know that if necessary those weapons will be used. The best weapon of any kind is one that's never used, and the best soldier is one that never dies in war.

But the only way I know to maintain peace for my country and for those who depend on me is to be strong and to let potential attackers know that if they should attack us their attack would be suicidal.

AUTOMOBILE INDUSTRY

Q. Mr. President, the new K-Car Chrysler, there little itty-bitty cars are going to cost $6,000. Do we get any quid pro quo from the automobile industry, or can your administration—you've given them billions of dollars in the past year or so and, I think, a half billion dollars more today from air pollution. They've dropped the airbag. Can the consumer get any break in giving out all these Federal funds?

THE PRESIDENT. It's important to America for us to have modern-design cars, small, efficient, that comply with air pollution standards and are safe. As you know in the past, with extremely cheap gasoline, the efficiency of an automobile, its mileage per gallon, was not very important to the American consumer, because gas was so inexpensive.

Lately there has been a change in buying customs by America. There is no doubt in my mind that the automobiles produced today are much more efficient, much more clean-burning, and becoming more safe than they have been in the past, and I don't have any doubt that in 1985 they will continue that steady progress toward a clean-burning, efficient, safer car.

We have provided increasingly stringent standards for safety and for efficiency and for air pollution standards. And I think that's going to continue. But I don't look upon our Government as subsidizing or paying the automobile industry to make these changes.

We have made available loan guarantees to Chrysler because they were on the verge of bankruptcy. The reason the Congress did this, with my full support and approval, was to avoid the loss of hundreds of thousands of American jobs among automobile workers and to keep a highly competitive automobile industry in our country. These loan guarantees are sound investments by the American Government. We do not anticipate any loss of funds from taxpayers' money with this loan guarantee.

PRESIDENTIAL CANDIDATES' POPULARITY

Q. Mr. President, the opinion polls indicate that you've made quite substantial gains in recent as against Governor Reagan—according to one, marginally ahead; according to one, marginally behind—but certainly in a lot better position than you seemed to be a few weeks ago. Could you give us your analysis of why you think you've made these gains? To what extent you think now that John Anderson will be a factor and your analysis of what you expect to happen in this very volatile period of the next few months, politically speaking?

THE PRESIDENT. Well, I think you all have seen in the last year the extreme volatility of public opinion polls, perhaps more than has ever been the case in the

past. I would guess they would be up and down between now and November 4.

My belief is that in a general election campaign for President there is a unique situation that's not extant in the election of any other official in our country nor the nominating process by the Democratic and Republican Parties even for President. As we approach November 4 there is a continual sobering among individual Americans as they approach a decision who is going to control the affairs of this Nation from the Oval Office for the next 4 years and realization that that choice is a profoundly important one for them individually, for their family, for their community, in economic life, the quality of life, war or peace. The issues begin to become paramount.

The personal characteristics of the candidates, as far as attractiveness or speaking style and so forth, in my opinion become less important and the questions come down to: Who cares more about me and my family and my future? Who can deal with the inevitable crises in a more calm and effective way, and who is most likely to keep this country at peace?

So, I don't know what's going to happen in the future. I'll just do the best I can. I think that the essence of it, though, is that the election will be decided ultimately, however, by that very calm, very reasoned, very sober analysis of the issues and the difference in the stand of the candidates on the issues, and not by the excitement or sometimes even the frivolity of the election campaign during the primary season.

THE NATION'S ECONOMY

Q. Mr. President, based on guidance you were given by your economic advisers and other information that's available to you, do you think that the country is now out of the recession or that it will be before the November 4 election?

THE PRESIDENT. Some of my economic advisers have told me within the last 2 days that the recession might very well be over. I don't know. Only in retrospect, several weeks after something occurs, can you be sure of that. The technical definition of recession with which you are familiar is really of not much significance. The point is, I believe that we'll have ups and downs during the next few months.

We still have an unemployment rate, although below 8 percent, which is too high. The chances are that it won't vary much for the rest of this year. I believe that the inflation rate, which is still too high, will stay below double-digit inflation the rest of this year. Recovery of our economic system seems to be progressing very well, with housing starts going up, investments going up, and with the number of jobs available to the American people continuing to rise. It's just hard to predict; but I believe that we will have a stable economy with statistics fluctuating from one month to another.

The thing that we must do, though, is to realize that the election pressures cannot be permitted to shape economic policy. We have got to keep inflation under control while we deal with the increase in productivity over a long period of time in the future; build permanent jobs for people in the private industry sector, not in make-work jobs that are very expensive to the American taxpayer; continue to deregulate the American free enterprise system, getting government's nose out of the affairs of American business and American families. These kinds of basic things—to increase productivity, to increase investment, and to have long-range, permanent jobs—are the major challenge

that I face as President, and not to have an election-year-type quick fix by promising a major tax decrease that might simply be repaid to the working families of this country by increased inflation in the months ahead.

THE MIDDLE EAST

Q. Mr. President, yesterday, after meeting with Foreign Minister Berg of Israel and Hassan Ali of Egypt, you said without elaboration that unanticipated progress had been made in restarting those trilateral talks here in Washington on Palestinian autonomy.

THE PRESIDENT. Yes.

Q. But Foreign Minister Berg said today those initial discussions would not include the issue of Jerusalem. Given the importance of that issue, what progress has been made this week, and what's the cause of your optimism?

THE PRESIDENT. When Sol Linowitz went to Jerusalem and to Egypt a few weeks ago and met with Foreign Minister Shamir and with General Hassan Ali, and also with Prime Minister Begin and President Sadat, we were pleasantly surprised after a fairly long dearth of direct contacts between Isreal and Egypt to find both nations eager to get back to the negotiating table.

Yesterday, after they left my office, Sol Linowitz, Mr. Shamir, General Ali, sat down to continue top-level negotiations to try to find a basis for carrying out the comprehensive peace.

Following Sol Linowitz' trip to the Mideast, President Sadat announced, both before and after he arrived, that he was eager to see a summit conference later this year. Prime Minister Begin had not until that time made that statement. Prime Minister Begin called me on the telephone to say that the Linowitz mission had been remarkably successful, to thank us for what he had contributed, and to say that he would be eager to meet with me and President Sadat at a summit conference either before or after the American elections were concluded.

We will work that out. I am determined that the prospect for a summit meeting will not interfere with the substantive negotiations that must precede it. And I think the fact that yesterday and today the Foreign Ministers of the two countries are negotiating again in the presence of the American Ambassador assigned that task is indeed encouraging in itself.

RONALD REAGAN

Q. Mr. President, you have been asked several times about some tough language you used in Atlanta regarding Ronald Reagan, and to be fair to you, and before I ask my question, we should point out that some tough language has been used against you in the past by Mr. Reagan and other of your opponents. I recall during an interview with Mr. Reagan he said that you had let our defenses slide and that was a great danger to war. So, I'm not impugning, putting upon you the exclusive use of tough language. But nevertheless I'd like to return to Atlanta and ask this question.

You have said here today that you do not consider Mr. Reagan a racist.

THE PRESIDENT. That's correct.

Q. I believe that to be true. You have said that you do not think he's running a campaign of hatred or racism. But you used all three of those words in connection with the discussion of Mr. Reagan. Do you regret that, or could you tell me how this could happen if you don't attribute any of those characteristics to Mr. Reagan?

THE PRESIDENT. I was speaking to a

group at Ebenezer Baptist Church, leaders of a black community all the way from Maryland to Texas, leaders who had been involved in the civil rights movement in years gone by in the fifties and sixties, who had endangered their very lives to bring about equality of opportunity and an end to racial discrimination. Those people understand the code words, the use of the words "Ku Klux Klan" and the use of the words "States rights" in the South, and my message to them was that the Presidential election is no place for the reviving of the issue of racism under any circumstances. And that's the way I feel about it. It ought not to be a part of the Presidential race.

I was asked later by a newsperson as I was getting on the plane, "Do you think that Governor Reagan is a racist?" And I replied, "No." And I do not. And I would hope that from now on after this news conference that we could leave out references to allegations that anybody thinks that I'm a racist or that any of the other candidates in the race for President are racists. I don't believe they are, and I believe it ought to be dropped.

Q. Mr. President, it was your own Cabinet Secretary, Patricia Harris, who first interjected the KKK into the Presidential race. She said in Los Angeles essentially that Governor Reagan was running with the endorsement of the Ku Klux Klan and raised the spector of white sheets. So then, how can you blame Governor Reagan——

THE PRESIDENT. I am not blaming Governor Reagan. That's just exactly the point. The press seems to be obsessed with this issue. I am not blaming Governor Reagan.

Q. You accused him of interjecting the Ku Klux Klan into the campaign.

THE PRESIDENT. The only thing that I said Governor Reagan injected into the campaign, was the use of the words "States rights" in a speech in Mississippi.

I hate, here on national television, to go through the procedure again. What happened was that the Ku Klux Klan endorsed Governor Reagan and stated that the Republican convention could have been written by a Klansman. Governor Reagan subsequently rejected, wisely and properly, any endorsement by the Ku Klux Klan. That was what injected the Klan into the Presidential race.

I regret it. I wish it had not been done. I would like to see it eliminated from the Presidential race. I do not blame Governor Reagan at all for the fact that that endorsement was made, and I admire him for rejecting the Klan endorsements.

HELEN THOMAS [United Press International]. Thank you.

THE PRESIDENT. Thank you very much.

NOTE: The President's fifty-ninth news conference began at 4 p.m. in Room 450 of the Old Executive Office Building. It was broadcast live on radio and television.

United States Ambassador to Singapore

*Nomination of Harry E. T. Thayer.
September 18, 1980*

The President today announced that he will nominate Harry E. T. Thayer, of Washington, D.C., to be Ambassador Extraordinary and Plenipotentiary of the United States to the Republic of Singapore. He would replace Richard F. Kneip, resigned.

Thayer has been in the executive seminar in national and international affairs at the Foreign Service Institute during 1979–80 and has been a Foreign Service officer since 1956.

He was born September 10, 1927, in Boston, Mass. He received a B.A. from Yale University in 1951. He served in the U.S. Navy from 1945 to 1946.

Thayer was a researcher and writer for Newsweek from 1952 to 1954 and a reporter for the Philadelphia Bulletin from 1954 to 1956. He joined the Foreign Service in 1956 and served in Hong Kong and at the State Department. He took Chinese language training from 1961 to 1963 and was economic officer, then political officer, in Taipei from 1963 to 1966.

Thayer was desk officer for China from 1966 to 1968 and Deputy Director of the Office of Asian Communist Affairs at the State Department from 1968 to 1970. From 1971 to 1975, he was Deputy Principal Counselor to the U.S. Mission to the United Nations.

From 1975 to 1976, Thayer was Deputy Chief of Mission in Beijing. He was Director of the Office of the People's Republic of China and Mongolia Affairs at the State Department from 1976 to 1979.

Constantino Brumidi Day

Proclamation 4794.   September 18, 1980

By the President of the United States of America

A Proclamation

On September 18, 1852, a noted Italian artist named Constantino Brumidi arrived in this country as a political exile.

He spent the remainder of his life embellishing the United States Capitol with magnificent works of art and truly earned the description "Michelangelo of the Capitol of the United States."

Mr. Brumidi's gratitude for the liberty this nation provided to him and his contributions to our national heritage are a source of inspiration for all of us.

In tribute to his achievements, the Congress of the United States of America, by House Joint Resolution 594, has requested the President to proclaim Thursday, September 18 as Constantino Brumidi Day.

Now, THEREFORE, I, JIMMY CARTER, President of the United States of America, do hereby designate Thursday, September 18, 1980, as Constantino Brumidi Day.

IN WITNESS WHEREOF, I have hereunto set my hand this eighteenth day of September, in the year of our Lord nineteen hundred and eighty, and of the Independence of the United States of America the two hundred and fifth.

JIMMY CARTER

[Filed with the Office of the Federal Register, 10:55 a.m., September 19, 1980]

Congressional Hispanic Caucus

**Remarks at the Annual Dinner.
September 18, 1980**

Chairman Roybal, distinguished Members of Congress, honored guests: Es un gran placer para mi y para Rosalynn estar aquí con muchas de neustras amistades. Siempre nos sentimos bienvenidos entre los hispanos no solamente por su colorosa amistad si no tambien por su lealtad a neustros principios democraticos. [It's a great pleasure for me and for Rosalynn to be here with many of our friends. We always feel welcome among Hispanics, not only for your warm friendship but for your loyalty to our democratic principles.]

It's especially good to be with Congressman Ed Roybal. He has a great influence over the President. You see, among other duties, he's the chairman of the subcommittee that controls the White House

budget, so I have to be a good President or Congressman Roybal *podría hacer que me cortar en el agua.* [*Laughter*] Or for the benefit of those few people in the United States who don't speak Spanish, since he controls the White House budget, he could cut off my water. *Puedo hablar un poquito de inglés tambien* [I can also speak a little bit of English]—[*laughter*]—and so I will speak the rest of my time in English.

I come from Georgia, a part of the Nation that was founded and settled by brave Spanish explorers about a hundred years before the pilgrims landed at Plymouth Rock. And if the history books had been written in Spanish instead of English, we would all have known that without my telling you.

It's a real pleasure and honor for me to speak to you at this third annual dinner to honor the achievement of the Hispanic Caucus in the United States Congress, the contributions of your chairman, Ed Roybal, Bob Garcia, Baltasar Corrada, Kika de la Garza, Manuel Lujan have served this country well, and you and I and 240 million Americans can truly be proud of them.

I've looked forward to a chance to speak to this banquet, because I want to express to you my concerns about our country and the human fabric that binds us together in our diverse Nation. The diversity of our country is a major element of what makes us strong. This Nation has indeed drawn heavily from its Spanish heritage, for too many of us forget what you and your ancestors and your families and those who look to you for leadership have contributed. The achievements are too numerous for me to enumerate tonight. But we should especially be thankful for the basic traditions that you've contributed—a belief in strong, loving families, a belief in hard work, a deep and enduring belief in

God, and a burning commitment to freedom and to justice for all people.

This dinner comes at a critical time. In less than 7 weeks the American people will choose not just the next President, but the choice will be more than between two men, more than between two parties. It'll be the choice between two very different futures. When you sort through the many specific issues before us, the choice will be this: Will we continue to strive toward justice and fairness, or will we turn away from that long struggle that's been such a vital part of your lives? I know which choice you would make. The formation of the Hispanic Caucus, the issues that you have championed in Congress, and your individual careers all testify to an unwavering struggle for justice. In that struggle you've championed not only the cause of Hispanic Americans, but you have actually enriched the strength of all this Nation and I'm grateful to you for it.

The Hispanic Caucus and I joined forces 4 years ago to bring our country closer to economic justice. We made a commitment that every person who lives in this country would have a chance to work, to feel useful, and to have a decent life. Together we've expanded jobs and training programs. We've targeted hundreds of millions of dollars in direct assistance for Hispanic workers, and we've sent to Congress now—and it's making good progress—a major new youth employment program which is nearing passage. The sum of these efforts, new jobs, is a proud accomplishment for us all.

Since I took office, in spite of very difficult, worldwide economic problems, 1.2 million more Hispanic men and women now hold fulltime jobs. Nearly 5 million Hispanics are employed in this country, and one out of every five of those jobs was created in the last 3½ years. With your help 2 years ago we enacted into law the Humphrey-Hawkins act, and now we have a chance, building on our energy program, to rebuild the economic base of this country and guarantee that full employment.

Our new program to revitalize American industry will create a million additional jobs above and beyond all the programs now authorized, above and beyond all programs proposed to the Congress today, and above and beyond the jobs that will come from normal economic recovery—jobs in growing, competitive industry; not make-work jobs, permanent jobs, real jobs, jobs for a lifetime's career. This program will increase productivity, encourage innovation, and help communities and families that might otherwise suffer with inevitable changing times brought about by new technology, new buying habits, and new opportunities for progress.

Our commitment to jobs and justice demand that we help modernize American industry, but we must solve our economic problems with careful regard for human consequences. We're determined to share the burdens equally and to protect the poor and the elderly. We recognize that economic progress in this country must go hand in hand toward economic and social justice as well.

As long as I'm President we will enforce civil rights laws. These are crucial to you and crucial to all those who look to you and me for leadership, because they permit people who are sometimes without influence, without good education, without wealth, without social status, to work to their full capacity to find decent housing, to eat in any restaurant they choose, to vote, and to be free from abuse. As a result of this commitment of mine, which I know you share, all Americans now know that the Government of the United States is on their side and will stay there.

And I'm equally determined to ensure justice in the Federal court system. With your help, I have been able to quadruple the number of Hispanic Federal judges in less than 4 years. I'm proud of the fact that I've been able to appoint more Hispanic judges than all other Presidents combined in the 200-year history of our Nation. And I'm not done yet.

And I might add, parenthetically but importantly, as we have made these appointments, maintained the highest possible standards, of professional competence, and dignity, and ethics, and integrity in the judicial system. It's been a credit to the judicial system to have these appointments. As you all know, these appointments are for a lifetime. And these judges will exert their influence on our system of justice for many generations to come.

I'm committed to securing for all the children in America an equal chance to learn and to dream and to excel. There's a a saying in Spanish, *"Negar la educación a nuestros hijos es la ruina de las naciónes"*—"To deny education to our children is the ruin of nations." That's why Federal aid to education in the last 3½ years is up 73 percent. We've increased education spending for Title I, Head Start, college student aid—program after program to help disadvantaged children get an equal education. That's where the need was greatest, among those children who had not had an opportunity to take the talent and ability that God gave them, and have it nurtured and expanded for their own well-being, and for the better life of all Americans in our great country.

And that's why I put such a firm commitment behind you, in your effort toward having a good system of bilingual education forever in this Nation, as long as it's needed. Too many children do not learn, too many are scared to speak up in class, too many drop out of schools where their language is not spoken. Working together, we've doubled requested funds for bilingual education in the last 3 years.

And let me add that I stand with you against the Ashbrook Amendment. As you all know, this amendment would prevent the Department of Education from enforcing regulations on bilingual programs, even after the Supreme Court of the United States has ruled that children have a right to such programs. This is a disgraceful attempt to play politics with the civil rights of our children, and I will work with you to beat it.

The threats to programs in which you deeply believe are very serious. The undocumented workers issue is one of the most difficult and important which faces this Nation. That's why I've asked Father Hesburgh to head the Presidential commission developing recommendations on this subject. I've not seen their recommendations yet, but I can assure you that under my administration there will not be a *bracero* program.

It's very important that this commitment that I have, under my sworn oath to uphold the laws of our country, must be done in a humane way, an understanding way, respecting the rights of all those who reside in our country. I must have Government officials working with me who understand the diverse needs of our people. I've appointed more than 200 Hispanic Americans to top posts in my administration, more again than any other President. It's not enough yet, but names like Castillo, Hidalgo, Garcia, Torres, Rios, Marrero, Olivarez, many others are heard now—those names are heard in the top levels of Government, where policy is made and where direct access to the President is guaranteed, and where Congress Members, business leaders, labor leaders, and others can listen to their voice—working with me and with the Hispanic Caucus members to give all Americans a better life.

And I also made a commitment to achieve an accurate census, and now we must begin the next step, ensuring fair apportionment of legislative districts to allow full participation of Hispanic citizens in our system of government—especially in Congress. The Hispanic Caucus in Congress is ready to grow some more.

None of these challenges can be met adequately if you're satisfied only to attend the Hispanic Caucus banquet every year, and not work every day between times for the banquet. The Hispanic Caucus, I know from experience, are constantly at my door at the White House saying, "These are the needs of the people we represent, but they must be supported by you." You must become full partners with them and me, to make sure we protect these programs so vital to the people who have too long in this country been deprived.

And finally, let me mention that for the last 3½ years, our Nation has been at peace. We pursued peace not only for ourselves but for other nations as well. We took the historic steps toward a new relationship, based on mutual respect, by concluding the Panama Canal Treaty. In the Middle East, we brought a historic treaty of peace to two ancient enemies, Israel and Egypt. And we've once again raised the banner of human rights and given hope to all those who love freedom. Our principles of human rights extend to the people of Puerto Rico and their right to self-determination. I've made my position clear, and I'll repeat it tonight. I will support the decision of the people of Puerto Rico about their future status. And when that decision is made, I will also do my utmost to make sure that Congress carries out that decision also.

When more than a hundred thousand Cubans fled oppression, we treated them with compassion and decency, under the most difficult possible circumstances—at the same time trying to enforce our laws against those who would exploit the yearnings of divided families. We've not forgotten the burden on communities affected by the sudden influx of Cuban refugees. We're committed to providing the assistance needed by communities to ensure a workable, humane resettlement.

In our own hemisphere the United States was once identified, as you know, with the status quo and with dictatorships more interested in stability than in justice. Now we are once more identified with ideals, human rights, social justice, peaceful and democratic change. Because we have shown respect to others, we can now receive respect. This has done more to enhance United States influence in Latin America than just brandishing a big stick.

I'm pleased especially with the mutually beneficial, constantly improving relationship that we're developing with Mexico. I was proud to appoint—and I'm sure the people of Mexico were proud to receive—the first Mexican American ever to be serving as our Ambassador in Mexico, Julian Nava.

And let me add, with emotion, that tonight I met with 6 of the 36 Hispanic-American recipients of the Congressional Medal of Honor. They escorted me to this dais. These heroes remind me of the great contributions made by Hispanic Americans, and what sacrifices may sometimes be demanded of us all as we keep our commitment to freedom, to justice, and to equal opportunity.

Let us remember the words of Robert Kennedy when he said, and I quote: "Nations around the world look to us for leadership, not merely by strength of arms but by the strength of our convictions."

We not only want but we need the free exercise of rights by every American. We need the strength and talent of every American. We need, in short, to set an example of freedom for the world—and for ourselves.

We have not yet realized all our dreams for the American people, yet we've come too far now for any of us to turn back. We've worked hard together, you and I, to put our hearts into this struggle which so far has realized great success. Let's rededicate ourselves tonight and join together in making even greater the greatest nation on Earth.

Thank you very much.

NOTE: The President spoke at 9:33 p.m. in the International Ballroom at the Washington Hilton Hotel.

National Advisory Council on the Education of Disadvantaged Children

Reappointment of Five Members.
September 19, 1980

The President today announced the reappointment of five persons as members of the National Advisory Council on the Education of Disadvantaged Children. They are:

CLEO HOLT, a public school reading teacher in Mt. Vernon, Ill.;

ANNETTE DROZ FUENTES, a classroom teacher in the Bronx, N.Y., public schools and a specialist in bilingual education;

ROBERT H. KOFF, dean of the School of Education, State University of New York at Albany;

LUCILLE L. SANTOS, deputy assistant superintendent of special programs with the San Antonio (Texas) Independent School District;

RICHARD ST. GERMAINE, tribal chairman and director of education of the Lac Courte Oreilles Tribe in Hayward, Wis.

Regulatory Flexibility Act

Remarks on Signing S. 299 Into Law.
September 19, 1980

THE PRESIDENT. First of all, I want to welcome all of you here. This is a very good day in the economic history of our country. As a small businessman myself, as one who's been intimately involved in the development of the White House Conference on Small Business, and as the leader of this Nation, trying to search for the proper delineation between regulation on the one hand, and the utmost competitiveness and freedom for our free enterprise system, I'm delighted to participate in this ceremony.

I do want to welcome all of you here, especially the Members of Congress, who are on the platform with me, who worked so hard to pass this legislation. I especially want to recognize John Culver, Neal Smith, Gaylord Nelson, Andy Ireland.

In a few minutes I will sign into law an important element of my program to cut back on excessive regulations—a bill known as the small business Regulatory Flexibility Act. This law recognizes the fact that small businesses are vital to the growth and to the future of our country. It recognizes that Government regulation can impose a disproportionate and unfair burden on small businesses. This law requires agencies to tailor their regulations to the size and the resources of the affected business without sacrificing legitimate regulatory goals.

Politicians have talked about regulatory reform for a long time—for decades. We've acted on it. This is the fifth major regulatory reform bill that I have been able to sign—the broadest reform program in history. We have deregulated airlines, trucking, banking, and fossil fuels, and I hope to sign a railroad deregulation bill before this Congress adjourns.

I've ordered Federal agencies to analyze all the costs and benefits and to choose the least burdensome way to meet their legal objectives. These measures that I've just outlined to you so briefly are increasing competition and helping us fight inflation at the same time, without sacrificing environmental quality or the protection of the health and safety of Americans and other vital public interests.

These steps correspond to the major regulatory concerns that were expressed to me and to the public by the White House Conference on Small Business. In May, Chairman Arthur Levitt presented me with the Conference Commission's report. Since that time, my administration has already acted on many of the recommendations we received.

Let me tell you very quickly how we followed other recommendations of the Conference in addition to those that I've outlined and which will be encompassed in this bill.

A major concern was capital formation and the retention of capital by small businesses. The economic revitalization program that I announced on August the 28th directly addresses the most important recommendations. My program will help to create—above and beyond existing programs, normal recovery, and even all the proposals on Capitol Hill—a million new jobs in the next 2 years and will increase productivity of American workers without rekindling inflation. As a matter of fact, the total program to revitalize industry and create all those jobs will be anti-inflationary in its impact.

One half of the benefits of this program are incentives for business investment—especially helpful to small businesses. I'll describe some of them very quickly.

We will make accelerated depreciation of capital goods available to many more small businesses by simplifying and liberalizing existing rules. On the constant rate depreciation, small businesses can use the same depreciation methods as the large businesses, without having to hire an army of accountants. All those here, like myself, who are involved in a small business know that the extremely complicated depreciation rules in the past have almost made it impossible for us to utilize, without a staff of accountants, those opportunities in the tax laws. This will correct that defect.

The investment tax credit will be partially refundable for the first time—especially beneficial to new businesses and struggling businesses which are attempting to become financially solvent but which have not had a substantial income in the preceeding year. New businesses would be assisted with improved tax flow by my proposal to deduct start-up costs over not less than 5 years. Offsetting social security tax increases with refundable tax credits will increase the ability of small businesses to keep current workers employed and to hire new ones.

At the urging of Senator Sam Nunn and others, I'm directing that OMB, the Office of Management and Budget, and the Small Business Administration study the use of loan guarantees, at no cost to the Federal Government, in conjunction with local development companies and private lenders to finance plant expansion and renovation.

We're increasing the share of Federal procurement going to small business—especially those owned by minorities and by women. Purchasing from minority-owned firms, as a matter of fact, was only about $1 billion when I became President early in 1977. We expect to reach my goal of tripling that amount by the end of this fiscal year, and we hope to triple again the dollar volume of minority procurements.

Further, I've accepted the Commission's goal that contracts and subcontracts to minority firms account for 10 percent of all Government procurements by the end of this decade. We expect to double the current level of $200 million in purchases from women-owned firms by the end of fiscal year 1981. And my goal is that the Federal procurement from women-owned firms will be tripled again, to reach $600 million in fiscal 1982.

The experience we've had so far with this program, although predictions were made to the contrary, have been very good. I participated early this week, parenthetically, in the dedication of the new Atlanta International Airport—a major project, the largest airport in the world, advanced design, high quality workmanship. More than 25 percent of all the contracts in that airport were to minority-owned businesses. The results have been outstanding. As a matter of fact, in airport construction, 80 percent of the minority contracts were concentrated in that one project alone.

The same White House Conference that has made all these recommendations which we are trying to carry out as rapidly as possible encouraged the Small Business Administration to expand its $3 billion a year loan guarantee program—establishing targets for minority-owned and women-owned firms. We've already more than doubled funding for small business programs, and we'll propose further expansion.

We've been able to act quickly under sometimes almost emergency circumstances when necessary. To help revitalize the automobile industry, for instance, the SBA worked closely with local banks this summer to lend over $100 million to more than 500 automobile dealers so that they could stay in business.

The Office of Advocacy of the SBA has been strengthened, and its mission has been broadened. You can see that we have begun to implement many of the Conference recommendations in this short period of time, and we're not through yet. I intend to reconvene the Conference and its leadership in 1982, to review the progress made by that time, to reassess priorities which were set this year to see how much progress we have made, and to establish new goals, as appropriate, for future years.

In closing, let me say that the economic initiatives that I've outlined to you can help to revitalize our national economy, which is so reliant upon the vitality of small businesses. I recognize as an engineer, some experience in science, and as a small business leader of my own, and as a President, that quite often the innovation, the dynamism, the entrepreneurial attitude of American free enterprise system is concentrated in the small business. And all of these programs are designed to revitalize and to stir up competitive spirit—which is the foundation of our free enterprise system—in the years ahead.

I want to call all of you to help me in this ambitious program and to put it into action next year. John Culver and Andy Ireland invented the regulatory flexibility concept encompassed in this bill and worked long and hard to reach this day.

I will now sign the legislation into law, following which I would like to ask John Culver and then Andy Ireland to respond.

SENATOR CULVER. *Thank you very much, Mr. President. Members of the Congress and ladies and gentlemen:*

This is a very exciting moment for so many of us in the Congress who have worked hard, along with so many of you here in this room, in the development and the formulation and the final enactment of what I think is very landmark legislation as far as this country is concerned.

It clearly is a victory not only for small business, but I think in a real sense, for a stronger economy and for a better Government. As we're all painfully aware when we apply uniform regulations, they unquestionably have fallen disproportionately hard on small business in their costs and in the resource difficulty in compliance.

This legislation, I think, is desirable because it's not a quick fix. It's not any easy remedy. But it really goes to the heart of the problem. It attacks it at its source. And it creates a reform of the process itself. So that in institutional terms, from this day forward, every agency of our Federal Government will necessarily be increasingly sensitive in the formulation of rules and regulations to deal with and meet and dove-tail with the particular entity being regulated, whether it's a small business or a small community.

And I would like to also say that in my judgment, this will help make possible the creative energies of small business in job creation and will also increase competition and, certainly, innovation where our small businesses have really been the heart of America's great economic strength.

And in closing, I want to also express my appreciation to Senator Gaylord Nelson, who with me, 3 years ago, began the long trek with this bill on the Senate side of the Congress; and also Senator Paul Laxalt from Nevada, who worked long and hard on this; and certainly Congressman Ireland; my colleague from Iowa, Congressman Neal Smith; and Congressman Kastenmeier as well. But finally, I wish to express to all of you my admiration, my respect, and appreciation, because in a very real sense, although the White House Small Business Conference was crucial, Milt Stewart's cooperation was indispensable, the work in the Congress was of course necessary, this legislation is really your creation and it's really your victory.

Thank you very much.

REPRESENTATIVE IRELAND. *Mr. President, distinguished colleagues from the Congress, ladies and gentlemen:*

When I introduced in the House the concept of regulatory flexibility for small business in 1978, I knew it would be a long, long struggle to see it enacted. With the help of the friends of America's small business, most of whom I believe are represented here today, it has become a reality.

We have thrown a regulatory lifeline to the millions of small businesses, organizations, and small governmental units which have been slowly sinking under an ocean of Federal regulation and paperwork. President Carter put us on the right road last year when he issued an Executive order encouraging the use of regulatory flexibility. Now, we've all joined together and have made it the law of the land.

The small business person in this Nation represents the independence, the freedom, the perseverance that have long been identified with the American way of doing things. Small business means innovation, it means productivity, and it means jobs. We have bettered the environment for all three of these by what we have done here today.

My thanks, on behalf of 13 million small businesses in the United States, to everyone who made this day possible. Thank you.

MR. WEAVER. I'm Vernon Weaver, Administrator of the Small Business Administration.

Mr. President, Members of Congress:

Last January when the White House Conference on Small Business came to a close, the delegates elected a unity council and charged it with helping and implementing the delegates' recommendations. It's my pleasure to introduce to you a small business person, who is the chairman of that council, for a presentation—Mr. Bob Carr.

MR. CARR. *Mr. President, Members of Congress, ladies and gentlemen:*

You don't know how proud I am to be able to fulfill one of our top resolutions of the White House Conference. Specifically, the delegates to the White House Conference on Small Business, representing the needs, the views, concerns of more than 12 million small businesses, overwhelmingly adopted a resolution to congratulate and extend their appreciation and support to President Carter for his efforts to make 1980 the beginning of the revitalization of small businesses in the United States.

President Carter's concern, foresight, and initiative for protecting small businesses led to his calling the first ever White House Conference on Small Business to allow the small business people the opportunity to develop legislative proposals to resolve the problems facing small businesses. Small businesses across the Nation are encouraged by and appreciative of President Carter's efforts in the progress to implement the recommendations of the White House Conference on Small Business.

September 19th, 1980, bears witness to President Carter's efforts on behalf of small businesses and marks the realization of the dreams and hopes of 12 million small business owners and their 100 million employees, with the signing by President Carter of S. 299, legislation which enacts one of the recommendations of the White House Conference on Small Business.

THE PRESIDENT. There are very few secrets kept around the White House; this is one of them.

I think all of you know, from the comments that I have made and the comments of Congressman Ireland and Senator Culver, Bob Carr and Vernon Weaver, that this is a partnership. We have a long way to go, because for too many years the small business community in our Nation had its values underestimated in the strengthening of our economy, the innovation which is the spirit of America, and the contribution that can be made if the detriments and the handicaps in the way of small business progress can be removed.

We recognize that we have a long way to go. But this partnership, which has paid such rich dividends in the brief period of time it's been formed, I have no doubt will make our Nation realize a brighter future, a more prosperous future for our economic system and a better life for every American. I'm very grateful to be part of it.

Thank you very much, Bob Carr.

NOTE: The President spoke at 1:32 p.m. at the signing ceremony in the East Room at the White House.

As enacted, S. 299 is Public Law 96–353, approved September 19.

Regulatory Flexibility Act

Statement on Signing S. 299 Into Law.
September 19, 1980

I have today signed into law S. 299, the Regulatory Flexibility Act. The Regulatory Flexibility Act provides vital help for America's small businesses.

Small businesses are crucial to a competitive, healthy, and productive economy. However, regulations often impose heavier burdens on small organizations than on big ones. The Regulatory Flexibility Act recognizes that regulations need not be uniform to be effective. It requires agencies, whenever appropriate, to tailor their rules to the size and resources of those affected.

Under this bill, agencies will assess the impact of their rules and paperwork requirements upon small businesses and other small organizations and government jurisdictions. These agencies will publish advance notice of proposed rules and will include, for public comment, possible approaches such as exemptions and reduced requirements that would eliminate the rule's disproportionate impact upon these smaller entities. Agencies will also publish similar notices in business and trade journals in order to help those affected by the rules to participate in the review process. The agencies will also reexamine existing rules every 10 years to see if their impact on small entities can be reduced.

This bill will not sacrifice the legitimate goals of regulation. It recognizes instead that many of those goals can be achieved without imposing rigid, uniform requirements.

This process is already working. I consulted with the sponsors of this bill last year when developing a directive to the executive agencies instructing them to use flexible approaches in regulations, and already dozens of rules have been adjusted. For example, the Environmental Protection Agency varied a rule on solid waste to exempt small entities. This change exempts 91 percent of those who would have been covered by the regulation, but it exempts only 1 percent of the waste.

The bill was carefully drafted to avoid new costly rounds of litigation. The regulators who write the rules are charged with adjusting them. I will use my Executive authority to ensure that they do so,

and my administration will work closely with the sponsors of the bill, who plan vigorous oversight.

This bill adds another piece to the far-reaching regulatory reform record that we and the Congress are building. Major reform legislation has been passed covering the airlines, banking, trucking, and natural gas. I urge Congress to continue this impressive record of progress by passing railroad deregulation, paperwork reduction, and other pending regulatory reform measures.

I congratulate Senators John Culver and Gaylord Nelson and Congressmen Andrew Ireland and Neil Smith for their leadership in developing and passing this legislation.

NOTE: As enacted, S. 299 is Public Law 96–353, approved September 19.

Explosion at a Titan Missile Site in Arkansas

Remarks to Reporters on the Incident.
September 19, 1980

THE PRESIDENT. Concerning the Titan missile explosion, I have stayed in close contact all throughout the morning with the Secretary of Defense. We deeply regret the casualties from the explosion. The situation is under control. There is no indication of radioactivity at all. The crews have performed superbly and with courage. I have asked Secretary Brown to give me a complete evaluation of the cause of the accident and also the Titan missile sites throughout the country, to make sure there is no repetition of this accident.

Those are the comments that I have.

Q. Mr. President, are the Titan missiles a part of our—are they a useful part of the Triad now, or are they possibly defective?

THE PRESIDENT. These missiles are the oldest part of our Triad, as you know. We have now 52 or 53 missiles of the Titan class still in stand-by for use if necessary. They are an integral part of the Triad.

Q. Are they too old, Mr. President; should they be replaced with solid-fuel rockets?

THE PRESIDENT. Well, obviously we are getting ready to move into the MX missile program, which is a solid-fuel rocket, and of course, the Minuteman are solid-fuel rockets as well. But the Titans still serve a useful deterrent purpose. But we have been aware of the fact that they are older missiles, and through a normal evolutionary process they will be replaced with a new missile.

Q. What were the odds on a nuclear disaster in a situation like that?

THE PRESIDENT. Extremely low. As I say, we've monitored the site very carefully. There is no indication of radioactivity at all.

Q. Has the warhead been removed?

THE PRESIDENT. The—everything is safe.

NOTE: The President spoke at 2:07 p.m. at the South Portico at the White House.

International Communication Agency

Nomination of John William Shirley To Be an Associate Director.   September 19, 1980

The President today announced that he will nominate John William Shirley, of Chicago, Ill., to be an Associate Director of the International Communication Agency (ICA). He would replace Harold F. Schneidman, resigned.

Shirley has been Counselor for Public Affairs at the U.S. Embassy in Rome since 1977. He has been with ICA and its predecessor agency, the United States Information Agency (USIA), since 1957.

Shirley was born August 18, 1931, in Hailsham, Sussex, United Kingdom. He received a B.S. in international relations from Georgetown University School of Foreign Service in 1957. He served in the U.S. Air Force from 1952 to 1956.

Shirley joined USIA in 1957 and served in Zagreb, Belgrade, Trieste, Rome, and New Delhi. From 1968 to 1969, he was a policy officer in USIA's Office of Near East and South Asian Affairs. In 1969–70 he took Polish language training at the Foreign Service Institute.

From 1970 to 1972, Shirley was First Secretary for Press and Cultural Affairs at the American Embassy in Warsaw. From 1972 to 1975, he was Deputy Assistant Director, then Assistant Director, of USIA for Soviet Union and East European Affairs. From 1975 to 1977, he was Assistant Director for European Affairs.

National Highway Safety Advisory Committee

Appointment of R. Todd Renfrow To Be a Member.   September 19, 1980

The President today announced his intention to appoint R. Todd Renfrow, of Springfield, Ill., to be a member of the National Highway Safety Advisory Committee for a term expiring in 1983. He will replace Rebecca Young, whose term has expired.

Renfrow is president and owner of Uptown, Inc., an automobile parts company, and former president of the Springfield Safety Council, where he initiated a program in the schools on safety.

Digest of Other
White House Announcements

The following listing includes the President's public schedule and other items of general interest announced by the White House Press Office and not included elsewhere in this issue.

September 13

The President met at the White House with Zbigniew Brzezinski, Assistant to the President for National Security Affairs.

September 17

The President met at the White House with:

—David L. Aaron, Deputy Assistant for National Security Affairs;

—the Democratic congressional leadership;

—Frank B. Moore, Assistant to the President for Congressional Liaison;

—Roy Orr, president of the National Association of Counties;

—Ambassadors Ephraim Evron of Israel and Ashraf Ghorbal of Egypt, Foreign Minister Yitzhak Shamir of Israel, and Kamal Hassan Ali, Deputy Prime Minister and Minister of Foreign Affairs of Egypt.

In a ceremony in the Oval Office, the President, Honorary Chairman of Boys' Clubs of America, presented the Clubs' 1980 Boy of the Year award to Jace L. Smith, 17, of Massillon, Ohio.

The President announced that he is withdrawing the nomination of Fred D. Gray to be United States District Judge for the Middle District of Alabama, at Mr. Gray's request.

The White House announced that, based on relevant laws and Executive orders, the Attorney General and the Director of the Central Intelligence Agency have been asked to investigate the matter of a forged document, labeled Presidential Review Memorandum/NSC–46, dated March 17, 1978, concerning black Africa and the U.S. black movement, which was circulated to members of the press on September 16.

September 18

The President met at the White House with:

—Dr. Brzezinski;

—Congresswoman Elizabeth Holtzman of New York;

—Mr. Moore;

—representatives of the International Association of Operating Engineers.

The President announced that he will nominate Robert Alan Frosch, Administrator of the National Aeronautics and Space Administration, for the rank of Ambassador while he serves as Head of the U.S. Delegation to the United Nations Outer Space Conference, to be held in 1982.

September 19

The President met at the White House with:

—Dr. Brzezinski;

—Secretary of State Edmund S. Muskie, Secretary of Defense Harold Brown, Deputy Secretary of State Warren M. Christopher, Lloyd N. Cutler, Counsel to the President, and Dr. Brzezinski;

—a group of consumer advocates;

—guitarist Chet Atkins;

—Olin Robinson, Head of the U.S. Advisory Commission on Public Diplomacy, who presented the Commission's 2-year report to the President;

—Paul A. Volcker, Chairman of the Board of Governors of the Federal Reserve System, Secretary of the Treasury G. William Miller, Charles L. Schultze, Chairman of the Council of Economic Advisers, James T. McIntyre, Jr., Director of the Office of Management and Budget, Alfred E. Kahn, Advisor to the President on Inflation.

The President left the White House for a stay at Camp David, Md.

NOMINATIONS SUBMITTED TO THE SENATE

The following list does not include promotions of members of the Uniformed Services, nominations to the Service Academies, or nominations of Foreign Service officers.

Submitted September 15, 1980

The following-named persons to be Representatives of the United States of America to the Twenty-first Session of the General Conference of the United Nations Educational, Scientific, and Cultural Organization:

ROBIN DUKE, of New York
BARBARA W. NEWELL, of Massachusetts
ELIE ABEL, of California
JOHN E. FOBES, of North Carolina
JOHN HOPE FRANKLIN, of Illinois

The following-named persons to be Alternate Representatives of the United States of America to the Twenty-first Session of the General Conference of the United Nations Educational, Scientific, and Cultural Organization:

SANDRA LOPEZ BIRD, of New York
JOSEPH D. DUFFEY, of the District of Columbia
KATHLEEN NOLAN, of California
BEATRICE RANIS, of Hawaii
ROGER REVELLE, of California

Submitted September 17, 1980

MYRON H. THOMPSON, of Alabama, to be United States District Judge for the Middle District of Alabama, vice Frank M. Johnson, Jr., elevated.

RALPH W. NIMMONS, JR., of Florida, to be United States District Judge for the Middle District of Florida, vice a new position created by P.L. 95–486, approved October 20, 1978.

ISRAEL LEO GLASSER, of New York, to be United States District Judge for the Eastern District of New York, vice a new position created by P.L. 95–486, approved October 20, 1978.

PHILIP WEINBERG, of New York, to be United States District Judge for the Eastern District of New York, vice Jacob Mishler, retired.

NOMINATIONS—Continued

Withdrawn September 17, 1980

FRED D. GRAY, of Alabama, to be United States District Judge for the Middle District of Alabama, vice Frank M. Johnson, Jr., elevated, which was sent to the Senate on January 10, 1980.

The following-named persons to be Associate Judges of the Superior Court of the District of Columbia for terms of 15 years:

DOROTHY SELLERS, of the District of Columbia, vice Edmond T. Daly, deceased.
RICARDO M. URBINA, of the District of Columbia, vice Normalie Holloway Johnson, elevated.

The following-named persons to be members of the Board of Directors of the National Railroad Passenger Corporation for the terms indicated:

WILLIAM T. CAHILL, of New Jersey, for a term expiring July 18, 1982, vice Robert G. Dunlop, resigned.
W. HOWARD FORT, of Ohio, for a term expiring July 18, 1984, vice Harry Edwards, resigned.

Submitted September 18, 1980

The following-named persons to be members of the Board of Directors of the United States Railway Association for terms expiring July 8, 1986:

STANTON P. SENDER, of the District of Columbia (reappointment).
FRANKLIN D. RAINES, of Washington, vice Samuel B. Payne, term expired.

HARRY E. T. THAYER, of the District of Columbia, a Foreign Service officer of Class one, to be Ambassador Extraordinary and Plenipotentiary of the United States of America to the Republic of Singapore.

ROBERT ALAN FROSCH, of Virginia, Administrator of the National Aeronautics and Space Administration, for the rank of Ambassador during his tenure of service as Head of the United States Delegation to both the preparatory meetings and the subsequent United Nations Outer Space Conference as well as to related meetings of the United Nations Committee on the Peaceful Uses of Outer Space and its two subcommittees.

JOHN A. GRONOUSKI, of Texas, to be a member of the Board for International Broadcasting for a term expiring April 28, 1983 (reappointment).

NOMINATIONS—Continued

Submitted September 19, 1980

John William Shirley, of Illinois, to be an Associate Director of the International Communication Agency, vice Harold F. Schneidman, resigned.

The following-named persons to be members of the Board of Directors of the United States Synthetic Fuels Corporation for the terms indicated (new positions):

John D. DeButts, of Virginia, for a term of 1 year.

Catherine Blanchard Cleary, of Wisconsin, for a term of 2 years.

Frank Savage, of New York, for a term of 3 years.

Cecil D. Andrus, of Idaho, for a term of 4 years.

Joseph Lane Kirkland, of the District of Columbia, for a term of 5 years.

Frank T. Cary, of Connecticut, for a term of 6 years.

The following-named persons to be the Representative and an Alternate Representative of the United States of America to the Twenty-fourth Session of the General Conference of the International Atomic Energy Agency:

Representative:

Gerard C. Smith, of the District of Columbia

Alternative Representative:

Joseph Mallam Hendrie, of New York

Withdrawn September 19, 1980

The following-named persons to be the Representative and an Alternate Representative of the United States of America to the Twenty-fourth Session of the General Conference of the International Atomic Energy Agency which were sent to the Senate on August 26, 1980:

Representative:

John C. Sawhill, of the District of Columbia

Alternate Representative:

Gerard C. Smith, of the District of Columbia

CHECKLIST OF WHITE HOUSE PRESS RELEASES

The following listing contains releases of the White House Press Office which are not included in the issue.

CHECKLIST—Continued

Released September 13, 1980

Advance text: remarks at the National Italian-American Foundation's Third Biennial Tribute Dinner

Transcript: informal remarks at a Carter/Mondale reception at Merriweather Post Pavilion, Columbia, Md.

Released September 15, 1980

Fact sheet: H.R. 2538, concerning illegal drug traffic on the high seas (Public Law 96–350)

Advance text: remarks at a town hall meeting in Corpus Christi, Tex.

Released September 16, 1980

Advance text: remarks at the Ebenezer Baptist Church in Atlanta, Ga.

Advance text: remarks at the Hartsfield Atlanta International Airport, Atlanta, Ga.

Advance text: remarks to textile workers at Startex Mills, Startex, S.C.

Released September 17, 1980

Fact sheet: U.S.-China relations

Announcement: nomination of Philip Weinberg to be United States District Judge for the Eastern District of New York

Announcement: nomination of Ralph W. Nimmons, Jr., to be United States District Judge for the Middle District of Florida

Announcement: nomination of Israel Leo Glasser to be United States District Judge for the Eastern District of New York

Announcement: nomination of Myron H. Thompson to United States District Judge for the Middle District of Alabama

Advance text: remarks at signing ceremony for United States-People's Republic of China Agreements

Released September 18, 1980

Announcement: administration's plan to ease the strain of the Cuban/Haitian influx in south Florida

Advance text: remarks at Third Annual Dinner of the Congressional Hispanic Caucus

Released September 19, 1980

Fact sheet: Regulatory Flexibility Act of 1980

ACTS APPROVED BY THE PRESIDENT

Approved September 15, 1980

H.R. 2538_____ Public Law 96–350
An act to facilitate increased enforcement by the Coast Guard of laws relating to the importation of controlled substances, and for other purposes.

H.R. 4627_____ Public Law 96–351
An act to authorize the enlistment of citizens of the Northern Mariana Islands in the Armed Forces of the United States of America.

Approved September 17, 1980

H.J. Res. 607_____ Public Law 96–352
A joint resolution making an urgent supplemental appropriation for the Veterans Administration for the fiscal year ending September 30, 1980.

Approved September 19, 1980

H.J. Res. 594_____ Public Law 96–353
A joint resolution to authorize and request the President to issue a proclamation designating September 18, 1980, as "Constantino Brumidi Day".

S. 299_____ Publc Law 96–354
Regulatory Flexibility Act.

United States Policy Toward Iran

White House Statement In Connection With a Newspaper Column. September 20, 1980

Jack Anderson's latest column alleging that the United States plans to attack Iran and that Soviet leaders believe in the seriousness of such plans is as false, grotesque, and irresponsible as were his columns a month ago on the same subject. The latest charges are complete inventions which can only damage efforts to obtain the prompt and safe release of the American hostages in Iran and the prospects for peace in that region. What is true, however, is that Soviet propaganda has exploited Anderson's similar false allegations to inspire anti-American sentiments in Iran and elsewhere, to prolong the hostage crisis, and to construct pretexts for aggressive Soviet actions.

NOTE: The column was distributed by United Features Syndicate for publication on September 22.

Niles, Illinois

Remarks at the 100th Anniversary Dinner of the Polish National Alliance. September 20, 1980

President Mazewski, Mayor Byrne, Mayor Blaise, Congressman Dan Rostenkowski, John Berry, former Congressman Roman Pucinski, Francis Meehan, our new American Ambassador to Poland, ladies and gentlemen:

I knew that when I welcomed the Pope to the White House for the first time in America's history and spoke Polish in my welcome that everybody was going to do what I did and take the glory away from me as being the only one to welcome someone in the Polish language. It was easy for me to understand what he said. I could get the words very clear—Taft, Carter, Brzezinski. [*Laughter*] And I noticed that many of you were in about the same shape I was. [*Laughter*]

I do want to thank your great president, Al Mazewski, for that fine introduction. In his capacity as president of both the Polish National Alliance and the Polish American Congress, Al is a frequent visitor at the White House. He knows how to get things done. He knows how to get reelected. [*Laughter*] So far he's in his fourth term; I'll settle for two. [*Laughter*] And I might say it is good to see him again and also so many other leaders of the Polish-American community. I cannot recognize you all, but there are a few that mean a lot to me and to this Nation, and I would like to recognize their presence.

I may repeat some of the things that the Governor and the mayor have said. But I come here in a unique role as President of our great country, representing almost 240 million Americans, and I want to say those things, because they're important to me, to our Nation, and perhaps to you.

I want to recognize the national president of the Polish Roman Catholic Union, Joseph Drobot; the president of the Falcons, Bernard Rogalski; the chairman of the board of Alliance College, Hilary Czaplicki; and the vice president in charge of the women's division of the Polish Na-

1851

tional Alliance, Ms. Helen Szymanowicz; and also the president of the Polish Women's Alliance, Mrs. Helen Zielinski. The motto of her organization, as you know, is "The ideals of her women are the strength of a nation," and I agree with that statement. And someone else who would agree with that statement is the mayor of the world's second largest Polish city, Mayor Jane Byrne. As you know, Chicago is also known as "the city of the big shoulders," and during the early years of Chicago and of our Nation, the tough years of building, those were Polish shoulders, here and in many other cities in our country.

And it would be a mistake for us to forget the tremendous contributions of artists and thinkers such as Nobel Laureates Henryk Sienkiewicz—right on; is that right?—and Madame Curie and Joseph Conrad, Arthur Rubenstein, Ignacy Paderewski, one that I can pronounce very easily, Hyman Rickover, who I might add, was my old boss. And of course, we've already had mentioned Secretary of State Ed Muskie and Zbigniew Brzezinski, who are so close to me.

As you know, with Zbig in the White House and Ed Muskie in the State Department, I'm getting used to hearing jokes about the "bipolar" foreign policy. As a matter of fact, with Clem Zablocki, chairman of the House Foreign Affairs Committee, what we actually have is a "tripolar" foreign policy. And other nations know that when we speak around the world, we speak with a deep commitment that's been characteristic of the Polish people down through the centuries, which is also the character of America, and I'm proud of that.

Danny Rostenkowski, as you know, is one of the great leaders of the Congress. I meet with him regularly as one of the small, elite, extremely influential group,

who has been elected by his own peer group, the other Members of Congress, as their leader. What we have in Washington now is a Polish-American contribution, unprecedented in modern history at least, which is a benefit to all Americans.

It's been estimated that about 30 percent of all Americans can trace at least one of their ancestral lines back to Poland. And for generations, the Polish National Alliance has been the mortar that has held the Polish-American community together. Your first meeting was held in Chicago a hundred years ago, and I'm honored, as President, to join you in celebrating your hundredth birthday. And I'm sure this second century will be just as successful as the first one.

As Al mentioned, I'm only the second President in history to appear before you. The first, William Howard Taft—as Al mentioned in passing—was a Republican. And I'm proud to be the Democrat who's evened the score. I'm not going to talk politics tonight, but I can't help noticing an interesting coincidence. When President Taft spoke to you, it was also an election year, 1912. [*Laughter*] There was also one Democratic candidate and two Republican candidates, just like this year. And here's the coincidence that I particularly like—the Democrat won.

I'm sure you know your history, but I'd like to point out this other part. The winner of that election, President Woodrow Wilson, played a decisive role in the history of Poland. He made Poland's freedom one of his Fourteen Points. And because of Woodrow Wilson's deep commitment and because he accurately expressed the sentiments, at that time and now, of America, after more than a century of foreign oppression Poland's existence as a state was restored.

I have a special feeling for the sons and daughters of Poland. Poland was the first foreign country that I ever visited* as President of the United States. And I've been inspired by the fact that the Polish people have been among the earliest and most consistent fighters for human rights, not just for a year, not just for a hundred years, but for a thousand years. The entire world was reminded of this fine heritage last year when Pope John Paul II visited our country .

When Pope John Paul II came to the White House, it was the most exciting and gratifying day of my life. It was a beautiful occasion in our country. What a tremendous impact this good and holy man had on all our people. His spirit, his kindness, his personal warmth, his radiance conquered our hearts. That was a proud and a special moment for all Americans. It was doubly so, I know, for Polish Americans. Pope John Paul II, a faithful son of his nation and of his church, became a living symbol of Polish contributions to our common values. The Pope is only the latest of the millions of Poles who have come to America, as visitors and as immigrants, bringing with them a love of human rights.

My second daughter-in-law lives in Pulaski County, Georgia, named after Count Casimir Pulaski. And everyone in my State, and indeed the entire Nation, knows that Thaddeus Kosciuszko was also there, with courage and commitment and the deepest sense of freedom, to help America win our independence. What most people do not know is that Kosciuszko did a noble thing when he left this country. Just before he returned to Poland to fight for freedom in his own homeland, he had a large sum of money coming to him from the Continental Con-

gress. He left that money with Thomas Jefferson, with instructions to Jefferson to purchase the freedom of as many black slaves as possible. That great Polish general very simply believed that slavery was as repugnant here in America as in his own country.

Let me remind you of one more incident in the long history of Polish Americans and human rights. Mayor Jane Byrne mentioned it in passing, but I'd like to elaborate just for a moment. This goes back a long time, more than 350 years, but it's just as fresh as today's newspaper. In 1608, in what is now Virginia, Captain John Smith brought a small group of Polish glassmakers to Jamestown to set up the first factory in America. But the Polonians, as they were then called, were denied the rights of free citizens.

These proud people endured these indignities for 11 years. Then finally in 1619 they staged the first sitdown strike in American history—not for money, but for freedom and for human rights. And because of that, the House of Burgesses, the first legislature in America, passed a bill giving the Polonians the right to vote and the other rights of free people. Think of that, three and a half centuries ago, and then think of the Gdansk workers of 1980. The spirit of the Jamestown Polonians is very much alive here in this room and also across the ocean, and I'm thankful for it.

I was reviewing my notes on the way here early this evening from Camp David, and I thought about my being a southerner and, as a southerner, knowing what it means to be the butt of jokes. It's especially revolting among great and proud people, and I know you share my disgust with this ill-considered habit. For such remarks to be made about the home of a Pope, the home of modern and ancient freedom-fighters, the home of Nobel scientists, the home of the world's greatest

---

*The sentence should read, "Poland was the first foreign country to which I made a state visit as President of the United States." [White House correction.]

musicians, the home of great statesmen, there and here in our country, and of heroes who helped give birth to our Nation is especially incomprehensible to me as President of this country. The joke is on those who are crude and ignorant enough to indulge in such slander. And as an American and a southerner and an admirer of the Polish-American people and the Polish people, I resent it very much.

The events of recent weeks in Poland have indeed inspired the world. During this period of exciting change in Poland, the United States Government, advised very carefully by your own president here, has pursued a careful policy, a policy based on the need for a calm atmosphere, free from outside interference. We will not interfere in Poland's affairs, and we expect that others will similarly respect the right of the Polish nation to make its own decisions and to resolve its problems on its own. It appears, and we pray God that it will be, on its way to a peaceful and a constructive resolution.

But Poland's economic problems remain very severe. Besides the dislocations, there have been terrible floods. Poland needs food. That's why I ordered quick approval of Poland's full request of $670 million in new credit guarantees for 4 million tons of American grain and other farm products. This is the largest such guarantee we have ever made. And also, as you know, we have also, as you know, substantially increased Pacific coast allocations of fish to Poland.

These steps, urged by many of you here tonight, are intended to meet an urgent and a basic need for food. They are also intended to show our admiration for the dignified manner in which the entire Polish nation is conducting itself in this time of wrenching and positive change. And they are intended to demonstrate to the new leadership of Poland our desire for better relations. We want to strengthen even further the human ties of blood, kinship, and friendship that tie our two nations together.

The shipyard workers in Gdansk, the coal miners in Silesia, the store clerks and workers in Warsaw, and the authorities in Poland who responded to them have sent a powerful message around the world. Poland has reminded us that the desire for human rights and human dignity is universal. Freedom of thought and expression, freedom from arbitrary violence, freedom from violations of personal integrity, due process, participation in government, civil and political and economic rights—these are the very stuff of human rights. And tonight I pledge to you this: As long as I am President, this Nation will stand for its beliefs, will stand for its ideals, will stand for its values. We will stand up for human rights.

To those who criticize our human rights policy and say it is not in our national interest, who say it hampers American foreign policy, I say: How can we, as free people, be indifferent to the fate of freedom elsewhere? How can we, as people with the most abundant economy on Earth, be indifferent to the suffering of those elsewhere who lack food and health care and shelter? We cannot be indifferent. And we will not retreat one step from our human rights policy, because human rights is the very soul of the identity of this Nation.

We support human rights, yes, because our conscience demands it, but the fact is that our human rights policy, specifically and in general, also pragmatically serves our national interest. Both our Nation and the world are more secure when basic human rights are respected.

Our words and our actions have left their mark in many places on Earth. Governments have released political prisoners, lessened political repression, eased economic misery. Hundreds of thousands of people have immigrated to freedom from the Soviet Union, from Cuba and elsewhere. Increased trade with African and Third World nations has resulted in part from the growing trust generated by America's human rights policy.

The Soviet Union may not like our human rights policy. Some generals and colonels and dictators in other countries may not like it. Those who tyrannize others will always fear the ideas of freedom and human dignity. But the people in the villages, the factory workers, those who farm the land and who populate the cities—they care and they applaud and they pray that Americans will never abandon them.

Here at home, our Nation's commitment to fundamental values is strengthened by advancing human rights. When we advance human rights overseas and stand firmly for the principles on which our Nation was founded, we help to guarantee equality, freedom, and the respect for individual human beings here in the United States. The rights of all Americans, regardless of color or national origin or language or sex, must be preserved.

That commitment makes us proud to be Americans, and it makes us realize that America's foreign policy in the 1980's will always emanate from those basic values which do not change. We cannot return to the days when we too often gave unquestioning support to repressive regimes. We cannot return to the days when secrecy in foreign policy was used to hide policies and acts which the American people would never have supported had they known what was going on.

We must continue to strengthen our defenses. Our military might must be unquestioned in order for us to keep our Nation at peace. We have had a steady increase in our commitments to a national defense every year since I became President, and we will continue to do the same in the future. But we cannot sap our strength by returning to the days when some would advocate a military solution to every international disturbance. We've learned too much from the last 20 years. Too many American families have made too many sacrifices for their leaders to have their vision blurred by nostalgia for a world that no longer exists. I say to you that America's military might should be used to seek peace and to avoid war. The best weapons are those so formidable that they need never be fired in anger, and the best soldier is one that's not killed in battle.

And I also say to you that America's human rights policy should be used to pierce the curtain of oppression, to throw the searchlight of the world's conscience on those who would smother the winds of freedom. The cause of human rights is a slow process. Results are not always immediately evident. Progress is often painfully slow. Sometimes there are delays, sometimes disappointments, sometimes reverses. But when the cause finally triumphs and the winds of freedom blown, no power on Earth can withstand their force.

We will stand up for human rights in Madrid at the European Security Conference, and Al Mazewski will be there as a member of the American delegation to make sure my promise to you is kept. I pledge to you that as long as America stands true to itself and as long as I'm President, our voice of liberty will not be stilled.

In closing let me say this: America is human rights. That's what America was meant to be. That's what America has meant to the rural people of Poland, to the potato farmers of Ireland, to the Jews of Eastern Europe, to all who were oppressed or seeking a better life, who built and peopled our country. Those inalienable human rights of life, liberty, and the pursuit of happiness, so eloquently written by Thomas Jefferson and honored by Kosciuszko and Pulaski, so profoundly demonstrated by the Polish workers—they will endure. They will endure for a thousand years.

Thank you very much.

NOTE: The President left Camp David, Md., early in the evening for the trip to Illinois. Following his arrival in Chicago, he attended a reception for supporters at Heuer's Restaurant. Following the reception, he went to the House of the White Eagle in Niles, Ill., where he addressed dinner guests in the Dining Room at 8:45 p.m. Following the dinner, the President returned to Camp David.

Channel Islands Marine Sanctuary

Statement by the President.
September 21, 1980

Today I have approved a proposal by the Department of Commerce to designate the 6-mile area surrounding Santa Barbara Island and the Northern Channel Islands as the Channel Islands Marine Sanctuary.

Congress passed the law authorizing marine sanctuary designations—the Marine Protection, Research and Sanctuaries Act—in 1972. It recognized that while the ocean frontier is developed to meet our Nation's diverse needs, we must bear in mind the lessons of past development on the land. We cannot ignore the environmental consequences of our activities. We must temper those activities with prudent environmental safeguards.

Much of the impetus for the law came from the disastrous Santa Barbara oil spill in 1969. Congress developed the marine sanctuary idea as a way of identifying unique ocean areas that deserve special status and making sure that any activities carried on in those areas are consistent with their long-term health and preservation.

More than a century ago, Americans with a clear vision of the future began to set aside as national parks our land's most magnificent natural wonders. Today, in this Year of the Coast, it is most fitting that we demonstrate our concern for future generations by extending comprehensive protection to the marine equivalents of Yosemite, Big Bend, the Great Smokies, and the Everglades.

When I entered office, little had been done by the executive branch to use this important new tool. Since the program began in 1972, only two sanctuaries had been designated. In my 1977 environmental message to Congress, I therefore indicated that I had instructed the Secretary of Commerce "to identify possible sanctuaries in areas where development appears imminent, and to begin collecting the data necessary to designate them as such under the law." I also asked the Secretary of the Interior to work closely with the Secretary of Commerce as he identified potential sanctuaries in areas where offshore hydrocarbon leasing appears imminent.

Since then, my administration has been working to locate areas appropriate for sanctuary designation. We have been doing so in close cooperation with local and State governments and concerned citizens. The Santa Barbara sanctuary is an excellent example of this close working relationship. It was originally nominated by California's Resources Agency, Santa Barbara County, and the National Park

Service. It is supported by Governor Brown, Senator Cranston, and members of the California congressional delegation. Much of the public dialog about the proposal was carried on through the California Coastal Commission, and the sanctuary will include State waters.

The area clearly deserves marine sanctuary status. The islands and surrounding waters are an exceptionally productive ecosystem. They provide feeding and breeding grounds for one of the largest and most varied assemblages of seals and sea lions in the world. They are one of the richest resource areas in the United States for marine birds, including the endangered brown pelican. The area has become particularly important as the pressures of human development have driven these species from one refuge after another on the mainland. It will complement the Channel Islands National Park that I recently approved.

The sanctuary will not inhibit activities around the islands such as fishing, recreational boating, and existing hydrocarbon leases but will prohibit new oil and gas leases within the sanctuary boundaries. These and other aspects of the marine sanctuary will provide important protection for the wildlife, marine animals, and flora and fauna of the islands. The area within the sanctuary has low hydrocarbon potential, and therefore this designation will not be detrimental to our efforts to meet energy needs.

The Channel Islands Sanctuary demonstrates how we can work together to manage our environment prudently without major economic sacrifices. It will be a model for other sanctuaries to follow and, once again, California has been a leader in this effort as it has been in so many other efforts to achieve this balance.

Suspension of Certain Armed Forces Promotion and Disability Separation Limitations

Executive Order 12239.   September 21, 1980

By the authority vested in me as President of the United States of America by Section 10 of Public Law 96–343 and having determined that certain promotion limitations applicable to the Navy and Marine Corps should continue to be suspended, and having determined that the new statutory conditions authorizing a continuation of certain existing disability separation practices in the Armed Forces should be effective, it is hereby ordered as follows:

1–101. For the period beginning on October 1, 1979 and ending on September 30, 1982, the application of the following provisions of Title 10 of the United States Code is suspended.

(a) Section 5707(c), restricting the number of Navy and Marine Corps officers who may be recommended for promotion from below the appropriate promotion zone.

(b) Section 5751(a), requiring Marine Corps officers serving in the grade of brigadier general to have completed three years' service in grade to be eligible for consideration for promotion to major general.

(c) Section 5751(b), requiring certain officers to have completed specific years of service in grade before being eligible for consideration for promotion to the next higher grade.

(d) Section 5751(e), precluding officers designated for limited duty who are below the appropriate promotion zone from being considered for promotion.

(e) Section 5770, requiring certain officers to have had at least two years' sea or foreign service in grade before they may be promoted.

1–102. For the period beginning on September 15, 1978 and ending on September 30, 1982, the conditions provided for by the following provisions of Title 10 of the United States Code are effective:

(a) Section 1201(3)(B)(iv), authorizing the retirement for certain disabilities of at least 30 percent which were incurred in line of duty.

(b) Section 1203(4)(A)(iii), authorizing separation for certain disabilities of less than 30 percent which were incurred in line of duty.

(c) Section 1203(4)(C)(iii), authorizing separation for certain disabilities of at least 30 percent which were not incurred in line of duty.

1–103. Executive Order No. 12082 is hereby revoked.

JIMMY CARTER

The White House,
    September 21, 1980.

[Filed with the Office of the Federal Register,
    11:51 a.m., September 22, 1980]

NOTE: The Executive order was released on September 22.

National Day of Prayer, 1980

Proclamation 4795. September 22, 1980

By the President of the United States of America

A Proclamation

Our Nation's current electoral process is both testimony and example of the power of free men and women to govern themselves. Our forebears, drawing from a faith in the people rooted in a firm faith in God, launched this grand experiment in responsible self-government. In the days ahead, no matter what our individual political convictions, we can all be grateful for the honor and integrity of this noble process.

Without trying to impose our will on other nations, let us continue to hold high the torch of liberty and democracy that has illumined our land. Laying aside arrogance and false pride, let us continue to urge self-determination and human rights as the best way for peoples everywhere to realize their own full destiny.

Let us pray that freedom, in all its manifestations, may be the reality of the present and the wave of the future. Let us pray that people everywhere will be free— free even to make their own mistakes as they struggle to build a life of material security and spiritual satisfaction.

As we pray, let us never forget the American citizens in Iran who remain hostages in fundamental violation of the teachings of the world's religions. Let us also pray that harmony and stability will come to the people of Iran, leading both to the safe return of our brothers and sisters and to a better life for all in that troubled land.

Recognizing our need for prayer, the Congress, by Joint Resolution, approved April 17, 1952 (36 U.S.C. 169h; 66 Stat. 64), has called upon the President to set aside a suitable day each year as a National Day of Prayer.

Now, THEREFORE, I, JIMMY CARTER, President of the United States of America do hereby proclaim Monday, October 6, 1980, as a National Day of Prayer. I further ask that all who so desire make this a Day of Fast as well. On that day, I ask Americans to join me in thanksgiving to God for His blessings and in earnest prayer to Him for His protection in the year ahead. Finally, may He grant freedom to all unjustly held captive, and may He grant us His vision of a world at peace.

IN WITNESS WHEREOF, I have hereunto set my hand this twenty-second day of September, in the year of our Lord nineteen hundred and eighty, and of the Independence of the United States of America the two hundred and fifth.

JIMMY CARTER

[Filed with the Office of the Federal Register, 11:52 a.m., September 22, 1980]

International Atomic Energy Agency

Nomination of U.S. Representative and Alternate Representative to the 24th Session of the General Conference.
September 22, 1980

On August 26, the President nominated John C. Sawhill as Representative of the United States to the 24th Session of the General Conference of the International Atomic Energy Agency, and Gerard C. Smith and Roger Kirk as Alternate Representatives. The Conference is being held September 22 to 26 in Vienna, Austria.

Mr. Sawhill has requested that the President withdraw his nomination, as he will be unable to attend the Conference. The President has done so and has nominated Mr. Smith as the U.S. Representative. To replace him as Alternate Representative, the President has nominated Joseph M. Hendrie, Commissioner of the Nuclear Regulatory Commission.

Federal Drug Program

Message to the Congress Transmitting a Report. September 22, 1980

To the Congress of the United States:

Pursuant to Sec. 4 of the Drug Abuse Prevention, Treatment, and Rehabilitation Amendments of 1979 (P.L. 96–181; 21 U.S.C. 1117), I transmit herewith the Annual Report of the Drug Policy Office of the Domestic Policy Staff.

This report reflects the nature and accomplishments of the drug abuse policy coordination function and highlights the major activities and accomplishments of the Administration in reducing the effects of drug abuse in the United States. As we move forward in the decade of the 1980s, I pledge my continued support to our fight against drug abuse.

JIMMY CARTER

The White House,
September 22, 1980.

NOTE: The 45-page report is entitled "Annual Report on the Federal Drug Program."

United Nations

Nomination of Five U.S. Representatives and Five Alternate U.S. Representatives to the 35th Session of the General Assembly.
September 22, 1980

The President today announced the nomination of five persons as Representatives and five persons as Alternate Representatives to the 35th Session of the General Assembly of the United Nations. They are:

Representatives

DONALD F. McHENRY, U.S. Representative to the United Nations;

WILLIAM J. VANDEN HEUVEL, Deputy U.S. Representative to the United Nations;

HANNAH D. ATKINS, Oklahoma State representative;

JACOB K. JAVITS, United States Senator from the State of New York;

PAUL E. TSONGAS, United States Senator from the State of Massachusetts;

Alternate Representatives

NATHAN LANDOW, president, Landow and Co., Bethesda, Md.;

United States-Spain Treaty of Friendship and Cooperation

Nomination of Jack B. Kubisch for the Rank of Ambassador While Serving as U.S. Special Negotiator of a Successor Agreement or Treaty.   September 22, 1980

The President today announced that he will nominate Jack B. Kubisch, of Pinehurst, N.C., for the rank of Ambassador while he serves as U.S. special negotiator of a successor agreement or treaty to the current U.S.-Spanish Treaty of Friendship and Cooperation.

The current treaty will expire in September 1981, and negotiations will begin this fall.

Kubisch, 58, retired as a Foreign Service officer in 1979. During his career in the Foreign Service he served as Assistant Secretary of State for Inter-American Affairs, Ambassador to Greece, and Vice President of the National Defense University at Fort McNair. Since his retirement he has served as a consultant to the State Department.

United States Ambassador to Malawi

Nomination of John A. Burroughs, Jr. September 22, 1980

The President today announced that he will nominate John A. Burroughs, Jr., of Temple Hills, Md., to be Ambassador Extraordinary and Plenipotentiary of the United States to the Republic of Malawi. He would replace Harold E. Horan, who is serving as Deputy Assistant Secretary of State for African Affairs.

Burroughs has been Deputy Assistant Secretary of State for Equal Employment Opportunity since 1977.

He was born July 31, 1936, in Washington, D.C. He received a B.A. from the University of Iowa in 1959.

From 1960 to 1963, Burroughs was a passport examiner with the State Department and from 1963 to 1964, he was Assistant Chief of the Special Services Branch of the Passport Office. From 1964 to 1966, he was administrative assistant in the Bureau of Economic and Business Affairs.

From 1966 to 1970, Burroughs was an employee relations specialist with the Department of the Navy. From 1970 to 1977, he was special assistant for equal opportunity to the Assistant Secretary of the Navy.

United States Ambassador to St. Lucia

Nomination of Sally Angela Shelton. September 22, 1980

The President today announced that he will nominate Sally Angela Shelton, of Bellaire, Tex., to be Ambassador Extraordinary and Plenipotentiary of the United States to St. Lucia. She would be the first American Ambassador to St. Lucia and would serve in this position concurrently with her positions as Ambassador to Barbados, to Grenada, and to Dominica.

National Urban Policy

*Message to the Congress Transmitting an
Executive Summary and Report.
September 22, 1980*

To the Congress of the United States:

I am pleased to issue the Executive
Summary of the Second Biennial Report
on National Urban Policy, as called for
by Congress in the Housing and Urban
Development Act of 1970, as amended in
1977.

In 1978, I committed my Administration to implementing in cooperation with
the Congress the nation's first comprehensive urban policy. Our efforts have yielded
important benefits to cities, urban counties and their residents. It is my hope that
this Executive Summary, and the full
Biennial Report on which it is based, will
help us define this nation's urban policy
agenda for the 1980s.

JIMMY CARTER

The White House,
   September 22, 1980.

NOTE: The reports are entitled "The President's National Urban Policy Report, 1980"
(Government Printing Office) and "Executive Summary—The President's National
Urban Policy Report, 1980."

National Urban Policy

*Announcement Concerning the 1980 Report.
September 22, 1980*

The President today transmitted to
Congress the second biennial National
Urban Policy Report. The report presents
key accomplishments in the last 2 years in
carrying out the objectives of the President's urban policy announced in 1978;
analyzes trends and patterns affecting
urban, suburban, and nonmetropolitan
areas; reaffirms the President's commitment to American communities; and sets
out an urban policy agenda for the 1980's.

The report, required every 2 years by
Congress, was prepared by the Depart-
ment of Housing and Urban Development
(HUD).

The report provides an extensive list of
specific legislative initiatives and administrative actions that have been taken to implement the 1978 urban policy. These
include:

—action to target Federal aid to distressed communities;

—the community conservation guidelines, which require impact analyses of
Federal actions leading to large commercial developments;

—Executive orders targeting procurement to distressed areas, encouraging Federal agencies to locate in urban areas,
initiating urban impact analyses of new
Federal policies and programs, and creating a formal urban policy coordinating
group;

—legislation to change the tax code
(e.g., targeted jobs credit, rehabilitation
tax credit) and to expand social service,
education, and housing aid;

—steps to strengthen fair housing, equal
opportunity and affirmative action regulations and enforcement.

The major portion of the report presents a detailed analysis of economic,
population, employment, and numerous
other trends and their effects on central
cities, suburbs, and nonmetropolitan
communities.

The study confirms recent census findings that many older cities are losing
population, but shows that neighborhood
and housing conditions are generally improving throughout the Nation. It concludes that population shifts between
regions of the country continue, especially
between the Northeast and North Central regions and the South and West, although migration has slowed compared
with the years 1965–75. The study documents the growth of nonmetropolitan
and suburban areas, and indicates that

while national rates of poverty have diminished, they have increased in central cities.

The study shows that while cities' needs were increasing, the Federal response was also increasing while targeting resources to needy urban areas and the poor. Growth in Federal aid to States and localities has increased from $59.1 billion in 1976 to $88.9 billion in 1980.

The report demonstrates the value of Federal programs and agencies such as HUD's Urban Development Action Grant (UDAG) program, the Commerce Department's Economic Development Administration (EDA), the Department of Health and Human Services' public health services in urban areas, the Environmental Protection Agency's changes in regulations to deal with urban problems, and the Department of Transportation's shifts of highway and transit programs to older, distressed cities, and urban impact analyses on new highway projects.

The UDAG program has brought enormous private financial resources to bear against such urban problems as unemployment and disinvestment, with a minimal amount of budget expenditure. To date, the program has attracted more than $8.6 billion in new private investment to cities which qualify as needing assistance the most. This is roughly six times the amount of HUD's Action Grant expenditure. In addition, the program will create 234,000 permanent jobs in the private sector while increasing the participating cities' annual tax revenues by over $250 million.

EDA has moved from an agency primarily concerned with rural problems to a balanced economic development agency. Half its funds are now distributed to urban areas.

The third section of the report reaffirms the administration's commitment to the 1978 urban policy and presents an urban policy agenda for the 1980's. Specific actions and strategies are grouped under five general policy goals:

—to strengthen urban economies and assist distressed communities to compete successfully for households and jobs;

—to expand job opportunities for the structurally unemployed where they live and increase their mobility to communities where jobs are available;

—to promote fiscal stability by assisting cities to strengthen their tax bases and meet urgent revenue needs;

—to eliminate discrimination and increase access for all population groups to good quality housing, pleasant neighborhoods, and needed community services;

—to encourage energy-efficient and environmentally sound urban development patterns without limiting mobility or economic development.

Springfield, Illinois

Remarks to Lincoln Land Community College Students and Local Residents. September 22, 1980

I'm really delighted to be here at Lincoln Land College. I've just had a chance to have a personal introduction to one of the gasohol plants here—ethanol. I've also been told by Dr. Poorman that there are windmills on the campus. He says the electric bill goes down greatly when political speeches are made. [*Laughter*] We sometimes get enough to light up half the city of Springfield. So, I'm glad to be here today as a student and a promoter of new energy sources, and I guess I'm delighted to be an energy source today.

Alan Dixon is a great public servant of Illinois, and I want to express my deep personal thanks to him for his introduction. I was not in the car 5 minutes with him before he pointed out that although Illinois has one of the greatest records of any State in contributing to our national treasury, according to his figures it ranks 50th in getting Federal funds back to help the people of Illinois. I have no doubt that when Alan Dixon gets to the United States Senate that he and I will make a good partnership for the State of Illinois next year. He's already gotten me to promise to meet with him and with the Secretary of Transportation, Neil Goldschmidt, to look into the problem of Highway 51 from Rockford to Cairo and also the Central Illinois Expressway from Quincy eastward across the State.

Transportation is crucial in a modern society. And today I want to confine my own remarks to that of energy. I'll be going from here to California and then to Oregon and then to the State of Washington. One of the most important things that we can remember is the importance of addressing serious problems in a courageous and united way. Energy security is crucial to the well-being of every family in this country and crucial to the well-being of our Nation as it faces the years ahead.

We face the possibility of two different energy futures in the years to come. It's a choice that will affect all of us in this audience. It's a choice that will affect the grandchildren that we will have in the years ahead. It will determine the kind of world that we'll have and the kind of role that the United States of America will play in that world. It will determine to some extent whether or not we live at peace. Let me put the choice to you as simply as possible. Will America have a secure future based on reliable sources of energy, from sources both as old as the Sun and as new as the new synthetic fuels we're producing, or will we face a pre-

carious dangerous future at the mercy of uncertain supplies and uncontrollable prices?

What I've seen today here on this campus and across the land in recent weeks convinces me that Americans are ready and eager and capable of reversing our unwarranted dependence on foreign oil to give us a secure nation in the future. If you'll help me, we'll do that together. From the very moment I assumed the Presidency of this Nation and took the oath of office, this has been one of the major themes that I have described to the American people. I have maintained that the energy problem is a clear and a present danger to our lives and also to our livelihood, both as individuals and as a nation.

We're at the receiving end of a 12,000-mile supply line. And as you know, at the other end of that supply line is danger and uncertainty and turmoil, and until this year at the other end of that supply line was one-half the oil that we used. That imported oil in 1980 will cost us $85 billion. That's hard to envision, but it means that every man, woman, and child in the United States of America will send overseas to buy foreign oil $400 this year. That's more than the net income of the top 500 corporations in the United States. The scope of it is sobering and emphasizes the importance of it.

Just as foreign oil drives our cars, its ever-increasing use drives inflation. And along with inflation and oil which we import, we also have been importing unemployment, declining productivity in this country, and scarcity and poverty and even the downfall of government in the less developed countries of the world. It's impossible to overemphasize the seriousness of this threat and the greatness of the opportunity involved. Inflation brought about by foreign oil purchases affects the quality of our schools, our tax burdens, our health care, and other social services. It shakes the security of retired Americans, and it makes less hopeful the future of young Americans. It hurts all of us, not just by causing inconvenience but by undermining our society itself.

These are not pleasant facts; they're hard facts, and it's been hard for America to face them. After the first big OPEC oil price increase in 1973, along with an Arab oil embargo, the administration which was in power then declared that the energy crisis was over and did absolutely nothing to prepare us for the long, hard struggle ahead. The result was predictable. Between 1972 and 1977, our oil imports just about doubled, from 4½ million barrels a day to 8½ million barrels of foreign oil bought per day. While domestic production of oil—particularly of oil—declined year by year, America did not search for more oil and natural gas. America did not develop alternative sources, and America did not develop a good conservation program.

Now, finally, we have a national energy policy, and its results already are a fact of life for Americans. We are proving in this country already that we can produce more, discover more, create more, and conserve more energy, and we can use American resources, American knowledge, and American labor to do it. That's a major step forward. Thanks to you, our country is on the right road to security and to more progress.

Just a few quick figures. At the last count there were more than 3,000 drilling rigs operating in the United States, more than at any time in the last 25 years. More new oil and gas wells will be drilled in 1980 than in any other year in the history of our country. We've launched a massive synthetic and renewable fuels program to turn our coal and shale and farm products

into fuel for our cars and trucks and to turn the light of the Sun into heat and electricity for our homes. There are 10 times more homes in the United States now using solar power than there were just 4 years ago.

Our strides in energy conservation are just as noteworthy. Net oil imports are down 1½ million barrels per day, which means that this year we'll buy 20 percent less oil from overseas than we did last year. And every day we'll buy between 1½ million and 2 million barrels less oil from overseas than we did just a year or so ago. And during the most recent weeks we have actually imported one-third less oil than during the same time last year.

The American people have come to learn that energy saved means money saved, for ourselves as individuals, for our families, and also for our Nation. The soul of our energy policy is this—that there are a lot of different, complex, but exciting roads to energy security, and they must all be explored.

I also want to point out here in Illinois that we are mining more American coal in 1980 than in any other year in history, and we're exporting vast quantities of it. What I want to see in the future is for OPEC oil, as a major world energy source, to be replaced with Illinois coal. With the synthetic fuels program, as you know, high-sulphur coal—in the past has been difficult to burn because of air quality standards—can be made into clean-burning oil and natural gas.

We also have a major goal that 20 percent of all the energy used in the United States by the year 2000 will come directly from the Sun, either through growing crops or from solar heat—energy that's renewable, nonpolluting, and of course, it cannot be embargoed. In 1981 alone, we'll spend more than $1 billion on energy research from the Sun. In 1975, 2 years after the oil embargo, the previous administration spent only about $50 million on solar power. This means that in that brief period of time, because the American people have awakened to the opportunities of solar power, we have multiplied that program 20 times over.

We've been blessed by God with tremendous natural resources. All the Arab OPEC nations put together have about 6 percent of the world's energy reserves. The United States of America has 24 percent. We've got, as you well know, more oil locked up in our shale plus a lot more locked up in coal than three Saudi Arabias put together, and through our new synthetic fuels industry, we can tap that resource now, efficiently and competitively.

Our strong emphasis on gasohol will make farmers more self-sufficient and all Americans more secure. Eighteen months ago virtually no gasohol was being produced in this country. We now have the capacity to produce 135 million gallons of ethanol, and by 1981, next year, we should reach 500 million gallons of ethanol. My goal is that by the end of 1990 we'll produce enough alcohol fuel to replace 10 percent of all America's gasoline use. I want to be sure that you understand the advantage not only to our country but to Illinois, because growing crops, with your beautiful productive land and extremely high deposits of coal here, will open a vista of a new life of prosperity and excitement and achievement for the people who reside in the great State of Illinois.

I'm not going to take more time to emphasize to you the production of new energy. I would like to say this, though: It's vital that we increase conservation, that we use energy more efficiently. The quickest, cheapest, and cleanest energy is the energy that we do not waste. And at the same time we must conserve the quality of our air and our water and our land. All the programs that I've described to you will be carried out without lowering at all the standards for environmental quality. In our haste to develop, we must not weaken our environmental standards. We must not forget that whenever we dig coal or shale or tar sands that we dig into the living earth and that wherever we produce waste, we affect the water that we drink and the air we breathe.

But the new Republican leaders, they have a hard time believing that this program is effective and that it cannot be defined in very simple terms. Their energy program, I'd like to point out to you, has only two parts. First is to turn the oil companies loose. They'd like to do away with the windfall profits tax and trust the major oil companies to take care of our energy problem. And the second one is worse—to ignore or to reverse our hard-won gains in solar energy, gasohol, synthetic fuels, and conservation.

They fought the windfall profits tax every step of the way. Their vision of the future does not include research and development on new sources of energy or the revival of old ones such as small hydroelectric dams. They apparently do not understand that we must wage our energy fight on many fronts, public, private, and individual. They seem to want us to solve the energy crisis the same way they want us to fight inflation, by just consuming more and letting the future take care of itself. That's exactly how we got in trouble in the first place. As for nuclear waste, they simply say all the waste in a year from a nuclear powerplant could be stored under a desk. They seem to be content to let it go at that.

For the first time in 35 years, we have now proposed to the Congress a comprehensive program for permitting our nuclear industry to continue as it does in

Illinois and at the same time take care of nuclear waste disposal, with the State playing the major role. Nothing about this entire program is simple. It's complicated; it's interrelated. But we're well on our way. We spent the 1970's getting this program intact, going through very difficult times.

Now, on the energy program that I've described to you so briefly, we can build the industrial complex of our Nation with modern tools, modern factories, an exciting life, secure families, secure nation, to give us the challenge which America has always been able to meet. It's not a time to eliminate conservation, to stop making sure that homes are efficient, or to eliminate the 55-mile-per-hour speed limit, which even the oil companies support. Nothing could be a sharper contrast concerning the future.

I want the private sector, the free enterprise system of our Nation to play the major role in our energy future. In fact, all of the actual production that I've outlined to you today we envisage as being in the hands of private enterprise, not the Federal Government. But I want us all to participate in our national energy policy, not only myself as President but every one of you. All of us can contribute to it; all of us can benefit from it. Our goal is nothing less than changing the way America produces, uses, and even thinks about energy, and that's the most exciting single undertaking in the last part of the 20th century.

In the past when we switched from wood to coal and then later on from coal to oil, those changes brought only better things to Americans, better lifestyles, more leisure time, essentials like electricity and heat. Now as we switch from foreign oil to American fuels, we stand only to gain again, for our economy, our security, and our confidence.

Let me say, in closing, this: It's exciting for me to come here to be with you to describe as President one of the greatest challenges our Nation has ever faced. We are at peace. We have kept our Nation at peace. But we also must prepare for the future and have a nation that's secure. As long as our industrial system depends upon foreign oil 12,000 miles away, we rob ourselves of money, of jobs, of a better life, and we make our Nation vulnerable to blackmail and the interruption of our foreign policy by that excessive dependence.

When I made a speech in April of 1977 and called the energy crisis the moral equivalent of war, a lot of people did not believe it, but it was true. And now the American people and the Congress have put together an energy policy for our Nation that will stand us in good stead. Our country has never failed to answer a question, to solve a problem, or to overcome an obstacle when we could understand the challenge clearly and work together toward the future. That's where we've come already. And I'm determined that the future of this country will be a bright one, exciting, dynamic, challenging, unifying, and that we approach that future with confidence.

I'm determined, with your help, in energy and other elements of American life, to make sure that in future years the greatest nation on Earth will be even greater.

Thank you very much.

NOTE: The President spoke at 10:06 a.m. in the dining room of Menard Hall at the Lincoln Land Community College. In his remarks, he referred to Alan Dixon, Illinois secretary of state and Democratic candidate for the United States Senate.

Prior to his remarks, the President viewed a demonstration of a corn mash gasohol still, a student energy conservation project headed by Dr. Robert L. Poorman, president of the college.

Springfield, Illinois

*Remarks to Democratic Leaders From
Downstate Illinois. September 22, 1980*

How many of you believe the Democrats are going to whip the Republicans in Illinois—*[applause]*—and all over this country? I believe this is going to be true.

I came here for a couple of reasons. I wanted to associate myself politically with Alan Dixon and with the Springfield Redbirds—I figured that would help me all through this country—and secondly, to be with my good friends behind me on the platform. David [1] rode in with me from Washington this morning on the plane. He's going to make a wonderful new Democratic Congressman, and I look forward to being with him in January. And Roland Burris and Jerry Consentino, Todd Renfrow, and Speaker Redmond— all of you have an eager ally in me in bringing that victory to Democrats at the local, State, and of course, the Federal level in November.

I'm not going to talk very long to you, because I want to shake hands with as many as possible. But I would like to say this: This is a year of crucial decision for our country, and as we approach November the 4th, it's important for us to remember two things. One is the character of the Presidency itself. It's the most important elective office in the world. It's the kind of position that can arouse the hopes and inspiration and confidence and progress of our Nation or have the opposite effect, as we've seen in recent years under previous administrations.

There's a place in the Oval Office where decisions are made that are very difficult. There are no easy answers to

---

[1] David Robinson, Democratic candidate for Congress from the 20th Congressional District of Illinois.

questions that arise in the Oval Office at the White House. If the questions can be answered easily, then the answers come in a private person's life or within a home or in a county courthouse or city hall or at the State legislature or in the Governor's office. If the answers don't come to any of those places, they arrive in the Oval Office for me and the Members of Congress to try to address. It's a major, heavy responsibility, but an exciting opportunity to see our Nation grow and prosper and to stay at peace.

Advisers help; I doubt if there's ever been a better Cabinet than the one I've put together, from Ed Muskie, Harold Brown on down. This is very important to a President. But I have found that the most difficult decisions and the ones that are most important are the ones where your advisers are split almost 50–50. And in that condition, the President, and no one else, has to make that tough decision, deal with that crisis, hopefully so that the crisis that I have on my desk is never even known by you, because a crisis managed well is not catastrophic to our Nation. A crisis that is not handled well can become a crisis for the entire world.

So, the nature of the Presidency itself is important for us to remember during this election year. And the second point I want to make is this: The future of our Nation is at stake. I doubt if there's ever been a sharper difference between two major candidates than between myself and the Republican nominee. The only possible exception that I can remember was when Goldwater ran against Lyndon Johnson earlier in the sixties, 1964. Now that choice is not only between a candidate, a party, but also between the two futures that our Nation faces.

We've made a lot of progress in this last 3½ years. We've added 8½ million more jobs. We have more agricultural exports this year than ever before in history. We set a world's record in '79, a world's record in '78, a world's record in '77. This year we have increased agricultural exports, even in spite of the restraint on Soviet sales, by 8 million tons—$8 billion, $40 billion in exports this year. And I see your State playing the major role in our Nation's progress and prosperity in the future, with the rich land that God has given you and the enormous supplies of coal, for instance. We have an opportunity to address our energy problems, but also give the families of this Nation confidence in the future.

We've kept our country at peace, through strength. As long as I'm in the White House, our country will stay militarily strong, and my top responsibility will be the security of this country and peace for all Americans.

And finally let me say this: There is no way for a President to be elected in this country without help from people like you. I've got confidence in what you can do. I've studied the election results many years back, and I've always seen the crucial nature of Illinois in the outcome of an election and also the closeness with which the decision is made in your State.

This meeting with me this morning, I hope, will be constructive for our country. It's certainly an exciting thing for me to be with you. And I believe that together, you and I will see new Democratic Congressmen and women, a new Democratic Senator from this State to Washington, and the reelection of Fritz Mondale and me, to give our Nation a better future with a Democratic administration that has confidence in people, confidence in our Nation, confidence in the peace process, and confidence in even a better prosperity for the greatest country on Earth in the years ahead.

Thank you very much. God bless you.

NOTE: The President spoke at 10:57 a.m. in the auditorium of Logan Hall at the Lincoln Land Community College.

Los Angeles, California

Informal Exchange With Reporters.
September 22, 1980

Q. Mr. President, did you hear anything more on the Iranian-Iraqi situation?

THE PRESIDENT. Well, I've been getting reports in from NSC and the State Department in the trip from Illinois here. We've been monitoring the situation very closely. The reports are that Iraq has made several attacks on Iran, by air primarily. We don't know the extent of the ground force engagement.

Our only hope is that the two nations can resolve the disputes between them peacefully. We'll do everything we can to contribute to that peaceful resolution. We're not taking a position in support of either Iran or Iraq except just to encourage them, through the United Nations and through other means, to end the conflict and to minimize any bloodshed that might occur.

Q. In the past Iran has threatened that if it was attacked by Iraq that the American hostages would somehow pay. Are you worried about that?

THE PRESIDENT. Well, I've always been concerned about the hostages, but not because of this.

NOTE: The exchange began at 1:15 p.m. following the President's arrival at the Los Angeles International Airport.

As printed above, this item follows the text of the White House press release.

Torrance, California

Remarks and a Question-and-Answer Session at a Town Meeting. September 22, 1980

THE PRESIDENT. Thank you very much, Jerry Brown.

Governor Jerry Brown, Mayor Jim Armstrong:

It's a real pleasure for me to be here with you at North High, the home of the Saxons, who haven't been scored on yet. First, I'd like to make a few remarks about a subject of great importance to you and to our Nation, and then we'll spend the rest of the hour with my answering your questions about things of interest to you.

CAMPAIGN ISSUES

Six weeks from now our Nation will make a very critical decision. This decision will set the course of your life and of our Nation's life not just for the next 4 years but for many generations to come. It will help to decide what kind of world we live in. It will help to decide whether we have war or peace. It's an awesome choice. And in this great and free land of ours, the choice is made not by me, not by my opponents, not by other candidates, not by Members of the Congress, not even by Governors, but by you. Americans have an inalienable right, a very precious right, to choose your own future and to set your own course as a free people.

Having served as President now for 3½ years, I have a very optimistic vision of America's future, because I feel the strength and the good sense of the citizens of our Nation at townhall meetings like this. I believe this is my 26th townhall meeting, and I've had 60 press conferences. Over 500 times I've met with the news media for different kinds of interviews to present my case to the American people.

When people of this country are told about a clear challenge or a problem or an obstacle and they understand what is at stake in the history of our Nation, America has never failed. We are ready now to do the right thing, to make a good investment on your part and on mine in a bright future for this country. There are indications now that our economy is improving very rapidly, much more rapidly than the economists thought was possible. But my strongest source of optimism is not on statistics about the economy, but in the American people and how you've responded to some of our Nation's very serious challenges.

As a farmer, as a businessman, I know that there is no way to turn a profit and have a better life without making a good, sound investment at the beginning. If you want to get something out, first you've got to put something in. The same goes for a family that buys a precious possession or that puts money into an education investment. If you want to have a bright future, you have to invest in it, and you have to work for it. And the same thing goes for our Nation.

Our land has faced some very tough, difficult challenges in the last 4 years. For the first time in memory, we have had to confront a major economic threat from outside—the challenge by the OPEC nations on our economic independence from uncontrollable oil prices and threatened shortages. For too many years we've been importing that very high-priced oil and at the same time importing inflation and unemployment, and we've exported the economic power that it takes to create jobs and a better life for American people.

Three and a half years ago, in April of 1977, I called the energy crisis the moral equivalent of war. Many people were skeptical. They said that dealing with our energy challenge was politically infeasible, that it would be unpopular, and that the American people would never respond. The skeptics were wrong. Dealing with our energy challenge has not been easy. Certainly it has not been all that popular. But it has been necessary. The people have come to see in our energy program that we've hammered out with Congress the soundest possible investment in our Nation's future, and we're just beginning to see some early returns on that investment.

This year the United States will consume an average of 1½ to 2 million barrels of oil, imported oil, less every day. We've had a reduction of about 24 percent in oil imports this year compared to preceding years. We are drilling more oil wells and natural gas wells this year, 1980, than ever before in history. American coal production is the highest it's ever been in history, and 10 times as many homes now have solar power than 4 years ago. So, we're making good progress.

And finally let me say that we are looking to the future with confidence, because we're taking the profits that formerly went to the OPEC nations and investing those profits in American enterprise, American technology, American fuels, American jobs, to give us in America a better life in the future. We're ready to revitalize American industry across the board. And this particular community and your State is crucial to that future progress, because here you're on the cutting edge of change. Californians have never been afraid of change. You have had the pioneer spirit ever since the first settlers came here. And you know and I know that in technology and new ideas, new concepts, new ways of life, this has been an exciting part of the greatest and most exciting nation on Earth.

A generation ago America set a goal to go to the Moon. Today we face challenges and opportunities much greater in scope than even putting the first men on the Moon. The new energy program for conservation and the development of energy in our own Nation is greater financially than the entire Interstate Highway System, the entire space program, and the Marshall plan that rebuilt Europe, all put together. This can give us a challenge, yes, but an opportunity for ingenuity and sweat and accomplishment and a better life than we have ever yet known.

Americans have always met challenges. We've always overcome obstacles. We've always resolved difficult questions and carved out a better future for ourselves. And I have absolutely no doubt that the 1980's will see that exciting life that will make our Nation in the future even greater than it has been in the past.

And now I'd like to answer your questions.

QUESTIONS

NATIONAL DEFENSE

Q. President Carter, let me be first, Betty Quiroz, to welcome you to Torrance.

THE PRESIDENT. Thank you, Betty.

Q. My question is, What is your opinion between the B–1 bomber and the B–1— I mean the B–52—sorry—and the B–1 bomber?

THE PRESIDENT. All right. What we need to do in our Nation is to stay ahead of the threats that are mounted against us. The B–1 bomber is a superb penetrating bomber, quick to take off, more heavily armed, much smaller in cross-section to radar than was the B–52. The problem has been that the Soviets have invested tens of billions of dollars in ground-control radar and anti-aircraft capability that would have made the B–1 bomber obsolete or obsolescent as a penetrating device carrying missiles by the time it was fully deployed.

So, I made the judgment, which I'm sure was the right one, to shift instead to the air-launch cruise missile, a relatively inexpensive, small, effective weapon that can be carried several hundred miles from the shores of the Soviet Union, launched with pinpoint accuracy, which is almost invisible to the Soviet radar, and can penetrate much more effectively without the threat of the loss of life of American pilots. So, the B–52 carrying the air-launch cruise missiles, with the followup, more modern bomber to come later to carry those cruise missiles, is the best approach.

In addition to the air-launch cruise missile, which is a highly effective new weapon—and we'll be producing 3,000 of those this year; it's not way off in the distant future—plus the Trident submarines and Trident missiles and the MX missiles—those three will keep us in a competitive position with equality and an ability to withstand the threat from the Soviets.

We have got to keep our Nation strong. For the 8 years before I became President, 7 of those years we went down, down, down in our commitment to a strong national defense. We've reversed that trend now, and we've had an increase every year since I've been in office in national defense capability. That's going to keep on to keep our Nation strong and at peace. The best weapon is the one that's never fired in combat, because we're so strong we keep the peace. And the best soldier is one that never dies in combat, because we're strong enough to keep the peace.

Thank you very much. Good question.

SOCIAL SECURITY SYSTEM

Q. Mr. President, my name is Ray Hawkins, and I live in the wonderful city of Torrance. And my question to you, sir, is: What is your position on taxing social security?

THE PRESIDENT. I'm against it.

Q. That's very good, sir. Thank you.

THE PRESIDENT. As long as I'm President, we're going to keep the social security system sound. We're not going to tax social security income. We're not going to reduce the social security program to, quote, "its original concept" of the 1930's and eliminate SSI and all the benefits that have been done. We're going to continue to index social security so that as inflation goes up, the social security payments will stay in touch with the changing cost of goods. And we're not going to reduce the age at which social security recipients have to retire to get benefits or raise the age either. So, we're going to protect the social security system as you know it, and we will not tax the social security income.

Thank you very much.

CAMPAIGN DEBATES

Q. My name is Marc Brown. I'm from Harbor City. Mr. President, the general consensus among the informed voting public is that John Anderson, with a moderate stance on most issues, would draw more votes away from your candidacy than from Ronald Reagan. Is that why you will not debate with Mr. Anderson and Mr. Reagan on the same platform?

THE PRESIDENT. I think your analysis is right. As you know, Anderson and Reagan are both Republicans, and Anderson's voting record the 20 or so years he was in Congress is very similar to the positions that have been staked out by Governor Reagan. In the campaign Anderson, however, has taken some extremely liberal positions on a few highly publicized points.

I have no objection at all to debating both Reagan and Anderson, but the first debate that I want to hold is a one-to-one, man-on-man debate with Governor Reagan. That's what I want, and that's what I determined to get. Marc, I might add one thing. Following that debate with Reagan, man to man, I'll be glad to debate Reagan, Anderson, Clark, Commoner, anyone who has a theoretical opportunity to be elected President. I'm not trying to avoid debates. I'm eager to see them.

VIEWS ON THE PRESIDENCY

Q. My name is Marissa Fruchter, and I'm 16 years old. And I'm in the alternative program here at North High School. You must have had some idea of what the Presidency would be like before you were elected President. How have your feelings changed on this issue?

THE PRESIDENT. Marissa, there is no preparation for being President. I was on a local school board during the integration years in Georgia. I was in the State senate for two terms. I was Governor of a State. And I campaigned for President for 4 years and got to travel all over this Nation and to learn about its problems and to study what I might do if I should become President.

The job is unique. Even a Vice President, in my judgment, cannot prepare adequately for being President, because in the Oval Office, under the most difficult circumstances, when a crisis arises or a difficult question comes, you're on your own. The issues that come to me as President are not easy ones. I never get an easy question or an easy problem, because if a question is easy, it can be solved by you or your parents in your home or in a local city hall or a county courthouse or in a State legislature or Governor's office.

But if those problems can't be solved in any of those places, then they come to me as President, and I share them with the Congress.

Also, I've found that the more difficult a question is and the more vital it is to the American people, the more likely my advisers are to split almost exactly 50–50. Half say do this; half of them say do that. I have to make the ultimate decision.

I deal with a lot of crises every week. Most of them you never know about. If I handle them well in the Oval Office, then they don't become worldwide crises separating our Nation from a chance for peace or adversely affecting your life. If I meet a crisis improperly and don't handle it well, then it becomes a crisis for the entire country or maybe sometimes for the entire world. So, there's no preparation for President.

On the other hand, it's a good job, because it's the best elected office in the world. And in a democracy the President doesn't feel alone, because I have the support and the confidence and sometimes the criticism and sometimes the advice of millions of people who share the same beliefs and the same goals and the same ideals and the same principles that I do.

And the history of our Nation is such that as I live in the White House and realize that Thomas Jefferson and Andrew Jackson and Abraham Lincoln and, of course, more recently, Harry Truman and Franklin Roosevelt lived there and dealt with problems much worse than the ones I face, it's a reassuring feeling, because the underlying strength of this Nation is so great that it can accommodate a President who is fallible and who does sometimes make mistakes.

So, although there's no preparation for it, it's a great and exciting job and a great and exciting nation. And the support of people like you make my job easier, sometimes under the most difficult circumstances. I like the job, and I intend to keep it for 5 more years.

CAMPAIGN DEBATES

Q. Hi, I'm Noelle Naito, from Costa Mesa. And any time you're in Orange County, my dad says don't hesitate to drop in for dinner, but my mom says think twice, because you'll have to cook and clean. My question is: What was your reaction to the debates last night? Did you find yourself agreeing more with John Anderson or Ronald Reagan? [*Laughter*]

THE PRESIDENT. How do you know I didn't watch "Midnight Express"? [*Laughter*] I watched them. I watched the debate, and I thought it was very interesting between the two. I think it would not be appropriate for me to say who I think won or lost. My judgment is that John Anderson's wife thought he won and Ronald Reagan's wife thought he won. [*Laughter*] And I'm not going to get in an argument between the two wives.

I think the debate process is a healthy one. I believe that the debate between myself and President Ford in 1976 was very constructive, not only for me and President Ford but for the country. I believe it is good to have the major emphasis on the debates, at least in the initial stages, between the nominee of the Democratic Party and the nominee of the Republican Party.

As you know, Congressman Anderson ran as a Republican. He never won a primary, even in his home State. He never won a caucus contest, even in his home State. And after he was defeated or eliminated as a Republican, then he decided to run as an Independent.

In my judgment it's better for the Nation and for my campaign and for, I believe, Governor Reagan's campaign to have the sharp issues drawn in the minds of the American people between the two candidates who do have a chance to win. And so that's why I look forward to debating Governor Reagan on a one-on-one basis to sharply define those issues between me and him. Following that, as I said earlier when Marc asked me the question, I'll be very glad to debate Anderson as well.

But I don't want to answer your question by saying who I think did best and who I think did worse. I think I came out okay last night. [*Laughter*]

Thank you very much.

EDUCATION

Q. Mr. President, my name is Sharon Dezutti, and I'm from Redondo Beach. You are known as one of the best friends of education. And I would like to think about that topic for a minute and ask you to share with us, when it comes to education, why you are the far better choice than the other two.

THE PRESIDENT. Well, I started my public career on a local school board in Georgia, and I saw during those difficult years between 1955 and 1962 the tremendous opportunities that existed in my own State that were not being realized. And ultimately, when the politicians and the churches and others were too timid to move forward and change the South and eliminate racial discrimination, it was the teachers and the school boards and some of the courageous parents that made those social changes that opened up to the Southland a new opportunity or new era for us all. I would not be President today had that change not taken place. So, as a dynamic force in America I saw the courage and the commitment, sometimes the sacrifice, that was exhibited in the lives of those deeply involved in education, particularly those who are professionals, classroom teachers and administrators.

When I became Governor, Georgia had a long way to go, and I think we made a lot of progress. I spent about 25 percent of my time as Governor trying to improve the educational system of my State, because it was so far behind. When I became President finally, I only spent 1 percent of my time, roughly, in a Cabinet meeting on education, because about the only questions that came to me were lawsuits between individual citizens and a local school board or between a local school board and the State legislature or something of that kind involving the relationship between students.

I felt that it was important for us to have a Cabinet officer there so that a parent or a student or a teacher or an administrator or a State legislator or a State school superintendent could know which person in Washington was specifically responsible for education, because in the past, with health, education, and welfare in one department, education was buried under health and welfare. So, I looked around the Nation to find the best person I could find to be responsible for the education system in our country. I came to California, found a woman named Shirley Hufstedler, a great judge, and asked her to be Secretary of Education. Now I believe that we have a bureaucracy, in the finest sense of that word, ready to make major strides forward in education.

We have had since I've been in office a 73-percent increase in Federal funds for education, channeled to those kids that needed it most. We have now arrived at the point so any child in this country, any young man or woman can go to college if they are academically qualified, regardless of the income level or the social status or the net worth of their family. And we've expanded greatly the emphasis on educa-

tion for those past the college age who might want to use their lives in a constructive way as adults or even senior citizens.

And the last point is we've emphasized youth programs. We have a major youth bill in the Congress now, a $2 billion bill, which is very vital, to make sure that a young person who graduates from high school or from a vocational, technical school or community college or senior college will be matched with the jobs that are open in that particular community. In the past there's not been a good relationship between the Labor Department, that was trying to fill jobs, on the one hand and the education system that was turning out graduates. In the future we want to be sure that those jobs seeking persons are matched with persons seeking jobs and that any defect in a person's education is overcome, preferably at the senior high school level, so that the young person who graduates will have a career waiting for him or her and not just a life of idleness or unemployment.

Those are a few of the things, just offhand, that come to my mind about education. My heart is in it. I think we've done a good job so far, a better job in the future.

REGISTRATION AND THE DRAFT

Q. God bless you, *señor*. My name is Santana Mata. I live in Torrance, and God bless you.

THE PRESIDENT. *Gracias, señor.*

Q. What are you going to do with the draft? [*Laughter*]

THE PRESIDENT. We're not going to have any draft, in my judgment, any time in the foreseeable future. The only circumstance under which I would recommend to the Congress new legislation to implement a draft would be if I was convinced that my Nation's security was actually threatened.

What we have done is to pass through the Congress a law permitting young men to register for the draft so that we could stop the long delay, which would be 90 or 100 days, if there is an opportunity or a need to marshal our forces. We had a remarkable response from our young men. About 93 percent signed up in the original sign-up period, and thousands are signing up now every day to bring this very high percentage on up higher. You might be interested in knowing that 15 percent of those who did sign up to register for the draft indicated that they would like additional information about the career opportunities in serving in the military forces.

So, I believe in a volunteer military force. I believe the registration for the draft will strengthen the voluntary military force. It will help with recruiting for young people looking for a career in the military. It will help to encourage those to reenlist when they are qualified technically to do a better job for the military. It will help to keep our Nation at peace and help to avoid any need for a mandatory draft in the future.

Q. I don't think so. You're doing a good job. God bless you.

THE PRESIDENT. Thank you very much.

MORAL PRINCIPLES

Q. Mr. President, my name is Myrna Loy Sampson. I'm from Torrance. Welcome.

THE PRESIDENT. Thank you, Myrna.

Q. I appreciate the interest that you've shown in the moral fiber of American families as you evidenced in the White House Conference on Families. I'd like to know, are you planning to declare all-out war on the moral disintegration that

we're seeing in our cities? Last night three human lives were lost across the street from the campus I attend. I'm frightened, Mr. President. What can I do as an individual citizen to combat this horror?

THE PRESIDENT. Thank you, Myrna. You have a very famous name, and you're very beautiful.

Q. My dad liked her, too. [*Laughter*]

THE PRESIDENT. The longer I'm in the White House as President, the more I realize that the basic structure of our Nation is founded and must be preserved not in a government bureaucratic system, even at the local and State level, but in the individual family structure and magnified from there into the community structure as well. Strong families, strong communities are the basis for a safe life and a good life for our people. I believe there's been a move back toward a deeper commitment to moral principles in our country.

We did have a very serious shock to our country and to our beliefs and to our ideals with the Vietnam war, with the revelations about the CIA violating American law, and during the Watergate era, when Americans lost faith in their own government, lost faith in truthfulness, and also lost faith to some degree in one another. I think we've helped already to repair that damage.

Also, I have seen in recent years, since I've been in the White House, remarkable demonstrations of a need for American people to cling to those principles and ideals that never change, because in a rapidly changing, fast technological world, when people are uncertain about what's going to happen next year in energy or what's going to happen next year in where they live, educational systems, and so forth, there are some things that don't change. Religion is one of them.

Everybody was shocked when Pope John Paul II came to our Nation, traveled around our country, and had an unbelievable outpouring of respect for him, respect for what he advocated, and also for one another during that period. I think the most exciting day I've spent as a President, although I'm not a Catholic, was the day that Pope John Paul II came to the White House. And a million and a half people went to see him and listen to him and have Mass at a park in Chicago. I think that this is something that indicates the hunger of American people for those finer elements of American life.

One of the things, finally, to abbreviate my answer, is that we've got to alleviate the problem that alienates particularly young people from the system within our society. If a young person finishes high school and searches for a job and can't get it, it's a very severe blow to that person's self-respect. And over a period of time, there's a sense of discouragement and despair, anger, and then later comes alienation when that young person turns against his own parents and turns against the school system and turns against the police and turns against the local officials and turns against his own country.

And that's why I think it's extremely important for us to strengthen our education system, tie that educational system to job opportunities, have this new youth bill passed, which will add hundreds of thousands of new jobs for young people and let them know that when they get out of high school or out of junior college or whatever that they can have a productive life and be part of our societal structure. I think that'll go a long way to eliminating the violence that sometimes results because those young people don't feel that they are part of the investment in a safer and more sound future.

Yours is an excellent question. It's one that addresses my thoughts every day, and I'm grateful to you for it.

Q. Thank you very much.

THE PRESIDENT. Thank you very much.

HISPANIC AMERICANS

Q. Hello, Mr. President. My name is Mike Caudillo. I live here in Torrance. And also I'm a disabled person and a Chicano at that. I was wondering if your attention was drawn to the immediate problems with the Hispanic communities of perhaps all the killings and shootings that go on throughout the barrios of California—and here in the Southwest we're now the majority, not the minority—and if perhaps you might know of civil servants that are drawn to this attention and perhaps may have watched a televised program on August the 11th on "PM Magazine" that addressed the immediate problems within the communities.

THE PRESIDENT. Thank you, Mike. *Esta ciego?* Mike, are you blind?

Q. Yes, I am.

THE PRESIDENT. I thought so.

Q. I was wondering, well, if perhaps you could comment on the issue, though.

THE PRESIDENT. Yes, I'll be happy to.

One of the serious problems that we face in this country, Mike, is the assimilation into our society of newcomers to our Nation. I would guess, unless there's some native Indians here, that all of us and our families were immigrants to this country, coming here for a better life, a better opportunity, for freedom, for a chance to worship as we chose, and all of our ancestors, or maybe some of us, felt strange and alienated when we first came. We didn't know the language. We didn't know how to get along with our neighbors. We didn't know how to accommodate this great and exciting and changing new free world.

Now we're going through a stage of trying to accommodate civil rights improvements in our country. I mentioned earlier that I'm from the South. I don't want to go through that again, because I've already covered it. But in the Southwest and in the western States, we've had a problem, certainly before I became President, of equality of treatment of Chicanos and other Spanish-speaking citizens. In the Department of Justice, there were examples of a lack of equitable justice and a sense in the Hispanic community that they were not treated fairly, or you were not treated fairly by the Federal Government.

I think we've corrected that to a major degree. We have an advisory committee made up of Hispanic leaders now who work directly and personally with the Attorney General. We have a prosecuting attorney in the Justice Department who is a minority citizen himself, Drew Days. In addition to that, we've tried to move towards the appointment in the judicial system of highly qualified minorities as judges so that they can bring not only wisdom and integrity and experience and sound judicial temperament but also a special sensitivity about minority groups.

And I'm glad that although I've only been in office 3½ years, that I've appointed more women judges, I've appointed more Hispanic judges, and I've appointed more black judges than all the other Presidents in the 200-year history of our country. This will help a great deal to alleviate some of the problems that you've described, Mike.

Thank you very much.

Q. Mr. President, I'm Fred R. Booth. I'm from the city of Torrance. Sir, I would like to ask you, are there any new items of interest for the retired and the active duty personnel, such as commissary privileges and so forth, in the Navy at Long Beach?

THE PRESIDENT. No. I don't know of any. I just signed this month another in a series of bills that would improve the pay, the moving expenses, the living expenses, and the reenlistment benefits of people who are still in active duty or coming into the military. But I don't know of any plans at this time to change the privileges of retired military personnel at the commissaries and so forth.

You want to ask another question? Go ahead.

Q. To additional statement, they keep telling the retired personnel there was going to be new, additional commissaries built here. There's literally thousands of retired personnel in this country, and we don't have the space available for those people.

THE PRESIDENT. Let me see if I can discover the answer to that question and write you or either call you on the phone no later than Wednesday.

Q. Thank you, sir.

THE PRESIDENT. We've just had passed through the Senate the military construction bill, and I'm not familiar enough with it to know about specific locations as to whether the money will be used for commissaries and so forth. But if you'll come up here to the front and give your name and address and your telephone number to one of my staff members, we'll give you a telephone call Wednesday and answer your question specifically. I don't know the answer at this point.

Thank you, sir.

FAIR HOUSING LEGISLATION

Q. Mr. President, Kay White, League of Women Voters, Torrance. I'm a resident of Torrance.

THE PRESIDENT. Good to see you, Kay.

Q. Faced with growing resistance to local communities to provide affordable family housing, what steps would your administration take to strengthen the enforcement of fair housing laws?

THE PRESIDENT. I'm very glad that lately, in the last 4 weeks, we've had a steady increase in the number of housing starts in this country—up now to a rate of about 1.4 million homes being built per year, which is a very good recovery.

We still have a problem in the legal ability to enforce the existing fair housing legislation that was passed in 1968, as you know. The House of Representatives has passed a fair housing bill, which we sponsored, to give us the administrative authority to enforce the existing law. That legislation has now passed out of the Judiciary Committee, the chairman of which is Senator Ted Kennedy, and is ready to be voted on in the Senate. I support that legislation very strongly and hope it passes. Later on this afternoon, in Los Angeles, I will be with Senator Kennedy at a joint political event, and we'll be discussing it then.

But I hope that the fair housing legislation does pass. It will be another major step forward to provide equality of opportunity and also fairness to the people of this country.

Thank you, Kay, very much.

NATIONAL HEALTH INSURANCE

Q. Good afternoon, Mr. President. You look very well today.

THE PRESIDENT. Thank you.

Q. I'm Coralee Randall, from the 10th—[*inaudible*]—district of Los Angeles, California. I'd like to know, what is your feeling about some type of socialized medicine in the near future?

THE PRESIDENT. Coralee, I'm not in favor of socialized medicine, but I am eager to see a nationwide comprehensive health insurance plan put forward through the Congress, phased in very carefully, with the emphases as I'll describe very briefly: first of all, on controlling the rapidly increasing hospital costs for all Americans; secondly, to have an emphasis on prevention of disease rather than the emphasis on the treatment of an illness once a person gets it; also, an emphasis on outpatient treatment, whenever that's feasible, for a given affliction rather than the placing of a person in a hospital, which costs a lot.

I'm also very committed to the fact that each person in this country ought to have the complete freedom to choose one's own physician, either a family doctor or a physician, to treat a special illness. In addition to that, we want to make sure that as much as possible the private insurance sector is involved in the insurance program. And it ought to be emphasized as we phase in those who need it most.

At the present time, with Medicare and Medicaid there's a fairly good insurance program for the elderly and also those who have very little, if any, income, in the welfare category. This new program ought to be phased in, I'd say, first of all to strengthen the health care given to women and tiny babies, even those in the prenatal stage, and for the first year or 2 years or 5 years of their life and then constantly expanded until eventually the health insurance program would cover all Americans.

In my judgment, it would be cheaper than what we spend now, it would prevent a lot of illness instead of just treating illnesses after they occur, and it would mean that in a given community you'd have much better cooperation in providing a healthy environment in which to live and hospitals to treat illness at a much lower cost if one does get a serious illness. It would also include a catastrophic health program so that if a family did have a very expensive illness, say, the husband of the family had terminal cancer and had to linger for months and months in the hospital, that that cost would be paid.

Those are the principles of the health program that I envision, that I believe the Congress will pass in my second term. But I am not in favor of socialized medicine, where the Government takes over the medical establishment and runs it for the private sector.

Thank you, ma'am, very much.

INFLATION

Q. Good afternoon, Mr. President.

THE PRESIDENT. Good afternoon.

Q. Thank you for coming to the South Bay.

THE PRESIDENT. I'm glad I came.

Q. My name is John Mandell, and I live in Harbor City. And, Mr. President, opinion polls show that voters now consider inflation to be the major problem confronting all Americans and, also, many of these same voters believe that Government deficit spending is the root cause of inflation, not OPEC, not union wage contracts, not corporate pricing structures. I would like to know what specific steps you now propose to take to eliminate inflation or at least reduce it and why you believe these actions might succeed at this time, when your prior efforts during the last 3½ years have actually resulted in accelerating inflation.

THE PRESIDENT. Well, as a matter of fact, my efforts have not resulted in an accelerating of inflation. What's inflicted the entire Nation and indeed the entire world with inflationary pressures has been an increase in the price of OPEC oil of 120 percent in only 1 year. The price of oil on a nationwide basis in 1979 went up more than the price of oil had increased since oil was first discovered back in the 1880's. And that has permeated our entire economy and caused a tremendous increase in the price of all goods.

In March, if you remember correctly, after that tremendous series of increases in the price of energy, I imposed on the Nation some anti-inflation measures. The interest rates dropped about 1 percent per week for a long time, and inflation decreased dramatically. The last figures that we have for inflation showed that the inflation rate was zero. We had no increase in inflation in July. I don't anticipate that continuing in August, because it was probably an aberration, but at least it's the first time in 13 years that we have had zero inflation in any particular month. There's no doubt that inflation has come down, and I believe it'll be out of the double-digit figure for the rest of this year.

There are two or three things that must be done. One is to increase the productivity of American workers. We now have the highest productivity among our workers of any nation on Earth. But our plants and our tools are becoming obsolescent, and our productivity is not increasing as much as it is in nations like Germany and Japan, where their industrial complex was destroyed in the Second World War and they are more modern. Now that we've got the energy program intact and ready to implement, we are now ready to revitalize American industry and create new jobs, by better tools and better factories for American workers, not only in basic industries like steel and automobiles but also the high-technology industry that's so important here in California, particularly in your own community.

Another thing is to be responsible in dealing with tax reductions. As you know, the Reagan-Kemp-Roth proposal would slash income taxes, primarily for rich people, over the next 7 years a total of a thousand billion dollars, a trillion dollars. This is similar to what the income tax reduction was under Proposition Nine that the Californians wisely rejected in a recent referendum. But if we have that tremendous slash in income taxes, with great benefits going to rich people, then that would be highly inflationary in nature.

The tax proposal that I have put forward would actually be anti-inflationary in nature. It would primarily result in investments in new machines, new jobs, new industrial capability, and would help to offset the built-in increase in social security payments to keep the social security system sound, and in that, would be actually a contributing factor toward decreased inflation in the years ahead.

So, higher productivity, a balanced tax program, that I've put forward that won't be implemented until next year, and the removal of our excessive dependence on imported oil—those are the things that I believe would contribute to controlling inflation in the months and years ahead. We'll do all three of them if I'm elected, and I intend to be elected.

Q. Thank you.

THE PRESIDENT. Thank you, sir.

CUBAN REFUGEES

Q. Mr. President, welcome. I'm Jim Logue of Carson, and on June 5th you directed the Department of Justice to look into all Cuban aliens with criminal backgrounds. Two thousand had gone to Federal prisons for investigation. Over 200 have been expelled back to their country, but they haven't left our country yet. When is the date for that? And we have to stop all this hijacking with these people.

THE PRESIDENT. We now have a massive force of Coast Guard ships and Navy ships between the coast of Cuba and the coast of Florida to stop the illegal aliens coming in here from Cuba. I can understand their desire to escape from communism. We've got 3 or 4 million refugees around the world who are escaping from various elements of totalitarian persecution, not only in Cuba but also in Cambodia, Afghanistan, Ethiopia, and other places with which you are familiar.

It's my responsibility as President to enforce the law. Once these people arrive at our shores, then I have to be responsible for making sure that the law is carried out in accordance with my oath.

We have placed now over a hundred thousand of the Cuban refugees in communities in our country. They're doing very well. As you know, the Cubans are a highly motivated, very good workers, very competitive. And the ones who escape from a communist system most often are the ones that have some freedom desire in their hearts and some competitive spirit about them to escape from government control. So they are competitive, and as you know, they've done very well.

The second point is, the last point I want to emphasize is that we are doing the best we can to work with the officials in Cuba to stop this illegal flow into our country. It was announced in Cuba the first of last week, last Tuesday, that any hijackers who took a plane to Cuba would be immediately returned to the United States for trial and they'll be given the maximum sentence under the law, or they'll be executed by the Cuban officials themselves. In my judgment, this would go a long way towards discouraging hijacking in the months ahead.

So, to stop the illegal flow, to treat those that are already here humanely and assimilate them into communities where the unemployment rate is ultimately low and where they have families, to punish the hijackers severely, and to work with the Cuban officials to stop any illegal aliens coming in in the months ahead—those are the things we are doing in accordance with the law. And I believe we're having increasing effectiveness, although it is a messy business. It's been a very time-consuming thing for me, and I can't tell you that we've handled it perfectly so far. We're making progress on it, and I believe that we are doing the best we can.

That's a good question and a difficult one to answer.

Thank you, Jim.

Yes, ma'am.

AMERICAN HOSTAGES IN IRAN; IRANIAN REFUGEES

Q. Good afternoon, Mr. President. My name is Patricia Phedey. I'm from Carnes, California, and I'm concerned about the effects a war between Iraq and Iran will have on our hostages. And I would also like to know why Iranians are still allowed by Immigration to enter this country.

THE PRESIDENT. I've been monitoring all day from Air Force One, with messages and telephone calls, the developments in Iraq and Iran along their border. Apparently, Iraq has decided to mount air strikes against several places in Iran and has done some damage, the extent of which we don't yet know. I'm also not familiar yet with accurate reports about the degree of ground force involvement.

I don't believe that this altercation between Iraq and Iran will have any predictable effect on the lives or safety of the hostages. It could cut both ways. It could convince Iran that they need peace with their neighbors, they need to be part of the international community, they need to be able to have a strong and viable economy, they need to get spare parts for their military weapons, and so forth, and therefore induce them to release the hostages. I'm not predicting that, but it's a possibility.

The most important thing in Iran is that they finally have a government. They finally have a President, a Prime Minister. They finally have a cabinet. They have a speaker of the Majles, and they have a parliament. This has not been the case in the past. I can't predict to you a rapid movement toward release of our hostages. I pray that it will happen. I cannot predict that it will yet. But I can tell you that the signals coming out of Iran lately— and they've all been public signals—have indicated some new desire on the part of the Iranians to resolve the problems between ourselves and them.

We have a very restrictive policy now between ourselves and Iran. We are not permitting any Iranians to come here from that country to the United States. There were some Iranian refugees who had already left their country and moved to different places in Europe, to Austria or to England or a few other countries, that we do permit to come in here, only on a very serious hardship case. I won't belabor the point, but just let me make one example. There are some fervent religious believers, for instance Jews, who were persecuted in Iran under the revolution, who escaped from Iran to Europe with the idea of coming here to join their relatives. A person like that is given a hardship permit to come into our country, and those are the only ones now that we are permitting to come here from Iran.

I hope we'll get the hostages back safe. We've had two policies ever since this happened. One is to protect the honor and integrity and the best interests of our country. The other one is not to do anything to endanger the lives or safety or the hope for freedom of the hostages themselves. That's our unchanging policy, and I'm committed to that. And I believe that we will see the hostages come back to freedom in the future; I can't say when.

Thank you.

Q. Thank you, Mr. President.

ENERGY

Q. Hello, Mr. President, my name is Tim Good. I live in San Pedro, which is about 10 miles from here. In your opening remarks you called for an increased investment in our economic capabilities. Why then don't we make more than a token investment in solar power instead of going to the quick fix of nuclear energy, which is the most polluting technology ever devised?

THE PRESIDENT. Tim, in 1975, 2 years after the Arab oil embargo, we were only spending about $50 million on solar research and solar power development. We are now spending a billion dollars a year on solar power. This is a 20-fold increase over what was the case in 1975, in just 5 years. We now have 10 times as many homes using solar power as were using it 4 years ago.

This commitment of mine to solar power will be extended throughout the end of this century, when we have a very noble goal, which I believe we can meet, of having 20 percent of all our energy used in this country come from the Sun, either directly from the Sun's rays or from growing crops, indirectly—converted into fuels from the growing crops. That's a major commitment, and it's second only to the commitment to conservation.

If there's one thing better than solar power to meet our needs, it is to save energy and not waste it. So, the emphasis on conservation and the emphasis on solar power are two major components, and they have been increased more than any other element of the energy production cycle. However, I want to point out to you that the energy complex is very broad and far reaching and has many facets to it—the production of synthetic fuels from coal, the production of synthetic fuels from oil shale and tar sands, the production of energy from hydroelectric, particularly the small dams, from temperature gradients in the ocean. All of these kinds of things are an integral part of producing more energy in our country.

There are only two ways to cut down on imports. One is to produce more energy in the United States, and the other one is to save more energy and to cut out waste. You might be interested in knowing that this year we have more oil and natural gas wells being drilled than any other year in history. This year we're producing more coal in the United States than any year in history. And of course, we have much more commitment to solar power and to conservation than any year in history. Those are the kinds of things that we're having to do. I think we'll be successful in the long run.

Thank you very much.

LABOR

Q. Mr. President, Eugene R. Anderson, from Torrance. Mr. President, the organized labor feels that the Carter administration has been unsympathetic to its needs. What are some of the programs you will introduce to gain support of labor, such as enacting the situs picketing bill and the continuous enforcement of the Davis-Bacon Act?

THE PRESIDENT. Eugene, I think that it's accurate to say that the vast majority of labor organizations in the Nation have already endorsed me and Fritz Mondale, and I'm very grateful for that support.

I am supporting Davis-Bacon. I will not permit Davis-Bacon to be destroyed. If the Congress should act to eliminate Davis-Bacon, I will veto the legislation when it comes to my desk. Secondly, I have supported situs picketing, and I am also strongly in favor of labor law reform. And my hope is that next year we will have the votes in the United States Senate to pass labor law reform legislation.

The most important element of my program that will benefit labor, however, is to have a high quality of life for Americans and high employment in the new technologies that are inevitable in our country following the establishment of an adequate national energy policy.

We have a vision of the future, as I said earlier, that is very optimistic. We've been through terrible times in the last few years in trying to accommodate these changes that were forced on us. But our Nation has always been able to accommodate change. We've been on the cutting edge of progress. And what we do in this Nation, in providing for new jobs in energy, high technology and otherwise, will set the tone not only for ourselves but for the entire world.

I've got a good partnership with labor. I'll be leaving here this afternoon, going to speak to the State AFL–CIO group. And I'll be meeting Senator Kennedy there, and he'll also be on the program with me. I think that labor will give me strong support in the future, and I hope and pray that I'll continue to deserve it.

Q. Thank you, Mr. President.

THE PRESIDENT. Thank you very much. I'm sorry to say that our time is up, and I won't have a chance to take any more questions. But let me make a few comments in closing.

I don't know of anything that's more beneficial to a President than to have a chance to come to a community like yours, to stand here and answer questions—I have no idea what you're going to ask me—that I feel are the most important to you in your lives. We've had questions from retired military people. We've had questions about education. We've had questions about morality in America. We've had questions about our future. We've had questions about energy. We've had questions about our hostages. We've had questions about the strength of our military. We've had questions about the draft. We've had questions about the duties of President. We've had questions about the campaign itself. We've had questions about medicine. We've had questions about fair housing. We've had questions about Chicanos. These are the kinds of questions, coming from your heart, that are very important to me.

And I believe that we can look to the 1980's in this great country with confidence and a sense of unity of purpose and a belief that our lives, already the best on Earth in my judgment, will be even better in the future in the greatest nation on Earth.

Thank you very much. God bless you all. I've enjoyed being with you.

NOTE: The President spoke at 2 p.m. in the gymnasium at North High School.

Los Angeles, California

Remarks at the California State AFL–CIO Convention. September 22, 1980

Leaders of the organizations of working people for California, my good friend Jack Henning:

That's one of the best introductions that I have ever heard—beautiful. I, too, am familiar with being quoted out of context by the same crowd. And these are the same people, as you know, who said there are two ways to deal with facts: You can look them up, or you can make them up. Well, now they've found a third way: You can botch them up. And they've really botched this one up. Thank you, Jack. But I don't think you ought to feel too badly about it, particularly since you give a good explanation as you just did. You're the only leader in America, because they've used you in the advertisements, to collect residuals from the Republican National Committee. And if they pay you for using your name, I hope you'll let me know when you collect, because you'll be the first person and this will be the first time that the Republicans have ever done anything in meeting an obligation to the working people of this country. You'll be the first.

I'm grateful that you've let me drop by to interrupt your important proceedings, because it means an awful lot to me to be with you. This is an important State in determining the outcome of this election. I do not intend to lose California. If you'll help me on November the 4th, we'll win.

I've only got a few minutes, so I'll be brief. But there are a few things that I wanted to say because, although you may have heard them from other people, I want you to hear them from me as the President of the United States, as a nominee of the Democratic Party, and as the one that you've endorsed for reelection.

Six weeks from now, the American people will make a very profound choice— a choice not just between two men or two parties but between two futures. And what you decide on that day, you and those who listen to your voice, will determine what kind of life you and your families will have, whether this Nation will

make progress or go backward, and whether we have peace or war. It'll be a choice between two very different futures.

We've had five decades, since Franklin Roosevelt's time, of steady progress, interrupted on a few occasions by Republican administrations in the White House. We need to continue what the Democratic Party means for this country and what the labor movement of America has meant to the strength of this Nation, not only to your own members, whether this Nation will stand firmly by its commitments to justice, to equality, and to freedom. In keeping these commitments for the last $3\frac{1}{2}$ years, we've faced some of the most difficult problems that this Nation has seen. We have stayed at peace through strength. We've faced up to the first time I ever remember when an outside force could exert economic pressure on our great country.

The energy problem is profound. We've taken action, and now oil imports are down 24 percent. We've got over 3,100 oil-drilling rigs running right now. We'll have more oil and natural gas wells drilled in 1980 than any other year in the history of our country. We're producing more coal this year than any other year in the history of our country. We've got 10 times as many homes using solar power today as we did just 4 years ago.

This steady progress, which comes in recent months, can profoundly affect the quality of your life, because in the 1970's, in the late years, we have been successful in meeting this challenge on energy, which is crucial, and now we're ready to rebuild the industrial complex of this country.

As you know, the American worker is the most productive worker on Earth. But the American worker has too long been saddled with obsolescent tools and obsolescent factories, and we've got to have the investment going to give you the tools and the factories and the opportunities to continue to be the most productive workers on Earth in the years ahead. We will revitalize America, look to the future with confidence and with commitment and with unity and with courage in the process, above and beyond normal economic recovery and above and beyond the programs that are now in the halls of Congress. We'll add a million new jobs in the next 2 years, jobs in growing and competitive industry.

It's crucial to me, as President and as Commander in Chief, to keep our Nation's defense structure strong. For the 8 years before I became President, 7 of those years we had a decrease in the commitment of American budget funds for defense. Since I've been in office, every year we've had an increase in commitment in real dollars, above and beyond inflation to American defense. And as long as I'm in the White House, this country will be strong, second to none in military power. And you can depend on it. And that's the reason we stay at peace—because we are strong. American people know we're strong; our allies know we're strong; our potential adversaries know that we are strong. We're developing advanced weapons, but I think it's good for us to remember that the best weapon is the one that's never fired in combat, and the best soldier is one that never sheds blood on the battlefield. And that can only come about if our determination to keep America strong never waivers.

It's important for us to strengthen our basic industries—steel, automobiles, mining, transportation—also to encourage high technology industries, to expand research and development, to rebuild our transportation system, and to expand exports. And we'll give direct aid to communities and workers that are hit by changing times. Because change is inevi-

table, we cannot stop and freeze the societal structure of our country. But as those changes take place, it's important to me, and my responsibility along with yours, to make sure that families don't suffer and, as a factory or plant is phased out because of changing circumstances, that we have jobs come into that community to tide those families over for new and productive careers.

The American economy must and will be a full-employment economy, and the American worker will continue to outwork, outproduce, and outcompete workers in every other nation on Earth. That's my commitment to you. That is not enough. I listened very closely to Jack Henning when he pointed out what Reagan had done here in depriving labor of an adequate voice in matters that are crucial to you and to your families. We need a new consensus that recognizes that labor ought to be represented at the major decision tables when the future of our Nation is shaped. We are in danger of having some of those important considerations decided against labor unless we've got a President in the White House who can stand in partnership with you. I'm still with you on common situs, and I will veto any attempt to repeal or to modify Davis-Bacon against the interests of the working people of this country.

And I might add one other thing. I don't get in political campaigns to lose. Sometimes there is a delay in victory. But I'm still committed to you, and I will support, for your interests and for our national interests, labor law reform. And I believe we'll have it in the years ahead.

There's another point I want to make very quickly, and that is that when we rebuild our economy and as we give labor a firm voice in shaping the future of America, we must also expand social and economic justice in America. We must sustain programs for the poor and the unemployed and the elderly and the afflicted and the weak. We need to enact national health insurance. And we need to enact welfare reform and expand youth employment. These kinds of things give us an unfinished work agenda that will be very challenging and also very exciting in the years ahead.

In these last 3½ years we've laid a good foundation for a future of an expanding economy, a just society, and a secure nation at peace. In contrast to that, we face a Republican candidate and a Republican Party that offer this country a counterfeit future. The Republicans promise the same Republican formulas that long ago failed the majority of Americans, and the majority of Americans, when reminded, remember.

We've heard the Republicans praise the newborn free trade unions of Poland. Don't you wish they were as enthusiastic about free trade unions in America? They oppose the minimum wage. They support the so-called right-to-work laws. They support including unions in antitrust laws. They opposed and still oppose Humphrey-Hawkins. They support repeal of Davis-Bacon. They oppose labor law reform. They were against Medicaid and Medicare. They call for making social security voluntary. We've heard that unemployment compensation is, and I quote, "little more than a paid vacation for freeloaders." Yet after all that, they now campaign under the guise of being a friend of the working people.

To solve our energy problem, they have a very simple answer: Just turn it over to the oil companies; they'll take care of our needs. "Trust them," they say, "to conserve our scarce oil resources and develop alternative energy sources. Let's do away with the windfall profits tax. Let the oil companies keep that money and make a decision on how it should be spent." They deny the need for energy conservation, and they deny any notion that oil is a scarce resource and ought to be conserved. They fought against and still fight against the windfall profits tax.

They have another very simple answer to all our economic problems—a massive tax cut that would be a windfall for the rich and would rob the working man and woman with rapidly increasing inflation in the future. Only one-tenth of that tax cut would go for job-producing investments. The rest of it would set off an inflationary whirlwind.

There's nothing in these simple answers for rebuilding our ports, our railroads, for research and development, for retraining workers, for aid to cities or communities hit by economic change. That's the kind of future that the Republicans hold out. And that's the reason you and I in this next 6 weeks must work with determination and fervor in a sacrificial way with the majority of American workers who share our commitment.

We need to work together, to turn out the Democratic voters in California, the working people, who've been the backbone of social and economic progress. Let's rededicate ourselves to this task and join the struggle for justice and human dignity. Let's join together in sweeping California on November the 4th and making this great country of ours even greater in the future. You do your share. I'll do my share. We'll have a great victory in November.

Thank you very much.

NOTE: The President spoke at 4:13 p.m. in the Neill Petrie Hall at the Los Angeles Convention Center. He was introduced by Jack Henning, executive secretary/treasurer of the California State AFL–CIO.

Beverly Hills, California

Remarks at a Democratic National Committee Fundraising Reception. September 22, 1980

Senator Kennedy and Governor Brown, Tom Bradley, Lew Wasserman, Chuck Manatt, Edie, and all of you who've come here tonight:

It's indeed a pleasure to be introduced in such a forceful and effective way by Senator Kennedy. He has a lot of friends in California. I can certainly vouch for that. [*Laughter*] I haven't always been pleased with that fact, but tonight I'm delighted. And I might say that had we had this kind of unity all the year, I would have had a much more pleasant springtime. [*Laughter*]

But as Senator Kennedy pointed out, it's important to the Democratic Party, it's crucial to the future of our Nation that issues that are troubling to our people and to the people throughout the world be clearly aired, that the issues be sharply defined, that hopes be raised, that confidence be restored, that unity be ensured, and that the doubts and trepidation and embarrassments that have been with us under the Republican Party in the past and as a prospect for the future be eliminated.

I'm particularly glad to come and meet with average families, common, run-of-the-mill Americans to get your views here at the Beverly Hilton in Hollywood. [*Laughter*] That's been the source of my political strength in California— [*laughter*]—and I think it's the source of American strength in the future to have you and others like you throughout the country on our side.

I want to say two or three things to you this evening that are important to me and, I believe, to our country. Ted Kennedy, Jerry Brown, and I share a common faith in the future, a common vision of what our Nation ought to be and will be, a belief in a Democratic Party that has an open heart, that's deeply concerned about principle, about compassion, and about concern for those who are aged, poor, who don't speak English well, who've been deprived in the past of an adequate opportunity for progress in their own lives, who've been deprived quite often of a chance for equal justice and of the proper self-respect that was guaranteed to all Americans by the original founders of this country.

In addition to that, we are committed to peace. We've had 3½ years when our Nation has been at peace. Not a single soldier has been sent into combat, and I pray God we'll have the same success in the next 4 years. And we've had that peace through strength. Our Nation is the strongest nation on Earth—militarily, politically, economically, and I believe morally and ethically.

I have no apology to make for keeping our Nation's defense strong. We had a steady decrease in commitment to American defense during the 8 years prior to my own administration. Since then we've steadily increased our commitment to defense—still only about 5 percent of our gross national product. And I believe that's the best way to ensure not only peace for our country but for our allies and friends around the world. The best weapon, as I said at Torrance early today, is the weapon that's never fired in anger, and the best soldier is one that never sheds blood on the field of battle. And as long as we know that we are strong and our allies know our strength and our potential adversaries respect that strength, our Nation can maintain its commitment to peace.

We've had notable success the last 3½ years in addressing, I believe courageously—the Congress, the Governors, and also myself—issues that in the past had been ignored. I won't name them all, but just one or two.

Energy is a subject that permeates the consciousness now and for a long time the lives of every family in this country. For a long time it was ignored. And now America has recognized that for economic progress and for an exciting, dynamic life in the future, we must reduce our unwarranted dependence on foreign oil. We've been remarkably successful in the brief months since the Congress passed legislation establishing an energy policy for our country for the first time in its history.

This year we will import about 6½ million barrels of oil per day—2 million barrels each day less than we did when I first became President. At the same time, we have a massive commitment to conservation. We already have 10 times as many homes using solar power as did 4 years ago. We've multiplied by a factor of 2,000 percent the commitment of our Nation to research and development in solar power. We have more oil wells and gas wells being drilled this year than any year in this history of our Nation, and we're producing more coal in our country this year than any year in the history of our Nation.

And this is just the beginning of a wonderful era working toward energy independence for our country that will be vital to the American people. And on top of that foundation, we're now ready to make sure that the tools and factories of our Nation are modern and that the workers, who are now the highest and most productive in the world, stay competitive with any other nation on Earth. These kinds of economic progress opportunities will give our Nation the strength to continue through the 1980's with the hope that it lives in our hearts intact.

Finally, I'd like to say that we have a great obligation to our allies and friends. One of the most gratifying experiences of my Presidency has been the ability to work toward a comprehensive peace in the Middle East. I recognize that when I contribute to the peace and the security of Israel, I make a direct contribution in a magnified form to the peace and the security of the Nation that I have been elected to lead. My goal in the next 4 years is to continue this progress. And with Sol Linowitz' help, President Sadat, Prime Minister Begin are now arranging for continued negotiations. The Foreign Minister of Israel and the Minister of Foreign Affairs for Egypt were in my office last week on the second anniversary of the Camp David accords and met for hours with Sol Linowitz to lay the foundation for more progress.

After this election year is over on November the 4th, then our prospect is that President Sadat, Prime Minister Begin, and myself would have another summit meeting to pursue the progress that we've made so far and bring about a realization of the hopes and dreams of the Israeli people, the Egyptian people, and in my judgment, a vast majority of the people in the other surrounding nations adjacent to Israel, for a comprehensive peace in the Middle East with the security of Israel intact. This is important to us and to all the people on Earth.

And finally, let me say that I deeply appreciate the confidence and help that you've given me. California is a crucial State. The outcome of the election could very well depend upon the electoral votes from California. This will not be an easy campaign, to beat Ronald Reagan in his home State. That is a noble goal, which I'm sure you share with me. And I do not intend to lose this election.

I'll be back here as often as I can. My wife will be here, my children will be here, my mother will be here, Fritz Mondale will be here. [*Laughter*] I don't want you to get tired of the Carter family, politically and blood-kin, but we intend to carry California, because I know from experience, the last 3½ years how important the occupant of the Oval Office can be. It's one of the most gratifying and exciting jobs on Earth.

The Presidency of the United States is held in great reverence and respect by people in every nation on Earth. The decisions that come there are crucial decisions. There are no easy answers in the Oval Office. If the answers are easily derived, they are found within a person's own life or within a family or a home or a county courthouse or a city hall or a State legislature or a Governor's office.

If, in that process, they cannot be resolved easily, then those questions come to the Oval Office. Advisers are valuable. I would challenge anybody to compare the Cabinet quality that I have now with any Cabinet that's served this Nation down through history. But I've also found that when the issue is of the utmost importance to the American people and perhaps the world and it's most difficult to resolve that that's when advisers are highly likely to be evenly divided in the counsel they give to the President. At that time it's a lonely job. And a sensitivity to the hopes and ideals of the American people, a knowledge of the facts, an awareness of the interrelationship of our country to all the other countries on Earth, a knowledge of the personal characteristics of leaders of those foreign countries, an intimate, detailed study of the bureaucratic structure of our Federal Government and its interrelationship with local and State governments—all those factors come into a decision in the lonely confines of the Oval Office.

I've had, with your help, 3½ years of experience. I've been a good student. I don't claim we've never made mistakes, but we've made steady progress. We've carved out for this country a great vision of the future, and we've kept our Nation at peace. I've dealt with many crises during the last 3½ years, and I'm thankful that most of those crises—that you never knew about them. Had I handled a crisis improperly or had I made an incorrect judgment, that crisis would be a vivid issue in your mind and perhaps would have endangered the safety and the peace of the entire world.

I don't claim to be infallible, but I have a reassuring belief that the intimacy with which you give me your support and your counsel and your advice and your criticisms makes you a partner with me in shaping the future of our country and ensuring that the United States of America, the greatest nation on Earth, will be at peace and even greater in its influence in the years ahead. That's my prayer. With your help, we'll make that prayer come true.

Thank you very much.

NOTE: The President spoke at 6:45 p.m. in the Grand Ballroom of the Beverly Hilton Hotel.

Following the reception, the President went to the Century Plaza Hotel in Los Angeles, where he remained overnight.

Los Angeles, California

Remarks in an Interview With Reporters From Newscenter 4, KNBC–TV. September 23, 1980

IRAQI-IRANIAN SITUATION

AMERICAN HOSTAGES IN IRAN

Q. Mr. President, the war between Iran and Iraq seems to be escalating by the hour. Can you tell us at this point what you think the impact will be on the hostages in Iran and on the shipment of oil through the Straits of Hormuz?

THE PRESIDENT. Early this morning I've talked to Dr. Brzezinski, the national security adviser, and to Secretary Brown and also communicated with Ed Muskie, who is now at the United Nations. Our own position is one of strict neutrality. And we're doing all we can, through the U.N. and through other means, to bring a peaceful conclusion to this combat that seems to be waged so far—most of the action seems to be by air or naval forces and with a minimum involvement at this point, so far as we know, of ground forces.

I don't see any way at this time that this altercation between Iran and Iraq will affect the safety or the lives of the hostages nor the date of their release. But it's too early to assess that with any sort of final conclusion.

Q. Well, would you still be able to say that if it appeared that the Government of Iran had become unstable as a result of the conflict, if it were likely to fall?

THE PRESIDENT. Well, there's no indication of that at all so far. Iran has come through a very long and tedious and extended period of forming a government. They've elected the members of their parliament. They now have for the first time a Prime Minister and a speaker of the parliament plus a President. They're putting together the final identity of the Cabinet. And of course, Khomeini still enjoys a great influence on the entire process. So, I believe that the likelihood of a destabilization of the Iran Government is not very great.

CHARGES OF GOVERNMENT RACISM

Q. Mr. President, news reports this morning quote the Iraqi Government as saying that its objective is to break what it calls "the racist government of the Aya-

tollah Khomeini." Do you accept that characterization?

THE PRESIDENT. No. I think obviously the difference in religious beliefs would incur that sort of statement on both sides, but no, I wouldn't ascribe any sort of racism to either government. They have their fervent beliefs, well known to their own people, and I think both governments are acceptable to their people.

INTERRUPTION OF OIL SHIPMENTS

Q. Mr. President, with regard to this country's position of strict neutrality with regard to that conflict and with regard to the fact that the Straits of Hormuz are extremely strategic in terms of oil shipments for this country, you and your administration have said in the past on several occasions that we are committed in terms of strategic commitment to that area of the world.

THE PRESIDENT. Yes.

Q. Do I assume that that has not changed?

THE PRESIDENT. Well, Iraq has been exporting lately, I think, about 3 million barrels of oil per day. Iran's export has been down to about 500,000 or half a million barrels per day. Obviously with the Straits of Hormuz and also the other areas that are closed—Shatt al Arab— closed or at least restrained, this will have an adverse affect on oil supplies in the world market. Although no interruption of oil supplies is good for us, this is a better time, if we had to choose one, because there is a large supply of oil on world markets (relative to demand)* at this particular moment, and also we (in the U.S.)* have perhaps the highest reserve supplies of oil on hand that I can remember.

So, a temporary interruption of oil

_____
*White House clarification.

shipments from Iraq and Iran will not be very serious, but the prospect of an extended interruption would be very serious to us. However, the only solution to this for us is certainly not any sort of engagement between Iran and Iraq by our own forces, but simply an effort to bring a peaceful solution to this problem.

Q. But in terms of defending the Straits of Hormuz to ensure oil supplies continuing, has that commitment on the part of this country changed, and for example, do you take seriously Iran's threat to blockade the Straits?

THE PRESIDENT. We have never taken a position that Iran or Iraq should be a threat to which we would respond with our force or might. The principle that I've described is if the Soviet Union should move into that area, it would be a threat to our vital needs in this country. That's the principle that I described in my State of the Union speech, but not involving Iran and Iraq's control over their own waterways.

Q. Mr. President, you said that a temporary cutoff of oil supplies would not be too serious, because of the supply situation now. Suppose it persists. Would that lead to undermining the whole energy conservation program and the energy management program that you've tried to develop and require you to ask the American people to make new sacrifices, lead to new lines at the gas stations, that sort of thing?

THE PRESIDENT. This threat to the oil supplies from Iran and Iraq is a vivid demonstration of the need for the exact energy policy that my administration has put through the Congress and now has implemented. Every day this year we are importing 1½ to 2 million barrels of oil from overseas less than we did just a year ago. This is a notable achievement by the American people, based upon the new energy policy that we've put forward. If this interruption of supply should continue, then I would have to call on the American people to restrict their consumption of oil even more severely on a voluntary basis, which I think would be adequate, with a patriotic tone to it.

But there is no doubt in my mind that we must continue to move forward in strict conservation measures in this country and also in the production of more American energy of all kinds. That's exactly what we have done since the first day I came into office, and the Congress has responded very well.

This interruption in the Persian Gulf region could become important not only to our own country in the future but to all the major consuming nations. And at Tokyo and also at Venice, at the economic summit conference, with six other major developed nations, we jointly committed ourselves to strict conservation measures, which have been implemented, and we also agreed that if there is a severe interruption of international oil supplies that we would consult very quickly and share the shortage among ourselves in an equitable way. That mechanism has been put into place. It's ready to be used, if it must be used. I hope it will not be necessary.

U.S. NONINTERVENTION POLICY

Q. Before we get away from Iran completely, back again to the question of the hostages. If there appears to be instability of the Government in Iran, if it appears to be threatened by the Iraqis or by anybody else, is there any possibility that this country would consider any sort of military action to go and get the hostages out of there, lest their lives appear to be threatened as well?

THE PRESIDENT. The worst thing I could do as President would be to escalate this disruption or altercation between Iran and Iraq to an even greater international crisis because of ill-considered decisions by myself. What we want to do is to calm the situation and not aggravate it. And so any comment by me about the use of American forces would be completely inappropriate.

Our forces have been built up in the Indian Ocean and in the Persian Gulf region to protect our interests and to let the people there know that the fate of the hostages is very important to us, and stability and peace in the region are very important to us. But I have no inclination to act precipitiously or to take any action that might aggravate an already dangerous situation.

We'll be calm, steady, open in our diplomatic posture, and working as best we can with other nations and with Iran and Iraq to resolve this entire problem peacefully. The basic decision, of course, is within the government structure of Iran and Iraq. We'll offer our good services to enhance peace, and if it's accepted, we'll be gratified. But we're not going to interfere.

OIL PRICES

Q. Will you comment, Mr. President, on Senator Percy's comment yesterday that if the conflict continues he believes that gasoline prices in this country would raise to $4 to $5 a gallon, that home heating bills this winter would be as much as a thousand dollars a month?

THE PRESIDENT. I think that's an exaggeration.

FOREIGN POLICY AS A CAMPAIGN ISSUE

PRESIDENT'S RECORD

Q. Mr. President, the current headlines which report war, however limited it may be at the moment, are disconcerting to people. In the past day, when you campaigned here in the Los Angeles area, you said several times that the issue of the election this year is nothing less than the question of war and peace. Are you suggesting that only by voting for you can the American people assure that there will be peace?

THE PRESIDENT. No, I'm sure that anybody who's in the White House as President would want to maintain peace.

It is true, however, that in the last 3½ years we've kept our Nation at peace. This has not been the record of very many Presidents in this century. And I'm committed to keeping our military forces strong, our political and diplomatic relationships with other nations intact, our alliances commonly committed to the preservation of peace, and to using the strength of our country with reticence and with calmness, so that we don't aggravate potential crises into a warlike environment which might lead to combat. This is very important.

And I believe that the American people must realize that the identity of the President and the strength of our Nation, our relationship with our allies, our relationship with potential enemies, and the rhetoric that's put forward by a President all are factors in the maintenance of peace. I'm committed to this, a continuation of what I've done the first 3½ years. And my prayer is that when I go out of office at the end of two terms, I hope that our Nation will have been at peace throughout that period.

RONALD REAGAN

Q. You've gone so far as to say that the real issue in this election may be the difference between war and peace. How far are you willing to go with respect to your opponent, your principal opponent, Ronald Reagan, in saying that his election might be a threat to peace?

THE PRESIDENT. Well, I think it would

be better for the news media and for the American public to analyze some of the statements that Governor Reagan has made in the past calling for a blockade of Cuba, calling for the use of American military forces in Lebanon, calling for the American military forces to be used even off the western coast of South America. I think in 8 or 10 different instances in recent years he has called for the use of American military force to address problems that arise diplomatically between nations.

I don't know what he would do if he were in the Oval Office, but if you judge by his past highly rhetorical calls for the use of American military forces in these altercations, it is disturbing. I'll let him answer that question. But I know that I'm committed to the use of American strength for the maintenance of peace and not to inject American military forces into a situation when it's not necessary in order to protect American interests.

U.S. MILITARY STRENGTH

Q. He says what he has in mind is the adoption of a policy of strength in order to maintain peace.

THE PRESIDENT. But there's a difference between keeping a nation strong militarily and using those strong military forces in combat, and that's a distinction that a President alone must exercise.

My record as President has been to keep our Nation strong. After 7 years of downward commitments to American military capability, in 7 out of 8 of those years that the Republicans were in office before me, we had a decrease in American budget commitment to our military strength. We've been going upward every year since I've been in office, and we'll continue to do that to keep our Nation strong.

That strength must be used, however, with great reticence and great care and

great calmness and great deliberation, not to create combat by getting our military involved in the use of weapons, but to let people know we are a peaceful nation, but if we are attacked or if our interests are threatened, we can use that military force in a crisis. The best thing a President can do is to avoid that crisis and to avoid the use of military forces, keeping them there. As I said yesterday in Torrance in a town-hall meeting, the best weapons are the ones that are never used in combat, and the best soldier is one that never sheds his blood on the field of battle. But to have strong military forces ready to use if necessary is the best deterrent to anyone who wants to challenge us and precipitate war.

RONALD REAGAN

Q. You're not saying that Governor Reagan has ever advocated combat, though?

THE PRESIDENT. I'll let you examine what he has called for. I've outlined it in general terms. But the record's there. To call for the use of military forces in a very dangerous situation has been a repeated habit of his as a Governor and as a candidate for President. What he would do in the Oval Office I hope will never be observed by the American people.

CAMPAIGN STRATEGY IN CALIFORNIA

Q. One brief question, also, on something else. You said yesterday that winning California is a "doable" cause as far as you're concerned between now and the end of the campaign 6 weeks from now. Specifically, how do you plan to defeat Governor Reagan in his home State, where, of course, he has never lost? Specifically.

THE PRESIDENT. Well, times change, and my belief is that I can carry California on November the 4th. We have now in place an extensive campaign organization, which I have never had in California before, but which we have had in place in other States in 1976 and in the primaries in 1980. Also, there are many people in California who know Governor Reagan's record concerning the aspects of life that are important to a family or to a person.

I believe the combination of our comparative commitment on issues that are crucial to the California people plus an all-out effort by me to win the State on November the 4th, with Fritz Mondale as my running-mate, will prove that our prediction of victory is true. I don't intend to lose California.

Q. Thank you, Mr. President.

NUCLEAR WEAPONS

TITAN MISSILE SILO EXPLOSION

Q. There's great concern about the incident that occurred last week in Arkansas. Can you tell us if, in fact, a nuclear warhead was ejected from the Titan silo; if so, how badly it was damaged and what has happened to it since?

THE PRESIDENT. We have a policy of not confirming or denying the location of nuclear warheads, but let me say this. There was never any danger from radioactivity. There was never any radioactivity present in the area. And I can say this morning that there are no components of a nuclear warhead at the site at this time.

NUCLEAR ACCIDENTS

Q. What can you say to allay the concern of people who are worried because one of the most destructive weapons in the world has itself been destroyed by a chain of events which seems to have begun so simply as by a workman dropping a wrench?

THE PRESIDENT. The design of nuclear warheads is such that there is no way for

it to be exploded accidentally. There has to be a series of events, carefully controlled, in order for a nuclear warhead to be put into an explosive state. An outside explosion or the dropping of a nuclear device from an airplane and so forth could not possibly precipitate an explosion. So, although it is a matter of concern to people, because of the design of these devices there is no danger under the circumstances that I've just described.

Q. Mr. President, the Titan case is not the only one. In the past year or so there've been several instances of SAC bombers being put on alert because of malfunctions of the warning system, sometimes, we are told, a 50-cent part. What does this say about the vulnerability and the integrity of our whole defense system, if it can be subjected to accidents of this sort?

THE PRESIDENT. Well, you can't prohibit by even the most careful design some sort of malfunctions that exist inside a computer or in an airplane or in a fueling device. The fact is that in our own society, a democratic society with freedom of the press and a maximum desire on my part and those who work with me to let the American people know what happened when an incident does occur, the American people know about it and the world knows about it.

We have never had a situation in this country, either before or since I've been in the White House, where in my opinion any sort of danger existed (of a nuclear explosion or a nuclear exchange caused by a malfunction).* We have fail-safe devices that have always functioned. We have personnel highly trained to prevent any sort of incident that might lead to a nuclear explosion. And the design of the weapon system, the design of the control

---

*White House clarification.

system, and the training of the personnel are such that we have never approached the point where any sort of danger existed.

TITAN II

Q. Specifically about the Titan II, is it time for it to be phased out, or is it your opinion that it is still necessary for our national security to have those missiles?

THE PRESIDENT. Well, as I mentioned earlier about weapons systems, the best weapon is one that's never used.

The Titan is a very large missile. It's a missile that we've had deployed more than 10 or 15 years. It's a missile that has a liquid propellant system instead of a solid propellant system, which the most modern American missiles have, and that's proven to be very safe. I might also say that the safety devices assigned to the Titan, both with its own internal system for explosions if it should be used in combat and also to propel it, are safer than they were when the Titan was first deployed a number of years ago.

We don't have any present plans to phase out the Titan until the MX missile comes on production line—comes off the production line. The liquid propellant itself is not necessarily an obsolescent system. The most modern Soviet missiles, the SS–18 for instance, has a liquid propellant system. We opted 10 or 15 years ago to go toward a solid propellant system.

But the Titan is still a formidable missile. It has its great deterrent value, which is the reason for having the entire nuclear weapons system—to deter a war and to make sure that if the Soviets are tempted to make any attack on us with nuclear missiles that they realize that this would be suicidal in nature. So, as part of an overall deterrent system on a balanced basis with the Soviet Union to prevent nu-

clear war, the Titan has a role to play, and for the next foreseeable number of years, they will continue to be deployed.

INFLATION

Q. Mr President, on another subject, the Government reports this morning that the cost of living went up again, the price index went up seven-tenths of 1 percent during the month of August. The prediction is that it will go up somewhat more than that during this month of September. Does that mean that your effort to control inflation and to manage the economy is again in jeopardy?

THE PRESIDENT. Inflation is an ever-present threat, not only to us but to all the nations on Earth. We have gone through 1979 with a 120-percent increase in the price of oil for the world, including of course our own country. This has been highly inflationary in nature.

As you remember, back in the first part of March we were faced with an inflation rate of 18 or 20 percent and interest rates of 18 to 20 percent. Since then that circumstance has improved. In July the inflation rate was zero, the first time in 13 years. This past month the inflation rate was up around 8 percent. My hope is that the American people will be persistent and will join me and the Congress in taking steps to control the rate of inflation.

One of the things that the American people can do is not to insist on a highly inflationary tax reduction program as has been advocated by the Reagan-Kemp-Roth procedure, very similar to Proposition Nine, by the way, which was rejected by the California voters in a recent referendum. If we have this highly inflationary giveaway program for rich people, it would mean that the average working family, under Reagan-Kemp-Roth would be severely impacted next year by increased inflationary pressure.

So, as we go through this time of revitalization of our American economy with an emphasis on new jobs, new technology, new confidence about the future, new investments, modernization of our plants, we've got to do it in such a way that we control inflation. The entire economic package that I have proposed to be implemented next year is anti-inflationary in its consequence. In other words, it will tend to reduce inflation rather than increase inflation. The Reagan-Kemp-Roth proposal would be highly inflationary in nature and would have a minimal impact, practically no impact, on the revitalization of American industry and the creation of new jobs and technology for the future. That's the difference between us. And I think that we've got to keep in mind the fact that inflation is a constant threat to us and to other nations on Earth.

SCHOOL INTEGRATION AND BUSING

Q. Mr. Carter, as you know, we have a controversy going on in Los Angeles with respect to busing for school integration. You said recently in Texas you didn't think that busing for school integration was a very good idea.

THE PRESIDENT. That's right.

Q. But under your administration the Justice Department has defended judicial authority to order busing in a number of cities around the country. Does your public statement suggest that you are withdrawing from the position of leadership in that area and that the Justice Department policy consequently will change?

THE PRESIDENT. No. I noticed a comment made by Congressman Jim Corman this morning very similar to mine. I'm against busing, and Jim Corman is against busing, and others are, too. I have never

known a massive busing system that was mandated in this country to work with effectiveness. Both the minority parents and students and those in the majority races in a particular community soon find out that the mandatory massive busing programs just do not work.

What is necessary under the American law and the Constitution is that if the school boards and the parents and the teachers cannot come up with a way to treat the minority students fairly and equitably and give them equal quality of education, then the courts move in as a last resort and mandate that students be bused to one another's schools. That's a last resort that ought to be avoided. And in my judgment, the best thing that parents and teachers and others can do to avoid the injection of the Federal courts into the situation is to guarantee equality of opportunity in the school systems as they exist.

But I'm against massive busing, do not think it works, and have to acknowledge the fact that as President I'm sworn to uphold the law once it's implemented by the courts. That summarizes it. And my hope is that in Los Angeles and other places this massive busing can be avoided.

Q. In those places where the courts have ordered busing, will the Justice Department continue to support it as it has in the past?

THE PRESIDENT. Yes. The Justice Department must enforce the American law and uphold the American Constitution. The optimum way to run the American schools—what I'm for and what almost every Member of the Congress that I know is for—is for the local people to resolve the issue outside the Federal courts and not require the Federal courts to move in to guarantee equality of opportunity. This is the important issue to be drawn.

I might also add that a United States Congressman like Jim Corman or myself as President has no authority and no direct responsibility over what is done by the local school officials or the Federal courts. That's outside of our authority, but it becomes a burning issue in many communities when busing does become controversial. And my hope still is that this massive kind of court-ordered busing can be avoided throughout the country.

Q. Mr. President, thank you very much.

THE PRESIDENT. It's been a pleasure.

NOTE: The interview with Saul Halpert, Warren Olney, and Tricia Toyota began at 7:05 a.m. in the President's suite at the Century Plaza Hotel.

San Jose, California

Remarks at City Hall. September 23, 1980

Thank you very much, Mayor Janet Hayes, Congressman Norm Mineta, Congressman Don Edwards, and distinguished members of the county and city governments who've come here to make me feel at home and to welcome me:

This morning it's extremely important for me as President to acknowledge what is being accomplished here in the Santa Clara Valley in preparing our Nation for the future, which could be very troublesome for us unless we learn from the experience that you have given the Nation. This valley is indeed a fine example for us all. Your technology and the innovation that you've expressed is the cutting edge of our economic progress.

It's absolutely crucial in these troubled times, when overseas oil supplies are uncertain and their price is rapidly escalating, for us to be energy-secure here in the United States. There are two ways, and

only two ways, that we can do this: One is to conserve energy—to save energy, to cut out waste—and the other way is to produce more energy of all kinds here in the United States.

Industrial change is inevitable; it's good. There is no way to avoid it, and Americans have never been afraid of change. We are an innovative, pioneer-spirit people, and you have made this clear here in San Jose and throughout this valley. We must have economic health, with new jobs, new opportunities for American workers to remain the most productive on Earth. And of course, our national security itself is at stake. These are also the keys to the future of this city and this region of our great country. Now that we have an energy policy in place, after long and laborious effort by the Congress, we have a chance to literally revitalize the entire American industrial complex.

You have indeed made this valley hum with activity. You've made great progress, and you've set an example which I'm sure the rest of the Nation will be eager to emulate. As you know, the same state of art of the computer systems which formerly would have filled a file cabinet or even a room can now be used as a pocket calculator and can also be inserted on an automobile, in a traffic light, in a home, to make sure that efficiency of operation of our entire energy-consuming society is increased substantially. We have an opportunity now also to reduce pollution and to make sure that the quality of our lives is constantly enhanced. Technology is indeed the key, and your technology in this valley has been an inspiration to us all.

Our goals have been spelled out very clearly in the Global 2000 report, which indicates to us the challenges to the world society unless we address these issues directly and take action to prevent the catastrophes which could occur from a burgeoning population throughout the Earth, constant depletion of our reserve supplies of oil, coal, and other fossil fuels, and a failure to move forward on technology that gives us renewable supplies of energy derived directly or indirectly from the Sun.

We have made great progress in a brief period of time. In just 3½ years, since I've been in office, with the good help of the Congress, we have spelled out for ourselves now in law an opportunity to reduce our dependence on overseas oil. Today and every day this year, we will import 2 million barrels of oil less than we did just a year ago. This is good progress. It's because we've had a 20-fold increase in the allotment of Federal funds for solar power research and development. And because we now have, compared to just 4 years ago, 10 times as many American homes using solar power.

I just visited a very exciting exhibit, which will be open to all of you, that shows some of the new ideas that can be put into practical application in your own homes, your own automobiles, and your own communities. This kind of innovation gives a bright hope for Americans and indeed the rest of the world in the years to come.

The Sun, with which we're so generously blessed today, will indeed open up an opportunity for excitement and a better quality of life for Americans in the future. And our goal is that 20 percent of all the energy we use in this country by the end of this century will come directly from the Sun. We've been blessed, as you know, not only with a good climate but with very rich oil, and growing crops can take the Sun and indirectly convert it into energy that we can use, of all kinds. Solar cells, photovoltaic cells, the focusing of the Sun's rays to heat liquid—these kinds

of technologies are already known to us. And as the years go by and the price of oil continues to go up, which it will, these will be increasingly economically competitive with the alternative sources of oil.

I might say a couple of other things, and that is that the wind, the water, growing crops, indirect beneficiaries of the Sun's rays, have not yet been adequately tapped by the American public. Farmers can move forward with decreased tillage, a minimum amount of cultivation for their crops, and therefore to save fuels that had been used for unnecessary cultivation with tractors. Crops can be cured with direct rays of the Sun instead of using oil, natural gas, and other heat sources.

This next year, we'll spend about a billion dollars on solar energy, whereas 5 years ago we were only spending about one-twentieth that amount. This year we're also increasing the search for American energy supplies of a conventional nature. We'll have more oil wells and natural gas wells drilled this year, 1980, than any other year in the history of our country. And you may be surprised to know that this year we'll produce more American coal than in any other year in the history of our Nation.

We're exporting large amounts of coal now and can export more in the future to nations overseas when we improve the quality of loading facilities in our ports and our rail and transportation systems on the highways to take that coal to be shipped overseas. In the future, as a major energy source for other nations, I would like to see OPEC oil replaced with American coal. And obviously in every element of life, in our own families and families around the seas, American technology and the use of American inventions can provide millions of new jobs for American workers and at the same time improve the lives of people all over the Earth.

We're using agricultural products, as you know, already for gasohol, methanol, and ethanol directly and to make other fuels. This opportunity is burgeoning so rapidly it's almost indescribable. A couple of years ago we had practically zero production of gasohol from the ethanol/methanol process. This year we'll produce about 135 million gallons. In 1981 that will leap to 500 million gallons. And I have no doubt that that upward trend in producing fuel for automobiles and other vehicles directly from growing crops will be one of the most exciting opportunities for us in the future.

Basic research goes far beyond energy itself. Your valley and our Nation have benefited from a major commitment to research and development, both in private technology and also through the defense commitments of our country. I'm very deeply committed to keeping our Nation strong militarily. And our commitment this year for research and development through the Department of Defense helps you directly, creates new jobs, and gives us the foresight to expand from defense to domestic technologies, at the same time keeping our country strong.

I'm grateful that, as President, we've kept our Nation at peace. I have not been required to send a single American soldier into combat. And I pray God that when I go out of office at the end of 5 more years that we will still have a nation at peace.

I might add one other point, and that is that the peace of our own country, of our allies, and indeed of the entire world depends upon our Nation being militarily strong. We must know of our strength. Our allies must know of American strength. And political adversaries and potential military adversaries must know that any threat to attack the United States of America would be suicidal on their part. As I've said many times, the best weapons are those that are never fired in combat, and the best soldiers are those that never shed their blood on the field of battle. And to keep our Nation strong and at peace is the major responsibility that I have as President of the United States.

In closing, let me point out to you that what has happened in this wonderful community is not only good for yourselves but is an indication of what can happen throughout our Nation, with the new technological advances now being opened to us, with my determination to revitalize the economic system of our country based on an adequate energy policy.

When I was running for President in 1976 and came to California, the unemployment rate here throughout your State was almost 10 percent—9.8 percent. That is 58 percent higher unemployment rate than it is now. It's now not much more than 6 percent—still too high—but in the process we have been able to create in California alone 1,461,000 new jobs. This shows what can be done with American ingenuity, a competitive American free enterprise system, getting the government's nose out of the affairs of private citizens and private business through deregulation, and the search for the future that can be opened up to all of us with confidence and with unity and with deep commitment.

With your help, I'm determined to see our whole Nation benefit as your community has benefited and to make the greatest nation on Earth, which we love very dearly, even greater in the future.

Thank you very much. God bless you all.

NOTE: The President spoke at 10:40 a.m. outside City Hall. Prior to his remarks, he attended an energy/technology briefing in a conference room and then viewed energy/technology exhibits in the courtyard of City Hall.

San Jose, California

Informal Exchange With Reporters.
September 23, 1980

THE PRESIDENT. I just wanted to say very briefly that I have stayed in touch this morning with Dr. Brzezinski, with Harold Brown, the Secretary of Defense, and have recently communicated with Secretary of State Muskie, who is at the United Nations in New York. We all are doing everything possible, through international means and also through individual countries' contacts, to help terminate the conflict that presently exists between Iran and Iraq.

Apparently air strikes against one another have increased today, with some reports that I've had that the oil refineries both in Iraq and Iran have suffered some damage. Also Baghdad has been attacked through aerial means. So far most of the conflict has been through air and naval forces, but there has been some movement apparently of ground forces from Iraq into the Iranian territory. We are concerned that this might escalate further between the two countries.

We urge all nations, the Soviet Union and all nations, to refrain from any interference or involvement in this conflict. We will certainly observe that mandate meticulously.

We are concerned also that the supply of oil to the Western World and to the rest of the world might be interrupted or reduced. In recent months Iraq has been producing and shipping out about 3 million barrels of oil per day, Iran only about a half-million barrels of oil per day. But some nations, not ourselves, are heavily dependent on these shipments of oil. We hope that the countries involved will honor the international nature of the passage for ships through the Straits of Hormuz, and we will, of course, restrain ourselves and do everything that we can do to minimize any further danger of further escalation of the conflict.

Q. What will happen if they close the Straits of Hormuz?

Q. Any effect on the hostages, Mr. Carter?

THE PRESIDENT. I don't know.

Q. What will the United States do?

Q. What will be the effect on the hostages of any——

THE PRESIDENT. Well, we hope and we expect that the conflict between Iran and Iraq will not have any effect on the safety or lives of the hostages. We will be consulting with other nations about the international straits. As I say, we buy very little oil directly from either Iraq and none from Iran. But countries like Brazil, Japan, Italy, France are heavily dependent on shipments of oil from Iraq. We'll be consulting with others. We do have military forces in the area, but we don't anticipate at all the use of American military forces.

Q. Have you had any contact with Iran, sir?

Q. Mr. President, have any American military forces been moved at all, any carrier dispositions?

THE PRESIDENT. No.

Q. Do you have any contact with Iran on this, directly or indirectly?

THE PRESIDENT. I think I'd better restrain my answers to those I've already given.

Thank you very much.

NOTE: The exchange began at 11:10 a.m. at the San Jose Municipal Airport, prior to the President's departure for Oregon.

As printed above, this item follows the text of the White House press release.

Portland, Oregon

Remarks at a Democratic National Committee Fundraising Reception. September 23, 1980

First of all, let me say how delighted I am to be with all of you and to thank John Schwabe and Jean and all their family for making this event possible.

Also it's very exciting for me to come to Portland and be with famous people like Neil Goldschmidt. [*Laughter*] Sometimes you get an exalted opinion of yourself. I was going down the line a while ago shaking hands with some high school students, and I heard one jump up and down and say, "Oh, isn't it wonderful to be near such an exciting and internationally famous celebrity?" And the other little girl said, "You mean Phil Donahue is back in town?" [*Laughter*] Well, a lot of things happen to a President to take him down a notch, but one of the things that has taken me up several notches is being able to go on this trip.

The main emphasis of my journey to four different States has been the energy crisis and what it means for our Nation and how well Americans have done already, in a very brief period of time, to make our lives more pleasant, to add an exciting dimension for the 1980's, to acknowledge that we have a foundation now on which we can build a revitalized financial and industrial system, and to take advantage of the free enterprise system of our country, our advances in research and technology, and the entrepreneurial spirit or the pioneer spirit that's made America great.

I just want to make a couple of points, and then I would like to shake hands with each one of you individually, thank you, and have a photograph made if you'll honor me with that occasion.

First, a word about the Presidency. I've been President now for more than 3½ years. And before I went to the Oval Office, which occurred after I was elected President, for the first time, I was already filled with a reverence for the job itself, an acknowledged awareness of the importance of the position of President and how much the future of this Nation and the well-being of our people and the peace of the world depended on it.

It's an exciting and challenging job, the highest elective office, certainly in the free world, and one that puts a heavy responsibility on anyone who serves there. The job is not only exciting but very sobering. The questions that come to me at the Oval Office are difficult ones. They are, I guess, the most difficult that arrive at the desk of anyone in this country. If a question can be answered more easily, it's answered by you personally or within your home or at a city hall or a county courthouse or by a State legislature or by a Governor. If they can't be answered anywhere in those places, then they come to me.

And the choices that I have to make affect the future of this Nation. I consult with the Congress, consult with my excellent Cabinet, and make the best judgments I can. I've also found that the more important a question, more vital to our Nation's future the question might be, the more likely my advisers are to be split 50–50. So, eventually the loneliness comes back in an overwhelming degree, and I have to make the ultimate decision.

I have to deal with crises with which I'm aware and potential crises for all of you. If I handle a question well, then perhaps you don't ever know about it. If I don't handle a question well and the crisis becomes real for our Nation or for the world, then the consequences could be catastrophic. So, I have a sober and excited awareness of what the Presidency means to this country.

One of my major responsibilities is looking to the future, to have a vision of what our Nation can be. And my own vision of the future of America is indeed optimistic. We've never failed to answer a difficult question or to resolve a difficult problem or to overcome an obstacle if the Americans could see clearly what it was and if our Nation was united. My judgment is that we've been making now that kind of progress.

We have hammered out for ourselves the best solution, perhaps of any nation, to the very difficult and trying challenges of extraordinary increases in the price of oil. We've already made major achievements in reducing our dependence on foreign oil. This day and every day this year, we are buying about 2 million barrels of oil less overseas than we were a year ago. That's a remarkable achievement. There's only two ways that that can be done. One is to conserve energy—to eliminate waste, to be more efficient—and the other way is to produce more American energy. We're doing both things.

This year we'll have more oil-drilling rigs running, more oil wells, natural gas wells dug in our Nation than any year in history. And this is combined with the fact that we're producing more coal, strangely enough, in our Nation this year than ever before in history. A lot of that coal is being exported, and a lot more in the future will be exported—not only coal but other products.

One of the most exciting things is that we've opened up a billion new customers in the last few months to American supply of goods and friendship, in the sharing of strategic responsibilities in the eastern part of Asia and the western part of the Pacific, with China. And all of your lives will be improved because of this brand new billion addition among our friends.

The last thing is that I see a future of peace. We've been successful the last 3½ years at keeping our Nation at peace. I've not been required and have not decided to send a single soldier into combat. Very few Presidents in the last—none in the last 50 years, by the way, can make that same statement. And I pray to God that I'll go out of office, hopefully at the end of 5 more years, still with our Nation at peace.

I don't see any way to keep our country at peace except to keep it militarily strong. We faced, when I became President, a constantly decreasing commitment of our national resources to defense expenditures. Since I've been in office, we've had an annual increase every year in real terms, above and beyond the inflation rate.

And I think the best guarantee of peace for ourselves, for the Middle East, for our other allies and friends is to keep our Nation militarily strong. The best weapon is one that's never fired in combat, and the best soldier is one that never sheds his blood on a field of battle. And if we know we're strong and our allies know we're strong and our potential adversaries know that any attack on us would be suicidal in its consequences, then that's the best way to keep our country at peace. Well, the issues are so multitudinous and so interrelated, I don't want to pursue them any further.

Today I've been monitoring very closely and dealing to some degree with the combat between Iran and Iraq. It's a disturbing thing. I've just been on the phone—the secure telephone that has encoded voices, going back and forth—with Dr. Brzezinski and earlier with Secretary Brown and also exchanging messages with Secretary Muskie, who's at the United Nations. We hope that this combat will be quickly terminated and that peace can be restored between Iran and Iraq.

Baghdad has been bombed. The refineries built in Iraq and in Iran have been damaged, and we are very deeply concerned about the free movement of oil. As you know, we don't buy much oil from Iraq and none from Iran, but some of our allies and our friends in this hemisphere and in Europe and in Japan are heavily dependent on that kind of shipment. So, we'll do everything we can in a peaceful way to add our voice to that of other nations to resolve this issue without further bloodshed. And we will not become involved in the combat, and we are urging and insisting that the Soviet Union and other nations do not interfere in this very dangerous situation around the Persian Gulf.

Well, I don't want to bore you with further details, but I did want to point out to you the importance of the Presidency and the importance of his influence in the shaping of our future. The reassuring thing is that I have the advice and counsel and support, sometimes the criticism, of people like you. And that's important in a democracy for a President to feel that he has partners in Portland and in other places in the country that share a common belief, common principles, and common goals for our great country. And with your help and with your support, I believe we can prevail and realize the hopes that we all have—a peaceful nation and making the greatest nation on Earth even greater in the years ahead.

Thank you very much, again. God bless you all.

NOTE: The President spoke at 2:23 p.m. at the residence of John Schwabe, a Portland attorney.

Earlier in the afternoon, the President visited the Buckman housing project, consisting of 10 energy-efficient rowhouses, and took part in an energy roundtable discussion with local residents. Secretary of Transportation Neil Goldschmidt also participated in the discussion.

Tacoma, Washington

Remarks to Employees at the Continental Grain Terminal. September 23, 1980

Thank you, my good friend Marvin Williams.

It is great to be in Washington—the real Washington, that is—and to see your beautiful weather, which I understand you have 365 days a year. Right? That's what they told me in the car on the way out. As a farmer myself, as a businessman and a former professional naval officer, and now as President of our country, it's indeed a pleasure and a pride for me to come here to this beautiful facility. I'm also happy to join your next Governor, Jim McDermott, who's with me this afternoon, and to express my deep thanks to Scoop Jackson for those kind words.

This morning on the way from Los Angeles to San Jose, I called Dixy Lee Ray to express my appreciation and admiration for her, to let her know how much I appreciated what she has done in the past with the Mount St. Helens explosion and all the other difficulties that an incumbent must face. A few minutes ago, after we left Portland, we got permission from the air controllers, after my request was recognized, to fly over Mount St. Helens. It was a remarkable sight. The destruction and devastation there are truly awe-inspiring, and the contribution that all of you made to stability and to keeping your wits about you and to facing the future with confidence in one another and with a sense of unity indeed was a pleasure for me as President and an honor, I think, for our country.

I'm also here to salute two of Washington State's most important products—grain and Warren Magnuson. Maggie has done a lot for this State and also for this Nation, and as you know, now being chairman of the Appropriations Committee for the Senate, he has the power and the influence to do a lot more in the future. The appropriations legislation, at this moment, to finance all the functions of the United States Government is being debated and considered by the Congress. Senator Magnuson is in charge. He and I agreed yesterday in a telephone conversation that he ought to stay there in the Senate, not just for this crucial week but for 6 more years.

I'm here today, not by accident, but to call attention to the whole Nation to what has been truly the great wonder of the world, and that is American agriculture. It's a wonder of Providence what God has given us, with productive land and with innovative producers as stewards to care for that land and to strengthen our Nation in every possible way. It's a wonder of man's hard work to produce. And I think that you know that this grain elevator behind me—this terminal—is now loading more grain than it ever has since it was first built. It's a wonder of American industry and experience and knowledge.

Since I became President, United States farm exports have set new world records in 1977, in 1978, in 1979, and again in 1980. And this year we're going to set—we're going to break every record that's ever been set in American agriculture. In 1980, as a matter of fact, U.S. farm exports will reach $40 billion, up $8 billion above last year—the greatest 1-year increase in history. And today American agricultural strength, as you know, is unsurpassed throughout the world.

We're by far the world's largest agricultural exporter. We account for 60 percent of the world's grain exports, 80 percent of the world's soybean exports. These startling figures, almost too high to believe, continue to improve every year. To paraphrase Winston Churchill, never in history

have so many been fed by so few. Our success in exporting U.S. farm products is a direct result of aggressive sales and promotion by representatives of the American farmers, producers, shippers, and the Government and of completing a multilateral trade negotiation, within the last few months approved by Congress, which opens up new opportunities for us to sell all kinds of American products with a minimum of interference all over the world.

In addition, a great benefit to every person listening to my voice, to your families now and in the future, has been the normalization of relationships between our Nation and the People's Republic of China. This is a major step forward in preserving peace throughout the Pacific region and the Asian region. It's a major step forward in diplomacy, and it's a major step forward in trade, giving Americans jobs now and in the future. A billion new friends, a billion new consumers, a billion eager buyers for all kinds of American products are now available to us because of those normalized relationships. And I might add parenthetically that our relationship with Taiwan has not suffered at all. Our trade with Taiwan at this moment is at an alltime high.

The ship behind me will be carrying American corn to Japan. We've opened up trade offices to sell American products in major buying centers throughout the world. We've increased export credits to let sellers of American grain finance those sales on a sound basis to foreign buyers. And we've improved grain inspections, Federal and State grain inspections, to make sure that when customers do buy American grain, they get the highest possible quality and come back again and again to make additional purchases.

I'm not only the President, but I'm also the Commander in Chief of our Armed

Forces. I want to make sure our Nation is strong. And therefore I would like to certify to you that we need to have a strong American merchant marine fleet to help us to deliver agricultural and other products abroad, and I'm committed to ensuring that we have such a fleet now and in the future.

Sometimes we Americans take our abundance for granted. It's human nature to complain about things if they are not absolutely perfect. But I think during this election year it's a good time for us to stop and say, "What has God done for us?"— not only freedom, not only a chance to make our own voices heard, not only a chance to be world leaders in raising high the banner of human rights and letting democracy and our way of life be known about throughout the world. Sometimes we take these basic rights for granted.

Events recently in Poland, for instance, and our careful, considered, proper response to those moves toward freedom have helped to remind us of our own basic rights. Recently I directed the U.S. Department of Agriculture to extend $670 million in new agricultural credit assistance to Poland. This is the largest such assistance in the history of our country. It means that American farmers will provide some 4 million tons of grain and other farm products to the people of Poland. This demonstrates not just the power of our agriculture but the power of our commitment to human rights around the world.

You've benefited greatly in this particular region from the advances that we have made in the last 3½ years. Since January of 1977, in spite of some setbacks because of the unprecedented increase in world oil prices, unemployment in the State of Washington has gone down 17 percent. In Tacoma City unemployment has gone down, measured up to last month, by 27 percent. Employment in Tacoma, in the metropolitan area, has gone up 20,000 new jobs, and of course, employment in the whole State of Washington has gone up 26 percent in just 3½ years.

When we overcome, which we are doing very rapidly, the adverse impact, the damage that was done to our economy by seeing the price of oil jump 120 percent in 1 year, the chances for a better life for all Americans in the years to come are obvious to us. We need to look to the future, to have confidence in the greatness of our country, pull ourselves together in a spirit of unity and conviction and also anticipation and hope, and realize that we can make the greatest nation on Earth, with which we have been blessed, even greater in years to come. If you'll help me, I'll help you make that dream come true.

Thank you very much.

NOTE: The President spoke at 4:56 p.m. outside the Continental Grain Terminal after touring the facility.

Tacoma, Washington
Remarks in an Interview With KOMO–TV.
September 23, 1980

SITUATION IN IRAN AND IRAQ

MONITORING OF SITUATION

Q. Thank you very much for joining us this afternoon, Mr. President. I'd like to begin first of all with the most pertinent question, of today anyway, and that is the situation in Iraq and Iran. And I'd like to know, first of all, where the United States stands on that right now?

THE PRESIDENT. Well, I've been monitoring the situation, obviously, very closely, because it's important to us, talking to the Secretary of Defense and the Secretary of State, who happens to be at the United Nations headquarters in New York, and to Dr. Brzezinski, and my other advisers.

We have a deep concern about the conflict between Iran and Iraq. The chance of that conflict spreading further in those two nations and maybe involving others is a very important consideration for us.

We hope that there'll be a termination as soon as possible to all the bloodshed and the fighting and also that the supplies of oil are not interrupted to other nations. We buy no oil from Iran and very little, if any, from Iraq.

Our position is that we will not get involved in the conflict at all. We are staying neutral completely. And we expect other nations, like the Soviet Union, also to stay out of any involvement in this area. We'll do everything we can through the United Nations and through other international fora and working with individual countries in the Moslem world and in that region to try to bring a quick end to the combat between Iran and Iraq.

This is a very important region strategically to us. So far as I know, there is no direct effect on the life or safety of the hostages.

OIL SUPPLIES

Q. It's particularly important to American allies, some of that oil that comes out of Iran and Iraq.

THE PRESIDENT. Yes.

Q. What is the United States at this time prepared to do should that situation escalate slightly and maybe close the flow through the Gulf of Hormuz?

THE PRESIDENT. What we've been doing since I've been in the White House is crucial now—and I think it's demonstrated vividly with this potential inter-

ruption of supplies—and that is to reduce drastically the amount of foreign oil that we buy and use. This day, in fact every day this year, we are buying about 2 million barrels of oil less from overseas than we did a year ago. This new energy policy that we've put through for conservation and producing more American energy is paying off for us.

We don't get much oil from Iraq. They produce about 3 million barrels per day, shipped heavily to countries like Brazil, France, Italy, and Japan, and of course Iran is producing very little oil for export, only about a half million barrels per day.

THE PRESIDENT. We have an arrangement, worked out by me and other leaders in Tokyo, and later in Venice, among the major consuming nations, to share any shortage equitably among ourselves, so that there will be a minimal adverse impact if the supplies are interrupted to us.

Q. So that would be our contribution, rather than any kind of military consideration?

THE PRESIDENT. I see no chance that we will put military forces into action there. I think the best thing for me to do is protect our national interest with caution and with forbearance and with using our great influence to bring peace between the two warring countries.

SAFETY OF AMERICANS IN IRAQ

Q. Earlier today there was a report that on Iraqi soil, as I understand it, there was a bombing raid by Iranians and that four Americans, three or four Americans, and four British petroleum workers were killed in that raid——

THE PRESIDENT. Yes.

Q. —— and as I got this report, then the British had moved their people from that dangerous area near the Iranian border to Kuwait where it might be more safe.

THE PRESIDENT. Yes.

Q. Are we doing anything of the same for American people in Iraq?

THE PRESIDENT. Yes, we're doing the same thing. You know we don't have diplomatic relations with Iraq; however, we do provide a large technical service to the oil-producing nations, including Iraq. One of the refineries in Iraq was attacked, and some Americans there who were workers for oil companies were killed. I understand that they have been moved to safety and I think the—I understand, I don't have this confirmed—that the refinery is not producing at this time.

Also, the Iraqis attacked the major oil refinery in Abadan in Iran. These refineries are primarily for producing products like kerosene and gasoline that are used within those two countries, not used for export.

NEUTRALITY OF UNITED STATES AND SOVIET UNION

Q. We're in, of course, a difficult position there, and it would be made more so by a build-up of Soviet forces in that area, and that was somewhat of a surprise in the Afghanistan situation. If that should happen again, are we in a position to move either way, for or against Iran or Iraq?

THE PRESIDENT. Well, I'll do everything I can to avoid any military combat but, as I said in my State of the Union speech, we have vital interests in the Persian Gulf region. To repeat myself, we are committed not to intervene in the internal affairs of those two countries, not to be embroiled in the combat, and we insist that the Soviet Union honor the same commitment.

Q. Militarily, now, we are a bit more prepared in that area than we had been, say, prior to November 4th of last year.

THE PRESIDENT. Yes, but the best way to avoid military action, quite often, is to be prepared.

AMERICAN HOSTAGES IN IRAN

Q. Now, what situation would we confront with the hostages in Iran? Are we just monitoring again through Iranian channels that as this continues, because the parliament now has dropped their consideration, apparently, of the hostage situation while the war goes on? Are we on hold also?

THE PRESIDENT. We've never been on hold. This is a problem that's always on my mind. We've had two basic commitments since the first day the hostages were taken. The first one is to protect the honor and the integrity of our Nation and to protect our own vital interests and, secondly, to avoid taking any action on my part that might endanger the lives or the well-being of the hostages or their chance, ultimately, to come to freedom. We're still pursuing that policy, steadily and cautiously, but firmly.

We also use every possible avenue of communication with Iranian officials, and we've been waiting until Iran has a government established. The delays have been aggravating and very discouraging to us, but they are approaching now a time when their government will be established. They have a President elected who is in favor of releasing the hostages. They've had a Foreign Minister now, an acting Foreign Minister, Ghotzbadeh, who does want the hostages released. They have a Prime Minister and a speaker of the Majles, or the parliament, and they've elected all the parliament members. The only thing they lack now in completing their government is the choice of the remaining members of the cabinet, and I hope that'll be done within the next few days.

I don't predict any early release of the hostages. I don't want to build up unwarranted expectations. But we will fervently pursue, through every possible avenue, a resolution of this problem and a return to safety and freedom of the hostages. In the meantime, we will not do anything to endanger their lives.

U.S. AUTO INDUSTRY AND INTERNATIONAL TRADE

Q. I'd like to move to another international question. The situation—well, it's international in that we have to relate to Japan on this, and it's the auto industry, which has been in serious trouble, of course, of late, in the last few years, and they're in the process of retooling to meet that problem.

THE PRESIDENT. Yes.

Q. Are we now considering any more stringent action on the Japanese auto industry at all——

THE PRESIDENT. No.

Q. ——ever, or not? I mean, is a quota system a realistic approach to that—higher tariffs, anything of that sort?

THE PRESIDENT. No. It would be counterproductive for us to start a trade war with Japan or other countries. I just visited a grain loading facility here, Continental, in Tacoma, and one of the best things that's happened to us in recent years has been the lowering of tariff barriers that would let us have freer trade between countries.

This not only applies to overseas shipments, which is making the West Coast ports very vital to our Nation's economic prosperity as we open up new vistas of trade with Taiwan, with Japan, our old customers, and also with new customers like the billion people who live in China, but it also strengthens our chance to preserve peace throughout the Pacific region.

We will sell to Mexico this year about 10 million tons of grain. Formerly, they've not been that good a customer. In fact, we've tripled trade with Mexico the last 4 years. So, we are moving to export as much American products as possible.

With the increasing cost of oil and gasoline, American buying preferences for automobiles have simply shifted very quickly to the smaller and more efficient automobiles. There's no doubt in my mind that American automobile manufacturers can meet this consumer demand. Now, every American car that's produced, that's small and efficient, that meets our environmental standards, can be sold without delay. And, of course, recent tests have shown that the American cars are safer than the imported cars with equal operating efficiency.

So, we are going through a difficult transition period brought about primarily with changed buying habits, where Americans are getting out of the gas guzzlers and going to the smaller and more efficient cars.

I was pleased that the government officials in Japan announced unilaterally that their export of cars to the United States the last half of this year will be maybe 200,000 cars less than was the case even in 1979. So, this is encouraging.

Q. It's their decision?

THE PRESIDENT. It's their decision.

Q. No pressure came to bear, right?

THE PRESIDENT. It's their decision. But the thing that I want to avoid is a trade war where we raise barriers to their products and they, in return, raise barriers to our products. Sooner or later all of our consumers and all our producers and all our workers suffer, and nobody gains.

But I was very pleased that they will lower their exports of cars to us to help us go through this transition period, because, to repeat myself, we can sell all of the American cars that are produced, more of the more popular sizes and with the high efficiency.

———

NUCLEAR WEAPONS

TITAN MISSILE

Q. Just a few days ago, we had the problem down in Arkansas with the Titan missile in the silo down there and the liquid fuel, the older Titan system. I know it's been said that the Titan system is one that we have to keep viable in the American defense armaments. Do you feel that it's something that should be phased out slowly, though?

THE PRESIDENT. Well, over a period of time, if and when the missile is replaced by the MX or the more modern missile, it's likely to be phased out because of common constraints which the Soviets have to observe as well.

The Titan is still important to our strategic forces. Its purpose is to deter a Soviet attack on us, and its deterrent value is very good because it's such a massive missile.

The liquid fuel in itself is not an indication of obsolescence. The most modern Soviet missile, for instance, the SS–18, uses a liquid propellant system. We use a solid propellant in our Minuteman and will use that solid propellant in the MX, as well, in the future.

We have a very strong and a very sound Triad: the land-based missiles like the Titan and the Minuteman, the upcoming MX; also, the Cruise missiles, the air-launched Cruise missiles that are small, very efficient, highly accurate, relatively inexpensive, and can penetrate any Soviet air defense; and also the new Trident sub-

marines and the Trident missiles that go with them, which are major breakthroughs—all three, in making sure that we have a strategic nuclear arsenal that would prevent any attack on our country. That's the purpose of the entire nuclear intercontinental system, is to prevent any adversary, the Soviets or others, from daring to attack us, knowing that it would be suicidal if they do.

DEFENSE POLICY

Q. During this campaign you have had to address the military situation as has candidate Ronald Reagan, and there has been because of that, primarily because of Governor Reagan's stance, a lot of tough military talk that's come out of this. In a world where you have to strive continuously for peace, is it not difficult or dangerous to come out with such tough military talk on both sides? Is that not a dangerous trend to get involved in?

THE PRESIDENT. No, it depends on the judgment and the general philosophy of the President. My own belief is that a President ought to be the representative of a strong nation that's confident; that the use of American military forces should be a very rare thing. And I'm convinced that the best way to preserve peace and to keep our Nation out of war is to be militarily strong.

The new weapons systems are important because they let our own people, our allies, and our potential adversaries know our capability. We've always been in the forefront of technological change. We've developed a weapon type; many years later, the Soviets and others develop a similar-type weapon.

I intend to stay this way. We will spend in the future about five percent of our gross national product on military budget items. Seven of the 8 years before I became President, under the Republican administrations, we had a decrease in the amount of real money we spent for our Nation's defense. We were getting quite vulnerable to Soviet threat. Since I've been in office we've had a steady increase in real dollars, above and beyond the inflationary values, for military defense. And we're going to keep it that way. We'll continue the next 5 years with a steady, predictable, sure increase in our commitment to a stronger defense.

I've said many times—and I think it's good for everybody to remember—that the best weapons are the ones that are never used in combat, and the best soldier is the one who never sheds his blood on the battlefield. The best way to avoid combat that could kill tens of millions of Americans is for us to be strong and sure about our strength, but also that the President in the White House uses sound judgment and insists upon the maintenance of peace. I've not had to send a single military person into combat since I've been in the White House. I'm the first President who can say that, by the way, in 50 years, and I hope and I pray that if I should be able to serve as President for 5 more years that I can still say that we have kept our Nation at peace when I go out of office.

RONALD REAGAN'S POSITION

Q. If, you know, militarily we are superior or equal and certainly in a comfortable situation, is Ronald Reagan then trying to overshoot the mark? I mean is he instigating, were he to become President at any point, a build-up in an arms race that is, in fact, unnecessary since we already hold such a strong position?

THE PRESIDENT. Yes. Some of the philosophy that he's expressed, some of the commitments that he's made, some of the promises that he's expounded to the American people disturb me very much. Every President since Eisenhower, Democrat or Republican, has believed that nuclear weaponry should be controlled that there should not be an arms race to see which nation can produce more nuclear missiles, but that we should have SALT agreements with the Soviet Union so that we can have a damper on that build-up and have equal but reducing commitments to military weapons of a nuclear type.

Reagan has reversed that philosophy—a radical departure from the philosophy of his own party. He says we've got to be superior to the Soviet Union in that kind of weapon. If we are superior to the Soviets as a national commitment if Reagan should become President, God forbid, then the chance to negotiate mutual controls on nuclear weapons would be gone.

Also what concerns me about Governor Reagan—I think he would try for peace, but if you look at the record over the last number of years, when he has been a major spokesman for himself and the Republican Party, he has repeatedly called for the use of American forces in times of strain or dispute with other nations, some very small nations, some large nations. But this inclination on his part to use military force instead of diplomatic resolution of differences is deeply concerning to me. He's advocated using military forces in Cyprus; he's advocated using it in Lebanon, in Peru, in our own country with a naval blockage around Cuba. He advocated the using of American military forces in Angola. This repeated call for Reagan to use military force to resolve differences is of great concern to me, and I think it's a legitimate campaign issue to be raised in the minds of the American people. He ought to explain what he means.

1980 PRESIDENTIAL CAMPAIGN

DEBATES

Q. Did the American people learn more about Ronald Reagan as a candidate and John Anderson as a candidate through the debates on Sunday night, do you feel?

THE PRESIDENT. I don't know. I watched the debate. I was interested in it. It's hard to say what was learned there. My own assessment is they basically repeated their standard campaign statements that they had made for many months.

Q. I think the question being is the debate valuable in form of——

THE PRESIDENT. I think so. The debate would be very valuable if Reagan would accept my challenge to debate me. He's not willing to do that. It doesn't help to have a forum with three people or four people or five people on the stage when you just answer—like a "Meet the Press" sort of thing. What is important is for the Democratic nominee, who has a chance to win, and the Republican nominee, who has a chance to win, to debate each other to let the American people know the sharp differences that exist between me and Reagan and between the Republican and Democratic Party.

To have a third candidate, a Republican, who entered the Republican primaries and caucuses, who never won a single contest, even in his home State, now come as a defeated Republican and seek equal status along with the Democratic and Republican nominees is what I object to.

After I debate with Reagan, man-to-man, at any place in our country——

Q. Do you expect this to happen?

THE PRESIDENT. I hope so—then I will be glad to debate Anderson plus Mr. Clark plus Mr. Commoner and Reagan all together in the kind of a forum arrangement. But I think that wouldn't be nearly so valuable to the American people as a direct debate between the two people that have a chance to be elected President.

TAX CUT ISSUE

Q. One thing that was talked about during the debate is the tax cut and the talk of a tax cut, and Ronald Reagan again stated that he is planning that tax cut. John Anderson was opposed to that. Are you still behind a tax cut this year?

THE PRESIDENT. Not this year. I don't even want the Congress to consider a tax cut this year. What I want are the tax changes that I advocated, a tax system that would stimulate increased investment and better jobs for American people. It would add a net of a million new jobs in the next 2 years, and that would be anti-inflationary in its character. That is what I advocate.

What Reagan advocates is the so-called Reagan-Kemp-Roth proposal with a reduction of a thousand billion dollars between now and 1987, which would be highly inflationary in nature, designed almost exclusively to reward rich people at the expense of high inflation, which would hurt the working families of this country. There's a sharp difference between what we advocate. He wants a tax cut right now, in an election year. I think it would be ridiculous——

Q. Both being tax cuts, but achieving very different goals?

THE PRESIDENT. Absolutely.

DEMOCRATIC PARTY

UNITY

Q. Mr. President, Senator Kennedy has become much more visible in your campaign in the last few days. Has there been a change between yourself and the Senator at all?

THE PRESIDENT. You know, Ted Kennedy and I have always gotten along very well personally. The first year I was in the White House as President, his voting record in support of my programs was the highest of all 100 Senators. It was the top. And even the last 2 years, the second and third year I was in office, it was within the top three or four. So his commitment to my programs and my basic philosophy has been very helpful. During the primary season the differences that do exist between me and him were sharply exaggerated.

Q. It had to happen?

THE PRESIDENT. Well, that's part of the process of politics. But he has been very helpful to me. This week he was in Los Angeles at a joint fundraising effort and, by the way, Jerry Brown was there. We had the three of us together.

But, in my opinion, the unity that presently exists within the Democratic Party is remarkable and maybe even unprecedented. This show of support for my campaign by Senator Kennedy and by Jerry Brown is very valuable to me all over the Nation. I'm indebted to him and believe that it bodes well for the Nation in the future, if and when I'm reelected.

FUTURE CANDIDATES

Q. Are you in a position, in a reciprocating manner, to say that, then, Senator Kennedy might be the personification of the future of the Democratic Party in future years?

THE PRESIDENT. Let me wait until later to decide what to say about that. He is obviously one of the major potential candidates in the future to replace me as President, but I don't want to ignore Governor Brown and Vice President Mondale and others who might have ambitions that I don't even know about.

WASHINGTON STATE

NORTHERN TIER PIPELINE

Q. Right. Okay. On a local level, the Northern Tier Pipeline has been a large issue in the Seattle area—a pipeline that would go to Minneapolis or into Minnesota. You were behind that program at one time, and I'm curious if there is still the need, if the administration still sees the need for such a thing in light of the fact that oil demand has dropped and is expected to remain at a slightly lower level or, hopefully, at a lower level for the next, say, 10 years?

THE PRESIDENT. Yes, I am strongly in favor of it. The demand that we want to see drop is the demand for overseas or foreign oil that we have to buy and pay for. This is what imports inflation and unemployment. To have a more effective way to transfer, say, Alaskan oil, to the areas in our Nation where oil is needed or consumed is important to us. The Congress has not yet appropriated the money that would be necessary to go ahead with the Northern Tier Pipeline project. And of course, we must resolve the environmental questions that would relate to the quality of life in Puget Sound, particularly the threat of water pollution. But when those questions are resolved, we are strongly in favor of going ahead with the project.

PRESIDENT'S CHANCES OF WINNING IN STATE

Q. Now also, in 1976 you lost the State of Washington by a narrow margin, as well as other Western States. What are you bringing to the party, to the Nation, to those voters in 1980 that is different or enough to change that outcome?

THE PRESIDENT. I think the 3½-year record as President has been a good one. We've been able to add 8.5 million jobs. Since I've been in office the employment rate—unemployment rate in the State of Washington has dropped 25 percent. I notice in the Tacoma metropolitan area, for instance, the number of jobs added had been 20,000.

We've opened up new avenues of trade between our country and the Orient, for instance, that are unprecedented. We've kept our Nation at peace. We've kept our Nation strong. I think there has been a remarkable repair of the damage that was done by the Vietnam war and by the CIA revelations and also by Watergate, under my administration. We have a good working relationship between myself and the Congress. We've weathered the shock that came to the entire world with oil prices more than doubling in 1 year, in 1979. And we have an energy policy now that will give us security in the future and an exciting life in the 1980's.

Obviously, some things could have been better, and we recognize those very clearly. But we've spelled out our positions very cogently and so that the American people can understand them.

Another thing is that in an election year, there is a time of inventory of what our blessings are, what our Nation has accomplished, and the challenges that open up an exciting vista for the future. And also there's an inclination to compare not just a President against a theoretically perfect leader—the combination of George Washington and Thomas Jefferson and Abraham Lincoln and Harry Truman and, perhaps, Franklin Roosevelt—but to compare me against my opponent, Ronald Reagan, and to decide,

"Who could take better care of this Nation, who could provide more assurance of peace, who is more interested in economic progress, who will be best for my own family?" This is the kind of question that I think will be addressed in 1980, and it gives me every assurance that I'll be reelected, and I believe that we have an excellent chance to carry the State of Washington.

THE PRESIDENCY

Q. Also—and, I think, finally now; we don't have a lot of time left—the Presidency, as you certainly have found out is not an easy job. Why again? Why continue? I mean there's so much difficulty with it.

THE PRESIDENT. It's a difficult job; it's a challenging job, and on the most crucial issues of life or death, peace or war, progress or retrogression, it's a lonely job. The man in the Oval Office has a lot of problems that come to his desk and a lot of questions that need to be answered. They are the most difficult problems and the most difficult questions. If a question can be answered easily, it's answered in a person's life inside a home or in a county courthouse or a city hall or a State legislature or Governor's office. If it can't be answered in any of those places, it comes to me. And the decisions that I make I realize affect the lives, perhaps, of all people who live in this country and, indeed, the entire world. I've also noticed that the more crucial the issue, the more difficult the question, the more likely my advisers are to be evenly divided. So the President, in a lonely way, has to make that decision.

And the last thing is, when I address a crisis or potential crisis, my hope is that it will not become a crisis for our country and that you and the news media and the American people never even know about it. If I handle it well, a potential crisis, it doesn't become important to you. If I should make an error in judgment, then a potential crisis could become a very serious threat to the existence of people's lives and to the future of our Nation and even to peace throughout the world.

So, the challenges are great, the loneliness is sometimes great, but, in return, in this democracy, the respect for the office of Presidency and the support and the common principles and ideals that I share with the American people, the history behind us and the strength of our Nation all are very reassuring. So, it is a challenging job, but it's an exciting and dynamic opportunity to be part of making a great nation even greater. So, in that respect it's a very good job.

Q. Thank you very much for being with us. It's been our pleasure.

THE PRESIDENT. I've enjoyed it very much, David. Thank you very much.

NOTE: The interview began at 5:48 p.m. at the Tacoma Bicentennial Pavilion.

Tacoma, Washington

Remarks at a Democratic National Committee Fundraising Reception.
September 23, 1980

Mr. Mayor, Chairman Murphy, Dale Carlisle, and other friends that have assembled here to help me and the Democratic National Committee with a very important element of politics, and that is to finance an adequate campaign:

It's important to the American people to know the facts about our Nation, its past, its present, and its future. And I'm delighted to be with you here today. I've

had a good visit to Tacoma. The crowds on the street were much larger than I ever dreamed, and the excitement and fervency of their support is very good.

I'm sorry that Maggie [1] couldn't be with us today. He wanted me to express his apologies. But as you know, he is *the* person responsible for the appropriations of funds for the entire Federal Government. He's there taking care of the State of Washington; he's there taking care of the entire Nation. And I advised him, although I'd like to have him by my side here, to stay in Washington, where he means so much to our entire Nation. I appreciated Scoop Jackson sending a congratulatory message to me for being back in Tacoma and expressing the wish that he could be here. As you know, the Congress is going to adjourn very shortly, and the last minute crush of business for them is all-consuming.

I'm also glad to be with Ted McDermott, who will be the next Governor of the State of Washington. I've been looking at some of the poll results, and they're very exciting. And I would guess at this moment that it's a tossup. And what happens to Ted, in spite of enormous influx of money, is very important to all of you. And I hope that, Ted, you'll be very successful in your campaign. Good luck to you. I mean—Jim—Jim McDermott. Excuse me. Jim is very important to me, too. He rode in in the car with me, and we had a chance to talk about the future of this State.

Dixy Lee and I had a good conversation on the phone this morning. I called her as we were leaving the State of California on the way to Washington and expressed my appreciation for what she has meant to your State with the catastrophe

[1] Senator Warren G. Magnuson, chairman of the Senate Appropriations Committee.

that was imminent with the explosion at Mount St. Helens. And to work with her has been a gratifying thing to me.

As you know, Jim, Maggie, I, and the Democratic ticket I think will make a good combination this year. And if you all will continue to help us, we'll have a great Democratic victory.

I want to say just a couple of things to you in closing. One is that the office of the Presidency is a major and vital force in the life of every human being in this country and every family, perhaps in the entire world. The decisions that come to the Oval Office have a profound importance to us all. The decisions are not easy. If they are easy, they would be resolved somewhere else.

It's sometimes a lonely job, but the life or death of many people are at stake. If sound judgment is used and the strength of our Nation is wisely applied, our Nation can make progress, lives can be enhanced, the quality of American life can be preserved, and peace throughout the world can have a better chance to persevere.

I'm grateful in the last 3½ years there has been no American troop or soldier sent to endanger his or her life in combat against another nation. And I pray that we can stay strong enough and have sound enough judgment in our decisions that we will remain a nation at peace for the next 5 years, as long as I'm in the White House.

The other point I'd like to make is this: A President is responsible for the future of this country. We've made great progress so far in building a sound basis for the resolution of a very challenging problem of energy. The achievements have been notable. This year we'll buy 2 million barrels of oil less per day than we were buying a year ago. We are drilling more oil and natural gas wells this year than any

other year in the history of our Nation, and you might be surprised to know that we are also producing more coal than any other year in the history of our Nation. We have 10 times as many homes now using solar power as used solar power just 4 years ago.

And that commitment to the new forms of energy and to conservation give us a chance to have a springboard toward an exciting, dynamic, challenging, fruitful, and successful future. We now must take the tremendous opportunities that we have been given in this country, invest it in a structure of our industrial society to keep the American worker the most productive on Earth, with new tools and new factories and new trade opportunities throughout the world.

We are rapidly increasing exports of American products. We are opening up new customer opportunities for us in China, keeping those in Taiwan, increasing those in Japan, opening up new ones in Mexico, so that the American workers will have a ready product [market] for what we produce, both on the farm and in our factories. And in technological advances, new discoveries, new ideas, new products, we will stay on the cutting edge of progress as an inspiration to people all over the world.

This bright future, of a nation strong, secure, prosperous, united, proud, raising high the banner of human rights, and a nation committed to peace—that's the vision I have for the future. It's a bright future, an optimistic future. And I look forward to sharing that future with other Democratic candidates like Maggie, like Jim McDermott, if you'll help us between now and November the 4th. We'll have a great victory, thanks to you.

God bless you.

NOTE: The President spoke at 6:23 p.m. at the Tacoma Bicentennial Pavilion Rotunda.

Rural Development Policy Act of 1980

Remarks on Signing S. 670 Into Law.
September 24, 1980

THE PRESIDENT. *Senator Leahy and Congressman Wes Watkins, Congressman Nolan and others who are assembled here, ladies and gentlemen who are interested in the future of rural America—future of America:*

This event brings back very special memories to me. In 1972 when I was a Governor, I was privileged to appear in Tifton before Senator Talmadge and Senator Hubert Humphrey, who were having hearings then on the Rural Development Act of that year.

It was an exciting thing for me to meet with these two leaders and to see the enthusiasm with which the people of south Georgia, the rural area of my State, welcomed an opportunity to spell out their own needs to the Congress of the United States with a hope that some of their ideals and some of their dreams could be realized. That landmark bill, as you know, expanded the rural development mission of the Farmers Home Administration and gave the Secretary of Agriculture responsibility for developing and coordinating rural development activities throughout the Federal Government.

Many of you here were involved in the evolution of that legislation. Unfortunately, the opportunity which was presented for the Rural Development Act of 1972 and what it offered to those who supported it has never been fully realized, and its full impact has never been grasped. The basic reason was a lack of commitment to creating a comprehensive rural policy throughout the executive branch of Government and a lack of vision to see the tremendous potential for our entire Nation—not just for rural communities—and for the land and the urban communities of this country.

When I took office with this memory fresh in my mind, I took action to correct this defect in our societal life, to establish consistent and overall approaches to the needs of both our cities and our rural areas. No one in contemporary America articulated the need for this balanced approach more eloquently nor more fervently than did the late Senator Hubert Humphrey. And I appointed men and women to my own administration, including the Vice President and certainly the Secretary of Agriculture, who shared Senator Humphrey's sense of the interdependence between urban America on the one hand, and rural America on the other.

The pride which all of us feel today in what we have accomplished is not only well-justified but is also deeply personal for many in this room. This is a bright prospect for our country. I know how important this gathering is because I know how important rural America is to our country. As a farmboy myself, as an organizer and administrator for a number of years of a seven-county rural development planning commission, as a State senator representing a rural district, and also as a Governor representing a predominantly rural State and, of course, as President, I believe I know rural America very well.

I know its greatness, I know its beauty, and I know its strength. I know its resilience in time of trouble and trial and testing, and I know the character of the people who live in rural America and the critically important role they play in the production of food and fiber, of energy, of wood and minerals.

I've just finished a trip to some of the key States of our Nation—to Illinois, to

California, to Oregon, to Washington—
and everywhere I went I saw vividly displayed the contribution to our Nation's
strategic strength of our agricultural production, particularly with the exports to
foreign countries which are rising so
rapidly.

I understand the ultimate strategic
value of our land and what it means now
and what it can mean in the future as a
force for peace, for extending the benef-
icent influence of our country in a constructive and a peaceful way throughout
the other nations of the world.

I also know the problems of rural America: the relatively low quality of housing
for many who are poverty-stricken; the
isolation of a rural family; the absence of
any sort of public transportation; and the
deprivation of services that most of us
take for granted; the very high incidence
of some kinds of disease; the lack of adequate medical care for those who suffer;
the lack of facilities for the aged; and the
fragmentation of families, because of
poverty, with shrinking landholdings and
very high requirements for investment in
farm machinery to stay economically viable. The rapid changes taking place in
rural America, some of it uncontrollable,
some of those changes not adequately
assuaged in the lives of people most directly affected, the hardships and deprivations are vivid memories in my mind.

Some of you have heard me say that
the greatest single event in my life was
not being elected President, but when the
lights were turned on in our house by the
REA. Our life was transformed; a family
that had been burdened down with literally 16 or 18 hours of hard work per day,
with little opportunity for outside interest except to go to school and to go to
church, was certainly broadened with
some leisure time and some responsibility,
on a national basis, to protect that vital

program which had been so hard in being
born.

This kind of advance has also been important to me, and just as we counted on
the Rural Electrification Administration
to light up rural America 40 years ago,
so today we're counting on that same
agency and hundreds of rural electric cooperatives across this Nation to help us
achieve a future of energy independence.

Those rural electric co-ops, with the
intimate involvement of the customers
who comprise them, can be on the cutting
edge of advances so important to us in
energy conservation and, therefore, increasing the security of our country. You
might be interested in knowing that 44
percent of all the rural electric loans ever
made by REA have been made during the
last 3½ years since I've been President.

I also know, personally, the tremendous help that the Farm Security Administration and its successor, the Farmers Home Administration, have been in
providing credit to buy land, to plant
crops, and to modernize equipment.

Today, the Farmers Home Administration is assisting rural families both on
and off the farm to build or to rehabili-
tate their homes, to build water and sewer
systems, and to obtain the necessary
credit to own and to operate job-producing businesses, primarily on the farm; in
some cases, through cooperative efforts
off the farm.

The Farmers Home Administration, in
cooperating with other Federal and State
agencies, is financing the building of
clinics to make health care more accessible and affordable for isolated rural
residents, the building and rehabilitation
of transportation systems, and the construction of gasohol plants—I visited one
in Springfield, Illinois, this week—and
other energy facilities. To help it undertake these new and expanded ventures,

while still meeting its traditional mandate to serve family farmers, we provided resources to the Farmers Home Administration equal to half of all the loans and grants ever made during its 44-year history.

This deep commitment on the part of my administration, with the good assistance of the Congressmen here and others with them, is an indication of the importance that we attach to the REA and its various programs and the Farmers Home Administration. The rural resources of the Economic Development Administration have nearly doubled during the last 3½ years.

But most important of all, this administration has forged the Nation's first comprehensive small community and rural development policy. We've already made significant strides in accomplishing many of the initiatives—such as those I've described in energy, health, housing, transportation, and services for the elderly—called for in that policy hammered out, not by us in an isolated environment of the White House or the Congress, but hammered out with full consultations among rural leaders from throughout this country, who have assembled in their own regions and who came to the Cabinet Room or the Oval Office and met with the congressional leaders on the Hill. This is indeed a rural program of comprehensive development, initiated and controlled and forged at the grassroots level.

We've entered into a close partnership with the Nation's Governors and with local officials and with private leaders to make sure that the success of this program is guaranteed. Today I am pleased to sign the Rural Development Policy Act of 1980, which places into law many of the reforms that were developed by this rural policy. It also creates the position of Under Secretary of Agriculture for Small Community and Rural Development.

This legislation will enable the Farmers Home Administration to assist small communities in establishing circuit-rider programs, to provide assistance in economic and community development. I'm today directing the Farmers Home Administration to act promptly to make funding immediately available for these circuit-riders, who will go into a community, assess what can be done, that the initiative be from the local people, but provide counsel and assistance as necessary.

This bill also extends our authority to conduct rural development research and extension activities. While we've made good progress in identifying our objectives and charting our course, all of us know that much remains to be done. With the tools provided in this bill and with the continued support and dedication and hard work of all of you and the people whom you represent in the small towns and communities in the countryside of rural America, we'll make even more progress in the future.

After I sign this bill, in the next few minutes, I would then like to call on Senator Leahy, one of the sponsors of this measure and a champion of rural development in Congress to say a few words. And substituting for Tom Foley, the Chairman of the House Agriculture Committee, I'd like to call on Congressman Wes Watkins, who's the Chairman of the Rural Caucus to say a few words, outlining from their points of view how important this legislation is to rural America, all those who live there, and what their contribution is to our great country.

Thank you very much.

SENATOR LEAHY. Thank you very much, Mr. President. You know, as a Vermonter, I naturally feel a great thrill any time to come to the White House.

Quite frankly, sir, the two most thrilling times that I've felt were last December when you and I talked about the rural policy statement and today, actually see it signed into law.

I think that of all the many things that you can be proud of, and there are so many, that for all of us who live in rural America, whether it's in Vermont or Georgia or anywhere else in the country, you can be most proud of this. Everybody looks for a way to reduce Federal waste, to cut redtape, to improve program efficiency, to expand services to the needy, without causing large increases in the Federal budget. But in this, not only have we done that, not only have we removed a great deal of bureaucracy, but what we have done far more, Mr. President, is that we've moved on to help those 4 million rural households without running water for sewage facilities, the 20,000 small towns with no public transportation system, the 26 million rural Americans living in medically underserved areas. What we've done really, no less than to say to one-third—one-third of the people of our great country—that they are indeed part of our great country. And, Mr. President, we all owe you a great deal of thanks for this.

REPRESENTATIVE WATKINS. I would like to express my thanks to President Jimmy Carter, my colleagues, and many of you who've supported this particular piece of legislation. And I think it's only fitting that a chapter secretary of the Plains, Georgia, FFA signed into law a major piece of legislation for this country.

I'd like to make a point. I hope this is not missed by the media here—the significance of this bill as far as this particular Congressman goes.

How many of you read the book by John Steinbeck, "The Grapes of Wrath"? Well, some of you may not have read between the lines, but this movement that occurred at that time, Mr. President, was the largest movement of people ever recorded in history, the largest migration of people, the largest uprooting of families ever recorded in the history of our country.

At the same time this was occurring on up in the forties there, our country saw fit to write the Marshall plan, to rebuild the economic base of Europe. Twenty years later, during the riots of the sixties, Mr. President, our country—and probably rightly so, where many of our loved ones had gone—saw fit to write a massive urban renewal program. But, Mr. President, our country has never seen fit to write a program to rebuild rural America. And I think this is the significance of this particular piece of legislation.

This is a piece of legislation that will grant us, for the first time, a voice in Federal Government—to speak out for equity and fairness in the programs. And we've got a lot to do, when only 17 percent of the money from community development bloc grants goes to communities of less than 50,000 while only 25 percent of UDAG moneys go to people in communities of less than 50,000; where only 7 percent of the money for handicapped children in education goes to rural America, and our children are handicapped also out there.

So, Mr. President, I want to say thank you for a beginning, for a step forward, and we look forward to working with you for 5 more years in doing the job.

THE PRESIDENT. I know all of you appreciate these two excellent statements, obviously from the bottom of the hearts of those who made them. And I agree with Wes Watkins that this is a long-delayed step in the right direction toward giving equality of treatment to the millions of families who live in rural America, whose voice has not always been as strong as it might have been where the organizational cohesiveness has deprived them of an adequate voice and influence.

But I believe, in the future, that what we do for these families and for these communities will pay rich dividends for our country. And as Pat Leahy pointed out, this is not an additional bureaucratic structure, not a massive allotment of new Federal funds, not a very costly program. It will be an additional burden for the taxpayers of this Nation, but a coordination of programs as they presently exist and an establishment of a degree of equity and fairness that is indeed long overdue.

An ancillary part of this bill which I've just signed will provide good water resource supplies for South Dakota. It just happens that these two issues have been brought together, and Congressman Daschle and Senator McGovern deserve a lot of credit for that, to make sure that water resources money is spent wisely and effectively, so that the ill-advised project is being phased out, and a very badly needed project in that State is being approved.

Again, let me express my deep thanks to the Members of Congress who've been so instrumental in making this progress possible, and particularly to thank all of you who helped to forge this project and whose success will depend upon how well you perform your jobs in the future.

I don't have any doubt about the success. It's a good day for rural America, indeed, for America. Thank you very much.

NOTE: The President spoke at 1:48 p.m. at the signing ceremony in the East Room at the White House.

Following the President's departure from the East Room, Assistant to the President Jack H. Watson, Jr., and Deputy Secretary of Agriculture Jim Williams addressed the audience. The remarks of Mr. Watson and Deputy Secretary Williams are included in the White House press release.

Rural Development Policy Act of 1980

*Statement on Signing S. 670 Into Law.
September 24, 1980*

I am today signing S. 670, the Rural Development Policy Act of 1980. This legislation is the culmination of a joint effort by the Congress and the administration to fashion a process for building sound and comprehensive strategies for the development of rural America. In modern times, rural and smalltown America has suffered a heavy loss of population and seen a decline in the number of family farms. Today rural America is entering a new era of opportunity for growth and progress. However, widespread need still exists for economic diversity, job opportunity, modernized housing, community facilities, and other amenities that measure up to recognized American standards.

Last December 20, I announced my small community and rural development policy. It is a plan for generating a real and productive partnership among Federal, State, and local governments and the private sector to enhance the development of rural areas and to improve the quality of rural life.

The Rural Development Act of 1972 gave the Secretary of Agriculture primary responsibility for marshaling Federal resources to support development efforts in rural areas. The bill I am signing today strengthens the Secretary of Agriculture's role in this endeavor and provides for annual reports to Congress of the Federal Government's rural development strategy and progress. It creates an Office of Under Secretary of Agriculture for Small Community and Rural Development. The Under Secretary and my Special Assistant for Intergovernmental Affairs will serve as cochairmen of the Federal Executive Working Group that I have established to coordinate Federal participation in rural development.

The bill authorizes grants of $15 million a year through the Farmers Home Administration for planning and technical assistance and for the establishment of a circuit-rider program to facilitate the delivery of Federal programs to rural areas. It also provides for dissemination of more information to the rural public about the availability of these programs.

This bill will improve the Federal Government's capacity to meet the needs of our small towns and country areas. It will move us from a protracted period of analysis to a program of active involvement in rural and small-community development.

Finally, the bill's authorization of the WEB project, coupled with the pending deauthorization of the Oahe project, upon which completion of WEB depends, represents a major step both for rural development and for water resources policy in South Dakota. By this step, rural development prospects are advanced, and the economic inefficiences and adverse environmental effects of the Oahe plan are avoided. With the guidance of Senator McGovern and Congressman Daschle, the local supporters of the WEB project worked closely with the administration to secure the authorization of this important project. The administration can now fully support the necessary steps toward economically efficient and environmentally acceptable water resources development in South Dakota.

NOTE: As enacted, S. 670 is Public Law 96–355, approved September 24.

Situation in Iraq and Iran

Remarks Concerning the Conflict. September 24, 1980

THE PRESIDENT. I've met this morning with my principal advisers to review the very dangerous situation created by the conflict between Iran and Iraq. Although the United States is in no way involved in this dispute—and charges to the contrary are obviously and patently false—it is important to make clear our position in this matter.

The fighting between Iran and Iraq is causing needless hardship and suffering among the people involved. It represents a danger to the peace and stability of the region. There should be absolutely no interference by any other nation in this conflict. The fighting should be promptly terminated. Any grievances between Iran and Iraq should be settled at the negotiating table and not on the battlefield.

We strongly support international efforts, both the statement made by the Secretary-General of the United Nations and also by the President of the Security Council of the United Nations, to bring this fighting to a prompt end and to obtain a negotiated settlement. Secretary Muskie, in New York, has consulted with a number of foreign ministers in the last several days, and he's continuing these contacts this afternoon and tonight. I am also in contact with other nations, through our embassies abroad and directly between me and the leaders of some of those nations. We will continue to work vigorously with as many nations as possible and also with international institutions who seek, as we do, a speedy end to the conflict.

I know that the conflict has caused considerable concern that world oil supplies might be severely reduced, therefore driving up oil prices and endangering the economic security of the consuming nations. This concern is not justified by the present situation. It is true that oil companies and shipments relating directly to Iran and Iraq have been interrupted or suspended during the outbreak of the hostilities. But even if this suspension of Iran and Iraqi shipments should persist for an extended period of time, the consuming nations can compensate for this shortfall.

Oil inventories in the world's major oil-consuming nations are now at an alltime high. The world's margin of oil supply security is much greater today than in the winter of 1978 and '79, when the Iranian revolution reduced oil supplies at a time when reserve oil supplies were very low. Our greater security today is due in part to energy conservation and also the substitution of other fuels for oil, both in the United States and in other consuming nations. This has facilitated the building up of reserve stocks to much more satisfactory levels than did occur in 1979. Hence, there is no reason for a repetition of the shortages or the price escalations that resulted in 1979.

Of course, a total suspension of oil exports from the other nations who ship through the Persian Gulf region would create a serious threat to the world's oil supplies and consequently a threat to the economic health of all nations. Therefore, it's important that I add my own strong support and that of my Nation to the declaration which the nine European Community nations made yesterday. Freedom of navigation in the Persian Gulf is of primary importance to the whole international community. It is imperative that there be no infringement of that freedom of passage of ships to and from the Persian Gulf region.

Let me repeat that we have not been and we will not become involved in the conflict between Iran and Iraq.

One final point, very important to Americans, is, in our concern for the dangerous situation created by this conflict, we have not forgotten for one moment the American hostages still held captive in Iran. We continue our work for their prompt and safe release, and we continue to hold the Government of Iran responsible for the safety and the well-being of the American hostages.

Thank you very much.

REPORTER. Mr. President, would you do anything to keep the Gulf open? Would you take any actions if necessary?

THE PRESIDENT. We're consulting the other nations about what ought to be done to keep the Strait of Hormuz open and therefore access to the Persian Gulf.

Q. Mr. President, if Iran asked for spare parts in return for releasing the hostages, would you go that far?

THE PRESIDENT. We're consulting through every means with Iran, as we have been for many months, to try to seek the release of the hostages, but that particular point would perhaps be better for me not to single out from the others.

Thank you.

NOTE: The President spoke at 3:16 p.m. to reporters assembled in the Briefing Room at the White House.

Shipment of Nuclear Fuel to India

White House Statement on Senate Approval of Fuel Shipments. September 24, 1980

We are pleased that the Senate, in a display of bipartisanship, has supported the President's decision on shipment of fuel to the Tarapur Atomic Power Station. The Senate action will help further the administration's policy of seeking to prevent nuclear proliferation and adds support to our discussions with the Government of India toward bringing all of that nation's nuclear facilities under international safeguards.

The Cyprus Conflict

Letter to the Speaker of the House and the Chairman of the Senate Foreign Relations Committee.   September 24, 1980

Dear Mr. Speaker: (Dear Mr. Chairman:)

In accordance with the provisions of Public Law 95–384, I am submitting the following report on progress made during the past 60 days toward a negotiated settlement of the Cyprus problem.

Intercommunal talks between the Greek and Turkish Cypriots resumed in Nicosia on August 9 under the auspices of Ambassador Hugo Gobbi, the Special Representative of the United Nations Secretary General on Cyprus. At the August 9 session, Ambassador Gobbi read a statement outlining the Secretary General's understanding of the common ground between the parties and the matters which will be discussed in the negotiations. (A copy of the opening statement is attached.)

The parties agreed to meet on a weekly basis with the following major subjects to be dealt with in rotation:

(A) Reaching agreement on the resettlement of Varosha under United Nations auspices;

(B) Initial practical measures to promote goodwill, mutual confidence and normal conditions;

(C) Constitutional aspects;

(D) Territorial aspects.

The first substantive meeting was held September 16 to address the issue of Varosha. The meeting was characterized as having been a good beginning on this issue. The negotiations will return to this topic after having dealt in turn with the other three major subjects noted above in weekly sessions. The next meeting will take place on September 24.

I welcome the resumption of the Cyprus intercommunal talks. The painstaking efforts of the Secretary General and United Nations' Secretariat officials are to be commended. We hope that the resumed talks will be conducted on a serious, sustained and productive basis and will lead to a just and lasting settlement of all outstanding issues.

Sincerely,

JIMMY CARTER

OPENING STATEMENT AT INTERCOMMUNAL TALKS

BY AMBASSADOR HUGO GOBBI

August 9, 1980

I note that both parties have indicated their readiness to resume the intercommunal talks, which were recessed in consultation with the parties on 22 June 1979, and to do so within the framework of the good offices mission entrusted to me by the Security Council and on the basis of the high-level agreements of 12 February 1977 and 19 May 1979.

Both parties have, in this regard, signified their intention to carry out the resumed talks in a continuing and sustained manner, to get down to concrete negotiations, discussing constructively, and giving full consideration to, all aspects of the Cyprus problem.

In this connection, I should like to outline the Secretary General's understanding of the common ground that was worked out in the course of consultations which took place over the past several months:

(A) Both parties have reaffirmed the validity of the high-level agreements of 12 February 1977 and 19 May 1979;

(B) Both parties have reaffirmed their support for a federal solution of the constitutional aspect and a bizonal solution of the territorial aspect of the Cyprus problem;

(C) Both parties have indicated that the matter of security can be raised and discussed in the intercommunal talks. It is understood that this matter will be discussed, having regard to certain practical difficulties which may arise for the Turkish Cypriot community, as well as to the security of Cyprus as a whole;

(D) Both parties have appealed to the Secretary General for the continuation of the intercommunal talks.

The practical implementation of the concepts in (B) and (C) above will be dealt with in the context of the substantive consideration of the constitutional and territorial aspects and will be reflected in the substantive positions and proposals of the parties concerning the various items of the agenda.

Concerning the matters to be discussed, the Secretary General understands, on the basis of the 19 May agreement, that these will include the following subjects:

(A) Reaching agreement on the resettlement of Varosha under United Nations auspices, in accordance with the provisions of point 5 of the 19 May agreement;

(B) Initial practical measures by both sides to promote goodwill, mutual confidence and the return to normal conditions, in accordance with the provisions of point 6, which states that special importance will be given to this matter;

(C) Constitutional aspects;

(D) Territorial aspects.

Concerning procedure, it is understood that the four items above should be dealt with concurrently in rotation at consecutive meetings. At an appropriate early stage, committees or working groups will be set up by the interlocutors.

NOTE: This is the text of identical letters addressed to Thomas P. O'Neill, Jr., Speaker of the House of Representatives, and Frank Church, chairman of the Senate Foreign Relations Committee.

Foreign Ownership of United States Real Estate

Message to the Congress Transmitting a Report. September 25, 1980

To the Congress of the United States:

Today, I am transmitting to the Congress a report required under Section 4(d) of P.L. 94–472, as amended, the "International Investment Survey Act of 1976." The report, entitled "Monitoring Foreign Ownership of U.S. Real Estate—A Report to Congress", was prepared by the Secretary of Agriculture with oversight and review provided by an interdepartmental committee under the chairmanship of the Office of Federal Statistical Policy and Standards, Department of Commerce. The report addresses the feasibility of establishing a system to monitor foreign direct investment in agricultural, rural, and urban real estate property; including the feasibility of establishing a nationwide multipurpose land data system.

The study examined the feasibility of four methods of obtaining foreign ownership data:

1. A centralized compulsory Federal registration system that is exclusively devoted to reports filed by foreign owners of U.S. real estate.

2. A compilation of data on foreign holdings of U.S. real estate from Federal offices such as the Bureau of Economic Analysis, the Securities and Exchange Commission, and the Internal Revenue Service. These agencies already require reports on foreign investment, income, or other related matters.

3. A multipurpose, all-encompassing land information system using information collected at the local level. This system would serve a wide range of local, State, and national information needs.

4. Nationwide, periodic surveys of all domestic and foreign land ownership. Foreign ownership information is presently being collected through compulsory registration and reports (Methods 1 and 2).

Although all four methods are deemed technically and legally feasible, I am not proposing the development of new or additional reporting systems. I believe that necessary information on foreign ownership of U.S. real estate can be acquired at less cost than Method 3 or 4 would entail.

JIMMY CARTER

The White House,
September 25, 1980.

National Advisory Council on Economic Opportunity

Message to the Congress Transmitting a Report.   September 25, 1980

To the Congress of the United States:

In accordance with Title VI, Section 605 of the Economic Opportunity Act of 1964, I am transmitting herewith the Twelfth Annual Report to the Congress of the National Advisory Council on Economic Opportunity.

This report reflects the Council's views in its role of examining programs authorized by the Economic Opportunity Act of 1964, and their impact in alleviating certain problems confronting low-income people. There are a number of interesting and challenging recommendations contained in this report which we shall consider in the future.

JIMMY CARTER

The White House,
September 25, 1980.

National School Lunch Week, 1980

Proclamation 4796.   September 25, 1980

By the President of the United States of America

A Proclamation

The future of our country lies in our children. Nutrition is vital in insuring

that they reach their full potential—physically, emotionally and intellectually.

The National School Lunch Program provides nourishing lunches to 27 million children every school day. Studies show that nutritious meals help increase the attention span and learning capabilities of students. School lunches also help children learn good dietary habits. Cafeterias can become learning laboratories, especially when menus are related to nutrition instruction in the classroom.

Recently, many changes have been made to improve the lunch program in American schools. Thousands of people have contributed to this effort. Principals, teachers and parents, Federal, state and local officials have joined school food service personnel in improving the quality, appearance and nutrition of school meals. Students themselves have been involved through youth advisory committees. I want to recognize these individuals for their concern and their work in over 95,000 schools across the country. Their continued involvement will contribute to a healthier generation.

In recognition of the School Lunch Program's contribution to America's youth, the Congress, by a joint resolution of October 9, 1962 (76 Stat. 779; 36 U.S.C. 168), has designated the week beginning the second Sunday of October in each year as National School Lunch Week, and has requested the President to issue annually a proclamation calling for its appropriate observance.

Now, THEREFORE, I, JIMMY CARTER, President of the United States of America, do hereby urge the people of the United States to observe the week of October 12 as National School Lunch Week and to give special attention to activities that will promote good nutrition to America's youth.

IN WITNESS WHEREOF, I have hereunto set my hand this twenty-fifth day of September, in the year of our Lord nineteen hundred and eighty, and of the Independence of the United States of America the two hundred and fifth.

JIMMY CARTER

[Filed with the Office of the Federal Register, 3:27 p.m., September 25, 1980]

United States Ambassador to Czechoslovakia

Nomination of Jack F. Matlock, Jr. September 25, 1980

The President today announced that he will nominate Jack F. Matlock, Jr., of Coconut Creek, Fla., to be Ambassador Extraordinary and Plenipotentiary of the United States to the Czechoslovak Socialist Republic. He would replace Francis J. Meehan, who has been appointed Ambassador to Poland. Matlock has been Deputy Director of the Foreign Service Institute since 1979 and a Foreign Service officer since 1956.

He was born October 1, 1929, in Greensboro, N.C. He received an A.B. from Duke University in 1959 and an M.A. from Columbia University in 1952.

Matlock joined the Foreign Service in 1956 and was posted in Vienna, Oberammergau, Moscow, Accra, and Zanzibar. From 1969 to 1970, he was Deputy Chief of Mission in Dar es Salaam, and in 1970–71 he took the executive seminar in national and international affairs at the Foreign Service Institute.

From 1971 to 1973, Matlock was country director for Soviet affairs at the State Department, and from 1973 to 1974, he was Director of the Office of Soviet Affairs. From 1974 to 1978, he was Deputy Chief of Mission and Minister-Counselor in Moscow. In 1978–79 he was

diplomat in residence at Vanderbilt University.

Overseas Private Investment Corporation

Nomination of Two Members of the Board of Directors. September 25, 1980

The President today announced that he will nominate two persons for reappointment as members of the Board of Directors of the Overseas Private Investment Corporation. They are:

James M. Friedman, of Shaker Heights, Ohio, a partner in the Cleveland law firm of Guren, Merritt, Sogg & Cohen. He is general counsel of the Lake Erie Regional Transportation Authority and former chairman of the Ohio Civil Rights Commission.

Edward L. Marcus, of Branford, Conn., an attorney in New Haven, Conn., specializing in real estate, corporate, and commercial law. He was a member of the Connecticut State Senate for 12 years and served as chairman of Connecticut's Commission on Intergovernmental Relations.

Foreign Claims Settlement Commission of the United States

Nomination of Ralph W. Emerson To Be a Member. September 25, 1980

The President today announced that he will nominate Ralph W. Emerson, of Washington, D.C., to be a member of the Foreign Claims Settlement Commission for a term expiring in 1981.

Emerson is president and chairman of the board of Emersons, Ltd., general counsel and executive vice president of

U.S. Bank Note, and an attorney with the Johnson, Tenn., firm of Emerson & Emerson. He has served as commissioner of commerce for the State of Tennessee and as a consultant to the U.S. House Small Business Committee.

National Endowment for the Arts

Nomination of Arthur I. Jacobs To Be a Member of the National Council on the Arts. September 25, 1980

The President today announced that he will nominate Arthur I. Jacobs, of Fernandina Beach, Fla., to be a member of the National Council on the Arts for a term expiring in 1986.

Jacobs is an attorney with the firm of Frates, Jacobs & Farrar and county attorney for Nassau County. He is chairman of the Fine Arts Council of Florida and a member of the board of directors of the Southern Arts Federation. He is active in community and educational affairs.

Uniformed Services University of the Health Sciences

Nomination of Doris A. Evans To Be a Member of the Board of Regents. September 25, 1980

The President today announced that he will nominate Doris A. Evans, of Cleveland Heights, Ohio, to be a member of the Board of Regents of the Uniformed Services University of the Health Sciences for a term expiring in 1983.

Evans is a pediatrician and executive director of the Glenville Health Association in Cleveland. She is an assistant professor of community health and pediatrics at Case Western Reserve University School of Medicine.

Country Music Month, October 1980

Message of the President. September 25, 1980

I feel a special pride and nostalgia each year as I issue this message designating October as "Country Music Month."

Growing up on a farm, I learned to appreciate firsthand the sounds coming from the fields, hills and valleys of our country during harvest season. I grew to know and share the emotions, hopes and dreams of the men, women and children of rural America. And every time I listen to Country music I am reminded of the timeless values by which they live.

During this traditional observance, I want to salute Country music as the purest echo of rural America at work to help build the progress and well-being of our land.

This is why I welcome this opportunity to applaud the gifted artists who devote their finest talents to ensure our continued enjoyment of Country music and the dedicated fellow citizens who bring their performances to the widest possible audiences.

JIMMY CARTER

Congressional Black Caucus

Remarks at a White House Reception for Members of the Caucus. September 25, 1980

THE PRESIDENT. First of all, let me say that it's very good for me to get such a good welcome in my own house. [*Laughter*]

We have some very distinguished guests with us this afternoon, whom I'll recognize in a few minutes, but first I'd like to say that this afternoon the League of Women Voters invited me and Governor Reagan to participate in a one-on-one debate, to be followed later by a multi-candidate debate. I have already accepted the invitation and look forward to a good debate on the issues that are important to you and important to our country, and I hope that Governor Reagan will do the same and accept the debate request. If he does accept we'll have an opportunity to meet one on one with the nominees of the Democratic and Republican Parties, and that's essential. It's what I've wanted from the very beginning. And I hope that this acceptance by Governor Reagan will be prompt, that we can go ahead and schedule the debate and have the debate about the debates ended, at least for this election year. [*Laughter*]

I might say, too, that it's always a pleasure to be with the Congressional Black Caucus. This is the first time we've had this kind of invitation extended to you. It's because I have such a special friend who's the chairman. I invited Cardiss Collins to come over, and she said she'd like to bring a few friends with her. [*Laughter*] So, I'd like to welcome Cardiss Collins and about 2,000 of her close friends. [*Laughter*]

As you may or may not know, yesterday was Cardiss Collins' birthday. And, Cardiss, I'd like to give you a rose now, since my wife's not here.

Ms. COLLINS. Oh, thank you, Mr. President. Thank you. Thank you very much.

THE PRESIDENT. I'm sorry we couldn't get together yesterday. We could have hired the RFK Stadium and gotten all of Cardiss' friends in there together. [*Laughter*]

Any time a President or any other leader gets together with the Congressional Black Caucus, it's a special occasion. And although there's no way for a President and the members of this caucus to agree on every detail of method and timing, we do share a common commitment to freedom and to justice and to opportunity for all Americans and also for people throughout the world. Because of deep conviction, compromise is not always possible. But the members of this caucus and those of you who depend upon it and upon its members to represent your interests—there has never been any hesitation to share your concerns with me. Cardiss Collins, as the chairman, has been a strong and persistent and an effective voice in keeping your goals constantly before the Nation.

We are especially privileged to have two outstanding leaders of the new Africa with us: President Siaka Stevens of Sierra Leone—we are very pleased to have you, President Stevens; and also President Habyarimana of Rwanda is here—we are very proud to have you, sir—with his beautiful wife. He's been a very strong promoter of the cause of human rights in Central Africa. And as you all know, President Stevens is also the Chairman of the Organization of African Unity, representing 50 nations in that great continent, having an important voice in mending regional and bilateral disputes, trying to carve out the ideals and hopes of the people of Africa, and playing a very significant role in the affairs not only of his continent but indeed of the entire world. President Stevens has just made a very important address in the United Nations General Assembly and President Habyarimana will be speaking to the United Nations General Assembly tomorrow.

With the help of Secretaries of State Vance and Muskie and of our own Ambassadors, Andy Young and Donald Mc-Henry, at the United Nations, my own administration, aided and supported by the Congressional Black Caucus, has carved out a new American foreign policy, which we consider to be of great interest to the people of Africa and indeed of the entire developing world.

With the needs and the rights of people of all nations in mind, one of my earliest goals as President, supported by many of you and spoken to the world by Andy Young and Secretary Vance, was to have a peaceful and a just settlement in Zimbabwe. And as you know, just a few weeks ago the new Prime Minister of that great country, a new democracy, was here in this same room to celebrate in an emotional way the birth of additional freedom and human rights and equality and the end of racial discrimination in that country. We are very proud of that development.

America's influence is never stronger than when we are meticulously true to our own highest principles. There is no way that a country even as strong as ours can force peace on the rest of the world. But we can be a powerful force for peace when we act to help other nations whose people are committed to resolve their differences in a just and fair manner without war or combat. This is our aim in the Middle East, and this is also our aim in Africa.

The United States supports the political, economic, and social justice in southern Africa through peaceful efforts by the people of southern Africa themselves. We are particularly eager to work with these two great leaders here, with the Congressional Black Caucus, with our State Department, and with our representatives at the United Nations to bring about democracy and freedom for the people of Namibia and to eliminate apartheid throughout the southern part of Africa in the early future, not in the distant future.

And of course, I've recognized these two national leaders and the members of the Congressional Black Caucus, but I also want to acknowledge the leadership that's played by many of you here who will be attending, this weekend, meetings with the Congressional Black Caucus. This is a social occasion, but I do want to take this chance, as President, to ask you to help with two very crucial decisions now in prospect in the Congress of the United States, two projects on which the Congressional Black Caucus and I have been embarked for many years, and lately in a concentrated fashion.

One is to implement a bill that was passed in 1968 to guarantee Americans equality in seeking adquate housing. We must have enforcement powers for the Fair Housing Act. This is the most significant civil rights legislation of the last 10 years, and I ask you to help us all get it passed through the United States Senate before this Congress adjourns for the year. It's crucial. We must have it.

And the other request I have to you is to remember that although we've made great strides forward in making available to Americans 8½ million more new jobs, 1.3 million of those jobs being for black people, we still have an extremely high unemployment rate among young minority citizens of this country. We must provide additional help for them, because as the economic recovery takes place, many people can go back to the jobs they had, but too many young black Americans have never had a job to which they can return. And a $2 billion program on our youth bill now before the Senate must pass. That's the other item on the agenda that I want to discuss with you, and I ask you to join with me as a full partner in getting this legislation passed.

And finally, let me say that it's an honor

for me to be with you. Our country's ideals and hopes, our country's concerns and fears are always present in the minds of people who are most deprived, who've suffered from years of discrimination, who've not yet realized the hopes and dreams that you and I have realized who are in this room.

Progress is still there to be made. It can only be made with commitment, with tenacity, with cooperation, and with courage. In years gone by, in the fifties and sixties, many of you in this room exhibited extraordinary courage in freedom marches and in insisting that the discriminatory laws of our Nation should be removed. That was a great achievement, but it is not enough. We must continue to reach the Promised Land and the land of great promise. In better health care, more equitable taxes, the control of inflation, the provision of jobs, better housing, better transportation to and from work, the care for the aged, better education—these kinds of programs are still being challenged as we try to make progress toward a better future.

With your help and your commitment and the courage that I've already described and with close cooperation, we can make these dreams come true. Some of us have realized these dreams already in our own lives, but there are millions of Americans looking to you for leadership. And with the partnership between you, the Congressional Black Caucus, and with me as President, there's no doubt in my mind that in the future we can make those dreams come true.

Coretta Scott King, come on up. Miss Black America, Miss Wright, come on up. These are two of my sweethearts. I want you to see them.

It's a pleasure for me to be with you. My wife won't be back until about 9 o'clock tonight, but she said to give you her best regards. And you can look on the stage and see why I was not concerned to know that she would be gone. [*Laughter*]

Thank you very much.

NOTE: The President spoke at 6:07 p.m. in the East Room at the White House.

Situation in Iraq and Iran

White House Statement.
September 26, 1980

Over the past several days, as the President noted in his statement of September 24, the President and the Secretary of State have exchanged views with key friends and allies on a wide range of issues related to the conflict between Iran and Iraq. We have consulted with a number of friendly nations about the status of oil supplies and international shipping in the Persian Gulf area. In view of the importance of minimizing the economic effects of the conflict on international shipping and world petroleum markets, the United States has indicated that it would be willing to host a meeting to review these issues if that should seem desirable. If it is determined that a meeting of experts is required, we will work out timing and location. No such meeting has been set. In the meantime, our consultations are continuing.

Libraries and Information Services

Message to the Congress.
September 26, 1980

To the Congress of the United States:

I am pleased to transmit to you the Report of the White House Conference on

Libraries and Information Services and my own recommendations on public access to information, as required by Sec. 1(d) of Public Law 93–568 of December 31, 1974.

Information is the essence of education and the lifeblood of democracy. People need accurate information to make the personal and political decisions that will shape the country's future. The production and distribution of information is a significant factor in our economy. A technological explosion is reshaping the way information is stored and communicated, while rising costs and limited resources strain the public institutions that make information accessible.

The White House Conference considered all these issues. It examined our information needs and problems and the key role of libraries in meeting them. The delegates included librarians, information specialists and community leaders. They were selected at conferences in every state and territory, through a process that involved 100,000 people. I wish to commend the National Conference on Libraries and Information Services for their key role in making the Conference a success. The Conference theme was "Bringing Information to the People." Its recommendations will help us frame an information policy for the 1980's.

THE IMPORTANCE OF LIBRARIES

Since the beginning of our Nation, libraries have played an important role in providing citizens with the information they need to guide our destiny. Our First Amendment rights have been strengthened by the independent status of libraries free from government control. By preserving the records of our history and culture, libraries serve as a door into our past. As a source of the information we

need to direct our lives, they also serve as a door into our future. As we plan for the information requirements of the 1980's and beyond, we should acknowledge the contributions that libraries have made and ensure they remain vital.

Most libraries are local institutions, under local control. State and local governments bear the responsibility for supporting and operating public and school libraries. I agree with the White House Conference that this principle must be maintained.

At the same time, the Federal Government has assumed a special role of helping libraries provide access to information for all. The Government also provides leadership in developing new technologies and services, and encouraging resource sharing among all types of libraries. This Federal role complements the basic responsibilities of state and local governments. My Administration has worked with Congress to fulfill that role.

To ensure that library programs get the attention they deserve, we created an Office of Libraries and Learning Technologies in the new Department of Education, headed by a Deputy Assistant Secretary.

Overall Federal support for libraries has increased by almost 30% since the beginning of my Administration. We proposed improvements in the Higher Education Act to strengthen support for library research and demonstration and training programs and for college and research libraries. We supported literacy and school library and media programs through our 1978 amendments to the Elementary and Secondary Education Act.

My 1982 budget request to Congress will reflect our response to the Conference recommendations for increased budgetary support for resource sharing among libraries; research and development in information technologies; and research libraries.

The Conference recommended a new National Library and Information Services Act to redefine the Federal role. I will submit new legislation to replace the Library Services and Construction Act which will expire in 1982. This legislation will include such issues as:

- barriers to information access for the handicapped and disadvantaged;
- library networking and resource sharing;
- the role of large urban libraries and research libraries as centers for library resource networks; and
- new information technologies.

I urge the Congress, the library community, and the public to join in the discussion during the next year on the priorities among these important concerns.

GOVERNMENT INFORMATION

The Federal Government has a special responsibility to ensure that its information is made available to the people. Open government is vital to democracy. We must also recognize the constraints of national security, privacy, efficient decision making, and costs.

We are working to address these concerns in a way that increases access to information. A new office has been established in the Office of Management and Budget to develop Federal information policy. This office is working closely with the agencies, libraries, and private sector to develop a policy on the management and dissemination of information by Federal agencies. This policy will affirm the key role of the Federal depository libraries as centers where citizens can obtain free access to government publications.

The policy will also stress the special role libraries can play in helping Federal agencies disseminate information that people need. We should not create new delivery systems when libraries, with strong community bases, can do the job. The Denver Public Library is one example of a library that is working closely with several agencies to make consumer and environmental information available. I encourage and support cooperation like this. To foster such partnership, I have directed the Administrator of the General Services Administration to work with the library community and the Department of Education to select three to five Federal Information Centers and locate them together with libraries. If this cooperative effort is as successful as I expect, I will expand the program.

My Administration has also taken a number of other initiatives to improve and enhance public access to government information. For example:

- We revamped the security classification system to eliminate needless initial classification and reduce the time that documents remain classified while strengthening protection for necessary secrets. About 250 million pages of documents will be released because of this change.

- The Freedom of Information Act is being administered fairly. The Department of Justice has instructed agencies to release information that could legally be withheld if the release could not be clearly harmful.

- Our policy on industrial innovation calls for an improvement in the dissemination of patent information, which will make over 4 million patents accessible.

- The National Technical Information Service has expanded the indexing and dissemination systems available to scientists and engineers.

- Increases were requested for the National Commission on Libraries and Information Sciences, an agency which has a vital leadership and coordination role in library and information science at the national level.

THE NEEDS OF THE DISADVANTAGED

The Conference report serves as a reminder that too many of our citizens are cut off from the information available to most of us. One of the greatest barriers is functional illiteracy. To overcome this problem, I have directed the Department of Education to take the lead in coordinating Federal efforts to eliminate functional illiteracy. Their task will be to identify methods and programs of demonstrated value and to work with local education agencies, libraries, and voluntary organizations to implement these programs. Twenty percent of our Americans are functionally illiterate, and we must expand our commitment to helping these people obtain the basic skills they need.

Under my Administration, a new Basic Skills Improvement Program was authorized in 1979. Its overall objective is to bring about national improvement in student achievement in the fundamentals of education—reading, writing, speaking and mathematics.

We are working to assist disabled Americans. At my request, the broadcasting networks helped establish a pilot closed-captioning television system to permit the hearing-impaired to share the educational and entertainment shows available to everyone. In addition, the Library of Congress and the Department of Education are working to provide special materials, equipment and services for those with physical handicaps and learning disabilities.

Another frequently overlooked barrier to information is geography. Many Amer-

icans are denied access to information because of where they live, such as an Indian reservation, a Pacific Island, or an isolated area. To address these problems and those of other persons isolated from information due to their location, I am directing the Department of the Interior to analyze these issues and provide recommendations to me.

I will soon send to the Senate a protocol to the Florence Agreement of 1952 further liberalizing the exchange of books and information and reducing barriers to international understanding. The National Commission on Libraries and Information Sciences has already begun working with the International Federation of Library Associations.

THE NEW INFORMATION AND COMMUNICATIONS TECHNOLOGIES

New technologies are revolutionizing the ways in which we create, store and disseminate information. For example, the text of 3,200 books can now be stored on a 12-inch videodisc which costs $20. In the library computers are replacing the card catalog. The sum of changes like these will have a major impact on our lives.

My Administration is actively encouraging the creative application of these technologies for the benefit of all individuals. As the largest user of computer technology in the world, the Federal government plays a major role in deciding how this technology is applied everywhere. We are using technology to provide government services, including information, in new and better ways. A number of agencies are actively involved in conducting or supporting research and development into new technologies and their application. We shall aggressively pursue such research. We also have a program to develop standards which will enhance our ability to transfer technology.

We have worked to remove regulations that prevent competition and constrain application of the new technologies. The Federal Communications Commission is completing a dramatic overhaul of its regulations, opening up competition and promoting diversity. Recent actions are creating 1000 new radio stations and a whole new class of community TV stations. We developed a program which has doubled minority ownership of broadcast stations. We are working with Congress to pass legislation to reduce regulation and promote competition in telecommunications. The explosion of outlets in the electronic media provides special opportunities for libraries. For example, libraries can work with cable TV systems to program public service channels. Competition will stimulate innovation, increase productivity, and make the communications industries more responsive to consumer demands.

Actions we have taken to realize the public dividend from the new technologies include:

—My space policy, which is helping public service producers use satellites to cut their communication costs. The Commerce Department is responsible for this program, and I am directing them to work with the library community to make satellite and other emerging communication technologies available where it is cost-effective for networking and other purposes.

—The Department of Education will support a conference of independent experts to develop an agenda for library research in the 1980's.

—The library and information science communities will be encouraged to pro-pose technology assessment studies for consideration by Federal agencies.

As our society expands use of the new information technologies, we must protect our personal privacy. Last year I proposed the Nation's first comprehensive privacy policy. Five privacy bills are now before Congress, covering medical, bank, insurance and other types of records. Their passage is an essential ingredient to an information policy of the 1980's.

The biggest challenges rest with the library and information community. These institutions are run by talented and dedicated people with strong bases in their communities. They have contributed much, and they can do even more to meet people's needs in coping with the problems we face in the 80's. I believe we have viewed libraries too narrowly. The needs of the public who must cope with our increasingly complex society can only be met by libraries actively providing access to the great variety of information they have. Libraries can provide information to individuals about jobs and education opportunities; information to families about social services and energy; and consumer information to small business on marketing and technological innovation. Americans must be able to obtain this information in convenient, accessible, community institutions like the library. To survive as community institutions, libraries must be strengthened and the public made more aware of their potential.

We expect that the libraries will help to teach people the value of energy conservation and the ways to accomplish it; help the American people protect themselves from inflation by informed purchasing; help them to see that we live in an interrelated world which requires both America's strength but also American patience and American understanding; and, help them most of all to learn that we have to look at the world as it is and not as we remembered it 25 years ago. I have every confidence that you will meet these challenges as you have others in the past. Libraries will continue to be a critical ingredient in building a stronger, a more vibrant, a more informed America that we all hope for.

JIMMY CARTER

The White House,
    September 26, 1980.

Nuclear Safety Oversight Committee

Executive Order 12240.   September 26, 1980

By the authority vested in me as President by the Constitution of the United States of America, and in order to provide for the extended life of the Nuclear Safety Oversight Committee to the extent that funds are to be made available therefor, it is hereby ordered as follows:

1-101. Section 1-303 of Executive Order No. 12202 is amended by adding thereto the following sentence: "Beginning October 1, 1980, such support shall be provided in accordance with Section 213 of the Independent Offices Appropriations Act, 1945 (31 U.S.C. 696).".

1-102. Section 1-402 of Executive Order No. 12202 is amended to read, "The Committee shall terminate on September 30, 1981.".

1-103. In Section 1-102 of Executive Order No. 12202 the words "The membership of the Committee shall be composed of five persons" is amended to read,

"The membership of the Committee shall be composed of six persons."

JIMMY CARTER

The White House,
    September 26, 1980.

[Filed with the Office of the Federal Register, 4:45 p.m., September 26, 1980]

Advisory Council on Historic Preservation

Appointment of Steven F. Arvizu as a Member. September 26, 1980

The President today announced the appointment of Steven F. Arvizu, of Sacramento, Calif., as a member of the Advisory Council on Historic Preservation.

Arvizu is an associate professor of anthropology at California State University. He is director of the Cross Cultural Resource Center and president of the Council on Anthropology and Education. He was chairperson of National Education Task Force De La Raza from 1970 to 1973.

Committee for the Preservation of the White House

Appointment of Marjorie Fry Davis as a Member. September 26, 1980

The President today announced the appointment of Marjorie Fry Davis of New Orleans, La., as a member of the Committee for the Preservation of the White House.

Davis is a trustee of the New Orleans Museum of Art and a life fellow of the Metropolitan Museum, the Newark Museum, and the New Orleans Museum. She is active in numerous civic activities related to the arts. She owns an extensive art collection, which tours to benefit communities throughout the State.

Interagency Committee on Emergency Medical Services

Appointment of David B. Horner as a Member. September 26, 1980

The President today announced the appointment of David B. Horner, of Santa Monica, Calif., to be a member of the Interagency Committee on Emergency Medical Services.

Horner is a practicing orthopedic surgeon who also serves as an assistant clinical professor of orthopedic surgery at the University of Southern California Medical School. He is president of the Los Angeles County Medical Association and a member of the Health Advisory Council for the State of California.

Infant Formula Act of 1980

Remarks on Signing H.R. 6940 Into Law. September 26, 1980

This signing ceremony for the infant formula bill is particularly gratifying to me as President for several reasons. One is it shows the influence that just one or two private citizens can have if they feel very deeply about an important subject. Lynn Pilot and Carol Laskin were concerned about the fact that in the past some of the infant formulas sold in this country to trusting parents for their dear children, babies, were lacking in certain food ingredients and caused very severe damage to the children's or babies' health.

A reporter, Lea Thompson, became interested in this subject and let the public become aware of it, and then later, of course, Senator Metzenbaum, Congressman Gore, Congressmen Mottl and Tim Lee Carter, who happens to be a doctor himself, Congressman Waxman, and then, of course, Senators Baucus and Leahy and others became interested in this problem. As a result of that, we've now had a bill passed that would set very rigid standards for the quality and the adequacy of infant formulas and, secondly, would let the Department of Health and Human Services monitor very carefully this quality, to raise its standards or modify them as research results indicated, and provide for a testing program for the health of the children and also the adequacy of formulas in the future.

As you may or may not know, the Department of Agriculture now also has centers wherein the nutritional value of foods sold and the needs for food products by children and older people, retired people can be tested.

I'm very grateful that this fine work has been done, appreciate the dedication of these parents, the news media, and the Members of the House and Senate on a bipartisan basis, and am very gratified as President to sign into law now the infant formula bill, which will guarantee to the children of our Nation in the future that they can be healthy, that they can indicate their strength and their health even in the presence of the press and the President. [*Laughter*] This is the way a free society ought to be, and I'm very grateful for it.

[*At this point, the President signed the bill into law.*]

It makes me feel at home. It also reminds me of my own grandchildren, who are dear to me.

I'd like to ask Senator Metzenbaum if he'd like to make a comment, representing the Members of the Senate who worked on this bill, and then I'd like to ask Congressman Gore if he would make a statement, representing the House of Representatives.

NOTE: The President spoke at 1:30 p.m. in the Cabinet Room at the White House. Following the bill signing, there were remarks by Senator Howard M. Metzenbaum, Representative Albert Gore, Jr., Secretary of Health and Human Services Patricia Roberts Harris, Lea Thompson of NBC News, and Representative Tim Lee Carter. The President also had a conversation with mothers attending the ceremony with their children. Their remarks are included in the White House press release.

As enacted, H.R. 6940 is Public Law 96–359, approved September 26.

Infant Formula Act of 1980

Statement on Signing H.R. 6940 Into Law. September 26, 1980

I am today signing H.R. 6940, the Infant Formula Act of 1980. This legislation recognizes that our most important resource for the future—our children—should be afforded safe and nutritionally adequate formulas during a critical period of development. Infant formulas are uniquely important to the health of our children, because for many infants they are the sole source of nutrients for the first several months of their lives. The proper growth and long-range health of children are determined to a large extent by the quality of the nutrition they receive during these first vital months.

H.R. 6940 is designed to ensure that commercially produced and marketed infant formulas meet accepted nutritional standards and that consistent quality is maintained in their preparation. This bill, which resulted from reports during 1979 that more than 100 infants became seriously ill as a consequence of using soybean-based formulas marketed with an insufficient amount of chloride, establishes a statutory requirement that formula manufacturers include chlorides as well as other essential elements in each infant formula preparation sold. It also gives the Secretary of Health and Human Services (HHS) authority to adjust nutritional standards to conform to the best available scientific knowledge. In addition, the bill requires manufacturers to test infant formulas on a periodic basis and to notify the Secretary promptly whenever formulas do not meet nutritional requirements.

The enactment of this legislation represents the work and cooperation of many individuals and groups, including concerned parents, Congressmen Henry A. Waxman, Albert Gore, Jr., Ronald M. Mottl, and Tim Lee Carter, Senator Howard M. Metzenbaum, the infant formula industry, and officials of this administration. H.R. 6940, together with existing authority under the Food, Drug and Cosmetic Act, will aid in ensuring that both the Federal Government and the private sector meet their responsibilities in providing for the quality of infant formula preparations.

NOTE: As enacted, H.R. 6940 is Public Law 96–359, approved September 26.

National Aquaculture Act of 1980

Statement on Signing S. 1650 Into Law. September 26, 1980

I am pleased to be able to approve enrolled bill S. 1650, the National Aquaculture Act of 1980.

Almost 2 years ago, I reluctantly disapproved an aquaculture bill that authorized major new Government financial programs without, in my opinion, an adequate demonstration of need. In my memorandum of disapproval of the 1978 bill and in separate correspondence with several Members of Congress, I promised to work with Congress to strengthen Federal aquaculture programs and to fashion aquaculture legislation which I could approve.

Since that time, we have established highly effective mechanisms for interagency coordination and joint endeavors, and we will soon publish the first phase of a national aquaculture plan that has been developed in close cooperation with the aquaculture industry. We have also initiated studies designed to provide solid information on the financial and regulatory barriers to the expansion of commercial aquaculture in this country.

I am most pleased that the bill I am signing here today formalizes the interagency coordinating mechanism which is working so well and calls for the formulation of a long-range national aquaculture plan. It also requires the development of strategies to meet the recommendations of the studies on financial and regulatory constraints. Perhaps most important, S. 1650 authorizes funds for the support of research, development, and technology transfer by the Secretaries of Agriculture, Commerce, and Interior.

Although commercial aquaculture development is clearly the responsibility of the private sector, the Federal Government has a role in conducting and supporting research and in establishing, through a national plan, a framework for cooperation between Government and the public sector.

The Government also has a strong interest in developing new sources of food for this country and for the poorer nations of the world. Many developing countries have already recognized the potential benefits of aquaculture. In China, for example, where fish is a staple, aquaculture accounts for a major portion of the seafood consumed. Here at home, an expanded aquaculture industry can help overcome a trade imbalance caused by the importation of some $2 billion of seafood each year. Since only 3 percent of our current domestic seafood supplied are produced through aquaculture, there is considerable potential for expansion. I believe that this legislation will greatly benefit the many farmers of this country, who will be encouraged to grow fresh-water fish in their lakes and ponds. At the same time, commercial fishermen will see larger stocks of wild fish as a result of increased commercial aquaculture.

In signing this bill into law, I wish to thank leading Members of the Congress, particularly Senators Magnuson, Inouye, Stone, Cannon, Cochran, Bentsen, Pryor, Stewart, and Talmadge and Representatives Foley, Murphy, Breaux, de la Garza, Forsythe, and AuCoin, for working with us on this important legislation.

I would also like to make note of the contribution of Dave Wallace. Until his death last year, he was Director of International Fisheries in the Department of Commerce and longstanding advocate and tireless worker for an expanded United States aquaculture program. His leadership, wisdom, patience, and skill were the driving forces behind the coordinated effort to strengthen Federal aquaculture programs. I wish to acknowledge his dedication and perseverance and dedicate this act to his memory.

NOTE: As enacted, S. 1650 is Public Law 96–362, approved September 26.

Department of Agriculture

Nomination of Alex P. Mercure To Be Assistant Secretary for Small Community and Rural Development. September 26, 1980

The President today announced his intention to nominate Alex P. Mercure to be Under Secretary of Agriculture for Small Community and Rural Development. This is a new position created by the Rural Development Policy Act of 1980, which the President signed on September 24.

Mercure has been Assistant Secretary of Agriculture for Rural Development and a member of the Board of Directors of the Commodity Credit Corporation since 1977.

He was born June 30, 1931, in Lumberton, N. Mex. He received a B.S. from the University of New Mexico in 1958 and an M.A. from New Mexico Highlands University in 1961.

Mercure was a teacher at Chama High School in Chama, N. Mex., from 1958 to 1962 and a counsellor at Los Lunas Public Schools in Los Lunas, N. Mex., from 1962 to 1964. From 1965 to 1971, he was executive director of the home education livelihood program of the New Mexico Council of Churches.

From 1971 to 1974, Mercure was president of the New Mexico Technical Vocational School in El Rito, N. Mex. He was vice president and assistant provost of the University of New Mexico, in charge of regional and community affairs, from 1974 until his appointment as Assistant Secretary of Agriculture in 1977.

1980 Hispanic Democratic Victory Dinner

Remarks at the Dinner.   September 26, 1980

It's also a long way from Plains, Georgia, to the White House. [*Laughter*] And I wouldn't be in the White House if it weren't for a lot of you who had confidence in me 4 years ago and who still express your confidence in me and Fritz Mondale and the principles of the Demo-

cratic Party by coming here tonight.

Esteban, I appreciate the introduction that you gave me. There is no doubt that you meant what you said, and the friendship that you've expressed for me in a personal way is the same feeling that I have for you. Governor Jerry Apodaca, who is here and who was a friend of mine as a common Governor—at the same time I had Georgia, he had New Mexico. Secretary of State Pedro Vasquez was going to speak to this group after supper tonight. He is not going to speak, and I'll have some comments to make about that later on. I think the sense of equality of opportunity and the sense of equality of responsibility is important for us all to understand, and I have no hesitancy about substituting at least to some degree for him.

I'm very proud that the Vice Chairperson of the Democratic National Committee, Carmella Lacayo, is here. She's been very important to me and to the Democratic Party. And I'm very thankful for Ed Romero; I've been watching him for years. He's a little too timid, a little too quiet—[*laughter*]—he ought to smile a little bit more. [*Laughter*] Other than that, he's just a great man, and I'm grateful to be with him.

Tonight, the money that you are raising with your generosity is very important, as Chairman John White would acknowledge, for the Democratic National Committee and for the Democratic Party and, I believe, for our Nation. It's also a tribute to Hispanic Americans and to your commitment to the principles that are important to me, to the great founders of this Nation more than 200 years ago, to our party. I'm grateful for your contributions, your time, your hard work, and your common commitment.

It's good for me to stand here feeling a sense of brotherhood and sisterhood with you. And I'd like to outline tonight, in just a few moments, some of the responsibilities that I have as President and how they relate directly to you and to the leaders among the Hispanic-American community.

Your dedication and the fact that the Democratic Party accurately represents your hopes and dreams and aspirations is why we're going to whip the Republicans on November the 4th.

If you analyze all the things that are important to you personally, all the things that were important to your mother and your father when you were a child, all the things that are important to your children and the generations to come, I think you will see that there is more at stake than just a contest between Jimmy Carter and Ronald Reagan, there's also more at stake than just a contest between the Democrats and Republicans. What is at stake is the honoring of those ideals and commitments and hopes and dreams and the shaping of the future of our country not just in the next 4 years or 8 years, but the shaping of our Nation for the balance of this century and perhaps even beyond.

I spoke to the Hispanic Caucus dinner last week. Many of you were there. It shows your loyalty and your dedication and your unselfishness to come to two events in this short a period of time, at great expense to you. I'm not going to repeat what I said then. But I have come here tonight with one assignment only, and that is to pay tribute to the Hispanic men and women who have served so well in my administration and who epitomize, personally, the challenges that we face to a common degree.

I learned a long time ago that the best intentions of an executive officer—and I hold the highest executive position in the free world—is shaped by those who are chosen or recruited to serve with him. That's why when I took office I sent trusted representatives, some of you here tonight, throughout the Hispanic communities of this Nation, to talk some, but primarily to listen, because there obviously are things that are in my own background as a naval officer, as a farmer, a businessman, a State senator or Governor or candidate for 4 years that I knew about and understood about this country. But there are some special aggravations and special problems that relate to people just because their culture and background, religion, habits, and their hopes for a family or hopes for a community are different. And I don't have that special sensitivity as an Anglo President that I consider to be vital for me to do a good job as President of all the people of this country.

Rosalynn, my wife, is a sensitive person. She understands people. She also listens. And when I have to be in the White House dealing with Iraq, Iran, Afghanistan, SALT, Congress, other things that are pressing on me, she, quite often, as you know, is in communities listening to your people and bringing those messages back to me so that I can be a better President.

It's important for me within the White House itself to have someone on whom I can depend, at my shoulder day in and day out, to give me advice on matters that relate directly to you, uniquely, and the people who look to you for leadership. And that's why I asked Ambassador Esteban Torres to come there and serve with me, and I'm grateful that he's there at my shoulder giving me guidance to do the right thing as President.

As you know, many of the recent immigrants to our country, particularly those who speak Spanish, have settled in our major cities—not in the most elite suburban areas of those cities; in neighborhoods that formerly were deteriorating. And when I traveled this country in '75 and '76, campaigning for President, a common concern or complaint from almost every mayor that I met and local official that I met, Democratic or Republican, was, "Something must be done to restore the integrity and the life and the quality [of life] of the people who live there in those urban areas."

In the Housing and Urban Development Department of our country, the Under Secretary is Victor Marrero, a great man who's serving with me and I'm grateful to him. And the Assistant Secretary, as you know, is William Medina, and I'm thankful to him as well.

One of my additional responsibilities is to deal with many other countries from all over the world—China, Russia, Yugoslavia, the European countries, the 52 countries, in Africa, Latin America, Australia, New Zealand, Japan. It's not an easy task. There has to be a special sensitivity there about people who are different from us, whose relatives have moved here as immigrants. It's important that I have in that key diplomatic post a Chief of Protocol who when those visitors come to our Nation are treated with respect and with understanding and with sensitivity and with friendship. And I'm very grateful that Ambassador Abelardo Valdez occupies that position.

You think I asked him to serve because he's so well qualified; that's not the case. He knows why I asked him to serve as protocol officer. I'd like for his wife to stand up. Our Nation got two for the price of one—[*laughter*]—and I'm grateful for them.

There's a department in our Government, not very well known, that has one specific assignment, and that's to deal with the poor, the unfortunate, those in particularly dilapidated homes where medical services might be scarce, where the roads in front or the streets in front may not be well paved, where the distances to schools might be very great, where job opportunities are not readily apparent. That's the Community Services Administration, and as you know, I've had a very fine woman who served there earlier and now a very fine and highly qualified man, Richard Rios, and I'm very grateful for him.

In the rural areas, we can't overlook that important position. The primary Department responsible for the rural areas, as you know, is the Department of Agriculture. This is an area which is rapidly growing in importance for the Federal Government. I signed a major bill this week establishing for the first time in the history of our country an Under Secretary for Rural Development, and I've asked and just promoted or recommended Alex Mercure to serve in that position, and he will be doing a good job.

If I were to ask a hundred Americans, "What's the most important single domestic problem that we've had to address in the last $3\frac{1}{2}$ years?", the answer would be energy, because it permeates our lives. The excessive dependence on foreign oil has given us too much inflation, too much unemployment, and shocked our economic system. But there's a specil element of energy that must be addressed humanely, and that's how these serious problems— that might be accommodated by rich people or those even with moderate means and a steady job—and that is the minority impact of energy problems. And I've asked Louis Moret to serve in the Department of Energy specially [as] director for the minority impact.

In Health and Human Services, there's a special category of human development, the development of human beings, to permit each person to take what talent God might have given that person and to let it be growing and expanding and to be used in a productive way for our country.

And Cesar Perales serves in that position, and I'm very grateful for him.

Education's a new Department, a burning issue in the Hispanic-American community. We have a deep commitment to bilingual education, as you know, and a wonderful Secretary of Education. But the Assistant Secretary at the Department of Education—John Gabusi, and I'm very grateful for him.

I'm not going to go down the entire list of people. I would like to just mention two or three who are of special importance to me and ask them to stand if they will.

Francis Garcia—Francis? She's a commissioner of the Coypright Royalty Tribunal. And as you know, the Federal Cochairman of the Southwest Border Regional Comission is the Federal representative who ties together the Southwestern States, relates them one to another, to Mexico as well, and to our Federal Government. And Cristobal Aldrete is the Cochairman representing the Federal Government, and he administers that major responsibility.

The President must have a lawyer. The lawyers in the White House must be superb, because I get most of the problems that you could possibly imagine in my life in that position. And Patrick Apodaca is one of my legal counsels. Patrick?

All these things are important to me, but there's one thing that's particularly important during the next 6 weeks, and that is my campaign. And I wanted the best trained person who knew me very well to serve in that position and, as you know, formerly of my staff and now deputy chairman of my entire reelection campaign, Rick Hernandez. Rick, *gracias.*

I'm not going to go down the entire list of the 200 people that I've appointed in positions of major responsibility who happen to be Hispanic Americans, but I think it is very good for me to point out that these persons have been selected because of their own innate qualities. It's never been necessary for me to lower the standards of excellence and professional qualification in order to fill these posts.

We've had 17 town meetings around the country to try to discern the special problems that address those who look to you and me for leadership, and it's very important for me to understand that not just in the administrative branch of Government but also in the judicial branch of Government these special needs existed. I wasn't quite aware of it, I have to admit to you, when I began running for President. I was aware of the special legal problems of black people in the Southeast, the Deep South. But I didn't know fully about the discrimination that had been existing in the Federal judicial system against Hispanics until I approached the office of President.

I think you know that we've made good strides there. I have quadrupled already the number of Hispanic Federal judges, including the first Hispanic woman Federal judge, Carmen Consuelo Cerezo. And this, as you know, will have a major impact on the attitude and tone, not only in the court itself but in the entire communities where they serve, not just during my term of office, no matter whether it's 4 or 8 years, but for a long time, for a generation.

And we have set a standard now in this administration that subsequent Presidents will have to meet. And I ask you as a special favor to me to make darned sure that in the future that Presidents do at least as well as I do on these appointments, and I hope even better if it's possible.

Immigration, naturalization—a burning issue with you and with me and with our Nation, and I asked to serve as Commissioner of that entire major department

Leonel Castillo. He did a superb job. And I've now nominated, as you know, Matt Garcia from Texas to take that position, and I hope he'll be confirmed very shortly.

I'm not only President, I'm Commander in Chief of the Armed Forces. It's my duty to keep this Nation strong. It's my duty to make sure that those who serve in the Armed Forces feel that they have a legitimate responsibility and a privilege to be patriotic soldiers or sailors or marines—those who serve in the Coast Guard are great; Air Force. One of those major departments, the one that's dearest to my heart, as you know, is headed up by a very fine man who's highly qualified, who did an absolutely unbelievably good job in a lower position, but now is Secretary of the Navy, Ed Hidalgo. I don't know if Secretary Hidalgo is here tonight.

But as Charlie Duncan knows, when I became President—Harold Brown became Secretary of Defense; Charlie Duncan became Deputy—one of the major elements of our Armed Forces that was aborted in its progress was the Trident submarine system, the submarines and the missiles themselves, and there was an unbreakable deadlock between the major shipbuilding yards of our Nation and the Navy and, therefore the Federal Government, and, therefore, the Commander in Chief. And Ed Hidalgo was the one that broke that deadlock. And the remarkable progress now being made with the Trident submarines, now he's the Secretary of the Navy, is a great tribute to him.

One other person that I want to mention, and then that's all. We've got special relationships with many countries. No closer relationship exists than the one that must be maintained with our neighbor to the south, the great nation of Mexico.

This has not always been an easy relationship. But the ties of blood kin and the common challenges and opportunities grow month by month. Growing pains are sometimes difficult to accommodate. We've made great progress. Mexico is a wonderful trade opportunity for us. As a farmer, I'm grateful that now we will ship to Mexico this year 10 million tons of American grain. In the last 4 years we have tripled trade with Mexico. That's good. But we also have a lot of human interrelationships and, in the past, there's been kind of a prohibition—for some reason; I don't understand it—in trying to send someone who couldn't speak Spanish down to Mexico. I've changed that, and I'm very grateful that I have. And Julian Nava, a great American, is now serving as Ambassador to Mexico.

And now I'd like to say something about Puerto Rico and why one of the great leaders of Puetro Rico decided not to speak to you tonight. It's not a pleasant thing, but it's one of the duties that I have as President. We've had in the last few months, 120,000 Cubans to come to our Nation, above and beyond the immigration quotas, above and beyond those permitted by the law. I've done the best I could, under one of the most difficult possible circumstances, to accommodate these newcomers to our Nation who came here seeking freedom.

We are placing those new Americans in homes and in communities and in jobs as best we can. It is a very difficult thing. I have at the same time a responsibility to make sure that Americans accept them, as you were accepted and as my ancestors were accepted when they came here, and as other Americans—all except the American native Indians—had their families accepted. Sometimes it wasn't easy. When the European Jews came here, when the Italians came here, when the Irish came here following the potato famine there was a lot of obstacles there, and people didn't like it. And when we started taking in new Americans from Indochina, it wasn't easy.

We still have a problem in that—although we are placing these new Cubans, Cuban Americans now, as rapidly as we possibly can in a humane and legal way—we've had an influx of about 150 per day ever since we stopped the massive influx which was running 3 or 4 thousand per day.

Jack Watson, sitting here, and Esteban Torres know how much I have worried about this problem. We still have a few thousand not yet placed.

Last night, and I'm thankful for it, the Cuban officials, Fidel Castro announced to the ship or boat captains in Mariel Harbor that no more would be permitted to carry out Cubans, but he would take the names of those who had families here and later arrange for them to leave Cuba in a legal way.

So we've got now the first prospect in months and months and months of handling this problem to its conclusion, because we'll re-double our efforts to settle those who are still in camps, rapidly, in their own permanent communities.

We've had tens of thousands of those newcomers in Florida, in Arkansas, in Wisconsin, and other States in the Nation. It's been a very difficult thing for me. The adverse reaction has been unbelievable. And now, searching about for a place to put a few thousand, 3 or 4 thousand, where they would be accommodated in a military base, I decided to put some in Puerto Rico. The people in Puerto Rico do not like it. The politicians don't like it, and the people don't like it. The politicians, I guarantee you, in Florida didn't like it, and in Arkansas they didn't like it, in Georgia they didn't like it, and in Wisconsin they didn't like it. The Spanish-American community wants to be treated—and I've tried to

outline to you how we are treating the Spanish-American community—Hispanic Americans—with equal and growing responsibilities and, I hope, the end of discrimination.

But it's necessary for me to treat the people in Puerto Rico the same way that I treat the people in Wisconsin or Florida or Arkansas. I wish that we had all the Cubans settled already; that's not possible.

And Secretary of State Vasquez feels very deeply that those Cubans should not come to Puerto Rico. Now that the stream of Cubans has been cut off and we're not receiving those 150 per day, the problems that we anticipated will not be nearly so severe as we thought. Isn't that right, Jack [Watson]?

But during this transition phase, I will have to put a few, as small a number as possible, in Puerto Rico. We will not put anyone down there who's undesirable, we will not put anyone down there who's been a prisoner in Cuba, we will not put anyone down there who has mental problems—those are in places in the continental United States. But there will be a few put there. And I know that many of you are Puerto Ricans and perhaps you would rather me not put anyone down there, but I don't want to mislead you. It's something that I have to do. And I hope this small group, highly dedicated to me and to my party and to my election, will help me to explain this problem to the people of Puerto Rico.

I tried to explain it to the Secretary of State, but he felt very emotional about it, and I sympathize with him. I stand here not to criticize him—God knows I don't criticize him—but to sympathize with him. And my heart goes out to him and to the Governor. He's facing a re-election just like I am, and we'll have to share this responsibility. He helped me carry Puerto Rico, as you well know, in the primary season.

But I wanted to explain to you why he will not be here after your banquet, and to let you know, I think in the most vivid possible way, that we're all in it together—I and the people of Puerto Rico.

[*At this point, the President made a brief closing statement in Spanish.*]

NOTE: The President spoke at 7:41 p.m. in the State Ballroom at the Mayflower Hotel.

Digest of Other White House Announcements

The following listing includes the President's public schedule and other items of general interest announced by the White House Press Office and not included in this issue.

September 21

The President returned to the White House from Camp David, Md.

September 22

The White House announced that on Saturday, September 20, the President declared an emergency for the State of Maine as a result of an outbreak of toxic shellfish poisoning, beginning on July 30.

The White House announced that the President will meet with President Shehu Shagari of Nigeria on October 7 at the White House. President Shagari will be in Washington on an official visit from October 6–8. While in the United States, President Shagari will visit New York City from October 3–6, where he will address the United Nations General Assembly on October 6.

The White House announced that the President has signed a determination authorizing the use of an additional $11.6 million from the United States Emergency Refugee and Migration Assistance Fund

for the purposes of processing, tranportation, caring for and resettling Cubans and Haitians arriving in the United States, and for associated administrative expenses.

September 24

The President met at the White House with:

—his national security advisers, to discuss the situation in Iran and Iraq;
—Stansfield Turner, Director of Central Intelligence, Zbigniew Brzezinski, Assistant to the President for National Security Affairs, Jack H. Watson, Jr., Assistant to the President;
—Clark Gruening, Democratic candidate for the U.S. Senate from Alaska.

September 25

The President met at the White House with:

—Dr. Brzezinski;
—the Democratic congressional leadership;
—Frank B. Moore, Assistant to the President for Congressional Liaison;
—President Siaka Stevens of Sierra Leone;
—a group of senior citizen leaders.

The White House announced that the President will meet with President Mohammad Zia-ul-Haq of Pakistan on October 3 in Washington. President Zia will be in the United States to address the United Nations General Assembly in his capacity as Spokesman for the Islamic Conference.

September 26

The President met at the White House with:

—Dr. Brzezinski;
—Vice President Walter F. Mondale, Secretary of State Edmund S. Muskie, Secretary of Defense Harold Brown, Deputy Secretary of State Warren M. Christopher, Lloyd N.

Cutler, Counsel to the President, Dr. Brzezinski, and Mr. Watson;

—Representatives Mario Biaggi of New York and Kika de la Garza of Texas;

—Mr. Moore;

—Rev. Jesse Jackson, president of Operation PUSH (People United to Save Humanity);

—Larry Lucas, 5½, of Cleveland, Ohio, the 1980 Sickle Cell Anemia Poster Child;

—Vice President Mondale.

The President announced the appointment of Zane G. Smith, of San Francisco, Calif., as U.S. Government Representative on the Governing Board of the Lake Tahoe Regional Planning Agency. Mr. Smith is the Agriculture Department's regional forester for the Pacific Southwest Region and administers the National Forest lands which make up 65 percent of the Tahoe Basin.

The President announced the persons who will represent the United States at the Brazzaville Centennial celebrations, to be held October 2–4 in Brazzaville, People's Republic of the Congo. J. Bruce Llewellyn, President of the Overseas Private Investment Corporation, will head the delegation, attending as personal representative of the President. Mrs. Llewellyn will accompany Mr. Llewellyn. The additional representatives of the President will be:

LANNON WALKER, Deputy Assistant Secretary of State for African Affairs;

HENRY L. MARSH III, mayor of Richmond, Va.;

CLARENCE MITCHELL III, State senator, Maryland;

DONALD B. EASUM, president, African-American Institute;

MARTIN LOWELL ANDREAS, president, Archer Daniels Midland Foods;

DR. JAMES CHEEK, president, Howard University;

B. L. BESSINGER, ABF Ltd.;

MARTIN LUTHER KING III, student;

MILDRED ROBBINS LEET, consultant, Women in Development;

SARAH VAUGHAN, singer.

By participating in the Centennial ceremonies, the United States wishes to underscore improving relations with this important central African country.

The President declared a major disaster for the State of Texas as a result of Tropical Storm Danielle, intermittent rains and flooding, beginning on or about September 5, which caused extensive property damage.

In the evening, the President left the White House for a weekend stay at Camp David, Md.

NOMINATIONS SUBMITTED TO THE SENATE

The following list does not include promotions of members of the Uniformed Services, nominations to the Service Academies, or nominations of Foreign Service officers.

Submitted September 22, 1980

The following-named persons to be Representatives of the United States of America to the Thirty-fifth Session of the General Assembly of the United Nations:

DONALD F. McHENRY, of Illinois

WILLIAM J. VANDEN HEUVEL, of New York

JACOB K. JAVITS, United States Senator from the State of New York

PAUL E. TSONGAS, United States Senator from the State of Massachusetts

HANNAH D. ATKINS, of Oklahoma

The following-named persons to be Alternate Representatives of the United States of America to the Thirty-fifth Session of the General Assembly of the United Nations:

NATHAN LANDOW, of Maryland

BARBARA NEWSOM, of California

RICHARD W. PETREE, of Virginia

JOAN EDELMAN SPERO, of New York

H. CARL McCALL, of New York

JOHN A. BURROUGHS, JR., of Maryland, to be Ambassador Extraordinary and Plenipotentiary of the United States of America to the Republic of Malawi.

NOMINATIONS—Continued

Submitted September 22—Continued

SALLY ANGELA SHELTON, of Texas, now Envoy Extraordinary and Minister Plenipotentiary of the United States of America to Saint Lucia, to be Ambassador Extraordinary and Plenipotentiary of the United States of America to Saint Lucia concurrently with her positions as Ambassador to Barbados, to Grenada and to the Commonwealth of Dominica.

JACK B. KUBISCH, of North Carolina, a retired Foreign Service officer, for the rank of Ambassador while serving as United States Special Negotiator of a successor agreement or treaty to the current United States-Spanish Treaty of Friendship and Cooperation.

Submitted September 25, 1980

JACK F. MATLOCK, JR., of Florida, a Foreign Service officer of Class one, to be Ambassador Extraordinary and Plenipotentiary of the United States of America to the Czechoslovak Socialist Republic.

RALPH W. EMERSON, of the District of Columbia, to be a member of the Foreign Claims Settlement Commission of the United States for the term expiring September 30, 1981 (new position—P.L. 96–209).

The following-named persons to be members of the Board of Directors of the Overseas Private Investment Corporation for the terms indicated:

JAMES M. FRIEDMAN, of Ohio, for a term expiring December 17, 1982 (reappointment).

EDWARD L. MARCUS, of Connecticut, for a term of 3 years expiring December 17, 1983 (reappointment).

ARTHUR I. JACOBS, of Florida, to be a member of the National Council on the Arts for a term expiring September 3, 1986, vice Gunther Schuller, term expired.

DORIS A. EVANS, of Ohio, to be a member of the Board of Regents of the Uniformed Services University of the Health Sciences for a term expiring May 1, 1983, vice Philip O'Bryan Montgomery, Jr., term expired.

CHECKLIST OF WHITE HOUSE PRESS RELEASES

The following listing contains releases of the White House Press Office which are not included in this issue.

CHECKLIST—Continued

Released September 20, 1980

Advance text: remarks at the 100th anniversary dinner of the Polish National Alliance in Niles, Ill.

Released September 22, 1980

Advance text: remarks to students and local residents at the Lincoln Land Community College in Springfield, Ill.

Advance text: opening remarks at the town meeting in Torrance, Calif.

Released September 23, 1980

Advance text: remarks to employees at the Continental Grain Terminal in Tacoma, Wash.

Released September 24, 1980

Fact sheet: Rural Development Policy Act of 1980

Released September 25, 1980

Advance text: remarks at a White House reception for members of the Congressional Black Caucus

Released September 26, 1980

Fact sheet: Infant Formula Act of 1980

Announcement: appointees of the Speaker of the House, the President of the Senate, and the Chief Justice of the United States to the Commission on Executive, Legislative, and Judicial Salaries

ACTS APPROVED BY THE PRESIDENT

Approved September 24, 1980

S. 670_____ Public Law 96–355
Rural Development Policy Act of 1980.

S. 1625_____ Public Law 96–356
An act to amend the Act of December 20, 1944, as amended.

H.R. 5766 _____ Public Law 96–357
An act to authorize additional Reserve Officers' Training Corps scholarships for the Army, to authorize the Secretary of the Army to provide that cadets awarded such scholarships may serve their obligated period of service in the Army Reserve or Army National Guard of the United States, to authorize the Secretary concerned to require an individual furnished post-secondary education by an Armed Force to reimburse the United States for the cost of such education in the

ACTS APPROVED—Continued

Approved September 24—Continued

event such individual fails to comply with such individual's active-duty obligation, to provide that certain full-time training duty of members of the National Guard shall be considered as active duty for training in Federal service for certain purposes, and for other purposes.

Approved September 25, 1980

S. 261_____ Public Law 96–358
Agricultural Subterminal Facilities Act of 1980.

Approved September 26, 1980

H.R. 6940_____ Public Law 96–359
Infant Formula Act of 1980.

H.R. 3210_____ Public Law 96–360
An act to terminate the authority to make grants to the Las Vegas Valley Water District under the Act of August 27, 1954.

ACTS APPROVED—Continued

Approved September 26—Continued

H.R. 6511_____ Public Law 96–361
An act to designate the building known as the Federal Building in Morgantown, West Virginia, as the "Harley O. Staggers Federal Building".

S. 1650_____ Public Law 96–362
National Aquaculture Act of 1980.

S. 2223_____ Public Law 96–363
An act to permit any Indian to transfer by will restricted lands of such Indian to his or her heirs or lineal descendants, and other Indian persons.

H.R. 3904_____ Public Law 96–364
Multiemployer Pension Plan Amendments Act of 1980.

S. 215_____ Private Law 96–60
An act to provide for the relief of Renuka Pavla.

S. 1125_____ Public Law 96–365
Federal Crop Insurance Act of 1980.

○